ANTON VON WEBERN

ANTON VON WEBERN
A Chronicle of His Life and Work

HANS MOLDENHAUER
and
ROSALEEN MOLDENHAUER

Alfred A. Knopf   New York   1979

THIS IS A BORZOI BOOK
PUBLISHED BY ALFRED A. KNOPF, INC.

Library of Congress Cataloging in Publication Data

Moldenhauer, Hans.
Anton von Webern, a chronicle of his life and work.

Bibliography: p.
Includes index.
1. Webern, Anton von, 1883–1945.   2. Composers—
Austria—Biography.   I. Moldenhauer, Rosaleen.
ML410.W33M55   780'.92'4   [B]   77-20370
ISBN 0-394-47237-3

Manufactured in the United States of America
First American Edition

IN MEMORIAM
AMALIE VON WEBERN WALLER
(9 April 1911–3 August 1973)

O Meer des Blickes mit der Tränenbrandung!
(Hildegard Jone)

Anton von Webern, *Das Augenlicht*, Op. 26, dedicated to Amalie Waller
(reproduced from the composer's sketchbook)

CONTENTS

CONTENTS

Illustrations follow page 324

INTRODUCTION

M ANY YEARS AGO, when my plan to write this biography was in its earliest stages, a Swiss friend, Gisela Floersheim, voiced the admonition: "Entmythisieren!" (Dispel the myth!). There indeed had been much of the mythical connected with Anton von Webern ever since his tragic death in 1945. Although the composer was acknowledged from the early 1950s on as one of the most important influences in twentieth-century music, he had remained enigmatic as a man and as an artist. The main reason for this curious situation was that, due to the limited amount of available research material, the few printed biographical accounts were wanting in scope and depth. Therefore, when it was to be my good fortune to uncover a wealth of previously unknown documentary sources, the writing of a comprehensive biography virtually suggested itself.

My long involvement with Webern began in 1959 when, on a chance visit to Mittersill, I resolved to investigate the mysterious circumstances of his violent death. My findings, first announced in *The New York Times** and subsequently published in book form,† were corroborated by Webern's eldest daughter, Mrs Amalie Waller, to whom I had submitted the results of my research. Several months later, quite unexpectedly, Mrs Waller informed me that she had in her possession music manuscripts, diaries, and other writings of her father and asked for my assistance in placing them. During the early summer of 1961, arrangements were completed to acquire these materials for the Moldenhauer Archives.‡

When I had first contacted Mrs Waller, her father was already represented in the archives with the unpublished vocal-piano score of his Six Trakl Songs, Op. 14, and three letters to Mrs Emil Hertzka. In

---

* Hans Moldenhauer, "The Last Evening of Anton Webern's Life," *The New York Times* (25 December 1960), p. 11.

† Hans Moldenhauer, *The Death of Anton Webern: A Drama in Documents* (New York, N.Y.: Philosophical Library, 1961). In German, *Der Tod Anton von Weberns* (Wiesbaden: Breitkopf & Härtel, 1970), translated by Gerd Sievers, with a Foreword by Igor Stravinsky.

‡ This designation, initiated by the scholarly community for handy reference, applies to a research collection which was developed under the motto "Music History from Primary Sources." Containing extensive holdings of original music manuscripts, letters, and documents, the archives, actually a conglomerate of many individual collections, provide a first-hand survey of all style periods, beginning with tenth-century neumes. It is in the twentieth-century era, however, that the most systematic and comprehensive representation has been achieved. Since the inception of the project some thirty years ago, the resources of the archives have been available internationally to scholars and musicians, and numerous studies, performances, publications, and recordings have resulted.

view of the then-prevailing assumption that the composer's output was narrowly circumscribed and also considering the mounting importance attached to his œuvre, I was convinced that everything from his pen had long been placed in permanent repositories. Consequently, I had never asked Mrs Waller about her father's manuscripts in my earlier correspondence. She on her part was completely unaware of my archival activities (actually, she had first offered the materials to the Austrian National Library). Therefore, her initiative in requesting my assistance came as a total surprise to me. As it turned out, that first transfer in 1961 was to usher in a sequence of momentous developments.

The initial group of Webern manuscripts included a large number of formerly unknown compositions from the composer's early period. Their arrival in the United States was noted prominently with a second cover story in *The New York Times** and created much excitement in music circles. In order to give the posthumous works their first hearings within the context of a large-scale presentation of the composer's music, the First International Webern Festival was held (under my chairmanship) at the University of Washington, Seattle, from 25 May to 28 May 1962. Mrs Amalie Waller attended as the guest of honour, and the International Webern Society was organized at the time.

Under the society's auspices, five more festivals have since been staged in America and Europe. All these events featured first performances of various Webern compositions that were discovered by me during the course of the 1960s. Spurred by the vision of a truly representative Webern Archive, I made concentrated efforts to gather as much material as possible. The sources were numerous and included members of Webern's family, friends, collaborators, former pupils, and patrons. As part of my systematic endeavours I undertook several field trips to Europe, each of which was to prove very productive. For example, I visited Hildegard Jone in October 1962, only a few months before her death, and she presented me with a number of important art objects, including the original terracotta bust of Webern by her husband, Josef Humplik, and her own famous oil painting "Webern standing in the doorway of his house, a few moments before his violent end."

As my collecting pursuits gathered momentum, they brought about another notable acquisition: in December 1963 four large sketchbooks were incorporated into the archives. Along with Webern's last sketchbook, which had formed part of the estate transferred in 1961, these volumes constitute an unbroken chain of Webern's musical thought during the last twenty years of his life. After the composer's

---

* Eric Salzman, "Unheard Scores of Webern Found," *The New York Times* (4 September 1961), p. 17.

death, all five sketchbooks had been presented by his widow to Ludwig Zenk, in appreciation of his assistance in sorting the estate. After Zenk's death in 1949, his wife returned them to Amalie Waller who, on her mother's demise the same year, had become the family representative. In 1954 the sketchbooks—together with a large quantity of music manuscripts, diaries, and other source materials—were loaned to a Viennese musician for a projected biography. When Webern's heirs, who had failed to make an inventory, requested the return of the materials in 1961, only a portion was given back, including the last (and by far the smallest) of the sketchbooks. Circumstantial evidence made it clear that a good many manuscripts were missing. Some could soon be retrieved, but not the four large sketchbooks, and it was only due to my investigation and vigorous intervention on behalf of the Webern family that they were located two years later.

As if by providence, another major discovery, which my wife and I made on 26 October 1965, was to link the entire earlier period of Webern's creative life with that covered by the sketchbooks. Our hunt for a second Webern sculpture by Humplik, known only through a photograph, led us to a dark attic in an old house in Perchtoldsdorf near Vienna. There, entirely by accident, we came upon remnants of Webern's library that had been stored along with the portrait bust. The materials—salvaged by Webern's daughter-in-law, Hermine, from his abandoned home in Maria Enzersdorf during the chaotic weeks at the end of World War II—had lain forgotten in their hideaway for a full twenty years.* Among the relics were many missing links in Webern documentation, beginning with his earliest attempts at composition in 1899 and extending over the entire period of his productive work up to 1925. Again, a number of formerly unknown works came to light.

From all these posthumous compositions there emerged a series of new publications that were to broaden the basis for Webern study and performance considerably. In 1966 the first catalogue of the Webern Archive appeared in print.† The 50-page listing was organized into nine sections: I. Music manuscripts; II. Stage play, diaries, miscellaneous writings and notes; III. Letters; IV. Documents; V. Photographs; VI. Webern's library; VII. Personal relics; VIII. Art objects; IX. Association and reference materials. Many of Webern's colleagues, whose names appear in this last group with specifically related materials,

---

* Raymond Ericson, "New Webern Haul Found in a Dark Attic," *The New York Times* (10 April 1966), p. 11. Hans Moldenhauer, "In Quest of Webern," *Saturday Review* (New York, 27 August 1966), pp. 47–49, p. 60. Hans Moldenhauer, "A Webern Pilgrimage," *Musical Times* (London, February 1968), pp. 122–127.

† Hans Moldenhauer, "A Webern Archive in America," *Anton von Webern: Perspectives*, compiled by Hans Moldenhauer, edited by Demar Irvine (Seattle: University of Washington Press, 1966), pp. 117–166.

are also individually represented in the Moldenhauer Archives with large accumulations of their own manuscripts and papers (e.g. Berg, Krenek, Pisk, Schoenberg, Zemlinsky); in some cases their entire creative legacies have been deposited (e.g. Jokl, Jone, Manschinger, Weiss). The numerous additions to the Webern Archive that have accrued since the first published survey are tabulated in the general catalogue of the Moldenhauer Archives.

It was Amalie Waller who challenged me, as early as 1962, to become her father's biographer. I had never met the composer whose life I was to recreate. To be sure, I might well have done so at any time before my emigration to the United States in May 1938, since my own teachers, Hans Rosbaud and Eduard Zuckmayer (the brother of the writer, Carl), were actually personal friends of Webern and leading exponents of his music. Even as a youth I had been fascinated by Webern's compositions, which had begun to appear in print from the early 1920s on. I can still remember how, on my way home from the Altes Humanistisches Gymnasium in my native city of Mainz, I would stop at the retail store of B. Schott's Söhne behind the Stadttheater and browse through some of Webern's scores. I was awed by a music that I realized was wholly apart from the mainstream, a music that then was as elusive for me as it was formidable.

Once I had overcome my reluctance to turn from archivist to chronicler, it was only natural that the character of the biography would be determined largely by the wealth of documentary materials from which I was able to draw. The book, in fact, evolved along the lines set by the intrinsic philosophy and structure of the archives. It had always been my policy in collecting to concentrate on preliminary sketches and intermediate drafts, from which the composer's working method and the evolution of a particular opus might be traced. In this respect, Webern's musical estate proved to be especially illuminating: there exists an almost complete record for each project, from the germinal ideas through the formative stages to the finished product. The evidence found in the music manuscripts is supplemented by copious references in Webern's letters. Since he was unusually diligent as a correspondent (his letters to Arnold Schoenberg alone cover several thousand pages), the information drawn from the rich storehouse of his communications forms an essential part of the documentation. Webern's style was so vivid that I have made it a point to weave frequent quotations into the text in order to give the reader a direct insight into the facets of his personality and temperament. Generally, my work was greatly aided by the fact that the composer seems to have been possessed by a profound sense of destiny as to his place in music history. He kept virtually everything: not only that which pertained directly to his music, but also whatever held any personal significance, such as the flowers he gathered on mountain heights or at the gravesites of his parents or the train ticket he purchased for that last fateful journey to Mittersill. The immediacy of all these memorabilia gave me a real sense of closeness to my subject, whom I came to know far more intimately than might have been expected.

As any biographer, I was confronted with the problem of combining the aspects of a narrative with those of a documentary, but my chief difficulty lay in selecting and organizing the abundant source materials at my disposal. This obvious necessity was, in my case, vastly hampered by a handicap to which I will refer at the close of this Introduction. Since it was my policy to let Webern speak for himself throughout the text, there is much of the autobiographical in the book, which was generally conceived as a strict chronicle of the composer's life and work. The chapters given over to Webern's compositions therefore are to be considered as work histories, rather than as theoretical or aesthetic discussions. Here my explicit purpose was to trace the genesis of each creative project and to supplement the account with the composer's own commentaries. Despite these self-imposed limitations, it is hoped that the information provided in the work chapters will prove useful to the scholar and stimulate him to further exploration. The detailed Work List (Appendix 1) may also serve that end.

All German language sources appearing in the text were translated by the authors; existing English translations were compared with their own.* Printed sources are credited in the appropriate places, and the kind cooperation of the respective publishers is gratefully acknowledged. My special thanks go to Alfred Schlee of Universal Edition, Vienna, and to its London affiliate for permission to quote from three basic sources: *die Reihe 2, Anton Webern; Anton Webern, Letters to Hildegard Jone and Josef Humplik*; and *Anton Webern, The Path to the New Music*. I am further indebted to Universal Edition for allowing me to study the voluminous correspondence between Webern and Berg and to quote various passages.

Amalie Waller, who inspired this book and who regarded it as the authorized biography of her father, actively assisted in many details and lent her constant moral support. She did not live to witness the completion of the task. For her comradeship and loyalty to the cause, the work is dedicated to her memory. Of the various members of Webern's family who also collaborated in the project, I am particularly grateful to the late Rosa Warto, the composer's younger sister, to Maria Halbich, his second daughter, to Hermine von Webern Weissenberger,

---

* For all original German quotations, see the German edition of the present book: *Anton von Webern: Chronik seines Lebens und Werkes* (Zürich: Atlantis Verlag, 1979).

his daughter-in-law, and to Doris Brehm Diez, the daughter of Ernst Diez, Webern's favourite cousin.

I am deeply indebted to Gertrud Schoenberg, the widow of Arnold Schoenberg, for giving me exclusive permission to use the still unpublished letters which Webern wrote to her husband, a correspondence that proved especially informative. My sincere thanks also go to Lawrence Schoenberg, who authorized me to draw from his father's published letters and notes. Pia Gilbert, a close friend of the Schoenberg family, was ever-helpful in furthering the project. Helene Berg, Alban Berg's widow, and Hildegard Jone lent invaluable assistance by sharing their reminiscences with me.

Numerous friends, pupils, and associates of Webern communicated their recollections in personal meetings or in letters and memoirs written especially for this book: Anton Anderluh, Cesar Bresgen, Mark Brunswick, Gordon Claycombe, Marcel Dick, Stella Eisner, Arnold Elston, Paul Emerich, Samuel Flor, Elsie Fritzenwanger, Felix Galimir, Rudolph Ganz, Felix Greissle, Karl Amadeus Hartmann, Ruzena Herlinger, Josef Hueber, Hans Humpelstetter, Rudolf Kolisch, Louis Krasner, Ernst Krenek, Rudolph Kurzmann, K. H. Lehrigstein, Roland Leich, Kurt Manschinger, Siegfried Oehlgiesser, Paul A. Pisk, Josef Polnauer, Franz Rederer, Willi Reich, George Robert, Hans Rosbaud, Paul F. Sanders, Julius Schloss, Humphrey Searle, Eric Simon, Georg Skudnigg, Peter Stadlen, Eduard Steuermann, Gunter Waller, Adolph Weiss, Egon Wellesz, Stefan Wolpe, Maria Zenk, and Donna Zincover. I also acknowledge the support of Lisa Jalowetz Aronson, Robert Craft, Marius Flothuis, Wolfgang Fraenkel, Walther von Gelmini, Wallace McKenzie, Edward Reilly, Albi Rosenthal, Nicolas Slonimsky, Leonard Stein, Alan Stout, and Bernice Thomas (the widow of Guido von Webern). To all these collaborators and to others whose names appear within the text, I express my most sincere gratitude. I am equally indebted to various institutions, notably the Library of Congress (William Lichtenwanger, Wayne Shirley, and Edward N. Waters), the Pierpont Morgan Library (Herbert Cahoon and Rigby Turner), the Spokane Public Library (Janet Miller and Marjorie Pitner), the Österreichische Nationalbibliothek (Franz Grasberger), and the Vienna Stadtbibliothek (Ernst Hilmar and Fritz Racek).

Wallace McKenzie, Paul A. Pisk, Zoltan Roman, Albi Rosenthal, and Isabel d'Urbal read the script and made helpful suggestions. Zoltan Roman assisted with the Work List (Appendix 1), translated Webern's analysis of his String Quartet, Op. 28 (Appendix 2), compiled the Bibliography and prepared the Index. Egon Batai made the graphic reproductions. I am deeply grateful to all of them. Finally my profound thanks go to my publishers for their constant support and patience:

William A. Koshland of Alfred A. Knopf, Inc., New York, and Livia
Gollancz of Victor Gollancz Ltd, London.

Throughout the evolution of the biography, my progress was greatly
obstructed by a physical difficulty: I have had to depend, ever since the
mid-1950s, on outside assistance for all reading because of a severe
visual impairment (retinitis pigmentosa). This underlines the all-
important rôle of Rosaleen, my wife and colleague of many years.
The book could never have been written without her full collaboration
in every aspect, from research to proofreading. It was she who constantly
encouraged me by her own patience and endurance, by her faith and
devotion, and by her acceptance of a challenge which, under the
circumstances, seemed a foolhardy undertaking. In the end neither of us
dared to let the other down. Through our joint labours we endeavoured
to carry out what our Swiss friend had urged us to do at the outset:
"Dispel the myth!" It is our hope that we have furnished an accurate
chronicle of Anton von Webern's life and work and, equally important,
that our factual account is pervaded by the deep humanity of the man
and artist.

Hans Moldenhauer
Spokane, Washington
13 August 1976

ANTON VON WEBERN

PROLOGUE

Genealogy

THROUGHOUT HIS LIFE, Anton von Webern treasured an heirloom, a miniature portrait painted in dark-hued oils on an ivory base. The oval picture, in a square ornamented gold frame, shows a young man attired in the fashion of the late eighteenth century. The eyes gaze quietly, yet inquisitively, upon the onlooker. The black hair falls in strands over the high forehead. Long sideburns frame and project the narrow face. Its features are handsome and refined. The total appearance is that of an aristocratic gentleman, an impression heightened by the ornate lace collar and the ranks of gold buttons on the blue coat.

The miniature depicts Josef Eduard von Webern, Anton's great-grandfather, and is the earliest extant likeness of a family ancestor. The portrait always hung above the composer's desk, and he frequently pointed it out to his children as he impressed upon them their noble heritage with all its privileges and obligations.

The baptismal certificate of Josef Eduard von Webern was issued on 20 March 1778 at Salurn (Salorno)[1] in Southern Tyrol. That village by the Etsch (Adige) River, a short distance upstream from Trent, has been a place of historical and cultural significance since antiquity. It lies by the "Salurner Klause," a shadow-filled narrow gap between steeply rising mountain walls that forms the gateway between north and south.[2] Long a frontier of the Bavarian and Austrian domains, the Salurn region underwent a period of intensive settlement by German immigrants. Among them were the forefathers of the Webern family who, bearing the name of "Weber," came from the Egerland, a region of Bohemia, during the fifteenth century. Documents in the Museum Ferdinandeum in Innsbruck confirm that settlers called Weber had been authorized to clear the woods and establish homesteads in the province of Tyrol. The Weber clan first made its home at Altrei in the district of Bozen (Bolzano), then branched out to other communities in the vicinity, including Branzoll, Cavalese, and Salurn.

In 1574, Emperor Maximilian II bestowed nobility upon two Weber brothers, assigning them a coat of arms. Subsequent endorsements of the decree were issued by Emperor Rudolf II (to Christopher Weber in 1598) and by Emperor Matthias. To replace these earlier letters of nobility, which had been lost, Emperor Charles VI issued another decree, dated 15 August 1731, at Vienna. This document still exists.[3] It contains a complete account of the family's noble history. Specifically listing the initial act of Emperor Maximilian II and its subsequent extensions, the 1731 decree elevates two brothers, Johann Jakob and Joseph Antonius Weber, to the rank of "Edle von Webern." According to the citation, the brothers had shown themselves "loyal, industrious, and obedient." Also mentioned are the merits of their late father and his older brothers, who in 1701 had "offered their substance and blood" in the defence of their native Tyrol against the invading Bavarians. The document not only reaffirms the knighthood bestowed on earlier generations, but expressly re-creates noble rank for the two recipients and their descendants.[4]

The decree is prefaced by an exquisitely painted full-page illustration of the coat of arms. Its shield is divided into pairs of red and blue fields. The red fields display a golden lion rampant, a sickle in the left paw and a vine laden with grapes in the right; in the blue fields a white fish is poised as if swimming upstream. Crowning the coat of arms is a helmet, out of which rises the half figure of a man in a richly ornamented surcoat. The man, like the lion, holds a sickle and grapes.

The insignia are symbolic of the occupation of the recipients. Implements of harvesting indicate that the family owned vineyards by the Adige River, the latter being represented by the fish. This particular region of the southern Tyrol has always been famous for its wine production, from which a large part of the population derives its livelihood up to this day. The 1731 decree gives the official status of Johann Jakob as "beyder Rechten Licenciat, Fiscal in denen Gerichtern Bozen und an der Etsch" (licentiate of the civil and ecclesiastical laws, fiscal at the courts of Bolzano and Adige) and of Joseph Antonius as "Wechsel Gerichts Beysitzer zu Laibach in Crain" (associate judge at the claims court in Ljubljana in Carniola). Of the two, it is Johann Jakob who ranks as the first-known ancestor in the composer's direct lineage. He was Anton von Webern's great-great-great-grandfather.

No birth or death records exist for this family patriarch, but his spouse, Maria Clara Margarita, née An der Lan von Hochbrunn, is listed in the parish books of St Josef's Church in Salurn as having died, at the age of 68, on 9 September 1764. She was buried in the village cemetery of St Andrew. The parish records also give the names and baptismal dates of each of the couple's four sons. The eldest, Johann Anton Joseph, was baptized on 8 June 1729. He married Catherine Mayer (called "Mayrin" according to the usage of the time) and they had four children, a daughter (baptized Clara Catherine Crescentia on 25 November 1762) and three sons. In March 1778 two of the sons (Joseph Carl Sebastian and Joseph Anton Urban) died prematurely.[5] During the same month that brought the parents such grief their third son was born. He was baptized on 20 March by the parish priest, Ignaz von Gstirner, who had officiated at the funeral of the two little boys. Standing as godparents were Carl Wilhelm An der Lan von Hochbrunn and Nothburga Lutterotti von Cazzolis und Langenthal. The child was christened Josephus Franciscus Xaverius Georgius, shortened in use to "Josef Eduard." It was he who became Anton von Webern's great-grandfather, and it was his likeness that looked down on the composer from the miniature oil portrait.

Josef Eduard's godparents belonged to the numerous titled families residing in southern Tyrol at the time, a good many of whom lived in or near Salurn. The setting of the small community—in the sun-drenched valley by the rushing stream, among fertile fields and vineyards, sheltered by the southernmost ranges of the Alps—is inviting enough. The village is dominated by Castle Salurn, an ancient fortress perched daringly on a rocky spur that rises in an almost vertical sweep several hundred feet from the valley floor.[6] The assertion made by some writers that Castle Salurn was the original seat of the von Webern family is purely conjectural, however. It is certain that, once it had outlived its usefulness as a military bastion, the fortress became unfit for habitation by the end of the sixteenth century. When Marx Sittich von Wolkenstein wrote his descriptive account of southern Tyrol, a work dating from 1600, he described the fortress as "a handsome little castle and very solid to look at," but he also remarked that "now they let everything go and fall apart, the chapel included."[7] Even today, it is obvious that this audacious stronghold, while offering a challenge to knights and their soldiers, could hardly have provided an abode for women and children. A picturesque and historic landmark, the castle was valued as a symbol of prestige by generations of successive proprietors. Nowhere in the annals of ownership, however, is the name von Webern to be found.

On the other hand, the family name occurs quite frequently in the communal registers of Salurn and its vicinity, variously appearing as "Weber," "von Weber," "Weber von Webern," and "von Webern." Johann von Weber is given as the owner of the "Thurnwirtshaus" (Thurn Inn) in which a fire broke out on 9 March 1785, destroying 35 houses, as well as St Josef's parish church. This Weber was the father of Josef Eduard. His spouse, Catherine, died thirteen days after the

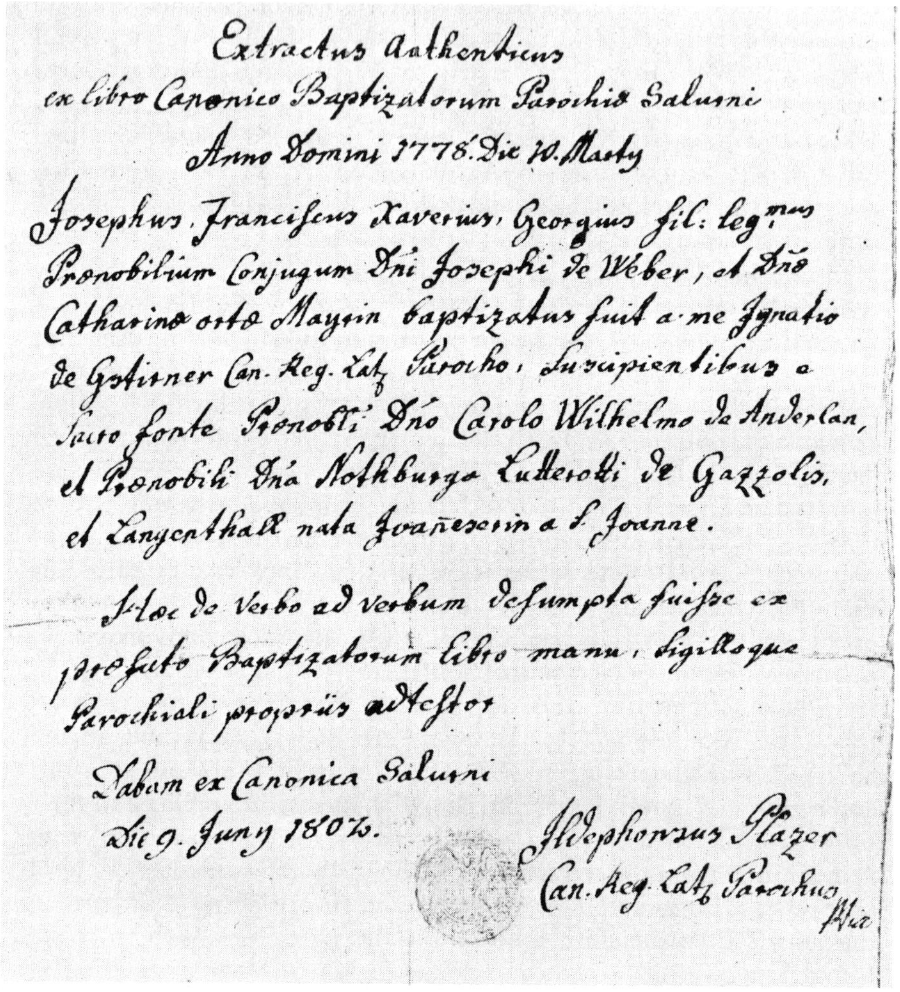
Extractus Authenticus
ex libro Canonico Baptizatorum Parochiae Salurni
Anno Domini 1778. Die 10. Martij
Josephus, Franciscus Xaverius, Georgius fil: leg.mus
Pronobilium Conjugum Dni Josephi de Weber, et Dnae
Catharinae ortae Mayrin baptizatus fuit a me Ignatio
de Gstirner Can. Reg. Lat. Parocho, Suscipientibus e
Sacro fonte Pronobili Dno Carolo Wilhelmo de Anderlan,
et Pronobili Dna Nothburga Lutterotti de Gazzolis,
et Langenthall nata Joanesorin a S. Joanne.

Hoc de verbo ad verbum desumpta fuisse ex
praefato Baptizatorum libro manu, sigilloque
Parochiali propriis attestor

Dabam ex Canonica Salurni
Die 9. Juny 1802.
Ildephonsus Plazer
Can. Reg. Lat. Parochus
Mia

Baptismal certificate of Josef Eduard von Webern

conflagration. She was only 46 years of age, and her early death may well have been connected with the disaster. She was buried by the same priest, Ignaz von Gstirner, who ushered so many of the Webern family both into life and into the hereafter.

By the end of the eighteenth century, branches of the von Webern family had spread far beyond their original dwelling places in southern Tyrol to other provinces of the Habsburg monarchy, with a goodly number living in the Krain as well as in the capital city of Vienna. The *Max von Portheim Nobility Catalogue* in the Vienna Stadtbibliothek, which contains mainly names from the second half of the eighteenth century, lists no fewer than twenty members of the clan, including the two brothers elevated to nobility in 1731.[8]

Not mentioned in that register is Heinrich Carl von Webern, the first of the family known to have reached the shores of the New World. He was a professional soldier in the employ of the Landgrave of Hesse-Cassel, holding the rank of captain in the Third Battalion of the Regiment of Guards. His name appears in an officers' roster of that regiment, published in 1779. When King George III of England hired Hessian troops as mercenaries in his attempt to suppress the rebellious American colonists, Captain von Webern became a member of the expedition, headed by Prince William Henry. He is mentioned in a report from New York dated 26 March 1782, written by Major Baurmeister, then serving as Adjutant General of the Hessian forces in America: "Twice a week Admiral Digby gives a great dinner to which all the officers of the garrison down to the rank of captain are invited in turn, and once a week a concert is given in his quarters, on which occasions Captain von Webern is as well liked as he is indispensable."[9] Unfortunately, no clue is given regarding Heinrich Carl von Webern's particular musical skill.

Many details of the family history related thus far probably were quite unknown to Anton von Webern. However, following Hitler's annexation of Austria in 1938, he was compelled to establish his genealogy. In compliance with the Nuremberg Laws, all citizens had to furnish proof of Aryan descent in order to escape discrimination. It was required to document the direct lineage only back to one's grandparents, but Webern, once involved in the tedious and difficult task, carried it through with characteristic thoroughness. He established a complete family tree, with all its rambling branches, back as far as Josef Eduard von Webern. That handwritten document was supported by a dossier of 45 birth, marriage, and death certificates, of which Josef Eduard's baptismal record of 1778 was the earliest.[10]

Nothing is known about the first 34 years of Josef Eduard's life except that he was left motherless at the age of seven. He next appears on record

in Marburg an der Drau (Maribor on the Drava River) far beyond the
alpine ranges of his native Salurn. A marriage certificate, dated 27
August 1812, gives his first name simply as "Eduard." His father is listed
as "Edler von Webern." The bride was Aloisia, age 24, the daughter of
Franz Mally, "landowner," and his wife Maria Anna née Heinzlin. The
certificate states the groom's occupation as that of "rosoglio manufacturer." (Rosoglio is a fine Italian liqueur, similar to maraschino,
that is prepared from fruits or flowers, most frequently orange
blossoms.)

The newlyweds resided in Marburg for at least five years. The third of
six children (the first of two sons) was born there on 17 May 1817.
Baptized Anton Eduard, he was to become the composer's grandfather.
Judging from the various birthplaces of the next three children, the
family moved rather frequently. By 1819 they lived in Steinamanger, by
1822 in Fürstenfeld, and by 1824 in Pettau (where their second son
Moritz was born that year). Apparently, Josef Eduard von Webern had
given up his Marburg business, becoming instead a tax assessor (the
profession listed on his death certificate). He was only in his 53rd year
when he died on 1 January 1831. Among extant family relics is an
engraving by Josef Eduard, done in 1830, which reveals him as an
accomplished artist.[11]

Josef Eduard's widow, Aloisia, who survived him by almost 39 years,
died on 12 September 1869, at Buchscheiden, where she had gone to live
with her son Moritz, a mining official. She had been a native of Bleiburg,
a market town in Carinthia, situated east of the provincial capital of
Klagenfurt and close to the village of Schwabegg. Nearby lies the
Preglhof estate, which was to become the property, through marriage,
of her older son, Anton.

This Anton is known to have begun his career at the age of 22 in the
mines of Liescha and Prävali.[12] (A citation, issued on 5 January 1879,
gives testimony to the 40 years he spent in faithful service. During that
time, he advanced to the position of general administrator of the
combined enterprises.) When Anton von Webern married at the age of
29, he was an official in the Liescha mine, owned by Rosthorn and
Dittmann. Franz Rosthorn, one of his employers, was a witness at his
wedding, which took place at Liescha on 7 October 1846. The bride,
Maria Gabriele Ulricka Isopp, was born on 5 July 1823, and was the
daughter of Karl Isopp (also spelled "Issopp"), landowner and manager
of estates in the Bleiburg district, and his wife Maria Anna née Writz. The
young couple went to live in House No. 9 at Liescha, and it was there
that all five of their children were born during the thirteen years and
seven months of their marriage. Maria Gabriele was only 37 when she
died at Liescha on 7 April 1860.

Through his wife, Anton von Webern inherited the Preglhof, a large country estate owned for generations by the Isopp family. The property is mentioned by name as far back as the Thirty Years War.[13] Beautifully set amidst the rolling hills of Lower Carinthia, the 500-acre estate (200 hectares) has remained intact to this day. Fertile fields surround the stately manor house, about which cluster an array of buildings, including quarters for the hired hands, barns, and sheds. The farmlands merge into extensive forests that cover the adjoining mountain slopes.

This was the setting in which two generations of Webern families held sway and which also provided a happy youth for a third, including the composer. To be sure, both the elder Anton von Webern and his son, Carl, who inherited the estate, spent only holidays and vacation periods at the Preglhof, since their professions fully absorbed them otherwise. The year-round management was delegated to others, among whom relatives figured prominently. They included Anton's unmarried sisters, Ida and Justine. The latter assumed the upbringing of her brother's five children, left half-orphaned after their mother's early death.

The first-born was a son, who arrived on 27 May 1850, and was baptized Carl Eduard Johann. Another son, Josef Eduard, was born on 5 March 1852. The only daughter, named Maria Luise, arrived on 29 September 1854. She was followed by Franz Moritz, born on 7 July 1856, and Anton Alois, born on 12 March 1859. The father had the satisfaction of seeing all his sons attain respected places in their chosen professions and his daughter provide him with a son-in-law who was a colleague in the mining field. Of all his children Carl had the most outstanding career. Following in his father's footsteps as a mining engineer, he rose steadily on the ladder of success to high positions in the government. As to the other sons, Josef Eduard became a commissioner of forestry, Franz Moritz a court assessor, and Anton Alois a warrant officer in charge of provisions in the Imperial Royal Army.

The elder Anton von Webern could not anticipate that three of his children would in turn become the parents of eminent sons. Carl fathered Anton, the composer to whom this book is devoted. Among the offspring of Josef Eduard was Guido, who was to become a very successful inventor in America.[14] The oldest of the first cousins destined for fame was Ernst Diez, son of Maria Luise von Webern and Friedrich Diez. He achieved renown as an authority on Asian art and contributed to that field of knowledge books of lasting importance.[15] Five years older than Anton, he shared with the composer an abounding love for both music and nature, affinities that made them life-long friends.

The cousins were among the many relatives who flocked to the Preglhof for family gatherings during the closing years of their grandfather Anton's life. The patriarch retired to the estate sometime after the 1879 celebration of his 40 years' service as mining administrator. As a testimonial of their respect and affection, his employees had presented him with a large leather-bound photograph album on which the family crest, artistically executed in metal, was mounted.[16] During the ensuing decade, the album was quickly filled with portraits of various family members, providing a rich pictorial documentary. A group photograph, taken on 17 May 1887, in front of the Preglhof's manor house, included nineteen members of the clan, presided over by grandfather Anton. The three-and-a-half-year-old future composer is seated at his feet.

The elder Anton von Webern died, in his 72nd year, on 15 January 1889, at his beloved Preglhof estate. He was buried in the family plot he had established in the nearby cemetery of Schwabegg, next to the little village church. There a good many members of the Webern clan were also laid to rest, including three of the patriarch's sisters, his brother-in-law, Johann von Tieffenthal (the husband of his sister Karolina), his son Franz, and his daughter-in-law Amalie, the composer's mother. Among the dead from following generations were to be Amalie's first-born son, Carl, and Theo Clementschitsch, one of the composer's nephews, whose early death was to affect him deeply. Many of Anton von Webern's strongest creative impulses were connected with that small churchyard of Schwabegg, which remained for him a place of pilgrimage for many years even after the Preglhof had been sold by his father.

By the time Carl von Webern, as the eldest son, inherited the estate in 1889, he was far along in his career. After graduating from the Klagenfurt Gymnasium, he studied law and political science at the universities of Graz and Vienna, and then, from 1871 on, attended the School of Mining at Leoben, from which he received an engineer's diploma in 1874. While at Leoben he met his future wife, Amalie Geer, born in Vienna on 13 May 1853; she was the elder of two daughters of Anton Geer, a landlord and master-butcher, and his wife, Amalie Elisabeth née Fetzer, in whose home the mining student had rented a furnished room. Carl and Amalie were married at Leoben on 8 October 1877, despite the reluctance of the groom's family to accept that of the bride as equals. Her forebears, both paternal and maternal, formed an assortment of tradespeople, including a grocer, a cheesemaker, a blacksmith, a miller, and a mason. Such differences in social status notwithstanding, the marriage was a happy one, although it was beset by frequent infirmities on Amalie's part. By the time she was 45 she had developed diabetes, and she died of the disease at the age of 52 on 7 September 1906 at the Preglhof.

The year of his marriage brought Carl von Webern the first in a long series of professional promotions, an appointment as Commissioner of

Mining at Olmütz (Olomouc). A year later, in 1878, he participated as First Lieutenant in the occupation of Bosnia and Hercegovina. Upon his discharge from the army in 1881, he was decorated for outstanding service and bravery in combat. Called to Vienna in 1883, he served in the Ministry of Agriculture and was then appointed Chief Commissioner of Mining. A transfer to Graz, in 1890, was combined with a promotion to Councillor of Mining, and a subsequent transfer to Klagenfurt in 1894 with the elevation to Chief Councillor of Mining. Another call to Vienna was to lead him to the summit of his profession: re-entering the Ministry of Agriculture, he became Ministerial Councillor in 1902 and Chief of the Ministry's Department of Mining in 1905. The same position was accorded him in 1908 within the Ministry of Public Works.

By that time, Carl von Webern's health had been undermined by overwork and grief over his wife's death, and he decided to resign. Withdrawing to the Preglhof, he soon recovered. But in 1912 he sold the estate and spent his last years in Klagenfurt, where he pursued his interest in mining to the end. He assisted in the re-opening of mines and in the establishment of new plants in the region, thereby aiding his country's war effort during the 1914–1918 struggle. The collapse of the Austrian empire and the breakdown of the Habsburg monarchy, with the consequent abolition of hereditary titles, were a severe blow to Carl von Webern, who had taken such pride in his noble ancestry. Saddened at seeing his old world crumble, he died in Klagenfurt on 10 August 1919, and was buried in the nearby cemetery of Annabichl.

The many official accolades received throughout his career[17] were summed up in his obituary, published in the *Montanistische Rundschau*, the journal of his profession. Extolling his "devotion, circumspection, most laudable zeal and industry," the article also praised him for his "expert adroitness, always honourable bearing, exemplary faithfulness to duty" and for being "a noble, selfless man, an Old Austrian official of iron industry, above partisan leanings . . . always endeavouring to be useful to his government, his profession, and his beautiful homeland."[18]

CHAPTER I

Youth

(1883–1902)

CARL AND AMALIE von Webern had five children. The first two, who died in infancy, were a daughter, Caroline, who did not live beyond her second year,[1] and a son, Carl, who was born in Vienna on 7 July 1878 and died on 4 April 1882. The boy was buried in the family plot at Schwabegg, in the same grave where his mother was laid to rest years later. The next three children survived: Maria was born at Olmütz on 26 October 1880, Anton in Vienna on 3 December 1883, and Rosa at the Preglhof on 2 August 1885.

The records show that the composer was delivered by a midwife at Löwengasse 53a in Vienna's Third District, then the family's residence. He was christened Anton Friedrich Wilhelm and baptized on 9 December in the Roman Catholic faith. Standing as godfather was his maternal grandfather, the master-butcher Anton Geer.

Owing to the various posts of duty assigned to Anton's father during his career, the family changed residence repeatedly, living in turn at Olmütz, Vienna, Graz, Klagenfurt, and again Vienna. At all times the Preglhof estate provided a cherished retreat for holidays and vacation periods, forming an anchor during the years of the family's frequent moves.

Young Anton's elementary education began in Vienna in 1889. The following year his father was transferred to Graz, and the boy's primary schooling continued there until 1894. Graz, the ancient capital of the province of Styria and the second largest city in Austria, was always rich in tradition and culture. During the years he lived in this picturesque town, the impressionable youth developed strong ties that continued long after the family moved on to Klagenfurt.

The stay at Klagenfurt, lasting from 1894 to 1902, was the most extended one of Anton's formative years. Like Graz, Klagenfurt is beautifully situated. The provincial capital of Carinthia, it lies not far from the eastern end of the famous Wörthersee. The Webern family lived first at Südbahnstrasse 9 (1894–1896), then at Bahnhofstrasse 47 (1896–1898), and finally at Hasnerstrasse 5 (1898–1902), a patrician grey stone house in which they occupied a large apartment on the third floor.

In Klagenfurt, Anton attended the Bundesgymnasium for the full eight years of its humanistic curriculum. The school, founded in 1563, was also his father's alma mater. Academic disciplines included Latin and Greek, and historical and cultural subjects were emphasized. The complete records of Anton's studies, containing his grades and the names of his principal teachers, are preserved. All in all, he was a satisfactory student. Of the academic subjects, he obviously preferred German, Latin, geography, and history. His achievements in Greek were uneven, those in mathematics and physics of barely passing quality. His handwriting, termed "exemplary" during the first school years, later was graded "sufficiently neat," dropping during one term to "untidy." Anton's deportment ranged from "satisfactory" to "appropriate"; his industry varied from "sufficient" to "consistent," with "satisfactory" predominating. To judge from his grades, he seems to have enjoyed gymnastics.

Significantly, young Anton received at all times high marks in singing. The tradition of the Humanistic Gymnasium has always included music as an integral part of education, and during the frequent singing periods much choral literature is covered. This training helped to foster Anton's musical inclination, which had already manifested itself in his early youth when the family still lived in Vienna. Long afterwards, his sister Rosa wrote in her memoirs:

> Our mother was very musical. She played the piano very well and also sang. It was she who awakened Anton's interest in music. When still a little boy, he very often sat next to her as she played the piano; then he would try to play also. It was she, too, who gave the five-year-old his first formal piano lessons. The little boy's Christmas wishes were always for instruments. He first received a drum, then a trumpet, and later, when he was a little taller, a violin. When his mother played the piano, he often begged her for melodies from the opera *Hansel and Gretel*, from *Puppenfee*, and from the opera *Lohengrin*. He would then sing along quite accurately. He also enjoyed dancing with his sisters to the tunes of the *Puppenfee*.[2]

Anton's mother had received a good musical education in her own youth. A large manuscript volume once used by her was preserved by the composer as a treasured relic in his library. The book, entitled

Compositions by Eduard Brunner for Amalie Geer, 1866, contains a collection of piano pieces that the teacher had written out for the then thirteen-year-old girl. Brunner's compositions—a sonata, a fantasy, and numerous genre pieces with flowery titles—attest to the considerable skill which Amalie must already have attained.

The future composer had his first experience in chamber music playing within the family circle. His sister Rosa recalled:

> Our older sister, Maria, also played the piano. After father's transfer to Klagenfurt, Anton continued his studies in piano and also took cello lessons from the music professor, Dr Komauer. I myself played the violin half-way tolerably, and so our family trio came about. It provided us with many happy musical evenings, during which our parents enjoyed listening to us. Mozart and Schubert—and Beethoven too—were on our programmes. As a result of the more advanced instruction that my sister and brother received, they later played more by themselves, either piano duet or piano and cello. Thus there were always very enjoyable musical soirées in our family.

In play, as in music, the trio of Webern children formed a merry team. Their youthful years at Klagenfurt were to provide them many happy memories. Rosa painted this vivid picture: "In winter it was a special pleasure for us to skate on the frozen Lendkanal all the way from Klagenfurt to the edge of the Wörthersee. When we were small children, our parents always sent us ice-skating on Christmas Eve while the Christmas tree was being decorated at home."

The Preglhof estate, lying within easy reach of Klagenfurt, ranks prominently in Rosa's reminiscences: "We stayed there very happily during our summer vacations and also at Eastertime. We spent the whole day in the meadows, fields, and forest. We made excursions into the surrounding countryside, riding in a small wagon which we took turns pulling. My brother had as much fun at this as the other children who often came visiting." A favourite spot for the children was the "Huben," a high meadow reached by a steep dirt road from the manor house. Cattle were put to graze there during summertime, and the children liked to call on the herdsman who lived in a small cottage in the middle of the pasture. The view sweeps down to the Preglhof and the church steeple of Schwabegg beyond, ranging unobstructed across the plains to the mountains which now form the Yugoslav border. This haunt, breathing peace and serenity, was the setting in which many of young Webern's first musical ideas were to be cradled.

Rosa further recounted:

Once every summer a fair was held in Bleiburg, a small town nearby. To our joy, we were always allowed to ride there in our carriage, drawn by two horses. A merry-go-round, puppet show and all sorts of other attractions provided great entertainment for my brother. His supreme joy was being allowed by the coachman to drive the horses himself. In order to save sugar cubes for "his" horses, he was willing to drink his coffee bitter. At hay harvesting time, he worked industriously with the others and rode home in the evening high atop the laden wagon.

The Preglhof was the scene of an incident that Rosa remembered throughout her long life:

My brother and I once bathed in a small pond near our estate. My brother sat on the meadow bordering the pond, and I went alone into the water. Careless enough to venture too far in, I lost my footing and went under. Seeing this, my brother at once bravely jumped in after me. He pulled me out and saved my life. Since he was only nine years old, his action was especially courageous. My parents were of course overjoyed, and he was much praised, admired, and rewarded.

Rosa related another Preglhof incident that occurred some years later:

At the age of seventeen, Anton shared in the experience of a big fire which destroyed the entire summer crop. The estate lay so far away from Bleiburg that the fire brigade arrived much too late. Consequently, everyone who could had to help in extinguishing the flames. My brother assisted very vigorously in this, pouring water from a bucket onto the manor house. The fire excited him so much that for many nights afterwards he got up in his sleep and doused the walls of his room with water from the pitcher.

At the time of this experience Anton had already consciously assumed the rôle of a young musician. Not only did his growing proficiency as pianist and cellist give him various opportunities to perform, but he also began the serious study of musical theory and engaged in his first creative efforts. He was fortunate to find a competent and enthusiastic teacher in Edwin Komauer, a native of Klagenfurt, who was still in his twenties when Webern came to study with him. Komauer had received his initial musical training from his parents and had composed his first sonatina at the age of eight. Despite the boy's apparent talent, however, his father, himself a piano teacher, vetoed a musician's career for him and prescribed instead the study of law at the University of Graz. At the age of 24, Edwin duly emerged as a Doctor of Law and henceforth made his living as an official in the Klagenfurt Finanzlandesdirektion, the main fiscal agency of the province. Music, however, remained his consuming love. Since his daily office duties were over by two o'clock in the afternoon, he found ample time to indulge his predilection and assumed a leading position in Klagenfurt's musical affairs. He became the artistic director of the Richard Wagner Society's Klagenfurt branch, acted as accompanist for noted visiting artists, participated regularly in chamber-music organizations, and acquired a reputation as a conductor and as the town's leading music teacher. He still found time to turn out a good number of his own compositions. They included several stage works (his opera *Frau Holde*, which had its première in 1911, ran for seven performances at Klagenfurt and two at Graz), symphonies, many choral and chamber compositions, songs, and piano pieces.

Komauer had been steeped in strict counterpoint during his early musical training. As a law student in Graz, he had helped prepare the Graz Singverein in performances of Bach's Mass in B minor and other masterworks.[3] He ascribed his preference for polyphony, and for Bach in particular, to that experience and insisted that his own pupils also lay a solid foundation through the study of polyphonic music. Such pedagogic principles were to have a lasting influence upon young Webern.[4] In addition to a thorough appreciation of Johann Sebastian Bach as the supreme master of musical art, he acquired from Komauer a familiarity with what was then considered modern music. Unquestionably, the student's admiration for Richard Strauss and his passion, bordering on idolatry, for Richard Wagner were fired by the teacher's own enthusiasm.

Anton's studies under Komauer were happily complemented by his apprenticeship in orchestral playing. In 1898, the fourteen-year-old student was accepted into the cello section of the local Konzertverein orchestra. There he gained first-hand acquaintance with orchestral literature and the rehearsal routine of a large ensemble. (Many years later he wrote to Paul Königer, the husband of one of his wife's sisters: "Orchestral playing is great pleasure. For years, I played in orchestras myself—for four years in Klagenfurt and afterwards occasionally in Vienna.")[5] To his cousin Ernst Diez, he reported on 8 December 1901: "We now rehearse intensively Handel's oratorio *Samson*, which contains many sublime passages. The orchestra is truly excellent and numbers about 40 members, with the wind instruments very well represented, for instance: three clarinets, four horns, three trumpets, three trombones, one tuba."

A kaleidoscope of Anton's activities is revealed in his youthful letters to that first cousin, the eldest son of his paternal aunt Maria. Four and a half years older, Ernst was Anton's closest friend from early childhood on, though Ernst's two younger brothers were closer to Anton's own age. One of the family anecdotes, as later related by Ernst's daughter, Doris, describes how "Toni" would await his cousin's arrival at the Preglhof during vacation time. Trembling with impatience, the small boy would watch from his window for the carriage bringing the Diez family from the Bleiburg railway station. When it finally came into sight, he would race down the staircase at breakneck speed and, ignoring all others, jubilantly greet his beloved companion. "Ernst was his chosen friend," wrote Doris. "He looked up to him, and there was nothing that he would not do for him. Later, too, when with their growing years the difference in age became irrelevant, it remained that way."[6]

During Anton's last years in Klagenfurt, Ernst was enrolled at the University of Graz, devoting himself to the study of art history. He was a lover of good music, playing the piano very well himself, and this common bond encouraged his younger cousin to keep him abreast of all his activities. A few excerpts from Anton's letters to Ernst reveal the intensity of that early friendship. It gave the budding musician an invaluable opportunity to air his thoughts freely, to test his critical views, and to receive in turn the stimulation of the older cousin's opinions. A letter of 15 November 1900 is characteristic:

Last Sunday we had a Musikverein concert, with a very tastelessly arranged programme: "Elsa's Dream" from *Lohengrin*, Mendelssohn's Violin Concerto and—now comes the idiocy—some songs, and then Beethoven's Ninth Symphony with omission of the final movement for lack of chorus and soloists. The individual numbers are grand, but their juxtaposition is horrible. How can one sing, in so large a hall, songs with piano accompaniment before the Ninth! The latter was well rendered, notwithstanding a few hardly noticeable uneven spots, which had not been done away with because of weak rehearsal attendance. Of course, I played in the orchestra. But the indifference of people is stupendous. They must not have the slightest conception of what it means to perform Beethoven's Ninth. Neither before nor after was there a report in the newspapers, an evaluation of the work. The people simply go there, listen as if a salon polka was being played, and leave again without any sign of excitement. If everyone had felt what I as merely one of the players felt! Often I believed—without exaggeration—that I was about to cry. To be sure, the first movement is really terrifying, these tones of infinite grief, with such a colossal build-up! Then again the moving Adagio.[7] And the Scherzo, so throbbing and then again wildly furious. There the kettledrums beat like crazy—this is a hellish dance that makes one shudder.

Anton went on to speak of the growing demand for his musical talent: "Recently, I was asked to join a string quartet, but I had to decline because of my dancing lessons. I was also asked by Eintracht, the men's choral society, to accompany the singers during rehearsals for Max Bruch's *Frithjof*. This I accepted and I am already looking forward to it." He also gave Ernst an account of his instrumental progress: "I am now practising a piano concerto by Weber and I am still working on Svendsen's magnificent concerto for violoncello. My teacher is very satisfied with me and affirms that I play some places in Svendsen's concerto very beautifully."

A year later, on 8 December 1901, he could report:

On the piano, I am playing Clementi études, Bach, and Beethoven; on the cello Bach's suites for violoncello solo. Dr Komauer apparently is quite satisfied with me. It is sheer bliss to play Bruckner (the Eighth Symphony) with him in a four-hand piano arrangement. . . . You certainly seem to be making great progress on the piano. Grieg, Niels Gade! Heavens, I must hurry so that you will not overtake me. But you should not resent what I have just written, as if I were an overly ambitious person who gets annoyed if another can do better.

Uncertain of his own pianistic future, he exclaimed: "My God, if I could only amount to something! But I just have such small hands, and my memory is weak, too. It is difficult for me to memorize. This causes me much worry and sorrow."

Early that year, on 20 February, Anton had written: "This season's piano lessons are for me, without exception, something sublime. Komauer also is very content with me. On Monday, Madame Fregi will sing here. She has a magnificent programme, *five* Wolf songs, among others. I hope I will be permitted to turn pages for Komauer, who accompanies her, so that I can become personally acquainted with the artist." The same letter mentions Gustav Mahler for the first time:

At long last, I had the opportunity to become familiar with one of Mahler's symphonies, of course in a piano reduction. I liked it very much. Naturally, if one plays Richard Strauss right after, or vice versa, one is bound to notice a great difference. The themes of Strauss are much grander, more ingenious, more powerful. Mahler's music makes an almost childlike impression, despite the quite enormous orchestral apparatus. He uses, for instance, two orchestras—no fewer than *ten* horns, the woodwinds in groups of six and five each. I am mad with curiosity to get to know his Fourth Symphony.

The work on which the eighteen-year-old student commented was the Second Symphony. In a diary entry dated January 1902 he took issue with Mahler's musical language at greater length:

When playing the score through for the first time, I was perplexed by the work; then I gradually became more detached and recognized that, while it has various beautiful aspects, chiefly in the first movement, in general much is affected and bizarre. Nevertheless, the spiteful criticisms, like those now being heaped upon the artist on the occasion of the first performance of his Fourth Symphony, appear very unjustified to me since, quite simply, the composer is not being understood, nor does anyone wish to understand him. The assumption that Mahler is writing parodies and is poking fun with his symphonies, or similar nonsensical statements, seem to me completely ridiculous. For me, he stands as a great and highly gifted conductor and as a serious, deeply introspective composer whom I regard with veneration. I am filled with a burning desire to get to know his further works.

Such discussions with himself show the emergence of young Webern's independent thinking. Aesthetic contemplation and critical judgements abound in his two earliest diaries. In all, eight notebooks are extant, covering some 45 years of the composer's life. The first two diaries were kept concurrently, with one appearing to have been begun as early as 1898, although the first specific date occurs only on 29 October 1900. That entry records Webern's impressions of a chamber-music concert and establishes the form in which he relates numerous similar events later on: first the programme and performers' names are listed, then comments are made on both works and artists. Interspered among these notes is a wealth of other material, including poems and articles that captured the young musician's imagination. Some of the essays Webern so avidly transcribed and absorbed are very extensive: those on Wagner's *Rheingold* and *Siegfried* cover 21 closely written diary pages, that on Strauss' *Don Juan*, copied from the *Grazer Tagespost* (following a performance on 26 January 1900), fourteen pages. There is also a lengthy extract from Felix Weingartner's evaluation of the Second Symphony of Brahms.

Jänner 1902.

Endlich wurde es mir zuteil ein Werk
Gustav Mahlers, wenn auch nur am Klavier
kennen zu lernen, seine II. Symphonie in C moll.
Beim ersten Durchspielen, erblühte mich das
Werk; dann wurde ich allmählich mißtrauisch
und erkannte, daß es zwar manche schön-
heiten besitzt, namentlich im ersten Satze,
daß aber im allgemeinen vieles gesucht und
bizarr ist. Trotzdem schienen mir diese
gehässigen Kritiken, wie sie jetzt anläßlich
der Erstaufführung von Mahlers IV. Symphonie
sich über den Künstler erhoben haben, sehr
unberechtigt, da man ganz sicher den Compo-
nisten nicht versteht oder verstehen will; wollen
sie lächerlich erscheint mir die Annahme, Mahler
schreibe Parodien, und mache sich einen Spaß
mit seinen Symphonien, oder dratige Absichten.
Mir scheint er als ein großer, genialer Dirigent
und ein ernster, tiefinnerlicher Componist vor

Texts of songs that had especially impressed Webern are written out, such as O. J. Bierbaum's "Traum durch die Dämmerung" (the first of the *Drei Lieder*, Op. 29, by Richard Strauss) or Eduard Mörike's "Gesang Weylas" and "Verborgenheit" (two of Hugo Wolf's most famous musical settings). Other poems copied are indicative of the young student's predilections. They deal with the mystic forces interweaving nature and the human soul. There are lyrics by Ferdinand Avenarius, the poet who inspired Webern's own first song, and by Hermann Ubell. Two additional poems by Mörike are "Auf das Grab von Schillers Mutter" and "Neue Liebe." Webern's first encounter with Stefan George falls into this early period; he quotes extensively from the poem "Indes deine Mutter dich stillt."

The diaries also contain excerpts from the writings of various philosophers and novelists. Webern obviously identified himself with these sentiments, and the passages he copied attest to his leaning towards serious meditation, his longing for intellectual penetration and articulation. His mind was captivated by the pronouncements of Nietzsche, whose thoughts on "Sternen-Freundschaft" in *Fröhliche Wissenschaft* form the opening entry in one of the diaries. The quotation was to prove, in some ways, strangely prophetic of the great friendship of Webern's future life, that with Arnold Schoenberg. Other literary excerpts range from E. v. Wolzogen's *Das dritte Geschlecht* and F. v. Hausegger's *Das Jenseits des Künstlers* to O. J. Bierbaum's novel *Pankraz- ius Graunzer*. Some quotations are of a curiously pessimistic nature, such as a line from the poet Gustav Falke: "Happiness consists in longing; fulfilment is death." One month after his seventeenth birthday, Webern jotted down an Indian prayer: "O Fate, if you will consent to be merciful, do not assign to me human birth once again! But if it must be, then do not afflict me with love, and if that yet must be, then do not instil me with love for someone whom I can never attain." A long quotation from Karl Hauptmann's *Tagebuch* is typical of the erotic impressionism marking the literary fancy of the times. The allusions of such writings quite naturally attracted the adolescent, and two of his own poetic attempts during that period are likewise strongly sensual. This phase passed quickly, however, and Webern's tastes turned fully towards the realms of emotional and spiritual sublimation.

Webern's handwriting in these notebooks developed rapidly from a carefully executed calligraphy in the earlier pages to a penmanship which, by the time he reached seventeen, shed the last traces of infantility and assumed the definitive characteristics of his mature style. Webern preferred the Gothic script; by comparison, his occasional use of Latin script appears stilted and even laboured. The chief features of his mature penmanship are neatness and clarity, conveying an impression of great orderliness and meticulous attention to form.

It is apparent from the diaries that the young artist's literary and musical preferences were for the "moderns" of his own time. All the writers and composers he cited in the diaries are either his contemporaries or of the immediately preceding generation. Some of the poets quoted were not to achieve a status of the first rank, but their style and sentiments were completely typical of the *fin de siècle* and thus bound to affect the sensitive student. Perhaps the severe academic discipline of the Gymnasium, centring on ancient and time-proven classics, provoked, by way of reaction, Webern's preference for contemporary poets and composers. Among the latter, it must be remembered, Richard Wagner was still a controversial figure, and Hugo Wolf, then living out his years in an insane asylum, was barely known. It is noteworthy that, out of the large quantity of music literature recorded in the diary reviews, Webern was always most deeply impressed by compositions that have since emerged as classic masterpieces, even though they were novelties at the time. His judgement proved equally unfailing in his assessment of composers who have since become obscure, such as Lange-Müller, Bungert, Hermann, and Sommer, whom he either ignored or denounced for their inferiority. For example, he called Heinrich Hofmann's *Nornengesang* for solo, chorus, and large orchestra, which formed the centrepiece of a Musikverein concert on 10 March 1901, "very feeble and without effect," while he exulted over the "Funeral March" from Wagner's *Götterdämmerung* as music "of unspeakable beauty," and also declared great liking, although not entirely without reservation, for Joachim Raff's symphony *Im Walde*, both included on the same programme.

The vigour of the musical life then prevailing in the small provincial town of Klagenfurt can be seen in the offerings of a single season (1900–1901), enumerated here as they appear in young Webern's diary. Some of his comments are included. They demonstrate his growing musical acumen, no doubt fostered by the emphasis on critical thinking that forms one of the main tenets of humanistic education in the European Gymnasium. In his intellectual approach to music, Webern manifested, at the age of seventeen, a fully professional attitude.

A chamber music programme, heard on 29 October 1900, offered a fare of Beethoven, Spohr, and Brahms; the latter's Piano Quartet in G minor, Op. 25, was termed "a wholly powerful tone poem," whereas the performance of Beethoven's String Quartet in F major, Op. 18, No. 1, was felt to be "wanting in some respects." The Musikverein concert on 11 November, in which Webern himself participated, has been described already in his vivid letter to Diez. On the 29th of the same

month, he heard the American mezzo-soprano Edyth Walker and
singled out as his favourites: Brahms' "In Waldeinsamkeit," Schubert's
"Die Allmacht," and foremost the "wonderfully deep-felt" "Zur Ruh',
zur Ruh'" by Wolf, while ignoring various offerings from the works of
Massenet, Franz, and Rubinstein. A joint recital given by the violinist
Franz Ondříček and the pianist Wilhelm Klasen on 11 December
enraptured him; Bach's Air and Liszt's Ballade in B minor elicited his
special praise. On 16 December the local Musikverein performed
Mendelssohn's oratorio *Lobgesang*, which Webern termed "a rather
insignificant but pleasing work." On 15 January 1901 he recorded a
"failure of an evening" during which Dvořák's String Quartet, Op. 106,
and Beethoven's Septet were played, along with vocal offerings by a lady
to whom the young critic granted "some full tones in the middle range
but nothing otherwise." By contrast, the 25 January recital of Johannes
Messchaert, with Brahms' friend Julius Röntgen at the piano, was "an
exquisite artistic pleasure." Hugo Wolf's "Gesang Weylas" was
declared "especially beautiful, noticeably moving the audience." On 11
February he praised Lillian Sanderson for her vocal technique and
masterly interpretation, and on 1 March another song recital, presented
by Lula Gmeiner, equally delighted her young listener. Wolf's
"Verborgenheit" touched him deeply, and he was impressed by the
simplicity of Strauss' "Du meines Herzens Krönelein." There followed
the Musikverein concert of 10 March mentioned earlier.

At the end of this season, during Easter week, the young devotee
experienced his first actual encounter with a Wagnerian music drama.
His diary noted that, on 2 April, he took the train to Graz, leaving
Klagenfurt "at 2ʰ 18'." This entry first displays the curious attention to
railway timetables that persisted throughout Webern's life. Never
failing to give the departure and arrival time to the minute, such records
reflect his high sense of order and exactitude.

It is easy to imagine the eager anticipation with which he rode the
train that day. For years he had steeped himself in the art of the revered
master. The Graz performance of *Tristan und Isolde*, conducted by
Weissleder and featuring the famous Hermann Winkelmann in the title
rôle, aroused the young disciple's boundless enthusiasm. "The
impression that I experienced was an overwhelming one," he wrote in
his diary. "If I am to enumerate what made the greatest effect upon me,
it was the scene in which they drink the love potion, then the love duet,
Tristan's question whether Isolde will follow him into the 'dark-nighted
land' and Isolde's answer, and finally the entire third act with its
gripping climaxes. Winkelmann's Tristan is unique; his interpretation,
especially during the last act, is magnificent." After speaking of the other
singers and the orchestra, not without some critical reservations, he

concluded: "Sitting in the first row of the parquet, I could enjoy everything wonderfully, having thoroughly studied the score beforehand, and thus I had an indescribable and unforgettable experience."

Although Anton was by now quite conscious of his calling as a musician, his ideas about the practical aspects of that profession were still nebulous. In his uncertainty, he opened his heart to his ever sympathetic cousin and friend Ernst Diez, writing on 22 July 1901, not long after that *Tristan* experience:

Now I come with a request. You know how doubtful I am concerning my future profession and how undecided I am where to turn. Perhaps you can find out how the so-called College of Music in Berlin or the Royal Academy of Music in Munich operates. What one learns there, who attends, etc. The purely theoretical, scientific study of music history naturally interests me very much, but my ideal is really practical activity—specifically as a conductor. Probably one just has to enrol in a conservatory and study an instrument—the cello, in my case—until one achieves mastery or at least a high level of proficiency, then one joins an orchestra and, if he succeeds, automatically becomes a conductor. So I imagine it to be. Nikisch, for example, made his career that way. Naturally I would like to embark immediately on such a course, but my father raises doubts about my talent, making me doubtful myself. Of course, in speaking of orchestras I mean only large ones, either concert or opera orchestras, in Dresden, Munich, Leipzig, Berlin, and other big cities in Germany. To be sure, I could not then devote myself to the affairs of the Preglhof. I have no idea what to do with the estate—lease it, sell it? It is father's wish that I study at the College of Agriculture and then settle down at the Preglhof. Oh, my God! And what about Art, which means everything to me, for which I would be ready to sacrifice myself! What I imagine to be so beautiful is just this: namely, that I will not occupy the most brilliant position at first but will live exclusively for art, and not *from* art only to earn money. What plans I so often make, such beautiful ones—but perhaps I suffer, too, from megalomania! I do· not comprehend my own self.

Conspicuously absent from Webern's discussion of a career in music is any mention of composition, though he had tried himself in creative endeavours from the age of fifteen. The decision as to his future profession was postponed for another year, during which he had to complete his Gymnasium education. That final year in Klagenfurt brought increased academic rigours at school, but Anton's preoccupation with music continued. Despite his artistic leanings and aspirations, however, there was nothing of the precious or effeminate in this young son of the Muse. He enjoyed life to the fullest in all its aspects, joining in the social activities of his fellow students and displaying a hearty appetite for fun, with an attendant interest in the opposite sex. Ernst Diez is made the confidant of some of his exploits. On 15 November 1900, a few weeks before his seventeenth birthday, Anton wrote:

Sad times, very sad ones indeed! At half-past two o'clock I was caught by some of my professors in the coffee house where I had gone after the dancing lesson. Consequences: four hours of incarceration[8] and—now comes something terribly sad—I am not allowed to continue my dancing lessons. My friend Supersperg is my fellow sufferer. My mood is horrible. You may not believe that I am so addicted to dancing, but—there is Stanzi [Constanza]! I am quite crazy about her. She is an enticing girl, full of temperament. Now I will probably see very little of her. The thought drives me mad! Only yesterday I danced with her so gaily, had such a marvellous time with her. She is also rather well disposed towards me—right now this can be stated as a matter of fact. And just when I have made such a splendid start, everything is to be over. Damn that coffee house! In my last dancing lesson I also had the pleasure of dancing with Frieda Hibler. My God! How dashing she is, if she only were a little prettier. But she is racy and dances with utter abandon, in short: elegant!

Intimating at some length that Frieda has voiced interest in Ernst, Anton urged his cousin: "If you do not find Frieda too 'schiach' [homely], I definitely advise you to take her, but you must leave Stanzi for me. However, enough of women! As it stands now, everything has come to an end anyway. . . . Cordial greetings from your deeply saddened and unhappy cousin Toni."

Apparently Ernst's greater age and wisdom did not prevent him from following his young cousin's suggestion, but whatever romance ensued, it was over by 20 February 1902 when, writing at Frieda's request, Anton asked that all her letters and her photograph be destroyed or returned to her. Now mid-way through his final Gymnasium year, he added a report on his social life: "I have spent this year's 'Fasching' [carnival] very merrily. I was at three parties where I had a very good time and danced the whole night through. I am now very enthusiastic about waltzing. It is simply wonderful to turn round and round to the tune of the 'Fledermaus' waltz. Now I shall be very good and serious-minded again. I just *must* be——"

Aside from such frolics, the correspondence between Anton and Ernst records a constant exchange of their ideas in the cultural sphere, each being as interested in the other's news as in giving his own account. The letters happily supplement young Webern's diaries, which, for that matter, contain only a few entries of strictly private nature. One of these concerns the wedding of his older sister Maria and Paul Clementschitsch[9] on 19 January 1901. The detailed diary account of the nuptial festivities culminates in Anton's admission that he indulged in too much champagne. "Consequence: intoxication," he placed on record.

Early in 1902 Webern's father was called to the Ministry of Agriculture in Vienna. In order to establish the new household, the entire family spent the Easter holiday in the capital city. The stay provided Anton with two great musical experiences. The first of these was a performance of *Götterdämmerung* on Palm Sunday. In his extensive diary account, the young musician congratulated himself on being able to hear the work performed with a stellar cast. It included Erik Schmedes (Siegfried), Anna von Mildenburg (Brünhilde), and Edyth Walker (Waltraute). Franz Schalk conducted. His orchestral crescendos and decrescendos were described as "simply marvellous achievements." Burning with enthusiasm, Webern declared *Götterdämmerung* his favourite of the Ring cycle. He was enraptured by the purely orchestral portions of the music drama, such as the first sunrise after the Nornen scene, Siegfried's Rhine journey, and the "Funeral March." The final scene, "something so immense and super-human," overwhelmed him. He professed that he trembled from emotion even when he played the music on the piano, and that he considered himself totally unworthy to play it at all.

Coinciding with this boundless veneration of Wagner was a growing admiration for another master. During the same week, young Webern attended a performance of Franz Liszt's oratorio *Christus* by the Singverein under Ferdinand Löwe.

The work is sublimely beautiful [he wrote into his diary]. Now I am even more enthusiastic about Liszt. I consider it an ideal task to bring the music of this great master to the widest public and to secure for him the general recognition which, curiously enough, has not yet been accorded him. The blood rises to my head if I hear it said that Liszt did not possess any power of invention, but that he only understood how to orchestrate skilfully. The devil! One should take, as an example, the march of the holy three kings from this oratorio. My God, what supremely glorious melody blossoms forth here. Or consider the altogether incomparable "Beatitudes." With a genius wholly beyond compare, Liszt has woven into his oratorio elements of the old church music. The entire work is pervaded by the glow of the most exalted Christian fervour, leaving a tremendous impression.

The Easter trip also brought an experience of quite another sort, one that planted the seed of a decisive influence in Webern's life: he looked for the first time with the eyes of a young man at his cousin, Wilhelmine, who resided in Vienna. Her mother, Maria (the sister of Anton's mother), was married to the notary Gustav Mörtl. They had five children (two sons and three daughters), the third of whom was Wilhelmine. Born at Raabs in Lower Austria on 2 July 1886, she was two and a half years younger than Anton and almost sixteen at the time when the cousins encountered each other again in Vienna. Their meeting kindled a deep attachment, destined to blossom into love and marriage in years to come. A wistful diary entry a few weeks later, penned at the Preglhof during the Pentecost vacation, reads: "The trees may be in bloom, but there is not much feeling of spring. It rains constantly—and yet I was so full of joyful anticipation. Everything here excites in me a sweet melancholy, an indescribably sweet nostalgia. Such dear, beloved images arise before my soul, and I feel always as if a lovely, cherished countenance were greeting me from far, far away—— "

When the Webern family moved to Vienna that May, Anton stayed back in Klagenfurt as a boarder to finish his last months at the Gymnasium. His time was fully given over to intensive preparation for the final examinations. Only those acquainted with the unrelenting strictness and gruelling academic standards of such institutions can appreciate the apprehension of the candidate. The fear of not passing was increased by the knowledge that social disgrace would befall the entire family in the event of failure. Many a hapless pupil was led to desperate acts of escape or even suicide (Alban Berg attempted to end his life when he failed his comprehensive examinations the first time). In this light, one can grasp something of the exuberance radiating from Anton's diary record, which is accorded a full page in celebration of the momentous event. Suddenly freed from the confines of the cloisterly Gymnasium, he and the other graduates, who were issued a "Certificate of Maturity to attend the University," now could anticipate an exciting student's life in that promised land of liberty. The jubilant diary entry read:

> On the 11th of July 1902 in the forenoon
> successfully passed *Matura*.
> HURRAH!
> Freedom at last!
> Vivat Life and the Future!

CHAPTER II

University years I
(1902–1904)

THERE WAS AN immediate reward in store for young Webern when he reached his first important academic goal, even though his achievements during the final Gymnasium year had been none too brilliant.[1] His father, despite his own wishes for Anton's future, had always been tolerant of the boy's artistic inclinations, and he now fulfilled Anton's most ardent wish: a visit to Bayreuth, the shrine of worship for all Wagnerites.

Apparently the trip had been anticipated for some time. As early as 1901 Webern had devoted three full pages in his diary to that year's schedule of Bayreuth Festival offerings, replete with names of performers and conductors. The annotations for the coming pilgrimage were even more detailed, down to train schedules and fares. "My First Bayreuth Journey" is the title of Anton's extensive diary account. It is prefaced by a musical motto, a quotation of the "Liebesmahlspruch" from *Parsifal*. The trip, beginning on 29 July 1902, was made in the company of Ernst Diez. Webern confided to his diary that excitement had kept him awake all the previous night. The beautiful landscape of the Salzkammergut, which he saw for the first time from the train window, intrigued him. At Passau the travellers reached German soil, and Webern, used to the quiet Klagenfurt, exclaimed: "O glorious Bavaria! Here there is still life! The splendid beer, the inexpensive meals, the conviviality of the people, the enormous traffic, all this makes this country enchanting to me!"

As the tedious train ride neared its end, Webern could hardly contain his impatience: "The longer the journey became, the faster my heart beat. At last—at last—Bayreuth!" By afternoon of the same day, 31 July, the cousins were ascending the hill to the festival hall. Webern was at once impressed by the multitude of visitors coming from all corners of the world to take part in the Wagner cult. Soon summoned to his seat by

Meine erste

Bayreuther Reise.

August 1902.

Nach schlaflos verbrachter Nacht fuhr ich Dienstag den 29. Juli 1902. vom Haghof am Schlatterhof um mit Robert zusammen zu kommen. Von hier bayrisch. Glandorf fuhren wir um Mitternacht weg nach Selzthal, von hier durch herrliche Salzkammer gut bis Altnang. das Salzkammergut ist reizend. Herrlich liegt der Hallstädter See, mit dem gleichnamigen Ort dessen weiße Giebelhäuser mit den grünen Fensterläden einen ungemein lieblichen Anblick bieten. Auch der Traunsee mit dem ... bei ... den ... köstlichen Reiz. --- Von Altnang ginng die Fahrt weiter über Ried, Schärding nach Passau. In Passau betraten wir bayrischen Boden. O herrliches Bayern! das gibt es nur Einen!

Diary account of pilgrimage to Bayreuth (August 1902)

the fanfare (the "Liebesmahl" motive from *Parsifal*, the work given that day), he was transported into ecstasy by the performance: "To find words for such impressions is an impossibility! In the face of such magnificence, one can only sink to one's knees and pray in silent devotion."

Webern's account of the experience is eloquent and graphic. Karl Muck conducted; Erik Schmedes (Parsifal) and Theodor Reichmann (Amfortas) sang the music drama's chief rôles. Equally enthusiastic is Webern's report of the following day's performance of *The Flying Dutchman*, attended by the friends after they had paid a reverent visit to Villa Wahnfried and Wagner's grave at noon. In that performance, Theodor Bertram sang the title rôle, and Emmy Destinn and Ernestine Schumann-Heink carried the female leads. His eyes as wide open to the stage effects as his ears to the music, Anton vividly portrayed one of the scenes: "The end of the first act is ingenious. Gaily the south wind swells the white sails of the Norwegian ship. As its crew rejoices it heads for the open sea. A wonderfully blue sky arches above the scene."

The two festival performances lifted young Webern's idolatry of Richard Wagner to its zenith. The diary account is climaxed by an impassioned outburst:

I saw clearly that Bayreuth has already become a fad. What appears to me almost impossible is that the ladies, in their ostentatious finery, with their eternally smiling faces, or these gentlemen in patent leather shoes, displaying the most expensive ties, could have even the slightest notion of where they really are or of what constitutes Bayreuth's enormous significance. This audience is as ill-mannered as that in a provincial town. It is revolting to see that people cannot keep quiet in the festival hall even after the music has begun, or while it still plays after the curtain has closed. Hardly has the crowd left the temple when laughing and idle chatter start again, when each one inspects the other's wardrobe and behaves as if he had not experienced at all something that transports our kind out of this world. And then! There was, on top of it, applause! If people start to applaud after the end of *Parsifal* it cannot be anything but a display of the greatest rudeness. Do they wish to prove, perhaps, that they have most graciously taken pleasure in the performance? This is really ridiculous to a gigantic extent. But, away with these thoughts!

The following day, 2 August, was spent at Munich, where the cousins indulged in visits to three art museums; at the Neue Pinakothek, a Segantini landscape made a special impression on Webern. That evening, at the Prinzregententheater, they saw Schnitzler's *Liebelei*, which elicited the diary comment: "A play that grates on the nerves." Riding the train through that night and all of the following day, Anton reached the Preglhof by evening. He admitted that he was "completely exhausted" but concluded: "Thus I have attained what seemed to me so unattainable! Now again the banal workaday. But this is a certainty: I will think of this all my life, my first Bayreuth pilgrimage."

After that stimulating experience, the summertime routine at the isolated Preglhof indeed seemed drab and banal. However, by the time the harvest was in, an important decision had been reached: Webern's father agreed that he could pursue a career in music. Doris Brehm-Diez related in her memoirs:

This was by no means a foregone conclusion. His father and the entire family naturally wanted the only male heir to study at the College of Agriculture so that he could take charge of the Preglhof's adminis-tration. But Toni was firmly resolved to live only for art. His determin-ation led his father to call in for advice a number of "musically knowledgeable" acquaintances who subjected the eighteen-year-old to an examination of sorts. In particular, he had to play for them something he had composed. He later confided to his friend Ernst that he had used in that "composition" some melodies pleasing to the ear in order to be quite sure that it would appeal to the gentle-men. At any rate, he passed the test and was given permission for a musical career, with the condition that he would study music history at Vienna University.

At summer's end the Webern family returned to Vienna. Their apartment was located on the third floor of the house at Ferstelgasse 6, close to the Votivkirche and a mere five-minute walk to the university. The latter's Musicological Institute was headed by Guido Adler, a noted scholar, under whose guidance musicology had developed into a respected academic discipline. The complete course of studies in which young Webern matriculated is on record. Most of his instruction was supervised by Dr Adler himself. Subjects taken included general courses such as "Style Periods in Music" and specialized topics like "Richard Wagner." Correlated with the strictly musical studies was a broad variety of lecture courses in philosophy and literature, with notable emphasis on the key figures of German thought. The range of the instruction is exemplified by such topics as "Kant, Herder, Schiller, Schopenhauer, Nietzsche and Music" and "Albrecht Dürer and his Time," while individual courses were devoted to Goethe, Schiller and Grillparzer. Webern's course in "Analysis and Evaluation of Art Works" continued through three of the four years.

Assisting the institute's chairman in the students' intensive technical training were two distinguished composers: Hermann Graedener, who had been appointed to the university in 1899 as lecturer on music theory, and Dr Karl Navrátil, the Czech composer of operas and symphonic works, who had himself studied under Adler and Franz Ondříček. After the rather rudimentary initiation into the secrets of musical craft provided by Edwin Komauer, Webern now engaged in systematic studies of harmony under Graedener and of counterpoint under Navrátil. At first he was bewildered by the multitude of tasks confronting him. Of the three courses that he took under Adler he found one seminar particularly demanding. In an extensive report to Ernst Diez on 5 November 1902, soon after the beginning of the autumn term, he described that class:

> In the institute are mostly older people, two with doctorates, and otherwise upper division students. There are only three young ones. The older ones give reports about theoreticians from the thirteenth, fourteenth and fifteenth centuries. They are assigned the translation of passages from their works, which they then have to explain. We young ones keep up as well as we can. My task is, for the time being, to cram into my skull as quickly as possible mensural notation and one of Riemann's works about this old music. A horribly dry and troublesome chore, for you just have no idea how many rules there are.

The pressure of academic duties seemed at first all the greater because young Webern, after the intimacy of life in Klagenfurt, suddenly found himself exposed to a cosmopolitan mixture of strangers. "The members of the institute include seven Jews, a Jewess, four Poles and four Germans," he wrote to Diez in that informative letter, confessing: "When I went to the institute for the first time I shuddered at the many difficulties. I would have liked best to quit right then, the Jews were all so unfriendly, etc. By now, I have already grown used to it."

One must read such remarks in the context both of attitudes prevailing at the time and of Webern's own previous experience, which had included almost no social contact with Jews. After the first few months in Vienna, such references disappear from Webern's letters and diaries, and Jewish fellow students like Heinrich Jalowetz and Karl Horwitz soon became his good friends.

Webern resumed private lessons on the cello and piano when he entered the university. His instructors were Josef Haša,[2] second solo cellist of the Konzertverein orchestra, "a young, very nice musician," as he told Diez in his letter of 5 November, and a young American woman, herself a Leschetizky pupil and an excellent pianist (whose name was not mentioned). She assisted the Webern family in the selection of a Dörr grand piano, which Anton described to his cousin as "a very carefully built piano, with English action I believe, and with a very pleasing tone." On 14 November, he reported to Diez about his piano studies: "For the second time, I have to change technique completely. Wrist low, hand hollow, knuckles poised outward, and the movements of the hand during arpeggios, etc., as natural as possible—a very sensible method, that of Leschetizky. But till one gets used to all this again! My teacher is a very dear, not exactly pretty, yet charming young woman who takes great pains with me. She is studying for a career as a dramatic singer."

Webern spent most of the day in the Musicological Institute, where he had a good library and a "magnificent Bösendorfer" grand piano at his disposal. Formal studies were supplemented by the concert and opera life of the metropolis, resulting in a most conducive blend of academic training and artistic experiences. Young Webern flung himself enthusiastically into the myriad of offerings, conscientiously recording each event in his diary. But after only a few weeks, he vented his exasperation:

Now the tidal wave of the concert season roars with terrible force. Too much, too much! Every day there are at least three concerts—violin virtuosi, piano virtuosi, male singers, female singers, orchestral concerts, etc. Mostly miserable programmes! Only now and then a newspaper review—every concert overcrowded with people who applaud after each number, not caring whether it was good or bad. Probably, nay certainly, the people can no longer perceive any difference. Their capacity to absorb, their ability to enjoy is lessened more and more by the over-abundance of what they hear, and their taste is continually corrupted by the miserable programmes and the witchcraft of the virtuosi. There is no rigorous, castigating criticism, either. What if this continues?

Webern blamed the city's musical leadership for the situation and pleaded for fewer offerings:

This could be put into effect by the concert direction. Such a concert manager should be an artistically well-bred man. Should a virtuoso come along with a horrible programme that is bare of any style, then out with him! What is one to say when a singer like Theodor Bertram includes in his programme, between Schumann and Schubert, songs by Bohm—no, these are not songs, but languishing shreds of nauseating sentimentality. Is there no criticism that rises angrily against such a crime?

Webern's attitude is so severe only when his discriminating senses are badly offended. He is quick to burst into rapturous approval when convinced by the music or performance: "A bright point in the darkness of our concert life recently was the concert under Siegfried Wagner. With how much warmth and love he conducted Beethoven's Seventh and Liszt's grandiose *Mazeppa*. It was the first time that I heard Beethoven's Seventh. What gaiety and charm! How happy and content Beethoven must have felt in his heart! This is a symphony from the realm of joy." In rapid succession Webern heard several other Beethoven symphonies, but none impressed him more than the Ninth: "O, divine Beethoven! It was the most sacred hour of my life up till now," he exulted in his diary on 25 January 1903, and on 18 February he wrote to Diez: "Even Bayreuth has not made such an effect on me as the last movement." In the same letter he extolled Bruckner's Ninth Symphony, the world première of which he had just attended:

The work is dedicated "dem lieben Gott." With the Adagio, Bruckner bade farewell to the world—and really, if you listen quite attentively, you imagine at the Adagio's end, which is wonderfully gentle and transfigured, seeing the dear man ascend to heaven, ever farther and higher, until the heavenly abode opens itself to him with the last, softest, long, long held E-major chord of the tubas (five!) and horns. There can hardly be anything more beautiful than this Adagio.

The first performance of Bruckner's Ninth was coupled with one of his *Te Deum*, in which several Vienna choruses, including the Academic Richard Wagner Society, participated. Webern had already been initiated into that group on 30 October 1902, at the beginning of the season. He was heartened by the friendly reception given him and thrilled by the presence of Siegfried Wagner when he first attended. Founded largely through the efforts of Guido Adler during his own student years, the Society's Vienna section was to afford young Webern many inspiring opportunities. The gatherings consisted of choral rehearsals, in which he soon joined, as well as a variety of musical programmes.

In that first season, Webern grew familiar with symphonic and chamber-music literature largely unknown to him before. On 5 January 1903, he attended a concert under Felix Weingartner with Berlioz' *Symphonie fantastique* and Liszt's *Dante* Symphony on the programme. "Both works are colossal," went his enthusiastic report of 18 February to Diez. "Liszt is probably one of the greatest; for me, the line from Beethoven goes on to Liszt and Bruckner. To be sure, Wagner, as dramatist, stands entirely apart."

Webern's addiction to Wagner was fully gratified that season. He attended performances of the entire *Ring* cycle, as well as of *Tannhäuser*, *Flying Dutchman*, *Tristan und Isolde* and *Meistersinger*. The latter work he saw five times within the first four months. After his first encounter, on 28 September 1902, he was so moved that he penned a long essay in his diary, opening with a musical quotation of the chorus "Wach' auf! Es nahet gen den Tag!" in the last act. "This tears one away from this earth. One would like to sing out loud with them. . . . O God, words fail me," he wrote, and in his 5 November 1902 letter to Diez he exclaimed: "Ernst, this *Meistersinger* is beautiful enough to drive one mad!"

After the glorious Bayreuth experience, however, the Vienna performances were a let-down. Webern was intolerant of any other standards. "I find the opera here simply abominable. I just did not expect such a difference," he told Diez in that same November letter, denouncing "the nauseous, pompous theatre, the visible orchestra, etc. Then the shameful performances! I always thought, God knows, I would experience such glories here. Now, such disappointments." Already on 14 September, after *Götterdämmerung*, he had noted in his diary: "The phrase 'One hears it in the Vienna Opera just as beautifully as in Bayreuth' is sheer nonsense," and a performance of the *Flying Dutchman* the following week (20 September) aroused his special indignation: "Was that supposed to have been the *Dutchman*?!!! O dear heaven! Is there no critic in Vienna who takes issue with something like this?"

Other experiences quickly appeased the young fire-brand. Of a triple bill on 4 October, two works delighted him: Mozart's *Zaide* ("Genuine Mozart, lovely and tender, so clear and simple, like a bright summer day. Such music makes one feel so good that one wishes for nothing else") and Bizet's *Djamileh* ("Music saturated with oriental ardour, full of ingenious rhythm, enchantingly orchestrated. Gustav Mahler conducted. I saw the man for the first time. An artist! Long black hair, closely shaven face, eye glasses. How he leads the orchestra! He extracts everything from the score"). Only the evening's closing ballet, *Harlekin as Electrician* by Joseph Hellmesberger, failed to please ("An idiocy of the first rank. Boring. The music is hardly attractive. Why did that 'Schmarren' [ordinary cheap stuff] have to be added?"). Then Webern heard operas by Gluck and Weber which completely intrigued him. In his diary, he described Gluck's *Orpheus and Eurydice*: "This is grandiose music of unapproachable greatness. I place the work side by side with the most sublime creations of Wagner and Beethoven." In his 5 November 1902 letter, he raved to Diez about Edyth Walker, who sang Orpheus: "I do not believe that there exists in the whole world a woman who possesses a more beautiful voice." He was equally entranced by

Berta Foerstrová-Lauterová in the title rôle of Weber's *Euryanthe*, an opera hailed as "gorgeously beautiful" and as heralding Wagner's ideas: "We already find in *Euryanthe* the motivic treatment of certain especially striking and expressive tone sequences, which are most intimately connected with the various characters. The music is purely dramatic, but rich in lyric beauty." At the same time the young critic lamented that the "cursed libretto" prevents the opera from ever holding a prominent place in the repertoire.

Only cursory notice is given to much of the standard operatic fare that winter, from Wilhelm Kienzl to the exponents of the Italian verismo school, but Webern was thrilled by Marie Gutheil-Schoder's performances in Bizet's *Carmen* and Nicolai's *The Merry Wives of Windsor*. He was an avid opera-goer, despite his small student's budget:

> I am mostly in the fourth balcony and always have to stand in line at the box office [he wrote to Diez on 28 December 1902]. The pushing and shoving is great, sometimes one's life is at stake. And then the race up to the fourth floor! To me, it is amusing. While waiting in line, one hears interesting conversations that in time arouse disgust. Every "Judendirndl" [Jewish girl] dares to pass judgement on the greatest artists. It is often really incredible what people wantonly talk about. Each and every singer is being called on the carpet and criticized to the point of life or death. . . . Every "Schusterbub" [shoemaker's apprentice] here knows Walther's *Preislied*. Recently, a Jewish boy stood behind me in line; he had attended the *Meistersinger* 30 times already!

On 21 February 1903 Webern attended a new production of *Tristan und Isolde* under Gustav Mahler's direction. The performance inspired a long and colourful diary account, evoking the very sensuousness of the music drama. The following day, Hugo Wolf died after years of suffering. Webern's diary description of the funeral service, held in the Votivkirche on 24 February, ended with the closing words from Goethe's *Faust*: "The trace of his days on earth cannot perish in æons."

Though coming close to Hugo Wolf only in death, young Webern was privileged repeatedly to see two other great composers of his day, Gustav Mahler and Richard Strauss, in action. The latter conducted his tone poems *Aus Italien* and *Tod und Verklärung* at the close of that season, inspiring Webern's comment on 4 March 1903: "Strauss' works are magnificent, highly inventive creations of a true genius."

The calendar of the student's activities during his first year in Vienna included, beyond the abundant musical events, various plays in the venerable Burgtheater and visits to the city's museums and art exhibitions. The diary records for the following season (1903–1904) become sparser, whether because Webern took in fewer events or because he found less time or motivation to keep up his notes. The latter do contain, however, a complete listing of the Philharmonic concert series that featured such famous conductors as Muck, Nikisch, and Schuch. Webern evaluated virtually every piece with critical vignettes, a sampling of which follows here. Concerning the orchestration of an organ toccata by Bach: "I am an enemy of such experimentation. There really exists not the slightest necessity for it." On the *Roman Carnival Overture* by Berlioz: "A work of overwhelming charm, confounding the senses, but full of spirit and fire." Just one word for Schumann's Fourth Symphony: "Boring." About Mozart's *Jupiter* Symphony: "One of the greatest art works of all time." As to Weber's *Konzertstück*: "We probably are already past this music. After all, times change and so do the demands of man, and what does not prove itself great must perish." On an all-Russian programme: "Glazunov's symphony is smooth, pleasing music, not at all specifically Russian. Scriabin's *Reverie* is languishing junk. Rimsky-Korsakov's *Scheherazade* is an ingeniously orchestrated tone poem, really strange music, so dreamy." About a concert in which Nikisch conducted the Third Sympony of Brahms and Wagner's *Faust Overture*, along with Beethoven's Eighth: "Brahms and Wagner are two men who probably do not belong on one programme. Such contrast! Brahms' Symphony is so restrained, cold and without special inspiration, everything brooding like a frosty November day, badly orchestrated—grey in grey. Wagner's Overture is full of the deepest passion, of scorching ardour, of uprooting power." On Schubert's C Major Symphony: "It shone in fullest warmth and most sublime radiance. Such splendour of melodious invention, such healthy sensuousness; now a sweet dreaminess, then again the brightest, most joyful jubilation. So genuinely 'wienerisch' [Viennese]."

The steady growth of Webern's critical faculties was fostered by his rapid progress in the musical disciplines. During the first year, on 18 February 1903, he had been able to tell Diez that, with his studies in counterpoint "blooming and flourishing," he had successfully completed the assignment of scoring Jean Brassart's *Sacris solemnis* from mensural notation,[3] and that the transcription had turned out "so beautifully that it is to be published in the *Denkmäler der Tonkunst in Österreich*. You can imagine how my courage has risen, for it certainly was no easy task."

The young musician's mounting confidence in the handling of his craft led him to renewed efforts in original composition. He had actually been composing sporadically for five years, and in the summer of 1904, at the end of his second university year, he attempted his first more ambitious essay: the orchestral idyll *Im Sommerwind*.

CHAPTER III

Early compositions I
(1899–1904)

THIS AND SUBSEQUENT chapters devoted to Webern's compositions will provide an account of the genesis of his works. The history of each project will be traced, as far as is possible, from original manuscripts, correspondence, and other primary sources.[1] No detailed analyses will be undertaken, but theorists may derive useful information from the data concerning a composition's evolution. With each "work biography," first performance and publication dates generally are included only if they fall within the composer's own lifetime; otherwise, they are found in the Work List (Appendix 1).

Fortunately, Webern dated most of his compositions, so that the sequence, and often also the locale, of their origin can be established. The initial sketches underlying his projects have largely survived and afford glimpses into his working method and the genesis of individual compositions. Included in the survey are works that, because of the loss of manuscript portions in the turmoil at the end of World War II, are extant only in a fragmentary state. Drafts of projects that never reached fruition are also examined; they, too, help to fill in the picture of Webern's total output, formerly thought to be of much narrower scope.

Webern's first known compositions, discovered only in 1965, are two pieces for violoncello and piano. Both marked *Langsam* (Slowly), but otherwise untitled, they are in the keys of F major and G major. The manuscript of the latter piece gives "Preglhof, 17. Scheiding [September] 1899" as place and date of origin, whereas the F major piece is simply marked "1899." Clearly of the same vintage, the pieces are gentle soliloquies for the solo instrument, with the piano providing a simple chordal accompaniment. The music is marked by quiet poise and restraint; though romantic, it is pure in line and free from sentimentality. The fifteen-year-old composer wrote out the cello parts separately, and one can visualize how he himself performed these first essays, with his mother or sister at the piano, in the idyllic setting of the Preglhof.

All further compositions during the Klagenfurt period were to be songs with piano accompaniment. The first of these, based on the poem "Vorfrühling" by Ferdinand Avenarius, was written out several times. One copy is marked "Klagenfurt, 1899," another "Klagenfurt, 12 January 1900." The duplication of manuscripts, frequent also with subsequent compositions, indicates that Webern had actual performances in mind, for which both singer and pianist needed copies. As the diaries reveal, Webern developed an early and marked affinity for the lyric muse of Avenarius, and no fewer than seven song settings bear witness to his continuing enthusiasm.

"Vorfrühling" could well stand as a motto for the spirit and substance of the musical world that has since become associated with Webern. The short poem provided the composer with an ideal vehicle:

"Vorfrühling"	"Earliest Spring"
Leise tritt auf——	Softly enter——
Nicht mehr in tiefem Schlaf,	No longer in deep sleep,
In leichtem Schlummer nur	In light slumber only
Liegt das Land.	Lies the countryside;
Und der Amsel Frühruf	And the blackbird's early call
Spielt schon liebliche Morgenbilder	Already blends lovely morning images
Ihm in den Traum.	Into his dream.
Leise tritt auf——	Softly enter——

The gentleness of the text is matched by its musical realization. Webern's conception is clear from his initial marking *Durchwegs zart* (Tenderly throughout). The dynamic shading, beginning with *pianissimo*, never rises above *piano*, only to withdraw at once to the *ppp*, so characteristic of Webern's utterances. Ending *so zart als möglich* (as tenderly as possible), the song has no instrumental postlude and dissolves with an up-sweep of the human voice like a breath in the pure air of early spring. The conciseness of diction and the compression of form in this first song (it comprises only 22 bars) foreshadows, and indeed already consummates, the stylistic ideal for which Webern was to become known.

One of the manuscripts of "Vorfrühling" contains the draft for an accompaniment consisting of oboe, two horns, and harp. Although abandoned after four measures, the attempt at scoring for chamber ensemble reveals Webern's predilection, even at that early time, for the combination of the voice part with a small but colourful group of solo instruments. That such a concept existed from the very start is already hinted at in the preliminary pencil sketch of the song.

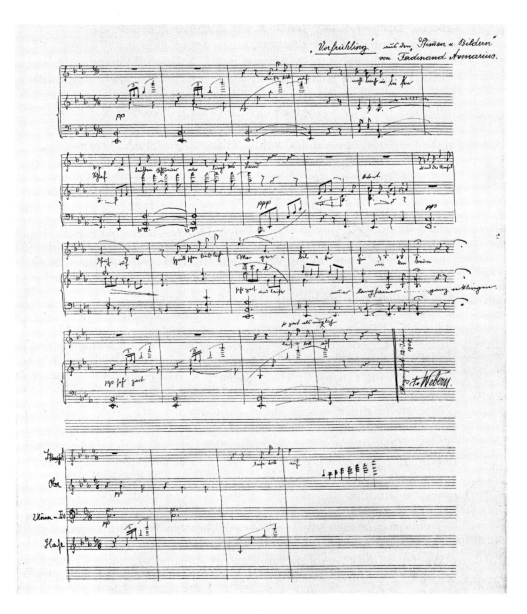

"Vorfrühling," for voice and piano

"Vorfrühling" is actually only the first in a cycle of poems published by Avenarius under that title. Webern undertook also the setting of the second poem,[2] beginning with the words "Doch schwer hinschnaubend durchs dampfende Marschland. . . ." The pencil draft is complete. Although undated, it no doubt originated soon after the first song.

Another setting of an Avenarius poem, entitled "Wolkennacht," is dated "Klagenfurt 1900." It constitutes one of only two songs with piano accompaniment specifically conceived for a man's voice, as is indicated by the use of the bass clef. The fourth of Webern's songs based on an Avenarius poem is "Wehmut," fully sketched out on 15 July 1901 at the Preglhof. Three months earlier, on 21 April, he had composed at Klagenfurt the song "Tief von fern," the first of a total of eight musical settings inspired by the poetry of Richard Dehmel. Like Avenarius, Dehmel is a supreme painter of the glories and secrets of nature, but he is more sensuous and passionate. In the realm of sensitive word painting he has no peer; his poems evoke moods ranging from melancholy and yearning to joy and serenity. "Tief von fern," like "Vorfrühling," is a nature image compressed into eight short lines, and the young composer, no doubt attracted by the poem's capsule form, matched it with a song measuring only eighteen bars.

That the young musician was by then beginning to think consciously of himself as a composer is evident from a diary entry headlined "Op. 1, 4 Lieder." Listed are, in the order of origin: "1. 'Vorfrühling' (E flat major) 2. 'Wolkennacht' (D flat major) 3. 'Tief von fern' (E major) 4. 'Wehmut' (B flat major)." That ink entry is supplemented by a pencil addition reading "5. 'Fromm' (E flat major)." The latter song was composed at the Preglhof on 11 September 1902, almost fourteen months after "Wehmut." The poet of "Fromm" is Gustav Falke, whose volume *Mit dem Leben* was among young Webern's favourites. The eight-line poem again answered what apparently was the composer's basic desire for maximum expressive force concentrated within the briefest space. Beginning and ending with the softest dynamic nuance, "Fromm" is characterized by hymnlike stateliness and solemnity. Considering that the composer was only eighteen, the maturity manifest in the strength and assuredness of the tonal projection is remarkable.

Written at the close of the summer holiday period and immediately before Webern entered Vienna University, "Fromm" marked the end of the Klagenfurt years, with their first attempts at original composition. Taking note of these early efforts, Ernst Diez had presented his younger cousin on his eighteenth birthday with a volume of selected poems by Richard Dehmel, writing on the flyleaf, "To my dear Toni for essays in composition." Confronted by demanding school work during his last year at the Humanistisches Gymnasium, Anton had acknowledged the gift in his letter of 8 December 1901 with the comment: "As far as the attempts in composition go, they are not being realized. Alas, I cannot get anything together." But when Webern did resume composing towards the close of his first university year, he used two poems by Dehmel as vehicles for musical setting. The first, "Nachtgebet der Braut," was written at the Preglhof and bears the date "Charfreitag [Good Friday], 10 April 1903." (A fair copy is marked "Vienna 1903.") Webern then placed this song in the centre of a cycle that he entitled *Drei Gedichte*; he designated "Vorfrühling" to open that group and "Fromm" to close it. "Nachtgebet der Braut," 75 measures in length and Webern's most extended single song, stands in stark contrast to its companions in the cycle. While the Avenarius and Falke poems are tender and pensive, Dehmel's text is full of passion, evoking Webern's equally tempestuous setting. Marked *Sehr erregt und leidenschaftlich* (Very excitedly and passionately), the music opens *fortissimo* and abounds in dynamic climaxes, to subside only at the very end as if such relentless vehemence had exhausted itself. The severe demands on the voice include a high C sharp and sustained *fortissimo* singing. If the song, appearing between the calm and introspective "Vorfrühling" and "Fromm," seems uncharacteristic of Webern's general expressive tendencies, it is perhaps because he had just gone through a period of intensive exposure to the powerful genius of Richard Wagner, prompting him to explore for himself the expressive limits of the human voice.

On 12 August 1903, during his summer stay at the Preglhof, Webern composed "Aufblick," another song using Dehmel's poetry. The mood is marked as *Klagend* (Lamenting), and the plaintiveness of the music is heightened by strong chromaticism. On 7 September of that year, also at the Preglhof, Webern gave "Sommerabend," a poem by Wilhelm Weigand, a musical setting that reflects the peacefulness of the landscape and the young composer's fervent mood. Marked "Preglhof 1903," and probably also originating during that summer, is the song "Gebet," based on a text by Ferdinand Avenarius, two more of whose poems Webern set to music early in 1904: "Freunde" on 6 January and "Gefunden" on 5 April. Composed towards the end of Webern's second university year and still many months before his meeting with Schoenberg, "Gefunden" is remarkable for its harmonically progressive features. The song, in its conscious application of tonal duality, anticipates a sense of key function expanding beyond traditional concepts.

A high degree of harmonic restlessness, manifested in frequent modulations, marks "Heimgang in der Frühe," composed in Vienna on 21 November 1903. The poem is by Detlev von Liliencron, and its romantic revelry is emulated by the music. Comprising 66 bars, the song is one of Webern's longest. In sharp contrast stands "Der Tod," composed only three days later. The text is taken from *Des Wandsbecker Boten Gedichte* by Matthias Claudius, a small volume that Webern treasured in his library. The grim and gripping tale compressed in the poem's four lines is projected in a highly dramatic setting of only fourteen measures. Sketched out on 24 November 1903 at Vienna (the finished score is dated 1904), this song is the shortest of all of Webern's early compositions, years before his "aphoristic" period. In "Der Tod" harmonic pungency is achieved through the striking contrast between a low C octave in the piano, persistently repeated as pedal point from beginning to end, and the strident harmonies in the upper voices. Another short song, "Blumengruss," is marked "Vienna 1903." Compelling in its purity and romantic lyricism, it is the first of Webern's compositions inspired by Goethe's poetry.

Dated 1904, but without month and day, is a setting of Nietzsche's poem "Heiter," a carefree ditty by the generally so austere German philosopher. Webern's realization, marked *Anmutig gehend* (Gracefully moving along) and in lilting 6/8 metre, captures the mood of Nietzsche's poem within nineteen measures. Only two measures longer is the song "Bild der Liebe," based on a poem by Martin Greif from his collection *Neue Lieder und Mären*. The composition, dated "Preglhof, 11 September 1904," is one of the last Webern wrote before his association with Schoenberg. This song, the image of loveliness, shares with many others from that early period the elements of chromaticism, stated or implied pedal points, and static harmonies. Undated, but probably close to the time of "Bild der Liebe," is the setting of another poem by Martin Greif entitled "Hochsommernacht," composed for vocal duet with piano accompaniment. The treatment of the voices is canonic and their skilful blending produces euphonious effects reminiscent of the melodious echo songs heard in the alpine countryside. This vocal canon is the first in a form that Webern was to employ with special skill in years to come. Two pencil sketches evidence his preliminary occupation with the project.

There exists also the rough draft of a setting of Hans Böhm's poem "Liebeslied." Dated 24 April 1904, the song is sketched throughout, but it is not sufficiently complete to be performed. Three other song projects, extant only in either unfinished or fragmentary form, are based on lyrics beginning with the words "Du bist mein, ich bin dein," (Minnelied, *ca.* 12th century), "Du träumst so heiss im Sommerwind" (source not identified) and "Im Sessel du und ich zu deinen Füssen." The latter poem, "Dämmerstunde" by Theodor Storm, is among the many that Webern copied out in his youthful diaries.

One of these diaries also contains the first of Webern's original poems. With his inclination towards lyric literature, it was only natural that he would try his hand at verse. These early poems reveal the sensitivity of the youth and his urge to embrace the universe through what he saw in nature. Like all who worship nature in its tiniest manifestations, he sensed that man is but part of the cosmos and that he must immerse himself in that wellspring for constant rejuvenation. Webern's poems, all short, radiate his abounding desire to communicate what he so deeply felt. Although the Preglhof is specifically mentioned in only one of them, they all were inspired by the beauty and solitude of that cherished retreat.

"Sonnenaufgang"	"Sunrise"
Herrlich strahlt sie empor,	Gloriously he sends his rays on high,
die Siegerin,	The conqueror,
wie unter Jauchzen	As if millions of voices
von millionen Stimmen.	Were rejoicing.
Ja, nun taucht sie in leuchtende Flut	Yes, now he plunges the world
die Welt.	Into a shining flood.
Gewichen das Dunkel——	The darkness has yielded——
Licht, allüberall Licht!	Light, everywhere light!
"Waldweg"	"Forest Path"
Auf grünem Moos mein Tritt . . .	On green moss my step . . .
Der Waldbäume und Eriken Duft	Fragrance of forest trees and heather
wogt weich um meine Glieder.	Floats softly round my limbs.
Die Sonne ist schon versunken,	The sun has sunk already,
ihr letztes Rot	Its last red glow
leuchtet	Shines
durch die dunklen Stämme,	Between the dark trunks,
die wie im Traum ihre Wipfel wiegen	Which cradle their treetops as in a dream
. . .	. . .
Meine Seele ist ruhig.	My soul is at peace.
"An den Preglhof"	"To the Preglhof"
Irgendwo,	Somewhere,
ganz fern,	Quite far away,
liegt ein liebes, liebes Haus.	Lies a dear, dear house,
Hohe, schlanke Pappeln	Tall, slender poplars
umsäumen es.	Surround it.
So lieblich schaut es in die Welt,	So lovely it gazes upon the world,
die selber wieder lieblich.	That is so lovely in itself.
Weich weht der Wind dort,	Softly the wind is blowing there,
dort ist die Ruhe.	There is tranquillity.
Tiefer Friede herrscht.	Deep peace reigns.
Mein Herz sehnt sich dorthin,	My heart longs to go there,
über die Berge hin bis zu	There beyond the mountains to

jenen Pappeln, jenen	Those poplars, those
hohen, schlanken,	Tall and slender ones
die das liebe Haus umsäumen	That surround the dear house
—Irgendwo—	—Somewhere—
Ganz fern——	Quite far away——

Two more youthful poems spring from Webern's yearning, repeatedly expressed in his letters to Ernst Diez, for a woman who might become his Muse. Even these shy blossoms of awakening eroticism are, however, sublimated in imagery drawn from the beauty of nature, which Webern held divine throughout his life. One of these poems, entitled "Traum," is filled with sensuous ardour. It portrays a woman standing naked on a lonely meadow in the forest; she sings dolefully to the moon above as the world sleeps. While this poem is tentative and awkward, the second one is more assured. It reads:

"Frauen-Schönheit"	"Woman's Beauty"
Wie weicher Mondesglanz	Like the moon's soft beam
auf duftenden Rosen,	On fragrant roses,
wie ein träumender Brunnen	Like a dreaming fountain
unter einer Trauerweide	Under a weeping willow during a
in heller Sommernacht,	Luminous summer night,
wie die Frühlingssonne	Like the spring sun
am strahlenden Morgen,	On a radiant morning,
wie ein Duft von blauen	Like a scent of blue
Veilchen, die im Frühling träumen . . .	Violets that dream in spring . . .
Ach, wie das unsagbare	Ah, like the unspeakable
Wehen von weichen Palmendüften,	Breezes of soft palm fragrances,
So, so bist du, Frauenschönheit.	Such, such art thou, woman's beauty.

Unlike other short poems he wrote a decade later, Webern gave none of these early lyrics a musical setting. The source of inspiration for his songs lay rather in the rich storehouse of German literature. His work was not long confined to vocal music alone, however. Under the supervision of Graedener and Navrátil at the university, he produced a wide range of instrumental compositions, as a wealth of surviving manuscripts reveals. Aside from formal exercises in counterpoint, there are numerous piano pieces, consisting of short self-contained movements and studies in variation form. One of the latter comprises 21 numbered variations and another, on the folksong "Der Winter ist vergangen, ich seh' den Maienschein," was drafted not only for piano but also for string quartet. In that idiom Webern practised extensively, drafting a great variety of movements. One of these is a Scherzo and Trio in A minor, extant in two slightly divergent ink scores.

The diligent student soon advanced to larger ensemble forms. His assignments included, besides essays in original composition, orchestrations from the works of such masters as Beethoven, Schubert and Wolf.

Of the Schubert transcriptions, those of five well-known songs are extant: "Romanze" (from *Rosamunde*), "Ihr Bild," "Der Wegweiser" (from *Die Winterreise*), "Du bist die Ruh," and "Thränenregen" (from *Die schöne Müllerin*). Webern orchestrated the piano accompaniment with pairs of flutes, oboes, clarinets, bassoons, and horns, and the usual strings. This instrumentation, patterned after the typical Schubert orchestra, in no way detracts from the intimacy of the songs, but heightens their loveliness and deepens their dramatic impact.

The same orchestral complement was applied to three of Schubert's piano sonatas, scores that are preserved, however, only in fragments. These include bars 1–52 of the second movement from the Sonata in A minor, Op. 42; bars 1–36 of the third movement from the Sonata in E flat major, Op. 122 (the Minuet without the Trio section); and bars 1–13 of the second movement and bars 1–53 of the third movement from the Sonata in D major, Op. 147. This early practice in scoring was to stand Webern in good stead much later when, in 1931, he was commissioned to orchestrate a set of Schubert's newly-discovered German Dances.

There also exist three arrangements of songs by Hugo Wolf. The instrumentation for two of them is identical with that employed for Schubert. Unfortunately, the opening page of "Lebe wohl" is missing, and the manuscript of "Der Knabe und das Immlein" is likewise fragmentary. "Denk es, o Seele" is complete, however. Here the orchestral apparatus is much larger, with two trumpets, three trombones, harp and percussion added to the "Schubertian" complement. The manuscript is dated "Preglhof, 16 April 1903." Webern worked out the orchestration during his Easter vacation, under the fresh impressions of Hugo Wolf's funeral on 24 February and a memorial concert on 29 March.[3] (The latter served the purpose of raising funds for a suitable gravestone.) The orchestration of "Denk es, o Seele" was Webern's homage to the master whose music exerted one of the earliest and strongest influences upon him.

Later that year, Webern completed the composition of *Siegfrieds Schwert*, dating the manuscript at the end "Preglhof, 25 September 1903." A ballad for voice and orchestra, the work is based on the well-known text by Johann Ludwig Uhland, one of the most popular German poets of the Romantic period, who wrote the majority of his lyrics during his youth. One of these was "Siegfrieds Schwert," a blend of the naïve and the heroic, and Webern's musical setting radiates the same exuberant spirit as the text. Considering the degree of sophistication that the young composer had attained by then, the naïveté and simplicity of the music must be considered a deliberate attempt to capture the essence of the poem. The balladesque or folktune-like character of the melody is matched by an harmonic background of simple tonic-dominant variety, with hardly a dominant seventh occurring even at the cadences, and the squareness of form is in keeping with the poem's primitive structure. The voice part, written in the treble clef and within the range of either a male or female singer, relates the poetic tale in a straightforward manner in accordance with the direction marked at the beginning *Frisch und keck, ziemlich lebhaft* (Fresh and bold, rather lively). The score employs a large body of instruments, including pairs of flutes, oboes, clarinets, and bassoons, contrabassoon, four horns, three trumpets, three trombones, timpani, triangle, cymbals, and the full complement of strings. Reflecting the character of the lyrics, rather than hinting at Webern's own personality, the music has an almost Handelian flavour.

Another somewhat enigmatic orchestral song, possibly of later date, bears a large headline *Zum Schluss*. Unfortunately, only a four-page torso of 22 measures is extant. The text of the unidentified poem begins:

Wen'ge sinds, die mich verstehen,	Few they are who understand me,
die mich nehmen, wie ich bin,	who take me as I am,
die das Wort mir nicht verdrehen,	who do not turn around my words
das ich sprach mit leichtem Sinn. . . .	that I spoke in carefree mood. . . .

The texture of the composition is highly contrapuntal and the tonal idiom progressive. The orchestration, even fuller than in *Siegfrieds Schwert*, is for pairs of flutes, oboes, clarinets, bassoons, and trumpets, as well as English horn, bass clarinet, contrabassoon, four horns, three trombones, bass tuba, timpani, harp, and a full body of strings. On the back cover of the manuscript, a string quartet movement of 26 bars is sketched out. Bearing the key signature of B flat major, this undated draft, marked *Schwer* (Gravely), tends away from a fixed tonality and, like *Zum Schluss*, displays canonic features.

Beyond the early exercises in string quartet writing already referred to, a large number of other compositions in the chamber music and orchestral media have been preserved. Most of them are incomplete, but some of the fragments are quite extensive, such as two movements for large orchestra in F major (marked *Kräftig bewegt*) and D major (marked *Sehr bewegt*), orchestral variations in D major–D minor, and a movement for string orchestra in D minor that has been worked out in ink score for 142 consecutive measures. Among the chamber music projects are numerous quartets and quintets in various instrumental combinations. This entire area of Webern's youthful creative legacy still awaits more intensive scrutiny.[4] It reveals, besides many aspects of a strictly musical nature, the amazing industry of the aspiring composer, a characteristic prevailing throughout his formative years. Because of the absence of dates, the origins of this large body of compositions must be conjectural.

No such uncertainty exists, however, about the last of Webern's major creative efforts before he met Schoenberg. That work was the symphonic poem *Im Sommerwind*, subtitled "Idyl for large orchestra" and inspired by a poem by Bruno Wille. A contemporary of Webern, Wille was a North German writer who became widely known as a social philosopher and liberal thinker. The poem "Im Sommerwind" was contained in his *Offenbarungen des Wacholderbaums* (*Revelations of a Juniper Tree*), then one of Webern's favourite books. The second edition, published in 1903, was in Webern's library, and from it he copied several passages into his diary, using one quotation as a motto for a string quartet he composed in 1905.

The extensive poem "Im Sommerwind" is interpolated into Wille's essay "Erkenne dich selbst" (Know Thyself), one of the book's major sections. It is a pæan to nature, an impressionistic description of a summer day in woods and fields. The ecstatic quality of the lyrics excited Webern's musical imagination. The poem's changing moods and currents are not followed in a quasi-programmatic sense, however, in that their loose sequence is converted into a rather tight symphonic structure, subject only to the dictates of musical proportion. The principal motives, interrelated by organic transformation, are introduced by various solo instruments in a treatment foreshadowing the composer's later style. The themes then appear in combinations which exhibit Webern's already considerable contrapuntal skill. A few thin places in the orchestral texture suggest that the score might not have been finished completely; however, such a notion is offset by the abundance of explicit directions for performance, from the opening tempo indication *Ruhig bewegt* (Calmly animated) to the final dynamic prescription *bis zu gänzlicher Unhörbarkeit* (down to total inaudibility).

Webern composed his symphonic poem during a summer vacation at the Preglhof. A first draft, in condensed score, was completed on 5 August 1904. Among the preliminary sketches is the initial concept of the coda section, pencilled out on pocket-size notepaper, and one can readily imagine the young composer jotting down his inspiration for that lovely music on one of his walks through the meadows and forests surrounding the idyllic country seat. The full score required several additional weeks for its completion; it is dated at the end "16 September

1904." A large orchestral apparatus is called for: three flutes, two oboes, English horn, four clarinets, bass clarinet, two bassoons, six horns, two trumpets, timpani, triangle, cymbals, two harps, and a string section large enough to allow subdivision into sixteen parts. The employment of six horns is noteworthy, all the more since trombones and tubas are absent. Colouristic solo passages alternate with chorale-like sections in the brass and massive tutti climaxes. Despite some idiomatic allusions to Liszt, Wagner, and Strauss, *Im Sommerwind* impresses one as a fully original musical creation already containing characteristic features of Webern's emerging artistic profile. As his own hymn to nature, it is imbued with the dominant traits of his musical personality: sincerity and independence.

For the young composer, then at the half-way point of his university training, *Im Sommerwind* certainly was no mere exercise in orchestration, but a conscious creative endeavour, conceived as such and therefore to be considered valid in its own right. While he never heard the work performed, and though his aesthetic course was soon to lead him on to new horizons, Webern is known to have shown the manuscript often to students in later years as proof of his own tradition-bound development. *Im Sommerwind* represents the culmination of his formal training received up to that point. The tutelage of Arnold Schoenberg, so decisive in its consequences, lay just ahead. The composition is therefore important for its position at the juncture between conservative and progressive influences.

CHAPTER IV

Arnold Schoenberg—University years II (1904–1906)

WEBERN'S GROWING URGE to create is amply documented by the steadily mounting number of compositions he wrote during 1903. His sense of calling became so articulate that he began looking for a mentor who might help him in the crucial process of developing his artistic individuality. Academicians like Graedener and Navrátil, routinely imparting the standard classroom curriculum, did not answer that need. Only one man then living in Vienna might have inspired him: Gustav Mahler. But Mahler was far too absorbed by his duties as the director of the Court Opera and by his own gigantic creative projects to have energies to spare for teaching.

Other towering figures of the day were Richard Strauss and Hans Pfitzner. The latter's music had traits very much akin to Webern's own at that time, an affinity which actually prompted him to seek this master's tutelage. Details of their meeting were later related by one of Webern's close friends, Josef Polnauer. According to his account,[1] Webern and Heinrich Jalowetz, a fellow student at the university, travelled together to Berlin during the late spring of 1904 for an audience with Pfitzner. At first, the master questioned the two young men on their knowledge of musical literature. However, when they mentioned the names of Mahler and Strauss, he made disparaging remarks. Webern, upon hearing his idols attacked, became so angry that he rose from his chair, took Jalowetz by the arm and stomped out of the room, abruptly ending the interview. Considering the expansiveness of Pfitzner's musical rhetoric, one can only muse over the direction Webern's style might have taken had he actually become Pfitzner's pupil.

It was in the autumn of the same year, 1904, that the decisive encounter with Arnold Schoenberg took place. The Vienna newspapers carried advertisements for courses to be given by Schoenberg at the Schwarzwald School. This was a private secondary school, at

Wallnerstrasse 9, founded by Dr Eugenie Schwarzwald. She was the wife of a high official and widely known as a philanthropist and pedagogue. Gathering around herself a number of leading artists and scientists, she opened the facilities of her school for extracurricular lectures and special courses. For many years Dr Schwarzwald and her stimulating group of friends convened every Sunday evening. The circle included such prominent personalities as the painter Oskar Kokoschka and the architect Adolf Loos. Alexander von Zemlinsky, who taught musical form and instrumentation at the school, brought Schoenberg to Dr Schwarzwald's attention, and she offered him the auspices of her institution for courses in harmony and counterpoint.

Following the public announcement, Webern at once seized on the opportunity to meet personally the composer whose music had already aroused his interest. During his first university year, a senior student, Karl Weigl, had brought the score of *Pelleas und Melisande* to the Musicological Institute. A glimpse of it had fascinated Webern. "The devil knows," he later wrote Schoenberg (on 2 September 1907), "the thing never let go of me after that. I could not stop wondering what this music might be like. I still remember how, during the following summer, I was almost exclusively possessed by this thought." During the 1903–4 concert season, he had heard, besides some Schoenberg songs, his string sextet *Verklärte Nacht*. "The impression it made on me was one of the greatest I had ever experienced," he recalled in the same letter. "The following year I wanted to go to Pfitzner, but I had hardly reached Berlin when it became fully clear to me that this was absurd and that I must return to Vienna in order to become your pupil."

Schoenberg himself then stood at the threshold of his career. Born in Vienna on 13 September 1874, he had just turned 30. His emergence as a musician had been slow and difficult; for a time he was compelled to earn his living by working in a bank. His earliest attempts to compose were those of an autodidact. He then gained some fundamental concepts from discussions with three friends of his own age: Oskar Adler, David Josef Bach and, in particular, Alexander von Zemlinsky, who counselled him in the theoretical and practical aspects of the craft. This was the extent of Schoenberg's training, but his brilliant mind enabled him, even without formal schooling, to develop rapidly as a creative musician. A string quartet, written in 1897, had a favourable reception when performed at the Vienna Tonkünstlerverein. Twelve songs (Opera 1 to 3) were composed between 1898 and 1900; the adverse reaction to a performance of some of these songs in December 1900 marked the beginning of the controversy that was to surround Schoenberg's work throughout his life. The string sextet *Verklärte Nacht*, based on a poem by Richard Dehmel, was written in three weeks during September 1899. It was premièred on 18 March 1902, by the Rosé Quartet (Webern heard it for the first time at a repeat performance during the autumn of 1903). In March 1900, Schoenberg embarked on his *Gurrelieder*, a cantata of enormous dimensions; while the work was drafted within a year, its orchestration was not to be completed until 1911. After his marriage to Zemlinsky's sister, Mathilde, in 1901, Schoenberg moved to Berlin in quest of a better livelihood. However, he found only hack-work as a conductor of operettas and low-brow musicals, and as a copyist. Yet it was during this period (1902–3) that, encouraged by the interest of Richard Strauss, he composed the symphonic poem *Pelleas und Melisande*, Op. 5, inspired by Maeterlinck's play (he apparently was not aware of Debussy's opera [1902] on the same subject). In 1903 Schoenberg returned to his native Vienna. During the following year he worked on the composition of songs and a string quartet. This was the point at which he stood when Webern first met him in the autumn of 1904, just after he himself had completed *Im Sommerwind*. It is important to remember that Schoenberg's musical concepts at that time still lay entirely within the confines of established tradition. The initial adherence to that tradition, the long groping for other modes of expression, the crisis, and the final break-through into new spheres, all were to be shared, step by step, by Schoenberg and his circle of disciples, among whom Webern was to be a prime moving force.

That Schoenberg could attract followers at a time when his reputation rested on a mere handful of works attests to the strength and magnetism of his personality. So immediate and dynamic was its impact upon Webern that, in the autumn of 1904, he decided to become his student, although Schoenberg at the time was only nine years his senior and lacked all the usual academic credentials. Webern was probably the first of Schoenberg's private pupils in Vienna. He was soon followed by his friends, Karl Horwitz and Heinrich Jalowetz. Sometime later, during the same autumn, Alban Berg and Erwin Stein joined the little band. In October 1905 Egon Wellesz, induced by Horwitz, also became a pupil. By then, Schoenberg had stopped teaching at the Schwarzwald School and had set up his home studio at Liechtensteinstrasse No. 68–70.

Each member of that initial group of Schoenberg disciples in due time attained prominence in his own right. Horwitz, only a few weeks younger than Webern and especially close to him during the early years, was to have a promising career as a composer, and he distinguished himself as an organizer of the Donaueschingen and other contemporary music festivals.[2] Both Jalowetz and Stein were to be highly successful conductors in various German opera houses. In 1924 Stein became artistic adviser of Universal Edition in Vienna, a post he held until 1938; when the advent of the Nazi régime forced him to go to London, he joined the publishing house of Boosey & Hawkes. While doing little composing of his own, he made important contributions as a writer and editor. Egon Wellesz, who matriculated in 1904 as a law student, soon followed his true bent and entered the university's Musicological Institute. He was to become both an outstanding musicologist and one of Austria's major composers. Wellesz' influence continues to the present day through the International Society for Contemporary Music, the basic idea and organization of which were conceived by him, in collaboration with Rudolph Réti, in 1922. Wellesz first met Webern at the univeristy in October 1904. Later he recalled:

We used to play together on the piano the Third Symphony of Mahler, which was to be performed that season. We went together to all the rehearsals that Mahler conducted of that symphony and, in later years, to those of the Fifth and Sixth Symphonies. In Professor Adler's seminar we played Beethoven's last quartets on the piano and analysed them. Working together, attending the same concerts and the same operas and, above all, studying with Schoenberg—all this created a bond that was to survive the years at the university and the different courses our lives were to take.[3]

Alban Berg was brought to Schoenberg through the initiative of his older brother Charly, who followed the same newspaper advertisement that had attracted Webern and submitted some of Alban's compositions to the prospective teacher. Musically self-taught and considered by his parents to lack sufficient talent for a musical career, Berg had entered government service as an unpaid apprentice. The meeting with Schoenberg was to change his life's course. He and Webern, his elder by fourteen months, quickly established close personal bonds. Their friendship, based on like tastes and sympathies as well as complementary temperaments, was to be an enduring one.

All of Schoenberg's disciples shared an enthusiastic and even fanatic loyalty to their leader. Such unity was essential for a movement that was destined to shape the course of twentieth-century music. The group's emergence was timely: the *fin de siècle* had brought unrest in all fields of art, and rebellion was brewing against established standards. The young generation asserted itself in its quest for new horizons, and the inevitable conflict with the "Philistines" ensued.

One of Schoenberg's first public activities in Vienna was particularly suited to enlist the support of aspiring composers. Together with Zemlinsky, Karl Weigl, Rudolf St. Hoffmann, and others, he founded the Vereinigung schaffender Tonkünstler (Society of Creative

Musicians), whose explicit purpose was the promotion of contemporary music. Gustav Mahler was honorary president. A lengthy circular setting forth the society's objectives was issued in March 1904, and this manifesto probably was instrumental in attracting the interest of the university students who later formed the nucleus of Schoenberg's following. The society had but one active season, during which it gave five highly successful concerts. For one of them, on 25 January 1905, Schoenberg conducted the first performance of his *Pelleas und Melisande*. Four days later a "Liederabend" was entirely devoted to Gustav Mahler, including songs from the *Wunderhorn* cycle, the *Kindertotenlieder*, and other songs based on poems by Friedrich Rückert.

On 3 February 1905 a repetition of that Mahler concert was followed by a social gathering in the Annahof. Webern was privileged to sit close to Mahler and hear him expound his views. The seriousness with which each word was absorbed is graphically reflected in a long diary entry:

These hours spent in his presence will always remain in my memory as exceedingly happy ones, since it was the first time that I received the immediate impression of a truly great personality. Almost all his words that I could hear are embedded in my memory, and so I want to note them down in this book that is so dear to me. At first there was a discussion of Rückert's lyric poetry. Mahler said: "After *Des Knaben Wunderhorn* I could not compose anything but Rückert—this is lyric poetry from the source, all else is lyric poetry of a derivative sort." He also mentioned that he did not understand everything in the *Wunderhorn* texts. The discussion turned to counterpoint, since Schoenberg said that only the Germans knew how to handle counterpoint. Mahler pointed out the old French composers, Rameau, and so on, and admitted only Bach, Brahms and Wagner as the greatest contrapuntalists among Germans. "Nature is for us the model in this realm. Just as in nature the entire universe has developed from the primeval cell, from plants, animals, and men beyond to God, the Supreme Being, so also in music should a larger structure develop from a single motive in which is contained the germ of everything that is yet to be." With Beethoven, he said, one almost always finds a new motive in the development. The entire development should, however, be carried out from a single motive; in that sense Beethoven was simply not to be considered a great contrapuntalist. Variation is the most important factor in a musical work, he stated. A theme would have to be really especially beautiful, as some by Schubert are, in order to make its unaltered return refreshing. For him, Mozart's string quartets were over at the double bar (of the exposition). The task of contemporary creative musicians would be to combine the contrapuntal skill of Bach with the melodiousness of Haydn and Mozart.

These recollections were prefaced by Webern's detailed and in part critical assessment of Mahler's songs heard during the evening's concert.

Curiously enough, apart from the brief reference in the foregoing account, neither Schoenberg personally nor his music is ever mentioned in the diary, which continues till the Christmas of 1906, well into the third year of Webern's acquaintance with Schoenberg. Only one other entry (an earlier one) appears during the 1904–5 season, when the combined demands of university and private studies apparently left no time for recording any but the most memorable impressions. Webern described a Philharmonic concert on 6 November 1904, in which Felix Mottl conducted Mozart, Pfitzner, and Beethoven. His extensive remarks on the *Eroica* Symphony are summed up in this personal testimony:

The genius of Beethoven reveals itself more and more clearly to me. It gives me an elevated strength—the experience, the final experience when one veil after the other is torn away, when his genius shines for me ever more radiantly—and one day the moment will come when I am directly imbued, in brightest purity, with his divinity. He is the comfort of my soul, which searches, cries for truth. I long for an artist in music such as Segantini was in painting.[4] His music would have to be a music that a man writes in solitude, far away from all turmoil of the world, in contemplation of the glaciers, of eternal ice and snow, of the sombre mountain giants. It would have to be like Segantini's pictures. The onslaught of an alpine storm, the mighty force of the mountains, the radiance of the summer sun on flower-covered meadows—all these would have to be in the music, born immediately out of alpine solitude. That man would then be the Beethoven of our day. An "Eroica" would inevitably appear again, one that is younger by 100 years.

Eight months after penning these lines, Webern set to work on a string quartet for which a Segantini painting actually provided the model (see Chapter V). That quartet was but one in a profusion of compositions produced during this period, in a burst of creativity no doubt inspired by Schoenberg. The nature of the teacher's methods can best be described in Webern's own words, written for a collection of testimonials in 1912:

One might think that Schoenberg teaches his own style, and that he forces the pupil to adopt that style for himself. This is entirely false. Schoenberg teaches no style at all; he preaches the use neither of old artistic devices nor of new ones. He says: "What sense does it make to teach the mastery of common situations? The pupil learns to employ something that he should not employ if he wants to be an artist. It does not give him what is most important: the courage and the strength to confront things in such a way that everything he looks at becomes an exceptional case by virtue of the *way* he looks at it." It is this "most important" endowment, however, that the Schoenberg pupil receives. Before all else, Schoenberg demands that the pupil should not write just any notes to comply with a school formula, but that he should perform these exercises out of a necessity for expression. Consequently, he actually has to create, even from the most primitive beginnings of shaping a musical syntax. All of what Schoenberg then explains to the pupil, on the basis of the latter's work, results organically from it; he brings no doctrine to it from without. Thus, Schoenberg actually educates through the creative process. With the greatest energy he searches out the pupil's personality, seeking to deepen it, to help it break through—in short, to give to the pupil "the courage and the strength to confront things in such a way that everything he looks at becomes an exceptional case by virtue of the *way* he looks at it." This is an education in utter truthfulness with oneself. Besides the purely musical, it embraces also all other spheres of human life. Yes, truly, one learns more than rules of art with Schoenberg. To him whose heart stands open, the way to the good is shown here.[5]

This glowing tribute conveys the spell of Schoenberg's personality and its power to open up ethical as well as aesthetic perspectives. It was that ethical concept of an artistic mission that bound the little fraternity together in its pioneering quest, a course beset by opposition, derision, and many a public scandal.

The spring of 1905 brought Webern a personal experience of lasting significance. During the Pentecost holiday, he went on an outing with his cousin Wilhelmine. The five-day excursion took them to the Waldwinkel, a picturesque region of Lower Austria. From Rosenburg, reached by train, the young couple hiked through the valley of the Kamp River to Zwettl and finally to Allentsteig. Webern's diary description of the journey was ecstatic. He revelled in the beauties of the landscape, marvelled at the old castles and cloisters, and exulted in the magnificence of springtime. "The sky is brilliantly blue," he wrote. "To walk forever like this among flowers, with my dearest one beside me, to feel oneself so entirely at one with the universe, without care, free as the lark in the sky above—O what splendour!"

With open soul, the young man drank in all of nature's beauties. His impressions of the next two days were recorded as follows:

After a brief shower, a rainbow arched its shining band of colours peacefully across the landscape. We had walked all day, again through the fresh green of fields and meadows, through fragrant forests, past quiet villages and dreaming mills. And the sun's shining radiance above everything! The next day it was gloomy outside, the heavens tearful. My heart, however, was jubilant. I spent wonderful hours during the forenoon. . . . When night fell, the skies shed bitter tears, but I wandered with her along a road. A coat protected the two of us. Our love rose to infinite heights and filled the universe! Two souls were enraptured!

A sense of fulfilment pervades the following day's account:

We wandered through forests. It was a fairyland! High tree trunks all around us, a green luminescence in between, and here and there floods of gold on the green moss. The forest symphony resounded. O, infinite beauty of nature—"and everything now belonged to me and I belonged to it, a secretly preserved sweet treasure of the heart." When evening fell, the skies cleared up more and more—and then the moon rose, its silvery beam lit up the dreamy world—what came now was a dream—a dream. A walk in the moonlight on flowery meadows— Then the night—"what the night gave to me, will long make me tremble."—Two souls had wed.[6]

Perfect happiness radiates from the following diary pages, and each entry fused Webern's young love with his passion for nature. He described rapturously, and with obvious literary aspirations, the seclusion of a forest meadow near Mödling. He copied out the gay lines of "Ging heut Morgen über's Feld," second song in Mahler's *Lieder eines fahrenden Gesellen,* and he painstakingly wrote down three long poems by Falke that clearly reflected his own state of mind during that most romantic period of his life. In June, he composed *Langsamer Satz* for string quartet, pure and exalted love music. When the school year closed and Webern had to leave Vienna for the Preglhof, he nostalgically confided to his diary the bittersweet pangs of parting from his beloved: "Once again a year has ended. It has brought me manifold and significant experiences. I have found my happiness—— All bliss, all torment that I suffered, now radiate in the light of our love—— Now I am separated from her. I am in the solitude of forests and mountains, and my soul longs for her, for her love. O, could the wings of my yearning carry my love to her! How painful parting is!" (10 July 1905). On the flyleaf of a small volume of John Ruskin's essays,[7] which he presented to Wilhelmine that summer, Webern wrote as dedication a quotation from the work: "There is no other wealth than life itself; life that encompasses all forces—love, joy, admiration. . . ." The love affair with Wilhelmine is the only one that Webern is known ever to have had, but the romance was not to be consummated by marriage until six years later.

Towards the end of that summer, during which Webern composed an expansive string quartet, he journeyed to Salzburg and Munich. A special notebook, dedicated to Wilhelmine, contains many vignettes of that trip, which lasted into early September. Seeing Salzburg for the first time, Webern vividly described an enchanting morning at the castle high above the city and visits to the Mozart and Paracelsus houses. Detailed accounts of his experiences in Munich follow. Since art history was Webern's secondary field of study at the university, he devoted special attention to all important museums, galleries, and exhibitions. A member of the Albrecht Dürer Society since 1903, he was particularly intrigued with the artist's self-portrait in the Alte Pinakothek, "the ideal image of the German man," as he called it in his lengthy description of the picture. In the International Exhibition of Art at the Glaspalast, only paintings by Fritz Hodler and two others could please the young critic, who otherwise condemned that show: "Whole rooms full of the most dreadful pictures from which one flees in horror. *Is that supposed to be Art?*" In the Neue Pinakothek he liked only paintings by Böcklin, Kalckreuth, Schwind, and Segantini, his verdict being that "everything else is inferior or even trash." In a Lenbach exhibition, Webern found the portraits magnificent, yet rather uniform, and in the Schack Gallery he admired, besides works by Böcklin and Feuerbach, especially Schwind's "Des Knaben Wunderhorn"; to this painting he devoted a long description, ending: "One cannot imagine anything lovelier than this picture." In an exhibition of applied art, he was intrigued by models of a private music room and a home library. Every detail was noted in the diary, no doubt for Wilhelmine's benefit and with a view to their own future household.

During his stay in the Bavarian capital, Webern attended a *Meistersinger* performance in the Prinzregententheater. He came away little satisfied, blaming, among other shortcomings, the acoustics of the house and the conducting of Artur Nikisch, who took all tempi "incredibly fast." For him, Bayreuth still meant perfection, but after the

Munich performance he found himself more kindly disposed towards the offerings of the Vienna Court Opera.

Another theatrical experience of the stay in Munich was Frank Wedekind's *Hidalla* in the Schauspielhaus. Webern discussed the play at great length, coming to grips with the weighty problems it raised. Wedekind, a dramatist of revolutionary views and controversial status, was a forerunner of the expressionists; his tragedies criticized the existing social conventions and advocated a new sexual morality. The performance of *Hidalla* impelled Webern to set down his own thoughts about the relationship between the sexes. In his discussion of the subject, the young man of 21 displayed responsibility and uncompromising zeal, as when he assailed "the greatest barbarisms of our culture: (a) the old spinster (what could be uglier than an old maid, for the sole reason that she is unnatural to the highest degree?) (b) the high esteem accorded to virginity before matrimony (c) the contempt and persecution levied on the whore." The tirade culminated in an impetuous attack on the bourgeoisie:

> How I hate them, these Philistines, who cannot get beyond their cursed conventions and even are conceited about them. In the shortest time, their enthusiasm is over, their inspiration finished. They cease to search and to struggle, they content themselves with something inferior, they marry and suffocate in laziness and become Philistines. These peasants, whose malice stinks like a cadaver! Where is a single one who would sacrifice his life for a good deed? Lazy, immovable, full of dullness, without emotion, without enthusiasm, without courage, they waste away and do not perceive beauty.[8]

On his return from Munich to Vienna, Webern stopped off in Alt-Aussee. For three days he explored the magnificent Salzkammergut, a countryside studded with lakes and mountains. On the last morning, he stood before sunrise on the summit of the Loser, and a glowing diary account describes the birth of the new day in the rarefied sphere of rock spires and glaciers. The diary of the journey ends with a tribute to the beauty of the alpine regions and the splendour of nature.

With the autumn term of 1905, Webern entered the last phase of his university training. The field of his concentration, musicology, was expanded with studies in art history and philosophy under Professors Dvořák, Müllner, and Wickhoff. By June 1906 Webern had submitted his doctoral dissertation and was diligently preparing for the comprehensive oral examinations. As the dreaded "rigorosum" approached, his apprehension grew. On 11 June Wilhelmine left Vienna for a three-month stay in Geneva to further her knowledge of French.

Two extant letters, written by Webern over a number of days, provide diary-like accounts of his thoughts and activities during that time. The first, dated 11–16 June, reflects his melancholy over his sweetheart's departure. He recalls the hour of their sad farewell; he visits her home and sits longingly in her room before giving Leopoldine, her younger sister, a piano lesson; he follows her in thoughts on the various stations of her journey. Then he tells her: "In writing to you, I always use the *Tristan* score as a base. . . . When I think of you I will never know what you are doing at that moment. Only when night comes, at 11 o'clock, then I know what you are doing, and I imagine that maybe you can see me in a dream. The cherished dream, perhaps it will bring you to me tonight, my Minnerl!"

In that letter Webern also reports on his concentrated preparation for the final exams. He studies Raphael, Titian, and Michelangelo and reads biographies of Gluck and Mozart.

When Mozart composed *Figaro* and *Don Giovanni*, they let him starve [he writes]. That is the way it goes in this life—the great among mankind are treated with contempt as long as they are alive because shabby people cannot stand it when someone who lives among them is superior to them. When he is dead, of course, then they favour him with compassion, just as they gladly remember a danger once it has passed, while during it they tremble—thus indeed it appears to me. But despite all afflictions, Mozart's soul calmly wandered along its starry path. This is the marvel!

An unexpected complication had arisen:

Today I learned of something disagreeable. As you know, my dissertation must be approved by Adler and Wickhoff. Now Wickhoff does not want to go along with it; he says that he does not understand the subject matter and that he will not sign his approval to it.[9] As a consequence the whole business is to come before the Ministry of Education, in order that Adler's sole commendation can suffice. If only my examination day is not delayed by this; otherwise the whole thing is really immaterial to me. I have asked my father to go to the Ministry and to expedite the matter. It is curious that things always have to happen to me differently than to others. Basically a very laudable principle, but now and then less propitious.

Webern's doctoral dissertation was approved on 20 June, with Hofrat Professor Dr Wickhoff co-signing after all. Dates for the final orals were set. In his next letter to Wilhelmine, again spread over several days, 22–24 June, the candidate's nervousness approaches fever pitch. He spends all day at the Musicological Institute reviewing what he has learned, and in the evening his cousin Ernst coaches him in the various branches of art history. He is mustering confidence, telling Wilhelmine: "This you know, too, that the professors are well disposed towards me, especially Adler." He will have a talisman along to give him courage for the test: "Immediately before, when I am already at the university, there in the staircase leading up from University Street, I will take a last look at your picture, the one where you sit in the Preglhof garden and look towards me, not the one where you read a book. There in the staircase it is always rather quiet and empty. Nobody will see me. There I will also write to you the postcard that will tell you how I have fared."

Webern's oral examination in musicology was held on 26 June under Professors Adler, Wickhoff and Jodl, who found the candidate's knowledge "sufficient." With the passing of the final test in the secondary subjects on 10 July (Professors Jodl and Müllner, examiners), the last hurdle was surmounted, and the Doctor of Philosophy degree was bestowed upon "Antonius de Webern" (as he was named in the Latin text of the diploma).

The university years behind him, but his head still spinning from the final rigours, Webern retired for the summer to the Preglhof. Schoenberg, vacationing at the Tegernsee, congratulated him on his academic achievement. Webern's reply, dated 29 July 1906, is the first extant letter in what was to become a voluminous correspondence.

> You admonish me to work [he wrote]. Yes, I would like to work the whole day through, but I cannot. My brain acts up in such a way that I have to spare myself as much as possible or else I will not have recovered by September. I live here as healthily as I can, but it is of no use—on the contrary. And if I come to Vienna in this condition I might end up not being able to work during the winter as I intend. Not that I am idle now. Each day I harmonize a chorale, play the piano, read, and so on. I am reading Kant's *Metaphysics of Ethics*, something quite marvellous. Kant's elevated philosophy makes me happier day by day. I do not know whether and how much you have occupied yourself with this man, but I can only wish that you would do so. . . .

The summer days at the Preglhof were overshadowed by Webern's mounting worries about the health of his mother. She had long been ill with diabetes, and in the days before the discovery of insulin the disease could not be arrested. Despite his anxiety, Webern returned to Vienna at the beginning of September, but he was called back to the Preglhof almost at once. Amalie von Webern died on 7 September 1906 at the age of 53. She was laid to rest in the family plot at the nearby village churchyard of Schwabegg.

Webern, who loved his mother beyond measure, never ceased to grieve for her. Six years later, on 17 July 1912, he wrote to Schoenberg: "I would like to tell you that the grief for my mother grows within me more and more. Almost all my compositions have originated in her memory. It is always the same thing that I want to express. I bring it to her as a sacrificial offering. The love of a mother is the highest form of love." (One of the works to which Webern alludes is his Opus 6, the Six Pieces for Orchestra, which, as will be seen, was conceived as a memorial to his mother.) He visited her grave as often as he could. At first, numb with sorrow, he resolved to dedicate all his creative life to her memory, to build out of his grief a testimonial to her spirit. This resolution gave him solace in the months and years to follow, and in it he found his Wilhelmine's full support. At Christmas 1906 she wrote to him: "My love cannot replace for you the love of your mother, but it will help you to create a beautiful life. And to assist you in reaching the highest goal as man and artist is the most beautiful content of my own life. I want to preserve your mother's memory in you."

In Wilhelmine, Webern had gained the most loyal of allies, lonely as his artistic mission was destined to be. Sensing this destiny, he wrote that same Christmas a closing entry into the diary that contained so many impressions of his formative years. His sentiments, rising from the depths of despair, affirmed his solemn dedication: "What I can write down here is really nothing—and what indeed should I write? And yet I want to record in this book something of my feelings. The following is clear to me: that my youth in the narrower sense is over, and that before me lies only a life of uninterrupted striving for the heights, and that the first consideration will always be to preserve, ever holier, my mother's memory.—Thus may this book be concluded."

As if fortifying himself for the future upon leaving the land of his youth behind, Webern added a postscript that was to become the motto of his life: "Through our great, deep love we will become perfect humans who live only for their inner being, guarding and cultivating their souls."

CHAPTER V

Early compositions II—Opera 1–2
(1905–1908)

To COMPREHEND FULLY the technique and style of Webern's own creative work, one must turn to his doctoral dissertation, an edition of the second volume of the *Choralis Constantinus* by Heinrich Isaac.[1] That Netherlands polyphonist was born about 1450 in Brabant and died in 1517 in Florence. In the course of his career, culminating in the position of court composer for Maximilian I in Vienna, Isaac assimilated the musical influence of the various countries in which he lived, and his music thus reflected the Netherlandish, Italian and German styles as they flourished in his day. His works include masses, motets, psalms, and secular songs. Isaac's crowning achievement was the three-volume *Choralis Constantinus*, a monumental collection of the church Offices in polyphonic settings. The work's second part, edited by Webern, comprises 25 graduals for two to six voices *a cappella*.

In his long introduction, Webern points out some salient features of the old master's music:

> Here we experience the wonderful effect of polyphonic art, achieved through the way in which the voices proceed alongside each other in complete equality; nevertheless, as an individual voice begins to gain importance during its development, it comes to the fore. Then, as that voice recedes, another starts to become more prominent— in short, the effect is achieved through subtle organization in the interplay of parts. . . . Isaac has realized in a wonderful way the ideal of the most lively and independent voice leading. Each voice has its own development and is a completely self-contained, separately comprehensible, wonderfully animated structural unit. . . . To the ideal of making each voice an independent, highly individual entity, Heinrich Isaac devotes every artifice of counterpoint. It is from this ideal that the boldness of his technique springs. . . . In the second

part of his *Choralis Constantinus*, Isaac uses artful canonic devices in the greatest profusion: two-voiced canons at the unison, the fourth above and below, the fifth and octave, or the twelfth. Then it may happen that one voice is so derived from another that, entering at the same time as the latter, it imitates it in notes of double the value or, likewise starting at the same time, transposes the other to the third above. . . . Isaac further constructs three-voiced canons, one of four voices, three double canons, and finally two crab canons. More distant or closer imitations, stretti, augmentations, diminutions are found time and again in the Offices; it is imitation that constitutes the point of departure for each voice. . . . It is admirable what variegated tonal effects Heinrich Isaac achieves with the means at his disposal. Added to this is the keenest observation of tone colourings in the various registers of the human voice. This is partly the cause of the frequent complete interlacing of voices and of their movement by leaps. . . . It should be kept in mind that the chant continually winds its way through Isaac's music in the *Choralis Constantinus*, and despite all alterations is always recognizable to one engaged in comparative study; to the listener, however, it is only rarely distinguishable from the other voices because of its intimate wedding with them. What is so marvellous is how Heinrich Isaac grasps the spirit of the chant with the greatest insight and so absorbs it into himself that the chant appears in his music not as something foreign to its nature but welded into the highest unity with it—a splendid testimony to the greatness of his art.

What Webern, the musicologist, observed in Isaac's four-centuries-old art was to be applied by Webern, the composer. Already at 22 he had mastered the intricacies of the contrapuntal discipline enough to become one of the editors for what, in Isaac's day, had been a polyphonic encyclopaedia. There was little that he had not yet acquired in basic musical craftsmanship. Even in the autumn of 1904, when he first came to Schoenberg, he certainly was no novice needy of preliminary instruction. Schoenberg's foremost rôle in Webern's life was to be that of instigator and supervisor, and later that of colleague and friend.

From all appearances, Schoenberg advised Webern, when he came to him with the just completed symphonic score of *Im Sommerwind*, to forego large-scale orchestrations for a time and to apply himself first to writing in the classic discipline of the string quartet. The many pieces soon emerging in that medium may be considered the first valid evidence of Schoenberg's tutelage. Numerous extant string quartet studies, comprising several self-contained short movements, obviously served as stepping stones towards *Langsamer Satz*, the first major work of that initial period.

The autograph score of *Langsamer Satz* bears the date "June 1905." Besides the full score, a set of parts in the composer's hand exists, an indication that the piece probably was played within the Schoenberg circle.[2] Written in Vienna at the end of Webern's third university year, the work radiates the joy and exhilaration he felt during a Pentecost outing, when he had fallen in love with his cousin Wilhelmine. The music is pervaded by a sweet poignancy; serene happiness rises to triumphant ecstasy in the coda. The quartet is traditional in structure. The working out of the motives shows the influence of Brahms, whose technique long served Schoenberg as a model. The principal theme is partly mirrored in the second subject; transformed by means of key and rhythmic changes, it emerges in an altogether new and perfectly contrasting character.

Immediately after composing *Langsamer Satz*, Webern set to work on a more expansive and ambitious essay in the same genre. An elaborate formal outline, dated "Preglhof, 13 July 1905," prefaces the earliest sketches. Drafted on small-sized notepaper which the composer could easily carry in his pocket on walks around the estate, the heading reveals that he received his inspiration from a painting, Segantini's tryptich "Werden-Sein-Vergehen" (Evolving-Being-Passing Away).[3] Ever since he had seen Segantini's "Alpenlandschaft" in Munich in 1902, Webern had felt a strong affinity for the subjects and symbolism of the painter's sombre world. An *Eroica* performance on 6 November 1904 had prompted him to a long diary discussion in which he envisaged a composer of Segantini's expressive powers as the Beethoven of the twentieth century. Now, eight months later, he found in Segantini's tryptich the inspiration for a broadly-conceived string quartet. The finished score bears the date of 25 August 1905; a change of the ending, made after Webern returned from the Munich journey, is dated 12 September at Vordernberg, the parental home of Ernst Diez. This one-movement work, entitled simply "Quartet," corresponds structurally to its pictorial model, with three clearly discernible sections. Harmonically, strong chromaticism effects in places the loosening of traditional tonal concepts. For this reason, the work has been heralded as the actual beginning of "atonality."[4] Certainly, every aspect of the composition shows a remarkable progressiveness compared with *Im Sommerwind*, written only a year earlier. The opening three-note phrase is reminiscent of the "Muss es sein" motive in Beethoven's Quartet, Op. 135; in the light of Webern's earlier diary entry, the reference to Beethoven was probably as deliberate as that to the Segantini painting. After the romantic mood of *Langsamer Satz*, the composer now plunges into depths of brooding. Strife and struggle are relieved only in the finale, when peace dispels the gloom like rays of sunlight breaking through the clouds after a storm in the mountains.

To express his spiritual involvement with the work, Webern prefaced the finished score with a quotation from the writings of the German religious mystic Jacobus Boehme (1575–1624). The excerpt is the one that Wille had used as the opening motto for his novel *Offenbarungen des Wacholderbaums*, and it now appeared to the composer as a fitting literary formulation of everything that his music, evoked by Segantini's art, was trying to convey: "The sense of Triumph that prevailed within my Spirit I cannot write nor speak about; it can with naught be compared, save only where, in the midst of Death, Life is born, like unto the Resurrection of the Dead. In this Light did my Mind forthwith penetrate all Things; and in all living Creatures, even in Weeds and Grass, did I perceive God, who He may be and how He may be and what His Will is."

Aside from the two string quartets of 1905 and two works still to be described—the quintet of 1907 and five settings of Dehmel poems, written between 1906 and 1908—there exists a multitude of undated compositions from this period. Their sequence of origin must remain conjectural, but it can be safely assumed that most of these works came into being only after the summer of 1906, since the final year of Webern's university studies was far too demanding to allow him much time for creative activity. His remarks to Schoenberg, quoted earlier, leave no doubt that his energies still needed regeneration when he retired to the Preglhof for a summer's rest. Webern's only compositional work that summer was the harmonization of German chorales, an assignment that Schoenberg had given him and Horwitz for the vacation period. On 29 July, he asked Schoenberg:

> Am I to harmonize the chorales simply or am I to treat them also contrapuntally? I understood that I was to work out the chorale melodies in a manner similar to the chorales in the *St Matthew Passion*, in four voices with a few passing notes. What Horwitz assumes, however, is that they should be done in the manner of Bach's chorale preludes: in one voice the chorale, in the others canons or developments of one or more themes. Please write to me whether I am to do both or only one of the two.

No fewer than eighteen of these harmonizations, carried out in both styles, are extant. With the exception of the canonic "Komm heil'ger Geist, du Tröster mein," written out in ink in full score, they are preserved only in pencil sketches, the four parts drafted on two staves.

All the settings are highly chromatic, projecting the traditional tunes in the harmonic idiom to which Webern had advanced by then. Among the ancient melodies he chose were some of the best-known, such as "Christ lag in Todesbanden," "Nun komm, der Heiden Heiland," "Wenn wir in höchsten Nöten sein," and "Nun ruhen alle Wälder."[5]

The crisis into which the established harmonic concepts had then entered, under the relentless probing of Schoenberg and his circle, is best described in Webern's own words. A quarter of a century later, in a lecture given on 4 February 1932, he said: "Today we shall examine the state of tonality when it was in its last throes. I want to furnish you with proof that it is really dead. Once that is proven, there is no point in dealing any more with something dead." After illustrating the nature of the impending "catastrophe," Webern goes on: "Relationship to a keynote became ever looser. This brought on the situation in which one could ultimately dispense with the keynote. . . . We—Berg and I—have lived through all this with complete personal involvement. I say this, not so that it will get into my biography, but because I want to show that it was a development achieved through bitter struggle and one which was definitely necessary."

The remarks that follow are of particular importance in connection with Webern's posthumously discovered manuscripts:

In 1906 Schoenberg came back from a stay in the country, bringing the Chamber Symphony. The impression was colossal. . . . I immediately felt: "You must write something like this, too!" Under the influence of the work I wrote a sonata movement the very next day. In this movement I reached the farthest limits of tonality. . . . Schoenberg and I sensed that in this sonata movement I had broken through to material for which the situation was not yet ripe. I wrote the movement to the end—it was still related to a key, but in a very curious way. Then I was supposed to write a variation movement, but I invented a variation theme that really was in no key at all. Schoenberg called on Zemlinsky for help and he dealt with the matter negatively. Now you have an insight into the struggle over all this. It was not to be stopped. To be sure, I then wrote a quartet that was in C major—but only in passing. The key, the chosen keynote, was invisible, so to speak—"suspended tonality!" But it was all still related to a key, especially at the end, in order to establish the tonic. The tonic itself was not there, however—it was suspended in space, invisible, no longer necessary. On the contrary, it would have been disturbing if one had truly taken one's bearings by the tonic.[6]

The hints provided in the foregoing remarks could fit several of Webern's posthumously discovered compositions. Each of them reflects the restive atmosphere of the time and the ferment in harmonic concepts that soon led to the overthrow of traditional tonality. Internal evidence still has to establish the definitive chronology of all these musical essays. Two short piano pieces, one marked *Langsam* and the other *Schnell*, are no doubt of earlier vintage. More advanced is a piano piece in C minor, a full-page section of which is extant in finished ink score. Then there are three expansive compositions for piano solo. One of them, *Satz für Klavier*, is modelled after the classic sonata-allegro form and contains a harmonically turbulent development section. This piece has been known since 1956 from a manuscript copy made by Friedrich Wildgans from Webern's autograph score, which was last in Wildgans' possession and has meanwhile disappeared. However, Webern's original sketches, discovered in 1965, could be used along with Wildgans' copy for publication of the composition.

Also found in 1965 was the ink and pencil score of another lengthy piano movement. The title page of the original manuscript bears the inscription *Sonatensatz für Klavier*. That designation, written in ink, was later amended in pencil to *Rondo*. The formal structure of the piece bears out Webern's second thoughts. Several harmonic aspects of this work again reflect the searching spirit of the period.

The earliest sketches of the *Sonatensatz (Rondo)*, as the piece is called in compliance with both of Webern's titles, appear on the same page as the ending of an extensive piano piece in F major. In ternary form, but freely rambling like a romantic barcarolle or intermezzo, the music is melodically and harmonically alluring. It stands in contrast to the aggressive mood of the *Satz für Klavier* and the dramatic impulse of the *Sonatensatz (Rondo)*, movements that are oriented, despite their chromaticism, to C as tonal centre. The appearance of the first ideas for the *Sonatensatz (Rondo)* immediately following the draft of this untitled lyrical movement suggests that Webern may have had in mind a three-movement sonata, for which the *Satz* conceivably could have been the beginning.

Also preserved is the extensive torso of a movement for violin and piano. One hundred and thirteen measures are fully worked out in ink score, in addition to many pencil sketches. The metre is 3/4, the tempo marking *Sehr lebhaft* (Very lively), and the key E minor. This tonality, implied by the opening motive, is not further definable, however, since extreme chromaticism soon leads the ear afar, precluding conventional harmonic analysis.

The crucial "quartet that was in C major—but only in passing," singled out by Webern in his lecture, may well be identical with a string quartet for which 45 pages of sketches were located in 1965. Among them is a draft of 82 consecutive measures in full score, opening in *Alla breve* time and marked *Sehr bewegt* (Very animatedly). Although clearly geared to the tonic C at first, the harmonic development soon takes the course of "suspended tonality," and the closing chords, in particular, appear to corroborate Webern's description. Certainly the entire work mirrors the rebellion against key hegemony of which he spoke. An abundance of triplets in cross rhythms adds to the turbulence. On one of the pages is a lengthy schematic outline; it illustrates how the composer planned the course of musical events ahead of time, anticipating the details of structure and harmony with his inner ear.

There exists another string quartet, bearing no key signature, that might also be the work which Webern described. However, this quartet ends rather strongly in A minor, though the key relationships in the themes and their development are full of ambiguities, defying definition. This particular work was completed and prepared for performance, as is evident from the fair copies of the violin II and cello parts, written out by the composer and containing rehearsal numbers (there are also pencil annotations by the players). Unfortunately, the violin I and viola parts have not survived, but they could be largely reconstructed from the sketches of the full score, preserved for all but 68 out of a total of 269 measures.[7] The quartet is in one movement. Among its remarkably progressive features are motivic concentration, complex rhythmic juxtapositions, and unusual sound effects. Perpetual development is the governing structural principle in this taut, highly dramatic piece, with its starkly dissonant physiognomy. Embodied in this work is the entire fertile and exciting phase of experimentation. That the new ideas were not formulated without a struggle is proven by the composer's five extant drafts of the opening section.

As to Webern's mention of a "variation movement," abandoned because of Zemlinsky's negative verdict, this could possibly be another essay for string quartet, of which the draft of a fifteen-bar theme, three completed variations, and sketches are extant. Although both the key signature and the close of the theme's statement assign it to the key of C sharp minor, its melodic and harmonic chromaticism virtually prevent orientation in any specific direction. Like the two string quartets just discussed, this composition probably came into being sometime in 1907. Regardless of whether or not it is the variation movement rejected by Webern's mentors, it constitutes a bold reach into the unknown.

Less daring than the music of that fragment is another work for string quartet, entitled Rondo. Together with the holograph, a complete set of parts in the composer's hand has been preserved, again indicating that within the Schoenberg circle compositions were frequently tested for their actual sound. Although supposedly in D minor, judging from such features as key signature and closing tonic, the Rondo strains the seams of tonality, its extreme chromaticism conveying an almost anguished intensity.

Somewhat less marked by the zealous striving to break away from conventional sounds is the Quintet for two violins, viola, cello and piano. Prior to the discoveries beginning in 1961, this work generally had been considered Webern's only representative early composition. Conceived as the first movement of a presumably larger opus (the programme for the première specifically lists it as "I. Satz"), its broad structure follows the traditional sonata-allegro pattern. A sweeping cello melody ushers in the exposition, not unlike the opening of the Trio, Op. 8, by Brahms. The bravura treatment of the piano part, certain rhythmic features, and the general rhetoric and sonority likewise point to that German master, but the special string effects, such as the *tremolo sul ponticello* that opens and closes the development section, fore-shadow in their eeriness of sound the Five Movements for String Quartet, Op. 5, composed only a few years later (1909).

The Quintet, whose holograph score bears the date "Spring 1907 Vienna," won Webern his first critical notice as a composer. On 7 November 1907, in the Gremium hall of the Wiener Kaufmannschaft, the Quintet formed part of a programme that featured compositions by eight of Schoenberg's pupils (Alban Berg, Karl Horwitz, O. de Ivanov, Heinrich Jalowetz, Erwin Stein, Wilma von Webenau, Webern and Rudolf Weirich). Webern's Quintet was performed by Etta Jonas (piano), Dr Oskar Adler (violin), Dr Georg Heim (second violin), Heinrich Jalowetz (viola), and Heinrich Geiger (cello). (The set of string parts prepared for this performance survives; it contains changes in the music as well as additional interpretative directions in Webern's hand.) Only invited guests were admitted to the concert, among them the critic Gustav Grube. His review, appearing in the *Neue Zeitschrift für Musik* (Leipzig) that November, generally denounces Schoenberg's "pernicious influence," but is perceptive in singling out the creative gifts of both Webern and Berg:

It is not at all customary that student concerts are reviewed here. However, in this case something so unusual is at hand that I feel impelled to report a few details about it. Arnold Schoenberg's school of composition can by all rights be called the "high school of dissonance," since in just that domain hair-raising results are achieved by the "master" as well as by the pupils. If I want to judge on the basis of short essays, then there were only two out of the eight pupils to whom I would grant talent. These were Alban Berg and Dr

Anton von Webern. As with all the pupils, the pernicious influence of
Schoenberg's compositions made itself felt with these two. The
principal theme of the Piano Quintet by Dr von Webern, while not
badly invented, lost itself very soon in wild confusion. Here and there
the players seemed to find their way together as if by chance, so that
one could sigh with relief and tell oneself "well, finally." Regrettably,
such "glimpses of light" were brief and rare in this chaos. What has
been said here about Dr von Webern applies, as far as style of
composition is concerned, to all the others.

Even during his later years, the composer's estimate of the Quintet
movement was sufficiently favourable that he contemplated its
publication. Mindful of this, his widow released the work in 1949 to
Kurt List, one of Webern's pupils, who had approached her on behalf of
the American publisher Boelke-Bomart. The subsequent edition was
based on Webern's holograph. The latter contains a number of
suggestions in Schoenberg's hand. Sparse as these annotations are, they
represent almost the only visual evidence of Schoenberg's supervision;
hardly any of the other manuscripts bear written suggestions or
corrections. If as a teacher Schoenberg generally refrained from the
didactic imposition of his views, he obviously found in Webern so well
grounded and gifted a disciple that whatever comments were necessary
could be passed on orally.

Webern's last three works still anchored in tonality are the Five Songs
after Poems by Richard Dehmel, the orchestral Passacaglia, Op. 1, and
the chorus *Entflieht auf leichten Kähnen*, Op. 2. The Dehmel cycle, for voice
and piano, represents the culmination of the composer's spiritual
kinship with the German writer, three of whose lyrics he had set to music
before. His early affinity for Dehmel's world had no doubt been
deepened by Schoenberg's occupation with that poet. According to
Webern's library catalogue, he owned no fewer than ten volumes of
Dehmel's works. Of the poems used for the Five Songs, "Nächtliche
Scheu" is taken from the collection *Aber die Liebe*, all the other from *Weib
und Welt*. The texts are largely concerned with night and its mysteries;
they are shadowy in mood and saturated with great, though always
subdued, intensity of feeling.

While the songs came into being over a span of several years, Webern
clearly intended to form them into a cycle, giving their order on a
separate manuscript page as "Ideale Landschaft," "Am Ufer,"
"Himmelfahrt," "Nächtliche Scheu," and "Helle Nacht." The opening
"Ideale Landschaft" was composed in Vienna at Easter time 1906.
"Nächtliche Scheu," fourth in the cycle, was written in 1907. The other
three songs are dated 1908, the year of the Passacaglia and *Entflieht auf*

leichten Kähnen. Partly overlapping the composition of the Stefan George song cycles, which opened the epoch of "atonality" in Webern's œuvre, the Dehmel songs occupy a crucial position on the threshold of a fundamental change in harmonic concepts. Incongruously, they came to light only in 1961, but they have since added a new dimension to that era of crisis and transition. Aside from their historic importance, the Dehmel songs form a distinct contribution to the literature, heralding Webern as a foremost exponent of the genre of the German *Lied*. They are significant also because they reveal, even at this early stage of Webern's association with Schoenberg and Berg, marked stylistic differences from the music of these two colleagues. Avoiding repetition, the composer aims for conciseness; he prefers transparency of texture to opulence. With a pronounced tendency towards asceticism in formal rhetoric and harmonic idiom, Webern sheds, earlier than either Schoenberg or Berg, the residues of the late Romantic style. The voice part, sometimes awkward in its relationship to the piano accompaniment in Webern's earlier songs, is now fully integrated, so that the three tonal levels—voice, upper and lower piano parts—can be seen abstractly as a composite design. All the songs are contrapuntal in fabric, but the one that closes the cycle, "Helle Nacht," in its elaborate employment of double and even triple counterpoint, especially displays Webern's already consummate mastery of that craft.

The same high degree of contrapuntal skill distinguishes the works long known as Webern's Opera 1 and 2, cast in the forms of passacaglia and double canon, respectively. The Passacaglia is Webern's first full-scale work in the orchestral medium since *Im Sommerwind*. There exist, however, a number of earlier drafts for orchestra. Among them are three short but complete movements in A minor, based on a ground and in 2/4 metre, that may be considered preliminary studies for the Passacaglia. This form has challenged composers through the centuries, since it requires adherence to a steady ostinato pattern as the structural base and, simultaneously, the display of melodic fantasy in the concertizing registers. The creative problem is, in short, to combine discipline with imagination. As in writing fugues, success depends on the intangible qualities distinguishing genius from mere craftsmanship.

Webern's realization of the time-honoured form looks both back to tradition and forward to the future. In some ways, the work is strongly reminiscent of Brahms (the finale of the Fourth Symphony immediately suggests itself), and the prevailing mood—austerity alternating with poignancy, bleakness with flashes of brilliance—cannot but bring to mind the world of that German master. On the other hand, the unmistakable Webern physiognomy is already there: soloistic use of instruments; economy and transparency belying the large orchestral apparatus; contrapuntal invention producing a wealth of thematic transformations; extensive use of triplets; subdued dynamics; and, finally, silence as a structural element. That silence is an integral feature of the eight measure passacaglia subject, in D minor, stated in unison by plucked strings:

An analytic synopsis of the work was provided by the composer on the occasion of its performance in Düsseldorf in 1922.[8] Webern first points out that his subject, in 2/4 time, deviates from the traditional triple metre. He then outlines the form as comprising, after the initial statement of the theme, 23 variations (eleven in minor, four in major, and then eight more in minor) followed by a "development-like" coda. These general remarks are supplemented with more detailed explanations:

> The first variation brings the fundamental harmonization of the principal theme and a counter-theme. Thereby, the two basic figures of the piece are given. Everything that follows is derived from them. Thus right away, in the second variation, the melody in the clarinet reveals itself as a transformation of the counter-theme. This becomes the theme of the third, fourth, and fifth variations and one of the most important factors for the further proceedings. The same also applies to a figuration formed out of the principal theme, which appears in the next (sixth) variation, which in itself has the character of a bridge. From it develops, in the following (seventh) variation, a theme in Allegro tempo, which returns reprise-like in the coda. Heard simultaneously in the eighth variation are: the original form of the principal theme (violins), a transformation (frequently recurring from here on) of the figure cited in example 4 (double basses) and, in the brass, a variation of the counter-subject that assumes great thematic importance. The ninth, tenth, and eleventh variations lead to the D major variations and work in the motives and combinations that were formed in the eighth variation.   The first variation in the major key has an introductory character. In the second, the clarinet melody appears in a new form, which provides the theme for the third and fourth variations. The eight variations in the minor key that follow result from canonic and multi-faceted imitative formations

based mainly on a figure derived from the principal theme. In these variations a great build-up takes place, which culminates in the last (23rd) variation, a repetition of the eighth variation in altered form. Then follows the coda. It brings, as introduction, a minor form of the first major-key variation and then, leaving the main key, constructs development-like sections using principally the theme established in the second major-key variation. These sections lead in a direct build-up to the reprise-like repetition of the seventh variation. Figurations of the eighth variation conclude the piece.

Webern does not comment on the nature of the principal theme itself, which has aroused considerable controversy among theorists. Some discover in it structural characteristics of the mature Webern, while others deny this and link the Passacaglia rather with the Beethoven–Brahms tradition. To the composer himself, certainly the Passacaglia meant but a step in a continuing evolution, a process by which the old forever procreates the new, and the future remains firmly grounded in the past. Webern's music presents the theoretician with many enigmas from the early works on, but it must always be viewed with the principle of progressive tradition in mind.

With a length of 269 measures, played mostly in moderate tempo, the Passacaglia is one of the largest single movements among Webern's works. Only the String Quartet (1905), with 280 measures, exceeds it in size (by comparison *Im Sommerwind* numbers only 253 bars). The development of Webern's style following the Passacaglia was to lead quickly to an ever greater compression of form.

The work is scored for three each of the woodwinds, four horns, three trumpets, three trombones and a bass tuba, timpani, percussion, harp, and the usual strings. Such an orchestral apparatus approaches that employed by Richard Strauss, but it falls short of the huge instrumental forces called for in Mahler's Eighth Symphony and Schoenberg's *Gurrelieder*, works originating during the same era. It is evident from the sketches that the Passacaglia attained its final shape only gradually; there are many alterations, often involving deletions of entire pages. The work's exact date of origin cannot be ascertained from either the composer's preliminary drafts or the finished score. It can be assumed, however, that it was completed by late spring of 1908. That summer, before going to Bad Ischl for his first conducting engagement, Webern had already begun an operatic project, and this would presuppose that the Passacaglia was finished. Also, since the work was premièred in the autumn there would scarcely have been enough time to prepare the orchestra parts had the score not been completed at an earlier date.

The Passacaglia received its first public hearing in an afternoon

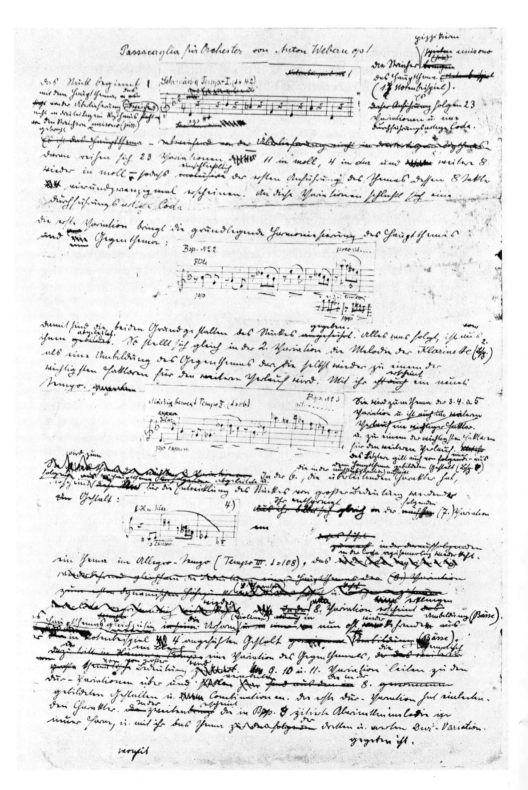

Analysis of Passacaglia, Op. I

concert on 4 November 1908. Schoenberg's pupils, who had presented their compositions the previous year before an audience of invited guests, ventured this time into the august main hall of the Musikverein. For the orchestral numbers, which occupied only half of the programme, the Tonkünstler orchestra was hired, and Webern himself appeared as the conductor of his work. Alban Berg was represented by his *Zwölf Variationen und Finale über ein eigenes Thema* for piano; other Schoenberg pupils whose compositions were played that night included Karl Horwitz, O. de Ivanov, Viktor Krueger, Erwin Stein and Wilma von Webenau. In Ivanov's Suite for piano, four hands, the concert's opening number, Webern shared the keyboard with Etta Jonas-Werndorff.

The music critics were invited and reported almost unanimously in the most derogatory terms. The reviewer of the *Wiener Illustriertes Extrablatt* (5 November) spoke of the overwhelmingly evident Schoen-berg influence: "Like their master, Messrs Erwin Stein and Anton von Webern seek confusion, cacophony at any price, dissonance not for the sake of necessity but for amusement. . . . Mr von Webern writes a passacaglia which hardly justifies the name any longer. Respect for form, without content." The one notable exception to the negative appraisals was an account by Elsa Bienenfeld in the *Neues Wiener Journal* (9 November) which devoted by far the largest space to Webern's work:

The talents of the young composers vary in strength and type. Common to all is a quite extraordinary assuredness in the technique of composition. Anton von Webern, whose Passacaglia for orchestra was performed, appears as the most significant and mature. The work consists of a series of variations on an eight-measure theme. Similar in construction to the fourth movement of the E minor Symphony of Brahms, the series of variations has an uninterrupted form that at the end merges into a development section. Webern's technique is uncommonly complicated as a result of the peculiar melodic inventiveness, the free harmonic treatment, and the manifold interlacings of counterpoint. The composition, surprising in its curiosities of tonal combinations and their progressions, nevertheless convinces through the depth of the moods evoked. Nothing appears accidental, nothing forced by a mania for originality; least of all is anything conventionally imitated. The moods are *felt*, the sounds *heard*. Especially characteristic is the instrumentation; its original tone colours and novel mixtures of instruments, some of which assume a solo function, indicate that everything is invented orchestrally, rather than having been converted from a piano sketch into an orchestral score.

The Passacaglia, published only in 1922, was among the first of Webern's works to be taken under contract by Universal Edition of Vienna.[9] By then the composer had developed his technique and aesthetic ideals to so advanced a stage that he was more concerned with bringing out the works following his "Opus 1" than those antedating it, such as the Quintet or the five Dehmel songs. As will be seen, Webern's designation of opus numbers for his compositions remained in flux until publication standardized them.

Late in 1918 the composer arranged the Passacaglia for two pianos, six hands, so that it could be played in Schoenberg's newly organized Society for Private Musical Performances. Webern listed the projected date in his notebook as 26 January 1919, then changed it to 2 February. The arrangement was publicly heard on 6 June 1919, when it was included in the last of "Four Propaganda Evenings" presented by the society at the close of its first season. Paul A. Pisk, who participated in the preparation, later reported: "Eduard Steuermann played the first piano alone. The principle was that he played the leading voice (Hauptstimme), and it was explicitly said that he should have more freedom of phrasing and punctuation than the accompanying voices, condensed in the second piano. Ernst Bachrich and I, playing the second piano, four hands, were following and adjusting to the melody parts like real accompanists. The arrangement was by Webern himself, who coached the rehearsals."[10]

Unfortunately, the manuscript of that version of the Passacaglia subsequently disappeared, but Webern's skill as an arranger is amply displayed in many other transcriptions. Among these is one of the composition to be discussed next, the *a cappella* chorus *Entflieht auf leichten Kähnen*, Op. 2. In 1907 Schoenberg had written a work in the same medium, *Friede auf Erden*, Op. 13, based on words by C. F. Meyer. Webern not only knew the score but actually copied it out for himself. His manuscript is dated "September 1908." It may well have sparked his own first effort in the choral idiom; if this is so, his chorus would have originated later that year. Webern's own work-list merely states "1908 Vienna."

The text used by Webern appears in the cycle *Traurige Tänze* by Stefan George and is part of the poet's collection *Das Jahr der Seele*. George had become the leader of the revolt against realism in German literature. In the creation of his aesthetic doctrine, he was greatly influenced by Baudelaire, Mallarmé, and other French symbolists. George's poems—always beautiful and melodious, though often esoteric and austere—added a new dimension to the concept of classicism. They influenced an entire generation of poets, Rainer Maria Rilke being the most notable. By 1907 most of George's major cycles had been published, including *Das Jahr der Seele* and *Der siebente Ring*. That year, Schoenberg had begun his Second String Quartet in F Sharp Minor, Op. 10. Adding a part for soprano voice to the strings in the last two movements, he used the texts of two of George's poems, "Litanei" and "Entrückung." The opening words of the latter, "Ich fühle Luft von anderen Planeten" (I sense the air of other planets), were prophetic. In that movement the harmonies are kept suspended and unresolved for long stretches, disregarding the dictates of traditional harmonic function and thus heralding the transition from "extended tonality," as Schoenberg called it, to the period of "atonality" which was about to commence.

Keeping closely abreast of Schoenberg in the exploration of the new tonal idiom, and at times even venturing ahead, Webern shared with his master the inspiration provided by Stefan George's poetry. In all, he was to set no fewer than sixteen George texts to music, the last of them (for voice and orchestra) in 1914. It is likely that one or another of his fourteen George songs for voice and piano came into being before the choral piece under discussion. (For that matter, it must remain uncertain which is the last of Webern's compositions to bear a key signature: this chorus, the George song "Erwachen aus dem tiefsten Traumesschosse," or one of the three Dehmel songs written in 1908, all of which still display the traditional emblem of tonality.)

The melodious word imagery of George's poem "Entflieht auf leichten Kähnen" (Take flight in light barks) was eminently suited to evoke musical ideas. Like the text, Webern's composition falls into three sections. Both rhythmic propulsion, 6/8 metre, and tempo, *Zart bewegt*, (Gently animated) suggest a barcarolle. The piece is cast in the form of a double canon, that most rigorous of contrapuntal disciplines. It opens in two parts, the pairs of upper and lower voices being alternately doubled in thirds and sixths. In the middle section (which uses, because of its quickened pace, not only the poem's second strophe but also the first two lines of the last), the voices appear in a four-part canon. The reprise of the first section, built on the poem's last two lines, ingeniously establishes proportion by a number of repetitions of the phrases that form these two lines. Submitting to the severe discipline of canonic writing, Webern displays in this chorus his training in the music of the early Netherlands school. His fondness for such contrapuntal formulas persisted through the changing harmonic phases of his work—tonal, atonal and serial—up to the last. The closing movement of his Second Cantata, Op. 31, is a chorale in canon form. In the fifth movement of that work, the style of choral writing in parallel intervals practised in Opus 2 recurs, except that the intervals became major sevenths.

Such theoretical aspects aside, the music of the chorus is hauntingly beautiful, pervaded by the same gentle melancholy that characterizes the lyrics. The final pure G-major tonic chord is startling as it emerges from the extremely chromatic vocal web. This chromaticism posed such difficulties of intonation that choral groups of the time were hardly prepared to cope with them. It was therefore not until two decades later that Webern could write in his diary, under the date of 10 April 1927: "Première Opus 2 *Entflieht* . . . in Fürstenfeld." The composer did not attend that first performance, which occurred in "a little place in eastern Styria," as he wrote the director of Universal Edition, Emil Hertzka, on 6 December of the same year. In that letter to his publisher, Webern called attention to a guest performance by the Hugo Holle Chorus on the following day, and on the evening of 7 December he recorded in his diary: "*Entflieht auf leichten Kähnen* performed for the *first time* in Vienna by the Stuttgart Madrigal Society. I heard the chorus for the first time after almost *twenty years*! Performance not good."

If the quality of that rendition disappointed the composer, some kind words from Alban Berg were to warm his heart. The day after the concert, Berg wrote: "I want to tell you quickly in writing how *much* your chorus delighted me despite the mediocre performance. What a wonderful melody it has!! And how beautiful it is when the F sharp of the first soprano is first avoided in the repetition, only to be produced later with mysterious power (*ppp*) at figure 5. Not to speak at all of the low G of the basses. It made me shiver with awe before this mystery of nature—no, of your art!"

The fact that the chorus, published by Universal Edition in 1921, had been available in print for several years before anyone ventured its performance reflects the problems of intonation mentioned above. Schoenberg had faced the same situation with his *a cappella* chorus *Friede auf Erden* prior to its Vienna première under Franz Schreker on 9 December 1911, and to circumvent the difficulty he had added a complement of assisting instruments (pairs of woodwinds and French horns, as well as strings). That orchestral backing was, however, intended only as an optional crutch for the singers, as Schoenberg took pains to make clear in his Foreword to the work. In the spring of 1914, Webern had been prepared to provide a similar support for his chorus when, at Schoenberg's suggestion, he submitted it to Schreker, the director of the Vienna Philharmonic Chorus. Optimistic about the prospect of a performance, Webern had written to Schoenberg on 4 June: "The copy for Schreker also contains a piano reduction. I told him, too, that I would, if desired, write out an instrumental assistance." Although Webern had considered Schreker "amicably disposed" towards him, the project never reached fruition. Nonetheless, Webern had gone ahead and prepared the instrumental score. The latter, discovered only long after the composer's death, employs a group of solo instruments: violin, viola, violoncello, harmonium, and pianoforte. This small ensemble, quite unlike Schoenberg's fairly large orchestration for *Friede auf Erden*, is fully in keeping with the subdued character of Webern's chorus. Rather than tracing the vocal lines throughout, the instruments limit their support to brief segments. These segments, which are carried successively by various players, form a highly transparent and colouristic background. The delicacy of treatment raises Webern's arrangement far above its utilitarian purpose, and the score attests to the spirit of creativity with which the composer approached every task at hand.

The holograph of this arrangement is one of the most exquisite of Webern's many strikingly beautiful manuscripts. His scores graphically convey the hallmarks of his art: meticulous workmanship, formal assuredness, lucidity, and refinement.

The chorus *Entflieht auf leichten Kähnen* constitutes Webern's last work written under Schoenberg's supervision, not the Passacaglia that has been dubbed by many as his "Gesellenstück" (journeyman's piece). This fact is documented by the composer himself. On 10 June 1914, when Schoenberg had replied favourably to Webern's question whether he considered the chorus still worthy to be submitted to Schreker, Webern wrote to him:

How am I to thank you for your exceedingly beautiful and kind words about my chorus! I must read them over and over again. They are just too beautiful! They give me infinite joy. I am overflowing with gratitude. I thank you a thousand times. How your words strengthen my confidence in my composing! I cannot say how happy they make me. I wrote the chorus six years ago under your direct guidance during the year when I last came for lessons with you. I would like to tell you again how beautiful the memory of those times is for me. I believe that I can still recall every one of your words. I believe I can remember each single lesson. All that you told me is of immeasurable value to me. How you have unveiled everything for me. Through you I came to know "how things really are." And whatever happens to me in life, I will at once orient my conscience towards you. Thus it shall remain forever. You are set up in my heart as my highest ideal whom I love more and more, to whom I am more and more devoted.

CHAPTER VI

Inauspicious beginnings (1906–1910)

WEBERN'S ASSOCIATION WITH Schoenberg had a profound psychological effect upon him. Formerly quite self-assured and independent, he completely surrendered to Schoenberg's overpowering personality once he entered into the rôle of apprentice. He followed Schoenberg's every suggestion. Even after attaining the doctorate in musicology, he arranged to continue his private studies under his chosen mentor. In the summer of 1907, when a stint of army duty loomed and threatened to interrupt his lessons, Webern discussed the problem with Schoenberg, whom he visited at his vacation retreat in Traunstein. On 2 September, he wrote to him:

> Am I perhaps now at the end of my regular study time with you? Since you allow it, I would like to come to you whenever I have composed quite a bit. . . . I feel that the moment has arrived when I must offer my thanks to you. I do not know how to put it into words. I would only like you really to believe how grateful I am to you—I can say: in every respect. As far as I am concerned, there is nothing in the world about which I did not learn something from you. I cannot express at all what you mean to me, though I perceive it quite clearly.

Such testimonials were to typify Webern's relationship with Schoenberg, whom he idolized to the point of utter subservience. He was as eager to please as he was afraid to antagonize the man whom he both loved and feared. His personal dependence deepened with the years and at times amounted to an obsession. The realization that he owed to Schoenberg his decisive impetus and direction as a creative artist, as well as the encouragement to chart his own individual course, forever bound him in ties of gratitude and loyalty. Paradoxically, the more self-willed Webern grew in his own musical language, the more he professed his personal indebtedness to the man who had shown him the path to his artistic destiny.

After completing his university studies, Webern had expected to embark on a conducting career. However, aside from a few vague references in his letters to Schoenberg, there exists no tangible record of his activities in this field before the summer of 1908. If he was connected with any theatre before that time, it was probably in the rôle of an assistant coach at the Volksoper, the Vienna opera house ranking second to the Court Opera. That institution is mentioned repeatedly in the correspondence, and the fact that Schoenberg's brother-in-law, Zemlinsky, was first conductor there during 1906–8 supports the likelihood of Webern's association. Whatever connection he might have had with the theatre during his last two years of study with Schoenberg, it certainly was limited to occasional work. The flood of compositions pouring from his pen during that time indicates that he was mainly absorbed in creative endeavours.

In the summer of 1908, Webern received a job offer from Bad Ischl, a fashionable spa.[1] His position was to be that of coach, chorus master and assistant conductor at the summer theatre, as well as second conductor for the Kurorchester, whose function was to provide daily entertainment for the guests. Soon after beginning work, Webern was disenchanted and in utter disgust he wrote to Ernst Diez on 17 July:

> I would welcome it beyond measure if you would come here. You would lighten my stay in this hell. My activities are horrible. I find no words to describe such a theatre. May the world be rid of such trash! What benefit would be done to mankind if all operettas, farces and folk-plays were destroyed. Then it would no longer occur to anyone that such an "art work" had to be produced at any price. If, like myself, one has to cope with this stuff all day, it is enough to drive one mad. But through hell into purgatory and finally into heaven—such is the path I must travel. I am kept very busy. Composing is out of the question. I have not conducted as yet. The first conductor takes care of this. But perhaps I will get a chance at it soon.

Webern's reaction to this professional engagement, the first on record, foreshadows the pattern that was to unfold over the next five years. His ideals, fostered since early youth and intensified by the close association with Schoenberg, were forever bound to collide with the harsh realities of the theatrical business. How he fared during the remainder of his Bad Ischl stay is unknown, but by the autumn he was back in Vienna preparing the première of his Passacaglia. On 4 November he mounted the conductor's podium in the large hall of the

Musikverein to preside over the work's baptism. That autumn, Webern's father decided to resign his high post in the Ministry because of failing health, and he was soon to dissolve his Vienna household and retire to the Preglhof. It therefore became mandatory for his son to strike out on his own. In order to promote his chances for employment, Webern travelled to Berlin. On 8 December he reported to Schoenberg: "Yesterday I called on an agent. Naturally nothing—hardly a prospect. He said that here well-known conductors walk around without jobs. I have not heard anything about the Braunschweig prospect, either."

If Webern was unsuccessful in the main purpose of that trip, it did not dampen his zeal to explore every cultural opportunity offered in the German capital. His days in Berlin were crowded with concerts, operas, and plays. He described to Schoenberg in great detail such varied impressions as a rehearsal of the Königliche Kapelle under Richard Strauss, the plush interiors of the Kammerspiele theatre, and a *Meistersinger* performance under Leo Blech. The greatest experience, however, was Debussy's opera *Pelléas et Mélisande*, which enthralled him so much that he attended two performances. "O God, I cannot express how beautiful it was. I have surrendered unreservedly to this impression," he wrote to Schoenberg on 6 December. Two days later he followed up with a minute description, devoting special attention to the novel staging technique. He found Debussy's music "very fine, often very strange, in places wonderfully beautiful," adding: "The ending is one of the loveliest that exists. And the instrumentation—simply magnificent. I was entranced, for Maeterlinck's drama also possesses such unheard-of beauty—such atmosphere, such tenderness, then again so much passion. . . . The new stage art is something quite glorious, and therefore I must stay with the theatre. It is marvellous! Oh, how grateful I am that I may be occupied with these things, that I may sacrifice my life to them."

In a third letter to Schoenberg from Berlin, dated 13 December, Webern alluded to his father's intercession with Karl von Weiner, the president of the Vienna Academy, in order to secure a teaching post for Schoenberg, a prospect materializing not long afterwards. Webern also referred to Schoenberg's suggestion that he call on Richard Strauss while in Berlin and volunteer his services as an assistant in the preparation of the forthcoming production of *Elektra*.[2] Timid about approaching Strauss, he asked Schoenberg (who was then on very friendly terms with Strauss) for a letter of introduction: "I do not know why I am so stupidly shy. This is also why I have not as yet called on Marschalk.[3] If I had a song collection all prepared I would, but as it stands there is nothing he could take on at the moment. On the one hand I would like to, but on the other hand——"

Webern returned to Vienna in time for the première of Schoenberg's Second String Quartet on 21 December 1908. Like the premières of the First String Quartet and the First Chamber Symphony the year before, this performance, by the Rosé Quartet, provoked a hostile demonstration. Webern reacted bitterly to the public rebuff, writing the same night to Schoenberg: "I am still totally upset and now am trying to remove from my thoughts this unspeakable, horrible experience, so that I can think again quite clearly about your exceedingly beautiful work. To me it is a marvel." On 27 December he vented his rage in a long polemic epistle sent to Schoenberg from his Christmas retreat at the Preglhof. The tirade culminates:

> Nothing is now more important than showing those pigs that we do not allow ourselves to be intimidated. The other day I had the impression that everything was lost again for years to come, and this was deadly. . . . Suddenly it is respectable to make noises and to hiss. The "high-class" part of the audience formed the opposition. . . . Well then, so youth is pro and the old men in the parquet contra. Those fellows can never do anything but come up with the past. All right, they should finally have comprehended that everything significant has such a fate; how idiotic that they are taken in over and over again. They see, after all, that their colleagues in Beethoven's time disgraced themselves. . . . One cannot conceive of the idiocy of men, it is really beyond measure. It is horrible! God, it is not worth getting so upset, but it is frightful! Everything in me reacts convulsively when I think of that evening. I am glad that I could escape right away the next day. Here it is glorious; I spend the whole day out of doors—a marvellous winter. If you could be here, you would feel so well. An ideal "cloister." And if one stands still, one hears nothing but a rustle once in a while in the forest—and this quiet is something really glorious, really remarkable, because in the city one hears bustle and noise continuously. It is sublime. If nothing happens earlier with the Volksoper, I will come to Vienna only on Epiphany Day.

The closing remark hints at a connection, hoped-for or real, with that opera house.

Since Webern was in constant personal contact with Schoenberg during the winter of 1909, there is a half-year gap in the correspondence, that important source for biographical information. In the spring he joined his father at the Preglhof. By the time he wrote to Schoenberg again, on 16 June, he could inform him that he had already completed "a string quartet" (Five Movements, Op. 5) and now anticipated writing "a few songs and then an orchestral work." The death and funeral of his maternal grandfather, Anton Geer, intervened. On 10 July Webern tells Schoenberg that he has been able to compose only one Stefan George song, but now is about to write several more. Apparently he was then unaware of a theatre engagement that was to take him to Innsbruck only a few days later. No doubt he was called there to substitute in an emergency. The job was to prove as short-lived as it was unexpected, however.

On 25 July Webern dispatched a message of distress from Innsbruck to Schoenberg, who was then vacationing at Steinkirchen. The letter, penned in a highly nervous scrawl, conveys the writer's extreme excitement and frustration:

By God, dear Mr Schoenberg, it is impossible for me to remain here. I have already written to Mr Zemlinsky in regard to the Volksoper. It just has to work out. At any rate, I will run away from here. My God, it is terrible. Perhaps when I am calmer I can write to you more. Just think: a young good-for-nothing, whom I know from Vienna, [is] my "superior!" From him I have to take orders. It would be a sin against the Holy Ghost if I remain here. It is dreadful! And anyway, what do I have to do with such a theatre? O my God, do I have to perform all this filth? It cannot be. What will become of me? If I think of my ideals—or whatever they are called—I would have to perish! I would like to flee—I know not where. The change was too sudden—I cannot endure this. Please, Mr Schoenberg, send me a few lines—Hotel Grauer Bär, Innsbruck. I am sure to die here. I am being murdered here.   Your Webern.
Please talk to Mr Zemlinsky and as quickly as possible.

Webern's threat to flee from his Innsbruck job was meant literally. Three days later, when he wrote again to Schoenberg, he had already returned to the Preglhof. Curiously, he makes no reference whatever in this letter to the calamitous affair. This is typical of Webern's reaction to all the catastrophic experiences in his life. Blotting them from his consciousness, he was loath ever to discuss them again. Seventeen years later (on 14 December 1926), however, he did refer to the Innsbruck episode when he wrote to his pupil Ludwig Zenk, warning him not to resign from a hated theatre post at Znaim:

Whatever may happen, I beg you to endure it. I once wailed to Schoenberg; he then wrote to me Strindberg's motto: "Cancel out and keep going!" I did not follow, i.e. I cancelled out so thoroughly that I stole away one night. Therefore, believe me: under no circumstances follow that example. As it is, half the season will soon be over. Do not allow yourself to be angered too much. And even if you give up sleeping and eating, it will not make a decent tenor out of the individual you have to deal with there, nor will it help with this or that female singer. It is of no use. Remember what I told you about Mahler. Once when the basso Kraus appeared as a guest in *The Magic Flute*, he took all tempi much slower than Mahler wanted. Then Mahler found the way out—he conducted the entire opera more slowly. This a man like Mahler had to do at the Court Opera in Vienna. And Mr Demuth, who did not want to wear the beard that Roller had designed for the rôle of Wotan, also got his way, etc. There is nothing that can be done. How Mahler had to suffer in Hamburg under Pollini for so many years! Therefore, patience, patience!

The wisdom Webern could preach to his former pupil had been gained from the bitter experience of many years. At the time of his flight from Innsbruck, however, he felt only angry frustration. Characteristically, to regain his composure he went on a mountain climb, carrying his woes to the purifying air of the high Alps. Back home at the Preglhof, further adversity awaited him: the prospect of a position at Mannheim had suddenly vanished. "What a mess I find myself in again," he wrote to Schoenberg on 28 July, only three days after his desperate outcry from Innsbruck. "The director at Mannheim has been discharged and with him all his staff, me included. So I am again without a position. Now the mess can begin all over. . . . Today I came down from the Hochschober.[4] And now this stupid news. When one descends to the valley—up there, in the heights, there one should stay."

Despite his débâcle at Innsbruck and his continuing frantic efforts to secure a position for the coming season, Webern turned the summer of 1909 into a creatively most productive one; his desire to compose evidently outweighed all concern about his future. The Five Movements for String Quartet were followed by several song settings of Stefan George texts and the complete draft of the Six Pieces for Orchestra. Webern's elation over his artistic fertility was dampened only by the vicissitudes of job hunting. Several agents provided him with leads to theatres in Troppau and Marburg an der Drau, and his friend Jalowetz with another in Koblenz. Schoenberg was perturbed by Webern's difficulties in establishing himself, and when he heard of the Koblenz opening, he sharply reproached him for failing to apply by telegram. Hypersensitive to any reprimand from the master, Webern laboriously defended himself. A seven-page epistle, dated 30 August 1909, reflects his obsessive need to dispel Schoenberg's irritation; to that end, he virtually prostrated himself. A submissive postcript reads: "Believe me,

Mr Schoenberg, this I always endeavour to do: to keep distance, to show respect, to take nothing for granted, to render honour——"

The remarks emphasize the autocratic position that Schoenberg occupied within his circle of disciples. In return for their absolute reverence and loyalty, however, his followers could reap the full benefit of belonging to the entourage of a man who associated with the leading spirits of the day. Thus Webern had been privileged, even in the first year of his studies under Schoenberg, to become personally acquainted with Gustav Mahler with whom Schoenberg was on intimate terms.

When Mahler left for America on 9 December 1907, Webern helped to organize an impromptu farewell gathering, since the Court Opera had failed to arrange any official function to honour its departing director after a decade of artistic triumphs under his leadership. A committee, headed by Webern, issued the following invitation to selected persons:

Dear friend,

The admirers of Gustav Mahler will meet for a final farewell on *Monday the 9th before 8.30 am on the platform of the West Station.* You are cordially invited to attend and to inform people of your acquaintance. As this is meant to be a surprise for Mahler, you are earnestly requested not to take representatives of the press into your confidence.

> Dr Anton von Webern
> Dr Karl Horwitz
> Dr Paul Stefan
> Heinrich Jalowetz

As a result of this invitation some 200 devotees of Mahler, including many leaders of Vienna's intellectual and artistic life, assembled at the train station to pay their homage. The display of loyalty must have been heart-warming for Mahler, who had resigned his powerful position because of long-festering intrigues.

Mahler returned to his native soil regularly for summer holidays. On one such visit an episode took place, for which Willi Reich cites Alban Berg as a witness. Mahler, the story goes, asked Zemlinsky and Schoenberg one evening to meet him in the Grinzing inn Zum Schutzengel and to invite also "the young people," since he enjoyed being with them.

They came [writes Willi Reich], found a separate room, and listened, for it was Mahler who spoke. He alone spoke, and hardly anyone dared to interject a word. It was not long before he referred to his revered Dostoyevsky. But it became apparent that he was not properly understood, for hardly anyone present possessed a close knowledge of Dostoyevsky. He said: "You must change this, Schoenberg! Let your pupils read Dostoyevsky, this is more important than counterpoint!" Silence—then Webern raised his hand like a small schoolboy and said quite softly: "Please, we do have Strindberg, after all." General laughter.[5]

Webern clearly felt compelled to rally to Schoenberg's defence even if it meant publicly disagreeing with a man of Mahler's stature. That he upheld Strindberg as a literary idol was the consequence of his intense occupation with this author's works. In 1908 he had glowingly described to Ernst Diez, in a letter of 17 July, his discovery of the "wonderful poet," possessed of such "marvellous intelligence," whose "phenomenal *Zones of the Spirit*, something entirely sublime" he was then reading, having already absorbed *The Red Room* and *The Black Flags*. During the summer of 1909, he read *Ghost Sonata* and *A Dream Play*, telling Schoenberg of the enormous impact that they made on him. His enthusiasm for Strindberg was to continue for many years.

The Swedish writer was but one of several contemporary authors who attracted the sympathies of the musical avant-garde at that time. Schoenberg maintained close contact with the brilliant essayist and poet Karl Kraus, a leader in Vienna's intellectual world, and it was through Schoenberg that Webern met Kraus. Webern likewise owed to Schoenberg an acquaintance with several painters who later became world renowned. Schoenberg himself was active as a painter, achieving in that medium a style and expressive force characteristically his own. His output had already assumed such proportions that a one-man exhibition of his pictures was held at Hugo Heller's Bookstore in early October 1910. For the opening, the Rosé ensemble performed Schoenberg's String Quartets, Opera 7 and 10. At that occasion, Gustav Mahler, who was aware of Schoenberg's economic plight, purchased three of the pictures with the stipulation that his name not be disclosed. (After Mahler's death Webern revealed this fact to Schoenberg.) Fully convinced of the artistic merit of his work, Schoenberg kept company with such painters as Gustav Klimt, Oskar Kokoschka, Egon Schiele, and Emil Stumpp, all of whom Webern came to know intimately. The three last-named actually became his portraitists. Webern was also friendly with the painter Max Oppenheimer ("Mopp")[6]—they addressed each other with the familiar "Du"—and when Mopp presented him with a picture in the spring of 1909, Webern wrote to him on 28 April in characteristic fashion: "Believe me, I always ardently try to appreciate an artistic achievement. Hardly anything is more nauseating to me than the matter-of-fact attitude that the Philistine brings to a work of art. Therefore, please believe in my sincerity, in the midst of this queer mendacious world." Such allegiance to a fellow artist reflected the spirit of the group. All its members felt themselves as brothers-in-arms against the bitter opposition that their avant-garde tendencies so frequently inspired. The group's solidarity was shared by men of diverse talents, such as Adolf Loos, the architect, and Peter Altenberg,[7] the poet, who was Alban Berg's special friend.

On 30 August 1909, Webern wrote to Schoenberg from the Preglhof that he would return to Vienna in the middle of September. After this letter, the correspondence again ceases until spring. Therefore, records of Webern's activities during the winter of 1909–10 are meagre. The 1909 Theaterband (theatre yearbook) of the Vienna Volksoper lists his name, along with that of Alexander von Zemlinsky, but it does not state in which capacity he served. Probably he was an assistant coach. Since his family had relinquished its Vienna apartment, Webern had to live by himself for the first time. A letter from his father, written on 2 January 1910, discloses that the elder Webern provided his son with financial assistance. That Christmas, Webern had been unable to spend the customary holiday at the Preglhof because of his theatre duties. Concerned about his well-being, his father offered his counsel:

> I beg you most urgently always to keep your health in mind, i.e. to eat and dress properly and not to strain yourself too much. If the director is so niggardly and pays you nothing, then you should at least make the duties somewhat easier for yourself. I would tell him, for instance, that you cannot be present at the performance *every* evening since you are compelled to earn something elsewhere and that you need for this at least three evenings weekly. The other coaches, who are being paid, are to do the stage duty. You really render enough service if you hold rehearsals during the daytime. If you are asked how you can earn something, just say "by giving lessons." . . . It would be very nice indeed if you were to obtain the conductor's post at the Volksoper in Berlin. Would it not be good if Zemlinsky would write out for you a report on your present activity?

On 14 January 1910 Webern participated in a concert given under the auspices of the Society for Art and Culture. The event featured the first public performances of Schoenberg's Three Piano Pieces, Op. 11, the song cycle on Stefan George's *Das Buch der hängenden Gärten*, Op. 15, and a piano reduction of an excerpt from the still unfinished *Gurrelieder*. (This gigantic project, begun in 1900, had been laid aside in 1903, but the success of the performance of the excerpt encouraged the composer to undertake the completion of the score that same summer.) Schoenberg had entrusted to Webern the reduction (for two pianos, eight hands) of the orchestral Prelude and Interludes. This was the first in a series of transcriptions that he assigned to him over the years. Pianists at the historic performance included, besides Webern himself, Etta Werndorff, Dr Rudolf Weirich, and Arnold Winternitz.

Several months after this concert, on 10 April, Webern sent Schoenberg his first written message since the preceding summer. Announcing a visit for the following evening, he cryptically remarked: "I have much to tell you. For me each day is more terrible than the one before." The complaint may or may not have had to do with his theatre work.

Shortly afterwards, Webern secured an engagement as second conductor at the Civic Theatre in Bad Teplitz, a well-known spa in northern Bohemia (site of the famous meeting between Beethoven and Goethe in 1812). He found the resort beautiful and his lodgings, in the home of Johann Korb at Stephansplatz 14, very nice. However, he took a dim view of his future when writing to Schoenberg on 13 May: "It appears to me more and more improbable that I should remain with the theatre. It is all so terrible. . . . Also I can hardly ever adjust to being away from home." The next postcard, dated 19 May, showed a marked improvement in his outlook. He had received various conducting assignments, including Leo Fall's *Geschiedene Frau* and *Dollarprinzessin*. He also expected to be in charge of Strauss' *Fledermaus* and he was particularly looking forward to conducting Schumann's stage music to Byron's play *Manfred*.

All was well when Webern wrote again on 25 May. By then he had made his conducting début in *Geschiedene Frau*, and the newspaper report had praised his "sensitive, devoted guidance" of the operetta.

I fared very well in my conducting [he related]. Nothing at all went wrong. On Saturday I will have *Walzertraum* [an operetta by Oscar Straus]. The orchestra is good, though very small (22 men). . . . I am only curious as to how it will be with the operas, for with such an ensemble I cannot perform any Puccini operas. The singers are to be engaged for July and August. Next week I will have *Dollarprinzessin* and *Geschiedene Frau*, then *Luxemburg* [*Der Graf von Luxemburg* by Franz Lehár]. By autumn I will have had much experience. Once one conducts [a performance], rehearsing is quite different. The responsibility heightens the pleasure. The personnel is very nice and does everything I want. I learned much again during winter. I am definitely already on top of things.

A postcard sent to Alban Berg the same day likewise shows Webern in good spirits, the fare of frothy operettas he had to deal with notwithstanding. But his anticipation that he might soon test his capabilities on greater tasks was to be crushed, for the Teplitz engagement, like that at Innsbruck, ended in a sudden and complete fiasco. Writing to Schoenberg from Klagenfurt on 14 June, Webern plunged into the middle of things:

> The matter in Teplitz was so: I had to do the *Dollarprinzessin* with a guest from Berlin. The next day, he complained to the director that I was not giving him any cues, and if I were to conduct the next performance (*Geschiedene Frau*), he would have to have an orchestral rehearsal. Now this operetta was allotted to me; I had already conducted it. However, since no orchestral rehearsal was possible on the day of the performance, and also not earlier, the director simply took the operetta away from me. This is certainly no way for a director to behave. Either the conductor is acceptable to the guest, or the guest is thrown out. The director is, after all, responsible for the conductor whom he has engaged. And this man tells me without hesitation, as if this were a foregone conclusion, that I had to step back. Without further explanation. This put me in such a rage that I walked out without any further discussion. At that, the performance of the *Dollarprinzessin* was entirely faultless on my part, and generally quite good considering the short rehearsal time. The newspaper review again prominently singled me out for special notice. This behaviour was therefore totally without justification. Moreover, I was told from two quarters that the orchestra spoke very well of me. The singers also were enthusiastic about me, and somebody told me that the singers all preferred me to the other conductor. And then this conduct on the director's part! Abominable! . . . If I obtain a good winter engagement, nothing is really lost. On the contrary: now I can compose during the summer. Believe me, it was quite terrible for me that I constantly had to face not being able to work during the summer.

The Teplitz affair forms but one link in the chain of Webern's unhappy experiences in the theatre. Already in the letter describing his latest calamity, Webern, undaunted, asks Schoenberg's assistance in securing the post of chorus master at the Court Opera in Mannheim (Schoenberg's friend, Artur Bodanzky, was music director of that theatre, and Zemlinsky had gone there from Vienna). While waiting for an opening, Webern settled down at the Preglhof for another productive summer. On 23 June, he told Schoenberg: "I have already composed something here: a cycle of four pieces for violin and piano." The satisfaction of being at work compensated him for his failure at Teplitz. "It often saddens me that I left there," he commented, "but still I am glad that I can compose and in that way continue to think." The summer's output was to include, besides the violin and piano cycle (Op. 7), two orchestral songs on Rilke poems (Op. 8). There were also sketches for an opera based on Maeterlinck's *The Seven Princesses*. However, Webern's work on this project was interrupted by an assignment from Schoenberg, who asked him to make a piano reduction of his Six Orchestra Songs, Op. 8. (All these works will be discussed in the following chapter.)

That Webern regarded his music as integrally connected with ethos becomes evident from some remarks to Schoenberg, penned at Klagenfurt on 10 August. About to set out on a mountain climb with his brother-in-law, Paul Clementschitsch, Webern wrote:

> I will ascend the Triglav, a very high and rather difficult peak. Perhaps you find it ridiculous that I do something like this, but what attracts me is the unique atmosphere on the heights of the mountains, its delicate and pure quality. True, the hiking itself is dull—but to be up there! One danger exists for me: I am getting farther and farther away from the theatre,[8] from companionship with people in general. It gives me such a disagreeable feeling to be away from our estate, to find myself immersed in the stream of people. I hardly understand all this any longer, or else I understand it only too well. The solitude and the striving for God. To cast off all that is impure. Whenever I think of my works, I feel better. I have become conscious that they are good. I mean good also in other respects. But perhaps this is only a delusion. There still is much that is bad in me. But since I perceive it already, it may well disappear soon.

That mountain excursion (on which the summit was attained) was the only interruption in Webern's stay at the Preglhof that summer. The pastoral seclusion allowed him to immerse himself in music, literature, and philosophy. The book *Über die letzten Dinge* by Otto Weininger[9] occupied him intensely and caused him to ask Schoenberg on 23 June: "Tell me, can one at all denote thinking and feeling as things entirely separable? I cannot imagine a sublime intellect without the ardour of emotion. This is certainly the case with Weininger—and with Strindberg, Plato, Kant, Kraus?[10] It simply flows directly out of these human beings. I presently keep thinking of the following men: you, Kokoschka, Mahler, Kraus, and Weininger."

In an attempt to apply his philosophical outlook to Mahler's music, Webern, writing again to Schoenberg two weeks later, speculated:

If one did not know his life, one could reconstruct it from his symphonies. They really must be most closely connected with his inner experiences. I also see a development: from the most intense worship of nature to an ever more spiritual, more detached content. This is, time and again, my compelling impression, regardless of whether it is justified or not. This quality of abstraction in an art work is more important for me, however, than, say, the assessment of technical skill. I can make such an assessment with Richard Strauss. With Mahler it never enters my mind. Here as there, of course, the man lies behind the work, but something ethically higher speaks from Mahler. The difference exists at any rate. Is it not a value difference?

Mahler was in Toblach that summer of 1910, and when Webern congratulated him on his fiftieth birthday, he received a friendly reply. Like everything else that moved him, this was shared with Schoenberg. The latter, on his part, drew Webern increasingly into his confidence, keeping him abreast of the progress of his *Harmonielehre* and sending him the recently completed libretto of his opera *Die glückliche Hand*, which only Zemlinsky had been allowed to read before. He also informed Webern immediately when he was appointed that summer to become lecturer in composition at the Vienna Academy.

On 27 July Webern excitedly wrote to Schoenberg of "a fabulously beautiful prose book by Rilke, just published, *Die Aufzeichnungen des Malte Laurids Brigge* [*The Notebook of Malte Laurids Brigge*]." A week later, he described the work rapturously and singled out one of the passages which then held profound meaning for him: "He [Rilke] makes, for instance, the distinction between fate and life, connecting the rôle of the man with the former and that of the woman with the latter. . . . 'Always, she who loves surpasses him who loves, since life is greater than fate. Her devotion wants to be immeasurable: this is her happiness. The unutterable sorrow of her love has always been, however, that she is asked to limit this devotion.'"

So immediate and consuming was the impact of Rilke's book on Webern that he spontaneously set to music two short poems interpolated in the narrative. These lyrics were singularly pertinent to his personal situation at the time. During the summer weeks of 1910, his love affair with Wilhelmine entered a crucial phase. Their intimate relationship had led to consequences which would make marriage mandatory. Their parents, however, were strictly opposed to a union. Anton's and Wilhelmine's mothers were sisters, and the Roman Catholic Church forbids marriage between first cousins.

The two Rilke poems abound in allusions to the predicament in which the young people found themselves. As matters stood, they fully belonged to each other, though they could not be united before the eyes of the world. Rilke's verses express that paradox of greatest closeness yet insurmountable distance. The lyrics therefore particularly affected Webern, who saw his own dilemma reflected in them. And like every true artist he sought liberation from his anguish through creative work.

CHAPTER VII

Opera 3–8—Two opera projects (1908–1910)

O N 1 7 J ULY 1908 Webern wrote to Ernst Diez from Bad Ischl:

It pleases me very much that you want to write an opera libretto for me. I believe I already wrote to you that I have begun with the composition of Maeterlinck's *Alladine and Palomides*. This will be my first opera. Schoenberg is very satisfied. Your opera libretto then could be used for the second opera. However, I make the following conditions: *no procession, no combat, nothing of the sort that in any way requires* "illustration." I need nothing but a few characters. By no means a theatrical piece. To a certain extent Maeterlinck writes in this vein. But I want it even more so. Just get away from everything that is now called theatre. The opposite. Do you understand me? If your libretto turns out that way, then it will be all right with me. Everything else repulses me to the highest degree.

While no record remains of whether or not Diez took up his cousin's suggestions, there does exist some evidence of the opera project *Alladine and Palomides*, the text of which forms the second of Maeterlinck's *Three Mystic Plays*. (That trilogy of short dramas opens with *The Seven Princesses*, to which Webern turned two years later.) The mystical and metaphysical writings of the Belgian author, Maurice Maeterlinck, exerted a strong influence during the *fin de siècle*. His works include many critical essays, but he attained fame chiefly for his symbolist dramas, among which *Pelleas and Melisande* is one of the best known. Since Schoenberg and Debussy had already used this subject, Webern looked for another Maeterlinck text. Characteristically, he chose the short play *Alladine and Palomides*—a drama closely akin in substance and symbolism to *Pelleas and Melisande*, but written two years earlier.

Judging from Webern's optimistic report to Diez, the project seems to have progressed to some length. However, only a single-leaf sketch, containing a short prelude and the beginning of Ablamore's monologue opening Act I, has survived. The scenario is identical with that of Maeterlinck's play. Details of instrumentation (oboe, muted trombone, timpani) already appear in the condensed score. The sketch bears the key signature of three sharps, a detail important to note since the year of its composition, 1908, opens the period of "atonality," to be discussed shortly. Other works originating that year—three of the five Dehmel songs, the Passacaglia, and the chorus *Entflieht auf leichten Kähnen*—likewise still employ key signatures, but the George songs, with the exception of one, do not. Much later (in a lecture given on 12 February 1932) Webern himself said of this transitional phase that the presence or absence of a key signature had ceased to be the criterion for a fixed tonality. "In this musical material," he stated, "new laws asserted themselves that made it impossible to designate a piece as being in one key or another."[1]

With the fourteen settings of poems by Stefan George for voice and piano Webern consciously crossed the borderline separating functional tonality from the still uncharted domain of "atonality." That controversial term, though conceded to be a misnomer, has been generally if reluctantly used to designate the harmonic situation that evolved when standard procedures of traditional harmony were being rendered increasingly obsolete. (Schoenberg's suggestion of the name "pantonality" did not find favour.) The most obvious feature of atonality was, in Schoenberg's coinage, the "emancipation of dissonance," bringing out the establishment of dissonance as a new unit, if not principle, of sound. This development was more a gradual transition than a sudden upheaval. Heralded already in the music of Alexander Scriabin and in the later works of Max Reger, the tendency towards atonality is likewise apparent in the early compositions of Béla Bartók. It was, however, the combined efforts of Schoenberg, Webern, and Berg that precipitated a full awareness and an attending articulation of the new harmonic concept. Among its characteristics were shifting chromaticism and the absence of triads, so that analysis in the conventional sense was no longer applicable.

In another of his lectures (on 15 January 1932), Webern vividly described that period of transformation and its effects:

The fact that cadences were shaped ever more richly, that instead of chords of the sub-dominant, dominant and tonic one increasingly used substitutes for them and then altered even those—it led to the break-up of tonality. The substitutes became steadily more independent. It was possible to go into another tonality here and there. The substitutes became so predominant that the necessity of returning to the main key disappeared. [Webern then focussed on the fundamental problem:] Where was one to go and did one in fact have to return to the relationships implied by traditional harmony? When we considered these things we felt: "We do not need these relationships any more, our ear is satisfied without tonality, too." The time was simply ripe for the disappearance of tonality. Naturally this was a fierce struggle. Inhibitions of the most frightful kind, the fear, "Is this at all possible?" had to be overcome. And so it came about that gradually a piece was written, assuredly and consciously, that was not in a definite key any more. You are listening to one who has experienced all these things and shared in the fight for them. All these events followed each other precipitately; they happened to us unselfconsciously and intuitively. And never before in the realm of music has there been such a resistance to these things. Naturally it is nonsense to advance "social" objections. Why do people not understand this? It was for us a push that *had* to be made, a push the like of which just had never happened before. With each work we must, in fact, arrive at another destination—each work is something different, something new.[2]

In their exploration of a terra incognita, the musicians were inspired by the poets. When Schoenberg's song cycle based on George's *Das Buch der hängenden Gärten* was first performed in Vienna in 1910, the composer acknowledged in the programme notes that the poems had been instrumental in opening up new vistas for him. Stefan George was also Webern's literary model. Selections from the cycles *Das Jahr der Seele, Der siebente Ring*, and *Das Buch der Sagen und Sänge* furnished the texts for a total of sixteen musical settings. Besides the chorus *Entflieht auf leichten Kähnen* of 1908 and the orchestral song "Kunfttag III" of 1914, fourteen songs with piano accompaniment were composed during 1908 and 1909. Of these, only ten were known before 1965: Five Songs from *Der siebente Ring*, Op. 3, and Five Songs, Op. 4.[3] The other four songs, discovered posthumously, were published in 1970 as Four Stefan George Songs.[4]

Webern's original plans for these fourteen voice–piano settings are revealed in two title pages accompanying the manuscripts. His first intention was to combine seven songs as his "Opus 2," [*sic*] with the sequence:

1. "Eingang"
2. "Dies ist ein Lied"
3. "Erwachen aus dem tiefsten Traumesschosse"

4. "Im Windesweben"
5. "Kunfttag I"
6. "Kahl reckt der Baum"
7. "Im Morgentaun"

The other plan, entitled "Seven Songs, Op. 4," stipulated:

1. "Trauer I"
2. "Ja Heil und Dank dir"
3. "Noch zwingt mich Treue"
4. "An Bachesranft"
5. "Das lockere Saatgefilde"
6. "So ich traurig bin"
7. "Ihr tratet zu dem Herde"

Several subsequent changes in the title listings bear witness to Webern's continual preoccupation with the grouping of the songs. One designation reads "Nine Songs on Poems of Stefan George." To this heading the composer added in pencil "Op. 6," but he did not give the individual titles which were to comprise that group. On the right hand upper corner of the page, Webern wrote "100—150—200 copies," an indication that he was making plans for publication. The entire concept was crossed out, however, and a later note on the same page reads "Five Songs, Op. 4." The manuscripts of the songs themselves also contain evidence of revisions and regroupings. For example, one of the copies of "Noch zwingt mich Treue" bears the marking "Op. 3, No. 5." "Erwachen aus dem tiefsten Traumesschosse" was designated as "Op. 5, No. 2," and "Im Morgentaun" as "Op. 3, No. 6."

When the cycles were finally published, more than a decade after their composition, two songs from each of the original title listings were omitted. Several of the other ten songs were interchanged, so that their definitive order was established as Opus 3: 1. "Dies ist ein Lied" 2. "Im Windesweben" 3. "An Bachesranft" 4. "Im Morgentaun" 5. "Kahl reckt der Baum," and Opus 4: 1. "Eingang" 2. "Noch zwingt mich Treue" 3. "Ja Heil und Dank dir" 4. "So ich traurig bin" 5. "Ihr tratet zu dem Herde." For the four posthumously published songs the composer's original sequence was retained: 1. "Erwachen aus dem tiefsten Traumesschosse" 2. "Kunfttag I" 3. "Trauer I" 4. "Das lockere Saatgefilde." Webern wrote out the last two songs in large notation for performance purposes, an indication that he himself considered them fully valid. If he did this also for the other two, the manuscripts are not extant.

Of particular importance is the composer's own date "1908–9" on his

Opus 3 cycle, since it conflicts with that given in the literature as
"1907–8." The last song in the Opus 4 cycle is marked at the end
"1908–9," which obviously applies to the entire group. In a later
handwritten work list encompassing his Opera 1 to 22, Webern further
confirmed the period of origin for the two cycles as "1908 and 1909."
The list also reveals that the songs were written partly in Vienna and
partly at the Preglhof. None of the individual songs bears a date. The
only reference to their origin occurs in Webern's letters to Schoenberg,
where he speaks of three of them as having been composed during the
summer of 1909. He gives no titles, however, and merely comments on
20 August concerning the last two that they had turned out "again quite
different than heretofore."

In considering the genesis of the fourteen George songs, it should be
kept in mind that they came into being as one complex, and that the
contents of the three printed editions are not in chronological order.
It might be conjectured that "Erwachen aus dem tiefsten
Traumesschosse" was written first, since it is the only song still
employing a key signature. However, that key signature of four sharps
(omitted in the printed edition) is hardly operative.

In May 1912 "Ihr tratet zu dem Herde" (later assigned the closing
position in the Opus 4 cycle) was included, with songs by Schoenberg
and Berg, in the publication Der blaue Reiter, edited by the painters
Kandinsky and Marc, both of whom were friends of Schoenberg. The
volume, a literary platform dedicated to a new aesthetic credo, was
singularly appropriate for bringing the musical avant-garde to public
awareness. The song (then marked "Op. 2") was the second of Webern's
compositions ever to appear in print (the first of the Four Pieces, Op. 7,
had been published two months earlier).

In 1919 the Five Songs, Op. 3, were printed by Waldheim Eberle,
Vienna, under the nominal auspices of the Society for Private Musical
Performances, but Webern no doubt assumed the cost himself.[5] Soon
thereafter, Universal Edition signed its first contract with Webern, and
Opus 3 and Opus 4 were brought out (in 1921 and 1923, respectively)
under its imprint. The composer worked on revisions up till publication
time. One title page contains the note "Op. 4 (5 songs) definitive version
1920." This work was dedicated to Werner Reinhart, a Swiss patron of
the arts, who by then had repeatedly given Webern financial assistance.
(The Variations for Orchestra, Op. 30, were likewise dedicated to him.)

Some songs on George texts were first performed in early 1910, along
with Webern's Five Movements, Op. 5, according to a short review
appearing in Der Merker, a Vienna journal for art and music.[6] No details
of the concert were given, but the precise date, 8 February, was recorded
in the 1911 edition of the Musikbuch aus Österreich.[7] The first public

ANTON WEBERN

FÜNF LIEDER

AUS

„DER SIEBENTE RING"

VON

STEFAN GEORGE

FÜR EINE SINGSTIMME UND KLAVIER

OP. 3

PREIS K 3.60

Herrn Alexander Zemlinsky.
in Verehrung und Dankbarkeit

A Webern

AUFFÜHRUNGSRECHT VORBEHALTEN

SELBSTVERLAG

EIGENTUM DES »VEREIN FÜR MUSIKALISCHE PRIVATAUFFÜHRUNGEN«

WIEN

Fünf Lieder, Op. 3, first edition

rendition of the complete Opus 3 cycle took place on 6 June 1919, in the
last of "Four Propaganda Evenings" presented by Schoenberg's Society
for Private Musical Performances. Felicie Hüni-Mihacsek was the singer
and Eduard Steuermann the pianist. The concert concluded with the
songs, which followed the piano reduction of Webern's Passacaglia.

As to the Opus 4 cycle, the earliest recorded performance of "So ich
traurig bin" (No. 4) occurred on 18 January 1925 in New York's
Aeolian Hall under the aegis of the Franco-American Musical Society.
Webern's song, paired with Alban Berg's "Dem Schmerz sein Recht,"
appeared on a programme that also included works by Debussy,
Stravinsky, and Charles Griffes. The artists were Greta Torpadie and
Rex Tillson. Such pioneer performances of Webern's compositions were
few and far between. During the late 'twenties and early 'thirties, Ruzena
Herlinger introduced individual songs to Paris and London audiences.
The first ascertainable performance of the complete Opus 4 cycle took
place, in the composer's presence, on 10 February 1940, in a concert of
the Basel section ISCM (International Society for Contemporary Music).
Marguerite Gradmann-Lüscher sang and Erich Schmid was at the
piano. In a letter to Willi Reich preceding that concert Webern had
recommended the performance of selected songs from various cycles;
he proposed a group consisting of Opus 3, Nos. 1 and 5, Opus 4, No. 5
or No. 1, and Opus 12, Nos. 1 and 4, in that order. This suggestion,
from the composer himself, deserves special attention, since it has
become established practice to render the song cycles unbroken. In that
letter of 20 October 1939, Webern had commented that "So ich traurig
bin" had "*never* been sung before." He obviously had forgotten the New
York performance fifteen years earlier, which he had recorded in his
diary.

In the George songs, Webern stepped over the threshold of
conventional tonality to explore the expressive dimensions of a novel
idiom. The new musical language required a form of its own, and a
technique of new units of sound developed as a result. In structure, as in
harmonic treatment, the tenets and patterns of the past are drastically
altered. The use of sequence is now shunned. The former concept of
symmetry, which governed the welding together of various structural
elements, is abnegated by avoiding repetition. Motivic working has
replaced conventional thematic development. The motives themselves
derive largely from the components of chords: spatial sound is
converted into time, the vertical becomes horizontal. Prominent among
the dissonant intervals employed is the minor second, an omnipresent
Webern hallmark that serves to heighten tension. Voice and piano parts
are fully integrated, each generating the other. The voice is treated in
recitative style and moves with conciseness and certainty towards the

natural high points implied by the texts. Syllabic synchronization of word and tone gives way to florid passages only at moments of emphatic significance. The high degree of momentum in the flow of the music is balanced by the sense of destination sustained in such climaxes. The wide vocal leaps so characteristic of Webern's later style are already in evidence. Subdued, atmospheric and transparent, the songs are the distillation of the purest lyricism.

Before the last George songs were composed, an instrumental work in the new atonal idiom had come into being. On 16 June 1909, Webern reported to Schoenberg from the Preglhof: "I have already written an entire string quartet. It has five movements: the first fast, the second very slow, the third very fast, the fourth slow, the fifth a slow 6/8 metre. The movements are all short. . . . If I cannot see you for some time, I would like to send you my quartet." The work so announced is now known as the Five Movements, Op. 5. Webern first designated it "Opus 3," and then expanded that opus in 1911 and 1913 with two further sets of string quartet movements. These later components were eventually consolidated into the Six Bagatelles, Op. 9, and the original quartet was labelled "Opus 5." On the back of one of the title pages the composer writes "for 2 July 1909" (Wilhelmine's birthday). With the exception of an earlier version of the first movement, breaking off after six measures, the work appears to have been written in one sweep, assuming definitive shape from the start.

At Schoenberg's suggestion, Webern wrote out the parts and sent them in early September to Arnold Rosé. However, it was not the Rosé Quartet but another ensemble, probably improvised for the occasion,[8] that played the work for the first time in a concert taking place on 8 February 1910. (The aforementioned notice in *Der Merker* of February 1910, which reported the quartet's performance, along with that of selected George songs, does not give the names of the artists.) On 20 September 1910, in a letter to Alban Berg, Webern indicated that the Rosé Quartet once again had the score and parts. Webern, Berg, and Horwitz were then planning to subsidize a concert of their own compositions. That programme was given on 24 April 1911, under the aegis of Vienna's Society for Art and Culture, and included the Five Movements. However, the Rosé Quartet, to the composer's great disappointment, was unable to participate and a substitute ensemble, consisting of Fritz Brunner, Oskar Holzer, Bernhard Buchbinder, and Josef Haša, had to be recruited. The Rosé Quartet did perform the work in a concert in Vienna on 29 June 1912. During the 1919–20 season of the Society for Private Musical Performances, the work (then announced as "Fünf Stücke" (rather than "Fünf Sätze") was played by the Feist Quartet. In 1922, the Five Movements incited a major scandal when performed during the first ISCM festival at Salzburg (see Chapter XV). To coincide with the Salzburg performance, Universal Edition published the score both in a large size, suitable for use by the players, and in a pocket edition.

If the quartet proved difficult to comprehend even for the audience of seasoned musicians assembled at Salzburg thirteen years after its composition, this was chiefly because of the startling brevity of some of the movements (the third lasts only 35 seconds) and their motivic concentration. The tonal fabric is so tightly interwoven that a high degree of structural condensation results; the textural intricacies, aurally elusive, can be fully grasped only through analysis. Para- doxically, this aphoristic style was born amidst the lush and over- grown manifestations of the late Romantic era. Such emancipation from structural models notwithstanding, the first movement can be traced along the outlines of the sonata-allegro form. In his treatment of the string instruments, Webern, himself a cellist, employs a great variety of devices: frequent changes of arco and pizzicato, abundant use of col legno and sul ponticello, harmonics and tremolos. All these techniques assume importance as structural elements, and each tone thus becomes a building block within the tiny cells that make up the total texture. Among the chief characteristics of these pieces are highly individualized timbres and dynamic and rhythmic differentiation. The harmonic web presents a contrapuntal kaleidoscope, abounding in imitation and inversion. The motivic use of dissonant intervals adds to the sense of dramatic tension.

Almost two decades after the composition of the Five Movements, Webern decided to transcribe them for string orchestra. He used as a basis the large printed score of the quartet, indicating the changes in red ink and indelible pencil and noting on the cover "First draft, Summer 1928." Apart from a few octave doublings in the upper strings, the arrangement affected mainly the cello section, parts of which were assigned to the newly added contrabasses. There appeared also indications for divisions into soli and tutti passages.

That first version was supplanted by another, the manuscript sketches of which were marked "Second draft, January–February 1929." The reason for the revision is given in a letter to Schoenberg, dated 19 February 1929:

In early January, I had already started intensive work on my new composition [the Quartet, Op. 22]. All of a sudden it became clear to me that the string orchestra arrangement of my first string quartet, which I had made during the summer of 1928 and had already turned over to Universal Edition, was not the right thing. During all the intervening time I had had a bad conscience, and so I took the arrangement back again and now I am making a new and *entirely different* one. The work—I will have finished it shortly—gives me much satisfaction. Only now is it becoming a true orchestra setting. I am using the original solely as a sketch for the full score. I lay bare the *motivic structure* (in doing so, I often come to fourteen staves) and with this, I believe, I offer proof that I have understood your former method of arranging Bach compositions. I am looking forward very much to showing you this work. The picture of the score turns out to be very good.[9]

After completing the transcription, Webern wrote to Josef Humplik, his sculptor friend, on 4 March 1929: "What I have succeeded in makes me very proud."

The first performance of the arrangement, noted in Webern's diary, took place on 26 March 1930. It was given by the Philadelphia Chamber String Sinfonietta under Fabien Sevitzky in the ballroom of the Bellevue-Stratford Hotel in Philadelphia. One year later, on 8 May 1931, Webern himself conducted the transcription in a BBC concert in London. The first movement was omitted because of lack of rehearsal time. In 1944, when Willi Reich tried to promote a performance in Switzerland, the composer wrote him about the work on 23 February:

It must be played by as large a body of strings as possible [in an earlier letter, dated 10 January, Webern envisioned "about 80 players," adding, "but naturally it will also go otherwise"], so that the constant subdivisions (from tutti to half to solo) stand out in a clearly audible way. It has really turned into something entirely new! In regard to the sound effect! I can only say: "How much those gentlemen conductors allow themselves to miss!" I am very glad that it is you who will now take the initiative! I believe that people will be amazed.

Webern, so convinced of the merits of his transcription, was not to see it published during his lifetime. Only in 1961 did Universal Edition release the printed score.

In the same letter (16 June 1909) in which Webern had informed Schoenberg of the completion of his Five Movements for String Quartet, he announced his intention to compose, after a few songs, a work for orchestra. "I can hardly wait to start it," he commented. The project, so keenly anticipated, was repeatedly delayed by the summer's events, culminating in the disastrous theatre experience in Innsbruck at the end of July. From that depressing fiasco Webern fled into creative work. On 20 August he informed Schoenberg: "Meantime I have written two songs and two orchestra pieces. The songs are quite different than heretofore. Of course, this goes also for the orchestra pieces." On 30 August he reported: "I have now finished five orchestra pieces. The instrumentation of the fifth is not completed as yet (that of the others is already done). Tomorrow I will finish it. . . . I am writing a cycle of orchestra pieces; rather, I should say, it just happens to turn out this way. There will be six pieces. In the instrumentation, almost entirely pure colours. Just as it comes about."

Before Webern left the Preglhof for Vienna that year, the draft of his Six Pieces, Op. 6, was completed.[10] In the work's first version, the fourth movement is marked *Langsam, marcia funebre* (Slowly, funeral march). That programmatic designation, though later dropped, is significant, for the funereal character of the cycle's central piece epitomizes the atmosphere of tension and melancholy hovering over the entire work. The lasting sadness which sank upon the composer with his mother's death in 1906 was repeatedly referred to by him, and many of his compositions are marked by the shadow of that fundamental experience. On 13 January 1913, a few weeks before the first performance of the Six Pieces, Webern described, in a letter to Schoenberg, the moods and scenes underlying the various movements:

> The first piece is to express my frame of mind when I was still in Vienna, already sensing the disaster, yet always maintaining the hope that I would find my mother still alive. It was a beautiful day—for a minute I believed quite firmly that nothing had happened. Only during the train ride to Carinthia—it was on the afternoon of the same day—did I learn the truth.[11] The third piece conveys the impression of the fragrance of the Erica [a kind of heather], which I gathered at a spot in the forest very meaningful to me and then laid on the bier.[12] The fourth piece I later entitled *marcia funebre*. Even today I do not understand my feelings as I walked behind the coffin to the cemetery. I only know that I walked the entire way with my head held high, as if to banish everything lowly all around. I beg you to understand me properly—I am myself trying to gain clarity about that peculiar state. I have talked to no one as yet about it. The evening after the funeral was miraculous. With my wife[13] I went once again to the cemetery and there straightened out the wreaths and flowers on the grave. Always I had the feeling of my mother's bodily presence—I saw her friendly smile, it was a blissful feeling that lasted moments. Two summers after that [actually it was three] I was at our estate again for an extended period; this was the time when I wrote these pieces at summer's end. Daily, towards evening, I was at the grave—often in deep dusk.

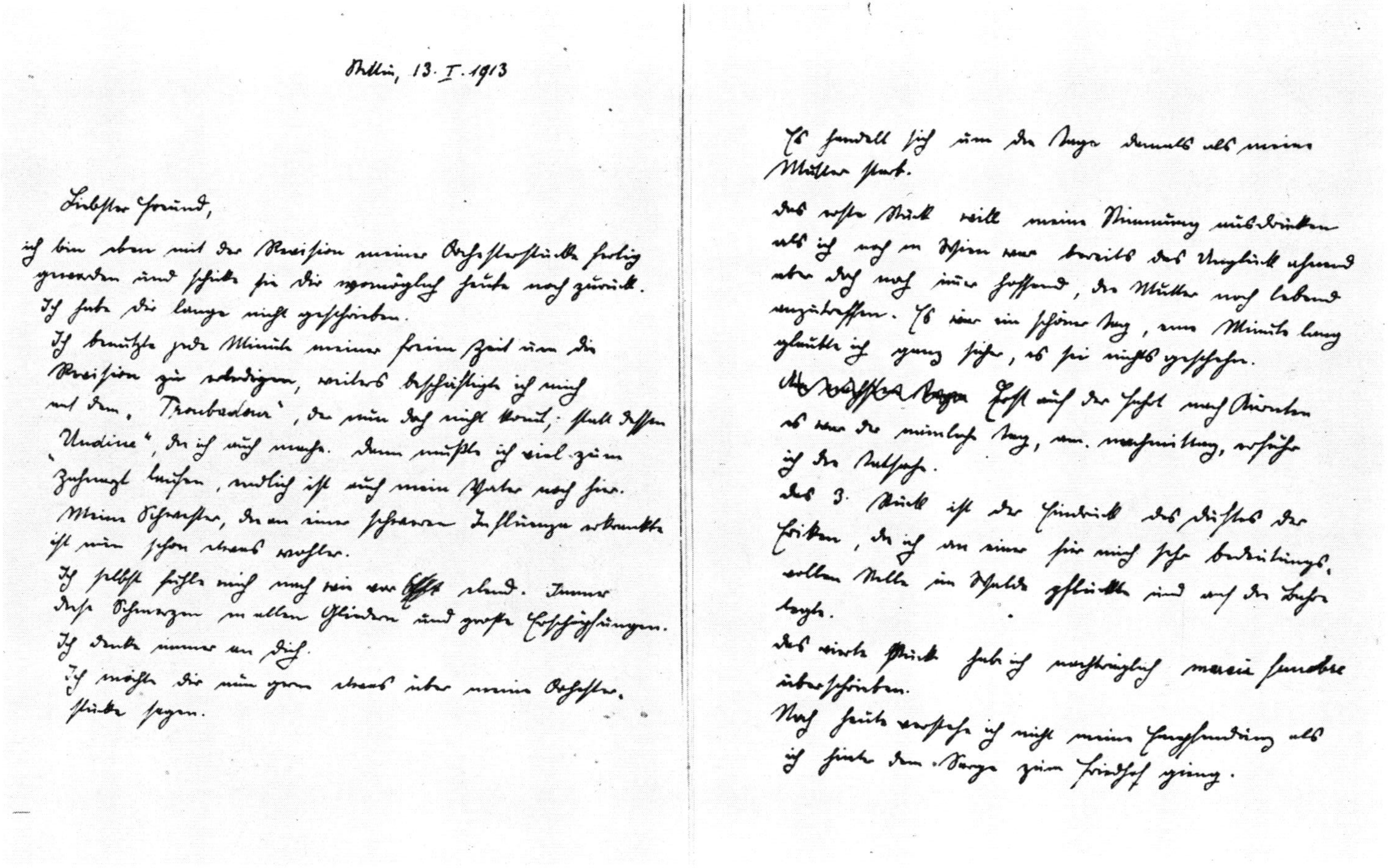

Stettin, 13. I. 1913

Liebster Freund,

ich bin eben mit der Revision meiner Orchesterstücke fertig geworden und schicke sie dir womöglich heute noch zurück.
Ich habe dir lange nicht geschrieben.
Ich brauchte jede Minute meiner freien Zeit um die Revision zu erledigen, weiters beschäftigte ich mich mit dem „Troubadour", der nun doch nicht kommt; statt dessen „Undine", die ich auch mache. Dann musste ich viel zum Zahnarzt laufen, endlich ist auch mein Vater noch hier.
Meine Schwester, die an einer schweren Influenza erkrankte ist nun schon etwas wohler.
Ich selbst fühle mich noch sehr elend. Immer diese Schmerzen in allen Gliedern und große Erschöpfungen.
Ich denke immer an Dich.
Ich möchte dir nun gern etwas über meine Orchesterstücke sagen.

Es handelt sich um die Tage damals als meine Mutter starb.
Das erste Stück will meine Stimmung ausdrücken als ich noch in Wien war bereits das Unglück ahnend aber doch noch immer hoffend, die Mutter noch lebend anzutreffen. Es war ein schöner Tag, eine Minute lang glaubte ich ganz sicher, es sei nichts geschehen.
Erst auf der Fahrt nach Kärnten, es war der nämliche Tag, am Nachmittag, erfuhr ich die Wahrheit.
Das 3. Stück ist der Eindruck des Duftes der Eriken, die ich an einer für mich sehr bedeutungsvollen Stelle im Walde gepflückt und auf die Bahre legte.
Das vierte Stück habe ich nachträglich marcia funebre überschrieben.
Noch heute verstehe ich nicht meine Empfindung als ich hinter dem Sarge zum Friedhof ging.

Letter to Arnold Schoenberg (Stettin, 13 January 1913)

In 1933, when Webern's Opus 6 was placed on the programme of the 63rd Tonkünstler Festival of the Allgemeiner Deutscher Musikverein, to be held in Dortmund during June,[14] the composer provided a short commentary that was published in the *Zeitschrift für Musik*:

> The pieces originated in 1909. . . . They represent short song forms, in that they are mostly tripartite. A thematic connection does not exist, not even within the individual pieces. I consciously avoided such connections, since I aimed at an always changing mode of expression. To describe briefly the character of the pieces (they are of a purely lyrical nature): the first expresses the expectation of a catastrophe; the second the certainty of its fulfilment; the third the most tender contrast; it is, so to speak, the introduction to the fourth, a funeral march; five and six are an epilogue: remembrance and resignation. In 1928 the pieces received a new instrumentation, which, compared with the original version, represents a substantial simplification and is to be considered the only valid one.[15]

The première of the Six Pieces, Op. 6, took place, under Schoenberg's direction, in Vienna on 31 March 1913. (The dramatic circumstances of the concert, which ended in a riot requiring police intervention, will be related in Chapter X.) To coincide with the first performance, Webern arranged for the publication of 200 copies of the full score, at his own expense and under his own imprint ("Im Selbstverlag des Komponisten"), through the printing house of Straube. He then gave the work the designation "Opus 4" and dedicated it "To Arnold Schoenberg, my teacher and friend, with greatest affection."[16] In 1961, that handsome first edition was reissued in pocket score by Universal Edition.

As noted in Webern's remarks of 1933, the instrumentation of the original version was substantially condensed by the composer in 1928.* According to his diary entries, he began the rescoring in early August and finished it on 4 September; he handed over the revision to Universal Edition three days later, together with the score of his just completed Symphony, Op. 21. The reduction primarily affected the wind instruments. Webern had approached the task of pruning the ensemble as a real challenge and registered his satisfaction with the outcome in a letter to Schoenberg on 20 August: "Everything extravagant is now cut (alto flute, six trombones for a few measures, and so on). Now I can represent all this much more simply. Beforehand, I had a discussion with Hertzka [the director of Universal Edition]. He was very happy over my intention (the unusual orchestration was perhaps a contributing reason for the rare performances) and will publish the new edition

* The orchestration of each version is specified in the Work List (Appendix I).

already this autumn." On the same day, Webern wrote to Alban Berg that he thought it now looked "like an old Haydn score." The final instrumentation took him considerably longer than expected, and it was 4 September before he could inform Berg of its completion. While he had not changed any notes, he had made other adjustments, so that certain relationships within the music were made clearer. He commented to Berg that the job had cost him a great deal of deliberation, particularly because he had had to make himself rethink again in his mode of expression of twenty years ago. But, after all, he had recently read in the published letters of Goethe to Schiller that Goethe spent weeks revising his little poems in order to improve the prosody. It was that "prosody," in the transferred sense, which Webern said had occupied him so much in his pieces.

The revised version, which the composer himself wished to be considered the only valid one, was first heard in Berlin on 27 January 1929, under the baton of Hermann Scherchen. A pocket score was published by Universal Edition in 1956.

Among the remnants of Webern's library, discovered at Perchtoldsdorf in 1965, were the composer's autograph parts for a chamber orchestra arrangement of the Six Pieces. The instrumentation includes flute, oboe, clarinet, violin I, violin II, viola, harmonium, pianoforte, large drum, triangle, tamtam, and bells. The cello part, referred to by cues in various other parts, was missing, but could be reconstructed from the 1909 score on which Webern had based his transcription. The choice of instruments followed, by and large, the model known as "Parisian ensemble," a widely used orchestral surrogate, frequently employed in the concerts of Schoenberg's Society for Private Musical Performances (see Chapter XIV). Webern's chamber arrangement of the Six Pieces was listed in the society's announcements, but it is questionable whether it was ever played. On 6 January 1921, Webern briefly mentions to Schoenberg that the arrangement was in the rehearsal stage, and many pencil notations appear in the parts of the players. However, those closely connected with the society's affairs such as Paul A. Pisk, Josef Polnauer and Josef Rufer could not recall an actual performance.

The Six Pieces are all brief. Their total playing time barely exceeds nine minutes. The third piece, comprising only eleven measures, is the shortest and takes a mere fifty seconds to perform. Within this limited span, there occur no fewer than eight changes of time signature. The fourth piece, comprising 40 measures, is the longest and lasts about three and a quarter minutes. Because of its brevity and the concentration required from the listener, the work has often been played twice in succession during the same concert.

Writing these pieces only two months after the Five Movements for String Quartet, Webern applied the new concepts of contour and colour for the first time to a full orchestral apparatus. Actually, he himself considered the pieces "a supplement to what was said in the String Quartet" (as he wrote to Schoenberg on 31 May 1911). To the elements of atonality, motivic telescoping, highly differentiated timbres, and dynamic contrasts, a further dimension was added: *Klangfarben-melodie*. In this device a single melodic line is assigned to a number of different instruments; only a few successive melodic components, or sometimes even a single one, are allotted to each player. Obviously, the effect is highly colouristic. *Klangfarbenmelodie* (which can operate also in the harmonic dimension) can be perceived as consisting of multi-coloured links in a continual chain.

On 23 May 1909 Schoenberg had completed his Five Orchestra Pieces, Op. 16, in which the technique was first employed. Webern, who was familiar with Schoenberg's experiments (he later made a two-piano reduction of Schoenberg's pioneering Opus 16), enthusiastically seized on the new expressive idea. It is already manifest in the opening phrase of his Six Pieces: within three measures, the melody is alternately carried by first flute, first trumpet, then again first flute, and finally third horn. Harmonic background and colouring are supplied first by two soft celesta chords, followed by three more chords played by muted violas and cellos. Brass instruments are consistently muted. However, at the same time that the inherent loudness of the brass is subdued, unusual tone colours and novel mixtures are created, such as muted trumpet with low flute. Although the total orchestral complement is massive, Webern deploys the individual parts in chamber-music fashion, with instruments playing in smaller groups or even soloistically. In contrast to the thick textures in earlier symphonic literature, which included much doubling of parts and heavy layers of inner voices, the emphasis is on transparency. The new aesthetic ideals are lucidity and conciseness of musical diction.

The winter of 1909–10 seems to have produced nothing tangible beyond Webern's reduction for two pianos, eight hands, of the Prelude and Interludes from Schoenberg's *Gurrelieder*. The manuscript of the arrangement is dated 1910, but since the transcription was played on 14 January (see Chapter VI), Webern no doubt carried out his assignment sometime during the autumn of 1909. The sketches of two undated piano pieces of his own, found posthumously, may also fall into that year. Both are in 3/4 metre and atonal in idiom; one extends over nineteen bars, the other over seven.

Webern's creative work during the summer of 1910 began with the composition of his Four Pieces for Violin and Piano. They were written at the Preglhof, where he had gone at the end of May after abruptly disengaging himself from the theatre job at Bad Teplitz. When he announced the new opus to Schoenberg on 23 June, the composition was already completed. The pieces form the first in a series of musical essays in which Webern carries the aphoristic style to its extreme. If his music generally shuns rhetoric, the works of that period, which extend through Opus 11, represent the consummation of his striving for the utmost concentration in substance and form. The first piece is only nine bars long; the others twenty-four, fourteen, and fifteen bars, respectively. The work presents a veritable kaleidoscope of violinistic effects, both in expressiveness and virtuosity. Wide intervallic leaps, frequent tempo shifts, and sudden changes of dynamic levels demand the performer's full technical control. The sequence of the movements provides a maximum of contrast: the slow, subdued first and third pieces alternate with the dramatic, dynamically explosive second and fourth. The motives are compressed into the briefest possible shape. Sometimes even isolated single tones assume an independent expressive function.

Several original manuscripts of the work, now known as Webern's Opus 7, are marked "Op. 6, No. 1." The composer obviously shied away from declaring so short a work a self-contained opus (this reluctance persisted even a decade later). One of the title pages of the Four Pieces bears the pencil note "Definitive version, summer 1914," evidence of the composer's continuing revisions. At that time, there was a prospect of publication by Universal Edition, but World War I intervened and the score came out only in 1922. Actually, the first of the Four Pieces had been published already in March 1912 as an insert to the second issue of the short-lived periodical *Der Ruf*, an organ of the Academic Society for Literature and Music in Vienna. This was the first time that a piece by Webern had appeared in print.

The first performance of the Four Pieces took place in Vienna on 24 April 1911 in the concert in which Webern, Berg, and Horwitz presented their own works. Arnold Rosé, supposed to give the première, cancelled shortly before the date of the programme, and it can only be assumed that Fritz Brunner, first violinist in the substitute quartet recruited for that concert, played instead and that Etta Werndorff was the pianist. Rosé did perform the pieces in Vienna on 29 June 1912, with the composer himself at the piano (see Chapter X). During 1919 the work, then designated "Op. 7, No. 1," appeared in several announcements of the Society for Private Musical Performances, with Dr Oskar Adler and Eduard Steuermann as performers. It was also included in the society's 23 October 1919 concert in honour of Maurice Ravel, who was present. The work was then played by Rudolf Kolisch and Eduard Steuermann.

On 10 July 1910 Webern wrote to Berg that he was at work on a "big project." Four days earlier he had reported to Schoenberg: "I am writing something for the theatre. It is a Maeterlinck subject. Once I am farther along with it, I will write to you what it is." On 16 July he disclosed: "I have begun *The Seven Princesses*. Work proceeds well." Schoenberg's request for a piano reduction of his Six Orchestral Songs, Op. 8, intervened, however. Webern mentioned his opera again when writing to Schoenberg on 10 August: "In July, while I was making the piano–vocal scores, I had to interrupt my work. Then I resumed by orchestrating what had been finished of the opera, in order to get fully into the swing again. Suddenly, however, I felt I must write an orchestral song on a text by Rilke. The poem compelled me, for it corresponded so completely to my thoughts. I composed it and orchestrated it quickly. Once I get back, I will again proceed with the opera." Webern's progress report continued on 30 August: "I have now written another orchestral song after Rilke. It belongs with the first. I have recently had some doubts about my opera. I shall speak to you about it." No sketches are extant for the projected opera which, like the one of 1908, was never completed. Webern still referred to it when he wrote to Schoenberg on 9 November 1910 from Danzig: "The other day I looked at my opera. I feel terrible that I cannot work." Much later, he mentioned to Berg, in a letter of 12 July 1912, that "several scenes" had been completed.

The assignment from Schoenberg that had interrupted the progress of the opera during July was carried out in short order. Within a fortnight, the piano reductions of the six songs were on their way back to their composer. Writing to Schoenberg on 27 July 1910, Webern deemed "Sehnsucht" as the best of his arrangements, and he commented on the unavoidable pianistic difficulties of "Das Wappenschild." Two weeks later, Schoenberg returned the manuscripts with his criticisms. On the cover of "Natur" he penned a caustic remark that the song was better than the arranger seemed to think. Webern, deeply wounded, responded in his letter of 15 August: "This was a severe blow. I do not understand how I could give you cause to make such a remark. This to *me*, who admires these things day after day and who wanted to make everything as beautiful as possible." Defending himself, he referred to Schoenberg's explicit direction to make the arrangements as simple and easily playable as he could. Despite his hurt feelings, Webern instantly set to work on the suggested revisions, adding a number of his own. By 22 August, he had returned the arrangements, which now met with the master's approval. Early the following year (1911) Universal Edition brought out the piano reductions, publishing each song singly (the full score appeared in print only in 1913). Aside from Webern's edition of Isaac's *Choralis Constantinus*, his doctoral thesis published in 1909, the piano–vocal scores of Schoenberg's Six Orchestral Songs, Op. 8, constitute the first printed music on which Webern's name appears.

The summer's work of 1910 culminated in the Two Songs on Poems of Rainer Maria Rilke, Op. 8. As Webern wrote to Schoenberg, the first had been completed by 10 August, the second by 30 August. The songs were composed under the fresh impression of Rilke's recently published *Notebook of Malte Laurids Brigge*. Considered the poet's most important prose work, it foreshadowed by decades the writings of the existentialists. The story's hero sees himself confronted with borderline situations of human existence: loneliness, disgust, fear, menacing insanity. The clinical analysis of fear, in particular, makes this work a path-breaker in literature at a time when psychoanalysis itself was still in the pioneering stage.

The two love poems that evoked Webern's instant response are interpolated into the prose of Rilke's story and form part of the action during which a girl sings "an unknown German song." The poet himself sets the stage and controls the mood of the scene. He describes the character of the voice, specifies the manner of delivery, and even designates the moment of pause. The commentary is a virtual prescription for musical realization. According to Rilke, the girl's voice sounds "strong, full, and yet not heavy; of one piece, without a rent, without a seam." The first song is delivered "with singular simplicity, like something inevitable." When the voice breaks out from the silence the second time, it is "decisive, broad and intense." Such precise directions for the interpretation of the lyrics were bound to influence Webern's musical conception.

The feverish urgency with which the composer felt compelled to express himself through these two Rilke poems sprang from his self-identification with their content. The lyrics, however enigmatic to others, directly reflected his own dilemma—that of a man deeply in love with a woman whom he could not claim as his own before the world. During that summer, Webern's long-standing affair with his cousin Wilhelmine had reached a critical phase. The enforced secrecy caused anguish and frustration to the lovers, and it was in Rilke's poems that Webern found the vehicle to sublimate his tortured emotions.

"Are there not violent reverberations of the soul that are yet very gentle?" Webern mused when, on 10 August 1910, he announced to Schoenberg the composition of the first Rilke song, a creative impulse so overwhelming that he had to set aside his operatic project. To that rhetorical question he added: "What the orchestra possesses in expressive possibilities is limitless." The "orchestra" employed in the Rilke settings is actually an ensemble of solo instruments: clarinet (also bass clarinet), horn, trumpet, celesta, harp, violin, viola and cello. While sparse in size and scoring, the instrumental ensemble is extremely subtle and perfectly complements the vocal part. As love songs, Webern's settings are the tersest professions imaginable. There is none of the voluptuousness and exultation commonly associated with that genre, and the songs avoid also the bittersweet melancholy implied by the lyrics. In gesture and diction they are concise and withdrawn, so detached as to appear aloof. Yet behind the ascetic façade glows a burning intensity, an almost desperate urgency. Like Rilke's verses, the music radiates both warmth and coldness and seems at the same time very near and very remote. The voice recites the lyrics straightforwardly, utterly free from sentimentality; yet, that chastity of declamation could not be more intimate and emphatic.

To facilitate rehearsals for the singer, Webern himself provided a piano reduction (unpublished) of the orchestral score, a practice followed in all his later vocal works employing larger instrumental ensembles. Before the full score was published by Universal Edition in 1926, Webern subjected the work to repeated revisions, noted in detail on the title pages of subsequent holographs. One marked "first version" was designated "Op. 7, No. 1" and specifies the vocal part as "for a lower voice." In another manuscript, this was changed to "medium voice," and the opus number 8 was established. Dates for later revisions read: "Spring 1921, new instrumentation (third version)" and "January 1925, newly revised for publication (fourth version)." The numerous changes and additions are doubly remarkable considering that the songs had come into being in a veritable burst of inspiration. The date of the work's first performance is obscure; the archives of Universal Edition list only "about 1927, Brussels?" and no other data can be ascertained.

To appreciate fully the radical advances displayed in the Four Pieces, Op. 7, and the Two Songs, Op. 8, one must project these works against the background of the general musical scene in 1910. That year Stravinsky completed his *Firebird* and Richard Strauss his *Rosenkavalier*; Mahler's Eighth Symphony and Massenet's *Don Quixote* had their first performances. With such forces dominating the field, Webern's creative direction seemed doomed to failure. Yet, like many a daring and uncompromising pioneer, he was destined to become the prophet of a new era.

CHAPTER VIII

Danzig
(1910–1911)

"ALAS, THE SUMMER is over. For me it is always the most beautiful time and the richest," Webern wrote to Schoenberg from the Preglhof on 30 August 1910. Still, returning to Vienna meant resuming the daily personal contact with his friend, whom he had missed so much during the months of their separation. Since there was as yet no definite prospect of a job during the coming season, Webern used the time of waiting to carry out a long-anticipated plan—a trip to Munich for the première of Mahler's Eighth Symphony, scheduled to take place on 12 September under the composer's direction. After the dress rehearsal he dispatched a rapturous report to Schoenberg, extolling in great detail the beauties of the symphony and quoting Mahler as having said: "The passage *accende lumen sensibus* forms the bridge to the concluding section of *Faust*. This spot is the cardinal point of the entire work."

The days at Munich provided Webern with his last opportunity to talk to Mahler, who had always been kindly disposed towards the younger musician. One of Webern's most cherished possessions was a manuscript given him by the master as a memento and token of encouragement. Entitled "Lob der Kritik," the three-page ink sketch is an early version of the song "Lob des hohen Verstandes."[1]

Webern had been back in Vienna only a few days when an opening for a position in Danzig (Gdansk) suddenly arose. Heinrich Jalowetz was second conductor at the town's civic theatre, and it was through his mediation that Webern was offered the post of assistant conductor. He went to Danzig immediately. At first the newness of the landscape and the professional challenge filled him with vitality and confidence. "Danzig is a beautiful big city, teeming with life," he wrote to Schoenberg on 24 September, adding: "The first sight of the ocean is almost frightening. This immense expanse of water! It is a pity that one cannot see beyond the horizon. I live at Pfefferstadt 52, Pension Arendt." He only regretted that, because of the hurried circumstances of his appointment, he had to leave Vienna just at the time when Arnold Rosé, for whom he had played his Five Movements for String Quartet on the piano, voiced interest in performing the work.

Optimism and satisfaction still pervaded the letter to Schoenberg dated 8 October:

> Tomorrow I will conduct here for the first time the operetta *Försterchristl* [by Jarno George]. Today's dress rehearsal turned out quite well. It is something quite different here: a complete orchestra, with the strings well-staffed for operetta performances—five first violins, five second, three violas, three cellos, three contrabasses. Even in the Volksoper they do not have more players for operettas. The musicians are very willing. To be sure, they have no idea of *forte* and *piano*. The operetta is staffed almost entirely with personnel from the opera. This, too, is quite good. The director is wholly delighted with Jalowetz and me. . . . I conduct several times each week. Thank God that I am at last on the right track. From now on things will go ahead quickly.

In another letter to Schoenberg, dated 16 October, Webern reported that he was faring "half-way well" in Danzig. What with a poetry reading by Richard Dehmel, an orchestral concert under Richard Strauss, and the series of regular symphony concerts that opened with a programme of Brahms, Bruckner, and Beethoven, he conceded that the city was "not quite outside the world." At the same time, however, he was already homesick, and disillusionment was manifest in his letters to Berg, to whom he confided as early as 13 October that he was "often completely despairing, completely so."

On 31 October, Schoenberg's *Pelleas und Melisande* was performed in Berlin in the composer's presence. Webern, granted leave from his theatre duties, made the seven-hour train trip to the German capital. The occasion filled him with new inspiration, although his hope of having a long talk with his friend was not fulfilled. When writing again on 9 November, Webern at first told Schoenberg that no other music besides that of Beethoven and Mahler moved him so much as his. He then shifted abruptly to a description of various physical discomforts, an ominous prelude to the sudden outpouring of his complete disenchantment with his situation. Simultaneously, he drew a blueprint for his life's true course: "I maintain almost unshakeably the stand of wanting to dedicate my work exclusively to my compositions. I could entirely forswear every worldly position. If I could only halfway find a subsistence in any kind of job that does not take me away from composition, wholly and completely, for months on end. As it is, one must kill off what wants to come forth. This is the difficulty, and it makes me very unhappy."

Webern's fundamental resistance to any extended interference with his creative endeavours soon took the form of a violent revulsion against Danzig and the mentality prevailing there. On 13 November, just six weeks after his confident beginning, he told Schoenberg: "If I stay with the theatre, I would nonetheless not want to remain here. The orchestra here is very unreliable and the public on the whole dreadful. I had always believed it to be different in the German provinces than in ours—better. But it is quite the opposite. . . . The population here is repugnant to me to the highest degree." His antipathy mounting daily, Webern wrote to Berg a week later how much he envied him for being able to make the piano reduction of the *Gurrelieder*. For such an opportunity he would gladly give up the whole theatre business which he loathed more and more. He professed that, for the sake of pursuing his creative work, he would renounce any position. "Thus I am in an eternal discord that exhausts me," he lamented, "here in this strange city that I hate so much." While he found his situation "barely endurable," he did not want to "run away again." As it was, he felt "only half alive" and the state of his nerves was growing more and more miserable. The terrible thing was that he could not talk to Schoenberg, with whom he had spent such beautiful hours during their walks together, especially that September. "If I stay with the theatre, this will never happen again," he anxiously commented.

The regret at being separated from Schoenberg and from the daily happenings in Vienna runs like a *leitmotif* through Webern's letters. Berg provided him regularly with extensive reports from home, but his glowing descriptions of the hours spent with Schoenberg, and such commiserating remarks as "how sad you will probably be again to have to dwell so far away from these divine experiences," could only increase Webern's longing. For a while, he fastened all his hopes on Schoenberg's plan for a Volkskonservatorium (People's Music School), of which he and Berg were to be co-directors. The project, outlined in detail, came to naught when Schoenberg became embroiled in personal difficulties that caused him to leave Vienna the following summer. Meanwhile, the mere prospect of such close collaboration excited in Webern the resolve to leave his Danzig post at once should it materialize. In essence, however, he wanted to dedicate himself to what he recognized as his life's mission and destiny.

For the creative person, there is probably only one thing that is important—to produce over and over again. What then happens with his work is almost a secondary consideration [he wrote to Schoenberg on 4 December]. I only want to express, all my life, without interruption, that which fills my soul. I do not want anything else. And if I cannot do this, I get sick—just as I am now. You once told me of Mahler's remark that I should not go to the theatre since I would not find time to compose. I cannot get this out of my head any more. . . . I think it would be wonderful to stay in Vienna and to make my living just by giving lessons and by taking on literary and other jobs. As it is now, I cannot exist. I come to no thought, to nothing serious. And I would much rather have entirely different things in my head from what now fills my thinking. . . . Do you believe that in the immediate future any work that yields some revenue might come up? It is mainly because of my father. Can I make piano reductions of your orchestra pieces or of your Chamber Symphony?

The urgency of this plea sprang not from artistic considerations alone, as Schoenberg was aware by then. Webern's situation was vastly complicated by concerns of a nature so intimate that at first he had not dared to confide them to anyone. When Heinrich and Johanna Jalowetz, who did their best to befriend him during the months at Danzig, became parents of a daughter, Webern had written to Schoenberg on 13 November: "It must be quite beautiful to be a father. I will probably never experience this." But Webern knew even then that Wilhelmine was pregnant. At summer's end she had gone to Paris to study French, which she hoped to teach later on. An exchange of letters from that period reveals the tribulations suffered by the lovers. These two letters,[2] filled with tenderness, are touching in their almost childlike quality. On 30 October, a Sunday evening, just before he left for the theatre to conduct, Webern began his diary-like epistle. He related his thoughts and activities of that night and of the following forenoon, when he travelled to Berlin for the *Pelleas und Melisande* performance. Rilke's *Notebook of Malte Laurids Brigge*, so meaningful to Webern, served him as a writing desk during the train ride. He alluded finally to Wilhelmine's predicament: "Indeed, I know by and large how matters stand with you. That it had to happen this way——. I always think of you."

During those autumn weeks, Wilhelmine desperately tried to do something drastic about her condition, but her attempts all failed. Confronted with the inescapable reality, Webern at last bared his heart to Schoenberg. In a long letter, dated 28 November, he described the agonies so heroically undergone by Wilhelmine and declared his intention of marrying soon, come what may. Despite his aversion to marriage between relatives, the decision had been forced on him by circumstances.

Wilhelmine, also ready by now to face the inevitable, still had to inform her family, whose reaction she greatly feared. On 30 November, she wrote to the prospective father, who had suggested that she return home: "My parents would never want this because they pay too much attention to what people say about them. And then they will always consider it a disgrace—even once I am married—that this has happened. This shame they will want to hide from other people at all costs. I know my parents only too well and realize that the most terrible thing for them would be for their fellow men to gossip about them and me." Despite all her worries, Wilhelmine looked forward with great joy to the child and trusted that her mother would be reconciled in due course by her own maternal feelings.

The pair had hoped to be married in Vienna early in December, but matters were delayed by the rule of the Roman Catholic Church that special papal dispensation had to be granted for marriage between first cousins. An application was filed immediately, but week after week passed by without response from the clerical offices. Meanwhile, the parents on both sides, all staunch Catholics, remained adamantly opposed to a wedding outside the church. Finally, only six weeks before the child was expected, the marriage had to be performed in a civil ceremony. It took place on 22 February 1911 in the Courthouse of Danzig, with the ever loyal Heinrich and Johanna Jalowetz as witnesses. (The union was solemnized by the Church only in 1915, after three children had been born.)

The trials endured by Wilhelmine during all these months can only be imagined. After leaving Paris she went to Berlin, then came to Danzig for the marriage, only to return to Berlin again to await the delivery. Meanwhile, all Webern's hopes for an early return to Vienna were frustrated. The Advent season, usually so full of joyful anticipation, was sad and oppressed that year. Rejected at home, Webern wrote a nostalgic Christmas letter to his younger sister Rosa, poignantly describing his longing for Vienna. He recalled their apartment window facing the house where Beethoven had died, the Kahlenberg (a mountain in the Vienna Woods) beyond, and the family outings their mother had enjoyed so much. Thinking of Schubert and Beethoven, he said: "Only in this mild, glorious air, in this magical landscape are such phenomena possible, nowhere else. Only Vienna is so rich in really great artists."

On Christmas Eve, Webern informed Schoenberg that he had returned the corrected proofs of his piano reduction of Schoenberg's Six Orchestral Songs, Op. 8, to Universal Edition, having been able to attend to the task only late at night because of his long hours at the theatre. He reported that Berg had given him much joy with his

photographs of some of Schoenberg's paintings, sent as a Christmas
surprise. Of that friend, Webern had written to Schoenberg shortly
before, on 28 November: "He becomes ever dearer to me. He is a whole
human being; the others—I like only Jalowetz as much. When men
begin earning a living and become involved with external matters, they
all get a hole inside. That passionate devotion is not there any longer.
But with me, I assure you, that devotion grows ever greater; with every
hour, I find it more difficult to get along in this world."

Such personal confessions alternated in Webern's letters with lengthy
musical discussions, news of the day, and polemics. The latter ranged
from a description of Mahler's Seventh Symphony, which had just met
with a hostile reception at Berlin, to an account of the sensational
success of *Der Rosenkavalier* by Richard Strauss and the phenomenal rise
of the thirteen-year-old Erich Wolfgang Korngold. "Publishers,
performances—the boy has everything. I will become old before that,"
Webern grudgingly commented in his letter of 13 November. He was
curious about Delius, whose name was becoming known, and inquired
about that composer's *A Mass of Life*, as well as about Zemlinsky's latest
work *Psalm* and his opera *Kleider machen Leute*. His enthusiasm for
Balzac's *Seraphita*, which he was reading, was surpassed only by that for
Schoenberg's Second String Quartet, which continued to arouse his
ecstatic admiration.

As the year 1911 dawned, there was still no sign that the families might
relent. On 17 January Webern told Schoenberg: "I am not permitted to
come home on account of the premarital child." If only because that
avenue was barred for the time being, life in Danzig temporarily
appeared more bearable. Webern's spirits were also raised by the
performance of his Passacaglia on 10 January, in the third symphony
programme of the Danzig concert season. The theatre orchestra's
principal conductor had generously invited the composer to lead the
work himself, allowing him four rehearsals for preparation. Webern was
pleased with the outcome and wrote to Berg on 18 January that the
performance had come out "quite well, astonishingly so." While the
strings had not quite managed their task, the winds had been very
satisfactory. He had come away with the renewed conviction that his
piece was good. On the night of the performance, he told Schoenberg:
"I got more out of the winds than in Vienna. It was really well done." To
Schoenberg's subsequent inquiry about the work's reception, Webern
responded on 19 February: "There was hardly an audience—only a
handful of people. There was no opposition. The newspaper critic
declared me insane, asserting that as a conductor I was 'liked and
valued' by the Danzig people, but as a composer they would have to
reject me completely." On that programme, featuring contemporary

compositions, there also appeared works by Debussy and Thuille and Mahler's *Kindertotenlieder*.

As conductor of theatrical performances, Webern was kept very busy during his tenure at Danzig. By the time he left his post in April, he had led over 60 performances. Besides the opera *Der Waffenschmied* by Lortzing, which he enjoyed, he was assigned such light standard repertoire as *Der Zigeunerbaron* and *Die Fledermaus* (J. Strauss), *La belle Hélène* (Offenbach), *Geisha* (Sidney Jones), *The Merry Widow* (Lehár), and Flotow's stage music to Shakespeare's *The Winter's Tale*. In addition, he had to contend with several lesser operettas and farces. By contrast, Jalowetz, in his position as second conductor, could preside over performances of Mozart's *Magic Flute*, Wagner's *Meistersinger*, Weber's *Freischütz*, Rossini's *Barber of Seville* (a work Webern liked very much), Thomas' *Mignon*, Flotow's *Martha*, Lortzing's *Zar und Zimmermann*, Halévy's *La Juive*, Meyerbeer's *Les Huguenots*, Gounod's *Margarethe*, and Offenbach's *Tales of Hoffmann* (another production delighting Webern).

Obviously, the Danzig theatre season was a very lively one and offered Webern plenty of opportunity to gain varied experience. Nevertheless, his attitude towards the theatre remained, aside from temporary fluctuations, negative. He recognized it as a necessary source of steady income if he was ever to become independent of his father's support. At the same time, every fibre of his being revolted against the entire routine. He realized only too well the conflict between economic imperatives and his pure ideals and, finding them irreconcilable, suffered much mental anguish and confusion. His letters read like soliloquies, in which he seeks to find a way out of his dilemma. The mere fact that he took time to pen one long epistle after another, when the theatre demanded all his energies for day-long rehearsals and nightly conducting or stage assignments, indicates his nervous state. He alternately takes positions contradictory in themselves, as in his letter of 18 January to Berg when he professed that, for the moment, his attitude was "somewhat milder." Because the activity in the theatre was so engulfing, it was actually stimulating his interest. As long as he had to be in that "whirl," it was "either, or." Nevertheless, he longed to get out of it so that he might concentrate exclusively on his own "cause." As to this cause, he saw his mission clearly. "I do not want to live any biography—but think of Beethoven. I am confused all over again—influenced by ambition. Ambition. It is exactly this earthly striving that I must leave behind. But if I persist in this point of view, then I must leave the theatre."

Three weeks later, on 7 February, Webern wrote to Berg in mounting discouragement that Schoenberg had recently refused to advise him either for or against and that he should do what he had to. As a result, he was very much out of sorts, and the indecision was making him ill. "O God, how often would I like to get out of my skin," he exclaimed. The mere thought of having to finish out the season burdened him "like lead, like an immense weight." And afterwards what then? It would only be the same story over and over again. "Am I thus to spend all my years—feeling redeemed each evening that another day has passed? Does this make any sense?" He could see nothing bright in his situation, nothing that could console him, and this was mainly because he was forced to barrenness. "I am growing old and am nothing and have nothing and accomplish nothing, or better, cannot accomplish anything," he bitterly complained.

Webern's letters to Schoenberg reflect the same conflict. "I work myself up firmly to the idea of doing well at the theatre," he wrote on 19 February. "I muster every thought about this that ever moved me. Then I get into a state of excitement that fortifies me, but suddenly I feel an inner rupture and I sense only the horror of unsatisfied creativity."

Although Webern had already decided to give up his Danzig position, and despite Wilhelmine's encouragement that he leave the theatre for good, the prospect of soon having to provide for a family led him to apply elsewhere. He entered into actual negotiations with the city theatre of Plauen, where the post of second conductor was vacant, and he also tried for the first conductorship at Klagenfurt. The latter position particularly attracted him, both because of the opportunity to direct music dramas by Wagner and because of his home ties with Carinthia. While exploring these prospects (neither materialized), Webern resigned his Danzig post, effective in the spring. He justified his action by pointing out the limitations of a job that would afford him neither an increase of salary nor the hope of conducting anything besides operettas in the coming season. Erwin Stein was engaged in his place.

On 9 April Wilhelmine gave birth to a daughter in Berlin. "When the child came into the world, the morning of Palm Sunday was just dawning," Webern wrote to Schoenberg that day. "It was a gloriously beautiful warm day; moreover, the moon was waxing and it was spring. I take this as an omen for the child's favourable development." Webern saw his daughter for the first time ten days later, when he came to Berlin from Danzig. The girl was christened Amalie in honour of Webern's mother. The happy event had reconciled the Mörtl family; Wilhelmine's mother came from Vienna to be at her daughter's side. Webern's father, too, accepted the accomplished fact; a few weeks earlier, he himself had taken the initiative in having wedding announcements printed and mailed.

From Berlin Webern proceeded to Vienna, where he participated in rehearsals for the concert subsidized by himself, Berg, and Horwitz and featuring their own compositions. It took place on 24 April 1911 in the Ehrbar Hall, under the auspices of the Society for Art and Culture, which counted Webern, Jalowetz, and Horwitz on its board of directors. Arnold Rosé and his quartet had been engaged to play, and their reputation augured well for success. However, five days before the concert, they cancelled their participation, and a substitute ensemble of professional musicians (Fritz Brunner, Oskar Holzer, Bernhard Buchbinder, and Josef Haša) had to be hastily assembled. On the programme were Berg's Piano Sonata, Op. 1 (played by Etta Werndorff) and his String Quartet, Op. 3, a string quartet by Horwitz, Webern's Five Movements for String Quartet, Op. 5, and his Four Pieces for Violin and Piano, Op. 7. The results appear to have been less than completely satisfying, for Webern wrote to Berg on 7 May how much he regretted that Rosé did not play. He felt that the performance "would surely have turned into something quite different." The event provoked a review in the *Wiener Extrablatt* in which the critic, Dr Paul Stauber, attacked Schoenberg, as the teacher of the three composers, with such insults that Schoenberg's followers jointly addressed a letter of protest to the Association of Vienna Music Critics.

When Webern met Schoenberg in Vienna on that occasion it was only with great apprehension. Several weeks earlier, he had learned through Jalowetz that Schoenberg had taken offence with him for failing to acknowledge with sufficient promptness a letter of personal advice that Webern had solicited. Schoenberg, while generally playing the rôle of a benevolent father to his charges, could on occasion be quite irascible. When he himself was confronted with hostilities on all sides, he tended to withdraw into brooding isolation. An inadvertent lack of attention on the part of one of his disciples, or the slightest misunderstanding, could arouse his suspicion and bring on his wrath. Webern, Berg, Stein and others of his flock, each in his turn, had to undergo such trials. Inevitably, however, these episodes ended in reconciliation once the offender had amply proffered his repentance and assured Schoenberg of his undying devotion.

"I am so glad that you feel entirely friendly towards me again. The first days in Vienna I was very unhappy," Webern wrote to Schoenberg on 1 May from Berlin, where he had gone again to join his wife and infant daughter. He reported that the little family was temporarily settled in an apartment at Habsburgerstrasse 11, complete with a "pianino" and with Schoenberg's self-portrait standing on the desk. Horwitz was accompanying him on his daily rounds to the agents, and applications had been filed for positions at Braunschweig, Zittau, Lucerne, Aachen, and Münster. With the assistance of Schoenberg and

Zemlinsky, the possibility of an engagement in Prague was also being explored. Having just been restored to Schoenberg's good graces, Webern was punctilious in keeping the master informed of his every activity and sentiment; he wrote no fewer than nine times during the five weeks in Berlin. An extensive account was devoted to Max Reinhardt's production of Goethe's *Faust*. "There is probably nothing in the art of poetry approaching its marvels. At the end, I continually heard Mahler's music," Webern exclaimed in his letter of 1 May. In that of 4 May he raged over a performance of Mozart's *Don Giovanni* under Leo Blech: "It was horrible . . . One must not think of Mahler's rendition at all, else one would have to die from anger."

As Webern's thoughts turned towards his idol time and again, Mahler himself lay mortally ill in a sanatorium near Paris. After being ignominiously treated by the directors of the New York Philharmonic Orchestra Society, he had returned to Europe, broken in health and spirit. From Paris he was taken to Vienna, the city that had witnessed so many of his triumphs and tribulations, and there, on 18 May 1911, he died. Webern, who like every member of the Schoenberg circle had written to the master in his last illness, was deeply shaken. He hurried to Vienna for the funeral, which took place at the small cemetery of Grinzing. The narrow confines of the chapel made it necessary to limit admission to holders of special permits. As privileged friends, Schoenberg and his disciples were in the procession of mourners who followed the coffin to the grave.

Back in Berlin, Webern immediately wrote again to Schoenberg. His letter, dated 24 May, culminated in a declaration of loyalty and faith:

Mahler's death makes me sadder every day. But it was certainly predestined. You said that you also have the impression that his work was fully completed. I have the feeling that Mahler knows how much we grieve for him. I will always think of the cemetery up there where his body now rests. Do you still sense that enigmatic silence when his coffin was lowered into the earth? Never to see him again! That time in Munich, as the train departed, he looked long at us through the window.[3] It was the last time I saw him. . . . I will forever preserve in my heart your indescribably kind words to me after Mahler's burial. . . . The past days are of immense significance to me: Mahler's death and the certainty that I possess your friendship forever. Gústav Mahler and you: there I see my course quite distinctly. I will not deviate. God's blessing on you.

At Schoenberg's suggestion, Webern tried to compose an essay on Mahler, but by 5 June he had to admit: "I become more and more timid and nothing appears good enough to me. I am very unsure of myself when writing." He was likewise dissatisfied with his first draft of an article on Schoenberg himself, one of a number of testimonials that were to appear the following year in book form under the title *Arnold Schoenberg*. The project, initiated by the master himself and first discussed during the days of Mahler's funeral, was intended to advance Schoenberg's standing as a teacher, on which his livelihood depended. To that end, his pupils were to testify what Schoenberg meant to them. First conceived as a mere pamphlet, the brochure soon assumed the dimensions of a small volume (see Chapter IX).

Freed from the fetters of his theatre work, Webern threw himself into these literary projects and turned again to his own compositions. He wrote out anew the score of his Passacaglia, incorporating minor changes in instrumentation derived from his recent experience of conducting the work in Danzig. He also made a fair copy of his Six Pieces for Orchestra, to be presented to Schoenberg, who had agreed that the work might be dedicated to him. In addition to pursuing these tasks and looking for a job, Webern was actively exploring prospects in Berlin for Schoenberg, who might there escape from the persistent hostility encountered in his native city. To Webern, it seemed a foregone conclusion that Schoenberg could be very successful in the German capital. Webern had recently met Edward Clark, a 21-year-old Englishman, who was so enthusiastic over Schoenberg's music that he contemplated going to Vienna to study. Clark was intimate with Oskar Fried, an influential conductor whom Webern visited several times to urge performances of Schoenberg's works, and Fried in turn was close to Ferruccio Busoni, one of the real powers in Berlin's musical life. These men, as well as the pianist Egon Petri, promised assistance in launching a promotional campaign, with advertisements in the newspapers and in the periodical *Pan*. Teaching fees could be substantial (30 marks per lesson),[4] expenses low, and living conditions in the western suburbs, where Webern himself then lived, most attractive. These optimistic reports laid the ground for Schoenberg's decision to move to Berlin a few months later.

During his last week in Berlin, Webern submitted to the Dreililien Verlag, Schoenberg's publisher, his Five Movements for String Quartet, the Four Pieces for Violin and Piano, and ten of his George songs. The summer now was ahead. Much as Webern liked Berlin, he eagerly anticipated seeing the mountains again and happily accepted his father's invitation to bring his new family to the Preglhof. There, the couple settled down for a belated honeymoon, moving into a small cottage a short distance down the road from the manor house. The summer brought one of the most extended periods of good weather Europe had known in many years. Webern revelled in the beauty and seclusion of the estate, and a burst of creative activity soon ensued. "I am glad to be able to compose again," he wrote to Schoenberg on 9 July.[5] The products of that summer were two groups of compositions, each augmented in 1913 and assuming final shape only more than a decade later. First came seven pieces for orchestra, two of which were later incorporated into Opus 10, and then the "II. Streichquartett," four short movements that subsequently became part of Opus 9 (see Chapter XII).

That summer Webern also read the proofs of Schoenberg's *Pelleas und Melisande*. The task inspired him to suggest to Schoenberg that he make a piano reduction of the lengthy score, if none of his prospective theatre engagements should materialize. Hamburg, Prague, and Graz were possibilities. The director of the Graz theatre offered the position of coach and assistant to the principal conductor, at a year-round salary of 150 kronen[6] a month (with one month paid vacation), but with the proviso that Webern begin on 1 August and agree to stay through the following summer. Declaring the definition of his conducting responsibilities too vague, Webern turned down the job. Most likely, his decision stemmed rather from reluctance to give up his newly-gained freedom so soon. At the end of July, he had a rendezvous with Jalowetz and Horwitz at Veldes, from where the trio set out for a mountain tour. Then Jalowetz came to visit at the Preglhof. Webern next accepted an invitation to the Berghof, the property of Alban Berg's mother at the Ossiachersee.

During June and July, Berg had suffered under Schoenberg's wrath, having failed to inform the master promptly enough of his presence in Vienna during a temporary return from the country. Webern, who had been passing through Vienna himself at the time, had been told by Diez that he had seen Berg on the street in Hietzing. Inadvertently, he had carried the news to Schoenberg, who angrily reacted to what he considered a severe breach of Berg's obligation to him. Crushed, Berg poured out his heart to Webern, who took it upon himself to bring about a reconciliation with Schoenberg. This was achieved by the time Webern visited Berg, for the latter had just received the preface to Schoenberg's recently completed treatise *Harmonielehre* (Theory of Harmony). This work, dedicated to Gustav Mahler, had been long in coming, and for months Webern had eagerly inquired about its progress. After reading the preface, in which Schoenberg paid tribute to his pupils as the source of his inspiration, Webern lost no time in writing the author on 19 August in a surge of emotion: "You thank us?! Whatever I am, everything, everything is through you; I live only through you. That you could use us for practice was our limitless good fortune, a boundless blessing for us."

The fanatic loyalty and solidarity of Schoenberg's pupils were put to a special test during the weeks to come. Towards the end of July, Schoenberg had hinted to Webern about grave personal difficulties. While often exposed to critical invective on professional grounds, he had lately found himself also the victim of anti-Semitic harassment from a man living in the same apartment house (Hietzinger Hauptstrasse 113). The animosity of this individual (an engineer by the name of Wouwermans) grew daily, leading to open displays of hostility. Distressed by the constant insults and threats, Schoenberg finally decided to leave the city and seek temporary refuge with his brother-in-law, Zemlinsky, who was vacationing at the Starnbergersee. At the moment of departure, only the presence of Josef Polnauer warded off a physical attack by the rabid neighbour.

Schoenberg was so unnerved that he was unwilling to return to Vienna. His immediate need was financial assistance, for his principal source of income, teaching, was now cut off. "Be assured, we will help you," Webern wrote him on 11 August. "If I only had a little money at my disposal, I would give it to you. But, as you know, I live from what my father gives me monthly. . . . Just trust in us. May what I say now not appear ridiculous to you: I believe that the disciples of Jesus Christ could not have felt more deeply for their Lord than we for you. God protect you." The same day, Webern began to rally his friends to Schoenberg's rescue. A sum of money, in which he and Jalowetz shared with 200 kronen each, was dispatched immediately. Assuming the rôle of treasurer, Webern then wrote to Berg, Horwitz, and Stein, asking for like contributions, and the emergency fund soon reached the total of 1,000 kronen. That initial act of support quickly assumed larger dimensions. In September, Berg issued an urgent appeal, circulated in the form of a printed leaflet to more than 100 potential donors. It bore the endorsements of 48 signers, including, besides Schoenberg's disciples and close friends, such prominent personalities as Guido Adler, Peter Altenberg, Hermann Bahr, Julius Bittner, Artur Bodanzky, Engelbert Humperdinck, Wilhelm Kienzl, Gustav Klimt, Julius Korngold, Karl Kraus, Adolf Loos, Artur Schnitzler, Franz Schreker, Richard Strauss, and Bruno Walter. By the time this action produced results, Schoenberg had decided to turn his back on Vienna altogether and move to Berlin.

CHAPTER IX

Berlin

(1911–1912)

WHEN WEBERN LEFT the Preglhof the first week of September 1911, he could not realize that his parting was to be permanent, that the time of many a happy holiday on the idyllic estate had drawn to a close. With his wife and child, he went to Vienna, taking up temporary residence with his parents-in-law at Ruckergasse 12. After the remoteness of his country retreat, he enjoyed anew the offerings of Vienna's musical life. On 8 September he wrote to Schoenberg: "I recently attended *Pelléas et Mélisande* (Debussy) at the Opera and once again received a wholly strong, wonderful impression of the work. By contrast, the *Rosenkavalier* pleases me less and less. I am inclined to pass the harshest judgement on it, but on the other hand there does indeed exist with Strauss such an immense virtuosity in everything, which Pfitzner and Reger, for instance, do not possess. At any rate, he certainly amounts to more than they."

All summer long Webern had aimed for a theatre position in Prague, offering his services regardless of compensation. Now that Zemlinsky asked him to come there as his personal assistant, he was not at all sure he wanted to go, since Schoenberg's plans were still hanging in the balance. Building his psychological fences, he had told Schoenberg on 23 August: "To be sure, it is terrible for me to think that again a winter will come without my producing anything. Really, if I do not sense how something works within me, how something new originates and is born, then I do not exist." Despite such misgivings, Webern travelled to Prague on 13 September, only to inform Schoenberg apologetically a mere five days later:

> I am again in Vienna. Please do not be shocked, I have not deported myself improperly. I have gone through a bitter struggle. The position that I could have obtained in Prague would have been quite

nice— I would even have received a monthly salary of 100 kronen. But as never before, the idea of leaving the theatre overwhelmed me. I have been completely frank with Mr Zemlinsky. For hours I walked around in Prague, considering and considering. I do not know what it is. . . . Above everything: I would like to be with you. I picture the winter thus: I will be in whichever city you are in and will mainly make reductions of your works.[1] Naturally, I would like to compose as much as possible. What will you say to my being in Vienna again? Mr Schoenberg, these hours in Prague were certainly not easy. Mr von Zemlinsky was extremely kind to me. I am so sorry that I prevailed on him so much in the matter. I only hope that he will not think badly of me.

Considering the prestige of the Deutsches Landestheater in Prague and the protection afforded by Zemlinsky's presence, not to speak of economic considerations, it is difficult to comprehend that Webern would decline this opportunity. Since Schoenberg's future course was still uncertain at the time, his decision appears the more reckless. Only his blind faith in Schoenberg's mission and his personal dependence upon him can explain his willingness to throw in his lot with that of the master, wherever this might be.

During the crucial month of September, Webern's letters to Schoenberg followed each other in quick succession; he wrote every two or three days, sometimes twice in one day. The correspondence included all the current news. At the request of Alfred Kerr, the editor of *Pan*, Webern sent him the third movement of his Opus 6 and the first piece of Opus 7. He began work on a biographical sketch of Schoenberg, including analyses of the works and the projection of Schoenberg's aesthetic precepts. The essay had been asked for by Dr Gerhard Tischer, the music publisher and editor of the *Rheinische Musik- und Theaterzeitung*. Webern was given access to Schoenberg's abandoned Vienna apartment so that he could study the music directly from the manuscripts.

By the end of September, Schoenberg had found suitable quarters in Berlin, and Webern immediately resolved to follow. There ensued feverish activity. Webern, Berg, Horwitz, and Polnauer joined forces in clearing Schoenberg's Vienna apartment. It took several days to pack the library, paintings, and household goods. Schoenberg's and Webern's belongings, filling two vans, were shipped together, but only after a last-minute complication was overcome: Schoenberg's rent had to be paid up until the following February before the landlord would sign the necessary clearance papers.

On 6 October Webern arrived in Berlin and stayed at first with Schoenberg, who had rented an entire floor in the spacious Villa

Lepcke, a baronial residence, with park-like grounds and a pond, in the suburb of Zehlendorf. "It is marvellous," he wrote to Berg on 10 October. "I am overjoyed finally to be with Schoenberg again. Here it is totally like being in the country, in the forest. Just like the Berghof, only in the plains, of course." A few days later, Webern moved to an apartment of his own, also located in Zehlendorf (Wannseebahn, Hauptstrasse 7, Gartenhaus, fourth floor). He was soon joined by Wilhelmine and their child. "It is very beautiful here where I live. I have absolutely no complaints. . . . Schoenberg is in good spirits. Regrettably, we live rather far from each other—twenty minutes by foot. There is practically no possibility of public transportation," he reported on 17 October to another Vienna friend, Paul Königer (a Schoenberg pupil then studying under Berg), adding: "I already have a pupil for coaching sessions, 5 marks per hour. If I get others, I will earn quite nicely." That prospect prompted the immediate acquisition of a small black Ibach grand, the first and only piano that Webern could ever call his own.[2] Schoenberg helped in the selection. The purchase price of 1,400 marks was paid in cash, ample indication that Webern was financially well off because of the dowry received from Wilhelmine's parents. The acquisition delighted Webern. "I inaugurated the grand piano with Schoenberg's second *Klavierstück* [from Opus 11]," he informed Berg on 24 October, after giving him a rapturous description of his purchase.

Letters to such intimate friends as Berg and Königer (who was soon to marry Wilhelmine's older sister, Maria, formerly the wife of the painter Commerlohr) provide a graphic account of Webern's stay in Berlin. It was to them that he first confessed his essential homesickness for Vienna, a longing besetting him even during his first month away from his native city. On 1 November he told Berg that he had come to Berlin only because of Schoenberg and certainly would stay on as long as the master was there. But under other circumstances he would not remain a minute longer. He found everything so uncongenial that most of the time he stayed home, where he felt best. The outcry: "Oh, how I envy you that you can be in Vienna," summed up his feelings.

For a time, Webern's nostalgia was alleviated by an exciting event. The first performance of Mahler's *Das Lied von der Erde* was scheduled to take place in Munich on 20 November under Bruno Walter's direction, and Webern persuaded Berg and Königer to join him for the première. The stay in Munich became one of the high points of his life. He arrived there ahead of his friends, found quarters at the Peterhof, and took in several rehearsals preceding the performance. The letters that Webern sent to his friends following the days in Munich are effusive and ecstatic in their veneration for Mahler's genius. On 23 November he wrote to

Königer: "*Das Lied von der Erde* is the most marvellous creation that exists. When one is dying, images of one's life are said to pass before one's soul—so it is with this work. It cannot be described in words. What power exerts itself here!" On the same day, Webern penned a long letter to Berg, dwelling on various details of the score, and professing that, when he heard a certain phrase for the first time during rehearsal, he would have liked to breathe his last right then. (He referred to the contrabassoon passage at "Aus tiefstem Schauen lauscht' ich auf.") Enthralled with the work's beauty, he felt humbled to the point of asking whether they were entitled to even hear it at all. But there was one thing for them to do, he resolved, "to strive in such a way that we merit it." To that end, they would have to reach into their hearts and rid themselves of all that was unclean. "Ever higher! '*Sursum corda*' says the Christian religion. Thus Mahler lived, thus Schoenberg," he concluded triumphantly.

The day before he wrote to his friends, Webern had played *Das Lied von der Erde* for Schoenberg on the piano. Schoenberg's diary record of 22 November noted that they were both deeply touched: "We could not speak!" Although Schoenberg had been invited by Webern and his friends to be with them in Munich at their expense, he was unable to go, as he was just starting a lecture series in Berlin.[3] Entitled "Aesthetics and the Teaching of Composition," the course was held under the auspices of the Stern Conservatory. The lectures were an attempt to improve Schoenberg's position in Berlin. Although his arrival had been auspicious enough—several patrons of the arts had presented him with a munificent welcome gift (2,000 marks), and the promotional articles appeared as planned—private pupils were quite slow in coming. Now the lectures, too, after an initial success, failed to attract a sufficient audience; one of the sessions was attended by only five persons.

Urged on by Webern, Schoenberg had completed the gigantic *Gurrelieder* score on 7 November. But he then fell into a state of depression that lasted into the new year and temporarily rendered him incapable of doing any creative work. Webern visited him daily and tried to be of service in every conceivable way. In letter after letter, each many pages long, he exhorted Berg to find a way for Schoenberg to return to Vienna, whether as conductor of the Singakademie (a post Bruno Walter was expected to relinquish soon) or as a faculty member at the Music Academy (where Fuchs and Graedener were retiring). The Vienna fund-raising campaign, begun in September, was continued, and Webern offered all sorts of suggestions for solicitation of potential patrons.

Most of the correspondence with Berg, however, dealt with the preparation of the literary homage for Schoenberg, first conceived at the time of Mahler's death. Discussions of the project reached a well-nigh incredible volume, with Berg at one time writing a 30-page letter. For all practical purposes, Webern and Berg acted as editors, although in the end, at Webern's insistence, the volume gave no editorial credit to anyone. The tremendous efforts going into the little book lasted all winter. Concurrently, Webern laboured over his Schoenberg essay for the *Rheinische Musik- und Theaterzeitung*. An early draft was discarded altogether, and the article was rewritten and polished until it met with Schoenberg's approval. "I am unhappy that everything I extract from myself is so little compared with what I believe myself to perceive, to feel. Especially, of course, when verbal language is involved. Then I can project nothing," Webern wrote in a downcast mood to Königer on 13 January 1912, when the article had finally gone to press. Webern's time and energies were so absorbed this winter by his endeavours on Schoenberg's behalf that, paradoxically, the Berlin sojourn, confidently expected to be a fertile time for composing, went by without the birth of a single new work.

At the end of November Webern fell very ill with bronchitis. Headaches and high fever kept him confined to bed for over a week, and his recovery was slow. Schoenberg came to visit him every evening. On one of his calls he brought along the first copy of his just published *Harmonielehre*. Webern's enthusiasm was boundless. "Since Wagner, nothing like this has been written in the German language. Perhaps not even since Schopenhauer," he exulted to Berg in his letter of 8 December. Soon afterwards he sent Berg Kant's *Letters* as a Christmas gift. "There are few such marvellous events as Christmas," Webern wrote on 21 December. "One must consider: after almost 2,000 years, the night when a great man was born is still celebrated by almost all the people on earth as a moment during which everybody says only kind things and wishes to do good to all. This is truly wonderful. Should not Beethoven's birthday be celebrated the same way?" Webern went on to indulge his penchant for metaphysical correlations: "It is remarkable that Beethoven and Kant on the one hand, and Wagner and Schopenhauer on the other, lived almost simultaneously. I always sense a spiritual communion there. Indeed, the influence of Schopenhauer on Wagner was really considerable. And with the other illustrious pair I sense a concord of minds, although an influence of Kant on Beethoven did not exist at all, in the sense that it did with the other two. And Strindberg and Mahler? Maeterlinck and Schoenberg? Also Strindberg and Schoenberg! Rays of God!"

Berg gave Webern a work by Baudelaire that Christmas, and Schoenberg presented him with a cordially inscribed copy of his *Harmonielehre*. Webern reciprocated with Plato's *Republic*. At the turn of the year, Schoenberg's spirits were at their lowest ebb, and in an unrelenting stream of letters Webern implored Berg to help pave the way back to Vienna for their master. Without an official call, Schoenberg would absolutely not consider returning, since the lack of artistic appreciation, added to his economic plight and the anti-Semitic pressures, had thoroughly disgusted him with his native city. Writing to Berg on 11 January 1912, Webern stated that he was more than ever convinced of the "surpassing importance" of Schoenberg and that he ardently wished for a happier time, "one in which Schoenberg fares well." As hardly ever before he anticipated spring, hoping that it would bring light into the darkness. Indeed, Beethoven had been denounced in his time, and Mahler still was being rejected. But it was "frightful" to witness such a fate at close range. It was enough to make him want to "die from anger and indignation."

Only a few days later, there was a turn for the better. After Hertzka had declined Schoenberg's Five Orchestra Pieces, Op. 16, for publication by Universal Edition, they had been offered to C. F. Peters, the renowned Leipzig house. The work was accepted and a first payment of 600 marks sent at once. The score was prepared immediately for release, and the publisher asked for a four-hand piano reduction. Suggesting that this be arranged for two pianos, Schoenberg promptly delegated the task to Webern. On Sunday, 4 February 1912, Webern was one of the participants in a Berlin performance of the work in a transcription for two pianos, eight hands, based on an earlier arrangement by Erwin Stein. It was included in a matinée concert, held in the Harmonium Hall, that featured Schoenberg's compositions. Eduard Steuermann, who was sent by his teacher Busoni to Schoenberg for theory lessons, manned one piano together with Louis Closson, also a Busoni student. Webern shared the other keyboard with still another Busoni pupil, the American Louis Gruenberg, who made his début with the Berlin Philharmonic that year. Only the first, second, and fourth movements were played. Schoenberg conducted.[4] Webern reported to Berg, on 5 February, that the performance went very well. The planned first rendition of Schoenberg's *Herzgewächse*, Op. 20, however, had to be cancelled because the singer, Martha Winternitz-Dorda, was "not sufficiently disposed for such heights" that evening. The omission disappointed Webern in particular, since he had been put in charge of the harmonium part.[5] He had practised diligently on the instrument, finding it "delicate" and capable of "the most marvellous sound effects," as he wrote to Berg.

While that concert went by without adverse reaction to Schoenberg's music[6]—largely because sympathetic colleagues like Busoni and Oskar Fried[7] and a good number of personal friends and supporters were in the audience—a performance of *Pelleas und Melisande* in Prague soon after, on 29 February, aroused public controversy. Accompanying Schoenberg to Prague a week ahead of the concert, Webern attended the long and arduous rehearsals (which took place in the Ständetheater, where Mozart had first conducted his *Don Giovanni*). Webern first stayed with Horwitz, who had assumed the Prague theatre post Webern had declined, then he moved to the Hotel Blauer Stern. As the performance approached, Berg, Königer, Linke, and Polnauer arrived, and so did Webern's and Königer's wives, the sister pair. The event became a reunion of the Schoenberg circle, "like the old days in Vienna," as Berg wrote to his wife, Helene, whom illness had prevented from coming. In the first half of the programme Schoenberg himself conducted a Bach suite (arranged by Mahler from two of Bach's orchestral suites) and his own 50-minute-long symphonic poem. This latter work, new to the Prague public, provoked demonstrations that lasted all through the intermission period. Only with some difficulty could the rest of the evening get under way. It included cello concertos by Haydn and Saint-Saëns, played by Pablo Casals, with Zemlinsky conducting the orchestra.

On this occasion, the little fraternity of disciples presented the master with the first printed copy (specially bound in blue leather) of their literary tribute, *Arnold Schoenberg*.[8] Its primary intent was to open the eyes of the musical world to the significance of Schoenberg as a composer and teacher, such promotion being deemed necessary because of the overwhelmingly hostile attitude of the press. Webern had been the driving force behind the production of the volume, which was published by R. Piper, Munich. His essay, "Schoenberg's Music," encompassing almost a third of the book's 90 pages, was by far the longest of the contributions. Also included were articles by Jalowetz ("The Theory of Harmony"), Kandinsky ("The Pictures"), and Gütersloh ("Schoenberg the Painter"), as well as a section, "The Teacher," in which Schoenberg's pupils[9] joined in a series of testimonials. A brief biographical sketch, referring to Schoenberg's strained relations with the Vienna Academy, opened the slender volume, followed by a list of Schoenberg's compositions up to Opus 19 and an introduction by Karl Linke. These preceded Webern's essay, which had also just appeared, virtually unaltered, in the *Rheinische Musik-und Theaterzeitung*[10] under the title "About Arnold Schoenberg." In his study Webern surveyed Schoenberg's principal compositions up to that time and said of his master's artistic perception: "It creates entirely new expressive values; therefore it also needs new means of expression. Content and form cannot be separated." Webern's remarks on Schoenberg's Opera 10, 15, 16, and 19 could readily serve as commentaries on his own compositions originating during the same period.[11]

The book of homage was illustrated with reproductions of several of Schoenberg's paintings. That same spring one of his pictures also appeared—among those of such masters as Cézanne, Gauguin, Matisse, Picasso, and van Gogh—in *Der blaue Reiter*, the volume edited by the avant-garde painters Kandinsky and Marc. Kandinsky was genuinely interested in music, advancing theories that linked colours with tonal sonorities. (An analysis of Scriabin's *Prometheus*, a work experimenting in this sphere, was included in the volume; it met with Webern's stern disapproval.) In order to demonstrate the corresponding advances in music and art, Kandinsky invited Schoenberg, Berg, and Webern to contribute some of their work to the publication. The three compositions, appearing as inserts, were Schoenberg's *Herzgewächse*, Op. 20, Berg's "Warm die Lüfte," Op. 2, No. 4, and Webern's George song "Ihr tratet zu dem Herde," Op. 4, No. 5. This was the second time that a work by Webern appeared in print. The Dreililien Verlag, to whom he had offered some manuscripts in June of 1911, had returned them "with regret." At the outset of his stay in Berlin he had submitted to Tischer & Jagenberg, at Dr Tischer's request, several of his compositions. These included nine George songs, the Five Movements, Op. 5, and the Four Pieces, Op. 7. This prospect also proved barren. Disappointed, Webern wrote to Dr Tischer on 2 January 1912: "I regret very much that you are not accepting my compositions for publication. Perhaps some day you will take a friendly view of them."

With the coming of spring, Schoenberg's fortunes were markedly improving. Performances of his *Pelleas und Melisande* were scheduled in cities as widely separated as Amsterdam and St Petersburg. In February he had received a commission of 1,500 marks for a work for the gifted actress Albertine Zehme, and by 30 March the first song of the *Pierrot Lunaire* cycle was completed. Schoenberg's position in Berlin was growing firmer; when an invitation to teach at Vienna's Academy was at last tendered him in late spring, he turned it down. Webern, on the other hand, was feeling increasingly obliged to seek the security of salaried employment. Once more, he steeled himself for the same course that had proven so unsatisfying before. " I am returning again to the theatre," he had written to Königer on 11 January 1912. "It is no use: I must conduct. Ever since I could think, I have wanted it. I cannot renounce it. I must perform Schoenberg and Mahler and everything that is sacred." Aiming anew for a position in Prague, he approached Zemlinsky, also offering to play the celesta part in Mahler's Eighth Symphony, scheduled for performance in Prague at the end of March.

Earlier that month, the work had been given twice in Vienna. Webern travelled there on 6 March and stayed for more than two weeks.[12] He had arranged beforehand with Königer to buy tickets for the two scheduled performances for his father and sister. Königer was to keep the plan secret, however, since Webern's father was bound to object to the extravagance of hearing the same work twice when tickets were so expensive. Webern confided that, by impressing his father with the grandeur of Mahler's "Symphony of a Thousand," he hoped to convince him that his choice of a career in music was the right one after all.

From Vienna, Webern proceeded to Prague for the rehearsals and two performances of the Eighth Symphony under Zemlinsky's baton. Schoenberg also came to deliver a lecture on Mahler. On 29 March Webern wrote to Berg of his regret that they could not be together in Prague. The performance was "incomparably finer" than the one in Vienna, and he especially enjoyed participating at the celesta. In the same letter, he informed Berg of a sudden development that had set off "a thousand conflicting emotions" in him. "I am confused, afraid, joyful, enthusiastic, everything at the same moment." He had just accepted a conducting post in Stettin (Szczecin), which he was to assume as early as 1 July.[13] Webern's decision was made somewhat easier by the fact that Jalowetz would again work side by side with him, but his signing up was nevertheless beset by misgivings, ranging from regrets at having to lose a summer of creative work to sadness at having to miss the Vienna première of Mahler's Ninth Symphony.

On his return to Berlin, there was a flurry of visitors (first the Königers, then Webern's father and sister), but by 10 April work on the two-piano reduction of Schoenberg's Five Pieces for Orchestra, Op. 16, could begin in earnest. It was not laid aside until completion, just before Webern's departure from Berlin in the middle of May. The only interruption was a trip to Stettin to rent what he described to Berg as "a really very beautiful apartment—probably *beyond* my means." As the Berlin episode drew to its close, the parting became difficult. "Here in Zehlendorf it is glorious now," Webern wrote Königer on 5 May. "Under my window are many trees in bloom. The air is full of fragrance. The way to Schoenberg is lined with blossoming fruit trees. At night the nightingales sing. This, too, I have never heard before. In short, it is wonderful here. I am with Schoenberg daily."

During the months in Berlin, Webern's friendship with Schoenberg had been officially sealed by the older man's offer of the familiar address "Du," henceforth used in all their correspondence. (That privilege was extended to Alban Berg only six years later.) As if trying to perpetuate the constant personal exchange of news and ideas, Webern dispatched to Schoenberg no fewer than twelve letters during the single month that he spent in Austria before going to Stettin. This time, his way home did not lead to the Preglhof. Early in the year, Carl von Webern had sold the estate. He gave the high cost of upkeep and the heavy taxation as reasons for his decision, but it was more likely due to the awareness that his son was incapable of managing the property. This realization had been growing with the years, and it now was compounded by Anton's having taken on the responsibility of a family while still depending on his father's financial assistance. There appeared little prospect that this situation would change substantially in the foreseeable future. No doubt the resolve to give up the beloved estate caused the patriarch much anguish.

After the sale was completed, Carl von Webern allotted to each of his three children the sum of 50,000 gold kronen.[14] Anticipation of this bequest spurred Webern to have some of his compositions printed at his own expense, an idea in which he was encouraged by both Schoenberg and Berg. "I have recently been rejected by publishers for the third time," he had written to Königer on 29 February 1912, reporting that he planned to have his Passacaglia, his First String Quartet (Op. 5), and "the older six orchestra pieces" (Op. 6) printed. The reproduction was to be done by the Straubedruck (Schoenberg's Second String Quartet had appeared under the same imprint). The publication programme was soon partly carried out: within a year, the full score of the Six Pieces for Orchestra was available, to coincide with the work's first performance in Vienna. Subsequently sent to a number of prominent conductors, this score helped to introduce Webern's name. Thus the sale of the Preglhof enabled Webern to become his own advocate at a time when publishers did not yet recognize the value of his work.

The Preglhof had been the focal point of Webern's youth. Future summers would lack the beauty and serenity of long weeks spent in meadows and forests, the peacefulness so essential to Webern's creative inner being. Lamenting his loss, Webern penned a nostalgic letter from Stettin, telling Schoenberg on 17 July 1912:

> I just wrote to you, but I must still tell you how, almost daily, the longing for our estate simply overwhelms me, especially now in summer. I grieve for it as for a dear departed. . . . Often I wish I could go there and acquire it again. I now see everything in a transfigured light. And in my memory it appears to me like a lost paradise. I cannot imagine that I should never live there, compose there any more. I am overwhelmed with emotion when I imagine everything there as it is now during summer. My daily way to the grave of my mother. The infinite mildness of the entire countryside, all the thousand things there. Now everything is over. . . . If only you could once have seen all this. The seclusion, the quiet, the house, the forests, the garden, and the cemetery. About this time, I had always composed diligently.

After selling the Preglhof, Carl von Webern rented a spacious villa in Klagenfurt. He shared the house, located at Schiffgasse 14, with his older daughter, Maria, and her family, and with his still unmarried daughter, Rosa. Webern, delighted with the residence and its large garden, spent three weeks there after leaving Berlin. Indulging in the glories of springtime, he made a mountain excursion for the explicit purpose of seeing the narcissus fields in bloom. "For me, this is a spiritual matter," he wrote to Berg on 4 June, the eve of his outing. "From time to time, I must breathe this air, this rarefied air of the heights. Does not everything lie in these words? Transparent, clear, pure—the heights. All this must mean something. I have to seek these regions periodically."

Earlier, Berg had come from the Berghof to Klagenfurt for a visit.[15] The well-known photograph, which pictures the friends standing in a meadow, was taken at that time (see insert). During Berg's visit, the pair tried out Webern's just completed two-piano arrangement of Schoenberg's Five Orchestra Pieces. Much of their meeting was devoted to discussions of a special project then approaching realization: two concerts scheduled for 25 and 29 June as an unofficial adjunct to the first annual Vienna Festival Weeks. The programmes, first conceived in a conversation between Schoenberg and Webern, were to constitute a "counter-festival," since the festival directors had totally ignored works by living Austrian composers. (The Festival Weeks did include the posthumous première of Mahler's Ninth Symphony under Bruno Walter.) The two concerts were organized under the nominal auspices of the Academic Association for Literature and Music and were to include works by Schoenberg, Schreker, Zemlinsky, Novák, Suk,[16] Berg, and Webern. The Rosé Quartet promised to collaborate with the string quartets by Schoenberg and Zemlinsky. Arnold Rosé also planned to perform Webern's Four Pieces for Violin and Piano, Op. 7, having been unable to give their première the year before.

A 32-page brochure, listing both programmes, was published by the sponsoring agency under the title "Das musikfestliche Wien." The editor, Paul Stefan, described in his article "The 'Dead' and the 'Living'" the curious situation prompting the apparent competition with the official festival. Other contributors to the brochure were Franz Schreker and Stefan Zweig. Of particular interest was the essay "Anton von Webern and Alban Berg," the first critical study to be accorded the two composers. It was written with sympathy and understanding by Karl Linke, a comrade in the Schoenberg circle. Webern, commenting to Schoenberg on the article in his letter of 7 July 1912, found the distinction between the essentially introvert nature of his music and the more extrovert quality of Berg's somewhat "contrived," but he was pleased on the whole. Although the essay was written at a time when the two were just beginning their careers, Linke's observations have proved to be particularly perceptive, and they retain validity even today.

From Klagenfurt Webern went to Vienna. Everything in him strained against his contractual obligation to be in Stettin before the two concerts took place. For a while he hoped that Steuermann could participate in his Four Pieces for Violin and Piano, but that prospect came to naught because the budget did not allow the pianist to be brought all the way from Berlin. Webern coached his work with the substitute pianist, Richard Goldschmied,[17] only to tell Schoenberg apprehensively on 13 June: "Up to now, he still does not have the slightest notion of it. I am somewhat worried because of Rosé. If only he will play my pieces!" Amidst these concerns, Webern had to leave Vienna. On his arrival in Berlin on 19 June, he spent some precious hours with Schoenberg (staying two nights in his home) and arranged for the transport of his household to Stettin. There he, his wife, and their child made their entrance on 21 June, the day before he had to report for duty.

CHAPTER X

Stettin

(1912–1913)

WEBERN'S APARTMENT IN Stettin was located on the fourth floor of the house at Dohrnstrasse 1. The spacious residence was much to his liking and was destined to provide him with a haven during the difficult months that followed.

The beginning was auspicious enough: the theatre director, having received a request from Arnold Rosé that Webern participate in the 29 June concert in Vienna, generously released his new assistant, despite the fact that he had barely made his appearance and was scheduled to conduct *Ein Walzertraum* (Oscar Straus) on 30 June. Encouraged by Schoenberg, Webern quickly waived all misgivings about leaving his new post so soon. On 28 June he wrote his friend a postcard from the Himmelhof Inn in the Vienna district of Ober St Veit. That afternoon, he told him, he had played with Berg and Jalowetz through the score of Mahler's "inexpressibly beautiful" Ninth Symphony (the première of which, on 26 June, he had had to miss). The concert of 29 June featured Schoenberg's Second String Quartet, with Martha Winternitz-Dorda assuming the vocal part, Berg's Piano Sonata, played by Richard Goldschmied, and Webern's Four Pieces, performed by Arnold Rosé with the composer at the piano. Webern's father, in Vienna on business, was present. The concert was a great success, and everyone was in high spirits at the party which followed. Webern penned an exuberant note to Schoenberg: "Dearest friend, if only you were here! It was wonderful, glorious!" Alma Mahler added "Yes! yes! yes!," while Oskar Kokoschka made the frank if undiplomatic comment: "Today I believed in you for the first time!"[1] to which Frau Winternitz-Dorda attached her testimony: "I believed always!" The postcard made the rounds until virtually every member of the inner circle had signed.

Back in Stettin, Webern wrote Schoenberg two long letters, dated 3 and 7 July, in which he reported in great detail on the evening's proceedings and his own impressions. Most of the commentary in his first letter was devoted to Schoenberg's quartet, which had been received with shouts of bravo and, this time, without any trace of disapproval. He could not say quite the same of the performance of his own work:

> It was Schreker's wife who, sitting in the first row, emitted sounds of barely suppressed laughter. Otherwise, it was quiet. At the end, Loos[2] is said to have shown someone the door. I myself heard nothing. Rosé played my pieces marvellously, and I only regret so much that I was not better. In the rehearsal during the forenoon, it had gone so well. Even now, I am still very depressed over it. I was terribly excited. I apologized to Rosé. He said that we would find another opportunity to play the pieces again. I hope so.

In his second letter Webern remarked: "Your quartet touched my father deeply. He also liked Berg's sonata. My pieces are too 'nervous' for him. 'It is always all over before it starts,' he says."

The feature article devoted to Berg and himself in the programme booklet "Das musikfestliche Wien" caused Webern to muse in his letter of 7 July to Schoenberg: "All these honours accorded one are depressing. I am more unhappy than glad over something like this. On such occasions, I sense all the more distinctly how little I myself am responsible should I really produce something good. I am only the instrument of a higher power. Myself, I am nothing." The day earlier, he had written to Berg how wonderful it was for him to know that Berg held his music in the same high esteem as he did his. Therefore, they would never have to consider the "disconcerting effect" that their works made upon the rest of mankind.

After the uplifting experience of the Vienna days, the humdrum routine in Stettin came as a shock. "I must be in the theatre all day long. What use is my beautiful apartment to me," Webern complained to Schoenberg on 3 July, the third day after his return. The daily grind of rehearsing music he could only loathe made him revolt, and he began complaining of physical troubles:

> As to health, I feel worse than ever. I really do not know whether I can endure it. I get into such a state of exhaustion that I cannot move. Then my feet ache so maddeningly that I can hardly walk. I cannot think any longer, not at all. I live like a beast. I have often thought that I will have to give up the theatre simply for the reason that I cannot withstand the fatigue. . . . I do not see my wife and child, and I am stuck in a "Schmiere" [cheap vaudeville] of the most horrible type,

among the scum of men. Do not be angry that I write you all this. It does me so much good to tell you about it. I despair more every day, and by now so does my wife, although she always helps me to keep going.

This litany of woes, beginning at the very outset of the months in Stettin, becomes a perpetual theme with variations. On 4 July, the day after baring his soul to Schoenberg, Webern wrote to Berg in similar vein. He deplored having to be occupied with the "silliest type of music" and groaned: "I am suffocating!" If it were not for his apartment lease binding him for the year's rent of 1,300 marks, he would be ready to leave at once and bring Erwin Stein in as replacement.

On Sunday, 7 July, Webern made his first Stettin appearance as conductor of an afternoon performance of the popular operetta *Der Vogelhändler* by the Viennese composer Karl Zeller. He conceded to Berg that the work was "quite nice." His dislike for the genre of the operetta notwithstanding, he was not completely averse to the lighter vein. Two works done in Stettin later that season excited his unreserved enthusiasm. One was *Eine Nacht in Venedig* ("This is such fine, delicate music. I now believe that Johann Strauss is a master," he told Schoenberg on 6 October); the other was Lortzing's *Zar und Zimmermann*, which was to remain one of his favourites. Operettas like *Ein Walzertraum*, on the other hand, elicited his disgust ("If only this music were not so nauseating," was his comment to Schoenberg on 12 July.) He particularly despised cheap farces, writing to Berg on 15 August that he was just leaving for the theatre where he had to conduct "something abominable, a Berlin farce called—do not vomit—*Autoliebchen* [*Darling of the Automobile*]."[3] His only consolation was that "everything eventually passes." A month earlier, on 19 July, he had told Berg: "As a non-participant, I would flee a theatre such as the one where I am at present as if it were a place infested with the plague, and now I myself must help to stir the sauce. Often I am ashamed, I appear to myself like a criminal even collaborating in this hell-hole of mankind. I can hardly await my deliverance from this morass."

Webern's revulsion against his work was bound to transfer itself to his personal relationships within the theatre. "The director is a cretin beyond compare. A man with no understanding at all. A fop. His main concern seems to be that the conductors should always be well shaven," Webern had told Schoenberg on 17 July, a mere two weeks after entering into his engagement. He had offered to conduct *Walzertraum*, an operetta already known to him, without any rehearsal. All went well, but Webern felt slighted by the director:

At first, he kept saying: "Yes, but will you not wreck the performance?" Now that I have not "wrecked it" would it not have been proper for him to make up for his doubts with at least a word? No, nothing whatever. He only said after the second act: "Well, *little man*, how do you feel about yourself now?" To be sure, he is six times bigger than I, but certainly innumerable times more stupid. On the whole, I have never seen such untalented, vulgar personnel. But only now and then do I get worked up over such matters any more. I have firmly resolved not to look right or left and I do my duty, may they think of me what they wish.

This determination was no doubt bolstered by Schoenberg's fatherly admonitions. Alarmed, he had urged Webern not to jeopardize his position, since it meant a livelihood if nothing else.

During his two-month stint in the summer theatre, Webern conducted 30 performances in all. He pinned his hopes on receiving more satisfying assignments once the regular season in the Civic Theatre began on 15 September. In the meantime, he continued giving vent to his frustration in frequent and long epistles. It was Alban Berg, in particular, who provided him with a sympathetic ear, and in his letters to him Webern conjured up all that he now felt deprived of. He dreamt of the mountain heights, to which he attributed unlimited powers over body and mind and which he missed with every fibre of his being. So vivid were the images of his fantasy that one can sense with him the sun's radiance reflected by the glaciers, see the varied hues of blooming meadows, smell the fragrance of a forest after rain, drink from fresh mountain streams, or breathe the pure air of the heights. During these months in the northern plains, Webern steeped himself in the writings of Peter Rosegger, with whom he shared a fundamental love for the seclusion of the mountains, and whose simple philosophy had a lasting appeal for him.

To Schoenberg, too, Webern confessed his longing. He visualized a retreat in the mountains, a certain place within view of the Preglhof, an hour and a half's walk from the railroad station: "This is where I would like to build a house for myself so that I could spend the largest part of the year up there," he wrote on 23 July. "I picture for myself everything in the smallest detail. The land would be cheap there, living still cheaper, and thus I could get along with my money and that of my wife. To think of this most extreme contrast to my present life is the greatest comfort for me now. You will thoroughly scold me, but I cannot feel otherwise."

That summer Schoenberg was on holiday at Carlshagen, a resort on the Baltic Sea about a three-hour trip from Stettin. At the end of July, Webern succeeded in obtaining a short leave so that he could spend a precious 24 hours with his friend. Also present were Jalowetz and Stein, who gave a champagne supper in celebration of the reunion. "It was wonderful. Schoenberg was in high spirits. . . . We bathed in the sea and sailed in the afternoon. On the following morning I walked with Schoenberg on the beach," Webern told Berg in his detailed report of 2 August.

It was during that visit that Webern was encouraged by Schoenberg to submit some of his compositions to the publisher Simrock. He chose the Passacaglia, the Five Movements for String Quartet, and the Four Pieces for Violin and Piano (he contemplated also a selection from his fourteen George songs). The initiative, carried out in early August, was to produce no result, although Schoenberg had written to Simrock on 4 August by way of introduction: "Webern is my pupil. He who penetrates more deeply will soon see that we are dealing here with a really great, truly outstanding, independent talent who in many respects surpasses my attainments and is clearly a fresh, original artist."[4]

Webern had returned invigorated from Carlshagen, but he quickly sank into depths of depression even greater than before. "Conditions at the theatre are becoming more and more horrible," he complained to Schoenberg on 31 July, his second day back. He alluded to personal tensions: "Fundamentally, I think badly of no one, wish well to absolutely everyone. Why do they treat me so rudely? After all, I do no harm to anyone. Well then, what do they want from me? This has never happened to me before. But it will pass."

Two weeks later Webern's spirits were lifted when Schoenberg and his family stopped over in Stettin on their way back to Berlin. This gave Webern and his wife an opportunity to reciprocate the hospitality that the Schoenbergs always extended to them. Schoenberg was able to observe Webern in action as conductor in a performance of Fall's *Dollar Princess*, and he combined his approval with some practical advice.

Further encouragement was provided by the promise of more challenging tasks during the oncoming winter season. In mid-August, Webern was assigned the chorus rehearsals for *Fidelio*. The performance was to be conducted by Jalowetz, who continued in Stettin the successful pattern of his tenure in Danzig. That season he led such operas as *The Marriage of Figaro*, *Ariadne auf Naxos*, *The Flying Dutchman* and *Tannhäuser*. In the preparation of these works, Webern learned a great deal while functioning as solo coach and chorus master, and he gained additional experience by serving backstage during performances. His expectation of better conducting assignments was not as yet to be fulfilled, however. Up until Christmas, the only opera entrusted to him was Lortzing's *Waffenschmied*. Even that much anticipated performance, on 16 November, brought him a disappointment. Writing to Schoenberg a day later, he cited the fact that he had had only one rehearsal, and he especially blamed the orchestra: "It is really quite miserable. Its incompetence is beyond compare. . . . The performance in Danzig was much nicer and therefore, although I was much more insecure at the time, I was then in the right mood. Here not at all. On the contrary, I longed for the end; I was actually bored because I thought to myself before every number: 'How miserably are they going to play that again!' I was very depressed and still am."

Within the strict theatre discipline, Webern's great sensitivity rendered him especially vulnerable whenever there was a personal confrontation. On 19 October an incident so much upset him that he poured his heart out to Berg: "My dear good friend, I thank you a thousand times for the picture of Mahler's grave. I had just come home from the theatre in deepest disgust. An operetta stage director barked at me as if I were a dog because I had come to the rehearsal a few minutes late. You see, even things like this are happening. And now came your letter and the picture. With it you made me deeply happy. You think of me, you love me. I am no dog *after all*. Tomorrow I will go to a doctor, I will let him give me a sick leave, and then away, away."

Webern's desperation had been deepened by a special event: the first performance, on 16 October, of Schoenberg's *Pierrot Lunaire*, the penultimate work in the composer's period of free atonality. Although it meant forfeiting a chance to conduct Louis Maillart's opera *Das Glöckchen des Eremiten*, Webern travelled to Berlin for the signal occasion. The première—conducted by the composer, who had prepared it in 40 rehearsals—created a sensation and left no doubt that, despite some audience opposition and unanimous rebuke by the dumbfounded music critics, Schoenberg's star was on the rise. Webern's faith in his master was beginning to be fulfilled. Besides an influx of new pupils, there soon ensued for Schoenberg many performances of his works and engagements as conductor and lecturer.

The impression left by *Pierrot Lunaire* was so overwhelming that Webern, on his return to Stettin, became obsessed with the thought of finding an escape from what he called the "wasteland" of his own existence into the loftiness of spirit that Schoenberg's world represented. For him, the summer had always been a fertile time to compose, and he bitterly regretted that this year no musical ideas had been allowed to germinate and reach fruition. All that he had been able to do, amidst the constant pressure of theatre chores, was to proofread his two-piano arrangement of Schoenberg's Five Orchestra Pieces (the printed score appeared in September). Webern was painfully aware of his unproductiveness. The day after the *Pierrot Lunaire* première, he wrote to Schoenberg: "What I would like best is to go away for a month to recuperate and then come to Berlin in order to compose again, at long last, after almost a year and a half."

From the very start of his Stettin engagement there was hardly a letter in which Webern had not dwelled on his frequent spells of indisposition. "Perhaps you think that I am a hypochondriac," he had written to Schoenberg on 23 July, "but I am not. I am decidedly feeling very ill." By 12 September he confessed to him: "I am often in complete despair about myself, about my talent, about my character, about everything. Just recently I have suffered through hours of deepest depression." On 2 October, Webern's morale had sunk even lower:

I have passed two horrible nights. And I dread the night to come. Convinced by Strindberg, I can think nothing else but that I am being punished. . . . That I amount to nothing as yet as a conductor is, after all, primarily my own fault. It is only my devilish nervous weakness, or whatever it is. You know that even when I studied with you, I suffered from constant headaches. Now it has seized my whole body. Head, arms, and legs ache terribly. And now insomnia has gripped me again. I cannot lie down. I must get up, pace back and forth. My dear friend, you can imagine that in such moments I long only for rest or for a situation which could free me from my idiotic sufferings. I would like to hide away somewhere in the mountains and only reappear as a respectable human being.

Three weeks later, on 23 October, Webern added dejectedly: "I recently saw a physician. He told me that I should talk myself out of my attacks of indisposition, then I would be cured. If only it were so simple! What a night I had again."

The same letter included a bitter tirade against Stettin and its "scandalous" music public. Following the Berlin première of *Pierrot Lunaire*, Schoenberg took the work on tour to Vienna, Breslau, and Hamburg, but performances projected for Stettin and Danzig had to be cancelled because of insufficient advance ticket sales. "Oh, if only I were not here. Damn it!" Webern raged.[5] In his irritated frame of mind, he soon became embroiled in a conflict with the theatre director who threatened to cancel his conducting assignment for *Waffenschmied*, claiming that he had not sufficiently devoted himself to another work, the stage music for a play. "That was not true at all. I was so furious that I would have liked best to walk out on the spot," Webern wrote to Schoenberg on 16 November as he described the incident, during which he actually dared the director to dismiss him.

In his despondency and overpowering desire to leave Stettin, Webern showed little concern for his economic future, despite the fact that his wife was pregnant again and that the unexpired lease and new moving expenses would cost him dearly. Apparently he relied entirely on his share from the sale of the Preglhof. Small wonder that his father—a hard-working, practical, and conservative man—was greatly alarmed. He urged his son not to throw his career away and, if Stettin were so unsatisfactory, to seek an engagement elsewhere. Actually, Webern went through the motions during the ensuing weeks, letting a Berlin agent file applications for positions at Düsseldorf, Dortmund, and Bochum. He refused even to consider an opening at Riga because it called for operettas only. In the end, none of these applications led to anything. Meanwhile, all the signals of the losing battle that Webern had been fighting in Stettin virtually from the outset were apparent in his correspondence. As early as 24 October he told Paul Königer: "I am becoming more and more discontented here, and the point when I simply get out is no longer far off."

Late in November, Webern went to Zehlendorf for two days to confer with Schoenberg before the latter left for Holland, where performances of *Pelleas und Melisande* were scheduled in Amsterdam and The Hague. The following month, Schoenberg was invited to St Petersburg to conduct the same work. Webern followed his friend's successes with enthusiasm. He himself had returned from Berlin with a more constructive attitude and felt temporarily encouraged by the outcome of his second *Waffenschmied* performance: "It was much better than the first, incomparably so," he wrote to Schoenberg on 4 December. "And this time I had great joy. I had the first concertmaster at his desk, and as a result the orchestra was virtually transformed. Thus I could really make music and entered more and more into the right mood."

By 13 December, however, he again could report only adversity: "Already I lie sick in bed again. My nerve attacks become more and more acute. For several nights by now I have had almost no sleep; the night before last I even had a fever. As a result, I am so exhausted that yesterday towards evening I went to bed instead ⸱of conducting *Waffenschmied*. What ill luck I have!" The doctor prescribed sleeping medicine, pine-needle baths thrice weekly, and massages. He was sufficiently convinced of the seriousness of the patient's condition to suggest a sick leave as well. "You see, my lamenting was not unfounded," Webern's letter continued. "Now it has simply come to the point that I can hardly go on any more. I believe that it makes no sense to try to gloss over the matter further. I have done this for many years. But now it does not work any more." A few days later Mathilde Schoenberg came with her two children for a visit and confirmed Webern's sad state of health, writing to her husband, who was on his Russian concert tour: "He looks frightful and is unbelievably weak. When he climbs the stairs he has to hang on to the railing with both hands; in the room he staggers from one chair to the other."

In his agony of mind and body, Webern had begun linking each adverse incident with supernatural causes. On 17 October, after a closing theatre curtain had shattered his eyeglasses, injuring him slightly, he remarked to Schoenberg: "Such strange things happen continually. Illness and misfortune." When he described the same accident to Berg, he interpreted it as an "omen" that he should not be in theatre work at all. Hoping to bolster his son's morale, Carl von Webern, accompanied by his daugher Rosa, came to Stettin at Christmas time. During his visit, Webern's father had the satisfaction of seeing him conduct *Waffenschmied* and the stage music to a Christmas play.

On New Year's Day of 1913, a year that was to be crucial in Webern's life, he penned a wistful letter to Königer in which he took stock of himself:

Thinking of your life always has a special attraction for me. It calms me. From the excess of diversion and outside activity (which the physicians always recommend to me as a cure, whereas in reality I almost perish because of it), I flee in thought to a life that is quieter on the outside but has more movement within. It is strange: I dry out in this flood of music, excitement, and so on. Mahler once wrote that he needed this commotion, or rather the conducting of works by others, in order to have a counterweight against his inner turmoil. I suffocate in it. I am so torn apart and cannot concentrate. I do not feel well. I already moan again. It seems to me that I am always writing you the same thing. I myself do not know any more what I want. And I am always ill. I have less and less strength to resist within myself. And therefore I like to think of your life that is so quiet on the outside.

The end of the season was only four months away, but Webern's indispositions had become so incessant and his mood so despondent that by now his father and Schoenberg were convinced that he needed a rest. Even the prospect of conducting Boieldieu's *La Dame blanche* and Verdi's *Il Trovatore* in January could not lift his depression. Completely exhausted, he requested sick leave on 17 January; the attestation submitted by his doctor prescribed a month of complete rest. For a week, Webern had to await the approval of the theatre director, who was out of town. In the meantime, he was released from his duties and confined to bed. His father and sister left Stettin on 20 January; their prolonged stay had been forced by attacks of influenza, attributed to the moist and mild climate.

On 24 January Webern informed Schoenberg that he would arrive in

Berlin the following day en route to the Semmering, where he planned to take his rest cure. (On the last day in Stettin he had submitted, at Schoenberg's suggestion, a selection of his George songs to Cadow at Hildburghausen in another vain attempt to interest a publisher in his work.) His sick leave having been granted, he now felt infinitely relieved and yet at the same time very depressed. He fully expected to return to his post within the month. Wilhelmine, who was awaiting her second child in February, stayed behind.

The Semmering is a fashionable mountain resort close to Vienna. On 1 February Webern wrote to Berg from Dr Vecsey's sanatorium, to which he had been admitted, that it was "glorious" there, and that he was "faring brilliantly." He was confident that he would recuperate in time for the first performance of Schoenberg's *Gurrelieder*, scheduled to take place on 23 February in Vienna. In the invigorating air of forests and mountains, his condition at first seemed to improve. However, he soon lost confidence in the method of treatment. In his frequent letters to Berg, he complained about the same old symptoms that had plagued him for "almost ten years" by now. Berg, himself always of uncertain health, was sympathetic and, responding on 25 February, questioned whether Webern's ill health came "*only*'(!) from the nerves." He speculated that the nerves are the organs which connect soul and body, and this would explain why so little is known about them, almost as little as is known "about the soul itself." Berg recommended a full six months' rest, and this suggestion met with Webern's own decision, arrived at by late February, not to return to Stettin at all but to have his family join him in Vienna once he was released. The family now included a second daughter, Maria, born in Stettin on 17 February.

Dr Vecsey's sanatorium was governed by strict regulations, and its patients were supposed to devote themselves to absolute rest. While the doctors were not satisfied that Webern's condition justified his discharge, they yielded to his pleading that he be allowed to attend the 23 February première of Schoenberg's *Gurrelieder*, an event of utmost importance to him. The performance had been preceded by uncertainties due to tensions between the composer and the concert organizers. As late as 6 February Schoenberg had pugnaciously challenged the Vienna Philharmonic Chorus to cancel the whole project.[6] The difficulties could be resolved, however, and the performance, directed by Franz Schreker, turned into a triumphant success, climaxed by the presentation of a laurel wreath to the composer. The work's apparatus, calling for 400 participants on stage, approached the dimensions of Mahler's Eighth Symphony. It included an orchestra of 140 musicians, an ensemble of soloists,[7] and four choruses.[8]

Greatly inspired, Webern returned to his confinement at the Semmering. During his stay in the sanatorium he prepared the score of his Six Pieces, Op. 6, for their première in late March. The preceding autumn, Schoenberg had first projected the idea of a "novelty concert" in Vienna, which was to include compositions by Webern and Berg. During his trip to Russia, he had written to Webern of his intention to conduct the Six Pieces himself. At Schoenberg's suggestion, Webern then proceeded to have the score reproduced in the Straube facsimile process, after incorporating some minor changes in the third and fifth movements. (He ordered 200 copies, which cost him 80 pfennigs each.) In his letter of Christmas 1912 to Schoenberg he had dwelt on the deep significance this work held for him:

> Dearest friend, permit me to place Rosegger's book, *Waldheimat*, under your Christmas tree. It describes Rosegger's youth. The last chapter is entitled "About my Mother." It contains these words, which are for me inexpressibly beautiful: "At last came the tear: the tear which a mother's heart sent with us into the world to soothe us in sorrow and as our only consolation when our soul despairs of hope for salvation, when friends do not understand us, and when a mother's heart is broken. O be hailed, you rich, eternal heritage!" If the unheard-of good fortune that you will conduct my orchestra pieces should really be granted to me, I beg you to think of these words.

On 9 March Webern was discharged from the sanatorium. Returning from his enforced solitude to the hustle and bustle of Vienna, he was beset anew by his ailing nerves. "Everything irritates me to the highest degree," he complained to Schoenberg on 13 March. His depression was deepened by loneliness. "It burdens me like the weight of a tree," he told Schoenberg four days later. "The long separation from my family causes me to suffer so terribly, as if it were a crime. Strangely enough, it affects me particularly now just as it comes to an end. Never again in my life will I do this. I could perish from longing for my Mali [his little daughter Amalie]. On Wednesday they will be here."

The concert date was set for 31 March. Preparations for the performance of the Six Pieces posed some problems: the copyist first employed for the orchestral parts decided that he could not cope with the job and returned the score after precious time was lost. But Webern succeeded in finding another. On 17 March he reported to Schoenberg: "Everything is in order for the concert. All the instruments are being procured, including the alto flute. It comes from Germany, and a member of the opera orchestra will play it. Such an expenditure because of a few measures! I almost have pangs of conscience, but I am full of joyful anticipation just the same." For the event, presented under the auspices of the Academic Association for Literature and Music, the large hall of the Musikverein was rented. Six orchestral rehearsals were arranged, the final one to take place on the morning of the concert. Schoenberg, arriving from Berlin for the first rehearsal, assumed command of the entire programme. It consisted of Webern's Six Pieces, followed by Zemlinsky's Four Orchestral Songs on Poems of Maeterlinck, Schoenberg's First Chamber Symphony, the second and fourth of Berg's Five Orchestral Songs on Picture-Postcard Texts by Peter Altenberg, and Mahler's *Kindertotenlieder*.

The concert occasioned one of the greatest scandals in the history of music. (Two months later, on 29 May, the première of Stravinsky's *Le Sacre du printemps* in Paris was to be similarly disrupted.) It was provoked by an apparently organized clique of reactionaries who spread disquiet from the start. In a newspaper article headlined "Tumult in the Large Musikverein Hall," a reporter described the occurrences as follows:

> Yesterday's concert of the Academic Association for Literature and Music degenerated into unprecedented scenes of scandal. Things could not have been worse at a turbulent meeting of voters in a proletarian district—the contrasting views of the opposing parties could not have been more brutally expressed—than at yesterday's concert conducted by Arnold Schoenberg. Immediately after the first part of the programme, an orchestral work by Anton von Webern, there was a confrontation lasting several minutes between the applauding and hissing factions of the audience. But this still remained within the bounds of the demonstrations with which we are all too familiar from other Schoenberg concerts. After the second orchestral piece, a storm of laughter went through the hall. This was drowned out by thunderous applause from admirers of the tension-laden and provocative music. The other four pieces also—the composition consists of six little pieces without titles—contributed to a mood in the hall which led one to fear the worst. Four beautiful orchestral songs by Alexander von Zemlinsky, based on poems by Maeterlinck—we are reserving critical discussion of all offerings—apparently calmed the heated and belligerent spirits. After Schoenberg's Opus 9, his Chamber Symphony that was rejected years ago, the furious hissing and clapping was intermingled, regrettably, with the shrill tones from house keys and whistles, and in the second balcony it came to the first fisticuffs of the evening. From all sides the respective positions now were aired in rude shouting, and during this unnaturally prolonged interval the opponents clashed vehemently. It

was, however, the two orchestral songs by Alban Berg, on picture postcard texts by Peter Altenberg, that robbed even the hitherto judicious listeners of their composure. The first poem reads: "Did you see the forest after the thundershower? Everything rests, glistens, and is more beautiful than before—Behold, woman, you too need thundershowers." The music to this absurd text exceeded everything heard up till then, and the fact that it was received with no more than hearty laughter must be ascribed to the good-naturedness of the Viennese. However, since Schoenberg stopped in the middle of the piece and shouted to the audience words to the effect that he would have everyone disturbing the quiet evicted by means of official force, there erupted anew agitating and wild invectives, face slappings, and challenges to duels. Herr von Webern also shouted from his loge that the entire "baggage" was to be thrown out, and from the audience there came the prompt response that the followers of the disliked musical idiom should be committed to the Steinhof insane asylum. The raging and screaming in the hall could now no longer be stopped. It was not at all unusual to see some gentleman in the audience climb, in breathless haste and with ape-like agility, over several parquet rows in order to box the ears of the object of his fury. The intervening police officer could achieve nothing in this chaos of wildly incensed passions. If he wanted to intervene and restore quiet in any one group of brawlers, the sound of face slaps was heard at the same time from all sides. Finally, the president of the Academic Association stepped up onto the conductor's podium and begged the audience to honour Mahler's memory and listen to his *Kindertotenlieder*. This misplaced request—for Mahler would only have suffered shame that evening rather than being honoured—provoked somebody to shout a vicious insult, for which the Herr President again reciprocated with face slaps. All kinds of people now stormed the musicians, who were deathly pale and trembling from excitement. They exhorted them to vacate the stage and terminate the concert. Nevertheless, it still took perhaps half an hour before the last rioters noisily left the hall. Mahler had been honoured and *not* performed.[9]

The scandal had a rather anticlimactic aftermath in one of Vienna's civil courts. Two of the chief combatants were fined 100 kronen each; lesser penalties were meted out to several others. The press naturally relished the sensational aspects of the affair. One newspaper article went so far as to suggest that Schoenberg had performed the works by Webern and Berg only because these composers had financially supported him. Outraged, Berg wrote to Webern in early April that the whole thing was so abominable that he would like best "to flee far away." This is precisely what Webern did. On 7 April, he replied from Portorose on the Adriatic Sea that he felt "almost redeemed from all these nauseating matters." To his thinking, the whole affair was not really a battle about art; the perpetrators of the scandal were not the kind of opponents worth speaking about. To the press the cause itself mattered little; all the reporters wanted was to delight their readers with "muckraking," and the greater the "filth" the more satisfying it was for them. In this context the composers and their works were completely "incidental." As for himself, he had fully regained his composure, and he admonished Berg not to dwell on the affair any longer, but rather on such "marvellous things" as "the beautiful time of the rehearsals, the Chamber Symphony, the glorious evening with Altenberg, and the Loos villa." He and Berg should resolve to go to work immediately, writing "still better compositions" instead of allowing "such filth" to distract them.

CHAPTER XI

Vienna—Illness
(1913–1914)

WHEN WEBERN RELINQUISHED his post in Stettin, he did not intend to abandon a theatre career altogether. During his confinement to the sanatorium at the Semmering, he corresponded with Zemlinsky concerning prospects at the Deutsches Landestheater in Prague. In March an understanding was reached whereby Webern was to assume a position at the beginning of the next season. With this objective in mind, he decided to devote all the remaining months to the restoration of his health.

Immediately after the tumultuous concert of 31 March, Webern went with his wife and children to Portorose, a sea-coast resort near Trieste. They found lodgings in the Villa Hansi. The spa, noted for its hot salt-water baths, had been recommended to Webern, and the cure, administered by a physician, proved beneficial. Webern's hope of basking in the southern sun was disappointed, however. The weather was so cold and rainy that, on 23 April, he broke off his sojourn and took his family to Klagenfurt for an extended stay in his father's house. There he spent most of each day working in the garden, an occupation he enjoyed very much because it brought him close to the soil and soothed his nerves. But whatever improvement he could note in his health was to be only temporary. On 15 May he wrote to Schoenberg: "Lately, I feel worse again. Sometimes not much different than in Stettin. What am I to do! In no time I will be in Prague. And there? I am often in despair." The following day he told Berg that the mental conception of his next composition was "already quite far matured," but that he still did not have "sufficient strength to deliver it" since he had begun to feel quite ill again of late. Willing to try anything, Webern, an avid smoker, gave up cigarettes, but even this sacrifice brought no relief.

Since his father's bustling household, made up of several family units, did not offer sufficient quiet, Webern looked for summer quarters elsewhere. A trip to Niederdorf in the Pustertal, a region of Tyrol, did not produce anything suitable. But an invitation to Mürzzuschlag in Styria provided the solution, and he moved there in early June. Webern had always liked the countryside surrounding this popular resort town, to which family ties had occasioned many visits. In the house at Wienerstrasse No. 104, his wife's paternal grandfather had carried on his trade as butcher. Webern had repeatedly referred to him in terms of the highest esteem, commenting to Berg on 23 May, that while it might be colloquial to say "he acts like a butcher," this particular butcher was "like a sage." The house and business had been inherited by Wilhelmine's aunt, Leopoldine Schmid, who offered her hospitality for the next two months. However, since Webern needed seclusion for his creative work, he rented for himself an attic room in a villa high up on the mountainside. Spending much of the day in this retreat, he composed the Three Pieces for String Quartet (see Chapter XII).

"Now that I am working intensively, I feel better. Often I am quite tired, though," Webern wrote to Schoenberg on 28 June, reporting on the progress of his composition. It was to be the only creative product of that vacation period, during which he made frequent excursions, as if to make up for the dismal summer of the year before. Together with Jalowetz and Stein, he ascended the Rax on 5 June. In July he repeated the climb in the company of his father. The Rax remained one of Webern's favourite mountain goals; hardly a year passed without his visiting its high meadows, during summer a wonderland of alpine flora. Webern also took long walks in the vicinity. On one occasion he made a pilgrimage to the birthplace of Peter Rosseger (a peasant hut nestled "in the most unheard-of solitude, high up on the mountain," as Webern described it to Schoenberg in his 28 June letter) and to the schoolhouse founded by the writer in the same remote region. Webern loved to tread the ground his idols had walked. In May, another pilgrimage had taken him from Klagenfurt to Gustav Mahler's former summer home by the Wörthersee. From the villa, he had made the ten-minute climb to the little stone house where the composer had retreated for his work. Webern peered through the window into the cabin's single room. Still in place were the table and chair Mahler had used while his inspiration soared to gigantic heights.

In his leisure time Webern fertilized his mind by devoting himself to the world of literature. During a brief stay in Vienna in early June, he was deeply impressed by Frank Wedekind's play *Francisca*, in which the author himself appeared as one of the actors. Webern's reading included Maeterlinck's *Vom Tode* and a half dozen of Strindberg's books. He gave Schoenberg some of his reactions in a letter of 18 June: "How marvellous the *Fröhliche Weihnacht* is. Hardly ever before was

Strindberg's thought clearer to me than in this play. Because he observes earthly affairs from such height they become transfigured. I cannot help myself—if Strindberg speaks of servants, one feels infinitely elevated, but when Maeterlinck speaks of eternity, one does not at all." Webern's aversion to Maeterlinck was of recent date. Earlier, he had been so inspired that he had wanted to set two of Maeterlinck's plays to music. The concepts of atheism and materialism expounded in *Vom Tode*, however, conflicted so sharply with his own views of eternity that they appeared to him "almost like a blasphemy," as he told Berg on 23 May.

That summer the two friends shared great concern over Schoenberg, who was again embroiled in various difficulties. Siegfried Ochs, the founder-conductor of Berlin's famous Philharmonic Chorus, had severely insulted him during a financial dispute connected with a projected *Gurrelieder* performance. Schoenberg related the confrontation in minute detail to Webern, who promptly and indignantly passed the complete information on to Berg. Schoenberg was also waging a legal battle in Vienna. While he had been there early in the year, the father of his former pupil, Paul Königer, had instituted an action against him which not only led to the confiscation of some of his personal effects but also deprived him of most of the revenue from the *Gurrelieder* première. The drawn-out proceedings kept tempers aroused and strained Schoenberg economically. Webern, referring in his letter of 28 June to this "all-surpassing most infamous, most criminal mean act," begged his friend to allow him to assist. The offer was accepted, and on 1 July Webern sent off an undisclosed amount of money. In the accompanying letter, he exclaimed: "I only thank God that I can and may help you."

The idyll at Mürzzuschlag came to an abrupt end just when Webern was about to visit Berg at Trahütten. If the restfulness of those weeks had done much to restore Webern's nerves, he was severely upset by a stroke of fate dealt to the family of his older sister, Maria, and her husband, Paul Clementschitsch. The couple had three sons, of whom the eldest, Theo, was Webern's favourite. While on holiday at an Italian resort on the Adriatic Sea, the twelve-year-old youth died suddenly from a ruptured appendix in spite of a last-minute operation. "It grieves me terribly; I liked the child so much," Webern wrote to Schoenberg on 17 July from his father's home in Klagenfurt. "At Pentecost this year I sponsored him at confirmation. He would have entered the third Gymnasium class. He was very talented. Now everything is over—it is not to be comprehended."

As if the shock of his nephew's unexpected death were not enough, the circumstances preceding the funeral were such as to leave Webern distressed and shaken just at the time when he needed strength and confidence for his new position in Prague. On 20 July, after his return to Mürzzuschlag, he gave Schoenberg a depressed report:

> I was away for almost a week—a dreadful time. There was s u h an accumulation of nerve-racking events that it was hardly to be endured. The uncertainty during the trip there, the news, then the wait for my sister, finally her arrival. Then again the wait for the body and the burial. What dreadful agony the boy's poor parents had to go through until the body was up there. These Italians! Imagine, customs had to be paid for a dead child—300 lire! They refused to carry the body out of the house unless so much was paid in tips, and so forth. I have a horror of this country. The papers went astray, so that the body was not permitted to cross the border, or was it for another reason? In short, it lasted endlessly. It was horrible and still is. It affects me so frightfully that the boy had to die. This on top of my stupid nerves—I am completely exhausted.[1]

It only added to Webern's anxiety that he had to face the immediate future. "The summer is already over for me. Every year, this makes me sad in itself, and now this ending," he wrote to Berg on 24 July, confiding to him that sometimes he was so overcome that he absolutely did not know any more where he belonged. What sense was there in his going to Prague at all? The purpose of his life could be fulfilled only through creative productivity. He begged Berg not to consider this attitude arrogant: "I am not conceited. It is a necessity that I must obey."

On 25 July Webern and his family left Mürzzuschlag for Vienna. Three days later, he informed Schoenberg from Prague that after much searching he had found an apartment. He was not pleased with it, but there was no other choice. His theatre job was to begin only on 4 August. He did not know as yet what his exact duties would entail, but early in June Zemlinsky had informed him that he was to assist in rehearsals for a *Parsifal* production and that he also might be entrusted with the complete preparation of a stage work. Inordinately fatigued, Webern returned to Vienna and arranged for the immediate transfer of his furniture. Everything was set for the move and the opening of a new chapter in his professional life.

At this juncture, a dramatic upset of all his plans occurred. On 31 July, only two days after he had written from Prague, Webern sent Schoenberg a desperate letter. Ill and more miserable than ever before, he felt himself incapable of assuming his post the following Monday and pleaded for advice: "Whatever am I to do? I beg you, what am I to do? . . . Am I once again to suffer through something like Stettin? Have

to go to bed every week? That I cannot do. I beg you, what am I to do?"
Without Webern's knowledge, his wife, frantic with worry, sent a
telegram to Schoenberg, also seeking his counsel in the distressing
situation. Schoenberg wired back that Webern was not to go to Prague
as long as he was not well and that he should consult a top-rank
specialist.

During the first days of August, Webern made the rounds of several
Vienna physicians. On the recommendation of Dr Werndorff, he saw Dr
Gross, a nerve specialist, who gave him a thorough examination, only to
conclude that no trace of disorder in the nervous system or in any of the
organs could be found. His advice to the patient was that he should help
himself by the application of strict self-discipline. Dismayed, Webern
returned to Dr Werndorff. At that moment, Dr Oskar Adler happened
to come by, and the two doctors agreed that perhaps only the new
method of psychoanalysis could get to the source of Webern's
symptoms.

> There were only two physicians in Vienna who could come into
> question for me, Freud and a certain Adler [Webern reported to
> Schoenberg in a long letter, dated 5 August]. The latter, a friend of Dr
> Werndorff, was telephoned at once, and I was able to go to him
> yesterday at seven o'clock in the evening. After I had told him all, he
> began at once with questions about everything, just everything. He
> voiced the opinion that he could cure me, but I would have to come
> daily to him for a month. Some of what he said was indeed
> astounding, and it appears to me, too, as if one could find out
> through analogies the real connections that uncover the cause. To be
> sure, I still have reservations and a strong antipathy towards it all. For
> the time being, I want to go to the fellow a few times; I will then see
> what develops. I can always quit.

The "certain Adler" was Dr Alfred Adler, who later attained fame as
the founder of the school of individual psychology. In contrast to Freud,
whose theories were strongly oriented towards sex, Adler maintained
that all personality difficulties have their roots in a feeling of inferiority
derived from physical handicaps or from conflict with an environment
that restricts an individual's need for power and self-assertion. He saw
behaviour disorders as over-compensation for deficiencies. Webern's
treatment is a classic example of Dr Adler's method. The patient himself
revealed his case history, step by step, in a series of letters to Schoenberg.
On 6 August he wrote:

> Well then, yesterday I was for the second time with the psychoanalyst.
> I just do not know at all what he is driving at. Yesterday, by means of a

thousand questions, he tried to establish how much of the effeminate there is in me. Ah, what sense does all this make! I then went to Adler [Dr Oskar Adler] in order to ask him again whether some good could come from the treatment, and how I am to get well from it. He thought that I should at any rate try out the method. He himself believed in it. Namely, if one could find through such "analyses" the reason for my attacks of indisposition, I would be almost cured already. The reason or cause would turn out to be something trifling. This realization would be sufficient to bring about the cure. No, I do not understand all this. He also could not express it clearly. I asked him again for another doctor, whether he knew of a Frenchman or an American—I spoke of your idea. He said that he knew of none and that, besides, he was convinced that these people, too, practise the Freud method. And, as a matter of fact, in Stettin one wanted to treat me in this manner, in Portorose likewise, here now the third. Nothing but psychoanalysts!

At first, Webern instinctively resisted Dr Adler's approach. In the same letter to Schoenberg, he argued in terms that reflected his strong leaning towards metaphysical explanations: "I do not believe that these pains are self-produced, but that they are inflicted." He cited the philosophical formulae of Strindberg and Swedenborg, and he argued that the adversities in his conducting career and his frequent illnesses were all predestined: "Look, when I went to the theatre for the first time my mother died, when I had the idea the second time my father became so ill that he had to retire. When I went to Danzig, I was forced to abandon my wife who was expecting Mali—she in Paris, I in Danzig. There I went through many frightful hours of suffering." Webern went on to enumerate the series of ill omens during the Stettin period: the accident with the curtain, his daughter's continuing illness, his own nervous condition bringing on his sick leave, the separation from his wife just before she gave birth to their second child, his nephew's death at the very time when he himself was about to assume his post at Prague, and finally his falling ill at the moment of his arrival there.

Reluctant as he was to accept Dr Adler's method of therapy, Webern was yet persuaded to submit to the treatment. On 13 August he attempted to describe to Schoenberg the physician's diagnostic procedure:

I go every day to Dr Adler. I have to tell him everything, simply everything. There is not much left in my life that he does not know by now. From it all he concludes always the same thing: my spells of indisposition were a transference of the battleground from the real world into that of illness. From the beginning, I needed something in order to delay decisions. To that end the body was unconsciously generating pains and was attaining therein a high degree of virtuosity. This seems to mean also that my body could not stand the slightest deliberation or worry. If I only imagine "how will this be?" I fall ill, and thus what I was worrying about cannot take place at all. . . . Some of this seems to me forced and following a scheme. But I nevertheless believe that there is sense behind it. It is very interesting to talk to Adler. If only it were not about myself—this is really terribly dull for me.

Only gradually did Dr Adler overcome Webern's scepticism and win his full collaboration. On 21 August Webern gave Schoenberg another progress report:

After everything that I told him of my illnesses and of my life from childhood on, he has arrived at the following conclusion: the cause lay in too tendentious a desire to be "on top," in a mania not to let myself be guided under any circumstances. I had set for myself a high goal in all respects, in my career, in married life, and so forth; on the other hand, however, I shrank from decisions because of a timidity —yes, indeed, a softness and exaggerated sensitivity—beginning in childhood. In order to delay such decisions, my body created these symptoms of illness so that it could offer, as it were, an excuse for my backing away. Now since I did not want to let myself be guided by anyone, so naturally I did not wish him [Adler] to lead me either. And the culmination of the cure, its goal, consisted in my overcoming this, too, in my convincing myself that he was right. The knowledge of the cause would already encompass the cure. At best I can comprehend all this only theoretically, my feelings have not responded so far. I do not sense as yet how a cure can be achieved.

By the end of the month Webern believed sufficiently in the validity of the theory that he was resolved to go through with the treatment. It was to last a full three months. The strain of the daily sessions taxed his patience, but the growing awareness that, being organically sound, he could become capable of overcoming his nervous disorders fostered his determination. On 10 September he observed to Schoenberg: "I am already able to ignore my attacks, when they come up, in such a way that the trouble decreases." On the same day, Webern could report his return to creative work, and the fact that he was able to compose again completely convinced him. "I now believe implicitly in the possibility of healing through such a cure," he wrote to Schoenberg on 16 September, relating Dr Adler's diagnosis of his case:

From earliest childhood on, a too single-minded striving for an almost abstract goal, and wherever I meet resistance in real life, the inclination to withdraw. And in order to make possible, to justify this retreat, the body produces the illness. A quite concrete example of this disposition is, incidentally, "claustrophobia," at which, the doctor says, I would soon have arrived. In my endeavour to accomplish the best in everything I do, I was showing the tendency to dodge wherever I believed it perhaps could not turn out that way (without this necessarily being true), and in order to do that and to calm my conscience, as it were, I was falling ill. This now applies to everything that happens in my life. And the cure: it consists in getting rid of the fear of "blue spots," as the doctor says, to have the strength to risk and to go my way without the "reassurance" of illness. . . . The doctor traces my endeavour to govern all situations, or better said, to seek out, with the help of my illness, only situations in which I "am in control," to my childish mania to surpass my older sister. There I must have learned all these "tricks," as he says. While this happens to everyone, the adult simply has to discard the tricks and reach his goal without them.

By 29 September Webern could report to Schoenberg that he was feeling "almost excellent." The few remaining references to Dr Adler's therapy were equally positive, and he announced completion of the cure on 30 October: "Since Tuesday I have finished with the doctor. I believe that he has helped me very much. I feel fine." His spirits revived, Webern threw himself with vigour into constructive activities. So wholesome was the transformation of mind and body that he thought of resuming his theatre work. In early August he had requested, not without great embarrassment, a sick leave from his contractual duties in Prague, with Dr Oskar Adler providing the necessary affidavit. Zemlinsky, acting in close rapport with Schoenberg, then had encouraged him to take the entire season off instead of only two or three months as he asked for. Deeply touched by so much goodwill, Webern had thanked Schoenberg profusely for acting as intermediary, acclaiming him the "guardian angel" of his life. When he subsequently converted the leave of absence into a formal resignation, the theatre director in Prague politely expressed the hope of seeing him join the staff at a future time.

Now, three months later, Webern was preparing himself anew for a conductor's career. His ambition, after all, had always been to preside over presentations of the works of the masters. Moreover, he was now confident, thanks to Dr Adler's clinical analysis of his nervous disturbances, that he could meet the demands of the theatrical

profession. Thus he concentrated on the prospect of going to Prague the
following year. In the meantime, he sounded out Jalowetz about the
possibility of returning to Stettin, despite all the tribulations that had
beset him there. In a constructive spirit, he threw himself into the study
of operatic scores. Charpentier's most recent work, *Julien*, impressed
him favourably. He also found a new love: "Of late, I have become
enthusiastic over Verdi," he told Schoenberg on 12 October.
Nonetheless, when Steuermann advised him of an opening in Aachen,
Webern failed to make the quick decision that was required. To
Schoenberg he justified his reluctance with a variety of reasons.
Primarily, he felt obligated to Zemlinsky, who, expecting changes on the
staff in Prague, had indicated that Webern might be assigned to conduct
operas there on a regular basis. Also, he resented the fact that his
application in Aachen two years earlier had not even been considered.
Then there were economic grounds, including new moving expenses
and the existence of a rental contract he had entered into only recently in
Vienna.

The misadventure in Prague at the end of July had cost Webern
dearly: three months' rent for the apartment he never occupied, not to
speak of the dispatch of a moving van containing his possessions. These
had to be held in storage for a month at a daily charge of seven kronen.
When Webern and his family first came to Vienna from Mürzzuschlag,
they had moved in with his parents-in-law at Ruckergasse 12. At the end
of August, when the prolonged treatment under Dr Adler necessitated
their finding quarters of their own, the family had taken up residence in
an apartment on the second floor of a new house located at
Kremsergasse 1, in the district of Hietzing; it was near the home of Paul
Königer and his wife, Wilhelmine's older sister. The apartment was
small (two rooms, kitchen, and bath), but the family appreciated its
privacy after so many months of living with one relative or another.
Webern, in particular, enjoyed getting established in his own little castle
once again. He loved being surrounded by his scores and books, with
the grand piano forming the centre of his sanctum. Thus inspired, he
soon began to work creatively. Between September and December he
composed a series of orchestra pieces, including an orchestral song, and
during October he wrote *Tot*, a stage play in six scenes. The surge of
renewed creative power was to carry him on to a multitude of other
projects during the early part of 1914.

It is interesting to note that Webern, although free from professional
obligations and financially independent, this time did not follow his
often professed yearning to hurry to Schoenberg's side at Berlin. His
decision to stay on in Vienna was no doubt prompted by Dr Adler. The
psychiatrist, aware of the dominant influences in his patient's life,

probably tried to show him the road to complete self-reliance. To be sure, Webern maintained as intensive a correspondence with Schoenberg as ever. The letters encompass the whole gamut of what he experienced, thought, and felt. Once again partaking, if only as a consumer, in Vienna's rich concert and theatre life, he was the most discriminating of observers. He denounced the bad taste in which a new concert hall was decorated (for its opening Richard Strauss had written a Festive Prelude) and he was outraged that the sixteen-year-old Erich Wolfgang Korngold had his Sinfonietta performed by the Philharmonic Orchestra under Weingartner ("Those dogs who never play a note by you!" he ranted in his letter of 30 November). By contrast, a performance of Mahler's Fourth Symphony on 11 December elicited a glowing report the next day ("My most decided impression of it, as with all works of such elevated nature, is: this is dictated. And I could die of love and reverence for him who is so endowed by a higher grace").

On 30 November Webern sent a postcard to Schoenberg from his favourite mountain: "This morning, all alone, I ascended the Rax. Up here, deep winter reigns already. It is indescribably beautiful." At Christmas time, there was a family reunion, for which Webern's father and sisters came up from Klagenfurt. The recent death of Maria's son Theo still cast its shadow over the holiday gathering, but otherwise the year, marked by so many trials, drew to a peaceful close. For Webern, who had just passed his 30th birthday, it had been a time of greatest tension. "The evil number 1913 will soon be over," he wrote to Schoenberg on 30 December, sending New Year's wishes. The letter also expressed his elation that Schoenberg had found the new orchestra pieces he had recently sent so good that he wanted to perform them.

On New Year's day, at noontime, Webern called on Alma Mahler, who, during the months to follow, invited him and his wife several times for tea or supper. "I really do not know how I come to this," he later remarked in a letter of 9 June 1914 to Schoenberg. "But the association gives me joy, especially because it is so wonderful to be in the room where there is still so much of Mahler, his books, scores, his piano, and many other things."

The love affair between the young widow and Oskar Kokoschka (who had painted her as his "Windsbraut") was the talk of the town at the time. Webern could not refrain from observing that the painter was conspicuously absent from the New Year's reception in Alma Mahler's salon, that the famous beauty looked thin and pale, and that the romance might be over. As he once remarked to Berg, Webern felt "a gigantic sympathy" for Kokoschka. He knew enough to appreciate the painter's artistic greatness despite the sensationalism surrounding his private life. The rapport with Kokoschka led to Webern's sitting for two

portraits: a pen and ink drawing in 1912 and an oil painting in 1914.[2]
Both portrayals are bold expressionistic conceptions.

Alma Mahler was present on 12 January when Erwin Stein conducted
her husband's First Symphony. On that occasion Webern was greatly
impressed by the ability of his former study friend. Stein was to join
Webern, Berg, and Königer when they travelled to Prague for a reunion with Schoenberg, whose Six Orchestral Songs, Op. 8, were
scheduled by Zemlinsky for a concert on 29 January.[3] Intimately
familiar with the score because of his piano reduction of it, Webern
greatly looked forward to hearing the work and, in particular, to the
hours with Schoenberg, whom he had not seen for a full ten months.
However, illness marred his stay. "Webern is very sick: during the last
few days he had such a terrible fever that he wanted to return home. And
now angina. He can hardly drag himself around," Berg wrote on 27
January, in one of the long reports he always gave his wife whenever they
were separated.[4]

Back in Vienna, Webern recovered. He immediately assumed the
leadership in organizing another initiative to help Schoenberg, whose
financial situation continued to be strained despite his growing
international reputation (on 17 January, he had made his first London
appearance as conductor of his Five Orchestra Pieces, Op. 16).
Arrangements for a monthly subsidy of 500 kronen were made, to
continue for the next two years and possibly beyond. The extent of
Webern's share is not disclosed in the correspondence, but it most likely
formed a substantial portion of the total guarantee. Although he was
earning nothing at the time, Webern still fitted the contribution into his
limited budget. A tax declaration, dated 5 May 1914, lists his annual
income as 3,820 kronen.[5] Of this amount, 1900 kronen came from
interest on a savings account of 40,000 kronen. The balance represented
a monthly allowance of 160 kronen given the family by Webern's father-
in-law, the notary Gustav Mörtl.

In early February Webern had his first opportunity to hear Mahler's
posthumous Ninth Symphony. Long familiar with the score, he
attended all the rehearsals and the performance, conducted by Oskar
Nedbal. His rapturous report to Schoenberg on 16 February closed with
a description of the ending of the symphony: "[It] is really like a greeting
from above. Mahler then was already far, far away from us." A few days
later, Webern denounced a *Parsifal* performance at the Court Opera as
"musically base, a disgrace for this institution." During the first part of
March, Schoenberg was scheduled to conduct his *Gurrelieder* in Leipzig
and the Five Orchestra Pieces in Amsterdam. Webern and Stein
accompanied him on this concert tour. While in Leipzig, where the
friends arrived on 28 February, Webern was the house guest of Albertine

Zehme[6] (who had commissioned *Pierrot Lunaire* and sung in its première). The two-week trip, which included a stop in Berlin, provided Webern with a wealth of impressions, not the least of which was his first view of the Atlantic Ocean.[7] On 15 March, the day of his return to Vienna, he summed up his musical recollections in a long letter to Schoenberg: "The *Gurrelieder* and the Orchestra Pieces—ten years of your life separate them. In ten years, such a revolution of the musical language! I believe nothing like this has ever happened before."

Just then, rehearsals for another *Gurrelieder* production under Franz Schreker in Vienna were in progress. As usual, Schoenberg's disciples attended the sessions. During one of them, Webern and his friends found themselves the centre of "a horrible row," related to Schoenberg in minute detail on 26 March. For whatever reason, the orchestra manager, whose name Webern only abbreviates as "Höll.," had told Berg that, since the instrumental parts had now been corrected, his presence and that of his friends was "superfluous" at the rehearsal. Berg and Stein were standing in the aisle outside the concert hall when Webern arrived. Ignoring the order, Webern and Stein entered and stood in a wing. After intermission, Schreker asked Webern to listen instead from the auditorium. There the friends were joined by Berg and Königer.

Shortly before the end of the rehearsal [Webern reported], this gentleman appears high up by the contrabasses and, disturbing the rehearsal, yells something like: "This is shocking indeed. Have I not asked the gentlemen to go away, and yet here they are again!" Then I got into a fit of anger and yelled to him across the whole orchestra that Professor Schreker had requested us to sit in the parterre. He retorts that we were to go or else he would send an attendant. We stay. The attendant approaches timidly. I tell him to report that we are here on Schreker's invitation. He leaves, returns with the same message. Then Schreker calls to him to keep quiet. Thereupon, Höll. appears again at the door to the parterre and calls to us to leave. The orchestra has meanwhile begun to get restless. I hurry over to Höll. and tell him the same thing over and over. The others follow me, and so we were actually outside.

The dispute continued. The orchestra manager was, in Webern's words, "white with rage" by then. "Such a pig!" Webern fumed to Schoenberg. When aroused, he could be quite pugnacious. "Afterwards, we apologized to Schreker, he to us. But the whole affair was abhorrent. What treatment we were given, by contrast, in Leipzig

and Amsterdam! I was so terribly upset and still am beside myself,''
he concluded.

That distasteful experience notwithstanding, the *Gurrelieder* performance on 27 March completely satisfied Webern. A few days later, Franz
Schreker presented another monumental work of the choral–orchestral
literature—Mahler's Eighth Symphony. Webern, who had been present
at the 1910 première under the composer's own direction, was again
enthralled by the work. Describing to Schoenberg, in his letter of 8
April, the ever-mounting ecstasy in the first movement, he related an
interesting detail: "Schreker carried out the following idea of Mahler,
communicated to him by Mrs Mahler, to assign the great bass solo in the
second part (*pater profundus*) to a group of voices! This was most
remarkable. At first I did not know that the idea was Mahler's own, but it
was clear to me at once: this is an excellent, sublime idea. One could
hear every sixteenth note, everything was so clear, and the sound was
oddly rugged and exciting."

Webern, previously highly critical of Schreker's very successful
operas, had begun to soften his attitude: "I have drawn much closer to
Schreker recently," he remarked in the same letter to Schoenberg.
"Who else is in Vienna at present who would do something like these
two performances?" Encouraged by this new sense of affinity, Webern
carried out Schoenberg's suggestion of submitting to Schreker his
chorus *Entflieht auf leichten Kähnen*. To facilitate intonation he added a
complement of supporting instruments.

Besides completing this arrangement, Webern composed several
orchestral songs and pieces for cello and piano during the spring. He
also drafted a chorus for women's voices based on a text from
Strindberg's *Ghost Sonata*. Webern's ever-increasing admiration for the
Swedish author resounds in letter after letter. In February he had seen
Frau Margit, one of the dramas from Strindberg's early period, and in
May he attended *To Damascus*. Shortly before, he had been at a
performance of Ibsen's *Peer Gynt*. Strongly partisan, Webern ranked
Ibsen far below his idol Strindberg. In his letter to Schoenberg of 23
May, Webern told him that he found Ibsen's symbolism "unclear" and
"confusing" compared with that of Strindberg, whose characters "say
the simplest things, and the most extraordinary insight is revealed
thereby." Besides Strindberg, other literary influences fertilizing
Webern's imagination during that spring were Karl Kraus and Hans
Bethge. Webern also followed the dramas of Frank Wedekind with keen
interest, finding his latest work, *Simson* (in which the playwright again
appeared as actor), "something quite unusual."

At Easter time, Webern and his family spent a fortnight in his father's
house at Klagenfurt. Working in the garden, he felt reborn after his

long and vexing illness. As always when visiting Carinthia, he made a pilgrimage to his mother's grave and to the Preglhof, the happy retreat of his youth. He also accompanied his father on a prospecting tour that took them into the mountains for several days (although officially retired, Carl von Webern continued to seek out sites rich enough in ore to warrant mining operations).

On 23 April Webern signed a contract with the Stettin theatre, ratifying his renewed engagement there. Negotiations had been in progress since January, when Webern had learned through Jalowetz that the post of second conductor would become vacant. At first Webern clung to the prospect of working under Zemlinsky in Prague. However, since the expected position there remained only vaguely defined, Schoenberg strongly recommended that he seize the Stettin opportunity. His duties were to commence in June, but he succeeded in persuading the theatre director to postpone the starting day until 20 August. As a proviso, Webern himself was to find a summer replacement. In consultation with Schoenberg, whose advice he solicited at every turn, he proposed Stein. After much back and forth, however, the theatre director engaged someone of his own choice.

That spring, Emil Hertzka had suggested that one of Schoenberg's disciples write an article on the master's eminence as a conductor. Webern, under the fresh impression of the concert tour to Leipzig and Amsterdam, sprang to the task. After many revisions, his essay, entitled "About Arnold Schoenberg as Conductor," was completed in May and submitted to the periodical *Die Musik*. Simultaneously, Webern mailed a copy to Schoenberg. Probably finding the article too polemic, Schoenberg rejected its publication.[8] This disappointment aside, Webern had much cause to feel indebted to Schoenberg, who had set out actively to promote his compositions. Following the visit to Amsterdam, Webern had sent the printed score of his Six Pieces, Op. 6, to Willem Mengelberg, conductor of the Concertgebouw Orchestra. When Schoenberg returned to Amsterdam in June to prepare a *Gurrelieder* production (for that occasion he asked Webern to make further corrections in the parts), he relayed the news that prospects were favourable for performances of the Six Pieces not only in Holland but also in London, where he had interested Sir Henry Wood, conductor of the Promenade Concerts. Webern was overjoyed: "Often it seems to me that I am only dreaming all this. Oh, how kind it is of you to have done this for me," he wrote to Schoenberg on 2 July, informing him that he would send the orchestra material to Wood before the week was out. Another contact established by Schoenberg was with the American violinist Arthur Hartmann, then in Paris, to whom Webern submitted, besides the printed score of his orchestral Six Pieces, a manuscript copy of the Four Pieces for Violin and Piano (for which he employed the services of Karl Kornfeld, a noted professional copyist).

At this point, perhaps the most important of all Schoenberg's recommendations was that to Emil Hertzka, the director of Universal Edition. During a personal visit, Webern was cordially received and virtually promised publication of several of his compositions for the following year. Hertzka also wanted to take over the distribution and promotion of the Six Pieces, Op. 6. It did not dampen Webern's elation that Hertzka qualified his assurances with the customary condition that nothing unforeseen should intervene. There seemed no cause for concern. Europe's cultural life was riding the crest of an unprecedented prosperity, and the future appeared peaceful and bright. However, that universal sense of security was shattered on 28 June by the shots at Sarajevo. The political murder of Archduke Franz Ferdinand, heir to the throne of Emperor Franz Josef, marked the beginning of an international crisis that was to erupt in war one month later.

At the end of June the Webern family gave up their Vienna apartment in anticipation of their move back to Stettin. Attending to the packing with mixed feelings, Webern used the occasion to make a detailed inventory of all his books and printed music. Webern's library contained not only the mainstays of classic and contemporary German writing, partly in complete editions, but also a wide cross-section from the literature of other nations, such as works by Balzac and Baudelaire, Emerson and Thoreau, Dostoyevsky and Tolstoy, Stendhal and Swedenborg, Dickens and Wilde. The music section displays a similarly wide range.[9] Especially identified as autograph music manuscripts were the piano–vocal reduction of Berg's Altenberg songs, Op. 4 (Nos. 2, 3, 4, and 5), Schoenberg's "Alle welche dich suchen," Op. 22, No. 2,[10] and Mahler's "Lob der Kritik."

"Summer is a glorious time. Now that I am well, I am enthusiastically absorbing this warmth and everything else, just everything," Webern wrote serenely on 24 June to Schoenberg. He had signed a lease for an apartment that Jalowetz had located for him in Stettin, and the moving van with his belongings was ready for transport. On 5 July, Webern and his family went to Klagenfurt for a last visit before the new working year. Father and son set out on another prospecting trip into the mountains. Their relationship had grown closer with the passing years. In the solitude of the remote alpine regions, Webern pondered anew the innermost nature of the man whose life appeared to him so "terribly tragic" and whose precepts filled him with awe. "My father's sense of duty is so infinitely high that, compared to it, I feel like a criminal," Webern told Schoenberg on 13 July, in a long and touching letter. He tried to clarify his feelings towards his father, concluding: "I know only this one thing: I am completely devoted to him and I believe unconditionally in him."

On 20 July Webern sent Schoenberg postcard greetings from the Klagenfurt Hut, where he stopped after an ascent of the Hochstuhl (2,236 m.). Thrilled by the uplifting experience, he wrote: "One of my most ardent wishes is to see something like this with you someday. Perhaps it will come to pass this time in Murnau." That village on the northern slopes of the Bavarian Alps, where Kandinsky lived, was the site of a rendezvous planned for early August. Kandinsky had invited Schoenberg to spend the summer with him. Jalowetz, Stein, and Webern intended to be there also. Webern envisaged an ascent of the mighty Zugspitze, to initiate Schoenberg properly into the wonders of the alpine world. From Murnau, Webern meant to accompany Schoenberg back to Berlin, before proceeding on 19 August to Stettin to assume his new post.

All these plans suddenly came to naught, however. On 23 July Austria–Hungary delivered a stiff ultimatum to Serbia. Momentous events followed in quick succession, stunning millions of people who, like Webern, had been unaware of the seriousness of the situation. On 28 July Austria–Hungary declared war on Serbia. This set off a chain reaction in the alliances holding Europe in a precarious balance of power. When Russia began massing troops along the German frontier, Germany declared war on Russia on 1 August, and on France two days later. After German armies marched into Belgium, violating that country's neutrality, England entered the war on 4 August. The conflagration soon enveloped so many nations around the globe that it was to go down in history as World War I.

CHAPTER XII

Opera 9–11—Other works—Tot (1911–1914)

In a letter to Berg, written from Stettin on 12 July 1912, Webern described his approach to composition: an experience would go around in his mind until it became music, "music that quite decidedly had to do with the experience—often down to the details." With the exception of his violin pieces and some of his last orchestra pieces, all his compositions related to the death of his mother—the Passacaglia, the quartet, most of the songs, the second quartet, the first set of orchestra pieces, and the second (with some exceptions). "Only one summer," Webern told Berg, "when I composed the violin pieces, was there something else in my mind; then I also wrote the two orchestral songs and several scenes of an opera (*The Seven Princesses*)."

The quartet first mentioned refers to the Five Movements, Op. 5, the first set of orchestra pieces to the Six Pieces, Op. 6, and the two orchestral songs to the Rilke settings, Op. 8. The second quartet and the second set of orchestra pieces will be discussed in this chapter, which deals with the works representing the culmination of Webern's aphoristic style. Epitomizing this style are the Six Bagatelles, Op. 9, for string quartet. The date of their origin has been given generally in the literature as 1913. However, the work actually evolved in two separate stages. One set of four pieces was composed during the summer of 1911 at the Preglhof. Webern entitled this group (encompassing the later Bagatelles Nos. 2, 3, 4 and 5) "II. Streichquartett," then considering it a fully self-contained work.

In the light of Webern's remarks that his musical ideas were the crystallizations of personal experiences, it may be appropriate to relate the following in connection with the genesis of that composition. The summer of 1911 had been unusually hot and dry. In letter after letter, Webern had complained about the prolonged drought. On 7 August he told Schoenberg: "I am now writing a string quartet. . . . It is out and out dreadful that it does not rain. Everything dries up here." The intense heat affected everyone. Even at the peaceful Preglhof tensions ran high, and when violence erupted, Webern was deeply shaken. "I had to be an eye witness when a drunken farm-hand stabbed our foreman twice in the back," he wrote to Schoenberg on 23 August. "It was horrible. We at once rendered assistance to the poor fellow, dressing his wounds and bringing him to town. I was present again as he was sewn up, and so forth. The wounds are incredibly deep. I hope that the spinal cord has not been injured, for his feet are still paralysed. Now I am calmer, but that moment the deed was done! O God, why is there so much misery?! I am fearful of this eternally burning sun. No rain, no coolness."

In this same letter Webern announced that he had finished his string quartet, which he was anxious to show Schoenberg. Obviously the composer then regarded the work as complete in itself. He still did so as late as 23 May 1913 when he informed Berg: "During the next few days, I will send you my quartet. You must look closely at the instrumentation. You have to imagine very precisely these mixtures and alternations of the various bowing possibilities (col legno, sul ponticello, naturale, etc.)."

Shortly after, on 3 June, Webern wrote to Schoenberg from Mürzzuschlag, where he had just settled down with his family for an extended vacation: "I hope to have soon gained the strength to carry out what has been prepared in my mind in every detail for a long time—a string quartet." By 28 June he could announce: "My string quartet will soon be complete. It will consist of three movements or pieces, rather short, but not as short as the last, and on the whole quite different again. The middle one is with voice (the words are by me)." On 10 July Webern reported to him: "My quartet is already finished." He gave his new work the title Three Pieces for String Quartet. The outer movements were later to become the Bagatelles Nos. 1 and 6. The middle movement was never published. In it the voice line was partly to be sung and partly treated in the manner of the *Sprechstimme*, introduced by Schoenberg in *Pierrot Lunaire* the year before. The text, beginning with the words "Schmerz, immer blick nach oben," is the shortest of three brief poems written by Webern during the summer of 1913, the others being "O sanftes Glühn der Berge" and "Leise Düfte" (discussed later in this chapter). The loose form of the verses, as well as their intensity of feeling, makes them closely akin to some of Mahler's poetic utterances. The expressive concentration in Webern's words is matched by that of the musical images with which they were fused.

For the autumn of 1913 a concert in Berlin was being planned. It was Schoenberg's idea that the programme was to include only compositions by Webern and Berg. Writing to Schoenberg from Vienna on 7 October, Webern suggested as his share the following:

> . . . the three groups of quartet movements. These are a) the five movements that were played here already [later Op. 5, 1909] b) the four pieces that I once showed you in Berlin [1911] and c) the three pieces (the middle one with voice) that I wrote this summer. These three groups belong together as to content, and I would also like them always to be played in sequence. I have combined them into one opus. The pieces of groups b) and c) are, moreover, so short that it would not make good sense to perform one of these groups alone.

Although the project fell through, elaborate preparations for the concert (the cost of which was to be underwritten by Berg and Webern) continued well into the autumn. On 12 November Webern mentioned sending a voice–piano reduction of "Schmerz, immer blick nach oben" to Steuermann so that the pianist could coach the singer Zlodmicka. He also mailed a fair copy of the Three Pieces to Schoenberg, asking for his opinion. Schoenberg replied that his erstwhile pupil no longer needed criticism from him. Responding in a state of high emotion, Webern implored the master never to withdraw his counsel. In that letter, dated 24 November, he confided:

> Perhaps I succeeded halfway with the last piece. I would like to tell you something about it. First a word: angel. From it comes the "mood" of this piece. The angels in heaven. The incomprehensible state after death. I come more and more to the absolute belief in these things: heaven and hell. But not in the transferred sense: hell on this earth, a condition in this life. No, really only after death. However, I would not like to separate the "here" from the "beyond." Not at all. To be sure, what use are all the angels if my piece is bad! I have the feeling that my orchestra pieces, which I am now writing, are much better. I hope that I have brought out much more in them. The shortness of my quartet pieces is embarrassing to me, too. My orchestra pieces are much longer.

Regarding the three groups of quartet movements written between 1909 and 1913 as one intrinsically coherent work, Webern at the time gave it the opus number 3, designating the groups as Nos. 1, 2, and 3. The fair copy of the Three Pieces sent to Schoenberg was thus marked "Op. 3, No. 3." An early facsimile reproduction of the autograph score of one of the 1911 pieces is entitled "No. 3 of Four Pieces for String Quartet." Later to be the fourth of the Six Bagatelles, it was published in

May 1913 as an insert to the fourth and last issue of *Der Ruf* (in which the first of the Four Pieces, Op. 7, had been introduced to the public the year before).

It is not known when and why Webern abandoned the original Opus 3 concept and established the two entities now known as Five Movements, Op. 5 and Six Bagatelles, Op. 9. A holograph score entitled "6 Sätze für Streichquartett" contains the latter work in the definitive sequence, combining the Second String Quartet (1911) with the first and third of the Three Pieces (1913). Although this manuscript bears an inscription "for 2 July 1913"—the birthday of the composer's wife—it is certain that it was written out later, since on that day the Three Pieces were still being composed.[1] The Six Movements were first designated "Opus 3." Subsequent changes on the title page read "Opus 5," then "Opus 7," and ultimately "Opus 9," bespeaking a long period of deliberation. The omission of the vocal movement in the former Three Pieces was prompted no doubt by practical considerations. The same probably holds true for the title Six Bagatelles adopted for the work's publication. It could well have been suggested by Emil Hertzka in order to project the miniature nature of the pieces. For the composer himself, though, these superlatively concentrated essays certainly were no "trifles." Be that as it may, the pieces entered the literature as Bagatelles when they were published by Universal Edition in 1924, on the occasion of their première during the Donaueschingen Festival. The composer was present when the Amar Quartet (in which Paul Hindemith played the viola) introduced the work in the matinée concert of 19 July. The same programme also included the first performance of Webern's Six Trakl Songs, Op. 14.

For the printed score of the Bagatelles, Arnold Schoenberg contributed an eloquent foreword, meant to serve the better comprehension of Webern's music:

> Though the brevity of these pieces is a persuasive advocate for them, on the other hand that very brevity itself requires an advocate. Consider what moderation is required to express oneself so briefly. Every glance can be expanded into a poem, every sigh into a novel. But to express a novel in a single gesture, joy in a single breath—such concentration can only be present in proportion to the absence of self-indulgence. These pieces will be understood only by someone who has faith in music as the expression of something that can be said only musically. They can face criticism as little as beliefs of any kind. If faith can move mountains, disbelief can deny their existence. Faith is impotent against such impotence. Does the player know how to play these pieces, does the listener know how to receive them? Can

believing performers and listeners fail to surrender themselves to one another? But what shall one do with the heathen? Fire and sword can keep them down; but only believers can be kept under a spell. For them, may this stillness ring!

Schoenberg wrote these words in 1924, the year after he enunciated the dodecaphonic method of composition. His music had fore-shadowed the principles of that system from 1914 on, but Webern's string quartet pieces were probing in the same direction even earlier. Webern himself referred to these experiments long afterwards, in a lecture on 12 February 1932:

> About 1911 I wrote the Bagatelles for string quartet, all very short pieces, lasting two minutes; perhaps they were the shortest pieces in music so far. Here I had the feeling that when the twelve notes had all been played the piece was over. Much later I realized that all this was part of a necessary development. In my sketchbook I wrote out the chromatic scale and crossed off individual notes. Why? Because I had convinced myself, "This note has been there already." It sounds grotesque, incomprehensible, and it was incredibly difficult. The inner ear decided absolutely rightly that the man who had written out the chromatic scale and crossed off individual notes *was no fool*. (Josef Matthias Hauer also experienced and discovered all this in his own way.) In short, a law came into being. Until all twelve notes have appeared none of them may occur again. The most important thing is that each successive "run" of the twelve notes marked a division within the piece, idea, or theme.[2]

In 1924 Webern presented the printed edition of his Bagatelles to Berg with a dedication that epitomized their essence: " '*non multa sed multum*' [not much in quantity, but much in content]. How happy I would be if this maxim could apply here."

The genesis of Webern's Five Pieces for Orchestra, Op. 10, is no less involved than that of the work just discussed. They actually represent an extract from a total of eighteen aphoristic pieces, seven of which were written in 1911 and eleven in 1913. The dates of composition for the five movements forming Opus 10 were given by Webern himself as follows: I. 28 June 1911 II. 13 September 1913 III. 8 September 1913 IV. 19 July 1911 V. 6 October 1913.[3]

The first mention of the project occurs in a letter Webern wrote to Schoenberg from the Preglhof on 6 July 1911: "I have already written two orchestra pieces. They are very brief. Nothing long occurs to me. There will be a number of short pieces that I shall call *chamber pieces for orchestra* in order to indicate that they should not be played in a large hall. Until now the instrumentation has been very small, a fact that gave me this idea. Basically it is yours. In a large hall one would hardly be able to hear anything of the music." The first group of orchestral miniatures soon grew to seven. No doubt they were already completed by early August, since Webern had then commenced work on the string quartet discussed above. The latter was finished by 23 August, when Webern informed Schoenberg that it consisted of four short movements: "I can hardly wait to show you these and my seven orchestra 'chamber pieces.' What will you say to them? They consist of a change of colours in sixteenth and thirty-second notes."

A two-year interruption in the work on the orchestra pieces followed. Webern anticipated that his stay in Berlin during the 1911–12 season would give him an opportunity to fulfil his creative aspirations. However, he produced nothing more than a reduction for two pianos, four hands, of Schoenberg's Five Orchestra Pieces, Op. 16, a task assigned to him by the composer when the work was accepted for publication by C. F. Peters of Leipzig. Webern's masterly arrangement was begun in early April 1912 and completed by the middle of the following month. On 7 May he had commented to Berg that he was totally engrossed in his work on the piano reductions. They were turning out well and Schoenberg was very satisfied. Schoenberg's approval is evident from Webern's autograph draft of the arrangement, for it shows only minor corrections in Schoenberg's hand in the second and fifth movements. The draft designates the five pieces merely with Roman numerals, and not with the titles later associated with them: 1. "Vorgefühle" 2. "Vergangenes" 3. "Farben" 4. "Peripetie" 5. "Das obligate Rezitativ." Actually, Schoenberg established these titles only on the special request of his publisher in connection with the appearance of the work in early 1913.

From the summer of 1912 on, Webern's dissatisfaction with his theatre position in Stettin, the constant attacks of illness bringing on his resignation, and the subsequent months of convalescence stifled his creative energies. Only in June of 1913 did he begin to compose again (the Three Pieces for String Quartet). However, the severe setback in his nervous condition that led him to submit to psychiatric treatment in early August caused another interruption. The beneficial results of that treatment soon inspired him to resume his creative work. On 10 September he wrote to Schoenberg from Vienna: "I am again composing orchestra pieces. A kind of symphony. I mean a series of movements belonging to each other." On 12 October he reported: "I am now working on a cycle of orchestra pieces and am at present on the sixth. The fifth is with voice. Again I have written the text myself ["O sanftes

Glühn der Berge"]. Since I am only too eager to know what you think of it, I am enclosing it. For the time being, I am too biased to have a proper perspective."

During October a literary venture, the stage play *Tot*, temporarily delayed Webern's work on the orchestra pieces. By 6 November, however, he could write to Schoenberg: "Now I am at work again on my cycle of orchestra pieces and have arrived at No. VIII. Relatively longer movements are forming themselves again for me now." In another letter, dated 24 November, he mentioned that he planned to extend the cycle to nine pieces. On 22 December he reported that he had composed a total of eleven pieces since autumn. Of those, the one dated 2 December 1913, the eve of Webern's 30th birthday, probably constitutes the last to be written. It is extant only in a condensed score.

That Christmas, Webern sent Schoenberg fair copies of four of the pieces, including the orchestral song "O sanftes Glühn der Berge." In his accompanying letter, dated 22 December, he wrote that he had selected these from the total group. The others did not "suit" him any longer. "But these four, I believe, belong firmly together." Schoenberg was so impressed with the pieces that he announced his intention to conduct them, a prospect which greatly elated Webern.

The four pieces copied out for Schoenberg were marked "Opus 6." The purely instrumental movements, Nos. I, II, and IV, constituted early versions of what later became Nos. II, III, and V of the Five Pieces, Op. 10. Nos. I and IV of that work were chosen from the group of seven orchestra pieces composed in 1911. Exactly when Webern made his definitive selection is uncertain; most likely he did so in connection with the chamber version that was performed during the 1919–20 season of the Society for Private Musical Performances. The whereabouts of all other movements indicated in Webern's letters remained unknown until 1965, when a cache of manuscripts was discovered in Perchtoldsdorf. It contained, besides drafts for the orchestral song "O sanftes Glühn der Berge," full ink scores of four pieces for orchestra (undated but marked III, IV, V, and VI, designations later altered) and the condensed score of another movement (dated 2 December 1913, but not numbered). A separate sketch to the piece marked IV was dated 21 September 1913, clearly indicating that the four consecutively numbered pieces originated during that autumn. Unfortunately, the ravages to which Webern's manuscripts were subjected at the end of World War II caused the loss of the closing bars from two of these otherwise finished movements. On the other hand, the dated condensed score was so explicit that it could easily be realized in full orchestration. (This movement, as well as those originally numbered III, IV, V, and VI, have since been published as a group.) Various fragments and sketches, included with

Orchestra Piece, Op. posth. (1913)

the manuscripts found in 1965, undoubtedly relate to the remaining pieces written in 1911 and 1913 that are not accounted for in the foregoing survey.

From the whole complex, these publications have emanated: Five Pieces, Op. 10 (Universal Edition, 1923), five posthumous Orchestra Pieces (1913) (Carl Fischer, 1971) and "O sanftes Glühn der Berge," No. 3 of Three Orchestral Songs (1913–14) (Carl Fischer, 1968). All these pieces are in the aphoristic style for which Webern became the chief exponent during this period. The fourth movement of Opus 10 has long been known as the most minute in orchestral literature. Encompassing only six measures, it lasts, according to the metronome direction, a mere nineteen seconds—a *non plus ultra* of formal compression and emotional concentration, the very antithesis of the expansive rhetoric of the late Romantic era. To be sure, the composer himself felt that he had reached a pivotal point when he told Schoenberg on 6 November 1913 that "relatively longer movements" were "forming themselves again." Thus, the fifth piece of Opus 10, composed on 6 October, extends over 32 measures, and the orchestral song "O sanftes Glühn der Berge," first sketched out on 30 September, over 35 measures. Whether diminutive or more expansive, all the pieces have in common a unique variety of novel colour combinations. Supercharged with intensity, they run the gamut from atmospheric suspense to explosive vehemence.

The unprecedented brevity of the music could not but startle those who first heard it. Webern himself conducted the première of the Five Pieces, Op. 10, on 22 June 1926, during the fourth festival of the International Society for Contemporary Music in Zürich. Played by the city's Tonhalle Orchestra, the work created the sensation of the festival and brought the composer world-wide notice. The same year, on 19 November, Koussevitzky introduced it to America. Actually, an arrangement of the Five Pieces had already been heard during the 1919–20 season in the concerts of the Society for Private Musical Performances. They were then played under Webern's direction in Vienna and Prague, in a reduction for piano, harmonium, violin, viola and cello (see Chapter XIV). In that version, made by the composer himself and designated "Op. 7, No. 4," the individual pieces bear the following titles: 1. "Urbild" 2. "Verwandlung" 3. "Rückkehr" 4. "Erinnerung" 5. "Seele." These headings, which do not appear in the published score, were probably inspired by the model of Schoenberg's Five Orchestra Pieces, Op. 16. Willi Reich, then close to Webern, said of the titles that the composer "did not wish to give any programmatic explanation by them, but only to indicate the feelings that ruled him while composing the different pieces."[4] A clue to some of these moods was provided by Webern himself in a long and beautiful letter written to Schoenberg on 23 April 1914, in which he dwelt with nostalgia on the perceptions of changing generations in a landscape saturated by recollections common to all.

A focal point in that landscape was for him the family plot in the little cemetery by the village church of Schwabegg, and it formed the setting for his orchestral song "O sanftes Glühn der Berge." Webern's intense occupation with the memories associated with that quiet gravesite also sparked, immediately after completion of the song, an ambitious literary project. As Webern recovered from his long illness in 1913, a burst of creative energy was released. On 30 October of that year, after telling Schoenberg of the successful termination of his treatment under Dr Alfred Adler, he described a new undertaking: "During the last few days I have written something for the stage, in words only. It consists of six scenes. For some years now, I have had the notion of something for the stage. Once I also spoke to you about it. Now this idea has taken shape, but it has turned into something entirely different. I have the most ardent desire to show it to you immediately."

Webern called his work *Tot, Sechs Bilder für die Bühne* (Dead, Six Tableaux for the Stage). The date "October 1913" is prefaced "*in memoriam*"; Webern explained, when he sent Schoenberg the manuscript of the play on 6 November, that "it came into being out of my grief for my nephew who died this summer." Apprehensive of Schoenberg's judgement, he stressed that he had conceived the work in a spurt of "sudden inspiration," writing down the first half at one sitting. The death of Theo Clementschitsch three months earlier had shaken Webern to the depths of his soul. To see one so young abruptly torn away brought him face to face again with the issues burdening him ever since his mother's death in 1906. Webern now contemplated anew the ultimate destiny of human existence, posing a challenge to all moral precepts and religious tenets, indeed to the entire philosophical structure of his own life, including his rôle as husband and father.

Providing him with a vehicle for that crucial debate over the meaning of life and death, the play was an attempt at clarification and, ultimately, catharsis. Although couched in allegory throughout, *Tot* represents Webern's own credo, a compound of very personal ideas and severe dogmatism. Naïve faith, pantheism, and a leaning towards mysticism—fundamental qualities of his own makeup—combine with the influences of Roman Catholic teachings and the ideologies of the eighteenth-century scientist and philosopher Emanuel Swedenborg,[5] about whom Webern wrote to Schoenberg on 30 October: "I am now reading Swedenborg. It takes my breath away. It is incredible. I had expected something colossal, but it is even more." An extensive quotation from Swedenborg's *Vera religio*, dealing largely with the doctrine of "correspondences" through which divine matters are represented on earth, forms the main body of the last scene of *Tot*.

Since the play is unpublished and since it so completely reflects Webern's artistic personality, a description of its character and a synopsis of its contents are deemed appropriate within this work chapter. The literary conception is utterly "musical." There are directions for the gradated dynamics of the spoken words, for the tempi of their delivery, and for the use of silence, which is frequently employed as a component of the dramatic context. No less explicit are the prescriptions for staging and lighting, for gesture and movement. Written in red ink, these instructions, on which Webern lavished minute attention, often occupy more space than the text of the spoken word (written in black); they tend to assume preponderance, just as in his compositions the element of tone colour frequently prevails over other components of the musical fabric. In a given scene, the text often dwindles to only a few words, but these are pregnant with implications that find their correlatives in stage setting and lighting. The text therefore often merely complements the general mood of a scene. The drama is psychological, and action as such is absent. What little motion there is serves merely to underscore the symbolism of the whole.

The autobiographical nature of the play is readily evident. It mirrors, above all, Webern's consuming love for all the phenomena of nature in the high mountain regions. Characteristically, the play takes place "in the Alps." The dramatis personae are four: the husband, his wife, a boy (representing their dead child), and an angel. As the following synopsis attempts to convey, the six scenes are infinitely varied in shading. The first is set in a peasant hut high in the mountains. The only words are spoken by the couple's dead son, who appears as an apparition. Assuring his parents of the magnificence of his new abode, he beckons: "You must come soon—a beautiful path leads here." As the light surrounding his figure fades away, the stage is left in darkness.

In the second scene, the husband and wife are ascending a steep mountain path. It is early morning in the forest. For the man, communion with nature is a ritual: "I sense the blessing of this air. When I am in the sun, among these herbs and flowers, a miraculous feeling comes over me." He contemplates the inherent healing powers of alpine vegetation. Through immersion in nature, the couple seeks a feeling of closeness to their lost child. Resigned to God's will, the husband assures his wife: "Whether here or there, we are where he is now."

The third scene finds the pair at timberline. Here Webern's worship of nature reaches its most ecstatic expression. The mountain flora, regarded by him as the incarnation of creative beauty, is fervently extolled. In a symbolic act, the man falls on his knees and buries his head in a bed of alpine roses. The scene is pervaded by the distant sound of cowbells. The husband then speaks of the divine origin of all basic things and utters the warning: "What is generally popular must not confuse us." A discourse on the Edelweiss develops into metaphysical speculation: "How wonderful that these flowers of the earth growing closest to the stars have assumed the shape of the stars—earth's last, most elevated greeting, sent skyward, towards the homeland." The vista point where the couple stands is termed by the husband "the dwelling place worthiest of man." Beholding the dark blue sky, he proclaims: "We are already closer to the mystery."

In the fourth tableau, the two pause by a mountain spring on their descent. Darkness is settling in the forest. Deep silence alternates with the wind's rustling in the trees and a bird's evening song. For the first time, resignation gives way to vehemence. In a tense and dissonant monologue, the husband castigates himself for failing to be loving and understanding enough: "One must flail oneself, subdue oneself until all impurity is expelled. To believe always that one is better! No, no, away with imperiousness, haughtiness, only seek the good—humility, humility." After the outburst, the mood turns serene again. The darkening forest is projected against a red sky, and the murmurs of the spring mingle with the sounds of the evening bell tolling in the distance.

The village cemetery, in which the fifth scene takes place, is clearly reminiscent of the churchyard of Schwabegg. It is All Souls' Day, late in the afternoon. In a soliloquy, the mother, alone this time, gives vent to her grief. Unable to submit to God's will, she asks for His forgiveness and the cleansing of her soul. Her rebellion against fate alternates with self-pity. As night settles, the boy's guardian angel appears in the pale light above the grave. Sent to console her, he brings a message from heaven: "Believe that he lives in peace and that he is with you always." The scene closes with two strophes of a poem in free verse, spoken by the angel in a barely audible voice.

The sixth scene, set again in the peasant hut, opens with the husband reading from "an ancient book." He recites an extensive passage from Swedenborg, who believed that human generations living prior to the Flood had been able to speak with the angels in heaven through "correspondences," which enabled them to attain so high a degree of wisdom that all their earthly experiences were spiritual and in direct communion with the divine. Turning from the book, the husband voices his fervent hope that mankind might again reach so exalted a state. While beholding flowers, he has himself always sensed such correspondences: "The blossom embodies the inexplicable beauty, tenderness, holiness of God. Through the blossom I came to the vision of God." The death of their child, the fruit of conjugal love, also can be

der Mann stellt ~~sich wieder~~ sich jetzt recht
(aufspringend), sieht zum Heldenstein
rechts hinauf. Plötzlich geht er eilenden
Schritten aufwärts und verschwindet.
Ruhe. Man hört das Klingen der Herden-
glocken.
Jetzt kommt der Mann wieder zurück in
der Hand 3 Mann Edelweiss. Er läuft
zur Frau und hält die Blüten vor ihr
Angesicht. Er wendet sich und blickt sie
an.

Der Mann :

Diese Blüten umgibt ein Nimbus,
der veranlassen könnte nicht an
sie zu denken.
Aber das ist falsch.
Es bleibt alles unberührt und so rein
wie zuvor. Nur das ist wichtig,
was etwas thut.
Die allgemeine Beliebtheit darf
uns nicht irre machen.
So ist es mit allem; mit Sitten
Gebräuchen, Einrichtungen, ~~....~~
~~..~~
und mit der Natur.
Und ich glaube was grundlegend
war, ist göttlichen Ursprungs.

From the stage play *Tot* (1913)

understood only through correspondences. The parents now recognize eternity in this act of Providence. As the sun breaks through the clouds, the scene closes with the husband whispering slowly: "O deepest meaning of sorrow, pointing to the highest happiness—Lord, O my God, I see you."

Schoenberg wrote that he found the play "wonderful" in places, but questioned whether the inclusion of a long verbatim quotation from Swedenborg was a legitimate procedure for an author to follow. Replying on 10 November, Webern defended his borrowing the passage, since it bore out so perfectly everything he himself had tried to express in the first five scenes. He confessed that he had come upon the words quite accidentally, as if by providence, when he opened the book at exactly that place at the very hour when he was about to write the concluding scene. All his own ideas about flowers, herbs, mountain springs, and wind were confirmed by Swedenborg, who held "that in all things of this earth the reality of God made itself manifest through correspondences."

Webern made no further use of *Tot*, though he told Schoenberg in his letter of 10 November: "Now I know it can somehow stand, even if it is full of mistakes." Probably his extreme sensitivity led him to suppress anything that met with the slightest criticism from Schoenberg.[6] The musical imagery implicit in the play would seem to have predestined it for a libretto. However, an extant outline for musical realization points to a purely orchestral rather than vocal work. The one-page draft is indicative of how Webern envisaged that various characters and ideas occurring in *Tot* could be woven into a kind of symphonic drama. The project was never carried out, but Webern attached so much significance to *Tot* that he preserved the manuscript throughout his life.

Closely akin to the setting and mood of the fifth scene of *Tot* is the orchestral song "O sanftes Glühn der Berge," based on Webern's own text. Indeed, the whole concept of *Tot* may well have germinated from that song, which came into being as part of the series of eleven short orchestra pieces composed during the autumn of 1913. The initial sketches, dated 30 September, differ considerably from a second undated draft in short score, which served as the basis of the finished score Webern sent to Schoenberg at Christmas-time. The song then was designated as No. III in the set of four selected orchestra pieces. Shortly thereafter, Webern altered his plan of organization and separated the song from the purely instrumental movements, for he had begun, early in 1914, a new project within which the song was to find its place. On 26 March he told Schoenberg: "I have meanwhile written another orchestral song (my own text)." This was "Leise Düfte," a draft of which is dated 23 March 1914. On 2 May Webern sent Schoenberg the finished manuscript of the song, along with another entitled "Die Einsame," both of which he labelled "Opus 7." ("Die Einsame" later became the second of the Four Songs, Op. 13.) In the letter accompanying the manuscripts, Webern hinted at having written still another orchestral song. That allusion was to "Kunfttag III," based on Stefan George's poem from the cycle *Maximin* in *Der siebente Ring.* (Years earlier, Webern had made a setting, for voice and piano, of the companion poem "Kunfttag I.") Dated 2 April 1914, the song is extant only in a condensed score, which, however, was sufficiently detailed to permit realization.[7]

That three of the songs under discussion were considered by the composer for inclusion in one cycle is evident from a cover page to "Die Einsame," where Webern outlined several ideas occupying his mind at the time. He then envisaged "Three Songs, Op. 9," stipulating their sequence as 1. "Leise Düfte" 2. "Kunfttag III" 3. "O sanftes Glühn der Berge."[8] In another plan, drafted on the same page, Webern thought of "Five Orchestral Songs, Op. 8," combining the same three songs with his two Rilke settings (the latter were subsequently published by themselves as Op. 8). He did not stipulate which sequence of songs he intended.

It is difficult to imagine why Webern refrained from bringing out these exquisitely beautiful songs. The fact that he sent two of them to Schoenberg indicates that he considered them valid creative products, and Schoenberg's reaction was so favourable that it should only have encouraged him. Apparently, he was so self-conscious about his poetic efforts (including also *Tot* and "Schmerz, immer blick nach oben") that he withheld them from a wider public. Terse and emotionally intense, the songs seem to express what Webern had written to Schoenberg a year earlier, on 12 September 1912: "When I read letters from my mother, I could die of longing for the places where all these things have occurred. How far back and how beautiful. How unfathomable is everything that has happened. Often a quite soft, tender radiance, a supernatural warmth falls upon me—this comes from her, from my mother."

Such sentiments underlie the two song texts that Webern himself wrote. "O sanftes Glühn der Berge," in particular, is an invocation of his mother, who appears to him as an apparition, now transfigured into the Mother of Grace. The use of whispered *Sprechstimme* and the chiming of the church bell add eerie touches to this gripping drama in miniature. The trance-like quality is heightened by the treatment of the orchestra: the instruments play mostly muted, and the dynamic indications never rise above a "*p.*" Admonitions such as "like a breath," "fading away," "softest tone possible," "disappearing," and "until inaudible" constantly remind the players of the composer's attempt to capture the visionary. The effect is one of hypnotic concentration.

"Leise Düfte," tender and ethereal, likewise conjures up a dream-like image. "Kunfttag III," the last of Webern's sixteen settings of texts by Stefan George, celebrates the coming of spring. The songs richly illustrate an assessment of Webern by Erwin Stein: "Ecstasy was his natural state of mind—his compositions should be understood as musical visions." Common to all three songs are the severe demands of the vocal part, with its wide range and virtuoso leaps. The highly colouristic orchestration lists such instruments as guitar, mandolin, harmonium, celesta, harp, sleighbells, and cowbells.

The harmonium is likewise included with the group of supporting instruments that Webern scored that spring for his chorus *Entflieht auf leichten Kähnen*, Op. 2. Also originating during the early part of 1914 were several songs, later incorporated into Opus 12 and Opus 13. These cycles mark the opening of an extended period in Webern's development devoted almost exclusively to vocal writing (see Chapter XVI). His last purely instrumental essay before that creative phase was his Op. 11, the Three Little Pieces for Cello and Piano. The diminutive work came into being almost incidentally. The violoncello and the piano were the two instruments on which Webern had achieved a measure of proficiency as a performer. During his Gymnasium days at Klagenfurt he had played the cello in the civic orchestra and thereafter frequently in string quartets. His early interest in the instrument had been fostered by his father. From the elder Webern came, during that spring of 1914, a suggestion about which Webern wrote to Schoenberg on 26 May: "I shall now write a major piece for cello and piano. My father asked me to do it. He likes cello music. For me, however, his wish becomes the occasion to find at last an approach to longer movements again—your idea."

The closing remark suggests that Schoenberg, upon receiving Webern's last brief musical essays, had recommended that he try to write again in more extended forms.[9] The draft of the "major piece," to which Webern refers, is entitled Cello Sonata. One movement, dated 9 May 1914 at the concluding double-bar, was fully sketched out when Webern wrote to Schoenberg on 26 May. He obviously still intended to proceed with the work. However, he suddenly yielded to another creative impulse, resulting in the Three Little Pieces for Cello and Piano, which he offered to his father as a belated birthday gift.[10] Fearing that Schoenberg might be annoyed by his failure to have produced a more extended work, he informed him from Klagenfurt on 16 July:

I am sending you by the same mail a copy of what I last wrote (still in Vienna). I beg you not to be indignant that it has again become something so short. I should like to tell you how this happened and thereby try to justify myself. I already had the quite distinct conception of a major two-movement composition for cello and piano and began working it out at once. However, when I was fairly far advanced with the first movement, it became more and more compellingly clear to me that I had to write something else. I felt with complete certainty that I would leave something unwritten if I suppressed the urge. Thus I broke off the major work, although my progress in it had been smooth, and quickly wrote these small pieces (that is, I actually had already written the first earlier, besides another that I discarded, however). This is how these three pieces originated, and rarely have I felt so certain that something good has come into being.

Two weeks after Webern penned these lines, World War I broke out, and the composer, caught up in the general tumult, never returned to his former project, the Cello Sonata.

Embodying the concept of the aphoristic style in its most extreme form, the Three Little Pieces extend nine, thirteen and ten measures respectively, and their total playing time is about two minutes. They are the ultimate manifestation of Webern's striving for compression of form and substance. The melodic sparseness here is tantamount to asceticism: the texture consists of motives encompassing two, three, or at the most four notes. The idea of using all twelve tones of the chromatic scale, first pursued in the string quartet movements, is further and more intensively explored, especially in the last of the three pieces. The brevity of the pieces, superficially perhaps appearing idiosyncratic, is in fact the result of Webern's pioneering experiments, his thrust towards a new technique, the twelve-tone system, formulated only a decade later by Schoenberg.

The Three Little Pieces, Op. 11, were published by Universal Edition during August of 1924. On 2 December of the same year, they were first performed publicly in a concert of the Society for New Music at Mainz by Maurits Frank, cellist of the Amar Quartet, and Eduard Zuckmayer, pianist. It is remarkable that the première should have occurred only a decade after the work originated, and that the pieces are not listed at all in the annals of the Society for Private Musical Performances, where a good many of Webern's compositions were heard. A performance in Vienna did take place on 10 February 1925, given by Maurits Frank and Friedrich Wührer. Alban Berg reported on it to the composer, who was not present (see Chapter XVII). A performance in Berlin in 1926 by Gregor Piatigorsky elicited laughter from the audience. Such reaction deepened Webern's awareness that the time for his pieces had not yet come. As late as 20 October 1939, he advised Willi Reich in the preparation of a concert planned for Basel: "The violin pieces would be

No. 1 of Three Little Pieces, Op. 11, for cello and piano

more suitable than the cello pieces. Those preferably *not at all*! Not because I do not think they are good. But they would just be totally misunderstood. Players and listeners would find it hard to make anything of them. *Nothing experimental!!!*"

The extant movement of the Cello Sonata, discovered only in 1965, was first heard on 3 June 1970, when the same Gregor Piatigorsky, who had pioneered the Three Little Pieces almost half a century earlier, played it with Victor Babin at the Cleveland Institute of Music.[11] The piece bristles with energy and abounds in sudden contrasts. Its length of 41 measures (nine more than the Three Little Pieces taken together) makes it a milestone in the composer's development. It marks Webern's deliberate effort towards formal expansion at the height of that unique epoch of musical aphorism, a genre both cultivated and consummated by him.

CHAPTER XIII

First World War—Prague—Mödling
(1914–1918)

As WAR BROKE out in mid-summer of 1914, a tidal wave of patriotism swept across the land. During the days of mobilization there was a tremendous surge of excitement. Caught up in the mass psychosis, with young men all around him rushing to arms, Webern, too, felt the urge to volunteer. He feared, however, that his poor eyesight would disqualify him, since an earlier examination had declared him "unfit to bear arms."

The rapidly unfolding events were discussed in a flurry of letters to Schoenberg, whom Webern still hoped to join at Murnau. By 1 August, however, the telegraph service was interrupted, and civilian train services between Austria and Germany were temporarily halted because of troop transports. All mail delivery in Germany stopped, to resume only gradually and under stringent censorship. Unknown to Webern, Schoenberg had left Murnau at the outbreak of the war and returned to Berlin. It was not until 19 August that a telegram from Schoenberg re-established the cherished communication. Meanwhile, Webern had kept on writing. Proclaiming his pan-Germanic sentiments, he told Schoenberg on 11 August: "I do not know at all any more how peace-time really was. Where was this dreadful hatred hidden before? . . . I implore Heaven for victory for our army and that of the Germans. It is really inconceivable that the German Reich, and we along with it, should perish. An unshakeable faith in the German spirit, which indeed has created, almost exclusively, the culture of mankind, is awakened in me."

Even though the first casualty reports included names of some of Webern's own acquaintances, his patriotic enthusiasm was boundless. As he witnessed the frequent swearing in of recruits in Klagenfurt's main square and heard the mass singing of the national anthem resounding through the streets, his emotions were aroused to a high pitch. "Oh, it is so marvellous!" he wrote to Schoenberg on 28 August. "I am so depressed at the thought that I cannot join in." Unbridled chauvinism reigned everywhere. Webern, too, was blindly partisan and echoed the official propaganda of the Austro–German coalition. Formerly quite sceptical of the German mentality, especially that prevailing in the northern provinces, he now acclaimed the might of Germany and denounced all its foes. Convinced of the higher mission of Europe's Central Powers, he wrote to Schoenberg on 8 September:

> I can hardly wait any longer to be called up. Day and night the wish haunts me: to be able to fight for this great, sublime cause. Do you not agree that this war really has no political motivations? It is the struggle of the angels with the devils. For everything that has revealed itself about the enemy nations during the course of these weeks really demonstrates only one thing: that they are liars and swindlers. Nothing but infractions of international laws: the apparently long, long accomplished mobilization of the Russians, the deceitful negotiations, the bribes among each other, the dum-dum bullets, etc.—what nauseating filth! By contrast, the open, honourable position of our nations. Lord, grant that these devils will perish. God indeed ordains it already. This victory march of the Germans towards Paris. Hail, hail to this people! A thousand times already I have apologized in thought for having sometimes been a little suspicious, especially of Protestantism. But I must say that I have come closer to it during these times. Catholic France! They have raged against Germans and Austrians like cannibals. Those left behind are interned somewhere in southern France—hard labour, bread and water their lot. And the most ridiculous of all—these Englishmen! They who up to now have only intrigued and who, once they were in battle, ran away so fast that the cavalry could not keep up. Perhaps, as I am writing to you, the Germans are already in Paris. And the Russians, too, will soon be chased away. . . . Oh, everything will end well. . . . The courage of our soldiers in the face of death and their daredevil fighting spirit are said to be without example. If only I could soon take part. How gladly.

The war thwarted several auspicious professional prospects for Webern. Among them was an August performance of his Six Pieces, Op. 6, under Sir Henry Wood in London. The most immediate and serious consequence, however, was the cancellation of Webern's engagement in Stettin. The theatre there at first closed down entirely, and when it re-opened in mid-October the staff was reduced and salaries were cut. Prompted by Jalowetz, Webern had informed the management that he would accept a lower remuneration, but he was nonetheless advised that his re-engagement was impossible under the circumstances. This unexpected turn of events posed severe problems. Webern had given up his Vienna apartment at Kremsergasse 1 at the beginning of summer. All his household goods, prepared for shipment in early August, had to remain in storage. He had signed a lease for the Stettin apartment for a full year and paid three months' rent in advance. The landlord now insisted on fulfilment of the contract. Assisted by his father-in-law, the notary, Webern argued that he neither had a job nor could even leave Austria under prevailing military regulations, but the landlord remained adamant and demanded at least another three months' rent. Yielding in the end, Webern suffered a sizeable financial loss.

With the Stettin plans frustrated, Webern tried for a position in Prague, but Zemlinksy could only promise to watch for an opening. On 2 September Webern and his family had returned to Vienna after their two-month stay in Klagenfurt. With the future so uncertain, they again moved in with his wife's parents at Ruckergasse 12. Webern's military status as "Landsturmpflichtiger" made him subject to call-up at any time. His impulse still was to volunteer, but he was dissuaded from this by his father, his parents-in-law, and especially his wife, even though they were all ardent patriots. The women in the family were busy knitting socks, mittens, and snow caps for the soldiers at the front. Webern's sister Rosa, trained in first aid, entered service with the Red Cross. Webern himself, joined by Stein and Polnauer, signed up for a two-week course that prepared civilians to serve as assistant male nurses. Besides learning to make beds and air rooms, he was instructed in the rudiments of anatomy and the dressing of wounds. Immediately afterwards, in early November, he enrolled for another two-week course, directed by an army captain, that provided pre-induction training.

Although the battles in the open field proved inconclusive and the front lines gradually hardened to warfare in the trenches, Webern's optimism remained unshaken. For him, the outcome of the contest was beyond doubt. When Maeterlinck issued an anti-German manifesto, calling for the extermination of Prussian militarism, Webern turned violently against him. His wishful thinking was to continue long after the hurrahs and fanfares had begun to subside, when the struggle turned into a war of attrition destined to last a full four years, and the promise of glory gave way to the bitter necessity of survival. With the nation's energies fully devoted to the defence of the fatherland, artistic aspirations seemed to lose their significance. Each member of the Vienna circle was affected. From Altenberg, Kokoschka, and Loos to Schoenberg and his disciples, the only matter of importance now was the individual's rôle within the war effort. When a physical re-examination found Webern fit for duty, he signed up as a volunteer. This allowed him to state his preferred branch of service. Inducted in February 1915, he joined the Landwehr Infantry Regiment No. 4, a Carinthian troop with headquarters in Klagenfurt. On 22 February he wrote to Berg that he was already in the midst of regular barracks life. He reported "all kinds of funny things," such as his having to fetch his food in a bowl that he had to clean out afterwards and sleeping away from home.

On the last day of February, Webern was transferred to Görz (Gorizia), a town on the Isonzo River, 27 miles north of Trieste. There he was to be stationed for over two months. On 20 March he described to Schoenberg some of the harsh aspects of basic training:

> I lie on the floor on a straw mattress, in dust and dirt, crowded together with other 'Einjährige' [recruits of higher education who ordinarily had to serve only one year]. This is really terrible and truly not necessary, for how much more efficient one would be if one could live privately in cleanliness. Now I can appreciate a clean bed, a private room, etc. . . . The rigours to be endured are really great. But I do not mind. . . . Indeed I lead a life as if I had spent weeks on a cross-country hike or something similar. On Sundays, my wife brings me fresh linen and something to eat. Tomorrow will be again such a joyous day.

In the same letter, Webern gratefully acknowledged a gift with which Schoenberg had just surprised him: a seven-page manuscript, bound by Schoenberg himself in dark blue linen, containing the song "Alle, welche dich suchen" (published later as the second of Four Orchestral Songs, Op. 22). The composer dedicated this song, on a poem from Rilke's *Das Stundenbuch*, "To my dear Anton von Webern" (though that inscription does not appear in the published score). Webern's joy was boundless, and he described the present in detail when he wrote to Berg on 7 April. He had then been confined to bed for ten days with laryngitis. His sick leave was to continue for several more weeks. His wife (now expecting another child) had come from Klagenfurt to nurse him, and the little family lived privately at Corso Franz Joseph 25 until the end of April.

In early May Webern was transferred to Windisch Feistritz, a small town south of Marburg. He was billeted privately at Frau Troyer's, at Burggasse 60, while he completed his training. On 10 May he reported to Berg that he had been promoted to the rank of corporal and that he much preferred his new location to that at Görz. Another transfer, in early June, brought him to Frohnleiten near Bruck on the Mur River. On 8 June he was advanced to cadet aspirant, a rank equivalent to that of sergeant, and he was now entitled to wear the small sabre of a mountain troop officer. He was placed in charge of training older recruits (aged 37 to 42) and enjoyed experimenting with some of his own pedagogical ideas. "I would like to accomplish my purposes without yelling, and all that," he wrote to Schoenberg on 8 June. "I am using the experience I gained in choral rehearsals. Theatre and military procedure indeed have much in common. I try to make everybody take things as seriously as possible. The relevance of everything is explained, even if it looks like mere drill. The best of sense really governs each detail. That sense they are to comprehend."

Renting quarters at Mauritzen 85, Webern was again joined by his wife and children. The countryside was beautiful, and for two months he enjoyed a pastoral idyll despite the grim overtones of war. "The existence here is truly a relief to me after what I have been through," he confided to Schoenberg. His situation continued to be relatively comfortable when he was assigned, in early August, to another post at nearby Niklasdorf, where he and his family lived pleasantly in the House No. 21. On 24 August he told Schoenberg about a new aspect of his life as a soldier that answered, at least partly, his thirst for musical activity: "Twice weekly so far, I have played quartets. Late Beethoven included. It gives me great joy. However, yesterday two of the players went off to the front. I am hoping for substitutes. I have a ravenous appetite for music."

A week later, the Niklasdorf garrison was suddenly disbanded, and Webern was transferred to Leoben. He found private quarters for himself and his family at Krottendorfergasse 11, in the home of Frau Sectionschef Zechner, the wife of one of his father's colleagues. Although he took pride in belonging to a crack battalion of the Carinthian Mountain Troops, he realized more and more the limitations of his reserve status. On 5 September he wrote to Schoenberg: "I now long for a type of duty in which I can, in quietude, direct my thoughts again to that which is really my calling. And thus I could perhaps await the end [of the war] more patiently." When two men in the battalion, both orchestra musicians, were released on request of the Klagenfurt theatre, Webern was quick to eye a similar course for himself. He wrote an express letter to Zemlinsky in Prague offering his services there even if it were to be only as a coach. Enlisting the theatre director's support, Zemlinsky immediately took the initiative: a formal petition to have Webern placed on leave of absence was submitted to the military authorities. Confident of his early return to musical life, Webern began practising. On 27 September he wrote to Berg that he had just rented a piano and that, for the first time since February, he was able to play again.

At the end of September Webern's wife returned to Vienna for the delivery of their third child, a son, born on 17 October. The boy was christened Peter. It had been the parents' wish to name him Carl, but they were dissuaded in this. "My father does not want our son to be called after him," Webern explained to Schoenberg on 31 October. "He says that no good luck is connected with the name Carl. I am so sorry about this, but yet I can understand him: two of his children who bore this name, a son and a daughter, Caroline, died early." Avoiding all names of other family members, the parents then chose from the Christian calendar the one closest to their son's birthday that they found to their liking.

While Webern awaited his release from army duty, Schoenberg had to prepare for induction. There had been vigorous intervention on his behalf all through the preceding months. Writing to a high official in the Ministry, Webern had pleaded, in the name of all friends and disciples of the master: "It is so very clear that the State must be concerned about protecting the work and creative strength of this artist, especially in this difficult time, and it must not sacrifice them to a law which, while indispensable and enormously beneficial in itself, must indeed in this case make an exception."[1]

All petitions, including those by influential patrons, proved to no avail. Schoenberg received his induction notice on 3 November, and on 15 December he entered service in the Deutschmeister Regiment, stationed in Vienna. Dismayed by the very thought that Schoenberg should have to don a soldier's uniform, Webern fought to the last. When the inevitable happened, he anxiously and solicitously advised his friend at every turn, even in such prosaic matters as how to procure the best equipment: "When you are being outfitted in the barracks," he wrote on 2 December, "give a little tip (say two kronen) to the sergeant-in-charge, then you get good things."

The request from the Prague theatre to have Webern placed on leave of absence from the army was long bottlenecked in bureaucratic channels. The application, requiring another physical examination, was endorsed by the War Ministry, but the orders to release Webern until 5 April were slow in reaching his command post at Leoben. It was the middle of December before the furlough took effect.

The Christmas holidays back home in Vienna were highlighted for Webern and his wife by a special event. By now the parents of three children, they at last received papal dispensation to have their civil marriage of 1911 solemnized by the Roman Catholic Church. The ceremony took place on 26 December at the parish church of Ober St Veit in Vienna, with Gustav Mörtl and Arnold Schoenberg as official witnesses.

The first weeks of 1916 saw Webern active as a coach at the Deutsches Landestheater in Prague. Since suitable lodgings could not be found, he established himself in the Hotel Schwarzes Ross am Graben. Living there was so convenient and inexpensive that he soon sent for his wife and children. Professionally, he felt challenged by such tasks as assisting in the preparation of Mozart's *Così fan tutte* and Schumann's *Faust*. About the latter work he wrote to Schoenberg on 16 January: "For me, there is much in it which ranks with the most beautiful music I know."

For a symphony concert on 27 January, Zemlinsky assigned Webern the re-orchestration of certain passages in the "Lied der Waldtaube" from Schoenberg's *Gurrelieder*. Originally the Chamber Symphony had been scheduled, but Schoenberg vetoed the performance on the grounds that he did not want to excite an aesthetic controversy now that the national emergency took priority over everything else. "In peacetime—which means wartime for me—I am quite prepared to go back to being everyone's whipping boy," he remarked.[2] Schoenberg was unable to be present at the concert, but Webern sent him, on 29 January, a glowing report on the success of his music. His words of admiration for Schoenberg's work contrasted sharply with the critical comments in the same letter on the *Alpine* Symphony by Richard Strauss, scheduled for an early performance in Prague: "I have to think of wall-size *Kitsch*-paintings as they can be seen in museums," he concluded.

From the beginning of his Prague engagement, Webern suffered qualms over his release from military duty at a time when Schoenberg had to lead a soldier's life. So compulsive became his sense of guilt about his civilian status that he himself took steps to have the leave terminated before its expiration date. When the adjutant of his reserve battalion in Leoben at first expressed doubt that his recall could be hastened, Webern, feeling like an "outcast," wrote to Schoenberg on 16 January: "I feel like a criminal. I would like to bury myself until April. It is madness to play theatre now. It is dreadful. And I assist in it. In the autumn when I wrote to Zemlinsky, I had such an overpowering longing to be able to occupy myself with music again. And I gave in to that longing. If only I had never done it!"

Webern's démarche, undertaken without Zemlinsky's knowledge, brought quick results. His leave was cancelled in late January, and the action elicited an official protest from the unknowing theatre director. In early February, Webern returned to his former command post in Leoben. Because of an outbreak of smallpox in the town, his family followed only in March. They again established living quarters at Krottendorfergasse 11. During the interim, Webern had lodged at the Hotel Krempl, which he praised for its "comfort and cuisine." His military duties were light and occupied him only during the mornings. He therefore had ample time to concentrate on what he made his chief objective—to secure Schoenberg's release from the army. Irked that

virtually every other musician of note was freed from military service, he
wrote voluminous letters urging all his friends to action. "Lehár, the
swine, he was discharged at once. Arnold Schoenberg is not. How can
one comprehend this? Must the great suffer in this respect also? Here,
too, no differentiation, no understanding?" he wrote to Zemlinsky on
25 February. To Hertzka he pleaded on 5 March:

> Reger, Pfitzner, the composers, the conductors in Vienna and Berlin
> —not a single one is serving. Therefore I ask you, Herr Director,
> to take steps to see that Schoenberg is released. . . . It is indeed a
> disgrace that he was called up at all, whether it was done in ignorance
> of his personality or in spite of it. To remove such a man from his
> work is the worst kind of cultural damage the State can inflict. If
> anyone is "indispensable" then it is Arnold Schoenberg.[3]

While his friends pressed for his release, Schoenberg stoically
endured the hardships of life in the barracks. To be thrown into close
company with wholly unsympathetic men was most trying for someone
of his aesthetic sensitivity and high intellect, his patriotic convictions
notwithstanding. Webern did his best to comfort him. He himself now
had to contend daily with an individual whom he loathed as his partner
in the training of recruits, "a middle-school professor, a cynical,
horrible man, a ruffian entirely impossible to stomach," as he told
Schoenberg on 21 April. In the middle of March, Schoenberg had been
delegated to a reserve officers' school in Bruck an der Leitha. Webern
sent him boxes of cigarettes he himself had handrolled and constantly
tried to hearten him by his own confidence in an early end of the war,
little as the situation warranted such faith. On all fronts, the struggle
between the opposing armies had entered a stalemate, and the scarcity
of basic necessities was spreading, especially in the larger cities.
Frequently, Webern's wife sent provisions to Schoenberg's family in
Vienna, and on one occasion a pair of "war shoes" (with wooden soles)
was included for Görgi, Schoenberg's son. The longing for peace was
general by now, but perseverance in one's patriotic duty was staunchly
upheld as an absolute imperative. "I am striving for the keenest, most
exact understanding of the obligations that have now become necessary,
to relate everything to them, to live in the most pious submission only to
this: to the rescue and the victory of our fatherland," Webern wrote
to Schoenberg on 21 June, after visiting him in Vienna (Schoenberg had
been stationed there since the middle of May).

Thus resolved, Webern braced himself for the possibility of being sent
to the front, especially since a new eye examination had found him "fit
for war service." For the next three months he waited for the decisive

orders. During that period, he was assigned to another unit, designed to prepare young recruits for combat. "These young soldiers interest me very much. It is nice working with them," he told Schoenberg on 7 July. Six days later he described his strenuous schedule: "Within the last week: a two-day manoeuvre on a 2,000-metre peak, followed immediately by barracks inspection, then an exercise on a 1,600-metre peak, then a whole day's drill in the valley, also combined with mountaineering. In between, giving commands on the drill grounds the whole day and running in the full heat of the sun. That was a little too much. Today, an exercise of about eleven hours, from half past two in the afternoon until one o'clock at night."

This intensive training continued all through the summer. Webern expected to be sent to Bruck an der Leitha in early autumn and to be attached to a special corps of machine gunners, a prospect that he was actually looking forward to since that unit, equipped for mountain warfare, used horses for transportation. In September he was given a furlough, which he spent partly in Vienna, celebrating Schoenberg's birthday with him, and partly in Klagenfurt with his father. On 1 October he had to report to headquarters in Graz for still another eye examination. This time the outcome again disqualified him for front-line service because of extreme near-sightedness. He was immediately reassigned to the reserve unit in which he had first begun his stretch of duty at Leoben. There he participated in an advanced course for officer candidates; it consisted of making sorties into the terrain, map reading, and drawing sketches—activities that suited his predilections.

With his change in status, Webern's schedule once again allowed him an abundance of free time. It was channelled into a most cherished activity. "Here I often have the opportunity to play chamber music," he wrote to Schoenberg on 10 November. "Recently the great Trio in B Flat Major by Beethoven. Only today do I understand this music fully. More and more clearly does this most sublime heart reveal itself to me—this inexpressibly elevated thinking." Ever since coming to Leoben, Webern had played the cello in a chamber group organized by the battalion's adjutant, Captain Hermann Hein. In civilian life a prominent functionary (Ministerialrat) in the Ministry of Finance, Dr Hein was an enthusiastic amateur musician, proficient in both violin and viola. He always saw to it that suitable instrumentalists were assigned to his detachment so that he could enjoy frequent ensemble playing. Anton Anderluh, later a gymnasium and college professor in Klagenfurt, was also a member of the group that met at Dr Hein's Leoben home two or three times weekly. The repertoire, sometimes extending to quintets and sextets, ranged from Haydn, Mozart, and Beethoven to Schubert, Brahms, and Hugo Wolf (the latter's *Italian Serenade* and posthumous quartet were on their list). Anderluh, who joined the group in the spring of 1916 on his return from the front, recalled in his memoirs Webern's special love for Schubert, whose quartets in D minor and A minor and the *Trout* Quintet were played.[4] Among his souvenirs was a photograph showing the Leoben chamber ensemble during rehearsal, with all its members in uniform.[5] Not until much later did Anderluh realize that Webern was a composer himself. His own music was never mentioned, although the conversation frequently dwelt on Schoenberg.

Dr Hein was among those whom Webern induced to petition for Schoenberg's release from army service. The combined efforts of so many eventually succeeded and, on 20 October, Schoenberg was given leave for an indefinite period. Webern was jubilant. At the same time, though, he was now losing his own incentive for staying in the army. Disillusionment and futility speak from his letter of 7 November to Schoenberg: "I have completely lost my earlier optimism. I often sink into such awful depressions. . . . It is really as if Christ had never existed. 'Eye for eye, tooth for tooth'—the ancient law of the Old Testament alone has validity."

It was not long before Webern, too, professed the wish to get out of uniform. Since he could not muster sufficient courage to prevail again on Zemlinsky, he asked Jalowetz, who also was now at the Deutsches Landestheater in Prague, to intervene on his behalf. As he waited for the outcome, his army life became markedly more difficult. A new company commander drove him hard and assigned him all sorts of disagreeable chores, such as inspecting uniforms for spots and missing buttons, supervising the kitchen, and checking on his platoon even during night hours. "I am being held responsible for everything, simply everything," he wrote to Schoenberg on 3 December. "I could not endure this for long. But it will not be necessary, for, as I heard today, on 1 January I will definitely be sent to Graz for eight weeks to attend a quarter-master's course. Subsequently, I will be stationed somewhere behind the front and will receive the rank of Fähnrich [commissioned officer]."

Webern wrote this hopeful letter on his 33rd birthday. Two weeks later, the expected transfer was called off. Webern begrudged the missed chance for promotion, not suspecting that the change of disposition was connected with his permanent discharge. It came suddenly on 21 December, when he was declared unfit for service because of deficient eyesight. Two days later he was released. The event was recorded as the first entry in a small notebook, used by Webern as a diary from then until 1939. Bound in leather and brocade, the ornate little volume was no doubt a Christmas gift that year.

In early January 1917, Webern and his family returned to Vienna and took up residence in an apartment at Auhofstrasse 136. In addition to their upstairs flat, Webern rented basement quarters so that he could have a quiet workroom for himself. On New Year's Day he had written to Schoenberg: "I envision now a time of introspection, of writing music. I have ideas for a quartet." Webern's creative output during the next seven months is ample evidence that he lived up to his aspiration, after the virtual stagnation of his creative work while he was in uniform for almost two years. He was stimulated by the long-missed artistic climate of the capital and, especially, by the personal contact with Schoenberg and Berg. He had only recently healed a severe break in his friendship with the latter, which had lasted from the autumn of 1915 to that of 1916. Although the exact reasons for their falling out can no longer be ascertained, they probably had to do with Berg's irritation at being reproached for ineffectiveness in representing Schoenberg's cause. (The promotion of their master's personal affairs had filled much of the correspondence preceding the break.) This is implied when Webern, who had vainly attempted a reconciliation at Christmas 1915, wrote to Berg on 13 October 1916 that his own "ill humour" naturally had been increased because Schoenberg had been very annoyed with Berg at the time. "For what offends him offends me, too," Webern stated. But he went on to assure Berg that all the time he had grieved over what had appeared to be the end of their friendship. He pleaded for its renewal for the sake of "someone infinitely sublime"—Arnold Schoenberg, for whose sake they should outdo each other in devotion and love.

In early March Webern went with Schoenberg to Prague for a concert. At that time he made arrangements for a position with the Deutsches Landestheater, to begin in August. Two months later he returned briefly to rent an apartment. On 24 May, after giving up his Vienna household, he moved to his father's home in Klagenfurt for the two remaining months before his engagement. In the Carinthian countryside, where he felt so much at home, the flow of his creative work continued, and by the time he had to leave for Prague four new orchestral songs had been composed. Considering the stringent wartime conditions governing most of the beleaguered nation, life at Klagenfurt still seemed idyllic. Only on one occasion did the distant rumble of the guns at the Italian front, not far away, reach Webern's ears. For a while, he tried to persuade Schoenberg to come for a holiday, giving an alluring description of a boarding house only five minutes away from his father's home. But once again Schoenberg was embroiled in personal difficulties, which made it necessary for him to stay in Vienna.

Webern and his family left Klagenfurt on 30 July. After a week in Mürzzuschlag they proceeded to Vienna, where he, his wife, and their infant son were house guests of the Schoenbergs, who then lived at Gloriettegasse 43. During that week-long visit, Schoenberg spoke a great deal about *Die Jakobsleiter* (his oratorio then in progress) and about his plans for the future. They so inspired Webern that he wrote to Berg on 18 August of his longing for "a beautiful house in the country, next to Schoenberg" and of his desire to be able to work in close touch with nature. He then mentioned Schoenberg's idea of founding a "colony," in which Berg, too, was to participate. Little did Webern realize that all these hopes would find a measure of fulfilment within the year.

Webern arrived in Prague on 12 August and established quarters on the fourth floor of the house Am Riegerpark 20.[6] Despite rumours that fuel shortages might force the closing down of the theatre during winter, rehearsals for the season got under way. Webern was involved in preparing the chorus and soloists for *Lohengrin* and for Méhul's *Joseph*. During the autumn, *Don Giovanni* and *Parsifal* were added. At first there was little prospect of a conducting assignment (the staff that season included no fewer than eight conductors), but Zemlinsky promised to give him the earliest possible chance. In a letter to Schoenberg, on 7 December, Webern described his daily schedule: "In the morning I have usually an hour or two of chorus rehearsal, followed by rehearsals with the soloists. I share these with the coach. Then I play for stage rehearsals. I also have stage service during performances. All this is for operas only. I have nothing to do with operettas. . . . My present subordinate rôle, however, is really difficult to bear. I feel this more and more."

The same routine was to continue into the new year. Finally, beginning on 16 January 1918, Webern was given the opportunity to conduct Lortzing's *Zar und Zimmermann* four times. Stella Eisner, a young and beautiful singer from Vienna then scoring her first triumphs, participated in those performances.[7] In early December Webern had accompanied her in a recital that included several songs by Schoenberg. He believed in her artistic future, and their musical association continued after both returned to Vienna.

During the winter of 1917–18, the long war entered a critical phase. After the United States of America had joined the Allied cause in April of 1917, German prospects for victory waned. The bitter conflict began to tighten its grip on the populace at home no less than on the embattled armies at the front. Scarcity of fuel paralysed community life. Early in the autumn of 1917, Webern had reported to Schoenberg that five of the larger towns in Bohemia were without light. On 7 December he described his own plight: "I am greatly worried over our coal supply. I received very bad coal, and the apartment is miserable to heat. In order to save a room, we changed the entire apartment around. Windows and doors close so badly. I am afraid that we will not receive any more coal.

The supply is dwindling fast. What am I to do when it comes to an end? I do not know what will happen then. In the theatre everyone freezes, too. It is heated only in the evenings. I rehearse in my overcoat in icy rooms." Food supplies likewise were severely rationed. Webern spoke of the "starved chorus" with which he had to work. He and his family had to get along with three pounds of meat a week, and their chief diet consisted of bread and starch products, supplemented by occasional food packages from Klagenfurt.

Despite the hardships of daily life, cultural activities, considered essential for the upholding of civilian morale, continued. In the fourth Philharmonic concert of the season, on 28 February 1918, Zemlinsky scheduled Schoenberg's *Pelleas und Melisande* as the principal work on the programme. On the preceding Sunday morning, 24 February, Felix Adler gave an introductory lecture in the Holzner Lyceum for Girls, in which Jalowetz and Webern assisted, playing excerpts from the work in piano-duet form.

When Webern had last seen Schoenberg in Vienna, his friend had been besieged by economic worries. His funds were depleted, and he faced not only eviction from his apartment but also an early recall into army service. In mounting distress, he had phoned Webern in Prague early in September. With a passionate vow to help in any way he could, Webern again stepped to the fore and began to organize support: he suggested to Alma Mahler (remarried to the architect Walter Gropius) a permanent subsidy for Schoenberg and asked her for her intercession in securing a large advance payment for a projected *Gurrelieder* performance. He exhorted Berg to assist him in his endeavours. He himself immediately placed 1,000 kronen at Schoenberg's disposal, to which Jalowetz was willing to add 2,000 kronen. Stein was approached to pledge himself to monthly payments, and Königer was asked to solicit a rich uncle.

Such energetic efforts were to bring results in due time, but Schoenberg's crisis appeared so desperate at the time that Webern seriously considered investing all of his and his wife's funds (a total of 40,000 kronen in war bonds) in a farm. "Then I could work and handle the chores so that you and I could have the food supplies. Perhaps it would even be possible for you to live there," he wrote to Schoenberg on 22 September, adding three days later: "I am firmly decided to purchase a farm—at the earliest possible moment. I have already written to my father. . . . Since I had the good fortune to receive some money, am I to sacrifice it to the profiteers? If I buy myself a property, I can save it for my children." Webern's reasoning was to prove only too correct, for a disastrous inflation wiped out his financial resources not long afterwards.

At this juncture, Schoenberg was recalled into the army. He had just issued a prospectus soliciting enrolment in a seminar to begin on 27 September in the Schwarzwald School. A diversity of subjects was offered for professional musicians as well as for amateurs. But before the first session could take place, Schoenberg was back in uniform, despite the frantic efforts of his friends to prevent the renewed draft. As it turned out, his stint of duty was to last only two months. During that time he was assigned to the Exhibition Orchestra, organized to provide concerts for the troops. Among its ranks were many of Vienna's most accomplished musicians. In early December, Schoenberg was permanently discharged. He decided to move to Mödling, an historic township outside Vienna, where he found an apartment in a large villa at Bernhardgasse 6. The news instantly filled Webern with longing. "When we read that you are moving to Mödling, we had only one thought: we must go there, too. As soon as possible! We are already making plans for it," he wrote on 7 December.

Schoenberg, sensing Webern's restiveness, urged him to stay at his post in Prague, and Webern promised to hold out. However, reports of the capacity enrolment for Schoenberg's seminars, now commencing at the Schwarzwald School, increased his impatience to be at the master's side. Closing his eyes to the relative security of his theatre position, he told himself and his father that he was being "exploited" in Prague. The elder Webern, greatly alarmed by what he recognized as the symptoms of an impending change, warned him against taking an ill-considered action. *"The theatre offers you, after all, the sole possibility of earning!"* he wrote from Klagenfurt on 18 March 1918, with thinly-veiled anxiety. "From what else could you and your family live? Schoenberg can really advise you only in regard to your future aspirations, but not about the manner in which you can procure for yourself an assured income, for, alas, he himself has none and has to live off the charity of others. God preserve you from this!"

The father's admonitions were of no avail. An entry in Webern's diary, dated 14 April 1918, notes: "Resolution reached to leave Prague. Apartment in Mödling rented by telegram." The decision came as a result of a trip to Vienna shortly before. Webern had gone there for some concerts organized by Schoenberg, and he undoubtedly found the apartment in Mödling at the same time. Still hesitant to take so far-reaching a step, he let more than two weeks go by before writing in his diary on 2 May: "Notice to relinquish Prague apartment given." The next entry reads: "Beginning of June, moved to Mödling—Neusiedler-strasse 58." The new apartment, situated within a five-minute walk from Schoenberg's home, comprised the entire second floor of a stately house with a spacious garden. It was to remain the family's residence for well over thirteen years.

CHAPTER XIV

Society for Private Musical Performances
(1918–1922)

The first weeks in Mödling augured well for the fulfilment of Webern's long-harboured hopes of finding the ideal setting for his creative activities. When Berg wrote to him that he had resumed work on *Wozzeck*, Webern replied on 8 August 1918 that he, too, was composing: "So far not too productively, but I feel that it will soon be different." His happiness during those summer months seemed complete: "I am with Schoenberg daily. At five o'clock in the afternoon, I call on him. Then we go for walks or we play piano, four hands. After supper, we are *always* together, too. As of late, we play card games (Whist or Tarock)."

Schoenberg, too, was in a serene mood. His financial situation had substantially improved. In the spring he had been awarded the Mahler Memorial Prize (2,500 kronen) and towards the end of the season, at the final rehearsal for a performance of his Chamber Symphony, a lady had handed him an envelope containing 10,000 kronen with a note from an anonymous donor reading "To the great artist from an admirer, a Jew." Thus he was secure for the time being. Webern's financial outlook, on the other hand, was far from inspiring confidence. All that Schoenberg could offer him was participation as an aide in his seminar classes at the Schwarzwald School and in the Society for Private Musical Performances, which was about to be launched. The latter would guarantee him a monthly salary of 100 kronen. Potential additional revenues, to be derived from such chores as orchestrating operettas, might bring Webern's monthly income, in Schoenberg's opinion, to between 300 and 500 kronen.[1] Such meagre prospects made Webern quite apprehensive. The heavy expenses resulting from his frequent moves during the last few years had greatly shrunk his capital. Now the constantly rising cost of living, combined with the substantial annual rent of 2,000 kronen for his Mödling apartment, gave him real cause for worry. Increasingly, Webern wondered whether he might not have forfeited his Prague position too rashly, as his father had warned, and he now began to ponder how he could reverse that decision.

Webern at first kept his predicament from Schoenberg. About mid-September, however, he wrote to him from Mürzzuschlag (where he was on a brief holiday and no doubt consulted with his father) inquiring what he would think of his making another attempt to build a career as theatre conductor (actually, he had already asked Jalowetz to petition on his behalf in Prague). Schoenberg, who had spent countless hours making plans for their joint activities in the autumn, was highly irritated. He informed Webern rather curtly that he did not wish to influence his decisions further in any way, having "wasted," time and again, days and weeks in the discussion of the pros and contras of his disciple's professional course. The coolness of this reply so wounded Webern that he virtually broke off relations with Schoenberg. In a short message, he announced his resolve to prove to him that all his guidance had not indeed been "wasted."[2] Although the engagement in Prague had turned out to be impossible after all, he had decided to leave Mödling and move back to Vienna. He and his family took up residence there with his mother-in-law at Schönbrunnerstrasse 23 while they looked for an apartment.

Berg, who had followed the entire episode at close range, described its development in minute detail in frequent letters to his wife (she was spending the summer in the country while he was confined to a clerical job in the War Ministry, having been found unfit for other military duty). As the little drama reached its climax, he exclaimed to Helene on 16 September: "Now the most incredible thing has happened. Something that I would not have believed possible any more than, say, that Lloyd George had travelled to Berlin in order to smother Kaiser Wilhelm with kisses: Webern has served notice on Schoenberg—quite simply, with a few words—of the termination of their friendship." The crisis was to last for well over a month. On 23 September Webern had a meeting with Berg, who reported to his wife the following day:

> To describe all we talked about, even to give only the main contents, is very difficult. The fact is that I now see the matter in a different light and that I consider him [Webern] by and large innocent. Even his letter [to Schoenberg], which heretofore had seemed brusque to me, appears to me far more understandable now that he has explained to me how Schoenberg's letter hit him hard—like a kick—and how his own letter really meant only that he was going into voluntary exile. The reasons for his renewed resolve to take up theatre work again were indeed always clear to me. They are purely financial and, as

such, most urgent if he does not want to risk actually becoming insolvent, perhaps within a year.

The break was made worse by the attitudes of Webern's and Schoenberg's wives, who, instead of trying to mediate, adamantly sided with their husbands. Berg related to his wife a petty dispute involving some food supplies, sent by Wilhelmine from Mürzzuschlag at Schoenberg's earlier request and returned by Mathilde without comment.

> The second "kick in the teeth," as Webern terms it [Berg wrote]. The comical aspect of the matter is that Webern naturally cannot find an apartment in Vienna and is moving back to Mödling again today, and that he does not know how he can avoid meeting any of the Schoenbergs, who, as you know, live in the closest vicinity. For, now and in the foreseeable future, he cannot at all imagine their getting together again. He became quite enraged at that thought, just as he was when defending his position earlier. Generally speaking, he appeared to me at times—even in his appearance—much more manly, more self-confident, more unyielding, harder. He does not want to stay in Mödling, however, but is still trying to obtain an engagement. Should this not be possible, though, he will look for a little house way out in the country, in Styria, where living would hardly cost him anything.

Webern was absolutely serious about this. An entry in his notebook—undated, but immediately following a detailed scenario for a *Don Giovanni* performance given the previous season in Prague—lists various household goods to be shipped "to Ettendorf," a small village south-west of Graz, not far from the Preglhof. Webern's father seems to have been in accord with the plan, since among the furniture listed were a sofa and two beds with night stands designated as coming from him. Before the move could take place, however, the differences between Webern and Schoenberg were resolved. Towards the end of October, there was an exchange of messages, most likely initiated by Schoenberg, who, in his ambitious plans for the Society for Private Musical Performances, relied on Webern as one of his chief aides. Webern readily showed himself conciliatory, and the end of the dispute was heralded when Schoenberg wrote to Webern on 1 November:

> My very dear fellow, your letter shows that you are well on the way towards getting a picture of the real issue and, what matters to me more, that you have regained your trust in my friendship for you. In

other words, you once more realize that, despite any wounded feelings, you could always have trusted blindly in my friendship. I have not many friends, it is true, but the few I have can rely on me entirely. If, after all this, I tell you that we still have to have a thorough talk to clear up some points that I think you still do not see in the right light, now at any rate you have enough trust in me again to know that it is not that I am trying to make use of you, but that my aim is to make a clean sweep so that we can make an entirely fresh start. So do come and see me as soon as you possibly can. Today if you like—but anyway, for the next few days I shall always be at home here in Mödling. Come soon. Very best wishes, Yours ever, Arnold Schoenberg.[3]

The reconciliation was followed immediately by the launching of an important enterprise: on 23 November 1918, the Verein für musikalische Privataufführungen (Society for Private Musical Performances) was officially founded. Its birth coincided with the end of the war and the downfall of the old régime. On 4 November, after the Italian victory at Vittorio Veneto, Austria surrendered, and on 11 November Germany also capitulated and signed an armistice. Supplies were exhausted, and the breakdown of morale made the countries ripe for revolution (the monarchies were overthrown and republics established). While the end of hostilities brought a general feeling of relief, the consequences of the four-year struggle were to inflict severe hardships upon the defeated nations.

For Schoenberg and his circle, the end of the war was the signal for speedy resumption of artistic activities. Although world famous as a stronghold of music, Vienna had always been loath to admit progressive trends. Schoenberg's organization proclaimed as its chief purpose the systematic introduction of contemporary music, more specifically the music written during the early twentieth century. A manifesto, published on 16 February 1919, set forth the society's aims and established stringent conditions for its musical presentations. Special requirements were that all performances had to be "clear and well rehearsed," that works were to be "repeated frequently," and that "performances must be removed from the corrupting influence of publicity, i.e. they must not be competitive and must be independent of applause or disapproval."

The duration of each programme was not to exceed 90 minutes. Introductory lectures were to accompany many of the musical performances. The ruling that neither approbation nor disapproval could be displayed was meant to enable listeners to form an unbiased opinion of each work. Likewise, no critical reviews were to be permitted to appear in the press, in order to ensure the freedom of individual response. The audience was to be limited to registered members of the society; they were required to carry identification cards, and the admittance of guests was subject to strict regulations. Dues, established in four categories, ranged from a nominal minimum to as high an amount as patrons wished to contribute. The fees in turn determined the seating arrangement in the hall. While the society's sessions were first held in the Schwarzwald School and in the Kaufmännische Verein, the strong response soon enabled the group to stage their events in the small halls of the Musikverein and the Konzerthaus. Each member had to subscribe to a full season's concert series and attend the weekly meetings. No advance announcement of the musical fare comprising each concert was issued, so that members were prevented from choosing one programme over another.

Schoenberg's leadership of his society was absolute. The organization's by-laws provided that the president, Schoenberg, was to have unlimited tenure.[4] The administrative committee, consisting of ten to twenty members, was chosen by the general membership, but was subject to Schoenberg's approval. All artistic and financial matters were under his direct control. Trusted pupils and friends formed his staff of officers: Paul A. Pisk, Josef Rufer, and Rudolf Wenzel served successively as secretaries, Ernst Bachrich and Josef Travnicek as keepers of protocol, and Dr Arthur Prager as treasurer. Josef Polnauer held the position of archivist and also headed a corps of assistants who checked admittance and kept order in the hall.

While Schoenberg himself did much of the coaching, he relied on the assistance of several music directors, called Vortragsmeister, for the thorough and authoritative preparation of each work. From the start, Webern, Berg, and Eduard Steuermann were these appointed aides. Later, Erwin Stein and Benno Sachs were added. With them, Schoenberg also shared the laborious task of making arrangements, either for piano or for small chamber ensemble, of works whose apparatus exceeded the society's resources.

During a directors' meeting, held before each concert, Schoenberg remained the final authority for the clearance of any scheduled performance. The Vortragsmeister were in their turn assisted by a staff of Vorbereiter who did the preliminary coaching. Among these assistants were Ernst Bachrich, Fritz Deutsch, Olga Novakovic, Paul A. Pisk, Karl Rankl, and Josef Travnicek. Viennese composers, whose works were scheduled for performance, also frequently shared in the rehearsals. They included Julius Bittner, Josef Matthais Hauer, Egon Kornauth, Carl Prohaska, Karl Weigl, and Egon Wellesz.

Many accomplished young performers rallied to the cause, including
the pianists Rudolf Serkin and Eduard Steuermann, the violinists
Gottfried Feist and Rudolf Kolisch, the singers Stella Eisner, Arthur
Fleischer, Marie Gutheil-Schoder, and Felicie Mihacsek, the actress
Erika Wagner, and the actor Wilhelm Klitsch. All were professional
performers with the exception of the physician Dr Oskar Adler, a
childhood friend of Schoenberg, who enjoyed general respect as an
excellent amateur violinist. All these names, and many more, appear in
the two notebooks that Webern kept on the society's activities.[5] These
records also contain outlines of programmes given, or planned to be
given, and the names of coaches, arrangers, and performing artists. A
significant entry (on page 38 of Notebook I) stipulated the policy
governing the rendition of works and their repetitions. That statement is
co-signed by Schoenberg and Webern.

In retrospect, the awesome amount of work invested in the activities
of the Schoenberg Society cannot but excite admiration. During the
opening season, 1918–19, no fewer than 26 concerts were presented.
They included a total of 45 compositions, most of which were heard
more than once because of the policy of repetition. Indicative of the
society's standard of excellence, pursued with an almost fanatical zeal,
was the very first concert, in which Mahler's Seventh Symphony, in a
piano-duet arrangement, was the featured work. The players, Bachrich
and Steuermann, were coached by Schoenberg in twelve rehearsals
averaging four hours each, and for a subsequent performance two
additional rehearsals were deemed necessary. (In that historic first
concert, Steuermann also played the Fourth and Seventh Sonatas by
Scriabin.)

Considering   the   uncompromisingly   progressive   idiom   of
Schoenberg's own music, the society's programming policy was
remarkably broad-minded. Some telling statistics are contained in No.
12 of the Society's frequently published *Mitteilungen* (Newsletters). That
issue lists 100 compositions that either had already been performed or
were contemplated for future programmes. The composers included
represent a wide range of tendencies, from the conventional to the
progressive: Bittner, Casella, Charpentier, Delius, Dukas, Finke, Fuchs,
Hába, Janáček, Jemnitz, Kornauth, Korngold, Labor, Lajtha,
Malipiero, Marx, Milhaud, Mraczek, Mussorgsky, Novák, Ostrčil,
Petyrek, Pfitzner, Pijper, Pisk, Prohaska, Réti, Satie, Schmidt, Schreker,
Scott, Sekles, Toch, Weigl, Weingartner and Wellesz.

Further statistics appear in issue No. 24 of the *Mitteilungen*, published
in April 1921. This list discloses that of the altogether 226 compositions
performed by then, 34 were by Reger (still hardly known at that time), 26
by Debussy, twelve each by Bartók and Ravel, eleven by Scriabin, ten by

Mahler (mostly in transcriptions), nine by Stravinsky, seven each by Busoni and Richard Strauss, six each by Hauer and Szymanowski, and five each by Suk and Zemlinsky. Performances of compositions by Schoenberg and his disciples were relatively few; as a matter of fact, Schoenberg would not permit any of his own works to be played until late in the second season. In the end, the annals recorded fifteen titles by Schoenberg, five by Berg, and nine by Webern.

It must be borne in mind that not all compositions projected for performance actually received a hearing, for the *Mitteilungen* announced works already performed alongside those still in preparation.[6] A case in point is the listing of the nine works by Webern, referred to above. They are the Passacaglia, Op. 1 (transcribed for two pianos, six hands); *Entflieht auf leichten Kähnen*, Op. 2; Five Songs, Op. 3; Five Movements for String Quartet, Op. 5 (then listed as "Stücke" rather than "Sätze"); Six Pieces for Large Orchestra, Op. 6 (arranged for chamber ensemble); Four Pieces for Violin and Piano, Op. 7 (then designated as Op. 7, No. 1); Six Bagatelles, Op. 9 (then entitled "Sechs Stücke für Streichquartett"); Five Pieces for Orchestra, Op. 10 (arranged for chamber ensemble and designated as Op. 7, No. 4); and Five Songs on Poems by Georg Trakl (no opus number was given by the composer at that time; the Trakl cycle, Op. 14, eventually included six songs). Since no individual programmes were printed for the society's closed concerts, it is difficult to verify exact performance dates or to ascertain whether certain of the projected works were actually played. For example, there is no conclusive evidence that Webern's chamber arrangement of his Six Pieces, Op. 6, ever went beyond the rehearsal stage (see Chapter VII).

Characteristic of the society's choice of repertoire were the programmes for the Four Propaganda Evenings, presented at the end of the first season for the purpose of attracting a wider membership. The large poster that served as an invitation to the general public is reproduced overleaf.

On 9 June Webern gave Berg (who had left for the country) an account of these Propaganda concerts:

> The evenings had increasing success. The last was overcrowded. Many had to be turned away. There was no more room in the hall. It was completely sold out. Stravinsky was magnificent. These songs are wonderful. This music moves me completely beyond belief. I love it especially. The cradle songs are something so indescribably touching. How those three clarinets sound! And "Pribaoutki." Ah, my dear friend, it is something really glorious. This reality (realism) leads into the metaphysical. My works, too, have gone well.[7]

VEREIN FÜR MUSIKALISCHE PRIVATAUFFÜHRUNGEN
LEITUNG

ARNOLD SCHÖNBERG
4 PROPAGANDA ABENDE

KLEINER KONZERTHAUSSAAL

I. Samstag, den 17. Mai 1919, abends halb 7 Uhr

GUSTAV MAHLER: *VII. Symphonie. Bearbeitung für Klavier zu vier Händen von Casella*
MAX REGER: *Klarinetten-Quintett. Op. 146*

II. Freitag, den 23. Mai 1919, abends halb 7 Uhr

MAX REGER: *Sonate für Klarinette und Klavier. Op. 107*
GUSTAV MAHLER: *Fünf Lieder aus »Des Knaben Wunderhorn«*
ALEXANDER ZEMLINSKY: *II. Streichquartett. Op. 15*

III. Freitag, den 30. Mai 1919, abends halb 7 Uhr

ALBAN BERG: *Sonate für Klavier. Op. 1*
FERRUCCIO BUSONI: *Sechs Elegien für Klavier*
CLAUDE DEBUSSY: *Proses lyriques. Vier Lieder — Ile joyeuse. Klavierstück*
JOSEF HAUER: *Sieben kleine Stücke. Op. 3 und Tanz, Op. 10. Klavierstücke*
MAURICE RAVEL: *Gaspard de la nuit. Drei Klavierstücke*
ALEXANDER SKRJABIN: *Sonate für Klavier.*

IV. Freitag, den 6. Juni 1919, abends halb 7 Uhr

BELA BARTOK: *14 Bagatellen. Op. 6*
ALBAN BERG: *Reigen. Op. 6, Nr. II. f. gr. Orch. Bearbeitung für 2 Klaviere. 8 händig*
IGOR STRAWINSKY: *Berceuses du chat. Vier Lieder für eine Singstimme und drei Klarinetten*
» » *Pribaoutki. Vier Lieder für eine Singstimme und Geige, Bratsche, Violincello, Kontrabass, Flöte, Oboe, Klarinette und Fagott*
JOSEF SUK: *„Erlebtes und Erträumtes." Klavierstücke*
ANTON WEBERN: *Passacaglia f. gr. Orch. Op. 1. Bearbeitung für zwei Klaviere, sechshändig*
» » *Fünf Lieder. Op. 3*

Änderungen der Programme sowie deren Reihenfolge bleiben vorbehalten

MITWIRKENDE

Die Damen: Frl. Ceula Dische, Fr. Emmy Heim, Frl. Felicie Mihacsek (Mitglied des Wr. Operntheaters) Frl. Olga Novakovic und das Quartett: Fr. Paula Bene-Jary, Frl. Annie Baradieser, Frl. Anna Fried und Fr. Maria Lazanski · Das Feist-Quartett: Die Herren Professor Gottfried Feist, Franz Poleany, Ernst Moravec und Wilhelm Winkler und die Herren: Ernst Bachrich, Hugo Burghauser, Simon Danzer, Karl Fiala, Arthur Fleischer (Mitglied der Volksoper), Karl Gaudriot, Hugo Gottesmann, Hugo Kauder, Rudolf Mayer, Franz Prem, Rudolf Serkin, Eduard Steuermann, Gustav Vogelhut u. Viktor Zimmermann

ZWECK

dieser Konzerte ist, die Musikfreunde auf das Bestehen und die Ziele des Vereines aufmerksam zu machen und durch die Programme eine auszugsweise Übersicht von den bisherigen Leistungen zu geben. Deshalb werden die bezeichneten Abende ausnahmsweise Gästen zugänglich gemacht.

Karten für Gäste ab 9. Mai zu K 2·–, 4·– und 6·– per Abend und Prospekte an der Tageskassa des Konzerthauses

Druck der Gesellschaft für graphische Industrie, Wien VI.

Poster announcing four concerts by the Society
for Private Musical Performances (1919)

For Webern, the epoch of the Society for Private Musical Performances constituted the most stimulating and satisfying phase of his professional life up to that point. In many ways, his position of leadership and authority as Vortragsmeister meant a coming of age. On the other hand, the heavy schedule of rehearsals, meetings, and assorted tasks so fully consumed his energies that, apart from transcriptions such as the one of his Passacaglia, he was unable to turn to any creative work. Only in July 1919, during a vacation at Mürzzuschlag,[8] did he have the necessary leisure to follow his innermost calling. As always, he found his inspiration in the seclusion of the high alpine regions, and in quick succession he produced a number of new compositions.

In a letter to Berg, dated 1 August, Webern articulated the philosophy governing his personal and artistic aspirations:

I have been to the Hochschwab. It was glorious, because this is not sport for me, not amusement, but something quite different: it is a search for the highest, a discovery of correspondences in nature for everything that serves me as a model, a model for all that I would like to have within myself. And how fruitful my trip was! These high ravines with their mountain pines and mysterious plants. The latter, above all, touch me deeply. But not because they are so "beautiful." It is not the beautiful landscape, the beautiful flowers in the usual romantic sense that move me. My objective is the deep, unfathomable, inexhaustible meaning in everything, especially in these manifestations of nature. All nature is dear to me, but that which expresses itself "up there" is dearest of all. I want to progress, to begin with, in the purely physical knowledge of all these phenomena. That is why I always carry my botanical lexicon with me and look for any writings that can help to explain all these things. This physical reality contains all the miracles. Studying, observing amidst real nature is for me the highest metaphysics, theosophy.

The creative impetus of those summer weeks at Mürzzuschlag was suddenly interrupted. Towards the end of July, Webern's father, now 69 years old, had fallen ill with severe dysentery and been admitted to the provincial hospital. On 5 August, Webern hurried to Klagenfurt, where he stayed at the apartment (Bahnhofstrasse 53) of his sister, Rosa, who meanwhile had married Otto Warto, a clerk at the local savings bank. Carl von Webern's illness, first considered a passing indisposition, was to prove terminal. His zest for living had been undermined by the collapse of the Habsburg régime and the attendant downfall of the standards and loyalties in which he had believed all his life. Klagenfurt had been occupied by enemy troops until 31 July 1919, and the mining districts in which he had formerly pursued his cherished activities now belonged to the Slovenians. Broken in health and spirit, he died on the evening of 10 August. Two days later he was buried in the cemetery at Annabichl, just outside Klagenfurt. He would doubtless have preferred being laid to rest beside his wife and infant son in the family plot at Schwabegg, next to the beloved Preglhof, but expediency had to prevail at a time of general curtailment. The gravestone bears the inscription "Sektionschef Dr. mont. Carl von Webern 1850–1919."[9]

Thanking Zemlinsky for his words of condolence, Webern wrote to him on 26 August from Mürzzuschlag: "Because my father permitted me to pursue my inclinations with such complete freedom, and because he never, never had even the slightest doubts in them—although for him my paths, on the surface, certainly were rather new and unfamiliar—I must be grateful to him forever."

A few days later, Webern and his family returned to Mödling. There were forebodings of a grim winter ahead, with threats of severe shortages of food and fuel. Webern's apprehensions about the care of his family were further increased by the rapidly declining purchasing power of his remaining funds. In addition, a fourth child swelled the number of his dependants. The new daughter, born on 30 November 1919, was baptized Christine. The record of "Christl's" arrival constitutes Webern's only diary entry during the entire year.

That winter of 1919–20, hunger and cold became harsh realities for most of the population, especially in the metropolitan areas. A few young friends assisted the Webern family in whatever small measure they could. Erwin Ratz, the son of the owner of a large bakery, often furnished supplies, and Kurt Manschinger, whose father was connected with the administration of the former imperial hunting grounds, occasionally contributed a rabbit, a much-relished delicacy. The situation soon grew so severe that the Webern parents, doting as they were, felt forced to take an emergency step, about which Berg commented to his wife on 1 February 1920: "Webern's fate is terrible. What a decision it must have been to separate himself from all his children." The oldest girl, Mali, and the son, Peter, had been sent to Hennersdorf, where they stayed with the family of Wilhelmine's sister, Maria Königer, until August. Mitzi, the second daughter, was placed for a similar period with the relatives in Klagenfurt. Only the infant stayed in her mother's care. The bitter cold, combined with exhausted fuel supplies (gas and electricity were curtailed to a few hours a day) even compelled the Weberns to abandon their Mödling home for a time and seek shelter with Wilhelmine's mother in her Vienna apartment.

Such general tribulations notwithstanding, the Society for Private Musical Performances launched energetically into its second year. Emboldened by the success of the opening season, Schoenberg had planned for the summer of 1919 nine public Propaganda concerts with large orchestra, to be directed by him.[10] Although this ambitious project failed to materialize, the scope of the society's activities was greatly extended during the new season. In addition to the regular closed concerts and various public presentations, a selected performing group went on tour to acquaint progressively-inclined audiences elsewhere with the society's objectives. Between 7 and 14 March 1920 four concerts were presented in the Mozarteum Hall in Prague. Steuermann and Serkin pioneered such new works as Schoenberg's Three Piano Pieces, Op. 11, and Debussy's two-piano suite *En blanc et noir*. On 13 March, Schoenberg himself presided there over his Five Orchestra Pieces, Op. 16, in a reduction for chamber ensemble, and Webern conducted his own Five Pieces for Orchestra, Op. 10, in a transcription for violin, viola, cello, harmonium and piano. The first performance of Webern's Opus 10 arrangement had actually already taken place in Vienna on 30 January.[11] "My pieces came out very well," Webern had written to Berg on 15 February in one of his detailed reports on the society's affairs.

Berg had left Vienna at the beginning of that year to take care of the Berghof, his mother's property on the Ossiachersee. Since he did not return for the rest of the season, Webern's burdens and responsibilities in connection with the society's operation were immeasurably increased. His involvement in Schoenberg's affairs then also included acting as principal assistant in the preparation of two *Gurrelieder* performances at Vienna's State Opera during early June (given within a three-week festival organized by David Josef Bach). Schoenberg himself conducted and scored a triumph.

That climax of the season was preceded by another great experience: "May 1920, attended the Mahler Festival concerts in Amsterdam," reads one of the few brief entries in Webern's diary of that year. Universal Edition, Mahler's publisher, had made available "for a Viennese musician" 100 guilders to help defray the expenses of a trip to the festival. Schoenberg was offered this money, but since he had already been invited to the festival as a guest, he recommended Webern in his stead. The festival was being held on the initiative of Willem Mengelberg, then celebrating his 25th year as conductor of the Concertgebouw Orchestra. All of Mahler's works were to be presented in nine concerts from 6 to 21 May. A series of lectures on Mahler and five chamber music recitals dedicated to contemporary music were also part of the festival. Schoenberg's Two Songs, Op. 14, was the only work by a Viennese composer appearing on these programmes.[12] (In March Schoenberg had gone to Holland from Prague to conduct three concerts including some of his own works. His success had led not only to his being invited back for the Mahler Festival but also for a six-month engagement during the following season.) For Webern, the strong impressions received during the festival served as the impetus for his own active championship of Mahler. Not long afterwards he himself began conducting memorable performances of Mahler's symphonies.[13]

At the end of June Webern once again sought recreation in the mountains. After a traverse of the Hochschwab he wrote to Berg on 14 July that the effect nature had upon him could only be comprehended "in the spiritual realm." Therefore, his ecstasy over a mountain stream ("crystal clear down to the bottom") would have to be understood in that light, and likewise his rapture over the fragrance of flowers, the tenderness of alpine blossoms, the shapes of trees at timberline, the air, the rain, and everything else "up there." Two weeks later Webern enthusiastically commented to Berg on the art and personality of Gustav Klimt, in whose work he recognized the equivalent of his own nature worship. The painter seemed to share with him the belief in "correspondences," which link the material world with that of the metaphysical. Webern professed to Berg that no pictures had ever affected him so much before as Klimt's. They made "an indescribable impression, that of a luminous, tender, heavenly realm." He extolled the artist: "What a soul this is that arrives at such visions of gentleness and light."

The year 1920 brought a most important development in Webern's career. Emil Hertzka, who had been prevented by the outbreak of war from placing some of Webern's works under contract with Universal Edition, now finally signed agreements for the publication and distribution of Webern's Opera 1, 2, 3, and 6. This recognition by the well-known firm became a turning point for the composer. The Passacaglia was soon to be heard in several major cities, including Leipzig (1921), Düsseldorf (1922), and Vienna and Berlin (1923). Webern was invited to conduct some of these performances. Contracts for the publication of other works followed in quick succession. With Universal Edition as his agent, Webern could be relieved from the odious necessity of self-promotion and the chores of sending out copies of his music to prospective performers. In the beginning, royalties were meagre, but what counted immeasurably more was the prestige of association with the influential publishing house.

To be sure, the mounting economic calamities of the defeated nation made revenues of any sort largely illusory. For a time, it remained financially questionable whether the Society for Private Musical

Performances could enter upon its third season at all. During his guest appearance in Prague in March, Webern had observed the relative prosperity of that capital (after the war Czechoslovakia had become an autonomous state). With the encouragement of Schoenberg, who foresaw a bleak future for Austria, Webern had then inquired into the possibility of returning to the Prague theatre. Zemlinsky's ever-faithful support resulted in the actual signing of a contract, according to which Webern was to assume his post on 1 September. With high determination, Webern thanked Zemlinsky on 15 June: "Believe me, I am fully conscious of your tremendous patience and of your loving indulgence towards me. And I promise that I will not disappoint you any more. I will hold out. . . . I envision and resolve that, this time, I will enter upon this course in order really to attain what, from the beginning, was my ideal: to become a good conductor, so that I will yet be able to interpret well the music for which I live."

Webern's ardent desire to succeed in a conducting career was actually to be fulfilled before long, but not in the theatre. His diary contains only this terse record: "From the end of August until the beginning of October 1920 in Prague at the theatre." That short tenure was to constitute his last association with the world of the operatic stage, upon which he had once fastened his youthful dreams. A number of unforeseen difficulties caused the early termination of his engagement: the necessity of leaving his wife and children behind because of visa technicalities, the virtual impossibility of locating an apartment in Prague (during his stay, Webern had to live with Jalowetz), and the disappointment that a teaching position at the German Music Academy (held out to him by Zemlinsky as a probability and quite essential to supplement his theatre salary) was denied him rather curtly at the last minute. Finally, there was an unexpected curtailment of his own activities at the Deutsches Landestheater when the Czechs took over the house for three days weekly.

After this distressing interlude, Webern was quite ready to return to Mödling. The Society for Private Musical Performances had managed to embark on its third season only because of the loyal support of its membership, which had agreed to a drastic increase in dues. That autumn of 1920, Webern again took on the duties of Vortragsmeister, joined by Erwin Stein and Alban Berg. The latter, after his long absence in the country, had been induced to return and assume the administration of the society's affairs during Schoenberg's six-month engagement in Holland. While Webern's activities within the valiant group barely provided him with a means of subsistence, his work was at least artistically satisfying. What the society offered him, above all else, was the opportunity for some memorable performances of his own music.

Another of the society's attractions for its participants, financially ill-rewarded as they were for their enormous investment of time and effort, was the chance to associate with visiting colleagues from abroad. On 23 October 1920 a special concert was dedicated to Maurice Ravel, who then was visiting Vienna (he was the house guest of Alma Mahler for three weeks). Webern's Four Pieces for Violin and Piano, Op. 7, were on the programme, as were works by Berg and Schoenberg. Music by the honoured guest included *Gaspard de la nuit*, *Valses nobles et sentimentales*, and his String Quartet. It should be remembered that Ravel was at that time considered avant-garde, and that his work was still relatively unknown.[14]

Many years later Eduard Steuermann recalled some of the exciting events of those days:

> Milhaud once came to Vienna. He had performed *Pierrot* in Paris, and Mrs Mahler gave a reception for him and Poulenc at which I played my *Kammersymphonie* arrangement and Schoenberg conducted *Pierrot*. Then Milhaud responded by conducting parts of *Pierrot* to show how he had done it. My most unforgettable memory, however, was that Milhaud and Poulenc invited me to the Hotel Bristol for a wonderful lunch. It was 1920 [actually 1922] during the inflation, and there was practically no food in Vienna; this was my first real meal in years! I also met Ravel during that period [1920] and even played four hands with him. We met at Mrs Mahler's and played through *Ma Mère l'Oye* and the *Rhapsodie Espagnole* for the conductor, Oskar Fried, who was planning a Ravel concert and always wanted to hear new pieces played first on the piano. By the way, Webern once did the Mallarmé songs; he adored them, especially the last, which is very close to Schoenberg.[15]

The special Ravel concert on 23 October actually formed the second of six Propaganda events which the society, endeavouring to improve its fortunes, presented to the public during that precarious 1920–21 season. Among the highlights of those concerts were Mahler's Fourth Symphony in a chamber orchestra version by Erwin Stein, four performances of Schoenberg's *Pierrot Lunaire* during early May 1921, a reading of his text to the oratorio *Die Jakobsleiter* by the actor Wilhelm Klitsch (22 May), and a "Walzerabend" (27 May). The latter, billed as "Extraordinary Evening," was explicitly intended as a fund-raising endeavour in the face of the catastrophically deteriorating monetary situation. Designed to attract the largest possible audience, the special programme, held in the Festsaal of the Schwarzwald School, featured four popular Johann Strauss waltzes in settings for "salon orchestra" (piano, harmonium, and string quartet). Schoenberg himself provided the arrangements of "Roses from the South" and of the "Lagoon Waltz" (from *A Night in Venice*). Berg transcribed "Wine, Women and Song" and Webern the "Treasure Waltz" (from *The Gypsy Baron*). To add to the personal character of the affair, the three composers themselves played in the ensemble. It consisted of Eduard Steuermann (piano), Alban Berg (harmonium), Rudolf Kolisch and Arnold Schoenberg (first violins), Karl Rankl (second violin), Othmar Steinbauer (viola), and Anton von Webern (cello). At the end of the evening, the four original manuscripts of the waltz transcriptions were put up for auction, the proceeds to benefit the society's depleted treasury.[16] The society's regular closed concerts of that third season ended on 8 June with a programme comprising music by Busoni, Satie, Stravinsky, and Webern, for whose Four Pieces, Op. 7, Rudolf Kolisch was the violinist and Steuermann the pianist.[17]

In addition to his exacting duties as Vortragsmeister, Webern had been working as a private teacher and coach. Soon after he had settled in Mödling, three young musicians had begun lessons with him. They were Kurt Manschinger, Ludwig Zenk, and Hans Swarowsky. Manschinger, who first had been recommended to Schoenberg by Zemlinsky, in turn was sent to Webern, with whom he studied from 1919 until 1926.[18] Zenk, whom Webern later considered his most accomplished pupil, was to become a lifelong friend, sharing with his teacher the love of mountain climbing and gardening. Zenk's cousin, Hans Swarowsky, became in due time prominent as a conductor. Also belonging to that initial group of disciples was the singer Stella Eisner, whom Webern had prepared for the rôle of Sophie in *Der Rosenkavalier* during his 1917–18 season at Prague; she engaged him to come to her mother's home for daily coaching sessions in the literature of classical and modern songs throughout the winter of 1919–20.[19] In addition, when Schoenberg had left for his prolonged stay in Holland in the autumn of 1920, he assigned three of his students to Webern. They were Hanns Eisler, who was to attain distinction as a composer, Karl Rankl, later musical director of Covent Garden Opera in London, and Josef Travnicek. With characteristic conscientiousness, Webern sent regular reports about the progress of his charges to Schoenberg.

Schoenberg's seminar classes had also been continued during his absence.[20] "In the conducting course, we are now doing *Freischütz* and Beethoven's First," Webern related on 6 January 1921. "The last named gives me the opportunity to say many things about projection, etc., primarily and *particularly* how the conductor is enabled, through purely *musical-technical* terms (dynamics, bowing technique, etc.), to impress upon the players what he has in mind." In his frequent letters to

Amsterdam Webern could also reassure Schoenberg, who was to direct a *Gurrelieder* performance there in March, that his own preliminary coaching of the two Vienna participants (the singer Bauer, cast for the Waldtaube part, and Wilhelm Klitsch, again assuming the speaker's rôle) was proceeding well.

   Never could a leader rely on more loyal vassals than Schoenberg. Despite the dismal economic conditions, his followers forever mustered fresh enthusiasm and energy to carry out their master's plans. One of these entailed a society-sponsored contest for a new chamber music composition. Serving on the jury, Webern could only register disappointment when he wrote to Schoenberg on 3 July 1921: "Regrettably very unenjoyable things. Mostly quite childish stuff."

   Webern's chief task that summer was a reduction for chamber orchestra of Schoenberg's musical drama *Die glückliche Hand*, Op. 18, intended for performance during the society's forthcoming season. Also projected for that fourth year, and so announced in the *Mitteilungen* No. 27 of 18 September 1921, were "ballet scenes" with music by Webern and Berg, to be staged as theatre performances, along with ballets by Debussy and Bartók. "I am sorry that I have not as yet found a subject for a ballet," Webern wrote Schoenberg on 3 July. "I am already a little uneasy about it. I would be so glad to carry out this work. If only there were someone who could provide me with a suitable idea. I cannot think of anybody."[21] Berg confessed that he was confronted with the same problem. However, the society's waning fortunes, obvious from the outset of the new season, were to relieve the friends of their assignments.

   For Schoenberg, that summer had begun with a very disagreeable experience. Immediately after the close of the society's third season, he had taken his family to Mattsee near Salzburg, where he had family ties through his brother's marriage to the daughter of the town's mayor. He should have been assured of an atmosphere conducive to his creative work (at the time he was engaged in the composition of *Die Jakobsleiter*), but an unexpected incident soon upset his peace of mind. Anti-Semitic sentiments had always been widespread among the peasantry, but this had never prevented summer resorts from welcoming Jews as well-paying guests. That summer, however, the township of Mattsee took a step that set an ominous precedent a dozen years before Hitler's rise to power in Germany and a full seventeen years before the Nazi takeover of Austria: a poster was publicly displayed asking all Jews to leave Mattsee immediately. Schoenberg was enraged. While a convert to Protestantism, he was proudly conscious of his Jewish heritage. On 30 June the scandal reached the newspapers. The *Neue Wiener Presse* of that date printed this account, in the section "Kleine Chronik," under the heading "The Baptismal Certificate of the Composer."

Our correspondent from Graz reports a significant experience of the well-known composer Arnold Schoenberg. The artist had chosen Mattsee as his summer residence. A few days ago, he was requested by the community officials there to furnish documentary proof that he was not a Jew. If he were, he would have to leave the village at once, since, according to a resolution, Jews were not permitted to stay in the community. Although Schoenberg could prove that he was a Protestant, he has decided to leave Mattsee. It is hardly astonishing that the artist preferred to avoid further discussions with the community council; but the question remains open whether the federal laws may be ignored in so unabashed a manner by a place like Mattsee.

To Schoenberg, this sort of publicity was extremely odious. His Vienna friends were beside themselves, and Josef Polnauer, who a decade earlier had personally protected Schoenberg from the attacks of an irate anti-Semite, hurried to his side. Some attempts were made to hush the matter up, but the atmosphere at Mattsee had been so poisoned for Schoenberg that, by the middle of July, he moved to nearby Traunkirchen. There, the sympathetic Baroness Anka Löwenthal placed at his disposal her summer home, Villa Josef, complete with private beach, dressing cabin, and boat. This arrangement was to prove so congenial for creative work that Schoenberg extended his stay far into autumn.

On 16 August Webern went to visit Schoenberg in Traunkirchen, and the three days that he spent there as Schoenberg's guest were the highlight of his own brief vacation (16–26 August). It included also an ascent of the Ankogel (3246 m.), a prominent summit of the Hohe Tauern group, and visits to Klagenfurt and the beloved Preglhof. The journey, short as it was, so invigorated him that, after his return to Mödling, he produced in quick succession two orchestral songs (later incorporated into Opus 15). For Schoenberg's birthday on 13 September, Webern returned briefly to Traunkirchen to present him with a collection of Klimt prints, a joint gift from all his disciples.

With the onset of the autumn season, Webern found himself harnessed into a working schedule that demanded more of his time and energy than ever. During the summer, he had accepted appointments as chorus master of the Vienna Schubertbund and of the Mödlinger Männergesangverein, new tasks adding heavily to his schedule as a private teacher and his continuing duties as Vortragsmeister of the Schoenberg Society. That organization now entered upon what was destined to become its final phase. At first, activities continued in accustomed fashion. On 17 October 1921 Webern recorded in his diary, using red pencil to commemorate the signal event, "100th evening," listing the programme as Schoenberg's *Pierrot Lunaire* and Berg's String Quartet. Eleven days later, he sent this progress report to Schoenberg: "In the society I am rehearsing Reger's *Passacaglia*, a piano solo piece by Novák with Miss Novakovic,[22] and a Beethoven sonata for the Sonata Evening (Steuermann, Kolisch). With Miss Eisner I am preparing a classic Lieder Evening: Schumann (*Frauenliebe*) and Hugo Wolf. In addition, five songs by me. Then various other works."

These are the last references to the society's activities in Webern's letters to Schoenberg before the latter returned to Vienna in November. Performances of *Pierrot Lunaire* are recorded as having taken place that autumn in Prague on 28 November (Erwin Stein conducting) and in Vienna on 5 December. However, Schoenberg's insistence that his musicians should always receive payment for their professional services, combined with the ever-worsening economic situation, now resulted in a rapid dwindling of the society's offerings. (The erosion of monetary values was becoming so disastrous that, on 1 December 1921, the frustration of the populace actually exploded into a devastating riot in the streets.) In the entire year following the society's hundredth evening there were only twelve more concerts given in Vienna, according to a letter from Schoenberg to Zemlinsky of 26 October 1922.[23] The letter gives a retrospective survey of the society's activities: 151 individual works had been programmed in a total of 360 renditions (209 of these being repeat performances). Despite such impressive achievements, the society fell victim to the general fiscal collapse. No exact date can be ascertained when the group finally disbanded. Early in 1922 a society patterned after the Vienna model had been organized in Prague. Schoenberg was named honorary president, but on 14 January 1923 he notified Georg Alter, secretary of the Prague chapter, that he felt compelled to devote all his energies to the composition of new works. For the same reason, Schoenberg had withdrawn, ever since the early autumn of 1922, from active leadership in the Vienna organization. Stein and Webern then had been made directors, but their main activity seems to have been the coaching of performers scheduled to appear in concerts of the Prague branch.[24] When the Vienna group was finally liquidated, Stein took over its entire library.

At its height, the Society for Private Musical Performances numbered, in Schoenberg's own words, "300 members, 200 of them good ones."[25] The ideals and activities of the small fraternity, which had to operate under the most adverse conditions, can hardly be overestimated. Within its brief life span, the society richly fulfilled its principal objective: to present a multitude of contemporary composers who, according to Schoenberg's postulate, possessed "physiognomy or name." It also provided a platform where men of diverging aesthetic tenets could meet, compare ideas and receive stimulation. Consciously designed as an institution of learning, the society bestowed rich dividends on all its participants. In addition, the initiative generated by that pioneering group was to have far-reaching effect: the society was the forerunner and prototype of various organizations that were to spring up soon after, such as the International Society for Contemporary Music (1922), the International Composers' Guild (1922), and the League of Composers (1923). The annual Donaueschingen festival, first held in 1921, subscribed to similar ideals. Claude Debussy, whose works ranked so prominently on the group's programmes, once had envisaged just such a "society for musical esotericism," one that would be concerned with "the purity of art" and would serve as "a school at last re-establishing respect for art, which is contaminated by so many people."[26] The French master died on 25 March 1918. Had he but lived to the end of that last war year, he could have witnessed his utopia becoming a reality.

CHAPTER XV

Rise to recognition
(1921–1924)

At the beginning of the same season (1921–22) that witnessed the decline of the Society for Private Musical Performances, Webern assumed an appointment as musical director of Vienna's prestigious Schubertbund. This long-established men's choral society, numbering some 400 members, had formed part of the massive chorus participating in the two *Gurrelieder* performances given in June 1920, under Schoenberg's direction, at the Vienna State Opera. As the composer's appointee, Webern had then coached the chorus in the final rehearsals, which had been of crucial importance, since the Schubertbund was actually about to abandon the project at the last minute. In the end, it yielded only to Schoenberg's urgent personal pleas and the management's threat to hold the club financially responsible if its withdrawal caused the expensive production to fall through. The society's annals note the "excellent manner" of rehearsal by their guest conductor and state that "without Dr Webern's outstanding coaching the Schubertbund would not have had a share in the surpassing success of this magnificent work."[1]

Because of the good impression Webern made on that occasion, the Schubertbund called on him in July 1921 when its conductor, Hermann Schmeidel, resigned to accept a position in Elberfeld. From the start, Webern had misgivings; the appointment was on a year's trial basis, and it stipulated that he would have to share the podium with Schmeidel for the season's two major public performances, including the annual gala concert with orchestra. Furthermore, the pay was low in view of the many services entailed; the club not only appeared in Vienna, but also frequently went on tours. Nevertheless, following Schoenberg's advice, Webern accepted. At first he enjoyed the association. "The sound of this chorus, comprising several hundred singers, often is extraordinary. And I see how they themselves rejoice over what I am already achieving at times," he told Schoenberg on 28 October, commenting on the excellent rehearsal attendance, the high degree of attention and seriousness, and the spontaneous applause accorded him after the work sessions.

On 9 November Webern made his début. The concert, billed as "Liedertafel" included choruses by Schubert, Schumann, Reger, Mair, Pilz, Kirchl, and Marschner. The Sophiensaal was overcrowded, and the evening was a great success. For the Schubertbund's annual gala concert, in which the Vienna Symphony Orchestra participated, the large hall of the Konzerthaus was the setting. In that concert, presented on 13 February and repeated two days later, Webern shared the conducting with Ferdinand Grossmann (the delegate for Schmeidel, who could not obtain leave from his Elberfeld post). Works by Schubert, Strauss, Othegraven, Brahms, Grieg, Volbach, Cornelius, and Wolf composed the programme, which also included two of Mahler's orchestral songs. Hermine Kittel from the State Opera was the guest soloist. The cordial public response should have been gratifying to Webern, but the club's historian relates that "despite the success of both concerts, a certain mood of crisis concerning Dr Webern had broken out." In consequence, a special meeting of the general membership was called on 24 February, during which Webern announced that he was resigning because he "felt himself not suited for the leadership of a men's chorus." There were hints of intrigues. Webern's demanding thoroughness and the intense rehearsal procedure were found too severe by many of the men, to whom choral singing meant primarily an evening of recreation. Since his successor was introduced the same night, Webern's resignation had obviously been pre-arranged. At any rate, the merits of the departing chorus master, who had worked with the group only five months, were recognized by the award of the silver Schubert medal and an extra honorarium of 50,000 kronen.[2]

This abrupt termination of his work with the Schubertbund was somewhat eased for Webern by the much happier association into which he had entered, also during the autumn of 1921, with the Mödlinger Männergesangverein. That group numbered about 60 male singers and, despite its name, supported a women's auxiliary of about 40 voices. The two groups often joined as a mixed chorus, and in due time Webern achieved with them notable performances of masterpieces by Schubert and Bruckner. From the start, he found it congenial to work with this amateur singing group of his own township and to introduce the best of choral literature to its members. Beginning with compositions by Schubert, Schumann, and Mendelssohn, he went on to stage, at Easter of 1922, a "Brahmsfeier" in commemoration of the 25th anniversary of the composer's death.

Also during the spring of 1922 Webern received his first engagement to conduct a Workmen's Symphony Concert. These concerts had been instituted in 1905 by David Josef Bach, who made it his life's mission to bring culture to the working classes. Before the revolution of 1918, such aspirations drew scorn from aristocratic and bourgeois circles. Yet the Workmen's Symphony Concerts had been distinguished from the start by unhackneyed programming and carefully rehearsed performances. Besides Ferdinand Loewe, who led the majority of concerts, conductors included such notables as Richard Strauss, Wilhelm Furtwängler, Georg Szell, and Franz Schalk. In 1917 David Josef Bach had become editor-in-chief of the literature and art section of the widely-read Vienna *Arbeiterzeitung*, and from that vantage point he was able to project his views to a broad public. When the Social Democratic Party rose to power after the fall of the Habsburg régime, the time for more effectively realizing Bach's visions had arrived. The party-sponsored Kunststelle (Arts Council) became the central agency for numerous and diversified cultural activities, and the working classes were now systematically exposed to the best in art and literature. For example, certain performances in the Opera and Burgtheater were specially reserved for them. The number of annual Workmen's Symphony Concerts increased to an average of six and, during the 1921–22 season, the hundredth such concert took place.[3]

It was soon after that anniversary observance that Bach called upon Webern to conduct a performance of Mahler's Third Symphony. Since the enthusiastic response to the concerts generally produced overflow audiences, two performances, on 27 May and 29 May, were scheduled in the large hall of the Konzerthaus. Participants were Emilie Bittner, soloist, the Philharmonic Chorus, the Boys' Chorus under Peterlini, and the Tonkünstler orchestra. Webern notes the event only tersely in his diary; as usual, he does not remark on success or failure. That his success was in fact great, establishing beyond any doubt his reputation as an orchestral conductor, can be learned from several accounts given by Berg to his wife. "Webern was like a king; never before have I seen a happier man than he was afterwards," he commented on 24 May following one of the rehearsals. And after the first public performance he wrote: "Last night the Third Mahler.[4] You just cannot imagine this. Without exaggeration: Webern is the greatest conductor since Mahler—in every respect. After the first and last movements, I felt exactly as one would after an adrenalin injection. I could not stand up. In the evening, I almost forgot about supper. It occurred to me only in bed, and I fetched a can of sardines and bread. I am almost afraid of Monday, it was so exciting."

At that repeat performance, Arnold and Mathilde Schoenberg also were in the audience. Berg's account to Helene of 30 May conveys the astonishing impression that Webern's conducting made on all his friends: "In some respects, it was still more beautiful. This time especially the second section. I sat with Schoenberg. He had not thought it possible. Webern's achievement is such that it can only be compared with that of Mahler himself, and such that all doubts, even those of Mathilde, were swept away to be replaced by unreserved admiration." Webern's unqualified success in this first appearance under the aegis of the Workmen's Symphony Concerts was to earn him the lasting confidence of David Josef Bach. It ushered in an epoch of close artistic collaboration and enduring personal friendship between the two men.

A few days after this triumphant début Webern was on his way to Düsseldorf where he was to conduct his Passacaglia during the Allgemeine Deutsche Tonkünstlerfest.[5] Included in the festival programme were also the Violin Sonata of Paul A. Pisk and the orchestral song cycle *Vom Tode* by Karl Horwitz, Webern's friend from university days. Pisk shared the long train ride to the Rhenish city with Webern. He later vividly recalled Webern's adverse reaction to the lowlands, voiced in his soft Viennese dialect: "Da kann ma nit atmen, dös is unterm Meeresspiegel" (Here one cannot breathe, this is below sea level).[6] Although he was with friends, Webern was so oppressed that he poured out his heart in a postcard to Berg, sent from Düsseldorf on 4 June. He spoke of his "terrible homesickness," which was growing "worse and worse." Never before had he crossed the border with such a heavy heart; never before had he felt so unhappy in a foreign country. And this although the occasion was an auspicious one. For him it simply was "another world." Having a presentiment of what would happen he had taken Rosegger's book *Summer in the Alps* along on the journey to give him "the strength" he needed.

The performance of the Passacaglia took place on 5 June. The programme book contained an analytical synopsis of the piece, furnished by the composer (see Chapter V). In his 19 June report to Berg, Webern called the rendition "rather good," despite insufficient rehearsal time for "so difficult a work," and he added that the reception was "quite warm," especially on the part of the performing musicians. The printed score of the Passacaglia had been released by Universal Edition in time for the occasion.

On his return to Düsseldorf, Webern found a letter from Zemlinsky promising an early performance of the Passacaglia in Prague, a plan to be fulfilled before the end of the year. During the early summer another auspicious development occurred: the Konzertverein, an important institution in Vienna's musical life, asked Webern to conduct the Wiener Symphonieorchester (now the Wiener Symphoniker) in a series of their

17. Jahr · Arbeiter-Sinfonie-Konzerte · 1921/22

SAMSTAG, DEN 27. MAI, UND MONTAG, DEN 29. MAI 1922,
ABENDS 7 UHR, IM GROSSEN KONZERTHAUSSAAL MIT
UNTERSTÜTZUNG DER GEMEINDE WIEN

GUSTAV MAHLER

(GEBOREN AM 18. MAI 1860, GESTORBEN AM 23. MAI 1911

DRITTE SINFONIE

AUSFÜHRENDE:

FRAU EMILIE BITTNER (GESANG), DER PHILHARMONISCHE
CHOR, DER KNABENCHOR DES PROF. PETERLINI, DAS
SINFONIEORCHESTER (KONZERTVEREIN-TONKÜNSTLER)

DIRIGENT: DR. ANTON WEBERN

Preis dieses Programms 100 Kronen

Programme of a Workmen's Symphony Concert (27 May 1922)

popular Sunday afternoon concerts. The invitation was prompted by Webern's recent success with Mahler's Third Symphony. The engagement, to begin in September, would be converted into a permanent appointment if the first three "trial" concerts proved satisfactory.

Greatly heartened by this opportunity for both artistic and financial reward, Webern turned his thoughts to taking a much-needed vacation. Since the summer of 1919, when his stay at Mürzzuschlag had been overshadowed by his father's death, he had toiled steadily without an extended break. Inflation had eaten up his savings, and whatever he earned from professional activities was instantly absorbed by living expenses. The financial situation had become so precarious that Wilhelmine felt compelled to share in the burden. Not only did she forego household help, then considered indispensable by any middle-class family with children, but she also took on work for a Vienna shop specializing in knitted wear. She laboured every spare moment; even when she took the children on an outing, she could be seen making ladies' sweaters and other garments. Although the remuneration was poor, she continued this extra work for several years; in 1924, when Webern began listing the sources of his income in an account book, his wife's earnings still were shown alongside his own. During the worst years of inflation, 1922–4, Webern was forced to supplement the family income by sacrificing from time to time many cherished books from his library. Several of these sales are recorded in his library catalogue—in 1922, for example, he parted with a nine-volume deluxe edition of Shakespeare.

During the spring of that year Schoenberg came to Webern's aid. Wanting to reciprocate for the unstinting help he himself had received in times of emergency, he wrote on 9 June to a patron living in Prague: "May I turn to you on behalf of my friend, Dr Anton von Webern? . . . He is faring very badly! Despite the greatest toil he is incapable of earning what one needs today for a wife and four children. Especially now, however, he sees himself confronted with a summer without income."[7] The initiative apparently brought quick results, for by 19 June Webern could tell Berg that his worries for the summer had been "diminished quite considerably" by a patron's generosity.[8] The gift allowed him to realize his foremost wish: to spend a long vacation with Schoenberg in Traunkirchen. The master had returned there for the summer, this time taking up quarters in the Villa Spaun. Webern and his family rented an inexpensive apartment (including a pianino) near by. They stayed from the middle of July until early September. The idyllic setting, combined with the stimulation of regular evening meetings with Schoenberg, was ideal for a happily productive sojourn. Writing to Berg on 22 July, Webern delighted in the mountains, meadows, and invigorating climate, all of which had a regenerative effect on him. "Yes, in such surroundings, I can collect my thoughts much faster," he told Berg, referring to one of his Five Sacred Songs composed that morning.

Interrupting his stay at Traunkirchen for almost a week, Webern went to Salzburg for a performance of his Five Movements for String Quartet, Op. 5, scheduled within an international festival of contemporary music held 7–10 August. Presenting works by 54 composers of fifteen different nationalities in seven matinée and evening concerts, the festival was to be a blueprint for those henceforth sponsored by the International Society for Contemporary Music, an organization officially founded on 11 August.[9]

Webern's Five Movements were to be played at the 8 August concert, along with compositions by Nielsen, Rangstroem, Ravel, Busoni, Szymanowski, Wellesz, Finke, and Pijper. Coming next to last on the programme, the work was played by the Amar Quartet (Licco Amar, Walter Casper, Paul Hindemith, and Maurits Frank), and it excited a riot that could be subdued only by police intervention. The disturbance was started by Wilhelm Grosz, a Viennese composer seated in one of the front rows. Across the aisle from him was the architect Adolf Loos, Webern's staunch supporter.

> It was during the quiet fourth movement that a loud outcry "furchtbar!" [terrible] was heard [related the pianist-composer Rudolph Ganz, an eye witness]. It was Herr Grosz objecting to the new music. From the other aisle came the equally forceful "Maulhalten!" [Shut up]. Grosz insisted that he had paid for his ticket and was entitled to his opinion, whereupon both men rose and went for each other. Half the audience got up and took an active part in the mêlée. The quartet had fled by this time and police rushed in from all sides. . . . There was hissing and applauding from the different camps, when—suddenly—Anton von Webern appeared atop the orchestra staircase, listening to the overpowering bravos of the progressives and all those who were horrified by the inexcusable incident. The battle of applause lasted at least ten minutes, when it was announced from the stage that the programme would not continue. Anyway, the hall had been ordered cleared by the guardians of the law. . . . Next day some 50 musicians were invited to hear the quartet in its entirety in a special performance in a smaller hall one hour before the evening concert. It was an unforgettable revelation.[10]

In his own report to Berg, written on 12 August after his return to Traunkirchen, Webern told his friend:

In regard to my quartet: rendition very good, really played as music. Unfortunately, however, there was a scandal again. The entire performance was disturbed by laughter. *Constant laughter.* Herr Grosz (the "composer") had a special share in this, so that Loos, when the battle raged between hissing and clapping, jumped on the podium and spoke roughly as follows: "This man has disturbed the performance by constant laughter. For this, he deserves to be publicly branded." I know all this only by way of report. I immediately left the hall. I finally had to appear on the podium. This I did in order to shake Loos' hand *publicly* for his wonderful words. My quartet was repeated the following day for a closed circle. The attending Frenchmen (Honegger, Poulenc, Wiéner) and Englishman (Bliss) were very nice and expressed many cordial sentiments to me.[11]

The international press was quick to report details of the scandal. Indulging in the journalistic aspects of the affair, the correspondent for the London *Daily Telegraph* (9 September 1922) described Webern's appearance on stage at the height of the tumult: "I never saw an angrier man; he is about 35, dry and thin as though pickled in perennial fury, and erect as a ramrod. It was amusing to see him face up to each of his executors as if he were going to kill them, then relent, wring his hands bitterly, glare defiance at the audience, and rush off stiffly into the artists' room." After reporting the calamitous affair in detail, the writer concluded: "But for these ever-recurring scenes, the school, whom no one takes seriously, except Schoenberg, would have fizzled out long ago."[12] The views of most of the other music critics were likewise negative, whether they concentrated on aspects of Webern's music or on the sensationalism of the affair.

On 11 September Webern wrote to Berg from Mödling that the summer had not been very productive for him. The Salzburg affair had put him "out of sorts." Webern had returned from Traunkirchen a few days earlier to make final arrangements with the Konzertverein for the forthcoming three trial concerts that were to precede an engagement for the full season. In formulating the programmes, he wisely chose standard repertoire since only a single rehearsal was allotted to each concert. The first was scheduled for 17 September, but a printers' strike forced its postponement to 24 September. On the following day Berg, who had attended the performance with Schoenberg, wrote to his wife: "The concert was sublime. Webern is the greatest living conductor, since Mahler the greatest altogether. It is indescribable what he achieved in that *one* rehearsal. The *Meistersinger* Prelude was as exciting as a first or last symphony movement by Mahler, and Beethoven's Fifth! The success was colossal. A completely sold out house."

That first programme also included, between the two works mentioned, Schubert's *Unfinished* Symphony. The following Sunday's concert, too, went well. It consisted of Mozart's *Jupiter* Symphony, Wagner's *Siegfried Idyll* and Bruckner's Fourth Symphony. For the third programme, Webern chose Beethoven's *Coriolan* Overture and Violin Concerto, as well as Brahms' First Symphony. However an ear infection forced him to forfeit conducting not only that concert, although he had already rehearsed it, but also the one scheduled for the following Sunday. When he returned to rehearse the 22 October programme, his hopes for a permanent engagement (which seemed already assured by the success of the first two concerts) were suddenly dashed. Webern described the circumstances of his abrupt resignation, when he wrote to Heinrich Jalowetz on 16 November:

> . . . It was during the rehearsal for the next concert—Schubert's C Major Symphony, Mozart's Violin Concerto (with Kolisch as soloist) and Bizet's *L'Arlesienne* Suite—that the incident occurred. I was just rehearsing the Bizet Suite—it *went really very badly*—and was explaining something to the first violins. At this point, the first trombonist rose and gave a speech telling me that I was wrong, I was *not* in a *music school*, I was insulting the orchestra with every word, that this was no way to rehearse, and that I should go to a movie house in order to acquire the necessary routine for myself. I beg you to understand, though, that up to this moment the rehearsal had gone perfectly quietly. I did not have the impression, either, that there was any aversion to it. . . . I answered the speech of the trombonist quite calmly and objectively and conducted the rehearsal to the end (the incident was right at the beginning). Rehearsing proceeded with the *greatest of attention* and in *deadly silence*. Probably they had noticed how deeply hurt I was. During intermission a deputation from the orchestra (among them the trombonist) came and tried to conciliate and to *apologize*. But my decision had been made: after consultation with Schoenberg, I telegraphed the Konzertverein that, because of this incident, I would not conduct the orchestra any more and that I was cancelling the concerts (including the coming one).

Webern told Jalowetz that, subsequently, both the Konzertverein and the directorship of the orchestra formally apologized in writing. But his wounded feelings were not to be soothed:

> I could not go on after this all-surpassing rudeness. Yes, this I must still add: the *first* sentences of the speech-maker were approvingly backed by some members. . . . But there was no enthusiastic general

agreement. I was told that they had great respect for me. And why then had I resigned? Alas, these people absolutely do not want to rehearse. Was I not to be permitted to use fully even this single rehearsal? No, then finish. What this fellow understands to be routine, this I hope *never* to acquire, and certainly not in a movie house. God preserve me from it.[13]

The affair, which shocked all his friends and caused much talk in Vienna, long oppressed Webern. To distract himself, he took up a challenging task: the reduction of Schoenberg's Chamber Symphony, Op. 9, for the same small instrumental ensemble used for *Pierrot Lunaire*. The suggestion had come from Schoenberg during their joint stay at Traunkirchen, and its purpose was to enable the scheduling of both works on one programme.

In mid-December, Webern went to Prague with Polnauer and Steuermann for a performance of his Passacaglia on 17 December.[14] Zemlinsky, who conducted, paired the piece with Beethoven's Ninth in one of his regular symphony concerts. Webern was gratified by this great distinction. After the concert, he sent an enthusiastic message to Schoenberg. Zemlinsky added a note confirming the acclaim that Webern's "extraordinary" work had received. The active promotion of Webern's compositions by Universal Edition was beginning to show results. Schoenberg, too, was trying to further his disciple's career. In a letter of 23 August to Josef Stransky, conductor of the New York Philharmonic Orchestra, he had praised both Berg and Webern as "two real musicians—not Bolshevik illiterates, but men with a musically educated ear!" Specifically recommending the Passacaglia, he wrote that it had been "repeatedly performed with unmitigated success" and that it was "not yet such a 'dangerous' work."[15]

Schoenberg's assessment was apparently shared by Franz Schalk, who conducted the Passacaglia on 17 February 1923 in one of the concerts of Vienna's select Gesellschaft der Musikfreunde. It was a homecoming of sorts, for in the same large hall of the Musikverein the music had first been heard on 4 November 1908, when a group of Schoenberg's students hired an orchestra to present their compositions, in an early bid for public notice. In the fifteen years since, Webern's Opus 1 had come to life only on a few occasions, primarily when he himself conducted. It was most gratifying for him to hear it interpreted now by such acknowledged masters as Zemlinsky and Schalk. The signal recognition by his home city's leading orchestra augured well for a brighter future. Also, the reaction of both audiences and newspaper critics had markedly changed since 1908, when the première of the Passacaglia had met with noisy disapproval. Now, on 19 February, the reporter of the *Neues Wiener*

Tagblatt wrote: "A work full of warmth and enterprise, kept together by the clasps of form." Noting that the piece was "received with enthusiasm" and that "the composer was called onstage," the reviewer added: "One regrets that this first work remained an Opus 1, that not six or twelve such works followed it: Webern would now be in a leading position."

This critic, who only voiced the attitude of the perennially conservative majority, would no doubt have been alarmed to learn of an event that coincided, quite by chance, with the Vienna performance of the Passacaglia: One morning that same February of 1923 Schoenberg assembled his closest associates in his Mödling home[16] and revealed to them for the first time the fundamental principles of his "method of composition with twelve tones related solely to each other," a technique that was to add a new dimension to the craft of writing music (see Chapter XVIII). The revolutionary theory had been in the process of evolution for many years. Various composers, including Josef Matthias Hauer and Webern himself, had experimented, simultaneously and independently, with the same idea. (During the summer of 1922, Webern had actually written out, in connection with one of his compositions [Op. 15, No. 4], a twelve-tone row with its further functional possibilities of inversion, retrograde, and retrograde inversion.) The new method answered the quest for an expansion of musical organization. With its adaptability to canonic and other contrapuntal devices, it was to prove especially suited to Webern's particular genius.

That historic meeting was, to be sure, but one of many gatherings at Schoenberg's home, which stood open to his friends at virtually every hour. It is certainly the greatest homage to Schoenberg as a teacher that his pupils continued to seek his inspiration and guidance long after they had become independent and recognized in their own careers. As frequent guests at his table, they participated in the many searching discussions, in which new ideas were put to the test. The foremost criterion for the validity of these ideas was their link with tradition, and actual music-making in the Schoenberg home was also anchored in that foundation. Polnauer confirmed this when he recalled those days: "In the house Bernhardgasse 6, chamber music was played every Sunday afternoon except during the summer vacation. Without exception, only works of the classic masters were played. Arnold Schoenberg sat at the violist's desk. Anton Webern was the cellist. The first violinist was usually Rudolf Kolisch, and at the grand piano was Eduard Steuermann."[17]

The early months of 1923 brought Webern satisfaction both as a composer and a conductor. The Havemann Quartet,[18] an ensemble renowned for its exemplary renditions, performed the Five Movements,

Op. 5, in several concerts in Berlin and elsewhere, undeterred by the scandal excited by the work at Salzburg the year before or by the derision most music critics continued to heap on it. As conductor, Webern, after his ill-fated experiences with the Schubertbund and the Konzertverein, now concentrated on his work with the Mödlinger Männergesangverein. In commemoration of its 75th anniversary, he prepared with the group Schubert's Mass No. 6 in E flat major, "the most magnificent work that exists," as Berg wrote to his wife in anticipation of the performance, which took place in Mödling's historic St Othmar Church on the morning of Sunday, 13 May.[19] Noting the event in his diary, Webern added: "Mother's 70th birthday." Seventeen years after her death, Webern thus celebrated his mother's memory with this royal offering.

Two weeks later, Webern readied himself to travel to Berlin. There, Heinrich Jalowetz and Paul Pella had organized an Austrian Music Week. Jalowetz was to conduct Schoenberg's *Gurrelieder* and Pella Mahler's Eighth Symphony in two performances each. For a special "Novitäten-Abend" (Evening of Novelties), Orchestra Songs by Bittner, Steuermann's piano reduction of Schoenberg's Chamber Symphony, Op. 9, Zemlinsky's Maeterlinck Songs, Op. 13, the world première of Berg's Three Orchestral Pieces, Op. 6, and Webern's Passacaglia were scheduled. At Berg's request, the festival organizers assigned his pieces to Webern, who also was to conduct the Bittner songs and his own work. While in Berlin, Webern stayed at the home of Dr Curt Sachs, the musicologist. He related the week's happenings in three reports to Schoenberg, who was about to return to his summer retreat at Traunkirchen in early June. The orchestra was described as "grand" and "admirable in its stamina during indefatigable rehearsing." Webern found Berg's Three Orchestral Pieces "infinitely difficult" and he briefed Schoenberg (to whom they had been dedicated as a 40th birthday offering) on a "painful situation" which had arisen: "I will be able to do only *two* (Nos. 1 and 2)," he wrote on 3 June.[20] "By no means did I want this to happen. But Berg himself begged me to render the first two as clearly as possible rather than to have all three unsatisfactory. Time is *absolutely* lacking to bring out all three clearly. You will be angry about this. But it is really so: the work is too difficult—such a completely incomprehensible muddle would be left that Berg could not get anything at all out of it." The concert, which took place on 5 June in the hall of the Philharmonie, was a great success in every way, as Webern reported to Schoenberg the following day. "Berg had to appear several times on the podium," he wrote with satisfaction, adding: "My piece also went very well."

With the coming of summer, Webern once again faced an extended

period without any prospect of gainful employment. What little money
he had earned during the season had vanished through the ravaging
inflation, which was defying all attempts at control. In desperation he
turned to Schoenberg, who was in a more fortunate position. Enjoying
wide-spread fame by now, Schoenberg received income from many
different sources, which included some in countries not affected by the
monetary erosion. It attests to his high character that his own relative
security only spurred him on to wield his influence for the good of less
fortunate fellow musicians. When he heard of the Friends' Relief
Mission, a Quaker-sponsored charity administered by the Philadelphia
publishing firm of Theodore Presser, he submitted the names of Berg,
Webern, and Hauer as needy and worthy recipients. He even turned
over his honorarium for an article published in the Paris periodical
Courrier Musical to a fund established by the municipality of Mödling to
aid deserving artists. Acting specifically on behalf of Webern,
Schoenberg wrote from Traunkirchen no fewer than three eloquent
letters on a single day (9 July 1923) to Mrs Renée Hendsch of Geneva,
one of his own supporters; a Mr Boissevain, a Dutch patron of the arts;
and Werner Reinhart of Winterthur.[21] The latter, a wealthy businessman
and excellent amateur clarinetist (Stravinsky dedicated his solo clarinet
pieces to him), was not only a leader in Swiss musical affairs but was also
active in furthering deserving composers in other countries. Two of the
patrons solicited, Mr Boissevain and Dr Reinhart, acted immediately,
the latter with the substantial sum of 500 Swiss francs. Webern's
gratitude to Dr Reinhart was expressed by the dedication of his Five
Songs, Op. 4, which appeared in print on 23 August. (That spring
Universal Edition had released the Five Pieces for Orchestra, Op. 10,
following publication of Opera 1, 5 and 7 the year before.)

Because of his economic plight, Webern could not afford an extended
vacation like the one in Traunkirchen the summer before. Only at the
end of July did he take his wife and the two younger children (the two
older children were sent to relatives in Vordernberg and Klagenfurt) for
a week's stay at the Bürgeralm, an alpine meadow at timberline, high
above the village of Afflenz. There living was "exceedingly cheap," he
wrote somewhat apologetically to Schoenberg, who had just completed
his intensive money-raising efforts on Webern's behalf.

> Perhaps you found it frivolous that I dared, in such uncertain times,
> to undertake a tour of several days with my family. But, by God, the
> extra expense, compared to staying at home, was quite insignificant
> [he commented on 30 July after returning to Mödling]. I knew this
> would be so beforehand. Nevertheless, my wife was entirely against
> the idea. But I wanted to give her and the children a little pleasure;

therefore I did not give in to her. . . . It is impossible to describe what a beneficial influence the stay at such height has had upon all of us. Without exaggeration: the purest physical rebirth. . . . I carried Christl across snow fields, in an icy mountain storm, almost to the summit of the Hochschwab. In a shepherd's hut we warmed our frozen limbs by the fire. Never before has it seemed to me as beautiful "up there" as this time with my family.

From that summer of 1923 on, Webern systematically preserved picture postcards of places he visited. He noted details of his holiday activities on the back of the cards, which he kept in specially designated envelopes.[22] Pressed mountain flowers, in tiny, neatly inscribed folders were often added. These envelopes constituted Webern's cherished "album" of souvenirs. His love of the mountains and their flora is also reflected in his personal diary, which he kept up more regularly from 1923 on, after making only sparse entries in preceding years. Notes on professional activities are comparatively few and limited to highlights. Most of the diary space was devoted to family events and to records of mountain excursions. These were the pivots around which Webern's private world revolved, and they provided the inspiration for his creative impulses. There are entries on family happenings which might appear trivial to others, but were important to him, such as the day when Peter began to walk, or the dates when the children, one by one, went to school for the first time, properly attending special Mass beforehand. The purchase of a pair of "Lederhosen" for "Peterl," or "Christerl's" first attempt at ice-skating, all rate separate entries. Notes like these appear in the diary until the children were fully grown. They show, perhaps better than anything else could, the love and care that Webern lavished on each member of his family. One of the most touching entries, written in March 1924, concerns "Peps," the family dog, to whom Webern devotes a long and tender obituary.[23]

During the summer of 1923, Webern composed three of his Five Canons on Latin Texts, Op. 16. Before his activities with the Mödlinger Männergesangverein began again in the autumn, he went in early September to Traunkirchen to offer Schoenberg birthday congratulations. Not long afterwards, Mathilde Schoenberg, who had been ailing for some time, had to be brought to Vienna. A month later, on 22 October, she died. The widower took the loss very hard. Zemlinsky, his brother-in-law, tried to help as much as he could, and so did the entire entourage of friends and students. But Schoenberg remained depressed, brooding, and irritable. The domestic situation was a heavy burden on him. His young son Görgi still needed care and supervision, and his daughter Trude, who had married Felix Greissle, had the responsibilities of her own household and could lend only limited assistance. Before a year had passed, on 28 August 1924, Schoenberg remarried. His new wife, Gertrud—the attractive, witty, and talented daughter of a prominent Vienna physician—was the sister of Rudolf Kolisch, who had been, since the days of the Society for Private Musical Performances, one of Schoenberg's most trusted friends.

Kolisch, a champion of new music from the outset of his career, had taken Webern's Four Pieces, Op. 7, into his repertoire. Accompanied by Erna Gál,[24] he performed the work in Vienna that autumn—"really excellently," as Berg wrote to his wife on 22 November 1923. The same autumn Webern's string quartet and George songs were heard in concerts of the Prague section of the Society for Private Musical Performances. His music was also included that season in a New Music cycle at Hamburg, organized by Josef Rufer and Hans Heinz Stuckenschmidt and patterned after the practices of the Vienna Society.

On 7 December Webern conducted the Mödlinger Männergesangverein in its annual autumn concert. A few days later, he began what was to be a very fruitful association with another choral group, the Singverein. This chorus had been founded in 1919, on David Josef Bach's initiative, as one of the special projects of the Kunststelle, the Social Democratic Party's cultural agency. Activities had been lagging, however, for want of a suitable director. Bach had attended the performance of the Schubert Mass on 13 May and had been greatly impressed by Webern's achievement with the Mödling society after only one season's training. Recognizing Webern's ability, he had contacted him concerning a project he had in mind: the development of the original Singverein into a large mixed chorus drawn from the working classes, a chorus that would be capable of joining in the Workmen's Symphony Concerts for the presentation of the most demanding masterworks. The ambitious plan called for the creation of a city-wide chorus that could take its place beside Vienna's established choral organizations, thereby proving that a group of amateurs from the proletariat could be moulded into an artistically satisfying unit. For Webern's first rehearsal, on 13 December, some 80 singers turned out[25] (the number soon increased).

Webern's association with the chorus was to constitute the happiest period in his career as an interpretative musician; encompassing a decade of success, it brought him ample recognition for his toils and aspirations. During the first season, the Singverein tried its wings publicly only in a limited way. On 10 April 1924 Webern notes in his diary its first appearance—as part of a concert given in the festival hall of the Hofburg by the Society for Popular Music Culture—in three Brahms settings of folksongs (*Abschiedslied*, *In stiller Nacht*, and *Schnitter Tod*).

On 4 June, in another guest performance, Webern conducted the group in a choral adaptation of *An der schönen blauen Donau* by Johann Strauss. The first full-scale public concert was not given until March 1925.

Webern's directorship of the Singverein improved his economic situation considerably. While the monthly salary was modest, it was substantially augmented whenever the chorus appeared in the Workmen's Symphony Concerts. The monthly revenue from the Mödling choral society was even smaller, but the two sources of income, added to that from private teaching, enabled Webern to weather the cataclysm then sweeping away every semblance of financial stability. During 1924 the depreciation of currency assumed fantastic dimensions. The havoc wrought by the runaway inflation could be halted only when the national treasury declared bankruptcy. The value of money was consolidated on a new basis as of 20 December 1924, when one million kronen became 100 schillings.[26] Webern lists his income in kronen in his account book through February of 1925; schillings are given thereafter.

Webern began his account book in January of 1924 and continued it systematically until February 1945. Each month the sources of revenue are detailed. Abbreviations are used throughout, but the names of individuals and organizations can be readily identified. At the outset of 1924, three private students were listed: Eisner, Manschinger, and Zenk. Both Manschinger and Zenk matched with their individual monthly fees the salary Webern was then receiving from the Singverein, namely, 500,000 kronen. Eisner paid considerably more: 800,000 kronen. By contrast, Webern received from the Mödlinger Männergesangverein 400,000 kronen a month. To these productive earnings were added contributions from the Presser Foundation (Webern listed $10 in his diary, giving the equivalent as 694,400 kronen) and from the Anbruch fund administered by Paul Stefan (350,000 kronen). Webern's total income for 1924 was 45,534,600 kronen. In January he had earned 3,744,400 kronen. During the following months, the picture fluctuated according to the number of pupils and some occasional extra sources of income. On 11 March 1924, for instance, Webern received from the Viennese nerve specialist, Dr Norbert Schwarzmann, an "Ehrenhonorar" of 3,000,000 kronen, almost the equivalent of an entire month's income from other sources. The occasion, listed in the diary, was an evening in Dr Schwarzmann's home during which his Five Movements, Op. 5, and Four Pieces, Op. 7, were played by Kolisch and his fellow artists, including the pianist Erna Gál. The evening had been suggested by Adolf Loos following a performance of these works in a public concert on 3 March. In a letter to Kolisch the next day, Webern voiced his distress when he spoke of this concert and of the "abominable" restaurant where they gathered afterwards: "I felt as if I were among madmen and ran away deprived of all my senses. Even today it oppresses me like a bad dream. . . . Last evening I could not listen at all while my pieces were being played: the entire row of people in front of me was bent over with laughter."

Dr Schwarzmann (to whom Webern later dedicated his Four Songs, Op. 13) was generous in his support of Schoenberg, Berg, and Webern. His home, at Krugerstrasse 17, was the scene of frequent musical soirées. Schoenberg's Serenade, Op. 24, was performed there for the first time on 2 May 1924, for an audience of invited guests.[27] Webern, who had coached the chamber ensemble, was remunerated with 6,000,000 kronen. The same spring, Webern received additional financial aid, coupled with the first official civic recognition of his status in Vienna's musical life: on 1 May he recorded in his diary that he received the "Prize of the City of Vienna" in the amount of 10,000,000 kronen. (He had petitioned for the award the previous autumn, along with some 500 other musicians.) The official notification, dated 29 April 1924, stated that Webern's selection by the jury—Julius Bittner, Joseph Marx, and Richard Strauss—had been unanimous. Since Berg, too, received the prize, the honour was doubly significant in its manifest encouragement of representatives of the avant-garde. The congratulatory message was signed by the mayor of Vienna, Dr Karl Seitz. He expressed the hope that the prize would fire Webern's creative spirit to ever greater achievements, bringing happiness not only to Vienna's art-minded populace but also to the entire German people and to the world. Flattering as the accolade was, Webern could not but ponder the anonymity of the bureaucratic process. Two weeks earlier, Berg, after attending the 10 April début appearance of the Singverein, had written on the back of his programme: "At this concert, Webern was presented to the mayor of Vienna, Dr Seitz, who asked him, 'Are you a professional musician?'" In connection with the awards, there was a small exhibition displaying the work of the prize winners in the various categories. Webern and Berg were represented with music manuscripts, pictures, and printed scores. A few months later the mayor sent each of them, as a souvenir of the festive occasion, the fascimile sketches of Mahler's Tenth Symphony, published under the auspices of the composer's widow.[28]

The recognition by his native city somewhat compensated Webern for a disappointment shortly afterwards. The manuscript of his Five Sacred Songs, Op. 15, mailed to America in early February as his entry for the Berkshire Chamber Music Composition Contest, was returned without having placed. On the other hand, he was heartened by the fact that two of his works, the Six Bagatelles, Op. 9, and Six Trakl Songs, Op. 14, were scheduled for first performances at the Donaueschingen festival in July. Before that event he travelled to Prague for the première of Schoenberg's monodrama *Erwartung* on 6 June. As the climax of an ISCM festival, the production was but one of several staged in honour of Schoenberg's approaching 50th birthday. After his return from Prague, Webern concentrated on coaching the ensemble he was to conduct in the Donaueschingen première of his Trakl songs. Clara Kwartin was the singer, and Rudolf Kolisch headed the instrumentalists.

Although then only in its fourth year, the Donaueschingen festival was already regarded as a favourite meeting place for both the musical élite and the international press. Presented under the nominal auspices of the Gesellschaft der Musikfreunde, the annual event enjoyed the patronage of Prince Egon Fürstenberg, who personally issued the invitations to participating artists and opened his stately castle for the receptions highlighting the social events. In 1924, Viennese composers on the programme included, besides Webern, Arnold Schoenberg (whose Serenade, Op. 24, was to receive its first public hearing) and Josef Matthias Hauer.

Leaving for Donaueschingen on the evening of 17 July, Webern travelled through the night and all of the following day. His two compositions were performed in the Sunday matinée concert on 20 July. The critics devoted long accounts to his works and were unanimous in recognizing him as a unique musical personality. One called him "a kind of musical Beardsley" (*Neue Zürcher Zeitung*, 25 July). Of the Bagatelles, it was observed that they "surpassed all that had gone before through their brevity, measurable only in seconds, and through their audacities of sound effects. . . . Emerging, so to speak, from the unconscious, they had something curiously compelling in them, though going beyond all usual concepts" (*Dresdner Neueste Nachrichten*, 25 July). Another critic saw in the quartet pieces "a concentration of musical thinking, a conciseness of expression that convinced even the unprepared listener of the spirituality of this introvert musician" (*Wiener Morgenzeitung*, 27 July). Regarding the Trakl songs, one reviewer held that "through their bizarre, jagged rhythms and melodies they do violence to the broadly flowing, darkly glowing music of Trakl's verses. However, if one disregards Trakl, Webern's songs create, in a purely musical respect, a highly original impression" (*Deutsche Allgemeine Zeitung*, 26 July). On 23 July, shortly after his return home, Webern reported to Berg:

The journey through the Tyrol and across the Lake of Constance—it was enormously choppy and is as large as a sea—was wonderful. The reception in Donaueschingen very cordial. Schoenberg stayed in the castle, I in a private home—excellent. We held various rehearsals. On Sunday morning my quartet pieces and songs were performed. Unfortunately, I could not rehearse any more with the Hindemith Quartet.[29] But the performance was very good all the same. After the first two movements there was laughter. I then considered not conducting my songs. Finally calm. The songs went excellently. Miss Kwartin performed brilliantly. She sang really beautifully, faultless in intonation, very convincingly, and had a very great success. On Sunday evening there was a truly splendid performance of the Serenade.[30]

That summer, Universal Edition, in accord with Webern's growing reputation, brought out not only the Bagatelles and the Trakl songs, but also the Three Little Pieces for Cello and Piano, Op. 11. In the autumn the Five Sacred Songs, Op. 15, followed. With obvious gratification Webern noted the various publication dates in his diary.

The diary also provides a detailed account of the ten-day vacation, begun on 25 July, that brought Webern and his family back to the Bürgeralm, the mountain retreat they had enjoyed so much the year before. A highlight of their stay was another ascent of the Hochschwab, minutely described in all its stages. Brief as that period of recreation was, Webern's notes radiate the zest with which he lived each hour in the alpine solitude, contemplating nature's singular manifestations at the last outposts of plant life. He had a faculty for making each excursion—even if it lasted only one or two days—an experience that revitalized his entire being. Fully aware of this secret source of energy, he went to the heights as often as possible. From spring to autumn, hardly a month was allowed to pass without an outing, and sometimes a climb was ventured even in the middle of winter. Webern visited most frequently the Rax and the Schneealpe, peaks closest to Vienna, but occasionally he sought more distant goals, even if they demanded all-night train rides. Despite Webern's restricted funds, such outings were by no means an extravagance, since their cost was quite negligible. Using the train was inexpensive, and so was the overnight stay in a hut. A hardy mountaineer, Webern was quite willing to sleep on a primitive mattress or a pile of hay. Self-sufficient and of frugal tastes, he carried all necessary provisions in his rucksack and was satisfied with a bowl of hot soup or a glass of milk even when prepared meals were available. The physical strain of climbing never deterred him, nor did inclement weather. Only another alpinist can appreciate the enthusiasm and stamina required to endure the hardships connected with mountaineering. Any full understanding of Webern's personality must take into account his passion for mountain climbing—a drive bordering on obsession. Behind his quiet gentleness there lay a dogged perseverance, a tough fibre that made him willing and able to undergo efforts considered futile or sheer folly by others. The analogy to Webern's life as a creative musician is obvious.

Back home on 4 August, Webern prepared for an arduous season. It began on 10 August with an appearance of the Singverein at a "Festakademie" in celebration of the 50th birthday of David Josef Bach (held in the Grünes Tor, Lerchenfelderstrasse 14), during which Webern conducted his chorus in Brahms' setting of *Abschiedslied*, Maier's setting of *Schatz, wo fehlt es dir?*, Strauss' *An der schönen blauen Donau*, and Mozart's *Scherzkanon*. "For me, composing is over for the time being," he wrote to Berg on 29 August, telling him that the choral rehearsals for Schoenberg's *Die glückliche Hand*, begun two days earlier, were being held daily and absorbed many hours. (In his income book Webern listed no fewer than 29 rehearsals in the Volksoper and fourteen in the Staatsoper, earning him 6,100,000 kronen.) Schoenberg's expressionist drama, based on his own text, was scheduled for first performance in Vienna's Volksoper on 14 October, almost eleven years after completion of the score. Fritz Stiedry conducted the première, and the composer himself a subsequent performance. Reporting to Zemlinsky on the work's "brilliant success," Webern mentioned that it was given on a double bill together with Schubert's "wholly delightful" opera *Der häusliche Krieg*, conducted by Jalowetz.

The Schoenberg première followed in the wake of the composer's 50th birthday celebration on 13 September. On that day, an official ceremony had been held in the Vienna Town Hall. It included a performance of the chorus *Friede auf Erden*, Op. 13 (sung by members of the State Opera chorus under Felix Greissle) and the première of the Wind Quintet, Op. 26 (played by an ensemble from the Vienna Philharmonic). The evening before, a private supper party had been given in Mödling,[31] during which Webern, on behalf of the circle gathered round the master, presented him with a leather-bound album containing a large collection of photographs of his family and friends. In Frankfurt, an entire series of festival concerts was organized in Schoenberg's honour, and many other performances of his music were given throughout the world. Universal Edition opened an Arnold Schoenberg Library for Modern Music, which made scores of contemporary music available for study. The *Musikblätter des Anbruch* devoted a special issue to him with articles and testimonials by his closest friends and colleagues. Webern's brief tribute summed up his sentiments: "It was just twenty years ago that I became Arnold Schoenberg's pupil. However, much as I endeavour to, I cannot grasp the difference between then and now. Friend and pupil: one was always the other. And this beginning . . . 'Jubilation: no beginning and no end!' (*Die Jakobsleiter*)."[32]

On 9 October, amidst the fever of final preparations for the première of *Die glückliche Hand*, Webern's Five Sacred Songs, Op. 15, received their first performance. The event is recorded in the composer's diary (for details, see Chapter XVI). Intensive coaching for the two premières, the regular rehearsals with the Singverein and the Mödlinger Männergesangverein, and Webern's private lesson schedule would seem to have precluded any thought of creative work. Nonetheless, the cycle of Five Canons, Op. 16, and Webern's first composition in strict dodecaphonic technique, the *Kinderstück*, were completed that autumn.

CHAPTER XVI

Opera 12–16—Unfinished projects—Arrangements (1914–1924)

THIS CHAPTER ENCOMPASSES Webern's creative work from 1914 to 1924, a period devoted primarily to the writing of songs. Because of the great number of compositions, both finished and unfinished, which fall into this time span, and because of their intertwining chronology, it is deemed advantageous, for the sake of clarity, to discuss the works in three groups. The completed song cycles (Opera 12–16) will be described first, then the numerous unfinished projects, and finally the arrangements both of Webern's own works and those of Schoenberg.

Opera 12–16

The Three Little Pieces for Cello and Piano, Op. 11, composed in spring 1914, were, strictly speaking, Webern's last utterances in the aphoristic style, with which he had been preoccupied for several years. Following Schoenberg's suggestion, he had already attempted a composition in more extended form, the Cello Sonata, only to lay it aside (after drafting one movement) in favour of the Three Little Pieces. Then, in the same spring of 1914, he entered upon a long period of vocal writing, which was to continue through the Two Songs, Op. 19 (1926), to be interrupted only by a few instrumental essays that were never completed. A poem obviously does not allow a musical setting to be terser than the span of its text. Therefore, by turning once again to the *Lied* at this juncture, Webern imposed upon himself a form of discipline that would help him break with his ever more compressed mode of expression and arrive at more extended musical structures.

Thanks to the composer's habit of dating his manuscripts, it is possible to reconstruct the genesis of the many songs originating from 1914 on. As will be seen, the cycles Opera 12 to 15 by no means evolved in a chronological sequence. Instead, the individual songs came into being at overlapping periods of time and apparently without a preconceived plan as to their ultimate place within a fixed work. For example, "Die Einsame," the first song of Opus 13 to be composed, was written early in 1914, a year before Webern finished two of the songs later finding their place in the Opus 12 set. The double canon "Fahr hin, o Seel'," eventually assigned the closing position in the Five Sacred Songs, Op. 15, actually came first in date of composition (1917), the other four being composed only several years later (1921–22). Another case in point is that of the six songs, all written in 1917, that were later to find their separate places in Opera 12, 13, 14, and 15. For the sake of an exact chronological survey, the origin of each individual song will be traced.

The trend towards longer compositions began with the Three Orchestral Songs (1913–14). On 2 May 1914, when Webern sent Schoenberg the manuscript of "Leise Düfte" (the song later accorded opening position in that cycle), he included with it the fair copy of another orchestral song recently composed. This song was "Die Einsame," based on words by Wang-Seng-Yu from *Die chinesische Flöte*, a collection of Chinese poetry freely transcribed into German by Hans Bethge. A sketch for "Die Einsame" bears Webern's note that it was written at Kremsergasse 1, Vienna, in 1914. The day is the 16th, but the month is undecipherable. Presumably it was February, since on the 18th of that month Webern informed Schoenberg that he was setting a poem from *Die chinesische Flöte*, as well as one from Strindberg's *Ghost Sonata*. The latter text was "Schien mir's, als ich sah die Sonne," for it appears in a draft dated "Winter 1913–14." Webern scored the Strindberg poem first for soprano and alto chorus, with the solo parts designated for boys' voices, and with instruments added in condensed score. The inspiration for this combination no doubt came from Berg, who had enthusiastically pointed out Strindberg's interpolation of musical situations in certain dramas, specifically mentioning a chorus of sopranos and altos accompanied by strings and harp.[1] Webern's first conception of "Schien mir's, als ich sah die Sonne" was sketched out for only five measures; he then transformed the basic musical idea into a setting for voice and piano (now known as Op. 12, No. 3). The draft in this form is dated 31 January 1915. During the same month, Webern had composed, likewise for voice and piano, "Der Tag ist vergangen" (Op. 12, No. 1), based on a folk text. The sketches are dated 13 January 1915. Into this period also falls, besides incomplete drafts of two Trakl songs, a first conception of "In der Fremde," a poem by Li-Tai-Po in *Die chinesische Flöte*. The sketches, dated "Hietzing 1915" (Webern's address before he joined the army in February) are for voice and instruments, but the initial musical ideas completely differ from the 1917 version.

The 22 months of Webern's life in the army—February 1915 to December 1916—were almost barren of creative activity, except for some attempts at composing "Wiese im Park," a poem by Karl Kraus. The extant drafts—two of which are dated "Leoben 1916"—are for voice with instruments and voice with piano, respectively. The settings show some similarities of approach, yet both differ substantially from the final version of 1917. The Leoben period formed for Webern the closing phase of his life in uniform. There he enjoyed a measure of privacy and had a piano at his disposal, very welcome after the many months of musical deprivation. He then also participated in a chamber music group, an experience that stimulated him to begin a string quartet immediately after his discharge, when he established residence in Vienna in early January of 1917.

The first composition completed that year was the song "Gleich und Gleich" for voice and piano, based on a poem by Goethe. The draft is dated 31 March. A few days later, on 10 April, Webern sketched out, also for voice and piano, his setting of "Die geheimnisvolle Flöte," another of Li-Tai-Po's poems from *Die chinesische Flöte.* With these two songs, the cycle of Four Songs, Op. 12, was actually completed, although it was not to be published until the summer of 1925. The work then appeared in the sequence: 1. "Der Tag ist vergangen" 2. "Die geheimnisvolle Flöte" 3. "Schien mir's, als ich sah die Sonne" 4. "Gleich und Gleich." The first song had an advance printing in May 1922 as an insert to the *Musikblätter des Anbruch.* Webern's copy of this publication, found in his estate, contains numerous corrections and additions. These were later incorporated into the Universal Edition release. Webern sent a copy of the latter to Berg, who responded on 12 October 1925:

It seems to me as if I see you in an entirely new light. What atmosphere in the Strindberg song. And altogether, what great diversity in the four songs! The last, for example: such charm is to be found nowhere else in all music. This kind of song by you is a veritable dispenser of joy for me, a distributor of delight that radiates through my entire being. It is as if on gloomy days the sun breaks suddenly through, and one does not know at all why one is suddenly happy. It is just the same with the scent of flowers. . . . .

In his diary, Webern notes the first performance of the Four Songs as having taken place during January 1927, but he gives no details. A diary entry of 1926 records: "In October, a Dutch singer performed 'Gleich und Gleich.'" On 25 October 1929, Ruzena Herlinger, with the pianist

Stefan Askenase, rendered a group of songs selected from the Opera 4 and 12 cycles at the Palais des Beaux-Arts at Brussels. The same year, three of the Four Songs were heard in Frankfurt. Webern marked his own copy of the printed work with durations for each song as follows: I. $2\frac{1}{2}$–3′ II. 3′ III. $2\frac{1}{2}$′ IV. 1′.

The creative flow that followed Webern's release from the army continued at Klagenfurt, where the composer moved on 24 May 1917, prior to going to Prague in August. During these weeks, early summertime and the serene landscape of Carinthia inspired a profusion of musical ideas. Webern tried to proceed with his string quartet, but vocal writing soon took precedence once again. On 1 July he told Berg that he again was deep in composition. At first he had experimented a great deal. But now two orchestral songs had come off "successfully." One was "Wiese im Park" by Karl Kraus, the other "Abendland III," based on a poem of Trakl. A week earlier, Webern had informed Schoenberg that he had been busy with the two songs, adding: "Gradually, I am gaining clarity again. How much I owe to your *Pierrot!*" On 13 June, he had mentioned that he had brought along the scores of *Pierrot*, *Erwartung*, and the George songs.[2] "I am occupying myself almost exclusively with your music," he wrote. "Every day I play in these works."

The draft of "Wiese im Park" (Op. 13, No. 1), the Kraus poem Webern had first begun setting at Leoben during autumn of 1916, is dated 16 June 1917. "Abendland III" was sketched out the following week. This poem by Georg Trakl was but one of many of the Austrian poet's verses inspiring the composer to musical realization.[3] There were, in fact, fifteen settings in all, but only seven were completed; of these, "Abendland III" (Op. 14, No. 4), drafted on 23 June 1917, was the first.

Webern's diary records a mountain excursion to the Klagenfurt Hut on 5 and 6 July. From there he sent Schoenberg greetings and reported: "I have completed a third orchestral song." The remark probably referred to "In der Fremde" (Op. 13, No. 3),[4] the poem which Webern had attempted to set in 1915. On 20 July the final draft of the double canon "Fahr hin, o Seel'" (Op. 15, No. 5) was finished. It was preceded by two preliminary sketches marked only "Klagenfurt 1917." On a piece of paper, later found inserted in his copy of Strindberg's *Blaubuch*, the composer had jotted down the verses, noting as source "P. R. *Erdsegen*, 13 June 1917, Klagenfurt," a reference to the book by Peter Rosegger. While Webern applied the term "orchestral songs" to all four compositions completed during that two-month period at Klagenfurt, the differences in their instrumentation eventually led him to place them into three separate cycles ("Wiese im Park" and "In der Fremde" in Op. 13, "Abendland III" in Op. 14, and "Fahr hin, o Seel'" in Op. 15).

On 18 August Webern wrote to Berg from Prague: "Now I am mourning the end of summer, i.e. the time when I could work. I have gone along the right paths. Schoenberg has confirmed this. Now I am writing quite differently. I have composed four orchestral songs. Homogeneous sounds, in part long themes, altogether something entirely different from before the war. I have felt this for some time. Now when I could have proceeded so well with my work, I must be in the theatre instead. . . . My conscience bothers me. It is our duty to compose." When Schoenberg commended his latest products, Webern modestly responded on 12 September: "This year I have in truth tried again to follow your *Pierrot* directly." With gratification he added: "Your judgement of my compositions tells me that I am achieving something really of my own."

The busy theatre season in Prague, which lasted through May 1918, did not allow Webern time for creative work. Only with the establishment of his residence in Mödling could he resume composing. During the summer and autumn of 1918, he tried to make up for lost time by undertaking several projects. After another attempt to proceed with his string quartet, he turned to a series of songs. They included three further Trakl settings, "Die Sonne," "Gesang einer gefangenen Amsel," and "Ein Winterabend," but only the last was fully drafted. It is dated 10 July 1918. That year, given in the printed edition, has been considered the year of completion. Actually, however, the 1918 manuscript of the song was marked "not to be used for publication—reworked 1922." The ink manuscript of the new version, done in March 1922 and forming the basis for the publication, displays so radical a revision that 1922, rather than 1918, must be considered the date of the definitive composition. At any rate, "Ein Winterabend" completed the series of orchestral songs that Webern now grouped together under the title Four Songs, Op. 13. The cycle was turned over to Universal Edition in February 1925 and published the following year in the sequence: 1. "Wiese im Park" 2. "Die Einsame" 3. "In der Fremde" 4. "Ein Winterabend." The first two songs employ thirteen instruments, the third nine, and the last ten. The work is dedicated to Dr Norbert Schwarzmann, Webern's patron and friend. Along with the full score, the composer's own voice–piano reduction was issued. Sketches for this arrangement are dated February 1924.

In the Four Songs, Op. 13, an increasing use of triple rhythms and a greater polyphonic density can be noted. The work had its première on 16 February 1928, in Winterthur, in a concert given in the Stadthaussaal under the auspices of the city's Collegium Musicum. Clara Wirz-Wyss sang and Hermann Scherchen conducted. The programme, which also included Schoenberg's Chamber Symphony,

Op. 9, was then repeated in Zürich. How far Webern's music was ahead of his time is evident from the review appearing in the *Neue Zürcher Zeitung* on 21 February 1928: "Employing cunning sound effects, leaving much to the listener's fantasy and reminiscent of late Schoenberg, the language is not suitable for musical lyricism. . . . It is curious that Webern did not choose more aphoristic poems than those of Kraus, Trakl, and from *Die chinesische Flöte*. Not the slightest trace of their thought and mood is evoked in the music. There can be no more mistaken lyricism."

The activities of the Society for Private Musical Performances, which began in November 1918, absorbed Webern's energies so fully during the group's existence that, aside from several arrangements made expressly for society performances, he found no time for creative work except during the summer recesses. After the arduous first season, Webern spent an extended vacation at Mürzzuschlag, where his pent-up urge to compose found release in a quick succession of works. He began with an orchestral song on a Kraus poem, but, leaving that project unfinished, he returned to the lyrics of Trakl. During July of 1919 he completed four settings: "Abendland II" (7 July); "Gesang einer gefangenen Amsel" (11 July); "Nachts" (18 July), and "Abendland I" (28 July). (Different conceptions of "Gesang einer gefangenen Amsel" date back to 1917 and 1918.) Webern was so elated over the steady flow of his inspiration that he informed Berg on 1 August 1919:[5] "I have written four songs on Trakl poems. With accompaniment for E flat, B flat and bass clarinets, violin and cello, in varying combinations; except for one ["Gesang einer gefangenen Amsel"], all are with three instruments. Two years ago, I composed a Trakl song in this manner; I have picked it up again, and so I have completed a cycle of five Trakl songs, up to now, for this small combination."

With the remark "up to now," Webern left open the prospect of augmenting his Trakl group. He had already begun work on several additional settings, but it was not until two years later that he finished "Die Sonne." This was, in fact, the first composition he had completed since July of 1919. In the busy summer of 1920, Webern had found little time for creative work. Frustrated, he had written to Berg on 17 August that he had produced "nothing" during that ordinarily so fertile season. "This gives me a feeling of guilt," he confessed. "But it was not possible."

In 1921, after devoting all of July to a chamber reduction of Schoenberg's *Die glückliche Hand*, Webern informed Berg on 6 August that he was now composing and that he hoped it would "continue to go well." The draft of "Die Sonne" is marked "Mödling, 12 August 1921." (An earlier sketch dates back to 1918.) Webern then proceeded to group the six completed Trakl songs into a cycle, placing "Die Sonne" first, followed by "Abendland I," "Abendland II," "Abendland III," "Nachts," and "Gesang einer gefangenen Amsel." The work was published in this sequence by Universal Edition at the end of July 1924 under the title Six Songs on Poems of Georg Trakl, Op. 14. Sending a copy of the printed edition to Schoenberg, Webern inscribed it "*post festum*," a reference to the work's première, which had taken place a few days earlier, on 20 July, at the Donaueschingen festival. That first performance was conducted by the composer himself, with Clara Kwartin carrying the vocal part and Rudolf Kolisch heading the instrumental ensemble. In his own copy of the published score, Webern gave the duration of the whole work as fifteen minutes, but the timings for the individual songs fell three minutes short of that total: I. 2' II. 2½' III. 2½' IV. 2' V. 1' VI. 2'. Among the extensive primary source materials for the Trakl cycle are two manuscripts of a piano reduction. One, comprising only the piano part, is marked "October–November 1923;"[6] the other, containing both voice and piano, is undated.[7]

The significance of Webern's Opus 14 within his entire development cannot be overestimated. Compared with his Opus 13, the songs show an advance in both vocal and instrumental treatment that is notable. The texture, woven in four and five voices, has become denser and more consistent in its contrapuntal application. Although this strictness of polyphonic structure suggests an affinity with *Pierrot Lunaire*, Schoenberg himself acknowledged that Webern's language was distinctly his own. The stylistic demands of the Trakl songs make the work's execution very exacting for performers. "My Trakl· songs are pretty well the most difficult there are in this field. They would need countless rehearsals," the composer wrote to Josef Humplik on 30 December 1929, discouraging a projected performance in Vienna.[8]

After composing "Die Sonne" in early August 1921, Webern went on a brief mountain excursion. At the end of the trip he visited his parents' graves and, under the impression of that experience, set to work on a new project immediately after his return home. In quick succession he drafted two orchestral songs: "Das Kreuz, das musst' er tragen," dated at the end 28 August, and "In Gottes Namen aufstehen," dated 3 September. On 27 August he informed Berg that he was composing songs again. After Trakl, he now was setting "old sacred chants," the texts of which had seized his mind. For the time being he would not compose anything else before he had finished them all, because the verses embodied "fitting perceptions" that touched him deeply. All he needed now was much more time. When he undertook the new project he had been in "terrible despair" and "horribly depressed." But now he could see the reason for this: "I need a certain period of time—especially at present under all these difficult living conditions, etc.—in order to arrive at the proper concentration," he told Berg. Now that he had reached this point, his free time was at an end again.

The fact that Webern composed "Das Kreuz, das musst' er tragen" and "In Gottes Namen aufstehen" within a week of each other demonstrates that, once his creative energies were given free rein after long periods of repression, he was capable of rapid production. The extended series of songs written within a short span of time during the summers of 1917, 1919, and 1921 amply document this observation. Unfortunately, with the onset of each new autumn season, the constant necessity of eking out a living had to take precedence over his creative impulses. He would then bitterly begrudge the loss of his momentum. As that summer of 1921 waned, he wrote to Berg on 6 September that he still intended to "assemble a collection of sacred songs," only to concede resignedly on 19 September that he again had to lay his work aside, something he found more difficult than ever before, because he had not found the time to "come to a conclusion."

The conclusion was to be reached only the following summer. Webern then went to Traunkirchen, greatly anticipating "the prospect of finally being able to work undisturbed for perhaps two months," as he wrote beforehand to Schoenberg.[9] On 22 July 1922, he reported to Berg that he was "faring very well" except that he was being bothered by much noise. However, he was sitting at his work the whole day and had just finished that morning another song in his cycle based on sacred poems. He told Berg: "A sacred cantata occupies me—I cannot get away from such texts. Further I have the idea to write a quartet (this already for a rather long time) and songs."

The song Webern had finished that morning was "Morgenlied," based on a text from Des Knaben Wunderhorn. Four days later, on 26 July, he completed "Mein Weg geht jetzt vorüber."[10] These two songs were to be the only creative products of the summer, for the scandal caused by the performance of his Five Movements, Op. 5, at the Salzburg Festival in early August left him out of sorts for the rest of his stay at Traunkirchen. Instead of pursuing his idea for a "sacred cantata," he proceeded to group the two new songs, the two written the year before, and "Fahr hin, o Seel'," composed in 1917, into a cycle. Under the title Five Sacred Songs, Op. 15, the sequence was established as 1. "Das Kreuz, das musst' er tragen" 2. "Morgenlied" 3. "In Gottes Namen aufstehen" 4. "Mein Weg geht jetzt vorüber" 5. "Fahr hin, o Seel'."

The instrumental complement comprises flute, clarinet (also bass clarinet), trumpet, harp, and violin (also viola). Density of polyphonic texture and subtlety of rhythmic treatment are even more pronounced than in the Trakl songs. "Fahr hin, o Seel'" is a double canon in contrary motion. One canon opens with the trumpet and clarinet, the

"Fahr hin, o Seel'," No. 5 of Five Sacred Songs, Op. 15

other with voice and violin. The remaining members of the ensemble join in later, sharing in the distribution of the canonic parts in *Klangfarbenmelodie* style. This piece was one of the composer's own favourites, as is evident from the number of manuscript copies he presented to his friends.[11]

Webern was so convinced of having achieved his best with this latest work that he entered it a year later into the Berkshire composition contest. This competition was held in conjunction with the Berkshire Chamber Music Festival, an annual event sponsored by Mrs Elizabeth Sprague Coolidge, the American patroness known for her generosity on behalf of contemporary music. The composer attached high hopes to his application, for he noted in his diary the date of mailing, 8 February 1924, as well as the code designation C+M+B under which the score was submitted. On 27 May, however, another diary entry records a disappointment: "My Sacred Songs returned from America." From the 104 manuscripts submitted to the jury that year, *La Belle Dame sans Merci* by Wallingford Riegger was chosen as the prize-winning composition, and *Two Assyrian Prayers* by Frederick Jacobi received honourable mention.[12] That same year, on 9 October, Webern conducted the first performance of his Five Sacred Songs in a concert at the Vienna Secession. Felicie Hüni-Mihacsek sang, and members of the Vienna State Opera formed the ensemble. The following month, Universal Edition brought out the score and parts ("magnificently engraved" as the composer had noted with satisfaction in a postcard to Berg on 29 August 1924, when he read the proofs). Webern's own voice–piano reduction of the work is still unpublished.

Many of the texts chosen by Webern for musical setting are religious in character, ranging from the liturgical to the pantheistic. While the poems for the Five Sacred Songs were of a devout folk-like character, those inspiring the composer's next work came directly from the Roman Catholic breviary, a book containing the daily offices and prayers of the church. On 30 July 1923, after a brief mountain vacation, Webern wrote to Schoenberg: "My work is, I believe, now under way. At first I experimented a good deal, discarding what I had begun. For this reason I have not given you details. Suddenly it was there again. It will become, so I hope, a cycle of Latin church songs. For this purpose, I have borrowed the breviary from the priest. It contains everything: hymns, psalms, and so forth. The breviary is a glorious work. Four volumes, a volume for each season." Selecting excerpts from this compendium, Webern wrote two canonic settings for voice, clarinet, and bass clarinet. "Crux fidelis," a hymn from the Good Friday liturgy, was completed on 8 August, and "Asperges me," a Psalm verse commonly used as an antiphon to the Sunday mass, on 21 August. These two canons joined

"Dormi Jesu," a similar setting based on a folk text from *Des Knaben Wunderhorn* that must have been composed earlier in the summer, since Webern, when informing Berg of his project on 21 July, had told him: "One is finished already."

On 23 August, two days after completing "Asperges me," Webern again wrote to Berg that, both because of his physical condition (Webern then suffered from infected tonsils and intestinal trouble) and his mental state, he had "passed some difficult hours (days, weeks)." He told Berg:

> Therefore, I have not accomplished much, even though I did not give in for a moment, as I may truly say (much was begun, some of it several times, and then left standing again). At any rate: the series of Latin songs numbers three by now. Probably this is the end of them. Now I want to work at something different. These three songs, for that matter, are canons. The first one ["Dormi Jesu"], a canon in the inversion, is for voice and clarinet, the second ["Crux fidelis"], a straight three-part canon for voice, clarinet, and bass clarinet, the third ["Asperges me"], a straight two-part canon for voice and bass clarinet. In sound, they are clearly differentiated from each other. The first is, textually, a kind of lullaby of Mary; the second an antiphon: song (prayer) to the crucifix; the third an invocation (holy water). Musically, the whole represents a unit in form and expression, I believe. Therefore, perhaps it will end with these three.

However, writing to Schoenberg a day later, Webern left open the prospect: "Maybe others will still be added to them."

The season's activities, more demanding than in preceding years and lasting throughout the following summer, once again forestalled Webern's creative endeavours. The draft of "Crucem tuam adoramus," a text from the Good Friday liturgy, is marked "begun August 1924," but it was not until 29 October—after the premières of his Five Sacred Songs, Op. 15, and Schoenberg's *Die glückliche Hand*—that this canon for voice, clarinet, and bass clarinet was completed. Sketches for earlier versions were marked, apparently retroactively, "already summer 1923?" As if to make up for lost time, the composer turned at once to another essay for the same combination. "Christus factus est," a text from Philippians 2: 8–9, used in the service as a Maundy Thursday Gradual, was finished on 12 November 1924. Deciding that the cycle was now complete, Webern placed the unit of three canons written the year before between the two last composed. Still titled *Lateinische Lieder*, Op. 16, in the original manuscript, the work was published in 1928 by Universal Edition as Five Canons on Latin Texts, Op. 16, in this sequence: 1. "Christus factus est" 2. "Dormi Jesu" 3. "Crux fidelis"

4. "Asperges me" 5. "Crucem tuam adoramus."[13] No performance during Webern's lifetime could be ascertained.[14]

The voice part, written for high soprano and demanding virtuoso technique, is so integrated into the overall texture that each canon gives the impression of an abstract instrumental invention rather than of a vocal composition in the usual sense. This effect is heightened by the fact that each canonic subject is first stated by one of the clarinets (in the opening canon by both clarinets) before the voice enters. Utterly concentrated in their contrapuntal density, the canons are all short, measuring only between nine and thirteen bars. While the time-honoured device of the canon had influenced Webern's creative thinking from the days of his doctoral studies on, it gradually became a governing feature of his technique. The Opus 16 ranks as a masterpiece of this ancient form, which has challenged composers of all generations by its exacting demands on both intellect and imagination.

The multitude of extant sketches for the Five Canons testifies to the intensity of concentration invested in them. Behind their deceptive brevity lies extraordinary craftsmanship. Webern himself was fully aware of his achievement as a creative artist. On 19 September 1923, after completing the first three canons, he copied into his diary a quotation from a letter written by Goethe to Schiller on 20 July 1799: "[I have] renewed the conviction: that we should do nothing but abide in ourselves, in order occasionally to bring forth something tolerable. Whatsoever is more . . . cometh of evil."

Unfinished projects

The evolution of the song cycles Opera 12–16 was intermingled with an abundance of other projects that were not completed. All were for voice except two. Some compositions were pursued to considerable lengths, others abandoned in the earliest stages. The following survey is necessarily confined to the most essential data. It should be borne in mind that the entire complex of unfinished projects dating from 1914 to 1924, because of its relatively recent discovery, is still largely unexplored in its theoretical aspects and implications. Detailed scrutiny will doubtless add new facets to the full understanding of this important phase in the composer's development.

While Webern usually dated his sketches, he never—with the exception of the song to be discussed first—indicated the title of a poem or its author. Thus, the identification of his literary sources for the post-humously-discovered songs has met with considerable difficulty. The only clues were the fragmentary and sometimes barely legible passages of text appearing in the sketches. Drafts for the orchestral songs all are in condensed score. This was Webern's habitual approach to composing.

The earliest unfinished project from the period under review is an orchestral song marked "1914 (Dante)". The text, beginning with the words "In einer lichten Rose . . . ," is the opening passage of Canto XXXI in Book III, *Paradise*, of the *Divine Comedy*, and the message of the words is closely related to Webern's own thoughts as expressed in *Tot* (October 1913). The two-page draft extends over twenty measures, fourteen of which are fully worked out, complete with detailed tempo and dynamic markings. The large and colourful instrumentation embraces the full orchestral palette, ranging from piccolo to contrabass and including harmonium, celesta, guitar, harp, glockenspiel, and triangle. This wealth of timbres makes the composition akin to "Die Einsame" and "Leise Düfte," other orchestral songs written in early 1914. Since Webern obviously bestowed much care on this unfinished Dante setting, it· is difficult to conjecture why he did not carry it to completion. The same enigma presents itself in connection with several other projects to be described below.

At the beginning of 1915, just before Webern enlisted for army service, he turned for the first time to the lyrics of Georg Trakl. Of fifteen settings of that poet's verses, eight were to remain incomplete. The first two of these were inspired by "In der Heimat" and "In den Nachmittag geflüstert." Webern noted on both sketches that they were conceived in the Vienna district of Hietzing in 1915. "In der Heimat" was scored for voice and piano and probably was intended for a group of songs that became Opus 12. Beginning with the tempo direction *Ruhige Bewegung* (Quietly moving), the draft is carefully worked out for 24 measures. It includes dynamic markings and even a pedal indication. The voice part continues for an additional four bars, and with this about one half of the text was realized. The other project, "In den Nachmittag geflüstert," was envisaged as an orchestral song, with English horn, clarinet, violin, and harp indicated. Marked *Sanft bewegt* (Gently animated), the draft extends over twelve measures.

In 1917 Webern occupied himself with four more Trakl settings, of which only "Abendland III" (Op. 14, No. 4) was completed. Early in the year, at his Hietzing apartment, he began drafting "Mit silbernen Sohlen" for a large orchestral ensemble, including trombone, celesta, tamtam, and timpani. The longer of two separate sketches extends over eleven measures. There also exist no fewer than five beginnings, each totally different from the other, for a setting of "Verklärung." The sketches, from four to thirteen measures long, are for voice with piano, as well as for voice with orchestra. Two of the latter drafts are marked "Klagenfurt 1917," which places them in the vicinity of the four songs finished there that summer (Op. 13, Nos. 1 and 3; Op. 14, No. 4;

Op. 15, No. 5). Dated 1917, but with no locale given, is the year's third unfinished Trakl project, a setting of "Siebengesang des Todes," for large
orchestra. Besides various brief sketches there is a draft of sixteen bars.

In 1919 Webern set four more Trakl poems. He continued to be
immersed in this poet's verses through the busy year of 1920, although
he was then unable to finish any composition. Two fragments are extant,
six and eight measures long, of a richly orchestrated draft of "Die
Heimkehr," as well as two different versions, four and nine measures in
length, of "Nachtergebung," also for orchestra. The only one of the
incomplete Trakl essays that uses an instrumental ensemble similar to
that of the Six Trakl Songs, Op. 14, is an attempted realization of
"Jahr." Dated 1921 and breaking off after only three measures, this
sketch is scored for voice, clarinet, viola, and cello.

The German thinker who exerted the strongest influence upon
Webern was Goethe, and of his poems no fewer than six inspired the
composer to musical settings. During the spring of 1917, "Gleich und
Gleich" (Op. 12, No. 4) was completed, and at about the same time
Webern began another song, also for voice and piano, based on
Goethe's "Gegenwart." The draft, marked "1917, Wien, Auhofstrasse,"
extends over 38 measures and covers two strophes and one line of the
six-strophe text. The bass clef for the vocal part indicates that it was
intended for a baritone. (The only other solo song in this range is the
early "Wolkennacht," 1900.) The piano accompaniment, largely
chordal, is well worked out. Here, as generally, detailed dynamic
directions show that Webern's earliest vision of a work already included
the last nuance of shading. In 1918, after settling in Mödling, Webern
turned to another Goethe poem, the "Cirrus" section from *Howards
Ehrengedächtnis*. The composer was thinking of an orchestral song
with large instrumentation, but did not get beyond several sketches
ranging from six to thirteen bars in length and representing varying
musical ideas. Although this project was abandoned, Webern returned
to the same text in the early summer of 1930, when he tried to cast it in
the dodecaphonic idiom (see Chapter XXV).

Karl Kraus excited Webern's admiration not only as a polemic writer
but also as a poet. Besides "Wiese im Park" (Op. 13, No. 1), the
composer undertook three more orchestral songs inspired by his verses.
The first of these unfinished works, "Vallorbe," originated at Mödling
during the summer of 1918, a year after "Wiese im Park." The draft of
63 measures realizes the entire poem and closes with a double bar,
followed by the date of 5 August 1918. Opening with the tempo
direction *Zart bewegt* (Gently animated), it calls for a large ensemble
including, for example, celesta, harp, glockenspiel, and timpani. There
exist two preliminary sketches, one appearing on the back of a draft of

"Abendland III" (Op. 14, No. 4). At Mürzzuschlag, in the early summer of 1919 and before composing the four Trakl settings later included in Opus 14, Webern again drafted an orchestral song based on a Kraus poem, "Vision des Erblindeten." Like "Vallorbe," it is fully sketched out for the voice part and a large ensemble of instruments. The draft, dated 2 July 1919 at the closing double bar, encompasses 39 measures. Still another Kraus poem, "Flieder," busied Webern the following year, 1920. This, too, he conceived as an orchestral song and made four separate attempts, each distinctly different. The fragments range from eight to fifteen measures. Two of them are worked out in great detail and call for a large instrumental complement. One of these drafts is marked "Mödling 1920," the other "1920 or 1921."

Just as Webern drew on texts of Trakl, Goethe, and Kraus much more frequently than is manifest from his finished compositions, so did he attempt more settings from Bethge's *Die chinesische Flöte* than those known from his Op. 12, No. 2, and Op. 13, Nos. 2 and 3. He intended also settings of "Nächtliches Bild" by Tschan-Jo-Su and "Der Frühlings-regen by Thu-Fu. The former was planned as a song with large orchestral ensemble. Two sketches, both marked "Mödling, autumn 1918," encompass a total of about 50 measures. "Frühlingsregen" was conceived both in a voice–piano seting and as an orchestral song. Dated 1920 and marked *Sehr fliessend* (Very flowing), the voice–piano version exists in two sketches, one four measures long and the other eleven. Each of these drafts, as well as the nine-measure orchestral sketch, displays altogether different conceptions of the music.

The lyrics of Detlev von Liliencron had inspired Webern as early as 1903, when he composed "Heimgang in der Frühe." A complete edition of that poet's works was in his library. Falling into the time frame under discussion is an undated nine-measure sketch, for voice and piano, of Liliencron's "Meiner Mutter."

Still to be mentioned are some of the vocal essays for which the textual sources have not yet been identified. Among them is a song beginning with the words "Mutig trägst du die Last," sketched out both in a version for voice and piano and in one that includes violin, oboe, and harmonium; the drafts are five and ten measures long. The words "In tiefster Schuld vor einem Augenpaar" open the text of a song fragment of nine measures, scored for voice, clarinet, violin, and harmonium. Another sketch, dated 1920 and extending over ten bars, is a voice–piano setting of a poem beginning "Christkindlein trägt die Sünden der Welt."

The last of Webern's unfinished vocal projects of that period is one of the most interesting. It stems from 1924, the year when the composer completed his Five Canons on Latin Texts from the Catholic breviary.

Curiously enough, at the same time he began setting a text occurring in the hymnal of the Austrian Evangelical Church, beginning with the words "Morgenglanz der Ewigkeit," an untitled poem by Christian Knorr von Rosenroth dated from 1684. One of three extant sketch-leaves is entitled "Prelude to 'Morgenglanz der Ewigkeit'." The condensed score, dated "Mödling, spring 1924," encompasses eight measures and calls for a large body of instruments. The tempo prescription *Sehr breit* (Very broadly), appearing on another draft of four measures, befits the chorale-like character of the text. The germinal musical conception is arrested with three-tone chords (largely major sevenths and minor ninths) noted under each syllable. For that matter, the musical ideas vary completely in each of the three versions. One of them displays wide leaps, both in the vocal line and in the instrumental parts. The "Morgenglanz" project belongs, together with the first and last of the Five Canons, to Webern's final pre-dodecaphonic essays. He adopted the strict twelve-tone system later that year, never to compose in any other idiom from then on.

On the evidence of Webern's published Opera 12–19, the period from 1914 to 1926 had long been considered one entirely devoted to vocal compositions. There exist, however, no fewer than six purely instrumental works that originated between 1917 and 1925. Only two of these will be discussed here, since the other four were conceived as twelve-tone pieces and will be taken up in Chapter XVIII.

On 13 June 1917 Webern wrote to Schoenberg from Klagenfurt: "I have begun a string quartet. I keep coming back to this time and again. I hope it will now progress." While the project was laid aside soon thereafter in favour of various vocal works, several layers of sketches prove that the quartet idea occupied Webern for a long time. Actually, he had begun the work early in the year: a section, on three pages and containing about 40 measures, is marked "End of January 1917, Vienna." Another draft bears the note "Klagenfurt 1917," relating it to the composer's announcement to Schoenberg. The composition, no doubt inspired by Webern's participation in a string quartet during the closing phase of his army life at Leoben, again busied him in 1918 when he first settled down to creative work after his theatre season in Prague. He then took up the earlier draft and wrote it out anew with the tempo marking *Sanft bewegt* (Gently animated). Another section, marked *Mässig bewegt* (Moderately animated) and dated "Mödling, 5 July 1918" is carried out for twelve measures. Among the various sets of sketches is one designated *Lebhaft* (Lively) and extending over twenty bars, which, judging from its idiom, could well stem from an earlier period. Four years later, on 22 July 1922, Webern wrote to Berg about his "idea to write a quartet," which he said he had entertained "for a rather long time." However, there are no sketches bearing the date of that year. The extant portions of the quartet are carefully worked out, making this project one of the most interesting of the composer's unfinished works. It demonstrates Webern's attempt to achieve greater formal expansiveness within a purely instrumental framework. Thus he continued the endeavour, first made with his Cello Sonata (1914), to break away from the aphoristic style.

Dated 21 August 1920 is the manuscript of another instrumental work, scored for clarinet, trumpet, and violin (the instruments make their entrance in that order). The movement, seventeen measures long, contains minute tempo and dynamic directions, an indication that the composer had reached a definitive conception of the music. The combination of the three contrasting instruments and their individual treatment produce a highly original effect.

Arrangements

Between 1918 and 1923 Webern made seven chamber ensemble reductions of orchestral scores. They were all prompted by the activities of the Society for Private Musical Performances and adapted to the limited instrumental resources of that group. Three of these reductions were of Webern's own works: the Passacaglia, Op. 1, for two pianos, six hands; the Six Pieces, Op. 6, for flute, oboe, clarinet, violins I and II, viola, cello, piano, harmonium, and percussion (large drum, triangle, tamtam, and bells); and the Five Pieces, Op. 10, for violin, viola, cello, piano, and harmonium. The Opus 1 and Opus 10 arrangements were heard repeatedly, but it is uncertain whether that of Opus 6 was ever performed.[15]

As his share in the society's "Walzerabend" of 27 May 1921, Webern set the "Treasure Waltz" from the *Gypsy Baron* by Johann Strauss for an ensemble consisting of a string quartet, piano, and harmonium. Incomparably more demanding were the three works that Schoenberg delegated to Webern for arrangement during that period. Announced in the *Mitteilungen* No. 24 (April 1921) is a projected performance of Schoenberg's Four Songs, Op. 22, for voice and orchestra, in Webern's reduction for violin, viola, cello, piano, and harmonium, a combination that he had employed in 1914 as an instrumental support for his chorus *Entflieht auf leichten Kähnen*, Op. 2. The whereabouts of Webern's manuscript of his arrangement of Schoenberg's Opus 22 is unknown, as is that of a much larger and more ambitious assignment. Throughout July 1921 Webern was occupied with a chamber orchestra reduction of Schoenberg's music drama *Die glückliche Hand*, Op. 18. While that work's public première occurred only in 1924, a first hearing, with a necessarily limited orchestra, was contemplated for the society's fourth (1921–22) season, but this project never materialized.

Several letters to Schoenberg disclose the progress and nature of Webern's work. On 3 July he announced: "I have already begun with the arrangement of *Die glückliche Hand*. Hertzka made the score available to me as a loan. So far, for about the first three pages, it is going quite smoothly. After first looking through the entire score, I chose the following instrumentation: flute (piccolo), clarinet (bass clarinet), trumpet, horn, harmonium (perhaps two, at any rate occasionally for two players), piano (likewise), two violins, viola, cello, and double bass." On 13 July, Webern could report:

> I have by now advanced quite far with the arrangement of *Die glückliche Hand*. I have arrived at measure 75. In all, there are 255 bars. Therefore, almost a third has already been completed. I am sitting at it the whole day, that is, for my entire free time. I want to bring the arrangement to its end in one sweep. It gives me extraordinary joy! Now I finally get to know your glorious work really thoroughly! Everything can be carried out very well. I am setting the stage music for two pianos (each four hands). On each stage will stand a piano, since the procurement of the pianos and their players certainly appears to me as something much simpler than the procurement of separate stage musicians (trumpets, etc.). At any rate, I retained the triangle and cymbal. This, combined with the manner in which I set the music for the pianos, should achieve very well the effect you intended.

Webern completed the transcription on 31 July, and on 6 August he wrote to Berg that his score covered 97 pages. He voiced the hope that the arrangement had turned out well and commented that it was "not easy to play, but not more difficult than the original, either." As in *Pierrot*, "only absolutely first-rank soloists" could be considered. Ten days later, he went to Traunkirchen for a three-day visit to Schoenberg and undoubtedly took the finished score along. It can only be hoped that the manuscript is still extant and will come to light some day.[16]

On 24 November 1922 Webern wrote to Zemlinsky: "At present I am working on an arrangement of Schoenberg's Chamber Symphony for the same ensemble as used in *Pierrot*. At the same time, it is to become one for string quartet and piano." Schoenberg's Opus 9, composed in 1906, employs fifteen solo instruments. Webern's reduction is scored for flute (or second violin), clarinet (or viola), violin, cello, and piano. Beginning on 3 November 1922 and working on it for a full three months, Webern accorded the task the same careful and devoted attention as if it were one of his own compositions. On 27 January 1923 he could inform Schoenberg: "A week ago, I finished the arrangement of the Chamber Symphony and now am revising this draft thoroughly. I hope to succeed in achieving what you expect from me in this regard. At any rate, I am aiming for it with all my strength." The extant drafts are proof of Webern's efforts, and the result attests to his great sensitivity and skill as an arranger. In the wake of the Webern renaissance during the 'fifties and 'sixties, Universal Edition brought out the transcription in 1968. It represents a distinct addition to the work catalogues of both Schoenberg and Webern.

CHAPTER XVII

Mounting success
(1925–1928)

On 13 and 14 March 1925, the Singverein gave its first full-length concert under Webern's baton. The programme included Beethoven's *Zur Weihe des Hauses*, Brahms' *Nänie*, Liszt's *Arbeiterchor*, Weber's *Konzertstück* for piano and orchestra, and Mendelssohn's *Erste Walpurgisnacht*. With its official début, the chorus at once drew favourable notice from the newspaper critics, one of whom hailed it as "new in every respect, fresh, vital, pervaded by youth and joy" (*Amtliche Wiener Zeitung*, 28 March 1925).

For the occasion, Webern had especially arranged Liszt's little-known *Arbeiterchor* for bass solo, mixed chorus, and large orchestra (see Chapter XVIII).[1] The spirit of the text made it eminently suited for a political manifesto of the Socialist cause. Notwithstanding the Singverein's alignment with and dependence on the Social Democrats, Webern managed to avoid deeper involvement in the pursuits and ideology of the party. It did not detract from his personal relationship with David Josef Bach, to whom he owed his position, that he showed little interest in the political aspects of the organization. According to Paul A. Pisk, a functionary of the Kunststelle and music reviewer for the *Arbeiterzeitung*, David Josef Bach was generally referred to as "Comrade Bach" and he himself as "Comrade Pisk," but a certain distance was always observed with Webern, who was never addressed other than as "Doctor Webern." Although several of his friends, like Josef Polnauer, were registered party members, Webern himself stayed clear of direct affiliation. Close as he felt to the people by virtue of his basic human sympathies and simple tastes, he always remained quite conscious of his family's aristocratic heritage. For a time, he even firmly believed in the restoration of the monarchy. In 1920, when his cousin Heinrich Diez (Ernst's brother) was allocated an apartment in the Hofburg, the former imperial palace, Webern actually warned him that the Habsburg rulers would be back.[2]

Whatever political notions Webern entertained from time to time, they never affected the mainstream of his thinking. Music was his calling, and the pursuit of his professional activities his only desire and objective. To that end, the aegis of the Socialist régime proved quite acceptable to him. On the other hand, his artistic integrity was so generally respected that the party demanded no special profession of political solidarity. On the contrary, Webern's aristocratic descent continued to be recognized, especially by friends and associates of long standing. For example, years after the legal abolition of nobility, Alban Berg inscribed a portrait photograph of himself: "To my dear Anton von Webern from Alban Berg, summer 1924."

Rehearsals for the Singverein's March concerts coincided with those for an important performance by the Mödlinger Männergesangverein: Bruckner's Mass in F minor, an ambitious undertaking for an amateur chorus. For the presentation, which took place on the morning of 10 May in Mödling's St Othmar Church, members of the Volksoper orchestra were engaged. Josef Hueber, an aspiring young bass-baritone, was among the soloists. Over the years, he became one of the singers Webern most relied on. Beyond their musical collaboration, during which Webern never accepted any compensation for the many hours of coaching, there developed a close personal friendship between the two men, enhanced by their common love of mountaineering and gardening.

In his memoirs, Hueber dwells on the difficulties encountered by Webern in coaching his choruses. Most members of the Mödling society, coming from the middle classes, had some knowledge of music, but those from the Singverein lacked this background, and their training had to begin with the most elementary instruction. "In order to acquaint the singers with a work," Hueber writes, "Webern first had to play and explain it at the piano. Then he began to rehearse voice by voice, demonstrating by singing single phrases himself, until the harmonization of voices was possible. Again and again, voice by voice, or a group of singers alone within a section, and then together again. With divided voices, for example, the upper tenors were taken together with the lower sopranos, etc., until each individual voice group 'heard' its part and became secure. In this manner, often barely twenty measures could be covered in two hours. There was the additional task of polishing the individual (mostly untrained) voices in order to obtain from them the best possible sound."[3]

The achievement of the Singverein in its first appearance that season, as well as the group's rendition of difficult choral works in the following years, must be viewed in the light of such tedious rehearsal procedure, which required Webern's tireless labours and limitless patience. Sensing their leader's struggle against discouraging odds, the singers reciprocated with loyal affection and a cheerful willingness to undergo many additional strenuous rehearsals before each major performance. The more sophisticated Mödlinger Männergesangverein was equally appreciative of its accomplishments under Webern's guiding hand. After the presentation of the Bruckner Mass, the club surprised him with a wooden music stand, artistically executed by one of its members, Obust Kreisler, a master carver. The stand, which bore the inscription "Kunst ist Gottesdienst" (Art is service to God), adorned Webern's study throughout his life, and the written testimonial of gratitude that accompanied the gift was kept among his cherished mementoes.

On 18 January 1925 Webern had recorded in his diary that the song "So ich traurig bin" (Op. 4, No. 4) was included in a concert of the Franco-American Society in New York. On 10 February the Three Little Pieces, Op. 11, for cello and piano (which Maurits Frank and Eduard Zuckmayer had premièred shortly before in Mainz), were played in Vienna for the first time by Frank and the pianist Friedrich Wührer in a concert of the local ISCM chapter. Webern, informed only at the last minute because of a mix-up in communication, could attend neither the rehearsal nor the performance, but Alban Berg was present and wrote to him on the following day how much the work had impressed him. From the first note, he stated, one could sense Webern's "so unique idiom." The audience was "spellbound" for the duration of the pieces, so that "all relativity of length and brevity was completely abolished." Like the fragrance of a blossom, however fugitive, the music conveyed "a breath of eternity." The rendition had not been bad, Berg reported. At any rate it had been clear, and the cellist, in particular, had brought out a good deal "surprisingly well." Berg felt that Webern, too, would have rejoiced in his harmonics, the like of which Berg had not heard before. The pieces had been played twice. This was a wise measure, since "the audience, which followed only with considerable astonishment the first time, was visibly moved the second." The rest of the programme had ranged from "mediocre" (Honegger) to "*far below* mediocre" (Delius, Miaskovsky), but Wellesz' Cello Suite was a "disgrace beyond discussion." In another Vienna ISCM concert, on 8 April, Felicie Hüni-Mihacsek and Eduard Steuermann performed Webern's George cycle, Op. 3.

Webern's diary accounts of mountain excursions are as detailed as his notes on professional activities are terse. On 13 April, Easter Monday, he made a solo climb to the Rax Plateau. Encountering still-wintry conditions in the upper regions, he failed to reach the summit, but was delighted to find some Erica amidst the mantle of snow. A later attempt to ascend the mighty Dachstein also ended short of its goal. That outing, in Ludwig Zenk's company, lasted from 28 June to 3 July, and the diary contains an enthusiastic description of the rich experiences along the way. This was Webern's third try to climb the majestic peak, and it was foiled only a short distance from the summit by treacherous going and by a dramatic incident: a member of another party slipped on the icy slopes and fell into a crevasse. While he was rescued unharmed, the experience sobered the two companions so much that they were prompted to turn back. Unlike the typical mountaineer, Webern was never a fanatic about attaining the highest point. His passion was not for conquest; he wished only to immerse himself in the wonders of nature and in the stillness of the heights. Another excursion in 1925, taking place 10–15 August, led to the alpine range called Totes Gebirge. Webern's family physician, Dr Cech, and his wife were his companions. Although no summits were reached, the usual observations of flowers and other natural phenomena were noted in the diary.

This journey was begun immediately after completion of a piece posthumously published as *Satz für Streichtrio*. During the summer recess, Webern had thrown himself into creative work. The three older children had been sent to Aunt Poldi in Mürzzuschlag, and the domestic quiet was conducive to concentration. Besides the string trio movement, one of two such essays originating in 1925, a piece for piano solo, published as *Klavierstück*, Op. posth., was sketched out, and work progressed on the song cycles Opera 17 and 18.

Despite Webern's gradually increasing earnings, the year 1925 still found him economically hard pressed. His account book reveals several private loans, an advance payment from Universal Edition, and a gift of 500 schillings from Werner Reinhart. The Swiss patron had been directly solicited by Alban Berg, who was disappointed that his appeal did not produce a more substantial sum. In July, Wilhelmine's knitting still figured as part of the family income, and during August and September a small revenue was derived from the rent of a room in their home. Also listed were 75 schillings from the sale of various personal articles, including shoes.

Webern's financial situation continued to be so precarious that, despite his former bad experiences, he once again considered a theatre position. He was serious enough to ask Hertzka, during the spring of 1925, to recommend him for an opening in the German city of Bochum. However, the prospect fell through, and by August Webern inquired about the possibility of giving courses at the University. Guido Adler, head of the Musicological Institute, had just asked him to edit the third volume of Heinrich Isaac's *Choralis Constantinus*, a task so time-consuming and financially unrewarding that Webern had to decline. But the invitation encouraged him to offer his services as lecturer, and he suggested in his letter of 20 August to Dr Adler the following two topics: "1. Analyses of modern music (Strauss, Mahler, Reger, Schoenberg) in the manner of a kind of *Formenlehre* [Doctrine of Form], entailing an examination of formal principles (musical logic) and their connection with those of the older masters, etc. 2. Modern Instrumentation (combined with instrumentation exercises)." Webern's letter closed: "I would like to confess quite openly that I have great hopes that these courses will materialize, not only for idealistic reasons, but also for purely practical, i.e. financial ones. . . . In this regard I also take the liberty of addressing you with the urgent plea to think of me when you advise your class members about teachers they should choose, or if some other opportunity should present itself to send a pupil to me."[4]

Webern had good reason to hope for Dr Adler's assistance, knowing that his former professor fully appreciated his capabilities. This fact is confirmed by Kurt Manschinger, a student at the university and one of Webern's earliest pupils. He related an anecdote concerning his qualifying examination for admission to the Musicological Institute:

We were about 25 candidates, and our assignment consisted of a chorale harmonization, a cantus firmus, a fugue exposition, and a figured bass. Adler examined all the papers and complained about the dismal results, since more than half had failed the test. Then he asked some of us with whom we were studying. Whenever a famous name was mentioned an incredulous "Oh" was heard in the classroom. Finally he said, "There were only two papers I really liked; one is by Mr Zenk, the other by Mr Manschinger. May I ask the gentlemen with whom they are studying?" When we both answered that we were students of Webern, his face beamed and he said, "There, you see!" He held Webern and his musicological abilities in great esteem and regretted it when Webern turned to private teaching instead of going on in research.[5]

Although Webern's erudition was generally acknowledged, he was never to secure a position at the university or at any other institution of higher learning. Schoenberg, on the other hand, even without Webern's academic credentials, was invited that autumn of 1925 to the Prussian Academy of Arts in Berlin as a teacher of advanced composition.[6] The terms of his appointment were most favourable for creative work, since only six months of each year were required to be spent in residence. After the many years of ceaseless struggle for a measure of economic security, Schoenberg was now finally assured of a comfortable existence. Moreover, the position spelled recognition and prestige, lifting him above the many petty intrigues and jealousies that had harassed him in the city of his birth.

Although Schoenberg's move to Berlin was delayed until January 1926 because of an appendix operation, he and his family left Mödling early in October of 1925 to take up temporary quarters in a Vienna pension. Thus the seven years during which Schoenberg and Webern had been close neighbours drew to an end. Their friendship had been tried repeatedly, but it had always triumphed over occasional frictions. For two decades, Webern had maintained almost uninterrupted personal contact with his revered mentor. Their constant interchange of ideas was, to a large extent, instrumental in the evolution of a new musical theory and aesthetic. Although they corresponded extensively whenever they were separated, musical problems, the topic of many an oral discussion, were hardly ever aired in their letters. Therefore, Schoenberg's departure from Mödling meant for Webern the beginning of complete artistic autonomy just at the point when he was delving into the newly formulated twelve-tone system of composition. All of his dodecaphonic works must be assessed in the light of this fact.

While Schoenberg reached the zenith of his career in Berlin, Webern's situation in Vienna never allowed him to attain more than limited success. However, in September 1925, shortly after his fruitless plea to Dr Adler, an unexpected source of revenue did open up. Heinrich Jalowetz had been asked to teach at Vienna's Israelitic Institute for the Blind, but when a successful guest appearance at the Cologne theatre won him a firm engagement there he recommended Webern for the Vienna position in his stead.

A private school supported by donations, the institute occupied a large building on the Hohe Warte near the district of Grinzing. It was attended by approximately 60 students, all boarders, including many from Poland, Hungary, and other countries. The pupils ranged in age from pre-school to twenty years or more. Each student could remain until his individual training was completed. The director, Professor Siegfried Altmann, was a noted Goethe scholar. Interested in music, he was sympathetic to Webern, often invited him to dinner in his private quarters, and assisted him with counsel in his new and unusual duties.

The remuneration from the institute was munificent when compared to Webern's other sources of income. While the monthly salary from the Singverein was 80 schillings and from the Mödling chorus 40 schillings, that at the institute amounted to 200 schillings during the first season, increasing to 225 schillings from the autumn of 1926 on. For this honorarium Webern coached the school chorus twice a week. He also taught several private piano pupils, for whom he was paid additionally. At a time when, according to his account book, he had no other source

of income than his choruses (Manschinger and Zenk, his only steady
pupils, had just terminated their studies in order to begin their own
professional careers), the unexpected job opening was indeed an
economic blessing. It was also to prove a moving experience. On 8
October Webern wrote to Berg that his work at the institute included
three hours of piano lessons each Monday and Thursday afternoon. The
instruction of the sightless deeply affected him. Among his pupils was a
fourteen-year-old girl who had been blinded only four months earlier
as a result of an explosion during a chemistry experiment in school.
When she had taken her last piano lesson she had still been able to see.
During her first session with him, Webern related to Berg, there had been
"a horrifying outburst of sorrow from the poor child." He could hardly
endure the agony and had only the one desire—that he might be able to
work "miracles." He felt increasingly that his call to the institute was a
mission, something that would have "deep meaning" for his life.
Moreover, it was an activity very much to his liking, because it was
"something that takes place in quiet and seclusion." Whenever his
situation compelled him to be exposed to the public, he wanted more
than anything just to be incognito. "For instance, to read my name on a
poster in the street has a quite terrible, crushing effect on me," he
confided.

The blind girl, whose fate affected Webern so deeply, was Donna
Zincover, who came from a wealthy family in Warsaw.[7] She recalled later
how kind and patient he had been with her. Over the years, she studied
Bach, Beethoven sonatas, Chopin études, and other works with him.
K. H. Lehrigstein, a junior teacher at the school, later described
Webern's method of instruction:

> He did not actually teach playing the piano, that is, as an instrument
> with its own technical requirements, but was concerned only with how
> a particular piece should sound. I would say he taught a Beethoven
> sonata as he would conduct a symphony. . . . Webern could bring out
> the musical aspects admirably, but he was not exactly interested in
> technical training. He gave the pupils the right things to play
> according to their state of technical advancement. He held, "It does
> not matter so much what they play but that they play it well.". . . He
> thought that sighted and blind people alike must learn to find their
> way about on a piano mainly by practising, and the will to express
> oneself musically acts as the stimulus and wellspring for deter-
> mination and perseverance. . . . I never heard Dr Webern correct
> a pupil or criticize him in a harsh or even unfriendly manner. With
> infinite patience he corrected and explained until he got the pupil
> to do a piece at least as well as he was capable.[8]

Webern's lack of attention to piano technique in time hampered the progress of his more advanced students. It also became apparent that he himself did not have sufficient proficiency for the demonstration of difficult compositions, indispensable for giving the sightless an aural grasp of the music. One by one his pupils were assigned to other teachers, including Steuermann, so that from 1928 on only the training of the school chorus was left in his charge. In this field, his ability was unquestioned. The chorus consisted of about 30 members of various nationalities, for whom high German was the common language for instruction. Webern's distinct Viennese dialect at times made communication difficult, but he endeared himself to the group by always proving good-natured and often witty in communicating his intentions. Works by Mendelssohn, Schumann, and Strauss were among those studied. When conducting the rehearsals, Webern did not use a piano accompanist, although Director Altmann had offered him one. He preferred to play himself, feeling that this way he could stay in closer contact with the singers and convey more directly what he felt. Lehrigstein, himself blind, remembered his almost hypnotic power to project the mood of a composition. He describes an episode following a rehearsal, when Webern, lighting a cigarette, sat down at the piano and began to play the chorale "Wenn ich einmal soll scheiden" from Bach's *St Matthew Passion*: "Now, that chorale was very well known to me. Yet I stood there and was deeply moved. Webern played it with so much expression and deep emotion. I could imagine so well what it would have sounded like if a choir had sung it under his superb vision. I could see one aspect of his personality I had not recognized before: that Webern was essentially a religious man."

Lehrigstein related several other anecdotes as well. Once, when his colleagues were discussing a performance of a Bruckner symphony under Bruno Walter, one of the teachers expressed disapproval of the interpretation, whereupon Webern retorted: "There is, strictly speaking, no such thing as how one should conduct Bruckner. There is really only a right or a wrong way." Lehrigstein comments: "This was characteristic of Webern. He felt so sure that there always was, at least in music, just one way of doing things. He could not make concessions of any kind and he felt quite certain that only the Schoenberg school knew the right way of understanding, performing, and, perhaps, even composing music. At the same time, Webern tried to be as tolerant as he could towards others. After all, it was not their fault that they did not know better. They had not been trained properly and this was what was wrong with them." On another occasion, when the appointment of a new president for Vienna's Music Academy was the topic of conversation, Webern acidly inquired, "Why did they not simply take the lowliest servant and make him director?" Lehrigstein observes, "Who would fail to see the contempt and bitterness reflected in that remark?" He also qualifies the widespread assumption that Webern was shy and unassuming: "Shy, I would not dispute this. But unassuming, that is not at all what I would say. On the contrary, I would go so far as to say that he was a fighter. He had to be. He felt superior to so many leading figures in the world of music."

Webern's estimation of his own worth was shared by many of his friends. Those who were influential tried to secure for him a position commensurate with his abilities. In early 1926 David Josef Bach recommended him for the post of chorus master at the Vienna State Opera. At about the same time, Hertzka intimated to Webern that he was being considered as principal conductor of the Konzertverein concerts, to succeed Ferdinand Löwe. Delighted with the performance of the Singverein at its début, Bach envisaged concerts in Moscow and Leningrad for the end of May. Webern wrote to Schoenberg in detail about these prospects, all of which failed to materialize.

However, the 1925–26 season was to witness one of the highlights of Webern's conducting career. After an October concert devoted to works by Johann Strauss, the Singverein concentrated entirely on a project of the first magnitude: a performance of Mahler's Eighth Symphony, the "Symphony of a Thousand," which was scheduled to celebrate the 200th event in the series of Workmen's Symphony Concerts. The combined forces of several additional choruses were mustered: the choral society of the Freie Typographia, the Philharmonic women's chorus, and a specially organized workmen's children's chorus. Even selected singers from the Israelitic Institute for the Blind participated. In addition, twenty male voices from the opera chorus were hired.

Many months were spent in arduous preparation. By early March, Webern was rehearsing the individual choral groups four nights weekly. On 31 March he reported to Schoenberg:

Yesterday I had the first combined rehearsal, with piano. Now the children's chorus and the seven soloists still have to be added. I must confess that I find myself in a state of considerable excitement! Unfortunately I am at this moment already rather worn out from the many rehearsals. To hold, *almost every evening* for weeks now (after *many hours* of other work), a strenuous choral rehearsal deep into the night, followed by the train ride to Mödling, only then to have supper, etc.—usually it is 2 am before I get to bed—this is really quite exhausting. The choruses go at it enthusiastically and indefatigably.

The two public performances, on 18 and 19 April 1926, took place in the large hall of the Konzerthaus and brought Webern a great personal triumph.[9] Amidst frenetic applause, he was recalled to the stage again and again. Finally, overwhelmed by the ovation, he spontaneously lifted the heavy score off the conductor's stand and, turning to the audience, held it high above his head, as if to signify that the public tribute belonged to Mahler rather than to himself.

In the memory of many who attended, this was the most stirring performance of the Eighth Symphony they ever heard. Despite the obvious success, a few of the newspaper critics were reserved in their judgement. The majority, however, outdid themselves in glowing reports. "With this achievement, Dr Webern, hitherto known only as one of the purest and most undaunted leaders in modern creative work, has placed himself in the very first rank as a conductor also," commented the *Wiener Zeitung* (21 April), and the *Arbeiterzeitung* (20 April), calling Webern's leadership "fanatic," concluded cryptically: "With this performance of the Eighth, Anton Webern would have become a famous conductor elsewhere, but here in Vienna . . ."

For Webern, the reaction of the press was all but anticlimactic. His satisfaction lay in the rendition of the great work itself. In the days following the concerts, his elation gave way to sober self-appraisal. On 27 April he penned his own account to Schoenberg:

I may well say that the performance, all in all, was successful. The choruses knew their parts really without a fault. And that I achieved this with these people—many, many of the almost 700 singers could not even read notes—this really satisfied me very much. The soloists were much less to my taste;[10] especially the tenor, who came only during the last days from Berlin, suited me very little. The orchestra did its share with much devotion, but in order to bring out what I had envisaged, especially in the second part, I would still have needed *many* rehearsals. I had two rehearsals with the orchestra alone, two combined rehearsals, and a dress rehearsal during which, however, I kept on polishing, although it was public. I had six rehearsals of the combined choruses with piano. Because of these circumstances I believe that the first part, which is exclusively designed for choral effect, was better than the second. I set a real *Allegro impetuoso*; in no time the movement was over, like a gigantic prelude to the second. The orchestra was—I may well say it—quite devoted to me this time. It acclaimed me, and individual members expressed themselves very warmly. I may therefore conclude that I have conducted well (although Miss E.B. [Elsa Bienenfeld] asserted the contrary, in the

most unheard-of manner, in the *Journal*). . . . What it is like to
conduct this work, dearest friend, I cannot describe. I always believed
I could neither physically nor emotionally endure it. But I was so well
trained by the many rehearsals that I mastered it. The great fugue in
the first part sat so well that, for all practical purposes, I would not
have needed to conduct it at all. The choral sound at the end of the
first movement was so strong—especially through the participation of
the children (*140* in number, they sang excellently)—that I, there on
the rostrum, hardly heard anything of the trumpets and trombones,
which were placed in *isolated positions*. The second part, too, came out
well; I could still have used several rehearsals of the entire ensemble
for it. . . . The number of participants was greater than ever before
during performances of the work in Vienna.

A few weeks after the great event, on 18 May, Webern joined a
delegation of members from the workmen's choruses in a pilgrimage to
the Grinzing cemetery, where they held a ceremony at Mahler's graveside in commemoration of the fifteenth anniversary of the composer's
death. David Josef Bach gave the oration and a wreath was laid.

Earlier that month, on 7 May, Webern had led the Mödlinger
Männergesangverein in a Schubert evening. The programme included
Der Gondelfahrer, *Trinklied*, *Nachtgesang im Walde* (in which the Stiegler
Quartet, a wind ensemble consisting of members of the Philharmonic
Orchestra, collaborated), and *Miriams Siegesgesang* (for mixed chorus,
soprano solo, and piano). For the last-named work, Josef Hueber's
sister, Berta, had been scheduled as soloist, but she fell ill and Webern
replaced her at the last minute with Greta Wilheim, a Jewish singer. That
choice aroused anti-Semitic sentiments in the group and precipitated a
crisis, described by Hueber: "The society had strong German
Nationalist leanings, and after the performance the majority of
members voiced objection. Webern's reaction to this was his immediate
resignation as chorus leader."[11] Satisfying as the short period of
association with the group had been, he did not hesitate to relinquish his
position at this challenge to his integrity as a man and an artist.

Webern was to mount the conductor's podium again within a month,
this time before a select audience and in the limelight of international
attention. He had been invited, largely through Werner Reinhart's
influence, to conduct the première of his Five Pieces for Orchestra, Op.
10, and a performance of Schoenberg's Wind Quintet, Op. 26, at the
ISCM festival in Zürich.[12] Schoenberg at first felt slighted that he had
not been asked to introduce his work himself. But after months of
grumbling and withholding his consent, he finally agreed to have it
performed under Webern, on whose conscientious and sympathetic

preparation he could depend. Webern requested from the festival officials ten rehearsals under his personal supervision, stipulating also that each player know his part thoroughly beforehand. The Austrian section of the ISCM subsidized his trip with 500 schillings, and his Swiss hosts assumed the expenses of his stay. Webern left Vienna on 5 June, travelling via Innsbruck and the scenic Arlberg (he saw this area for the first time, and it enchanted him completely). In Zürich he stayed in the Pension Wehrle, Bellerivestrasse 7. He found his quarters excellent and was delighted by the city's location alongside the large lake. Throwing himself at once into the rehearsals, he reported in minute detail to Schoenberg about their progress. On 15 June, four days before the Quintet's performance, he registered satisfaction that all his intentions were being carried out. About his own pieces, he wrote with equal confidence: "So far I have had three rehearsals and will have four more short ones. Enough, I believe. The pieces will turn out quite good. The co-ordination of the details caused many difficulties. As far as the sound effect is concerned, I am absolutely right. It sounds excellent. I believe that I may say this."

Webern's work was heard on 23 June in the closing concert of the festival; it was placed in the middle of the programme, which comprised a piano sonata by Miaskovsky, a septet for soprano, flute, piano, and strings by Arthur Hoerée, the Concerto for Violin and Woodwind Instruments by Kurt Weill, and the Pastorale and March by Hans Krasa. "Performance of my pieces: good," the composer noted tersely in his diary. The originality of the orchestral miniatures, conceived more than a dozen years earlier, was unanimously recognized by the international press. Tributes full of superlatives appeared in leading newspapers and journals. The *Berliner Tageblatt* (3 July), pointing out the long interval between the work's origin and its first public performance, commented: "The unexpectedly sympathetic participation of the audience is an obligation to disseminate these wonderful pieces." The report of the *Christian Science Monitor* (10 July) tried, as did numerous other writers, to convey the uniqueness of Webern's music:

> The last concert brought to many of us an unexpected and entirely delightful adventure. Anton Webern raised his baton before a chamber orchestra which included a guitar, mandolin, cow-bells, and that horrible instrument, the harmonium. From the silence there escaped into sound wafts of strangely beautiful colour. The ear caught wraith-like wisps of melody which, as smoke, eddied for a moment and then dissolved. A sudden shimmer of iridescence where form and colour became one—and then silence gently withdrew from us that of which we had scarcely become aware. Only a true musical poet could

give us these fugitive glimpses of a new and fascinating world of sound.

Webern's singular personality was sensed by many of his colleagues at the festival. Rudolph Ganz, then at the height of his career, later recalled: "His rehearsing was fantastic as far as sensitive demands were concerned, but there was much giggling among the musicians present over the small details he tried to impart. However, the general opinion after the concert was that the Opus 10 was the *real gain* of the evening."[13] The singer Ruzena Herlinger gave a sumptuous luncheon in Webern's honour at the fashionable Hotel Baur au Lac. She wanted him to meet some of the leading personalities in the world of music and invited Adolf Weissmann, the powerful critic from Berlin, Alfredo Casella, Edward Dent, Henry Prunières, and Egon Wellesz. At the table, Webern was overwhelmed by the luxuriousness of the setting. He loved good food, but this was the first time that he had ever been served lobster. In her memoirs the hostess recalled: "Suddenly Webern's voice 'Wie isst man dös?' ['How does one eat this?']. After a few minutes again, 'Dös is aber gut' ['This is surely good']. A similar comment accompanied the serving of the fine rosé wine. Everyone was charmed by Webern's unpretentious bearing."[14] During his stay, he was invited to participate in an automobile excursion that led via the famous Axenstrasse along the Vierwaldstättersee to Altdorf and beyond to Andermatt. The trip is vividly described in Webern's diary. At Tiefengletsch, on the way to the Furka Pass, the party had to turn back because the road was blocked by snow. The grandiose Swiss alpine scenery impressed Webern as "showcase, not landscape."

Webern had reason to be satisfied with the season's accomplishments, and he now anticipated the summer recess with a "sense of complete independence," as he remarked in his diary. The vacation period was given over to creative work, in particular to the String Trio, Op. 20. The only interruptions were a brief stay at Mürzzuschlag, 26–31 July, and a few mountain excursions, including an ascent of the Reichenstein with Ernst Diez. Lack of money prevented the outing to the Arlberg region that Webern had hoped to make with his wife.

As usual, the summer months were devoid of any income, and the outlay for the four children, all of whom were given the best of education, necessitated extremely close budget management. That year, Webern once again considered returning to the theatre and actually drafted an application to the artistic director of the Municipal Theatre at Graz.[15] In response to his plea to tide him over the critical period, Hertzka had consented to a monthly payment of 100 schillings from May through September. A few days before its expiration, Webern begged Hertzka to extend the subsistence, writing on 26 September: "I am now working on a String Trio, which I hope to finish in the course of the winter. . . . If only I could be more financially independent, so that I could devote myself to my work." Here Webern quoted a favourite maxim: Goethe's admonition to Schiller that only inner withdrawal could provide the fertile soil for creative productivity (see Chapter XVI). The request was granted, and payments from Universal Edition continued through the autumn. Hoping to secure a more permanent solution, however, Webern called personally on Hertzka at his home on 14 December. An agreement was reached that regular monthly payments of 200 schillings would be made throughout 1927. Hertzka also held out the possibility that more might be done in the future. Encouraged, Webern noted in his diary that day: "Arrived at satisfactory and auspicious arrangements."

Hertzka's confidence in Webern's potential was well founded. Performances of his compositions took place in growing numbers at home and abroad. Venturesome artists began programming his songs in their recitals. In Zürich the Six Bagatelles, Op. 9, were played in late October, in the wake of the success scored there by the Five Pieces, Op. 10. The latter work was conducted by Koussevitsky in New York during November. Another first American performance, given on 28 November in the same city, was that of the Five Sacred Songs, Op. 15. As a result of his growing reputation, Webern was named an honorary member of the New York Composers' Guild. On 10 December, in Vienna, he was able to hear his Five Movements, Op. 5. The Kolisch ensemble (then appearing under the name "Wiener Streichquartett") played the work "really quite fabulously," as Webern reported to Schoenberg. In January 1927 the Four Songs, Op. 12, were first presented as a complete cycle, and on 10 April the chorus *Entflieht auf leichten Kähnen*, Op. 2, written almost twenty years earlier, at long last appeared on a concert programme. That same season, the Passacaglia, Op. 1, was performed by the Philadelphia Orchestra under Stokowski (Ernst Diez, lecturing at nearby Bryn Mawr College, was present), and the Five Pieces, Op. 10, were given in Berlin, where Schoenberg heard them, delighting Webern with his high praise. The mounting recognition served to confirm the composer's conviction of his creative destiny.

As the summer of 1926 drew to a close, Webern was loath to put his work aside. On 26 September he wrote to Berg that he could not bear to look on when the leaves turned yellow. He then had only one wish—that the death of summer might be quickly over so that room would be made for new birth. "Once the old foliage is gone, you know, the buds are already there," he remarked. In January, amidst the most severe frost, the sap was gathering in the trees. These thoughts both comforted and excited him, for he could hardly await the coming of spring and with it the time of his own creative fertility. "If only it were that far along again," he exclaimed.

Shortly afterwards, Webern's melancholy over the passing of summer was lifted. On 14 October, Schoenberg and his wife stopped in Vienna on their way back to Berlin from Pörtschach, where they had spent their vacation, and there was a joyful reunion at Berg's home. By then Webern was already deeply involved again in his work with the Singverein. The chorus had resumed its regular Thursday evening rehearsals (held in the auditorium of òne of the city schools located at Stubenbastei 3) and was getting ready for two Workmen's Symphony Concerts on 10 and 14 November. Before public appearances, additional practice sessions became obligatory, three and even four a week being not unusual. About 125 chorus members regularly attended, and there was a small but reliable nucleus of good singers. One of these was the group's president, Felix Dantine, who was a railway official by profession, but a vocal expert by avocation. The November concerts comprised Beethoven's *Coriolan* Overture, Liszt's *Totentanz* (with the French pianist Lucie Caffaret), and Mahler's *Das klagende Lied* (in which the Singverein participated).

Another pair of Workmen's Symphony Concerts, on 19 and 20 March 1927, was dedicated to the Beethoven centennial. After the Second *Leonore* Overture and the Fourth Symphony, the Singverein joined in the *Consecration of the House*, Op. 124, and in the *Choral Fantasy*, Op. 80 (with Eduard Steuermann as soloist). The magistrate of Vienna sponsored a repetition of the programme on 21 March in the large hall of the Musikverein, to which the city's middle-school pupils were invited. So enthusiastic was the young audience and so stormy the applause that the *Consecration of the House* had to be repeated. In a letter to Schoenberg on 28 February, Webern called this work "an incomparably beautiful chorus . . . a serene, gentle, in part somewhat melancholy piece from Beethoven's last period." He added "*Brahms* is said to have been the last to do it in Vienna. Not even a piano–vocal score of it exists; it seems to be performed nowhere."

To Webern's great disappointment, the Beethoven concert was ignored by the press, probably because of the flood of events crowding the climactic centennial week. There was just one newspaper article, which was in general detrimental and did not even mention the conductor's name. Proud and sensitive, Webern bitterly complained to Schoenberg in his letter of 6 April: "This time I really was particularly angered. For who will want to make music with me or engage me as a conductor if, as a result, he is silenced to death or else torn apart?"

Webern's concern was unwarranted, however, since he found himself in steady demand. In January he had led a performance of Bach's Concerto for Four Claviers, and on 31 March he presided over the first performance of Alban Berg's Chamber Concerto for piano, violin, and thirteen wind instruments. This work, Berg's first in strict twelve-tone technique, had been completed early in 1925, the year of the *Wozzeck* première.[16] Dedicating the concerto to Schoenberg for his 50th birthday, Berg had used in the composition the letters in the names of Schoenberg, Webern, and himself, as far as they could be realized in musical notation, to form three themes that function prominently in the melodic development of the piece. With this allusion, Berg wanted to establish a monument to their creative triumvirate.

As with Schoenberg's quintet in Zürich, Webern considered it a holy mission to lead Berg's work to success.[17] He had strong allies in the soloists, Steuermann and Kolisch, and in a wind ensemble consisting of younger members from the Philharmonic Orchestra. The première, preceded by thirteen rehearsals, took place in an afternoon concert of the Vienna ISCM section at the Konzerthaus. Berg's concerto highlighted the programme, which opened with works by Beethoven (in observation of the centennial) and by Carl Prohaska (in homage to this Vienna composer who had died just three days earlier). Webern's report of 6 April to Schoenberg radiated satisfaction:

Kolisch and Steuermann were excellent. From rehearsal to rehearsal practising became more ideal. I have been able to rehearse as you did earlier with your Serenade and *Pierrot* ensembles. And this with thirteen wind players from the Philharmonic. From rehearsal to rehearsal they became warmer and more zealous. Berg was very content, I believe, and I am very happy to have succeeded so well in this eminently difficult task. The concerto is a magnificent piece and sounds really wonderful: the corner movements (Variations and Rondo) are tender, transparent, gay, and full of verve. The Adagio is deeply moving. How much would I have liked to introduce it to you!

On 1 May, the international workers' holiday, Webern conducted his first radio concert, with the Singverein participating. Opening with Richard Strauss' *Fanfares* for brass and drums, the programme included Scheu's *Sonntagslied* (a cappella), Liszt's *Arbeiterchor* (in Webern's arrangement), Beethoven's *Consecration of the House*, and Mendelssohn's *Erste Walpurgisnacht*. That same month, Universal Edition brought out Webern's Three Songs, Op. 18. Fired by the rapid publication of his works, the composer now was bent on completing his

String Trio, Op. 20, begun the year before. The two movements comprising the printed opus were completed by the end of June, but Webern had a third movement in mind on which he worked during July and August, only to abandon it unfinished.

Webern spent the summer of 1927 in the Krumpen Valley at Hafning near Vordernberg. On an outing during Pentecost of the preceding year, he had first come upon this "ideal landscape," as he called it in his diary. In May of 1927 he returned there and rented for the summer three rooms and a kitchen in a rambling old farmhouse (Krumpen No. 3). On 9 July, he and his family moved in for a stay that was to last until 30 August.

The prolonged sojourn was made possible by favourable arrangements with a pupil from America, Maurice Kaplan, a violist in the Philadelphia Orchestra and a participant in the recent Passacaglia performance under Stokowski. He had approached Webern for lessons after finding Schoenberg's honorarium too high for his pocket.[18] Kaplan and his wife arrived in Hafning three days after Webern and rented quarters in the same house. In his diary, the composer expressed his instant liking for the Americans, who were included in most of the family activities. Lessons began immediately; a piano had been rented for the purpose and brought up from Leoben. The steady revenue from Kaplan, totalling 420 schillings, made Webern's productive and carefree holiday possible.

Serenity pervades the entries in Webern's diary of those summer weeks. At the end of the first day, he enthusiastically noted: "Beautiful evening. Impression: as in a shelter high on the mountain. Wonderful air coming down from the Reichenstein." He revelled in the nearness of the alpine peaks: "Daily view of the mountains! At all hours, in all types of weather." Enthralled with the beauty surrounding him, he copied an excerpt from Goethe's *Annalen 1817*: ". . . the mysterious clear light, as the highest energy, eternal, singular and indivisible." The "Tagesordnung" (daily schedule) was outlined as follows:

Endeavoured to be at work at eight o'clock in the morning. In good weather, right out of bed for a dip in the Krumpenbachl [creek]. Work until about half past twelve. Staying in the room not very pleasant, cold and a little damp, somewhat cellar-like, especially on hot days. After lunch rest in the meadow behind the house, an hour at most. Sometimes bathe in the little creek with Minna and the children. Then work until Jause [coffee time], often also afterwards. Around six o'clock usually a walk in the Krumpengraben [valley] or in the surrounding forest, looking for mushrooms and berries. Minna and the children take many sunbaths, especially Mali.

Ernst Diez, after spending an academic year in America, had returned to his parents' home in Vordernberg, and it added to Webern's enjoyment of those summer days to have his cousin nearby. A joint ascent of the Reichenstein, graphically described in the diary, climaxed the many excursions. When the vacation idyll drew to its close, Webern nostalgically wrote to Zenk on 25 August: "Think once in a while of your old teacher, who, the older he becomes the more he likes to go to the mountains and ascend their heights, who is very unhappy to have to say farewell to them again so soon. What a climate this is, what an atmosphere—indescribable." A few days later, the weather broke, and when Webern and his family left Hafning on 30 August, the mountains lay covered with snow.

Back home, Webern could look forward to another reunion with Schoenberg. The master came to Vienna for his 53rd birthday and for the première, on 19 September, of his Third String Quartet by the Kolisch ensemble. By then, Webern had resumed rehearsals with the Singverein. For the group's first appearance during the 1927–28 season, the *Psalmus Hungaricus* by Zoltán Kodály was scheduled. It formed the closing number in a Workmen's Symphony Concert on 6 November. In that concert, Webern shared the podium with Stephen Strasser, who conducted the first part of the programme: Liszt's *Heldenklage*, Bartók's Piano Concerto No. 1, and Tchaikovsky's Fifth Symphony. Bartók himself was soloist in his concerto (which he had introduced in Frankfurt the preceding summer). His music fared no better with the Vienna press than that of Webern, Berg, and Schoenberg. "Easily one of the most indigestible works of today's literature," H.E.H. wrote on 9 November in the *Wiener Zeitung*. "Béla Bartók seemingly attempts in this work to beat even Schoenberg and heaps discord on discord, so that even the most undaunted champions of the creations of the 'contemporaries' shook their heads in perplexity and disappointment." In contrast, Kodály's work and its performance under Webern were accorded warm plaudits.

Two months later, on 8 January 1928, Webern took complete charge of the next Workmen's Symphony Concert, which was given in the large hall of the Musikverein. The programme included Goldmark's Overture *Prometheus Bound*, the *Song of Destiny* by Brahms (in which the Singverein participated), and Bruckner's Seventh Symphony. A glowing report in the *Arbeiterzeitung* spoke of the conductor's "dedication and enthusiasm" that captivated the orchestra, of his "unerringly sure feeling" for all aspects of the Bruckner Symphony, and of his unparalleled educational achievement with the Singverein. "It is astonishing with how much assurance and delicacy our comrades have conquered the exceedingly difficult *Song of Destiny* by Brahms," the critic wrote. In recognition of Webern's accomplishments, the Kunststelle presented him with a deluxe edition of the Bruckner score, with an embossed dedication commemorating the event.[19]

On 17 April, in one of the subscription concerts of Kolisch's Wiener Streichquartett, Webern conducted the world première of Schoenberg's *Herzgewächse*, Op. 20, for high soprano, celesta, harmonium, and harp. Marianne Rau-Hoeglauer was soloist. Meeting with great success, the work was played twice on a programme that also included Bach's *Brandenburg* Concerto No. 5, with Wangler, Kolisch, and Steuermann the featured soloists. "It was eminently exciting to hear *such* cantilena singing on so high a pitch. I revelled in this sound and that of the ensemble. The song is indescribably beautiful," Webern opened his 24 April report to Schoenberg, proceeding with a vivid account of every nuance of his rendition. As for his interpretation of Bach, he told Schoenberg that he based it on the *Urtext* instead of on Reger's edition, with which he disagreed. For Webern, distinct dynamic levels, rather than gradations leading from one to the other, formed the ideal Bach sound, and he felt that faithful adherence to Bach's original prescriptions made for *Buntheit* (variety of colours) rather than academic dryness.

On 1 May, Webern fulfilled his first conducting engagement under the auspices of Ravag, Austria's government broadcasting agency. Its director prescribed the programme, which included Liszt's *Festklänge*, Weber's *Konzertstück*, Mozart's *Jupiter* Symphony and Wagner's *Meistersinger* Prelude. Although he had only one short rehearsal, Webern was quite satisfied with the result. "The sound in the Studio-Room was not unsympathetic to me," he wrote to Schoenberg on 5 May about the then still novel broadcasting medium. "It is true that it was very dry, but on the other hand it was quite clear (something like piano playing without any pedal)."

During spring and early summer, rehearsals were in progress for the Workmen's Symphony Concert planned for November. Scheduled were Schoenberg's chorus *Friede auf Erden* and Mahler's Second Symphony. The intensity of preparations matched that for Mahler's Eighth Symphony and, as in the latter work, the Singverein joined forces with the choral society Freie Typographia, for a combined strength of some 350 voices. The intrinsic difficulties of Schoenberg's chorus offered Webern a special challenge. On 13 July he told the composer: "Today I had the last choral rehearsal before vacation. Since the beginning of July I have been rehearsing three times a week. Naturally, always your chorus. Now I am already somewhat reassured. The strophes in the middle are very difficult indeed for such choral groups. But presently I believe that things will turn out. At the end of August I will begin again."

Other projects also claimed Webern's attention during the first part of 1928. He had been called upon in the spring to serve as one of the judges in the awarding of the Vienna Music Prize. "A distasteful job," he wrote to Schoenberg on 24 April. "One gets to see really crazy things in the process. I would have preferred to win the prize again myself." Earlier, in February, the head of the Leningrad Philharmonic, Nicolai Malko, had appeared in Vienna as guest conductor of the Workmen's Symphony. He invited Webern to submit a number of sample programmes for a projected concert tour to Russia, but, much to the composer's disappointment, nothing came of this plan. Another possibility arose in early summer, when the singer Marya Freund transmitted an offer to Webern to come to Paris as first conductor of a private chamber opera theatre that had been in operation for six years. The monthly salary was to be 3,000 French francs (then corresponding to about 700 schillings in Austrian currency). Webern saw only risks in the proposition and turned it down, explaining to Schoenberg on 13 July: "As to chamber opera and theatre generally—I am glad that I now have time to compose again. It would be the same all over again. No, I believe that I must calmly hold out here for the time being and that I should leave only if something quite extraordinary presents itself. Only then could I feel justified in abandoning what has been begun here with Dr Bach."

Webern's determination not to allow any interruption of his creative work was furthered by the favourable financial arrangements in prospect for that summer. Maurice Kaplan, the violist from Philadelphia, returned for another period of study, lasting from 28 June to 1 September. This time he stayed in Mödling and, taking two lessons a week, contributed a total of 630 schillings to Webern's income. Additional revenue came from the singer Ruzena Herlinger, who was preparing for an autumn recital with Paul Amadeus Pisk in London's Wigmore Hall. (The programme was to include two of Webern's George songs, "Dies ist ein Lied" and "Kahl reckt der Baum".) She was also scheduled for the soprano solo in Mahler's Second Symphony. Her coaching sessions lasted from June through October, and when she took a holiday at St Wolfgang she invited Webern to come there for a week, beginning 16 July, at her expense. He was lodged in the famous resort hotel Weisses Rössl. Postcards to his children tell of his outings in the beautiful surroundings, of a dip in the lake at an hour when the beach was empty, and of the daily work sessions that formed the substance of that pleasant interlude. With characteristic thriftiness, he asked the children to preserve the picture postcards so that they might become part of his collection of holiday souvenirs.

Several brief outings during 1928 satisfied Webern's constant longing for the high regions. Time and again he went to his favourite mountain, the Schneealpe, a broad massif with a vast expanse of forests leading up to alpine meadows. He usually set out for the climb from Kapellen, ascending on the first day to the Kampl Hut, a rustic cabin offering shelter for the night. On the second day he would go on to timberline and the slopes beyond. Up there, amidst the abundant alpine flora, he found complete happiness and peace; leading those closest to him to the wonders of the heights gave him the greatest pleasure, and his diary reflects each cherished experience. One such tour was an ascent at night to the Kampl Hut, in November 1927, with Dr Norbert Schwarzmann, which was cut short by bad weather. In May, Webern began the climbing season of 1928 with another attempt on the Schneealpe. This time Dr Rudolf Ploderer came along. Wintry conditions still prevailed, and deep snowdrifts barred them from continuing to the summit. However, a few months later, in July, when Webern took his wife and children to the mountain, they had no difficulty in reaching the highest point, called "Windberg" (1,903 m.).

On a week's trip at the end of July, Webern went with his family to Vordernberg to help celebrate Ernst Diez's 50th birthday, and then on to Klagenfurt to see his sisters, Maria and Rosa. A pilgrimage to the Preglhof, on 30 July, evoked fond memories of his youthful years. Webern found the family burial plot at Schwabegg, which he had not visited since 1921, in good order, and he took some flowers from his mother's grave and also from that of his father at the Annabichl cemetery, where he went a few days later. He preserved these flowers in a tiny envelope, which he minutely inscribed, among his pictorial souvenirs of that summer.

A weekend climb of the mighty Hochschwab, on 11–12 August, was especially satisfying for Webern. The excursion, enhanced by excellent weather and magnificent alpine scenery, was made in the company of his thirteen-year-old son Peter and Dr Rudolf Ploderer. They saw many mountain goats as they traversed the high peak from Bodenbauer to Seewiesen, where they stayed overnight in the Schiestelhaus. It was the last outing of a summer that was especially fruitful. Webern completed his Symphony, Op. 21, and the rescoring of his Six Pieces, Op. 6. In addition, he began a transcription for string orchestra of his Five Movements, Op. 5.

Occasional fluctuations notwithstanding, Webern's economic circumstances remained straitened. As of September 1928, his monthly salary at the Israelitic Institute for the Blind was reduced from 225 to 100 schillings. Webern still had to make the long trip to the Hohe Warte twice weekly, although each time only an hour's choral rehearsal was involved. That autumn, he had only one private pupil, M. Hice, an

American from Philadelphia sent by Kaplan. Hice studied with Webern throughout the winter, coming once a week and paying $5 per lesson (amounting to 140 schillings a month).

A temporary source of additional revenue was provided by the Freie Typographia chorus, with which Webern had begun working in May. After the summer recess, at the end of August, rehearsals with that group and with the Singverein resumed. All efforts then were bent towards the November performance of Schoenberg's *Friede auf Erden* and Mahler's Second Symphony. With mounting enthusiasm, Webern kept Schoenberg informed of his progress in the difficult task of inculcating the music's intricacies to his amateur singers. (At the time, Schoenberg was still in his retreat on the French Riviera. He came to Vienna briefly for his 54th birthday, an occasion for a large celebration in the Rathauskeller with all his friends. Returning to Roquebrune Cap Martin, he remained there until February 1929, working on the libretto for *Moses und Aron*, then still planned as an oratorio, and on the opera *Von Heute auf Morgen*, for which his wife signed as librettist under the pseudonym Max Blonda.)

The difficulties of intonation in Schoenberg's *a cappella* chorus are such that the composer had provided an optional orchestral backing, consisting of pairs of woodwinds, two horns, and strings. Because of the limitations of his singers, Webern decided to rely on this support (enlarged for the occasion), although he was increasingly satisfied with the degree of security achieved during rehearsals. On 4 November, one week before the concert, he wrote to Schoenberg: "Unless everything deceives me, your chorus will turn out well. Now, I believe, all 350 singers have really learned it. Have you ever heard your chorus at all? Do you really know yourself how beautiful it is? Unprecedented! What sound! Exciting to the highest degree. I am always completely exhausted after we have taken it through without stopping. And the other day, when we had sung it through, Polnauer came up to me, trembling in every limb, incapable of uttering a word. Yes, such is this music!"

When Webern wrote this letter he was ill. He had been plagued by stomach troubles since early October, and the strain connected with the rehearsals now brought on an acute worsening of his condition. At first, ulcers were suspected and the necessity of an operation was contemplated, but an X-ray diagnosis disproved that theory. Instead, Webern was placed on a strict milk diet. In his weakened state, his energies were taxed to the limit. Becoming alarmed, his friends prevailed on Dr Norbert Schwarzmann to write to Schoenberg and urgently request that he prevail on Webern, who was obviously driving himself to exhaustion. Schoenberg complied at once. In his letter of 2 November, he begged Webern to spare his health not only for future concerts, but especially for the sake of his calling as a composer.

The concerts were set for 11 and 12 November in the large hall of the Musikverein, and the first was to be broadcast. Webern conducted the first of two orchestral rehearsals on the afternoon of Saturday, 10 November. Then the exertion took its toll. Feeling himself near collapse, he allowed his wife to summon Dr Cech, the family physician. The doctor forthwith ordered Webern to bed and forbade him to conduct the concerts. In the emergency, Erwin Stein leapt into the breach as conductor. Thanks to Webern's painstaking preparation, the choruses adjusted themselves with aplomb. The concerts were a great success, as reflected in long and favourable newspaper reports.[20] A brief excerpt from Der Tag (16 November) is characteristic: "Webern's fiery spirit, which had animated all participants and which had polished the workers' choruses into a most exquisite and noble body of sound, hovered directly over the magnificent performance. Erwin Stein had to do scarcely more than pull the stops of the giant apparatus and take care of the most important entries; thus the proportions of sound came about by themselves."

Sick and disappointed, Webern listened to the broadcast concert from his bed. He could think only of his loyal singers who, after months of devoted rehearsing, had been deprived of his leadership at the crucial hour, and in an eloquent letter, dated 15 November, he expressed his sentiments to the members of the Freie Typographia.[21]

His illness was slow in subsiding. The physician prescribed a three-week rest cure at Hof Gastein, where the Krankenkasse (compulsory medical insurance agency) maintained a convalescent home. Instead, however, David Josef Bach and Ruzena Herlinger initiated a collection to finance his admission to the fashionable Kurhaus Semmering. Staying there from 1 to 20 December, Webern found the privacy and personal attention conducive to his recuperation. He regretted missing another Workmen's Symphony Concert on 8 December, for which Erwin Stein again substituted as conductor. (That programme, held in the large festival hall of the Hofburg, was in homage to Franz Schubert, the 100th anniversary of whose death had occurred on 19 November.)

During those critical days, Webern's friends outdid themselves in spontaneous displays of affection and esteem, providing comfort and financial assistance. Among the contributions was one from the Vienna ISCM chapter, of which Webern was then a member of the board of directors. Representing that group, Paul Stefan also wrote of Webern's situation to Mrs Elizabeth Sprague Coolidge, the American patroness who had sponsored two chamber music concerts in Vienna the year before. She responded with a cheque for $100. Webern's income book meticulously lists the various donations, which included one by the ever-helpful Werner Reinhart. Schoenberg and Berg also assisted. The financial support, the numerous testimonials of friendship, and the invigorating mountain air on the Semmering, where the Kurhaus provided him with the best of care and unaccustomed luxury, quickly restored Webern's health and spirits. Home in Mödling by Christmas, he could look confidently into the future. In a cheerful letter to Schoenberg, dated 29 December, he outlined a number of new concert plans, voicing his special gratification that the Schoenberg–Mahler programme would be repeated in April. He was also elated that Klemperer, Scherchen, and Stokowski had all expressed interest to Universal Edition in his recently completed Symphony, Op. 21.

Performances and publication of Webern's compositions had been steadily increasing during the past twelve months. His Opus 2, the chorus *Entflieht auf leichten Kähnen*, unperformed for the two decades since it had been written, quickly found attention after its release in print. Following its première in a Styrian provincial town in early 1927, Webern was able to hear it himself for the first time on 7 December of that year, sung by the Stuttgart Madrigal Society in a Vienna concert (see Chapter V). On 8 February 1928 Margot Hinnenberg-Lefèbre and Eduard Steuermann performed songs by Webern and Berg, and in the same concert the Kolisch Quartet played Webern's Six Bagatelles, as well as Berg's Lyric Suite. Eight days later, on 16 February, Hermann Scherchen led the première of Webern's Four Songs, Op. 13, in a concert in Winterthur, with a repeat performance in Zürich immediately after (see Chapter XVI). At the end of April Universal Edition published the Five Canons, Op. 16, and the Two Songs, Op. 19. The String Trio, Op. 20, had been released earlier (November 1927), and the première of that work was given in Vienna soon after, on 16 January 1928, by members of the Kolisch Quartet. Performances of the String Trio in Berlin and Schwerin followed during spring, and another was given in September during the ISCM festival in Siena (see Chapter XVIII).

Webern was not present in Siena, but Hertzka was. The publisher's unerring faith in Webern's creative mission provided encouragement to the composer during the difficult years of his emergence into international prominence. A sense of solidarity with this friend and promoter speaks from Webern's letter to him of 6 December 1927. Thanking him for the extension of monthly payments and the recent publication of his Trio, he wrote:

> The faith you have again shown in my cause is my greatest support on a path that is certainly no easy one. But I should like to take this opportunity to reassure you by quite expressly pointing out that, particularly in the last years, a difficult but steady and uninterrupted

ascent of my cause can beyond doubt be observed. And is not this kind of success of more value than a rocket-like one? Every year the number of performances in each category of my works increases. I know, of course, that my work still means extremely little in purely commercial terms. But the reason for this lies in its hitherto almost exclusively lyrical nature: poems, to be sure, bring in little money, but after all they still have to be written.

CHAPTER XVIII

Twelve-tone method—Opera 17–21—
Other works—Liszt arrangement
(1924–1928)

IN OCTOBER 1902, at the outset of his university life, Webern had copied into his diary a passage from the writings of the Austrian architect and teacher Otto Wagner:[1]

> Every architectural form has evolved from construction and has successively turned into an art form. Therefore, there is always a constructional reason that influences the forms, and it can thus be deduced with certainty that new constructions must also give birth to new forms. Our most recent epoch, unlike any earlier one, has produced the greatest number of such constructions (one has only to think of the success of iron). What can therefore be more logical than to assert: If so many entirely new constructions are contributed to art, this in itself must cause a new formal concept, and gradually a new style, to evolve.

Webern's early preoccupation with such thoughts was to determine his entire creative career.

The year 1924 witnessed Webern's formal adoption of Schoenberg's "method of composition with twelve tones related solely to each other," a method that he henceforth employed exclusively in all his works and that he was to develop to its fullest potential. Erwin Stein published the first outline of the new technique in September 1924 (in *Musikblätter des Anbruch*), but its premises had been the subject of much prior discussion. As is the case with many revolutionary ideas, the creation of the dodecaphonic method cannot actually be attributed to a single intellect. Rather, it evolved from various currents of musical thought that gradually merged into one general trend. An early instance of a twelve-tone theme can be found in Liszt's *Faust* Symphony, and Richard Strauss concocted a twelve-tone series for the illustration of the section "On

Science" in his tone poem *Thus spake Zarathustra*. Scriabin developed a system of "synthetic chords," and the Ukrainian Jev Golyscheff wrote some works in pure twelve-tone style. In the second decade of the twentieth century, after atonality had abnegated the precepts of the traditional major–minor harmonic functions, composers consciously struggled for the formulation of a new musical syntax. The main thrusts were made, simultaneously but independently, by Schoenberg and Josef Matthias Hauer. In their common quest for the expansion of musical organization, Schoenberg was destined to outrank his close rival in the establishment of an autonomous twelve-tone technique.

Hauer, a man with a strong bent towards mathematics and metaphysics, developed a system of musical construction employing "tropes" (patterns within which no notes were repeated). These tropes added up to thematic formations of twelve notes. In Hauer's piano piece *Nomos* (Law), published in 1912, the germ of twelve-tone music is already embodied. He expounded his doctrines in several treatises, appearing between 1919 and 1926.[2] While Hauer's twelve-tone method, like Schoenberg's, does away with the hegemony of a tonal centre, his approach is quite different. In his *Tropenlehre* (Theory of Tropes), he arranges all possible combinations of twelve different notes into a convenient system of 44 groups. Each of these represents a field of sound, identifiable by the ear, similar to a definite key in the concept of the old tonal system, and the transition from one trope to the next is supposed to evoke an aesthetic experience in the listener.

The notion of replacing the seven-tone diatonic scale system with one based on all twelve tones of the chromatic scale had already been hinted at by Schoenberg in his *Harmonielehre*, published in 1911. His experiments led through a slow process of evolution to the establishment of the twelve-tone row as the fundamental principle of a new idiom. In Schoenberg's system, no tone has predominance. The former concepts of consonance and dissonance are abolished, along with the governing rôle of the tonic as a key centre and its consequent relationships. In row composition, no note is to be repeated before all twelve notes of the chromatic scale have made their entrance. A note can be sounded on any pitch level, however, and it may be re-stated immediately after its appearance, i.e. before the next note of the series is heard. The *Grundgestalt* (basic arrangement of the row) allows for three transmutations: inversion, retrograde, and retrograde inversion. Taking into account all transpositions available within the chromatic scale, these four forms of the basic row are capable of producing altogether 48 possibilities. Melody and harmony derive entirely from the row, while rhythm and other elements are treated freely.

Unlike Hauer, who demanded full awareness of the tropes and their sequences, Schoenberg did not wish listeners to be conscious of the tone row and its various modes of operation, and he expected composers to use the technique merely as another vehicle for musical thought. He himself infused it with expressive strength and succeeded in pioneering the revolutionary idiom despite initial difficulties with performers and public alike. In due time, dodecaphony came to be recognized as the greatest single influence in the shaping of twentieth-century music. Hauer, after an inconclusive theoretical controversy with Schoenberg, became quite bitter when the Schoenberg–Berg–Webern triumvirate took over the field, and when he saw his own unquestionable merit as an innovator condemned to almost total obscurity. Up to his death in 1959, he stubbornly maintained that pre-eminence in the domain of twelve-tone composition, as well as full credit for its invention, belonged to him. Missing no opportunity to claim his priority, he always signed as "Josef Matthias Hauer, the intellectual originator and, despite many poor imitators, regrettably still the sole expert and craftsman of twelve-tone music." This assertion (omitting only the offensive word "poor" in reference to his "imitators") Hauer even had made into a rubber stamp, which, from about 1937 on, he used on all his letters. In these, he constantly expressed his feelings of hurt and neglect, as for example when he wrote to Paul A. Pisk on 11 January 1935 concerning the forthcoming fiftieth birthday celebration for Alban Berg: "*My* 50th birthday was ignored by my colleagues, who are all, including Schoenberg, my pupils. This strongly smacks of politics! ! ! Alban Berg is very likeable as a person, but his psycho-pathological operetta successes impress me little."[3]

According to Schoenberg himself, his own twelve-tone theory had been in the process of development since 1914–15, but it was not until February 1923 that he officially announced its formulation to a close circle of associates. Later that year, on 1 December, he wrote to Hauer: "Admittedly I have not yet taught this method, because I must still test it in some more compositions and expand it in some directions. But in the introductory course for my pupils I have been using a great deal of it for some years in order to define forms and formal elements and in particular in order to explain musical technique."[4]

Ever since the early days of the breakthrough to atonality, Webern had been in the forefront of the revolutionary development, sometimes spearheading its harmonic and structural innovations. For more than a decade he had consciously experimented with twelve-tone fields himself, as in the Bagatelles, Op. 9. When the rules of strict twelve-tone composition assumed definitive shape, he was the first of Schoenberg's disciples to test their applicability in his own compositions. His preoccupation with the problem of systematic dodecaphony can be clearly traced in one of the manuscripts pre-dating his formal adoption of the method; on sketches to "Mein Weg geht jetzt vorüber," No. 4 of Five Sacred Songs, Op. 15, various row forms are charted, including inversion, retrograde, and retrograde inversion. There are two versions of the basic row, and Webern experiments with their transpositions. One of the rows is embodied in the first twelve notes of the song's vocal part and, in addition, three- or four-note segments of the series are worked, both horizontally and vertically, into the texture of the score.[5]

The song was conceived on 26 July 1922 at Traunkirchen, a period when Webern was in daily contact with Schoenberg. The fact that Webern actually did write out the four basic forms of a twelve-tone row that summer and that he consciously tried to apply the system shows that he was aware of the new method. This appears all the more remarkable in that Schoenberg later declared emphatically that he had not disclosed his system to Webern beforehand. The reference occurs in a note entitled "Anton Webern: Klangfarbenmelodie 1951," written by Schoenberg shortly before his death and published in the enlarged edition (1975) of *Style and Idea*. Taking issue with the assertion by Frederick Dorian-Deutsch that Webern was the first to use the technique of the *Klangfarbenmelodie*, Schoenberg states: "One thing is certain: even had it been Webern's idea, he would not have told it to me. He kept secret everything 'new' he had tried in his compositions. I, on the other hand, immediately and exhaustively explained to him each of my new ideas (with the exception of the method of composition with twelve tones—that I long kept secret, because, as I said to Erwin Stein, Webern immediately uses everything I do, plan or say, so that—I remember my words—'By now I haven't the slightest idea who I am')." Schoenberg's comment leaves no doubt that he deliberately avoided discussing the twelve-tone method with Webern, and the presence of Webern's fully developed row charts in connection with "Mein Weg geht jetzt vorüber," composed half a year before Schoenberg's formal announcement of the method, is therefore highly enigmatic.

Webern also wrote out row charts, with numbers for each of the twelve notes, in his sketches for "Crucem tuam adoramus" (Op. 16, No. 5), and on the same page where he drafted "Christus factus est" (Op. 16, No. 1), there is a sketch for a little piano piece in strict row style. It was at the time when he composed these last two of his Five Canons on Latin Texts, during October and November of 1924, that Webern embarked on the systematic use of the twelve-tone method, thenceforth employed exclusively for all his works.

During early 1924, Webern had been actively involved in the coaching of Schoenberg's Serenade, Op. 24, written in 1923 and scored for chamber ensemble and voice. In the fourth movement of this work, cast

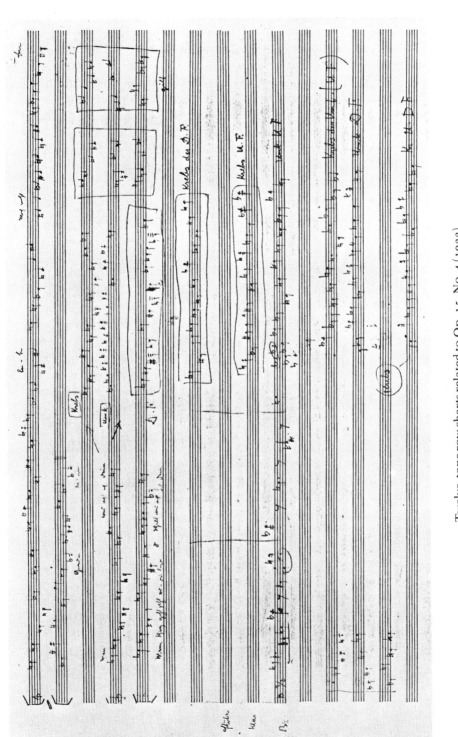

Twelve-tone row charts related to Op. 15, No. 4 (1922)

in the form of a classical suite, the twelve-tone procedure is firmly established for the first time: the theme, built on twelve non-repeated notes, appears in the voice as melody, in the accompaniment as motives, and in the harmony as complete chords. In preparing the performance, Webern had gained practical experience in the inner workings of the new technique. During autumn of the same year, he completed his own first musical essays based on tone rows. At the time, Hertzka had suggested to him a cycle of children's pieces for piano. A reference to that project is found in a letter written by Webern to his publisher on 3 January 1925:

> When you recently inquired, somewhat reproachfully, about the children's pieces that I have promised to write, I could not sufficiently explain in the rush why I have not made progress with them as yet. I would like to make up for this now. As much as it interests me to compose these pieces—I had in fact contemplated something of the sort before your suggestion—I had to interrupt my work on them, because I have been so busy with something else, which, contrary to my original intention, I shall now have to write before the children's pieces. I am working on a cycle of Latin songs and on songs with German texts. I should be very hurt if you thought me ungrateful for your well-meant proposal. No! Be assured that the opposite is the case, and that only my manner of production hinders me from writing these children's pieces in the meantime: for in this respect things never turn out as I wish, but only as is ordained for me, as I must.

When Webern "had to interrupt" work on the children's pieces, two of them actually had already been conceived. One was the aforementioned sketch of a little piano piece, appearing on the same page as the draft to the canon "Christus factus est." It is prefaced by a long list of standard forms from which an entire cycle or suite of pieces might be selected. Old genres like prelude, variations, fugue, passacaglia, and canon are enumerated, as are dance movements, from musette and minuet to mazurka, waltz, polka, Ländler, and Reigen. The multiplicity of moulds thus envisioned, including chorale variations and character pieces, shows that Webern approached the project with a large and imaginative storehouse of possibilities. His first attempt to realize one of the children's pieces extends for nine measures and ends with a double bar that could indicate completion of the conception. Two versions of the row are written out. One comprises twelve tones and is used in a preliminary sketch, the other contains only eleven. Curiously enough, the second, lacking the tone "a," was adopted for the piece; it is quoted six consecutive times. The work displays such hallmarks of Webern's style as widely spaced intervals and rhythmic intricacy, demonstrating the composer's conviction that his music could be fully comprehended even by a child, despite such technical difficulties as frequent crossing of hands and extreme range of note placement.

The character of this first piece, left in draft stage, is indicated by Webern's marking *Lieblich* (Lovely). The same designation is given at the outset of another composition, entitled *Kinderstück* and dated "Autumn 1924." This piece, Webern's first completed work in the twelve-tone method, was unknown until 26 October 1965, when a finished ink manuscript was discovered in Perchtoldsdorf among the remnants of Webern's library. Up till then, the Three Traditional Rhymes, Op. 17, had generally been considered his first twelve-tone work. But, as dated drafts prove, two of these songs were not completed before the second half of 1925. The *Kinderstück*, seventeen measures long, happily captures the spirit of childhood: it is charming, whimsical, and possessed of a quiet wit. The piece is especially interesting for Webern's handling of the twelve-tone technique in its characteristic early style. In the strict application of the method, all twelve notes of the chromatic scale must be introduced before any is sounded a second time, except when a given note is immediately repeated. This exception produces a "Morse code" effect peculiar to many early compositions in the idiom and conspicuous also in the *Kinderstück*.[6]

The same autumn of 1924, Webern employed the twelve-tone row in his song "Armer Sünder, du" (first of the Three Traditional Rhymes, Op. 17), although he did not treat the row in a strict serial fashion. As he wrote to Hertzka, it was this preoccupation with "songs on German texts" that interrupted his further work on the children's pieces. Six months later he turned to still another medium in which to test the new technique. Dated "Spring 1925" are the sketches to a trio movement, one of two essays for violin, viola, and cello undertaken that year. The draft includes two pages of row charts, in which various possibilities of the series are explored. The concept of the music is independent from that of another string trio movement composed later in the year and likewise from that of the String Trio, Op. 20, although the row is related to the one employed in the latter work. The piece—in 3/8 metre, marked *Ruhig* (Calmly)—comprises 24 measures. The row is used only in the original form and its inversion (no transpositions) in more than two dozen statements, the last of which breaks off after the eleventh tone of the series.[7]

Up to 1925, Webern wrote his sketches in loose-leaf form, and this was still the case with the string trio movement just referred to. Beginning with June of that year and for the remaining two decades of his life, the composer used sketchbooks for virtually all his drafts. There exists a total of six such sketchbooks, which Webern himself bound in simple grey cardboard covers. The first is the smallest, containing only 32 pages. The other five total 422 pages.[8] All are in oblong folio format. With the exception of the two published movements of the String Trio, Op. 20, the sketchbooks encompass all of Webern's works from Opus 17 to Opus 31, as well as numerous additional projects, some related to known compositions, others independent. Frequently, there are several layers of drafts clearly marking the stages of evolution. These sketches demonstrate the unending thought that Webern bestowed on every detail of his compositions. He approached music not simply as one who lavishes love and care upon the children of his muse, but in the spirit of a philosopher who labours in the unceasing search for truth. For Webern, the revelation of that truth lay in the achievement of perfection.

The sketchbooks will hereafter be referred to by the numbers I to VI. Since Webern's frequent dates provide an exact record of origin, all compositions, whether finished or unfinished, will generally be discussed in chronological sequence.

Sketchbook I, marked "begun June 1925," opens with a fragment of the song "Erlösung," the second of Three Songs, Op. 18, in an early version scored for voice, clarinet, bass clarinet, and viola. Further drafts of the Opus 18 cycle follow, as well as drafts of songs belonging to the Three Traditional Rhymes, Op. 17, and of the Two Songs, Op. 19. Sketches for other projects are interspersed. On page 11 appears a song fragment of seven measures based on a text beginning "Dein Leib geht jetzt der Erde zu." Identical scoring relates this song to the early draft of "Erlösung" (the instrumentation of both projects is the same as that employed in "Heiland, unsre Missetaten," Op. 17, No. 3). On page 15 a string quartet is begun. This draft breaks off at measure nine where there is a double bar with a repeat sign. It is dated 24 August 1925. On page 16 row charts appear, with attempts to form a theme. No instruments are indicated. Page 17 contains one measure of a string trio score, a twelve-tone row in its four forms, and the beginnings of a piano piece in several versions, based on this row.

Two formerly unknown compositions in Sketchbook I were considered sufficiently complete to be posthumously published (in 1966) by Universal Edition, under the titles *Klavierstück* and *Satz für Streichtrio*. The *Klavierstück*, marked by Webern *Im Tempo eines Menuetts*, was edited (by Heinz Klaus Metzger) from extensive drafts, found on pages 8–9, that include several beginnings, corrections, and deletions. Of two distinct versions, one reveals the plan of a three-part structure; the second, adopted for publication, is in binary form. (The first section, designated for repetition—with different endings—is nine bars long, the second eleven bars.)

The sketches for the *Klavierstück* bear no specific date (internal evidence places them in early summer 1925), but the draft for the *Satz für Streichtrio* (the second essay in the string trio medium that Webern worked on that year) is marked "Sunday, 9 August 1925, before departure for the Totes Gebirge." The conception, appearing on pages 12–14, displays, as do most of Webern's initial sketches, several starts and alternatives. This composition had already been edited (by Metzger), performed and engraved when the Perchtoldsdorf discovery of 1965 brought to light an ink manuscript in which the composer had worked out the movement definitively. So substantial were the differences between the early sketches and the final product that Universal Edition decided to make a new engraving. Comprising 24 measures, the piece is marked *Ruhig fliessend* (Calmly flowing). Within its 4/16 metre, only sixteenth, thirty-second and sixty-fourth notes occur, making for great density of texture, as is the case also with the preceding string trio movement. Both efforts in this medium must be considered preliminary to the String Trio, Op. 20, the composition of which Webern began the following year.

Shortly before the *Satz für Streichtrio*, Webern drafted two songs, which were combined with one conceived earlier to form the Three Traditional Rhymes, Op. 17. The year of origin for this work has erroneously been given as 1924 ever since it was so listed in the Index of Works compiled by Friedrich Wildgans and published in the Webern issue of *die Reihe* (1955). The following information, based on the primary sources, will clarify the situation: there are no extant sketches for "Armer Sünder, du," but Webern himself assigned the piece to "Autumn 1924" in a handwritten list designating dates and places of composition for all works from Opus 1 to Opus 22. At the end of the holograph score, on which the publication was based, 1925 is given for the entire work. "Heiland, unsre Missetaten," appearing on pages 3–5 of Sketchbook I, is dated at the end 11 July 1925. An early version of "Liebste Jungfrau," found on pages 6–7, was completed a few days later, on 17 July. This draft still deviates considerably from the final form, and the composer's laborious progress is evidenced by numerous beginnings, cancellations, corrections, and alternatives. Further versions of the song are found on pages 10 and 19.

In his definitive manuscript, Webern at first established the sequence of the three songs as 1. "Armer Sünder,· du" 2. "Heiland, unsre Missetaten" 3. "Liebste Jungfrau." Further thought caused him to reverse the order of the second and third songs, and he made a note to that effect in the score. All texts are anonymous folk poems of religious character. The instrumentation includes violin (changing to viola in

"Heiland, unsre Missetaten"), clarinet, and bass clarinet. Because it was believed to represent the first of Webern's dodecaphonic works, the cycle has been much discussed. Theorists agree that the composer made the transition to twelve-tone writing almost imperceptibly, without change in his basic approach and style. While there is some difference of opinion regarding the degree of mastery in his early handling of the row method, the consensus prevails that Webern, here as always, knew how to attain his expressive goal, technique becoming but the vehicle for his creative imagination.

Published only in 1955, the Three Traditional Rhymes, Op. 17, belonged to a group of six compositions that Universal Edition had not yet taken under contract at the time of Webern's death. The others were the Concerto, Op. 24, Three Songs, Op. 25, First Cantata, Op. 29, Variations for Orchestra, Op. 30, and Second Cantata, Op. 31. "Liebste Jungfrau," the second of the Three Traditional Rhymes, Op. 17, appeared in a separate printing as early as 1930 in *New Music*, an American quarterly devoted to modern compositions, founded and edited by Henry Cowell. Webern's song, submitted at the invitation of Adolph Weiss, yielded him an honorarium of $100. It was published under the title "Geistlicher Volkstext," without an opus number.

The creative momentum that had carried Webern through the summer of 1925 sustained him well into the new season, despite his demanding duties. By the end of October he completed another work, the Three Songs, Op. 18, for voice, E-flat clarinet, and guitar. The cycle consists of 1. "Schatzerl klein, musst nit traurig sein" 2. "Erlösung" 3. "Ave, Regina coelorum." The opening song is a gay love ditty, the second is taken from *Des Knaben Wunderhorn,* and the third is one of the Marian antiphons. The drafts of all three songs are contained in Sketchbook I, which opens with the previously mentioned early version of "Erlösung," scored for clarinet, bass clarinet, and viola. Several variants follow on pages 2, 3 and 19. The first sketches for "Schatzerl klein," also differing widely from the ultimate setting, appear on page 18; they continue on pages 19–21, with "10 September 1925, Mödling" given as the date for completion. The next two pages contain the final draft of "Erlösung," dated 27 September 1925. Pages 24–27 are given over to sketches for "Ave, Regina coelorum." Passing through several stages of development, this draft is marked at the end "Mödling, 28 October 1925." For this song, there also exist loose-leaf sketches.

Webern referred to the songs on 8 October 1925 when he enthusiastically responded to Berg's description of a mountain excursion. First Webern wrote of the "inscrutable meaning" of alpine flora. For him it was "the greatest magic." Behind it he sensed an unfathomable thought. "I have struggled all my life to reproduce in music what I perceive there," he said, and a major part of his musical production could be traced back to that endeavour: "Namely, just as the fragrance and the form of these plants impress themselves upon me—as a God-given gift—so *I would like* it to be also with my musical conceptions." He hoped that Berg would not find this aspiration presumptuous. He himself realized that it was "futile to try to grasp what cannot be grasped." In this light he wanted Berg to understand what he meant when he had given him as a hint for the comprehension of his recent folksong simply the name of the evergreen shrub Rosemary. Webern continued:

I have now completed the second of this song series: "Erlösung" from *Des Knaben Wunderhorn*. The third will be a Latin song (Song of Mary): "Ave, regina coelorum, ave domina angelorum—Hail, queen of the heavens, hail, lady of the angels." I will tell you in person some day what relationship exists for me between these three songs. I am at present working on the third. Twelve-tone composition is for me now a completely clear procedure. Naturally these songs are all written in this method. And the work at hand gives me pleasure as rarely any before. I am burning with desire to show you what has come into being and is still coming.

The relationship between the three songs to which Webern alludes is perhaps explained by an anecdote related by his eldest daughter, Amalie. When her father wanted to express special affection for her mother, he would call her "Minna-Mutter-Königin!" Minna (Wilhelmine) was for Webern, to begin with, the "Schatzerl" (sweetheart). Beyond this she represented the incarnation of motherhood and, symbolically, she reigned as queen over the family. The sequence of songs in the cycle follows these images. While none of Webern's compositions was ever officially dedicated to his wife, the present cycle, more than any other work, would appear to have been created in homage to her.

Outstanding characteristics of the Three Songs, Op. 18, are the extreme difficulty of the voice part, with its enormous leaps, and the contrapuntal and rhythmic complexity of the score's fabric. The work was published in 1927 by Universal Edition. Originally Webern meant to dedicate it to Emil Hertzka, as he indicated to Berg in his letter of 8 October 1925. It was to be his tribute to the director of the publishing house, in celebration of the firm's twenty-fifth anniversary on 25 January 1926. Instead, all composers then published by Universal Edition were asked for a manuscript specimen of their work, to be placed in a presentation album.[9] Webern's contribution was a beautifully written copy of "Schatzerl klein," which he then entitled "Volkslied."

On 25 October 1925, three days before he completed the draft of "Ave, Regina coelorum," Webern wrote to Berg that he looked back on the summer with nostalgia, difficult as that time had been "for external reasons and still more for *inner* ones." At the end he had felt so fortified in regard to his creative work, but by now he had "almost lost that assurance again." For him, it was an "eternal struggle." Added to this was the melancholy that always befell him with the onset of autumn.

Despite Webern's dejection, the flow of creativity continued. Before the year was out, he had embarked on his next work, the Two Songs, Op. 19, for mixed chorus, celesta, guitar, violin, clarinet, and bass clarinet. The texts were chosen from Goethe's *Chinesisch-deutsche Jahres- und Tageszeiten*. According to Webern's own work list, the composition originated "December 1925—January 1926," but dated sketches disclose a much longer span of evolution. The last five pages (28–32) of Sketchbook I are given over to the first song, "Weiss wie Lilien." Again, the composer experiments with several approaches. These drafts are continued in Sketchbook II, begun in January 1926, and are followed by those to the second song, "Ziehn die Schafe von der Wiese." On 9 February Webern mentions his work on this song in a letter to Schoenberg and he refers to it again on 8 May, after telling Berg a week earlier: "I want nothing else but time to compose." The date "Mödling, 8 July 1926," appearing on page 5, marks completion of the composition.

On the two pages immediately following "Ziehn die Schafe," a third chorus on a Goethe text is drafted. Although obviously undertaken as an extension of the cycle, this project was not finished. On the index page prefacing the sketchbook Webern gives "Autumn 1926" as the work's date of origin. Its tone row is identical with that of the two preceding choruses, but the scoring is confined to mixed voices *a cappella*. The short text, "Auf Bergen, in der reinsten Höhe, tief rötlich blau ist Himmelsnähe," evoked in Webern, the mountaineer and nature philosopher, so deep a response that he wrote the word "Motto" at the head of his musical realization. The words had already occupied him years earlier, for he had quoted them on 23 August 1920 in a letter to Berg, whom he then tried to persuade to join him on an outing into the mountains. The couplet (included in *Gott, Gemüt und Welt*) is one of sixteen written by Goethe at Weimar around 1810, in an apparent attempt to give poetic expression to the tenets expounded in his *Farbenlehre*. For Webern, as for Goethe, the wedding of nature's beauty to scientific principles was the magic key to the essence of art, and his quest for that elusive amalgam was perpetual.

"The *Farbenlehre*," writes Ernst Krenek in his commentary to *Sketches*, "was very close to Webern, who found Goethe's idea that all organic life originated from one germinal nucleus to be a notion related to the basic concept of the twelve-tone technique." Describing the chorus "Auf Bergen, in der reinsten Höhe," Krenek observes: "The sketch shows a contrapuntal treatment more characteristic of the later choral works from Opus 26 on than of the earlier settings of Opus 19."[10]

On the title page of the finished manuscript of the Two Songs, Op. 19, the composer indicated that the work might be performed by a quartet of solo voices in place of a full chorus. However, the parenthetical note providing for this alternative was later crossed out. In 1928, the full score, as well as a piano reduction, was published by Universal Edition. That Webern completed his voice–piano score only that year, is evident from pencil drafts of the choruses, which bear the date of 29 February for the first and 3 March for the second. Despite the early release of the work, no record of its first performance exists, and the same is the case for the Three Songs, Op. 18. Apparently both compositions were premièred only after Webern's death.

The Two Songs, Op. 19, are dedicated to David Josef Bach, with whom Webern was then working in close collaboration preparing a performance of Mahler's Eighth Symphony. No doubt Webern's active engagement in the field of choral literature inspired him to return to this medium, which he had not employed since his 1908 setting of George's *Entflieht auf leichten Kähnen* (Op. 2). Subsequently he was to produce three large choral works (Opera 26, 29, 31). The Two Songs opened a series of two-movement compositions, which included the instrumental Opera 20, 21, and 22. In each case, the composer originally envisioned a third movement, only to reach the conclusion that the principle of unity through variety had been amply fulfilled by the two finished movements. With the Two Songs, another dimension of unity was added: from that point on, the same tone row became the structural basis for all the movements within a cyclic work.

In the autumn of 1926, when Webern drafted "Auf Bergen, in der reinsten Höhe" as a potential third component of his Opus 19 cycle, he had already begun work on his String Trio, Op. 20, for violin, viola, and violoncello. The task was to keep him engrossed into summer of the following year. His prolonged effort is reflected in several letters. As early as 23 August 1926, Webern had written to Schoenberg: "I am relentlessly at work. The Trio goes very slowly, it is true, but I firmly hope to get over the hump with it this time." The closing remark refers to his two previous attempts in 1925 to compose in that medium. On 26 September, the same day on which he wrote to Hertzka pleading for financial assistance, Webern told Berg that he was continually and hard at work. He was busy with the development section of the first movement of his String Trio, and it made him feel very good to be able to write again "longer stretches of music," although he did not find it easy.

According to Webern's own records, two movements were completed by the end of June 1927. There are no extant drafts from which their evolution can be traced. Since, in Sketchbook II, the draft of "Auf Bergen, in der reinsten Höhe" directly precedes that for the Trio's abandoned third movement, it must be concluded that the two finished movements were sketched on loose-leaf pages that were later lost.[11]

As Webern settled down in his holiday retreat at Hafning that summer, he still was eager to carry out his original three-movement concept. On 11 July he wrote to Berg that he was working on the third movement, and that it would be the "last of the Trio." However, a doubtful note was sounded when he wrote again on 27 July. He then told Berg that he was still at the Trio. He had finished the second movement in Mödling, shortly before his departure, and by now he had almost completed the thematic exposition to the third. But he was not as yet "entirely certain" of his course. "Sometimes I have the feeling that there should be only the two movements," he confided.

Work on the third movement fills five pages in Sketchbook II.[12] Marked *Sehr lebhaft* (Very lively), it is carried through for 31 measures, plus a few additional notes in the cello part. Numerous preliminary versions, varying only minutely from each other, reveal how intensely Webern grappled with some intrinsic problems. How much this project weighed on his mind is evident from a diary note he made at Hafning: "After much deliberation, arrived at difficult decision to give up work on the third movement of my String Trio and to let it remain with only two movements. Fair copy of both of these."

The decision must have been made sometime in August, for on the 24th Webern announced to Berg that his Trio was finished and that it comprised only two movements after all. It had been a hard decision for him to "give up" the planned third movement. But he felt that he could not do otherwise. The "slow movement" now was to become the first, and the "fast one" that he had already shown Berg, the second. The character of the fast movement simply did not permit anything to follow it and, on the other hand, nothing could precede it but the slow movement. While the Trio as a whole had not turned out to be a "voluminous work," it nevertheless contained once again "more expansive movements of truly symphonic nature." The reason why it was "terribly difficult" to give up the work was that he harboured "quite a curious feeling towards the charts with the rows." He would have liked to work with them still further. "And why not, for that matter?" he asked, since "purely theoretically, nothing at all could really be said against it." This time, the *Bezeichnung* (designation of tempo and dynamic markings) had cost him real effort, because he needed at first a certain amount of time in order to understand entirely what he had written, or in Webern's words: ". . . what has been 'dictated,' as Mahler, I believe also Schoenberg, outright said it. Goethe, for that matter, too—naturally, how else could it be?" For this reason he liked to let an opus lie for some time until he was ready to have it published.

On the same day that Webern expressed these thoughts, he mailed the score to Universal Edition "for the purpose of having the parts made," as he noted in his diary. He wanted to have his latest composition released without delay this time because of a request from Kolisch to give the first performance a few weeks later, on 1 October, in Cologne. This prospect failed to materialize, but it may well have hastened Webern's decision to abandon the plan of a third movement.

The drafts of the third movement show the composer's system of numbering the row forms as they were being used. It was his custom to write out all 48 possibilities of the series and to hang these charts up around his desk for ready reference. The fact that Webern would establish the final sequence of movements in his cyclic works without regard for the chronological order of their origin has caused some confusion among theoreticians (who worked only from the printed scores) as to what constitutes the fundamental row.

In the case of the String Trio, the primary row is found at the outset of the second movement. As has been seen, that movement—in strict sonata-allegro form, with a slow introduction and complete with a repetition of the exposition section—was conceived as the first in the original three-movement plan. What was afterwards composed as the second movement—a classic rondo in slow tempo—subsequently was moved into opening position. The row which begins this movement is the 46th variant of the series, while that which is used at the start of the abandoned third movement is the 28th.

In November of the same year, 1927, Universal Edition published both the full score and the parts. Sending Schoenberg a copy, Webern wrote on 25 November: "Unfortunately a wrong metronome figure has remained in two places; correct: second movement, page 12, system 3 'sehr lebhaft' $\rtimes$ = 66 (instead of 60) and vice versa page 17, 4th system 'gemächlich' $\rtimes$ = 60 (instead of 66)." The two errors still appeared in the Philharmonia study score published in May of 1928 (they were not corrected in the 1955 re-issue, either).

This edition contained an Introduction by Erwin Stein who, no doubt in collaboration with the composer, provided some analytical comments:

The principle of developing a movement by variation of motives and themes is the same as with the classical masters. In his manner of developing his motives, however, and in the thematic treatment, Webern deviates far from the classical examples. Motives and themes are varied more radically here, and whenever they recur it is in a very modified form. One "tone series" furnishes the basic material for the entire composition, as in Schoenberg's "composition with twelve tones." The parts are composed in a mosaic-like manner from segments of the series. Thus ever new sounds originate through various combinations. The comparison with the kaleidoscope, which continually produces new images through manifold groupings of its colours and form elements, suggests itself.

A synopsis of structural elements follows. Obviously Webern was deeply concerned that his work should be comprehended. The composition is indeed a pivot in his development, heralding a transition in his architectonic and aesthetic outlook. After the long period of utmost concentration in thought and diction, he now consciously aspired to greater expansiveness. This deliberate trend towards enlarged constructions, fostered by the new technique with its multifaceted use of a basic idea, was hailed by Webern himself as a desirable development. In one of his lectures, on 2 March 1932, he summarized the completion of the cycle from the old tonal system to the twelve-tone technique via the aphoristic style: "As we gradually gave up tonality, the idea arose: we do not want to repeat, there must constantly be something new! It is self-evident that this does not work, since it destroys comprehensibility. At least it is impossible to write longer stretches of music in this manner. Only after the formulation of the law [the twelve-tone method] did it become possible again to compose longer pieces."[13]

The first performance of the String Trio was given in Vienna on 16 January 1928 in the small hall of the Musikverein. The ensemble consisted of members of the Wiener Streichquartett: Rudolf Kolisch (violin), Eugen Lehner (viola), and Benar Heifetz (cello). Webern, who had supervised the rehearsals, noted in his diary that the première "went very well." On 20 January, he thanked Kolisch and his colleagues by letter for the "brilliantly successful first performance," adding: "Everything came out so well, so convincingly, even if only a few of the listeners understood something of it. That I know."

The String Trio soon received widespread attention. Together with Schoenberg's Third String Quartet and Berg's Lyric Suite, it was given in a chamber-music programme in Berlin that spring. Webern's remark in his letter of 1 April to Schoenberg indicates that Schoenberg approved of the work: "I am very happy over what you have written me about my

Trio." The work was next given on 21 May during the Tonkünstlerfest of the Allgemeine Deutsche Musikverband in Schwerin. Performers were Licco Amar (violin), Paul Hindemith (viola), and Maurits Frank (cello), members of the Amar Quartet who had repeatedly championed Webern's then still quite provocative music. On this occasion the work met with almost unanimous rejection by the audience and newspaper critics alike. The latter heaped much abuse on the composer, charging him with "desolate eccentricity" (*Kreuzzeitung*, 25 May) and with writing "bloodless brain music" (*Chemnitzer Tageblatt*, 30 May). He was accused of playing a "bad joke with patient listeners" (*Hamburger Fremdenblatt*, 25 May) and of creating "sound phantoms which stand apart from all spontaneous music making" (*Zwickauer Zeitung*, 25 May). A spokesman from Webern's native Vienna called the work "completely incapable of survival" (*Neue Freie Presse*, 19 June). The reporter of the *Zwickauer Zeitung* likewise relegated "the piece that was buried under the jeering laughter of the majority" to certain oblivion. The critic of the *Hamburger Courier* (29 May), however, was less sure: "We smiled along with the others, for this perhaps someday one will smile about us. . . ." The lone voice of moderation and detachment belonged to Heinrich Strobel, later a prominent figure in the affairs of the musical avant-garde, who wrote in the *Dresdner Anzeiger* (30 May): "A work of imposing aloofness. . . . It is the summit of esoteric subjectivism. We admire the spirit that advanced to this frontier of music, even if we are not capable of following there."

If Webern's String Trio had, in Strobel's description, "half annoyed, half amused" the audience at Schwerin, it was to provoke undisguisedly violent reaction at the ISCM festival in Siena later that year. Alban Berg, as Austrian delegate to the preliminary board meeting in Zürich, had been instrumental in getting the work on the programme. It was played in the concert of 13 September, which included compositions by Frank Bridge, Heinz Tiessen, Manuel de Falla, and Robert Blum. The chamber music hall of Count Chigi-Saracini's palace was the sedate setting, and again the Kolisch ensemble appeared on stage to interpret Webern's work. The ensuing disturbances were fully exploited by the press, which obviously relished such sensational festival spice. According to Erich Doflein (*Breslauer Neueste Nachrichten*, 27 September), the representative of the Milan paper *Popolo d'Italia* shouted across the hall "barbarian music, Schweinerei [piggishness]," and the furor began. In the end the organizers and hosts had to apologize publicly.

Unable to attend the festival himself, Webern received a first-hand report from Kolisch, which he relayed to Schoenberg on 2 October:

Have you heard that there was a really full-fledged scandal in connection with my Trio in Siena? As Kolisch told me, it was like this: During the first measures of the second movement the restlessness became so great that he decided to interrupt. The ensuing demonstrative applause restored quiet, and Kolisch could once again begin the movement and play it to the end. But then things really broke loose, sparked by an Italian critic who declared that he would induce *Mussolini* to order the festival broken off. Such music should not be allowed to be played in Italy. Then a German critic, Springer by name,[14] retorted. Immediately after this the Italian critic went at him with his fists. Members of the audience jumped on the podium. At this point Casella and Dent gave speeches and ordered the *Italian out of the hall*. Whereupon the latter is said to have challenged Casella to a duel. And now the applause really set in, and for that matter very strongly, as Kolisch said, so that he had to return to the stage several times in acknowledgement. Hertzka also was present and wrote me a very kind postcard. This put me at ease, for I had already presumed an unfavourable repercussion on my relationship with UE from this affair.

When Webern penned this letter, his next work, the Symphony, Op. 21, had already been completed. On 25 November 1927 he had first mentioned to Schoenberg that he was busy with "something for orchestra, a little symphony." In Sketchbook II, drafts for the new project immediately follow those for the abandoned third movement of the String Trio. The initial heading reads: "Symphony for clarinet, bass clarinet, (2 horns), violin 1, violin 2, viola, cello, contrabass (possibly also tutti), and harp." Above the first musical sketch is the date "November–December 1927" and a structural concept, calling for three movements: "I. Rondo: lively—sun II. Variations: moderately III. Free form: very calmly—moon."

Five pages later (page 19), Webern jotted down another outline: "I. Variations II. Rondo (Scherzo, march-like) III. Slowly." By the time the second plan was envisioned, the composition of the variation movement was already under way. Its draft, including numerous starts and alterations, fills 22 pages and is dated at the end "Mödling, 27 March, 1928." On the 30th Webern wrote to Berg that the first movement of his work was done, that he was writing out the clean score, and that he was burning with desire to show it to him. He still had not decided on a title, however.

The following thirteen pages in the sketchbook are given over to what Webern then still planned as a second movement. The beginning is dated 11 May 1928. Again, various sections are drafted over and over

Coat of arms of the Webern family

Josef Eduard von Webern, the
composer's great-grandfather

The Preglhof estate

Family gathering at the Preglhof (17 May 1887). Sitting in the centre is Anton von Webern, the composer's grandfather, with young Anton at his feet. The parents, Carl and Amalie, are on the upper and lower right, with Webern's mother holding his younger sister, Rosa. His older sister, Maria, stands left of the family patriarch. Webern's cousin, Ernst Diez, is second from the left in the front row. The Diez parents, Friedrich and Maria, stand behind Ernst, his mother holding his younger brother, Heinrich

Amalie von Webern
with her children, Rosa, Anton and Maria

Wilhelmine Mörtl, Anton's
cousin and future wife (July 1901)

Carl von Webern,
the composer's father

Webern with Heinrich and Johanna Jalowetz (Danzig, 1911)

Alban Berg and Anton von Webern
(Spring 1912)

Anton von Webern
(Stettin, October 1912)

Webern during World War I,
with his wife and daughters, Amalie and Maria

Soldiers' string quartet,
with Webern as cellist (Leoben, 1916)

Anton and Wilhelmine von Webern
(Mödling, 1923)

Arnold Schoenberg

Otto Klemperer, Arnold Schoenberg, Webern and Hermann Scherchen
(Donaueschingen, July 1924)

Webern rehearsing the Wiener
Symphoniker for a performance of
Mahler's Sixth Symphony (Vienna
Konzerthaus, 23 May 1933)

Webern and Hildegard Jone (*ca.* 1928)

DRAWINGS OF WEBERN

By Oskar Kokoschka (1912)

By Emil Stumpp (1927)

By Egon Schiele (1917)

By Oskar Kokoschka (1914)

By Hildegard Jone (1945)

OIL PORTRAITS OF WEBERN

The Mödling residence,
Neusiedlerstrasse 58

Webern's birth house in Vienna,
Löwengasse 53a

The home in Maria Enzersdorf,
Im Auholz 8

At the graveside of Gustav Mahler. Webern and David Josef **Bach** (first
and second in the front **row**) with members of the Singverein
(Grinzing cemetery, 18 May 1926)

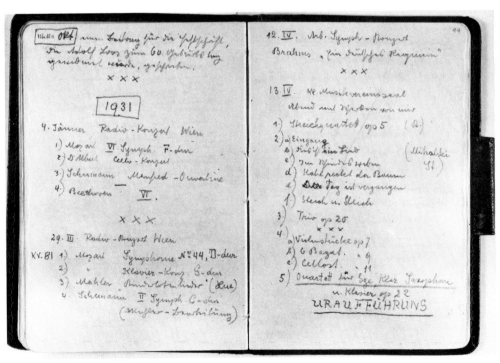

From Webern's diary (1930–1931)

Webern in his Mödling studio (Summer 1930)

Ernst Diez, Webern, Josef Hueber and Josef Polnauer
in the Kampl Hut on the Schneealpe (June 1933)

Webern in the Ötztal Alps (July 1937)

Webern (October 1940)

Webern with his son, Peter,
on the Schneealpe (July 1941)

Webern (1945)

The Mittersill house, Am Markt 101, where Webern was shot

1945–1955   1955–1972

THE MARKERS ON WEBERN'S GRAVE

The Ehrengrab (grave of honour) established by the
Mittersill community on 24 June 1972

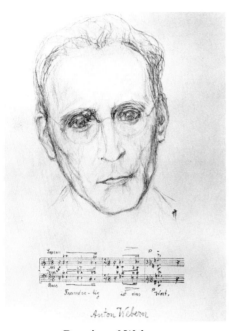

Drawing of Webern
by Hildegard Jone (1943)

Oil portrait of Webern
by Tom von Dreger (1934)

Anton von Webern. Terracotta bust by Josef Humplik (1928)

until the definitive form is attained. The close is marked "27 June—end of school for the children." On the same day, Webern informed Berg that he hoped to be finished "in a few days" with the second movement of his orchestral work, "an Adagio in canonic form throughout." The theme was a perpetual canon (double canon) with repetition. The middle part was a four-voiced (mirror) canon, followed by the reprise, which was again a double canon. While the movement was not a long one, working it out had been "tough" at times. He added that he had decided to call his composition a "Symphony" after all.

That summer, Maurice Kaplan, Webern's pupil from America, came to Mödling for an extended period of study. Staying home except for a few brief trips, Webern delved with vigour into a number of projects. Besides the Symphony, they included the reorchestration of his Six Pieces, Op. 6, and the transcription for string orchestra of his Five Movements, Op. 5 (see Chapter VII). Describing his work schedule to Berg on 13 July, Webern told him that his Adagio was finished, "really all finished: *written out in a clean copy* and *containing all the expression marks*—the latter was not so easy." Now he was turning to the third and last movement of his Symphony. However, he was not entirely certain as yet about the sequence of the movements.

The draft of the presumptive third movement (pages 51–53 of Sketchbook II) was begun on 3 August 1928.[15] In an undated diary entry Webern recorded: "The next few days occupied with the third movement of my Symphony, Op. 21. Arrived at the decision to remain with two movements." Having abandoned the tripartite idea, the composer reversed the sequence of the two completed movements, as he had done in his String Trio. The canonic Adagio—consisting of two sections, each repeated, and structurally resembling the earlier type of sonata form—was assigned the opening position, to be followed by the variation movement, containing the theme, seven variations, and a coda, each eleven bars long for a total of 99 measures.

On 20 August Webern wrote to Schoenberg:

I was again rather far along with a third movement. But whatever I sought to imagine as a supplement (before or after) or as a centre between the two movements disturbed me, and I recognized (after long deliberation) that the work should consist only of the two movements. The first is a slow movement that lasts almost a quarter of an hour; the second is the variation movement that I showed you earlier. In respect to form, I was finally put at ease by the example of so many two-movement sonatas by Beethoven and also by the two-movement orchestral works by Bach.

On the same day, Webern gave Berg a similar account, not without indicating, however, his difficulty in deciding against the third movement: "Again it was no simple, easy situation, but a hard, enervating struggle."

When writing to Schoenberg two weeks later, on 5 September, Webern added to his time estimate of "almost a quarter of an hour" for the first movement "about six minutes" for the second, "therefore about twenty minutes of music" for the entire work. The composer's assessment assumes special significance in the light of the widely differing conceptions by various conductors. The tempo problem is compounded by the fact that the catalogue of Universal Edition gives a duration of only ten minutes for the work. (Webern's tempo ideas were generally much slower than those followed in actual performance. In several letters to Edward Clark, for instance, he gave the timing for the Five Pieces, Op. 10, as ten minutes and that for the Five Movements, Op. 5, in the string orchestra transcription, as seventeen minutes. Usually these works are played almost twice as fast.)

Publication of the Symphony and the events leading up to its first performance were recorded by Webern in a series of diary entries. The final manuscript, bearing a dedication to his nine-year-old daughter Christine, was handed in to Universal Edition on 7 September. Nine months later, on 18 June 1929, the composer could hold the printed score in his hand. "Very beautiful. Unfortunately one printing error," he commented in his diary. Even before publication, he noted the possibility of an early première: "Letter from the League of Composers in New York arrived: they request a work for chamber orchestra. Delivery deadline early October; performance early December. Since meeting this deadline for a work to be newly written appeared impossible to me, I suggested (after long consideration and a conference with U.E.) my Symphony, Op. 21, for world première in New York by the L. of C. The amount offered to me for meeting the foregoing conditions: 350 dollars."

More than three months were to elapse before Webern could record in his diary: "Friday, the 20th of September, 12 o'clock noon, just now received the notification that the League of Composers in New York has acquired my Symphony, Op. 21, for world première." In his elation, Webern reiterated the circumstances of the commission and the honorarium offered, which, in his tight economic situation, seemed like a munificent sum to him. In the income book the conversion of the $350 into Austrian currency is registered: 2,472 schillings—an enormous amount compared to Webern's ordinary earnings.

The League of Composers had been founded in 1923 by Claire R. Reis, in collaboration with a number of leading musicians, for the purpose of promoting contemporary music. Programmes in the 1920s included such landmarks as Schoenberg's *Pierrot Lunaire* and Stravinsky's *L'Histoire du Soldat* and *Les Noces*. The League also took the initiative in commissioning new works at a time when that practice was virtually unknown, sponsoring a total of 110 compositions during its existence. Webern's correspondence went through Mrs Reis, the society's executive director. On 31 October 1929, he communicated the following instructions: "Please tell the conductor of my Symphony that each part for the string instruments in it may also be played in multiples (the occasional remark 'solo' in the score is thereby explained), for instance, about 4 first violins, 4 second violins, 3 violas, and 3 violoncelli (16 [*sic*] strings). However, it is of course entirely possible to play the work purely soloistically."

The première took place in New York's Town Hall on 18 December 1929, during the League's first concert of its seventh season. The programme, featuring works for chamber orchestra, consisted of Casella's *Serenata*, Hindemith's Concerto for Organ and Chamber Orchestra, Goossens' Concerto for Eighteen Strings, Webern's Symphony, and Gruenberg's *The Daniel Jazz*. Two of the composers, Goossens and Gruenberg, shared the conductor's rostrum with Alexander Smallens, who was in charge of the Webern opus.[16] Two months later, on 24 February 1930, the composer himself presided over the work's first European performance in Vienna (see Chapter XX).

The Symphony, Op. 21, constitutes a milestone in the development of serial technique. A generation later, Webern's rigid application of row patterns in this work was to have enormous influence on his followers, who saw in his example the point of departure for their own ideal of complete predetermination of all structural elements. Webern appears to have been deeply conscious of his progress in the direction of total integration. The tone row was for him the *Urpflanze* (primeval plant), and from it derived all components of the entire organism. Time and again he elaborated in his lectures on this principle: "Goethe's *Urpflanze*: the root is really nothing other than the stalk, the stalk nothing other than the leaf, the leaf again nothing other than the blossom: variations of the same idea."[17]

In the time-honoured variation form, Webern saw but a further application of the same precept: "This striving for unity, for relationships, leads of its own accord to a form that the classical composers often cultivated and which in Beethoven became truly predominant: to the variation form. A theme is given. It is varied. In this sense the variation form is a forerunner of twelve-tone composition. An example: Beethoven's Ninth Symphony, last movement: theme in unison; all that follows is based on this idea, it is the *Urform* (primeval form). Unheard-of things happen and yet it is always the same!"[18]

With obvious pride, the composer pointed out how all components in the variation movement of his own symphony were controlled through total discipline:

> The row reads: F–A flat–G–F sharp–B flat–A / E flat–E–C–C sharp– D–B. It has the peculiarity that the second half is the retrograde of the first. This is an especially intimate connection. There are, consequently, only 24 forms present, since two are always identical with each other. At the beginning the retrograde appears in the accompaniment of the theme. The first variation, in the melody, is a transposition of the series starting on C. The accompaniment is a double canon. Greater coherence cannot be achieved. Not even the Netherlanders have managed this. In the fourth variation there are constant mirrorings. This variation itself is the central point of the whole movement, and from there on everything goes backwards again. The entire movement thus represents in itself a double canon with retrograde motion. . . . What you see here (retrograde, canon, etc.—it is always the same) is not to be thought of as "Kunststückerln" [artistic tricks]—that would be ridiculous! As many connections as possible should be created, and you will have to admit that there are many connections here![19]

With the Symphony, Webern felt that he was close to the realization of his creative ideal, one in which art is governed by the same laws as nature. Sensing this breakthrough, he copied into his diary in the spring of 1929 (when his latest opus was about to make its way into the world) two excerpts from the *Italian Journey* by Goethe: "In art I must reach a point where everything becomes knowledge through observation, where nothing remains tradition and name (and I will of necessity extort this result in half a year)"; and ". . . for it now is unfolding, and art is becoming for me like a second nature, which, like Minerva from the head of Jupiter, is born out of the heads of the greatest men."

The same spring of 1929 Webern received from Berg a copy of Goethe's *Farbenlehre*, which, for him, was "the most sublime book of all time" (as he wrote Berg on 28 September 1929). Berg had underscored certain passages in the work's lengthy introduction, and Webern rejoiced at the fact that both of them concurred so fully with the poet's ideology. In Goethe's statement, "The same law will be applicable to all else *living*," Webern found the "infallible proof" of his analogy between the *Urpflanze* and the tone-row system,[20] the principle on which all his aesthetic thought now was based.

Not related to the twelve-tone method, but falling into the time span covered in this chapter, is Webern's arrangement of the *Arbeiterchor* by Franz Liszt. The piece was included in the Singverein's official concert début on 13 and 14 March 1925, and the Socialist message of the text (it calls for the worldwide solidarity of all working men) made it particularly appropriate for the occasion. Liszt's composition was scored for men's chorus with bass solo and piano accompaniment.[21] Webern arranged the work for bass solo, mixed chorus (soprano, altos I and II, tenors I and II, and basses I and II), and an orchestra consisting of pairs of woodwinds, 4 horns, 2 trumpets, 3 trombones, timpani and other percussion, and the usual strings. Although the conventional idiom of Liszt's original is followed closely, the largely expanded sonorities in both chorus and orchestra produce a strikingly new effect.[22]

CHAPTER XIX

International acclaim—Hildegard Jone
(1929)

THE YEAR 1929 began with severe and prolonged cold weather. Webern's diary lists temperatures of −30° Celsius (−22° Fahrenheit). Transport was bogged down by frost and heavy snow, and there arose almost catastrophic shortages of food and fuel. Webern noted in his diary that he needed to heat his home until the end of April, most unusual for the region, and that his son Peter came down with influenza and had to stay home from school for a full nine weeks. It was Webern's habit to place on record even the most ordinary occurrences in his children's lives, but when it came to an illness he went into great detail. The account of his son's appendix operation the year before, for example, takes three pages, and the events are covered virtually hour by hour: Peter's sudden illness during one of the Workmen's Symphony Concerts, the doctor's diagnosis, the rush to the hospital, the operation, the fever, the diet, the repeated change of rooms, the hourly schedule of the bedside vigil in which the parents shared, and so forth, up to Peter's return to school. Considering that during the same week Webern attended the rehearsals and first performance of his String Trio, Op. 20 (mentioned only in passing in the middle of the lengthy description of Peter's illness), this concern seems inordinate, but it reflects the preoccupation of the affectionate and conscientious father.

Early in January 1929, following his own illness and convalescence the previous autumn, Webern resumed his choral rehearsals. With the Singverein, he began the study of Bach's Cantata No. 106, "Gottes Zeit ist die allerbeste Zeit" (*Actus Tragicus*), and with the chorus of the Freie Typographia the preparation of the *German Requiem* by Brahms. His regained zest for work also carried over into the creative domain: he returned to a composition for violin, clarinet, horn, piano, and string orchestra that he had begun in September. This project, entitled "Concerto" (later Quartet, Op. 22) was interrupted in favour of a second and definitive version of the transcription for string orchestra of the Five Movements, Op. 5.

On 7 and 14 April, Webern was at last able to conduct Schoenberg's *Friede auf Erden* and Mahler's Second Symphony; in November he had had to relinquish his leadership of these works because of illness. This time the Freie Typographia assumed sponsorship, with the Singverein appearing as guest chorus. The concerts, held in the large Konzerthaus hall, met with resounding acclaim. The audience gave Webern an ovation, and the press lauded his achievement. One reporter commented:

> If workmen are successful in giving an exemplary rendition of so difficult a choral work as Arnold Schoenberg's *Friede auf Erden*, which was considered unperformable for decades, then truly the idea of the conquest of art by the people can take hold. Mahler's *Resurrection* Symphony, too, causes the singers of the Freie Typographia and the Singverein hardly any problems today. To be sure, a leader with the personality of an Anton Webern must know how to clarify, in month-long rehearsals, every detail of such complicated art works for the workers who perhaps cannot even read music well. . . . With fiery temperament he chiselled out the high point of the symphony. . . . One can hardly describe the impression that the concert made on its listeners.

On 18 April Webern registered his satisfaction to Schoenberg: "Finally it has come true, after all: I have performed *Friede auf Erden* twice. I believe that we succeeded beautifully. The chorus sang with great enthusiasm. It seems to me that I have really been able to bring the singers to the point of perceiving your work as I do myself."

In the same letter Webern relayed his deep impression of a recent *Pierrot Lunaire* performance given at the Music Academy by a group of students under the leadership of the composer Franz Schmidt, then the institute's director. At the close of his account, Webern could not help looking back to the work's scandalous première in Berlin in 1912: "How long has it really been since the good old Albertine Zehme, trembling and fearful, had to speak the Pierrot for an audience that deported itself in so beastly a fashion? And now recently: a young *Fratz* [brash girl] enthusiastically reciting your Pierrot, with what must almost be considered children at the instruments (the cellist played the Serenade as matter-of-factly as an old Haydn), and finally, a really enthusiastic audience (the hall was sold out). It was really beautiful and elevating!"

On 1 May, the Socialist holiday, Webern was asked again, as in the

GESANGVEREIN
FREIE TYPOGRAPHIA
VEREINSKANZLEI : VII., ZIEGLERGASSE 25

SONNTAG, 7. UND 14. APRIL
1929, ABENDS HALB 8 UHR,
IM GROSSEN KONZERTHAUS-
SAAL, LOTHRINGERSTRASSE

CHORKONZERT

SCHÖNBERG:
FRIEDE AUF ERDEN
GEDICHT VON C. F. MEYER

MAHLER:
ZWEITE SINFONIE

AUSFÜHRENDE:
Ruzena Herlinger (Sopran), Jela
Braun-Fernwald (Alt), Ehrhard
Kranz (Orgel), der gemischte Chor
der Freien Typographia, der Sing-
verein der Kunststelle, das Wiener
Sinfonie-Orchester

DIRIGENT:
Dr. ANTON WEBERN

Programme of a joint concert by the Freie Typographia chorus and the
Singverein (7 April 1929)

year before, to conduct a radio concert with the participation of the Singverein. After the opening *Egmont* Overture by Beethoven, the chorus appeared in the canonic *a cappella* setting of *Beherzigung* by Brahms. Based on a Goethe poem that invokes freedom from fear—"Feiger Gedanken bängliches Schwanken" (timid wavering of cowardly thoughts)—the work was adopted by the Singverein as its own political and artistic credo, to be repeated in many subsequent performances. The remainder of the concert consisted of Brahms' Three Folk Songs, with Vorsänger (leader) and piano accompaniment (Josef Hueber was baritone soloist), the fourth movement (*2. Nachtmusik*) of Mahler's Seventh Symphony, and Mozart's G minor Symphony, K.550.

Prior to this concert, Webern was informed that he was being considered for an executive position in the music department of the Ravag broadcasting system. He declined, despite the tempting offer of a monthly salary of 1,000 schillings, explaining to Schoenberg on 18 April:

> Since the matter has a political implication (I was to function as a "trustee" of the Social Democratic Party), I have refused. . . . No, I cannot enter into a position that would leave me almost no time for my work any more. Indeed, the contrary is what I would like: to be able to devote myself exclusively to composing. In that case I prefer to renounce a handsome income. But I hope more and more to be able to secure this for myself nevertheless through guest engagements outside Austria. This is my dream. . . . I would like best not to conduct in Vienna at all any more. It is getting worse and worse here.

Early in June, Webern was greatly heartened when he received an offer of a commission from the League of Composers in New York. (It was to lead to the acceptance and early performance of his already finished Symphony, Op. 21.) The same month, on the 22nd, the *Christian Science Monitor* published a lengthy feature article on his music by Erwin Stein. This essay was instrumental in spreading the composer's reputation in the United States. Such encouragement lent added impetus to Webern's work that summer. His projects included the repeatedly begun "Concerto," a song opening with the words "Nun weiss man erst" (Goethe), and a string quartet, but only the first was ever finished (see Chapter XXV, Quartet, Op. 22).

Extensive diary entries record Webern's mountain excursions that year. They included a traverse of the Schneealpe (5–6 May), an ascent of the Rax (22–23 June) with his son, Dr Ploderer, and Eduard and Hilda Steuermann, and a brief holiday (9–15 August) with his wife and the two youngest children in Vordernberg. There an outing was made each day, including a climb of the Reichenstein with Peter. The goal of the season's last excursion (5–7 October) was the Mödlinger-Hütte, a mountain shelter belonging to the Mödling Section of the German and Austrian Alpine Club. The occasion was the inauguration of the enlarged premises of the hut, combined with a celebration of the group's twentieth anniversary. Webern was an active member of the club, and he occasionally participated in its social functions with a musical offering.[1]

Following Webern's radio appearances during the May Day celebrations of 1928 and 1929, Ravag had begun to call on him for various conducting assignments. On Sunday, 21 July, he led a matinée concert with Mozart's Divertimento No. 11 in D major, the Serenade in E minor by Robert Fuchs, and Mozart's *Jupiter* Symphony. In a letter to Schoenberg on 8 July, Webern had called the Mozart Divertimento "a marvellous thing" and commented on the Fuchs Serenade: "I wanted once to conduct something from his work, but with closer study I have become very cool towards it." Another Sunday matinée radio programme conducted by Webern, on 22 October, included Wolf's *Italian Serenade*, Mozart's Piano Concerto in E flat major, K.271 (Eduard Steuermann, soloist), Milhaud's *Le Printemps*, and the Serenade, Op. 16, by Brahms. The payment for these concerts was quite small: 200 schillings, which included rehearsals. Nonetheless, Webern, always conscientious and thorough, gave much time and thought to the preparation of each performance,[2] which another conductor might have taken more lightly. For him, music-making never became mere routine.

In observance of the annual "Republik Feier," Webern conducted a Workmen's Symphony Concert, with the participation of the Singverein, on 10 November in the large hall of the Musikverein. The programme (repeated the following day) assumed special significance in that it featured the world premières of two works by Schoenberg: his orchestral transcription of J. S. Bach's Organ Prelude and Fugue in E flat major and two of his three settings of old German folk melodies for mixed chorus *a cappella*.[3] Since spring, Webern had made known to Schoenberg his ardent wish to give the first performances. In his letters he commented on the difficulties of the choral settings, their polyphonic intricacies, and the problems of intonation. These ultimately prevented, because of lack of rehearsal time, the rendition of the entire set of three.[4] The Bach transcription opened the programme. It was followed by a choral group consisting of *Beherzigung* by Brahms, Schoenberg's settings of *Schein uns, du liebe Sonne* (based on a melody by Antonius Scandellus, 1570) and *Herzlieblich Lieb, durch Scheiden* (a fifteenth-century tune), and two choruses by Hanns Eisler,[5] entitled *Naturbetrachtung* (based on a

poem by the composer) and *Auf den Strassen zu singen* (words by Weber).
The climax and close of the concert was Mahler's First Symphony.

As was the tradition, a high official of the Social Democratic Party
used the concert platform to deliver a speech commemorating the
founding of the Republic. The special occasion no doubt had prompted
the inclusion of Eisler's choruses on the programme, since their texts
were decidedly oriented to Socialist causes. Although Webern disliked
radical political messages, he was fond of Eisler's music and enjoyed
rehearsing it with his chorus. Since the singers had considerable
difficulty with the intonation, he had suggested to the composer that he
add an optional orchestral accompaniment similar to that in
Schoenberg's *Friede auf Erden*. In a long letter, dated 19 April 1929,
Webern pointed out that it was virtually impossible for any chorus to
stay on pitch during extended *a cappella* compositions: "If singing is to
be with force, the chorus rises, and vice versa. Therefore, the danger
exists that we end somewhere else than where we began. Indeed, I deem
it almost a foregone conclusion. *No chorus in the world* can avoid it with
certainty. Yes, there can be lucky instances. But then, why should I
render anything *false*? For me, impurity has become something utterly
dreadful."[6] Webern followed up with explicit suggestions for Eisler's
scoring of the orchestral ensemble, which was to support the chorus
effectively without ever becoming obtrusive.

The day after the concerts, the *Wiener Zeitung* printed a review
condemning Schoenberg's Bach transcription. The critic argued that, in
the first place, the organ idiom resisted adaptation to an orchestral
apparatus. Moreover, he felt that Schoenberg had injected his own
specific brand of instrumentation, thereby superimposing his
personality on Bach's. He was more favourably disposed towards the
Singverein's part in the programme and pointed out its "surpassing
precision, security, and musicality." On 13 November Webern gave
Schoenberg his own report:

The choruses sounded *incredible*! What I have done assuredly was
good, that I know. If you had only heard the two introductory
measures to the third strophe of *Schein uns*: "God's Will, God's
Will." Infinitely softer and ever softer and softer, and then the
entry of the sopranos. . . . We sang the song *Herzlieblich Lieb* without bar lines. I did not give a definite beat at all. The orchestra was
enthusiastic over your transcription [of Bach] and put forth every
effort. It was truly faultless. Rehearsing was splendid. After all, I could
spend only *two half rehearsals* on it. I could hear everything. Ah, yes,
how all this is scored! My God, how the end of the fugue sounds.

Two days after this account, Webern left for his first extended concert tour. Through the agency *Ithma* he had received conducting engagements in Munich, Frankfurt, and London. No doubt his growing reputation and his connection with Ravag had helped to open the door to invitations from abroad. Although loath to leave his home and family, Webern looked forward to the twenty-day trip, which seemed like a tremendous adventure to him. In his diary, he graphically recorded, day by day, his varied impressions and experiences. On the morning of his departure from Vienna's Westbahnhof he noted: "Happy feeling—love for the homeland." The crossing of the border shortly after Salzburg prompted the remark: "Farewell to the native soil." Frost and snow greeted him at Munich. He was met at the station by Fritz Kaltenborn, a Schoenberg pupil, who looked after him during his stay. After spending the first night in a "very bad inn," Webern changed to the Hotel Eden. The concert, given by the Munich Philharmonic, was one in a cycle similar to the Vienna Workmen's Symphony Concerts. Webern had only two rehearsals, on 16 November and on the morning of the concert, which was held on 19 November in the Tonhalle. In his diary Webern combined the programme listings with critical comments. The musical fare comprised Mozart's *Jupiter* Symphony ("The strings better than in Vienna"), Schoenberg's *Verklärte Nacht* ("Very good"), Wolf's *Italian Serenade* ("Very clean, clear; solo viola not so good. Nevertheless a good presentation"), and Johann Strauss' *Tales from the Vienna Woods* ("Had much joy. Orchestra followed well, above all in the spirit of the music itself. All-round presentation without doubt very good"). The choice of pieces, according to the diary, had "originated under much compulsion," meaning that an all-Austrian programme had been prescribed. Webern registered satisfaction with his own feelings on the podium: "No trace of nervousness or timidity. More secure than at home (in Vienna). Much joy and well-being."

After the concert, Kaltenborn took Webern to the Hotel Deutscher Kaiser for a farewell dinner (rated "very good" in the diary). The stay in Munich, which included a visit to a movie house ("Very bad impression!") was summed up: "Entire sojourn very nice. No significant disturbances. Munich a beautiful city, but provincial. Got along very well with the orchestra."

On the morning of 20 November Webern took the train to Frankfurt. There Theodor Wiesengrund-Adorno[7] awaited him at the station and brought him to the home of Dr Milton Seligmann,[8] Viktoria Allee 12, where he was "marvellously lodged and lived really exquisitely," as he noted in his diary. The accommodation had been arranged by Rudolf Kolisch, a close friend of the Seligmann family. Dr Seligmann held a high position in the Court of Justice, and his house was always open to visiting musicians. Alban Berg had enjoyed its hospitality years before and, in his letter of 15 December 1921 to his wife, had given this vivid description: "A little palace, incredibly distinguished. A colossal staff of servants. Mrs Seligmann, a very fine, very sympathetic and cordial person, who from far away still looks youthful. . . . A plate of cold cuts, a glass of Rhine wine, and then each to his room. Fabulously comfortable. Marble washbasins, warm water. . . . At 9.30, breakfast with Mrs Seligmann: ham and eggs, very good coffee, jam and butter."

Such unaccustomed luxury was also enjoyed by Webern during his Frankfurt stay. He spent the first two days studying his scores and taking walks through the city ("Unfortunately did not see the Goethe house," he noted in his diary). On the morning and afternoon of Saturday, 23 November, rehearsals were held in the broadcasting studio. "Orchestra quite good. Some wind players very good. Rapport quickly established." With a red pencil, Webern added that, after the practice session, his violin and cello pieces, Opera 7 and 11, were rehearsed under his supervision, in preparation for an ISCM concert in Frankfurt on 27 November. The broadcast began at 9.30 pm on Sunday, 24 November (Germany's Memorial Day). As before, Webern listed the programme in his diary, along with an appraisal of the performances: Mozart's Divertimento in D major ("Better than in Vienna"), Mahler's *Kindertotenlieder* ("Succeeded very well, conducted [the work] for the first time"), and Mozart's Symphony in G minor ("Very good").

Josef Hueber, who had come from Vienna to be the soloist in Mahler's *Kindertotenlieder*, related in his memoirs an incident connected with Webern's Frankfurt visit. After the concert a reception was held in Webern's honour, and the executive director of Radio Frankfurt was especially invited so that he might have an opportunity to discuss with Webern the possibility of more frequent conducting assignments. Some of Webern's friends had impresssed upon the director beforehand how great a gain this would be.

But the plan failed completely [Hueber recalled]. The director obviously waited, on the basis of his position of prestige, for Webern to broach the subject. Webern, in turn, was surprised that the director let the matter rest with only a few words of greeting, polite as these were. Dr Wiesengrund-Adorno, who accompanied me to my hotel after supper at the Seligmanns' the following day, informed me with regret of the failure of the plan, which certainly had been well intended. Later, at home, Webern on his part said something like, "If anyone wants to get something from me, then he has to approach me accordingly!"[9]

From each stopping place along his way, Webern sent brief reports to
Schoenberg. In Munich he expressed his joy at conducting, for the first
time, *Verklärte Nacht*, to which he had devoted most of his rehearsal time.
From Frankfurt he reported that William Steinberg was making
intensive preparations for Schoenberg's opera *Von Heute auf Morgen*,
scheduled for its première there on 1 February 1930. The next message
was mailed from Cologne, where Webern stopped for three days as the
guest of his old friend Heinrich Jalowetz, now an opera conductor in
that city. Together they went to a concert, a movie, and the opera.
Webern also spent an evening in the home of the composer Philipp
Jarnach. "Impression of Cologne: magnificent city, much life," he
remarked in his diary, adding: "When home, studied my Pieces, Op.
10."

That work was on the programme of the concert that Webern was to
conduct in London. He left Cologne in the early morning hours of 28
November and recorded his route in his diary:

> Via Aachen, Belgium, to Ostend. Rain. Disconsolate impression.
> From the train, Brussels did not make a good impression. German
> character (architectural style of the cities), here also not particularly
> different. At noon in Ostend, ate there. Then aboard ship. Crossing
> from 3.30 to 8 pm. First on deck, then slept two hours in the cabin.
> Awakened by storm. Quickly to the deck. Stood there two hours. The
> sea extremely rough. House-high waves. First felt miserable, but
> remained firm. Docked about 8 pm. Right away to the train. Arrived
> in London about 10.30 pm. Met by Clark.[10] With him to the Strand
> Palace Hotel in the city. Then to a party. Very tired.

On the following morning, a Friday, the first of three rehearsals took
place. It was entirely devoted to Webern's Five Pieces, Op. 10, which met
with "little understanding on the part of the orchestra." The difficulty
no doubt lay in the fact that Webern's English was insufficient, making it
necessary for his extensive and explicit comments to be relayed to the
musicians by an interpreter. The second rehearsal followed on Saturday
afternoon. This time Webern could cover more ground: his own
orchestra pieces, Milhaud's *Le Printemps*, and a portion of the Serenade,
Op. 16, by Brahms. Sunday was devoted to a sight-seeing tour of the
city, and in the afternoon Webern attended his first talking motion
picture which he "liked very much!" All meals and free time were
shared with his host. "Clark devoted himself to me in a touching
manner," Webern wrote to Schoenberg on 3 December.

The dress rehearsal was held on the morning of Monday, 2
December. In the evening of the same day, the broadcast concert took
place before an invited audience in a small theatre, which Webern

considered "unfavourable." The order of the programme was Milhaud, Webern, and Brahms. The official records of the BBC also list four orchestral songs by Gustav Mahler, to be performed second on the programme. Ruzena Herlinger was to be the soloist, but she was taken ill and this portion of the concert had to be omitted. In his diary Webern assessed the results: "My pieces came out well. About the same as in Zürich. Yet better there. Brahms was played dryly. Milhaud not very good either." The diary also recorded that Webern's Five Pieces were repeated for the studio audience after the broadcast. To the message Webern sent Schoenberg from the after-concert party, Clark added: "We are enormously happy over Webern's success as composer and conductor."

Early the next morning (it was his 46th birthday), Webern started on his way home. The crossing of the channel was smooth this time ("slept much"), and on the long train ride to Vienna there was another meeting at Cologne with Heinrich and Johanna Jalowetz, who came to the railway station despite the 1 am hour. On the evening of 4 December Webern was met at Vienna's Westbahnhof by his wife and the two youngest children. "Feeling of joy. Indescribably happy impression upon entering the apartment," were the sentiments he confided to the diary. Reminiscing on his first trip to England, he noted: "Not enchanted with London. Colossal traffic. But the entire character not very sympathetic. The same with regard to Clark and the orchestra. The social parties unbearable. Could hardly wait to leave. Strictly speaking, I was disappointed! Impression of the sea, the crossing, the coast: dismal! Fog, gloominess, longing for flowers in the mountains, for blue sky and clarity of the air. In general, however, felt physically well. Weather in London good."

Immediately after his return, Webern had to begin rehearsals for a concert on Saturday, 14 December. The Singverein and an amateur orchestra (augmented by wind players from the State Opera) joined with Eduard Steuermann and Josef Hueber as soloists in a programme consisting of Mozart's Piano Concerto in E flat major, K.271, the *a cappella* choruses by Schoenberg and Eisler that had been performed in the November concerts, Steuermann's piano solo rendition of a Bach–Busoni transcription, and Bach's *Kreuzstabkantate*.

At eight o'clock the following morning, Webern embarked on another trip, this time to Berlin, where he had been engaged to conduct a broadcast. Schoenberg, who had asked him to be his house guest, awaited him at the station. "Cherished, beautiful hours," the diary tells us about their reunion. The first rehearsal on 16 December was "not very favourable," the entire session being spent on Webern's Passacaglia. Only one more rehearsal, the following day, preceded the radio concert on the evening of 18 December.[11] Webern's diary lists the programme with his comments: Beethoven's *Coriolan* Overture ("not very good"), Brahms' Serenade, Op. 16 ("better than in Vienna and London, but also here hardly rehearsed. The beloved, sweet sound, which I expected, did not materialize here, either"), Mozart's Piano Concerto in E flat major ("Good"), and Webern's Passacaglia ("Realized to a considerable extent. Very satisfied with the work itself. Fluid expression. Difficult piece. Must be rehearsed a great deal. Regrettably this was not possible. All the same, quite satisfying").

After the concert, Schoenberg took Webern and Eduard Steuermann, the soloist in the Mozart concerto, to the famous Rheingold restaurant, and the three friends once again could indulge in reminiscences and discussions of musical affairs past, present, and future. The next morning, Webern secured a birth certificate for his eldest daughter, Amalie, born in Berlin almost nineteen years earlier. Taking the night train home, he arrived in Vienna on Friday noon, 20 December, and again was greeted at the railway station by the ever-faithful Wilhelmine—a fact worth recording in the diary, since this meant an hour's trip for her from Mödling into town.

Thanking Schoenberg for his hospitality, Webern wrote on 30 December: "Those days were wonderful, unforgettable ones for me. . . . How much I would like to be in Berlin permanently! The Funk-Stunde [Radio Berlin's classical music series] should engage me as a permanent conductor. Utopia. Here I can hardly expect anything any more. And I do need so urgently a position with a fixed income."

Despite the last remark, Webern could look back on a very busy and productive year. The concert tours had added substantially to his earnings, all of which are meticulously listed in his income book. The Munich engagement, for example, brought 700 marks which, after deducting the concert agency's commission, left a net of 530 marks. Similarly, the London concert netted £34 from a £42 gross honorarium. The grand total of the year's income amounted to 11,135.61 schillings, which compared favourably with the 9,714 schillings listed for 1928 and the 8,100 schillings earned in 1927.

That Christmas of 1929, Webern received two presents which particularly delighted him. With childlike joy he thanked Schoenberg on 2 January for the shirt of raw silk ("with a sewed-on collar!"), which for a man as unspoiled as Webern meant the height of luxury. He was equally exuberant over the other gift, a bust of Gustav Mahler by the sculptor Josef Humplik. Knowing of Webern's veneration for Mahler, the Humpliks had surprised him with a large plaster head, which was immediately given a place of honour in his home.

Webern had made the acquaintance of Humplik and his wife,

Hildegard, a few years earlier at the Künstlerbund Hagen,[12] an association of progressive painters and sculptors to which such men as Kokoschka and Schiele belonged. The headquarters of the group were located in the Zedlitzgasse, only a short distance from the Stubenbastei where Webern held his Singverein rehearsals. In 1926 Josef Humplik had given a one-man exhibition under the auspices of the Hagenbund. Webern came to see it, and on that occasion was introduced to the sculptor and his wife. Subsequently, Humplik created two busts of Webern. The first, larger than life and made of plaster, was done in 1927. For many years it stood in Webern's home.[13] The second, in terracotta, was created in 1928. This bust, life-size, was later cast in bronze and has since been reproduced in many publications. A superb work of art by any standard, it exemplifies Humplik's gift for capturing the spiritual qualities of his subjects.[14]

Humplik attained considerable renown in his profession.[15] He was one of the most representative members of the "Secession," a prominent group of Vienna artists. Exhibitions of his sculptures were held in the major cities of Europe and brought him international acclaim. Many of his works were awarded prizes. Particularly notable are his portrait busts of outstanding personalities. These include the writers and poets Ebner, Ficker, Kraus, and Trakl, the composers Mahler, Berg, and Webern, and the painters Moll and Klimt (Humplik's artistic tendencies were aligned with those of the latter).

The friendship that developed between Webern and the Humplik couple was close and enduring. The sculptor's wife, especially, was to become a major influence in Webern's life, for it was her poetry that inspired the entire vocal output of his last years. She was the daughter of the Austrian architect Huber.[16] Her mother's maiden name was Deym, and among her ancestors was the Countess Deym, famous for her friendship with Beethoven. Hildegard took up the study of art at an early age. Her teacher in sculpture at the Vienna Academy was Josef Humplik, whom she married on 29 March 1921. The couple first lived in Ried im Innkreis. Seeking her own realms of artistic expression, Hildegard soon turned from sculpture to painting and poetry. Although she produced a large number of oil paintings, drawings, and lithographs, she allowed only a few showings of her works. Similarly, only a small fraction of her prolific poetic output reached the public.[17] Because of her affinity with Attic culture, she adopted the pseudonym Jone, after the Greek word *Ion*. She combined deep religiousness, which bordered on mysticism, with the most acute perceptiveness in artistic and spiritual matters. These qualities earned her the confidence and personal friendship of men like Martin Buber and Ferdinand Ebner.[18] In May 1934 the Humpliks moved to Purkersdorf, an idyllic town in the Vienna Woods. There they lived and worked in a stately house (Wintergasse 31) surrounded by a park-like garden.

The kinship of ideologies between Webern and the two artists resulted in a constant exchange of thought. (After Webern's death his letters to the Humpliks were published and became an indispensable reference both for biographical data and for information concerning the genesis of his later works.)[19] The cordiality of Webern's letters attests to the sympathy he could be sure to find on the part of these friends. Hildegard Jone, in particular, became his Muse, in the fullest and purest sense of the word. Although she was not musically trained,[20] she inspired him to articulate the artistic and philosophical tenets of his work, and it was especially in his communications to her that he found the eloquence to formulate and project his innermost thoughts.

Excerpts from a letter written by Webern to Hildegard Jone on 6 August 1928, during the second year of their acquaintance, illuminate their spiritual relationship:

I understand "Art" to mean the faculty of bringing a thought into the clearest, simplest, i.e. "most comprehensible" form. In this sense, I cannot perceive the "Our Father" as something antithetical to art, but rather as its highest model. For here the greatest possible comprehensibility, clarity, and explicitness are attained. Therefore in this regard I cannot understand the view of Tolstoy and of all those who have expressed themselves similarly. But I do understand it when Beethoven drafts the main theme of the first movement of his *Eroica* over and over until it finally has the degree of comprehensibility comparable to a sentence from the "Our Father." This is my view of art. And for this reason I have never understood what classic, romantic, and the like are, nor have I placed myself in opposition to the masters of the past, but I have always only endeavoured to do exactly as they did: to represent as clearly as possible that which is given to me to say. This is, of course, quite a different matter than present day "classicism," which emulates the style without knowing its *meaning* (and this is what was hinted at above), whereas I (and Schoenberg and Berg) endeavour to fulfil this meaning—and it remains *eternally* the same—through *our* means. And what results in the end is hardly a copy, but something *most primary* and personal for just that reason. I am consequently also of your opinion when you said: "We must come to believe that progress is made only *inwards*." Yes, "Every heart colours its evening differently when it sets." Now let us hope that something will develop in regard to our joint work. From the fact that I have suggested it you may gather how very dear and really fundamentally related your way of thinking is to mine.

CHAPTER XX

Work and family

(1930)

AFTER THE EXCITING and rewarding last months of 1929, highlighted by the concert tours to London and Berlin, Webern found the beginning of the new year drab and unpromising. The only sources of income listed in his notebook during January and February were the Singverein and the Israelitic Institute for the Blind. Still excited by his meeting with Schoenberg, Webern grew very restless with his situation in Vienna. After reading in a newspaper that Heinrich Kaminski had been appointed successor to Hans Pfitzner at the Berlin Academy, he wrote to Schoenberg on 7 January:

> Is it really so unthinkable that such an appointment might come my way, too? It would be the most ideal solution to the problem of my livelihood! How much more would I appreciate such a position than, for example, a conductor's job, which hardly leaves one time for composing. Especially since I really like teaching better and better. Unfortunately, at present I do not have a single pupil. I therefore beg you sincerely to think of me when the occasion arises! Do not be angry with me for coming to you with this, but I am very anxious once again. And do not resent me for my fantasies.

Concerned over Webern's frame of mind, Schoenberg responded at once with fatherly counsel, admonishing him to be patient.[1] Apologetically, Webern replied on 16 January: "The deadly quiet here in Vienna was too dreadful after the exciting days of my trips, which filled me with hope, and especially after the stay with you in Berlin, which was so especially satisfying. Now I am gradually getting accustomed to it again and I am regaining my equilibrium."

The "deadly quiet" soon gave way to a spurt of new activity. No fewer than four concerts within three weeks were scheduled for February and

March, and in order to prepare them Webern had to abandon plans to attend the 1 February première of Schoenberg's opera *Von Heute auf Morgen* in Frankfurt. His decision was made easier because another conducting engagement, which he had asked Wiesengrund-Adorno to suggest to Radio Frankfurt to coincide with the Schoenberg event, could not be arranged. The first of Webern's four concerts—on 24 February 1930, in the medium-sized hall of the Konzerthaus—held special significance in that it featured the first Vienna performance of Webern's Symphony, Op. 21, under the composer's direction. Brahms' Piano Quartet in A major and Beethoven's Septet flanked the work on the programme, which was presented by the Kolisch ensemble and Eduard Steuermann under the auspices of the Wiener Konzerthausgesellschaft. The performers for Webern's Symphony included, besides the Kolisch quartet members and the violinist Elsie Stein, wind players and a harpist from the State Opera orchestra.

The event is recorded in Webern's diary as follows: "Much joy.[2] Came out quite beautifully. Better with multiple strings. Difficulties great. Held four rehearsals." As for the newspaper reaction, Josef Reitler's assessment in the *Neue Freie Presse* (3 March) was sympathetic but pessimistic:

> Besides the barbaric music of the primitive peoples, there has long existed one of the civilized. To Webern, also, *this* kind of soullessness is foreign. Perhaps it is that he wants to place something in opposition to the material sounds of machine music or to the confused rhythmic noises of a Stravinsky and Bartók, something that is dematerialized in sound, something dissolved in rhythm. The ecstatic manner with which the composer conducted his work compels at least the assumption of good faith. Sometimes, when we contemplate the development and practices of music outside Vienna, this Anton Webern appears to us like the eternally tragic figure of a sentry whom one has forgotten to relieve, and who now, as the last of the faithful, guards the precariously tottering edifice of an aesthetic which has long looked for escape and found *Jonny*.

(The closing remark alludes to Ernst Krenek's *Jonny spielt auf*, an opera employing jazz elements, which was then enjoying a sensational success throughout Europe.)

On 5 March Webern participated in another Kolisch–Steuermann concert of the Konzerthaus series. This time he was in charge of the first Vienna performance of Schoenberg's Suite, Op. 29. (On the programme were also Bach's *Brandenburg* Concerto No. 3 and Schoenberg's String Quartet No. 1.) "The last weeks of my work were devoted exclusively to the study of your composition," Webern wrote to Schoenberg as early as 7 February, before rehearsals with the ensemble actually got under way. "It is frightfully difficult. . . . Wherever I am, from morning till night, I practise these rhythms. *But what good fortune it was for me to penetrate this music!*" Nine rehearsals were held with the ensemble, which again included, besides Steuermann and the Kolisch quartet members, wind players from the State Opera orchestra. On 16 March Webern was able to report to the composer: "The success was extraordinary. I must confess that I was a little worried, for the conditions in Vienna are becoming more and more horrible." Deploring their separation, he added: "If only I could have produced all this *for you.* Be assured that for me it is always as though you were really present. But to have to miss you over and over again—this is so difficult. It becomes more and more unbearable for me. And I have only one wish, to be again, as soon as possible, where you are. So indeed I have always managed it and I hope that soon it can be this way again."

Only four days after that performance, Webern conducted a radio concert consisting of Brahms' *Tragic* Overture, Bach's *Kreuzstabkantate* (Josef Hueber, soloist; Eduard Steuermann, thorough-bass part), his own Passacaglia, and Beethoven's Seventh Symphony. Such broadcasts generally were allocated only two rehearsals of two hours each, a situation on which Webern commented in his diary: "Passacaglia much worse than in Berlin. Quite insufficiently rehearsed."

One week afterwards, on 16 March, Webern again appeared on the conductor's podium, this time for a Workmen's Symphony Concert. It included *Vorspiel zu einem Revolutionsdrama*, Op. 33, by Heinz Tiessen, a group of solo songs by Schubert and Wolf, Max Reger's Requiem, and Beethoven's Third Symphony. On the day of the concert, Webern wrote to Schoenberg about the Requiem: "It is a wonderful work in invention and expression. But what a curious 'representation' of ideas. The score is black from top to bottom, page after page." In his diary he noted that the performance "came out very well." The critic of the *Wiener Zeitung* (19 March) applauded the opportunity of becoming acquainted with the rarely heard work and spoke of Webern's "deep introspection and unconditional honesty" as a conductor. Erwin Stein, in an article published later in the *Christian Science Monitor* (2 August), compared Webern's performance of the *Eroica* with one just conducted by Toscanini and found it "more directly impressive." This accolade added to Webern's growing reputation in America, where, on 26 March of that year, the world première of his Five Movements, Op. 5, in the transcription for string orchestra, was given in Philadelphia.

On 15 March Webern received a six-month contract from Ravag for a position that he described to Schoenberg the next day as "a kind of

musical *Dramaturg* [programme supervisor]." Besides conducting, his
duties included making reports on new compositions submitted for
performance and suggestions for improving the quality of classical
music broadcasts. Julius Bittner and Rudolf Weirich (a Schoenberg
pupil) shared in these responsibilities. While Webern was disappointed
not to receive as many conducting assignments as he had expected, he
was satisfied to find a measure of economic relief in the fixed monthly
salary of 500 schillings. Before the season ended, he led two more radio
concerts: On 1 May the programme included *Vorfrühling* by Egon
Wellesz, Mozart's Symphony in D major (K. 84?), the *Adagietto* from
Mahler's Fifth Symphony, Bach's Concerto for Two Claviers in C major
(Eduard and Hilda Steuermann, soloists), and Beethoven's Eighth
Symphony. The broadcast on 22 June consisted of Schubert's Fifth
Symphony, three songs by Joseph Marx, Krenek's *Kleine Symphonie*, and
Mozart's Symphony in E flat major (K. 16?). Not convinced by Ernst
Krenek's earlier music (the composer adopted the twelve-tone
technique only with his opera *Karl V*, completed in 1933), Webern wrote
to Schoenberg on 1 July: "Krenek's *Kleine Symphonie*: they will not be
able to reproach me for not paying attention to it, now that I have, after
all, a little more free play as conductor. It was the first time that I *really*
concerned myself with his music. Much is frightening, some of it quite
amusing." Webern went on to tell Schoenberg that he had heard
Hindemith's *Lehrstück*, which he termed "horrible."

This verdict on Hindemith's music is indicative of the contempt in
which the members of the Schoenberg camp held certain colleagues
persevering in the traditional vein. Themselves constantly harassed by
vitriolic criticism, Schoenberg and his followers at times found it
difficult to be tolerant towards others. Moreover, they were utterly
convinced of the rightness of their cause and emboldened by the
growing attention accorded their works everywhere. Berg's *Wozzeck*, in
particular, reached wide segments of the opera-going public which had
never been confronted with atonal music before. Inevitably, heated
controversies resulted. After the first Vienna performance of the opera
that March, the opposition had attacked the new trends in music as
"l'art pour l'art" and "unsocial." On 19 April Webern gave his
commentary to Schoenberg: "Berg's *Wozzeck* has shaken me to the
depths. The production here was, I daresay, insufficient in every respect.
The success at the première really was quite tremendous. But this city!
Above all, the youth here! It really is not to be endured any longer."

The increasing international acceptance of the new school of Vienna
composers had been illustrated by a Viennese Chamber Music Festival
in Amsterdam during late March. In two evening concerts (24 and 25
March), works by Schoenberg, Berg, Eisler, Hauer, and Wellesz were

played, as well as Webern's Four Pieces, Op. 7, and Five Sacred Songs, Op. 15. Webern had been invited to preside over the latter work, but was not able to make the trip, partly because of his conducting engagements at home. He was gratified by their increasing number during the 1929–30 season (proudly he tabulated all fourteen of them in his diary), but he was disappointed in his hope of again receiving the Music Prize of the City of Vienna. Berg, a member of the jury, had vigorously promoted his name and secured the unanimous support of the other committee members. However, Universal Edition neglected to submit his application and scores in time, and regulations forbade overlooking this technicality.

That bad experience, made more ʻfrustrating by the loss of the monetary reward connected with the prize, is not even mentioned in Webern's diary, but the descriptions of his summer mountain excursions that year fill many pages. On 27 June, eager to show Hildegard and Josef Humplik the alpine flora of the high regions, he took them to the Rax, which they ascended by cable car. Webern found the ride "not very special," but he took pleasure in guiding his friends in a walk across the upper plateau. On 16 and 17 July he traversed the Schneealpe with Wilhelmine and Christine, spending the night before as usual in the Kampl Hut. Two days later Webern and Ludwig Zenk travelled to the mighty Dachstein (2996 m.). Approaching the mountain from the Schladming side, they spent the first night in the Austria Hut, and the second in the Südwand Hut (the last shelter at timberline below the precipitous cliffs of the towering peak). "Stay at the huts wonderful! Many alpine roses. Larch forest. Marvellous atmosphere. On Monday, a beautiful view of the Hohe Tauern, Wiesbachhorn especially clear," Webern noted in his diary. The climb to the summit was made on Tuesday, 22 July. Although rain and fog impeded the ascent, Webern was successful: "At last, really stood on the summit after three vain attempts,"[3] he recorded triumphantly. One week later, on 29 July, he was still brimming with enthusiasm when he described his impressions to the Humpliks:

The diffused light on the glacier (caused by the overcast sky and the fog) was quite strange. A *few* paces away the snow and fog melted completely into one indistinguishable layer. One could not perceive at all whether it went up or down. This was a situation most conducive to snow blindness. But it was marvellous, one felt like floating in space. And on the meadows of the south side! The contrast: the most luxuriant flora! Nothing but alpine roses in full bloom! And lower down the most magnificent stand of larches! Enormous trees, in the oddest shapes, with giant branches. You would have liked that.

The freedom of the heights, purchased at the cost of strenuous train rides at night to and from the mountain, had lasted only three days. Yet Webern noted "considerable regeneration" in his diary in summarizing the uplifting experience. After the Dachstein climb, Webern had only two more brief outings before the season resumed: with his daughter Maria he climbed the Schneealpe on 2 and 3 September, and on 8 September he and his family walked up the Anninger, a wooded hill above Mödling, which was a favourite goal for outings.[4] That the modest hike rated a diary entry this time marks it as a special occasion in a holiday period devoted largely to creative work (Webern's primary objective was the completion of his Quartet, Op. 22).

That summer, Arnold Schoenberg was at Lugano working on the music to *Moses und Aron*. From July on, an extensive correspondence between the two friends revolved around a special project: Webern, in his capacity as programme adviser at Ravag, had suggested that Schoenberg be invited to conduct a broadcast of his own works. While agreed upon in principle, the plan met with the major obstacle of Schoenberg's steep financial demands (1,000 schillings honorarium plus 500 schillings travel expenses). Acting as intermediary, Webern quickly found himself at odds with the directors. Naturally he sided with Schoenberg, although the management argued that Felix Weingartner had received only 800 schillings, the highest fee in Ravag history, and Franz Schreker 600 schillings. Negotiations dragged on, and the matter was still hanging in the balance in early September. Pressed by Schoenberg for a decision, Webern wrote to him in exasperation on 5 September: "With what sort of people have I become involved! . . . Now I only hope that it is still possible for you to wait a few days more and that, as far as Ravag is concerned, the fault lies only with this cursed Austrian characteristic of engaging in dilatory practices."

Webern's dilemma was compounded by the fact that his own contract with Ravag was due to expire on 15 September. He alluded to his troubles when he wrote to the Humpliks on 27 September: "During the last few weeks I had to go through such horrible things professionally, as perhaps never before! It cannot be put into words at all. And I really do not want to plague you with details. . . . Dear friends, things are getting worse and worse in the world, especially in the domain of the arts. And *our mission* becomes constantly greater and greater." Webern's worries for his own position were only too well founded: his contract with Ravag was extended for only one month, and thereafter the 500 schillings monthly salary ceased. However, Ravag did give Webern occasional conducting assignments up to the outbreak of World War II, and until the last year of his life he continued with the regular "Abhördienst," which entailed the critical survey, while listening at home, of live broadcasts of classical music. As he confided to Schoenberg on 2 April 1931, Webern found that chore "very torturous."

Thanks to Webern's efforts, arrangements with Schoenberg were finally consummated. The concert, on 17 October, was preceded by a lecture, "Arnold Schoenberg and His Work," by Paul Stefan. Performed by the Wiener Philharmoniker, the programme consisted of works from Schoenberg's early period: *Verklärte Nacht*, Op. 4, the Orchestra Songs, Op. 8 (Anton Maria Topitz, soloist), and the Chamber Symphony, Op. 9. Schoenberg's presence in Vienna provided the opportunity, all too rare since his move to Berlin, for a reunion of his old fraternity. Webern delighted in "being able finally to talk at greater length once again" with his friend, as he wrote to him on 12 November. During Schoenberg's stay, on 20 October, Webern went with him to Baden to see Adolf Loos, whom they found seriously ill. On the same evening they stopped at the apartment of Karl Kraus for a brief visit. Both calls are recorded in Webern's diary.

The architect Loos had long been a brother-in-arms of the Schoenberg circle, whose aesthetic was akin to his own.[5] A familiar figure in concert halls and a vocal supporter of avant-garde music, he had been in the midst of the scandals in Vienna (1913) and Salzburg (1922), firmly standing his ground in the battle. When his 60th birthday approached (on 10 December 1930), his friends, eager to show their loyalty, compiled a Festschrift,[6] to which Webern contributed. He quoted Loos' satirical remark "that he had to pull himself together to distinguish a violin clef (key) from a house door key" and alluded to the architect's book *Ins Leere gesprochen* (Spoken into a Void): "When he raised his voice [on behalf of the music of the New Vienna School], then it was no more 'spoken into a void' than was his entire doctrine." The dedication of his Quartet, Op. 22, was Webern's musical birthday offering to his revered friend.

During the month of October Webern gave two lectures for the International Pianists' Seminar. The founder and director of that organization was Paul Emerich, who had been coached by Webern in the days of the Schoenberg Society. He subsequently appeared as soloist under Webern in several broadcasts, performing such works as Reger's Piano Concerto in F minor and Weber's *Konzertstück*. Associates of the seminar included many pianists of high repute, such as Claudio Arrau, Erwin Schulhoff, and Eduard Steuermann. The headquarters were in Vienna, with branches in various capital cities. Webern's name was listed on the seminar's brochure, but his active participation appears to have been limited to the two lectures given in October, since his income book lists only the honorarium of 90 schillings received for these.

Webern's conducting activities during the autumn of 1930 were concentrated within a short period. On 10 November he led a broadcast concert consisting of Beethoven's *Consecration of the House* Overture, Mozart's Concerto for Flute and Harp, K. 299, and Beethoven's *Eroica* Symphony. On 28 November the Singverein participated in a function in the Hietzing district of Vienna, performing works by Brahms and Schoenberg, among others. The chorus also took part, on 13 December, in the "Renner-Feier," a large rally held in the Konzerthaus.[7] The Singverein's contributions were the choral settings of Beethoven's *Consecration of the House* and Johann Strauss' *On the Beautiful Blue Danube*. The fees Webern received for such occasional services (50 schillings for the Hietzing concert and 200 schillings for the "Renner-Feier") were a welcome addition to his restricted income.

On Sunday, 14 December, the day after the "Renner-Feier," Webern conducted Gustav Mahler's Sixth Symphony in a Workmen's Symphony Concert given in the large hall of the Musikverein. The programme opened with the Singverein's rendition of three mixed choruses *a cappella* by Hanns Eisler. The first of that group, *Gesang der Besiegten*, was a world première; the others—*Naturbetrachtung* and *Auf den Strassen zu singen*[8]—had already been performed by the group the year before. According to Webern's diary, there were only two orchestra rehearsals for the symphony, but this belies the degree of his preparation. "I am now entirely buried in the study of Mahler's Sixth. . . . To retain this giant complex with all its details in one's head is really no small matter," he wrote on 5 December to Schoenberg, with whom he had often played the work in piano-duet arrangement. Inviting Josef Humplik to attend the rehearsals, he confessed to him on 10 December: "My state of mind in the face of this *immense* task can hardly be described."

"Anton von Webern," a lengthy article by Willi Reich, did much to advance Webern's international reputation that year. Published in the August issue of the leading German periodical *Die Musik*, it also appeared in *De Muziek*, a Dutch journal. The editor of the latter, Paul F. Sanders, had asked Webern for a contribution to the special issue released on the occasion of the first Netherlands performance of Berg's *Wozzeck* (7 and 8 October) in Amsterdam.[9] Although Webern declined the request on the grounds that he was no writer, his letter itself rendered such homage to Berg that Sanders reproduced it in facsimile in the issue. That letter closes: "I can only stammer that *Wozzeck* moves me more and more and that I know with absolute certainty, rather than merely believe, that this work and all others by Berg, having sprung from the most sacred inspiration, will retain validity for all eternity."

While Berg was being fêted in Holland, Webern received from America the October issue of *New Music*, which contained the first printing of his song "Liebste Jungfrau," Op. 17, No. 2 (then entitled "Geistlicher Volkstext." The Sonata for Flute and Viola by Adolph Weiss and a piece called *36* by Carlos Chavez followed Webern's composition in this publication.[10] Adolph Weiss was then one of the men closest to the pulse of musical affairs in the United States. A disciple of Schoenberg, he was among the first, if not the very first, to employ the twelve-tone system in America. While studying in Europe, Weiss had become acquainted with Webern, whose work as composer and conductor he held in high esteem. After returning home he began at once to promote the cause of his European friends.

Shortly before Christmas, a surprise message from Weiss caused no little excitement in the Webern home. The diary records: "Monday, 22 December: Inquiry from America (Adolph Weiss) whether I would like to come for three months as conductor of a newly-founded orchestra in *New York*. Answered in an affirmative manner. Left the question of my salary open."

Webern was elated. Innately quite certain of his own worth, he suffered greatly from the lack of recognition in his native city. Although his abilities as a conductor were generally recognized, he never once was asked to lead the Vienna Philharmonic or to partake in any official function of the Music Academy, the University, or any other prestigious institution. The orchestra he directed for the Workmen's Symphony Concerts was specifically hired for each occasion under the sponsorship of the Social Democratic Party, and that political aegis carried a certain stigma with the upper strata of society. In his economic dependence, Webern frequently felt humiliated by powerful officials. Proud and sensitive, he was prone to both anger and dejection. Although always courteous and tactful, he was no diplomat and, because of his essentially independent spirit, he was averse to playing politics. Feeling suppressed in his own city, where petty rivalries and intrigues were notorious, he fastened his hopes on any encouragement coming from abroad. Calls to conduct in Switzerland, Germany, and England had confirmed his confidence that he might have a successful career anywhere but at home. Now America beckoned!

On 26 December Webern expressed to Adolph Weiss his general readiness to come to New York: "Believe me, not just considerations of a materialistic nature lure me over, but above all the hope of being able to find there a truly satisfying occupation, i.e. the faith that what I envision is perhaps still possible today only in America."[11] Raising a number of questions about the orchestra and his expected duties, Webern set forth his concerns: "Only when I know all these details, can I answer your question regarding my salary demand. To be sure, I am far from thinking of a 'star's' fee—I would never want to do that—but at any rate, I must be able to save something for myself, since, because of my prolonged absence, I will run the risk of losing some revenues here forever. Therefore, I must be protected and I must be able to cover myself in advance."

Except for these considerations, the tone of Webern's letter was quite positive. The Americans whom he knew personally had instilled in him a sympathy for their country, and the attention that his music was receiving across the Atlantic naturally fostered his enthusiasm for the proverbial "land of unlimited opportunities." Webern's faith in America and his belief that perhaps only the New World could provide a fertile ground for his ideas and intentions sounds prophetic in the light of what American initiative was to accomplish in the propagation of his work after his death (see Epilogue).

In this connection it is of interest that Webern kept in his library two books by American authors whose thoughts were akin to his own: *Walden* by Henry David Thoreau and *Society and Solitude* by Ralph Waldo Emerson. Certainly he could feel himself in accord with Thoreau's thought: "I went to the woods because I wished to live deliberately, to front only the essential facts of life, and see if I could not learn what it had to teach, and not, when I came to die, discover that I had not lived." It was Alban Berg who had brought this author to Webern's attention. On 26 April 1925 Webern wrote to Berg that he was just reading Thoreau's *Walden* and was "enthusiastic and refreshed." He added: "For this I thank you. A thousand times!!!"

One can only speculate how Webern might have fared had the prospect of his going to America indeed materialized. However, the inquiry by Weiss, issued at the instigation of Henry Cowell, had been quite tentative, for the orchestra in question was still in the planning stage and actually was never organized. At any rate, the closing days of 1930 were brightened by high hopes. On Christmas Eve, Webern's older sister Maria and her husband Paul Clementschitsch, who were visiting Mödling for a week, joined the family circle. Maria and Webern's younger sister Rosa continued to live in Klagenfurt. Despite the relatively short distance between the two cities, Webern and his sisters met only rarely. He wrote to them conscientiously on holidays and important occasions, but his correspondence does not give the impression of any real closeness.

By contrast, Webern's display of affection towards his four children was pronounced. Although his attention was bestowed equally on all of them, the first-born, Amalie, was his favourite. She was the only one to finish the Gymnasium and enter the University. With fatherly pride, Webern recorded in his diary her achievements during the final Gymnasium examinations, which she passed "with brilliant success."

He listed every grade in her closing report card, underscoring the best marks. He noted each party with which the graduates celebrated the end of their school days. The various stations of the journey to Holland, taken by the class as a group, were enumerated as if he himself had made the trip. Always including family news in his letters to Schoenberg, Webern reported on 1 July 1930: "Mali will prepare herself at the university to become a teacher of gymnastics and sports (secondary subject English). For four years: gymnastics, skiing, tennis, ice-skating, mountaineering, swimming, etc., in other words, everything that has always represented the 'ideal' of her father." That dream was soon dashed, however, since Webern had to record in his diary that Mali "was not accepted—reasons were not given." To Schoenberg he speculated on 12 November that "the main reason probably was that she does not wear pigtails or *'Schwesternschuhe'* [nurses' tie shoes] and the like."[12] Amalie, then nineteen, was very attractive, vivacious, and fun-loving. Webern took pleasure in being seen with her at concerts. He beamed with delight when on one occasion she was mistaken for his wife and addressed as Frau Doktor.

Possessed by an extreme sense of orderliness, Webern was quite pedantic about every detail of his domestic life, from the arrangement of the furniture down to the placement of household utensils such as the bread basket or the water jug. His study was the inner sanctum of the apartment. It was at the end of the corridor to ensure the greatest possible quiet. Except for his wife, only Mali was permitted there, since only she was considered reliable enough to preserve her father's concept of punctilious order. According to her, the pencils lay on his desk aligned according to length and colour, and when sharpening them she had to be careful to put them back into the same position. Webern's desk, incidentally, was left unpolished. Loving things in their natural state, he enjoyed seeing the original grain of the wood.

Webern's second daughter, Maria, two years younger than Amalie, resembled her father in appearance and her mother in temperament. Like Wilhelmine, she was very quiet and reserved. Although very intelligent, she did not pursue an academic career, but chose the profession of kindergarten teacher, specializing in gymnastics. Fond of adventure sports, she ran the white rapids of alpine streams in a kayak and ascended mountains like the Dachstein and Grossglockner on difficult routes. Although father and daughter shared a love for the mountains, they never climbed any major peak together.

Webern's son Peter, in his fifteenth year at this time (1930), bore his mother's facial features. Frequently ill, he caused his parents constant concern, reflected in Webern's numerous and infinitely detailed diary accounts. After his appendix operation of 1928, Peter was ill for several

months the following year and lost an entire year of school. There were
X-rays and injections, and the diagnosis was made that he had a slight
heart defect. In another extensive diary entry at the end of 1930, Webern
described his son's continuing ailments. Following a tonsils operation,
there were fever spells, relapses, and more injections. The account
closes: "Since the holidays he is quite well again. But great caution is
necessary for the time to come." Although Webern appears to have been
an indulgent, even doting father, it was he, rather than the mother, who
disciplined the children. That discipline could be quite strict. For
instance, in order to correct his son's slouching posture, Webern made
him hold a cane across his back on their Sunday walks. Spankings were
frequent while the children were small. Amalie remembers that she, as
the most mischievous, received a major share of them. As Peter grew up,
there were violent arguments between father and son because the youth
displayed no inclination towards any particular profession. Hampered
by many prolonged absences from school, he did not get beyond the
Gymnasium's fourth grade and finally contented himself with minor
clerical jobs for a livelihood.

The youngest child, Christine, was only eleven at Christmas of 1930.
Like Amalie, she was a very attractive girl (Josef Humplik portrayed her
in sculpture in 1932). Family life, from all accounts of the children, was
close and idyllic. Virtually every Sunday was given over to outings and
picnics in the neighbouring woods. Webern was a model father. For
instance, when the children were small, he sang them to sleep with a
lullaby, and for many years he read to them at bedtime. He played
pranks on them and amused them with his imitation of a village band,
simulating drum and trumpet. In contrast to her husband's gay and
lively nature, Wilhelmine was serious and withdrawn. Although she
displayed few outward signs of affection (Amalie does not remember her
mother ever kissing her), her devotion to her husband and children was
absolute and truly self-sacrificing.

During their childhood and adolescence, the girls took dancing and
piano lessons (Amalie recalled the "very strict lady piano teacher who
rapped our knuckles at each wrong note"). The violin was assigned to
Peter. Webern, horrified by noise in general and faulty musical sounds
in particular (according to Amalie "each wrong note drove him mad"),
could not bear to teach his own children, nor did he allow them to
practise while he was composing. Such practising had to be at set hours.
None of the children ever attained any degree of proficiency in music
and, as they themselves admitted, their desire to understand their
father's compositions began to develop only long after his death. They
were proud, however, to sit during concerts in the "Erste Künstlerloge"
(honour loge reserved for artists), "lined up like organ pipes" (in

Amalie's words), and to witness the clamour and applause of which their father was the centre. At such occasions, they caught a glimpse of his true domain, in which he rose before their astonished eyes like a reigning monarch.

Throughout his diary, Webern made a special note each time one of his children partook in the Mass traditionally held at the beginning of the school year. Similarly, he listed the dates of their confirmation and the details of the attendant family celebration. The consistency of these records would imply that Webern was a devout Catholic. So do the votive pictures found inserted between the pages of his books, and so does, in particular, his predilection for song texts expressing the Christian faith. However, Webern's religion stood above dogma. He refused to accept the authority of the clergy, denying any human being the right to act as intermediary between man and God. His wife felt even more strongly on this point. Consequently, both rejected the institution of confession. This was confirmed by Amalie, who did not remember ever seeing her parents receive Holy Communion. They would attend church services for such special occasions as their children's first communions and weddings, or for the baptisms of grandchildren. But the family never went to church together on holy days such as Christmas or Easter. On the other hand, Webern is known to have entered a church or wayside chapel to pray in solitude. His submission to a Higher Will was expressed in his custom of making the sign of the cross whenever the family sat down to meals. The gesture symbolized, if nothing else, an all-abiding faith. In a letter to Ludwig Zenk, written at Christmas 1930, Webern gave expression to that supreme trust in Providence. Zenk and his wife, Maria, had just lost their first child at birth. Offering his young friend the "brotherly 'Du'," he tried to comfort him with the words: "Be consoled. In everything that happens there lies hidden the deepest meaning, which we cannot unriddle, which we are not to know, but in which we must believe and to which *we can cling*! *I have already experienced this*."

CHAPTER XXI

Honour and notoriety
(1931)

Even though the prospect of a call to America, raised at Christmas-time, quickly faded, 1931 was to become a banner year for Webern. On 4 January he conducted a radio concert consisting of Mozart's Symphony in F major, K. 43, d'Albert's Cello Concerto, Schumann's *Manfred* Overture, and Beethoven's *Pastoral* Symphony. In another broadcast, on 29 March, he included Mozart's Symphony in D major, K. 81, and the Piano Concerto in G major, K. 453, followed by Mahler's *Kindertotenlieder* (Josef Hueber, soloist) and Schumann's Symphony No. 2. For the latter, Gustav Mahler's "Retouchen" (retouchings), as Webern called them, were used.

The major Singverein project during the early months of the year was the study of the *German Requiem* by Brahms. A plan of long standing, the performance was now scheduled for the last Workmen's Symphony Concert of the season. Webern approached the task with special dedication, devoting to it two chorus rehearsals weekly from mid-January on. To strengthen his forces, he invited Josef Polnauer, who had a powerful tenor voice, to participate in the performance. Keenly interested in music, Polnauer frequently attended the group's practice sessions and occasionally even substituted as conductor when Webern was on concert tours or ill.

Hans Humpelstetter, a Singverein member, later recalled a remark made by Webern, in his soft Viennese dialect, at the dress rehearsal on 11 April: "Da brauchert i hundert Proben, damit all's da is, was i ma da vorstell." ("I would really need a hundred rehearsals for everything to come out that I envision"). In his memoirs, covering many years of singing under Webern's baton, Humpelstetter cites another example of Webern's attitude towards rehearsals. For him they were an end in themselves: "Must it be the performance upon which everything finally depends? To get really immersed in a work, the rehearsals are the thing.

The fact that we eventually perform somewhere is a subordinate consideration. Recognition is secondary. It is in this spirit that the instrumentalists strive for complete virtuosity. We, too, must take this more to heart: to perfect our ability more and more."[1]

The performance of the *German Requiem*, which was broadcast over Radio Vienna, took place on Sunday, 12 April, in the large hall of the Musikverein. Two soloists of high calibre had been engaged: the soprano Margaret Philipsky from the Municipal Theatre of Magdeburg and the baritone Carlo Haas of the Metropolitan Opera, New York. As usual at these concerts, the hall was overcrowded, and the performance brought the participants a stormy ovation. The press reports hailed the success, of which the lion's share belonged to Webern. His achievement as conductor was likened to that of Furtwängler in *Der Wiener Tag* (15 April). The critic of that paper, Alfred Rosenzweig, admonished: "It is high time that also other concert organizations, such as the Gesellschaft der Musikfreunde or the Konzerthausgesellschaft, finally remembered that Webern is one of the few Viennese concert conductors of top stature, who, as no one else, would be qualified to preserve and add to the great tradition of Vienna's choral societies and to lead, at the side of Heger and other guest conductors, the representative choral concerts." The *Wiener Zeitung* (17 April) acclaimed Webern's "fervour" and accomplishment in equally glowing terms: "One knows how possessed this conductor is by every task." The reviewer of the *Allgemeine Zeitung* (15 April) spoke of "much spirituality, much genuine artistry" and declared that "uncommonly diligent, careful rehearsals and purposeful preparatory work have here achieved artistic perfection."

On the evening following the *Requiem*'s performance, Webern once again entered the Musikverein building. This time it was not to mount the conductor's podium in the large auditorium, but to mingle with the audience in the small hall. Although merely one of the listeners, he nevertheless was the centre of the proceedings, in that the concert was entirely devoted to his own compositions. This was the first such recognition accorded him. The programme of the notable event is reproduced overleaf.

Savouring the momentousness of the event, Webern noted the programme in his diary in complete detail, under the headline "Evening with works by me." In capital letters, he marked the "URAUFFÜHRUNG" (world première) of his Quartet, Op. 22. Although the audience consisted largely of friends and acquaintances, the reception was not free from dissent. The same critics who had acclaimed him as a conductor the preceding night were now unanimous in denouncing him as a composer. The *Allgemeine Zeitung* (15 April) said

KLEINER MUSIKVEREINS-SAAL

Montag, den 13. April 1931
abends halb 8 Uhr

KOLISCH-QUARTETT
EDUARD STEUERMANN

Mitwirkende: Aenne Michalski (Staatsoper), Prof. Johann Löw (Klarinette)
Leopold Wlach (Saxophon)

ANTON WEBERN:

1. Fünf Sätze für Streichquartett, op. 5
   Heftig bewegt – Sehr langsam – Sehr bewegt – Sehr langsam – in zarter Bewegung

2. Lieder aus op. 3, 4 und 12
   Eingang   Kahl reckt der Baum
   Dies ist ein Lied   Der Tag ist vergangen
   Im Windesweben   Gleich und Gleich

3. Trio für Geige, Bratsche und Violoncello, op. 20
   Sehr langsam — Sehr getragen und ausdrucksvoll; zart bewegt

4. Vier Stücke für Geige und Klavier, op. 7
   Sechs Bagatellen für Streichquartett, op. 9
   Drei kleine Stücke für Violoncello und Klavier, op. 11

5. Quartett für Geige, Klarinette, Tenor-Saxophon und Klavier, op. 22
   Sehr mäßig — Sehr schwungvoll   (Uraufführung)

Klavier: Steinway & Sons, beigestellt von der Firma Bernhard Kohn

Preis: 60 Groschen

Programme of the first all-Webern concert (13 April 1931)

of "this fanatic apostle of atonality," whose works could be measured only in seconds, that "such concoctions of horror, resulting from a musical mania that loses itself in chaos, have almost nothing to do any more with music." In *Der Wiener Tag* (15 April), Alfred Rosenzweig was more moderate but still reserved: "They [the compositions] are curious, crystalline formations out of the most secret and innermost laboratory of twelve-tone music, theoretical formulations by a fanatically serious musical mind, which follow no other practical purposes than to enlarge experimentally the perceptions of a new path. Although we have willing ears, we can hardly hear them." Dr Friedrich Bayer went on record with the most violent condemnation of all. In the *Neues Wiener Extrablatt* (16 April) he voiced his absolute disgust with Webern's music: "His pieces are noise-like injections of an extra-musical nature. . . .The musical excess reached its climax in the Quartet. This work is really a direct offence against good taste, since the squeaking, yelping, and gargling sound-scraps of the clarinet and the saxophone demonstrate amazing similarity to certain vital human utterances of an indecent nature. It would be interesting to learn what stimulated Webern to such a production and for what audience he intends his works. At least to the listeners with natural sensibilities, this mode of creation signifies a sin against the spirit of tonal art, which up to today, thank God, has remained still sacred to us."

Even Paul Stefan, although a partisan of the Mahler–Schoenberg camp since its early days, expressed his doubts regarding the course that Webern was following in his Opera 20 and 22. In *Die Stunde* (15 April) he warned: "These newest formulations, I openly admit, have progressed so far that I cannot follow them for the time being—they appear to be nothing but school-like constructions, and only the genius of Webern guarantees that probably more will have to be sought in them. . . . This music will probably never become an art for the masses. But also for the artist, for the common cause, such isolation can become a danger, a tragedy."

Webern remained undaunted in the face of such negative appraisals. Since the earliest years of his association with Schoenberg, he had learned to endure and even disdain the attacks of the press. With some justification, he regarded music critics as autocratic. Like any true professional, he believed in the absolute integrity of his work. By the same token, he was averse to convincing anyone with a few simplified explanations when the intricacies and complexities of his music demanded serious and patient study. Knowing the futility of short cuts in setting forth the principles of the new technique and aesthetic, he avoided being drawn into discussions if the circumstances were not conducive to understanding. His attitude in such matters is illustrated by an anecdote connected with the Vienna première of his Symphony, Op. 21. Humpelstetter relates: "After the performance, one of Webern's young singers from the bass section [of the Singverein] asked: 'If you please, Herr Doktor, could you not explain the work to us a little bit so that we are able to understand it better?' Webern jovially patted the young man on the shoulder and said to him and his friends, 'Just listen intently, Kinderl [children]!' With that the matter was settled for him."

If the Vienna dailies had disparaged Webern as a composer, there was an increasing number of voices being raised in his favour. Two articles, in particular, that appeared in professional journals during 1931 became mainstays in the early literature on his work. One was "Anton Webern" by Erwin Stein, published in the June/July issue of *Anbruch*. An expert musician himself, the author concentrated on the instrumental compositions up to the recent Quartet, Op. 22. Using carefully chosen examples, he emphasized the essentially melodic quality of Webern's music:

The intermediate stages of the development, precisely, are being omitted; only the essential, the point of departure and the result, is being said. Nonetheless, while listening, the inner connection is evident to one who knows Webern's music. True, not to one whose ear can orient itself only within an octave or who needs the crutches of the diatonic system in order to hear. But anyone who can at all comprehend intervals exceeding a tenth as tones of a melody will sense what tension-laden energy is inherent in such jumps. They are precisely what gives Webern's melodies their convincing plasticity. One must remind oneself of his progressions, striding downward in a far-flung arc, which sometimes have the effect of a closing cadence. Beyond any motivic connections, these short phrases become melody through the latent tension of their tonal relationships.

The second article was by Theodor Wiesengrund-Adorno, who, like Stein, was a qualified spokesman for the New Vienna School. It was printed in the January/February issue of *Modern Music*, a quarterly review published by the League of Composers, New York. Under the challenging title "Berg and Webern—Schoenberg's Heirs," Adorno traced the heritage of the two composers and outlined their essential differences:

The homogeneity which Berg and Webern share with Schoenberg is determined by a common level of knowledge, prescribing the radical patterning of all elements of composition, the shaping of which gives them common earmarks of style. Berg and Webern both may be said to present commentaries on Schoenberg, and by reason of this are assured of a place in the totality of history. Berg unites him with Mahler on the one hand and on the other with the great music drama and legitimizes him from this point. Webern pursues to its furthest extreme the subjectivism which Schoenberg first released in ironic play in *Pierrot*. He is the only one to propound musical expressionism in its strictest sense, carrying it to such a point that it reverts of its own weight to a new objectivity. Neither excursion is bound to the work of the master; in actual creation the original nature of the interpreter comes to light, just as in the great commentaries of philosophical literature, those of Plato and Aristotle, for example, the personality of each author breaks through the text.

Various newspapers, too, carried an occasional feature article drawing favourable attention to Webern's music. On 4 October 1930, the *Eisenacher Zeitung* (published in the town of Bach's birth) gave prominent place to an essay by Hermann Rudolf Gail, who ventured to give an appraisal of Webern's style: "'Wie wird mir zeitlos' [How timeless I feel] the text goes in one of the songs, *Wiese im Park*. One could write these words about Webern's total creative work. His music lacks every earthly heaviness. It is the most economical mosaic art. Glass-like, of sounding transparency."

Three weeks after the concert devoted to his works, Webern was gratified to receive a letter from the Mayor of Vienna informing him of the award of the city's Music Prize, annually given to distinguished men of his profession. (His application, submitted on 3 February 1931, to the directors of Vienna's Municipal Collections, had been accompanied by manuscripts of his Opera 19, 20, 21 and the string orchestra version of his Opus 5.) It was the second time that Webern was thus honoured and the stipend of 3,000 schillings was a great financial boon (the 1924 prize had been endowed with only 1,000 schillings). The award coincided with the May Day celebration. On that official holiday, Webern conducted a radio concert consisting of Beethoven's *Leonore* Overture No. 3, Mozart's Symphony (K. 81?), and two more Beethoven works, the Piano Concerto No. 5 (Eduard Steuermann, soloist) and the Fifth Symphony.

"On Tuesday, 5th May, 9.05 am, departed for London," reads Webern's diary at the outset of his second journey to England. The engagement to appear again with the BBC had been initiated by Schoenberg, who had conducted his monodrama *Erwartung* in the

English capital in January. Arrangements, concluded by Edward Clark, called this time for two concerts, both featuring Viennese music. In the first, popular classics were to be presented: Schubert's *Rosamunde* Ballet Music No. 2; Hugo Wolf's *Italian Serenade* and two Strauss waltzes, *Roses from the South* and *Tales from the Vienna Woods*. The second programme was to be devoted to the contemporary idiom: Webern's Five Movements, Op. 5, in his transcription for string orchestra, followed by two works by Schoenberg, the "Waldtaube–Lied" from *Gurrelieder* and the *Begleitungsmusik zu einer Lichtspielszene*, Op. 34 (first performance in England).[2]

Arriving in London late in the evening on 6 May, Webern was confronted with an extremely full schedule. The next day he held two rehearsals of three hours each. Two hours after the second one, the concert was broadcast from the BBC's Studio X. The next day was no less demanding. In the morning, Webern coached Enid Cruikshank, the singer of the "Waldtaube," and in the afternoon he held a three-hour rehearsal with the orchestra. The concert took place at nine o'clock that evening. After the broadcast, Schoenberg's *Begleitungsmusik* was repeated for the studio audience. "Since I had only two rehearsals for it (I hardly dare to say this), it naturally could not turn out perfect in sonority," Webern wrote to Schoenberg the next day. "But for my ears the main aspects had become very clear and the easier passages very beautiful also in sound. I have the feeling that I really made music. We played nine minutes (I say this because of the tempi). Did you perhaps listen in?" In regard to his own work, Webern felt somewhat frustrated. In his diary, he noted: "Of my Five Movements, Op. 5, I had to leave out the first. I saw at once that there would be no possibility of working it out with so few rehearsals. The others went quite well. Also the rest of the programme."

Allowing himself some relaxation after the exertions of the preceding two days, Webern spent 9 May in London visiting some sections of the old city that appealed to him. The next morning he travelled to Cologne to spend two enjoyable days with his friends Heinrich and Johanna Jalowetz. On the evening of 13 May he was greeted by his wife, who again came to the station to meet him. The closing remarks of the journey's diary, similar to those following his first trip to England, are revealing: "Made happy by impressions at home. Indescribable feeling of well-being to be again in my native country, which becomes ever dearer to me and appears more and more glorious. Weather like midsummer, blossoms in splendid abundance. Need for quiet and reflection."

So strong was that need for introspection that Webern forfeited the chance to return to England only two months later. His Symphony, Op. 21, was scheduled for performance at the ISCM festival, to be held in Oxford and London the last week of July. But the composer was apprehensive since recent press reaction, beginning with the all-Webern concert in Vienna, had been so totally negative. Following the first performance in Germany (under Johannes Schüler in Oldenburg) of the transcription for string orchestra of the Five Movements, Op. 5, the critic of the *Rheinisch-Westfälische Zeitung* (15 April) had called his music "bloodless, artificially construed foolishness!" On 10 April the Symphony, Op. 21, had been performed in Berlin under Otto Klemperer. The newspaper comments were devastating. "Artistically, Webern still lives in the inflation period of unhappy memories. At that time, perhaps one listened seriously to such a curiosity once, but nowadays it has an unspeakably ridiculous effect. What kind of a Vienna is this that sends us such symptoms of degeneracy under the label of 'music'?" (*Rheinisch-Westfälische Zeitung*). Another verdict was equally derogatory, terming the work "conceptions that cannot be grasped in their new meaning, that are being musically realized in dots and drops, without coherence, totally crumbled melodically-spiritually" (*Berliner Börsencourier*, 14 April).

Small wonder that Webern shied away from such notoriety. To Schoenberg, who was then at Territet near Montreux, he wrote: "I have a horror of the music festival and fear of having to go through a scandal again. It is quite clear to me that there will be one with my Symphony. Even here in the Steuermann–Kolisch concert (attended by what virtually was a former Verein audience) there was some objection. And above all I would like to use the summer for work. Therefore I am thinking seriously of declining the London project. What holds me back is the chance to earn."

In the end, financial considerations were the decisive factor. Although Edward Clark had secured for Webern an invitation from the BBC to conduct a popular concert on 20 July, so that he might preside over the performance of the Symphony the following week, the honorarium offered (£26) was far below that received in May (£75). Since it was Schoenberg who had prompted Clark to make the arrangements, Webern took pains to explain to him on 15 July: "Even with a much better honorarium it would not have been possible for me. These two weeks, including the journey and the stay in London, which is so expensive (plus the trip to Oxford, etc.), would have swallowed up too much. The income would have been too minimal in relation to the loss of time. And I had to think of that because, after all, I finally wanted to get to my work (in which indeed I am presently engaged)." Clearly, Webern preferred to stay at home for reasons other than purely economic ones.

The Symphony, Op. 21, was performed under Hermann Scherchen on 27 July in the Queen's Hall. It came second on a programme that opened with Symphonic Music by Roman Palester and continued with the Rhapsody of Virgilio Mortari, the Second Symphony of Vladimir Dukelsky, Music for Orchestra by Constant Lambert, and *An American in Paris* by George Gershwin. The reporter of the Berlin *Vossische Zeitung* (1 August) voiced the glib opinion that Webern's work "perseveres in the atonal twelve-tone system that at one time was celebrated and today has been laid *ad acta* with hardly a tear." Haddon Squire of the *Christian Science Monitor* (29 August) was more sympathetic, calling the Symphony "a sphinxlike work" and observing that "for all his technical skill, Webern is pre-eminently a poet of sound." As for Webern himself, he wrote to Schoenberg on 8 September: "I have had quite gratifying news about the performance of my Symphony in London." On 2 September he had informed Berg that, in addition to his Symphony, his Passacaglia had been conducted in London by Sir Henry Wood. Clark and Steuermann (who was giving concerts there) had written to him very nicely about it. "This was the third orchestra performance I have had in London within a few months," he commented.

That summer, Webern expected to participate as an instructor in the musical vacation courses held under American sponsorship at Mondsee. The project did not materialize, but the outline Webern made for his classes was to form the basis for his private lecture series that began in January of the following year. Having foregone trips to London and Territet (where Schoenberg had invited him for a visit), Webern used the time for creative work. First he carried out a commission from Universal Edition to orchestrate Schubert's German Dances, then he pursued the project of the *Orchesterstück (Ouvertüre)*, which he had begun that January and which ultimately resulted in the Concerto, Op. 24 (see Chapter XXV).

On 2 July the Singverein held a recording session in the Kasino Zögernitz in Döbling. The four choruses performed were listed in Webern's diary: 1. Brahms *Ich fahr' dahin [Abschiedslied]* 2. Schoenberg *Schein uns, du liebe Sonne* 3. Eisler *Auf den Strassen zu singen* and 4. *Der arme Kunrad.*[3] Only the recording of the first two numbers was released. Produced by Ultraphon, it became part of the series *Österreichische Volksmusik* and bore the label of the Kalliope Gramophone Company. The record was to be the only commercially available one ever made of a performance conducted by Webern. The sensitively-graded shading and freely projected phrasing demonstrate the high degree of discipline that the amateur chorus had attained under his leadership.[4]

26 May is recorded in the diary as the day when Alban Berg took Webern, his wife, and their two youngest children on an automobile excursion. They went to Heiligenkreuz and from there to Baden, places famous for their associations with Beethoven and other great figures. The preceding summer, Berg had purchased a small Ford, which was his pride and joy, and which provided him with relaxation during the sustained creative effort connected with his second opera, *Lulu*. While Berg shared with Webern the same novel and controversial musical idiom, the popular medium of opera inevitably brought him much earlier to wide public attention. Since its première in 1925, *Wozzeck* had made its way into many opera houses throughout Europe, and on 19 March 1931 the Philadelphia Grand Opera Company under Leopold Stokowski first performed the work in America. On 24 November the same ensemble introduced it in New York. *Wozzeck* by then was bringing Berg more substantial royalties than Webern could ever expect from his compositions, which, by their inherent nature, reached far more limited audiences.

During the spring and summer of 1931, Webern's diary abounds in the usual notes on family events and outings. When Maria graduated on 11 June from the Bundeslehranstalt, where she had completed her training as a kindergarten teacher, Webern recorded that he bought a bicycle for her (no doubt encouraged by the money received in connection with the Vienna Music Prize). On 2 July an entry, written in red pencil and prominently bordered—probably because it was Wilhelmine's birthday—lists the purchase, "in instalments," of another bicycle, this time for Amalie (twenty at the time). According to a note made on Tuesday, 11 August, Webern afforded himself a luxury: "Bought a typewriter: Remington Tabular-Portable." On 8 September he inaugurated it with a letter to Schoenberg: "As you see I was rather frivolous. I have acquired a typewriter. At a quite favourable price, it seems: with a ten per cent discount, as if it were a cash payment. But I can pay off the amount—513 schillings—in monthly instalments. The first letter I attempt is to be to you!"

On 13 and 14 June, Webern, accompanied by his daughter Maria and Eduard Steuermann, once again traversed the Schneealpe. From 11 to 14 July, he, Wilhelmine, Peter, and Christine spent a short vacation with the Diez family in Vordernberg, and on 16 and 17 August he went with David Josef Bach to the Hochschwab region. With this last entry, Webern ceased to use his diary systematically. Although there were many blank pages left in the little silk-bound book, to which he had confided his varied impressions ever since he was discharged from army service at Christmas 1916, only a half dozen sporadic notes occur between 1932 and 1938. The reasons prompting Webern to abandon his cherished diary habit are not known. Even without this important source, however, there exists ample documentation for the further chronicle of his life and work in the form of numerous diary notes appearing throughout his musical sketchbooks, extensive correspondence, miscellaneous loose-leaf notes, and the accounts of those who knew him.

Among the extant notes are several connected with an excursion Webern made immediately after his return from the Hochschwab tour. From 19 to 28 August he went with Wilhelmine to the Hohe Tauern, one of Austria's most scenic mountain ranges. Their children were given a day-by-day schedule with explicit instructions when and where they could reach their parents by telegram, telephone, or letter. For the eagerly anticipated outing, Webern had drafted a minutely detailed itinerary. From guidebooks, he copied trail directions, elevations, and distances to be covered. The various data were noted in black, red, green, and blue pencil. Such exactitude may appear exaggerated, but it is quite characteristic of Webern's painstaking preparation for everything he undertook. The highpoints of this week in Webern's life can be traced from the diary notes on the back of picture postcards collected as souvenirs during the trip. After canoeing at Zell am See, the couple spent four days hiking through the heart of the magnificent Grossglockner group. Ascending from the Enzingerboden to the Rudolfshütte, an outpost surrounded by glaciers, they continued via Kals to the Glocknerhaus, a shelter at the foot of the grandiose peak. On 24 August the pair stood on the Franz-Josefs-Höhe, a famous vista point, before descending to Heiligenblut, where the foot tour ended. The next day they visited Alban and Helene Berg at their summer home on the Ossiachersee; they then spent the last night with their relatives in Klagenfurt. "Truly magnificent," was the way Webern summarized his holiday experiences when he wrote to Schoenberg on 8 September.

The demands of the new season began immediately. For some time, Webern had rehearsed his Singverein in Bach's Cantata No. 106, "Gottes Zeit ist die allerbeste Zeit" *(Actus Tragicus)*. Because of greatly restricted finances, David Josef Bach was compelled to reduce the number of Workmen's Symphony Concerts that season from eight to only two. Webern was placed in charge of conducting both. The first was scheduled for All Saints Day, 1 November, and included Haydn's Symphony in D major *(The Clock)*, Mozart's Piano Concerto in G major, K. 453, and the first Vienna performances of Milhaud's Viola Concerto and Webern's orchestration of Schubert's German Dances, as well as Bach's *Actus Tragicus*. Webern's anticipation speaks from his letter of 22 September to Schoenberg: "I have never conducted

Haydn before. . . . The *Actus Tragicus* is indescribable. What sonority is contained in this choral writing!"

In October Webern fell ill. On the eighteenth he was supposed to conduct a radio programme including Schoenberg's *Begleitungsmusik*, but had to cancel it. Disappointed, he explained to Schoenberg that day the nature of his troubles: "Supposedly they are vascular disturbances (paralysis). This expresses itself in great fatigue, which last week progressed to rather painful manifestations. The doctor thinks that I should rest completely for some time, but this is, alas, impossible now."

Disregarding his physician's advice, Webern persevered with preparations for the Workmen's Symphony Concert. On Saturday, 31 October, he held the final rehearsal, but the next morning felt so exhausted that he had to stay in bed. Hoping to recover in time, he waited until the afternoon before informing David Josef Bach that he was unable to conduct the performance. The emergency was a twofold one, since the programme was to be broadcast by Ravag. Barely two hours before the concert was to begin, Bach succeeded in rallying two musicians to step into the breach. Erwin Leuchter, a young Kapellmeister, conducted the opening Haydn symphony. Meanwhile, Professor Oswald Kabasta, a member of the Ravag staff, used the precious minutes to hold a brief rehearsal with the soloists and chorus for the *Actus Tragicus*. The courage and achievement of both conductors were admirable, and the newspaper reviews justly spoke of a "Husarenstückchen" (Hussars' bravado exploit). Kabasta, in particular, distinguished himself by the aplomb with which he assumed the leadership in works that he had to conduct at sight: Milhaud's Concerto and the Schubert–Webern German Dances.

Considering the circumstances, the concert went well enough, but a veritable tempest arose in the press. Prior to the event, Rudolf Réti had published in *Der Abend* (21 October) an article entitled "The Programme of the Workmen's Symphony Concerts—a Disappointment," in which he denounced the concert fare as "bourgeois." He argued that, in view of the greatly reduced number of annual concerts, emphasis should be placed on works breathing the spirit of innovation rather than on those reflecting the tastes of a comfortable middle class. Réti was taking issue with David Josef Bach, who had set forth his justification for the choice of programme in the *Arbeiterzeitung*. In particular, Bach had argued that the beauty of the *Actus Tragicus* warranted the work's presentation even though its Biblical text might cause raised eyebrows on the part of some left-wing comrades who were opposed, on principle, to any intrusion of religious elements into a Socialist programme.

Although the controversy basically appeared to be between Réti and

Bach, Webern's sudden cancellation immediately made him the central figure of wild rumours and conjecture. It was pointed out that he had previously declined programming one of Réti's choral compositions, which he deemed too difficult for the Singverein, although that same piece was subsequently performed by another group in the Workmen's concert series. As a matter of fact, Webern had rehearsed the Réti work in January of 1929, but opposition from the singers was so strong that he had to confront Bach with the alternative of either taking the piece off the programme or facing an imminent break-up of the chorus.[5] Réti's attack therefore was construed as actually having been directed against Webern, who, as a result, supposedly had suffered what *Der Morgen* (2 November) headlined as "Nervous Collapse of Anton Webern before Yesterday's Workmen's Concert." The article alleged that "certain quarters" had inspired a demonstration during the Bach performance (actually a few members of the audience had noisily left the hall). Dr Réti, feeling personally accused, issued a denial on the same day in *Der Abend*, rejecting the innuendo as an "abject lie" and "cowardly slander." A composer and scholar of note himself, he took pains to stress his artistic solidarity with Webern, reaffirming at the same time that his opposition had been directed solely against David Josef Bach's programme policy.

A host of local newspapers soon joined the fracas. *Der Wiener Tag, Wiener Zeitung, Die Stunde, Arbeiterzeitung, Die Presse, Reichspost, Wiener Neueste Nachrichten*, and *Wiener Allgemeine Zeitung*, among others, all brought out their own versions of the controversy. A reporter from the last-named paper called at Webern's home and afterwards related: "The wife of Anton von Webern declares, upon our inquiry, that the ill feeling between Webern and the particular music critic could not be denied. There exists, however, no connection between this conflict and yesterday's cancellation by Webern, who really is seriously ill."

Above the confusion and polemics rose the voices of recognition and support. Paul A. Pisk (*Arbeiterzeitung*) and Paul Stefan (*Die Stunde*) spoke up for Webern, as did A. Rosenzweig, who wrote in *Der Wiener Tag*: "The Singverein offered the most astonishing achievement of the Workmen's Symphony Concert with Bach's deeply moving ode of sorrow, the *Actus Tragicus*. Over the performance reigned the artistic spirit of the ailing Anton Webern, who, in his fanatic striving for complete flawlessness, had impressed the seal of his perfection upon every measure and every phrase."

While the press was busily divulging the various aspects of the affair to the public, Webern lay confined at home. In a long letter, dated 13 November, he described his illness to Schoenberg:

The main cause of the illness that torments me so and in the end rendered me incapable of work seems to lie, after all, in the stomach, or rather in the duodenum. . . . They are not ulcers. A good number of doctors have examined me. Whatever their interpretation of the trouble, they all were of the opinion: take a rest immediately and undergo a cure. The latter will consist in my being put on a diet, in sunlamp treatment, and also in baths and massages, which are supposed to restore my strength in general. As early as summer I felt miserable. However, I did not want to give in, but finally I could not bear up any more.

Webern went on to tell Schoenberg about the controversy, saying of Réti's article, which originally sparked it: "The matter is really too stupid! I did not even read it." Concerning the crucial issue, the polemics against the performance of a sacred work on a platform supposedly serving revolutionary tendencies, he exclaimed:

O God! The *Actus Tragicus* too bourgeois! . . . Whatever was being gossiped to the effect that in my chorus, too, voices had been raised against the religious character of the Bach Cantata is completely trumped up. No, dearest friend, the people raised their voices only in order to sing this work with the greatest enthusiasm. And I believe that we learned it brilliantly. The last fugue flew by like a tempest, but every one of the sixteenth notes could be heard—it was really quite a virtuoso performance. However, in the end, I myself was not permitted to conduct. In the concert they did it by themselves, literally, for the conductor who stepped in for me (Kabasta)—or whoever it might have been—in reality could do nothing more than accompany the proceedings with simulated gestures.

Webern's letter was addressed to Barcelona, where Schoenberg had taken up residence a few weeks earlier. In May he had first gone from Berlin to Territet, Switzerland, and there he had resumed his work on *Moses und Aron*.[6] Because of a persistent cough, he then decided to stay through the winter in a warmer climate, and in early October he moved to Spain, establishing himself in Barcelona. "We occupy a small villa, situated on the highest point of a hill with a fabulous view over the city," he informed Webern on 11 October. In the meantime, he had sent him the libretto of *Moses und Aron*. Ailing and overworked at the time, Webern responded on 18 October: "You can well imagine how I have thrown myself into your poem and how deeply it has moved me. . . . What I would give if we, too, could be down there, if I, also, could work once again for a longer time without disturbance. This becomes more and more urgent. I must try to arrange things differently for myself."

Any such dreams were dashed by the harsh reality. On 14 November Webern entered the Sulz-Stangen Sanatorium, located near Hinterbühl, a short distance from Mödling. Under intensive treatment his health improved so rapidly that he was able to return home in time to celebrate his 48th birthday on 3 December.

A few days later, he travelled to Berlin as a delegate of the Vienna section of the ISCM to attend the meeting of the international jury in charge of selecting compositions for the society's next festival, to be held in Vienna during June of 1932.[7] The conference gave Webern the chance to intervene on behalf of Schoenberg, who had refused to collaborate with the ISCM ever since an incident at the Venice festival of 1925, for which he held Edward Dent responsible. Still feeling slighted, Schoenberg insisted on receiving a personal apology from Dent, who was now the society's president. On his return to Mödling, Webern could assure Schoenberg, when he wrote to him on 20 December, that satisfaction would be forthcoming:

> First of all I laid before the jury, i.e. before the president, the still unsettled case of Venice (before I entered into any other negotiations whatever) and I had him on his knees at once. He will write a letter to you and in it also ask for your consent that a work by you can be performed at the forthcoming music festival. . . . I hope that the letter will turn out to your satisfaction—the matter still arouses me, but I can assure you that I have achieved satisfaction: the man was annihilated and looked like someone hanging from the gallows.

In the same letter, Webern announced that he had been able to convince the jury to include in the festival programme works by two of Schoenberg's pupils: Roberto Gerhard and Norbert von Hannenheim. He could report that he had fully recovered from his protracted illness and that he was looking forward to an impending change of residence. For years he had been trying to find suitable quarters within the city limits of Vienna, to alleviate the loss of time and energy connected with his almost daily commuting from Mödling. At last, through Josef Hueber, he had learned of an apartment that seemed to answer his requirements. He described it to Schoenberg:

> We have found something very favourable, I believe, something that will not be more expensive than our home here. Neither will we have to sacrifice much of its rural setting because the house has a huge garden that we can use. It is not a rental barrack either, but a house of only two floors, in Hietzing to be exact (13th District),

Penzingerstrasse 82. . . . To be sure, the decision was not an easy one for us. God grant that we have come to the right conclusion. . . . The location of our new apartment (second floor) is completely quiet inside and outside, during summer certainly even more quiet than here. The street side faces south. Thus we will again be able to have much sun: therefore we are hoping for the best.

CHAPTER XXII

Hietzing—Maria Enzersdorf—
Lectures—Concerts—Illness
(1932)

T HE FAMILY MOVED to the new apartment on 5 January 1932. The day before, when Webern travelled by train to the city for the last time, he noted the event on the back of a picture postcard of a "Marterl" (a rustic roadside shrine). His high hopes connected with the change of residence were soon to be bitterly disappointed, however. The convenience of the location was offset by disadvantages that quickly became apparent: because of the lay-out of the rooms, Webern's studio was right above the street. Contrary to expectation, the noise was so disturbing for the sensitive man that it hindered him from work. Also, the large garden, attractive as it had appeared at first, did not provide the anticipated substitute for country living. By 20 January, a fortnight after the move, Webern indicated his dissatisfaction to Schoenberg, and on 1 February, he voiced his resolve to correct the situation as soon as possible:

> What I would give if I were still sitting in Mödling and could just work quietly! Because of my continuing indisposition—this is really getting to be a bad thing—everything becomes even more of a burden for me. Also that we have given up Mödling. Oh, if only I could undo this! We all wish it. And indeed set our will to it. Now admittedly I am more comfortable, but in return I have given up a *refuge*, which, after all, I cannot do without any more, nor would I like to do without it. . . . Therefore, we would like to move back, but not in order somehow to set the clock back arbitrarily, but so that we *really can start something new*!!!

The fact that his friend Josef Hueber now lived next door, and Alban Berg close by, did not ease Webern's qualms. Determined to escape the bustle of the inner city, he first attempted to return to his former apartment at Neusiedlerstrasse 58, but the landlord was about to sell the house and would not grant a new lease. By 17 March, however, Webern was able to inform Schoenberg: "We have the prospect of a little house outside town, quite splendidly situated and with a sufficient number of rooms (cheaper in rent than the present apartment). By summer, I hope, we will be out there again!" But Webern's patience was to be taxed. Not until five months later, on 8 August, could he write in his diary: "Rented apartment at Auholz 8." He was referring to the house in Maria Enzersdorf (a small community adjoining Mödling) that was to remain his home until a few months before his death.

Since autumn 1925, Webern's employment at the Israelitic Institute for the Blind, located on the Hohe Warte in the district of Döbling, had posed a major commuting difficulty. Ironically, his connection with the school ceased at the exact time when his move into the city brought him into closer range. According to his income book, he received, in December 1931, 300 schillings as "Ablöse" (severance pay). During the six years that Webern worked at the institute, its growing financial difficulties caused his salary to be gradually reduced until, in the end, the monthly remuneration of 80 schillings hardly made the twice-a-week trip worthwhile.

Webern's employment at the school actually constituted the one and only official teaching post he ever held. The Musicological Institute at Vienna University, his alma mater, did not avail itself of his services even when he offered them, and the Academy of Music simply ignored him. Berg, for that matter, fared no better. The forces of reaction remained too deeply entrenched in the proud capital of the music world. Schoenberg deplored the situation when he wrote to Berg on 8 August 1931: "It is really quite incomprehensible that once again neither you nor Webern have been approached for a professorship at the Academy. But believe me, you need not regret it; they are the ones who will regret it more some day!"[1]

Lacking the support of any institution, Webern thus had to depend on his own initiative when he embarked on a series of lecture courses in January 1932. The original idea for them dated back to 1929 when Webern had been asked by a Mr Krompholz to teach at the Austro-American Conservatory, a summer academy quartered in the castle of Count Almeida at Mondsee near Salzburg. Schoenberg, who had been invited to appear as a lecturer, had requested that Webern prepare the ground with an introductory course. Happy over the prospect, Webern wrote to Schoenberg on 30 August 1929: "I am thinking of 'Form Analysis' (as instruction in composition) and would like to analyse *works by you* also, and at the end I would like to speak about 'Twelve-Tone Composition.' I am supposed to give about *16 class hours*, two a week for eight weeks. But I can also compress them into a shorter period. . . . I was offered *20* or *25* schillings *per participant* for each *class hour*. As a condition that the course be given at all, it was stipulated that six students would have to sign up." Eventually the course was set for the summer session of 1931.

At the outset of that year, Webern began making preparations for his lectures and submitted his ideas to Schoenberg, who responded on 22 January:

> I find your plan for the Mondsee courses excellent in principle. Only I would recommend your arranging the analyses possibly in such a way (by the choice of works) as to show the logical development towards twelve-tone composition. Thus, for example, the Netherlands School, Bach for counterpoint, Mozart for phrase formation, but also for motivic treatment, Beethoven, but also Bach, for development, Brahms and possibly Mahler for varied and highly complex treatment. I believe that this outlines the most important points. The title could then be: "The path to twelve-tone composition."[2]

As late as 17 June Webern wrote to Schoenberg that he expected to go to Mondsee, since by 15 June, the stipulated deadline, he had received no information to the contrary. But four weeks later, on 15 July, he registered disappointment: "In the end, nothing has come of 'Mondsee' after all. Why, I would like to tell you in person sometime." The cryptic remark may be assumed to mean that the required minimum of students did not enrol, since Webern's course had been scheduled as an optional rather than a required one. That summer the faculty of the Austro-American Conservatory included the composers Béla Bartók and Paul A. Pisk, the Roth Quartet, and the pianists Josef and Rosina Lhevinne, among others. (Bartók, at his own request, taught only piano, while Paul A. Pisk was in charge of composition and analysis.)

The diligent preparation devoted to the aborted project was yet to bear fruit. Within a few months some of Webern's friends organized a lecture course, the first in a series that he was to give over the years. It began on 15 January 1932 and continued till 2 March. Following the third lecture, Webern reported to Schoenberg on 1 February: "At present I am holding here a very well attended course (about 30 persons) on the theme that you suggested for Mondsee at the time: the path to twelve-tone composition. This gives me much joy. I always speak without any preparation: after all, I only need to pass on what I have experienced since I have known you."

The weekly class met in the home of Dr Rudolph Kurzmann, a physician and music lover whose wife, Rita, was an accomplished pianist. The lectures were attended by students, musically interested laymen, and a few colleagues. Although the admission fee was nominal, Webern's revenue from the first lecture series amounted to 400 schillings. The second course, from 20 February to 10 April of the following year, was to yield considerably less (100 schillings). Each course consisted of eight lectures (presumably in conformity with the original Mondsee plan). The first series was entitled "The Path to Twelve-Tone Composition." Realizing that more fundamental information was needed for the thorough understanding of the twelve-tone idiom, Webern made the sequel course a basic survey on the general topic "The Path to the New Music." This title was also adopted for the posthumous publication of both lecture courses, in which the sequence of the two series was reversed.[3] The immediacy, conciseness, and eloquence with which the composer set forth his tenets make these lectures a mainstay in Webern literature. In his preface, the editor, Willi Reich, gives this first-hand account:

> They [the lectures] are reprinted here exactly according to the shorthand notes. . . . They give, simultaneously with their valuable content, also a highly life-like idea of Webern's curiously drastic and unforced manner of speaking and at the same time of his pure personality, which united marvellous erudition and most acute artistic thinking with an almost childlike expression of feeling. . . . The extraordinary brevity of some of the texts, particularly in the 1932 cycle, is explained by the fact that on those evenings Webern spoke less and played whole works or individual movements on the piano instead. The repetitions that occasionally occurred were used quite consciously by Webern to intensify and heighten his remarks, as were frequent long pauses and deep intakes of breath. All this was an essential factor in the unprecedented urgency of his delivery and in the deeply moving impression it produced on the listeners. . . . There is not a word here that Webern did not speak himself, in the fiery yet controlled way that made each meeting with him an unforgettable experience. These lectures are handed down to posterity as a reflection of those experiences; as a token of gratitude for all the beauty and profundity he gave us by precept and example; as documentation of his lofty spirit, as a monument to his noble humanity. He who has ears to hear, let him hear!

Webern's move to the city brought on an immediate increase of private students. There had been only two during the last year of his residence in Mödling, but with his studio more accessible their number increased to six in the first half of 1932. In his income book Webern listed the names of his students, along with all other sources of revenue, with abbreviations. However, these are not difficult to decipher, and the names of his pupils, as well as the time of their studies, can thus be readily traced. Not listed are students whom Webern instructed without compensation, since his income book primarily served as a record for tax purposes. (Stefan Wolpe, penniless at the time of his study, was one of those scholarship students.)

Not having appeared as conductor throughout the entire autumn of 1931 because of his illness, Webern found himself that much more in demand during the balance of the concert season. On Sunday, 31 January, he conducted a radio programme consisting of Schoenberg's *Begleitungsmusik* and Brahms' Serenade in D major. After two previous postponements of the Schoenberg work, Webern was elated to be able to report to its composer the next day:

> I believe that it was not bad. The musicians really exerted the greatest effort. In making music with them, I truly had the best rapport— almost as never before. Yes, naturally, I still envision your piece in another way—but, alas, one cannot secure the necessary rehearsals. By now, I could conduct it from memory. It is a wonderful piece, exciting beyond all measure. A marvellous sound. The structure of the ideas is magnificent. And the ending! The epilogue. Unprecedented, dearest friend! Totally overwhelming!

Webern's satisfaction was mixed with concern, however. After his return from the ISCM jury meeting in Berlin, he had placed the work on the programme of the society's June festival in Vienna and so informed the composer. At that point Schoenberg had balked. He had not received the requested apology from Edward Dent, and therefore continued to scoff at the inclusion of his works in any concert under ISCM auspices. Writing to Webern on 7 January 1932, he set forth— "mercilessly" as he said himself—his case in a six-point résumé, which concluded: "You will perhaps recall my declaring at the time that only if D. were thrown out of the committee could I consider having anything to do with this society. This has not happened and therefore the society does not exist for me. Please do not be cross with me: I cannot regard the matter otherwise!"[4]

Fully assured of his rôle in contemporary music, Schoenberg preferred the stigma of appearing difficult and petulant to sacrificing any of his principles. Once offended, he held his grudge and was quite unwilling to yield until the guilty party had been humbled. The correspondence with Webern, in which he expounded his views, is both tedious and voluminous. The matter was also to involve David Josef Bach, who, as president of the Vienna section, was in charge of programme arrangements, as well as Alban Berg, who was drawn into the exchange. The problem was compounded by Schoenberg's haughty attitude towards his native Vienna, which he felt had failed to recognize his worth. Webern virtually prostrated himself to make him change his mind, but it was not until their meeting in Barcelona during early April that a compromise was found: Schoenberg agreed that two of his works could be scheduled in a special Workmen's Symphony Concert to be given concurrently with the ISCM festival in June. Before this solution, however, Webern suffered much vexation: "I again beg you to say a few reassuring words to me," he wrote on 1 February. "*For I can really not exist* in the thought that you could not feel friendly towards me and that you were of the opinion that I, of all people, had made a mistake in this matter. This cursed society! If only I had not joined the jury. To this extent, I indeed deserve punishment!"

During these disturbing complications, Webern was engaged in preparations for a concert he had been asked to conduct for the Pan-American Association of Composers. That society had recently extended its activities to the European continent with an all-American concert in Paris.[5] Early in 1931, when Adolph Weiss corresponded with Webern about coming to America, he had presented the plan for a similar concert in Vienna. On 15 February Webern had written to him: "With pleasure I declare myself ready to conduct and, certainly, on the basis of a programme proposed by you. I am also prepared to repeat this programme possibly in Berlin." He recommended Steuermann as soloist if a piano concerto were considered, but ruled out the possibility of the Singverein participating. His budget for such a concert amounted to a grand total of "$800 maximum." The cost itemization included, besides advertising and the concert agency's commission, the hired orchestra (about $500 for two rehearsals and the concert), the hall (about $100), and his own honorarium ($100). He suggested the Vienna Symphony Orchestra, consisting of about 72 members, and the Vienna Konzerthaus Society for all arrangements, including the use of its hall. Displaying his astuteness in setting up the mechanics of a public concert, he even advised that the event be broadcast to help defray expenses, with a fee of $120 to be expected from Ravag.

By September 1931 the plan had reached the point that the medium-sized hall of the Konzerthaus was reserved for 15 November, but Webern's illness made it necessary to reschedule the event for Sunday, 21 February 1932. In the meantime, the original idea for an all-orchestral concert was altered. After examining the scores, Webern felt that it was impossible to do justice to so many difficult works with only two rehearsals. Over the objection of Henry Cowell, who had come to Vienna to make final arrangements, the concert was changed to include only those compositions that could be done with an orchestra of chamber size, i.e. without the full symphonic complement. The balance of the programme (reproduced opposite) was given over to small ensemble numbers.

Besides conducting the orchestral works by Ruggles, Weiss, and Cowell, Webern also directed the woodwind ensemble in Riegger's Three Canons. The Pan-American Association of Composers underwrote the expenses for the concert and signed as sponsor, with the Vienna section of the ISCM sharing in the nominal aegis. The US ambassador to Austria, Mr Gilchrist B. Stockton, lent his official patronage. At Henry Cowell's request, Gordon Claycombe, Webern's pupil from America, acted as co-ordinator, inviting the music critics and creating interest within the US Legation and the local American Women's Club. In his diary, Claycombe noted on 16 February: "First rehearsal . . . lasted the entire morning. Webern rehearses so thoroughly, every measure phrase for phrase." The comment on the second rehearsal was: "After three hours' work, Webern called it a day. A strenuous three hours!"

The concert was especially significant because a representative cross-section of American music was presented to the Vienna public for the first time. An introductory lecture by Dr Paul Stefan therefore had been deemed appropriate. A capacity audience attended the event, which met with resounding success. Claycombe recalls that Webern displayed no particular enthusiasm for any of the compositions, but that he fulfilled his responsibility with absolute competence. Webern himself was gratified with the results and described the concert in a long account to Weiss. The latter, incidentally—backed by the recommendations of Schoenberg, Berg, and Webern—had just received a Guggenheim Fellowship in music. He continued to promote Webern in the United States, and to this Webern alluded when he wrote on 7 May: "It is very good of you to make an effort on my behalf with the Philharmonic Society of New York."

That spring, the centenary of Goethe's death (22 March 1832) was commemorated throughout the German-speaking lands. On Sunday, 13 March, Vienna's Arbeiterschaft (council of labour unions) staged its own Goethe celebration by devoting one of the Workmen's Symphony Concerts to compositions based on texts by the great poet. The event was held in the large hall of the Konzerthaus. The Singverein's contributions to the programme included *Beherzigung* and *Gesang der Parzen* by Brahms, *Meeresstille und glückliche Fahrt* by Beethoven, and *Erste Walpurgisnacht* by Mendelssohn. In addition, Webern conducted Ernst Krenek's orchestral suite from the incidental music to *Triumph der Empfindsamkeit*. Included in the programme were solo songs and

PROGRAMM

1. Einleitender Vortrag von Dr. Paul Stefan

2. CARL RUGGLES: Portals

3. CHARLES IVES
   AARON COPLAND   } Gesänge
   A. GARCIA CATURLA

4. HENRY COWELL: Sinfonietta (2. Satz)

5. WALLINGFORD RIEGGER: 3 Canons für Holzbläser

6. CARLOS CHAVEZ: Sonatine für Violine und Klavier

7. ADOLPH WEISS: Kammersymphonie (2. Satz)

Sämtliche Werke sind für Wien Erstaufführungen

AUSFÜHRENDE:

Frau RUZENA HERLINGER (Gesang), KURT FUCHSGELB
(Violine), Dr. PAUL A. PISK (Klavier), Dr. ERICH SIMON (Klavier),
Dr. HANS LEWITUS (Klarinette), KAMILLO VANAUSEK (Flöte),
HANS HANAK (Oboe), OTTO SCHIEDER (Fagott) und ein
Kammerorchester
Dirigent: Dr. ANTON WEBERN

Programme of an American music concert (21 February 1932)

duets by Beethoven, Schubert, and Wolf. The success of the concert was confirmed by the press. The *Wiener Zeitung* (16 March) reported: "The Singverein surprised us especially in the *Gesang der Parzen* by its faultless intonation, precision, and musical temperament. Webern accomplishes these excellent performances chiefly by dint of his inner passion." On the following Sunday, 20 March, Webern participated in another tribute to Goethe (in the Deutsches Volkstheater), when he conducted the Vienna Symphony Orchestra in Richard Wagner's *Faust* Overture. When telling Schoenberg three days earlier of these activities, he complained about renewed ill health: "I continue to be in rather poor shape (the trouble is connected with my stomach!) and may finally have to take some thorough counter-measures during the summer."

First, however, Webern had to see the concert season through. On 1 April he left for Barcelona, sharing the long train journey with Eduard Steuermann. Upon Schoenberg's initiative, both had been invited to appear in the Spanish metropolis with the Orquesta Pau Casals, an ensemble founded by the celebrated cellist in 1919. Roberto Gerhard, one of Schoenberg's former pupils, had made all the arrangements.[6] Webern was to conduct two concerts, on 5 and 7 April. The programme for the first included Haydn's Symphony in D major (*The Clock*), Schubert's German Dances in Webern's orchestration, Webern's Six Pieces, Op. 6, and Passacaglia, Op. 1, and Beethoven's Seventh Symphony. The second consisted of Schubert's Symphony in B minor (*Unfinished*), Schoenberg's *Begleitungsmusik*, Beethoven's Piano Concerto in E flat major (*Emperor*), and Mahler's Fourth Symphony. Three rehearsals were allotted to each concert.

Webern and Steuermann arrived in Barcelona on 3 April, early enough to attend a concert conducted by Schoenberg that evening. On a picture postcard, dated 9 April, Webern conveyed some of his impressions of the following days to his sister Rosa and her husband: "I wish that you, too, could see this once! It is splendid here. Palms, olive trees, many evergreens and beautiful flowers. Yet it is really not especially warm. The concerts succeeded very well. A magnificent orchestra. . . . I stay here in a gorgeous hotel. Just think, the concerts start only at ten o'clock in the evening. The second that I conducted was over only at 1 am. Rehearsals, too, took place around midnight." On the same day, Webern informed Alban Berg: "Schoenberg's concert was magnificent; *Pelleas*, especially, I have never heard this way. The orchestra is really outstanding. The best I have ever conducted! And so my concerts, too, have turned out very beautifully, I believe. I am truly satisfied to the highest degree. Now a few days of recreation with Schoenberg. He lives in an indescribably beautiful setting."

Leaving Barcelona on 13 April, Webern first went to Paris, where the

Kolisch Quartet gave a concert on 15 April, including Schoenberg's *Verklärte Nacht*. Webern's presence in the audience occasioned an impromptu performance of three movements from his Opus 5. The following day he left for Vienna. Arriving home, he could look back on a completely satisfying trip, a highlight of which had been the long visit with Schoenberg, whom he had not seen since October 1930. In his income book he listed his net revenue from the Barcelona concerts: 2,140 schillings.

As on previous celebrations of May Day, the international workers' holiday, Webern was asked to conduct a radio concert. The 1932 programme consisted of Beethoven's Overture to the Ballet *Die Geschöpfe des Prometheus*, Mozart's Violin Concerto in D major, K. 211 (Oskar Adler, soloist), and Beethoven's Second Symphony.

A few days later, on 9 May, Emil Hertzka died. Universal Edition lost in him the founder and director who, by his progressive policies, had led the firm to international recognition. To the composers under his aegis, the publisher had been a true friend, and his death was widely mourned. Many musicians, including Webern, spontaneously joined in establishing the Emil Hertzka Memorial Foundation, a fitting homage in that it served the encouragement of aspiring young composers.

The same month, preparations for the approaching ISCM festival swung into high gear. Overburdened with rehearsals, Webern sought a brief respite. "I am now going to the mountains," he wrote to the Humpliks on 4 June. "I must walk to my heart's content for awhile. I will ascend to 'my' hut on the Schneealpe at night. Early tomorrow I will be on the summit." In his letters to these friends, Webern shared his every concern, from the artistic to the personal. Earlier that year, on 8 March, he had confided to them: "Here in Vienna the situation is becoming more and more terrible—what is inflicted on me almost daily is hardly bearable any longer. I received word again from Berlin. Perhaps my deliverance from these *dreadful Viennese* conditions will come from that quarter." What Webern alluded to was the possibility of a position that once again would bring him to Schoenberg's side. In his native city he had attained as much recognition as he could expect, but he knew full well that there the mainstream of musical life would always pass him by. True, his worth was appreciated within a limited sphere: that year the Vienna ISCM section elected him to succeed David Josef Bach as president, and on the festival's roster of conductors, which included men like Ernest Ansermet, he occupied a position of prominence.

In the opening concert of the Tenth International ISCM Festival, on 16 June, Webern introduced Roberto Gerhard's Six Catalonian Songs for soprano and orchestra, a work he had been instrumental in placing on the programme.[7] On the evening of 20 June, he conducted ("with extraordinary interpretative strength," as a critic commented) *Durch die Nacht*, a song cycle by Ernst Krenek based on Karl Kraus poems. The high point of the festival was the Workmen's Symphony Concert in the large hall of the Musikverein on Tuesday, 21 June. The programme, billed as "Wiener Konzert," had been arranged very much after Webern's own heart: Schoenberg's *Friede auf Erden* and *Begleitungsmusik*, Berg's *Der Wein*, and Mahler's Second Symphony.[8]

The concert scored an overwhelming success, which the newspapers unreservedly acknowledged. The *Neue Freie Presse* (26 June) spoke of the "fervour" and "ecstasy" with which Webern led Mahler's Second, remarking: "The zeal of the conductor drove all participants to the heights of extraordinary accomplishments." The *Wiener Freie Presse* (23 June) pointed out the sociological significance of the historic event in which members of the working classes shared in an ISCM festival, traditionally the preserve of more discriminating tastes. The *Wiener Zeitung* (23 June) similarly acclaimed the cultural aspirations of the group, praising Webern as a "fanatically dedicated" artist who was "willing to sacrifice."

Schoenberg's *Begleitungsmusik*, which Webern had introduced on 31 January over the radio, was being heard for the first time in a Vienna concert hall. So enthusiastic was the reception that the applause lasted long into the intermission, as Webern duly reported to the composer on 4 July. Berg's *Der Wein* was equally successful. This concert aria for soprano and large orchestra, based on three Baudelaire poems in Stefan George's translation, had been commissioned in 1929 by Ruzena Herlinger. Having premièred the work in 1930, she also gave the triumphant first Vienna performance, which was crowned by an ovation for the composer.

Mme Herlinger further took one of the solo parts in Mahler's Second Symphony (*Resurrection*), which brought the evening to its climactic finale. For this memorable concert, the Singverein again joined forces with the chorus of the Freie Typographia. Webern had rehearsed eight times with the latter group alone before getting the massed choir of about 300 singers together. Their appearance on stage—in Schoenberg's *Friede auf Erden* and Mahler's Second Symphony—was impressive. The *Wiener Freie Presse* reported:

> The conductor's extraordinary musicality, his talent as a leader, his interpretative strength, which grew in the Mahler symphony to giant dimensions, resulted in an exceptional achievement. He imbued the work with his intensity and led the chorus, soloists, and orchestra out of the depths of combat and struggle up to the pure height of a

common affirmation of unshakeable faith in a spiritual resurrection. The listeners, who filled the hall to the last seat—many had to be turned away because the tickets were sold out—were spellbound, deeply moved and elevated; their gratitude to the conductor and all participants was demonstrated in an outburst of jubilant acclaim.

Gratified as Webern must have been by such acclaim, his finest reward came when Schoenberg wrote to him on 12 August: "I have been told a great deal about the Vienna music festival, i.e. mainly about your accomplishments. Everyone is tremendously enthusiastic and nobody can understand that you have not been given an opportunity as yet to exhibit your abilities in Berlin. I still think very often of the two fabulous concerts you conducted in Barcelona; there is nothing that could be mentioned in one breath with that."[9]

Throughout the concert season, Webern had been plagued again by ill health. The festival preparations had taxed him to the limit of his endurance, and he suffered a fainting spell during the last rehearsal for the Mahler symphony. Ruzena Herlinger at once telephoned Professor Singer, one of Vienna's leading medical experts, who insisted on seeing Webern immediately. The consultation prompted Dr Singer to have the patient admitted to the Rudolfsstiftung hospital right after the concert. A thorough examination, lasting twelve days, revealed no organic ailment and produced the diagnosis that Webern suffered from a nervous condition involving the stomach and intestinal tract. An extensive cure was prescribed. Resignedly, Webern wrote to Schoenberg on 4 July from his hospital bed: "Unfortunately, I will have to use the summer for recuperation instead of for creative work. I cannot go on this way."

Dr Singer first ordered a prolonged stay at the Kuranstalt Friedmann, Vöslau-Gainfarn, close to Vienna, so that he could check frequently on the patient's progress. The treatment consisted of injections, medicines, baths, strict diet, and bed rest. Musing on his fate, Webern asked Schoenberg on 30 July: "What is it finally that causes these conditions, which recently again have tormented me so very much?" Schoenberg had a ready explanation when he replied on 12 August:

I believe (it sounds old-fashioned, but still I must say it, using the old-fashioned expression they had for it) that it stems from the *soul* [*Gemüt*]! I think you get too worked up about everything. Whether it is conducting, holding a rehearsal, having to gain a point, learning of a criticism, or whatever else it may be of countless other things: you always put too much heart into it. (If I did not know this about myself, I should not understand it so well in your case.) I believe: if for half a

year you had no annoyance and no agitations, that is, if there should
be no occasion for such, you would be well. Naturally this is not easy
in our profession. Still, it is not quite impossible.[10]

Staying at Gainfarn from 16 July to 6 August, Webern felt lonely and
missed his family. He worried about Amalie, who was suffering from a
kidney stone, the first severe manifestation of a chronic illness which was
to necessitate several operations over the years. Above all, there was one
great regret: it was summer, the only time for undisturbed composing.
And with the summer lost, it meant that an entire year would be
forfeited for creative work. At least there was no financial concern,
thanks to Dr Singer's generosity in waiving his fees[11] and to a special
contribution ("Kurbeitrag") of 1,000 schillings by the AKM, the Society
for Authors, Composers, and Music Publishers that administered
composers' royalties.

From Gainfarn, Webern was sent to the Kuranstalt Dr J. Arditti in Bad
Fusch, a beautifully located health resort noted for its radioactive
springs. Staying there from 12 to 28 August, he was able to recover fully.
Four days after his arrival he wrote to Schoenberg: "First, I would like
to let you know right away where I am: in the midst of the highest
mountains. In the immediate proximity of the *glaciers* of the Hohe
Tauern. I see them every day and breathe this indescribable air with the
greatest of reverence, as indeed I must say. You certainly know my
inclination in this regard. And this atmosphere works miracles! Now
things go forward with giant steps. I am rising like yeast dough in this
sun, in this air." On the same day, Webern described his treatment to
Berg: "In a tub made of larch-wood one lies down in this indescribable
water. One washes oneself with it in one's room, one drinks it in its ice-
cold state—then it is only 4° Celsius. It springs this way from the source
here. . . . I do not exaggerate, I already feel as I did once upon a time in
my childhood days. A long missed feeling."

Josef Polnauer, vacationing at nearby Uttendorf, came over to be with
Webern for several days. Another caller was Hans Rosbaud, then
conductor-in-residence of Radio Frankfurt, who was quickly establishing his reputation as a champion of contemporary music.[12] The
letters sent to various friends from Bad Fusch all attest to Webern's
growing confidence in the full restoration of his health. So invigorated
did he feel that he soon followed the lure of the alpine heights.
Rapturously he described one of his outings to Polnauer on 25 August:
"I have climbed the Kuh-Kar-Köpfel (to be pronounced quickly one
after the other). It is not quite as high as the Schwarzkopf, but has an
indescribable view. A panorama that at the first impact affected me in an
almost frightening way. My dear friend, the sight of the Hohe Tauern!

The Grossglockner, visible far down to the Pasterze base, towering above everything. It was a *cloudless* day! Just imagine this for yourself! I believe that *now* I am well."

In high spirits Webern left Bad Fusch on 28 August for Vienna. There he threw himself at once into the chore of moving from the Penzingerstrasse to his new home in Maria Enzersdorf. While still at Bad Fusch, on 25 August, he had given Schoenberg a vivid description: "It is a very nice villa. We will occupy the second floor and the attic (together they form the apartment). In addition a very nice (just big enough) garden with fruit trees, etc., *exclusively* at our disposal. The quietest location. . . . It is the slope below Liechtenstein [Castle Liechtenstein]. Our street leads straight to the mountain, so that our house, since it is the last on the street, stands directly at the edge of the forest, which stretches upward from there. In the immediate vicinity only villas with beautiful large gardens. So it will turn out to be pretty there, I think. More favourable than in the old apartment [in Mödling]."

The family moved into their new quarters on 5 September.[13] Webern made a special note of the event in Sketchbook III, where it appears amidst the long-dormant drafts for his Concerto, Op. 24, on which he was to resume work two weeks later. The move proved to be most fortunate. Whatever the following years were destined to bring Webern in growing professional and personal isolation, the house "Im Auholz 8" was to provide him with an ideal refuge. The garden, in particular, became the source of constant joy and inspiration. In the woods next to the house Webern could walk and find the serenity so essential to his mental well-being. "A splendid all-round atmosphere and absolute quiet. I feel in the best of spirits. Now I want to go to work," Webern wrote to Schoenberg on 13 September when extending birthday greetings.

The apartment consisted of five rooms, and the monthly rent (155 schillings) was modest. As in the old dwelling at Mödling, Humplik's portrait bust of Gustav Mahler found a prominent place in the dining room, where it stood on a beautiful Biedermeier style cabinet. Webern continued to champion Mahler's music, performing two of his symphonies that season, the Fifth in a Workmen's Symphony Concert and the Sixth in a Ravag broadcast. "It appears to me as if they were already beginning to trust me a little, after all," Webern ironically remarked to Schoenberg in the same birthday letter. He was referring to earlier broadcasts of a continuing Mahler cycle, which had been conducted by Bruno Walter, Oskar Fried and Oswald Kabasta.

In the Workmen's Symphony Concert, given in the large hall of the Musikverein on 26 November, Mahler's Fifth Symphony was preceded by a performance of Brahms' *Nänie*, in homage to that composer's approaching centenary. *Nänie*, for chorus and orchestra,[14] was then (as now) rarely performed, and it is a tribute to both Webern and Bach that they made it a policy to include such compositions in their programmes. The achievement of the chorus in performing the work was recognized by Paul A. Pisk in his review for the *Arbeiterzeitung*:

> It is a glorious deed of our Kunststelle that this piece—with its contrapuntal difficulties and its sonorities, which in many passages are hard to bring out clearly—was mastered. Anton Webern, who has already educated the chorus to the highest tasks, understood this time also how to lead the singers not only to a rendition of the notes but to the inner, spiritual experience of the music. Thus the members of the Singverein interpreted Schiller's verses with the deepest of sympathy, which aroused, on the part of the listeners, too, emotion and stormy applause.

Prior to that concert, Webern had conducted two broadcasts over Radio Vienna. The first of these, on 16 October, consisted of Reger's Piano Concerto in F minor (Paul Emerich, soloist) and Beethoven's First Symphony. The second, on 1 November, included Handel's Concerto in A major for organ and orchestra, Reger's Requiem for baritone, chorus and orchestra, and Beethoven's *Eroica* Symphony. Collaborating in this ambitious programme were the organist Franz Schütz, the baritone E. von John, the Singverein, and the Vienna Symphony Orchestra.

At the end of the year Webern went to Germany to conduct a concert for Radio Frankfurt, an engagement which Hans Rosbaud had arranged for him. The broadcast, on 29 December, included Schubert's *Unfinished* Symphony, Webern's orchestration of Schubert's German Dances, and Mozart's Symphony in E flat major (K. 16?). "In Frankfurt I had a very fine time," Webern reported to Schoenberg on 11 January 1933. "There was relatively ample rehearsal time. And thus I could achieve, I believe, quite good performances. My Schubert Dances, by the way, were recorded." About his host, who played several recordings of his own performances of Schoenberg works for him, Webern wrote: "The way Rosbaud makes music appeals to me very much. I have come to like him a great deal. He was extremely hospitable. *I was even his house guest*, and he really took a great deal of trouble on my behalf."

In that same letter, Webern informed Schoenberg that his Symphony, Op. 21, was performed in Brussels at the end of December. The close of the year 1932 also brought the composer an important literary tribute. Theodor Wiesengrund-Adorno published an essay entitled "Anton Webern" in the November issue of the *Schweizerische Musikzeitung und*

Sängerblatt. A perceptive student of Webern's music and an astute aesthetic philosopher, Adorno prophesied:

> During conversation, Alban Berg once said that Anton Webern's time would arrive only in 100 years; then one would play his music as one today might read poems by Novalis and Hölderlin. Nothing could more precisely characterize Webern's intrinsic nature than the extremes of lyric poetry, which, by the way it is cast, is so much hidden within itself that it unfolds only over a period of time and not in the first moment of its intonation. . . . One can readily imagine how Hölderlin's late verses withdrew themselves from his contemporaries. In like manner, Webern's music withdraws itself from us; it pricks the hand that gropes for it too hurriedly.[15]

Another testimonial had appeared earlier in the year. The third issue (March 1932) of the polemic music journal *23* contained Rudolf Ploderer's article "Ecce poeta!" in which the indifference of Vienna's official institutions to Webern was assailed with impassioned eloquence. Though the magazine's small circulation hardly allowed his voice to be heard, the author decried the "habitual local attitude" that was permitting "a gross injustice, for years being committed against one of the greatest and noblest artists, to continue." Ploderer emphatically declared:

> For once, it must be stated in all clarity and laid down as a confession of faith for those who neither want to hear nor see that we have in Vienna in the personality òf Anton Webern one of the really great musicians of the present time, a man who as creator of new, immortal works is no less great than as conductor. . . . Here, in quiet modesty, lives a conductor who barely twice or three times a year is being given the chance to put to use his powerful capacity as a leader, but who must absolutely be placed into at least the same rank as any of the "Dirigierkanonen" [fashionable star conductors] who enjoy world renown and for whose occasional appearance in Vienna all influential agencies make the most zealous efforts—a conductor who surpasses, however, these world-famous podium virtuosos through the incomparable musicality of a person who is a composer himself. But it is characteristic of Vienna that it hardly knows one of its best and most valuable sons. . . . Yet Webern's own creative work—in its mystic depth and tenderness, in its incomparable newness and the unrivalled originality of its artful construction—can be placed confidently beside the most uniquely profound musical creations of all time. Only later generations will be able to comprehend this œuvre in its entire depth and significance.

CHAPTER XXIII

Schoenberg's emigration—Webern's 50th birthday (1933)

1933. WEBERN HAD returned from his concert trip to Frankfurt in time to celebrate the dawn of that fateful year in his new home at Maria Enzersdorf. Although nobody could then foresee that within a few weeks the shock-waves of political upheaval would reverberate throughout Europe, eventually to engulf the entire world, there had been ominous forebodings for years. References to the prevailing situation had occurred in several of Webern's letters. As early as 22 September 1931, when asking Schoenberg for his opinion on the economic and political developments, he had voiced his concern: "What is still to come? I would like only to say that, to me, our rôle appears more and more meaningful, more important, more responsible."

Early in 1933, a rapid sequence of events took place in Germany, resulting in the establishment of the National Socialist régime and the dictatorship of Adolf Hitler.[1] A new flag was hoisted over the land. Its emblem, the swastika, lent official sanction to an overt anti-Semitism. Harassment of non-Aryans, which began with Hitler's take-over, became general after the discriminatory Nuremberg Laws were passed. A series of quick moves left no doubt that the revolution would encompass all phases of culture. On 11 March, just six days after Hitler gained a parliamentary majority, several of Germany's artistic leaders were dismissed for failure to meet the requirements of the Aryan clause of the National Socialist statutes. They included Carl Ebert, director of the Berlin Municipal Opera, and Fritz Stiedry, its conductor. The order was issued by Dr Paul Joseph Goebbels, Hitler's minister of Volksaufklärung (Popular Enlightenment)—later president of the Reichskulturkammer (National Chamber of Culture)—who wielded complete control over the theatre, cinema, radio, and press. On 15 March the head of Radio Berlin issued a ruling forbidding broadcasts of Negro jazz music.[2] One day later, the Leipzig authorities cancelled a concert under the Jewish conductor Bruno Walter, claiming that "public order and security" might be endangered. Wilhelm Furtwängler tried to intervene for him, as well as for other colleagues such as Otto Klemperer and Max Reinhardt, but his attempts at mitigation were of no avail.

On 1 April, a group of prominent musicians in the United States dispatched a cablegram to the German Chancellor urging him to desist from racial and religious discrimination. The message read in part: "We beg you to consider that the artist all over the world is estimated for his talent alone and not for his national or religious convictions. . . . We are convinced that such persecutions as take place in Germany at present are not based on your instructions, and that it cannot possibly be your desire to damage the high cultural esteem Germany, until now, has been enjoying in the eyes of the whole civilized world." Hitler's response was an order, issued on 4 April by the commissarial head of the government's radio department, outlawing broadcasts of compositions or recordings by any of the signers of the protest. These included Arturo Toscanini, Walter Damrosch, Frank Damrosch, Serge Koussevitzky, Arthur Bodanzky, Harold Bauer, Ossip Gabrilowitsch, Alfred Hertz, Charles Martin Loeffler, Fritz Reiner, and Rubin Goldmark. Toscanini, engaged to conduct at the Bayreuth Festival that summer, promptly notified the German government of his refusal to appear in view of the discrimination against Jewish musicians in Germany.[3]

The stunning speed with which the Nazi régime came into power, and the ruthlessness with which it seized control, could hardly have been anticipated by the populace. Over the years, the nation had become accustomed to constant tension, and frequent changes in government leadership were taken in stride. Even on that historic January day of 1933, when Hindenburg accepted Chancellor Kurt von Schleicher's resignation and appointed Hitler to form a new cabinet, the news had been eyed, if with anxiety, yet nevertheless with the vague hope that Hitler's followers would be tempered in their radical tendencies once they were charged with the responsibilities of leadership. Such self-delusion became quickly apparent, as virtually everyone found himself confronted with drastic changes.

The "purification" of German music was to be effected, on 15 November 1933, by the establishment of the Reichsmusikkammer (National Chamber of Music), a department subject to the German Ministry of Propaganda. Dr Goebbels himself announced the officers of this new clearing house for musical affairs: President, Richard Strauss;[4] Vice-President, Paul Graener; General Music Director, Wilhelm Furtwängler; Secretary, Heinz Ihlert.

In the course of all these developments, countless Jewish artists and intellectuals were dismissed from their positions. Arnold Schoenberg was one of the first to suffer. Webern had last seen his friend in April of 1932 in Barcelona. Late that year he had received from him as a birthday gift the orchestral and piano–vocal scores of *Von Heute auf Morgen*, both cordially inscribed. Webern's letter of 8 December, expressing his overflowing gratitude, as well as his subsequent letters to Schoenberg, reveal no trace of apprehension at that politically crucial time. As a matter of fact, he was rejoicing at the prospect of a position in Berlin. On 25 January 1933, Schoenberg, who was ill at home, asked Heinz Tiessen, his senate colleague at the Berlin Academy, to cast an electoral ballot on his behalf "in favour of Alban Berg's proposal that Dr Anton von Webern be elected into the place now vacant for a new member of the Academy."[5] Webern had already mentioned the possibility of the prestigious appointment to various close friends. But his hopes were soon to be dashed. The vote was negative, no doubt partly due to the prevailing anti-Semitic sentiments, which made no distinction between Jews and those closely associated with them.

On 12 February 1933, Schoenberg delivered over Radio Frankfurt a lecture on Brahms as his contribution to the composer's 100th birthday celebration. He then went to Vienna where, on 15 February, under the auspices of the Kulturbund, he presented another lecture, on the topic of "New Music, Outmoded Music, Style and Idea."[6] It was to be Schoenberg's last visit to his native city. His early symphonic poem *Pelleas und Melisande* was performed in his honour, and a festive reunion of his friends and former pupils took place in the Hotel Meisel & Schadn on the Neuer Markt. As Reich later recounted. Schoenberg was in the "gayest of moods," and those around him had no presentiment that many of them would never see their revered master again.

"How wonderful were the days of your visit in Vienna. If only our get-together could have been still more extensive. How we would have loved to have you and your wife with us in Maria Enzersdorf," Webern wrote to Schoenberg on 7 March, continuing: "*Pelleas* had an indescribable effect on me. I hardly even noticed that the presentation was not really good. I did not want to be concerned about it, either. During the performance I vividly thought of your first one, at the same place, almost *30 years* ago. Oh, dearest friend, what memories these are. What has unfolded since!"

As Webern wrote these lines he was unaware that a decisive turn in Schoenberg's fortunes had taken place. On 1 March, during a meeting of the Berlin Academy's Senate Council, its president, Max von Schillings, announced that Chancellor Hitler's newly formed government wished to see Jewish influence in the institution broken. Thereupon Schoenberg immediately rose and, declaring that he would never stay where his presence was not desired, left the room.

Under the impact of this news, Webern delivered on 14 March the fourth lecture of his series "The Path to the New Music." In a state of high agitation he voiced his indignation and concern:

What is going on in Germany at the moment amounts to the destruction of spiritual life! Let us look at our own territory! It is interesting that the changes made by the Nazis affect almost exclusively musicians, and one can imagine what is still to come. To what avail will our struggle be? (When I say "our" I mean the group which does not aim at external success.) . . . What is yet to happen? To Schoenberg, for instance? And though at present it is connected with anti-Semitism, in the future it will be impossible to appoint anyone capable even if he is not a Jew! Nowadays "cultural Bolshevism" is the name given to everything that is going on around Schoenberg, Berg and myself (Krenek too). Imagine what will be destroyed, wiped out, by this anti-culture force! But let us leave politics out of it! What, however, do Hitler, Goering, Goebbels imagine art to be? . . . It is so difficult to shake off politics because they are a matter of life and death. But all the more urgent is the task to save what can be saved. How everything is intensifying and changing! A few years ago, certainly, we saw changes happening in artistic production (art has its own laws, it has nothing to do with politics), but it was believed that things would still work out somehow. Today we are not far off a state when you land in prison *simply because you are a serious artist*! Or rather, it has happened already! I do not know what Hitler understands by "new music," but I know that for those people what *we* mean by it is a crime. The moment is not far off when one will be locked up for writing such things. At the very least one is thrown to the wolves, made an economic sacrifice. Will they still come to their senses at the eleventh hour? If not, spiritual life is heading for destruction.[7]

On 20 March, Schoenberg submitted a letter of resignation to the academy. In relinquishing his position, he demanded payment of his contractually assured salary up to 30 September 1935 and that he be compensated for his moving expenses. While official action was pending, he plotted ways and means of leaving Germany. He considered returning to Spain and asked Roberto Gerhard to secure concert and lecture engagements for him there. As a first step, however, he went on 17 May to Paris and lodged there at the Hotel Regina, Place des Pyramides. Two days later, he sent Webern a postcard with a cryptic message stating that Kolisch, in a telegram from Florence, had "urgently recommended a change of climate" and that he planned "a holiday of six months (at least)."

The "change of climate" was to be permanent and not, as Webern vainly tried to make himself believe, a temporary one. On 30 May, Arnold Schoenberg (along with Franz Schreker) was officially placed on "leave of absence" from the faculty of the Prussian Academy of Arts. In Vienna, the news was received with disbelief and horror. Was not Schoenberg the very exponent of Germanic music, deeply rooted in the ideologies of everything essentially German? Did he not represent and assure the continuing leadership of German music in the Western world? Webern, for one, was fully convinced of this. On 15 July 1931, he had written to Schoenberg: "We not only thank you for the German hegemony in music, but beyond this for *the rescue of the highest values altogether* from the general confusion of this time."

Schoenberg himself had repeatedly and unequivocally asserted his German heritage, tracing it from Bach and Mozart to Beethoven, Brahms, and Wagner. Though imbued with German traits, his art had not failed to exert its influence upon many composers of foreign lands. Maurice Ravel, but one of these, readily acknowledged his obligation to the Austrian master, as is clear from an episode related by Ruzena Herlinger in her memoirs. On the occasion of a concert on 7 February 1932 in the French Embassy in Vienna (at which Mme Herlinger performed Ravel's *Shéhérazade* with the composer at the piano), the singer arranged a luncheon in honour of the distinguished guest. Invited were the board members of the Vienna section of the ISCM, including Webern, Wellesz, D. J. Bach, Pisk, and Rita Kurzmann. During the conversation, Wellesz translated to Ravel a question posed by Webern as to what he thought of Schoenberg. Ravel replied: "Schönberg est important—je suis passé par Schönberg. Sans lui, je ne serais pas le Ravel d'aujourd'hui." (Schoenberg is important—I have gone by way of Schoenberg. Without him, I would not be the Ravel of today.)

Neither such recognition of Schoenberg's stature nor his avowed adherence to the great German musical tradition proved to any avail in Hitler's Germany. On 18 June Schoenberg explained to Webern the necessity of his decision. The long and pathetic letter read in part:

Dearest friend, you apparently have not understood my postcard. I myself never seriously considered it possible that I would have been allowed to stay on. What kind of a situation would that have been? I would not have had any performances, any publications, my name would not be mentioned! Is that any way for a composer to exist? But aside from this, can one swallow such insults? In the meantime, you probably have read that I have been given leave of absence. Unfortunately, however, I do not know anything at all as yet about the financial question, and even though Furtwängler intervenes on my behalf in an extremely decent manner it is still in no way assured that a satisfactory solution will be found. You surely know that heterogeneous forces are working against each other. Who knows who will gain the upper hand in my case. To be sure, I have learned with astonishment in what great esteem I am held in circles close to the government, and I know that my departure is being regretted very much by many. But I could not have stayed on! If I only knew already something definite concerning the financial aspect. From one day to the next good or evil can decide over me!

Schoenberg's future indeed appeared bleak: the publishers were reluctant to contract new works, Clark had not even replied concerning possibilities in England, and Gerhard had lined up only two concerts and lectures in Barcelona. "Aside from this," Schoenberg told Webern, "I have at present no prospects, but I have to wait here in this expensive hotel for a decision since I really cannot risk going to Spain without any assured existence. . . . Unfortunately, I am not well, either."

Webern's reaction was immediate and highly emotional:

How could I ever have thought that such a situation could at any time arise for you! [he wrote on 21 June]. I am so horrified and aroused that I cannot find words for it at all. Is this indeed reality that they let *you, you* go away instead of doing everything in order to prevent it? When this "system" took the helm, I felt somewhat similar to the time when the war ended: now this is probably the second stage—the destruction of the existing world order. I cannot comprehend it any other way. That is to say, it is a horror—I cannot express it differently! With terrible anxiety I have thought only of you. Now, however, I am filled with such disgust that I cannot expect anything else but that this time, too, the curtain of a temple will be rent, and the masters of the past will arise in order to bear witness for you because of such sinfulness! Oh, dear friend, I would not have thought it possible. Be assured of my faithfulness and know that I and my family stand ready to the last!

Responding to Schoenberg's plight, Webern spontaneously suggested that he re-settle in Mödling:

After all, here you could get along on *half* the cost in German money while living at least equally well. As far as I could observe on my trips abroad (England, France, etc.), we live here as in paradise, compared with conditions elsewhere. I know of a place, not far from us, which is more beautiful and favourable than can possibly be imagined: a villa in the Bergstrasse, *almost* as if it had been built by Loos, in complete quiet, situated in a large garden, the most beautiful I have ever seen. You could get a lease there at once. . . . A very sympathetic Jewish married couple with a boy lives in the attic apartment. The landlady, too, is exceptionally nice.

As to the political situation in Austria, Webern voiced confidence. All activities of the National Socialists had been banned as of the preceding day, and the government, backed by the Western powers, was doing everything to suppress the radical right.

The suggestion to move back to Mödling was the last of all possibilities that Schoenberg would consider. There was no doubt in his mind that Hitler would relentlessly pursue the political programme he had outlined in *Mein Kampf* and that sooner or later he would try to annex Austria. Like many Jews, Schoenberg had been a true patriot, never ceasing to uphold his allegiance to German culture. Now, however, seeing himself attacked as a member of the race that Nazi doctrine denounced as the mortal enemy of the German people, he decided to act accordingly. Renouncing the Christian creed to which he had been converted at an early age, he returned to the faith of his fathers. In a ceremony in a Paris synagogue on 24 July 1933, attended by the painter Marc Chagall, who signed as one of his witnesses, he formally re-dedicated himself to Judaism. This act meant for Schoenberg far more than a gesture. His faith in his own creative mission, to which he had felt predestined by virtue of his genius, was shaken to the depths. He therefore earnestly contemplated forswearing the pursuit of art, so that he might henceforth devote himself to the cause of his race. His specific aims were formulated in a long letter to Webern,[8] written on 4 August from Arcachon, an ocean resort near Bordeaux, where he had meantime moved. He remained there until the autumn, keeping Webern abreast of his difficulties. Dismay, dejection, and resignation echo from a letter of 16 September: "There are at present only unpleasant matters, annoy-ances and vexations with which one *is forced* constantly to occupy oneself." Despite his tribulations, Schoenberg had finished his Concerto for String Quartet and Orchestra after Handel's Concerto Grosso, Op. 6, No. 7. "It has caused me an extraordinary amount of trouble, and I have worked on these 400 measures intensively for ten weeks, whereas for my Third String Quartet I needed only five to six weeks," he commented.

On 20 September, the Berlin Academy of Arts converted Schoenberg's leave of absence into an official dismissal and granted him his salary only to the end of October, in violation of the contract, which guaranteed two more years' income. In his economic plight, Schoenberg had already pursued the possibility of moving to the United States. His plans included the establishment of a United Jewish Front, which, by means of its own newspaper, would promote the solidarity of the Jewish people throughout the world. For the moment, an invitation to join the staff of the Malkin Conservatory in Boston, a small music school with limited facilities, served as the tenuous bridge to the New World. In his letter of 16 September, Schoenberg informed Webern that he had accepted, despite the "very moderate conditions" offered.

Arrangements became definite by 1 October. Schoenberg, then in his 60th year, had no illusions about the hazards of so serious a step. In his farewell letter to Alban Berg on 16 October he wrote: "I would like to know, too, if I can do anything for you in America: always supposing that I should have the power, of course. For there is no knowing how disregarded, slighted, and without influence I may be there. I only hope that it will not be as in Holland, where I had the entire public against me from the moment I arrived, because everyone who feared me as a rival instantly mobilized the press and all the big battalions against me."[9] Nine days later, Schoenberg, his wife, and infant daughter embarked on the *Ile de France* for America. As the ship entered New York harbour on 31 October, the great musician, like countless others driven from their homeland, fixed his eyes and hopes on the Statue of Liberty, that symbol of freedom and opportunity in a new life ahead.

*   *   *

The same year, 1933, which produced such upheavals in Schoenberg's life, brought Webern comparative stability, however deceptive and short-lived it was to prove. Thanks to his treatment of the previous year and his basically resilient constitution, he had completely recuperated from his protracted illness. The quiet life at Maria Enzersdorf and the supreme joy in his new home and garden strengthened him physically and emotionally, so that he not only could withstand more readily the rigours of a demanding concert season, but also felt regenerated in his creative faculties.

On 1 February 1933, Webern began the draft of "Herr Jesus mein" (Op. 23, No. 3), the first setting he was to make of a poem by Hildegard Jone. His fresh urge to create was soon restricted, however, by a number of other activities. On 20 February he began his second lecture course in the home of Rudolph and Rita Kurzmann. The eight sessions, on the topic "The Path to the New Music," lasted until 10 April. On Sunday, 19 March, Webern conducted a Workmen's Symphony Concert in the large hall of the Konzerthaus. Billed as "Märzfeier" (commemoration of the March 1848 uprising), the event, with its left-wing political overtones, stood in glaring contrast to the right-radical revolution then sweeping Germany. The programme consisted of the first Vienna performance of Krenek's *Kleine Blasmusik*, Paul A. Pisk's cantata *Campanella* (after poems by the monk Campanella), and Hanns Eisler's *Das Lied vom Kampf* (a montage of song, chorus, and spoken word after poems by Bertolt Brecht). Press coverage was conspicuously absent; not even the partisan *Arbeiterzeitung* carried a review. Undoubtedly it was recognized that the concert bore the earmarks of a political demonstration (Eisler and his poet, Brecht, were known to be militant Communists, and Pisk a convinced Social Democrat). Censorship had just been imposed on all newspapers in an emergency measure to suppress the mounting political strife, and the tightening controls led the press to ignore the event.

Early in March, Amalie had fallen gravely ill and was hospitalized for several weeks with her chronic kidney ailment. In order to spend more time at his daughter's bedside, Webern had asked Ludwig Zenk to assist him with the solo rehearsals for the approaching Workmen's Symphony Concert. By the time Amalie began to recover, Webern had to leave, on 16 April, for his third concert tour to England. His schedule was an arduous one. "In London I have to hold an insane number of rehearsals; on one day as many as *8 hours*, otherwise *6 hours*, only on one day *just* 4," Webern had written Schoenberg the day before his departure. As on the previous tour, he was engaged to conduct two BBC programmes. The first took place on Friday evening, 21 April, and consisted of Berg's Lyric Suite (first and third movements only), Krenek's song cycle *Durch die Nacht* (Hedda Kux, soprano), and Berg's Chamber Concerto (Kolisch and Steuermann, soloists). In the second concert, on Sunday evening, 23 April, he conducted Beethoven's *Prometheus* Overture, his own orchestration of Schubert's German Dances, and Mahler's Fourth Symphony (Elsie Suddaby, soprano). On 3 May Webern reported to Schoenberg:

In London this time it was especially satisfying, though strenuous. In six days I had to hold *33 hours* of orchestra rehearsals and give two concerts. I believe that Berg's works turned out very well, at any rate they were clean throughout. They also met with great success. The first concert was for an invited audience in the hall of the BBC House. *The orchestra is really splendid.* How they played Mahler's Fourth! There was at times a quite fabulous sound, really and truly quite ideal. Marvellous in sonority. My Schubert Dances, too, came out very beautifully. The orchestra seems to have really enjoyed them. I might also report in all modesty that, from all appearances, I have had a very far-reaching effect on the orchestra (acclamations during and at the end of the rehearsals, a spontaneous storm of applause after the

Prometheus Overture, and after the second concert a veritable ovation). In short, dearest friend, I was really very, very happy. And Clark seems to have been happy, too. It is not easy to deal with him from a distance, but on the spot he is always a really splendid fellow, who knows absolutely and exactly what is involved, and who is full of the deepest faith in you and in us, too. Now I hope for a fortuitous continuation of my engagements there and also that eventually there can be more than only one a year. I need this so urgently. Things here really are becoming more and more impossible. Steuermann and Kolisch played splendidly. With the former I travelled via Paris. The return trip I made alone via Cologne and spent a few hours with Jalowetz.

Webern was back home on the evening of 26 April. Writing to the Humpliks on 3 May, he described his visit to the British Museum, which had left him with deep impressions: "... I saw the *Parthenon Frieze*! I stood in front of it for an hour and a half. It is an indescribable miracle. What a conception! Here is the most exact counterpart to our method of composition: always the same thing in a thousand forms. Overwhelming. Also comparable to Bach's *Art of Fugue*."

On 23 May, Webern conducted Mahler's Sixth Symphony in a broadcast concert in the Konzerthaus.[10] It had been a busy season. As newly elected president of the Vienna section of the ISCM, he had assumed many additional duties, which he carried out with characteristic conscientiousness. During the spring, he also had served on the jury for the Emil Hertzka Memorial Prize, awarded for the first time that May. His colleagues on the panel of judges were Gustav Scheu, chairman, Alban Berg, Ernst Krenek, Franz Schmidt, Erwin Stein, and Egon Wellesz. In all, 267 compositions were entered. Because of the high quality of so many of them, the jury decided to divide the prize money of 2,500 schillings into five equal parts. Recipients were the Schoenberg pupils Roberto Gerhard and Norbert von Hannenheim, the Berg disciple Julius Schloss, Pisk's student Leopold Spinner, and Webern's pupil Ludwig Zenk. The latter's entry was his *Klaviersonate*, Op. 1, subsequently published by Universal Edition (bearing the dedication "To Dr Anton Webern with warmest affection and veneration").

Webern considered Zenk his most gifted pupil. At Christmas-time that year, he wrote to Zenk's mother: "His latest works belong, for me, to the most important that the younger generation has produced. Indeed they are my personal favourites of them all. Moreover, he appears to me as the only one who *really* proceeds on our path. Yes, he is on that path. To be sure, it is not an easy one. But we want to do everything to facilitate it for him. ... Time to work, for which purpose we are here, is, above all, the most important thing for Ludwig. Everything else will fall into place. I am completely certain of this."

Performances of Webern's music during early 1933 included the Five Pieces for Orchestra, Op. 10, which Hermann Scherchen conducted in a Museum concert in Munich, and his *a cappella* chorus *Entflieht auf leichten Kähnen*, Op. 2. The latter was sung on 14 March in the Musikverein's small hall by the Neue Wiener Madrigalvereinigung under Hans Pless, in the second evening of a series devoted to Austrian composers. A performance of the Six Pieces for Orchestra, Op. 6, to have been conducted by Wilhelm Ludwig Sieben at the Music Festival of the Allgemeiner Deutscher Musikverein in Dortmund at the end of June, was cancelled, no doubt for political motives. The same pressures also caused the organization itself to be discontinued in 1936.

Settled in his new home, Webern thoroughly enjoyed the coming of spring. "We have never had it so lovely before," he declared in his letter to Schoenberg of 3 May. On the same day he wrote to Josef and Hildegard Humplik: "It is now indescribably beautiful out here. An unprecedented splendour of blossoms. We are completely buried in it! Your 'Spring', dear Frau Jone, hangs now in the middle of the most beautiful springtime. I look at the painting and then outside and back and forth again: it is the same."

With the rebirth of nature came a surge of creative inspiration. By 18 August Webern had completed two songs of the Opus 23 cycle, "Herr Jesus mein" and "Es stürzt aus Höhen Frische," and on 7 September he resumed work on the Concerto, Op. 24 (see Chapter XXV). His private pupils, growing in number that year, continued lessons deep into summer. All of them returned after the vacation (they included Buchman, Claycombe, Elston, Gelb, Cantor, König, Leich, Oehlgiesser, and Spira). On Friday, 21 July, Webern conducted a radio concert consisting of Schubert's *Unfinished* Symphony, Mozart's Violin Concerto in A major, K. 219 (Walther Schneiderhan, soloist), and Beethoven's Eighth Symphony. The broadcast, emanating from the medium-sized hall of the Konzerthaus, was given, as usual, for a live audience, and on such occasions Webern took pleasure in inviting his friends.

Immediately after moving to Maria Enzersdorf, Webern resumed his cherished excursions into the mountains. Apart from his own family, he preferred his musical friends as companions. In early June, he organized an outing to the Schneealpe with Diez, Hueber, Polnauer, and Zenk. Later in the summer he spent a week's holiday, from 6 to 12 August, with Hueber, who had access to a private ski hut located on the Untere Sintersbachalpe by the Jochberg near Kitzbühel. There the view sweeps from the spectacular rock spires of the nearby Wilder Kaiser range to the glaciers of the Hohe Tauern on the southern horizon. In his memoirs, Hueber described an ascent of the Gaisstein (2338 m.), including an episode that occurred on a mountain meadow at the outset of the climb. The story illustrates the extent of Webern's nature worship, which at times virtually amounted to a ritual:

> The meadow had just been mowed. The sun had already almost dried out the grass and flowers. An indescribably delightful fragrance rose from the ground. Webern stopped, gave me a rather peculiar look, then lay down with his face to the ground and dug his hands into the hay and the soft soil. Breathing deeply, he remained like this for some time. I sat down nearby and waited. Then he got up, brushed the grass from his clothes and said with a transfixed stare, "Do you sense 'Him' sometimes also as strongly as I, 'Him, Pan'?" With few words, but in a gay mood, we continued on our way at a brisk pace.

The radiant weather with which the day had begun changed by the time the companions reached the summit. The sky was overcast and the view was obscured. Webern's mood also had changed. He was "sad, oppressed, even irritable." The descent was made in haste and, quite unexpectedly, Webern cut his vacation short and left for home the following day.

The premature return to Vienna seemed to have been dictated by premonition. On 23 August, Adolf Loos died in Kalksburg (a Vienna suburb) where he had been a patient in Dr Schwarzmann's sanatorium for nervous ailments. Webern had been going to see him almost daily and was with him a few hours before the end. The day after the funeral, he wrote to the Humpliks: "Yesterday, Friday, the 25th of August, at 6 pm, we bore Adolf Loos in all privacy to his grave in the Kalksburg cemetery."[11] Karl Kraus felt strongly that attendance at the funeral service should be limited to those who had been sympathetic to Loos, and at his request Webern informed only such musical friends as Jalowetz, Ploderer, Polnauer, and Stein. The death of the great architect and innovator, while scarcely taken note of by the public at large, was deeply mourned by the inner circle. Upon receiving Webern's report at Arcachon, Schoenberg responded on 16 September with a poignant lament:

> For a long time, he really was not to be counted among the living any more, and as sad as the thought of this condition was—that the most productive brain of this epoch had come to a dreadful standstill—it is, on the other hand, consoling that he probably did not consciously perceive any more what was going on and is still bound to happen. So it is to be hoped! Just think, one calls the flat roof the "Palestinian

style of architecture'' and means something insulting by it! Now I also
know why I could not effect his becoming a member of the Berlin
Academy—just as I have always proposed you in vain. And now
everything that was stolen from Loos, and from which several pure
races could derive unbounded joy, amounts to nothing any more! It
no longer makes sense to live for art! What you have written to me
about the funeral I find very painful, too. A typical Vienna funeral,
in all quiet—just as it was with Mozart, Schubert, Mahler. All that is
missing is the mass grave. I am not at all of the opinion, either, that
one should allow Loos to sink into oblivion so silently. What I mean is
that his friends should do something quickly in order to compensate
him for the worldly honours due to him that he should not have to
renounce for all eternity.

On 29 August Webern wrote to Hueber from Bruck an der Mur: "I
have left once more—it was necessary after the difficult days of last
week when Adolf Loos died." He was on the way to join Ernst Diez in
Vordernberg. "We want to climb the mountains there," he announced.
As always in times of oppression, he found strength and comfort in the
solitude of nature.

Shortly after his return, Webern suffered another emotional blow. On
10 September Rudolf Ploderer, a close friend and staunch supporter of
the whole Schoenberg circle, died by his own hand, a victim of the
despair spreading in many quarters because of the tumultuous political
developments.[12] The suicide severely shocked all his friends. Ploderer's
keen intellect, wisdom, and helpfulness had endeared him to all,
particularly Webern and Berg. His death added greatly to the burden of
depression enveloping the diminishing band of Schoenberg's old
guard.

To those who were left Webern drew ever closer. In October he
visited Alban Berg at the Waldhaus, Berg's newly acquired country
home by the Wörthersee, where he had decided to stay throughout the
winter in order to complete his second opera. "It is gloriously beautiful
for him on his property. You no doubt know, too, that he is still there,
and that *Lulu* has progressed far by now. According to his last communication, he is already in the middle of the third act," Webern
wrote later that year (29 December) to Julius Schloss, Berg's assistant.

During the autumn of 1933, Webern conducted two Ravag concerts.
The first, on 28 September, included Beethoven's Concerto for Piano,
Violin and Violoncello, Op. 56 (Steuermann, Kolisch, and Benar
Heifetz, soloists) and Brahms' Fourth Symphony. The second, on 6
November, consisted of Schubert's *Rosamunde* Overture, Webern's
orchestration of that composer's German Dances, and the Serenade in

D major, Op. 11, by Brahms. Webern had hoped that the new season would bring another invitation to conduct in Spain. He had already submitted programme suggestions to Roberto Gerhard (Bruckner's Seventh Symphony, the first or second Beethoven symphony, and his own Five Pieces for Orchestra, Op. 10), but plans did not materialize. On 10 December Webern presided over a Workmen's Symphony Concert, which was billed as a "Festival Concert" in commemoration of the Singverein's tenth anniversary. The programme consisted of the Overture and "Tanzlied" from Beethoven's incidental music to the *Consecration of the House* (the rarely heard "Tanzlied" is scored for soprano solo, chorus, and orchestra), Mozart's Recitative and Rondo (concert aria for soprano, piano, and orchestra, featuring two Swiss artists, singer Alice Frey-Knecht and her husband, pianist Walter Frey), Brahms' *Song of Destiny*, and Schubert's Symphony in C major. The reviewer of the *Wiener Zeitung* (14 December) observed: "Actually, it was not only a celebration for the Kunststelle but also one for the conductor and composer Anton Webern, one of the best, though most self-willed of Austrian musicians. . . . With the *Song of Destiny* by Brahms he showed the astonishing level of accomplishment to which he has brought, over the years, the singing group entrusted to him."

Actually, Webern had intended a performance of Beethoven's Ninth Symphony for that festive occasion. As early as 26 June, he had written to Roberto Gerhard of his plan to conduct the monumental work on 3 December, apparently envisioning a double celebration of the Singverein's tenth anniversary with his own 50th birthday. Rehearsals of Beethoven's Ninth were in progress for some time, as were those of Bach's *St John Passion*, the other masterpiece of choral literature that it had long been Webern's consuming ambition to conduct. Because of Webern's insistence on perfection, the Beethoven work could not be prepared in time and, as it turned out, the concert on 10 December was to be the Singverein's last.

During that evening, in the august large hall of the Musikverein, Hölderlin's portentous words at the close of "Hyperions Schicksalslied" (Hyperion's Song of Destiny) became the swan song for the chorus:

Doch uns ist gegeben,	But to us it is given
Auf keiner Stätte zu ruhn.	On no spot to rest;
Es schwinden, es fallen	Suffering mankind
Die leidenden Menschen	Vanishes and falls away
Blindlings von einer	Blindly from one
Stunde zur andern,	Hour to the next,
Wie Wasser, von Klippe	Like water flung
Zu Klippe geworfen,	From rock to rock,
Jahrlang ins Ungewisse hinab.	Endlessly down to the unknown.

3 December 1933 was Webern's 50th birthday. This milestone was made the occasion for a number of celebrations. On 27 December the composer, for whom recognition and honour were rare occurrences, reported to Schoenberg with obvious satisfaction:

My 50th birthday has brought me much gratification. Upon Bach's initiative there was a festivity on the afternoon of 2 December in the small hall of the Musikverein, with a very beautiful address by Dr Bach, followed by the performance of some of my works. In the evening a gathering took place at a restaurant. Messages arrived, including some from official quarters, among them a letter from the mayor (who came in the evening, too) that really gave me much joy; by the way, the letter has also been published. The afternoon celebration was attended by various officials from the government, the city, the Party, the Ravag, the Gesellschaft der Musikfreunde, etc. Do not be cross with me because I tell you this. I only want to report to you how it was. There were also notices in various newspapers. Jalowetz wrote very beautifully in the *Anbruch*, Wiesengrund-Adorno in a Berlin newspaper, Jemnitz in one in Budapest. On 1 December, the Kolisch ensemble played my Quartet in a public BBC concert (in October they played it in Prague). I could even hear a little of it. On 3 December, in an afternoon concert with the new Wiener Konzertorchester, Jalowetz conducted my Schubert Dances (as well as Bruckner's Fourth, etc.). For that matter I could do the Dances myself at the beginning of November in a Ravag concert. In Prague my Symphony was performed (broadcast), in Winterthur my Saxophone Quartet. Thus there were some performances recently, after all. Schubert's German Dances, incidentally, still are being done quite often. Also, on 5 December, Ravag broadcast some of my songs and the Quartet, as well as songs by Berg and his Piano Sonata. Finally, there was a small festivity in the house of an American, at which my Quartet and the Bagatelles for string quartet were played. These Vienna performances of my quartets were done by the very young, but really very talented Galimir Quartet. Perhaps you have already heard of them: they are a family team. First violin is played by the brother, second violin, viola, and cello by the sisters. They are Jews who migrated here from Poland during the war.

The private birthday party mentioned by Webern was organized by Mark Brunswick, a New York-born composer, then living in Vienna with his wife, a psychiatrist trained by Freud. Their home was noted for its hospitality, and men like Klemperer, the writer Jakob Wassermann, and the cellist and philanthropist Felix Warburg were frequent guests.

Brunswick, who first met Webern through the Hungarian violist and composer, Marcel Dick, often invited him for dinner. Impressed with the sumptuousness of the home, Webern always enjoyed the good food tremendously. On this particular evening, he did not suspect that a special birthday surprise was in store. Upon entering the large salon, he and his wife were suddenly greeted by a group of their close friends (including Bach, Krenek, and Wellesz), who had been hiding in a side room. The climax of the evening came with the performance of Webern's Opus 5 and Opus 9 quartets by the Galimirs.

The official celebration, under the auspices of Vienna's ISCM section, took place in the small hall of the Musikverein on Saturday, 2 December, at five o'clock in the afternoon. It opened with a formal address by David Josef Bach.[13] The musical programme that followed included *Entflieht auf leichten Kähnen*, Op. 2 (Wiener Madrigalvereinigung under Hans Gál), Four Pieces for Violin and Piano, Op. 7 (Dea Gombrich and Rita Kurzmann), Three Little Pieces for Cello and Piano, Op. 11 (Joachim Stutschewsky and Olga Novakovic), selections from the song cycles Opera 3, 4, and 12 (Anne Michalsky and Eduard Steuermann), and Five Movements for String Quartet, Op. 5 (Galimir Quartet). The works chosen were all of earlier vintage, while, curiously enough, those in the dodecaphonic idiom, in which Webern had been composing for the last decade, were not represented at all. After the concert a large group of well-wishers congregated socially in the Melker Stifts-Keller.[14]

Among the many birthday greetings received by Webern was a large inscribed portrait photo of Franz Schreker. On 27 March 1934, six days after Schreker's death, Webern described to Berg the "unusually cordial dedication," which had been for him "an especially happy surprise." A few days after Schreker had sent the photo, he suffered a stroke. Now that he was dead, it was "extremely comforting" for Webern to know that their relationship, "though outwardly not very close, had come to such a beautiful conclusion."

Perhaps the brightest prospect on his 50th birthday was that of a professor's title, which his friends were promoting at the time. Alma Mahler, in her birthday message to him, referred to the advanced stage of these efforts: "Your professorship should be favourably settled around Christmas-time."[15] But the honour, so keenly anticipated, did not materialize, no doubt owing to political considerations in the Ministry.

Among the literary birthday offerings was a special issue of *23*, released somewhat belatedly at the end of February 1934. It was the first time that the periodical had been devoted entirely to a single personality. The 24-page publication, entitled *Anton Webern zum 50.*

Geburtstag, opened with an introduction by Willi Reich, the editor, and a reprint of Webern's homage to Schoenberg, "Der Schönbergschüler," written in 1912. The contributions that followed—by Theodor Wiesengrund-Adorno, Ernst Krenek, Hildegard Jone, Josef Humplik, Ludwig Zenk, and Franz Rederer—all radiate the veneration in which Webern was held by his friends, as well as their conviction that he was a great artist and the prophet of a new music.[16] They point out the isolation in which he had to live and create, and the lack of public acceptance and official recognition. At the close of the tributes stood a partial reprint from an earlier issue of *23* of Rudolf Ploderer's essay "Ecce poeta!," followed by a eulogy for that recently departed friend by Willi Reich, which read in part: "What I have to thank you for most is, besides our beautiful personal relationship, the understanding of the man Anton Webern, whom you have perceived with such clarity and love that others, too, could partake of your passionate perception."

The booklet contained two illustrations: a photograph of Josef Humplik's Webern bust (1928) and a portrait drawing done from life by Franz Rederer, a Swiss painter who spent a few months in Vienna in 1933 and became friends with Webern, Berg, and their circle.[17]

Reich felt that Schoenberg should not be prevailed upon for an original essay at a time when he was burdened by the problems of emigration, and the birthday issue therefore contained only a reprint of his preface to Webern's Six Bagatelles, Op. 9. Conspicuously absent from the list of contributors was the name of Alban Berg, although he actually attended to the final proof-reading.[18] On 10 December 1933, he had told Reich that, being deeply involved in the composition of *Lulu*, he could not afford to lose momentum by devoting eight to ten days to the kind of searching and comprehensive study that he intended to do on Webern some day, and he refused to just dash off some facile words of appreciation: "To write only a few warm and enthusiastic lines is impossible for *me*, from whom one justly expects the most extensive and significant contribution, and it would also amount almost to an offence to Webern." Instead, Berg had a special surprise in store: the dedication to Webern of his just completed "Lied der Lulu," the superb virtuoso aria that forms the dramatic climax to the opera's second act, when Lulu kills Dr Schoen. In his birthday letter, Berg said that these 50 measures were "perhaps the most important of the entire opera" and as such were not only placed in a central position, but also were to be considered as "a self-contained entity." He added: "Naturally, their dedication to you will be noted in the manuscript and in the printed editions as a small outward sign of our inner solidarity."[19]

A more regal gift could not have been devised, and Webern's delight at the dedication was boundless. He admired Berg's genius without

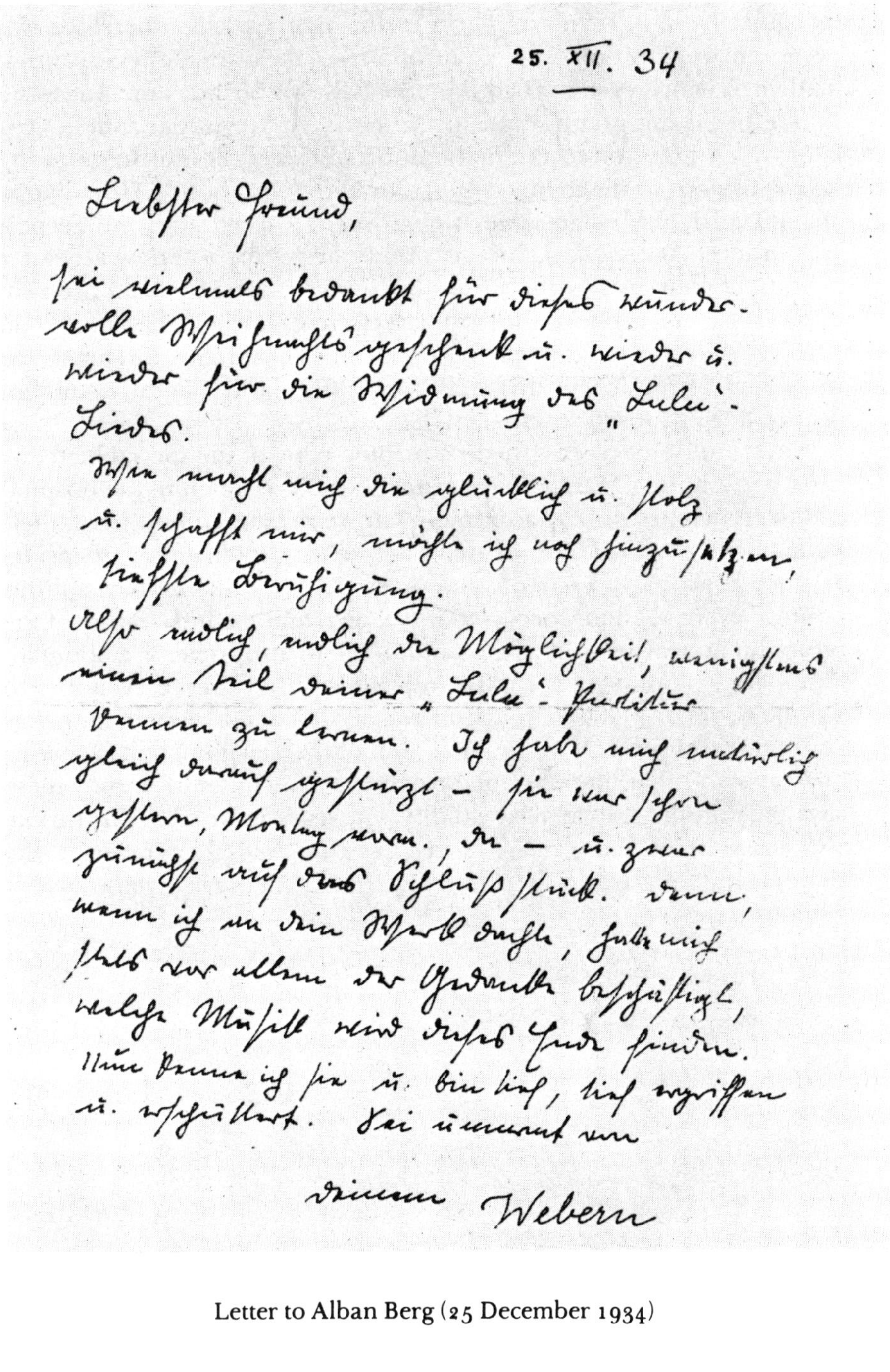

25. XII. 34

Liebster Freund,

sei vielmals bedankt für dieses wundervolle Weihnachtsgeschenk u. wieder u. wieder für die Widmung der „Lulu"-Lieder.

Sie macht mich so glücklich u. stolz u. schafft mir, möchte ich noch hinzusetzen, tiefste Beruhigung.

Also endlich, endlich die Möglichkeit, wenigstens einen Teil deiner „Lulu"-Partitur kennen zu lernen. Ich habe mich natürlich gleich darauf gestürzt – sie war schon gestern, Montag vorm. da – u. zwar zunächst auf das Schlußstück. Denn, wenn ich an dein Werk dachte, hatte mich stets vor allem der Gedanke beschäftigt, welche Musik wird dieses Ende finden. Nun kenne ich sie u. bin tief, tief ergriffen u. erschüttert. Sei innigst umarmt von

deinem Webern

Letter to Alban Berg (25 December 1934)

reservation, although it expressed itself through channels quite different from his own. Berg's esteem for Webern was based on an equal capacity for objective appreciation. Their enduring friendship therefore was never impaired by the complete autonomy of their artistic personalities, neither of which ever rivalled the other. Berg's birthday present was a source of lasting gratification for Webern. At Christmas time a year later, when he received the first edition of the orchestral score of the *Lulu* Suite, he again thanked Berg for the dedication: "How happy and proud it makes me, and it gives me, I should add, the deepest reassurance. At long last, the possibility of getting to know at least a portion of your *Lulu* score. Naturally I threw myself into it at once and, to be exact, I started with the closing section. For, when I had mused on your work, the thought that occupied me always and foremost was what kind of music will this ending produce. Now I know it and am deeply, deeply moved and shaken."[20]

Webern did not receive the first printed copy of the special birthday issue of *23* until 3 March 1934. Amalie, who was again in the hospital with a recurrence of her kidney ailment, remembered how her father, radiant with pride and joy, brought the slender booklet to her bedside. To each contributor he wrote a personal letter of thanks. Momentous political events had just occurred in Vienna, and the uncertainty of the future hung heavily on Webern's mind. He was apprehensive about an imminent extension of the crisis into the cultural sphere. Alluding to this, he wrote on 6 March to Ernst Krenek:[21] "Your 'avowal of faith' has given me extraordinary joy, your avowal of the viewpoint that art has its own laws and that, if one wants to achieve something in it, only these laws and nothing else can have validity. However, as we recognize this we also sense that, the *greater the confusion becomes*, the graver is the responsibility placed upon us to safeguard the heritage given to us for the future."

CHAPTER XXIV

Turn of fortunes
(1934)

W EBERN'S 50TH BIRTHDAY found him at the zenith of his professional
career. After the holiday recess, he had resumed his weekly rehearsals
with the Singverein, concentrating on Bach's *St John Passion*.[1] On 28
January he conducted a broadcast concert consisting of two of
Mendelssohn's works: the Violin Concerto (Christa Richter-Steiner,
soloist) and the Third Symphony (*Scottish*), in commemoration of the
125th anniversary of the composer's birthday. One day earlier,
Webern's Five Movements, Op. 5, were performed in Vienna.
Expressing his gratification to Berg, Webern wrote: "The Kolisches
played my Quartet this time nothing short of perfectly. There was really
nothing left for me to wish. I was also glad that the work for once stood
between classics—in a standard programme. Thus it was, I believe,
effective this time." In the same letter of 31 January, Webern discussed
his plans for a performance of Berg's *Wozzeck* Suite at an ISCM festival in
Florence at Easter time. The new year also held prospects for conducting
engagements in Rome (in conjunction with his Florence appearance), in
Lemberg in March, and in Amsterdam following another tour to
England in April.

Suddenly, however, that bright outlook changed completely. The
political situation in Austria, long taxed by strife and turmoil, came to a
showdown during February of 1934. Engelbert Dollfuss, the Christian
Socialist who had been appointed Chancellor in 1932, had obtained a
badly needed international loan in return for a pledge to maintain
Austria's full independence. He stood firm in this promise but, because
he was uncertain of his slim majority, he discarded parliamentary
government on a technical pretext and assumed quasi-dictatorial
powers. Soon he found himself in the squeeze between the rising
Austrian National Socialist party, backed by Nazi Germany, and the
Social Democrats, with whom he was unwilling or unable to cooperate.
More and more, he relied on an alliance with the Austrian Fascists under

the leadership of Ernst von Starhemberg. Receiving little support in his foreign policy from the Western powers, Dollfuss staked the preservation of Austrian independence on his friendship with Italy. On 12 February there was an uprising of the Social Democrats in Vienna, with bloody fighting in the streets. Seventeen thousand government soldiers and Fascist militia directed artillery fire on installations and apartments of the workers. When the slaughter ended on 15 February, 1,000 men, women, and children had been killed, and another 3,000–4,000 wounded. The Social Democratic Party was promptly declared illegal and all its organizations abolished, including the Kunststelle, which administered both the Workmen's Symphony Concerts and the Singverein. In April the Dollfuss régime was superseded by a one-party system under a "cooperative" constitution drafted by Kurt von Schuschnigg. Making an unsuccessful attempt to seize power, the Nazis brutally assassinated Dollfuss on 25 July.

As an immediate result of the political upheaval, the very basis of Webern's existence crumbled. His monthly salary of 200 schillings from the Singverein and his revenues from the periodic Workmen's Symphony Concerts were eliminated overnight. To his loss of position was added the loss of many close personal associations, such as that with Paul A. Pisk. An active Social Democrat, Pisk resigned that season as secretary of Vienna's ISCM chapter, a post he had held since the society's founding in 1922.[2] Many of similar political convictions and especially those of Jewish descent, realizing what had already happened in neighbouring Germany, prepared for emigration. Webern did his best to pave their way. On 21 May 1934, he approached Roberto Gerhard, urging him to investigate the chances for the Galimir Quartet in Barcelona and to try to secure an assignment for David Josef Bach as a music correspondent for one of the Spanish newspapers.

With the consolidation of the political overthrow in Austria, Webern grew increasingly dejected. Later that year, on 17 September, when he sent Ernst Diez (who had left for another teaching engagement in America) the printed birthday tributes by Bach and Jalowetz, he wrote: "This, dear Ernst, as a farewell from our country, so that you will not go away from us with only this terrible impression of the political events, but will know that *despite all* that is happening in the world, it is *exactly here* where, quietly, a few people have remained conscious of the responsibility which has been given to them: a responsibility that grows greater with every hour."

Webern for the first time now seriously considered leaving his native land. Pinning vague hopes on following Schoenberg, to find for himself a place in the New World as well, he addressed Adolph Weiss on 21 March 1934:

Very upsetting events have occurred here right along, events of a completely unimaginable sort, by which much has been totally changed, so that it was difficult to write. Yes, dear Mr Weiss, horrible things have happened in our country, and we still continue to be completely under the impression of these events. From Schoenberg came, thank God, highly enjoyable news, but the activity over there is probably very strenuous for him. Otherwise I am happy over it and *wish very much for myself also to be able to be in America soon*!!! (Or at least to be able to appear there as a guest.) For here it becomes more and more difficult for me. As a result of the events at which I hinted, I have lost my chorus and with it a fine sphere of activity that I have toiled to build up and enlarge for a *decade*. Naturally, I also lost a substantial part of my income. There is virtually no prospect that the organization will be restored as it last existed. What they have destroyed for me, dear friend! With cannons! We were just studying the *St John Passion*!

When Webern wrote this letter to Weiss, Schoenberg was about to move from Boston to New York. His first winter had not been an easy one, although, to be sure, the New World had welcomed him with a flurry of professional honours and engagements. On 11 November 1933, ten days after he had set foot on American soil, the League of Composers in New York had celebrated his arrival with a concert of his chamber music. Then the Boston Symphony Orchestra invited him to be guest conductor in a pair of concerts featuring his works, scheduled for 12 and 13 January. But Schoenberg, suffering under the rigorous New England climate, was ill for an entire month and did not appear with the Boston Symphony until 16 March (the programme featured his *Pelleas und Melisande*). Before that he fulfilled an engagement with the Chicago Symphony, on 8 and 9 February, conducting his own works: Five Orchestra Pieces, Op. 16, the transcription of Bach's Organ Prelude and Fugue, and *Verklärte Nacht*. Regarding the latter he commented on 31 January to Webern: "Hereabouts this is a sort of Tchaikovsky piece." Several weeks later, on 12 April, he reported: "Much went wrong in the first concert, also with me personally, for I mounted the rostrum expecting to conduct *Verklärte Nacht* and 'tuned in' for it, only to see one second before I had to start that I had to begin with the Orchestra Pieces. This was such a shock that I spoiled the whole first piece and almost caused a breakdown. Only in the fourth piece was I again entirely in command. But in the second concert everything went fabulously well."

Besides these concerts, there were invitations to lecture at various universities, including Princeton. Apart from such high points,

however, Schoenberg's efforts to establish an existence commensurate
with that left behind were excruciating. Some details of his struggle are
poignantly described in his letters to Webern. Because of the
arrangement with the Malkin Conservatory, Schoenberg first settled in
Brookline, Massachusetts. But what he found at that small music school
was disappointing. There were not even enough instrumentalists to
form a student orchestra, and the number of private pupils was so small
that Schoenberg was forced to supplement his income by travelling to
New York City every weekend to teach another group of students. The
fatigue of the long train rides, his continuing indispositions, and the
impossibility of working creatively so disheartened him that he soon
took steps to try to improve his situation.

During Schoenberg's first two months in America, he had sent
Webern only two postcards, but on 1 January 1934, he wrote him a long
letter, his first of the new year:

Beloved, dearest friend, before I give any lengthy explanations, let me
most fervently wish you on your 50th birthday whatever good there is
for men like us: health, joy in work, creative strength, happiness, and
the contentment of one's family and friends. I know, I understand
you: as for me, so there would be for you hardly any other wishes
besides these, were it not that the world is such a "Jammertal" [vale
of misery] and were it not inhabited by beings whose nature is so
entirely different from ours. And so I have to wish you, in addition, all
that is required for the fight against such disgusting ones.

Apologizing for not having been on time with his birthday wishes,
Schoenberg came right to the point:

I want to say it openly—there was a reason. Namely: for at least five to
six weeks I have been upset and (I really must say) not only very
depressed but completely in despair because of you and Berg,
especially, however, because of you! For neither of you have written
me a word for almost two months (you last wrote about 12 October,
Berg about 8 October). And since, after all, we Jews have experienced
it a hundred times in these days that the unbelievable has happened,
that people had suddenly become Nazis who yesterday were still
friends, I could not at all explain to myself your silence (especially
Berg's) other than that you, too, had fallen in line. It seemed
incredible to me, but you both have always spoiled me with letters,
and how else should I have explained it to myself, especially now
when I really need reports from *those who have remained faithful* more
urgently than ever! And when one learns that people such as

Hauptmann [the writer Gerhart Hauptmann] have gone over to the other side! I do not know how you think about this, but I find it shocking that a man like Hauptmann today approves of a party that not only has such a programme but really carries it out. And this programme purposes no more and no less than the *extermination* of all Jews! How one can consent to this is explainable to me only by cowardice and low character. I could not comprehend it, nor could I believe that both of you would also go along with such endeavours. But you will understand that I waited to see whether any communication would come from you, after all, that could remove my doubts. Now finally, a few days ago, a letter arrived from Berg who, in answer to my direct question (jokingly put), clearly says "no." And now I naturally regret a thousand times more that I have neglected your birthday and must console myself with the fact that it was not only for the above-mentioned reason, but also because of my great fatigue, and that as of today it has been a full *four* weeks that I have been ill. . . . Even so, tomorrow I must be off to New York again where I have to teach every week for 3–4 hours, which, however, costs me 24 hours (5½-hour train ride each way, auto, etc.). For a long time, I have racked my brain about what I should present you with on your birthday. My plan—oriented to this date for several years—to dedicate a major work to you cannot at present be carried out, for my larger works are related to Judaism. . . . There would be only a cycle of songs (3 numbers) and this I consider too small for you. Thus I am greatly embarrassed and must ask you to allow me some more time. Perhaps I shall still write a work worthy of our friendship.

That work, the Violin Concerto, Op. 36, was to be composed in 1936. It bears the simple dedication "To Anton von Webern," although Schoenberg first had asked Carl Engel (of the publishing house G. Schirmer, New York) to use the text: "To my dear friend Anton von Webern in cordial gratitude for his unsurpassable loyalty."[3]

Webern's own letter, containing the apology for his long silence and the description of the festivities surrounding his 50th birthday, crossed in the mails with Schoenberg's. He was quick to respond with an impassioned denunciation of the Nazi régime in Germany, writing on 17 January:

How can I possibly explain it to you in a completely convincing manner, dearest friend? I pride myself on having always thought in a *totally* opposite spirit. And the case of Hauptmann, for example, is to me exactly as *horrible* as to you. What do I say? For me, it has to be even more so. The greatest shame for a "nation"! But I really must say, too, that I have no feeling whatever for this concept [of race]; at most, I feel a sense of the most vehement aversion against my "own" since it thus displays itself. I get up and go to bed with the thought of how one could put an end to this reign of terror and what might rescue us!

Thanking Webern on 31 January for his "reassurance," Schoenberg declared: "Europe has lost every meaning for me if I do not have my faithful friends there, you above all!" On 25 March Schoenberg moved to New York City, taking up quarters in the Ansonia, an apartment-hotel frequented by musicians. "How my future here will turn out is still uncertain for the time being," he wrote to Webern on 12 April. "Up to now I do not have an engagement. This is because of the depression, the extent of which one cannot imagine in Europe, and in connection with it people are obviously afraid that I will make too high demands." Schoenberg was nevertheless confident that he could soon secure a good position with a university. Mindful of Webern's desire to come to America, he told him:

> You will believe me that I really rack my brain about how I can do something for you here. I also harbour some vague hopes: a few positions are open, but unfortunately there are so many applicants for them that the chances are very slim. But it is not out of the question. Only I must tell you right away: those fantastic salaries no longer exist here. One can get four to five hundred dollars on the average for a concert. Only once have I received more. . . . I most ardently wish I could procure something for you here. It would be very nice. Although, to be sure, I do not believe that you would like it very much here. . . . That you would have to consider. I know how unhappy you were in Holland and Spain where it certainly is much better than here.

Schoenberg remained in New York until June, teaching a small group of private pupils, some of whom made the weekly trip down from Boston. He had entered into promising negotiations for an institutional position. Two prestigious conservatories vied to have him join their faculties. One was the Chicago Musical College, whose president, Rudolph Ganz, always a staunch supporter of new music, offered Schoenberg an annual salary of $4,000. The other was New York's Juilliard Institute of Music, and Schoenberg considered that possibility long and seriously. When he finally declined, on 11 June 1935, he asked the president, Ernest Hutcheson, in his letter: "Would you not consider

Anton von Webern for the position? He is the most impassioned and intensive teacher imaginable and is at present not very satisfied with conditions in Vienna."[4]

It is admirable how Schoenberg, insecure as his own foothold still was, extended himself on behalf of his European friends. He had hardly arrived in the United States when Alban Berg asked for his help in securing financial assistance that would enable him to devote his undivided energies to the completion of his opera *Lulu*. Responding to the request, Schoenberg succeeded in interesting the Library of Congress in Washington, D.C., in acquiring the holograph score of *Wozzeck*, a three-volume manuscript. He also encouraged an influential patron of the arts in Philadelphia to organize an exhibition of the paintings of Oskar Kokoschka, whom he knew to be depressed and without funds because his works had fallen under the Nazi ban.

In quest of a climate more beneficial to his health, Schoenberg decided to settle in southern California in October. Before moving, he retired for the summer to the resort town of Chatauqua in New York State, where he quietly celebrated his 60th birthday on 13 September. A flood of congratulatory telegrams and letters brightened his day. He was especially gratified by the anniversay book *Arnold Schönberg zum 60. Geburtstag*, which had been completed in time for the occasion. Webern had functioned not only as compiler of the volume, but had also been active in raising funds for its publication by Universal Edition.[5] The Festschrift was first released in a limited number of 50 copies, each of which was personally designated by Webern with the recipient's name. Illustrated with a recent photograph of Schoenberg and manuscript facsimiles of his earliest song and of a page from *Moses und Aron*, the book contained testimonials by various friends and disciples. For Webern, assembling these tributes had been a true labour of love. He was particularly delighted with the message by Hildegard Jøne, to whom he accorded the honour of opening the parade of congratulants. Alban Berg was represented by an anagrammatic poem based on the trinity of Faith, Hope and Love. In addition, Berg planned the dedication of the still unfinished opera *Lulu* as his special birthday offering. As for Webern, he dedicated his Concerto, Op. 24, the draft of which was completed only nine days before Schoenberg's birthday.

For his own contribution to the Festschrift, Webern had collected salient excerpts from a number of Schoenberg essays that were scattered in out-of-print or hard-to-get early publications. In his introduction to the series of quotations, Webern defied the destructive forces then encroaching on man's free spirit and addressed himself directly to Schoenberg, stating: "Let me commemorate your 60th birthday by bringing to light some part of this treasure [of your thought]. For: 'Confusing doctrine linked with confused action reigns over the world' (Goethe, last letter). How much therefore is your word needed!''

Preoccupied with his move to California, Schoenberg did not thank Webern until 13 November, when he wrote: ". . . how glad and proud I am that our mutual feelings are being maintained, constant and unchanged, at the high level of our old and tested friendship, which cannot be shaken by anything. Now when everything goes to pieces and when one may rejoice all the more over the little that remains: it shows us the true values.''

In the ensuing years, Webern's loyalty to those values was to be subjected to severe trials. Following the loss of his activities sponsored by the Kunststelle of the Social Democratic Party, he faced a number of disappointments in 1934. None of his expected conducting engagements in Florence, Rome, Lemberg, and Amsterdam materialized. In Florence he had been scheduled to conduct Berg's *Wozzeck* Suite at the ISCM festival, but politics within the programme committee intervened, and in the end the work was withdrawn altogether. This caused so much resentment on Webern's part that he wanted to resign his presidency of the Vienna section, but David Josef Bach prevailed on him to stay on.

Under such depressing circumstances, the concert trip to London, on which his friend Josef Polnauer accompanied him, was bound to lift Webern's spirits. In his letter to the Humpliks of 21 April he was exuberant with anticipation: "I am conducting a Schubert symphony [the Fourth (*Tragic*)] and the two "Nachtmusiken" from Mahler's Seventh Symphony. I must show you these when you are here again. The second one especially is of indescribable beauty. What resounds there surely is nothing but love, love, love. It will be lovely to do this music with this wonderful orchestra." Webern's engagement at the BBC called for only one appearance this time, but the programme, stipulated by the management, could not have been more to his liking. He was given three rehearsals prior to the concert, which was broadcast on Wednesday, 25 April ("from 9.35 to 10.50 pm," as Webern wrote to Berg, so that he might tune in). An exhibition of Josef Humplik's sculptures in London, which included his bust of Webern, coincided with Webern's stay. In a letter to the sculptor on 15 May, Webern confirmed the affinity of their aesthetic concepts: "If you only knew, dearest Humplik, what a profound impression your heads made on me again. This mutiplicity of forms—what an expression of the most varied kind, in purest natural projection. There is no 'arbitrariness' here; it is, as Goethe extols it in the classics, only the purest representation!!! I must constantly think of it." On the way back to Vienna Webern stopped in Frankfurt to see Hans Rosbaud, a visit described to Berg as "exceedingly satisfying."

Early in May, the Emil Hertzka Memorial Prize was awarded for the second time. Webern, who again served on the jury, was delighted that composers employing the twelve-tone technique carried off the lion's share of the awards. His undaunted confidence in this idiom is reflected in a letter he wrote on 24 May to Otto Jokl, one of Berg's pupils and a prize winner: "The evening of 9 May made me very happy, not only because of the works performed! It appeared to me on that occasion as if a quite explicit affirmation of this music on the part of the audience manifested itself, an affirmation therefore of the only right path, of our path! And with this I conclude that perhaps things are not as bad with our contemporaries, after all, as it might seem. Therefore, my dear fellow: 'Nase zu und mitten durch' [Plug your nose and plough right through]"[6]

Thus Webern endeavoured to maintain confidence and to encourage the young at a time when his own situation was most precarious. Private teaching was then the sole avenue for him to earn money, but the income which he could derive from this source was neither sufficient nor stable. The group of faithful pupils who did not mind the long way to Maria Enzersdorf was small. At best, there were six within any given month that spring, and the fees they paid fluctuated in accordance with their financial ability. In June the number of students dwindled to three, and these stopped taking lessons altogether during summer. Webern's economic plight would have been desperate had it not been for the assistance of his friend Mark Brunswick, who perceived the emergency and, from April 1934 on, aided Webern with a substantial monthly subsidy. The income book shows that these contributions continued through April of the following year. In addition, Brunswick had sent him one of his own theory pupils, Margaret Cantor.[7]

Relief also was provided by a commission from Universal Edition, the result of an appeal Webern made soon after his return from London. On 5 May he had addressed himself to Mrs Emil Hertzka, the publisher's widow:

Because of a serious and drawn-out kidney ailment of my eldest daughter, I was forced almost to exhaust the modest reserves that I try to accumulate, as far as possible, for cases of illness and especially for the summer season, which is almost without earnings. Thus you will understand my worry. Since for about four years I have neither received nor solicited so much as a *Groschen* from UE, it should not appear as too immodest if I approach the publishing house once again with such a plea, after so long a time, and request that the one-time sum of about 500 schillings be placed at my disposal for the summer this year. This would help me considerably, and I therefore beg you cordially, dear Frau Direktor, to intervene accordingly.[8]

Mrs Hertzka was successful, and Webern, profoundly grateful, informed her on 12 July: "Just now I received the contracts: I shall arrange a classical work and receive immediately 500 schillings for it and later on a 5% royalty." The work that Webern selected for transcription was the six-voice Ricercar from J. S. Bach's *Musical Offering* (see Chapter XXV).

Over the years, the royalties paid to Webern by the AKM for performances of his works at home and abroad had become a source of income on which he increasingly relied. These revenues had been mounting steadily, from 846 schillings in 1930 to 2,735 schillings in 1933. During that critical year of 1934, however, the royalties dropped sharply to 1,544 schillings.

Webern's economic setbacks had one important positive aspect: the time formerly consumed by his various duties could be immediately converted into creative work, for which 1934 turned out to be a banner year. Having completed the cycle, Three Songs, Op. 23, on 20 March, he continued, after his return from England, with the Concerto, Op. 24, a project of long standing. It was finished on 4 September, the second and third movements being written with incredible speed. On 4 July, before starting the second movement of the Concerto, he had composed the first of the Three Songs, Op. 25. That cycle was finished by 15 November, and immediately afterwards he began his transcription of Bach's Ricercar, which was completed on 21 January of the following year.

The gathering momentum carried Webern from project to project. Once he had begun composing, he was loath to interrupt. Only the editorial chores for the Schoenberg Festschrift were permitted to intrude. "I must stay with my work continuously," Webern wrote on 11 July 1934 to Josef Hueber, who had suggested an outing to the Schneealpe. Towards the end of the month, however, he succumbed to the lure of the heights. Having just received the 500-schilling payment from Universal Edition and also a 100-schilling donation from a source listed in his income book as "anonymous" (Louis Krasner thought that it came from the American Quakers who conducted a relief action on behalf of the victims of the February revolution), Webern felt encouraged enough to suppress his monetary qualms and permit himself a single mountain excursion that summer.

The outing, made in the company of Zenk and Hueber, led to the Ötztal Alps, a range noted for its heavy glaciation and high summits. Punctilious as ever, Webern prepared a detailed itinerary. Written in black, red, and green pencil, the plan included train schedules, distances to be covered each day, time estimates, huts to be reached, glaciers to be crossed, and peaks to be ascended. Besides this, a list of equipment and foodstuffs was drawn up. For Webern, the expedition was a rather ambitious undertaking, in that it would keep him and his companions in elevations above timberline for several days.

The three friends left Vienna on the evening of 11 August and, after a stopover in Henndorf, reached the Ötztal on the night of 13 August. In his memoirs, Hueber provides a vivid account of the tour. On the morning of 14 August, they hiked from Zwieselstein to Vent, the last village of the high valley, and from there began the long ascent to the Breslau Hut, a shelter at an altitude of 2,848 m. The climb was slowed down by the afternoon heat and the heavy burden of provisions and mountain gear, including rope, crampons, and ice-axes. Zenk, who suffered from a chronic heart ailment, had to rest often and long. Concerned, Webern suggested that they turn back, but Zenk insisted on continuing to the hut. In the evening, the weather broke. It snowed throughout the night and well into the following day, but when the skies cleared in the afternoon, the friends decided that they would attempt the Wildspitze, a glacier peak of 3,774 m., the next morning. They were up before dawn on 16 August, feeling tortured after two nights on improvised beds, which was all the crowded refuge had to offer. It was a cloudless day, and glorious mountains rose all around. Zenk, an excellent amateur photographer to whose skill many pictures of Webern are due, was busy capturing the splendour with his camera. He had adjusted to the rarefied air and was eager to reach the summit. An ice wall, usually offering one of the climb's major obstacles, was ascended without difficulty. From the snow field above, the trio approached the Randkluft, a large crevasse below the slopes leading to the summit ridge. Suddenly Webern complained to Hueber: "I do not know why, but I do not feel quite well. Perhaps it is the height. For a little while I have had some difficulty in breathing. My stomach, too, rebels. And at home I had to promise my wife to turn back at the slightest feeling of uneasiness. What should I do? Poor Zenk, he is looking forward so much to making the summit!"

So brilliant was the day and so tempting the nearness of the goal that Webern, after a short rest, decided to continue. Now roped together, the party crossed the Randkluft and scaled the steep slope above. As they reached the crest, no further obstacles seemed to lie ahead on the ridge to the summit. Zenk was first, Hueber second, and Webern last on the rope. Hueber recalls: "At an elevation of perhaps 3,500 m. Webern tugged lightly on the rope to attract my attention: 'I cannot go any farther now, after all,' he said." Hueber was willing to abandon the climb, but Zenk, in the fever of pressing towards the summit, was greatly irritated and grumbled: "Never before was I on any mountain on so beautiful a day, and never will such a day come again."

Disappointed and downcast, the party returned to the shelter, continuing in the afternoon to the Vernagt Hut. The original plan had called for another glacier traverse to the Brandenburg House and an ascent of one or more of the surrounding peaks, but the experience on the Wildspitze had been so discouraging that the trio descended directly to the valley. Webern was home again on the morning of 19 August, four days earlier than intended.

The stop at Henndorf on the way to the Ötztal had as its special purpose a visit with David Josef Bach, whose 60th birthday was on 13 August. Bach was then a guest in the summer home of the late composer Carl Prohaska. Idyllically located by the shore of the Wallersee, the house was always kept open to fellow musicians by Prohaska's widow, Margaret. As a birthday gift Webern had brought along a fair copy of his Two Songs, Op. 19, which he had dedicated to Bach for the occasion.[9] He also presented to him a volume of congratulatory messages which Bach's friends had compiled as a display of their affection and esteem. In addition they had collected funds to assist Bach in his plight. "His financial situation is very oppressive. . . . Namely, he is at present, literally—since February!—without any income!" Webern had written to Schoenberg on 18 July. "Naturally I, too, have tried to procure aid for him in his efforts to secure his rights. But it all seems fruitless!"

In that letter, Webern alluded to the notorious "blood purge" of 30 June, with which Hitler had ruthlessly suppressed the opposition within his own party. Eager to declare his own position, he wrote to Schoenberg: "I would like to attempt to tell you what moves me increasingly and always more urgently in these days when it becomes ever darker and darker: the sense of accountability! Will the question not be posed: 'And where were *you* in these times?' I have the feeling that it becomes more and more decisive!"

As the summer waned, all hope of reorganizing the Singverein on a new basis had been given up. In early autumn, however, Webern was offered another opportunity: the conductorship of the Freie Typographia chorus. This singing group, consisting of members of the Vienna printers' union, had been in existence since 1890 and occupied a respected position in the musical life of the city. Unlike the Singverein, which was an offspring of the Social Democratic Kunststelle, the chorus maintained political independence. Webern had worked repeatedly with the group when it joined the Singverein for such performances as Mahler's Eighth Symphony and Schoenberg's *Friede auf Erden*. Heinrich Schoof, the Typographia's principal conductor since 1904, was retiring, and Erwin Stein, assistant conductor since 1929, had recently resigned. Numerous members from the defunct Singverein, eager to continue under Webern, joined the group when he assumed its leadership. Although the monthly salary of 100 schillings was only half what Webern had received from the Singverein, even that small income was important at a time when he was cut off from all his local conducting activities. Throughout that 1934–35 season Ravag did not give him any concert engagements, undoubtedly because of the stigma resulting from his decade-long association with the ousted Social Democratic Party. Performances of Webern's compositions in Vienna likewise suffered a sharp decline. Only two are on record for that autumn. The first was on 2 November when the Kolisch Quartet played the Five Movements, Op. 5. A week later, Webern wrote to Hildegard Jone about the work: "It is now just a quarter of a century since I composed it. However, up to the most recent time there has always been controversy in connection with it, so I actually do not have the feeling that it was so long ago. And I myself can only now give a more precise account of what I did then. And yet it seems to me I listened to it the other day no differently than 25 years ago!" The second performance took place during an ISCM concert on 17 December. The Five Songs, Op. 3, were done by Felicie Hüni-Mihacsek, with Eduard Steuermann at the piano. In Germany there was also a broadcast over Radio Munich of Webern's arrangement of Schubert's German Dances. Berg reported to him on 22 October from the Waldhaus that he had listened to it with keen pleasure.

On 14 December, Webern began another lecture course at the home of Dr Rudolph Kurzmann. This time he chose Beethoven as his subject, and the discussion was held on a level suitable for a general audience. Among the participants (on 18 January 1935 Webern wrote to Bach that they numbered "about 40") were several former Singverein members. They included Hans Humpelstetter and Rudolf Schopf, whom Webern invited to attend free of charge because they were university students with limited means. From an extensive notebook kept by Schopf, the proceedings of the course, which lasted until April of 1935, can be traced.[10] The series was entitled "About Musical Forms (Teaching of Form Based on Analyses)." In the opening lecture, Webern set forth these precepts:

All art, all music is based on laws. Goethe says that "laws have their origin in the ingenuity of man." *Music is communication, language.* The endeavour of each art form is to represent a thought. The representation of a thought in tones is tied to universally valid laws, which have been established and have become operative and perceptible. The fulfilment of the law lies in communicating something or in making something generally understandable. This is the case in language also. What I want to say I must clearly project, and it must be comprehensible. *Comprehensibility is the law*: therefore, the thought must be such that it can be grasped. Its beginning and end are already a primitive organization. As something takes on shape, it also becomes more distinct. The chaotic does not correspond with comprehensibility. *Organization* is one of the principal means of creating form. *Organization* is the subdivision into segments in order to keep the components apart from each other, in order to make the distinction between *principal* and *secondary* subjects. And nevertheless there must exist a coherence in order to make a thought intelligible.

During the course Webern guided his listeners through the structural intricacies of individual movements from Beethoven's piano sonatas. Frequently he referred to Schoenberg's teachings, stressing the continuity of tradition linking the present with the past: "After the classic masters, there certainly is no new principle of form to be found," he stated.

The lectures, which Webern illustrated with a wide choice of musical examples, were appreciated so much by his listeners that he continued them in following seasons. He then branched out to other composers and a variety of musical topics. K. H. Lehrigstein, Webern's former junior colleague on the teaching staff of the Israelitic Institute for the Blind, later recounted some details of the 1934–35 Beethoven course:

The whole setting was utterly devoid of the formal atmosphere usually associated with a lecture hall. This was of course partly due to the fact that the sessions were held in the living room of an apartment, but most of all it was because of Webern's own attitude. I had never seen him so relaxed, so really at ease, so jovial and witty. . . . Isolated and misunderstood as a composer, Webern derived much encouragement from speaking to a circle of people who respected his knowledge and ability as a teacher, even though they could only vaguely follow him on his pathways as a composer. Among the fifteen to twenty persons attending, there were several of Webern's private pupils who came out of respect for their teacher rather than to learn something new. For them, it was all very elementary and supposedly nothing new. In fact, when one of them once answered a question put to the audience, Webern cut him short and said: "Of course, the really smart ones know all that." Webern played the examples from Beethoven's piano sonatas himself. Because his analysis was so detailed, he never had to play as much as the exposition of a single movement. When he came to a technically more difficult bit, he was not perturbed. I remember one instance when he was confronted with a rapid passage leading into something he wanted to show. He simply gave a rough outline of that demanding passage and humorously commented "You know, some people can do it," saying it with such mock admiration that he made us all laugh.

In his analysis, Webern started with the most elementary facts. He pointed out that each composition presents first a basic musical idea consisting of a certain grouping of tones in a definite rhythmic pattern. These motives were dealt with exhaustively. At first, I sat there wondering why on earth did Webern spend so much time and energy on a point which, to me, seemed obvious. But Webern knew his audience better than I. From the answers they gave to his questions, I gathered that what they knew about music was rather hazy and really needed formulation and clarification. This is why Webern time and again expounded the concept of basic motives. He showed in many movements what he meant and, to my mind at least, he sometimes went almost to extremes with the splitting-up process. What impressed me so was this emphasis, this repetitive demonstrating, this untiring exertion to try to make clear what happens musically. Again and again he came back to the same thing, namely, that a composer does not just pile up idea upon idea but that he presents, in the first few bars, the motives which are actually the basic elements out of which the whole movement is constructed. . . . By way of this thematic development, I could very well recognize what Webern meant with his statement that modern music was based on the same principles as traditional music.

CHAPTER XXV

Opera 22–25—Schubert and Bach transcriptions (1928–1935)

INCLUDED IN THIS chapter are the work histories of Webern's Opus 22 to Opus 25, as well as those of his orchestrations of Schubert's German Dances and J. S. Bach's Ricercar from the *Musical Offering*. Four unfinished projects that interrupted the composition of the Quartet, Op. 22, are described together with that work.

The lengthy and involved genesis of the Quartet, Op. 22, began in the late summer of 1928. On 20 August, while working on the revision of his Six Pieces for Orchestra, Op. 6, and the transcription for string orchestra of his Five Movements, Op. 5, Webern reported to Schoenberg: "In two weeks I hope to be finished with these jobs and then I will undertake a new composition. I have various projects in mind, but have not decided as yet." Within a month, his plans had crystallized. On 19 September he wrote to Emil Hertzka: "I have turned again to a new work: a concerto for violin, clarinet, horn, piano and string orchestra—in the spirit of some of Bach's Brandenburg concertos."

The new project makes its appearance on page 54 of Sketchbook II under the date of 14 September 1928. Headed "Concerto (three movements)," it lists the same instrumentation that was given in the letter to Hertzka. It is evident from the sketchbook that Webern conceived no more than the initial plan at that time, further work being forestalled by his protracted illness. When he returned to the project on 17 January 1929, he elaborated on the first concept by drafting a schematic outline, interesting for its extra-musical associations:

1st movement: calm (Annabichl, mountains) perhaps variations
2nd movement: slow, introduction to the 3rd (Schwabegg), soloists only

A few days later, on 23 January, the outline was continued:

3rd movement: Rondo

Main themes	Secondary themes	
I		Coolness of early spring (Anninger, first flora, primroses, anemones, pasque-flowers)
	I	Cosy warm sphere of the highest meadows
II		Dachstein, snow and ice, crystal clear air
	II	Soldanella, blossoms of the highest region
III		The children on ice and snow
	I	Repetition of the first secondary theme (sphere of the alpine roses)
	II	Second secondary theme, light, sky
IV	Coda:	Outlook into the highest region

The outline of the third movement was followed by several annotations pertaining to its structural organization. The localities mentioned in Webern's plan are all places of significance to him: Annabichl and Schwabegg are the cemeteries where his parents were buried; the Dachstein, a majestic alpine peak, lured him time and again; and the Anninger, a prominent hill in the Vienna Woods close to Mödling, was a frequent destination for outings. It is important to observe that such programmatic associations appear at the very outset of Webern's musical conception and that these ideas form, as it were, the source of his inspiration. This fact can hardly be over-emphasized in the light of the seemingly abstract character of the music and the composer's mathematical procedure in creating it.

In the working out of his ideas, Webern first experimented with the row and its various possibilities. Because of his involvement with the Opus 5 transcription, a song project, and the concert season's demands, no appreciable progress was made before 10 May, when the first attempts at the actual working out of the row material were undertaken. On 27 May, the ultimate formulation of the series, which had undergone numerous transformations, was acknowledged by the comment: "rows noted down." On 3 June, he wrote to Schoenberg: "At last I can remain again more continuously with my work and am advancing well."

The original instrumentation, including French horn, still appears in the sketches up to the end of June. By the time Webern wrote to Berg on 8 August, however, he had changed his mind. He told him that he was "already quite far along" in his work. It would not become a concerto, as originally planned, but a quartet for violin, clarinet, tenor saxophone, and piano. "More than ever, I rejoice over all that the method of 'twelve tone composition' produces, really quite by itself, so to speak, what inter-relationships result from it, and how formally (in giving shape) everything falls into place so easily, etc.," he wrote.

The evolution of the work up to this point can be graphically traced in *Anton von Webern: Sketches (1926–1945)*. Also reproduced in this publication are the four extraneous projects intervening in the course of the quartet's genesis. The first of these (on pages 55–56 of the sketchbook) was a song with piano accompaniment on a four-line text by Goethe, beginning "Nun weiss man erst, was Rosenknospe sei." Written about 1823, the verses are contained in *Chinesisch-deutsche Jahres- und Tageszeiten*, a cycle of nineteen poems from which Webern had already drawn inspiration for his Two Songs, Op. 19. The sketches, dated 7 March 1929, do not develop beyond a fragmentary draft. A second short-lived project was a string quartet (pages 65, 66, and 68). Webern's concept is stated in the heading, dated 27 June 1929: "Quartet: I. Variations II. Intermezzo III. [blank]." The composer worked intensively on a seven-measure section, drafting it over and over, but after scoring it a last time on 30 June, he abandoned the enterprise.[1]

Shortly afterwards, Webern established the definitive instrumentation for what was to become his Quartet, Op. 22. Feeling sure of his direction, he worked throughout the summer on the Rondo movement (ultimately the work's second movement). Various dates mark the stages of his progress. On 3 August, a note was inserted: "In the evening Mali and Mitzi departed for Mondsee." The quiet domesticity of the vacation period was conducive to concentration, and the multitude of sketchbook pages covered mirrors the composer's steady advance. On 3 September, he wrote to Berg that he was working very diligently in order to finish the Rondo, "presumably the closing movement" of his new work, before the season began. He expected the piece to comprise about 250 measures. "Hence I can, it seems to me, compose quite 'long' again, too!" he commented. "Thanks to the twelve-tone technique, about which I really am becoming ever happier." He was eager to show Berg the movement very soon and summed up his experience during its composition: "I made the discovery that, basically, the instruments become more and more immaterial to me." Another report was given to Berg on 28 September, when Webern announced that only the "closing measures are still lacking."

An especially busy new season, including conducting engagements in Germany and England, again delayed progress on the composition. However, Webern worked on it sporadically throughout the winter.

Drafts for the Rondo movement fill the remainder of Sketchbook II. They continue on a number of inserted loose-leaf pages, one of which, leading up to measure 185, is dated 18 January 1930. In his Table of Contents prefacing the sketchbook, as well as in the draft itself, Webern explicitly calls the movement "3. Satz," obviously still adhering to his original formal outline. Sketchbook III, designated as encompassing "Christmas 1929 to August 1934," opens with the definitive version of measure 184. The end of the movement, at measure 192, is marked 12 April 1930.

Immediately following, the draft of a new movement appears. It is dated 6 May 1930. However, Webern interrupted his work on the Quartet once again and started two other projects, neither of which he was to carry to completion. Adolph Weiss had asked him to submit a composition for publication in *New Music*. After considering various possibilities, Webern informed Weiss on 13 July that, although he had "almost completed a new song for the purpose," he had decided to send "Liebste Jungfrau" (Op. 17, No. 2) instead. Two days later, he confided to his diary: "At first I wanted to send a new song, but met with obstacles in the already begun conception; also thought of choral settings and a piano piece."

Several pages in Sketchbook III reflect Webern's efforts to compose either a song or a chorus. For the song he returned to a Goethe text, beginning with the words "Doch immer höher steigt der edle Drang!" The poem, the "Cirrus" section of *Howards Ehrengedächtnis* (from the collection *Gott und Welt*), had occupied him as early as 1918 when he attempted to set it for voice and orchestra. This time his scoring was for voice and piano. The sketches, begun on 29 June, appear on pages 3, 4, 6, and 10 of the sketchbook. On the last page, dated 9 July, the first three verse lines are almost fully drafted, complete with tempo and dynamic markings, whereas the poem's fourth line and the beginning of the fifth are continued with the vocal part only. Concurrently with this song project, Webern worked on a "Chorspruch" (short choral piece), based on an excerpt from Goethe's *Der West-östliche Divan*. The text, beginning "Der Spiegel sagt mir: ich bin schön!" (recited by the poem's female principal, Suleika), was scored for four women's voices. The draft, begun on 7 July and covering pages 5, 6, and 8, did not develop beyond the first two lines of the poem and was abandoned by 14 July.

On 15 July 1930, Webern resumed work on the Quartet. His two older daughters were away for the summer, and the quiet of the household again enabled him to make fast progress. Within a month, on 14 August, he could record in his diary: "Finished second movement of my Quartet, Op. 22." That Webern framed the entry with prominent borders is indicative of his special sense of accomplishment. Still

pursuing the three-movement plan of the original "Concerto" outline
and having completed the "second" and "third" movements, he now
turned to the "first," beginning the draft on 20 August. The following
day he expressed to Schoenberg his "hope to have the entire work
completed soon." Eager to finish before the end of summer, he
undertook the new movement with great determination. The nine pages
of drafts, reproduced in *Anton von Webern: Sketches (1926–1945)*, reveal
the intensity of his effort and the degree of his progress. By 9 September,
however, Webern confided some doubts to Berg. He was deliberating
whether there should not be just two movements. "Once more," he
wrote, "I almost find the work complete—if I can say so—by reason of
the perfect opposition provided by the great contrast inherent, I believe,
in the two (already finished) movements. But I am nevertheless working
undauntedly on the rest—until my fate will have decided over me
again."

Three days later Webern attempted a new approach, only to note in
the sketchbook (page 38) his conclusion: "Arrived at decision to remain
with two movements——." A corresponding entry is found in the diary
under the date of 17 September. On that day, Webern told Schoenberg
of his difficult decision, adding: "I am already thinking intensively
about other compositions, and thus it appears to me almost like destiny
that my present work, too, is to contain only two movements."

Webern then assigned the definitive sequence to the two finished
movements: the one written that summer (*Sehr mässig*) was placed at
the beginning, and the movement evolving from the original
"Concerto" concept (*Sehr schwungvoll*) at the end. The printed score,
released by Universal Edition in 1932, is inscribed: "To Adolf Loos
on his sixtieth birthday." Originally, Webern had contemplated
dedicating the work to Mrs Elizabeth Sprague Coolidge, the American
patroness of music. Weiss had solicited her on Webern's behalf, but the
hoped-for sponsorship was not forthcoming, to the composer's great
disappointment.[2] Webern did not have to wait long to hear his new opus
performed, however. Its première took place in Vienna on 13 April
1931, during a concert devoted for the first time entirely to his own
music (see Chapter XXI). Performers were Rudolf Kolisch, violin,
Johann Löw, clarinet, Leopold Wlach, saxophone, and Eduard
Steuermann, piano.

Alban Berg repeatedly assured the composer of his special admiration
for this work. On 19 August 1932 he wrote: "This Quartet is a miracle.
What amazes me above all is its originality. One can assert with
confidence that there is nothing in the entire world of music production
that attains even approximately such a degree of originality, i.e. a full
hundred per cent." Schoenberg was equally impressed. On receipt of

the printed score he thanked Webern for the "fabulous piece." In view of the generally abusive criticisms heaped upon the work by journalists at the time of its première, such praise was especially heartening for the composer.

Today theorists recognize the Quartet as a masterpiece of formal construction. What, in the 'thirties, still struck the uninitiated as chaotic and radical has since revealed the secrets of its meticulous organization, comparable to that found in classical models. Webern himself likened the structural plan of the second movement to that of the Scherzo in Beethoven's Piano Sonata, Op. 14, No. 2.[3] Similar analogies between formal patterns in the music of the classical masters and that of Webern exemplify his loyalty to tradition and at the same time furnish a key to the true understanding and appreciation of his style. As to the composer's technique, the second movement of the Quartet furnishes an especially good example of his predilection for microscopic motives of one, two, or three notes.

Webern's Opera 23, 24, and 25 will be discussed here in numerical order, although there was much overlapping in the sequence of their origin. To illustrate: the germinal idea of the Concerto, Op. 24, actually makes its appearance in the sketchbook immediately after the abandoned third movement of the Quartet, Op. 22. The composition of the Three Songs, Op. 23, was intermingled with the extremely slow evolution of the Concerto's first movement, and a portion of the Three Songs, Op. 25, was conceived even before the second and third movements of that work were begun. Also concurrent with the genesis of the Concerto was Webern's orchestration of Schubert's German Dances, which will be described following Opus 25.

For three of the four projects interrupting the composition of the Quartet, Op. 22, Webern used texts by Goethe. Once he began immersing himself in the poetry of Hildegard Jone, however, it so completely evoked his sympathies that all his last vocal works (Opera 23, 25, 26, 29, and 31, as well as the presumptive Opus 32) were based on her texts. Although the poetess had never studied music, she possessed an intuitive perception of its essence. Webern recognized this in his letter to her of 3 November 1932 when he wrote: "It is quite clear to me that you really are able to follow musical thought." The composer found in her poems the realization of Goethe's *Farbenlehre*, the fusion of all the philosophical tenets in which he had always believed. The serenity and spirituality of her verses, their gently pulsating rhythm, glowing colours, and all-pervading nature worship made them singularly suited to his own sensibility.

Early in 1933, Webern began the first of his settings of Hildegard Jone's poems. Under the date of 1 February, there appear, on page 52 of

Sketchbook III, the opening measures of a song with piano accompaniment. The text begins with the words "Herr Jesus mein. . . ," an excerpt from the cycle *Viae inviae*, which had been printed in the periodical *Der Brenner* (Innsbruck). The composition, ultimately to become the last of the Three Songs, Op. 23, marked Webern's return to creative work after many months. The interruption had been caused by two changes of residence, a protracted illness, and a heavy schedule of rehearsals and concerts. Once he was settled in his rural retreat at Maria Enzersdorf, Webern begrudged it all the more when his creative urge was stifled again. "I feel very much under pressure: it depresses me more than ever that I do not have time to compose," he wrote to Hildegard Jone on 3 March. "Quite spontaneously one day I began the composition of your marvellously beautiful poem, but I soon had to interrupt, and it is now reaping its punishment that I have allowed myself to sit at my work *off and on* during January and February." Despite constant demands from the outside, Webern returned to the composition of "Herr Jesus mein" whenever he could. The sketches bear dates of 4 April and 31 May, but progress was visibly slow, amounting to only a few measures. With the coming of summer, however, the composer could muster the necessary concentration, and the song then proceeded quickly until its completion on 14 July.

Eight days later Webern commenced the setting of another excerpt from *Viae inviae*, about which he wrote to Hildegard Jone on 29 July: "I have been working well. Of your texts, which possess me more and more, one is already finished. . . . Now I connect the passage from 'Es stürzt aus Höhen Frische'—how wonderful this word-substance—to 'überglüht noch lange Glut' for a second song. But the sequence of the two songs will correspond to that of your poems. How deeply they touch me. And I am happy to be finally in a position to base a composition on your words. I have wished it for such a long time." The draft of "Es stürzt aus Höhen Frische," interrupted by a week's vacation, was completed on 18 August. Then the last illness and death of Adolf Loos cast a shadow over Webern's spirit, and it was not until early September that he turned again to composition, resuming work on the Concerto, Op. 24. He informed Hildegard Jone on 3 September: "*For the time being*, I have concluded the composition of texts from your 'Viae inviae.' . . . I say 'for the time being' because I have the feeling that I will soon have to come back again to words of yours. But I believe that at least for the present these two songs are to remain *by themselves*. Musically they combine to form a *whole*, in the sense that they constitute a certain antithesis. At the moment, I am back at a purely instrumental work that I began some time ago."

That autumn, circumstances did not permit Webern to carry his work on the concerto beyond a few pages. He had intended to send Hildegard Jone the manuscript of the two completed songs as a Christmas present, but lacked even the time to copy them out. On 6 January 1934, however, he suddenly announced to her: "Now at last I am back at work. 'Das dunkle Herz, das in sich lauschet' is evolving. . . .It seems to me as if I have never before experienced the state of creating as I do now. I hope that it can last for some time." The new setting was to become the opening of the cycle of three songs. According to the sketchbook, Webern started drafting the melody for the first four lines of the text on 3 January, adding the piano part two days later. On 14 February, the third day of the Socialist revolution, the composer gave the poetess a progress report, writing against the dramatic background of the street fighting in Vienna: "The upsets of the last few days are immense and are ever growing. It is hardly possible to formulate a thought. . . . Last week I again used every spare moment to continue work on the verses 'Das dunkle Herz.' I had a little free time once more. *And now again*, Frau Jone, thunder of cannon and rattle of machine-gun fire! I only want to quote your words: 'Dass wir auf Erden nicht allein, hat nur das Licht getan' ['That we are not alone on earth, is due only to the Light']. How could one say it more beautifully?"

On 20 February, after days of turbulence and anxiety, Webern wrote to Josef Humplik: "I am at work again, nonetheless. The more horrible things become, the more our task is weighted with responsibility." Despite the oppressive political developments, which destroyed the Singverein and with it Webern's only regular source of income, he persevered in his creative endeavour. The song (pages 65–70 of Sketchbook III) was finished on 15 March. Five days later, Webern tried to communicate to Hildegard Jone some aspects of the setting:

It has become rather long and in its musical form really constitutes a kind of "aria": consisting of a slow section and, from "Ich bin nicht mein" on, a faster one, which nevertheless bears the tempo designation *"Ganz ruhig"* [quite calm]. This second part is almost whispered. From this description you can perhaps infer approximately how I have interpreted your words, particularly in the second part: after a great upsweep in the first part, there is suddenly quiet, peace, simplicity. I think of using the following title: *Drei Gesänge aus Viae inviae* [Three Songs from *Viae inviae*].

Delighted about his new work, Webern described it on 27 March to Berg. Speaking first of the opening "aria" ("Das dunkle Herz"), he commented that the two songs originating earlier, too, were "really something other than Lieder, as far as form is concerned." Thus "Es

stürzt aus Höhen Frische" was "virtually a recitative with an arioso" and
"Herr Jesus mein," now the closing song, "a rondo." He felt that in this
opus he had come to grips with larger vocal forms "without really
having intended it." Humorously, he added: "In the end, I will yet get
to an opera."

The work, dedicated to Hildegard Jone, was published in the spring
of 1936 by Universal Edition, under the title Webern had mentioned in
his letter.[4] Almost eight years were to pass until the first performance of
the cycle, on 5 December 1943, in Basel. Then the local chapter of the
ISCM sponsored a concert devoted entirely to Webern's compositions
as a 60th birthday tribute. Marguerite Gradmann-Lüscher, soprano,
and Paul Baumgartner, piano, were the artists (for details, see Chapter
XXXI).

The Three Songs, Op. 23, constitute the first vocal work Webern had
completed since the Two Songs, Op. 19, eight years earlier. After the
sometimes problematic evolution of the intervening instrumental
compositions (Opera 20, 21, 22), the new work seems to have been
written with comparative ease. Here Webern asserted his sovereignty
over the mechanics of the twelve-tone method, making the technique
subservient to the free expression of his musical ideas. Moreover, his
identification with Hildegard Jone's poetic thought created an ideal
state from which flowed the fountain of his inspiration, her lilting words
begetting images in sound. Sensing the peculiar charm radiating from
the song cycle, René Leibowitz spoke of a "breath of Schubert" in
describing its "wholly singing character."[5]

Stylistically, the Three Songs reveal the metamorphosis that Webern's
music had undergone since his earlier vocal essays. The former
angularity, resulting from the extreme intervallic leaps typical of the
composer's expressionistic period, has given way to a calmer, more
conservative and therefore more easily singable vocal line. By its
structure, moreover, the tone row tends to evoke connotations of
harmonic relationships in the traditional sense. In the treatment of the
series, Webern assigns to the voice part a rôle independent from that of
the piano. The instrumental texture contrasts with the vocal line by the
use of closely spaced twelve-tone groups of a chordal nature.

Late in 1934, the year when the Three Songs were composed, David
Josef Bach published an article, "New Music by Berg, Webern, Krenek,"
in the American quarterly Modern Music. As Webern's close friend, Bach
had been one of the first to become acquainted with his latest opus.
Including it in his survey, he spoke of the "fortunate artistic union of a
real poet and a real musician." Schoenberg shared this impression.
When he received the printed score, he wrote to the composer from
Hollywood on 27 August 1936: "Naturally, I have a fabulous

impression of the songs. They contain a great wealth of moods and, it seems to me, you also have considerably expanded your expressive range. The wonderfully beautiful and profound words of Hildegard Jone have certainly been a rich source of stimulation."

On 16 January 1931, a full two years before the conception of "Herr Jesus mein" (Op. 23, No. 3), a project entitled *Orchesterstück (Ouvertüre)* made its first appearance on page 38 of Sketchbook III. Here lie the beginnings of a work that, after many interruptions, was not to be completed until three years and eight months later: the Concerto, Op. 24, for nine solo instruments. The earliest ideas for this composition occurred in the middle of a season that was the busiest and perhaps most satisfying in Webern's entire career. He had just been asked whether he might come to America to conduct a new orchestra, and it was in a spirit of hope and confidence that he launched into his new creative enterprise. As in the Quartet, Op. 22, Webern first drew up a literary outline, clear evidence that his musical thinking was associated with extra-musical experiences. The plan, designed for a one-movement overture, read:

Einersdorf, Schwabegg, Annabichl—Introduction: landscape
Schwabegg (Koralpe).   Finale: landscape Annabichl, M.P.

The autobiographical nature of this outline can readily be traced from Webern's diary notes. In the summer of 1928 he had last visited the graves of his parents at Schwabegg and Annabichl. (In a tiny, neatly inscribed envelope he preserved some pressed flowers taken from both sites.) "M" and "P" denote Minna and Peter, his wife and son; Einersdorf and Koralpe were among his favourite localities in the countryside.

Initial experimentation with various shapes of a highly chromatic tone-row soon led to the core of a special musical problem that Webern had set for himself: on the first sketch-page the word "Tenet" appears above a segment of the row, and on the following page, under the date of 4 February 1931, there unfolds a comprehensive attempt to realize a tonal equivalent to the Latin palindrome

SATOR
AREPO
TENET
OPERA
ROTAS

This ancient word square had long intrigued the composer. Its five-word components can be read in four ways: both horizontally and vertically, beginning both at the upper left corner and at the lower right.[6] The ingenuity of the "magic square," particularly its perfect integration of identical elements, challenged Webern because of its analogy to the dodecaphonic system. He valiantly struggled to invent a row in which the tones would interact in a manner corresponding to the textual model. "In the process he discovered a tone-row that must have appeared to him as an apex of constructive density. . . . It is a perfect case of total symmetry, wheels in wheels, tight as a Chinese puzzle," Ernst Krenek commented in his analysis of that all-important page.[7]

The row is divided into four groups of three tones each. In reality, its first three-note segment generates the following three subdivisions by using the same intervallic relations in retrograde and inversion. On 5 February Webern wrote the word "gilt" (valid) above the following row:

One day later he began actual composition with this series, already specifying some of the instruments. Little headway was made, however, and the last date (on page 42) is 22 February 1931. Feeling satisfied to have scored a break-through, Webern wrote to Hildegard Jone on 11 March: "At present I am again being very much prevented from working. But I believe I have laid a good foundation for something new (for orchestra). I have found a 'row' which in itself already contains very far-reaching relationships. It is perhaps something similar to the famous old saying." Webern continued with an outline of the palindrome and its possible manipulations. Beyond offering him a challenge and a model for his own aspirations, it served as an ideal example for the explanation of his theories. "As many connections as possible must be established," he remarked on 2 March 1932, in the last lecture of the series "The Path to Twelve-Tone Composition."[8] "An analogy can be found in language. I was delighted to notice that such connections also occur in Shakespeare, in the many alliterations and assonances. He even turns a phrase backwards. The linguistic art of Karl Kraus is also based on this. There, too, coherence has to be created because it increases comprehensibility." Webern concluded the lecture by citing the Latin word square.

Throughout the winter and spring, Webern was prevented from returning to his new composition. A commission to orchestrate Schubert's German Dances, which he received in May on his return from England, kept him busy until June. Declining the opportunity of returning to England to conduct his Symphony, Op. 21, during the

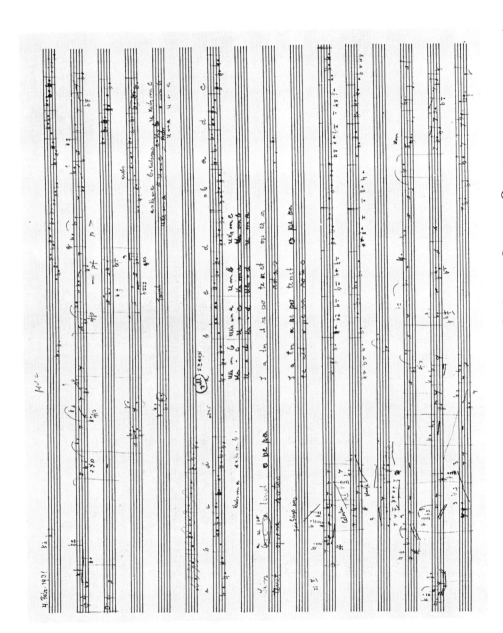

Orchesterstück (Ouvertüre), preliminary to Concerto, Op. 24

ISCM festival, he confided to Schoenberg on 17 June: "I finally must get to composing. In winter I began something new (for orchestra)." Writing out the row, Webern explained: "A is the inversion of the retrograde of B, the retrograde of C, and the inversion of D, and so forth with B, C, and D." On 2 July 1931, work on the orchestral piece was resumed. At this point, the concept changed from that of an "Overture" to that of a cyclic composition in three movements. On 7 July the title "Concerto, Op. 24," was first established and a formal plan drafted. The programmatic ingredients of the first outline were still present, but they were now expanded into a specific musical scheme:

I. Einersdorf 3/4 (animated, Introduction)
II. Schwabegg 2/4 (slow)
III. Annabichl 6/8 (2 x 3/8), flowing, secondary subject M., reprise P.

Two pages later, on 21 July, still another plan was mapped out. The title was modified to read "Piano Concerto." Among other alterations was a change of the time signature of the first movement to 2/4. In this movement, here designated as "Sonatensatz," the composer continued to have second thoughts about the tempo (it ranged from moderate to fast) and the tonal combinations and their instrumentation. The latter was to be reduced in the finished work to nine solo instruments: flute, oboe, clarinet, horn, trumpet, trombone, violin, viola, and piano. Some of these instruments had been indicated in the sketches to the erstwhile "Overture," along with cello, tambourine, and timpani. In early July, at the outset of the three-movement concept, there still appeared such parts as piccolo, harp, mandolin, celesta, and glockenspiel, as accessories to the opulent orchestral palette then envisioned. The evolution of the project up to this point (pages 38–40 of Sketchbook III) can be traced from the published manuscript facsimiles.[9] The rich "Piano Concerto" instrumentation was still pursued for two more pages, but Webern then began to prune it down to the more austere complement of the ultimate version.

The composer's work did not progress very far that summer. Various dates interspersed in the sketches reveal that his efforts were sporadic, and the movement did not develop beyond its early stages. On 8 September Webern admitted with exasperation to Schoenberg: "Regrettably, I was hindered rather frequently from composing during the summer months this time. It often drives me to despair that I cannot continue to work in one stretch." His innermost desires notwithstanding, a full year was to elapse before Webern could note in his sketchbook on 19 September 1932: "Work taken up again." Once again, however, circumstances prevented any sizeable progress, and when, in February of 1933, Webern did resume composing, he undertook an altogether different project: the setting of two excerpts from Hildegard

Jonc's cycle *Viae inviae*, which kept him engaged intermittently from February to August. It was not until 7 September, shortly after the death of Adolf Loos, that he returned to his instrumental work. On the following day he began drafting a section marked "Var.". Rudolf Ploderer's suicide, on 10 September, again temporarily unsettled the composer, but on 9 October he was back at his project. He then jotted down a totally new plan, which disclosed changes both in title and instrumentation: the piece was now called "Konzertstück," and eleven instruments were designated. Woodwinds, brass, and piano were the same as in the final version, but of the full string quartet included in this scoring only the violin and viola were to be retained in the end.

Returning to his work in early January 1934, Webern first completed "Das dunkle Herz" (Op. 23, No. 1), which kept him occupied until the middle of March. In the meantime, the February revolution shattered the foundation of his professional activities. The composer reacted by withdrawing more and more into his creative work, for which, in fact, the most fruitful period was now to begin. The concerto, a project of more than three years' standing by now, was to be completed that summer. So far its evolution had been extremely slow: of the 69 measures into which the first movement eventually grew, only 25 had been established. In the process, a veritable labyrinth of sketches had accumulated. For his own orientation, the composer found it necessary to employ numerous *vi–de* signs (the *vi* indicating the point from which a skip was made to a connecting passage at *de*). Graphic symbols, such as stars, circles, crosses, and lines, written in red, green, or blue pencil, distinguish one *vi–de* signal from the other. Without such aids, the maze of intertwining sketches would be virtually impenetrable. This is particularly true of the impasse apparently reached at measure 25, when Webern temporarily laid the project aside in favour of the setting of "Das dunkle Herz."

Immediately following the sketches to that song, a surprising turn in the concerto's development occurred, explainable only by the composer's continuing preoccupation with Hildegard Jone's poetry. On 11 May, soon after his return from a successful concert tour to London, Webern began drafting a four-part chorus based on a Jone text beginning "Wie kann der Tod so nah der Liebe wohnen? / Wie kann der Tod so ganz im Leben thronen?" ("How can death dwell so close to love? / How can death have its throne so totally in life?"). The verses were drawn from a cycle of poems entitled *Der Schnee*.[10] The tone-row employed is identical with that of the concerto, and the ensuing measures are consecutively numbered 26 to 36, clear proof that Webern meant to integrate this choral section into the composition already in progress. Within three or four days, however, he relinquished his astonishing excursion, to continue, on 15 May, with measure 26 of the original instrumental score.[11]

Whatever motivated that enigmatic choral concept, whatever caused it to be withdrawn almost as soon as it appeared, the crucial impasse at measure 25 was now readily resolved. As repeated cancellations and redraftings show, problems still arose, but no serious obstacles seem to have occurred, and the movement was completed on 25 June 1934.

To the number of different titles previously considered for the work another was added when Webern wrote to Berg on 7 July: "I believe I will call it 'Divertimento'." While enumerating the nine solo instruments, he explained his choice of the viola instead of the cello. The latter instrument had been omitted, he commented, because he found "ample resource in the piano's low register." He also objected to the inordinate effort required to produce high tones on the cello: "More and more the instruments possess too small a range for me."

The new idea of a "Divertimento" was also mentioned to Schoenberg when Webern informed him of the completion of the first movement. Before continuing with the work, however, the composer allowed himself a diversion, mentioned to Hildegard Jone on 9 July: "For reasons that I have yet to relate I have momentarily put another project in between—the composition of a short poem of yours, dearest friend: 'Wie bin ich froh!'" The draft of that song occupied Webern until 16 July. Immediately afterwards he returned to his instrumental work, sketching out the beginning of a movement in 2/4 time marked *Sehr rasch* (Very fast), which was obviously conceived to provide contrast to the more moderate tempo of the "Divertimento's" first movement. That idea was abandoned after only eight measures, however.

On 30 July Webern began a section specifically designated as "second movement," with the tempo *Ruhig* (Calm), which was changed to *Sehr langsam* (Very slow) in the final version. After the painfully slow evolution of the first movement, the second was realized with a speed and facility that must be termed phenomenal for Webern: he drafted its 78 measures in less than one week. The three-page draft bears witness to the spontaneous ease and assurance that carried the composer from beginning to end. Hardly any changes occur in the manuscript, and the printed score proves that the composer remained free from afterthoughts. The sense of having reaped the fruits of inspiration deeply gratified Webern and he expressed his satisfaction when he wrote to Hildegard Jone on 8 August: "It seems to me that the movement I have just finished expresses something similar to your picture with the harvest wagon."

With the second movement, Sketchbook III was filled. On 22 August Webern began the next sketchbook with the draft of the Concerto's closing movement. Having just returned from a week's excursion into the Ötztal Alps, he set to work inspired and refreshed. After some difficulty with the first three measures, he began on 27 August to write out the movement. For the first time the instrumentation, previously not clearly defined, was explicitly established. The movement of 70 measures was completed by 4 September. Like its predecessor, it was written in one continuous effort, though not with the same unerring sweep.

No doubt Webern was fired to such speed by his determination to finish the composition in time for a special occasion. Completed just nine days before 13 September 1934, the Concerto was dedicated "To Arnold Schoenberg on his 60th birthday." The première, conducted by Heinrich Jalowetz, took place on 4 September of the following year at the ISCM festival in Prague. The first performance in Vienna was scheduled soon afterwards (see Chapter XXVI). The Concerto, Op. 24, was published by Universal Edition only in 1948. The same year the firm also granted a licence to Editions Dynamo of Liège, Belgium, to issue the work in a separate publication, which included a commemorative message by Schoenberg, written in June 1947, and an essay, "Qu'est-ce que la musique de douze sons?" by René Leibowitz. Webern's manuscript, prepared for the publishers (it is now in the Pierpont Morgan Library, New York), bears his timings for the three movements: I. *ca.* 3–4', II. *ca.* 3', III. *ca.* 2'.

The formal complexities of the work have challenged numerous composers and theorists to attempt analyses. René Leibowitz (in *Schoenberg et son école*), Leopold Spinner (in *die Reihe 2*, 1955), and Karlheinz Stockhausen (in *Melos*, December 1953) were among the earliest proponents of intricate theories, some of which have been contested. Much lively controversy was sparked, in particular, by Stockhausen's assertion that the first movement contains the prime elements of total serialization and that it therefore represents the archetype from which the principles of electronic music may be deduced. All scholars agree that the theoretical examination of the Concerto offers many an intriguing problem, both in the overall structure of the work and in the nature of the tone-row governing every component.

As to form, the first movement has been called a "sonata model" (Adorno) and the second a "three-part Lied-form" (Spinner). The germinal character of the row had been aptly described by Roman Vlad as follows: "Here the idea of serial variation has invaded the detailed structure of the series itself, which reproduces in principle the whole structure of the twelve-tone composition. In the course of the whole concerto the systematic and exclusive use of this series, which in its turn is composed of four micro-series, leads of necessity to a constant invention on a single motive of three notes. It is as if the whole sound organism had germinated from this single cell, which constantly reproduces itself in different aspects and relations."[12]

Stockhausen's thesis elevates Webern's treatment of the row to a principle applicable to parameters beyond pitch, marking the Concerto, Op. 24, as the beginning of total permutation. Rather than placing such emphasis on purely mathematical formulas, others give priority to the intangible force of inspiration that soars above all dogmatic theory. They maintain that, ultimately, the emotional message of music must transcend its technical aspects. Winfried Zillig, believing that intuition is the mainspring of artistic creation, holds that the true criterion for the understanding of Webern's music rests on an equally intuitive capacity for its comprehension. "If one looks at the second movement of the Concerto more closely," Zillig writes, "one will find in this piece, which on the surface is unprecedentedly simple, such an abundance of secrets that one could devote many hours to the solving of the enigmas within these few measures alone. But even with the first glance it becomes apparent that the material of such structures once again consists of those mysterious interval numberings that enter so inexplicably like lightning flashes into Mozart's G minor Symphony."[13]

Realizing that the new idiom of row composition perplexed the traditionalists, Webern himself said on 2 March 1932 in one of his lectures: "We want to 'say in an entirely new way' what has been said before. But now I can invent more freely, everything has a deeper unity. Only now is it possible to compose in free fantasy, without constraint—except by the row. To say it quite paradoxically: only on the basis of these unprecedented fetters has complete freedom become possible!"[14]

With his Concerto, Op. 24, completed at long last, Webern once again turned to the verses of Hildegard Jone. Several times he had allowed them to divert his attention during the evolution of the instrumental work. After finishing its first movement he had spontaneously turned to the setting of "Wie bin ich froh!" which was to become the first of his Three Songs, Op. 25. The draft, for voice and piano, was begun on 4 July 1934 and completed by 16 July (Sketchbook III, pages 75–76). Numerous details in the conception differ from the published version, including the conspicuous tempo change from the original *Lebhaft* (Lively) to the final *Langsam* (Slow).

" 'Wie bin ich froh,' . . . 'noch überblühn die Blumen mir die Welt' ['How happy I am,' . . . 'for me flowers still bloom all over the world']: in this spirit I am setting out," the composer wrote to the poetess on 8 August, before leaving for the Ötztal Alps. Meanwhile he had completed the second movement of his Concerto and, after his return, he wrote the third. On 19 September he resumed work on the setting of "Sterne, Ihr silbernen Bienen," another Jone poem. He had busied himself with this text already in August, as is indicated by some initial formulations of the melody line appearing amidst the Concerto sketches. However, that earlier approach differed substantially from the definitive concept now taking shape. The draft (Sketchbook IV, pages 9–14)—disclosing several beginnings, various alternatives, and repeated changes in tempo—was finished on 8 October.

The creative momentum carried the composer without pause into his next song, "Des Herzens Purpurvogel." After some preliminary sketches of the vocal line, Webern began the full scoring on 24 October and completed it by 15 November. Again, the originally envisioned tempo underwent a change—from *Sehr ruhig* (Very calm) to *Fliessend* (Flowing). Webern's constant concern with nuance of every type resulted in many such differentiations. Characteristic was also his practice of deciding on the sequence of movements within a cyclic work only after completion of the whole. Thus in the Three Songs, Op. 25, the song composed last was placed in the middle, and the definitive order of the cycle became 1. "Wie bin ich froh!" 2. "Des Herzens Purpurvogel" and 3. "Sterne, Ihr silbernen Bienen."

The work was not published by Universal Edition until April 1956, 22 years after its completion.[15] No performance during the composer's lifetime is recorded. Actually, the première was scheduled for a concert of the Basel ISCM chapter on 5 December 1943. The day before, Webern wrote to the poetess: "Tomorrow, the *six songs* [Opera 23 and 25], the first that I wrote on your words, dear Hildegard, will be sung for the first time in Basel. It is a programme devoted exclusively to music by me, with which the people there commemorate my 60th birthday (let it be said in all secrecy)." However, only the Opus 23 cycle received its première at that occasion, the Opus 25 songs being replaced by the George cycle, Op. 3.

Closely related to each other in impulse and date of origin, the songs of Opera 23 and 25 are remarkable for their high degree of intimacy, delicate shadings, and ascetic sparseness. In the construction of the basic row for Opus 25, a strong sense of unification is achieved by means of transposed repetitions of the opening three-tone motive in the second and fourth segments of the twelve-tone series. Unmistakably, the composer so much enjoyed his virtuoso command of the new method that his handling of the row material appears playfully relaxed rather than severely systematic: with obvious abandon, particles of the series are freely passed back and forth between voice and piano, and the total effect is one of a triumphant fusion of intellect and emotion.

Immediately after completing the Three Songs, Op. 25, Webern began a transcription of the six-voice Ricercar from Bach's *Musical Offering*. It was the second of two orchestral arrangements he produced during the time span covered in this chapter. The first of these, based on a Schubert work, was completed during the initial stages of his Concerto, Op. 24. Shortly after his homecoming from the concert tour to England in early May of 1931, Webern received a commission from Universal Edition to orchestrate six German Dances of Franz Schubert. Their manuscript, dated October 1824, had recently been discovered in the archives of the Gesellschaft der Musikfreunde. Seizing on the find, Universal Edition immediately published the pieces in their original version for piano. Thinking of an orchestral setting as well, Emil Hertzka then approached Webern. According to the composer's diary notes, he accepted the assignment on 19 May 1931 and delivered the finished score on 17 June.

In his arrangement Webern employed the standard Schubertian instrumental complement in which he had gained practice during his early university years while orchestrating a number of the composer's songs and piano sonatas: pairs of flutes, oboes, clarinets, bassoons, horns, and the usual strings. On 17 June, the day when Webern handed in the score to the publishers, he wrote to Schoenberg: "I undertook this gladly. But I must confess that I had to give it much thought until I believed I had found the right way. . . . In the process, the problem of classical instrumentation confronted me in its entirety. I took pains to remain on the solid ground of classical ideas of instrumentation, yet to place them into the service of *our* idea, i.e. as a means towards the greatest possible clarification of thought and context." On 29 June, Webern described his arrangement to Berg: "It looks like a *classical* score, but still more like *one by me*: everything is unified and yet dispersed into a really *great* variety. . . . Now one sees most distinctly how these six dances (seemingly written so hurriedly) were produced in *one* cast. Lovely, tender, beautiful ideas! So much has become clear to me during this work."

For an idealist like Webern, the challenge of the task was paramount and his greatest reward was the approval of his friends. Schoenberg, who was more realistic, quickly realized the commercial potential of the orchestration and advised him to safeguard his interests. However, it was too late. On 15 July Webern wrote to him: "Naturally, dearest friend, you suspected it. I have contracted with Hertzka for my Schubert instrumentation in the most unfavourable manner imaginable: namely, for a one-time honorarium of 400 schillings. . . . Naturally, I will also receive the performance royalties from the Authors' Society." Schoenberg, long experienced in such matters, strongly urged him to try to change the business arrangements. But Webern admitted resignedly in his letter of 8 September: "I see with ever greater horror how clumsy my contract was. How stupid I was!"

Whatever his misgivings, Webern could console himself with the rapid production of the printed score, which appeared that same September, and with the warm words of approval from Schoenberg, who wrote to him about the arrangement on 11 October: "It really corresponds in every way with the expectations that one harbours with respect to your fine ear, and it must sound enchanting. At that, it is astonishingly simple, stylistically uniform, and delicate like a *genuine Webern, the best that one cay say!*"

The first performance of the Schubert–Webern German Dances was conducted by Hermann Scherchen on 25 October 1931 in a broadcast concert from the Volksbühne theatre in Berlin. "Webern achieves miracles of sound (for instance, through the use of a solo string quartet) that lie far above the sphere of what is merely colouristic," commented the critic of the *Börsenzeitung* on 3 November. The next day Scherchen introduced the work in Switzerland in a Collegium Musicum concert in the hall of the Stadthaus of Winterthur. In the ensuing years, Webern repeatedly included the German Dances in his concerts, displaying his own fondness for them, as well as for all music so essentially Viennese in grace and poignant lightheartedness. With satisfaction he could note that his arrangement made its way into the standard orchestral repertoire. Twice, in 1936 and 1939, his cousin Ernst Diez, then living in the United States, informed him that he had heard the piece in broadcasts of the New York Philharmonic Orchestra under John Barbirolli. Among the earliest commercial recordings bearing Webern's name was one of the German Dances conducted by René Leibowitz.

While Webern had orchestrated Schubert's German Dances at the specific request of Universal Edition, he himself chose the subject for his second transcription. The project resulted from a subsidy of 500 schillings granted Webern by the publishers in July 1934, when he was in financial straits (see Chapter XXIV). Deliberating upon which work to select, Webern wrote to Schoenberg at the end of August:

I have taken on the task of setting for orchestra a classical composition (from the clavier or organ literature). I am not quite decided as yet, but am thinking very much of the great six-voice fugue from the *Musical Offering* by Bach. . . . It would interest me extraordinarily to transform this abstraction (which probably has never been performed except perhaps occasionally by an organist) into an acoustically possible reality, if I may call it that. I do not have to be in a hurry and would be very glad to hear your opinion beforehand or to receive some advice.[16]

Schoenberg was absorbed by his move to California and did not reply until 13 November:

> This is no easy task, for these pieces are very little known, and if one wants to make them palatable to the public, it will probably be necessary to help somewhat through the manner of their presentation. Actually, I do not believe that this can be effected by merely bringing out the "entries" [of the subject]. We often have talked about this in connection with Reger's fugues. Offhand, I can say only what I have done myself in this regard in my *Präludium und Fuge*: I have, so to speak, modernized the organ, replaced its slow, rarely occurring change of colours with a more richly varied one that establishes precisely the rendition and the character of the individual passages, and I have given attention to clarity in the web of voices. In order to learn how one can secure a larger number of voices, such as is indispensable for a big orchestra, I studied the technique of Bach's eight-voice settings and then I could write quite easily in six to ten voices and could also attain enough voices to fill in. For this can hardly be achieved by doubling alone. To be sure, in the process I have taken the position that I am making a *transcription* and that I should be allowed to take for myself at least as much liberty as Bach permitted himself in chorale transcriptions, where he even completely recreated figurative and, especially, harmonic details—I have not gone so far, however. Perhaps if you had asked me earlier, I would have proposed to you the Trio Sonatas for organ or the Orchestra Suites, which, to be sure, already exist in orchestral transcriptions.

Meanwhile, in the middle of November, after completing his Three Songs, Op. 25, Webern had set to work on the orchestration of his chosen Ricercar from the *Musical Offering*.[17] The latter work, along with the *Art of Fugue*, represents the summary and culmination of two centuries of contrapuntal development. Both compendia were conceived primarily as abstract studies. In the *Musical Offering*, only the Trio Sonata (No. 5) and the Perpetual Canon (No. 6) contain specific instrumental designations; otherwise, no prescriptions whatever as to media, tempo, or dynamics are provided.

By disposition and training, Webern was attracted to the severe intellectual discipline exhibited in Bach's work. The contrapuntal prowess that he himself had attained during his university years had provided him with a solid foundation throughout his development as a composer. It supported him through the changing phases of his "atonal" period and became the mainstay of his structural thinking once he adopted the twelve-tone method as his exclusive idiom. In view of his own contrapuntal predilections, Webern was especially intrigued by the challenge of applying contemporary ideas and techniques to an abstract design written 200 years earlier by the supreme master of the baroque era. That he approached his task with a definite conception is confirmed by Arnold Elston, one of his students at the time: "Pointing to one of those long lines without pauses in Bach's score, Webern maintained that it was necessary to crystallize out the particles of such a line, to bring out the refined succession of impulses and articulations in the rhythm values and melodic intervals through changes of tone colour and fresh attacks by the instruments."[18]

Webern was to attain these objectives by a most judicious employment of the *Klangfarben* device, which proved uniquely suitable for the purpose at hand. "I am working on the Bach fugue day in and day out," he wrote to Hildegard Jone on 10 December 1934. If Webern made any drafts of the transcription, they are not contained in Sketchbook IV, where the conception of *Das Augenlicht*, Op. 26, immediately follows the Three Songs, Op. 25. The finished ink score that served for the publication is dated at the end 21 January 1935. As always, Webern subjected his work to intensive scrutiny. To Hildegard Jone, who inquired about his next project, he wrote on 7 February: "Until the day before yesterday I was still occupied with the Bach fugue: there is much that I have re-thought through time and time again!"

The instrumentation of the Ricercar arrangement consists of flute, oboe, English horn, clarinet, bass clarinet, bassoon, French horn, trumpet, trombone, timpani, harp, and the full complement of strings. Webern dedicated the score to Edward Clark, his English friend, who had been instrumental in arranging another trip to London for him that spring. On 25 April 1935 he led the first performance of the work in a BBC broadcast. Soon afterwards, on 13 July, he introduced it in Vienna in the last of the radio programmes that he was to conduct in his native city (for details of both concerts, see Chapter XXVI).[19] Later the same year the transcription was published by Universal Edition under the title "Fuga (Ricercata) a 6 voci, No. 2 aus dem 'Musikalischen Opfer' von Joh. Seb. Bach."

For Webern, transcribing Bach's music was an important creative act, much more so than the orchestration of Schubert's German Dances which could be classified as an arrangement in the customary sense. In the Ricercar, his own ideas were assimilated to such an extent that the original design was virtually transformed into a new organism, imbued with fresh creative elements that lifted Bach's intellectual *tour de force* from its relative obscurity. It was the *Klang*, that life-blood of musical reality, which always mattered most to Webern, and in the Ricercar he aspired to produce a sound matching his own aural image. The attention lavished on every detail of the transcription was fully equal to that given to his original compositions. The extent of this absorption is evident from a letter he wrote on 1 January 1938 to Hermann Scherchen, who was about to perform the work with the BBC Orchestra in London. Meticulous explanations of structural elements are combined with equally explicit directions for their realization in performance. Painstakingly detailed and exhaustive, the letter reflects Webern's unsurpassable conscientiousness in every musical aspect. The long account closes:

> My instrumentation attempts to reveal the motivic coherence. This was not always easy. Beyond that, of course, it is supposed to indicate the character of the piece as I feel it. What music it is! To make it accessible at long last, by trying through my orchestration to express my view of it, was the ultimate object of my bold undertaking. Indeed, is it not imperative to awaken this music, which lies asleep in the seclusion of Bach's own abstract presentation and still is simply unknown or at least totally incomprehensible to most men? Incomprehensible as music! Let me know about your impressions and experiences in London. I shall listen in! One more important point for the rendition of my arrangement: nothing must be allowed to take second place. Not even the softest notes of the muted trumpet, for example, must be permitted to be lost. Everything is of primary importance in this work and—in this instrumentation.[20]

Obvious as Webern's concern with the true essence of the music appears, it could not assuage the objections of the purists, who, as guardians of tradition, consider any arrangement of the classical masters suspect.[21] In the camp of the progressives, however, Webern's transcription was hailed as a distinct achievement. Providing a novel dimension to the time-honoured fugal essay, it opened up completely new vistas of both the past and the future. Webern himself was convinced that his orchestration would render exactly this kind of service. While seeking new horizons, he yet found it important to emphasize his allegiance to tradition at every opportunity. In that vein he wrote to the painter Franz Rederer on 16 May 1935, after returning from London, where he had just conducted the première of the transcription. Speaking of Bach's "totally unknown, wonderful piece," he described in detail its abstract nature and his transformation of the work into a living "Klangfarbenmelodie."[22]

Arnold Schoenberg, whose transcriptions of the old masters are less daring than the Ricercar setting, was reserved in his judgement when Webern sent him the printed score. "It is very hard to form a mental picture of this music," he wrote on 27 August 1936, "and it is extraordinarily difficult to find the thread of the individual voices and, once one has it, not to lose it. This piece is certainly only for playing, and hardly for reading. Perhaps this is the most important anyway: what sounds. I would like to listen to it and have requested Klemperer to play it through sometime."

In live performance, that ultimate criterion, the transcription emerges with the clarity and transparency of a chamber-music composition. The texture is a filigree of solo instruments, save for the *tutti* in the final climax. In general character, the arrangement is typical of Webern's entire orchestral style from the early *Im Sommerwind* on. The most striking aspect of the Ricercar, and the one most provocative to the purist, is the way in which Webern dissects the fugal subject and recreates it as a *Klangfarbenmelodie*. In this process of fragmentation, motivic relationships are translated into relationships of tone colour. The result is a "pointillistic" technique analogous to that pioneered in painting by Paul Signac and Georges Seurat. The melodic line is given over in its sub-divisions to several instruments, which enter in relay fashion, and this produces the effect of a tonal chain consisting of links of various colours. In the challenging problem of viewing the old through the prism of the new, the thinking of Webern, the creative musician, was permeated by that of Webern, the trained musicologist. In this connection, the question of whether his Bach transcription represents an "orchestrated analysis" or an "analytical orchestration" remains purely academic.[23]

The same year in which the Ricercar transcription made its appearance on the musical scene, Erwin Stein published a long article, "Bach via Anton Webern," in the *Christian Science Monitor*. He concluded: "It is apparent to everyone who knows Webern's music that the tonal concept he employs for Bach's music is entirely his own. It is amazing that two things, stylistically so far removed, should blend into a perfect artistic whole. We are, it is true, concerned here with a totally new interpretation of Bach. For those, however, who understand and admire Bach, it will be an experience, for once, to hear him through the ears of a Webern."

CHAPTER XXVI

Last conducting appearances in Vienna— Berg's death—Crisis at Barcelona (1935–1936)

HIS BACH TRANSCRIPTION completed in January, Webern immediately set to work on his next composition, *Das Augenlicht*, Op. 26.
With a mere handful of private pupils, one evening weekly for the
Beethoven course, and another for the choral rehearsal, he found
ample time for creative endeavours.

Only in spring was there a temporary increase in his activities. On 14
April 1935, the Freie Typographia chorus gave its annual public concert.
The choice of programme numbers, however, caused some preliminary
difficulties. Georg Skudnigg, a functionary of the chorus, later recalled:
"The changed political conditions of the time and the prohibition of the
Social Democratic Party induced the Typographia to schedule a
programme of defiance. The government then in power at first wanted
to forbid the concert, but then shied away from the embarrassment. At
any rate, official representatives stayed away from the event."[1]
Deliberately chosen as an act of protest, the programme comprised
Beethoven's *Chorus of the Prisoners* from *Fidelio*, Brahms' *Song of Destiny*,
Mendelssohn's *Festival Song of the Artists*, Scheu's *The Hope*, and Mendelssohn's *First Walpurgis Night*. Several of the works contained texts that
could be taken as allusions to the current oppressive conditions, and
the inclusion of Mendelssohn's music, which had been summarily
banned from German concert halls since the arrival of the Hitler régime,
represented a further challenge.[2] As Skudnigg reported, the hall was
sold out and the performance was enthusiastically acclaimed. But despite
this success, it was to be the last time that Webern appeared as a choral
conductor. According to his income book, his monthly salary from the
Typographia continued only into September. One explanation might
be that he found the financial compensation offered by the group
simply too small for the time and effort involved. On 13 February of the
same year, he had confided to David Josef Bach that he had never been

able to establish the kind of rapport with the membership that had made his work with the Singverein so productive.

Within a week of the concert, Webern was on his way to London for another engagement, his fifth since 1929. Edward Clark had arranged for a BBC programme on 25 April, which, aside from the opening *Unfinished* Symphony by Schubert, contained only works by Webern: his recently completed transcription of Bach's Ricercar (world première), the Six Pieces for Orchestra, Op. 6, and the Passacaglia, Op. 1. Only once before, during his 1932 appearance in Barcelona, had the composer been given a similar chance to present a cross-section of his orchestral work in one concert. Reciprocating royally Clark's faith in his music, he dedicated the Ricercar score to him.

A few weeks after returning from England, Webern was invited to conduct a broadcast concert. Ever since 28 January of the preceding year, he had not received an engagement from Ravag, the government-controlled radio station. Suddenly, however, it appeared that his former link with the Social Democratic Party was being overlooked. Pleasantly surprised, Webern wrote to Hildegard Jone on 2 July: "Here we go again, after all!" The programme, on 13 July, included his Ricercar transcription (in its first Vienna performance), followed by Mendelssohn's Violin Concerto (Wolfgang Schneiderhan, soloist), and the Serenade in D major, Op. 11, by Brahms. Despite Webern's optimism, it turned out not only to be the last time that Ravag was to assign any concert to him but also his final opportunity to conduct the Wiener Symphoniker, the orchestra he had led in so many distinguished performances over the years. No doubt his choice of the first two programme numbers caused him to be relegated permanently to the status of *persona non grata*. His Bach transcription was bound to alienate many purists, and the inclusion of Mendelssohn's music antagonized those already subscribing to the Nazi code. Henceforth, Webern's employment by the radio station was restricted to the menial chore of "Abhördienst" (listening service).

After his brief stay in England, where the spirit of freedom still reigned and his music was appreciated, Webern found the atmosphere at home doubly oppressive. "The battle with the phantoms surrounding us is worse than ever and sometimes really burdensome," he wrote on 16 May to Franz Rederer. The Swiss painter, with whom Webern had become very friendly, was soon to prove helpful in a family matter: Webern's daughter, Amalie, after spending several months in England, had returned home in need of another kidney operation. One of Rederer's Zürich friends was Dr Maximilian Bircher, a physician famous for his championship of organic foods. Webern, a firm believer in nature's healing powers, hoped that a "Bircher diet" (then as now widely followed) might forestall the operation. Rederer made arrangements for Amalie to live in Dr Bircher's own household and thus be under his direct care. While the cure did not avert the necessity of surgery for Amalie, her experience with the "Bircher diet" led the entire family to adopt it forthwith.

After her recovery, Amalie, a highly attractive and vivacious young woman of 24, married Gunter Waller, the son of a well-to-do family that lived at Im Auholz 2, only a few doors away from the Weberns. (Gunter was an energetic and successful businessman engaged in the distribution of Nu Enamel, an American lacquer product then sweeping the world market.) The wedding took place on 8 August in the Dorotheerkirche, one of the Protestant churches in Vienna. Despite their limited means, the Weberns outdid themselves in providing all the trimmings of an elaborate formal wedding, one that would befit their daughter's future social status. Amalie later recalled: "Our wedding dinner took place at the Hotel Imperial. Only the closest family members on both sides were present. My parents made a great sacrifice financially in offering me this dinner in so expensive a hotel. But Gunter's parents were very wealthy and looked down contemptuously upon the poor musician. Mother and father wanted to spare me any humiliation and thus this showy affair came about."[3]

Among the wedding guests were Webern's sister, Maria, and her husband, Paul Clementschitsch. The latter invited Webern to join him on a climb of the Gross-Venediger, a temptation proving irresistible. "The Gross-Venediger has haunted me too long and too much," Webern wrote to Polnauer on 10 August, the day before his departure for Klagenfurt. A mountain guide had been hired, and the party reached the summit of the mighty peak (3,660 m.) from the Defregger Hut (their overnight shelter) on 14 August. Elated, Webern sent picture postcards to Bach, Hueber, and Zenk. Knowing that Zenk had long wished to climb that monarch among glacier peaks, he wrote: "I do not want to make your heart heavy, but I was on top. . . . It was indescribable!"

Following the climb, Webern stayed a few days with Paul and Maria Clementschitsch at their holiday retreat in Virgen, and on 19 August, on his way home, he visited Alban Berg at the Waldhaus. Berg had just completed the orchestration of his Violin Concerto, a work requested earlier in the year by the American violinist Louis Krasner. Financially pressed, the composer had had to interrupt the instrumentation of his opera *Lulu* in order to carry out the commission. The untimely death, on 22 April, of the beautiful nineteen-year-old Manon Gropius, Alma Mahler's daughter from her second marriage, was the inspiration for the two-movement concerto, which Berg dedicated "To the Memory of an Angel." (The first movement portrays the young girl's nature, the second conjures up the catastrophe and release of death.) Working at a feverish speed (the condensed score was finished by 12 July, the orchestration by 11 August), the composer was not only creating a monument to the much-beloved girl, but was also, without knowing it, composing his own requiem.

At the time of Webern's visit, Berg was suffering from an abscess caused by an insect bite in the area of the lower spine. Nonetheless, he planned to attend the ISCM festival in Prague in early September. As late as 26 August, Webern instructed Polnauer to provide railway passes for Berg, Krenek, and Steuermann, all of whom were officially to represent the Vienna section. But at the last minute Berg was forced to cancel. Webern, despite his reluctance to interrupt his work on his new composition, *Das Augenlicht*, had agreed to conduct the première of his Concerto, Op. 24 (his name actually appeared on the printed programme), and Alois Hába had already notified him of the time of the first rehearsal. However, still annoyed over the society's politics, which had prevented his appearance at the Florence festival the year before, Webern suddenly decided not to go when a new irritation arose. "I will not make the trip and I have handed over my Concerto to Jalowetz," he explained to David Josef Bach on 26 August. "Finally and mainly because they have taken the *Lulu* pieces away from him. They will be conducted by Herr Szell!!! On Saturday, the 24th, word came from Hába, with the comment that *'for economic reasons and technical dispositions'* they had to make this decision and with the request that I was to give my consent. I declared that, in order to compensate Jalowetz in some measure, I now would transfer to him the conductorship of my work and that I would not come to the festival."

The first orchestral concert, on 1 September, opened with a symphonic work entitled *Miserae* by the young Munich composer Karl Amadeus Hartmann, who subsequently became one of Webern's disciples.[4] Webern's Concerto, Op. 24, was scheduled for the chamber music concert of 4 September. That programme also included works by Goffredo Petrassi and Wladimir Vogel, among others. Members of the Kolisch Quartet and Eduard Steuermann, who had been coached beforehand by Webern, participated in the ensemble under Jalowetz' direction. The critic Felix Stössinger, writing a special report for the *Pariser Tageblatt*, singled out Berg's *Lulu* Suite[5] and Webern's Concerto as festival highlights:

Both works show how wide and many-faceted Schoenberg's world is. . . . Webern's Concerto continues the style of a music in which two to three tones in themselves form an entity. An instrument or a group of instruments play them, or as one might say, arrange them spatially. Surely this is a music about which listeners lacking understanding laugh. But it was performed with such compelling brevity and plasticity that one was reminded of Chinese master drawings in which also nothing is to be seen except some bamboo leaves, distributed on silk in a seemingly senseless arrangement. Webern, an ascetic in Vienna, has reduced the music to silent but impressive glimpses.

In the audience for the Webern première was one of Italy's most promising young composers, Luigi Dallapiccola, then 31. On the evening of the concert, Dallapiccola noted in his diary:

> . . . a work of incredible conciseness (six minutes of music) and of unique concentration. Every decorative element has been eliminated. . . . I could not form a precise idea of the work, it is too difficult for me to understand; however, it seems to represent, without any question, an entire world. We find ourselves in the presence of a man who expresses a maximum of ideas with a minimum of words. Although I did not understand the work completely, I had the feeling of finding an aesthetic and stylistic unity as great as I could wish for. Many people in the hall smiled during the performance: our own delegation also seemed to be in a hilarious mood ("O Latin gaiety, you are not dead yet!" one can read in the *Chantecler*. But some laugh at anything). I have not heard the whole programme tonight. Webern compels me to meditate.[6]

With the coming of autumn 1935, Webern's sole source of income, apart from the Abhördienst, was private teaching. The number of his students remained small, seven or eight at best, and some of them paid minimal fees. However, they were devoted, came regularly, took their instruction seriously, and stayed on year after year. Besides those mentioned earlier, the names of Arnold Elston, Kurt List, and Willi Reich now made their appearance in the income book. Some of the students came to Webern's home at Maria Enzersdorf, others were taught in the dwellings of friends living in Vienna. Over the years, the Humpliks (who maintained a studio in the city), the Kurzmanns, Erwin Ratz, Greta Wilheim, and Webern's sister-in-law Leopoldine Gross generously placed their facilities at his disposal, which allowed him to schedule his lessons conveniently.

On Friday, 18 October, Webern again began a series of Beethoven lectures at Dr Kurzmann's home. The course lasted through April. Josef

Polnauer, a faithful factotum since the days of the Schoenberg Society, had assisted in organizing the small group of listeners. By disposition a perennial student, possessed of unbounded vitality and infectious enthusiasm, Polnauer attended almost every session. He also was a prominent member of the Verein für neue Musik, the Austrian ISCM section, whose activities then provided virtually the only outlet for contemporary music in Vienna. The board of directors, presided over by Webern, represented strongly progressive tendencies. It included at that time Bach, Jalowetz, Krenek, Polnauer, Reich, Steuermann, Wellesz, and Zenk. The few performances of Webern's compositions, as well as his conducting engagements abroad, were due primarily to this organization. In Germany the Nazi régime, suspicious of all foreign influences, had already suppressed the ISCM, along with other international societies such as the Freemasons and Rotary. Though increasingly conscious of its precarious position, the Vienna section continued to display its undaunted spirit. This was exemplified by the concert given on 21 November 1935 at the Hagenbund. The programme comprised Krenek's *Symphonische Musik für neun Instrumente*, the world premières of songs by Zenk and a piano quintet by Hauer, Schoenberg's *George Lieder*, and the first Vienna performance of Webern's Concerto, Op. 24. For the latter, the composer himself conducted the ensemble, with Steuermann at the piano, as he had been for the Prague première.

Shortly before the concert, Alban Berg had returned to Vienna from his country home. The infection that had afflicted him ever since August had spread and was gravely undermining his health. In addition, financial worries oppressed him (the royalty income from his works, *Wozzeck* in particular, was greatly curtailed as a result of the Nazi ban on his music). "Somehow or other, help *must* be provided!" he had written to Willi Reich from the Waldhaus on 4 November, adding words doubly ominous in retrospect: "*I still have enough to live on for one or two months*, but what then? I keep thinking about nothing but this and am weighing the possibilities—consequently, I am deeply depressed."

By the end of November, Berg's economic circumstances had deteriorated so much that he even considered selling his beloved retreat, the Waldhaus. In his letter of 30 November to Schoenberg he bitterly lamented:

At this point my morale is at low ebb. It will not surprise you to learn this from one who suddenly had to find out that he is not "of the soil" in his own country and, therefore, practically homeless. Add to this that such a state of affairs did not come about without friction or without deep human disappointments which, in fact, still continue.

But it is certainly not appropriate that I should tell you such things, you, of all people, who have lived through all this to such an enormous extent, compared with which my experiences are only pocket-sized. After all, I live in my homeland and may speak my mother tongue.

By the time Berg entered the Rudolfspital on 17 December for an emergency operation, the infection had spread throughout his body. He was given blood transfusions, and a second operation was performed, which still failed to locate the source of infection.[7] Berg's friends were unaware of the seriousness of the situation. On 21 December Webern wrote to Rederer that Berg's condition was "already much improved." The rally was deceptive, however, and on the following day the death struggle set in. Berg who, like Schoenberg and Webern, harboured certain superstitions, considered the number "23" his Schicksalszahl (fateful number), and 23 December therefore was ominous for him. "This will be a decisive day," he stated calmly in the morning. He did not live to see another dawn. The end came at 1.15 am on 24 December 1935. Polnauer later testified: "Webern was the only one of our circle of friends who spoke with him on the day of his death."[8]

In Hildegard Jone's estate was found the draft of her letter of condolence to Berg's widow. Her beautiful words expressed the sorrow felt by all his friends. Strongly inclined towards the metaphysical, the poetess firmly believed in extra-sensory perception, and her words of comfort culminated in the promise of lasting communion between husband and wife, which death could not destroy:

On the 24th, shortly before evening, I learned of the incomprehensible loss that has befallen you. For me the holy lights burned black that night—in the thought that for you the Christmas candles had become candles of death. I could think only of you! The communion between you and your husband was so dear to us; it stands inextinguishable before my soul. Greater than the greatest art is such unity of two human beings, which cannot be lost even in death. You have grown close to my heart, dear Frau Berg, more than almost any other human being. I believe I know you well, you who have lived so fully for your husband. And this I would like so very much to tell you, with all the strength of my heart: do not believe that your husband is dead. He is with "the father of heavenly lights," he will come close to you again, he will be wholly with you—this you will experience for certain. You will, when you quietly listen within yourself, perceive his voice and his words. This will not happen right away and perhaps not very soon (at first, you will only feel his having "passed away"), but it will certainly come about.

Hildegard Jone's prophecy was to be borne out. Helene Berg survived her husband by forty years, and for the rest of her life she professed to live in continual spiritual contact with him, undeterred by the scepticism that this belief occasioned. Holding firmly to her mission, she carried out what she considered Alban Berg's artistic will and testament. Thus she steadfastly refused to allow the orchestration and performance of the third act of *Lulu*, which had been left unfinished.

Berg was buried on the afternoon of 28 December in the cemetery of Hietzing. Ernst Krenek spoke at the funeral on behalf of the ISCM's Vienna section, performing this task in the absence of Webern, the group's president. Webern, though deeply shaken by the death (his daughter, Amalie, remembered him weeping unrestrainedly that sad Christmas eve), had felt obligated to go through with a trip to Barcelona, where he was to serve on the jury selecting compositions for the forthcoming ISCM festival there. He no doubt believed that he could best serve Berg's memory by persuading the jury to schedule the first performance of his Violin Concerto, and in this he succeeded. Leaving Vienna on 26 December, he wrote to the Humpliks that same day from Salzburg: "Despite everything, I had to make this trip. You can imagine what I have been through during the last few days. I can hardly wait to be home again."

Webern returned on 4 January. Berg's death increasingly engulfed him in gloom and despair. Sensing how deeply he felt the loss, his friends tried to console him. Schoenberg, in particular, clearly realizing the tragedy that was enveloping their individual and artistic fates, wrote to him a poignant letter on 15 January:

Dearest friend, I am anxiously awaiting a letter from you concerning the death of our poor, dear Berg. It has been so frustrating for more than three weeks now not to be able to learn anything here except the little that the newspapers bring, although they have accorded him relatively extensive coverage. So far, nobody from Vienna has written me details, which I cannot understand, for everybody must know how deeply this affects me. It is too horrible. There goes one of us (who were only a mere three), and now we two must bear this isolation alone. And the saddest aspect is—it had to be the one of us who had success, who could have at least enjoyed *that*. Had he lived on, he at least would not have had to suffer to the same degree the bitterness that would have spoiled for him all joy in the performances of his works and, consequently, in his own effectiveness, as the two of us have to. To be sure, he, too, had to suffer under the general pressure that burdened the three of us, under the hatred with which we are persecuted. But still, thanks to some ingratiating traits in his personality, people believed in him, and he could have enjoyed this. We have not heard from each other for an infinitely long time, and I am the more guilty: I have not written for at least a half year. But I have the excuse that, during this time, I have written to almost no one. . . . Please, do write to me again now, too. I myself will endeavour to write to you as often as possible. But I cannot promise this if things go on as they have until now, if my nerves continue to be strained to the limit. You ought to keep in mind, though, that this means no estrangement, and you will understand how much it pains me that I did not write sooner, if not to you, at least to poor Berg, to whom it surely would have given joy to hear from me once more, and to whom I had not written for so long. This, too, makes me very sad.

Another friend who felt moved to write to Webern was the singer Ruzena Herlinger. Long an active collaborator and generous supporter, she had moved back to Prague a few months earlier. On 14 January Webern responded to her condolence:

Indeed, it is unspeakable what has happened! I cannot get hold of myself and cannot find peace. I thank you from the bottom of my heart for your kind sympathy, and I respond to it in like manner, for I am fully aware of how hard it has hit you, too. For that, the *Wein* aria will give testimony forever. On 15 February, there will be a memorial to Alban Berg, consisting of his chamber music compositions. At the music festival in Barcelona during April, his last work, the Violin Concerto, will be played for the first time. In all probability this will be under my direction, as it will be on 1 May in a BBC concert in London.

Webern's participation in the ISCM jury meeting in Barcelona had resulted in a particularly strong representation of his Vienna colleagues in the festival, scheduled for 19–25 April. As an homage to Berg, not only the première of the Violin Concerto was to be featured, but also the three fragments from *Wozzeck*. Included further were three excerpts from Ernst Krenek's twelve-tone opera *Karl V*, the *Five Sonnets of Elizabeth Browning*, for soprano and string quartet, by Egon Wellesz, Two Movements for String Quartet, Op. 1, by Mark Brunswick, and the Piano Sonata, Op. 1, by Ludwig Zenk (the pupil whom Webern was trying to launch on his career).

In closest collaboration, Louis Krasner and Webern prepared the performance of Berg's Concerto, rehearsing at the home of the Kurzmanns. Rita Kurzmann had made the piano reduction of the work under Berg's direct supervision. It was she who related an anecdote about Webern that illustrates his remarkable power of inner concentration, which made him oblivious at times of actual physical phenomena: "Webern started out playing with full chords," the story goes (as retold by Webern's pupil Kurt Manschinger). "Then his accompaniment became lighter and lighter until it finally ceased completely. Krasner played on for a considerable length of time. Suddenly Webern stopped him, exclaiming, 'Halt, jetzt war' ma net beisamm!' [Stop, now we were not together!]"

On 8 April, Krasner and Rita Kurzmann gave a preview of the Violin Concerto in the chamber music hall of the Musikverein for a circle of friends and guests invited by Universal Edition. During those weeks, Webern was seized by a growing reluctance to go to Barcelona. The continuing depression over Berg's passing was deepened by his emotional involvement with his friend's last work, itself conceived with connotations of death. The responsibility of conducting its première increased his apprehensions, and by early April he had developed a strong aversion to going through with the task altogether. Alarmed, Bach and Krenek, then Polnauer, tried to prevail upon him. But Webern refused, insisting: "I cannot." Finally, Krasner went to see Webern at his home and spent the day pleading with him. Only when the violinist categorically stated that he would not perform the Concerto at all unless Webern conducted did Webern give in. The difficulty with which he had to be persuaded was an ominous foreshadowing of the dramatic events in Barcelona.

The Vienna delegation to the festival was a large one. Most of the members took the direct route to Spain through Switzerland, but Webern asked Krasner to travel with him via Germany, so that they might see for themselves what the conditions there were like under Hitler. Wellesz, who took the Swiss route, later recounted how he made the long train trip in the company of Helene Berg and Willi Reich.[9] In those days, they were all limited in funds and had to travel in a third-class compartment with wooden benches. At night, the men sat on their suitcases in the aisle so that Berg's widow could stretch out on the seat and rest.

At Barcelona, Webern was greeted by Roberto Gerhard, who had been instrumental in bringing him for a guest engagement four years earlier. Webern then had conducted the Casals orchestra in a pair of successful concerts, which included three of his own works. He had lavishly praised the excellence of the orchestra and the splendid collaboration of its members. This time things turned out to be drastically different. From the first rehearsal on, Webern ran into obstacles of communication with the musicians. The difficulty was intensified by his almost fanatic insistence on matching his mental image of Berg's score with the reality of sound. Felix Galimir later recalled: "He tried frantically in his Viennese German to explain the music to the orchestra, who understood neither his language nor the music."[10] In two sessions, only the beginning section of the first movement was covered. The third rehearsal took place on the morning of Saturday, 18 April, the day before the opening of the festival. Webern appeared extremely nervous. Again the rehearsal did not proceed significantly and, according to Wellesz, Webern became "rude" in dealing with the orchestra members. Convinced that the Catalan musicians were deliberately failing to understand or follow his directions, he abruptly announced: "The performance cannot take place." Thereupon he left the rehearsal hall and locked himself in his hotel room.

General consternation followed. The première of Berg's Concerto was considered the festival highlight, and everyone, from the officials to the composer's widow, was seized by dismay. Wellesz has described the course of events that followed: he and Helene Berg at once went to Webern in a desperate attempt to reason with him. If Webern was unwilling to conduct, he should at least relinquish the assignment to someone else. But Webern remained adamant and repeatedly exclaimed: "The performance *must* not take place. No, no, no!" Only the entreaties of Helene Berg could finally sway him. When she literally knelt before him and tearfully begged for his permission, he grudgingly conceded: "Meinetwegen dann" [All right then]. With that, he surrendered the conductor's score.

Immediately—it was noon—Wellesz hurried to Edward Dent, his close friend and the society's international president. The two deliberated, and Dent then called on Hermann Scherchen, whom he found busy correcting orchestra parts. Scherchen had not seen the score of the Concerto before, and it was with great reluctance that he consented to step into the emergency. While resting on the bed in his hotel room, he went over the work, which Krasner played through for him. A single rehearsal with the orchestra had to suffice. Krasner had intended to perform his part from the manuscript, but Scherchen made him play it from memory. During the rehearsal he swept the soloist's part off the stand, saying: "One does not play a thing like this from the music." He pointed out to Krasner that he had proved himself quite capable of memorized performance when he wandered away from the score while playing for him in the hotel room. The violinist submitted to Scherchen's dynamic will, and the first performance, on Sunday, 19 April, went off well enough, aside from minor shortcomings of which only the executants themselves were aware. At the last minute Ernest Ansermet assumed the responsibility for Krenek's three fragments from

Karl V, which Webern was supposed to have conducted in the same concert.

It is difficult to imagine Webern's state of mind during those trying days. Mark Brunswick went for long walks with him. He described Webern's behaviour as definitely pathological, a case of temporary paranoia—an opinion held by Brunswick's wife, a psychiatrist and pupil of Freud.[11] Webern's subsequent action would tend to support that view. He was supposed to proceed from Barcelona via Paris to London, with Krasner and Polnauer. Instead, in an obvious flight from the scene of his frustration, he discarded all his previous travel arrangements and went back to Vienna, a detour of hundreds of miles. The experience in Barcelona had so shaken him that he could think only of regaining his mental equilibrium in the shelter of his rural retreat, at the side of his infinitely understanding and compassionate wife. On 20 April he had announced his return to David Josef Bach, to whom he had poured out his heart in a long letter from Barcelona:

Dearest friend, unfortunately I cannot give you good news. *It has turned out badly for me here*. In contrast, in *terrible* contrast to what had been promised, the rehearsal possibilities were so limited that, 24 hours before the performance, I had achieved practically nothing. Then, when an ultimatum given by me did not bring results, I had to draw the consequences. *I could not have taken the responsibility for anything else*. However, what was impossible for me, Ansermet and Scherchen, not being fundamentally responsible, could carry through. That is the way it then was done: the performances were saved, but the circumstances almost ruined me. You can readily imagine this. So that in the end the stated reason (illness) corresponded with the truth. But I really knew it all beforehand. I am returning home today. . . . Then on Tuesday of the coming week I will travel to London. To think of this gives me comfort now. . . . Naturally, I would like to talk to you as soon as possible, in order to be able to tell you what was done to me here *in every respect*. And how no one considered at all, but really not at all, that the première of Berg's last work—in memoriam—was at stake. It was an *immeasurable torment*. A hell. I can take the responsibility for what I have done. The contrary, however, would not have been possible.

On 24 April Webern wrote to Polnauer, at the Paris address of Max Deutsch, that he would arrive at Victoria Station in London on the afternoon of 29 April, and that Krasner had reserved rooms for the three of them at the Bentinck Hotel. It was Webern's sixth and last concert tour to England. His engagement with the BBC orchestra called for two evening broadcasts, on 1 and 3 May. The programme for the first concert, dedicated to the memory of Alban Berg, included two movements from the Lyric Suite and the Violin Concerto. Although rehearsals began only one day beforehand, the performance proved to be excellent in the recollection of everyone who heard it.[12] Webern fully redeemed himself, refuting the accusation made by some that his failure at Barcelona was caused by inefficient rehearsing, compounded by emotional incompetence in coping with the task.

On 3 May Webern conducted the BBC orchestra in Bruckner's monumental Seventh Symphony. He could not know that he was standing for the last time at the helm of that great orchestral body, which had provided him with so much satisfaction over the years. Considering that he had to surmount the language barrier in his London engagement no less than at Barcelona, his débâcle with the Spanish musicians appears the more inexplicable.

The Barcelona episode was to have a disagreeable aftermath in Vienna. Ernst Krenek, as Austrian ISCM delegate, was asked to make an official report on the embarrassing affair. He later recalled: "There were several sessions of the board devoted to this matter until a compromise was found. Webern's claim that he behaved as he did because the Catalan people did not give him the rehearsal time they had promised was taken into account, even though the facts on record contradicted this."[13] According to Mark Brunswick, these committee proceedings were extremely painful for Webern. The whole experience left him at first with a sense of defeat and humiliation, much as he tried to suppress it. However, his characteristic reaction in the face of adversity was not to dwell on it. He assiduously avoided references to such setbacks both in his correspondence and in his diary notes. A constitutional optimism apparently enabled him to absorb emotional shocks with stoicism and resilience, so that he remained ever hopeful of a better future.

CHAPTER XXVII

Webern as a conductor—Schoenberg in Los Angeles—Before the Anschluss (1936–1938)

ALTHOUGH WEBERN WAS only 52 years of age and at the height of his powers at the time of his 1936 London engagement, his conducting career came to an end with that appearance. It may therefore be appropriate at this point in the narrative to let some of those who had observed him in action over the years provide their recollections.

"Without exaggeration: Webern is the greatest conductor since Mahler—in every respect," Alban Berg had written to his wife as early as 28 May 1922, after attending a performance of Mahler's Third Symphony. Two days later, after the repeat performance, he confirmed his judgement: "I sat with Schoenberg. He had not thought it possible. Webern's achievement is such that it can only be compared with that of Mahler himself." Of the three friends, Webern was the only one to attain real prominence as a conductor. Berg never attempted it and Schoenberg appeared only occasionally, mostly in performances of his own works. After one of them, the London production of *Erwartung*, Schoenberg implicitly acknowledged Webern's mastery when writing to him on 22 January 1931: "Never before have I worked so well with an orchestra, never before rehearsed so well, heard so well, given the beat so well as this time. To be sure, I was substantially better prepared this time than on other occasions, not without being influenced by your stern reprimand."

Berg's glowing assessment of Webern's prowess was shared by many. In an article, published in the *Christian Science Monitor* on 2 August 1930, Erwin Stein observed:

We have just had an opportunity of comparing the old and the new style of interpretation, Toscanini and Anton Webern having conducted most representative performances of Beethoven's *Eroica*. Toscanini's reading embodied the ideal of the old style of

interpretation: the changes of "tempo" were dictated by a splendid
sense of form: pathos and expression were never carried to excess, but
on the contrary informed by utmost subtlety and distinction. With so
high a level of interpretation, the old style can still delight us.
Webern's reading was less perfected technically. It suffered from lack
of time for rehearsing. And yet I found it more directly impressive. He
assigned a "tempo" to each movement and kept to it without
impairing one single contrast. The first "allegro" was full of
vehemence, and the lyrical elements in it fell quite naturally into place
without losing their character. The same unity prevailed in the other
movements: the "Marcia Funebre" was more flowing, less pathetic
than customary, and yet no less moving. Wonderful were the
variations of the Finale, taken really "allegro molto, sempre l'istesso
tempo," with telling impetus.

Eduard Steuermann, whose long collaboration with Webern included frequent performances of the classic masters under his baton,
has said: "For me, he conducted Bach best of all. He combined a
projection of the motivic structure, which made the music vibrant with
inner life, with a sense of the great line, always supported by simple and
clear dynamics. He influenced my approach to Bach strongly."
Steuermann, who took part in the first performances of Webern's
Quartet, Op. 22, and Concerto, Op. 24, recalled: "When the first
movement [of Op. 24] was finished, he played a little of it for me. . . . He
played so freely that I hardly could follow the music, but it was
extraordinary. When he conducted, however, he was not so free; I
suppose one cannot be, or at least he could not."[1] Steuermann also
commented on the enormous sensitivity of Webern's aural perception:
"It was so great that only one with a similarly good ear could hear the
same things he did."[2]

Felix Greissle, Schoenberg's son-in-law, esteemed Webern as one of
the best conductors he ever knew. In Greissle's opinion, "His Mahler
interpretations were superb,"[3] and Paul Stefan, following a presentation
of Mahler's Sixth Symphony, wrote in the Badische Landeszeitung (25
December 1930):

Webern as a conductor is a singular case. A musician of the greatest
purity of intent, of an incomparable emotional and interpretative
strength, he nevertheless is to be considered, perhaps for the very
reason of his ecstatic nature, as a man who would not be able to fit
himself into routine work. But each time he mounts the podium he
succeeds in a rendition of such beauty that one asks oneself in vain
why such a performance must remain the exception. At any rate, the

finale of the Sixth this time was a stirring experience, which has carved itself deeply into the memory.

Josef Polnauer, who regularly attended Webern's rehearsals and concerts, made this assessment:

> As a conductor, Webern was no "star" and also no virtuoso of the baton; all airs of this type were extremely repugnant to him. Nevertheless, his spiritual intensity and power of conviction enabled him—even with the usual minimal number of rehearsals—to attain superlative achievements of inspired delivery, such as are indeed only possible for a productive artist to whom ultimate insights and perceptions reveal themselves. Webern always prepared himself in the most careful manner through minute, but also time-consuming study of the text and structure of each single work.[4]

The singer Ruzena Herlinger, who repeatedly appeared as soloist under Webern, described his Mahler interpretations in her memoirs: "When he conducted, Webern conveyed such overwhelming strength that it seemed as if he transmitted rays. Even those members of the orchestra who were sceptical during rehearsal admitted after the performance: 'We have never played a Mahler Second like this one, not even under Bruno Walter.'"

All accounts agree that Webern's mannerisms as a conductor did not conform to the image of a typical maestro. "His gestures," according to Mme Herlinger, "had nothing of the classic. His whole body was in motion when he conducted." Another observer, Hans W. Heinsheimer wrote:

> Anton Webern, considered a serious-minded, shruggingly tolerated screwball, was permitted to make a bare living as conductor of the Workers Concerts. We always went to hear them, to pay homage to their thin, bespectacled conductor, whose stooped, slightly clumsy, professorial movements, his face deeply buried in the score, had only one purpose: to serve the music. My most poignant memory of this unique man is a performance of Mahler's Eighth Symphony. As the audience rose in applause, he lifted, not without difficulty, the huge, heavy score over his head. The work, not the conductor, was to be applauded. I have often thought of that gesture of proud modesty, never encountered again.[5]

The various reports concur in describing the intensity of Webern's manner of conducting.

What he lacked in routine he made up for by great musicianship and passionate enthusiasm [wrote Kurt Manschinger in his memoirs]. His concerts were always highly polished and made an electrifying impression. The eminent music critic Ernst Decsey called him "the finest craftsman with the least routine." He always came to the rehearsals well prepared, musically and technically. Once when he rehearsed Mahler's Third Symphony, the first trombonist was absent, so Webern sang the whole part during the rehearsal. While his voice never approached the volume of a trombone, it somehow sounded complete and satisfactory, and one became aware of the beautiful trombone part one had never noticed before. Whenever a concert was approaching, Webern was a bundle of nerves, and at the end he was completely exhausted. He conducted with such fervour that his shirt was soon drenched. His wife always waited in the dressing room with a clean shirt so that, in the intermission, he could change before continuing. . . . Although Webern knew the music he performed forwards and backwards, he never conducted without a score. He believed that the picture of the music should always stand graphically before the eyes even if one were able to conduct by heart.

Several instrumentalists who played under Webern have provided additional close-up views. Among them is the violinist Felix Galimir: "It was amazing how a man concerned with the smallest details never lost the big line of a work. He was not the routine or experienced conductor who would get the best results out of an orchestra in the shortest time. On the contrary, he needed time to explain, and especially time for the musicians to get used to his way of rehearsing. If he felt they understood him, he could do great things. If not, he was completely helpless." Galimir was coached by Webern in several performances of his own music: "We studied with Webern his Five Movements, Six Bagatelles, Four Pieces for Violin, the Concerto, and his Symphony. I remember at first our shock, a reaction almost prompting us to ridicule the sparsity of notes in each composition. After we worked with him for a little while, though, the proportions were so perfect that all length or shortness vanished. Of course, the minutest details were of greatest importance. How expressive every little miniature phrase became when he sang it."[6] The violist Marcel Dick has commented similarly: "His fanatic search and drive for perfection during every second of the rehearsal, his refusal to accept anything that had the slightest blemish (noticed only by one with his incredibly sensitive ear), the exaltation caused by performances of masterworks, be they his own or those of other composers, all were experiences to be remembered for a lifetime."[7]

Another instrumentalist, the clarinetist Eric Simon, found Webern "a strange conductor. It goes without saying that he was a superior musician. He knew his scores to the last note. Yet he did not take his eyes from the music and was very, very nervous. . . . He sometimes had great difficulty in making his wishes clear, but the performances were remarkable for their character, consistency, and musicianship."[8] Simon, as well as the violinists Kurt Frederick (Fuchsgelb) and Samuel Flor, confirm that Webern often spent an inordinate amount of rehearsal time on specific sections of a work, as he indulged in the rôle of pedagogue. This practice tended to evoke mild ridicule from some musicians who considered the rendition of standard works a simple routine and who had no patience with Webern's obsession for perfection. Webern's constant complaint that conductors were not given adequate opportunity for preparation was, in reality, a result of his painstakingly methodical and consequently slow approach, which often caused a disproportionate allocation of the available time. Ernst Krenek has corroborated this fact: "As an interpreter of music, Webern was an implacable perfectionist—an attitude characteristic of all of Schoenberg's disciples. . . . The demands Webern made upon himself and his musicians were so severe that frequently the purpose of such efforts, that is, the presentation of the music, was jeopardized."[9] On the other hand, Krenek has also said that when Webern conducted a Haydn symphony he made it sound in such a way that one felt one had understood it for the first time.

Webern was fully aware of the critical eye with which professional musicians watch conductors, and whenever he established an especially satisfying rapport with an orchestra he recorded it in his diary. He was free from such considerations when he stood before his amateur chorus because then he did not have to be concerned with any standards except his own. According to Josef Polnauer, "Each rehearsal became an elevating experience. Webern spent himself to the last at all times; he was always totally keyed up, encouraging, inspiring. But also inexorably exacting. He did not let the slightest inaccuracy or insufficiency slip through. At that, his patience was inexhaustible, again and again he resorted to friendly persuasion and encouraged improvement. Never a harsh word fell, let alone a hurtful one."[10]

Hans Humpelstetter, a member of the Singverein, called Webern "one possessed by his mission." Humpelstetter's memoirs include numerous anecdotes from the Singverein epoch. These stories point not only to Webern's devotion to the task at hand, but also to his dynamic leadership in lifting the chorus of working-class men above the cultural level of their background and education into the highest spheres of art. As he raised the comprehension of his singers he imparted to them the essence of his own convictions. While rehearsing the *Gesang der Parzen* by

Brahms, he told them: "A more modern, or shall we better say, a more 'futuristic' music has not yet been written." When giving his directions for the closing chorus of Mahler's Second Symphony, "Auferstehn, ja auferstehn . . .," he denied that it should be rendered in the manner of a slowly moving funeral march: "In this music there is no trace of sadness. No, to the contrary: it is light, serene, joyful." On another occasion he said of the same choral passage: "You must sing this like a folksong, for a folksong is *never* sentimental."

Humpelstetter recalled many more such incidents, some serious, others humorous, quoting Webern in his pronounced Viennese dialect. The vivid memoirs close with a portentous remark that Webern, sensing a dark future, made towards the end of the Singverein's existence: "Our task is *to carry forth what must stand absolutely above all things—the spiritual. When everything collapses* we will go and sing Schoenberg's 'Friede auf Erden' [Peace on Earth]."[11]

Another Singverein member, Hans Csap, later described their leader's achievement: "With true mastery and loving sensitivity, Anton Webern understood how to bring us workers closer even to a Schoenberg. The most important thing for us singers from the working classes was that we learned through such music to really hear for the first time, and this was the great merit of Anton Webern."[12]

Humbly as Webern stood before a great composer's genius, he was proudly confident of his own competence as an interpreter. This is illustrated by an anecdote told by Mark Brunswick, who once took Webern to a concert in which Toscanini conducted the Vienna Philharmonic. After the performance of Brahms' Third Symphony, Brunswick asked Webern how he liked it. The reply was: "Basically, as *I* am doing it."[13] Webern's self-assurance caused him to be critical or even disdainful of certain maestros whose mannerisms he considered as egotistical showmanship rather than as serving the ends of true interpretation. In a letter to Zenk on 17 December 1927, he advised him in his work as a theatre conductor at Meissen: "Just keep on as you are doing: pure objectivity must win in the end. It is frightful and abhorrent how, to a great extent, only the pose, the appearance, not objectivity governs almost all conductors of today and especially those of rank (yes, they indeed have risen for just that reason). Just look for once at the General Music Director in your neighbouring city (Dresden)![14] You will be quite astounded."

In his musical tastes, Webern leaned heavily on the German tradition and was ever critical of music from other national schools. Arnold Elston recalled that Webern, on hearing Toscanini conduct Debussy's symphonic poem *La Mer*, said, "Everything sounds like an introduction." Elston also related: "In either 1934 or 1935 the French

Embassy in Vienna invited Webern to conduct a concert of contemporary French music, which included Roussel's Third Symphony. Though the engagement would have brought him much-needed funds, he declined, declaring Roussel's work 'wretched.' To Webern the whole neo-classic movement was regressive and a mutilation of the great classical tradition."

Although he knew the music of Béla Bartók well, Webern apparently lacked affinity for it. Elston reported that "upon hearing Bartók's Quartet No. 4, Webern remarked: 'It is too cacophonous for me.' Evidently, Webern's aural sensibilities were such that, though he was fond of the most complex dissonant chords, he found the Bartókian clusters of minor seconds grating on the ear." On the other hand, he appears to have liked Leoš Janáček's music. "In view of their totally dissimilar styles and aesthetics," Elston commented, "it is curious that Webern always spoke of Janáček with respect. He may have known the composer personally and this may have coloured his judgement. Perhaps a certain rough-hewn quality, an ingenuousness of tone and a kind of homespun originality in the Czech composer stood for the diametrical opposite which attracts." Bach, Beethoven, Mozart, Schubert, Brahms, Bruckner, Mahler, and Schoenberg were Webern's idols. Best of all he loved the music of Gustav Mahler. While rehearsing Mahler's Sixth Symphony, Elston related, he once made the orchestra hold a certain chord for a seemingly endless time, apologizing to the musicians: "I simply must revel in this sonority for a little while. Who knows whether I shall ever hear the work again!"[15]

In the early 'twenties, Webern gave a conducting course at the Schwarzwald School. The class, which met in the gymnasium, was attended mainly by aspiring young musicians from Schoenberg's seminar for composition. Among the participants were several men who later attained prominence, such as Frederic Dorian (Friedrich Deutsch), Fritz Mahler, Karl Rankl, and Hans Swarowsky. Dorian later described the proceedings. The study programme included both operatic and symphonic repertoire. A piano and a small group of instruments served as a substitute orchestra. Illustrating operatic passages, Webern both played and sang. "He was no piano virtuoso," Dorian wrote, "but he played accurately and freely and he sang all the parts with passionate conviction, without ever 'simulating'. . . . He taught that beating time as such was 'like swimming' and he gaily commanded, 'jump right away into the water and start kicking.'" He held that the fine points of conducting technique could wait. "'The *Pinseln* [using the paint brush] is the least,' Webern said disdainfully, 'and any donkey can learn this.' Whoever has seen his gentle or sometimes ecstatically demanding manner of signalling knows how fundamentally different it was from

the choreographic style of the podium virtuosos, whom Webern liked to
call 'dancers.'" According to Dorian, the baton was obligatory even
during study. "He rejected as a futile venture the manner of conducting
from memory without a music stand, so popular nowadays, and
unmasked it as a pose of the conducting virtuosos."[16]

Beethoven was the central figure of the conducting course, which
began with the First Symphony and culminated in *Fidelio*. On 16
December, the anniversary of the master's birth, Webern reflected,
"Beethoven's birthday should be observed by all humanity as the most
important of holidays!" Dorian commented:

> Such views of general and deeply-human associations were typical of
> Webern's way of looking at things. He had a preference for symbol
> and metaphor. He discovered ever new inter-relationships between
> music and humanism. The frame of an individual musical discipline
> was kept as broad as possible. Thus the conducting course proceeded
> to an awareness of interpretation in the widest sense; basic as well as
> ultimate artistic concepts were discussed time and again. Every
> solution to a problem was supported by the ethic of an artistic attitude
> that had its deepest roots in Beethoven's ideal of humanity.

Besides Beethoven, Webern loved Mozart, whose music was closely
akin to his own sensibility and temperament. He gloried in every
manifestation of that supreme genius, in the perfect balance Mozart
achieved between the playfulness of the rococo style and such dramatic
elements as the spirit of revolution in *The Marriage of Figaro* or the
demoniacal aspects of *Don Giovanni*. Fritz Mahler later remembered that
Webern emphasized the "sensuous" quality of Mozart's music, which he
felt embodied, in the guise of pure beauty, the gamut of human
emotions.[17] When Samuel Flor, an orchestra musician who frequently
played under Webern, once asked him whom he considered the best of
all Mozart conductors, the reply was: "He who can laugh the most
heartily!"[18]

*   *   *

The cessation of Webern's conducting activities, which had been
precipitated by the February revolution of 1934, compounded his
economic plight. However, he was somewhat relieved by Amalie's
marriage to Gunter Waller, which alleviated the financial burdens
brought on by her chronic illness. Moreover, two of his other children,
Maria and Peter, were given employment in Waller's business.

That first year of her marriage, Amalie surprised her father at
Christmas-time with a brown and white checkered scarf, purchased at

C. & H. Habig, Vienna's most exclusive haberdashery. She remembered the child-like delight that the present excited, for her father would never have thought of buying even so modest an item at the fashionable store. Made of fine English wool, the scarf was cherished by Webern to his last days, and he can be seen wearing it in numerous photographs. As time went by, Wilhelmine's skilful fingers mended each worn spot.[19]

Totally unspoiled, Webern could become exuberant over any new acquisition. "I will initiate my new hiking suit. I am curious what you will say about it!" he wrote to Zenk on 1 July 1936, when asking him to decide on the destination for a proposed Sunday outing. "Let us get a really early start!" he urged. "At dawn if possible. And in any kind of weather! Any weather!!!" The tribulations of the Barcelona experience and its Vienna aftermath had filled Webern with a need to seek the healing embrace of nature. When conditions did not permit him to go to the high mountains, he loved to wander for hours in the hills of the Vienna Woods, with their many vista points and hidden meadows.

During that summer of 1936, Webern, disregarding his limited means, allowed himself a two-week holiday. On Sunday, 25 July, he, his wife, and their youngest daughter, Christine, left for Uttendorf, a village in the Pinzgau, a wide valley in the northern Hohe Tauern Range. Close by is Mittersill (where Webern later was to meet his tragic fate), and the family went there repeatedly on their walks. On the day they departed for Uttendorf, Webern had written to Hueber that he hoped to find "cheap, peasant-like and solitary" accommodation. His expectations were fulfilled, for on 31 July he reported to Zenk:

> I would like to say that I could not imagine a place more suitable for me. The extensive view up and down the valley, the snow-covered mountains, the tremendous expanse of forests enveloping the foothills, and those charming settlements: the ancient farm-houses, hay huts, etc. It is really magnificent, beyond all expectation. We are being taken care of in a simply ideal way. The meals are *incredibly* plentiful and *how good!* We are in fact quite alone here, and the innkeepers take care of us in the most touching manner. Last night it snowed even in the lower altitudes. For breakfast the room was heated for us—in July! Just as I wished it for myself!

The weather was changeable, and the plan of a glacier trip to the Venediger had to be abandoned. Only towards the end of the vacation period, on 5 August, could Webern make a mountain tour. With R. Maier, the innkeeper, he climbed to the summit of the nearby Brustkogel (2,302 m.). He savoured this experience to the last fibre of his being, as his description to Zenk a week later reflects: "It is a steep grass mountain. One often had to crawl on all fours, but this between Edelweiss and Kohlröschen! And up there! The most beautiful vista I ever had in the mountains. A monstrous knife-edged ridge, snow-white, could be seen. Unbelievable! . . . Yes, indeed, when one ascends a generally unknown mountain it always is a most beautiful experience." On 9 August, Webern returned home, refreshed in mind and body. On a picture postcard of the Bichlwirt Inn, kept among his souvenirs of that summer, he wrote longingly: "Have come to like the inn and the R. Maier family very much. Wish: to go there again."

Soon thereafter, a letter from Schoenberg arrived, the first in eight months.

It is so sad that we so rarely have letters from eath other [Schoenberg wrote on 27 August]. But I am convinced that, just as I write many letters to you in thoughts, you, too, discuss with me every interesting matter. Unfortunately, letters are a very inadequate surrogate. I would like very much to have you here, and I have made repeated attempts to get you for a couple of concerts at the Hollywood Bowl. Would you wish to do this even if you had only a small net gain? [Outlining financial details, Schoenberg summed up:] The net income would amount to about $1,000. This is little, but we would at least talk to each other once again to our hearts' content and you could be our guest as long as you like. In any case, I will try to start some promotion for you here—but naturally I cannot know whether it will be of any use. I only would like it so much. At any rate, I would like to know whether you would consider something like this. There is not much prospect for other concerts. In three years, I myself have conducted only five times, two of them here! . . . Now let us still hope that there will be no war; it is ugly enough in the world without one.

The correspondence between the friends had dwindled to a few letters each year. In the autumn of 1934, Schoenberg had moved to California. At first he had been enchanted with the southern climate and his new surroundings, but he was soon disillusioned in his hopes of having come upon a musical Eldorado. The prevailing concepts and standards of social and cultural life vexed him, and the customary methods for success were frustrating to one who had always obeyed only the dictates of his artistic conscience. Yet he never wavered in his self-assurance. Indomitable in spirit, he valiantly coped with the problems of building a new existence at an age when other men begin thinking of retirement. In a long letter, dated 15 January 1936, Schoenberg had brought Webern up to date. In that report, which was spiced with derogatory observations of the musical scene in Los Angeles, he related that, the preceding autumn, he had been appointed to the faculty of the University of Southern California, where he went twice weekly for lecture courses, but that he was already considering a change. The University of California at Los Angeles (UCLA) had offered him a tenured professorship, which he was inclined to accept. "To be sure, the pay is miserable," he wrote. "In purchasing power it is hardly a third of my Berlin salary, and it is difficult to make ends meet with it if I do not earn something on the side. Private lessons cannot be depended on . . . for professional jealousy rages here more vehemently than in Europe, and every little teacher of harmony sees in me a competitor whom he would like to get rid of."

In the same letter, Schoenberg described the annoyances he had encountered with a concert in which he conducted the Los Angeles Philharmonic Orchestra in a programme of his own works, including *Verklärte Nacht* and his new Suite in G Major for string orchestra.[20] The guest engagement had come about through the personal efforts of the orchestra's musical director, Otto Klemperer (who was to perform Webern's Symphony, Op. 21, in Vienna that autumn).

Schoenberg, much as he resented what he considered the lack of recognition accorded him in America, still tried to make his influence felt in the promotion of Webern. When Hermann Scherchen submitted to Schoenberg the programme outline for an international music festival, Schoenberg wrote to him on 16 March 1936: "It is obviously a very big affair indeed, and if there is anything I miss, it is Webern. I should be sorry if he, who, like myself of old, is always left out of things, would be given further cause for bitterness. He is, after all, one of the most original figures in the musical life of our time."[21]

In the autumn of 1936, Schoenberg moved to a stately house at 116 North Rockingham Avenue, close to the campus of UCLA. The university welcomed him to its faculty with a most distinctive tribute: during January 1937 the Kolisch Quartet, through the generosity of Mrs Coolidge, presented a series of four concerts, in each of which a Beethoven quartet was paired with one by Schoenberg. (The latter's Fourth String Quartet received its première during this series.) Such honour notwithstanding, Schoenberg was soon disenchanted again. On 30 April he wrote to Adolph Weiss: "This *Un-Universität* [non-university], as I call it, is a big disappointment for me. None of the promises made to me was kept. I, who can communicate to a certain number of 'masters' many a secret still unknown to them, remain a music teacher for beginners. And although I have indeed long been accustomed to strewing pearls before swine (almost always), this is really rather oppressive."

Despite such bitter remarks, Schoenberg stayed on with the

University, which permitted him to continue beyond the usual retirement age of 65, until 1944, when he turned 70. Finally obliged to leave, he was outraged, feeling that his unimpaired faculties of mind and body should not be subjected to the compulsions of a bureaucratic regulation. So much did he resent the affront to his dignity that he is said to have prevailed on his wife not to drive by the campus when they were out for a ride. He carried this deep resentment to his death. Nevertheless, the building housing the music department of the University of California today bears his name: Schoenberg Hall.

*   *   *

In October 1936, Otto Klemperer came to Vienna as guest conductor for two concerts, one under the auspices of the local ISCM and one with the Philharmonic (in the latter he and Krasner introduced Berg's Violin Concerto to Vienna). Undoubtedly due to the representations of Schoenberg, he had included Webern's Symphony, Op. 21, in the ISCM programme. Klemperer was familiar with the work (he had conducted it once before in Berlin in 1931), but Webern was nonetheless apprehensive. Press reviews had been generally derogatory and, worse still, the reaction of his friends after the Symphony's earlier Vienna performances had convinced the composer that his work was not properly understood. On 9 October Webern wrote to Polnauer: "The more I occupy myself with my symphony the more urgent does my wish become that at least the *very closest* of my friends might, through the coming performance, gain an appropriate impression of it, i.e. I have an abounding desire to explain it, above all, to *you and Zenk* as thoroughly as possible. So I request *you both most urgently* to come out to my home on *Sunday afternoon* so that I can play and explain the Symphony to you." A postscript ominously announces: "I have resolved to show and tell everything to Klemperer, as far as this is possible." Webern's sceptical attitude towards the eminent conductor can be explained not only by his consuming desire to see his work fully comprehended but also by the fact that there was little personal sympathy between the two men.[22]

At the rehearsals for his Symphony Webern appeared nervous. Besides his work, compositions by Schoenberg and Stravinsky were on the programme. Eric Simon, who then played clarinet in the orchestra, related this episode: "Webern was obviously upset by Klemperer's sober time-beating. He thought that if you did not go through physical and mental stresses and strains a performance was bound to be poor. During intermission he turned to the concert master and said: 'You know, Herr Gutmann, the phrase there in measure so-and-so must be played "Tiiiiiiiiii-aaaaaaaaa."'" Klemperer, overhearing the conversation, turned around and said sarcastically: 'Herr Gutmann, now you probably know exactly how you have to play the passage!'"[23]

Peter Stadlen, who sat with Webern at the concert, later provided a first-hand account of the composer's reaction after the performance: "Webern felt rather gloomy because the world-famous conductor had not spent nearly enough time discussing the work with him—and there had been occasional waves of mirth during rehearsals. The moment the performance was over, Webern turned to me and said with some bitterness: 'A high note, a low note, a note in the middle—like the music of a madman!'"[24]

Having definite concepts of the correct interpretation of his music, the composer could not help being exasperated by any rendition diverging from his own intentions. He was convinced that if his music were correctly projected it would elicit favourable response from the audience, and he felt that it was unnecessary for the listener to have prior knowledge in order to understand his music. This belief was expressed on 14 January 1937 in a letter to Nicolas Slonimsky, who had recently published the diminutive fourth movement from the Five Pieces for Orchestra, Op. 10, on the Children's Page of the *Christian Science Monitor*. Delighted, Webern wrote: "I am deeply touched that my music appears on the Children's Page. If only grown-ups were like children, free from prejudice against everything new!"

There were two other public performances of Webern works in Vienna that season. On 25 April 1937, Walter Gutmann, violinist, and George Robert, pianist, played the Four Pieces, Op. 7, in the third concert of the chamber music series, Konzerte moderner Musik.[25] Held in the Kleinkunstbühne ABC in the Café Arkaden, the concert was sold out and repeated on 2 May. On Friday, 14 May, the Kolisch Quartet played Webern's Five Movements, Op. 5, in a programme featuring the first Vienna performance of Schoenberg's Fourth String Quartet, composed the year before and premièred in Los Angeles. (The Schoenberg work was played twice, with Webern's quartet in between.)

To celebrate the 50th anniversary of the birth of Georg Trakl, the great Austrian poet who had died tragically at the age of 27, a memorial was scheduled for 15 March. Both Josef Humplik and Webern were asked to contribute to the event, the former with a display of his Trakl bust, and the composer with his Six Songs on Poems of Trakl, Op. 14, to be sung by Julia Nessy. On 23 February Webern wrote to the Humpliks: "If only I can get the songs worked out well. This is at present a grave worry for me. They are so difficult and conditions in Vienna are becoming more and more unsuitable for them. Yet, let us hope in the meantime that the project succeeds." As it turned out, various problems arose, causing the programme to be postponed and finally cancelled altogether.

During the year 1937, political conditions in Austria grew ever more critical.[26] Frequent and violent demonstrations by Nazi supporters revealed the government's weakness in dealing with the rising movement. As always during times of tension, Webern sought escape in nature. With Ludwig Zenk, he went for long hikes even in mid-winter. Zenk and Webern's cousin Ernst Diez were his companions on that year's major excursion, an outing into the glacier world of the Ötztal Alps, begun on 21 July. Webern's diary notes, giving a full account of the week's itinerary, include such details as the price for lodgings (as low as "Sch. 1, 60" at one of the stations), mountain peaks ascended (Seen-Platte and Hohe Mutt), flowers found, weather encountered, glaciers traversed, and huts used as shelters in the high regions. On 27 July, Diez and Zenk set out for a climb, leaving Webern back in the Remelhaus. When they returned in the afternoon, they were surprised to find a note from him saying that he had left for home. Webern's own chronicle records that he was "feeling ill," but to Polnauer he wrote that day from Obergurgl: "I will tell you verbally why I am coming home earlier than originally planned." The remark suggests that there may have been another reason. However, if there was dissension within the party, as can easily be caused by the strain of climbing in high altitudes, it was not serious, for in September Webern invited Zenk to a farewell party for Diez, who was leaving for another teaching engagement in America. The envelope with inscribed picture postcards from the Ötztal trip is the last in Webern's collection of mountain souvenirs that he had begun in 1923. Several photographs taken by Zenk during the tour are extant. These include one showing Webern with ice-axe and rucksack on the way to the Fidelitas Hut, silhouetted against the majestic backdrop of glaciers and peaks (see insert).

All through the year 1937, Webern worked on the string quartet he had begun two months after completing his Variations, Op. 27. In autumn, a commission from America fired his efforts to finish the composition. That season, the number of Webern's private pupils increased, to reach its highest level just before the Anschluss, the upheaval that temporarily wiped out this main source of his livelihood. Webern's income book lists another lecture course between December 1937 and March 1938. Among the listeners who made up his audience at Dr Kurzmann's home was Zenk's wife, Maria. Aside from the faithful Polnauer, there were only a few professional musicians in attendance. Consequently, Webern had to be more concerned with a basic introduction to musical form than with advanced analyses.

Webern's Piano Variations, Op. 27, published in early May of 1937, had their first performance by Peter Stadlen on 26 October (see Chapter XXVIII). A repeat performance took place on 30 October in a concert of the Verein für neue Musik. On 6 November, the reviewer for the *Neue Freie Presse* commented caustically: "Here the musical solution to the much contested problem of smashing the atom has succeeded."

This occasion was the last time that Webern was able to hear his own music publicly performed in his native city. As he well knew, it was already branded "degenerate art" in Germany. This terminology, of Third Reich coinage, stemmed from the cultural pronouncements in Hitler's *Mein Kampf*, and no time had been lost after the Nazi take-over ruthlessly to enforce the dictates of the Führer to their last consequences. The extremism of the new policies had been blatantly exhibited to the world as early as 10 May 1933 with an act of "purification." On that evening, some 20,000 books were publicly burned in Berlin under the approving eye of Dr Joseph Goebbels, Hitler's Propaganda Minister.[27] As the flames signalled the abolition of free intellect and speech, Goebbels jubilantly exclaimed: "The soul of the German people can again express itself. These flames not only illuminate the end of an old era, they also light up the new."

Despite that early sounding of the Nazi death knell to German culture, Webern's essentially optimistic outlook did not permit him to succumb to whatever apprehensions he may have harboured for the future. In conversation with his friends, especially those who were Jews, he maintained for years that Hitler, after satisfying his followers with an initial display of raw power, would moderate his policies. Steuermann engaged in heated discussions with Webern during those early years of the Hitler régime. On a stroll through the Schwarzenberg gardens, Webern voiced the firm belief that everything would work out eventually, an attitude Steuermann angrily condemned as complacent.[28] Felix Galimir related an episode that occurred in the Café Museum, where the group used to gather after concerts. One of the frequent political controversies arose: "Dr Bach at one point became very critical of the Germans' attitude towards the Jews. At that point Webern interrupted him: 'But David, not all Germans are Nazis!' Thereupon Dr Bach closed the discussion with the words: 'Every German who has not given absolute proof to the contrary is a Nazi.'"[29]

Louis Krasner, Galimir's brother-in-law, stated that Webern had persuaded him, in April 1936, to travel to Barcelona via Munich for the explicit purpose of stopping off in that hotbed of Hitlerism, just to prove to the American that life in Germany proceeded quite normally.[30] During those years, Webern still sincerely believed that the spreading stories of Nazi atrocities were exaggerated propaganda machinations of the radical left-wing opposition, and that the entire issue was beclouded by irrationality. With a naïveté as incredible in retrospect as it was tragic, Webern continued to assure his friends that the Nazi régime, were it to envelop Austria, would lead to a victory of the cultural precepts for which they had all been fighting for so long. Felix Greissle remembered frequent debates in 1936 and 1937 in which Webern steadfastly maintained that, with the coming of a new order to Austria, Mahler's music, too, would "arrive" at long last. Nothing could convince him that anti-Semitism held no regard for personal greatness, and not until reality proved him wrong was he shaken out of the illusion that the works of Mahler, Schoenberg, and Karl Kraus would be spared the fate heralded by the burning of the books. Hans Erich Apostel, Berg's pupil, recalled Webern saying: "One should attempt to convince the Hitler régime of the rightness of the twelve-tone system."[31] Such was Webern's blind optimism during a time when systematic moves to consolidate the Nazi-ordained cultural doctrines in Germany followed each other in quick succession.[32]

30 August 1935 was the date of a decree by the Reichsmusikkammer that non-Aryans could not be employed in German orchestras. This law affected not only Jews but anyone having one Jewish parent or even a single Jewish grandparent. On 12 October of the same year all jazz music was banned from the German broadcasting system "to do away with the last remnants of the culture-Bolshevist Jew." On 1 March 1936 *Die Musik*, Germany's leading music periodical, issued a special anti-Semitic number. Two of the articles bore the revealing titles "Mendelssohn, Mahler and We" and "The Jew as Musical Manufacturer." Illustrated with pictures of Mendelssohn, Meyerbeer, Offenbach, Mahler, Schoenberg, Toch, Weill, and Klemperer, the issue was prefaced by quotations from Hitler's writings on the subject of Jews in the arts. International activities of any sort were suspected of Jewish influence. One month before the 1936 ISCM festival at Barcelona, a music festival at Baden-Baden was given in undisguised opposition to it. The programme included only those foreign composers approved by the organizers. In order to crush the last remnants of free artistic spirit, the 76-year-old Allgemeiner Deutscher Musikverein was dissolved in a general meeting at Munich on 19 July 1937. It was claimed that the society was alien to the totalitarian philosophy of the Third Reich and incompatible with the musical ideals of the Hitler youth.

One day before that act, Hitler delivered a tirade on the subject of "degenerate art." The occasion was the formal opening of Munich's House of German Art, a dreary edifice in pseudo-classic style, which Hitler himself had helped design, and which he described as "unparalleled and inimitable" in its architecture. The Führer considered himself a genuine artist, although he had failed in his early attempts to become a painter. His tastes, determined as they were by political tenets, were now imposed as the absolute artistic law of the land. Some 6,500 paintings were removed from German galleries.[33] In his 18 July address, Hitler proclaimed the standards that henceforth were to govern all artistic expression:

> Works of art that cannot be understood but need a swollen set of instructions to prove their right to exist and find their way to neurotics who are receptive to such stupid or insolent nonsense will no longer openly reach the German nation. Let no one have illusions! National Socialism has set out to purge the German Reich and our people of all those influences threatening its existence and character. . . . With the opening of this exhibition has come the end of artistic lunacy and with it the artistic pollution of our people. . . . From now on we will conduct a merciless war of purification against the last elements of our cultural decomposition.[34]

In 1936, Hitler had fulfilled his promise to restore Germany's military might. Despite repeated professions that he wanted peace, he had ordered the occupation of the demilitarized Rhineland by German troops in early March of that year. The French, torn by internal strife and seized by a mood of defeatism, stood by as Hitler for the first time exerted brute force in his international relations. The Führer's next objective was to bring the German-speaking people of other countries into the fold of a greater Germany. Since he himself was a native of the Austrian border town of Braunau, he held that the incorporation of his fatherland was mandatory. Obsessed by this idea, he had worked towards its realization since the beginning of his reign as chancellor. After five years of plotting, subversion, and violence, he had brought Austria to the brink of a crisis. On 11 February 1938, the eve of the fourth anniversary of the bloody Socialist uprising, Hitler summoned the Austrian Chancellor, Dr Kurt von Schuschnigg, to the "Adlerhorst", his mountain retreat near Berchtesgaden. During a stormy meeting the following day, the German dictator, threatening military occupation of Austria, forced Schuschnigg to sign an agreement granting far-reaching concessions, such as the appointment of Arthur Seyss-Inquart as Minister of Security (and thereby Chief of Police), the admission of several other pro-Nazi members to the cabinet, and an amnesty for imprisoned Austrian Nazis. Triumphant at his success, Hitler broadcast a speech on 20 February that set off a series of Nazi demonstrations throughout Austria. Schuschnigg, gravely alarmed, addressed the Bundestag, warning: "Thus far and no farther." While conciliatory towards Germany, Schuschnigg vowed at the same time that Austria

would never voluntarily relinquish its independence. Referring to the
national colours, he exclaimed: "Red-white-red until we're dead!"

During this speech, relayed by broadcast, a wild demonstration took
place in Graz. A mob of some 20,000 Nazi supporters went on a
rampage, tearing down the loudspeakers in the city's main square and
hoisting the swastika in place of the Austrian flag. With Hitler's deputy,
Seyss-Inquart, in command of the police, no attempt was made to curb
the outbreak. Clearly, Schuschnigg's government was breaking down.
Since the February revolution of 1934, a one-party régime had ruled
the country. Schuschnigg tried valiantly to gain the support of the
Socialists, but it was too late. The political chaos was hastened by
economic pressures. There were wholesale cancellations of orders from
firms in foreign countries and the banks were besieged by withdrawals of
funds. The tourist trade, a mainstay of the country's economy, was in
jeopardy, with thousands of visitors leaving in haste.

In a desperate move, Schuschnigg announced in a speech given at
Innsbruck on 9 March 1938 that a plebiscite would be held on 13 March
to determine the will of the people to remain free. The surprise action
infuriated Hitler. He decided on military force to subjugate Austria. By
11 March, German troops were mobilized along the frontier and Hitler
urged Mussolini, his Fascist ally, not to counteract his intentions. On
that fateful day, Germany issued an ultimatum: the plebiscite must be
called off or there would be an invasion. When Schuschnigg submitted
to that demand, it was further stipulated that he should resign. He
complied.

Louis Krasner was present in the Webern home the afternoon of that
critical day, 11 March. Webern had turned on the radio, saying that
something important was about to happen. In the early evening,
Schuschnigg went on the air announcing his resignation as chancellor
and delivering a farewell address which was to become the obituary for
Austria as an independent country:

> I declare before the world [he climaxed his moving speech] that the
> reports launched in Germany concerning disorders by the workers,
> the shedding of streams of blood, and the creation of a situation
> beyond the control of the Austrian government are lies from A to Z.
> President Miklas has asked me to tell the people of Austria that we
> have yielded to force since we are not prepared even in this terrible
> hour to shed blood. We have decided to order the troops to offer no
> resistance. So I take leave of the Austrian people with a German word
> of farewell, uttered from the depth of my heart: God protect
> Austria![35]

On the morning of 12 March, the German Army crossed the border, and Hitler returned in triumph to his native soil. At noon, Goebbels read a proclamation that the Austrian people would now be offered the opportunity for a "real plebiscite" to decide their future destiny. The jubilation with which the German troops were greeted by those who believed that strong authority would put an end to the long turmoil encouraged Hitler to carry out his full intentions immediately. On the afternoon of 12 March he instructed his legal expert, Dr Wilhelm Stuckart, to "draft a law providing for a total Anschluss." (Originally, Hitler had thought only of becoming president of Austria.) The country's independence ended, in effect, the following day, 13 March, when the officials of the newly appointed government under Seyss-Inquart signed the draft into law. It was ratified on 10 April by a mock plebiscite, with pressure tactics and questionable procedures prevailing at the polls. The nation's name, Austria, was abolished and the country henceforth became merely an extension of the German Reich.

On 12 March 1938, that fateful day when the swastika flags were hoisted over Austria, when the goose-step of the German troops and the rumbling of their armoured cars resounded in the streets of towns and villages, when bands blared, and the brown-shirted storm troopers paraded everywhere, singing the "Horst Wessel-Lied" as their hymn of victory, Webern wrote to the Humpliks: "I am totally immersed in my work and cannot, cannot be disturbed." A note on page 90 of Sketch-book IV reads: "13th March, incorporation of Austria into the German Reich." It is impossible to imagine the emotions behind the terse statement with which Webern recorded this momentous event.

CHAPTER XXVIII

Opera 26–28
(1935–1938)

WEBERN HAD BEEN used to opposition on aesthetic grounds almost from the beginning of his career. But his struggle for independent artistic survival became hopeless when the issue was politically compounded. Although he was an Aryan and had always prided himself on carrying forth the great German tradition, his music was by now summarily dismissed in Germany as "cultural Bolshevism." Not for a single moment was he deterred from his course, however. Convinced of the infallibility of his chosen idiom, he continued to turn out work after work in which he perfected the new language of the twelve-tone method. With little hope of recognition or of hearing his music performed, he found joy and satisfaction in the lonely pursuit of his art, more specifically in the continual exploration of its still uncharted dimensions.

Having decided not to attend the Prague festival in early September 1935, Webern continued to devote himself fully to a work that had occupied him since February of that year: *Das Augenlicht*, Op. 26, for mixed chorus and orchestra. On 7 February, immediately after completing his Ricercar transcription, he had written to Hildegard Jone:[1]

You ask me what I intend to write next: originally, I thought, an orchestral piece; but I am also thinking of writing a *choral work with orchestra* on a text of yours, and at the moment this is uppermost in my mind. But I have not found the text as yet. I have looked through everything of yours that I possess with this in mind. It is not possible to describe what I envision. If the text is there, I will know it. . . . If only I could see your new works! . . . It is so urgent for me because I would like to—I must—go to work right away.

The composer's desire for a new poetic vehicle was soon satisfied. "I have found what I was looking for: *Das Augenlicht* from *Viae inviae*, and have started work already," he informed Hildegard Jone on 24 February.

The beginnings of the composition appear on page 22 of Sketchbook IV under the date of 19 February 1935. Drafting the row occupied Webern until 14 March, at which time he began working out the condensed score. After a few measures, however, his progress was interrupted by preparations for the Typographia concert in April and the subsequent trip to England. Not until 14 June could he write to Hildegard Jone: "Gradually things are easing up: I can now turn a little to my work again." A date in the sketchbook confirms that he resumed work on the composition the next day. By 17 June, the earlier sketches were amalgamated into a new and definitive beginning, which combined the choral parts with the condensed orchestral score. The tempo marking then was *Sehr fliessend* (Very flowing); curiously, this concept was changed to *Langsam* (Slow) in the final version. The composition appears to have proceeded steadily until completion of the draft (sketchbook page 42) on 13 September, always a special day for Webern since it was Schoenberg's birthday.

Diary notes interspersed in the sketches record family events: the end of secondary schooling for Peter, Amalie's wedding, and a mountain excursion to the Gross-Venediger. On 21 July, Webern wrote to Hildegard Jone: "Now, thank God, I can stay entirely with my work," and on 17 September, he informed her: "The *Augenlicht* is finished. Now I am writing out the full score in fair copy. How much I would like to show you what has come into being." Two days earlier he had written to David Josef Bach in a mixture of elation and self irony: "*I have finished my choral piece.* And I hope it is so good that (if people ever get to know it) they will declare me ready for a concentration camp or an insane asylum!" Completion of the final score was reported to Hildegard Jone on 29 September. Totally withdrawn while engrossed in the creative process, Webern doubly felt the need of communication once it was over. On 15 October, he wrote to the poetess:

I would like to tell you a few things, foremost among them something that I would have wished to give expression to *long ago* and especially at the time when you asked me: namely, how much your words again had meant to me! "O Meer des Blickes mit der Tränenbrandung!" [Oh, the ocean of a glance with its surf of tears!] (It lies just in the middle of the piece and constitutes at the same time its dynamic climax.) What a thought! And then in its continuation (musically, the greatest possible contrast follows *immediately*) you awaken an image that can only be the quintessence of all loveliness, all kindliness: "Die Tropfen, welche sie versprüht auf Wimpernhalme, vom Herzen und der Sonne werden sie beschienen." [The drops it sprays on the blades of an eyelash are shone on by the heart and the sun] Thus a mode of representation is provided that I can only regard as the highest: the tears, a drop of water, "shone on by the heart and the sun." And what makes them flow? The answer is no longer needed.

Das Augenlicht is inscribed "To my daughter Amalie Waller," a dedication no doubt commemorating her wedding. Amalie knew nothing of the honour until her father quite casually mentioned it that autumn at a "Heuriger" in the Hasenöhrl at Gumpoldskirchen. The family had been invited by the newly-weds to join in the popular Vienna pastime of spending an evening in one of the many small taverns where the new wine is served. At the gathering Webern spoke of Amalie's beautiful eyes, which shone so brightly when she was happy and were so indescribably sad when she cried. He dwelt on anecdotes from her youth, on the times when passers-by in the streets of Berlin would comment on her large eyes peering up from the baby carriage, or when he—as proud a father as ever lived—would receive admiring comments from total strangers as he carried her in his arms.

It should be noted that Webern dedicated only one other work to a family member, the Symphony, Op. 21, which was inscribed to his youngest daughter, Christine. Curiously, he never bestowed a similar distinction on his wife, although he is known to have often sought her response to his ideas while composing. None of his children ever showed the slightest interest in or understanding of his music, however.

The first performance of *Das Augenlicht* took place on 17 June 1938, during the ISCM festival in London, with Hermann Scherchen conducting (see Chapter XXIX). In order to provide choral parts for the rehearsals, Universal Edition hurriedly brought out, in April of 1938, a piano–vocal score prepared by Webern's pupil, Ludwig Zenk. It was the first and only time that the composer delegated such a task to someone else. There was a compelling reason, however: when Webern learned, in early February 1938, that *Das Augenlicht* had been placed on the ISCM festival programme, he had just begun the final movement of his String Quartet, Op. 28. The commission, recently received from Mrs Coolidge, stipulated that the work's first performance should take place in July of the same year. It was this deadline that caused Webern to entrust Zenk with the *Augenlicht* piano–vocal reduction.[2] The miniature edition of the full score was not published until 1956.

In his letter to Hermann Scherchen, dated 12 April 1938, the composer pointed out: "The work lasts approximately 10 minutes.

Nothing of the choral voices appears in the orchestra (this indeed presents the great difficulty). Everything is obbligato, in a purely polyphonic presentation. Orchestral complement: 4 woodwinds, 3 brass, harp, celesta, mandolin, a little percussion, and 8 violins, sub-divided, 4 violas, 4 celli, no string basses!"

In the printed programme for the London première, a short analytical description of the work appeared.[3] Textual references abound in the synopsis of the formal outline, which points out that the composition is a two-part structure, with the climax occurring in the second part, a modified recapitulation of the first.

Polnauer related that, soon after completion of the work, Webern played it several times for him on the piano. When Polnauer remarked that the music impressed him as being full of cadences, the composer was so overjoyed that he embraced him.[4] Arnold Elston, who studied under Webern at the time, provided this information: "Webern loved Brahms' music and often performed it. While he was composing *Das Augenlicht* he said: 'I am thinking of a cantata like Brahms' *Schicksalslied.*'"

Das Augenlicht, Op. 26, a single-movement work in motet style, is the first in a trilogy of choral pantheons which was to be continued with the cantatas, Opera 29 and 31. The vocal treatment alternates between homophonic and polyphonic passages, some of which are sung *a cappella*. Each voice line represents a complete statement of the twelve-tone row, and the strata of combined rows, often pitched note against note, produces euphonious effects. The orchestral texture, on the other hand, is woven according to the *Klangfarbenmelodie* principle, following the method employed in Webern's Bach transcription. Here the row is fragmented, with single tones or short motives of two or three notes assigned to various instruments. The woodwind and percussion parts are treated soloistically, and consequently the orchestral sound is one of great transparency throughout.

Although the work exemplifies Webern's severely contrapuntal style and abounds in canonic imitations, the effect is one of spontaneous freedom. If the purely instrumental works of the later period tend to make the listener aware of the composer's austere workmanship and supreme intellectual sovereignty, the vocal creations are imbued with the lyricism of the texts and thereby become readily accessible through the immediacy of their emotional content and simplicity of diction.

Webern's next work, the Variations for Piano, Op. 27, was to be rather short, but took almost a year to write. Although there were outside reasons for the slow progress, the composer believed that a creative product required its own time for the maturing process. As Webern was working on the Variations, Ludwig Zenk voiced exasperation over not advancing well with one of his own compositions. Webern reassured him, writing on 12 August 1936: "Naturally, it must be this way. The correspondences for which we aim often allow themselves to be realized only very slowly: whether more slowly or more quickly—you really do not need to be concerned about this. Goethe once told Eckermann that he had meditated over a poem for *40* years! Well then, what do you want!"

The chronicle of Opus 27 is graphically documented in Sketchbook IV (pages 43–56). Webern began his new project on 14 October 1935, signalling it with the title "Klavier-Variationen" and a first draft of the tone row. Two days later he started the actual scoring. During the next eight months only four and a half pages were to be covered. A long series of adversities, beginning with Berg's death, readily accounts for Webern's inability to concentrate. On 12 June 1936 he wrote to Hildegard Jone. ". . . Ever-renewed upsets of a professional sort and such as I have never previously had to endure do not allow me any peace. Thus, I am, apart from brief attempts, still not able to get down to work properly. But now at last it must proceed. Shake off everything, only this can help. But indeed it is often very difficult."

It was in this frame of mind that Webern again set to work on his Variations. After no fewer than seven separate beginnings, the movement (which was to become the closing section of a three-movement composition) was completed on 8 July. In the first draft, comprising 88 numbered measures, seven variations are designated. Two of these, IV and VI, were discarded in the final version.

Ten days later, on 18 July, Webern started another movement. On that day he wrote to the Humpliks: "I am working well at present. I have already finished one part of my new composition. I told you that I was writing something for piano. The completed part is a movement of variations; what is evolving will be a kind of 'suite.' In the variations I hope I have realized something I have envisioned for years now." Webern then cited Goethe's remark, quoted to Zenk, about the long inner preparation sometimes necessary for the ripening of a creative idea. The concept of a "suite" was also mentioned to Polnauer, to whom Webern wrote on 26 July, the day he left for a two-week holiday in Uttendorf: "During the last few weeks I was uninterruptedly at my work and now see that the *variations go on further*, even if they turn into movements of most diverse types."

The first sketches for the new movement, with dates of 18 and 22 July, reveal no fewer than four separate attempts to formulate the opening measures. Whatever problems existed, they were clarified during the composer's introspective sojourn in the Alps. After returning home, he started the movement all over again on 10 August. Work then proceeded smoothly to the last bar-line, dated 19 August. This section was later assigned the opening position in the work. Marked *Sehr mässig* (Very moderate), in 3/16 metre, the movement is clearly in A-B-A form. Constant tempo fluctuations give it an improvisatory character, which, as Peter Stadlen later related, Webern himself compared to that of an intermezzo by Brahms.[5]

"I have in the meantime finished another part of my new work. Now comes, I think, the third and final part," Webern wrote to Hildegard Jone on 23 August. Two days later he began sketching this section, which, in fact, was to become the middle movement. Again, some intrinsic obstacles had to be surmounted at the outset. Preliminary drafts were dated 25 and 29 August. When Webern set out on the definitive version on 1 September, however, he had worked it out so well mentally that it was completed the following day. By way of an afterthought, he revised the endings of the movement's two sections (each of which is repeated). The final date reads "5 September 1936."

In the original draft, Webern gave this movement the tempo designation *Rasch* (Quick). The notation was in quarter notes in *alla breve* time. In the printed version, however, the tempo marking became *Sehr schnell* (Very fast), and the notation was changed into eighth notes in 2/4 time. According to Stadlen, Webern compared the scherzo character of the movement "to that of the 'Badinerie' of Bach's B Minor Overture, of which he said he had thought when composing his piece."[6]

Offered the prospect of early publication, Webern subjected the first draft of his piano "suite" to a complete revision: the movement second in date of composition became a kind of prelude, the scherzo written last was placed in the centre, and the variations composed first were made the finale. In the latter, as in the scherzo, Webern altered the tempo and metre designations: the earlier *Fliessend* (Flowing) became *Ruhig fliessend* (Quietly flowing) and the 3/8 metre was converted to 3/2, all note values undergoing corresponding changes.

The work, published by Universal Edition in May 1937, bears a dedication to Eduard Steuermann. Steuermann later recalled: "Before Webern's Variations were published, Webern sent them to me with a very cordial dedication in a manuscript beautifully copied by Zenk." When asked why he never publicly performed the work, Steuermann claimed "personal reasons,"[7] alluding to the tragic political developments that caused his estrangement from Webern after a friendship of more than a quarter of a century (see Chapter XXX).

On 16 October 1937, Webern informed Josef Humplik: "On 26 October, a local pianist, who is very talented and with whom I am already working hard, will play my Variations for Piano (this is their first performance), and he is to play them again on 30 October in a concert of our Society for New Music, in which there will also be works by Schoenberg." The young pianist was Peter Stadlen. More than twenty years later, he described Webern's painstaking efforts during those rehearsals:

> For weeks on end he had spent countless hours trying to convey to me every nuance of performance down to the finest detail. As he sang and shouted, waved his arms and stamped his feet in an attempt to bring out what he called the meaning of the music I was amazed to see him treat those few scrappy notes as if they were cascades of sound. He kept on referring to the melody which, he said, must be as telling as a spoken sentence. This melody would sometimes reside in the top notes of the right hand and then for some bars be divided between both left and right. It was shaped by an enormous amount of constant rubato and by a most unpredictable distribution of accents. But there were also definite changes of tempo every few bars to mark the beginning of "a new sentence." Again, Webern's extreme demands for differentiation of sound, especially in the field of *pianissimo*, resulted at the time in a friendly rumour that he had introduced the "*pensato*." This meant that a note had to be so indescribably tender and soft that it was only allowed to be thought of.[8]

Dwelling on some of the pianistic details of the work, Stadlen referred to the awkward crossing of hands demanded for the proper execution of the scherzo movement: "Webern said that the inevitable difficulty in bringing it off would invest it with just the right kind of phrasing." Other observations deal with the difficulty of realizing highly syncopated rhythms within the metrical complex and with the abundant use of the sustaining pedal "not only as a means of varying the tone colour but also to make up for the angular thinness of the texture and to increase the sheer volume of sound in climaxes." The use of the sustaining pedal recommended by the composer is of particular importance, since the printed score contains no pedal indications whatever. This and other points caused Stadlen to conclude:

> If Webern omitted to write interpretation marks without which I know he considered his music meaningless, I suggest the reason lay in his dual attitude to his music: on the one hand his urge to express extra-musical contents went to such extremes that the notes had become almost incidental and were only regarded as carriers of expression; at the same time he strove to free music from this very bondage and to restore to it that autonomous structural sense it had

tended to lose during the romantic period. However this may be, it appears that an authentic performance of a Webern score is impossible without direct tradition.

Webern himself distinguished clearly between the craft of composition and the emotional impact of the music. According to Stadlen, he used to say to his pupils: "A composer must learn to listen to the basic series and force it to yield its secrets." As far as the performer and the audience were concerned, however, intimate familiarity with the manipulations of the row was deemed unnecessary. In Stadlen's account:

> Throughout all those weeks of instruction and preparation Webern never once touched on the serial aspect of his Piano Variations. Even when I asked him, he declined to go into it with me—because, he said, it was important that I should know how the work should be played, not how it was made. Nor did he give the impression of a *reservatio mentalis*, of holding something back—as if he thought that perhaps I or his potential audience were not yet ready for it. Indeed, he acted as if he himself were not aware of the serial aspect of his work, or at least never thought of it when playing or discussing it. He seemed to imply by his behaviour that both he and we need only be concerned with the *prima facie* appearance of the correspondences and structures as we see them in the score and as they are made to sound according to his instructions—and that knowledge of their serial implications was not required for a full appreciation of the music.

Webern's own attitude notwithstanding, the serial features of the Variations have made them a favourite object of scrutiny for theorists, who are primarily concerned with the inner workings of a musical organism. They have been intrigued by the geometrical aspects of the row treatment, such as the horizontal and vertical mirror symmetries, particularly developed in the first two movements. As the genesis of the works shows, these two movements evolved only after completion of the original set of variations ("I now see that the *variations go on further*," the composer had written to Polnauer on 26 July 1936), and close attention to the concluding bars of the third movement reveals how Webern was led directly to the configurations of the first movement. Thus the germinal idea procreated itself organically. Through a tradition anchored in Beethoven and Brahms and enforced by Schoenberg's tenets, Webern had made the principle of constantly developing variations so much his own that it had virtually become the generator of all his musical thinking.

While Webern was still working on his Variations for Piano, he briefly considered a proposal made by the violinist Louis Krasner, to which he responsed on 3 August 1936 from Uttendorf: "I can only tell you that I have already almost decided to write something in the spirit of your suggestions. In particular, the thought of a *solo violin sonata* occupies me." Webern asked Krasner to allow him some time, but there is no evidence that he pursued the project further, and in his sketchbook the draft of the piano variations is immediately followed by that of another work. Under the heading "Streichquartett, Op. 28" the new composition makes its appearance on 17 November 1936 (page 57 of Sketchbook IV). On that day both a tone row and an outline were drafted. From the start, the work was planned in three movements. Its formal structure and inspirational ideas were set forth as follows:

development

1. Langsam (slow): seed, life, water (forest)—Ma.
   blossoms—Minn.
   Sonata movement

3. Rondo: Glockner—Mi., Chri.—Annabichl
   Pe.—Finale (personal)
   Scherzando

2. Fuge: Koralpe, Schwabegg (as introduction to the third movement)

As has been pointed out earlier, the localities mentioned were those most cherished by Webern; as always, they include his parents' graves at Schwabegg and Annabichl. The abbreviations denote his wife (Minna) and his four children (Mali, Mitzi, Peter, and Christl).

Under the dates of 19 and 21 November, Webern set to work on a movement headed "I" (a designation later changed to "3. Satz"). He made several attempts to formulate melodic shapes from the row, assigning them to various instruments. Prolonged experimentation, during which the row was gradually transformed to its definitive melodic arrangement, absorbed an inordinately long time, for the next date, appearing towards the bottom of the second page, is 7 April 1937, almost five months after the inception of the project. If progress was slow, the composer was nevertheless constantly concerned with his work. On 3 February he wrote to Hildegard Jone: "I am working on a string quartet. Perhaps I will fulfil with it, in a quite special way, the principles that you formulated in your letter."[9]

Whatever external causes distracted Webern from his new work during that winter, they are not known. The only diary note from that period announces the birth of Amalie's first child, Michael, on 22 March

1937. A proud grandfather, Webern recorded the happy event both in his diary and in his sketchbook. In the latter, he also listed, on 9 May, the child's baptism.

On 7 April Webern began an energetic attempt to redraft the string quartet movement completely, assimilating various ideas from his earlier efforts. There were numerous fresh beginnings marked with dates in May and June. Each time, the composer tried to solve his problems by minor changes of metre and rhythm and, chiefly, by striving for a satisfactory assignment of the various forms of the tone row to individual instruments. The last date, 9 June, was followed by three more abortive starts until (on page 64 of the sketchbook) a definitive version of the beginning was finally attained. It established the contrapuntal allocation of the parts, but the metric designations still differed widely from the final scoring. The tempo, too, was to be changed later from the original *Sehr bewegt* (Very animated) to *Sehr fliessend* (Very flowing). On 20 July Webern informed Hildegard Jone: "I have worked diligently the last few weeks. I look forward to seeing your new pictures with the keenest anticipation and in the joyful expectation of seeing confirmed again what becomes apparent to me ever more clearly: how much our modes of representation resemble each other." The next day, Webern left for a week's excursion into the Ötztal Alps. Returning refreshed and inspired, he completed the draft of the movement on 20 August.

From 21 to 23 August, Webern was on holiday in his beloved Kapellen, the village by the Schneealpe, and on 3 September he launched into the draft of a variation movement (sketchbook page 74) that he designated as "II". (This later became the quartet's opening movement.) Again the creative process posed considerable difficulty. Many measures were crossed out and redrafted. While the 2/2 metre was established from the start, the note values first employed were later to be halved: whole notes were changed to half notes, quarter notes to eighth notes, etc. Accordingly, the 56 numbered measures of the first draft became 112 measures in the printed score, and the tempo marking, first given as *Sehr langsam* (Very slow), was adjusted to *Mässig* (Moderate). In the course of this movement Webern designated each of the variations. At measure 7, he clearly fixed the images of his associations: "K.A. [Koralpe]: spruce forest, source of a brook, garden—Schwabegg." (The two localities, Koralpe and Schwabegg, had appeared in the original outline.)

The composition of this movement was to keep Webern occupied for almost five months. It was far advanced when a letter from the United States arrived, bringing him a happy surprise: the offer of a commission from Mrs Elizabeth Sprague Coolidge. It had been prompted by Rudolf

Kolisch. After his Vienna concert in May 1937 (his quartet then played Webern's Five Movements, Op. 5, together with the first Vienna performance of Schoenberg's Fourth String Quartet, commissioned by Mrs Coolidge), he had suggested to the American patroness that she assist Webern, who was struggling in isolation and sorely needed moral and financial support. In her letter of 23 November 1937, Mrs Coolidge offered the composer a commission "for the writing of something for five wind instruments, preferably without piano."[10] But Kolisch could arrange that the string quartet on which Webern was then working would be acceptable instead and so informed him by telegram. Having experienced disappointment in his hopes for Mrs Coolidge's sponsorship before, Webern was elated. On 23 December he wrote to the Humpliks about the opportune development, which brightened his Christmas holiday: "With regard to the commission from America, some very welcome additional information has arrived: they now want a string quartet instead of some other ·kind ·of chamber music, as originally requested. With that, everything is beautifully resolved: for what I am working on now is a *string quartet*! I therefore do not have to interrupt my work, am not under pressure, and can finish on time without much trouble."

His spirits fired, Webern completed the variation movement on 21 January 1938 and informed the Humpliks on 9 February that he was "about to embark on the third and probably last section." When the composer set out to draft that "last section" on 17 February, however, he headlined it "first movement" (it was subsequently placed in the middle of the work). This movement, which is distinguished by its pizzicato character, is especially interesting in its rhythmic evolution. Webern originally drafted the first twelve measures in 3/8 time. The published version, however, is in 2/4 metre, and the same tonal material is distributed over eighteen measures. Obviously, the original approach sprang from a totally different concept of pulsation. Also, in the first draft no provision is made for a repetition of the movement's closing section; the first ending, appearing in the printed score, was added only later. Extensive revisions must have taken place as the movement was put into final shape. Its tempo, *Gemächlich* (Leisurely), however, was established from the outset.

Webern was in the closing stages of working out this movement when he inserted into his sketchbook the historic record of Austria's annexation by Germany on 13 March 1938. The day before he had written the Humpliks that he was deeply engrossed in his work and could not be disturbed. The draft was completed on 26 March, and with it the end of Sketchbook IV was reached. (On an added sheet, under the date of 1 June, Webern drafted four measures of a quartet scored in 6/8 time, using the same tone row. That afterthought was not used further, however.) On 15 April, the composer wrote to Hildegard Jone: "I have now completed my composition. How much I would like to show it to you. I have a good feeling about it and would like to try at least to tell you something about it at our next meeting." On 5 May, he added: "The score of my new quartet has been sent off to America." In a similar report to Reich, dated 29 April, Webern mentioned that the parts had been mailed to the Kolisch Quartet, then playing in London.

It was to Rudolf Kolisch that the composer first revealed some of the structural features of his latest opus, in a letter of 19 April 1938:

Once again, of course, it has not turned out to be a very extensive work—duration about twenty minutes—but I really have not made it easy for myself: perhaps I have succeeded to a large extent in combining the two styles—the "horizontal" and the "vertical," as Schoenberg calls them. . . . I must confess that hardly ever before have I felt so good about a work of mine (after its completion) as I do this time. It seems to me that I actually had just begun it. Naturally, it has become lyrical again. But in the middle there is a rather long movement: an adagio in a broad *alla breve*. Basically it is a variation movement, though *functionally* the individual variations correspond to the components of an *adagio form*, including *main subject, transitional secondary idea*, and *reprise* (coda); thus it is a fusion of the structural principles of a variation movement and an *adagio* form! Everything is purely polyphonic (canonic with augmentation and diminution, the two elements which control the entire movement).

Preceding and following this adagio are two movements that can be interpreted structurally in several ways. As it is, the one following the adagio brings about the formal fulfilment of the one preceding it. Basically, it is a scherzo, of which the development section, however, introduces a fugue (double fugue), with the *reprise* of the *scherzo-subject* appearing as its *third* exposition. (I would like to say that if ever a reprise was justified, it is this one.) A third exposition with a *double canon*—and, moreover, in *retrograde motion* (subject and counter-subject)—for an "*Engführung*" [stretto]! Thus the *subject* of this scherzo makes its appearance! As a finale, it, too, has become a rather long piece. I think that you will be amazed when I show you the relationships that exist in it (but I am convinced that you will naturally discover many things for yourself), and when you consider the *expression* and *character* of the piece in the face of these constructions. Everything is tender, completely tender!

As to the *first* movement, it is a miniature rondo or simply also a *scherzo with trio!* The first theme is a *perpetual four-part canon*, but nevertheless structurally a "subject" (following strictly classical principles) of eighteen measures; thus there is a combination of the two modes of representation here also, as everywhere else in the quartet. But, it is a canon in which, moreover, *everything* is mirrored in smaller dimensions; whatever moves forward, in the next instant goes backward elsewhere, and so on, but all in accordance with the construction of a "subject." (A constructive, *purely constructive* use of the "rows"—that is the key to everything!!!) Now comes the second theme of the movement—the trio, as it were. (A 3/8 in contrast to a 2/4—like a slow *waltz* to a *quite unhurried polka*; the tempo of this polka is very tricky, it must be *quite, quite "gemächlich,"* as my tempo indication reads.) As to this second theme: it has a *periodic* structure, but here, too, everything is *canonic*, self-mirroring, and so forth. It is immediately followed—with an especially effective connection, I believe—by the first theme. But now everything, just everything is transposed (incidentally, the same "rows" are used in all three movements of the piece). From a certain point on, everything runs in reverse as compared to the first time, except for the ending that here is transformed into a "stretta" with which the whole thing takes off on wings. As a whole, you must understand the quartet in its formal appearance like several of Beethoven's three-movement *piano sonatas*! It is in this sense that I have tried to shape it. (Do once examine the structures of these movements in Beethoven's work really thoroughly.)

At the time Webern wrote to Kolisch, neither the score nor parts contained the movements in their final sequence. The Kolisch Quartet performed the work several times in the succession of movements designated in Sketchbook IV: II, I, and III of the printed score. Rudolf Kolisch is known to have pleaded for keeping that original order, in which the movement marked *Gemächlich* preceded the two faster ones. However, the composer felt that the tempi were better balanced in the sequence he decided on for their publication.

The first performance of the quartet (with the earlier order of movements) was given at the Tenth Berkshire Festival of Chamber Music, a three-day event consisting of five concerts under the sponsorship of Mrs Coolidge and held at South Mountain, Pittsfield, Massachusetts. The work, played by the Kolisch Quartet, was included in the 11 am concert on 22 September 1938. The programme opened with Schubert's Quartet in A minor, Op. 29, followed by the premières of three works commissioned by and dedicated to Mrs Coolidge: Webern's String Quartet, Op. 28, Louis Gruenberg's Quartet No. 2, Op. 40, and Frederick Jacobi's *Hagiographa: Three Biblical Narratives* for string quartet and piano.[11]

Three weeks after the première, on 13 October, Webern wrote to
Polnauer: "I can show you a beautiful letter from Schoenberg about my
new quartet. The Kolisches have played it for him. About the Pittsfield
performance itself, indirect news—very enjoyable—also has arrived (via
Universal Edition). Stein, too, has come to the fore in the meantime. A
letter from the English publishing firm [Boosey & Hawkes] is already
here with various inquiries."

According to a note in Sketchbook V, the String Quartet had been
registered with AKM (Authors, Composers, Music Publishers) on 24 June
1938, prior to its first performance. By then, the "Gleichschaltung"
(synchronization) of all Austrian affairs with Nazi regulations had taken
effect. The Jewish executives of Universal Edition had been dismissed,
and the new directors were pledged to the cultural doctrines of the
Hitler régime. Accordingly, Webern's music was summarily classified as
"degenerate art," and for the remainder of the composer's life the
house that had pioneered his works published nothing more by him.

Erwin Stein, for many years on the editorial staff of Universal Edition,
had succeeded in being transferred to Boosey & Hawkes, with whom the
Vienna house maintained close connections through its London
branch. Stein's mediation led to an agreement by Boosey & Hawkes to
publish Webern's Quartet. On 16 November 1938 the composer
informed Stein: "When my contract with U.E. expired some time ago,
we *explicitly* agreed not to renew it any more, but rather to maintain a
kind of moral understanding. Therefore, from that quarter nothing
stands in the way of a contract between Boosey & Hawkes, or rather the
UE, Ltd., in London, and myself." Although the terms were less
favourable than Webern had hoped for, arrangements were concluded
by the end of the year.[12]

As soon as the contract was signed, the composer turned his full
attention to the production of the printed score, which, for the first time,
he would not be able to supervise personally. On 6 January 1939 he
wrote to Stein setting forth his explicit wishes, such as those for the
spacing of the musical score:

Please, not more than *three* systems on one page. . . . The systems not
too closely spaced, not too many measures in one line, but rather
following my manuscript model as much as possible! ! ! In the final
analysis, the entire layout, the *proportions within the measures*, should
comply as exactly as possible with my manuscript! While rhythmically
there are hardly any complications in my quartet, the idea
nevertheless has to be plastically projected through its image! What a
help this is for comprehension! I beg you to make this clear to the
publishers! This in case they want to be too thrifty.

Webern also stipulated the employment of German for tempi, title, and dedication, the use of antiqua (Roman) lettering for the text, as used in all his other scores, and the omission of any type of embellishment.[13]

Except for a decorative border on the cover and title–page, all instructions were carried out. "On 6 May 1939 received the printed score of my String Quartet, Op. 28," reads the last entry in Webern's diary, which from 1931 on had been used only sporadically for records of important family events. The composer was very satisfied with the publication and repeatedly expressed his joy to Erwin Stein. On 27 June he wrote: "The more I look at the edition, the more it appeals to me! The make-up, too! The Humpliks find the latter excellent, in accordance with genuine English tradition and in the spirit of old *Dickens* editions."[14]

Planning to promote the newly-published work in the Boosey & Hawkes periodical, *Tempo*, Stein had asked Webern on 29 April to give him "some pointers for the article: dates concerning the work's evolution and perhaps a few hints to facilitate the analysis." That simple request was to elicit a response far exceeding the expected dimensions. During May the composer wrote out, in longhand, so comprehensive and detailed an analysis that Stein was prompted to acknowledge it as "an illumination in every direction . . . a complete course in musical form." There exists a typescript of that exposition, which was made at the request of Webern, who had not kept a copy for himself and wished to show the analysis to some friends.[15] On 27 June he asked Stein to reproduce his letter in a few copies. "In doing so, however," he wrote, "the passage dealing with Polnauer's discovery (concerning my fugue subject: B-A-C-H) would most definitely have to be omitted. As far as I remember, this could quite easily be accomplished without destroying the continuity of my statements."

Apparently, the composer did not wish it to be pointed out that the intervallic relationships of the first four notes of the quartet's tone row represented an analogy to Bach's last utterance in *Die Kunst der Fuge*, although that parallel does indeed exist. The Quartet's basic tone row reads:

The first four notes are a transposition of the B-A-C-H sequence, the next four an inversion thereof, and the closing four a transposition of the first. In his treatment of the row, Webern not only employed the motives, or "Gestalten" as he liked to call them, in three groups of four, but also divided the twelve-note series into two groups of six. In the latter arrangement, the second six-note group forms the inverted retrograde of the first. In consequence, the inversion of the entire row is identical with its transposed retrograde. In his row charts, drafted into the sketchbook during the earliest stages of the composition, Webern employed both divisions, that into three times four notes and that into two times six. The dual ramifications of those initial drafts leave open the question whether the composer was actually conscious of the B-A-C-H connotation.

When Stein warned Webern that the article in *Tempo* would necessarily have to be limited in length, the composer was disappointed and pleaded with him to reconsider. In his letter of 27 June he maintained that everything was essential and reasoned:

> Only quite recently have I myself comprehended fully what is happening in the scherzo of Beethoven's Ninth. Basically, we already find here a synthesis of the two modes of representation: the combination of *fugue* and *scherzo* forms. Something similar, therefore, to the third movement of my quartet. But one must show how the inner laws of both modes are fulfilled, with Beethoven I mean. All this must be done first, at least should be done: for we are dealing here with the most important problems of our time, *generally speaking*!!! At last, at last, to open the eyes of people to *our* music.

Despite Webern's arguments, Erwin Stein's introductory article was brief. Entitled "Webern's New Quartet," it appeared in 1939 in *Tempo* (No. 7). The following year, after the outbreak of World War II, Egon Wellesz wrote about the work in another English periodical, *The Music Review*. Tracing the entire development of the Viennese School, he said: "We can see today that Webern drew the logical conclusions from the stylistic development in nineteenth-century post-romantic music with even more rigour than Schoenberg. A close study of the dates of their works and a comparison of their style might reveal to everyone the fact, known to all their friends, that Webern forced his former teacher into an attitude of musical radicalism alien to Schoenberg's earlier compositions." Wellesz' assessment was summed up in these thoughts:

> It is impossible to apply the usual standard to this new work of Webern. He is a musician of astounding originality, an artist *sui generis*, whose style is formed by his personality and therefore cannot be followed or imitated by anyone who has not had the same emotional experiences. It does not diminish the importance of the

composer when we see in his art a late and subtle blossom of a long evolution. It will only do justice to him and to his efforts, to fight against the torrent of time with unbroken confidence in his ideals.[16]

The String Quartet, Op. 28, was the last of Webern's works to be printed during his lifetime. Though political conditions necessitated its publication abroad, the composer was nevertheless immensely gratified because he felt that with this work he had achieved a most important step on the ascent of his own Parnassus. This was recognized by Theodor Wiesengrund-Adorno, who wrote: "To the String Quartet, Op. 28, in particular, he attached the greatest importance. He expected from it no less than that it would bridge the gap in the development of Occidental music, the gap between objectivity and the subject, which he deemed codified in the historic types of fugue and sonata."[17]

Whatever the stylistic implications of the Quartet may be, Webern's analysis of his work has unique significance for the comprehension of his whole mode of musical thinking. For this reason the full text is reproduced in Appendix 2.

CHAPTER XXIX

Consequences of the Anschluss— Webern as a teacher

(1938)

WHEN WEBERN NOTED in his sketchbook that Austria had been incorporated into the German Reich, he could not foresee the dire consequences that were to follow in the wake of this momentous event.

On the afternoon of 14 March 1938, Adolf Hitler made his triumphant entry into Vienna, the city of his frustrated early aspirations. The delirium of victory led the conquerors to an unbridled assertion of power: in short order, 79,000 persons were arrested in Vienna alone for being politically "unreliable." A much worse fate befell the Jews, who numbered at that time about 180,000 in the city. An eye-witness account is provided by the American correspondent, William L. Shirer:

> For the first few weeks the behaviour of the Vienna Nazis was worse than anything I had seen in Germany. There was an orgy of sadism. Day after day large numbers of Jewish men and women could be seen scrubbing Schuschnigg signs off the sidewalk and cleaning the gutters. While they worked on their hands and knees with jeering storm troopers standing over them, crowds gathered to taunt them. Hundreds of Jews, men and women, were picked off the streets and put to work where the S.A. and the S.S. were quartered. Tens of thousands more were jailed. Their worldly possessions were confiscated or stolen. I myself, from our apartment in the Plösslgasse, watched squads of S.S. men carting off silver, tapestries, paintings and other loot from the Rothschild palace next door.[1]

Few could flee in time, since the borders were almost immediately sealed off. The exodus henceforth was controlled by the Office for Jewish Emigration.[2] Until the outbreak of the war in September 1939, it allowed perhaps as many as half the Jewish population to purchase its way to freedom at the cost of forfeiting all property left behind.[3]

Among the first of Webern's friends to leave were Heinrich Jalowetz and Kurt Manschinger, both of whom slipped out by way of Prague, where they had relatives.[4] Eventually they made their way to the United States. Manschinger settled in New York and became an editor with a music publisher; Jalowetz secured a teaching position at Black Mountain College in North Carolina, Dr Oskar Adler and Egon Wellesz emigrated to England, the latter assuming a readership at Oxford University. Willi Reich fled to Switzerland and later became a music critic for one of the Zürich newspapers. Schoenberg's son-in-law, Felix Greissle, whom Webern assisted with packing, storing books, and settling money matters, departed with his family for New York, where he became an executive with a publishing firm. Foreseeing the inevitable, Eduard Steuermann and Paul A. Pisk had left Vienna as early as 1936, Ernst Krenek in 1937, and Mark Brunswick in January of 1938.

Each time Webern had to say good-bye to a friend, he suffered the same emotional pain as if he himself were leaving his homeland. One of these farewells was later recalled by Dr Rudolph Kurzmann, whose last meeting with Webern took place the day before he departed for America in July 1938:

> Since I had little time left, he accompanied me the entire morning on my errands. Then we had lunch on the terrace of a garden restaurant. During our hours together, we spoke for the first time in all these years about politics, i.e. about Hitler and his criminal helpers. In the restaurant he was so impassioned that I had to ask him to lower his voice in my interest, one day before my departure. An hour later, in the middle of the street, he suddenly gave me a manuscript, embraced me and disappeared.[5]

Not only Jews were trying to make their way out of the Hitler-dominated countries, but also many Gentiles who did not want to live under a rule that suppressed all freedom of expression or serve a régime that was clearly steering towards military conquest and the disaster of war. Every one of the tens of thousands who escaped did so under more or less adventurous circumstances. Even after they reached safety, however, enormous practical and emotional problems had to be faced. Uprooted from their familiar surroundings, deprived of their native tongue, all—intellectuals and labourers, the rich and the poor—were confronted at first with an uncertain future. Often arriving penniless, many had to accept the most menial occupations to earn their daily bread.

Small wonder that reluctance to endure such hardships caused many to remain behind, hoping that the storm would blow over or that pressure from abroad would temper the extremism at home. Such illusions were soon destined to wane, however. Wide segments of the populace, if not converted already to Nazism, were gradually reconciled to it by the positive aspects of the new régime: the end of the many years of turmoil, the restoration of order, however autocratic, and the almost immediate economic improvement, which did away with unemployment and produced increasing prosperity. Last but not least, a wave of Pan-Germanic patriotism swept away the bitter recollection of defeat in the First World War. Freed from the last shackles of the humiliating Versailles Treaty, most German-speaking people were soon prepared to follow their leader blindly into the glorious future that he held out to them so convincingly.

It was not long before virtually everyone who was free from the taint of non-Aryan descent had joined an appropriate party organization, whether out of political conviction, or for reasons of expediency or coercion. The young were the first to embrace the new national creed. Webern's daughter, Christine, became a member of the Bund deutscher Mädchen, the sister organization of the Hitler Youth. Just a few weeks after the Anschluss, on 2 June 1938, she married Benno Mattel, a zealous Nazi storm trooper. Webern stood as Trauzeuge (legal witness) in the civilian ceremony held at the Mödling Court House. The groom wore the brown-shirted party uniform, and above the proceedings hung the flag of the Third Reich. One can only imagine Webern's feelings as he gave his last-born child in marriage under the swastika, that symbol of sworn enmity towards his own best friends. Was the spectre of Schoenberg, to mention but one, haunting him during that solemn occasion?

As matters stood, the parents had little choice but to approve the match. Christine was five months pregnant, and her welfare and the family's honour outweighed all other considerations. The new son-in-law (the son of a Mödling veterinarian and an Italian mother) had been involved as a schoolboy in a shooting incident that had caused some notoriety at the time. Now he was headed for an influential position as a party functionary. Shrewd and astute in his personal affairs, he possessed all the qualities that would assure him of great material success in the various phases of his adventurous career. However, he was little liked by the family, as Gunter Waller, Amalie's husband, later candidly revealed.

Waller himself, to be sure, also joined the Nazi party, a formality then virtually mandatory for persons in all walks of life, especially for those in executive positions. Webern's son Peter, then 22 years old, had embraced the system even before it came into power. During his prolonged stay at Graz, where he operated a branch office of Waller's firm, he was thoroughly indoctrinated with Nazi ideology and had secretly joined the then still illegal party. With the Anschluss, he became an enthusiastic and outspoken proponent of the Neue Reich and its reforms.[6] Of the four Webern children, only Maria withstood the mass psychosis. For years, she had been in love with a young man of Jewish origin who was forced to emigrate. Maria had intended to follow him, but when the war broke out in 1939 she was unable to leave, and he eventually married another.

In the face of the intense political feelings within his immediate family circle, Webern followed a single policy. It was, as Dr Rudolph Kurzmann has related, dedicated to the "preservation of a pure family life."[7] He forbade any political discussion at home, and if Nazi sentiments were nevertheless voiced, he met them with silence.

Actually, with the new régime firmly in control, Webern found himself at a crossroad both as a private citizen and as an artist. What really were his chances under the new order? Webern, a pure-blooded Aryan, was the descendant of a family that had been raised to noble rank as early as 1574. Through the centuries his family had produced many men of distinction and of unquestionable patriotism. Webern's father had risen to the position of Chief of Mining in the Habsburg government. Webern's own military record during the First World War, though it did not include front-line duty, had been honourable. Certainly, he would have been found quite acceptable to the new authorities on the basis of purely personal qualifications. His former affiliation with a Socialist agency would have been readily overlooked if only he had declared his solidarity with the new order and tried to ingratiate himself with its officials. Men of lesser character had been quick to do so and reaped rich rewards. As a composer, Webern might have stooped to fabrications of music in the tonal idiom, thereby publicly renouncing his errant ways and simultaneously admitting the fallacy of Schoenberg's theories. He could have justified such action: had not Schoenberg himself coped with practical necessities when he produced some tonal works in America?

It was exactly in this realm, the test of his artistic conscience, that Webern rose to his full stature. If he had previously entertained the naïve hope that his music would in time prove acceptable to the new régime, that illusion was quickly destroyed. Soon after the Anschluss a propaganda exhibition under the banner "Degenerate Art" was put on view in Vienna's Künstlerhaus. This display, which followed the example of one mounted in Munich the year before, encompassed not only paintings, but literature and music as well. Webern was among those included and thus his work was clearly and officially branded. To the embarrassment of the organizers the show was attended by throngs of people, including many students, and queues formed far into the street. Whether such interest signified silent solidarity or mere curiosity made little difference to the artists who were being stigmatized as decadent and undesirable.

The unmistakable warning served by the new cultural dictators did not deter Webern, however. Not for a moment did he waver in his credo or deviate from his course. Josef Polnauer has testified that, despite the professional boycott confronting Webern, he was not at first discouraged. He still hoped that things would "calm down" and that he would yet come into his own.[8] Not even the take-over of Universal Edition by Nazi executives could shake that optimism, nor could the elimination of his compositions from performances in Austria or Germany, nor Ravag's failure to re-engage him as conductor, although with the barring of Jews there were opportunities aplenty. According to Polnauer, Webern only very gradually came to realize what was happening in the world around him. It took a full three years until his childlike faith in a brighter artistic future was definitely shaken. By then, of course, even those politically most unrealistic were beginning to feel the grim effects of a disastrous war.

Webern's last works are a testimony to his integrity and consistency of purpose. Wholly committed to his creative destiny, he accepted the fact that, for the time, he had nothing to expect in terms of recognition or support. The vacuum in which he was condemned to work was the price he willingly paid for artistic independence.

Up to the outbreak of the war, Webern might have considered emigration. There are allusions to that possibility in his correspondence with Arnold Schoenberg and Willi Reich. He also talked about it to Polnauer. It is to be seriously questioned, however, whether he would ever actually have undertaken so drastic a step. First of all, he was emotionally quite incapable of parting from his children. Likewise, he would have been most reluctant to bid a permanent farewell to his fatherland. So intense was his love for his native soil that on every trip abroad he counted the hours until he could cross the Austrian border again. Only in his homeland and, still more, within the narrowly drawn boundaries of his immediate vicinity did his sensitive soul feel sheltered. One needs merely to read his diary notes to sense the depth of that singular devotion. For Webern, the splendour of Paris could not begin to rival that of Vienna, and the palms of the Riviera were but a pale surrogate for the green forests of the domestic woods. He was quite homesick whenever he was away from his family, even if only a few days, and the mere thought of living in some distant land, uprooted like a plant from its natural habitat, was enough to terrify him.

Webern's overwhelming aversion to severing himself from everything to which he was so deeply attached decided for him the conflict between

reason and emotion whenever there was serious talk of emigration.
Instead he chose a double life. As a private citizen, he maintained the
principle, "One must obey authority," regardless of which system
authority was vested in. Paradoxically, he reconciled this philosophy
with an artistic temperament that had in fact made him a rebel from the
start. As a creative artist, he consciously entered an inward emigration,
devoting the last seven years of his existence to the ceaseless pursuit of
his visions. In that exile of a lonely spirit, freedom reigns. Why then
escape to foreign shores? Thus committing himself to a higher
Providence, Webern was resigned to await his day.

*   *   *

On 9 February 1938 Webern wrote to the Humpliks: "Our *Augenlicht*,
dear Hildegard, will have its first performance at a music festival [of
the ISCM] in London in July. I will not conduct myself since, after all,
I cannot really speak the language and therefore would have too many
difficulties in rehearsing the chorus. But I would like to go there anyway,
to listen and perhaps, indirectly, even be of help 'durch unsere offnen
Augen . . .' [through our open eyes . . .]."

Webern's hopes were not to be fulfilled—the rapidity of political
changes following the Anschluss in March upset all plans. One
immediate consequence was the suspension of all activities of
organizations not complying with Third Reich doctrines. Into this
category fell the Austrian ISCM section, of which Webern was still
president. With a heavy heart he wrote to Willi Reich on 29 April: "From
here nobody can go [to England]. I did receive an invitation, but I shall
hardly be able to get away. This time there will not be a 'delegate' from
the local section. Its future and that of the society itself are uncertain for
the time being. At any rate, it cannot be called (according to law)
'Austrian' any longer. At the moment I am solely reponsible for signing
everything."

Webern had last attended an ISCM festival in April 1936 in Barcelona,
when Hermann Scherchen had had to replace him as conductor of the
première of Berg's Violin Concerto. The deep humiliation suffered by
Webern at the time filled him with resentment, and there had been no
personal contact between the two men until late in 1937, when
Scherchen informed the composer that he would perform the Ricercar
transcription in England during January 1938.[9] Soon afterwards,
Scherchen also agreed to take charge of the first performance of *Das
Augenlicht*. On 12 April 1938 Webern wrote the conductor a long letter,
thanking him for his readiness to assume this difficult task.[10] While he
trusted Scherchen's comprehension of his new work, he nonetheless
hoped that there might be an opportunity to discuss the score with him

beforehand in Vienna. His chief concern was that the BBC chorus could be employed for the performance and that the text would be sung in the original German, a point which he took infinite pains to stress. All his wishes were to be fulfilled, and choral rehearsals began in May.

London's Queen's Hall, an auditorium seating 2,500, was the setting for the première, which took place on 17 June, during the opening concert of the week-long festival. *Das Augenlicht* was placed at the end of the first half of the programme and was preceded by compositions by Vitěslava Kaprálová, Josef Koffler, and Lennox Berkeley. After the intermission there followed works by Manuel Rosenthal, Julián Bautista, and Igor Markévitch. Webern's opus (for which he had provided a short commentary in the programme) scored an unqualified success. On the following day the critic of *The Times* wrote:

> By far the most genuinely modern and convincing work in this programme was that of the oldest composer represented in it, Anton Webern. His setting of a short lyric poem *Das Augenlicht* for choir and orchestra in a manner peculiarly his own, and distinct from that of the generality of composers who now claim what is called the "12-tone system," created a remarkable impression. Here at least is no furbishing up of old devices with additional instruments. Every note of the delicate instrumentation is in its right place, however strange that place may seem, and the poem is beautifully delineated in the vocal parts.

Other newspaper reviews read: "Webern, after all, appeared as the master, for all the eccentricity of his orchestral usage" (*Daily Telegraph*, 18 June). "The one thing in the programme that really commanded respect was Webern's work. Webern's mind is the queerest thing imaginable, so much off the beaten track that much study is necessary to enable us to see his music even approximately as he must have seen it himself: but at any rate there can be no doubt that it is a mind, which is more than I would venture to assert of one or two of the other cerebrating-boxes to which we were introduced" (*Sunday Times*, 19 June).

The professional journals were equally generous in their praise: "Webern's *Das Augenlicht* was convincing and moving, despite its strangeness of idiom. The performance of this work was miraculously good, and due credit must be given to Hermann Scherchen, who conducted, and the BBC Singers, a body probably unrivalled in Europe" (*Musical Times*, July 1938). "For all its unvocal intervals and seeming scrappiness, Webern's *Das Augenlicht* gained a number of converts to its composer's musical faith. Perhaps these uncanny, otherworld wisps of sound do mean something. They made their maximum effect in a wonderful performance" (*Musical Opinion*, July 1938).

Musicians from near and far attended the festival. From Florence came the composer Luigi Dallapiccola, who had been present at the première of Webern's Concerto, Op. 24, in Prague three years before. In a lengthy diary account written on the evening of the concert, Dallapiccola epitomized the impact of Webern's music: "The most powerful emotional impression I received from this work was the sound. A sound, by itself, that makes me consider *Das Augenlicht* as one of the fundamental works of our time."[11]

Prevented from being in London himself, Webern had been quite apprehensive about the rendition of his work. On 11 June he had written to Reich: "If you attend rehearsals of my choral piece, please write to me your impressions immediately! List and Searle,[12] who, to conclude from their communications, must already have heard some of them, have reported nothing as yet—is this a good or a bad sign? I am already somewhat nervous and at long last would like to know how the chorus is doing it, whether it is going at all! . . . Since the concert will be broadcast, perhaps I shall even hear one or two tones of my piece."

The expected broadcast was cancelled, however, and the composer was deprived even of that small satisfaction. So much the greater was his elation over the many favourable reports that were beginning to reach him. "Are 'miracles' happening?" he exclaimed to Erwin Stein in a letter of 23 June, and to Hildegard Jone he wrote six days later: "All the past week really most enjoyable news has arrived about the performance of our *Augenlicht* in London. There are words like 'veritable triumph,' 'jubilation and enthusiasm,' etc. Since you were *part of what sounded* there—it is *our 'Augenlicht,'* after all—it makes me especially happy and that is why it is permissible to quote such things to you. You must read some of them yourself."

In a letter to Scherchen, dated 1 July 1938, the composer eagerly inquired about the specific acoustical realization of his ideas (he himself was never to hear the work performed):

How did the orchestra sound? Did the complement of strings that I prescribed prove itself well in relation to the chorus (how strong was the group?) as well as to the other instruments? How did the high kettledrum work out? You see, I would very much like to know some more details. Is this not understandable? Therefore, do not mind my asking. I know that you have little time for writing. . . . Judging from all that I have heard, you have *in fact won a great "victory" for my work*—just as you held out that prospect to me in your first letter regarding it! All the news that arrived was most pleasing and is especially significant for me just now.[13]

On the same day that Webern wrote to Scherchen, he began the composition of his First Cantata, Op. 29. Not only did the success of *Das Augenlicht* inspire him to another work in the choral genre, but it also helped to reconcile him to a distressing occurrence, news of which had reached him from England earlier in the year. He had described the affair in a letter to Reich, written on 29 April: "Did you hear about the awful thing that happened when my String Trio was performed in London? The cellist got up saying 'I cannot play this thing!' and *walked off the platform*! Surely nothing like that has ever happened before!"[14] This incident, to be sure, was to be an isolated case and one quite uncharacteristic of Great Britain, where audiences showed a greater appreciation of Webern's music during his lifetime than in any other country. In 1938 alone, the composer could count with satisfaction performances of no fewer than eight of his works. They included his Bach transcription, the String Trio, Op. 20 (twice), the Five Movements for String Quartet, Op. 5, *Das Augenlicht*, the violin and cello pieces (Opera 7 and 11), the Trakl Songs, Op. 14, and the Symphony, Op. 21. The latter work, played in Birmingham, was relayed by broadcast.

Of two brief holidays Webern took with his wife that summer, the first (25–29 July) was spent with the Diez family in Vordernberg and the second (22 August–2 September) in Kapellen. Webern returned there again and again; he enjoyed the idyllic remoteness and, particularly, the absolute quiet. This time, they stayed at the rustic inn Zum Abendstern. The weather was bad, and an early snow fell on the mountains. Nevertheless, Webern felt content in his rural seclusion, as he reported to Polnauer on 24 August when he set a date for their next meeting.

The contact with Polnauer had grown much closer following the Anschluss. Webern was not deterred by the ever-increasing anti-Semitism, and numerous letters attest to his unstinting willingness to be of assistance to his Jewish friends. He furnished those who had emigrated with introductions and recommendations and, until the war terminated all correspondence, maintained a lively exchange of letters. Even from afar he tried to help in every way he could. For example, he counselled a young pupil, George Robert,[15] on 9 October 1938: "For your development as a pianist, as a musician, it is self-evidently 1,000 times better that you remain in the metropolis for the time being [Robert considered leaving New York, which was overcrowded with immigrant musicians]. . . . I imagine that you will at first work with Mr Steuermann again! I have not had any news from him for a long time, it is true, but I believe that I can assume he will again be in New York for the season." Then Webern pleaded that the younger generation be mindful of its obligation to champion Schoenberg, an admonition doubly touching in view of the ban that had long silenced such music in the Nazi domain:

> As your old teacher, I would like to impress upon you especially this *one* point: you must feel first and foremost that your mission is to stand up (as a *pianist* at first) *for what* out of the production of our time we have perceived and continue to perceive as valid for the future! It is high time that youth considers this, not for our sake, no, for its own sake. You must recognize, dear friend, that the terrible low–point of musical life today (everywhere in the world!) has its cause in the fact that nowadays, *as never before in history*, people sin against the *living*! It should be a matter of course that, when for example you perform today, you play *Schoenberg*! And your response to "possible astonish-ment" should only be: *"Well, what else should I play?"* It is *more than high time*! Otherwise, everything that is important to us in art would of necessity have to *perish*!!!

Such were the entreaties with which Webern followed his former pupils to their unknown destinies in foreign lands. Robert had been only one of the private students who provided Webern's chief source of income up to the Anschluss. Then, as if the bell of fate had tolled, the pupils had scattered in all directions. Those of Jewish descent, and they formed the majority, made haste to flee the country. The rest were caught up in the general anxiety. The weekly lecture course that Webern had given at Dr Kurzmann's home was suspended at the end of March. One month after the arrival of the Hitler régime, Webern told Reich in a letter of 29 April: "With the lessons, too, things are in such a state; at the moment I have only *one* to give. One must have patience." The lone pupil still pursuing his studies was Emil Spira. He, too, was to disappear from Webern's income book after "Kristallnacht," the pogrom against the Jews instigated later that year. As the Socialist revolution of 1934 had practically terminated Webern's conducting career, so the Anschluss brought his teaching activities to a virtual standstill. At the close of that portentous year, Webern's confidence appeared shaken as he wrote to Reich on 27 December: "As to pupils, I have lost almost everything. Sometimes I am very worried."

✻   ✻   ✻

Shortly after Webern's death, Alfred Schlee, one of the directors of Universal Edition, wrote of him: "His greatest influence was through his teaching, even though this reached only a small circle of private students who deified him and had made the pilgrimage to Vienna from many countries. He knew, as no other, how to make his inexhaustible learning accessible, nurtured young talent with paternal affection, and counselled the same seriousness and responsibility with which he himself composed."[16] In 1935 Arnold Schoenberg had called Webern "the most impassioned and intensive teacher imaginable."[17]

There is no better way to assess Webern's pedagogical methods and philosophy than from the accounts of those who studied under him.[18] The recollections of his pupils provide a cross-section of impressions that are at once intimate and comprehensive.

The first of Webern's students in Mödling was Kurt Manschinger, who came to him in 1918 as a youth of seventeen and remained under his tutelage for a full six years.[19]

> When I first met Webern [recalled Manschinger in his memoirs], his high forehead and unrimmed glasses gave me the impression of a very interesting and sensitive man. He was soft-spoken and always a little nervous, but underneath one felt his warmth. . . . He took his teaching as seriously as his composing and used to say: "If someone knows something, he has the duty to pass it on." He not only taught me theory, but urged me to take piano and cello with other teachers. He was always very concentrated when teaching and sought to explain everything very thoroughly and precisely. His uppermost principle in explaining was the same that prevailed in his composition: comprehensibility [*Fasslichkeit*]. When analysing a Beethoven sonata or a Brahms symphony, he found so many hidden connections which eluded others, and of which perhaps even the composers themselves might not always have been conscious, that it seems to me now that the idea of "total organization" was born already a century ago.
>
> His patience was limitless, and he was very generous with the time allotted to me. A lesson supposed to last one hour usually lasted two. Beethoven, of course, was his highest god, then came Brahms and Mahler, finally Schoenberg. He respected Stravinsky, but had no good words for Strauss (Richard, not Johann, by whom he was enchanted).[20] He was the first to call my attention to Debussy, whose *La Mer* I heard for the first time in a two-piano arrangement which was performed in Schoenberg's Society for Private Musical Performances, to which Webern had introduced me as a new member.
>
> The first compositions I showed him were wild and uncontrolled and, although he acknowledged the good ideas I had, he reproached me for attempting something I could not as yet master. Throughout the years I studied composition with him, he dissected every measure of my homework and criticized the smallest detail.

The last two years were given over to contrapuntal studies of the most severe order. Manschinger, whose sprightly temperament predisposed him to a spontaneous· conception of music, recalled that he felt "paralysed" by the austerity of that discipline. It took him some time to "emancipate" and to find his own style, one that assumed a Debussyan flavour. Webern himself, no doubt recognizing his pupil's basic disposition, discouraged him from writing in the atonal idiom. Nevertheless he remained interested in everything Manschinger composed later on. In 1932, when Manschinger played for him the score of his first opera *Madame Dorette*, he listened attentively from beginning to end, then nodded approval, saying: "This is not the kind of music I would write, but it is good." Manschinger added: "Webern even attended a concert of 'literary cabaret' songs, which I wrote for my wife, Greta Hartwig, and he did not hide his enthusiasm, to the dismay of some of the hard-core dodecaphonists around him."

Contrasting with Manschinger's expressive tendencies were those of Stefan Wolpe, who came to Webern in 1933 with the explicit desire to prune his style, then influenced by the lush orchestrations of a Debussy, Ravel, or Stravinsky.[21] Fleeing from Hitler's Germany, Wolpe had arrived in Vienna penniless, and Webern insisted on teaching him without a fee. This somewhat embarrassed Wolpe, especially since the lessons never lasted less than two hours and often were followed by lengthy conversations over coffee. "Webern's jovial manner changed to one of extreme intensity when he read or played music," Wolpe later remembered. On a train ride from Mödling to Vienna, Webern once told him: "You know, ever since I have worked with twelve tones, composing has become quite easy."

Siegfried Oehlgiesser studied with Webern from March 1932 until July 1938. His lessons were usually shared with Emil Spira.[22] Oehlgiesser has recalled their joint sessions:

I see him [Webern] before me with his habitual cigar stump, the massive lighter lying in readiness on the cover of the grand piano in the study at Maria Enzersdorf. He always insisted on our preceding him through the door. A word, a glance created warmth in the room, and work could begin. We had brought along our various composition assignments—attempts to develop an idea into a complete thought, to write a slow movement, or to exploit a theme in its full possibilities for variation. Webern's look told us, even before he spoke, whether our efforts possessed any merit. Truthfulness of musical diction was the most essential criterion. His extraordinary perceptiveness enabled him to realize what we actually had intended to say. A brief suggestion, "Was this not what you really had meant?"

would help a basically good idea towards its appropriately clear and comprehensible formulation. He was always right, but his teaching was never authoritarian. The personality of each pupil was respected. If an assignment was successfully carried out, it was always warmly praised, and Webern could become quite cordial on such occasions. He would then tell of his excursions in the Alps during holidays and of the creative idea and its organic development that he found manifested everywhere in nature; he compared the organic growth of a plant to the organic development of a motive. If he disagreed with the outcome of an assignment, he exposed its shortcomings, and intellectual and moral gain was the result. He had sympathetic understanding for everything except untruthfulness, such as attempts to dress up a theme by ornamentation or to simulate a pronouncement when there was actually no basic thought. If this occurred, it visibly caused him pain, and the student never forgot it. We learned mostly from our own original composition attempts, in which Webern showed us all that was necessary. To this came, always at the right moment, references as to how Beethoven would have done it—a Beethoven sonata furnishing the example—and at times he himself developed an entire series of variations on a theme furnished by the student, masterfully exemplifying the concept of the variation form. Unprejudiced, respectful of any real desire for expression, however awkward, objective in his criticism, though severely critical in the face of self-deception—this was Webern as teacher.

Arnold Elston was Webern's pupil from December 1932 to June 1935.[23] During that period, a close personal relationship was established, and Webern frequently invited him to join the family circle. Elston's observations reflect his own keen insights as a composer and pedagogue:

Anton Webern's activity as a teacher of composition reflected at every turn his own experiences as a pupil of Arnold Schoenberg, of whom he always spoke with utter devotion and unbounded admiration, both as artist and as teacher. Webern taught harmony from Schoenberg's *Harmonielehre*, strict counterpoint from Bellermann's *Kontrapunkt* (which Schoenberg had also used), and his beginning instruction in free composition generally followed the precepts laid down in Schoenberg's *Models for Beginners in Composition*, though the latter had not yet appeared while I studied with Webern.

Upon looking at my student efforts before I undertook work with him, Webern noted certain French influences attributable to Debussy and Ravel. His reaction surprised me at the time. "If we want to

understand philosophy," he said, "we must turn to the ancient
Greeks, and if we want to understand music we must turn to Mozart,
Haydn, Beethoven, and the other great masters of the Austro-
German tradition." This meant, in effect, that all material for analysis
and all models for the student-composer were exclusively drawn from
the Austro-German classics. One may look upon this as a most
confining attitude on Webern's part—not a single reference to Berlioz,
to Verdi, to Mussorgsky, or even to the Liszt–Strauss vein in German
music. But Webern's horizon was wholly filled by the music from
Bach, through the Viennese classics to Wagner, Brahms, and Mahler;
he found his complete personal affirmation as composer therein.
Occasionally he would analyse some early work of Schoenberg or
Berg, always eager to point out their ties to tradition. Of his own
work he spoke only rarely; indeed, he was apparently most reluctant
to discuss the constructive aspects of his music, but on a few
memorable occasions he played a new song for me on the piano. Such
a performance was always a revelation of the élan, of the intensest
expressivity which infused every note, so that one experienced a living
presence, and all questions of tone-row manipulations and
constructive devices seemed totally extraneous. I speak of this because
Webern is often considered as a constructivist. He did indeed aspire
towards the utmost crystalline clarity of form and the maximum
thematic strictness, especially in his twelve-tone works, but he
fervently believed that the greatest freedom of expression arose from
the greatest exercise of exactitude and rigorous control over the
imagination.

The lessons with him would begin with a prolonged, silent reading
of the music I had brought. When at length he began to discuss the
piece, he had penetrated it to its core, he had grasped my every intent,
he knew where I had had trouble and knew why I had chosen such and
such a way to extricate myself from the trouble.

It must first be said that his criticism never touched on matters of
style. My music could betray the influence of the First Chamber
Symphony of Schoenberg, or of the Seven Early Songs of Berg, and
though Webern must have looked upon such efforts as quite
conservative (after all, these works were by then 25 years old), he never
said so, nor did he ever prod me in any way to give up tonality, or
when my music broke away from tonality did he suggest that I should
organize it on a serial basis. His primary concern in criticizing my
music was to clarify the functional character of every phrase, theme,
section, and the organic relatedness of the parts to the whole. Did I
intend this to be a principal theme? He would thereupon probe it to
see why the motives developed rather rapidly, while the harmonic

rhythm showed no comparable increasing animation. If the music sounded flawed to him in some way, he could instantly reach to his music shelves and open a score of one of the masters which contained a similar type of theme and show how the composer had succeeded. His criticism, in short, went hand in hand with analysis of the masters, so that it conveyed a distinctly objective tone; it was really a Beethoven or a Brahms who showed one the error of one's ways, rather than the teacher who sat beside one.

Only on the rarest occasions did Webern attempt to emend what I had written, and this I suspect he did with much reluctance, for he knew that this amounted to the intrusion of a foreign aesthetic sensibility, and that somehow it constituted an act of violence to the student's own sensibility. Inevitably a composer with so pronounced a musical individuality as Webern could not help expressing some aesthetic predilections. "Pauses sound good," he would say, as he noted a passage of unrelieved dense texture in which the lack of rests resulted in a loss of articulation in phrase and motive structure. Or if a section seemed too short, for one reason or another, he would say, pointing to another section, "You should consider expanding this section to compensate for the brevity of the other." Webern was expressing here a sort of personal precept which he called "justice through compensation" and which guided his own creative endeavours. Nevertheless, he refrained from pointing to a specific solution, leaving this to the student to find for himself.

Essentially, Webern's scrupulous care not to influence the student in his choice of style showed his deep respect for the innate capacity of the student to discover himself, and this quest for the authentic musical self, which Webern so solicitously encouraged, eventually led far beyond one's efforts at acquiring an adequate technique. The student, once made aware of how the masters had obeyed the dictates of the spirit—even when it meant grappling with the most exacting technical problems and risking the leap over routine into that awesome *unknown* born of necessity—was learning the meaning of moral courage: he was to cast aside his bag of facile tricks and to confront his vision with bared soul, honestly and uncompromisingly. Thus Webern not only came to be a great artist and teacher to his pupil, but an exalting and purifying force which radiated deep into the heart.

Just as Webern's music at first found more appreciation abroad than at home, so was his work as teacher most highly valued by pupils from foreign lands. They formed a large contingent of his class. For example, from the United States came, besides Elston, Carl Buchman, Margaret

Cantor, Gordon Claycombe, Maurice Kaplan, and Roland Leich. Webern took a great liking to these Americans. Their freshness of spirit and open-mindedness, their generosity and helpfulness, which he also observed in friends like Brunswick, Krasner, and Weiss, fostered his faith in the New World. There alone, he once told Weiss, the realization of his visions and aspirations might yet be possible.

Roland Leich studied under Webern during the winter of 1933–34.[24]

At my first lesson [he related], I showed Webern some of my compositions, including a group of A. E. Housman songs (which had financed my visit to Europe by winning the Bearns Prize administered by Columbia University). He began his teaching by discussing the need for music to have "Fasslichkeit" in order to be intelligible to the "man in the street." This might come as a surprise to those bewildered by Webern's music. (In Philadelphia, I had heard Stokowski's performance of Opus 21, the audience reaction to which is still remembered as a public scandal.) Although my Housman songs showed a grasp of phrase and period structures, regular and irregular, Webern minutely analysed *Kommt ein Vogel geflogen* as an example of the period. New to me, however, was the distinction between period and "Satz," not normally covered by English-language textbooks.

At an early lesson, Webern lectured at some length on the utter supremacy of German music, emphasizing that leading composers of other lands are but pale reflections of Germanic masters: Berlioz a French Beethoven, Tchaikovsky a Russian Schumann, Elgar an English Mendelssohn, etc. To me this was both shocking and amusing, but I was much too diffident to offer any comment. . . . I deeply respected Webern's dignity and obvious integrity. Also I sensed that he was a dreamer preoccupied with his own thought and that he might have known more than his share of sorrows.

Gordon Claycombe, another pupil from America, studied under Webern from 1932 to 1934.[25]

Webern [he later wrote] was without question one of the most outstanding teachers I have ever had in any field of learning. Usually our lesson started almost from the moment I took out the music paper on which I had done the assigned exercises, the composition I was working on, or my volume of Beethoven's sonatas, one of which I had to analyse, from a structural point of view, for every lesson. I would sit next to Webern on the piano bench and we would review these materials together. The wonderful thing about Webern was his contagious enthusiasm for the work under study, whether it be Beethoven, Brahms, or Mahler. Though he had seen these sonatas or symphony scores hundreds of times before, one had the feeling that, during these lessons, he himself was always discovering something new in them. Webern did not teach by the clock, but continued each session until the subject under discussion was exhausted. At times, we would glance back to the works of Bach, Haydn, or Mozart, or forward to those of Brahms and Mahler, examining how each master handled the· three-part vocal form, or other standard mould. However, no matter where we might wander in our analyses and discussions, we always returned to the sonatas and symphonies of Beethoven! . . . Often, following my lesson, while relaxing over a cigarette, we would discuss many things not necessarily having to do with music, but matters concerning politics, the state of cultural affairs in Vienna, mutual friends, Zenk, Stein, Steuermann, Adolf Loos, and many, many other individuals and subjects.

British musicians, like their American colleagues, showed an early appreciation for the new style developed by Webern. Edward Clark had been the first to promote performances of his music in England. Subsequently, Humphrey Searle contributed greatly to its widespread understanding through his theoretical writings.[26] At nineteen, Searle had been deeply impressed by a broadcast of Berg's *Wozzeck*. In September 1937, after being awarded the Octavia Travelling Scholarship by the Royal College of Music, he went to Webern on the advice of Theodor Wiesengrund-Adorno, who then was living in Oxford. Searle's programme of study was particularly concentrated, and the monthly honorarium of 200 schillings that Webern noted in his income book for the six months of his tutelage was considerably higher than he had ever received from any other pupil.

In an article published during Webern's lifetime (1940) Searle wrote:

At our first lesson he said with great emphasis that music must express what it has to say as clearly as possible, but that complicated ideas naturally need complicated means of expression. . . . Webern invariably uses the piano when composing, and his sketchbooks are full of variants which would all be equally possible according to the twelve-tone technique; I suspect that he chooses the one of these which *sounds best* in the context, and therefore relies ultimately to some extent on his ear, which is, of course, astonishingly keen. He also used actually to play over my harmony exercises on the piano, though these were often quite simple chord progressions, and did this in a style rather resembling the sound of his own music, usually breaking the chords and mostly *pianissimo*, with sudden explosive *forte* outbursts.[27]

At that time, Heinrich Schenker's ideas had made their inroads into musical thinking, and Searle asked Webern for his opinion as to their validity. "He admitted that there was a great deal of good in Schenker's theories, and showed that, so far as classical music was concerned, Schenker and Schoenberg took up more or less the same position; but he naturally denied Schenker's assertion of the necessity of tonality and the omnivalence of his theories." Searle concluded his impressions of Webern: "His amazing sensitivity, combined with his sheer creative genius, obviously make him one of the few composers of today who really matter."[28]

Two decades later, Searle amplified these observations in another essay:

At my first lesson he talked absorbingly for an hour simply on the properties of the chord of C major: to him the laws of music were a living evolutionary process, not a set of abstract formulae laid down by theorists. This idea of evolution was very important to him and was the basis of his view of life and art; a fanatical lover of nature, he felt in the same way that music had developed along a logical evolutionary path which led from the Middle Ages through the works of the great classical and romantic composers to the twelve-note method. That is to say, he did not regard the music of Schoenberg and his followers as providing a contrast to that of the past, but rather as being a logical extension of it. In fact, he had a great admiration for some of the romantic composers with whom one would have thought he had little in common. I had gone through a period of adulation of Wagner in my school days, but by then was undergoing the inevitable reaction against him; but when I ventured to criticize Wagner, Webern soundly berated me. "Wagner was a great composer," he said, "and you cannot possibly say that you do not like him." Similarly, he greatly admired Bruckner, and we sometimes played his symphonies together as piano duets, Webern remarking on one occasion in the slow movement of the Seventh Symphony: "Could your Elgar write an arch of melody like that?"

After we had finished our study of the *Harmonielehre*, Webern analysed for me various twelve-note works, including his own recently-completed Piano Variations. He was prepared to do this for me as a composition student; but he felt that audiences and even performers did not need to know the technical processes by which twelve-note music is constructed. His approach was always practical rather than theoretical; he invariably used the piano while composing, trusting to his extraordinarily acute ear as well as to his knowledge of the laws of music. On this point he said to me once: "Don't trust your ears alone; your ears will always guide you aright, but you must also *know* what you are doing". These twin principles of knowledge and practice were, I believe, the basis of his approach to music.[29]

Reflecting on the scant recognition that Webern's music had found during the composer's lifetime, Searle concluded:

He would certainly have been astonished at his present world-wide fame. Nevertheless, such considerations did not greatly matter to him; he simply knew that he was doing what was right, and whether other people accepted this or not, was not of great importance to him. He was indeed an idealist, but one who remained very conscious of the world around him; he certainly did not shut himself up in an ivory tower. . . . Now at last his genius is universally recognized, and I for one will always be grateful to him for his guidance and his example.

By training and inclination, Webern was essentially an educator in all his activities. He preached with the missionary's zeal what he himself practised in the seclusion of his creative workshop. While he generally was loath to discuss his own compositions, he elaborated freely on every aspect of the music of the masters. Therefore, his pronouncements as a teacher yield important clues to the understanding of his own works. Friedrich Deutsch,[30] one of his students during the Mödling days, has illustrated this point with some specific observations:

Webern began his lessons conservatively. He taught strict counter-point according to the polyphonic masterworks of the sixteenth century. His rules generally agreed with those of the *Gradus ad Parnassum* by J. J. Fux. This eighteenth-century treatise is, of course, a digest of Palestrina's contrapuntal technique.

"The primeval source of musical experience is the tone," said Webern. "The individual sound is the latent force of all development." Webern explained why the question of the next step was all–important. It concerned the immediate rise or fall of the tone-line in the making. The logical evolution of all music thus depended on the correct answer to these earliest steps. Webern quoted the statement of Karl Kraus that the fate of humanity often depended on the correctly placed comma. Webern considered the transference of this idea—from literature to music—to be crucial.

Not only did he teach strict counterpoint, but the still stricter discipline of developing patience for the maturing of thoughtful, honest work. In general, his pedagogy was a mirror-image of his own creative process: a careful search for worthy tonal material, to be constantly tested on the gold-balance of the most refined stylistic sense and, above all, to be judged for its individual sonority. . . . Free counterpoint was taught according to the basic style characteristics of the Vienna Classical School. Here, Webern pointed to the sovereignty of the melodic element in many scores of Haydn, Mozart, and Beethoven. Nevertheless, the general texture abounded in polyphonic design. Everything was invested motivically, resulting in the complex of voices called "obbligato accompaniment." This term Webern took over from Guido Adler, his teacher in musicology at the University of Vienna.

Webern often tried to awaken in his students an appreciation for historical thinking, thereby objectively to support their sense of style through the knowledge of the past. Thus he helped me, too, to find the intellectual values and compensations of musicological research. . . . When I turned to him in doubt, he would earnestly say: "Later on you will understand my advice. For the time being you must have faith in me." Faith! This word was perhaps the most significant in Webern's rich vocabulary. It was the essense of his religious spirit, and it built the bridge to his art.[31]

CHAPTER XXX

Webern and "The Third Reich" (1938–1941)

EMBOLDENED BY THE easy success with which he had brought Austria under German domination, Hitler soon moved towards his next objective: the annexation of Sudetenland, Czechoslovakia's western territory, which was populated by a strong majority of German-speaking people. Following anxious weeks of international crisis, armed conflict seemed inevitable. Actually, mobilization was in progress not only in Germany, but also in France and England, countries linked to Czechoslovakia by mutual assistance pacts. In the last hour, war was averted when Neville Chamberlain, the British Prime Minister, and his French colleague, Edouard Daladier, acceded to Hitler's demands by signing the ill-famed Munich Pact of 29–30 September 1938. The hapless little nation of Czechoslovakia was abandoned by its allies for what Chamberlain, on his return to London, claimed to be "peace in our time." Winston Churchill, then still a lone voice in the wilderness, had clearer political foresight. Addressing the House of Commons a few days after the Munich surrender, he warned: "We have sustained a total and unmitigated defeat . . . do not suppose that this is the end. It is only the beginning."

The weakness displayed by the Western democracies convinced Hitler that he no longer needed to exercise any restraint in consummating his anti-Semitic programme at home. Having already established stringent laws eliminating Jewish influence from all walks of public life, he now ruthlessly set out to drive the Jews themselves from German soil. During the night of 9 November a notorious pogrom, which came to be known as "Kristallnacht" (Crystal Night) because of the wanton destruction of much precious crystal, was staged. Supposedly, the atrocities perpetrated were a spontaneous act of revenge on the part of the German people when they received the news of a political murder committed by a young Jew in Paris.[1] The day after the rampage,

Reinhard Heydrich (second in command after Himmler of the dreaded
SS and director of the equally feared Gestapo) reported to Goering the
first statistics: 119 synagogues and 171 apartment houses burned and
815 shops destroyed (the following day it was announced that 7,500
shops had been looted), 20,000 Jews, most of them wealthy, arrested,
and 26 killed.[2]

William L. Shirer described the pogrom as follows:

> On the flaming, riotous night of 9 November 1938, the Third Reich
> had deliberately turned down a dark and savage road from which
> there was to be no return. A good many Jews had been murdered and
> tortured and robbed before, but these crimes, except for those which
> took place in the concentration camps, had been committed mostly
> by brown-shirted rowdies acting out of their own sadism and greed
> while the State authorities looked on, or looked the other way. Now
> the German government itself had organized and carried out a vast
> pogrom. The killings, the looting, the burning of synagogues and
> houses and shops on the night of 9 November were its doing. So were
> the official decrees, duly published in the official gazette, the
> *Reichsgesetzblatt*, which fined the Jewish community a billion marks,
> eliminated them from the economy, robbed them of what was left of
> their property and drove them toward the ghetto—and worse. World
> opinion was shocked and revolted by such barbarity in a nation which
> boasted a centuries-old Christian and humanist culture. Hitler, in
> turn, was enraged by the world reaction and convinced himself that it
> merely proved the power and scope of "the Jewish world con-
> spiracy."[3]

According to many accounts, Kristallnacht (staged in Austria one
night later than in Germany) was especially horrible in Vienna. Jewish
homes everywhere were invaded under the pretext that a search for
weapons was being made. Even the public kitchens for destitute Jews
were raided. Thousands were arrested, thrown into jail, and herded off
to concentration camps. Many were so severely beaten that they died.
News of the horrors spread quickly. Early on the morning following
Kristallnacht, Webern hurried to the homes of David Josef Bach and
Josef Polnauer to convince himself that they were unharmed, an act
requiring great personal courage. Ever since the Anschluss, when social
intercourse with Jews had become a public offence, Webern had made it
a point to prove to his friends that he was unwaveringly loyal to them. In
this endeavour he was demonstrative and, on occasion, even provocative, such as when he allowed himself to be seen promenading along the
Ring arm-in-arm with Bach, whose appearance was decidedly Jewish.

The atrocities of Kristallnacht, the results of which were there for everyone to see, shocked Webern deeply. Hueber related that, when walking along the Enzersdorferstrasse some time afterwards, Webern made a deliberate detour around a synagogue which had been burned out by the Nazis. "I do not want to pass by there," he said. "You must understand that I have absolutely nothing to do with such people."

Webern's revulsion against these excesses spurred him to dedicated and tireless efforts on behalf of his persecuted friends. That same November of 1938 he wrote to Erwin Stein, imploring him to assist in finding ways and means for Polnauer to escape to England. When the Bachs left for London in January, Webern and his wife helped them to pack their household effects. As a farewell gift, he presented Bach with the manuscript of his String Trio, Op. 20. Similarly, he gave Hugo Winter, who was leaving for the United States after having been forced out of his position as director of Universal Edition, the autograph of his piano reduction of the Trakl Songs, Op. 14.

Webern was equally unstinting in his efforts for his younger colleagues. On 8 July 1938 he wrote an eloquent letter of recommendation on behalf of Otto Jokl, Alban Berg's former pupil and assistant, who wanted to emigrate.[4] When the necessary papers failed to arrive, Jokl tried to avert the full brunt of persecution by embracing Catholicism and asked Webern to stand as witness at his baptismal ceremony. "Of course," Webern wrote in response, and on 14 June 1939 he signed officially as "Godfather" in the register of St Ulrich Church in Vienna.[5] Jokl's plight continued until February 1940 when, with the war already blocking most escape routes, he finally succeeded in making his way to America.

Julius Schloss, Jokl's fellow student under Berg, was not so lucky. Arrested during Kristallnacht, he was taken to the notorious Dachau concentration camp. At that time some prisoners could be ransomed, and Schloss was rescued after five weeks through the energetic intervention of his family. From Genoa he embarked for China, one of the few countries with relatively simple immigration formalities. For eight years he eked out a living in Shanghai playing the accordion in a bar several nights a week and working as a copyist during the day. Finally, in the ninth year, he obtained a teaching post at the National Shanghai Conservatory of Music and resumed composing. A year later, the arrival of the Communist régime drove him to the United States.[6]

With almost all his old friends and pupils gone, life became very quiet for Webern. "We live completely withdrawn. I work a lot," he wrote to Franz Rederer on 3 February 1939. Correspondence meant for him, more than ever, a vital link with the outside world. Always a prolific letter writer, he now tried almost compulsively to maintain contact. On

27 July he informed Willi Reich: "My correspondence has grown really enormously as a result of the new circumstances. Every day, thank God, messages from friends arrive, all of which I would like to answer right away in most cases."

Ironically, it was only through his channels abroad that Webern learned of the continuing performances of his music, which had been totally silenced at home. In January 1939, Ernst Diez, who was teaching that season at Bryn Mawr College, informed him of a radio performance of his orchestration of Schubert's German Dances by the New York Philharmonic Orchestra under John Barbirolli. (Diez commented: "The announcer did not make the slightest mention that the arrangement was by you. You should have this prevented by your publishers.") Diez also wrote of a forthcoming performance in Philadelphia of the Five Movements, Op. 5, in the string orchestra transcription. The same month, Erwin Stein reported from London that there were a number of prospects for performances, including a repetition of *Das Augenlicht*. On 14 February Webern commented to David Josef Bach:

> The series of my London performances continues: on 21 January my Schubert Dances were played by the BBC, on the 27th Stadlen played the Variations, and on 7 February the Bach Fugue was done by the BBC (under Leslie Heward, of whom Stein wrote that he is called the *"coming"* man in London).[7] *This programme also was in time to welcome you.* Did you perhaps listen in? I could hear it quite well, but was disappointed. Again one has to say: these conductors—they are *basically no musicians*! In *Florence*(!) my Bach Fugue is to be performed shortly. Today I received Newman's "critique" of my Variations (*Sunday Times*, 29 January). It is brief, but states at the end: "and the odd thing about it is that in time one actually gets *to like it!*"

Another Webern work was played on 17 April in the Aeolian Hall; Humphrey Searle then conducted a string orchestra (newly founded by the composer Alan Bush) in the transcription of the Five Movements, Op. 5.

Most of these performances were due to the promotional efforts of Erwin Stein. It was he also who informed the composer on 22 February 1939 that his String Trio, Op. 20, had been recorded under the Decca label. This was the first time that a phonograph disc of any of Webern's compositions was made commercially available, a fact particularly notable because the work chosen remains up to this day one of the least accessible to performers and listeners alike. "Unfortunately it was not Kolisch who played, but the same people who performed the Trio in

December," Stein wrote Webern in regard to the Kathleen Washbourne Trio who performed on the recording. "Still this is a rehabilitation: a gramophone recording one year after a cellist declared that no one could play the work." The disc did not reach Webern until late October. By then the war prevented all direct communication between Vienna and London, so that Webern could air his reaction only to Reich, to whom he wrote on 9 December: "The recording of my Trio is, as a recording, very good. But the performance! I recognize the presence of diligence and the best of intentions, but not really my music. I am convinced, however, that it would have turned out much better if only one had given the players a few pointers. Nonetheless, I certainly respect the accomplishment."

Webern's most recently published work, the String Quartet, Op. 28 (released by Boosey & Hawkes in May 1939), quickly elicited widespread interest. The Kolisch ensemble, who had premièred the work in September 1938 at the Berkshire Festival of Chamber Music, introduced it in New York on 1 November and thereafter in London at a private concert arranged by Boosey & Hawkes. It was also scheduled to be played by the Ondříček Quartet of Prague on 17 April 1939 during the fourteenth ISCM festival at Warsaw, but that performance was cancelled at the last minute. Subsequent renditions were planned for Budapest and Holland. Aside from the political situation, everything augured well for the success of the quartet, and the composer felt greatly encouraged.

Regardless of whether the public accepted or rejected his music, Webern never ceased to be convinced that his creative direction was infallible. He, who was himself artistically banned in his own country, constantly tried to impart to his friends in exile confidence in the absolute rightness of their cause. On 27 July 1939 he wrote to Reich, who was struggling to establish himself in Switzerland: ".... we do have a 'stronghold', after all, and in my opinion an invincible one, so I have never for a single moment lost heart (either on my own account or in my concern for others). Yes, dear friend, this makes all the difference!!! Seen from this 'stronghold' the 'Herrschaften' [masters] you mention—that is what one has to call them—have *always* appeared to me as 'ghosts'!"

Such allusions to Nazi tyranny on the one hand and to the bond uniting the Schoenberg circle on the other recur frequently. On 3 February of the same year, Webern had again exhorted his former pupil George Robert, who was aspiring to a career as a pianist in New York: "Even though it may be difficult in this respect over there, you must, with inexorable *energy*, conquer the ground by playing Schoenberg, and so forth. Only in that direction does the path lead, there is only the one; with anything else one of necessity suffers bankruptcy!!! Noncompliance is bound to avenge itself in the most awful way."

This uncompromising faith in the course of new music rings like a *cantus firmus* through Webern's communications. On 29 June he admonished Robert anew:

> Remember and always keep before your eyes *solely* that there exists music by Schoenberg. He who thinks otherwise or does not muster the energy to overcome the outside resistance must *by way of natural law* remain stranded on the "track." *The indications for this are multiplying!* In three decades, after all, something has transpired, i.e. indeed after such a time span the situation already looks different! And now things will move *rapidly*! You must appear on stage primarily as one who plays Schoenberg! Onward into battle! The outcome is clearly assured!

Thus Schoenberg remained uppermost in Webern's thoughts. Letters from the master had become few and far between, but when he did write, his words proved that his feelings for Webern were as warm as ever, and that he esteemed him above all others. In 1939, Schoenberg was working on his textbook *Models for Beginners in Composition*. Thirty years earlier, Webern had belonged to the small group of disciples who had inspired the *Harmonielehre*. Now that Schoenberg was again absorbed in formulating a theoretical guide, he addressed himself to the one member of that old circle whom he could expect to be the most receptive and sympathetic to his ideas. In a long letter, dated 8 July, he outlined his new method. As in times past, the challenge of setting forth his precepts concisely fertilized his thought and made the teacher-student relationship a productive entity.

> I believe [Schoenberg wrote] that it will become something very good, aesthetically, theoretically, intellectually, and (I believe I do not have to boast about this) morally. Especially, however: pedagogically. . . . The examples I have constructed, which in part almost possess the validity of compositions (as far as this is possible without thematic originality), are based mainly on the idea of showing how many solutions, respectively continuations, can result from a certain situation. Thus, one motive, created out of a broken chord, goes through the entire book. From this motive hundreds of phrases, fore and after–phrases, periods and movements of varied character with diversified piano scoring are constructed.

Enumerating in detail the structural elements to be covered, Schoenberg quoted as examples such challenging topics for discussion as "Character," "Instructions for Self-Criticism," "Polyphony and Counterpoint in the Forms of Homophony," "Melody and Theme, Melodic and Non-Melodic," "The Tendency of the Smallest Notes," and "About the Climax." He was by then midway through the second draft of his treatise and admitted: "What the third draft will look like I cannot anticipate as yet. Unfortunately, it is indeed one of my short-comings that I keep improving on such things too long. One simply has to tell oneself at one point: now it is finished. I have the intention and the desire to do this earlier this time than with the *Harmonielehre*—I hope I can!"

In conclusion, Schoenberg told Webern: "Please do not say that I have become an old woman because I speak so long and extensively about my projects. My apology is not simply that you have asked me, but that it does me infinite good to be able at last to talk again to someone who understands what I mean and can evaluate it."

News of the successful London première of *Das Augenlicht* had reached Schoenberg, and he asked about the new cantata on which Webern was working. This project, begun in July of 1938, was to be completed in late November 1939. Diary notes interspersed with the musical sketches record what was happening simultaneously in Webern's family. On 9 January 1939 Peter left the work corps, to which he had been assigned, because the physical hardships proved too taxing for his health. A month later he secured an office job with the railway. On 27 March Amalie lost her second child at birth. The heartbreak felt by the Weberns was shared by Hildegard Jone, as had been the joy which the first two grandchildren, Amalie's son Michael and Christine's daughter Karin, had brought into the house Im Auholz.

The poetess, herself childless, had written perceptively to Webern about the cycle of generations on 16 January:

My whole life, dear friend, I have been involved with art, have really lived my entire life immersed in it. More recently, however, I see more and more clearly what is much greater than even the purest of art. For example, the wonderful matter of course manner with which your wife cares for her daughter's child and has so fully absorbed it into her own life. With you, too, we like this so much. After all, you two had slowly become accustomed to the quiet after your children's nursery had become empty as they grew up. But now new life resounds closely all around you again. This may not always be pleasant for you, especially not for your musician's ears. I believe, however, if one allows oneself to be disturbed in one's own work with loving resignation, *then this will not only result in the highest perfection of that work, but also in that of one's own life.*[8]

Hildegard Jone's sensitivity and clairvoyance were a constant source of inspiration to Webern, who corresponded with her intensively throughout the months of the cantata's composition. On 27 July 1939 he mentioned the work also to Reich: "I am already rather far along in my cantata. . . . Next week I will 'relax' a bit and go into the mountains." The holiday was to be brief (19 July–5 August) and in accordance with Webern's severely restricted funds. He spent a few days in Kapellen and then went to nearby Vordernberg to visit Ernst Diez, who had returned from America. On 4 August he hiked to the Leoben Hut, one of his favourite spots in the Styrian Alps.

That summer Webern spent much time and effort on behalf of his daughter Maria, who wanted to go to England to bid farewell to her Jewish friend before he emigrated to Australia. Because of Germany's stringent currency regulations, Webern asked Stein to give Maria £5 as advance payment on royalties for his String Quartet, Op. 28. In a series of letters, he also solicited David Josef Bach to assist his daughter with pocket money and guidance during her stop in London. On 12 August Maria returned home. Three weeks later she would have found herself stranded in England, as war flared up over Europe and the gates between the countries swung shut.

Political tension had long been approaching the breaking point. On 1 September diplomatic negotiations came to an end when German armies invaded Poland. Two days later England and France declared war on Germany, and all the members of the British Commonwealth, except Ireland, followed suit. Barely 21 years after the end of World War I, the nations again were locked in mortal combat, a struggle to become more ravaging than any in the history of mankind.

The outbreak of the war had an immediate effect on Webern. His employment by the radio station was abruptly terminated. While it had entailed no more than the routine task of surveying programmes, it yet had yielded, since March 1931, a small but steady income. So desperate was Webern's situation that Universal Edition agreed to step into the emergency. Beginning in October of 1939, the firm gave him periodic assignments such as examining new compositions submitted, proof-reading works in production, and arranging. His first job was the piano-vocal reduction of Rudolf Wagner-Régeny's opera *Johanna Balk*. Webern referred to this task when he wrote to Reich on 20 October: "Imagine, I now have to do work for U.E., a thick, thick piano reduction. (I am not disclosing more for the time being!) Yes, in September I lost my steady activity at the Radio: the post was liquidated. There I was—left sitting! So I had to take what there was quickly! ! ! It is a devil of a situation. At the moment I do not have a *single* pupil!" A postscript read: "Besides Polnauer, I see no one any longer! Except the Humpliks, of course."

Although the job provided Webern with a monthly salary of 150 marks from October 1939 to January 1940, his funds were so limited that he had to accept contributions from Maria and Peter, both of whom were employed in Gunter Waller's firm, but continued to live at home. Their small monthly shares are listed in Webern's income book, as is an amount of 20 marks regularly received from "Mutter," Wilhelmine's mother, who continued her support until close to her death in 1944.

During those dismal months, the prospect of a concert tour to Switzerland sustained Webern's spirits. Reich had informed him in early autumn that a performance of his Passacaglia was scheduled for 7 February 1940 in Winterthur. Erich Schmid, one of Schoenberg's former pupils, was to conduct. Reich suggested that the composer be invited not only for this concert, but also for a song recital featuring music of Schoenberg, Berg, and Webern, which the Basel ISCM section was planning in conjunction with the Winterthur event. Webern seized eagerly on these prospects. In his enthusiastic response of 20 October, he implied strongly to Reich that his coming might well lead to his emigration: "Under certain circumstances my visit could even be of *special consequence* for me! Its realization therefore is *very close to my heart*!!! I am delighted that you thought *of this*. Very good, my dear Reich! Thank you very much! Anything of the sort did seem quite out of the question for me! I take it as a good omen!"

Webern's letter contained detailed suggestions for the choice of compositions for the Basel programme. With marked concern for effectiveness, he recommended a selection of individual songs from various cycles for the vocal group, proposing this sequence: "Dies ist ein Lied" and "Kahl reckt der Baum" from Opus 3, "So ich traurig bin" or "Eingang" from Opus 4, and "Der Tag ist vergangen" and "Gleich und Gleich" from Opus 12. Should a string quartet be available, he recommended that at least the second, fourth and fifth movements, if not all, of his Five Movements, Op. 5, be included.

> This would certainly work! And well! [Webern wrote]. Otherwise the *violin pieces* would be more suitable than the *cello pieces*. Those preferably *not at all*! Not because I do not think they are good. But they would just be totally misunderstood. Players and listeners would find it hard to make anything of them. *Nothing experimental*!!! Create favourable conditions for the performance of the "Passacaglia"!!! Look, look, everything that I mentioned is already *three decades old*! And still I have to worry! As if "world premières" were at stake. If only I could at last be understood a little. . . . And as far as your lecture is concerned: *nothing theoretical*! Rather just tell *how you like this music*! People will believe you, and this way a favourable effect can be achieved.

Because of the war, stringent passport regulations were in force, and Webern had to obtain a special visa to enter Switzerland. To that end, an official invitation from the sponsoring Collegium Musicum in Winterthur was necessary. When it was slow in arriving, Webern grew very nervous. In time, however, the preliminaries were taken care of, and the travel permit was granted.[9]

In Winterthur, where he arrived on 4 February, Webern was the guest of his old benefactor, Dr Werner Reinhart. He thoroughly enjoyed the comfort and elegance of his wealthy patron's home. On 17 February, after returning to Mödling, he gave Hildegard Jone this enthusiastic description: "I was surrounded by wonderful exotic plants: orchids, African violets, primulae, narcissus, etc. It was really an ideal sojourn, primarily on account of the personality of my host."

The concert in Winterthur on 7 February was followed by the one in Basel on 10 February. Since 1936 Webern had not been outside Austria, and he was elated over the opportunity to hear his music played for an appreciative audience. Among those attending was his former pupil, Siegfried Oehlgiesser, who came over from nearby St Gallen for a joyful reunion. Two months later, on 21 April, Webern reported to another pupil, George Robert, about the rendition of the Passacaglia: "It was really an excellent performance, placed for that matter within a truly classical frame—with the Fourth by Brahms and the Cello Concerto by Dvořák.[10] After this, there was also an evening in Basel, exclusively with songs by Schoenberg, Berg, and me, which also succeeded very well. So these days in Switzerland were really enjoyable, giving me complete satisfaction and reassurance."

The song recital at Basel, which was held in the auditorium of the civic conservatory, was presented by Marguerite Gradmann-Lüscher, with Erich Schmid at the piano. Following songs by Schoenberg and Berg, Reich gave a lecture entitled "Arnold Schoenberg and his Vienna circle." The closing group, given over to Webern's music, included the complete George song cycle, Op. 4 ("So ich traurig bin," first performed in 1925 in New York, was erroneously billed as a world première) and three songs from Opus 12 (in the order Nos. 2, 4, and 1).

As Webern headed back the following day, a blizzard and arctic cold delayed his journey repeatedly and he did not reach home until the middle of the night of 12 February. The storm and snow made the stretch between the railway station and the house Im Auholz virtually impassable. Webern related all this to Reich in his letter of 8 April 1940, adding: "I must say that I have returned home really well pleased and have derived much peace of mind." Werner Reinhart's generosity contributed significantly to the composer's gratification. The honorarium of 1,000 marks is listed, circled in red, in Webern's income book.

Even more important than the financial gain was the encouragement Webern derived from the visit. As a consequence, he now began to focus all his hopes on Switzerland, the only island of peace left in Europe. In his letters to Reich he repeatedly asked about prospects for commissions, performances, and conducting engagements. Suggesting the première of his recently completed Cantata, Op. 29, he also inquired about the possibility of a subsidy for his current work on the Variations, Op. 30. Knowing that Paul Sacher had commissioned works by such composers as Hindemith, Honegger, Martinu, and Bartók, he urged Reich on 18 June 1940 to put in a word on his behalf:

> Do you think it possible that Sacher might give me a commission—in the way in which he has actually done it in other instances? You mentioned the case of Bartók.[11] I must confess to you that the matter is really urgent for me. But in the final analysis, it would be the most natural way of "earning" for people like us. In the past it was certainly frequently that way. Only nowadays is it practised so little. Would you be so kind as to look into the matter a little (perhaps very soon)? What I am working on at present possibly would be very suitable for just this purpose! It is something instrumental.

Although Webern kept pressing the matter for some time, nothing was to come of such a commission. He was also disappointed by Reinhart's negative reaction to his inquiries about conducting engagements. Reinhart no doubt had to take into account the stiffening anti-German sentiments of his Swiss compatriots who, completely surrounded by totalitarian powers, were fiercely determined to preserve their independence. Webern alluded to this when writing on 3 March 1941 to Reich, whom he considered his faithful agent: "At the end of November I received a very long letter from Reinhart. Among other things he told me that an appearance as guest conductor would not be possible under the prevailing conditions and he gave me the reasons for this in a thoroughly friendly way."

During 1940, while vigorously exploring avenues in Switzerland, Webern had ample time to concentrate on his new orchestral composition. The quiet domesticity, so conducive to his work, was temporarily interrupted that summer. On 19 June Christine gave birth to her second daughter, Ute, and she and the children moved in with the Weberns because her husband was stationed at an army post. Much as Webern missed his annual mountain holiday, he resigned himself: "We old ones will hardly be able to get away this year," he wrote on 25 July to Josef Hueber. "But where is it more beautiful during summer than here in the Auholz?" Ever since Hueber's induction into the army, the friends had maintained a lively correspondence. Hueber was assigned to a garrison in northern France after the German whirlwind victory in spring. Knowing Webern's passion for smoking, he frequently sent him cigars and tobacco out of his own rations.

On 16 September Peter was drafted into military service. Although he was released again by 19 November because of his heart trouble, there remained the lingering concern that he might be recalled at any time. The growing pressures of war had begun to reach into every family circle, and that grim shadow hovered over all of Webern's last years. Secluded as he lived, immersed as he was in creative endeavours, he, too, was to become irresistibly drawn into the tidal wave of dramatic events, which allowed nobody to remain indifferent or impartial. Like everyone else, he saw his fate and future projected against the huge tableau of the war. With Germany immersed in battle, the destiny of the fatherland naturally had become the first concern of every good citizen. Webern's entire make-up, from his aristocratic heritage to his almost chauvinistic belief in the supremacy of German music, predestined him to the kind of patriotism that, with the outbreak of the conflict, caused him to rally behind the national cause. Like most of his countrymen, he could not help but be blinded by the first sweeping conquests. The amazing resurgence of a Germany, which he had seen go down in defeat only two decades earlier, as a power that might dominate all of Europe was a triumph so overwhelming that it could not fail to thrill and intoxicate him. As Webern saw it, an early and complete victory seemed beyond question. Lasting peace and prosperity would be established for a Greater Germany, and with it all would turn out for the best for every-one. To that ideal, the momentary hardships of individuals had to be subordinated. For the welfare of all people, even a totalitarian form of government had to be accepted.

Such were the ideologies to which Webern, along with most of the German people, subscribed during the first years of the war. His patriotism grew to a degree so boundless that for a time it distorted even his cultural outlook. Proof of this tragic self-delusion is found in a series of letters he wrote to Josef Hueber, from which the following excerpts are quoted:

4 March 1940 [Webern comments on Hitler's *Mein Kampf*, which Hueber had given him]: The book has brought me much enlighten-ment. In reading it, I went through the period covered therein (up to 1930) with reference also to my personal experiences and again wondered how such opposites could have become possible next to each other. Yes, this is really something to "wonder" about. What

I believe I see at present makes me supremely confident! I see it coming, the pacification of the entire world. At first east of the Rhine as far as——yes, how far? This will depend on the USA. But probably as far as the Pacific Ocean! Yes, I believe this, I do believe, and I cannot see it any other way!

2 May 1940 [following Germany's surprise invasion, on 8 and 9 April, of Denmark and Norway]: Your explanations, partly only in the form of allusions, interested me extraordinarily. Some of them actually excited me. They were enormously important contributions for me. This all really falls in line with what I would like to see happening and with what is also to be expected. It fits exactly into the picture that I create for myself. And are things not going forward with giant steps?! (These last results! Magnificent!) But not only the outward process! Also the inner one! It is elevating! I have recently seen a so-called cultural film which shows life in a "pool" that had been placed under protection to preserve its natural state; it was magnificent! By that I do not mean so much the subject matter that was to be seen, but rather the level in word and picture displayed by such a film. This is the one thing for which we have always yearned. Since the main film *Befreite Hände* [Hands Unshackled] was also good, and the *Weekly News*, too, is now shown in a new, quite excellent manner, I left the cinema with the definite feeling: yes, if the audience is not totally insensitive, then such an evening would really have to have a purifying effect on the people. I would like so very much to believe this. And it is just this that makes the film so important, since it is capable of making an *effect* with a greater impressiveness than almost anything else today. Well, we have indeed often spoken about this. And what I expect for myself in this respect is already being fulfilled in part so beautifully. In this connection some other aspects would still have to be mentioned, which definitely indicate progress in the process of inner purification. This is Germany today! But the *National Socialist* one, to be sure! Not just any one! This is exactly the *new* state, for which the seed was already laid twenty years ago. Yes, a *new state it is*, one that has never existed before!! *It is something new*! Created by this unique man!!! Look here, you sense my concern: that one could (in the end) consider as matter of fact what has evolved in *so remarkable a way*, what indeed could spring forth only from *this nature*, what has for its originator this *singular* man. Do write to me *again* quite *soon* and report to me what you find out. Such commentaries as your last ones are enormously important to me! *Each day becomes more exciting*. I see such a good future. It will be different also for me.

7 July 1940 [France had capitulated on 22 June]: How much, how much indeed has happened in the meantime! About what will follow I have my special thoughts and I am curious whether some of them will come true. I really have not erred much so far. (Only perhaps sometimes I did not *say* everything just as I *secretly* had it in my heart!)

21 December 1940: I would still like to tell you that I have made really eminently interesting discoveries with Stefan George: in *Stern des Bundes*, in which he pronounces a *doctrine* that is now being realized in many ways—but already in *1914*!!!—and in *Das neue Reich* (1921), in which, fundamentally, things are directly spelled out: he speaks of the *"true symbol"* on the "people's banner"!!! Well, more about this orally sometime.

20 March 1941: It is getting more and more exciting. The two last speeches! Now we should soon experience it!

5 June 1941: I wonder whether the possibility of an early end to the war does not exist, after all. Today there has been news on the basis of which this possibility may be considered as really not so improbable! Nothing has been confirmed as yet, to be sure, but it could be at any moment. What I would like best is to sit by the radio all the time. If it is true, then, my dear fellow, the "riddle in the East" would also be solved! I must confess—and you are my witness—that this aspect *never* posed a question for me! The alliance against that power that alone is guilty! Did I not say after the termination of the Russo–Finnish war: what could prevent the alliance any longer? At that time I meant from the Rhine to the Pacific Ocean, but now it is from the Atlantic Ocean to the Pacific. And is it not only a question of time that the *entire* world will thus be linked together? This is my belief!!! It is coming! Let us calmly wait, each at his post! When do you think you will come on leave again, if it does not turn into an indefinite one earlier? You are not to laugh at me.

18 July 1941 [following Germany's attack on Russia]: That it had to happen this way, after all! Up to the last moment I had expected it to be otherwise. You know what I had in mind. Now the goal, about which I recently wrote again, simply has to be attained in this manner—but the goal is being reached, perhaps still more quickly now. It is hardly to be comprehended any more what is going on! And already new dangers threaten. It really seems that our *entire* globe must be ploughed up over and over. Have you read the utterances of the gentlemen from the Kremlin? How diabolical this plan is—but really, how *dilettantish*, how silly! And again *Providence* (this word I mean in its most literal sense, signifying that which "provides" or correctly foresees) is beating the "weapon out of the enemy's hand" (again in the literal sense of the words). And thus will it strike them all! It is stupendous, dear friend!

Christmas 1941 [Japan attacked Pearl Harbor on 7 December, precipitating the entry of the United States into the war]: Yes my dear fellow, what has happened again now! I perceived Japan's entry into the war as a *fundamental, decisive turn for the better!* A mighty event! I really cannot tell you how much this preoccupies me! For who knows what will yet come forth from these people! I must say that this thought fills me with a quite special confidence. For as I imagine them—the Japanese people—they appear to me as a *completely healthy race!* Through and through! Does not something new arise from that direction? Out of an *undamaged, age-old soil!* I can only perceive it *that way!* I cannot see it any other way! And I am happy over it!!! How much more would I still like to say about this. I shall do so when you are here again on leave!

25 February 1942: What is happening at present is really staggering! Around Christmas-time, to be sure, there were days full of the gravest concern! But now!!! What have I said of the Japanese? Well, is it not so? And the immense accomplishments of our own forces! In this winter, full of horror and suffering!

The year 1942 brought the first reverses in Germany's fortunes of war, and Webern's letters soon became more muted in their expression of confidence in early victory. Nevertheless, he long maintained his optimism, seeking nourishment for his faith in the mystical poems of Stefan George, whose ideologies had inspired him for well over 30 years. Now he recognized in George the prophet of a new German generation, united behind a leader chosen, as he believed, by Providence. Eager to share the spiritual source of his patriotism with his friends, he called their attention to George's writings. As early as Christmas of 1940, he had told both Hueber and a former Singverein member, Hans Humpelstetter, about his "most curious discoveries." Humpelstetter, a trained philologist, was then away at the front. He had always been a staunch Social Democrat. Therefore, Webern, when referring to George's *Stern des Bundes* and *Das neue Reich*, expressed himself guardedly: "Just look into these poems. I do not say anything further, but I am most curious how this '*doctrine*'—as one probably would have to call it—impresses you. I am not taking a position! I only point it out."

In *Das neue Reich* (The New Reich), section "Der Dichter in Zeiten der Wirren" (The Poet in Times of Confusion), Stefan George predicts the birth of a future leader and extols his deeds:

Der sprengt die ketten fegt auf trümmerstätten
Die ordnung, geisselt die verlaufnen heim
Ins ewige recht wo grosses wiederum gross ist
Herr wiederum herr, zucht wiederum zucht, er heftet
Das wahre sinnbild auf das völkische banner
Er führt durch sturm und grausige signale
Des frührots seiner treuen schar zum werk
Des wachen tags und pflanzt das Neue Reich.

(He bursts the chains, he sweeps order back unto ruined sites, he scourges home the lost to the eternal law where the great is great again, master again master, discipline again discipline, he fastens the true symbol on the people's banner, he leads, through storm and the awful signals of his faithful troops' early dawn, onward to the work of the full day, and plants the new empire.)

It was in such passages as these that Webern identified the poet's vision with the actuality of Germany's rise under Hitler. Unmistakably that "true symbol on the people's banner" was the swastika, which proclaimed national greatness through racial purity. How could Webern reconcile these Pan-Germanic ideals with his personal allegiances and artistic convictions, which were so inexorably bound up with each other? No one but he himself could answer this vexing question.

The dilemma was a crucial one, and Webern soon found himself walking a tightrope between his loyalties. His pupil and friend, Ludwig Zenk, formerly of radical leftist persuasion, had become an ardent National Socialist and tried to convert him to the cause. According to Brunswick, Zenk was the "dangerous intellectual Nazi type."[12] Realizing his indebtedness to Jews like Steuermann (whose playing of Zenk's Piano Sonata prompted Universal Edition to publish the work),[13] Zenk had devised for himself a "modified" brand of anti-Semitism, declaring men like Arnold Schoenberg, Karl Kraus, and Gustav Mahler "exempt by virtue of their art." (Just the same, Webern had found it necessary to relegate Humplik's Mahler bust, which for more than a decade had been prominently displayed in his home, to the seclusion of the bedroom to escape the watchful eyes of Nazi sympathizers.)

As political convictions hardened, tensions mounted, undermining the bonds of long-standing friendships. Polnauer related that he broke with Zenk in 1940, when during a chance encounter on the street, Zenk bluntly told him that the war *had* to be won. This sent Polnauer, a man of choleric temperament, into a rage. Hearing of the quarrel, Webern tried to mediate. But Polnauer reminded him that on Kristallnacht Zenk had proved indifferent to the fate of David Josef Bach, a man who had long promoted him, whereas "a certain Dr Webern" had at once come to his friend's aid. According to Polnauer, Webern let his head hang with an embarrassed smile and, disarmed, made no further attempt to reconcile the two.[14]

Ever since the Anschluss, Webern had made it a point to invite Polnauer regularly on Friday evenings for dinner. Even after social intercourse with Jews was forbidden he continued this practice. Such disregard of official directives meant serious danger for Webern, especially when, from September 1941 on, Jews were forced to identify themselves publicly by wearing yellow armbands displaying the Star of David. The humiliation was particularly distressing for Polnauer. A large man with blond hair and blue eyes, he conformed to the image of the Germanic type, and he himself had certain doubts that he actually was of Jewish descent. He suspected that he came from a line of Bohemian ancestors who, persecuted as Hussites, adopted the Jewish faith rather than submit to Catholicism. From Kristallnacht on, Polnauer tried desperately, with Webern's help, to get out of the country. Success seemed at hand in early 1940 when an affidavit from Brunswick enabled him to book a passage to America. At the last minute, however, his immigration visa was denied because of the German invasion of Holland in May, which caused the United States to allocate preferential quotas to Dutch refugees.

Despite Webern's display of loyalty to his Jewish friends, it quickly became known abroad that his family included active National Socialists, and by extension he himself also was suspected of sympathy with the new régime. Eduard Steuermann left several letters unanswered because he deeply resented that Webern appended to his return address the designation, "Deutsches Reich" (German Empire). Steuermann considered this an unnecessary and inexcusable affront to those who had been forced to leave Austria.[15] Thus Webern's pedantic compliance with postal regulations cost him, without his ever knowing it, Steuermann's friendship.

As far as Schoenberg was concerned, he knew Webern well enough not to be perturbed by the things that others resented. Always a realist, he understood Webern's impressionable nature and recognized the dilemma in which he was trapped. Their correspondence continued until all direct communication terminated with the entry of the United States into the war. Although most of Schoenberg's letters are no longer extant, a comment in a letter Webern wrote to Reich on 3 March 1941 reveals that Schoenberg kept him abreast of his activities to the end:[16] "News from Arnold: Krasner played his Violin Concerto—world première under Stokowski. There also was the world première of the just-finished Second Chamber Symphony, which he had begun already in 1906."

Torn in his fundamental loyalties as man and artist, Webern struggled to maintain a precarious balance between his allegiance to the fatherland and his solidarity with his friends. Agonizing as that conflict must have been, there was nothing ambiguous or compromising in the pursuit of his creative vision. To the end, it was made to serve the ideas for which he had fought so valiantly in phalanx with Schoenberg and Berg. To that mission and, through it, to his friends in exile and in death, he remained unwaveringly faithful, and therein lay his ultimate loyalty.

CHAPTER XXXI

Wartime vignettes—Webern's 60th birthday—Iconography (1940–1943)

WEBERN'S WORK ON his last three compositions (Opera 29, 30, and 31) was interrupted periodically by sundry assignments from Universal Edition. These jobs helped to relieve his financial needs and, as the war progressed, also protected him from being drafted into one of the branches of civilian service set up to support the national effort. Nevertheless, Webern heartily disliked the unwelcome duties, considering them far below his dignity. His letters to friends abound in plaintive references to what he called "Fronarbeit" (forced labour), jobs doubly loathed because they kept him from his own compositions.

"I would have written to you before this had not a compulsory job totally absorbed me for a full four weeks. I wanted to get it behind me as quickly as possible. Now it is done, and I can breathe a sigh of relief," Webern reported to Josef Hueber on 25 July 1940. He was then engaged in proof-reading his piano-vocal reduction of Wagner-Régeny's *Johanna Balk*. The score, published on the occasion of the opera's Vienna première on 4 April 1941, does not give Webern's name as arranger, but his conscientious workmanship is evident in every detail.

After *Johanna Balk*, Webern was called upon to make piano arrangements of Othmar Schoeck's opera *Das Schloss Dürande* (premièred in Berlin on 1 April 1943) and Alfredo Casella's *Paganiniana*, Op. 65 (an orchestral suite from the ballet *La Rosa del Sogno*). Schoeck's bulky score kept him occupied from August 1941 to February 1942. Webern referred to the tedious task when writing to Reich on 23 August 1941: "At present I must again slave over a piano reduction of an opera which is—please do not pass this on—by a Swiss 'master.' Woe to you if you let it out! (If other Swiss had shown some understanding, perhaps I would not have to do it!)" The closing remark alluded to Sacher's refusal to subsidize Webern's Variations for Orchestra, Op. 30.

In similar vein, Webern complained on 16 September to Hueber, apologizing for his delay in acknowledging a shipment of cigars: "Just then I sat from early till late with a job (for UE) that I had to take on for understandable reasons: again it is a piano reduction of what seems to be a terribly long opera. Fortunately, I now have a portion behind me and can look toward my *own* work again." The reference pertains to the Second Cantata, of which Webern had already completed one movement. Thwarted in his urge to continue with that project and embarrassed by having to stoop to doing another composer's chores, he lamented to the Humpliks on 7 December:

Things are not good for me, which is partly the reason why you have not heard from me for so long. It was against my nature to have to admit that for *weeks* now I have been tied down to the compulsory job that I mentioned when we last met. And it will still continue for several weeks more, so I can hardly hope to get to my own work before the new year. *But then!* Once the sun is on the rise again! This is a really bad situation. But I could not evade it. So I had to interrupt work on "Freundselig ist das Wort" as early as *November*! It was hardly to be endured any more! So I kept silent. But I finally had to tell you. In the end keeping silent also was unbearable.

In his Christmas message to Hueber, Webern voiced his determination to get the hated job over with as quickly as possible: "It will still require some weeks, however. My manuscript leaves stack up to hundreds already." On 24 February 1942 the "horrible job" was finished, as Webern informed Hueber the following day, and joyful release emanates from the letter he wrote to Reich on 28 February: "I have again cranked out a piano reduction, this time from a monster of almost 1,000 pages of full score! Do not inquire further, I do not care to talk about it and I do not want you to tell anyone about it either!!! After all, it is behind me by now! I feel reborn. . . . Therefore I can again turn to my true work. The interruption was bad."

That interruption was not without reward, however. "To be sure, I secured quite a good price for my work," Webern told Hueber on 25 February. According to his income book he received from Universal Edition, beginning in July of 1941, six monthly instalments of 100 marks each and a final sum of 900 marks in March 1942. The instalment payments were marked "R," an indication that Werner Reinhart may have had a hand in the assignment of the job. The published piano–vocal score of Schoeck's opera, like that of the Wagner-Régeny work, does not bear the arranger's name.

During the autumn of 1942 Webern entered two payments from Universal Edition, totalling 500 marks, for his piano reduction of

Casella's *Paganiniana*. (The Italian composer's symphonic suite was given in Vienna that year.) Webern commented on the arrangement in a postcard sent to Alfred Schlee on 17 October 1942.[1] Three movements were finished and he was then working on the lengthy fourth movement, which required, in his words, "especially much deliberation." Justifying his slow working method, he remarked: "Nothing would be accomplished by undue haste. 'Gut Ding . . .'" (an allusion to the German proverb "Gut Ding will Weile haben"—A good thing takes its own time).

Webern's painstaking care notwithstanding, Casella did not like the arrangement. According to Schlee, he found it too thin and wanting in its simulation of the brilliant orchestral score. Here, as in his other arrangements, Webern had confined himself to a delineation of the essentials, stripping the musical structure of everything he considered padding. He was not concerned with pianistic effectiveness, technically or acoustically, but only with the musical substance. As a result, what had sounded impressive in Casella's virtuoso orchestration lost much of its effect after it was pruned down to the bare ingredients. Webern's condensations, revealing as they do the basic features of a work, inadvertently also point up any shortcomings in inventiveness or construction. Casella himself seemed to realize this, and the piano reduction was never published.[2]

Besides employing Webern as an arranger, Universal Edition engaged him from time to time as a Lektor (reader) for new compositions submitted. If Webern was conscientious enough to invest all his diligence and skill in arranging works he did not care for, he was merciless in passing judgement on some of the insipid products he had to review. The prevalent musical taste of the time was neo-classicism, a style that Webern detested for what he considered its pseudo character and with which he took issue on numerous occasions. The following excerpts are characteristic of his appraisals, which were mainly negative. For obvious reasons, the names of the composers were not released.

> X. . . Tanz-Capriccio: Suffers from too many repetitions, and so appears somewhat primitive, but might—because of its tempo—be effective.

> X. . . Ballet in one act: Definitely more valuable than V's piece. But again the endeavour at primitive effects (so much unison!). One would need to know the "scenic" intentions.

> X. . . Four Songs: Amateurish throughout, miserable Kitsch! Indescribable!

> X. . . Violin Concerto: I cannot recommend it. Invention clearly based on Grieg, at least in the first movement. In the second and

third it is different again. Therefore: who knows whether the man really comes from up there? But further: how miserable it all is! Harmonically: constant, irrelevant modulations, but generally this is nothing but falling by a fifth, which is the easiest method. When he tries anything else he fails completely. Since there is constant meandering, no structure whatever evolves. Perhaps the theme of the second movement is not too bad. The opening is quite warmly felt; but nothing is done with it! The last movement is no good at all. The orchestration is very suspect. In all, then: dilettantism! This is only a general view—I could, of course, give you detailed reasons. I looked at the thing thoroughly. After all, I am personally interested in understanding these things.

X. . . Quintet for Winds: What is usually referred to as "shoddy."

X. . . Albumblätter: Impossible!

X. . . Prelude for large orchestra: One would have to see other compositions; ask him perhaps to submit chamber music, songs, etc.[3]

These were mostly harsh verdicts, but they were candid and unquestionably honest, and Universal Edition knew that they could rely on the integrity of Webern's advice. The relationship between the publishers and the composer remained completely cordial even though the ban on "degenerate" music prevented the firm from actively promoting his works. One distinct benefit Webern derived from his continued association with Universal Edition was that of being able to stay in touch with the musical trends of the day and on occasion to meet visiting musicians. When the Florentine composer, Luigi Dallapiccola, came to Vienna, Webern was included in an intimate gathering at Schlee's home. An ardent admirer of Webern's music, Dallapiccola had attended the premières of his Concerto, Op. 24 (Prague, 1935) and Das Augenlicht (London, 1938). Himself a victim of discrimination because of his marriage to a Jewess, he was fiercely opposed to Fascist tyranny, and the suppression of all art forms not complying with racial doctrines enraged him. In his diary, Dallapiccola described his meeting with Webern:

Vienna, 9 March 1942. A stop of twelve or fourteen hours in this dead city is inevitable for anyone who returns from Hungary to Italy. (Two controls by the police are mandatory.) However, I am happy this evening. In Schlee's home I had the good fortune to meet Anton Webern. A mystic, a short man, who talks with some inflection of Austrian dialect; kind, but capable of a burst of anger, cordial to the point of treating me like an equal. ("*Our common responsibilities,*" he says.) Without fear, without hesitation, we talk about the war. Among all topics, this is the most urgent in every country, and we readily understand each other. It is obvious on which side of the barricade we stand. . . . But we also talk about music. Since Webern has not witnessed the immense success of *Das Augenlicht* in London, I tell him about the great impression it made on me, and Webern immediately asks: "Were you impressed *by the sound* also?" (The sound! I understood it correctly.) While discussing problems of orchestral sonorities, the sensitive seeker (history will not ignore his enormous contribution to the formation of the new language) states: "By now I am unable to imagine a chord of three trumpets or four horns."

Incidentally, the name of Kurt Weill is mentioned and Webern suddenly explodes. He points his finger at me (but I had not been the one who uttered the name of the composer he disliked!) and asks me a very direct question: "What do you find of our great Middle-European tradition in such a composer—that tradition which includes the names of (and here he starts to enumerate them on his fingers) Schubert, Brahms, Wolf, Mahler, Schoenberg, Berg, and myself?"

I was embarrassed. I do not say that an answer would not be possible; but what confounds me most is that Webern used the term "tradition," a term which, knowing the scores of the Variations, Op. 27, the Cantata *Das Augenlicht* and, through a performance, the Concerto, Op. 24, I supposed had been eliminated from Webern's vocabulary. Not only that. But that he should consider himself an heir to tradition, that he should believe in the continuity of language. . . . And finally, that it should not be a question of aesthetics and of taste that separated him from Kurt Weill but rather the fact that Kurt Weill had refused the Middle-European tradition.

Webern impressed me very much also as a human being, and I think again of what Theodor Wiesengrund-Adorno wrote about him years ago: "*The assault that Schoenberg's constructivism launched against the walled doors of musical objectivism is (in Webern's songs Opera 14 and 15) just a vibration which comes to us from extreme distances. It is a solitary soul who trembles before the walled doors and clings to faith: nothing else is left.*"[4]

On his return to Italy, Dallapiccola proposed Webern's Passacaglia for the September 1942 programme of the Venice Biennale and suggested that the composer be invited to conduct. Curiously, the ban on Webern's music did not include his works that employed traditional tonality, but only those that were associated with Schoenberg's style and therefore considered products of a "Judenknecht" (serf of the Jews).

Performances of his Opus 1, of his Schubert arrangement and, oddly enough, of his Bach transcription were admissible. On 10 January 1941 Webern had written to Hueber: "Some time ago I heard over Radio Leipzig (as a *Reich* broadcast) my Schubert Dances in a performance that was not bad at all. During the summer they were broadcast once even over the Italian stations." A year later, on 25 February, he told Hueber: "You will be amazed: at the 'Contemporary Music Festival' here in May there is a possibility of a performance of my Passacaglia (Philharmonic Orchestra) under Furtwängler or Böhm." But on 3 June Webern informed his friend: "In Vienna naturally nothing materialized. Thank God, I must say—that was some programme!" However, Webern was to find new support for his unfailing optimism later in the year. "This Monday Rosbaud is performing my Passacaglia in Strasbourg," he wrote to Hueber on 12 December. Meanwhile, Dallapiccola's efforts had had results, about which Webern reported to Reich on 31 July 1942: "My Passacaglia was supposed to be played this September in *Venice* (at the 'Biennale') under *my* direction. Now it is postponed till *next year, for certain*! This is not unimportant! *Dallapiccola* has written to me about this in an *extraordinarily* nice way."

As late as 17 October 1943, when writing to Hueber, Webern was still confident: "In the autumn my Bach transcription will be performed in Berlin under Schmidt-Isserstedt, the new conductor of the German Opera. Something is stirring, after all." The composer's naïve hopes for a measure of recognition within the Third Reich were soon to be completely dashed, however. Beginning that summer of 1943, intensive air raids brought the war to every major city, including Vienna, and concerts became the first casualties in the ensuing disruption of public life.

During the earlier stages of the war, when the victorious German armies were occupying wide territories, the general confidence had created a degree of normality at home. Thus Webern had written to Reich on 30 October 1940: "I am holding a course again this year. Just think, it has become possible again, after all! I also have one (just one!) new pupil. Therefore—a slight improvement. Otherwise nothing new in this respect!" Earlier in the year, the possibility of employment at the Music School of the City of Vienna had arisen. Webern had had a conference with the conservatory's director, Othmar Steinbauer, as he informed Hueber in his letters. But no engagement resulted, and he continued to have to rely on his other sources of income. His lecture courses were held regularly on Friday evenings at the home of Erwin Ratz who, after Dr Kurzmann had emigrated, provided a base for Webern's teaching activities in the heart of Vienna. The series was so successful that it was continued, season after season, until the closing months of the war. In the autumn of 1942, Webern could report to Hueber that his class was "very well attended (about twenty participants)." Margaret Prohaska has related that one of Webern's lecture courses took place in her apartment at Maxinggasse 18 (where Johann Strauss once lived and composed his *Fledermaus*). Nazi surveillance had grown so stringent by then that the course participants left the house one at a time in order to avoid suspicion of a political conspiracy.[5]

As the class attending his lecture courses grew in size, there was a corresponding increase in the number of private pupils. Webern could list in his income book a good half-dozen through most of 1943 and 1944, including several from countries seized by Germany. Delighted that his reputation had spread so far, Webern wrote to Reich on 28 February 1942: "Just think, since autumn I have had two pupils from *abroad*: a *really young* Dutchman who strikes me as very talented and one from the Baltic region." On 17 October of the following year he told Hueber: "As of October all private lessons have commenced again and also a class course. The number of pupils has increased again. At present a *Serb*, too, is studying with me, an older man, who was a conductor at the Belgrade opera."

Webern's satisfaction in once more finding outlets for his inclinations as a teacher is vividly reflected in many letters to his friends. On 10 January 1943 he commented to Reich: "I believe I have again achieved rather good results in the 'Lehre' [Doctrine]. Especially in pushing on to the 'idea' of the various principles. Thus what I can tell the students—also in the course—is now based on other, better reasons! And yet this is but a beginning! For it seems to me as if with the explanation of the procedures followed in the music of the masters an explanation of the cosmos also would have to be given. 'Oneness diversified within itself,' as Hölderlin translates it." Webern prefaced this quotation with the original statement of Heraclitus, which he wrote out in Greek letters.

Teaching thus was for Webern a means of clarifying his aesthetic thinking, which was directed towards finding a common denominator that could encompass the universe. His absolute devotion made him enjoy his rôle as an educator far beyond any monetary rewards. The challenge of the task so absorbed him that he often completely forgot about time. Aware of this tendency, he could refer to it with irony, as for example when he wrote to Zenk on 15 November 1942: "Throughout last week I was very much detained by the visit of Hartmann from Munich who took a 'Stunde' [in German the word means 'lesson' as well as 'hour'] every day, which mostly extended to two hours."

The name of Karl Amadeus Hartmann, the young Bavarian

composer, had first appeared with that of Webern on the programme of the 1935 ISCM festival in Prague, when Scherchen premièred his *Miserae* symphony. Hartmann had already turned out a number of successful works[6] when, in the early autumn of 1941, he approached Webern about the possibility of having his compositions published by Universal Edition. Acting on Webern's advice, he came to Vienna that November and, although his mission with the publishers proved in vain, he found the personal contact with Webern so challenging that he returned the following year for a series of daily private lessons. Brief as that period of concentrated study was, it led to a lasting friendship. The letters that Hartmann wrote to his wife Elisabeth under the fresh impression of those days in Maria Enzersdorf contain many candid vignettes of Webern as a man and artist. Some excerpts follow here:

> You will ask what he looks like. Only one who has never seen him could claim that Webern looks like a small clerk. True, in group photographs he presents an unpretentious and bourgeois appearance. Actually he comes from an old noble family. . . . He is smaller than one imagines from the pictures. At the first meeting, when he put away his garden tools and led me into the house, a measure of coolness and objective severity was present in his face. When I had introduced myself this dissolved at once and gave way to a pleasant affability of the Viennese type. At that, much charm and distinction radiate from him without his seeming to be obtrusive or striking any pose. If one disregards the glasses, which easily make any face look severe, he appears warm-hearted and friendly. He is lean of countenance and has a sharp nose which juts out just under the metal bridge of his glasses. The glasses—I cannot get away from them—are of a touching simplicity as far as the frame is concerned and underscore what one has long known of him, that his demands are not focused on external things. The mouth, by the way, is somewhat thin-lipped. . . .
>
> In his painstaking manner he concerns himself also with the household and exerts a patriarchal influence over his small domestic circle. When I recently brought a little rainwater from the street into his room, the lesson did not begin until everything had been carefully wiped up. You can imagine my face as I stood there while he mopped around between my legs with a rag. In the end I will not only learn from him the braiding of compositional plaits but will also become an orderly human being in every respect. . . .
>
> It was largely my fault that the conversation kept returning to politics. I should not have steered it there, for I learned things that, in my strong leaning towards anarchism, I would rather not have heard.

This is because he seriously defended the viewpoint that, for dear order's sake, *any kind* of authority should be respected and that the State under which one lives would have to be recognized at any price. All the while, he comfortably smoked his cigar, and I had a hard time to restrain myself and not to become disrespectful. His benevolence towards those who push him against the wall is incomprehensible to me, but after all I have not come here to explore his view of the world. . . .

Here in Vienna there is a music festival, and I want to tell you about it. Yesterday I was with Webern at the State Opera and thought with much longing of the beautiful festivals in Prague, Paris, and London. The stage setting at the State Opera was overloaded as if to compensate for the wretchedness of the music. Just imagine, a contemporary music festival in Vienna without Schoenberg, Berg, and Webern, an event in which Webern goes about physically, but like a ghost whom nobody sees or knows. I can only be glad that no one asked *me* to participate because I would have felt like a traitor.

Webern is invited neither to a performance nor to other festivities, let alone to the reception by the governor. In the Opera none of the composers present recognized him, neither would they have found it worth the effort to seek his acquaintance. We—Webern, Hans Erich Apostel, and I—walked about the theatre like strangers and could rightfully feel ourselves to be outcasts. Webern bore it at first with equanimity and appeared indifferent. But during the intermission I experienced his one and only act of rebellion. Almost beside himself, he hurried towards me in the foyer and began to pour out his heart without considering those standing around. Like a madman he, who otherwise expressed himself only in a civilized and sedate manner, heaped Old Testament curses on the music performed and condemned all the triviality and pseudo-modernism that was promulgated with it. It was painful and redeeming to see how he suffered under the stupidity of this music and for once abandoned his reserve because of it.

This afternoon not a word more was spoken of yesterday's theatre evening. We worked on analyses and while doing so I felt that he was especially fond of me. How much I value this affection and how I respond in kind!

At the end of the lesson I still had a few questions concerning Schoenberg's *Erwartung*. I had brought along the score and opened it, although I had fatigued Webern enough with my queries. Unexpectedly, a lengthy discussion resulted from this. In the course of it he became more and more unrestrained and excited and finally spoke so glowingly about this work that I felt like the one whom Virgil guided through heaven and hell. He began to unfold the work before me, at first pointing out a few tones which express a great undefinable feeling and reveal a marvellous architecture. He continued by showing how the work grows organically in all directions until it has gained its full stature, and I had some inkling of the creative intoxication that must have seized Schoenberg. This was *his* festival performance in response to the insipid evening before. . . .

Now I have been here some time, and still have experienced no sobering of my high-pitched mood. Webern has at present no pupils, and I believe that not a soul is concerned about him. This can only suit me, for he devotes himself to me the entire afternoon, and with his concentrated working method the amount of material we plough through together is immense. Each session the work goes on intensively for three to four hours. After that, we converse about this or that composer, then he evaluates, propounds theories about the future of music and the like. We have thoroughly discussed my *Simplicius* and my First Symphony. In doing so, he went into the most detailed ramifications of form and thematic structure. Then we analysed classic works—Beethoven's Sonata, Op. 2, No. 3, and a string quartet by Reger. He esteems Reger highly, and it is very enjoyable to take apart under his guidance the String Quartet in F Sharp Minor. While doing so, he gives me the impression of a scientist who dissects an insect under a magnifying glass and takes pleasure in the changes of the wings and the multi-faceted eyes. While his estimate of Reger makes sense to me, I disagree with his rejection of Bruckner. He does not believe that Bruckner has accomplished anything for the development of music. Is Bruckner really so far distant from his beloved Mahler?

His relationship to Strauss stands in the shadow of his love for Mahler, and he has convinced me that Mahler is more important and direction-giving for us than Strauss. I, for one, cannot take so decided a position for either of the two. But in the end, Mahler meets my intentions more closely than the programmatic poet Strauss.

It gave me enormous joy that Webern considers Scherchen the best conductor for his works—no wonder, in view of their similarity, their open-mindedness to the new, and their readiness to promote us young people. Webern never lets you feel that he is the teacher. His temperament is well-balanced, controlled and amiable. Each time it is a ceremony, to which I look forward by now, when he carefully pulls open the drawer, takes out a folder, places it on the desk, then opens the folder, leafs through it, takes from it a sheet—the looked-for analysis—closes the folder, carefully puts it aside, and after the work is done, again follows all the steps of the ritual in reverse, with imperturbable meticulousness, in the manner of a retrograde canon. Each of his compositions is accompanied by painstakingly exact analyses and with charts of the transmutations of the tone row. He engages with me in precise investigations of the rhythmic, melodic, and thematic aspects of my works, giving the thematic the most attention. Today we discussed in a particularly intensive manner his Piano Variations, Op. 27, which I had to analyse. These variations are a miracle of sound, supremely constructed. If I could only learn, beyond the technique of these serial inter-weavings, how he accomplishes it, and whereupon it is based, that his music contains the divine breath!

Recently he told me in all candidness: "Sometime in the future even the postman will whistle my melodies!" I rather believe, for that matter, that the postman will whistle *at* his melodies. At the very least, the postman someday will have to bring him the mail from admirers all over the world, whatever he whistles while doing so.

In a quiet and unobtrusive way he finds words for his destiny and the position of his work within music history. In this respect, the adverse nature of the present external circumstances does not touch him.[7]

The story has been circulated, even printed,[8] that, during his last years, Webern was so impoverished that he was unable to purchase a ticket and had to stand outside the door of a Vienna concert hall to listen to a performance of Orff's *Carmina Burana* during a contemporary music festival. This is unquestionably a myth, however romantic. At all times and under any conditions, Webern remained the aristocrat, and any public admission of poverty would have been irreconcilable with his fierce sense of pride. Mark Brunswick recalled that Webern insisted on leaving a generous gratuity for the maid whenever he came to dinner, although he could scarcely afford such a display of social decorum even in his better years.[9] Another American, Adolph Weiss, related: "My meetings with Webern were usually in the Café Sacher, a very popular haunt for musicians. We had a cup of coffee or a glass of beer, but Webern would never let me treat him. He was a very proud man who always wanted to pay his own bill and be free of obligations to anybody."[10]

The dignity of Webern's personal bearing was matched by his self-sufficiency. Stemming from a family that traditionally practised frugality as a virtue, he made only the most modest of demands on life. Much as

he enjoyed the sumptuous comfort offered him on rare occasions
during a trip abroad, he was quite content with his spartan domestic lot.
Only for the sake of his family did he regret the limitations of his living
standard, especially when he saw composers whose integrity he
questioned enjoy the affluence that came with popular success. It
saddened him when at times he could not provide more than the bare
necessities. According to Amalie, the family meal frequently consisted
only of soup or potatoes. The table setting, with linen and silver, was
always meticulous, however.[11] Even in the few personal pleasures
Webern allowed himself, cigars and a little wine, he was extremely
moderate. Hueber recounted that, at social gatherings after rehearsals
of the Mödlinger Männergesangverein, Webern would confine himself
to an "Achtel" (a small glass) of wine.[12] Thrift dominated his home.
While the children were given every possible advantage, the parents,
particularly Wilhelmine, denied themselves most simple luxuries. Even
purchases of new clothes were rare events, and those of a bicycle or
typewriter were noted in Webern's diary as red-letter days. Despite the
frugality of everyday life, hospitality was an indispensable social grace.
Friends were always welcome, and the traditional "Jause" (afternoon
coffee and cake) or a small supper were never lacking.

Long accustomed to relative privation, the Webern household was
less affected than most by the hardships of a wartime economy once
shortages of food and fuel became general. Financially, the family's
situation remained dire. Webern eked out a mere subsistence, but
somehow he managed to maintain a small reserve in the Mödling
savings bank. His last account book, begun in August 1938, shows the
balance of Austrian schillings being converted to 1,400 German marks.
Although Webern frequently withdrew small amounts, the occasional
influx of major payments—such as those from Reinhart in 1940 and
from Universal Edition in 1942—increased his savings again. They never
exceeded 1,500 marks, however. In 1944 these reserves markedly
dwindled, leaving a balance of only 47 marks and 83 pfennigs in the
end. At no time in his life did Webern go into debt. While he was willing
to accept the all too rare subsidies from wealthy patrons as compatible
with his dignity as a creative artist, he never allowed the slightest in-
fringement on his independence. Economically and artistically, he
remained the sovereign.

Webern's income book records during the last years—besides
revenues derived from private lessons, class courses, and jobs for
Universal Edition—payments received from Stagma, the organization
that superseded the AKM as the clearing house for performance
royalties. These amounts, for obvious reasons, never totalled more than
a few marks, and they ceased completely by the middle of 1942. From

1940 to 1944 a sum of 50 marks is listed annually in the income book at Christmas-time under the designation "Künstlerdank," and a one-time subsidy of 200 marks is recorded, in October 1942, as "Künstlerhilfe Wien." Both payments represented relief measures during the wartime emergency.

Peter's small monthly contribution to the household, which he had made since the outbreak of the war, came to an end in 1941. On 5 April he married Hermine Schubert, a girl he had known since school days. She was the youngest of the six daughters of a master carpenter in nearby Perchtoldsdorf. The civil ceremony took place in the Liesing courthouse, with Webern standing as witness for Hermine, whose father had recently died. The marriage was solemnized in the Perchtoldsdorf parish church. Afterwards the two families gathered for a dinner at the bride's home at Hochstrasse 43, where the young couple was to occupy a small garden house following their honeymoon trip.[13]

Sensitive to the pre-eminent place of the family in Webern's life, Hildegard Jone wrote to him about the wedding on 23 April: "Here, too, another circle within your marvellous family unit has been closed in a wonderful way. You and your wife can take much joy in this, dear Anton. Not only has a *total* picture of your art developed for you, but most happily also the richest panorama of life. *All God's blessings on your house!*" Overflowing with gratitude, Webern responded on 3 May: "The way you understand us—we have heard these things from no other quarter. That you should express such a sentiment! Yes, it certainly contains my goal—a goal unattainable!"

On 19–20 July, Webern took Peter and his bride to his favourite alpine retreat, the Schneealpe. A photograph taken by Hermine (see insert) shows him happily leaning against his son's shoulder as they rested on a mountain meadow. Following that excursion, Webern stayed on in Kapellen, where one of his sisters from Klagenfurt was vacationing. From there he sent Polnauer a postcard setting up their next Friday evening meeting at his home. These regular visits continued into 1942, despite the latent dangers for both. Then anti-Semitism became so violent that Polnauer, fearing arrest and deportation to a concentration camp, went into hiding. For three years, beginning in May of 1942, a courageous woman (whom he later married) sheltered him in her home. Throughout that time he was provisioned by the intrepid Erwin Ratz, who also supplied several other victims of political persecution in their hideouts. Webern once came to see Polnauer, but refrained from further visits when Polnauer begged him to stay away for the sake of their mutual safety.

With Polnauer underground, Hueber in the army, and the Humpliks living too far away for frequent meetings, Webern drew closer and closer to Ludwig Zenk who, because of a heart ailment, was exempt from military duty. (He had become the musical director of Vienna's Theater in der Josefstadt; besides conducting, he composed incidental music for the plays given in that quaint old theatre.) The war had put an end to their far-ranging mountain excursions of former years, and the friends had to content themselves with long walks in the nearby Vienna Woods. They frequently went up to a hillside—referred to by Webern as "our meadow"—from where on clear days the Schneeberg, the easternmost spur of the Alps, could be seen.

Webern's consuming love for alpine flora, which in earlier years always made him yearn for the high regions, had found an ideal outlet when, shortly after his move to Maria Enzersdorf, he began to develop a garden in the yard behind the house. Planning and cultivating that cherished spot became his favourite recreation and an unfailing comfort when he was under emotional stress. "Today I worked in the garden quite early in the morning, digging around in the soil in order to free myself from yesterday's impressions. And it succeeded, of course," he once wrote to Polnauer.[14]

Before the garden could take shape, much preliminary work had to be done: the soil, consisting largely of clay, was treated until a fertile humus was developed, and trees and bushes which blocked the light were relocated. Several years passed before Webern's vision could be realized. Immersed in his project, he participated body and soul in the changing seasons as they were mirrored in the budding, blooming, and fading of the many varieties of flowers and shrubs he planted. For Webern, his garden was the source of purest delight during the closing years of his life. Characteristically, he infused his hobby with the scientist's zeal, studying books on horticulture and acquiring the Latin terminology for each of the floral species. Not satisfied with the local supply of seeds and young plants, he placed orders with Karl Foerster, a well-known garden specialist in Potsdam. With child-like exuberance, Webern described each new acquisition to Hueber and Zenk. Hueber, himself an amateur gardener, actually had been the one to stimulate Webern's interest in gardening when they were neighbours for a short time in the Penzingerstrasse (where Hueber took care of the large grounds for the landlord).

In his recollections, Hueber wrote of the enthusiasm with which Webern created his own floral microcosm:

> He worked in the garden partly in the early hours of the morning, partly when he took a break after lessons, or when he needed recreation or to refresh himself during composing. . . . The "peasant" in Webern, the friend of nature and flowers, felt

exceedingly happy there, regardless of the garden's narrow confines. He observed closely the change of seasons and the influences of the climate on the growth of his beloved flowers. He could not do enough to create for them ever more suitable conditions. And, during such activity, he was uncommonly happy.

In letter after letter that he sent Hueber during the war, Webern dwelt on the garden, his pride and joy. At one time he announced "the newest adornment, a Chinese *dwarf juniper*, a cherished present from Zenk" (20 June 1940), and at another the coming of spring: "I have discovered crocus shoots already!!!" (17 February 1941). Later he reported with satisfaction:

> I would have liked to show you my garden during the past weeks. Much of it was especially beautiful this year! What I had planned obviously quite correctly is now taking effect. In short, only now is the garden really *full*! I believe this should hold true for the whole year! Not only for the most favourable time locally. I have triumphed over the climate and soil. There are also beds of *lettuce* and other vegetables. I received plants from *Styria*: hence *real* vegetables at last!!! You understand—in this way I feel at home. But I do not want to make your heart heavy. Soon, soon, dear Hueber, you will be here again (5 June 1941).

As always, the fading of summer was lamented: "How different everything becomes once the sun has passed its zenith. I sense it more each year and grieve ever more" (16 September 1941). By Christmas-time that year, in the throes of winter, Webern hailed the coming resurgence: "Only a few days more and things will again begin to stir—*the great turning point* in nature, which I feel more deeply with every year. How marvellous!" (Christmas 1941).

As the war intensified, so did Webern's preoccupation with his garden: "One blooming follows the other. This year, too, everything is much better. As time goes by, I somewhat understand what gardening is all about. As for vegetables, I have planted onions, tomatoes, parsley, and radishes, and also started a *plot of poppies*! Everything thrives very nicely" (3 June 1942). Some alpine plants ordered from Foerster required special consideration: "I have already changed my beds around for them and have worked in the best fertilizer (out of the compost pile) very deeply. Therefore, I believe that my garden will *represent something completely different* from next spring on!!! If everything turns out the way I have figured (after very thorough reflection and taking into account blossom time, *colours*, etc.), I believe that you, too, will rejoice in it!" (16 October 1942).

Later that year Webern proudly enumerated his most recent
acquisitions:

Primarily I would like to name the "Silberwurz"-Dryas, a great rarity,
a plant from the highest alpine region, stemming from the Arctic, one
of the oldest on earth! The "*Dryas* Period" derives its name from it. It
is a rather low shrub that blooms *ivory–white*. Then a really wonderful
species of Steinbrech; even the seedling offers quite a peculiar sight: it
blossoms red like a mighty precious stone. Further to be named are
the Enzian bed and that of the Hungerblümchen (Draba, yellow), as
well as the Goldfingerkraut (Potentilla, orange) and four new types of
iris, a red Schafgarbe, a yellow Eisenhut, etc., and finally a dwarf iris
that blooms really early and consists of the tiniest deep-blue buds
and, lastly (the climax!!) the scarlet–red wild tulips! . . . Also, I have
planted two apple trees and four gooseberry bushes. The old pear tree
is gone, as well as the cherry tree by the gate. And my neighbour, Perl,
has created air space—all the birch trees have been removed. Now
there will be much more sun in the afternoon! And how beautiful the
unobstructed view is!! It will be a new garden when you come back!
(12 December 1942)

The profusion of plant varieties grew in the following year and by mid-
1944 Webern could write: "My garden looks good. Now it blooms
uninterruptedly, very much as a rock garden should and already much
closer to my vision of one, that is, in places it appears like a veritable
wilderness garden. . . . But, after all, I have toiled over these things for
more than ten years—finally some success!" (17 June 1944).

In stark contrast to such idyllic accounts are Webern's constant
references to the raging war. In 1942, the outcome of the gigantic
struggle still appeared favourable for the Axis Powers, and German
confidence in victory remained unshaken. On 3 June Webern wrote to
Hueber: "We probably have in the meantime come substantially closer
to the 'really great' decisions indicated by you, dear friend. I wonder if
the end is not already quite close at hand? Sometimes such a feeling
overcomes me, such hope!!!"

This letter was written on the eve of Webern's departure for
Klagenfurt where he visited his sisters, Maria and Rosa, whom he had not
seen for seven years. The trip also afforded him another opportunity for
a pilgrimage to the graves of his parents. Wilhelmine accompanied him,
as well as Christine and her two little daughters (a third daughter was to
be born that autumn). However, the holiday was interrupted when
Webern fell ill, and the family had to return home after only one week.

During the autumn, plans for the first performance of Webern's

Variations for Orchestra, Op. 30, entered into the final stages. After Sacher and Ansermet had shown no interest, the score had been sent to Scherchen early in the year. When Reich informed Webern that Scherchen hoped to be able to schedule the première for a concert in Winterthur, the composer had excitedly commented to him on 31 July: "I have not written to him [Scherchen] as yet. Why does he not write? Does he have nothing to tell me now that he has seen *this* score? Naturally, I am waiting for word. Of course it pleases me immensely in any case that he wants to study the piece with his orchestra. And if it then also came to a performance and I would be invited for it, this would really be very, very valuable to me! It certainly would be good if at last a plan could turn into reality again."

Soon after, Reich was able to let Webern know that the première was set for 9 December and that he was to attend. Webern was overjoyed. He asked Reich at once for an official invitation so that he could apply early for the necessary travel permit: "Again an affidavit regarding the necessity for my presence during the study of the work is required!!!" he wrote to Reich on 4 September, summing up his anticipation:

If one is approaching a first performance, especially an orchestral one, then one primarily (if naïvely) wonders: how will it sound? And one already looks forward to it, equally naïvely! But when one actually performs, then the right sensory impression must result, too. Revel in sounds, you conductors, then you do right! I hope that Sacher thinks this way also, if at last he wants to give me a try, too! As UE informed me, he has already written for the Passacaglia. Well then, perhaps something will really come of it this time. I am happy indeed and naturally would like to attend! Especially because of Alban's Violin Concerto!!! It would really be nice!

In his next letter, dated 11 November, Webern explained why he had not written to Reich sooner: "I had to 'slave away' once again and wanted to get this job over with as quickly as possible. In my present situation, this sort of thing simply becomes necessary from time to time." The disdainful remark referred to the piano reduction of Casella's *Paganiniana*, which Webern was then making. Meanwhile, the concert date in Winterthur had been postponed to 3 March. Webern kept urging Reich to prevail on Sacher to perform the Passacaglia in Basel during the same period. He would welcome an invitation to go there also and commented that it would be useful for him to have affidavits from two different sponsors because of the tightening scrutiny of visa applications.

Mail between the two countries had become exceedingly slow. When

Webern wrote to Reich on 10 January 1943 he told him that the last letter had taken three weeks to arrive. He was anxiously awaiting the necessary invitations from Scherchen and his Winterthur host, Reinhart: "I still have nothing in hand with which to pursue my trip abroad." The prospect of a Passacaglia performance had since faded and Webern remarked: "So Basel had to fall by the wayside," adding: "Das ist so eine Sache mit diesem Sacher! [a pun, freely translated: It's one of those things with Sacher!] His continual evasiveness annoys me by now." To the end, Webern was kept in uncertainty. "If everything works out I will travel to Switzerland the last week of February," he wrote to the Humpliks on 11 February. Finally, on the day of his departure, his passport was validated. The official visa specified the purpose of the journey as "participation in the rehearsals and première of an orchestral work" and was limited to ten days.

It was to be Webern's last trip abroad and also the last time that he would hear his music publicly performed. On 29 March he gave Hueber a detailed account of his experiences:

> I was in Switzerland, after all! At the very last moment permission arrived from Berlin. I left the evening of Wednesday, 24 February, and returned home again Saturday, 6 March. The performance of my Variations turned out quite well and the reception was gratifying beyond all expectations (I would almost like to say: against all expectations). Yes, dear friend, the point has now been reached, I believe, that they cannot easily ignore my cause any more. How I would have liked you to have been able to hear this work—I can truly say that from the first to the last moment it was a completely new sound constellation (also compared to my own earlier works)!
>
> Naturally I was again splendidly taken care of in Reinhart's house. Marvellous meals, glorious coffee, magnificent cigars (unlimited amounts!). There was an automobile outing to the Lower Lake of Constance, where Reinhart has a wonderful country home. So I have experienced much friendliness. Also certain prospects for the next season have emerged. Among others, the performance of one of my choruses by a society in Zürich, which is said to be able to master the most difficult tasks and which consists entirely of soloists. One of the sopranos is the singer Gradmann, who the last time (when I was there) and also afterwards sang some of my Lieder and who surprised me this time with the performance of my first song cycle on Jone texts. A very talented woman.
>
> Now, just think, I had hardly arrived in Winterthur when the German consul in Zürich inquired of Reinhart, in the friendliest manner, about me! He was present at the concert; before that we had

supper together at Reinhart's. To meet him in such a setting, and yet quite intimately, at home as it were, naturally meant a very welcome opportunity for me. After the concert he was also with us at a restaurant. And on the following day he *still* phoned *twice*!!!! He appeared to me very sympathetic, and I must confess that I was overjoyed—never before had it happened to me that a representative of my fatherland had paid any attention to me! Now just consider my present situation here at home! May the homeland be kind towards me only outside its borders? But I see it as a good omen and as a reward for my loyalty.

(Although Webern attached such great significance to the presence of the German consul, it probably represented little more than a diplomatic gesture at a time when relations between the countries were extremely tense.)

The concert, on 3 March, was under the auspices of the Collegium Musicum Winterthur and took place in the Stadthaus auditorium. The municipal orchestra, under Scherchen, was augmented for the occasion. Webern's Variations were heard between works by the Swiss composers Hans Studer and Conrad Beck. Schubert's *Auf dem Strom* (in Scherchen's arrangement for small orchestra) and Albrechtsberger's Symphony in C major followed.

So happy was Webern over the performance that it was still fresh in his mind when he wrote to Reich five months later, on 6 August:

It benefited me very much to be able to hear my piece. For it was very important for me to check personally what it has to say—I believe I was proven right. Namely, that when this kind of unity is the basis, even the most fragmented sound must have a completely coherent effect and leave hardly anything to be desired as far as "comprehensibility" is concerned. Is this not so? I believe the effect on the public has shown this, too! The performance, for that matter, turned out quite good in the end.

Since Switzerland had become the only country where his music could be heard, Webern desperately clung to that last remaining outlet. In the same letter to Reich, he voiced his hopes:

It is my great wish that in the coming season the opportunity might again present itself for me—if Scherchen would perhaps perform my Six Orchestra Pieces, Op. 6! These are the ones for which I re-worked the instrumentation some time ago. A copy of the full score is with UE; the parts also have been there for a long time. How long have

I been waiting for a performance of these pieces!!! In their effect they should be equivalent to the Five Movements for String Quartet which Rudi [Kolisch] has played so often. With this I want to say that the timidity of the Herren Dirigenten, which perhaps still exists, can have absolutely no further justification!

The same evening that Webern had left for Switzerland, his son was called into the army again. For a while his job with the railway system had been deemed sufficiently important to warrant deferment, but the reverses suffered by the German armies, culminating in the disaster at Stalingrad,[15] prompted a hasty call-up of reserves. Webern was glum as he saw Peter don his uniform. For the first time his belief in Germany's victory began to waver, but it was restored by the time he wrote to Hueber on 29 March: "I would like to tell you still, dear friend, how good it made me feel when, during our last conversations in which I expressed myself so gloomily, you held fast so unshakeably to your confidence!!!! And how happy I am that everything has now turned out quite differently again, just as your good faith let you foresee!"

These were idle hopes. The continuing setbacks of the Axis armies were the signal for the underground partisans in the Balkans, particularly in Yugoslavia, to begin waging major warfare. The unit to which Peter von Webern was assigned was stationed south of Belgrade and put in charge of guarding the railway lines that were under constant harassment by the guerrillas. Webern's deep concern is revealed in numerous entries in his sketchbooks. During the few months of his son's basic training at Olmütz and St Pölten, he noted each home visit. But when Peter was sent to Serbia in early July, his anxiety mounted and he recorded every date that he received a message. Webern's worries were reflected in his letters, which were now losing their patriotic zest. "When will it ever be *different?* Mankind delivered from these dangers!" he exclaimed at the close of a lengthy account of Peter's whereabouts that he gave Hueber on 17 October 1943.

The first air raids had taken place and the war was coming close to home in a very real sense when that letter was being written. Webern referred to the bombings, as he continued: "Since your departure a good many things have happened again, also to us directly: on 13 August and 1 October. On the latter day it was really very distressing here *in Mödling.*" Disenchantment and doubt had begun to creep into Webern's former blind confidence: "I just read the Goebbels article in the *Reich* of 10 October ('Clock of Fate'). Well, what does it mean that, for the first time, he raises the question how the war might be terminated!!!!! Is that not strange? What does it imply? Do we face something totally unexpected?"

On the day of the first bombing attack, Christine with her three children and her mother-in-law moved into the Webern home. Since it was located at the edge of Mödling, it promised greater safety than the inner city. The four stayed more than two months until the onset of colder weather prevented the children from playing out-of-doors and the living quarters became too confined. Before they left, there was another air raid. On 10 October Webern commented on it to Zenk: "The 1st of October was quite upsetting for us out here since some incidents took place in our immediate vicinity." In a letter written to Hildegard Jone the day after, he exclaimed: "To have to suffer such horrors with *small children* holding your hand!"

As the year 1943 drew towards its close, a gloomy mood spread throughout the land. Webern's 6oth birthday, on 3 December, came and went almost unnoticed in Vienna. Unlike a decade earlier, there was no formal observance, but only a small party given by his closest friends. Webern himself described the occasion to Reich on 10 January 1944:

We were together at Ratz' in the evening; it was in fact the day for the course. There were the course participants, the Apostels and—what gave me quite special pleasure—Frau Helene [Berg]. We—my wife and I—had already been with her in Hietzing during the afternoon, and afterwards she went along with us to Ratz' who had prepared a splendid buffet. So for once on a Friday (course day) evening there was more agreeable food than "scholarly" morsels. Now you know how it was! Frau Gradmann wrote to me very kindly, but that was *before* the Basel matinée, and a telegram arrived from Erich Schmid. However, I heard nothing from Scherchen and not from Reinhart, either. The UE wrote to me, but otherwise there was not a stir from more official quarters.

The matinée referred to was a concert by the Basel ISCM section. It had come about through the initiative of Reich and commemorated Webern's 6oth anniversary in the manner most to a composer's liking: a programme consisting entirely of his works. Planned originally as a vocal recital, the event was to have included two previously unperformed song cycles. Keenly concerned, as always, with every aspect of programme building, Webern had written to Reich on 23 October:

I fully approve of the idea that these songs—there are six of them (three each in Opera 23 and 25)—should be premièred in Basel; after all, they are already almost ten years old. I think it would be best to put these songs in the middle of the programme and to play the Piano Variations in between. Before and after this group, a selection from

the songs with piano, Opera 3, 4, and 12. Whichever suit Frau
Gradmann best. From Op. 3 perhaps Nos. 1, 4, and 5 (those are the
ones I would like, but I believe that Frau Gradmann has never sung
them before). Begin with these. From Op. 4 whichever she prefers,
and from Op. 12 perhaps Nos. 1, 2, and 4. Consequently, two groups
of four to five songs each. And that could make up the whole
programme; it would then last about an hour and that would be quite
adequate, my dear Reich! Not more! As far as the date is concerned:
under no circumstances tie yourself to that particular day! Do not
stage a direct birthday celebration—no, no, a performance! Do not
even mention that—— How unimportant, how irrelevant, for God's
sake! Fulfil this wish for me by all means!

In this letter Webern makes a point that is of vital significance to
performers, namely that he himself would allow the selection of
individual songs from various cycles, rather than insist on the rendition
of a complete cycle as an organic entity.

Contrary to the composer's modest plea, the concert, which took
place on the morning of Sunday, 5 December, was billed as a 60th-
birthday tribute. Participating artists included the soprano Marguerite
Gradmann-Lüscher, the pianist Paul Baumgartner, the violinist Walter
Kägi, and the cellist August Wenzinger. The programme opened with
the Piano Variations, Op. 27, followed by the Three Songs, Op. 23, the
Four Pieces for Violin and Piano, Op. 7, and the Three Little Pieces
for Violoncello and Piano, Op. 11. After an address by Willi Reich,
the concert continued with repeat performances of the three instrumental works, to which the Five Songs, Op. 3, were added. All the
offerings were first performances for Basel, and that of the Three Songs,
Op. 23, was a world première. Universal Edition had provided the
singer with a photocopy of the still unpublished Three Songs, Op. 25,
but the première of this cycle did not take place. It is interesting to note
that the cello pieces were included despite the strong apprehension
Webern had voiced to Reich four years earlier.

This birthday homage coming to him from abroad delighted the
composer. After Reich had sent him a report on the success of the
concert, Webern expressed to him, on 10 January, his deep gratitude for
his "unflinching, courageous, self-sacrificing loyalty" and for his "truly
magnificent championship." He closed with what meant for him, a man
of strictly formal bearing, the highest recognition: "So, dear friend, I
embrace you with my best sentiments. And these I would like to express
also by offering you the 'Du'."

Kurt List, another of Webern's pupils who had fled from Nazi
persecution, also commemorated his teacher's birthday, but in a literary

way. He published in America an article, "Anton von Webern," in the November–December issue, 1943, of the periodical *Modern Music*. The overtones of politics entered into the biographical portion of the essay, which, appearing at the height of the war, recognized the composer as "a tragic victim of present circumstances." List wrote:

As a conductor of the Workers' Symphony Concerts in Vienna, he allied himself to the Social-Democrats. But, being utterly ignorant of politics, he was a ready prey to the personal influence of family and friends. He lived in a state of perpetual confusion about the proper solution for the plight of impoverished Austria. Soon he abandoned his first allegiance in favour of more nationalist ideas. This new course may have saved him from the concentration camp but it did not preserve his music under the New Order. In recent years he has made his living as an orchestrator of operettas [*sic*]. To hear his works performed he must travel to Switzerland: at home his musical principles are attacked as "Jewish" and Bolshevist.

List's discussion of Webern's music was summed up in the statement: ". . . although this music represents the purest expressionism, even the orchestration being determined by thematic necessities, it often bears a resemblance in colour to the sound of the impressionists. What his music actually does, is to combine the substance of expressionism with the colour of impressionism." List's assessment concluded:

Webern's character is completely in accord with his style. Only a shy and retiring man could write such intimate and individual music. He exemplifies another of Schoenberg's maxims: "Have the courage and force to approach everything in such a way that it becomes unique through the manner in which it is seen." The very intimacy and conciseness of his music has been an obstacle to Webern's success. A world which has little regard for the individual, which is deafened by the thunder of war machines, is not attuned to the whisper of an artist's soul. Let us hope that at some saner, not too distant moment, Schoenberg's wish for Webern's music will be realized: "May this stillness ring."[16]

Webern was unaware of that tribute paid to him in a distant land. His heart was warmed, however, by letters he received from the handful of remaining disciples and friends, such as Hartmann, Hueber, Zenk, and Humpelstetter. The latter surprised him with a compilation of recollections from Singverein days, extolling the exploits of that by-gone time and bemoaning the lack of recognition shown Webern ever since. Thanking Humpelstetter on 14 December 1943 Webern proved reconciled to his lonely position:

> I enjoyed so much that in your comments you did not become *polemic* in any way. But of course I do not mean this just in connection with the present situation, since, to be sure, my battle has lasted almost four decades already. No, I mean it in a general sense: for only the positive counts. Naturally, it is better to look at what there is instead of at what there is not. And what there is, after all, is being seen—in my case by just a few (for that matter perhaps there are many more, only one does not know of them)—this fills one with joy, with reassurance, for which one is thankful.[17]

Webern rounded out the sixth decade of his life with a celebration of his own: the completion of what was to become the last movement of his Second Cantata, Op. 31. During the three years of the work's evolution, the composer had maintained the closest communion with Hildegard Jone. Curiously enough, the poetess was not among those who congratulated Webern on his 60th birthday. She simply forgot, being fully immersed in her own creative work. The day before, she wrote to him: "I have finished several lithographs which are close to my heart. I would like to *explain* them to you, not just hand them over in some strange place. Here at home, however, it is not really comfortable enough because the large room cannot be heated. Would it be possible nevertheless for one of you to come in order to receive the leaves?"

Among those leaves was a lithograph of Webern, perhaps Hildegard Jone's best effort. She had been secretly working on that drawing[18] when she asked Webern to send her a specimen of his musical handwriting. Without disclosing her purpose, she had written to him on 28 October 1942: "What I would like best is the passage 'Freundselig ist das Wort,' sung by the chorus. It is my aim to place a key passage of your music under a drawing. This small musical image would suit me perfectly. . . . This drawing, in particular, seems to me to have come out really well. What is at hand is not a religious subject, for which the music would provide the explanation, so to speak. Rather it is to be *a part of the picture itself*."

The finished lithograph incorporates, beneath Webern's portrait, the first three measures of the four-part chorus "Freundselig ist das Wort." The artist had painstakingly traced not only the passage, but also Webern's signature. Thus the two friends were linked in an art work celebrating the completion of the latest musical creation in which they had collaborated, the Second Cantata, Op. 31, "The Great Cantata," as it was subsequently called by Hildegard Jone. The lithograph, printed in a limited number of copies, has since become famous among portraits of the composer.

Webern iconography, while limited in extent, contains several works by noted artists: Oskar Kokoschka's often-reproduced drawing (1912) and oil portrait (1914), two pen-and-ink drawings by Egon Schiele (1917 and 1918), two lithographs by Emil Stumpp[19] (both dated Mödling, 13 February 1927), three pen-and-ink drawings by Benedikt F. Dolbin (1920 and 1924), a drawing by Franz Rederer (1934), and an oil portrait by Tom von Dreger (1934). All of these were done from life. Hildegard Jone's contributions include, besides the lithograph (1943), several pencil and charcoal drawings made after Webern's death. Also painted posthumously was her large oil "Webern standing in the doorway of his house, a few moments before his violent end" (1945).[20] This picture has been frequently reproduced, as has been Josef Humplik's portrait bust of Webern (1928). Another sculpture of the composer was done by Humplik somewhat earlier (1927). Among the posthumous portraits is a large woodcut (1964) by Franz Rederer.[21]

CHAPTER XXXII

Opera 29–31
(1938–1944)

WHEN WEBERN SET out to write the work that evolved into his First Cantata, Op. 29, he was to realize a plan that had lain dormant for over eight years. The basic idea was outlined in a letter he wrote to Hildegard Jone on 8 September 1930, long before he had begun to use her poems for his compositions:

> Ever since I have known your literary works the thought of setting some of them to music has never left me. . . . Now I am very much occupied with the idea of writing a cantata. And my request: would you consider undertaking a text of that kind for me? . . . The schema of a cantata (such as I intend) is approximately this: chorus, solo song, possibly another one, and then another chorus. For the solo voices I envisage a soprano and perhaps a baritone. (But none of this is binding.) So what is needed, since I am not thinking at all of long pieces of music, is basically very little text. And furthermore, in the choral movements words can be repeated. Frequently in Bach's choral works a huge movement is built on *a few words* (a single sentence). Think of the "Kyrie eleison, Christe eleison" in the Masses. But again this is just for your orientation.
>
> Now for what concerns the textual theme: I say straight out: the *Farbenlehre*! [a cycle of poems by Hildegard Jone] Send me a few sentences from your *Farbenlehre*! That is about the way I imagine this cantata text! Now surely you understand me! I want words that bring out something of these miracles. In so many of your poems natural phenomena have been given such extremely beautiful form. But the text certainly would not have to rhyme, nor be in any kind of "bound" form. This is why I say: just a few sentences from your *Farbenlehre*! I would be so happy if you could find what I envisage—I do not want to say anything further now. Do you feel like doing it? Once again the main point: brevity.

Although the final form of Webern's First Cantata was very close to that early conception, the actual genesis of the work was to be quite improvisatory and tentative (as was the case with virtually all of Webern's cyclic compositions from his middle period on). When the composer began he had neither selected the complete text nor was he fully certain of the ultimate character of the work. He in fact first headlined it "Symphony." This designation appeared on 1 July 1938, on the opening page of Sketchbook V, and was followed by various experimental drafts of the tone row.

The origin of Webern's new creative effort coincided with highly favourable reports reaching him after the London première of *Das Augenlicht*. The good news, coming at a time when the radical effects of the Anschluss were making themselves felt in ever-increasing measure, lifted him from the throes of depression and inspired him to new constructive activity. On 3 August, the definitive statement of the tone row (circled in red and marked "gilt") was set down in the sketchbook.

Throughout the period of composition, Webern maintained a close rapport with Hildegard Jone. On 20 July 1938 he informed her: "I am now composing 'Kleiner Flügel Ahornsamen, schwebst im Winde.' It is to become the key to a sizable symphonic cycle for solo, chorus, and orchestra, in which still more of your texts will appear. A kind of symphony with vocal sections."

With the exception of a brief vacation in Kapellen, Webern worked on the movement without interruption. Several dates reveal the stages of his progress. Interspersed among the sketches are various diary notes, such as his son's departure for a German work camp and the birth of his first grand-daughter, Karin (the child of Christine). Aside from small changes in the early stages, the draft of "Kleiner Flügel" proceeded smoothly to its completion on 14 December. The serenity of the music gives no hint of the horrifying experience of Kristallnacht, the pogrom that occurred while Webern was working on the composition.

As usual, he set to work at once converting the condensed score into its full orchestration. On 25 January 1939 he could write to Hildegard Jone:

> *By the same post* I am sending you what I promised for Christmas.[1] It has *long* been *finished*, but I still had to write out a copy (for myself); thereby the matter was delayed. Well then, it is the first full-score manuscript of "Kleiner Flügel Ahornsamen." May it be handed over herewith to you and Pepo [Josef Humplik]. I am convinced you will understand everything from the "drawing" that has appeared through the notes. But what seems to float around so freely there ("schwebst im Winde . . .")—possibly music has never before known

"Kleiner Flügel Ahornsamen," second movement of First Cantata, Op. 29

anything so *loose*—is the product of a *regular procedure more strict*, possibly, than anything that has formed the basis of a musical conception before (the *"little wings,"* "they carry within themselves" the "whole . . . Gestalt" [shape]—but really, not just figuratively— exactly as your words say it). But how *these words* have fostered my ideas!!

Although Webern knew that the poetess and her husband could not read music and therefore were unable to realize the implications of notation in sound, he nevertheless submitted all his scores to them as if believing in the interaction of optical and acoustical phenomena. In his dedications and letters are found many allusions to the essential relationship of eye and ear. This was in accord with his general philosophy, which centred upon a common source for all of life's manifestations. He could be certain of a sympathetic response from Hildegard Jone. Acknowledging receipt of the "Kleiner Flügel" manuscript, she commented: "I see the idea of your creation through the transparent picture of your notes. . . . *How good* that nowadays a symbol so pure, so full of grace, may rise in sound, may float heavenward!"[2]

In quest of a text for the next component of his "symphony," the composer again turned to the poetess. On 16 January 1939 she sent him a selection of distichs (her favourite form of concentrated poetic expression) from her unpublished cycle *Der Mohnkopf*. From that group Webern chose three: "Blitz und Donner," "Das Prisma," and "Doppelte Gabe."[3] As was his habit, he copied them out in longhand, imbuing himself with their lyric qualities in order to crystallize his musical thought.

On 11 February, Webern began setting the first of these distichs for mixed chorus and orchestra. Under the title "Second Symphony, Op. 29" (Sketchbook V, page 14), he drafted a schematic outline in which he tried to formulate the shape and structure of the entire cycle, then envisioned to be in five sections:

1. Little Rondo.   Adagio form (Allegro)
2. Brief development.   Adagio form (Adagio)
3. *Kleiner Flügel*.   Three part.
4. Scherzo (theme—secondary theme—theme)
5. Variations (chorus)

As has been seen before, such architectural outlines were typical of Webern's approach, although he frequently modified his ideas in the course of his work. On 15 March, the composer reported to Hildegard Jone on his progress: "In the meantime some of the *couplets* have already been set. I am amalgamating *three* of them into a *musical* unit. It will be for chorus and orchestra. And this planned cycle of movements will make up a cantata (i.e. exclusively vocal) on words by you!"

Here for the first time Webern applied the term "cantata" to his work. The draft of the new movement was completed by 25 April. On 14 May, Webern informed Hildegard Jone that he was working on the final orchestration, explaining: "I have not used all the texts that I originally planned to use; the musical form demanded something different, after all. There are some purely instrumental passages in it, with your couplet 'Lightning, the kindler of Being . . .' [the opening words of 'Blitz und Donner'] in the middle."

To this movement, which was to open the cantata, the composer proceeded to provide a counterpart, so that the orchestral solo song, "Kleiner Flügel," completed earlier, could be flanked by choral cornerstones. A section from Hildegard Jone's unpublished poem, "Verwandlung der Chariten," was chosen. Webern had first been drawn to this subject matter when the poetess expounded her concept of "charis" in the letter with which she thanked him for the manuscript of "Kleiner Flügel":

> The thought is so precious to me that "charis" means mercy and at the same time grace. I would not know of a better word than this to associate with your music. I have written a long poem this summer: "Die Chariten," which is close to me in many respects. You know that if one is enabled to perceive a miracle, then other miracles at once follow. Thus the Sanskrit root "har" means to glitter, to trickle, to spray, to gleam, to burn; "haritas" means stallions of the sun. With the latter, however, the colours of the spectrum are meant. *Glorious!*

As a lover and student of ancient Greece, Hildegard Jone found in that bygone culture a never-ending source of allegory. She was enchanted with the image and meaning of the Charites, the goddesses who, as muses of the arts, incarnated charm and eternal youth. In the double meaning of their name, Anmut (gracefulness) and Gnade (grace), she saw the embodiment of both physical and divine perfection. The lines that Webern chose from her poem are infused with dithyrambic fervour, and their impassioned strength no doubt reminded him of Hölderlin, whose writings he cherished in his later years. The peculiar quality of Hildegard Jone's poetry, which was both mystic and ecstatic, suited Webern's temperament. Time and again his imagination was stirred to transform her word-painting into the dimension of music. As he was copying out the "Verwandlung der Chariten" poem, he pondered its tonal realization, setting down a compositional outline on the margin of the text:

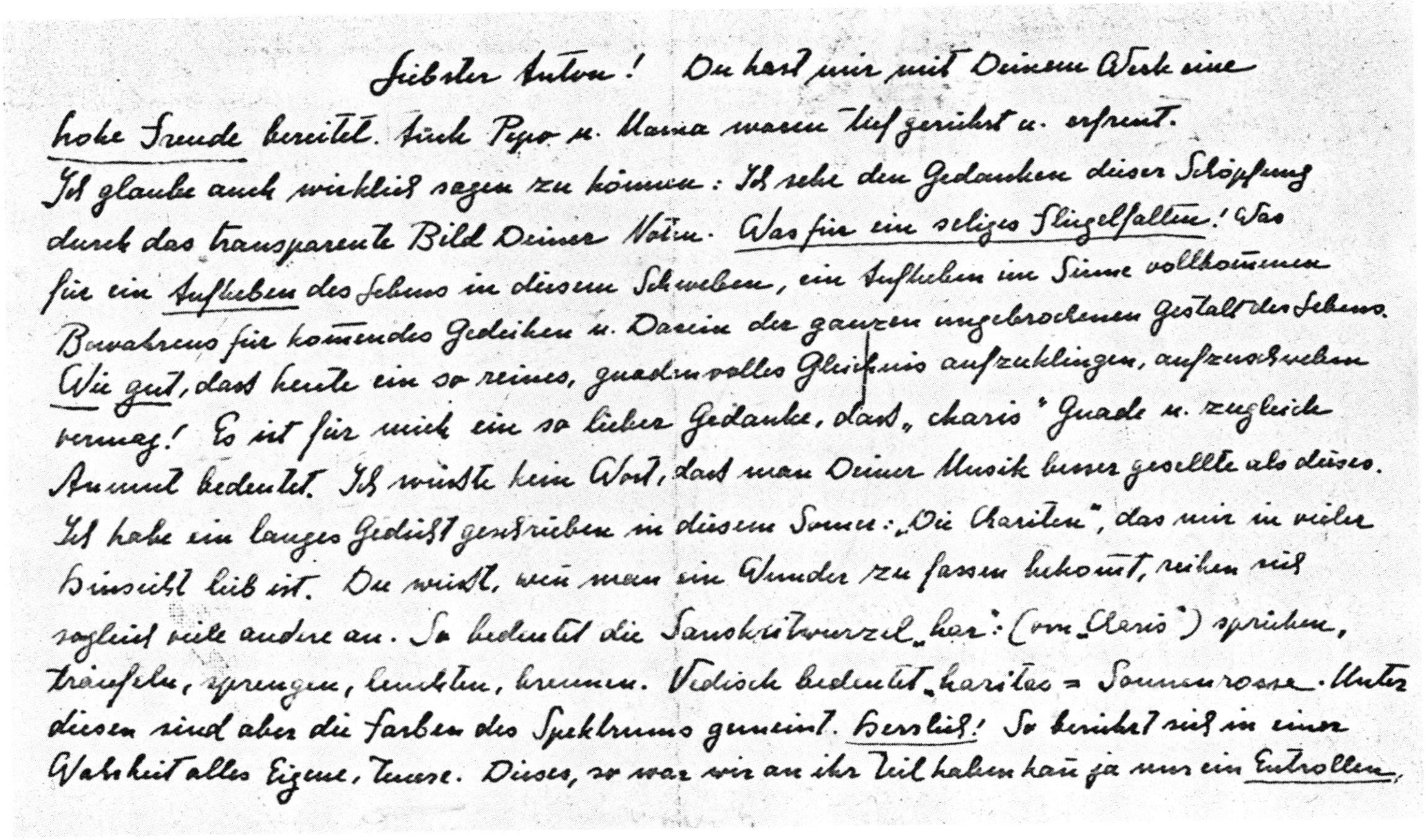

Liebster Anton! Du hast mir mit Deinem Werk eine
hohe Freude bereitet. Auch Pepo u. Mama waren tief gerührt u. erfreut.
Ich glaube auch wirklich sagen zu können: Ich sehe den Gedanken dieser Schöpfung
durch das transparente Bild Deiner Noten. Was für ein seliges Flügelfalten! Was
für ein Aufheben des Lebens in diesem Schweben, ein Aufheben im Sinne vollkommenen
Bewahrens für kommendes Gedeihen u. Darin der ganzen ungebrochenen Gestalt des Lebens.
Wie gut, dass heute ein so reines, gnadenvolles Gleichnis aufzuklingen, aufzuschweben
vermag! Es ist für mich ein so lieber Gedanke, dass „charis" Gnade u. zugleich
Anmut bedeutet. Ich wüsste kein Wort, dass man Deiner Musik besser gesellte als dieses.
Ich habe ein langes Gedicht geschrieben in diesem Sinne: „Die Chariten", das mir in vieler
Hinsicht lieb ist. Du weisst, wenn man ein Wunder zu fassen bekommt, reihen sich
sogleich viele andere an. So bedeutet die Sanskritwurzel „har" (von „Charis") sprühen,
träufeln, sprengen, leuchten, brennen. Vedisch bedeutet „haritas = Sonnenrosse. Unter
diesen sind aber die Farben des Spektrums gemeint. Herrlich! So bindet sich in einer
Wahrheit alles Eigene, Teuere. Dieses, so wie wir an ihr Teil haben kann ja nur ein Entrollen,

Letter to Weberb by Hildegard Jone (1939)

Introduction Theme	Tönen die seligen Saiten Apolls, wer nennt sie Chariten?
Addenda (Orchestra alone)	Spielt er sein Lied durch den wachsenden Abend, wer denket Apollon?
Development	Sind doch im Klange die früheren Namen alle verklungen; sind doch im Worte die schwächeren Worte lange gestorben; und auch die blasseren Bilder zum Siegel des Spektrums geschmolzen.
Reprise Coda	Charis, die Gabe des Höchsten: Die Anmut der Gnade erglänzet!
(the original introduction)	Schenkt sich im Dunkel dem werdenden Herzen als Tau der Vollendung.

[Hearing the blessed strings of the Sun god, who senses the Graces?
Echoes his song in the darkening evening, who thinks of Apollo?
Have not the earlier names all been gathered, lost in that music?
Have not the weaker words long ago perished, slain by the word's might?
Also the fainter image is melted as seal of the spectrum.
Charis, the gift of the highest: the grace of her favour is sparkling!
She comes in darkness, the ripening heart's gift, as dew of perfection.][4]

Webern began composing the text on 3 July 1939 (Sketchbook V, page 24). "Last week I was away for a few days. But otherwise constantly at work," he wrote to Hildegard Jone on 12 August, referring to his brief holiday in Kapellen and Vordernberg. In the same letter he told her for the first time which excerpt from her poem he had selected. For two months he struggled with some initial problems (the opening pages of the draft show much experimentation). Early in September he made a fresh start, from which he then carried on. A number of details differ considerably from the final version. It was while Webern was working on this movement that war broke out. Curiously, he made no mention of this world-shaking event, although his sketches are otherwise dotted with diary notes. Webern's progress on the movement was temporarily hampered when he was compelled for financial reasons to take on an arranging assignment (Wagner-Régeny's opera *Johanna Balk*) for Universal Edition. Referring to this task he wrote to Reich on 20 October: "As a consequence, unfortunately I had to postpone work on the cantata somewhat, otherwise perhaps I would have completed it already. But I hope nonetheless it will be possible soon." The draft of the movement was finished on 26 November 1939, a date that appears on page 41 of Sketchbook V as well as in the index that prefaces the book. However, five more pages were to be filled with revisions made in preparation of the final score.

Emerging from the seclusion of his creative workshop, Webern as usual felt the need to communicate with his friends. Predictably, the first whom he told about his new work were the Humpliks. On 2 December 1939 he wrote:

Dear friends, I would like to tell you that the "Chariten" are finished now! The piece was a lot of work. In construction it is a four-part *fugue*: but to regain all freedom of mobility within this strictness—so that there can be no question of constraint—was not easy. So in fact it turned into something completely different, a *scherzo form*, that came about on the basis of *variations*. But still a *fugue*! Now I am preparing the full score. This will still take some time—I want to attain a sound more manifold than perhaps anything I have imagined hitherto. That done, this cantata will be complete. I believe that the "Chariten" will have to be the first piece, for musical reasons, but also for *textual* ones. Do not the "Kleiner Flügel" and "Blitz und Donner" prove the answer to the questions posed in the "Chariten" verses, dear Hildegard? Are they not saying what is implied by the latter, by the "sound," the "word," the "seal of the spectrum"? Naturally, the "Chariten," too, are composed on the basis of the same sequence of twelve notes ("series") as the other two pieces. It is that "series" which has, as I told you already, the peculiarity that the second set of six notes is, in its intervals, the *backwards inversion* of the first set, so that everything that occurs can be traced back to a sequence of *six notes. Ever the same*: whether it is the "blessed strings," the "grace of her favour," the "little wings," the "lightning of life" or the "thunder of the heartbeat." Do these examples not reveal how well the text could be built into the said sequence? And it is also this way musically. And yet *each time something quite different*!

Surprisingly enough, Webern obviously had not yet decided on the definitive sequence of the movements. When writing to Polnauer on "Nicolo Day" (St Nicholas Day, 6 December), he affirmed his intention concerning the "Chariten" chorus: "It will be the first of the cantata." Only during the following weeks, while he orchestrated the "Chariten," did he decide on the ultimate order of the movements: 1. "Blitz und Donner" 2. "Kleiner Flügel" 3. "Verwandlung der Chariten."

A deep sense of accomplishment radiated from Webern's letter of 9 December to Reich. As in the description he had given the Humpliks, he dwelt on features of the "Chariten" chorus, but since he was writing to a trained musician, he could be more explicit: "Structurally it is a four-part double fugue. But the subject and counter-subject are related like antecedent and consequent (period) whereby, as a result, the elements of the other (horizontal) mode of presentation play their part."

As the picture of the full instrumentation unfolded, the composer could perceive graphic relationships and dimensions not apparent in the condensed score. He delighted in the appearance of the notation, which he considered a mirror of its musical contents. Excitedly he told

his friends about these visual aspects. On 27 December he wrote to
Reich: "Pictures result in the full score that surprise even me. The forms
accompanying my subject and counter-subject become, so to speak, the
'Continuo'." Similar comments were made in letters to Polnauer and
Hildegard Jone.

Webern's immersion in the orchestration of the "Chariten" movement continued into the new year. Only when he wrote to Hildegard
Jone on 16 January 1940 was the work completed and the right proportion between its components reasoned out:

> I have now definitely brought the full score of my cantata, i.e. the part
> I worked on last, into its final form. How I would love to show it to
> you. How your wonderful words, dear Hildegard, have turned out
> musically: "Charis, the gift of the highest: the grace of her favour is
> sparkling" or the preceding passage "Also the fainter image is melted
> as seal of the spectrum" or "She comes in darkness . . ." I have now
> placed this piece at the end of the cantata after all. Musically it has to
> be the conclusion. It lay in the plan, basically, and it has turned out
> exactly so. Musically there is not a single centre of gravity in this piece.
> The harmonic construction (as it results from the individual voices) is
> such that everything remains in a floating state.

A few days later, on 22 January, when Webern informed Polnauer
that his cantata was finished, his words could hardly hide his pride: "I
must confess that I am satisfied as hardly ever before. I believe you will
be amazed. This last piece—perhaps it is the best that I could achieve
up to now."

Shortly after, Webern made a brief concert tour to Switzerland. He
returned home greatly encouraged by the hope of an early première in
that country where "degenerate music" was not banned. On 19 March
1940 he wrote to Hildegard Jone: "I can report that the full score of my
cantata has gone off to Switzerland—it is possible that it will be
performed in Basel. Of course, the danger exists that they will shrink
from the great difficulties involved. But, after all, think what I was able
to impart to my chorus in the old days!"

The score had been sent to Paul Sacher, founder-conductor of the
Schola Cantorum Basiliensis. Willi Reich, then residing in Basel, acted as
intermediary, and when Sacher declined the work, he offered it to
Hermann Dubs. In the course of Webern's correspondence with Reich,
he declared his readiness to help overcome the difficulties of the choral
passages in the first movement by adding appropriate support from the
orchestra. On 3 March 1941 he even proposed: "If circumstances
require, one could also perform the last piece by itself."

Despite Webern's efforts, however, the first performance was not to take place until 1946, the year after his death.[5] During his lifetime, the composer had to content himself with introducing the work to a small circle of friends, who met on 18 August 1940 in the apartment of Ludwig and Maria Zenk at Stephansplatz 5. The window of their music room, high above the street, directly faced the magnificent spire of St Stephan's Cathedral ("The sight of this holy rock creates the impression of being on mountain heights," was Hildegard Jone's description).[6] When the bells tolled, as they did frequently, their sonorous ringing vibrated through the room, drowning out all other sound.

It was in this setting that Webern, playing and singing himself, solemnly initiated his friends into the mysteries of his cantata. The serenity of the hour deeply touched the members of the little group, as they found themselves in the embrace of something lofty and transcendental. For a short time their common anxiety over the war was removed. Hildegard Jone described her impression when she wrote to Webern on 27 August:

Dear Anton, it can happen in life that one hour encompasses so much concentrated living, that it throws its light with such illumination and penetration upon the past and also upon what is destined for the future, that we truly perceive it as the present at its most translucent. . . . It was just such an hour when—in the silent vicinity of the bells, close to the high steeple—you interpreted your work for us, which I found really an overwhelming musical pronouncement. I have known and loved your music for so long, but here something new has happened. I wished that all who have become shiftless as a result of our times could hear this work. Here is a view of the future and a way out: an answer. . . . Seppi [Josef Humplik] also was infinitely touched. He said that the music sounded like truly great classical music never heard before, that is, like *the* classical music of the future. What else should one say about it? *Thank you, dear friend!*[7]

In the autumn of 1944 Webern arranged a piano–vocal score of the cantata, in keeping with his practice of providing piano reductions for all his vocal compositions employing instrumental ensembles (the one exception being *Das Augenlicht*). The work was published only in 1954, in both full score and piano–vocal reduction, under the title First Cantata for Soprano Solo, Mixed Chorus and Orchestra, Op. 29. The orchestration consists of flute, oboe, clarinet, bass clarinet, horn, trumpet, trombone, timpani, percussion, harp, celesta, mandolin, and strings without double basses.

On 16 January 1940, when Webern informed Hildegard Jone that he had just completed the full score of his First Cantata, he also announced: "I have already turned to a new work; this time it will be purely instrumental."

This project was the Variations for Orchestra, Op. 30. If Webern was then actually making preliminary sketches for the composition, they are not extant. In February he was invited to Switzerland to attend performances of his works in Winterthur and Basel. The success of that journey led him to focus all his hopes on an early return engagement and, particularly, on receiving a commission for his new composition.

According to the date given in Sketchbook V, Webern began the actual draft of the variations only on 15 April 1940, when he set down an initial concept reading: "Theme: periodically structured from motivic elements. Repetition in a new form." Following this, a tone row was written out. Its second half was altered a day later, and the resulting form of the series became the definitive one. In the row, the last six notes are the retrograde of the first six, and the intervallic patterns themselves consist of micro–structures that afford a rich variety of manipulations. Essentially, the series operates in three groups of four notes each, which allow utilization motivically as well as harmonically, in the horizontal as well as in the vertical.

Aside from the interruptions caused by the assignments from Universal Edition, the composer's work on the project proceeded steadily. As so often, the manuscript draft took on a colourful appearance. Black, red, blue, and green pencil designated various rows, dynamic and tempo markings, time signatures, measure numbers, and instruments. On the fifth page of the draft a green pencil note "Anfang" signalled the amalgamation of all the preceding sketches into a fresh beginning. The earlier indication *Sehr bewegt* (Very animated) was changed to *Lebhaft* (Lively), which then became the definitive tempo. As usual, Webern's sketches were interspersed with sundry diary notes of family happenings, such as the birth of another grand-daughter, his son's induction into military service and subsequent release. Also recorded is Germany's sweeping victory in the Battle of France: "Friday, 21 June 1940, armistice negotiations at Compiègne. Tuesday, 25 June, 1.35 am, armistice."

That summer Webern took no holiday and remained at his work. On 1 August he reported to Hildegard Jone: "It is a purely instrumental piece; something very colourful, but based on the strictest discipline." In the course of the composition, six variations emerged, each of which Webern numbered with a different colour. By 30 October he could tell Reich: "Every so often I have thought of writing to you, but all the time my work absorbed me so much and it still does; the difference now, however, is that it is approaching its end. I am speaking of the orchestra piece I mentioned to you earlier—variations in the form of an 'overture.' The piece is becoming rather long and necessitates many sketches, etc. After that the full score will have to be prepared. How much is to be considered again in that connection!''

The draft of the condensed score was completed on 25 November 1940 (Sketchbook V, page 79). At this point, the composer embarked on a thorough revision, and it was not until mid-December that he could begin to write out the full score. It varied considerably from the first draft in metre, rhythm, and pitch fixation. On 21 December Webern informed Josef Hueber: ''I have spent all my time in the most concentrated work, have now finished, and at present am working on the full score. The piece has turned into variations for orchestra of considerable extent. And already my thoughts are on the next composition.'' A day later, he wrote out for Hildegard Jone two four-note groups from his work as a specimen of what he called the ''germ cells'' for the ''metamorphoses.''

The final orchestration occupied Webern far longer than he had anticipated. Only on 14 February 1941 could he notify the poetess: ''Things got delayed, although I was working constantly. It was a very difficult and tedious job, but the result is, I believe, something extremely simple. But now it is done. I am finished with it.'' The new child of his muse delivered, Webern, with fatherly pride, shared the news also with other friends like Humpelstetter and Hueber. To the latter he wrote on 17 February: ''Thus another opus has been brought to completion. For the time, probably scant notice of it will be taken. But I think everything will yet be 'justified.' ''

Wistful as the closing remark seemed, Webern was far from inactive in furthering his own music. He had known ever since the early years with Schoenberg that diligent and persistent promotion was essential for success. Throughout his career, he submitted his compositions to performing artists and conductors, although this involved, particularly at the beginning, the toilsome necessity of making manuscript copies. Even after Universal Edition became his publisher, Webern supplemented the firm's routine promotion by writing numerous letters to musicians and agents who might programme his works. Consequently, when he returned from Switzerland in early 1940, he immediately asked Reich to prevail on Paul Sacher to commission his new orchestral piece. There had been no response, however. Now that the score was finished, Webern brought up the subject again when he wrote to Reich on 3 March 1941. Before coming to the point he gave him some general information:

The piece lasts approximately a quarter of an hour;[8] almost throughout very quick in tempo, but sometimes with the effect of a sostenuto.
I settled on a form that amounts to a kind of overture, but based on
variations, and that is also the title, "Variations for Orchestra."
The orchestra is small: flute, oboe, clarinet, bass clarinet, horn,
trumpet, trombone, tuba, celesta, harp, timpani, strings, (with
double bass). Once again, there is a synthesis: in formal respects the
presentation is "horizontal," in all others "vertical." Basically, my
"overture" is an "adagio" form, but the recapitulation of the
principal subject is in the form of a development, so this element is
also present. Beethoven's *Prometheus* and Brahms' *Tragic*, for example,
also are overtures in adagio forms, not in sonata form!!! But with me
all of this evolves on the basis of a theme and a certain number of
variations.

Alluding to the commission he had suggested nine months earlier,
Webern then asked Reich outright if he could intervene personally: "I
do not know the exact procedure, but I can imagine it approximately.
That is to say, I would naturally find it most to my liking if the 'request'
would come from Sacher personally and directly. . . . Now let me have
your reaction, my dear, good friend, and make your influence felt, I beg
you. If only it could come to some consideration of my new work!"

To support Webern's efforts, Universal Edition made a photostat
of the score, which Alfred Schlee took with him on a business trip to
Switzerland. In order to prepare the ground, the composer supplied an
analytical outline. Although it took the form of a letter to Reich, it
actually was meant for the benefit of Sacher, whose predilections lay
with the more conservative trends in contemporary music. On 3 May,
the day Schlee left for Basel, Webern told Reich that he had "initiated
Schlee a little into the work so that he will not be so totally uninformed
when he hands it over." He added: "And now I would like to tell you,
too, quite briefly, something about it so that you can effectively refute
any objections Sacher may make."

The style in which Webern proceeded to explain the character and
form of his variations calls to mind his vivid manner as a lecturer in front
of a class of pupils. He posed rhetorical questions and immediately
countered with his own arguments. By this method, his skill as a teacher
was displayed no less than his authority as a composer, and the result
was a description both lively and thorough:

On first looking at this score will the reaction not be: why, there really
is "nothing in it"!!! Because the one concerned will miss the many,
many notes he is used to seeing otherwise, in R. Strauss, etc. Right!

But that in fact touches on the most important point: it would be vital to say that here (in my score) a different *style* is present. Yes, but what sort? It does not look like a score from the pre-Wagner period either—Beethoven, for instance—nor does it look like Bach. Is one to go back still further? Yes—but then *orchestral* scores did not yet exist! But it should still be possible to find a certain similarity to the mode of presentation that is associated with the Netherlanders. So, something "archaistic"? An orchestrated Josquin perhaps? The answer would have to be an energetic "no"! What, then? Nothing like any of that!

Now you would have to say unequivocally: this is music (mine) that is in fact based *just as much* on the laws arrived at by musical presentation *after* the Netherlanders, music that does not deny the development that came then, but tries on the contrary to continue it into the future, and does not endeavour to return to the past. What kind of *style*, then? I believe, to be sure, a new one. Following exactly, in its material aspects, natural law, as the earlier, preceding forms followed tonality; that is to say, *forming* a tonality, but one that uses the possibilities offered by the nature of sound in a different way, namely on the basis of a system in which the twelve different tones that have been used in Western music up to now "relate only to each other" (as Arnold has put it), but which just the same does not ignore (I should add to clarify things) the inner laws provided by the nature of sound—namely the relationship of the overtones to a fundamental. At any rate, it is impossible to ignore them, if there is still to be *meaningful* expression in sound! But nobody, really, is going to assert that we do not want that! A style, therefore, whose material is of that nature, and whose formal construction *relates the two possible types of presentation to each other.*

Now I would like to explain the piece to you from the score. But a few important things still, briefly.

The "theme" of the variations extends to the first double bar; it is conceived as a period, but is "introductory" in character. Six variations follow (each one to the next double bar). The first brings the principal subject (so to speak) of the overture (andante form), which unfolds in full; the second the bridge-passage, the third the secondary subject, the fourth the recapitulation of the principal subject—it is an andante form, after all!—but in the manner of a *development*, the fifth, repeating the character of the introduction and bridge-passage, leads to the coda: the sixth variation.

Now everything that occurs in the piece is based on the two ideas given in the first and second bars (double bass and oboe!). But it is reduced still more, since the second figure (oboe) is already retrograde in itself: the second two tones are the retrograde of the first two, but rhythmically augmented. It [the second figure] is followed right away again, on the trombone, by the first figure (double bass), but in diminution! And in retrograde as to motives and intervals. For that is how my row is constructed—it is made up of these thrice four tones.

But the succession of motives takes part in this retrograde, though with the use of augmentation and diminution! These two modes of alteration now lead almost exclusively to the respective variation idea, that is: a motivic variation happens, if at all, only within this frame-work. But, by means of all possible shifts of the centre of gravity within the two shapes, there is always something new in the way of metre, character, etc. Just compare the first repetition of the first figure with its first form (trombone and double bass respectively)! And so it continues throughout the entire piece, the whole content of which is already present, in germinal form, in the first twelve tones, that is to say the row! It is pre-formed!!! So are, in bars one and two, also the two tempi of the piece (pay attention to the metronome marks!).

Well, that was quite something. But now I must stop. I shall be glad to say more about it another time, however.[9]

In closing his discourse, Webern told Reich: "If you would convey some of it to Sacher, I really would welcome it very much. I hope that he will decide in the positive." The outcome was to be another dis-appointment: despite the combined efforts of the composer, Reich, and Schlee, the support of the wealthy Swiss conductor could not be won.[10]

The score of the Variations was submitted next, again unsuccessfully, to Ernest Ansermet. Early in 1942 it was brought to the attention of Hermann Scherchen, who conducted the first performance at Winterthur on 3 March 1943 (for details, see Chapter XXXI). The composer was present for the occasion, again at the invitation of Werner Reinhart, to whom Webern showed his gratitude by dedicating the work to him (as he had done earlier with his Opus 4). Universal Edition furnished the orchestral parts for the première, but the work was actually not placed under contract until after Webern's death, and the score appeared in print only in 1956.

The creative drive that produced the unbroken chain of Webern's last works culminated in the Second Cantata, Op. 31, the genesis of which was to absorb three full years. During that long time span there was a dramatic change in the course of the war that formed the background to the evolution of the composition: when the work was begun in 1941, Germany still entertained bright hopes for an early and victorious end to the conflict, but as the cantata neared completion in 1943, bombs had begun to rain on Vienna.

Webern turned to the new project soon after finishing the final score of his Variations for Orchestra, Op. 30, in February of 1941. Once more he found inspiration in the poems of Hildegard Jone. When writing to her on 11 March 1941, he gave the first hint that one of her lyrics again had ignited a spark in him: "*Never* have I gone looking, as it were, for a 'text' with the intention—indeed *I could never have such an intention*—of writing something vocal (a song, a choral piece). It was never this way, but *the text was always provided first*! Given a text, then of course 'something vocal' was bound to originate. . . . I really believe that your poem 'Freundselig ist das Wort' is once more something for me."

On 20 March Webern announced to Hueber: "Now I am about to start my next work." By 3 May he informed Reich: "I am at a new work and will write to you about it in the near future. It will be something vocal again." Judging from Webern's remark, he had made preliminary sketches which, however, no longer exist. The initial draft (Sketchbook V, page 82) is dated a few days later, 7 May. This draft discloses that the first movement of the evolving cantata was the setting of a text beginning with the words "Leichteste Bürden der Bäume . . ." for solo soprano with orchestra. Therefore, it was not "Freundselig ist das Wort," as various writers have presumed because of Webern's comment in his letter of 11 March to Hildegard Jone. The chronological sequence in which Webern composed the movements of this work, the most extensive of all his later compositions, may be anticipated here: the fourth, fifth, and sixth movements were written first, in that order, while the three movements ultimately assigned first, second, and third position followed. A seventh movement was abandoned. The sketches to four of the movements (IV, V, VI, and I) fill the rest of Sketchbook V; those for the other movements are contained in Sketchbook VI.

On contemplating the classic proportions of Webern's cyclic works, one is surprised to learn from the composer himself that there was nothing premeditated in his approach and that he allowed himself to be guided by intuition in his search for an ultimately satisfying form. Announcing to Hildegard Jone that he had embarked on his new creative voyage, he told her on 26 May: "Now it is 'Leichteste Bürden der Bäume.' I do not know at all yet where it will have its place; nor what there will be besides. But it is happening again. I feel it already—I am being guided again. Yes, how should I put this differently?" In a similar vein, Webern wrote to Hueber on 5 June: "I am in the process of laying the foundation for a new work—it must be accomplished soon—and this is always a time that absorbs me very much. It is again something vocal. Perhaps something very extended. But this still remains rather open. For the time being, I allow myself to drift." This last remark might befit the poet admitting dependence on inspiration, rather than the craftsman working at the draftboard of twelve-tone construction.

To be sure, Webern did not just "drift." His patient quest for inspiration forever aimed at harnessing musical ideas into a structural framework which in the end would embody the ideal of any true work of art: the interplay of imagination and skill. As he progressed with the movement, he realized that he was succeeding well. On 15 July, a few days before leaving for a short holiday in the mountains, he excitedly wrote to Josef Polnauer: "I must be diligent until my departure. I want to reach the end of a certain section in my work. Suddenly it has become clear to me that what is now coming into being is a rather extensive *recitative*, as far as the *form* is concerned. But in the construction it is stricter than anything I have written heretofore. It will open my new cantata." Three days later he wrote to Hueber: "I work uninterruptedly. I am reaping as long as I am permitted to."

The next day, Webern went to his beloved Schneealpe with Peter and Hermine. After a brief stay in Kapellen, he returned home on 24 July. Invigorated by his sojourn in the Alps, he brought fresh impetus to his work and completed the draft of the movement on 31 July. Actually, Webern sketched out the piece twice, but there are only minor differences between the two versions. It is interesting that both drafts employ eighth and sixteenth notes as units of measurement. These were changed to half and quarter notes, respectively, once the composer entered upon the final phase of his work on the movement. As a preparation for the full instrumentation, Webern wrote out a condensed score on six staves. He forwarded this intermediate manuscript, designated "Recitative," to the Humpliks and wrote to them on 13 August: "Dearest friends, by the same mail I am sending you the first piece of my new work. It is 'Der Wind.' As simple and unassuming as it looks, the constructive task I set for myself was an extremely difficult one. With 'the most delicate breath' it is to open the new 'cantata'—or whatever it turns out to be. . . . It is to be followed by 'Freundselig ist das Wort'—as a *choral piece*."

The title "Der Wind" actually appeared on the manuscript Webern sent the Humpliks. However, since he usually used only portions of Hildegard Jone's poems, all such titles were omitted from the final score. On 18 August, the poetess thanked Webern profusely: "Dear, good Anton, what great joy you have given me and Seppi with the manuscript of your new work. . . . Even if I cannot read the notes with real understanding, they nonetheless lie open to the inner eye perhaps more clearly than one would think. . . . This '*breath*' at the end of the text will no doubt be of unearthly tenderness and ring on like chimes of silence, for a long, long time."

Gratifying as the intuitive response of Hildegard Jone must have been to the composer, the scholar in him needed to communicate also with a knowledgeable musician. He was convinced that he held the key to an inner sanctum in which countless metamorphoses of a basic musical idea were about to unfold. On 23 August, he wrote to Reich that his new project might even exceed a cantata in extent, and in two later letters to Reich (28 February and 31 July 1942) Webern actually spoke of an "oratorio." Announcing that the first piece was ready in finished score, he discussed his work with the intensity of the creative artist who sees himself catapulted to unlimited possibilities:

Formally it is like an introduction, a recitative! But this section is constructed in a way that perhaps none of the "Netherlanders" ever thought of; it was probably the most difficult task (in this respect) that I have ever had to fulfil! The reason is that it is built on a four-part canon of the most complicated kind. But the way it is carried out was only possible, I think, on the basis of the law of the row, which is quite particularly in evidence here. In fact this may well be the first time it has been so completely operative. I have read in Plato that "Nomos" (law) is also the word for "Weise" (melody): Now, the melody the soprano soloist sings in my piece by way of introduction (recitative) may be the *law* (Nomos) for all that follows! In the sense of the "primeval plant" of Goethe: "With this model, and the key to it, one can proceed to invent plants ad infinitum. . . . The same law can be applied to everything else that lives!" *Is this not the meaning, at its deepest, of our law of the row?*

From the outset, the "recitative," whose row established the "law," was conceived as a unit with the movement to follow. Significantly, one of the two sketchbook versions of "Der Wind" ends with Webern's note "attacca No. 2." That "second" movement was to be a setting of "Freundselig ist das Wort."[11] The first sketch is dated 24 September 1941, but almost ten months were to elapse before this initial draft was completed on 2 July 1942. The long delay is explained by a major task that Webern had to carry out for Universal Edition in between—the piano reduction of Schoeck's opera *Das Schloss Dürande*, which occupied him from August 1941 through February of the following year. Greatly begrudging the time spent away from his own creative work, he told Hueber that he had just finished the first of the opera's four acts when he began the draft of "Freundselig ist das Wort."

The sketches reveal the difficulties that Webern, beset by continuing interruptions, encountered with his new movement. Sketchbook pages 89 to 94 contain his initial attempts, in which the metres and note values differ from those ultimately adopted. On page 95 the movement is started anew, in the rhythmic disposition of the final version. Numerous *vi–de* signs and copious changes occur throughout the draft. The only intermediate date, 24 June 1942, is found close to the end.

"Freundselig ist das Wort" was set for soprano solo, mixed chorus, and orchestra with solo violin obbligato. Again, Webern proceeded to write out an intermediate score, which he sent to the Humpliks. Before he had completed the movement, he wrote to Hildegard Jone on 3 June that it was conceived as an "aria," commenting: "In it I succeeded—I believe—in achieving what I might almost call a *completely new* style of representation: namely, on a *purely polyphonic* basis I arrive at what amounts to the most opposite kind of representation."

Whenever a work was in the process of evolution, Webern's references to it were generally terse and reserved, but they became profuse once he could contemplate the finished composition. His letter of 25 July to Hildegard Jone radiated his satisfaction:

> You ask about the "shape": at the centre are the words: "Because he fell silent on the cross. . . ." What went before is now repeated backwards. "*Repeated*": "All shapes are similar and *none are the same*"; thus the chorus points to a secret law, to a holy riddle! You know this pronouncement of Goethe! (Metamorphosis). But the fact that it was just those words that constitute the centre of the musical shape came about entirely of its own accord—indeed it could not be otherwise. The ending was difficult: "hostility" . . . "coldness": amidst the warmth and friendliness of your words!!! So here begins in the music (like a breath): "then we turn blissfully . . .". But that, too, I see only *now*—it also came about unintentionally.

Alluding to the arduous process of transformation from the first draft to the final score, Webern wrote to Ludwig Zenk on 30 July: "The problem of economic instrumentation (especially considering my style of expression) again could not be solved offhand. But I think that everything has become clear. What I really would like best is to do as Bach did in his *Art of Fugue*."

The following day, when describing the technical aspects of the movement to Reich, Webern largely reiterated the precepts expounded in connection with the preceding "recitative" movement. He again dwelt on the concept of "Nomos," with the "Weise" (melody) assuming the role of "Gesetz-Geberin" (law giver), and concluded:

This is how it has always been in the music of the masters! Whether I am succeeding as they did, only God knows, but at least I have recognized what it is all about! In my case nothing happens any more that is not predetermined by this "melody"! It is the law, hence truly the "Nomos"!!! But predetermined on a canonic foundation! Naturally, the "row" in itself already constitutes a law, but it does not also have to be the "melody"! But since in my case it in fact *is* the melody, the row assumes a quite special importance, on a higher plane so to speak, rather like the chorale melodies in Bach's arrangements. In general, the early stages of our technique are there, but I am returning to them, I believe, in a quite special way.

His high spirits carried the composer without pause through the next movement of the cantata. Within a month of completing the "second" piece, he finished the "third." It was a setting, for mixed chorus, of a poem entitled "Das Neugeborene," part of Hildegard Jone's unpublished cycle *Alltag.* Webern composed it as a four-part canon, in which the manipulation of the tone row produced double-canonic results. The draft of the chorus (Sketchbook V, pages 107–110) is dated at the beginning "August 1942." The first three pages were given over to experimentations with the melodic line and its metric allocations. On the fourth page, marked at the end "26 August 1942," the four choral parts were drafted in full, while the orchestral instruments, which actually trace the vocal lines note by note, were merely indicated by name. In this draft, the tempo marking is *Sehr fliessende Achtel* (Very flowing eighth notes), and various time signatures appear throughout: 3/8, 5/8, 6/8, 7/8, and 9/8. Shortly thereafter, however, Webern established the half note as the unit of pulsation, assigning its metric quantities to measures of varying length and discarding time signatures altogether. These changes appear already in the *a cappella* score of the chorus Webern sent to the Humpliks.

When he mailed the manuscript on 4 September, he told them that the movement was to be considered "a sort of 'chorale'" and that it completed the first "section" within his overall plan, a sequence consisting of integrally connected pieces (beginning with the soprano recitative "Der Wind" and followed by the aria with chorus "Freundselig ist das Wort.") He cautioned: "You should not think of the 'chorale' I mentioned in the *Bachian* sense, *purely musically,* I mean. It is something *quite different.*" Webern continued with a description of his choral treatment, but that aspect was set forth more explicitly when he wrote to Reich the same day. Discussing the "Chorallied" (chorale), which was to round out "the first part of the projected 'oratorio'," he pointed out the "relationships" in the polyphonic fabric:

The second part (alto) sings the notes of the first (tenor) backwards, the third (soprano) brings the inversion of the second, and the fourth (bass) is the inversion of the first, but moreover sings the notes of the third backwards! Therefore, a double interlinking: one and four, as well as two and three (by inversion), and again: one and two, as well as three and four (retrograde). I think you will be astonished by the appearance of this score. Long note values, but very flowing tempo.

As the composer reached the end of the first organic unit in his work, he saw the further structural scheme clearly before his eyes. There was no longer any "drifting." The sequence "recitative–aria–chorus" so completely satisfied his sense of balance that he decided to employ the same musical order for the next section, with contrast to be achieved through appropriate changes in media. He indicated this intention in his letter of 4 September to the Humpliks:

Now a *new section* begins; it will start with: "Schweigt auch die Welt, aus Farben ist sie immer . . ." and again it will be, to a certain extent, something like a recitative (for *bass* voice), followed by the "aria": "Sehr tief verhalten innerst Leben singt . . ." from "Die Stille um den Bienenkorb in der Heimat". . . . Unfortunately I now have to interrupt my work for a while—I am forced to earn my bread and butter.

This closing remark referred to Universal Edition's commission of a piano reduction of Casella's extensive orchestral score *Paganiniana*, a task which occupied Webern for over two months. According to the date in his sketchbook (page 111), he was unable to return to his own creative project until 16 November 1942. The next day, a diary note heralded the arrival of his daughter Christine's third child, Liesa. On 19 November Webern expressed to Hildegard Jone his joy over the eternal miracle of birth, alluding to her poem "Das Neugeborene" (The Newly-Born), the text for his "chorale" movement. He added: "Now for 'Schweigt auch die Welt.'" The verses are from the poem "Strahl und Klang," which forms part of the unpublished collection *Licht und Lied*. On 12 December the composer informed Hueber, his trusted baritone soloist on many past occasions: "Now I am writing something for you—within the framework of my new composition: a *recitative and aria for bass voice*. For the first time!!! Naturally the bass (as well as the soprano solo) will also take part in the action otherwise." (In actual fact, Webern had composed songs in the bass-baritone range before, the very early [1900] "Wolkennacht," based on an Avenarius poem, and an incomplete setting [1917] of Goethe's "Gegenwart.")

After three pages of preliminary sketches, the draft for his new "recitative" took on almost definitive shape. Tempo, metre and other details were virtually identical with the final version. The movement was completed on 21 January 1943 and Webern again proceeded to write it out in a short score, in which the orchestration was compressed into four staves. Sending the manuscript to the Humpliks on 11 February, he wrote:

"Strahl und Klang" is over and done with. The orchestral score, too. The piece took a relatively long time. I would like to explain the reasons for this to you in person someday. One reason, the main one, probably lay in the formal aspects: a form has emerged that must have lain dormant for a long, long time. But now, on the basis of our harmonic system, I have come as far as constructing twelve-tone chords in it, ". . . then it resounds. . . ." But above all I would like to tell you, dear Hildegard, the beautiful things I have discovered in the course of setting your poems to music: namely that—except for the last (fourth) movement (*musically* seen, this appears only self-evident in connection with the formation of the *ending*)—each of the three preceding movements contains the *same* number of syllables (16!). So that in my tone rows I arrive at the *same* spot at the words "Farben," "Farbenschimmer," "Farbige," and in the third movement (correspondingly) "das Aug mehr bindet" as well as the designation "so lang," "wenn nachts," "wenn nichts," and in the fourth movement (in keeping with the sense of fulfilment) "tritt das Bewegende"!!! Just think—what correspondence also in the musical setting!!!

Among the remnants of Webern's library were found the texts on which the cantata's six movements were based. Two of them, "Die Stille um den Bienenkorb in der Heimat" and "Der Wind," had been published in a cycle of fourteen poems, under the title *Das Feldpostpäckchen* in the July 1940 issue of the Catholic periodical *Die Christliche Frau*. The other texts were selected from verses that Hildegard Jone had submitted in manuscript form. All these sources bear Webern's annotations for musical setting. Ranging from syllable counts to indications of structural plans, they illustrate his preoccupation with intrinsic correlations of poetic metre and tone row, statements and retrograde relationships of tone sequences corresponding to their verbal equivalents.

On the evening of 24 February 1943 Webern left for what was to be his last trip abroad. He attended the rehearsals and première of his Variations for Orchestra, Op. 30, in Winterthur, Switzerland. Returning home on 6 March, he recorded the pertinent data on the opening page of Sketchbook VI, the last of his musical workbooks. On 1 April he resumed work on his cantata, sketching the melody line for the text of the projected "aria." As in the preceding "recitative," it is wholly given over to a solo bass voice. The poetic source of the new movement was revealed in Webern's letter to the Humpliks on 22 April. Writing out two short phrases of the melody with text, he told them: "'Die Stille um den Bienenkorb in der Heimat' has made a lot of progress. I hope to be able to send you the piece soon." The composer's expectation was not to be realized so quickly, however. On 18 May he explained to Hildegard Jone: "My work follows its course. What I am carrying out in the 'Bienenkorb' will, to be sure, again require a considerable amount of time."

The draft covers the first seventeen pages of the new sketchbook. Seventy-four measures in length, the movement was to become the most extended of the cantata. For the opening two verse lines, Webern first sketched the bass solo a minor third lower than the definitive pitch level that was established soon after. Definite time signatures, dropped in the finished score, occur throughout the initial draft. Rhythmic values show some variance from the final version.

The first two pages of sketches are studded with diary records: Amalie had to undergo another operation, and Maria married on 20 May 1943. Most of the notes refer to Peter. He had been called into active service on 24 February, and from that date his moves were traced in minute detail until he was sent to Serbia at the end of June. Webern's grave concern for his son contrasts starkly with the loveliness and tranquillity of the poem that served him as vehicle for his musical thought at that time.

The draft of the movement was completed on 6 July. In the ensuing intermediate score, the initial tempo marking *Sehr langsam* (Very slowly) was changed to *Sehr verhalten* (Very introspectively), in allegoric correspondence to the opening words "Sehr tiefverhalten innerst Leben singt/ im Bienenkorb in stiller Mitternacht" (Deep down the inner life sings/ in the beehive at midnight's quiet hour). In that short score, again sent to the Humpliks, the orchestral texture was condensed on three staves, with no instruments indicated as yet. On 6 August, after completing the full score, Webern described the new movement to Reich:

Everything has become even stricter, and for just that reason still freer, too. That is to say: I move with complete freedom on the basis of an "endless canon by inversion." By means of variation, diminution, etc., rather as Bach proceeds with his theme in the *Art of Fugue*. But formally the aria is ternary, with a circa 32-bar theme of periodic structure; so, once again, a very close inter-linking of the two types of presentation. In character, a kind of hymn: "Die Stille um den Bienenkorb in der Heimat" [The Stillness around the Beehive at Home].

Just one week later, on 13 August, that stillness was rudely shattered when the first bombs fell on idyllic Mödling. The dangers of the mortal struggle were beginning to reach from the battlefront to every doorstep throughout the land. Webern's home became a temporary refuge for his daughter Christine, her three children, and her mother-in-law. Apparently the composer stoically ignored the commotion, not permitting it to interrupt his work. On 16 August he wrote to the Humpliks: "The 'Bienenkorb' is now to be followed by 'Schöpfen aus Brunnen des Himmels . . .' It will be a big choral piece." On the same day, Webern began his musical setting of this poem, which Hildegard Jone had sent him in the autumn of 1942.[12] The dramatic character of the verses, which foretold the oncoming storm, fired the composer's imagination at exactly the time when the fury of the war was being unleashed before his very eyes. On 19 August, three days after beginning the composition, he wrote to Zenk: "The foundation should soon be laid. But at times it is getting really difficult to concentrate."

On 1 October, Mödling was the target of a heavy air raid. The experience sorely distressed the sensitive composer, but he nevertheless concentrated on his creative task, about which he wrote to Hildegard Jone on 11 October:

> I have been working without interruption: my new piece should soon be finished. It is "Schöpfen aus Brunnen des Himmels" for three-part *women's chorus* and *soprano solo* (with orchestra). Following after "Stille der Mitternacht," it will be a very animated piece. Yet not sounding so much *excited*, but rather (to express myself in Goethe's spirit) *"representing something excited"*—so at least I hope. Therefore, in the spirit of your wonderful poem: "Sturmläuten muss nun die Liebe" [Now Love must sound the alarm].

It was not the first time that Webern contemplated the medium of a women's chorus. As early as the winter of 1913–14, he had employed it in an early draft of "Schien mir's, als ich sah die Sonne" (from Strindberg's *Ghost Sonata*), but this initial concept was later converted into the song known as Op. 12, No. 3. During the summer of 1930, he had sketched out the beginnings of another women's chorus to the words "Der Spiegel sagt mir: ich bin schön!" (from Goethe's *Der West-*

östliche Divan). Now, in the last of all his compositions to reach fruition, he combined a three-part women's chorus with a solo soprano voice in a musical declamation full of strife and dissonance. It was an echo of the all-engulfing war, a foreboding of catastrophe, a fervent invocation to Love, which in the hour of doom must be both a requiem to the dead and the flame of hope in the last flicker of existence.

The initial draft of the movement (Sketchbook VI, pages 18–31) was begun on 16 August and completed on 3 November. The first few lines were given over to preliminary experimentations, in which the composer wrote out various row shapes denoted by numbers. Only then was the melody drafted, followed by attempts to work it out in contrapuntal scoring. Although smooth progress seemed assured, the ensuing sketches evidence obstacles. Numerous *vi–de* signs serve as guides through the maze of passages and their re-workings. Writing to Reich on 23 October, Webern spoke of "problems of the utmost difficulty."

In curious contrast to the intense intellectual effort revealed by the sketches is an entry at the bottom of page 27 where Webern wrote out a simple diatonic melody of nursery-tune character. Above the last five notes he penned the name Karin, obviously associating her with the motive. Circling the entire entry in red, he dated it 15 October, his grand-daughter's fifth birthday. With childlike innocence, gay as laughter, the bright little tune intrudes into the austere pursuits of the composer, who had interrupted his lofty project to celebrate the birthday of the little girl then living under his roof.

A few weeks later, on 3 December, Webern observed his own birthday—his 6oth. By the time he reached that milestone, he had finished orchestrating the latest movement, working again from a condensed score that he presented to Hildegard Jone at Christmas-time.[13] Another integral unit of three movements was now complete, and without pause the composer turned to the next segment of what he still envisioned as an "oratorio." He had already selected the text, drawn from Hildegard Jone's poem "Verwandlung der Chariten," an excerpt of which he had used for the last movement of his First Cantata.

Page 33 of Sketchbook VI contains the beginning of this seventh movement. Under the date of 18 December, Webern drafted the melody for the verse lines "Kleiner sind Götter geworden und wohnen in Kelchen der Blumen/wohnen in Kehlen der Vögel: denn einzig ist Gott uns geworden." The sketches continue with the working out, on two staves, of a four-voiced double canon for mixed chorus.[14] On 10 January 1944 Webern wrote to Reich: "I am working without pause: now I am on the seventh piece of the planned cycle. . . . More about it soon. At present my boy is here on leave!" (Diary notes on the lower

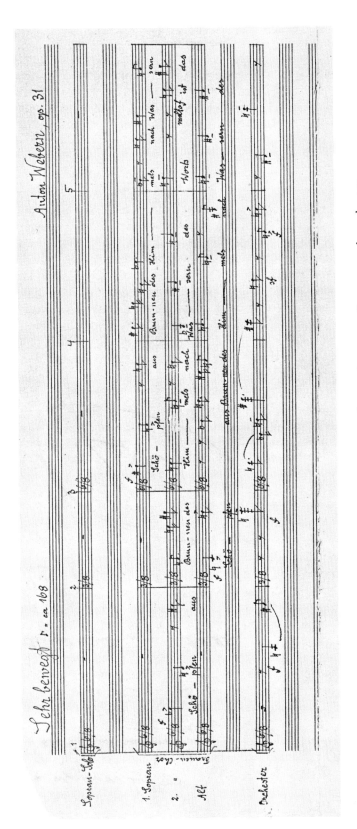

"Schöpfen aus Brunnen," third movement of Second Cantata, Op. 31, condensed score

margin of the sketchbook page record Peter's homecoming on 28 December and his departure three weeks later.)

Surprisingly, the projected seventh movement was soon abandoned. The composer gave his reasons to Hildegard Jone in a letter dated 28 January:

While I was working intensively on "Kleiner sind Götter geworden . . ."—I told you recently that this was to be the next piece; the foundation was already laid—I suddenly felt with absolute certainty—to be sure, there had been hints of it once or twice before—that this work *was musically complete* with the six finished pieces! I still hesitated, but I soon definitely decided to group these finished pieces together into a "cantata." I only needed (vis-à-vis the sequence of origin) to make a slight rearrangement—for *musical* reasons, but also for reasons of the textual continuity. The result satisfies me in all respects. Now look at the order: basically, has it not become a "missa brevis"?

1. "Schweigt auch die Welt . . ." (Bass solo), is that not a "Kyrie"?
2. "Sehr tief verhalten . . ." (Bass solo): the "Gloria in excelsis deo" of the stillness around the "Bienenkorb in der Heimat."
3. "Schöpfen aus Brunnen des Himmels . . ." (women's chorus with *soprano* solo). Is that not a "Credo"?
4. "Leichteste Bürden der Bäume . . ." (Soprano solo)
   and
5. "Freundselig ist das Wort . . ." (Soprano solo and mixed chorus) a "Benedictus, qui venit in nomine domini" and "Sanctus"?
   Is not that *"blessed"* which the wind carries through the "spaces" the "fragrances" the "gentle shape"? And holy, holy "the word" when it "knows all that is thine"? "Holy, holy": but when it soundeth once more in the morning hours, finally:
6. "Gelockert aus dem Schosse . . ." (Chorus): "Agnus dei"—the "Lamb of God."

I really believe that my selection displays cohesion. Now *you* say how you see it! What I am working on now is something *purely instrumental.* I hope to be able to tell you about it in more detail soon.

The closing remark refers to an instrumental "concerto" that Webern had begun two days earlier, a project he subsequently converted into another vocal work (see Chapter XXXV).

On 7 February Hildegard Jone wrote to Webern, endorsing his decision: "The new grouping of your cantata makes really wonderful sense to me. What magnificence is embodied in this work! 'Missa brevis'—that is what it is!" Webern's application of the liturgy to his cantata was bound to appeal to the poetess. Religious fervour and Christian symbolism, which are particularly manifest in the texts Webern used for the third, fifth and sixth movements, are dominant traits in much of her poetry.

On 23 February Webern informed Reich that the work was completed, adding: "It is my plan to send a photocopy of my new cantata to Reinhart so that it is preserved and safeguarded." The comment alluded to Webern's growing concern for the protection of his manuscripts from the ravages of the air raids. One of the photocopies that Universal Edition made of the conductor's large score was found in the composer's estate. It contained Webern's own indications for the duration of each movement: I–2', II–6', III–2', IV–4', V–7', VI–3'. The total of 24 minutes differs from the half hour Webern estimated in his letter of 23 February to Reich. Performance practice has fallen far short of these guidelines. The composer's own metronome markings notwithstanding, conductors have applied varying tempo interpretations.[15]

The performance time actually was lengthened somewhat when, six months after completion of the work, the composer had an afterthought. In the photostat score mentioned above, the closing movement still consisted of the original text of "Das Neugeborene," a single five-line stanza. (The typescript of the poems prefacing the score also contained only this one strophe.) As has been seen, Webern thought of the chorus from the beginning as a "chorale." But the concept of that term, generally associated with the tradition of sacred music, implies strophic repetition of the hymn tune. And so the composer decided to employ, for the first and only time in his entire musical output, a threefold reiteration. During the summer of 1944 he discussed with Hildegard Jone the possibility that she might extend the poem by two additional stanzas. The suggestion was quickly carried out, for by 12 September Webern could write to her: "I am deeply touched by the new verses, and am very happy to have received them so soon! They are wonderful and fit especially well into the musical context! My unending thanks!" A week later, Webern added: "I have already entered the new text into the full score: it fits marvellously."[16]

The orchestration of the cantata consists of piccolo, flute, oboe, English horn, clarinet, bass clarinet, alto saxophone, bassoon, horn, trumpet, trombone, bass tuba, glockenspiel, chimes, celesta, harp, and strings. Foreseeing the need for a piano–vocal score for study purposes, Webern prepared the reduction during the autumn of 1944, when he also provided one for the First Cantata. The piano–vocal score was not printed by Universal Edition until 1951 (the choral score was copyrighted in 1949, prior to the work's première in 1950); a pocket edition of the full score followed in 1956. Incongruously, the two publications list different performance times, the piano–vocal score suggesting about thirteen minutes, the orchestral score about sixteen. The official title reads Second Cantata for Soprano Solo, Bass Solo, Mixed Chorus, and Orchestra, Op. 31.

The Second Cantata was the crowning harvest of Webern's creative life. Considered a "breakthrough,"[17] the work has evoked numerous theoretical discussions. Its multitude of fascinating aspects encompasses both the archaic and the futuristic. That the concluding movement of the composer's last completed work should consist of a thrice-repeated musical stanza constitutes a phenomenon unique within his œuvre and one particularly striking, since by that final gesture he once again affirms his allegiance to tradition. With this strophic chorale, he embraces and reconciles the extremes of complexity and simplicity.[18] As a whole, the work stands as the epitome of Webern's style and genius. It is as emotionally affecting as it is intellectually rigorous.

CHAPTER XXXIII

The war comes home—Peter's death
(1943–1945)

"DAS NEUGEBORENE" (The Newly-Born), the poem that Webern used for the closing chorale of his Second Cantata, Op. 31, his last complete work, held more than symbolic meaning for him: its message was as real as life itself, and its significance grew to the degree that the war struck deeper into the roots of human existence. By 1944 Allied air raids were bringing devastation to the Nazi-occupied countries. That autumn, on 6 October, Webern wrote to Karl Amadeus Hartmann, announcing the birth of Amalie's second son, Christian:[1] "A sixth grandchild, a boy, has arrived. Let us be steadfast in keeping such happy events before our eyes. The final words of my Second Cantata are: 'Im Friedensschoss gestalten uns, weil ein Kindlein spricht, der Liebe Urgewalten' [In the womb of peace we are formed by love's primeval forces because a little child speaks]."

As the nation was gripped by a mood of oppression, Webern clung closer than ever to his family and his few remaining friends. One of these was Ludwig Zenk, to whom Webern had written at Christmas-time the preceding year: "In a few days there will be the turning point! [A reference to the change of season, heralded by the lengthening of the days.] The turning point—if only it would also come *otherwise*! May this be our thought at Christmas!"

That year (1943), for the first time, Webern and his wife did not celebrate Christmas in their own home since all their children had married and left. Instead they joined Christine and her three little girls in the Mattels' Mödling apartment. The grandchildren were a source of never-ending joy for Webern; he lavished on them the same tender affection that he had bestowed on his own offspring, and they now rank prominently in his diary notes: on 9 February 1944 he recorded the birth of Maria's first child in his sketchbook, and on 26 February the baby's baptism. The boy was named Peter, after Webern's own son.

Never was there a more devoted father and grandfather, and the family idyll would have been perfect in ordinary times. Amidst the strife of war, Webern's domestic life provided him with an island of peace and hope. It gave him the courage to face the increasing number of ordeals to which he was exposed, caught up as he was, like everyone else, in the mounting holocaust which was soon to bring on the disintegration of all normal life. Throughout this trying time, he staunchly upheld his confidence and never ceased to lay ambitious plans.

After the success of his concert tours to Switzerland in 1940 and 1943, Webern had reason to believe that he might be invited there again. Determined to maintain his only remaining link with the free world, he beseeched Willi Reich to promote performances of his works. In a letter dated 10 January 1944, he suggested that Scherchen schedule his Six Pieces for Orchestra, Op. 6, or the transcription for string orchestra of his Five Movements, Op. 5. He also asked about the prospects for a performance of *Das Augenlicht*, Op. 26, under Robert Blum in Zürich, and about Frau Gradmann's plans for a première of his Three Songs, Op. 25. According to Reich, the Basel ISCM chapter hoped to repeat the concert they had given in commemoration of Webern's birthday. Referring to all these possibilities, the composer concluded: "There certainly are enough plans on the horizon. I wonder whether any of them will come to pass and if perhaps I might even return. I am curious."

For Webern, optimism was a way of life and, correspondingly, constructive action constituted for him the appropriate form for living. His temperament and basic faith impelled him to uphold that attitude in the face of all obstacles. Writing to Reich on 23 February 1944, he quoted the axiom embodying the philosophy that helped him to pursue his path through all adversity:

Leben heisst, eine *Form* verteidigen [To live is to defend a *form*]—Hölderlin puts it some such way. I would like to tell you that for a long time I have been intensely interested in this poet. Imagine the effect on me when I found this passage in his notes on the translation of Oedipus: "Also other works of art lack *reliability*, compared with those of the *Greeks*; at least until now they have been judged by the impressions they make, rather than by their *ordered calculus* and all the other modes of procedure *by which beauty is produced*." Do I still need to say why I was so moved by the passage?

After this philosophical contemplation, Webern turned to practical matters: "Your suggestions and requests regarding parts and scores were at once discussed by me with UE." Various compositions were sent to Reich, as well as to Radio Lugano. To further matters, Webern urged Reich to act again as his intermediary with Scherchen and Sacher. In a postscript he remarked that, due to ever-tightening censorship, letters abroad had been restricted to two a month. Since the summer of 1943, Webern's letters to Reich had been stamped with a large grey "X" which signified clearance by the censor.

Such stringent security measures reflected the deepening anxiety created by the disastrous turn in Hitler's fortunes of war. Although a ring of steel was closing all around the homeland, and bombs rained unremittingly upon the hapless civilian population, there was no break in morale. For too long the Führer had demonstrated his invincibility, and his brilliant victories had instilled in the German people a blind faith in his military genius. Even the older generation, forgetful of the bitter lesson learned in the First World War, still believed in ultimate victory. Such delusion was as widespread as it was tragic. Characteristically, when Edwin Komauer, Webern's first music teacher in Klagenfurt, set down his memoirs at the end of 1943, he concluded:

It was a great joy for me when the Gaumusikpreis [District Music Prize] for the year 1943 was accorded me by the governor in October 1943 in recognition of my accomplishments as a music teacher, pianist, and composer. If I was allowed to witness the magnificent rise of our people under their leader Adolf Hitler, so it is now my most ardent wish and prayer that the Lord Our God may still permit me to live to the final victory of the German people in the present gigantic struggle between the nations.[2]

Komauer was spared the agony of disillusionment. He died on 20 March 1944. In his autobiographical sketch, which dwelt on music, his great love, he spoke of the pupils whom he was proud to have guided through the years. Anton von Webern's name was not mentioned among them. Ironically, none of the students Komauer enumerated as his most talented is to be found in any standard musical dictionary. Whether the omission of Webern's name was based on aesthetic or political considerations, it proved a fallacy as great as the old musician's glorious dream of a "Thousand-Year Reich."

As Komauer lay on his deathbed, that empire was sinking into débris and ashes all around him. Defences were crumbling under aerial bombardment, and civilians were recruited to cope with the dire emergencies on the home front. On Monday, 17 April 1944, Webern found himself suddenly drafted into the "Luftschutz-Polizei" (air-raid police), a civilian work corps organized to supervise air-raid shelters and the clearing of rubble after the bombings. He had to leave home that same night. Torn from his beloved domesticity, he reacted almost frantically, dispatching an urgent message to Zenk on 20 April: "I believe that you know already what has happened to me. I can only say that it is *Hell!* Just get me out of it! . . . I could not possibly let you know, it came so quickly." On the same day, Webern gave details of his situation to the Humpliks:

> I am "embarracked," am not allowed to *live at home* and hence snatched utterly from my work!!!! *Just try* to imagine this! My post is *Mödling*, the Gymnasium my billet, i.e. *my barracks!* And naturally I must be in uniform. From 6 am to 5 pm I grind away. Duties: roughly those of a *mason*—hauling sand and that sort of thing. Passes only once in *three* days, from 5 o'clock (till 10). But I can be visited on the other days from 5 o'clock on. And so on, and so on. . . . I am tired, spent!

After less than a week, Webern was temporarily released from duty when he became ill with influenza. He was allowed to recuperate at home, but the uncertainty of his future depressed him. Recognizing his desperation, Webern's friends rallied to have him exempted from service. A flurry of petitions went to the authorities, including one personally submitted to a high official by Josef Humplik. However, they were of no avail, and on 8 May Webern had to return to his post. The day before he went back, he wrote to Zenk: "You can well imagine that I am quite out of sorts because of all these obstructions. Just the same, despite everything, I have been working again for a few days."

Throughout that difficult period Hildegard Jone wrote frequently, lending her support and encouragement. In a letter of 10 May, she commiserated with Webern's wife over his renewed confinement: "It is incomprehensible that poor Anton again has to perform such terribly hard and unaccustomed duties. This spring the world is so beautifully green. One could really have been ready to let the joy in this friendly regeneration take full effect within one's own work—but then the alarm sounds *again*. That horrifying sound which signifies that in a few minutes all the people, who now look out on everything that blossoms and grows green, will be surrounded by night."

On 14 May, a Sunday which he had had to spend in the barracks, Webern thanked the Humpliks for their concern: "How good this makes me feel! What is being imposed on me now is really very disagreeable. Perhaps you cannot even imagine it in its full impact. . . . The worst thing is that instead of being able to *use* time, one wants it to pass as quickly as possible. In truth: 'a pity that the time is wasted.'" There was, however, one consolation. The school that served as the barracks was close to the Mattel residence: "Christl is living just a *couple of houses* away! The gardens adjoin. I can talk to the children over the fence and see them through the slats. At night they breathe *not far away from me!*"

At that time, one of Webern's pupils was Christa Fuhrmann.[3] Her father held a high position in the Mödling police department, and it was through his influence that Webern was finally released from active duty. As of 20 May, the composer was allowed to return home during the daytime, but he still had to spend his nights in the air-raid warden's station until his discharge became official on 1 June. "Well *that* ordeal is over!" he wrote to Zenk two days later, with obvious relief. To be sure, Webern and his wife had to participate whenever the populace was called upon to assist in clearing away the rubble after air attacks. Such raids now recurred with ever greater frequency. Webern alluded to them when writing to Hildegard Jone on 2 June: "I dare not touch on the storms of Wednesday last week, Monday, Tuesday, and the night between (something we luckily survived). All I can say is that we are thankful to God!"

The intensity of the bombings increased with the invasion of Normandy by the Allies on 6 June. The next day, Webern's daughters, Maria and Christine, left with their four children for the safety of the remote mountain village of Mittersill, where Maria's father-in-law, Major Halbich, owned a house, Burk No. 31, at the edge of town. Although Webern recognized the necessity for it, their departure was a severe blow to him. Still emotionally affected by his experiences in uniformed service, he now began to realize the vanity and hopelessness of the struggle. The tone of the letter he wrote to Hueber on 17 June—the last message to reach his friend before he was taken prisoner of war on the Western front—was noticeably muted. His allusion to the recent Allied landings in France ("So it has come to this point, perhaps it is decisive, after all!") admitted the possibility of defeat. According to Hueber, who had been home on leave earlier in the year, Webern had wept during their last farewell and, unable to surmount his depression, did not accompany him to the garden gate as was his custom.

So disillusioned and discouraged was he that he actually thought of leaving Austria. On 6 July he wrote to Reich that Alfred Schlee, who was on his way to Switzerland, would relate the details of his draft into war service:

He will also talk about a plan that I most urgently request you to consider and pursue. I do not imagine that it would be too difficult to find something appropriate: as a formality, it would have to be an appointment. Then there would be no difficulty whatever. As far as the people in Basel are concerned, I am already considered "popular." Perhaps one could approach the matter from that angle. The financial question would have to be solved by a private party (or parties).

By that time, the number of people fleeing into Switzerland from all parts of Europe had greatly taxed the hospitality of that small country, which was struggling to maintain its precarious neutrality. As the war approached its final stage, it became impossible for the Swiss to grant asylum to the countless refugees. Thus, Webern's last-minute cry for help came far too late.

In his letter to Reich, Webern still spoke confidently of new musical plans. Schlee was taking with him to Switzerland the score of the Second Cantata, and Webern had personally acquainted him with the essential features of his work. "What will you say of it? For instance, when you first see the notational picture of the sixth movement?" the composer asked. He was elated over the plan for a radio concert in Basel and suggested that the programme open with Schubert's *Unfinished* Symphony, followed by his own arrangements of Schubert's German Dances and Bach's Ricercar, with his Passacaglia, Op. 1, at the end. In his bid for refuge in Switzerland, Webern had set all his hopes on Basel, the city where his music had been heard repeatedly (Baumgartner had just played the Variations, Op. 27, again). He renewed his plea that Reich try to interest Sacher in the string orchestra transcription of his Five Movements, Op. 5, and he inquired again about the prospects for a performance of *Das Augenlicht* in Zurich.

In this letter, in which the composer also described his latest project (the presumptive Op. 32), reference was made to Arnold Schoenberg. Since 1941, the war had disrupted all correspondence between the friends. Schoenberg's 70th birthday was only two months away, and Webern asked Reich to relay to him a message. It contained a proclamation (the last he was to make) of his undying loyalty and affection: "Convey my most heartfelt remembrances, which possess me night and day, my inexpressible longing! But also my unceasing hopes for a happy future!"

On 14 July Webern wrote to his sister Rosa about new air raids that were so severe that he and Wilhelmine were forced to seek refuge in the public shelter near their home. Despite stringent travel restrictions, he and his wife were planning an early visit to Mittersill to see their daughters. They were looking forward to a much-needed respite from the constant nervous strain, which was aggravated by another heavy air attack on 16 July. According to notes in Webern's sketchbook, they left Vienna on the evening of 24 July and stayed in Mittersill until 16 August.

A postcard to Zenk, sent on 30 July, vividly reflects Webern's sense of liberation:

We travelled here by night as planned, by express train as far as Salzburg. It was all turmoil and confusion, but then, as we rode in the local train up the Salzach valley in the early morning, there was peace and quiet! How refreshing this was, bringing happiness—long missed—such as one can hardly imagine any more! I thought of you and wished that you could have such moments when one can breathe freely. It really was a breath of relief! And here it is as peaceful as ever. We have good accommodation. From the house we can look across the valley of the Salzach River into the Felber Valley and beyond to the Tauernkogel, an imposing peak high enough to *bear glaciers*. It lies in front of the Venediger and is surrounded by several summits which are also *snow-covered*. The sight is magnificent—one I have long missed, which now has a *particularly powerful impact* on me! The water, dear friend, that comes out of the Felber Valley! A marvel, which at present touches me perhaps most of all! Today the clouds are drifting around the Tauernkogel. For two days it has been overcast, which suits me in every respect. This is mainly because, after all, I am always thinking of home. [Air raids largely depended on good flying weather.] On Wednesday it must really have been bad again, particularly in the region of Mödling. Write soon! May God protect you. We are mostly in the company of our children and of the little ones, all of whom we found looking very well.

The majestic alpine scenery that impressed Webern so deeply was the setting in which he himself was to spend the last months of his life. His serenity of mind in this retreat (he had alluringly described the setting also to the Humpliks two days earlier) was marred by news of heavy air raids on Vienna. On 24 July Hildegard Jone reported to him that her husband's atelier, located in the Hofzeile in Vienna's Grinzing district, had suffered severe damage during the air raid of 16 July. The blast from a nearby explosion had blown out the large studio window, torn a hole in the roof, and affected several of the art objects, including the death mask of Adolf Loos.[4]

Such news, followed by a report from Amalie that Mödling had been hard hit on 26 July, greatly depressed Webern. He and his wife had intended to stay away a full month, but when he read in a Salzburg newspaper that the registration of all males for emergency labour was imminent, he felt compelled to cut short his visit. Resignedly he wrote to Hildegard Jone on 10 August: "At least we have had a beautiful time. . . . The flock of children around us is something so *reassuring*, so *elevating*! This helps one to go on! Let us continue to see only happiness before us."

Arriving home on the evening of 16 August, Webern found that his alarm over the notice of the expected call-up was premature. He did, however, anticipate the inevitability of being drafted into some kind of service, and he therefore discussed with Universal Edition how he might cope with this eventuality. On 19 August he informed Zenk that the necessary arrangements had been made. A few weeks later, when he actually had to register for a labour force, the publishers intervened, and he was exempted.

From October of 1944 on, when a regular job was required to qualify for exemption from war duty, Webern spent every weekday at Universal Edition, which was located by the Karlsplatz in the heart of Vienna. His various tasks ranged from proof-reading to the examination of new compositions. Always peculiarly sensitive in matters of personal pride, he kept his employment secret from all but his most intimate friends. The position, while paying very little, actually afforded him time to accomplish some work of his own. On 7 November, he reported to Humpelstetter: "The necessary concentration for composing is hardly possible any more. However, I am at present working on something long overdue, something for which I just had not taken the time as yet: *piano reductions* of my last vocal works. These are two rather extensive cantatas for soli, chorus, and orchestra. The notational picture that is evolving here is, I believe, really quite remarkable and novel."

Webern's work for Universal Edition also gave him the time to continue his teaching activities. His private pupils were few but faithful, and his class course was regularly attended by a small group of staunch disciples. Each Wednesday and Friday he taught in the afternoon and evening at Erwin Ratz' home, which for years he had used as a convenient studio in the city. Ratz himself was one of his steady private students. To the last, Webern enjoyed his rôle as an educator. The class course, in particular, gave him much satisfaction and stimulated him to ever new ideas.

All too often, these peaceful pursuits were disrupted by air raids. Webern's correspondence is full of references to the bombings, which by then had become almost daily occurrences. By temperament averse to indulging in the darker aspects of life, he alluded to the mounting tribulations only tersely and with obvious reluctance. Yet his brief comments are telling: "An ill fate has befallen Vienna, especially during the *last few* days," he wrote to Humpelstetter on 7 November. "Yesterday our district again. Let us keep up our hopes!"

Shortly before this, on 26 October, Webern had assured his sister Rosa that the building in which Universal Edition was housed had a bomb-proof cellar and he described some of the conditions. "Last week Meidling [the twelfth district of Vienna] suffered greatly," he wrote. "Poldi [Wilhelmine's sister, Leopoldine Gross] went through a difficult time. Nothing happened to her house, but there was a hit in the immediate vicinity. For a week the connection to Mödling was very difficult. It could hardly be managed in under two hours for each trip."

As death became a real threat, family members drew together as never before, and the safety of one's next of kin became the primary concern. Throughout the years, Webern's relationship with his sisters (neither of whom was capable of following him on his lofty path as a composer) had been more or less casual. But now that Klagenfurt was under constant bombardment from the air because of its strategic location at the crossroads of Italy and Yugoslavia, he maintained closer contact. On 6 November he reported:

My dear Rosi, after difficult days! We are well, however. On Monday it was bad again in our region, too. But in Vienna on Sunday! Since then I have stayed home because the train connections, too, have suffered. But it seems to be better now. You must bear in mind that, because of the many disruptions, *everything* is concentrated on a *few* connecting roads. There are masses of people. Yes, commuting, too, has really become very difficult. How are you faring? Do keep us posted. Just be careful, for God's sake! In Poldi's neighbourhood the bombs have been falling again. But we do not have any information yet about Sunday and Monday. One cannot telephone at present. There was also a bomb behind the Votivkirche, in the *immediate* vicinity of Beryl's apartment [Beryl Diez, the wife of Ernst]. We have not heard from her yet, either, how she is faring. . . . If only things could be easier again, at last! Let us hope for it!

It was about this time that Webern, fearing catastrophe, made out an inventory of all his works that had not yet been published. The list included the whereabouts of the original manuscripts, most of which were stored in the cellar of Universal Edition.[5] A few had been left for safe-keeping with individuals like Werner Reinhart in Switzerland. Such precautions were virtually imperative in the face of the spreading devastation. In one of the November air raids Josef Humplik's atelier was completely demolished.[6] The senseless destruction of their creative work was a cruel blow to the artists. Helpless in his impulse to assist, Webern could only vent his anguish when he wrote to Hildegard Jone on 18 November: "Our distress is beyond words. The ever more pressing question is, when will it all be over?"

Late that month, the antithesis to the grim drama of the time was embodied in an hour dedicated to spiritual pursuits. On Wednesday, 29 November, a small circle of guests gathered in a hall of the Archbishop's palace in Vienna, at Stephansplatz 3, for a programme billed as an "Evening of Contemporary Poetry." Dr Otto Mauer, a high-ranking clergyman, was the official host for the event, which was devoted exclusively to the lyrics of Hildegard Jone.

The project had been conceived during the spring and originally called for the reading of all Jone poems that Webern had set to music,[7] with some of his compositions to be included in the programme. Webern had proposed his Opera 23 and 25 cycles and suggested that a Swedish singer then living in Vienna be asked to perform. As accompanist he recommended one of his students from Holland, Free Focke, whom he described to Hildegard Jone on 27 June as "a *brilliant pianist* and excellent musician."

However, difficulties arose when, a few weeks before the event, the singer unexpectedly raised demands for an honorarium. It was Hildegard Jone who objected. On 11 October she informed Webern that she was unwilling to pass on the request to Dr Mauer at a time when the sponsoring church agency needed all its resources to alleviate the most urgent wartime needs. "It is, after all, almost like a performance at home, for mutual acquaintances," she wrote. "A person who demands money for her services does not fit in at all! How *much* we would like to hear the songs—this you must believe!"

As the programme had at first been conceived, Focke was supposed to perform the Variations, Op. 27. But when that plan foundered, Webern decided to make altogether different arrangements and he asked the pianist Olga Novakovic, a trusted friend since the Schoenberg Society days, to step into the breach. On 25 November, four days before the event, he explained his position to Hildegard Jone:

The *primary* reason for my having changed the *musical part* of the evening lies in my desire to ensure the most satisfying result possible for your evening. Nobody is to have cause for head-shaking, etc. This would have happened, *unavoidably*, had I kept to our original plan. I have considered it over and over: so I beg you, a thousand times, do not be disappointed!!! It is decidedly better this way, believe me. I have had enough experience. Had it been a matter of the songs, the situation would have been something else again! But an outside consideration also entered: Dr Mauer requested (as the pianist informed me) a musical number for the *beginning*. For this purpose I could choose only something *classical*. So the evening will open with a piece by *Mozart*, a rarely played Fantasia. Then, between the two poetry portions, there will be the Sonata by Berg; to include my Variations would result in altogether too much music for the evening. It is precious to me that I can allocate this place on the programme, which I *esteem so highly*, to my friend! Oh, you will certainly understand me. I am sorry myself, but it is done with the *best* of intentions. Be assured of this! Trust me!

Webern's self-effacement was to cost him his last opportunity of hearing his music performed. But he knew that the tastes of the audience, expected to be made up chiefly of clergymen, would be deeply rooted in the classic and romantic tradition, and his sole concern was that the evening, which was intended primarily as an homage to Hildegard Jone, would be a success. He had asked Werner Riemer-schmid, Josef Hueber's brother-in-law, who lived in his neighbour-hood in Mödling, to read the poems.[8] Dr Riemerschmid held the position of dramaturge at Radio Vienna and was a poet and an experienced actor. All the same, Webern took infinite pains to impart to him the nuances of the texts as he had perceived them in his musical realizations.[9]

Successful as the evening was, Webern sensed Hildegard Jone's disappointment that his music had been omitted. Feeling it necessary to explain his position once more, he wrote to her on 8 December:

My sole endeavour was to rid the evening of everything problematical and hence of anything that might be burdensome or disturbing! Believe me, I know it all: when suddenly everything begins to fall flat. *All my life* I have had to endure it, *all my life*. As far as I am concerned, it therefore would not have mattered much to experience it again. But on *this particular evening*, I could *not have stood* it, *on your behalf*, dear Hildegard. The *only thing* I had in mind was that nothing should disturb or detract from the *profound effect* of your words, in which I had complete confidence—and indeed it was so!

Although she persisted in her belief that the small circle would have been as responsive to Webern's music as it was to her poetry, Hildegard Jone was profusely grateful for the composer's efforts on her behalf. On 11 December, she summarized her impression of the evening in a letter to Webern: "Thus, indeed, the whole event was, in our unfathomably dark time, a welcome glimpse of light, which I am happy to remember."

It was Advent, and the poetess closed her letter with a Christmas message that transcended the anxiety and oppression of the time: "Let us hope that there will be another spring for us! Now would be the right time to express pure thoughts through tones, forms, colours, and words! *Let us, despite everything, grasp the light of Christmas as never before! I wish you, my friends, that it may shine deep in your hearts!*"

Of all the Christmas seasons since the outbreak of the war, that of 1944 was the most dismal. The German war lords, in a last attempt to extricate themselves from the stranglehold exerted on all sides by the Allies, engaged in a desperate gamble. On 16 December they launched a counter-offensive on the Western front. A strong force, spearheaded by armour, attacked the thinly-held American lines in the Belgian Ardennes sector. Taking advantage of the foggy weather and the utter surprise of the Allies, the German columns penetrated deep into Belgium and, by use of rocket bombs, subjected the Allied supply centres at Liège and Antwerp to intensive punishment. Only a small American pocket at Bastogne held out against the onslaught, during which both sides suffered from the severe cold and snow. After 24 December, improved flying weather helped the Allied counter-thrusts which, by mid-January 1945, cut off the German escape routes. Hitler's last daring offensive had turned into a complete rout.

Writing to Humpelstetter on 20 December, Webern expressed his Christmas wish: "Let us become more conscious than ever before of the *meaning of these holidays! Perhaps it will help!!* May God finally grant us better times!" It was only natural that Webern's deepest concern should be for the safety of his own flesh and blood. Ever since Peter had been sent to Yugoslavia in the early summer of 1944, he had worried constantly. His fears increased when the Yugoslav partisans intensified their harassment as the Germans began their withdrawal from the Balkan countries. Webern's letters to friends were full of references to Peter, and the pendulum of his emotions swung from the greatest anxiety whenever his son was in a danger zone to joyful relief when he returned home on one of his rather frequent visits.

Until the autumn of 1944, Peter had been stationed in the vicinity of Belgrade. Assigned to guard duty, he periodically had to accompany military trains running between Dresden and Belgrade. On one of these occasions, while reporting at the Vienna headquarters for army personnel in transit, he fainted. "On the trip back his *heart* trouble seized him again," Webern wrote anxiously to Ludwig Zenk on 4 October. "When he reported here at the arsenal, he collapsed! He is now in the arsenal's infirmary. We hope that he can remain here, that he will be sent to a hospital for treatment and not on any account be ordered to travel again! *Down there!* I hope it turns out well."

In spite of his father's prayers, Peter soon had to return to active duty. However, he had lost contact with his unit and, since he was unable to re-establish it due to the breakdown of communications, he was transferred from post to post during the next few months. His odyssey included a period of comparative quiet (from the end of November until February 1945) when he was stationed at a supply depot in Znaim, close enough to Vienna to visit home quite often.

Early in 1945 the plight of the German armies became generally apparent. Fighting merely delaying battles, they were being pushed back on all fronts. On 30 January Adolf Hitler spoke to the German people over the radio in a last desperate attempt to rekindle their faith in his leadership. The following day Peter wrote to Hermine: "Yesterday I was at a rally in Znaim, held in the riding arena of the Klosterbrugg barracks. The speaker was Comrade Frauenfeld, whom you perhaps will remember from the time the party was outlawed. He spoke very well and con-vincingly. A social gathering in the mess hall followed at 7 pm. Beer and wine were served and everyone got two pieces of buttered bread, thickly covered with ham, and a pickle. It was really nice, and we talked and sang. Since there was plenty of wine to go around, we got into quite high spirits." Thus did the army try to bolster morale.

Peter continued:

Work here is always the same—some days less to do and then sometimes so much work that the day is too short. But regardless of how much work there is here, it cannot be compared with the strain and deprivation which the soldiers at the front must endure. Yes, my dear Hermi, these are certainly very difficult and serious times, but despite everything we must not lose heart. For all of us now only one motto exists: "fight and work" with every effort until victory is ours. For victory will be ours. I still believe in this exactly as before. And today, after I heard the address of our Führer, I was even more strengthened in my faith. Therefore, my dear Hermi, do not be disheartened, do not lose courage, and do not allow yourself to be influenced by the gloom-mongerings of some people. For us, too, the sun will shine again, and once again we will have all that we must now do without. We will shape our life together beautifully and all our secret wishes will find fufilment. I love you infinitely and I think of you day and night, and you are really the most precious human being I possess in the world. Yes, I would like once to be able to tell you just how much I love you, but there are no words that can express this properly to you. I believe, however, that you must feel how much I love you, my Frauerl [little wife].

Two weeks later, Peter von Webern was dead. With some comrades from the Znaim detachment he had been sent to Dresden, where he received orders to proceed to Yugoslavia. On the evening of 10 February he arrived unexpectedly in Perchtoldsdorf, and the next morning he went with Hermine to visit his parents. He had to return to the barracks that evening and in the morning he boarded the train for Agram, Yugoslavia. During a long stop in Wiener Neustadt, he wrote to his young wife: "As far as Mödling I kept looking out of the window, and as I gazed at my native country I thought of how many beautiful hours I had spent with you in these surroundings. . . . Never before has parting been so difficult for me. I do not know why."

It was past midnight when the train left Wiener Neustadt. That day, 13 February, as Vienna reeled under especially heavy air raids, the troop transport rolled slowly towards its destination. Because the rails had been blasted by air and guerrilla action, the trip was repeatedly interrupted. Thus it was not until 14 February that the train reached the vicinity of Lindenkogel in Lower Styria, where it was surprised by a low-flying fighter plane. Three days later, Alfred Gundel, a comrade of Peter, sent this report to Hermine:

> On the route between Marburg and Agram, the train stopped shortly after passing through a tunnel. Peter sat beside me in a compartment of the first car behind the engine. Since someone in the compartment said that the train had collided with another one, we refrained from immediately jumping off. Only when we heard the aircraft approaching did we leap out, but in the excitement unfortunately on the wrong side. After I had jumped over the ditch along the track and ducked for cover, the first burst from the aircraft gun sprayed the engine, hitting along with it the first few cars. Peter, who just at that moment was either still jumping off or was already on the ground, was hit by a bullet that tore open his upper thigh rather badly. Our comrade Eckert was killed. Peter endured his pain very bravely and spoke very animatedly with me, so that I firmly believe he will be healed again completely, since within a short time he was transported for home in a military hospital train.

That letter, as well as a similar account from another comrade, Anton Schnabel, did not reach Hermine until 13 March. They had long been preceded by the official notification of Peter's death. When Hermine returned home from work on Saturday noon, 3 March, a letter from Major Goeser, the superior officer of the Znaim garrison, was awaiting her. It brought the news that Peter had succumbed to his injuries in the hospital train. In closing his expression of sympathy, the commandant wrote: "May you find consolation in the thought that your husband has served his fatherland by his ultimate sacrifice and by the highest fulfilment of his duty, and that his death will contribute to the final liberation of our people."

An hour later, the block leader of the Perchtoldsdorf section of the NSDAP (National Socialist German Workers' Party) called on Hermine, as it was customary that death notices be personally delivered by a party functionary. He brought the official report, which was issued on 21 February at Marburg/Drau. It stated that Peter had died on 14 February from a pulmonary embolism and that he had been buried on the 19th in the municipal cemetery "with military honours and in the presence of a Catholic priest, together with other comrades who had died during the air raid on Marburg."[10]

Although initially paralysed by shock, Hermine gradually realized that it was her duty to inform Peter's parents of the death of their son. With her sister, Lotte, she went the same afternoon to their home. Hermine later recalled how, under the impact of the tragic news, Webern first turned to his wife and took her in his arms.[11] But it was not he who dispensed comfort. His instinctive gesture was rather that of one deeply hurt, of one in need of help, who had to cling to someone strong for support so that he himself would not collapse. Thus, in his most difficult hour, Wilhelmine again became for Webern the trinity, for which he himself had coined the phrase: Minna, Mutter, Königin (Minna [Wilhelmine], mother, queen). And like the Queen of Sorrow, Pietà, the mother ministered her office.

Later, Amalie and her husband arrived, and the family's common grief helped to soothe their pain and anguish. The Weberns insisted that Hermine stay with them that night. She slept in Peter's former room on the upper floor. The next morning, a Sunday, Webern accompanied her back to Perchtoldsdorf. Hermine related that, as they parted, Webern embraced her and said: "After your father, you now have lost your husband, too. I want to be both to you from here on." In her grief, Hermine gained a deep sense of security from these words. Father and daughter-in-law stood for a long time in the street weeping openly as they held each other.

Hermine and Webern together attended to the sad task of preparing the death announcement. Because of the war, most printers had long ceased to function. Father and daughter-in-law went repeatedly to the monks of the Abbey St Gabriel, pleading with them to print the announcement. During one of these visits, which were to prove of no avail, they entered the darkened church to pray. As they walked up the centre aisle towards the main altar, the stillness was suddenly broken by the sound of the organ and the choir. It was Lent, and the monks were rehearsing for the services of the Passion and Resurrection. During that solemn hour, Webern's and Hermine's sorrow found relief in uncontrolled tears. Nobody was present to see them and the music drowned their sobs. For a long time they could not regain control of

themselves. At last, the same music that had so stirred their wounded
hearts enveloped them in a comforting mantle. Solaced and uplifted
they left the sanctuary.

In the end, the death announcement was printed in Perchtoldsdorf.
Due to the scarcity of materials, Hermine not only had to supply the
paper (from a stationery pad she found at home), but also had to ink in
by hand, with Webern's help, the black borders and the cross.[12] The text
read:

✝

Mein innigstgeliebter Gatte, unser Sohn und Bruder

Gefreiter P e t e r   v o n   W e b e r n

verschied nach schwerer Verwundung am 14. Februar 1945 im Alter
von 29 Jahren.
Er wurde am 19. Februar am städtischen Friedhofe in Marburg a/d Drau
zur ewigen Ruhe gebettet.
Die heilige Seelenmesse findet am 15. März um 7.15 Uhr in der
Pfarrkirche Perchtoldsdorf statt.

In tiefstem Schmerze

Hermine von Webern geb. Schubert

Dr. Anton und Wilhelmine von Webern

Amalia Waller, Maria Halbich und Christine Mattel

Perchtoldsdorf und Maria Enzersdorf, am 3. März 1945

A Requiem Mass for Peter was held on 15 March in the parish church
of Perchtoldsdorf. After the service the family went to the cemetery,
where Hermine placed a bouquet of flowers on the grave of her father
(who had died in 1939) in memory of her husband. It was the custom to
honour in this way those who had fallen far from their homeland. At
eleven o'clock that morning an air-raid alarm sounded. The family
spent the next five hours in a wine cellar, hewn out of the rocks. It
belonged to a neighbour of the Schuberts, who allowed them to use it
as a refuge although, officially, one was supposed to go to the nearest
public air-raid shelter. The cave-like chamber, its rock walls dripping
with moisture, affected Webern deeply.

When the alarm was over, the Weberns went with Hermine to the
small garden house which she and Peter had occupied during the few
years of their marriage. On the wall hung the oil portrait of Webern

which Tom von Dreger had painted in 1934, and which Webern had presented to the young couple for their first Christmas together in 1941. Sitting in the room where Peter had gone in and out, the three tried to soothe their sorrow with memories of better days. During the next weeks, the Weberns returned several times to the little house, as if unable to tear themselves away from the spot where their son had enjoyed his happiest hours.

CHAPTER XXXIV

Catastrophe and flight
(1945)

"Die arme Freude"	"Hapless Joy"
Der Mensch:	*Man:*
"Liebe Freude, gingst du aus?	"Dear joy, have you left?
Kommst du nimmermehr?"	Will you never return?"
Die Freude:	*Joy:*
"O, mich findet du und der.	"O, you and anyone else can find me.
Blieb im Lebenshaus,	I have remained in life's house,
auch in allerärgster Zeit:	even in the most grievous of times:
wohn in einer Kammer	I dwell in one chamber
mit der Schwester Herzeleid,	with my sister Sorrow,
mit dem Bruder Jammer."	with my brother Misery."

I T WAS A favourite practice of Hildegard Jone occasionally to include with her messages to Webern one of her newest poems. At times she would burst into spontaneous verse even within her letters. The little poem quoted above, reminiscent of the stark simplicity of a Matthias Claudius, sprang from such sudden inspiration. It appeared at the close of the last extant letter written by Hildegard Jone to Webern on 20 February 1945. In that letter, the poetess revealed the full stature of her humanity. Her ever-constructive philosophy triumphed over the onslaught of adversity, and with an all-encompassing love she clung to the eternal beauty of life. Extolling the courage of those near and dear to her in the face of overwhelming tribulations, she wrote: "Above all, let us contemplate the human spirit, which today thrusts upward like a pure flame out of the present conflagration! What vistas are revealed amidst all this obscurity. Before the new cold spell I found some primroses, between one alarm and the next. The joy over little things—how great it can be!"

Only a very strong soul could sustain the flickering light of confidence with such serenity. A weaker person might have despaired under any single shattering blow, such as the air assault that battered the doomed city the day after the poetess had written these lines. On 26 February, in the last letter to reach Humpelstetter before he was taken prisoner-of-war, Webern described the situation:

> You will probably learn what we have to go through here: last Wednesday, 21 February, a climax was reached! For a whole week I could not get to Vienna—there was no connection. When I was last in the city a week ago today, I had to make my way home on foot from the Meidling station of the Stadtbahn. I had a similar experience the week before that. It is really unimaginable what the calamitous traffic situation that results from such disruptions means for so large a city, quite aside from the scarcity of water, electricity, and gas. It is indescribable how this has already affected some districts. But I do not wish to burden you even more.

A postcard containing similar remarks, written by Webern to Ludwig Zenk two days earlier, did not arrive until 9 March (according to a note Zenk pencilled on the margin). The fact that mail delivery even within the city took thirteen days illustrates the existing chaotic conditions. During those trying times, Webern and Zenk met frequently, but their personal contact ceased with that devastating air raid of 21 February.[1] Zenk later recalled: "Webern suffered immeasurably during the time of the bombing! God knows—we all suffered!!! But Webern was very close to the breaking point."[2]

At the end of February 1945, Webern's earnings ceased. The last listing of his class course in his income book appears in January, and his records for February include only the tuition fees from two private pupils (Ratz and Leyer) and a payment from Universal Edition. Webern wrote the headline "March" in his notebook, but the space below remained blank, mute testimony to the soul-shaking sorrow that engulfed him with his son's death, word of which reached him on 3 March.

That month the war entered its final stage. The German armies, which had held out against the Russians, were retreating. On 7 March, the Western Allies crossed the Rhine after smashing through the strongly fortified Siegfried Line.[3] The climax of the long and torturous struggle was imminent. Since the summer of 1944 the aerial siege of Vienna and its environs had steadily intensified. The prevailing conditions were described by Hermine von Webern, who kept a diary during that time. Carrying the notebook constantly with her, she wrote many of the entries by candlelight in bunkers and cellars. Everyone relied on the radio for quick communication in those days. Before an air-raid alarm, "cuckoo" calls interrupted the programme in progress. The signal was followed by an announcement of the danger that menaced, including information on the direction from which the enemy squadrons were approaching and the districts most likely to be the targets. Then the electric current was switched off and the sirens began to sound in the streets. Failure to comply with the instructions of the air-raid wardens or to go to the nearest shelter was subject to severe penalty.[4] Each person kept in readiness a rucksack filled with warm clothing, a blanket, and emergency provisions, so that it was possible to hold out in the underground shelters, which were often damp, for a prolonged time if necessary. Towards the end of the war, gas masks were issued.

Under such conditions, Hermine's diary entries, concise and factual as they appear, assume a stark immediacy. From the multitude of her notes, made in early 1945, a few are quoted here:

Wednesday, 7 February: 11.40 am to 3.30 pm, alarm. Attack on Vienna: Ring, Gauhaus [party headquarters], Rathaus [city hall], Burggasse, Franz-Josef-Bahnhof [railway station], Westbahnstrecke [railway to the west], many squadrons, return flight over us, aircraft shot down, toys dropped [for propaganda purposes Allied planes occasionally dropped small children's toys].

Thursday, 8 February: 11.45 am to 2.15 pm, alarm. Rode home from work on my bicycle, was still in the living room when shooting started during the first wave of attack, heard loud detonations. Attack on Vienna.

Tuesday, 13 February: 11.30 am to 1.30 pm, alarm. Terror attack on Vienna: 10th, 5th, 11th, 3rd districts, etc., arsenal. 7.45 pm bombers flying from the direction of Carinthia, Styria, attack on Graz, bomb Rupp's house, small bomb, which did not explode, on house of Marz in the Hochstrasse [the street in which Hermine's home was located].

Friday, 16 February: No light, no gas, no streetcars, no sirens. Advance alarm 11.15 am to 1.30 pm.

Hermine's diary also lists the attacks that followed on 19, 21, and 22 February. In nearby Liesing, the supply depot and the building housing the Arbeitsamt (the agency to which Hermine had been assigned for war service) were hit. Seven died. During March the tempo of the air bombardment accelerated. Whatever Hermine recorded as happening in Perchtoldsdorf equally affected Maria Enzersdorf, only four kilometres distant. The Weberns and their daughter Amalie (who lived at Im Auholz 2, a few houses down the street) were assigned to the public shelter at Vorderbrühl, about a quarter of an hour's walk away. The shelter, which had been blasted out of the mountain, held about 2,000 persons. It has been described by Amalie:

> The refuge contained a Red Cross station for the special care of children and old people. As with all these shelters, there was the constant worry that the exit might be blocked as a result of a bomb. Inevitably this would have led to mass death. My father did not like this shelter. I was not often in it, either, because the trip there was so troublesome for me, first because of my pregnancy and afterwards because it was so difficult to walk there holding one child in one arm and another by the hand. Moreover, the nearby Ostmark Werke [an airplane factory] employed an artificial fog screen as a protection against the bombers, and this fog hovered in thick swathes over the path along the aqueduct that we had to use in order to reach the shelter. I do not know what kind of gas it was, but at any rate it stank terribly and we all had to cough violently. So we preferred to wait out the attacks at home. My parents always came to our house, not because it offered more protection, but because if something should happen, then we preferred to go all together.[5]

Even during the early morning hours, one could see mothers and children hurrying towards the air-raid shelters, convinced that there would be another alarm. They looked like tourists heading for a holiday in the country, but their rucksacks contained only whatever was most precious or essential to them, for nobody knew whether his house would still be standing on his return. For hours before the actual alarm, groups would form in front of the shelters. Everyone wanted to be assured of a good place. Earlier, the air assaults had been launched only during daylight, but in March they began to occur also at night. The Allies shared in the bombings: the American squadrons flew up from the south by day, and the Russian planes attacked from the east at night.

Webern, who was already grief-stricken by Peter's death, suffered untold mental anguish from the daily raids. The howling of the sirens, the constant crackling of the anti-aircraft guns, and the deafening explosions of the bombs were overwhelming to a man who was, even under normal conditions, unusually sensitive to noise. He, whose faith had always been unshakeable, began to doubt a higher providence. Amalie, who lived on the ground floor of the Waller home and often saw her father pass by, once heard him exclaim: "My God, how could you permit this?"

On the eastern front, the situation deteriorated rapidly. The German armies were in full retreat, and the Russians were closing in from Czechoslovakia, Hungary, and the Balkans. Rumours of the enemy's approach spread everywhere. While the radio reports continued to sound reassuring, the fact that the Russians had already penetrated into two Austrian provinces, Burgenland and Lower Austria, could not be denied. Towards the end of March, a mass evacuation of the civilian population commenced. The "U-Karte," an official authorization to move to another locality, became a new concept. At first it was issued only to women with children, then to the elderly and the sick.

The Weberns, with Amalie and her two sons, made plans to flee to Mittersill where Maria and Christine were already living with their children. On Tuesday, 27 March, Hermine wrote in her diary: "At 6 pm with my parents-in-law. Very sad. They have received U-Karte for Mittersill. Father accompanied me to the streetcar." At their parting, Webern beseeched Hermine to come with them. The next day, 28 March—it was five days before Easter—Anton and Wilhelmine came in the afternoon to Perchtoldsdorf to see Hermine and her mother once more. Hermine's diary entry of Good Friday, 30 March, read: "Very sad. Everyone cried in the street. Siebenhirten-Vösendorf [communities in the immediate vicinity of Perchtoldsdorf] evacuated. 10 am to 1.45 pm alarm, attacks on northern and north-eastern Vienna. Dug a hole with Lotte [to bury valuables]. Was in Vienna in the afternoon. Everyone in a turmoil because of evacuations."

The following day, Hermine noted: "10.30 to 4.30 pm alarm. Frau W. and her children left. In the morning, went to my parents-in-law, did not find them there any longer. At 5.30 am they had set out on foot for Mittersill. Amalie and the children evacuated. Digging and packing." Frau W., who lived next door to the Schubert family, was the wife of a high party functionary. For such people, holding out till the last moment was an absolute duty, and their hasty departure signalled "every man for himself!" Those who did not leave the sinking ship prepared for the coming of the Russians. Everywhere people dug holes to hide their belongings. In this way Hermine and her sisters concealed their sewing machines and bicycles, which first had to be dismantled, as well as their linen, clothes, and household articles. The young women had decided to stay with their mother in Perchtoldsdorf and there await their fate.

On 3 April, Gunter Waller, Amalie's husband, brought Hermine a farewell letter that Webern had written to her on the evening of Good Friday:

My dear, dear child! It has become a reality, after all—we *must* leave tomorrow! *On foot!* For there is no opportunity for us to get a ride! Mali and the little boys will travel in one of the buses which have been made available for the *women* with small children who are to be evacuated! Our town, as well as Mödling, will be evacuated tomorrow (Saturday) from 4 am on!!! It has happened so suddenly that we have to say goodbye to you and yours in this manner. We used all of today to put everything in order and to pack our things. Each of us has a rucksack. En route we hope to find space on a truck, etc., for at least part of the way. Perhaps farther west there will also be the possibility of travelling by *train*. Our goal: Mittersill! We have the papers for relocation, etc. Officially we are taken care of. This goes also for me; as a man! One is even *supposed* to leave. When will it be Perchtoldsdorf's turn? Presumably during the next few days. *Remain* in touch with the organization for *evacuees* in so far as it applies to you! I hope that all goes well. Write to us in *Mittersill*. Your mother and Elly [Hermine's sister Gabriele, who was paralysed by multiple sclerosis] certainly will be allowed to ride in an autobus! You others have bicycles, after all. If only we could stay together!!! How difficult this parting is! Under such circumstances! May God protect you and yours! Farewell! A thousand heartfelt kisses! Till we meet again—*we hope that it may be soon*!!!   Father and Mother

In a surge of fatherly love, Webern added: "Be embraced!"

By the time that Gunter delivered this letter, the beginning of the end was at hand. On Easter Sunday, the day after Webern's flight, the Russians were close to Baden, near Vienna. Hermine's diary entries report continual air assaults. On the evening of 4 April she saw from the Hochberg, a nearby hill, the conflagrations in Brunn am Gebirge, Maria Enzersdorf, and Mödling. On Thursday, 5 April, Mödling fell. On that day, Hermine's diary entry read: "Our wedding day (1941), the Russians in Maria Enzersdorf, Giesshübl, Triesterstrasse. Since 11 am artillery fire. Moved into Uncle Tastl's cellar. Wine, brandy, foodstuffs freely distributed. DAF building [Deutsche Arbeits-Front headquarters] in the Beatrixgasse blown up and set on fire."

The final crisis had arrived. Hermine's notes about the next few days speak for themselves:

Friday, 6 April: Strong artillery fire, bombs. Was in bunker at Schnötzingers [Hermine's sister and brother-in-law]. Slept in cellar.
Saturday, 7 April: Very strong artillery fire. Could not go out on the street any more. Only lukewarm meals. During afternoon direct hits and fires in the Hochstrasse. Windows in the living quarters shattered. Slept in cellar. Worst day thus far!
Sunday, 8 April: At night artillery bombardment. During day further strong bombardment. Spent all the time in cellar. 7 pm tank

spearhead. 7.15 pm Russian infantry from Moscow marched from the Semlergasse into the Hochstrasse.

Hermine observed the coming of the first Russian soldiers through a crack in the boarded-up cellar window. In the dark street they first appeared one by one, then in groups of two or three. They seemed like ghosts in their camouflage: brown- and green-spotted canvas cloaks were slung over their shoulders, and sand-coloured nets hung from their steel helmets which were covered with twigs. Rifles in readiness, they moved soundlessly from doorway to doorway, their backs against the house walls for cover. It was a fearsome sight.

Two days later, 10 April, Vienna fell. Much of the city lay in ruins, and some of its prized edifices—such as St Stephan's Cathedral, the Opera, and the Burgtheater—were virtually destroyed. It was the end of an epoch.

*   *   *

Late on 31 March, the day they had left home at dawn, Anton and Wilhelmine reached Neulengbach, a station on the railway line to Salzburg, not far from St Pölten. They had walked, burdened by their heavy rucksacks, the entire distance of about 25 kilometres. The fatigue and anxiety of that forced march can only be imagined. To be sure, Wilhelmine could have used the autobus that was available for the evacuation of women and children, but she refused to leave her husband by himself. In Neulengbach the couple was fortunate enough to get on a westbound train.[6]

Amalie Waller and her two small sons, who had left Mödling the same day on the bus, travelled with the group of refugees as far as Innsbruck. Their destination was Rosenheim, Germany, but Amalie decided to break away and head back to Mittersill. A train took her to Zell am See. There, on Easter Monday, 2 April, as she stood with her children on the platform waiting for the connecting train to Mittersill, she suddenly found herself face to face with her parents. She later described their reunion: "My father was so deeply moved that he embraced me with tears in his eyes and said: 'Mali, my child, this is a dispensation of God's providence. Now everything will turn out well.'"[7]

Together they boarded the little train that ran through the Pinzgau valley to Mittersill, where they soon were able to join Maria, Christine, and their children. In the shelter of the house Burk No. 31, the family awaited the collapse of the German empire. On 30 April, Adolf Hilter committed suicide amidst the burning ruins of Berlin. Germany's unconditional surrender was signed on 7 May in Reims and ratified the following day in Berlin.

For the Webern family, assembled in their remote refuge, anxious days were still to follow, days dominated by fear for the safety of the husbands of the three young women. Weeks went by until the first of them, Gunter Waller, was able to make his way to the village. His experience had been harrowing. Towards the end of March he had been recruited into the Volkssturm, a hastily-formed brigade of adolescents and invalid or overaged men who were called up for the last-ditch defence of the fatherland (earlier in the war, Waller had been exempted from service because of a permanent leg injury). At three o'clock in the morning, a soldier had aroused him from bed and given him orders to accompany him immediately. He and other men, most of them well over 60, were put into uniform and cursorily initiated into the rudiments of warfare. On 5 April, armed with bazookas, the use of which they had to study from a manual, they took up position on the Trieste highway, where a blockade had been improvised from newly-felled trees. Their task was to defend this barricade from the approaching Russian tanks. It was not long until a barrage of enemy artillery fire killed several Volkssturm men. The remaining unit was quickly pulled back and transported by truck to the Waldviertel, a district northwest of Vienna. During the night the officers abandoned their charges and fled, taking along the entire supply of petrol. Left to their fate, the men worked their way back to the vicinity of Linz, where the prisoners of the concentration camp at Mauthausen, who had just been set free, suddenly attacked them. Some were clubbed to death, others beaten unconscious, and all robbed of their belongings. Gunter, who had been left with nothing but his underwear, managed to make his way to a nearby house where a kindly woman took him in and cared for him. He then began his torturous trek to Mittersill. Along the way he was captured by American soldiers who brought him to a prison camp, from which he escaped by swimming across the icy Salzach River under a rain of bullets. After that he travelled mostly by night, relying on friendly peasants for food and shelter. To avoid the more populous valleys, he traversed the mountain slopes of the towering Hochkönig, sometimes waist-deep in snow. His boots had been seized during the attack by the concentration-camp inmates, and the thin leather shoes left in their place were a miserable substitute, hardly protecting his swollen feet.

In Mittersill, Amalie stood with her seven-year-old son, Michael, on the balcony of the house one day when a shabby-looking man staggered up the hillside. "A tramp is coming—he wants to take something away from us," the child cried fearfully. It was thus that Gunter Waller, whose hair had turned white during the ordeal, returned to his family.

The horrors of war continued long after the actual fighting had ended. Acts of violence occurred everywhere. Even in the peaceful valley of Mittersill, the atmosphere was laden with tension. The mountain peasants, rooted in their age-old customs, were ruggedly independent, cunning in their ways, and suspicious of any outsiders. As staunch Catholics, they had been stubbornly opposed to the virtual deification of Hitler and his régime, and before the collapse had had to be ruled by a detachment of SS men (the élite Nazi security corps). When the war ended, the French were the first to march through, spearheaded by Moroccan troops. Then the Americans arrived and stayed on, restoring a measure of stability. However, because of the general turbulence, the military had orders to remain on the alert. Many German soldiers and active Nazis were known to be still hiding out in the mountains.[8] Mittersill itself was crowded with refugees from many lands. Natives and displaced persons often found themselves embroiled in strange incidents. An American captain was killed by local men in a fight over a girl. A Romanian dignitary, the former Minister of Finance, was found slain in the forest, and a large sum of money that he was known to have carried disappeared.

Brutal acts of all kinds were frequent in the gradual transition from war to peace, particularly in larger centres such as Vienna. During the first days of the occupation, there were many excesses. Looting and rape were not uncommon, and scores of terrified civilians were driven to suicide. In numerous townships, such as Perchtoldsdorf, martial law was declared. There, as everywhere in the Russian-occupied zone, the populace lived through a period of constant fear and hardship. Hermine's diary records that her mother's home was plundered several times. Many a night she and her sisters hid themselves in a space between two firewalls to escape the attention of drunken soldiers. For six weeks they never undressed, and the first night they dared to spend in bed again merited special mention in Hermine's diary. The supply of gas and electricity was disrupted for months. So great was the famine that in late summer the women went out to glean the already-harvested fields.

Immediately following the occupation, the Russian military established a tailor's shop in Perchtoldsdorf to provide new uniforms for their officers. A local tailor, Johann Strasser, who could speak a little Russian, was put in charge of recruiting helpers, and Hermine and two of her sisters, Lotte and Grete, were fortunate enough to be given jobs. In a short time the sisters gained the confidence of their Russian supervisors. This enabled Hermine to carry out a plan that had been uppermost in her mind since the day her parents-in-law had fled: to find out what had happened to their abandoned apartment in Maria Enzersdorf. On 2 May, when work in the shop was discontinued early in the afternoon for a post-May Day celebration, Hermine, with the help of Strasser, the head tailor, persuaded the Russian officer in charge to conduct her and her sister Lotte to the house Im Auholz 8. Such escort was necessary in the face of the dangers still prevailing, particularly for young women, so soon after the take-over. The lieutenant ordered an armed guard to accompany them.

What they found at the Webern home was a scene of devastation. Successive contingents of soldiers had been billeted in the house. The doors had been broken open, and many of the family's belongings lay strewn around. In the search for valuables, sofas and mattresses had been slit open and wall panels ripped off. In the centre of the round dining table a hole had been sawed to hold a wash tub. For Hermine, the sight of the chaos in the formerly so well-ordered household was crushing. She immediately resolved to salvage whatever she could, and during the following weeks she trudged again and again the four kilometres between Perchtoldsdorf and Maria Enzersdorf, each time carrying a loaded rucksack back to her home. On a few occasions, her sisters and sympathetic women friends lent her a helping hand. At first a Russian soldier would still go with them, but as conditions gradually returned to normal, the women ventured on their way alone.

On 27 May, Wilhelmine's sister, Leopoldine Gross, came to Perchtoldsdorf for the first time since communications had broken down. Only then did she learn from Hermine that the Weberns had fled almost two months earlier. Learning of the salvaging action, Leopoldine offered to help and procured a small wagon so that they could carry bigger loads. This also enabled Hermine to transport larger pieces. By then, most of the furniture, household utensils, books, and music had been cleared out by the occupying forces, so that the rooms could be used for occasional mass billeting. Most of the things had been thrown in the cellar, and when it was full, the overflow was dumped outside.

Knowing that many people had buried silverware and other property in their gardens, looters had searched the grounds and discovered the hideaway under the small garden house where Webern had concealed some of his prized belongings, including a suitcase full of manuscripts. Taking what appealed to them, they left the rest scattered about. Weather and wind soon began to play havoc: books and music moulded from the moisture, and manuscript leaves were blown away.

Hermine often asked herself whether it was worthwhile to salvage some of the soiled and damaged items, but knowing how much her father-in-law had treasured each piece, she gathered all she could. From many of the larger volumes entire sections had been torn out, apparently to light fires. Thus the piano score of Berg's *Wozzeck*, beautifully bound in leather with gold embossing, was robbed of several sections. A handsome art book, *Die chinesische Landschaftsmalerei* by Webern's cousin Ernst Diez, had been mutilated when someone cut an insole out of the hard cover. Such was the disregard for any cultural values at a time when basic needs took precedence over all else. Whatever of Webern's belongings remained after the disaster is mainly due to Hermine's efforts. She stored everything in the attic of her mother's home: household goods, manuscripts and books, as well as such objects as Webern's cello, which had lain broken in the cellar, and several busts by Humplik (those of Mahler, Christine as a child, and the first of two Webern heads).[9]

In his refuge at Mittersill, Webern was unaware of what was happening. When the war ended, a demarcation line had been established between the Russian-held eastern territory and the American sector in the west. In the beginning there was no communication between the two zones, no postal service, no transportation. Whoever attempted to cross the border without proper authority faced mortal danger, since the frontier was closely guarded, especially by the Russians.

Because of these conditions, more than four months were to pass before Webern even learned that his daughter-in-law was still alive. In the meantime, he had had to endure much hardship. Major Halbich's home, high on a meadow above the Salzach River, with a sweeping view of the village and the glacier-crowned peaks beyond, would have provided the setting for a perfect idyll in more normal times. But with seventeen adults and children crowded together, nerves were taut, and although the family was grateful to be safe and together, friction could hardly be avoided. The situation was relieved somewhat when Benno Mattel (who had returned soon after the armistice) was able to find quarters for himself and his family elsewhere in the village. (Maria's husband was a prisoner-of-war in Yugoslavia and did not return until January of 1949.)

During the first few months, the shortage of food was critical, and mere survival was uppermost in everyone's mind. The American occupation forces did what they could, but supplies were scanty and had to be closely rationed. Cesar Bresgen, a young musician then living in the house next to that of Major Halbich, described how a long queue would form all around the church and down the street on the days when bread was distributed.[10] He often saw Webern standing in line, patiently awaiting his turn. The scarcity of fuel was equally severe. Amalie recalled how she, like the others, went to the woods to gather fallen branches. Tiny in stature, the young woman would weep from frustration as she struggled to hoist the heavy peasant's crate with its precious load on her back.

In May, nervous exhaustion and malnutrition took their toll on Webern, and he fell seriously ill. A violent dysentery weakened him so rapidly that the family began to fear for his life. There was no physician, and medicines were not available. It therefore seemed like a miracle when in June, after repeated set-backs, Webern began to recover. As a result of his illness he was severely emaciated, and his weight dropped to well below 50 kilos. A photograph taken at that time shows him changed almost beyond recognition. Grief for his son, the hardships of the last months, hunger, and sickness had etched deep furrows into his face. It was the countenance of a man who had suffered deeply (see Plate XIIa).

In the middle of June, Gunter Waller, anxious to look after his business affairs in Vienna, made his first attempt to cross the demarcation line. He carried with him a letter that Webern had written to his daughter-in-law on 13 June:

> My dear, dear Hermi! A thousand heart-felt greetings to you and yours! How we hope that Gunter will bring us *really good* news from you: news that you have had *good luck* in surviving those awful days!!! Oh God, how we think every day, every hour of you, dear beloved child! As soon as it is possible, we will immediately return home, hoping to find all our belongings still intact. . . . More from Gunter who is about to try his luck by venturing a trip to Vienna, and who intends to return here right away. You can imagine how we accompany him in thoughts, with what *impatience* and *excitement* we await his news, in particular and *above all* the news about you and yours! Our warmest greetings! Till we meet again soon! Embracing you with love and affection, Father and Mother.

Gunter's journey ended at Enns, the border of the American zone, where he was stopped for lack of the proper papers. He returned to Mittersill, but was ready to try again a month later. Webern then gave him another letter for Hermine, dated 13 July, which was to supplement his first one:

> At the beginning of this week we sent you *a postcard* (new Austrian stamp) through the *Red Cross*, for which this "one time" opportunity was offered! You can imagine with what eagerness we seized on it. We hope that the *ten words* that we were allowed to write really reached you.[11] If only we knew how you and yours are faring, how matters stand at our home! Were you over at the Auholz once? How does it look there? I am afraid to ask! Please, Hermi, give Gunter as comprehensive a report as possible about the critical days after Easter, etc. Also about the food situation!!! Here it is not so bad. Even wonderful *white* bread and flour have been available since last week. All in all, it really has become better already. We hope this is the case also in Vienna. But on that point one hears such conflicting

reports! Now, how is it really??? This is the burning question! Once Vienna is occupied by all *four powers*, then the time to return should finally be at hand!!! How we wait for that!!!

Five days later, on 18 July, Gunter handed both letters to Hermine. His journey had been full of adventure. Avoiding the check points, he had crossed the border at dawn by crawling through a culvert. He then walked to St Valentin, the first railway station inside the Russian zone, from where he caught a ride to Vienna on the roof of a freight car. His arrival in Perchtoldsdorf ended a long period of anxiety for Hermine who, since the end of March, had known as little of the fate of her parents-in-law as they of hers.

When Gunter returned to Mittersill shortly after, he was able to temper the bad news of the devastation in Webern's home with the report of an auspicious development in Vienna: on 24 May there had been a newspaper announcement that the Austrian section of the ISCM, which had been suppressed soon after the Anschluss in 1938, had been reorganized, and that Webern had been elected president of the provisional board of directors. In June, the first concert of the group had taken place, with works by Schoenberg, Eisler, Prokofiev, Hindemith, and de Falla on the programme. Gunter brought back with him a letter that Alfred Schlee, the director of Universal Edition, had written to Webern on 17 July: "We regret infinitely that you are not in Vienna. So much that will determine the future is now under consideration or being put into effect, that your presence would be of truly great, decisive importance. . . . Many other artistic tasks are awaiting you, too. As I said, all this can be decided only when you are here."[12]

This letter had been given to Gunter by Webern's sister-in-law, Leopoldine, through her husband, the violinist Wilhelm Gross, who was in contact with Universal Edition. Schlee's entreaties greatly increased Webern's desire to return to Vienna, not the least because he longed to establish again a home of his own. The overcrowded conditions in the Mittersill abode were particularly trying for him and his wife, who felt very uncomfortable at having to depend on the prolonged hospitality of the in-laws of one of their daughters. The prospect of regaining his privacy and independence lifted Webern's spirits and speeded his recovery. In her recollections of those days, Amalie wrote: "It seemed as if we had got over the worst."

CHAPTER XXXV

Mittersill notebook—The presumptive Opus 32 (1944–1945)

"THE WAY FROM fervour to greatness leads through sacrifice." A small piece of paper, on which Webern had written these words, was found after his death among his effects. He had added: "Quotation found in *Rilke and Benvenuta*,[1] 24 May 1945, Mittersill." It was Webern's life-long habit to extract from books passages that evoked in him a special response. He would commit them to his diary and thus preserve their spiritual essence long after the particular volume had been laid aside. Frequently he quoted such capsule thoughts in letters to friends, as if to justify or reinforce his own ideas and attitudes.

Webern was gravely ill when he copied the sentence from *Rilke and Benvenuta* that held so much significance for him. During his prolonged convalescence he excerpted other passages from various works, writing them into a slender notebook. In its pages are reflected the tenets and sentiments that occupied his thoughts during those last months at Mittersill. There he had ample time and leisure to immerse himself in reading and contemplation. The crystals of vision and wisdom that he selected from the writings of the poets he then favoured comprised a vade-mecum that accompanied him through the closing stage of his life.

As if baring his own soul, Webern quoted from Rainer Maria Rilke:

What is sacrifice? I believe it is nothing else than a person's *unbounded* resolve, no longer limitable in any direction, to achieve his purest inner potential.

. . . for poverty is a great radiance from within . . .

. . . whoever in art is satisfied with something below his present best is lost for the greatest.

. . . when music speaks, it speaks to God and not to us. The finished work of art has no relationship to man, except that it survives him. It is true that music has different laws from those of the other arts, but if we stand in its way it goes right through us.

. . . I was almost afraid of music, except when it was played in a cathedral and went straight to God, without tarrying with me on the way . . . and I understood it—that in the Old Kingdom (it is assumed) music was forbidden. It could only be performed before God, produced solely for His sake, as though He alone could bear the excess and seduction of its sweetness, and as if it were fatal to anyone else.

Other quotations copied into the notebook were from Hölderlin, with whose thoughts Webern had long identified himself. The poet's maxim, "To live is to defend a form," had become his guiding principle. It provided him with the fortitude to hold out in his lonely artistic post, hopeless as it had become in view of the political situation. Hölderlin's *Hyperion*, the impassioned plea of a sensitive soul confronted by indifference and abuse, who cries out against the ignorance and cruelty of the world, had long fascinated Webern. Small wonder then that he found comfort in the poet's compassion, and that he agreed with his scathing denunciation of the treatment accorded the prophet at home and in his fervent hope for a better future. In previous years, Webern had applied the meaning he derived from *Hyperion* mainly to the battleground of aesthetics. But now there was the far wider dimension of the political state within which, of necessity, the artist must live. Webern had seen the rise and fall of the Third Reich, that awesome Utopia which ended in disaster. His own son, but one among millions, had died for this hallucination, of which now only a smouldering heap of ashes remained. If Webern himself had fleetingly shared, however naïvely, in the great illusion, he had paid dearly. Like Hölderlin's "Hermit in Greece," he now stood divested of everything but his naked soul. And so he copied into his notebook the words from *Hyperion* that encompass the gamut of existence: from man's essential loneliness to his unceasing longing for kindred souls, from the true function of earthly governments to the divine illumination which forever remains the ultimate redemption. Webern's invocation of *Hyperion*'s spirit reads like a soliloquy, heightened in impact by the actuality of his experiences:

What is loss, when a man finds himself in his own world? In us is all. Why should a man care if a hair falls from his head? Why does he struggle so fiercely for servitude, when he could be a god?

There is a god in us, who guides destiny as if it were a river of water, and all things are his element. Above all else, may he be with you!

A friendly word from a valiant heart, a smile under which the searing glory of the spirit hides itself, is little and is much, is like a magical password that conceals death and life in its simple syllable, is like spiritual water that comes welling from the innermost recesses of the mountains, imparting the secret strength of the earth to us in its crystal drops. But how I hate all the barbarians who imagine that they are wise because there is no more heart left in them, all the vulgar monsters who slay and desecrate youthful beauty a thousand times over with their narrow-minded unreasonable discipline.

You accord the state far too much power. It must not demand what it cannot enforce. But what love gives, and spirit, cannot be enforced. That the state is to leave untouched, or we will take its laws and whip them in the pillory! By Heaven! He knows not how he sins, he who wants to make the state a school of morals. The state has always been made a hell by man's wanting to make it his heaven. The state is the coarse husk around the seed of life, and nothing more. It is the wall around the garden of human fruits and flowers.

. . . do you ask me when this will be? It will be when the darling of Time, the youngest, loveliest daughter of Time, the new Church, will arise out of these stained, antiquated forms, when the awakened feeling of the divine will bring man his divinity, man's heart its beautiful youth again—I cannot prophesy when this will be, because I can hardly surmise it, but that it will come, I know for certain. Death is a messenger of life, and that we now lie asleep in our infirmaries testifies that we shall soon awaken to new health. Then, and not till then, shall we exist, then the element of the spirits will have been found!

The last two entries in Webern's notebook once more were drawn from Rilke. The first is an excerpt from Robert Faesi's monograph on the poet, in which a fragment from one of Rilke's letters is incorporated:

The belief that God is not here yet, that he could not be here yet . . . "has freed me from the fear that God could be gone and used up; it includes the certainty that God will be created out of our functioning will, out of our age-old yearning. The lonely ones who reject all existing forms of God and all claims of possessing God, they are in the process of creating God with their hearts, their brains, their hands, be it that they form the things or the conditions. God becomes reality to the same degree that men fill life with soul, time with eternity."

The closing quotation is the last line from Rilke's poem "Requiem for Wolf Graf von Kalckreuth." Embodying resignation as well as final triumph, it stands as Webern's ultimate credo:

Who speaks of victory? To endure is everything.

There are various other entries in the notebook. Two pages list titles of works by Balzac and Thomas Mann. (Webern recorded that the fourth volume of Mann's *Joseph* tetralogy had appeared in Sweden in 1944—the Nazis had expelled the great author from the ranks of German writers.) Of particular interest is a page on which Webern made notes for a projected complete edition of his own compositions in five volumes. Obviously, he himself found the problem of organization difficult. No fewer than four alternatives, for instance, are envisioned as the contents of volume 1: one of them lists his early orchestral works (Opera 1, 6, 10) and the string orchestra transcription of Opus 5; another includes all songs with piano accompaniment; still another all the string quartets and the string trio; and a fourth some of the choral compositions (Opera 2, 19, 26). Webern's attempts to group his works, including the Schubert and Bach arrangements, remained inconclusive.

The Mittersill notebook contained, inserted between its pages, Hildegard Jone's manuscript of her *Lumen* cycle, the poems from which Webern drew for his last unfinished composition.[2] He had begun that project in January of 1944 and was still working on it, as he mentioned to Humpelstetter, in late February of 1945. But since the last three pages of sketches do not give any dates, the answer to the question of just when Webern actually ceased composing can only be conjectured. The following account includes all that is definitely known about his presumptive Opus 32, on the basis of the seven pages of drafts in Sketchbook VI and a number of references in his correspondence.

Before discussing the details of the project, it seems appropriate to refer to a statement made by Cesar Bresgen, Webern's neighbour, that has become the source of widespread speculation. In his article "Webern's Last Months in Mittersill," Bresgen wrote:

It seems certain that Webern committed no works to paper at that time. Yet I still remember distinctly that he was repeatedly busy at a crude little table with pencil and compass, occupied with geometrical figures or lines and signs. He explained to me once, too, that he no longer needed to hear his work performed; the work sounded "in itself"—he himself could hear it completely with his inner ear. Once it was committed to notation, if only on the bare table top, Webern deemed the real work completed. "The sound is always there," he said; a rendition could by no means recreate it so perfectly. In other words, Webern was then living more and more in a tonal realm of ideas which—and this seems to me important—he not only calculated in advance, but could actually hear.[3]

While some of the remarks ascribed to Webern are self-evident, in that any competent composer is capable of hearing his musical ideas with his inner ear, Bresgen's story of the abstruse table-top manipulations does not justify the conclusion that Webern might have abandoned conventional notation altogether for an esoteric manner of perceiving, constructing, and hearing music. Amalie and Maria, who had been familiar with their father's habits since childhood and were in a position to observe him daily in the confined quarters at Mittersill, emphatically deny any such behaviour. They disagree, however, on the crucial question of whether or not Webern had taken his sketchbook along on the flight to Mittersill. Amalie was positive that he did. But Maria held that her father would not have loaded his rucksack with anything but the barest essentials; she also maintained that Webern did not compose any more after Peter's death. It could be argued that the sketchbook, the thinnest of them all, was light enough, and that Webern certainly did take along a small diary and the *Lumen* manuscript. The presence of the latter in the Mittersill notebook suggests that he immersed himself in these verses no less than in the thoughts of Rilke and Hölderlin.

The roots of Webern's last creative project were anchored in January 1944. During the early part of that month, the composer was still engaged in drafting a seventh movement to his Second Cantata. However, he abandoned that undertaking abruptly in favour of an altogether new concept: on 26 January (the date appearing at the top of page 35 of the sketchbook) the title "Concerto" is given, followed by this brief outline: "1. Sonata 2. Adagio 3. Rondo." Two days later, on 28 January, the composer explained to Hildegard Jone why he had left the cantata in six movements, adding: "What I am working on now is something *purely instrumental.*" On 23 February, Webern wrote a similar letter to Reich concerning both the completion of the cantata and his new project, saying that the latter was to be "a multi-movement 'Concerto' for a number of instruments."

The evolution of the composition can be traced from the facsimile reproductions in *Anton von Webern: Sketches (1926–1945)*. On the first page of the draft, which bears the dates of 31 January, 2 and 4 February, the composer attempted to formulate the tone row. The series that he finally decided upon then was outlined in red pencil:[4]

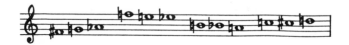

In his commentary to *Sketches*, Krenek remarked on the symmetrical nature of this row, stating that it "reaches out towards the boundaries of dodecaphonic possibilities . . . we have a tone-row that consists simply of four segments of the chromatic scale. Webern had ventured towards this point of no return before, and here near the unforeseeable end of his career, he again approached the extreme limit."

When Webern set out to assign the notes of the series to a melody line he placed the first F sharp in the position above high C, following it with a wide leap to the G below middle C. A similar musical gesture had characterized the first draft of the *Orchesterstück (Ouvertüre)* that later merged into the Concerto, Op. 24. On page 35, the first page of the draft, the composer sketched out the melody repeatedly, at one time designating the violin for the opening motive. (Diary notes on the lower margin record the birth and baptism of his grandson, Peter, on 9 and 25 February, respectively.) Webern continued on page 34, the left-hand page of the sketchbook, with extensive work on the melody. The wide leap characterizing the first sketches was then modified to the interval of a seventh. Another specific instrument, the viola, also makes its appearance. Several *pizzicato* and *arco* designations indicate that Webern was preoccupied with strings. Remarkable are the detailed prescriptions for execution that become an integral part of the musical formulation at so early a stage in the creative process. They include accents and sostenuto marks, as well as a variety of dynamic shadings in which abrupt changes from *sforzando* to *piano* occur frequently.

On 3 April 1944 Webern wrote to the Humpliks: "My work is progressing steadily. But all winter long I have been plagued with the necessity of giving lessons. Well, it has to be; it even has its benefits: in teaching, and often precisely through teaching, perceptions emerge." Two weeks later, Webern was suddenly recruited into service with the air-raid police. To comfort and encourage him, Hildegard Jone then conveyed to him some of her impressions of the First Cantata, derived from the evening in August of 1940 when the composer had introduced the work to his friends. Delighted, Webern wrote to her from his barracks on 14 May: "It is not so: that *I* have understood *you*, is proved to you by *my music*; and that *you* understand *me*, is proved to me by *your words*!"

In that letter, Webern announced: "Meanwhile a new plan has matured: just as soon as things are possible for me again I am going to compose your *Lumen* poems! The sketches I have been making since the Second Cantata will go into the first *Lumen* poem. That means that the foundation is already laid! But it has not happened all of a sudden: it was there from the start! I hope, therefore, that I can soon get down to it! Our path goes ever onward!" Hildegard Jone's response, on 22 May, was characteristically supportive: "My thanks, dear Anton, for your letter, which describes your new work so movingly to us. Oh what a glimpse of light in times of darkness! To a man, 'unheard-of' things occur—and *unheard-of* things begin to resound in him!'"

The *Lumen* cycle had been in Webern's hands since the preceding year. On 28 June 1943 he had written to the poetess exuberantly about it: "What a marvellous product of your thought and of your ability to give form to it! The way it leads one from the 'first glimmer of light' to 'complete clarity', from 'Helios' to the 'light of lights'!!!" The references characterize the nature of the work, a collection of poems extolling the manifold facets of celestial light, its reflection in colour schemes, and the philosophical implications of its divine origin. The influence of Goethe's *Farbenlehre* is obvious.[5] Hildegard Jone's *Lumen* is a literary pantheon in which descriptions of natural phenomena are blended with theosophic ideologies. The cycle opens with the words:

Das Sonnenlicht spricht:
Aufgeht der Vorhang der Nacht! Durch Licht wird die Herrlichkeit
sichtbar,
sichtbar die Säulen des Seins: Sehet, die Farben stehn auf![6]

(The sunlight speaks:
Up goes the curtain of the night! Through light the splendour becomes visible, and visible become the pillars of existence: Look, the colours are emerging!)

These verses apparently inspired Webern to convert his instrumental concerto into a vocal work. In making the decision, he probably did not know yet whether the composition would develop into another cantata or assume the dimensions of an oratorio, that more ambitious form envisioned earlier for his Opus 31. He would have again "permitted himself to drift," allowing his creative impulse to influence the direction, organization, and size of the work. "When I undertake a vocal work again it will be something altogether different," he had told Reich on 23 February 1944, reporting to him again on 6 July: "What I had sketched for an instrumental piece has been transformed into a setting of a very long poem by Hildegard Jone. The poetic form will be matched by a musical one correspondingly expansive and unified, the solution of which especially entices me. Again for soloists and chorus (with orchestra)."

The transition from the first concept of the work to the second was simple enough. What had already been sketched out for the "concerto" was incorporated into the new plan as an orchestral introduction to the first vocal entrance. Sketchbook pages 36 and 37 contain drafts for the setting of the opening verses of *Lumen*. The melody line for the full text passage, as quoted above, was definitively established. Webern then began working it out for mixed chorus.

Despite the difficulty of concentrating on his work because of the frequent air raids, the composer pursued his new project enthusiastically. Satisfied that he had made an auspicious beginning, he broke his customary reluctance to talk about a composition in progress and wrote to Hildegard Jone on 27 June:

> As you know, "Das Sonnenlicht spricht" is in the making. . . . Naturally this line, which is really placed at the head of your poem like a title, will also be included in the composition. . . . Here it is:

> But these six notes are the second half of the "germ" (i.e. of the twelve-tone series), or better still *two quarters*: for the last three notes are the "retrograde" of the preceding ones, a condition that also prevails in the first half [of the series]. "Motivically," too, these six notes are the product of an arrangement that is *very strictly controlled* from several points of view: so they stand there on a foundation of *laws*!

This was Webern's last direct reference to the composition in his correspondence. The final dates given in the sketchbook appear in the form of two diary notes at the bottom of page 37: on 7 June 1944 his daughters, Maria and Christine, departed for Mittersill and, between 24 July and 16 August, the Weberns themselves went there for a visit. The sketches continue on pages 38 and 39. They show the composer chiefly concerned with the scoring, for four-part chorus, of the text passage "Aufgeht der Vorhang der Nacht." The draft extends over eighteen numbered measures. On page 41 (page 40 is blank), a fresh start is made with what seemingly was meant to be the definitive version, but this auspicious beginning breaks off after only six measures. Four of these are given over to an instrumental introduction, confined to a statement of the row, followed by the opening words "Das Sonnenlicht spricht" assigned to the alto part. Throughout the sketches Webern explored, in conformity with his later choral style, both homophonic and contrapuntal possibilities. The rhythmic structure, which so often underwent alteration during the genesis of a work, this time remained consistent within a 2/4 metre.

During the autumn of 1944 the air raids on Vienna steadily increased. "The concentration necessary for composing is hardly possible any longer," Webern wrote to Humpelstetter on 7 November. At Christmas-time, he told his young colleague, the Munich composer Karl Amadeus Hartmann: "That you work *despite everything* is good, dear friend! Thus *we* have to get through."[7] On 26 February 1945, at a time when the bombing attacks had reached their full impact, Webern still tried to maintain confidence when writing to Humpelstetter: "Let us continue to hope! Spring is coming! I work whenever possible!" Only five days later, he learned that his son had been killed. Weeks of utter despair followed, and on 31 March he set out before dawn on his flight to Mittersill. Just when and where Webern last worked on his presumptive Opus 32 must forever remain an enigma, shrouded by the composer's death.

CHAPTER XXXVI

Webern's death
(15 September 1945)

———————————

"I WOULD LIKE to be buried here someday," Webern once told his wife as he sat on a bench behind the village church in Mittersill.[1] He is known to have particularly liked that spot, from where the view rises above the rows of graves to the shining snowfields and granite spires of the mountains beyond.

Both Peter Ehrenstrasser, the village priest, and Cesar Bresgen, who assisted in the daily celebration of the Mass, stated that Webern repeatedly attended early morning services, though he never came forward to receive Communion. In his recollections Bresgen wrote: "I made the attempt, with the church choir then entrusted to me at Mittersill, to introduce at early Mass a certain amount of Gregorian chant. Webern took especial delight in this. . . . After one such Mass he said: 'At last a pure line once more, this glorious monody—it is quintessential music, complete in itself.' "[2]

During that time, Bresgen played chamber music with another refugee, a violinist from Vienna, and on two or three occasions Webern attended their impromptu recitals. The programmes included music by the old masters, as well as works by Debussy, Hindemith, and Bresgen himself. Remarking on Bresgen's compositions, Webern noticed the continuing influence of Debussy, which had been especially strong upon Viennese composers since the early 'twenties. In this connection Bresgen recalled:

He expressed a keen but never wounding criticism. The formulation of his judgement was terse but never dispiriting. Of course, he proceeded from the premise that a completely new development of music would now begin. The future composer would grasp this "newness" of his own accord, however, would "breathe this fresh morning air and absorb it as a matter of course." "In fifty years at the most," he said, "everyone will experience this music as *his* innate music; yes, it will be accessible even to children—people will sing it.". . . This image was intensified by a pride born out of his conviction of the rightness of his new musical standpoint, and the permanence of his thought in the sense of a doctrine. Then the countenance of the man would light up in a strange way, such as occurs only with those who know ultimate truth.

Mittersill, which at first had been but a refuge for survival, soon became for Webern a haven for meditation. He derived consolation and regeneration from the wondrous beauty of alpine nature and he felt confirmed in his life-long belief that metaphysical forces were inherent in the air, sun, water, earth, and plants of the high regions. The pastoral landscape was a constant lure for extended walks. His favourite haunt was the evergreen forest above the picturesque castle of Mittersill. Bresgen recounted an incident that reveals Webern's fascination with the microcosm of nature:

During this lonely period, I liked to go mushroom hunting, and occasionally my path crossed Webern's. One evening, about ten days before Webern's death, has remained especially fixed in my memory. The master admired the contents of my well-filled basket, in which lay some rare and interesting mushrooms. Obviously stirred by the sight, he spoke admiringly of the rich variety of forms in nature. We fell to contemplating the remarkable qualities of fungi, mosses, and lichens, and I still remember that point in our conversation at which Webern broke off to scrutinize a curious lichen that had so covered a large stone that it looked like an etching. This extraordinary veined network both moved one to reflection and was somehow touching: after all, it was a part of life, growing organically according to a design, indebted to a high and hidden reason.

Bresgen, who always found Webern in a serene mood, described the atmosphere of the waning season:

Those days were filled with a late summer luminosity of a radiant nature: early snow on the northern slopes, but on those exposed to the sun still real summer, and a sky above as blue as it can be only in the high mountains. This purity of colour, as well as the peace that emanated from that harmonious valley scene, with its old peasant houses and churches, never failed to delight Webern. In the last days of his life, he must have felt this peace intensely, for the days were unusually tranquil and harmonious.

On 30 August, Webern and his wife made an outing to nearby Zell am
See, a small town renowned for its beautiful setting. From there he wrote
his last letter, which was addressed to his daughter-in-law:

My dear beloved Hermi, at long last another opportunity to send
news to you. After a four-week stay here in Mittersill, Gunter is *again
going back* [to Vienna]. How much we would like to do so, too! But
Mother and I cannot risk what he risks! We must wait until conditions
are different. However, unless all indications are misleading, this
should be possible relatively soon—perhaps within a *few weeks*.
Beautiful as it is here—at the moment we are sitting by the shore of the
Zellersee—we *constantly* think of the journey home, of *you*, dear child,
and we are so full of concern. From what one hears here about
conditions at home, one could despair!!! But in today's newspaper
from Salzburg (US zone), we read of the arrival in Vienna of the first
English convoy of food supplies. 450 tons: meat, flour, sugar,
potatoes, coffee! Yes, it must soon get better in Vienna, too!

To judge from what we hear, conditions are *probably better* here:
currently we are receiving at least a *little more bread* (5 kg. per month).[3]
In the city of Salzburg one can get magnificent pure-white rolls. Also
in Mittersill, for weeks now, blossom-white rolls! The meat ration has
been increased by about 10 dcg.[4] for the current period; coffee, too, is
to be available from next week on—what a sensation! Naturally, there
is only little, very little of everything! But one can get that little!

As I said, however, everything indicates that for Vienna, too, more
favourable conditions are *imminent*! Have you been to the Auholz
again to see how things are at our home? Of all our belongings, is
there not something or other still left and *possible to salvage*? The *electric
stove*, I understand, still stands in its place! I hope it, too, has not been
stolen in the meantime. Part of the books are said to lie in the cellar! If
you can, take some along, I mean put them in a safe place—perhaps
right away with one of the neighbours (Mr Gasteker or the *Perls*). Be
extremely careful, though!!! We will be eternally grateful to you for
saving even the smallest trifle. Has everything really disappeared from
the hideaway *under* the garden house??? The suitcase with the
manuscripts of my *youth*, the typewriter and—*just think!!—all our
"silver"*!!! We had stored there some clothes, linen, etc., the most
important and necessary things! Is everything gone??

Where will we live??? Problems in abundance! All depends, of
course, on what the immediate future brings for Vienna.

And how do *you* manage to get *through these horrors*? We speak
about it every day and imagine that at least your garden provides
some sustenance! Are you all well? Mother and I were plagued greatly

by dysentery. For four weeks, I, in particular, suffered repeated bouts, so that I have become *very, very weak. I creep about with difficulty!* Thank God, though, it gets better every day. And Mother, although very emaciated, is again quite well, the courageous, good, tireless one!

Now goodbye, until we meet again soon! Many regards to your family. Embracing you fondly, dear child, Your old father.

The next day, back in Mittersill, Wilhelmine added to her husband's letter one of her own. Both messages were to be delivered by Gunter Waller, who was about to attempt another crossing of the border. Wilhelmine explained to her daughter-in-law that the strain and risk of such a trip would be too much for Webern in his weakened condition. "He has grown frighteningly thin," she wrote, "but, thank God, he is gradually recuperating." On the food situation she commented: "For a monthly period, we each receive $\frac{1}{2}$ kg. butter, 30 dcg. food concentrates, $1\frac{1}{2}$ kg. white flour, $\frac{1}{2}$ kg. sugar, 40 dcg. marmalade, 6 kg. bread, 90 dcg. meat and, among additional supplies, either $\frac{1}{4}$ kg. fat cheese or $\frac{1}{2}$ kg. lean cheese." Confident of an early reunion, Wilhelmine closed her letter: "We must be together often, for us you are a part of our dear Peter."

The conditions prevailing in Vienna notwithstanding, Webern had good reason to look forward impatiently to his return. It had been intimated to him that he was to be offered a professorship at the State Academy, where he was to give a master-class in composition. He also was to be given a place on the permanent staff of conductors of Radio Vienna, a position that, according to Polnauer, would have allowed him complete freedom in the choice of programmes. Small wonder that he was eager to seize on these professional opportunities, which he considered long-due recognition by his native city and a measure of recompense for the many injustices he had had to endure throughout the years.

At that time, units of the US 42nd Division (the so-called "Rainbow Division," famous for its war exploits) were stationed in Mittersill. Because of the many refugees crowding into the region, stringent controls were established. Each resident of the village had to register and was given an identity card, printed in both German and English. Webern's listed his occupation as "composer" and described him as having "brown hair, grey eyes, weight 50 kg., height 161 cm." His card was dated 13 September 1945, only two days before it was to serve its last tragic function.

Soon after arriving in Mittersill, Benno Mattel had established contact with some American soldiers for the purpose of engaging in black-market activities. Endowed with an acute business sense, he soon found his dealings lucrative and was emboldened to trade not only in foodstuffs but also in American currency. His daring was bound to

Identity Card Nr. 439

For Mr. Mrs. Miss: Dr.Anton
.... Christian Name

W e b e r n
.... Surname

Date of birth: 3.Dezember 1883

in Wien

single, married, wid., div.: verh.

Occupation: Komponist

Address: Mittersill, Burk 31

Hair: br.m.   Eyes: grau

Weight: 50 kg   Height: 164 cm

Nationality: Austrian

Valid 6 months from date shown thereon.

Dr. Anton Webern
.... signature

Mittersill the 13.9.1945
Gendarmerieposten Mittersill
stam **Kreis Zell am See** Salzburg.

Ebner,gh.
signature of issuing officer
(Ebner,Gend.)

Identitätsausweis.

für Herrn/Frau/Frl. Dr.

W e b e r n
.... Familienname

geb. am 3.Dezembe ... .

r Wien

ledig, verh, verw., gesch.: verh.

von Beruf: Komponist

wohnhaft in: Mittersill, Burk 31

Haar: br.m.   Augen: grau

Gewicht: 50 kg   Größe: 161 cm

Staatsangehöriger: Österreicher

Gültigkeitsdauer 6 Monate vom Tag der
Ausstellung.

Dr. Anton Webern
Unterschrift des Inhabers.

Mittersill am 13.9.1945
Gendarmerieposten Mittersill
L. S. **Kreis Zell am See** Salzburg.

Ebner,gh.
Unterschrift des ausfert. Beamten.
(Ebner,Gend.)

Last identity card (tear presumably caused by a bullet)

attract attention, however. Andrew W. Murray, First Sergeant of Headquarters Company, 242nd Infantry Regiment, later testified: "Two or three days prior to 15 September 1945, Ray Bell [the company cook] came to me and advised of Mattel's approaching him wanting to purchase quantities of sugar, coffee, etc., and most of all American money."[5] Currency regulations were so strict at the time that even members of the military were not allowed to have US bank notes in their possession, but Mattel was aware that many soldiers still carried a bill or two.

Following Mattel's proposition, Murray and Bell went to their superior officers, who advised them to see the Counter-Intelligence Corps in Zell am See. Captain Richardson, the head of that agency, was confronted with a personnel shortage in his department, and for this reason he delegated the two soldiers to proceed with a simulated transaction and to arrest Mattel in the act. For their mission, the soldiers were permitted to take foodstuffs from the supply depot and authorized to carry revolvers. The fictitious deal was set up for the evening of 15 September at Mattel's apartment on the ground floor of the house Am Markt 101. Mrs Elsie Fritzenwanger, the owner of the house, who lived on the upper floor with her young son, was instructed by the military not to leave the premises that evening nor to talk to anyone about this special order.

That day, a Saturday, Webern and his wife had been invited by the Mattels for supper. It was for the first time since their arrival in Mittersill that the couple could plan an evening out. Webern's eager anticipation was described later by Amalie:

For my father this was a festive occasion. For days ahead, he looked forward to the pleasure which awaited him. . . . I was just bathing my child when my father took his leave from me for the last time. As always, he embraced and kissed me with all his fatherly love. He had to descend a narrow garret staircase; once more he turned around and waved to me. I saw him in that moment for the last time with his dear, kindly smile. . . . My sister Maria stood on the balcony when my father left the house. As she waved to him, he looked up at her and said the portentous words: "Do you know by any chance what an historic day it is today?" He meant this in reference to the first American cigar.

Benno Mattel had held out that prospect as a special attraction for the evening.

As Webern and his wife walked down the meadow-like hillside to the valley floor and from there the short distance to the house, fate was closing in on them. At that very hour, preparations were being made to apprehend Mattel during his black-market dealings. The account of what happened that night is compiled from the depositions of three persons present on the scene: Wilhelmine von Webern, Sergeant Murray, and Martin U. Heiman, a German-born soldier who was attached to the regiment as interpreter.[6] The sequence of events was as follows: Anton and Wilhelmine arrived at the house about 8 pm. The supper party was described later by Amalie (who based her story on her mother's account): "The meal at the Mattels' had been marvellous, and all were gay and in the best of humour. For my father, the concluding and crowning event of the supper was a magnificent American cigar. Father was a passionate cigar smoker, and this first cigar after so long gave him special joy."

In her official deposition, Wilhelmine said: "My son-in-law, Benno Mattel, told us that he expected Americans later in the evening. As soon as they arrived at about 9 pm, my husband, my daughter and I went to the neighbouring room where the children slept." That room opened to the right of the small entrance hallway, directly across from the kitchen where the supper had taken place. During the next hour, Webern sat with his wife and daughter beside the three peacefully sleeping children. Wilhelmine related the events that cruelly shattered the serenity of that hour:

At 9.45 pm exactly, my husband said we had to leave soon for our home (house No. 31), because we had to be there by 10.30 pm [the curfew hour for civilians]. He wanted to smoke the cigar that he had received the same evening from our son-in-law. He stated that he wanted to smoke it only partly ("einige Züge") and outside the room in order not to bother the children. This was the first time that he left the room. My husband was only outside for two to three minutes when we heard three shots. I was very frightened but did not think that my husband could be involved in any way. Then the door to our room was opened by my husband, who said "I was shot" ("Ich wurde erschossen"). Together with my daughter, I laid him on a mattress and started opening his clothes. My husband was just able to say the words "It is over" ("Es ist aus") and he started losing consciousness. I only saw a wound at the left side of the belly and at the stomach. I asked my daughter to do something and suggested a cold bandage around his head; then I went outside to get help. I saw the kitchen door open and my son-in-law standing inside with raised hands. Then I went upstairs to ask the people to fetch a doctor. When I came downstairs, my husband was lying alone in the room with the children. He gave signs of dying. My daughter was also in the kitchen by then with her hands raised high. Shortly afterwards, I asked an American for medical help; he answered that somebody had already gone for it. Then more Americans came, and I was taken into the kitchen and told to sit down.[7]

That evening, a dance was held at the Mittersill inn where the kitchen and supply depot of Headquarters Company were located. Close to 10 pm, Raymond Bell came running to fetch Martin U. Heiman, who was attending the dance. In his sworn statement Heiman related:

He [Bell] asked me to follow him to a nearby civilian home in order to help arrest a black-marketeer, Benno Mattel, and to act as interpreter in a shooting which had taken place in this connection. When I got there, I met the First Sergeant of Headquarters Company, 242nd Infantry, who kept Mr Mattel under guard. However, in the same house, on the ground floor opposite the kitchen where Mr Mattel was kept, a man was lying dead from newly-inflicted bullet wounds. It was Anton von Webern, Professor of Modern Music from Vienna. His wife, Wilhelmine von Webern, sat beside him in complete daze and shock. Their daughter, Mrs Mattel, was present, too. Presently more US Army personnel, officers, and medical men arrived. Upon instruction of the senior officer present, I had to take not only Mr Mattel but also Mrs Mattel into custody. She was a suspected accessory to her husband's contemplated or real black-market activities. However, after two days I succeeded in getting her released from the jail at Mittersill.

In the military investigation that immediately followed the shooting, Heiman was assigned to act as interpreter. Thus he became closely acquainted with every detail of the case. The tragedy so much aroused his sympathy that he retained in his possession a copy of the official deposition made by Wilhelmine during the inquest. The following is Heiman's description of what happened in the kitchen after Murray and Bell arrived at about 9 pm:

After some discussion, prices for the food and material were agreed upon, and Mr Mattel was about to pay for it. Thereupon the two US soldiers drew their pistols, dropped the pretence of cooperation and placed the surprised Mattel under arrest. It should be noted at this time that the cook involved was even normally a very nervous person, easily aroused and excitable, even though—according to my knowledge—not a bad character and sometimes helpful. After Mr Mattel was trapped, the cook left the room (kitchen) on the ground floor to go to the nearby restaurant in order to fetch the undersigned, so that I might take Mr Mattel into official custody and put him into the local jail, pending further disposition. The cook—already in a very excited state—stepped out of the hallway and the house into the darkness and promptly bumped into a figure by whom he felt himself attacked. He fired three shots "in self defence" and kept on going to the restaurant to get the undersigned.

Sergeant Murray's version of the evening's development was as follows:

Previous to going to Martel's [sic] house, neither I nor Bell had anything to drink, because we wanted full control of our faculties in undertaking the arrest. At the house No. 101 Mittersill, we accepted three drinks from Martel in the course of an hour. After getting the necessary evidence we wanted, we placed Martel under armed arrest. Bell and I had arranged a plan by which Bell would go out the door first to prevent any trickery from Martel in the close quarters of the hall and doorway. Once during the course of the evening, Bell had gone to a window at the front of the house and closed it. We had also heard footsteps in the hall leading outside. I stood in the room with Martel, his hands raised high over his head, clearly visible from the outside, front of the house. Bell went into the hall, and here my vision was obstructed. All that transcribed [sic] within the next 30 or 45 seconds can only be described by me through the distinct sounds I heard. The kitchen door had swung partially closed. I heard the hall door leading outside open; strike the wall as it swung back, fully open; a sharp outcry from Bell, best described by me as surprise; a scuffling of feet on cinders; and then three shots, fired rapidly. I heard no outcry after that except some hysterical shouting by a woman. I felt sure that Bell was the one who had been shot at. After the surprise of hearing shots left me, I called out for Bell, but received no answer. Then I was sure Bell had been shot. But I later learned he had gone for help. I then ordered Martel and his wife, who had come into the kitchen, to precede me through the door. I was taking them down the street, when I met Bell in the company of four officers and returned to house No. 101 with Lieutenant Shaneyfelt, Acting Regimental S-2. It was only then that I discovered that anyone at all had been shot. Upon entering the front door I looked into the room to the right and saw a man lying on a mattress with blood on his shirt front. An officer immediately sent for the medics.

After seeing her husband's body placed on a stretcher and carried away, and her daughter and son-in-law led off to jail, Wilhelmine spent that dreadful night alone with the three small children. Her daughter Amalie described how she learned of the tragedy the following day:

> Towards four o'clock in the morning, I was awakened by neighbours who informed me that I should go to the Mattels' because something terrible had happened. Since my sister, Mrs Halbich, was in the eighth month of pregnancy with her second child, I had to walk to the Mattels' alone. I waited, however, until seven o'clock since in those times the path through forest and field, alone at so early an hour, seemed to me too full of danger. When I arrived at the house, greatly worried, with no presentiment of what awaited me, the first shock was that I was not permitted to enter the house. It was surrounded by American military with fixed bayonets. Because of my questions and my consternation, I was allowed to communicate with my mother from the street across the garden. Mother looked terrible. There were no tears, no lament, but her features were marked by fear as she said: "Father was shot last night and was at once carried away by American soldiers. Please search for him. I have been locked up with the children. Christl and Benno have also been led away." I ran to the hospital in order to look for my father. It was Sunday, all the sisters were at church, nobody was there to give me information. Then I stood in front of the hospital, almost dying from fear and worry. Finally the sisters came back from church. None of them knew what to tell me. The night nurse ventured: "Well, last night an old man was brought in, but he was already dead when he arrived here. He lies in the morgue, look in there, perhaps he is the one whom you are seeking." And it was he. On a blanket, on the floor of the chapel, lay my father—dead. His eyes were open, dreadful terror stood in them.

The chapel that served as the morgue was the Annakirche, a small baroque edifice. The first parish church of Mittersill, it is located a short distance from the hospital where Webern had been brought.

The military investigation of the shooting was conducted by Major Cunningham, acting as deputy for the regimental commander, Colonel Norman C. Caum. It was concluded on 17 September. On that day, even before her husband had been buried, Wilhelmine was interrogated. When confronted with Bell's assertion that he had acted in self-defence, she simply stated: "My husband was convalescent and weighed only about 50 kilos; he was about 160 cms. tall. According to my belief, it would be against his nature to attack anybody, especially a soldier."

During the hearing, the company cook showed a wound on his shinbone and asserted that it had been inflicted by the man whose presence had surprised him as he opened the door and stepped into the darkness. To those present, however, it seemed quite unlikely that the wound could have healed so quickly, and there was suspicion that it dated from an earlier time. No doubt Bell had bumped into Webern, and the physical contact had startled him. On this point, Heiman commented:

Of course, he claimed self-defence, and in his highly emotional state no doubt he believed himself attacked at the time of the incident. I do not know what Major Cunningham's report stated about his innocence or guilt in the shooting. But shortly after the investigation was finished, his confinement to quarters was lifted; he worked again in the kitchen until he returned to the States a few months later. I also do not know what the investigation report stated about Mr A. von Webern's role—apart from the testimony of his wife. But to the best of my knowledge not the slightest proof existed that he attacked the cook, apart from the testimony of the cook, who was about two heads taller than Mr A. von Webern. I did not speak to a single officer familiar with the case who believed Mr von Webern was guilty of anything in this connection. Certainly in my opinion he was a completely innocent bystander. Almost everybody felt terrible about the tragedy, especially when it became vaguely known what an outstanding man and artist he was in life.

On the morning of 21 September, Anton von Webern was laid to rest in the cemetery behind the village church of Mittersill. The Requiem Mass was celebrated by Dean Peter Ehrenstrasser and two assistants, one of whom was Cesar Bresgen. During the rites, the strains of Gregorian chant, so loved by Webern, filled the sanctuary where his body lay. Bresgen recalled: "Outside there was again that radiant sky, and an early snow lay on the mountains. Quietly, and unspoiled by noisy or impure distractions, this hour produced a lasting impression." Only a handful of mourners accompanied the widow and her three daughters to the open grave close to the back wall of the churchyard.

Several weeks later, Benno Mattel was tried before a US military-government court under Lieutenant Friedman in Zell am See. Heiman stated: "During that trial, Benno Mattel received a jail sentence of one year for black market activities, but the death of Mr Anton von Webern was not part of the trial as such."

Despondent over the loss of her husband and distraught by the notoriety connected with her son-in-law's conviction, Wilhelmine refused to talk to anyone about the details of the tragedy. She pledged her daughters to preserve silence also. Consequently, many and widely-varying rumours sprang up. The first newspaper reports, published only a month later, stated that Webern had been killed in an accident, and that his son-in-law had been taken into custody.[8] Initially, these terse reports were interpreted as if Benno Mattel himself had shot his father-in-law "by accident." This rumour and several others persisted for many years. As a result, grossly differing stories appeared in print: in one version Webern was gunned down by a drunken soldier, in a second he was killed by a stray bullet, and in a third he was out in the street after curfew and, when challenged by an American sentry, failed to heed and was shot. Another account stated that he was mistaken for his son-in-law when he left the house which had been surrounded by guards, and still another that he was wantonly murdered by a trigger-happy soldier. All these rumours, circulating with ever new distortions, tended to shroud the affair in a veil of mystery, which was only lifted fifteen years later with the publication of the book *The Death of Anton Webern/A Drama in Documents*.[9] After the research for that documentary account was concluded, its findings were corroborated by the Webern family. Only one detail remains to be added: Mrs Elsie Fritzenwanger, in whose home Wilhelmine died, related that the widow tormented herself with remorse during her last years as it had been at *her* request that, because of the children sleeping in the small room, her husband had gone outside to smoke that fateful cigar.

This final link in the chain of events deepens the sadness of the dramatic plot that had unfolded with the inevitability of a Greek tragedy. A decade later, almost to the day, the man who had killed Webern himself fell victim to the sense of guilt from which he had suffered ever since that moment of panic. Raymond Bell died on 3 September 1955 from alcoholism. His wife, Helen, a school teacher in Mt Olive, North Carolina, wrote afterwards: "I know very little about the accident. When he came home from the war he told me he killed a man in the line of duty. I know he worried greatly over it. Every time he became intoxicated, he would say 'I wish I hadn't killed that man.' I truly think it helped to bring on his sickness. He was a very kind man who loved everyone. These are the results of war. So many suffer."[10]

Wilhelmine—Renaissance

A MONG THE FEW personal effects that Webern had carried in his
rucksack on his flight to Mittersill was a small diary, bound in leather
and brocade, to which he had committed, from 1916 to 1939, most of the
data that were important to him both as a man and as an artist. When the
little book was found later in his widow's estate, there was a final entry in
her hand:

1945
September 15th, 10 pm
Toni ✠ Mittersill
February 14th, Peter ✠ near Marburg
Everything lost, but must go on living as long as
Mizi, Christi, and their children need me.

With these moving words Wilhelmine von Webern entered upon the
last span of her life, a period overshadowed by grief, poverty, hard work,
and illness. Her daughter Amalie returned to Vienna with her husband
and two sons not long after Webern's death. Wilhelmine could have
joined them there, but she lived up to her resolve and stayed on in
Mittersill so that she could be of help to Maria and Christine. In October
of 1945, Maria gave birth to her second child, a daughter who was
named Johanna. However, it was to be more than three years before her
husband, Fred Halbich, could rejoin his family. He was detained in
Yugoslavia longer than other prisoners-of-war because he was a medical
doctor. These were hard times for Maria, and they were equally trying
for Christine. Benno Mattel served out his year's sentence in jail and
then went directly to Italy, his mother's native country. Christine and the
children could join him there only after a separation of three years.

Wilhelmine, although a tireless worker all her life, found herself pressed almost beyond endurance during that difficult time. Overwhelmed by grief, she was also constantly taxed by hard work. Her daughters, particularly Maria, were frequently ill, and she not only had to nurse them but care for her grandchildren as well. As of December 1946, she lived with Maria who, because of continual friction with her mother-in-law, had left the Halbich home and taken up quarters in House No. 119 in the village.

The widow was desperately short of money, although initially her situation was alleviated when Universal Edition contracted for Webern's posthumous Opera 17, 24, 25, 29, 30, and 31. After learning of the composer's death, the publishing house acted quickly to secure these works. They appointed Leopoldine Gross and Hermine von Webern to go to Mittersill and make the appropriate arrangements. In order to obtain a travel permit for the two women, Alfred Schlee wrote on 16 October 1945 to the State Office of the Interior:

Because of the death of the composer, Anton von Webern, the urgent necessity arises to safeguard immediately the manuscripts that were in his possession, manuscripts that not only have a significant cultural value but also are of the greatest importance for the export activities of our publishing house. Since we have learned that an English publishing firm is already interested in the legacy of Professor Webern, it is of the greatest urgency that the manuscripts be brought to Vienna at once. On the basis of verbal agreements, which because of the ban on Webern's works could not be ratified as yet in writing, we have secured the works in his estate for our publishing house. We place the highest value on having these works reserved for an Austrian publisher. In consideration of the international significance of Webern and the cultural as well as material value of the manuscripts, we beg you to approve of our dispositions and to issue to the above-named persons an affidavit confirming the urgency of their trip to Mittersill (Salzburg) and back, so that the necessary steps can be undertaken at once and the exceedingly valuable manuscripts neither get lost nor into the wrong hands.

On 26 October 1945 Webern's widow, who could advise UE that the manuscripts in question had been left in Vienna, signed the contract. It provided for a one-time payment of 1,000 Reichsmarks (US $399 at the time) and the usual royalties. The cash helped for the moment, but Wilhelmine did not live to derive any benefit from the royalties. On 14 September 1949, shortly before her death, she signed another agreement with Bomart, a small publishing firm in New York,[1] for Webern's early (1907) Quintet, a work that the composer himself had long wanted to see published. Kurt List, one of Webern's former pupils, served as the agent for the completion of the contract, which stipulated the nominal payment of $1, with royalties to follow as they accrued.

Two months after her husband's death, Wilhelmine made the first of several trips to Vienna in order to dispose of the household goods and other belongings salvaged from her home in Maria Enzersdorf. Overcome by anguish, she was incapable of coping with this sad task. In the spring of 1946, during another visit, she took some of the alpine plants from the garden, which Webern had cared for with such loving devotion, back to his grave in Mittersill. That autumn, a simple cross of larchwood, designed by Josef Humplik,[2] was erected as a marker. In May 1948, Hermine von Webern took the first known photograph of the grave.

After Christine and her children left for Italy in September 1948, Wilhelmine's days became ever lonelier. She greatly missed the three beloved grand-daughters[3] and was distraught over Benno Mattel's plan to emigrate to South America.[4] In August 1949, after Maria's husband had accepted a position at a hospital some distance away, Wilhelmine decided to stay on in Mittersill. She moved to a small upstairs room in the house Am Markt 101, owned by the kindly Mrs Fritzenwanger, who had rented living quarters to the Mattel family earlier. There, under the same roof where her husband had breathed his last, Wilhelmine, ailing and alone, spent the remaining months of her life. To the end she upheld Webern's artistic legacy, and her faith in his creative mission never wavered. She eagerly followed the all-too-rare news of performances of his works and diligently maintained an intensive correspondence with those who had been closest to him.

The deep sadness that had engulfed her spirit after her husband's death speaks from almost every letter. On 26 January 1946, after her first trip back home, she had commented to Hildegard Jone: "The stay in Vienna was so upsetting and without any consolation for me. To be so alone—I became so fully conscious of it there."[5] On 13 July of the same year, she told Hermine how sorrowful her 60th birthday (on 2 July) had been without her husband and son. The day before she wrote that letter, the première of Webern's First Cantata had taken place in London. The widow had been invited to attend, but declined for reasons explained to Hermine: "How painful it was for me that I could not be there. But I would not have received a travel permit and would have had neither the money nor the clothes for it. As so often before, I again had to just renounce being present." On 27 September she reported to Humpelstetter: "I have received news about the performance that shook me to the depths. It was a truly great success. That my husband could not have lived to experience this! It would indeed have been a satisfaction after the last frightful years during which his music was prohibited and held in contempt."

On 10 February 1947 Wilhelmine wrote to Ernst Diez in America:

You will have read the letters by Toni in the July issue of *Turm*. Did it not strike you as strange what the editor wrote by way of introduction: "Vienna has taken notice of the tragic death of the composer Anton von Webern some months ago only by way of a simple news item, but none of his works was performed in his memory. The man who was averse to all outside display has silently and unceremoniously departed from Vienna's artistic life." Is this not a dreadful observation, but it is true! London and America have commemorated him in a different way. In autumn 1945 a very beautiful memorial programme was broadcast over the BBC. Then, during the ISCM music festival this summer, there was the world première of his First Cantata, which is now to be repeated in February during a Webern concert by the BBC. On that occasion Toni's orchestration from "The Musical Offering" will also be performed. Dr Bach sent me the news and he writes, "nothing else will be played on the programme—the homage is to be to him alone. Here at least his friends and admirers have not forgotten him." From Guido Webern I received word that in New York "there was a concert in honour of Toni." These are the bare facts. It befits Toni's fate so much. These Viennese, these Austrians—and how he loved this city and this country. To be sure, during the summer of 1945 he became convinced that he could not live here any more. He was firmly resolved to go to England and he would have carried it out, too.

The BBC memorial referred to by Wilhelmine took place on 3 December 1945, the composer's 62nd birthday. David Josef Bach, Webern's long-time friend, delivered the commemorative address. He had been the first from abroad to re-establish contact with the widow. Responding to his inquiry about the circumstances of her husband's death, Wilhelmine had written to him in early 1946:

To my regret I cannot report to you how it all happened. . . . My husband's death was just too dreadful. If he had passed away peacefully as a result of an illness, then there would be only the grief, but as it is I am filled with such a horror that I sometimes believe I will go mad. Why did my husband have to suffer such a fate? How difficult the last eight years had been for him. My husband was so embittered that he had only the one wish: to flee from this country. But one was caught, without a will of one's own. . . . It was close to the limit of endurance what we had to suffer. And just when a better time was coming for him, the disaster had to happen.[6]

Early in 1947, when there was the prospect of a performance of the Passacaglia in Vienna, Wilhelmine commented to her daughter-in-law on 7 March: "Unfortunately I have heard from no one in Vienna when the radio performance of father's work is to take place. Probably it has been postponed again. Everything is so hurtful and sad." Later that year, on 2 December, she wrote to Hildegard Jone: "Tomorrow is his birthday. What a beautiful day this always was for me. How indescribably sad that everything is over. How beautiful was my life at his side."

Such fleeting moments of happy memories could not dispel Wilhelmine's sorrow and despair. On 4 May 1948 she told Hildegard Jone:

Unfortunately, at present there are no performances of Anton's work anywhere. I had hoped so much that in Vienna one of his large orchestral works would be played this season. His Passacaglia and the Six Pieces for large orchestra really are already classic works—they would not provoke the slightest objection. But no conductor will dare to do them. Are they afraid of this task or do they absolutely not comprehend Anton's works? I cannot understand it. It grieves me very much. Just one single conductor, whom I do not know at all, a pianist named Häfner, has performed the Sacred Songs (on 22 December in the Ravag).[7] In some cities—Munich, Mainz, Heidelberg, and Prague—they wanted to perform works by Anton, but this does not seem to have materialized, for I have received no information about it from the publishers. Should Anton have already been forgotten? Or is it the fault of the dreadful time in which we live? It is all so depressing. I can do nothing about it, although sometimes I would like to, but it would not be in accordance with Anton's wishes. Thus I must wait and hope that perhaps it will become different some day.

While the neglect of Webern's music in his homeland was to continue for some time, Wilhelmine could report to Ernst Diez on 11 February 1949 about several performances abroad:

Most of what is being done takes place in America, London, and Brussels. Radio Brussels is the most active. It seems that a very talented conductor, Paul Collaer, is there. He has made it his task to perform over the Belgian radio the complete œuvre of the composers belonging to the "Vienna School." Of Toni's works, the First Cantata was just played on 17 January, and the Orchestra Variations, Toni's penultimate composition, will be performed on 14 February. I have received the report that the performance on 17 January was a very great success. Is it not curious and so sad that this work was played on Toni's Saint's Day? And the performance on 14 February will be on the anniversary of Peter's death. On 14 April 1948 the piano variations and the violin and cello pieces were played during the Brussels Music Festival.

In France, too, interest in Webern's music was on the rise. Jean Louis Martinet, a young composer, came to Vienna to lay plans for several performances in Paris during the 1949–50 season.

> He wanted to visit me here [Wilhelmine informed Hildegard Jone on 14 September 1949]. I declined, although I would have liked very much to make his acquaintance. It is difficult in my situation. The paralysis in my foot makes me shy of people. Also my dwelling is really so primitive, one could almost call it wretched (after all, I have only one room). To me personally it does not matter—I have my books, the music of Anton, and pictures of my loved ones. For me these are riches. But I do not wish strangers to look in on me. . . . Martinet is said to be full of ardent veneration for Anton's works and for his personality. I am told that at Hueber's he played the First Cantata (which he has already performed over Radio Paris). He is supposed to have done it with such sensitivity and devotion that this wonderful music moved everyone. Martinet also related that Anton's music has many followers in France and that it corresponds in its nature to the French spirit much more closely than, for instance, the music of either Berg or Schoenberg, and that works by Anton are being performed time and again. And of this I did not have the slightest notion, although I have begged UE over and over to inform me of performances. How can one understand this?

Among the Webern works intended for performance during the autumn of 1949 in Paris was the première of the Second Cantata. The concert also was to be broadcast. "Now all my efforts are directed towards being able to buy a radio. I hope I will succeed. *I must be able to hear this work!*" Wilhelmine wrote to Hermine on 28 September. Her wish was to remain unfulfilled, however, since Martinet's ambitious project came to naught, and Wilhelmine was to die before the year was out. On 29 December 1949, at five o'clock in the afternoon, she succumbed to a stroke in the small upstairs room of the house Am Markt 101.

Wilhelmine was buried beside her husband. In 1955, the wooden grave marker was replaced by an ornate iron cross (ordered by Maria Halbich from a Salzburg artisan). The simple inscription read:

ANTON WEBERN

1883–1945

MINNA WEBERN

1886–1949

Years later, the family accepted an offer from the town council of Mittersill to establish an Ehrengrab (grave of honour) for the composer and his wife. It was officially dedicated on 24 June 1972. A large block of African marble marks the new site, which is more spacious and access:ble than the earlier one. The gravestone, ordered by Amalie Waller, has been controversial because of its modernistic design and lettering (see insert for the three grave markers).

✻   ✻   ✻

During the years that her mother-in-law's life was drawing to its close, Hermine von Webern bravely and quietly began to rebuild her own. The news of Webern's death, which followed that of her husband by only seven months, was shattering. Hermine had not learned of the tragedy until 3 October from Leopoldine Gross. Ironically, the ten-word Red Cross message, mailed by Webern to his daughter-in-law early in July, reached her only on 16 October. It read: "Auf Wiedersehen in allseitiger Gesundheit, sobald Reise möglich. Tausend Grüsse." (Till we meet again in good health on all sides, as soon as trip is possible. A thousand greetings.)

On 4 October, the day after she received the news of his death, Hermine, grief-stricken, went once again to the house Im Auholz. When she had last been there on 17 September, Russian soldiers had still been billeted in the apartment. This time, they were out of the house, and she carried away the large portrait bust of Webern by Josef Humplik, which had formerly adorned the living room.[8] On the following day, Hermine made another trip to Maria Enzersdorf. This time, Mrs Rose Kruppi, who formerly had lived on the ground floor below the Webern apartment, handed her a suitcase full of books, printed music, and manuscripts, which she had secured earlier from the house. Hermine's diary entry of 5 October read: ". . . leafed through the manuscripts until a quarter to midnight."

When Mrs Barbara Fasching, the owner of the house, learned that Webern was dead and that his widow would not return, she bluntly requested that the remaining "rubbish" be removed from the premises.

Despite all her efforts, Hermine had been unable to carry away more than relatively small portions of their belongings. Therefore, Mrs Fasching asked Dr Werner Riemerschmid, Webern's former neighbour, to go with her to the house and see what might be done. In a letter which he wrote later to Polnauer, Riemerschmid described the appalling conditions:

As to the beds, only the iron frames were left; large sections of the floor had been used for firewood; here and there were remnants of furniture. Parts of the library were moulding on the cellar staircase where they had been stacked in cupboards between old broken fruit jars. On a veranda, where the windows were shattered, lay heaps of scores—Schoenberg's *Gurrelieder*, conductor's scores, books, and pictures. Many covers were torn, soaked through, or crumpled up. She [Frau Fasching] showed me the little garden house, a "Salettl," through the roof of which the rain had soaked the letters that were strewn around. On a strip of the lawn, remainders of ashes could be seen: there, piles of letters had been burned. The landlady had stuffed the remainder into coal sacks for the purpose of starting the fire in her stove at home. I asked her to let me look through the coal sacks. There I found, between dirt, bones, dead mice, and epaulets from uniforms, about a thousand letters by Webern to his wife, manuscripts, composition sketches, several hundred letters by Alban Berg, Arnold Schoenberg, Alma Mahler, Marx, and so forth. I returned all the things that I had pulled out to Webern's widow on the occasion of her visit in Mödling. She left the letters by Berg and Schoenberg with me for the purpose of bringing them into order and for possible publication. The sorting will be completed in the near future. . . . In the approximately twenty coal sacks the letters had naturally been totally crumpled, in part the ink had run, some had been gnawed on by mice, everything was mixed up—portions of letters in this or that sack. Of some, only fragments are extant. Another group of letters had been thrown on the coal heap in the cellar, including letters belonging to the other inhabitants of the house. The job of sorting in the cellar, where there was only the light from a candle, lasted several days, that with the coal sacks about two weeks. It was indescribably sad to see this devastation of so precious a property.[9]

Later, it turned out that the materials recovered by Riemerschmid included 240 letters and postcards written by Berg to Webern and 29 letters from Arnold Schoenberg.[10] Dr Riemerschmid also found Webern's first sketchbook (1925). Subsequently, the widow presented it to him in recognition of his labours (it was later acquired by Universal

Edition). Only the letters that Webern had written to his wife, estimated by Riemerschmid to number close to a thousand, were taken back by Wilhelmine. According to Amalie, they were all burned on her mother's request, because she felt so strongly that their contents had been meant for her alone and should not be exposed to the curiosity of outsiders.

On a cold January morning in 1946, Hermine completed her mission. Assisted by relatives, she removed the remaining property and brought it to her home, using a horse-drawn cart for the transportation. When Wilhelmine thanked her on 22 January, she wrote: "I simply would not have trusted myself, regardless of the self-control I exercise in front of others. Here, however, I would have failed. My nerves would not have endured it. And also I would like to preserve our beautiful home in my memory as it had been and not keep seeing the destroyed one before my eyes."

Wilhelmine and Amalie subsequently came several times to Perchtoldsdorf to select from the stacks of materials the items they wished to keep. Ludwig Zenk assisted them in sorting the manuscripts and books. Dismayed by the sight of so many mementoes—damaged, stained, and in total disorder—the widow's first impulse was to eradicate it all from her consciousness. Thus she asked Hermine to do away with her husband's broken cello.[11] She arranged to have most of the furniture sold, and on 5 May 1947 she informed her daughter-in-law that she wanted "to bring as many of the books and scores as possible to the Dorotheum." The Dorotheum is Vienna's public auction house, and a good part of Webern's library actually fell under the auctioneer's hammer. Painful as this was for the widow, the small proceeds helped to relieve her pressing need. Webern's grand piano, which had been left standing in the apartment, was acquired by Alfred Schlee who had the damaged instrument repaired.

After her mother's death, Amalie Waller, as the eldest, became the family representative. Neither Webern nor his wife had left a will. On 26 May 1948, the District Court at Mödling made an official disposition of Webern's estate, assessing it at 1,168 schillings (then US $24.52) and naming the widow as the sole beneficiary. After Wilhelmine's death, a judgement by the District Court of Mittersill, dated 13 June 1950, designated the three daughters as heirs. Since Peter von Webern had died before his parents, Hermine was not included in the inheritance.

During the early 1950s, when interest in Webern's music began to rise phenomenally,[12] the royalties from performances, printed music, and recordings surged correspondingly. Amalie, who administered the revenues on behalf of her sisters, could write on 18 April 1967: "If father could only know what rich fruits his life by now bears in every respect, he would rejoice. My God, *how* he would rejoice! I can *only* be grateful."[13]

The recognition of Webern's genius, belated as it was, became worldwide and enthusiastic. Between 1962 and 1978 a series of six International Webern Festivals was held.[14] The crowning event of the second festival was the unveiling of a bronze memorial plaque at the house in Mittersill where Webern had died twenty years earlier. It was commissioned by the International Webern Society and created by Anna Mahler, the daughter of the composer so revered by Webern. For those attending, the dedication ceremonies were an unforgettable experience. They opened, on the evening of 4 August 1965, with a concert by the LaSalle Quartet in the Annakirche. Playing on the same spot in front of the altar where Webern's body had lain the night he was killed, the artists paid homage to his creative spirit with his String Quartet (1905) and the Six Bagatelles, Op. 9, together with music by Purcell and Mozart. Dean Ehrenstrasser, who had buried him, spoke words of remembrance and led the assembly in a *Pater Noster*. Permeated by the peace of the summer evening, that solemn hour in the little church, richly adorned with flowers and burning candles, encompassed everything that Webern himself might have wished in celebration of his memory.

On the following morning, after early Mass in the village church, a large group gathered at the graveside. Music by Michael Haydn was sung by the choir, a wreath was placed, and the poem "Gebet" (Prayer) by Ferdinand Avenarius was recited, verses that in 1903 had inspired the young composer to a song setting. The poem is an allegory relating the fertile soil to the human heart. Both must suffer the wounds of the plough before the sower, God the Father, can plant His seed.

The sower, as the originator of growth, also is the guiding spirit in the text of the memorial plaque that was unveiled shortly afterwards at the house Am Markt 101. High dignitaries were in attendance at the ceremony: the Cultural Minister of the Province of Salzburg extolled Webern's genius, and the Mayor of Mittersill joined in the accolades. The sound truck of the Austrian Broadcasting System and the press corps were on hand to relay the event from the mountain retreat to the world. But the sudden fanfare of public acclaim could not disturb the quiet dignity of the hour. From the room in which Webern had lain mortally wounded came the recorded sounds of his Bach Ricercar transcription. Then Ernst Krenek gave the memorial address, delving deeply into the meaning of the ancient Latin palindrome that had inspired the creative thought of the master. This ingenious word square forms the centre of the memorial plaque:

Along his lonely path, Webern, too, had been the sower. His prophecy of a new aesthetic became the hub around which fresh creativity was destined to rotate. During his lifetime it was not given to him to witness the harvest of his seed, but like the just of old he will live on by the strength of his faith.

NOTES AND SOURCES

NOTES AND SOURCES

Prologue: Genealogy

1. Geographical designations appearing in the text are those in use at the time of the events. The present names are given in parentheses.

2. This natural barricade was the scene of crucial battles throughout the centuries. In the year 580, the Duke of Trent defeated near Salurn an army of Franconians who had advanced from the north. According to some historians, that event first established Salurn as the southernmost outpost of German language and influence.

3. It was brought to America by Guido von Webern, one of the composer's first cousins. After his death at Dayton, Ohio, in 1962, it was transferred, along with other family relics, to the Webern Archive (henceforth WA), a division of the Moldenhauer Archives. See the Introduction for details.

4. The sixteen-page document sets forth, in elaborate calligraphy, the rights, privileges, and honours appertaining to the noble title. Commanding that these rights and distinctions be respected by all levels of society, the emperor declares that violations are subject to a fixed monetary penalty, proceeds of which are to be divided equally between the imperial treasury and the offended family.

5. They were buried together in St Andrew Cemetery on 1 March. The boys, whose ages were given in the death records as six years, one month, twelve days and two years, nine months, respectively, had "flown to heaven" ("coelum volarunt") within twelve hours of each other.

6. The origin of the castle dates back to Roman times, although it is first documented only in the *Chronicles of Benediktbeuren*, in which a story, referring to the year 1053, mentions "Castellum quod SALURNA dicitur." Many a saga has been woven around the proud citadel, a landmark in the countryside. "Haderburg" ("Castle of Contention"), the name popularly associated with the fortress in the region, reflects its defiant appearance.

7. *Salurner Büchl*, ed. R. Klebelsberg (Innsbruck: Universitätsverlag Wagner, 1956), p. 50.

8. Four men appearing in that catalogue were members of the clergy. Two attained the rank of canon, the others served as court preacher and castle chaplain. Two Webern women likewise took holy orders. Also listed were several military men, two of whom saw action in the Seven Years' War between Austria and Prussia. Another, Joseph Webern zu Treuenhausen und Postfelden, distinguished himself as a defender of southern Tyrol during the Napoleonic wars, as did other Webern men, whose exploits are described in documents preserved at the Ferdinandeum in Innsbruck. The family branch "von Webern zu Treuenhausen und Postfelden" can be traced from their own decree of nobility, dated 20 May 1705 and kept in the Adelsarchiv of Vienna. It was bestowed upon Georg Weber, councillor and customs collector at Leifers and Branzoll, and his three brothers residing at Bolzano, Cavalese, and Altrei, the original seat of the Weber family that once had immigrated from the Egerland.

A "Herr von Webern" figures in a letter written by Joseph Haydn to Count Anton Georg Apponyi on 2 February 1785. Haydn then was keenly anticipating his initiation into the Masonic Lodge Zur Wahren Eintracht of Vienna, the same to which his young colleague and friend, Wolfgang Amadeus Mozart, already belonged. Haydn's words "Just yesterday I received a letter from my future sponsor, Herr von Webern" refer to Franz Philipp von Weber, master of ceremonies at the Lodge. In the German usage of the time, the dative case of "Weber" became "Webern," and English translations erroneously took over that form of the name. A register of 1785 gives the name of Haydn's sponsor as "Franz Philipp Weber," without the predicate of nobility. The same register lists a Sigmund von Webern, attached as court councillor to the War Ministry.

9. *Revolution in America, Confidential Letters and Journals 1776–1784 of Adjutant General Major Baurmeister of the Hessian Forces*, tr. and ed. Bernhard A. Uhlendorf (New Brunswick, N.J.: Rutgers University Press, 1957), p. 498.

10. All these documents have been preserved. WA.

11. The engraving (WA), signed and dated "I. E. v. Webern, 1830," depicts the village of Therl, located in the province of Styria. Surrounded by forests and rocky cliffs, it is dominated by the ruins of Castle Schachenstein.

12. Coal was mined at Liescha, a settlement of about 100 people, and iron in the much larger community of Prävali.

13. Hieronimus Pregl is cited in a legal document dated 7 January 1643. WA.

14. Guido von Webern was born on 15 January 1888 in Judenburg. After his father's death, at the age of only 44 years, the widow, Elisabeth *née* Kleinpell, moved to Vienna so that her three children might enjoy greater educational advantages. In 1907 a relative who practised medicine in Chicago, Dr Henry Kleinpell, sponsored the family's move to America. Guido von Webern soon acquired a reputation as an engineer and inventor. Back in Vienna, while studying chemistry at the university, he had become acquainted with the just-evolving printing method of rotogravure. On 15 December 1912 he produced a section of the *New York Sun* in that process, the first time that the technique was applied in an American newspaper. After this pioneering feat, for which the inventor had to grind his own ink and prepare special plates, he further improved the method. Later, when his employer, the National Cash Register Company, wished to replace the ornate brass appointments of its machines with a plainer sheet steel, Guido von Webern invented the photographic process of wood-graining on metal. That technique was subsequently applied to several other uses, so that Guido von Webern's innovations have since played a part in the development of numerous industrial products, particularly plastics. In all, he registered 87 patents. His interest in engineering was matched by that in the natural sciences, primarily geology and botany. He had a passion for gardening, to which he gave full rein on his seven-acre plot near Dayton, Ohio. There he died on 21 December 1962. In his estate were several family relics that he had brought to America 55 years earlier, as well as many of his original drawings. The latter display the exquisite artistic taste and immaculate craftsmanship that this first cousin of Anton von Webern shared with the composer.

15. Ernst Diez was born on 27 July 1878 at Lölling, in the province of Carinthia. The family later lived at Vordernberg, Styria, where the father was a mining administrator. Attaining a doctorate of philosophy after studies at the universities of Graz and Vienna, Ernst Diez emerged as the most prominent pupil of the famous art expert Josef Strzygowski, who appointed him his assistant. Specializing in Eastern art, the young scholar undertook, before World War I, an adventurous expedition into the regions of northern Persia, then entirely unexplored by art historians. An inveterate traveller, he made field trips to India and China, and his reputation earned him professorships in the United States of America (including posts at Western Reserve University and Bryn Mawr College), as well as an extended tenure at the University of Istanbul, Turkey. Of his many published studies remaining valid and useful to this day, that on Islamic art is an outstanding example. Other treatises were devoted to Indian art and to the subject of Byzantine mosaics in Greece. In connection with the latter work, Diez pioneered the use of colour photography, then in its earliest stages, for the purposes of scientific publications. Among his books aimed at bringing art history close to popular understanding was *Entschleiertes Asien* (The Ancient Worlds of Asia), which became a world success and was translated into all major languages. Ernst Diez died in Vienna on 8 July 1961 at the age of 84, having continued his literary activities to the last and being universally recognized as the Nestor of Austrian art historians. His literary estate is in the Moldenhauer Archives.

16. The citation on the title page, in ornate calligraphy, was followed by a fine

coloured engraving depicting the small settlement of Liescha. The album was preserved by Guido von Webern. WA.

17. Among the honours bestowed upon Carl von Webern during his fruitful life was the Imperial Commander's Cross, including the star of the Franz Josef Order, with which he was decorated in 1907. The year before, his alma mater, the School of Mining at Leoben, awarded him the honorary doctorate of mining sciences (Dr mont. h.c.). Thanks to his influence, that institution, like the mining school at Pribram, had been elevated to full college status. Unchallenged as an authority, Carl von Webern had held numerous posts with industrial, educational and legal bodies, helping to bring about reforms and new laws.

18. *Montanistische Rundschau* 6 (1920), pp. 128–129.

Chapter I   Youth (1883–1902)

1. No records are available. According to Rosa Warto, Webern's younger sister, the child was born out of wedlock in 1876 in Vienna and was also buried there.

2. Memoirs of Rosa Warto. Manuscript. WA. The following quotations are from the same source.

3. At Graz, Komauer was a protégé of Dr Heinrich Potpeschnigg, Hugo Wolf's friend, who introduced him to the city's leading musical circles. He thus became assistant to Wegscheider, director of the Graz Singverein. Dr Potpeschnigg also recommended to the local section of the Richard Wagner Society that Komauer be given a stipend to attend two performances (*Parsifal* and *Meistersinger*) at the Bayreuth Festival. That pilgrimage generated in Komauer an enduring enthusiasm for Wagner's music.

4. In his published memoirs, Komauer summarized his teaching precepts:

I placed principal emphasis on achieving the warmest expressiveness possible, as well as on a strict legato style with exact observance of the prescribed phrasing marks. Also essential for me was the correct use of the pedal, in which I followed the directions of Hugo Riemann. I was enthusiastic about promoting piano-duet playing. My favourite areas of instruction, however, were the theoretical subjects, harmony and counterpoint.

Edwin Komauer, "Kurze Selbstbiographie," *Jahresbericht des Musikvereins für Kärnten* (1943), p. 11.

5. Letter dated 3 November 1910.

6. Memoirs of Doris Brehm-Diez. Typescript. WA.

7. Apparently, the sequence of the second and third movements was reversed.

8. Solitary confinement in a locked room was a form of punishment for disciplinary transgressors at the Gymnasium.

9. In the course of his career, Clementschitsch rose to the position of a superior judge at the provincial court in Klagenfurt and later was distinguished by the title of "Hofrat" (Court Councillor).

Chapter II   University years I (1902–1904)

1. As his graduation certificate shows, he earned just passing grades in two of the chief humanistic disciplines, Latin and Greek, and he fared no better in mathematics, physics, and natural sciences. On the other hand, he was decreed "laudable" in German, which, as the mother tongue, is held to be of prime importance in the Gymnasium curriculum. Anton's grades in history and geography likewise were "laudable," and those in religion and philosophy "satisfactory." The lone "excellent" in the report card was for singing;

this no doubt took into account the varied musical activities that had earned the student a certain reputation in the city.

2. According to Josef Polnauer ("Paralipomena zu Berg und Webern," *Österreichische Musikzeitschrift* 24, 1969, pp. 292–296). Webern also studied cello sometime during this period with the composer Franz Schmidt, then a cellist in the Vienna Philharmonic, but he had a falling out because of the teacher's attitude towards the music of Mahler.

3. Brassart was a fifteenth-century Netherlands singer and composer.

Chapter III   Early compositions I (1899–1904)

1. These materials are largely in the Webern Archive. For the history of the Archive, including the discoveries of many posthumous Webern compositions during the 'sixties, see Introduction.

2. Listed as "Vorfrühling II" in the Work List, Appendix 1.

3. The programme of that event was kept by Webern, who had a life-long habit of preserving such mementoes. It was found after his death between the pages of his *Tannhäuser* score.

4. A survey of these projects can be found in the Work List.

Chapter IV   Arnold Schoenberg—University years II (1904–1906)

1. Conversation with the author.

2. Horwitz' untimely death on 18 August 1925 followed the loss of his hearing from tuberculosis the year before. He was considered one of the finest of Schoenberg's early pupils.

3. Letter to the author.

4. Giovanni Segantini (1858–1899) was renowned for his portrayal of grandiose mountain scenery.

5. "Der Lehrer," *Arnold Schoenberg* (Munich: Piper 1912), pp. 85–87.

6. The first quotation is from Wille's *Offenbarungen des Wacholderbaums*, the second from Liliencron's poem "Heimgang in der Frühe," which Webern set to music in 1903.

7. Published in German under the title *Was wir lieben und pflegen müssen*.

8. In the same year that Webern was so strongly moved by Wedekind's new moral postulates, Alban Berg received, through Karl Kraus, the first inspiration for his opera *Lulu*, based on Wedekind's *Erdgeist* and *Büchse der Pandora*. Such ideological affinities cemented the friendship between the two young men far beyond their musical ties.

9. Webern's dissertation, an edition of Heinrich Isaac's *Choralis Constantinus*, Part II, will be discussed at the beginning of the following chapter.

Chapter V   Early compositions II—Opera 1–2 (1905–1908)

1. Its full title reads "Heinrich Isaac *Choralis Constantinus*. Zweiter Teil. Graduale in mehrstimmiger Bearbeitung (a capella), bearbeitet von Anton von Webern." Webern's edition was published in 1909 in the *Denkmäler der Tonkunst in Österreich* (the monumental work supervised by Guido Adler), where it appears in the first section of the sixteenth annual series.

2. In a letter to Paul Königer of 3 November 1910, Webern reminisced about such chamber music sessions:

Quartet playing is the most glorious music-making there is. In times gone by, we very often played quartets at Schoenberg's. Only in a small room does it become the real thing. We also played Schoenberg's quartets. When Marie Gutheil-Schoder first studied the second quartet, we accompanied her—Dr Adler, Jalowetz, myself, and a second violinist whose name escapes me. Schoenberg coached. That was wonderful then. Yes, these are beautiful memories. We rehearsed in like manner with Madame Winternitz, too.

3. The painting, depicting mountain scenes in spring, summer, and winter, had been commissioned for the Paris World's Fair but remained unfinished because of the artist's premature death.

4. The musicologist, Heinz Klaus Metzger, wrote in his programme notes to the LaSalle Quartet's recording of Webern's string quartets (Deutsche Grammophon 2530 284):

Webern's single-movement String Quartet of 1905, which was discovered only a few years ago, still contains tonal passages, but these are contrasted by extensive atonal sections. As the beginning of the Viennese atonal revolution has hitherto been attributed to Schoenberg and dated 1908—with the finale of his Second String Quartet, Op. 10—musical history must be rewritten in this respect, because the priority was not in fact Schoenberg's. Furthermore Webern's early Quartet is rich in precise structural pointers to later works: the unpretentious chromatic scale figures in contrary motion leading to the brief climax of the whole work were to become the germ cell for the last section of Schoenberg's monodrama *Erwartung*, and later also for the end of the second scene by the lake in Berg's *Wozzeck*. The motivic-thematic material of this Quartet is very largely derived from a three-note constellation heard at the outset; amazingly enough this is exactly the same group of intervals which, three decades later, constituted the basis for the constructive entity of Webern's Concerto, Op. 24. It is even more astonishing that as early as 1905 the fundamental notes were subjected to permutations of articulation as in the late String Quartet, Op. 28, written when Webern's constructive technique had attained its highest point of fulfilment.

5. For a complete listing of Webern's chorale harmonizations, see Appendix 1, Work List.

6. Anton Webern, *The Path to the New Music*, ed. Willi Reich, Eng. tr. Leo Black, p. 48.

7. The complete score was realized by Edwin Haugan.

8. Webern's analysis was published in the *Allgemeine Musikzeitung*, 49 (1922); the particular issue served as the festival programme book. It was reprinted in Rudolf Stephan, "Weberns Werke auf deutschen Tonkünstlerfesten," *Österreichische Musikzeitschrift* 27 (1972), p. 121. The first draft of this analysis is in the WA. The commentary shows many alterations and deletions in the text, which includes five musical examples and autobiographical data up to that time.

9. It was brought out on the occasion of the work's performance at the Allgemeines Deutsches Tonkünstlerfest in Düsseldorf (see Chapter XV).

10. Quoted in Hans Moldenhauer, *The Death of Anton Webern*, p. 39.

Chapter VI *Inauspicious beginnings (1906–1910)*

1. Bad Ischl was the seat of an imperial villa. Emperor Franz Josef and many members of the aristocracy frequented the resort.

2. Dresden, 25 January 1909.

3. Max Marschalk, director of the Dreililien Verlag, Schoenberg's first publisher.

4. A peak in East Tyrol (3,240 m.).

5. Willi Reich, *Alban Berg* (Zürich: Atlantis Verlag, 1963), pp. 30–32. (Both Paul Stefan and Richard Specht place the incident in 1909 or 1910.)

6. One of the best known of Mopp's paintings is his impression of Gustav Mahler conducting a symphony orchestra.

7. His real name was Richard Engländer.

8. "Theatre" is used here figuratively and implies the whole range of social activity.

9. Otto Weininger was a brilliant Viennese philosopher who in 1903 committed suicide at the age of only 23, shortly after the publication of his best-known book, *Geschlecht und Charakter*.

10. Webern was a regular reader of *Die Fackel*, the literary organ edited by Karl Kraus.

Chapter VII   Opera 3–8—Two opera projects (1908–1910)

1. *The Path to the New Music*, p. 51.

2. *Ibid.*, pp. 44–45.

3. The poems of Opus 3 are all found in the cycle *Lieder* contained in *Der siebente Ring*. In Opus 4, the first song is based on a poem in the cycle *Traumdunkel*, part of *Der siebente Ring*. Nos. 2, 3, and 5 use texts from the cycles *Waller im Schnee*, *Nach der Lese*, and *Traurige Tänze* in *Das Jahr der Seele*, and No. 4 appears in *Das Buch der Sagen und Sänge* under the sub-title *Sänge eines fahrenden Spielmanns*.

4. The text for No. 1 is from the cycle *Nachtwachen* in *Das Jahr der Seele*; the three others are taken from *Der siebente Ring*, Nos. 2 and 3 from the cycle *Maximin* and No. 4 from *Gezeiten*.

5. A copy of this early publication, bearing an autograph dedication to Zemlinsky, is preserved in the WA.

6. *Der Merker* 10 (February 1910), p. 37.

7. "Konzert—Novitätenschau Saison 1909–1910," *Musikbuch aus Österreich* 8 (ed. Hugo Botstiber), Vienna/Leipzig, 1911, Carl Fromme, p. 78.

8. According to a letter from Webern to Berg, dated 27 November 1912.

9. Webern frequently speaks of the appearance of his scores as "Partiturbild" or "Notenbild."

10. The date of composition later appeared in the literature erroneously as 1910, giving rise to speculation about the chronology of the first aphoristic orchestra pieces, since Schoenberg's untitled three small pieces for chamber orchestra are dated 8 February 1910. Webern himself confirmed the time of origin when he wrote to Berg on 20 September 1910 that he was copying the orchestra pieces he had composed "during the summer of 1909" in order to submit them to the Deutscher Musikverein.

11. This sentence refers to the second piece; the description following·that of the fourth piece applies to the fifth and sixth movements.

12. In a letter to Berg of 21 August 1913, Webern speaks at greater length about his inspiration for this movement.

13. Webern refers to Wilhelmine; since they married in 1911, she was his wife at the time he wrote the letter, though not at the time of the events described.

14. The performance of Webern's Opus 6 was cancelled in line with the cultural directives of the newly established Nazi régime.

15. *Zeitschrift für Musik* 100 (1933), pp. 566–567.

16. Webern presented Schoenberg with a fair copy of the manuscript, which was subsequently lost. An entry in Schoenberg's diary, dated 18 February 1912 at Zehlendorf, reads:

Webern with me during the forenoon. We search (also in the attic, in all crates) for Webern's Orchestra Pieces, which he has presented to me in a very clean and painstakingly executed autograph copy. . . . But it is not to be found. I am very unhappy over the fact that I, who guard manuscripts so scrupulously, have to inflict this on someone. . . . Finally we assumed that our former maid, Mathilde Stepanek, in her stupidity has either taken it along "as a souvenir" or has misplaced it.

Chapter VIII Danzig (1910–1911)

1. The manuscript, now preserved in the Moldenhauer Archives, was discovered twenty years after Webern's death among the remnants of his library.

2. Besides the two letters written by Webern to Wilhelmine in 1906, the letters of 1910 are the only ones to survive from the couple's voluminous correspondence, which was burned after the composer's death at the request of the widow.

3. In September 1910, when Webern attended the première of Mahler's Eighth Symphony.

4. About US $6 at the time.

5. In the same letter, Webern thanked Schoenberg for the wedding gift of one of his paintings.

6. About US $30 at the time.

Chapter IX Berlin (1911–1912)

1. It was Webern's plan to provide piano reductions of all of Schoenberg's works, beginning with *Verklärte Nacht*.

2. After Webern's death, the instrument was purchased from his widow by Alfred Schlee, director of Universal Edition.

3. Webern missed the first lecture because of his trip to Munich.

4. Ferruccio Busoni's impressions of this performance appeared in the next issue of *Pan*:

At the keyboards sit four youths with fine characteristic heads. The effect is almost touching as, with devotion and competence, they place their young intellects at the service of what is still enigmatic. In the background of the small stage two eyes glimmer restlessly, a baton moves about abruptly and nervously. One perceives the head and hand of Schoenberg, who exhorts the four valiant ones, communicating to them more and more of his feverishness. An uncommon picture, which, aided by the uncommon sound, exerts a fascination.

5. Schoenberg made the following note in his diary concerning the morning rehearsal on 3 February: "During the rehearsal, small conflicts between Webern and Clark. Webern becomes impatient when Clark does not pull the stops in time and is gruff. I mediate! It was really funny!" On 4 February, after the concert, Schoenberg wrote in his diary that Webern was "to me, as always, the dearest!"

6. There did ensue a polemical exchange in the press between Schoenberg and Dr Leopold Schmidt, critic of the *Berliner Tageblatt*, who was said to have heard only a small part of the programme and whose review deeply offended Schoenberg.

7. During his Berlin stay Webern became acquainted with these and other leading musicians. On 15 February 1912 Schoenberg introduced him to Richard Strauss after a concert in which Strauss appeared as guest conductor with the Berlin Philharmonic. Beyond this casual encounter, there apparently never was any further personal association between the two men.

8. During a reception in Zemlinsky's home, Webern made the formal presentation, which Schoenberg described in his diary: "How moved he was when he presented the book to me. Solemnly and yet so simply. Almost like a schoolboy, but one who has studied his part, so that he will not be overwhelmed."

9. Linke, Wellesz, Neumann, Stein, Jalowetz, Horwitz, Webern, Königer, and Berg.

10. XIII, No. 7, Cologne, February 1912.

11. Webern's article misspells Franz Schreker's name as "Schrecker" (p. 36), one of a

number of such errors to be found in his writings. These were not accidental mistakes, but misconceptions persisting through the years; he wrote "Mendelsohn," for example, all his life. If this seems curious for a doctor of musicology, Webern's frequent misspellings of quite common words is even more surprising in view of his thorough Gymnasium education. These errors may have been due to Webern's marked dialect, which altered the phonetics of some words. His misspellings became less frequent as the years went by.

12. Webern's departure at a time when a performance of Schoenberg's First String Quartet was scheduled in Berlin by the Rosé Quartet caused a controversy between Schoenberg and his wife. In his diary, Schoenberg noted:

He travels to Vienna in order to hear Mahler's Eighth Symphony. To be sure, I would like to do this also. Shows, however, that he is not as attached to me, after all, as he would like to make believe. Discussion with Mathilde about this in the evening. Result therefrom: we are half angry with each other. Naturally, she goes much too far; namely, for certain reasons (G) she has a need to hang something on Webern. I represented to her that, strictly speaking, I often did not behave better in my relationship with Mahler. That parents behave badly towards children and children towards parents. That good is an abstraction and nothing absolute. That there exist no absolutely good and blameless human beings. And that I do not want to forget in how many other cases Webern behaves excellently towards me. But this she does not want to admit. She holds rigidly to her assertion and hardly listens.

The initial "G" refers to Richard Gerstl, a painter for whom Mathilde temporarily left Schoenberg in 1908. She returned to her husband and two little children only upon the entreaties of friends, Webern foremost among them. Gerstl, who was only 25, committed suicide on 4 November of the same year.

13. Actually, Webern had to assume his duties as early as 22 June.

14. This was verified by Webern's younger sister, Rosa, who invested her share (about US $10,000 at the time) in bonds, only to see inflation wipe out the inheritance.

15. That spring Berg and Webern had attended together Strindberg's *Dance of Death* in Vienna. Only a few days before, on 14 May 1912, the great Swedish author had died. An unreserved admirer, Webern collected all of Strindberg's works in his library. The tortured human misery projected in the author's plays proved closely akin to the social and psychological problems of the time. Strindberg's dramas and other writings became widely fashionable, and Webern and Berg, along with many other creative artists, were deeply affected by his ideas.

16. The Czechs then belonged to the Austrian Empire.

17. A pupil of Emil Sauer, Richard Goldschmied then was a professor at the Vienna New Conservatory. Later a faculty member of the Hamburg Conservatory, he was deported in 1942 to Riga, where he was murdered.

Chapter X   Stettin (1912–1913)

1. Schoenberg was highly irritated over the remark and reproached Webern for mailing the card.

2. The architect Adolf Loos.

3. One of the numerous farces and revues by Jean Gilbert (pseudonym for Max Winterfeld).

4. Reprinted from H. H. Stuckenschmidt, *Schönberg*. The letter of Mathilde Schoenberg to her husband, also quoted in this chapter, is from the same source, as are the quotations from Schoenberg's diary.

5. Actually, Stettin's musical life seems to have been quite venturesome and

progressive, at least at the theatre. In December Jalowetz was to introduce Richard Strauss' *Ariadne auf Naxos*, following by less than two months the opera's première in Stuttgart. Webern, who coached the ensemble, concluded that the work was the composer's best, and he found many of its traits "delightful."

6. See *Arnold Schoenberg Letters*, pp. 37–39.

7. The part of Waldtaube was created by Marya Freund (1876–1966), who became an ardent champion of all progressive composers during her long and distinguished career.

8. Alban Berg assisted in rehearsing the chorus. Since it was his first such experience, Webern had volunteered his advice. On 27 December 1912 he wrote to him from Stettin that he should begin with each part by itself. Difficult passages should be sung by smaller groups, or even by single voices. Each part was to be rehearsed singly up to a sub-division of the composition, then the parts together, or first the women's voices together, then the men's voices. If things did not work, then the parts were to be taken singly again. Webern urged Berg to proceed very slowly, even if only a few measures were covered at the first rehearsal. These measures, however, should be brought into as finished a shape as possible. In this way, the chorus would have the feeling that it had learned something. To sing all the way through at the first session was impossible with a chorus. This would work only with an orchestra.

9. The article was reprinted in *Arnold Schönberg zum fünfzigsten Geburtstage, 13 September 1924*, a special issue of *Musikblätter des Anbruch* 6 (August–September 1924), pp. 321–323. This newspaper report is corroborated by the following unpublished eye-witness account made available to the author by Paul Amadeus Pisk. It is from the diary of the noted architect Richard Neutra.

> Tonight I was at the concert Schoenberg conducted. From the start, the people, that is, some people, began to boo, laugh, and shout. There was ceaseless talking, yelling, and tramping around. The rabble simply sensed that there was someone ready for easy slaughter, someone who was fair game. It all was quite natural, but revolting beyond measure to witness. People who relate to art as little as I to card games continually made jokes which were considered brilliant by their respective lady companions. At times I was almost beside myself. After the Schoenberg Symphony (which despite everything gave me an impression of power and of being a true work of art) a hellish noise broke out; on the second balcony a few persons were thrown out after a rough scuffle. For inexplicable reasons Berg's songs were interrupted by a resounding whinnying noise. Prior to that Loos had become so incensed that he almost committed acts of violence. Schoenberg shouted threats into the auditorium. The songs could barely be finished. Then all restraints broke down. People challenged each other, were forcibly separated by others, roared, laughed, whistled. Across from me Arthur Schnitzler quietly sat in the second loge. Somebody called to the audience to deport itself in a civilized manner or leave. Someone else yelled back "Lausbub." The first jumped down into the crowd and vigorously boxed the ears of the one whom he suspected of having insulted him. Everybody in the hall followed these events with fascination. Then more bellowing. A uniformed policeman shouted something. Everything seems comical to me now, but while I was there my whole body shook with anger. The musicians left the hall—the mob had succeeded in breaking up the concert. Down below they were quarrelling about something. Oscar Straus acted as mediator. The public is like a cowardly beast, foreign and hostile to art, which retaliates by shouting down and inciting others against what seems fair game because it is compelled to bow to whatever is generally accepted.

Chapter XI   Vienna—Illness (1913–1914)

1. Three months later, in October, Webern sublimated the morbid experience in a stage play entitled *Tot* (see Chapter XII).

2. The drawing was first published in Oskar Kokoschka, *Dramen und Bilder* (Leipzig: Kurt Wolff Verlag, 1913).

3. Actually, only three of the songs were performed: "Das Wappenschild," "Voll jener Süsse," and "Wenn Vöglein klagen." Soloist was Heldentenor Hans Winkelmann, the son of Hermann Winkelmann, a famous Wagnerian tenor.

4. This and subsequent quotations from Berg's letters to his wife are from *Alban Berg Briefe an seine Frau*.

5. About US $764 at the time.

6. She was the wife of the prominent lawyer Dr Felix Zehme.

7. There exist three snapshots showing Schoenberg, Webern, and Stein at Holland's North Sea coast. WA.

8. The essay was published in *Österreichische Musikzeitschrift* 27 (March 1972), pp. 127–130.

9. In subsequent years Webern added to his catalogue. As of 1929, however, when the last entries were made, the names of Bartók, Ravel, and Stravinsky were still absent from the listings of contemporary composers. The catalogue encompasses 129 pages. WA.

10. The whereabouts of the manuscripts by Berg and Schoenberg are unknown.

*Chapter XII　Opera 9–11—Other works—*Tot *(1911–1914)*

1. Another holograph, in the Pierpont Morgan Library (R. O. Lehman Collection), gives the year 1919 at the end. The work, then called "Sechs Stücke" appeared on the programmes of the Society for Private Musical Performances.

2. *The Path to the New Music*, p. 51.

3. Webern to Nicolas Slonimsky, 14 January 1937; quoted in Slonimsky, *Music since 1900*, p. 117. Webern speaks in this letter of "about twenty pieces" that he wrote between 1911 and 1913 "as expressions of musical lyricism."

4. "Anton von Webern," *Die Musik* 22 (August 1930), p. 814.

5. Emanuel Swedenborg (1688–1772) was a Swedish scientist whose theosophic beliefs led, after his death, to the founding of the Church of the New Jerusalem. His thought profoundly affected his contemporaries, including Kant and Goethe (the latter's *Urfaust* was influenced by him), and later thinkers such as Balzac and Strindberg expounded his theories in their own writings.

6. Berg does not seem to have shared Schoenberg's reservations; in July of 1914 he wrote to Webern and referred to *Tot* as "the theatre play that I have come to like beyond all measure."

7. By Peter Westergaard.

8. All three songs were discovered only posthumously. They were published in 1968 under the title Three Orchestral Songs (1913–14) in the sequence given by Webern.

9. In this connection, a note by Alma Mahler, dated March 1915, is of special interest: "Webern produced few but original compositions. He became ever more radical, and Schoenberg at one time complained to me and Werfel how much he was suffering under the dangerous influence of Webern and that he needed all his strength to extricate himself from it." (Alma Mahler-Werfel, *Mein Leben*, Frankfurt: S. Fischer Verlag, 1960, p. 77.)

10. The original manuscript (WA) bears the inscription: "To my dear father, for 27 May 1914, T[oni]."

11. It was published in 1970 by Carl Fischer, New York, in an edition by Friedrich Cerha.

Chapter XIII   First World War—Prague—Mödling (1914–1918)

1. The draft of this letter was found among Webern's papers. WA.

2. Schoenberg to Zemlinsky. This pungent letter, not included in the published correspondence, was printed in a Prague newspaper on 23 January 1916.

3. This and later quotations from Webern's letters to Hertzka are from *die Reihe 2, Anton Webern* (1955). Various quotations from Webern's letters to Berg and Scherchen are from the same source.

4. Memoirs of Anton Anderluh. Typescript. WA.

5. Besides this snapshot, there is another extant photograph showing Webern in the dress uniform of a Mountain Trooper, with cape and plumed hat. A third photograph from Webern's war years pictures him with four comrades on a mountain manoeuvre in 1915. WA.

6. Found among Webern's souvenirs was a picture postcard showing the attractive location of the house (in the district of Kral. Vinohrady). It contains Webern's handwritten record of the duration of his stay, "12. VIII. 1917—31. V. 1918." WA.

7. She was the sister of the concert pianist Bruno Eisner.

Chapter XIV   Society for Private Musical Performances (1918–1922)

1. These and other details were disclosed in a letter from Berg to his wife dated 13 September 1918.

2. The gist of Webern's note was conveyed by Berg to his wife on 16 September 1918.

3. Contents and tone of the letter, published as No. 32 of Schoenberg's *Letters* (p. 57), under the caption "To an Unknown Correspondent," leave no doubt that it was directed to Webern.

4. The by-laws were drawn up by Dr Ludwig Pisk, the father of Paul A. Pisk.

5. The first encompasses the period 1918–20, the second 1921. WA.

6. No comprehensive history of the society's activities has been compiled thus far, and there exist only short accounts by Paul A. Pisk ("Der Verein für musikalische Privataufführungen" in *Musikblätter des Anbruch* 6 (August–September 1924), pp. 325–326), and Leonard Stein ("The Privataufführungen Revisited" in *Paul A. Pisk, Essays in his Honour*, pp. 203–207), as well as assorted records and anecdotes by Reich, Slonimsky, and Steuermann, among others. The most recent account is contained in "Memories of Schoenberg" by Paul A. Pisk, published in the *Journal of the Arnold Schoenberg Institute* 1/1 (Oct. 1976), pp. 39–44.

7. The performance of the Five Songs Op. 3, occasioned the first publication of the work, under the nominal aegis of the society.

8. Webern and his family then lived again with Aunt Poldi (Leopoldine Schmid) at Wienerstrasse 104.

9. Subsequently his two daughters and their husbands were also buried in the plot.

10. The *Mitteilungen* No. 8, 4 May 1919, contained a subscription blank for the concerts.

11. The society's *Mitteilungen* No. 13, 21 November 1919, announced the performers as Rudolf Kolisch, Walter Seligmann, Maria Lazansky, Hans Neumann, and Karl Hein.

12. Other composers featured were Busch, Casella, Chausson, Debussy, Dresden, Halvorsen, Malipiero, Mussorgsky, Nielsen, Pijper, Ravel, Reger, Röntgen, Schmitt, Schnabel, Scott, Scriabin, Strässer, Stravinsky, and Suk.

13. Webern's copy of the richly executed 236-page Amsterdam festival book is extant. WA.

14. As late as 1923 Béla Bartók admitted to the pianist Rudolph Ganz (to whom Ravel dedicated the "Scarbo" movement of *Gaspard de la nuit*): "Of Ravel, I know nothing at all as yet" (letter Bartók to Ganz, 17 April 1923, Moldenhauer Archives).

15. Quoted from Gunther Schuller, "A Conversation with Steuermann," *Perspectives of New Music* 3 (Fall–Winter 1964), p. 22.

16. Webern's *Treasure Waltz* arrangement is now in the Vienna Stadtbibliothek.

17. The following year (1922) Kolisch founded his own quartet. It became the first ensemble to perform the classic standard literature from memory. It also championed contemporary music, giving first performances of works by Bartók, Berg, Schoenberg, and Webern, among others. Rudolf Kolisch (b. 1896) was one of the few professional violinists to bow with the left arm. He studied violin under Ševčik and composition under Schreker at the Music Academy. He also attended lectures by Adler at the University and studied privately with Schoenberg.

18. For biographical information on Kurt Manschinger see Note 19, Chapter XXIX.

19. Among Stella Eisner's contributions to the society's concerts was Mussorgsky's *Kinderstube* cycle. Her lively memoirs abound in musical details and personal anecdotes concerning Webern, Schoenberg, and their intimate circle. Typescript. WA.

20. Instructors included (besides Webern) Berg, Polnauer, and Stein. Founded by Schoenberg as a Seminar for Composition in the autumn of 1917, these courses continued to be held in the Schwarzwald School until they fell victim to the inflation early in 1923.

21. It is worth noting that, after Webern's death, several of his orchestral works became the basis of successful choreographic interpretations by Balanchine, Cranko, and others.

22. The pianist Olga Novakovic was one of Schoenberg's pupils and a noted astrologer.

23. *Arnold Schoenberg Letters*, pp. 79–81.

24. On 19 June 1922 Webern wrote to Berg that he was presently "very much harnessed" with work for the society's guest appearance in Prague; he specifically mentions rehearsing "a second *Pierrot* ensemble." In a letter to Zemlinsky, dated 24 November 1922, he speaks of having coached Felicie Hüni-Mihacsek for her rendition of songs by Zemlinsky. His own George Songs, Op. 3, were on the same programme.

25. Schoenberg to Raffael da Costa, *Deutsche Allgemeine Zeitung*, 18 June 1930, *Arnold Schoenberg Letters*, p. 142.

26. Quoted from Wolf-Eberhard von Lewinsky, "Young Composers, " *die Reihe 4*, (1958, Eng. ed. 1960), p. 2.

Chapter XV Rise to Recognition (1921–1924)

1. The annals were compiled by the society's secretary, Gustav Grainer.

2. This amount, although on the surface the same that Webern had received in 1912 as his share from the sale of the Preglhof, represented only a tiny fraction of its former value because of the devastating inflation.

3. The programme, comprising works by Beethoven, Weber, Wagner, and Hugo Wolf, was a replica of that of the very first concert, given on 28 December 1905.

4. Berg and Webern had previously played Mahler's Third Symphony in a piano-duet arrangement.

5. The work had been performed under Hermann Scherchen in Leipzig earlier in the season (15 November 1921).

6. Letter Paul A. Pisk to the author.

7. Quoted from J. A. Stargardt Auction Catalogue No. 574 (November 1965), p. 151.

8. There exists a letter of thanks, dated 27 January 1923, addressed by Webern to a Prague patron (the name is not given). Presumably he received a second contribution that winter.

9. The society was based on ideas first formulated by Rudolf Réti and Egon Wellesz. Edward J. Dent was elected its first president.

10. Memoirs of Rudolph Ganz. Typescript. WA. Among the Ganz memorabilia in the Moldenhauer Archives is his pocket score of Webern's Five Movements, Op. 5, which he used at that concert.

11. Francis Poulenc, who knew Webern from a visit to Vienna with Milhaud earlier that summer, presented him during the festival with a copy of his *Impromptus*, which he inscribed: "à Webern que j'admire comme Weber ce qui est à mon sens le plus joli compliment que je puisse lui faire. Bien amicalement, Francis Poulenc. Salzburg Août 1922" ("To Webern, whom I admire as much as Weber, which to my mind is the nicest compliment that I could pay him. In sincere friendship, Francis Poulenc, Salzburg, August 1922"). WA.

12. Schoenberg chose not to attend the festival, although his Second String Quartet was on the programme.

13. Unpublished letter. By kind permission of Mrs Boris Aronson.

14. As Webern announced to Jalowetz on 16 November 1922, his Six Pieces, Op. 6, were to be played in Bochum on the same day that the Passacaglia was performed in Prague.

15. *Arnold Schoenberg Letters*, p. 74.

16. The time has been confirmed by Josef Polnauer, who was present at the meeting.

17. Josef Polnauer, address at the unveiling of memorial plaques at Schoenberg's and Webern's Mödling homes, 6 December 1959. Typescript. WA.

18. Consisting of Gustav Havemann, Georg Kniestädt, Hans Mahlke, and Adolf Steiner.

19. A draft of Webern's own programme notes for the performance of the Schubert Mass was found among his papers. WA.

20. "Präludium" and "Reigen"; the concluding "Marsch" had to be omitted.

21. *Arnold Schoenberg Letters*, pp. 99–101.

22. There are in all sixteen such envelopes, commemorating the summer trips up to 1938. WA.

23. "Peps" was no doubt named after Richard Wagner's favourite dog. The diary account reads:

Tuesday, the 18th of March, 1924: Lost Peps. On Monday, January 29th, 1923, he came to us (through a school friend of Mali from Luxembourg). He fell ill the end of January 1924, became very weak. Got better again. But from then on appetite very poor. On March 2nd, worsening again. Sunday the 16th to the veterinarian. Hopeless disease diagnosed. Prescribed medicinal powder and bath salt (intestinal ulcers). Night from 17th to 18th very bad. Early on the 18th fetched veterinarian. Then brought Peps there, where he was delivered from misery at circa 10 in the morning. Two pictures of him: one with the children, one with Minna. We gratefully owe him many beautiful, happy hours. I also would like to write down that his boundless love and affection for Minna was so particularly beautiful. He followed her every step. And how he liked the children! How sweetly he played with Christerl. Farewell my dear Pepsi.

24. The sister of the composer and musicologist Hans Gál.

25. The event is recorded in Webern's diary, together with its locale, the Bürgerschule in the Stubenbastei.

26. About US $14 at the time.

27. The programme for this special occasion also included *Pierrot Lunaire*.

28. Webern's copy is extant, as are the official letters notifying him of the award of the music prize in 1924 and 1931. WA.

29. Webern means the Amar Quartet, in which Hindemith played the viola.

30. For Schoenberg and Webern it was a signal occasion to participate jointly in the prestigious event that united so many prominent musicians. A photograph taken during

the festival shows the two composers flanked by the conductors Otto Klemperer and Hermann Scherchen.

31. The menu of that supper, signed by Schoenberg, Berg, Webern, and other participants, is extant. WA.

32. *Arnold Schönberg zum fünfzigsten Geburtstage, 13. Sept. 1924*, p. 272.

Chapter XVI Opera 12–16—Unfinished projects—Arrangements (1914–1924)

1. Unpublished letter Berg to Webern, undated (August 1912).

2. *Das Buch der hängenden Gärten*, Op. 15.

3. The expressionist poet Georg Trakl (1887–1914) brought out his first volume of lyrics in 1913, shortly before his untimely death early in World War I. Now recognized as Austria's foremost elegist, Trakl reconciled his lamentations for the present by conjuring up the golden spirit of a pastoral past. The intensity of Trakl's verses, reflecting the poet's personal fate, could not but evoke a response in Webern, who was probably the first to set his poems to music.

4. The draft to this song, in condensed score, bears the date of 4 June 1917, but Webern undoubtedly meant this to read 4 July.

5. This was the same letter in which Webern, under the fresh impression of an ascent of the Hochschwab, explained to Berg that his passion for the mountains had metaphysical connotations (see Chapter XIV).

6. One leaf, containing the close of "Abendland II" and the beginning of "Abendland III," is missing.

7. In November 1938, Webern inscribed this voice-piano score as a farewell gift to Hugo Winter. Winter, having risen after more than 25 years of service with Universal Edition to the position of general manager, was deposed by the Nazi régime. He subsequently became vice-president of Associated Music Publishers, Inc., in New York. Quite possibly, Webern hoped that a printing of the piano-vocal score could be arranged for abroad—as was the case with his String Quartet, Op. 28—at a time when Universal Edition was subjected to cultural policies that classified his music as "degenerate art."

8. *Anton Webern Letters to Hildegard Jone and Josef Humplik*, ed. Josef Polnauer. All further quotations from Webern's communications to the Humpliks are from the same source. An Eng. tr. by Cornelius Cardew is published by Universal Edition, London.

9. Letter fragment, undated.

10. The sketches of that song hold special significance because they contain a chart of the twelve-tone row used, with its inversion, retrograde and retrograde inversion of the series (see Chapter XVIII).

11. One such copy was inscribed to Hildegard Jone on 25 June 1929. WA.

12. The jury consisted of Eric Delamarter, Carl Engel, Edward Burlingame Hill, Albert Stoessel, and Augustus Stephen Vogt.

13. A copy of the printed edition, given by Webern to Willi Reich, contains German translations of the texts in the composer's hand. WA.

14. When the composer Daniel Ruyneman organized a series of contemporary-music concerts to be given in Amsterdam during early 1930, his programme proposals to Webern included performances of the Five Canons, Op. 16, and the Two Songs, Op. 19. Webern rejected the plan, arguing that these works were too difficult to be undertaken without "many, many rehearsals" under his personal supervision and that the ground for the proper understanding of his music in the Netherlands would first need to be better prepared. To that end he recommended selections from his song cycles Opera 3, 4, and 12. (Paul Op de Coul, "Unveröffentlichte Briefe von Alban Berg und Anton Webern an Daniel Ruyneman.")

15. For details on these reductions, see Chapters V (Opus 1), VII (Opus 6), and XII (Opus 10).

16. The printed full score of *Die glückliche Hand*, which Schoenberg presented to Webern at Christmas of 1921, is extant. In a lengthy and whimsical inscription, Schoenberg, referring to the work's title, expressed the conviction that for men like Webern and himself happiness can find room on a single fingertip. WA.

Chapter XVII   Mounting success (1925–1928)

1. Walter Berry (not identical with the well-known baritone by that name) was soloist at the first performance.

2. The anecdote was related to the author by Doris Brehm-Diez.

3. Memoirs of Josef Hueber. Typescript. WA. Later quotations are from the same source.

4. Webern's letters to Adler are in the Guido Adler Collection at the University of Georgia, Athens, Georgia.

5. Memoirs of Kurt Manschinger. Typescript. WA. Later quotations are from the same source.

6. The professorship carried with it a voice in the academy's senate, where Schoenberg filled the chair left vacant since Busoni's death the year before.

7. After completing her training at the institute, she returned to her native city and, with the outbreak of the war in 1939, went into hiding. Surviving the horrors inflicted upon the inhabitants of the ghetto, she migrated in 1949 to New York, where she became a proof-reader at the Hebrew Braille Institute. A sensitive and highly intelligent woman, she personally communicated her recollections of Webern to the author in 1963.

8. Memoirs of K. H. Lehrigstein (real name Klapper). Typescript. WA.

9. At the second performance, the 200th Workmen's Symphony Concert was formally celebrated with addresses by the President of the Austrian Federal Republic and the Mayor of the City of Vienna. Before their speeches, Webern conducted *Fanfares* by Richard Strauss, for 24 brass instruments. Mahler's Eighth followed the official proceedings.

10. Maria Gerhart, Karl Ettl, Oskar Eisenberg, Sylvia Feller, Emilie Bittner, Max Klein, and Yella Schmeidl-Braun.

11. Letter to the author, 29 September 1972.

12. Composed in strict twelve-tone technique during 1923–24, the quintet was bound to have a provocative impact because of its still totally unfamiliar idiom.

13. Letter to the author, 4 August 1964.

14. Memoirs of Ruzena Herlinger. Manuscript. WA.

15. Reprinted in "Blätter aus Österreich," *Der Turm, Monatsschrift für Österreichische Kultur T/12* (Vienna 1945–46), pp. 390–391.

16. Berg's *Wozzeck*, an expressionist opera in atonal idiom, received its sensational world première on 14 December 1925. After no fewer than 137 rehearsals, it was staged under Erich Kleiber at the State Opera in Berlin. The controversy first surrounding it notwithstanding, the work constituted a momentous development in operatic history. It signified a break-through in bringing the atonal idiom to the stage and in subsequently making the music of the "New Vienna School" palatable to the widest international audience. Unable to attend the première for lack of funds, Webern had written to Berg on 6 December 1925 that he had recently looked through the score again and in the process had suffered such "emotional shocks" that he was concerned whether he would be able "to survive a performance." He admitted: "The older I grow, the greater my sensibility becomes. Often I cannot endure it at all."

17. The thoroughness of his preparation is evident from his conductor's score, which is covered with red, green, blue, and black pencil annotations. WA.

18. Schoenberg's monthly fee at that time was 150 marks for one weekly lesson and 250 marks for two. These terms were stipulated in a letter written from Beaulieu sur Mer on 10 February 1925 to the father of Julius Schloss (the latter subsequently became a Berg pupil). The letter is in the Schoenberg sector of the Moldenhauer Archives.

19. The score was used by Webern when he later conducted the work in London and bears his annotations in coloured pencil. WA.

20. The event was designated as "Republik-Feier," in commemoration of the tenth anniversary of the November 1918 revolution.

21. The letter is reprinted in *die Reihe* 2, p. 20.

Chapter XVIII   Twelve-tone method—Opera 17–21—Other works—Liszt
arrangement (1924–1928)

1. Otto Wagner (1841–1918) was at first much attacked for his progressive views. However, he later became widely influential and now is generally held to be a founder and leader of the modern movement in European architecture.

2. *Über die Klangfarbe* (1919), *Vom Wesen des Musikalischen* (1920), *Deutung des Melos* (1923), *Vom Melos zur Pauke* (1925), *Zwölftontechnik* (1926).

3. The letter is in the Hauer sector of the Moldenhauer Archives.

4. *Arnold Schoenberg Letters*, p. 104.

5. The particular sketches appear on the back of the draft of "Morgenlied," Op. 15, No. 2, composed on 22 July 1922.

6. The little piece, relegated to obscurity for over four decades, had its unlikely resurrection on the glamorous stage of Philharmonic Hall in New York City. The occasion was an Igor Stravinsky Festival, organized by the New York Philharmonic Society, for which the honoured composer himself chose the programme. In the particular concert, on 22 July 1966, the première of the *Kinderstück* was assigned, appropriately, to a nine-year-old pianist, Caren Glasser, a scholarship student at the Juilliard School of Music. The *New York Times* critic, Howard Klein, otherwise averse to the concert fare (Babbitt, Boulez, Carter, Foss, Stravinsky, and Varèse), singled out the *Kinderstück* as providing "the one moment of warmth." According to his review (*New York Times*, 23 July 1966), the youthful performer "pecked her way through the minute and forty seconds piano solo like an accomplished little musician." Receiving an ovation, she delighted the audience and at the same time complimented Stravinsky, present in the hall, by playing a short arrangement of the trumpet tune from *Petrouchka*. The critic's comment on the two Webern works played in that programme—the other was the String Trio (1925), op. posth.—read: "It took longer to set up the stage for each of his pieces than to play them. But Webern, who is one of the century's real innovators, holds up well within this delicate pointillism because of his compressed time span. In the short time he allots to the complete development of his materials, one never doubts the inevitability of what is coming. And when Webern ends, there is no doubting that, either." Soon afterwards, in 1967, publication of the *Kinderstück* (by Carl Fischer, Inc., New York) opened up to young performers for the first time the possibility of active participation in Webern's world of music.

7. The missing portion was realized in an edition by Wallace McKenzie.

8. These five sketchbooks are in the Webern Archive. The first sketchbook, formerly with Universal Edition, Vienna, is now in the Robert Owen Lehman Collection at the Pierpont Morgan Library in New York. This collection also contains most of Webern's works in fair copies, as he wrote them out for publication by Universal Edition.

9. Along with such members of the Austrian circle as Schoenberg, Berg, Krenek, and Zemlinsky, the international fraternity of creative musicians was represented. Composers included Casella, Janáček, Kodály, Malipiero, Milhaud, Respighi, and Szymanowski, among others. The presentation album was subsequently dismembered.

Some manuscripts, including those by Webern, Berg, and Schoenberg, were individually sold. The remaining bulk of 49 specimens was auctioned off by J. A. Stargardt, Marburg, on 23–24 May 1967.

10. *Anton von Webern: Sketches (1926–1945)*. Commentary by Ernst Krenek. Foreword by Hans Moldenhauer (1968). This volume reproduces, in facsimile, materials from Sketchbooks II, III, and VI that had been formerly unknown: projects never completed (such as "Auf Bergen, in der reinsten Höhe"), abandoned movements originally intended to enlarge known compositions, and initial concepts eventually evolving into works different from those first envisioned. The book, bound in a linen cover to simulate the appearance of the original sketchbooks, contains 47 plates.

11. An ink score of the two finished movements, in which Webern still made many alterations, was presented by the composer to David Josef Bach in 1939 and is now in a private collection in Basel, Switzerland.

12. A facsimile reproduction is contained in *Anton von Webern: Sketches (1926–1945)*, plates 4–8.

13. *The Path to the New Music*, p. 55.

14. Dr Hermann Springer, an ISCM official and chairman of the Association of German Music Critics.

15. It is reproduced in *Anton von Webern: Sketches (1926–1945)*, plates 9–11.

16. Smallens, a native of St Petersburg, was at that time assistant conductor of the Philadelphia Orchestra, which, under Stokowski, had already introduced Webern's Passacaglia to American audiences. The day after the première of Webern's Opus 21, the critic of the *New York Times*, Olin Downes, stated: "The Symphony is one of those whispering, clucking, picking little pieces which Webern composes when he whittles away at small and futile ideas, until he has achieved the perfect fruition of futility and written precisely nothing. 'The Ultimate Significance of Nothing'—this would be the proper title of this piece. The audience laughed it out of court, and this laughter could not be restrained, as Webern's little orchestra suggested nothing so much as a cat, that, arching its back, glared and bristled its fur, and moaned or growled or spat." Downes did not moderate his negative assessment of Webern's music in later years. After a performance of the String Quartet, Op. 28, he wrote on 22 May 1941, in the *New York Times* that the work was "Dead Sea fruit, and Dead End music . . . The windows were closed, because, as it was remarked, the delicate music of Webern could not be heard if they remained open. Not for this music the fresh air or the crude turbulences of the world. For it is the ultimate of orderly and deliberate disintegration . . . Is it any wonder that the culture from which it emanates is even now going up in flames?"

17. *The Path to the New Music*, p. 53.

18. *Ibid.*, p. 52.

19. *Ibid.*, p. 56.

20. Webern to Berg, 5 June 1929.

21. The history of the work and the source on which Webern based his transcription are obscure. The Vienna Stadtbibliothek houses a ten-page manuscript in Liszt's hand, in which only the first stanza is completely composed; thereafter the music is only scantily sketched. In an extensive preface to the 1954 publication of the work by Zeneműkiadó Vállalat, Budapest, Dénes Bartha wrote that no known printed copy of Liszt's original composition exists. Outside of the Vienna manuscript, the only other verifiable source material is kept in the Liszt Museum at Weimar. It consists of the proofsheets which bear Liszt's autograph corrections. Title and date are missing, but Liszt wrote to his publisher a note accompanying the proofs: "Since the circumstances of our time furnish a totally abnormal commentary to the problem of the working classes, it could appear more suitable to postpone the publication of this *Arbeiterchor*. Concerning this, I leave the decision to you." The note explains the possibility that the work was not released at that time. The Liszt biographer Peter Raabe has placed its origin before 1848. No doubt Liszt was inspired by the excitement of those politically

turbulent times, which saw a great rise in the social consciousness of the working classes. The author of the poem is unknown; Bartha advances the assumption that the poet was one of Liszt's acquaintances in Weimar.

22. The Singverein performed the *Arbeiterchor* a few times under Webern, but after the group was dissolved in 1934 the orchestra parts were lost. Possibly they were used for a performance that Dénes Bartha records to have taken place in Budapest on 11 December 1932 on the occasion of a "Jubiläumskonzert" given by the Hungarian Workmen's Chorus. The holograph of Webern's full score, located by this writer only in 1968, is still unpublished. Besides this score, there exists a lithograph copy of the piano-vocal reduction, with Webern's pencil annotations, as well as a set of the vocal parts. WA.

Chapter XIX   International acclaim—Hildegard Jone (1929)

1. Characteristically, Webern would prepare his programmes for such informal presentations as fastidiously as if they were major professional appearances. Typical for this is the proposal he made to Josef Hueber in his letter of 7 December 1927:

Would you have the time and inclination to perform *with me* a few songs at the Christmas party of the Alpine Club in Mödling? If yes, I suggest three or four songs—to be exact, by Wolf and Schubert. Of Wolf I would like to do the "Christblume I" (from the *Mörike Lieder*). This one should suit you excellently. It is rather long. Then perhaps another Wolf and a Schubert, or only Wolf. It would make me *very happy* to do this "Christblume" with you. The occasion is very nice and fitting. The song is perhaps the most beautiful that Wolf has written. Only we would have to be able to rehearse properly.

2. This is borne out by the numerous annotations Webern made in his study scores, of which several are extant. These include the Wolf and Mozart works performed in the 22 October radio concert. WA.

3. Published later as *Drei Volksliedsätze*.

4. Omitted was *Es gingen zwei Gespielen Gut*, a fifteenth-century tune. Fair copies of all three choruses in Webern's autograph are extant. WA. Those performed bear his markings of phrasing and dynamic shading.

5. Hanns Eisler (1898–1962), a pupil of Schoenberg, identified himself all his life with left-wing political causes. Even after he migrated in 1933 to the United States, where he functioned as musical assistant to Charlie Chaplin from 1942 to 1947, Eisler's radical views caused him eventually to submit to the terms of "voluntary deportation." Thereafter he lived in Vienna and from 1950 on in East Berlin. Several of his choruses for workers and the Red Army have become popular in Russia.

6. Reproduced in facsimile in *Tagebuch*, Vienna, 1957.

7. Theodor Wiesengrund-Adorno (1903–1969) studied with Bernhard Sekles in Frankfurt and with Alban Berg in Vienna, then worked in his native Frankfurt as music critic and as instructor at the university. After spending the years 1934–1950 in the United States, he returned to Frankfurt University, where he became professor of philosophy. From his American years on, he used the name of Theodor W. Adorno.

8. Dr Seligmann was an excellent amateur violinist and ardent chamber-music fan. One of his four sons was a Schoenberg pupil and subsequently became a conductor. Under the pressure of the Nazi régime, the family later migrated to the United States.

9. The story confirms the deep-seated sense of pride that prevented Webern from stooping to anyone except his idol Arnold Schoenberg. Julius Schloss, for years the pupil and assistant of Alban Berg, took part in another episode that illustrates the point:

After a concert, Berg suddenly asked:"Where is Webern, anyway? We all want to go to the café. Run to the train station and bring him along." I ran to the station and saw Webern as he was just about to go downstairs. Out of breath, I gasped, "Herr Doktor, Berg sent me and said that I am to bring you along to the café." Whereupon Webern said icily: "Nobody brings me along!", turned around, and descended the stairs to the railway. (Communication Schloss to the author.)

10. Edward Clark (1888–1962), a pupil of Schoenberg whom Webern had known since the early days in Berlin, had risen to an executive position in the British Broadcasting Corporation. It was he who had contacted Webern and arranged for his trip to the English capital.

11. On the same day, the world première of Webern's Symphony, Op. 21, took place in New York.

12. Hagen was the owner of an inn where the artists used to meet socially; hence the name "Hagenbund."

13. In 1945, at the end of World War II, Hermine von Webern, the composer's daughter-in-law, salvaged this bust, as well as that of Mahler, from the débris left at Webern's apartment and stored it in the attic of her childhood home in Perchtoldsdorf. Only in 1965 was it relocated by this writer. The bust (like that of Mahler) is now in the Webern Archive. A picture of it appears on the cover of the London periodical *Musical Times* of February 1968, in connection with a story describing the important manuscript discoveries resulting from the search for the bust.

14. The bronze head of Webern found its permanent place in the Historisches Museum der Stadt Wien, where it stands beside the bust of Gustav Mahler by Auguste Rodin and that of Hugo Wolf by Franz Seifert. The original terracotta was kept by the sculptor's widow, Hildegard Jone, in her Purkersdorf home until a few months before her death, when she transferred it to this writer, together with a number of other art works. They include her large oil painting "Webern in der Haustüre stehend, wenige Augenblicke vor seinem gewaltsamen Ende" (*Webern standing in the doorway of the house, a few moments before his violent end*) (1945), oil portraits of Schoenberg and Berg, and drawings of Webern, Schoenberg, Berg, her husband, and herself, Humplik's prize-winning model of the Schoenberg medal (bestowed by the Schoenberg Kuratorium on outstanding musicians), and his portrait bust of his wife. The latter, a masterpiece of sculpture, cast in bronze, is mounted on a fragment from an ancient Greek stone column. In severe classical style, the likeness captures the grace, beauty, and serenity of its subject.

15. Humplik was born in Vienna on 17 August 1888 and died there on 5 April 1958. Among the galleries permanently housing his sculptures are the Österreichische Staatsgalerie, the Belvedere, and the Historisches Museum der Stadt Wien. In the last-named stands "The Runner," Humplik's prize-winning entry for the Kunst-Olympiade of 1936 at Berlin. The Austrian government, after bestowing several state prizes upon the artist, honoured him with the title of professor in 1937.

16. She was born on 1 June 1891 in the Serbian city of Sarajevo (the town that became known for the events precipitating the First World War) and died in Purkersdorf on 28 August 1963.

17. Miscellaneous poems appeared in various journals. The slender volume *Selige Augen* (1938) was published in the series *Zeugen des Wortes*. A larger collection of her poems appeared in 1948 under the title *Anima, Gedichte des Gottesjahres*. Her vast literary estate, all in manuscripts distinguished for their graceful calligraphy, is preserved in the Moldenhauer Archives, where it forms a fitting adjunct to the Webern Archive. The archives also house her numerous memorabilia of Webern. These include manuscripts and published compositions with the composer's personal dedications; fair copies in Webern's hand of all Hildegard Jone poems that he set to music; her manuscript of "Passages that Anton Webern copied from Goethe's *Farbenlehre*"; "Vertonte Verse," her

own selection of excerpts from Webern's letters, made preliminary to Polnauer's edition; her personal copy of the published correspondence (into which she glued an unpublished letter, dated 7 July 1927, in which Webern thanks her for the gift of a painting); and a folder of newspaper articles pertaining to Webern.

18. After Ebner's death in 1931, Hildegard Jone took it upon herself to prepare his literary legacy for publication, a task completed after her death by her friend Dr Franz Seyr.

19. *Anton Webern Briefe an Hildegard Jone und Josef Humplik*, ed. Josef Polnauer; English edition, *Anton Webern Letters to Hildegard Jone and Josef Humplik*, tr. Cornelius Cardew.

20. When Webern presented her, in summer 1927, with the printed score of his Six Bagatelles, Op. 9, he inscribed it: "Dear, esteemed Frau Jone, I do not know at all whether you can read music, but if not: perhaps the 'image' which *these* notes form, in conjunction with Schoenberg's words that preface them, reveals to you something of what they contain. This would give me great joy. Yours devotedly, A. Webern." Two tiny notes were found in Hildegard Jone's copy of Webern's printed correspondence. On one he had written out for her a few rudiments of musical notation. On the other he had copied, in both Greek and Latin wording, the maxim "Harmonia est diversitas identitate compensata" ("Harmony is diversity with identity taken into account"), a variant of the principle for all artistic creation, "Unity through variety."

Chapter XX   Work and family (1930)

1. It is interesting to note that three months later Schoenberg, at Franz Schreker's suggestion, contacted Alban Berg about a position teaching composition and subsidiary subjects at the Hochschule. The position did not materialize, and nothing is known of a similar initiative on Webern's behalf.

2. Webern's pleasure was increased by the presence of Hildegard Jone, who made the occasion more memorable by surprising him with a gift of her oil painting "Winter." At a later concert, on 14 December of the same year, she presented him with the painting's counterpart, "Spring."

3. Here Webern lists August 1906 (Simony Hut), August 1915 (Gutenberg House), June 1925 (Ademek Hut).

4. According to a story told by Polnauer, it was on the Anninger that Schoenberg conceived his *Gurrelieder*, when, after a night of conviviality, he went there with his friends in the small hours of the new day.

5. Placing his emphasis on pure form and suitable materials, Adolf Loos (1870–1933) conducted vigorous polemics against superfluous ornamentation. He strongly influenced the development of the functional style, in which his pioneering ideas were realized. Frank Lloyd Wright credited him with doing for European architecture what he himself was accomplishing in the United States. A well-known example of Loos' style is the office building on the Michaelerplatz in the heart of Vienna, erected in 1910 and for a long time the topic of violent controversy among the staid citizenry. Two volumes of Loos' essays, entitled *Ins Leere gesprochen* (1921) and *Trotzdem* (1931), form a compendium of his thought. Webern's veneration for Loos was such that he preserved to the end of his life a small piece of paper on which the architect had written his name. The relic bears Webern's note of identification. WA.

6. *Adolf Loos Festschrift* (Vienna: Verlag Richard Lányi, 1930).

7. The celebration was in honour of Karl Renner (1870–1950), the Socialist statesman who, after the Revolution of 1918, was head of the provisional government and then became the first chancellor of the Austrian Republic. In December 1945 Renner was to be elected president after Austria's liberation from Nazi rule.

8. The scores of these two songs, with Webern's conductor's markings, are in the WA.

9. The production was staged by the visiting Aachen opera troupe under the auspices of the Wagnervereeniging, a Dutch society noted not only for performances of Wagnerian music dramas but also for those of important operatic works from all periods. Sanders, who had attended the Aachen performance of *Wozzeck*, was instrumental in bringing the work to Amsterdam. He and another Dutch composer, Willem Pijper, saw the opera again in Vienna when it was done under Clemens Krauss on the occasion of the tenth ISCM festival during June 1932. Sanders later related:

> Willem Pijper and I were invited by Alban Berg to sit in his loge during the performance of *Wozzeck*, that von Webern also attended. Both of them took us afterwards to a *Heuriger*. Our talks there led to my suggestion for a Webern concert in Amsterdam, which resulted in a formal invitation only one and a half years later. I invited von Webern to conduct a concert of the Concertgebouw Orchestra under our auspices, planned for June 1934, to be combined, if possible, with a radio concert. Alas, the political situation killed these intentions.

(Letter to the author, dated 18–19 January 1977.)

10. On the cover appeared a listing of *New Music*'s "Honorary Board of Endorsers." It included the names of the Austrians Berg, Krenek, Webern, and Wellesz, but that of Schoenberg was conspicuously absent. On the international roster of luminaries appear such names as Bartók, Bloch, Casella, de Falla, Kodály, Malipiero, Milhaud, Poulenc, and Roussel. The pioneering American composers of the day were in evidence with John Becker, Aaron Copland, Charles Ives, Carl Ruggles, and Edgar Varèse, among others. In growing self-reliance, the American contingent had founded, in 1926, the Pan American Association of Composers. This group, like the League of Composers, vigorously promoted contemporary music on a truly international scale. *New Music*, founded and edited by Henry Cowell, also served that end. In the Moldenhauer Archives is an undated letter by Charles Ives to Adolph Weiss suggesting Schoenberg, Berg, and Webern as "Honorary European-Americans" for the honorary board of directors of the Pan American Society.

11. The first page of Webern's letter is reproduced in facsimile in *Anton von Webern: Perspectives*, comp. Hans Moldenhauer, ed. Demar Irvine, p. 37. All of Webern's letters to Weiss are extant. WA. The complete musical estate of Adolph Weiss, including his correspondence, is in the Moldenhauer Archives.

12. Amalie did enter into premedical courses, but a chronic kidney ailment soon disrupted her university career. The information on Webern's family life was derived largely from her and Maria's communications.

Chapter XXI   Honour and notoriety (1931)

1. Memoirs of Hans Humpelstetter. Typescript. WA. Further quotations are from the same source.

2. Completed by Schoenberg on 14 February 1930, the *Begleitungsmusik zu einer Lichtspielszene (Music to accompany a Cinema Scene)* had been premièred the same year in Berlin under Otto Klemperer. The piece portrays cinematic emotions, as programmed in the subtitles: "Drohende Gefahr" (Menacing Danger), "Angst" (Fear), and "Katastrophe" (Catastrophe).

3. A tune dating back to the Peasants' War in the sixteenth century.

4. A copy of this recording was located in the 1960s on a bargain counter in a Vienna record shop by the son of Rudolf Schopf, a former Singverein member. WA.

5. Webern confirmed these facts in his letters to David Josef Bach, dated 26 January 1929 and 18 June 1929. WA.

6. In a letter to Webern on 12 September, Schoenberg had written about the "Dance round the Golden Calf," outlining his ideas about staging in general and the rôle of the dance in particular. Calling the stage directors "those new despots of the theatrical art," he said of the dance that "its 'beauty' is odious to me in its petrified mechanics." Therefore he resolved to replace "the traditional ballet caperings" with specific choreographic directions opening up "another domain of expression." *Arnold Schoenberg Letters*, pp. 152–153.

7. In its column "In Berlin traf ein" (Arrived in Berlin), reserved for celebrities, the *Berliner Tageblatt* of 11 December took notice of the visitor with a portrait drawing and a biographical sketch. Webern preserved the clipping among his papers. WA.

Chapter XXII   Hietzing—Maria Enzersdorf—Lectures—Concerts—Illness (1932)

1. *Arnold Schoenberg Letters*, p. 151.

2. *Ibid.*, pp. 146–147.

3. Dr Rudolf Ploderer, an attorney and one of Webern's close friends, took down the lectures in shorthand. The original plan to publish them in instalments in *23*, a music periodical owned and edited by Willi Reich, did not materialize. Reich emigrated to Switzerland with the arrival of the Hitler régime in Austria. Only long after World War II and Webern's death did he locate Dr Ploderer's stenogram among his old papers. At his initiative, Universal Edition published the lectures in 1960 (*Der Weg zur neuen Musik*; translated by Leo Black into English as *The Path to the New Music*, 1963). In a "Postscript," Reich provides some reminiscences from his private lessons under Webern, as well as excerpts from the letters Webern wrote to him between 1938 and 1944. Letters in WA.

4. *Arnold Schoenberg Letters*, p. 156.

5. Held on 6 June 1931 in the Salle Gaveau and conducted by Nicolas Slonimsky, the concert included works by Cowell, Ives, Roldan, Ruggles, and Weiss.

6. Excerpts from Webern's letters to Gerhard (WA) were published in *The Score* 24, November 1958, pp. 36–41. Roberto Gerhard (1896–1970), though of Swiss parentage and nationality, was prominently identified with Catalan music. A student of Pedrell and Schoenberg, he became a noted composer and scholar. In 1936 he emigrated to England as a result of the Spanish Civil War and settled in Cambridge, where he was made an Honorary Fellow at the university.

7. On 27 December 1931 after his return from the Berlin ISCM jury meeting, Webern had written to Gerhard: "I believe it was a good thing that the choice fell on this particular work of yours, because it will have a general appeal. . . . Personally I like all the works you sent me very much and I was determined to fight for them. But these songs are particularly lovely. And since the other members of the jury thought so, too, it seemed best to agree with full speed on *that work*."

8. The programme is reproduced in *die Reihe 2*, plate 8.

9. *Arnold Schoenberg Letters*, p. 166.

10. *Ibid.*, pp. 165–166.

11. Professor Singer had been advised by Ruzena Herlinger that Webern was short of money and too proud to have her pay the expenses. "Vienna always had doctors who were *doctors first*," Mme Herlinger relates in her memoirs. "A few months later, when Webern and I met accidentally in the Alps, he told me what a wonderful doctor Professor Singer was and how he never took a penny from him."

12. Hans Rosbaud (1895–1962), a native of Graz, Austria, studied at the Hoch Conservatory in Frankfurt. From 1923 to 1930 he was director of the Municipal School of Music in Mainz. His conducting career led him to positions in Frankfurt, Münster, Strasbourg, Munich, and Baden-Baden, where in 1948 he became music director of

Südwestfunk. He also conducted the Tonhalle Orchestra in Zürich and there directed the first stage performance of Schoenberg's *Moses und Aron* in 1957, having given the first concert presentation in 1954 in Hamburg. He was prominent in the development of the Aix-en-Provence Music Festival. Among his many guest appearances were regular engagements with the Chicago Symphony and the New York Philharmonic. He excelled in the presentation of Mozart operas no less than in that of contemporary music, introducing new works, from Hindemith and Stravinsky to Boulez and Penderecki. Rosbaud's entire musical estate is in the Moldenhauer Archives.

13. The house and its surroundings have remained virtually unchanged. Across the street stands the stately villa once occupied by Anton Wildgans, the noted Austrian poet. The lovely forest still borders the street and the picturesque Castle Liechtenstein dominates the pastoral landscape as it has for centuries. On 15 March 1972 a stone plaque was unveiled at the house during the Fifth International Webern Festival. Donated by the International Webern Society, it commemorates Webern's residence from 1932 to 1945. During the same festival, a plaque was affixed to the house in which Webern was born, Löwengasse 53a in Vienna.

14. Using Schiller's lament as his text, Brahms composed the work in 1880 as an offering of consolation to the mother of his friend, the painter Anselm Feuerbach, who had died shortly before.

15. The essay was first presented on 21 April 1932 as a radio lecture over Südwestfunk, Baden-Baden.

Chapter XXIII   Schoenberg's emigration—Webern's 50th birthday (1933)

1. On 28 January, after a long political struggle, Germany's president, the aged Field Marshal Paul von Hindenburg, summoned Adolf Hitler to form a new cabinet. Confident of an electoral victory, Hitler dissolved the Reichstag (Germany's parliamentary body) and set new elections for 5 March. On 27 February the Reichstag building burned down. Hitler immediately accused the Communists of having set the fire, and a wave of anti-Communist hysteria swept the country, which for weeks had been terrorized by brown-shirted Nazi storm troopers. As a result of Hitler's manoeuvres, the Communist Party was outlawed, and the National Socialists gained a parliamentary majority. On 23 March the Reichstag passed a law enabling Hitler to assume dictatorial powers. Germany's new overlord promised that the Third Reich, successor to the Holy Roman and Hohenzollern empires, would endure for 1,000 years. In a single-slate election in November of 1933, Hitler consolidated his absolute powers and, in 1934, after von Hindenburg's death, an 88 per cent majority of the German people voted in favour of the fusion of the presidency and the chancellorship in the person of the Führer of the National Socialist Party.

2. Such cultural chauvinism did not remain limited to Germany. On 31 December of the same year, an anti-jazz parade was held at Mohall, Ireland, with banners proclaiming "Down with jazz and paganism," and Sean MacEntee, Finance Minister, was denounced for his tolerance of jazz bands in the State Broadcasting System.

3. Toscanini had already been the central figure of an incident in Fascist Italy. On 14 May 1931 a political zealot had struck him for refusing to lead the orchestra in the Fascist hymn, "Giovinezza," at the beginning of a concert in Bologna. Four days later, the syndicate of artists and musicians of Bologna adopted a resolution condemning Toscanini's stand as "absurd and unpatriotic."

4. The presidency of Richard Strauss was to last only until 13 July 1935. Then 71, Strauss resigned, giving old age as his reason, but rumours ascribed his withdrawal to pressures resulting from his collaboration with Stefan Zweig, the Jewish librettist of his most recent opera, *Die schweigsame Frau*, premièred in Dresden on 24 June 1935.

5. *Arnold Schoenberg Letters*, p. 171.

6. Later published in Schoenberg, *Style and Idea*.

7. *The Path to the New Music*, pp. 19–20.

8. Alban Berg, to whom Webern showed the letter, copied it for himself, and from that source Willi Reich published an excerpt in his biography *Arnold Schönberg*, pp. 242–244. Quotations from Schoenberg's letters to Webern in this and following chapters were based on a transcript which Josef Hueber had made of the original letters, at the time in the possession of his sister, Mrs Bertha Riemerschmid. The letters have since been published by Ernst Hilmar under the title "Arnold Schönberg an Anton Webern: Eine Auswahl unbekannter Briefe" in *Arnold Schönberg Gedenkausstellung 1974* (Vienna: Universal Edition, 1974), pp. 44–67.

9. *Arnold Schoenberg Letters*, p. 184.

10. A photograph showing Webern rehearsing the Wiener Symphoniker for that concert is reproduced in *die Reihe 2*, Plate 7. Another snapshot taken at the occasion is to be found in the insert.

11. Later on, the remains of Adolf Loos were moved to an *Ehrengrab* (a grave provided by the municipality in honour of the departed) next to that of Karl Kraus in Vienna's Zentralfriedhof.

12. Gordon Claycombe described to the author the last evening of Ploderer's life. As so often before, Claycombe and Ploderer sat in the Café Museum until long after midnight. Their conversation dwelt first on Schoenberg's emigration and the gloomy future, then reached out to Plato and finally to Aristotle's *Nicomachean Ethics*. But there was no hint of impending doom. A few hours later, Ploderer made his quiet exit from the troubled world.

13. The text was printed and distributed by the local ISCM group in 1934. Both Bach's address and Jalowetz' article in *Anbruch* have been reprinted in the English edition of Friedrich Wildgans' *Anton Webern*, pp. 176–180 and pp. 171–172.

14. A postcard signed by Webern, Krenek, Reich, Steuermann, and Apostel was sent from the party to Julius Schloss by Hans Erich Apostel. WA.

15. Alma Mahler's letter and the inscribed photograph of Franz Schreker were found among Webern's papers. WA.

16. Hildegard Jone's and Josef Humplik's contributions to *23* have been reprinted in *Anton Webern Letters to Hildegard Jone and Josef Humplik*, pp. 67–68.

17. Both the Webern drawing and an oil portrait of Berg were in the artist's estate at the time of his death in 1965 in Zürich. The year before, Rederer made a woodcut of Webern's head. WA.

18. The galley proofs contain Berg's copious annotations. WA.

19. Webern's reply to Berg is not extant, but some weeks later, on 28 January 1934, Berg refers to a suggestion apparently made by Webern. It concerned a performance of the "Lied der Lulu" as a separate concert number in advance of the opera's completion. Berg's response to that idea was: "As soon as I have finished the entire opera, there will again be the possibility of performing excerpts from it, to include, besides *your* aria, a smaller or larger number of others, plus four interludes. To me, this would appear much more appropriate."

20. The letter, dated Christmas 1934, was presented to the author by Helene Berg on the occasion of the First International Webern Festival.

21. In 1933 Krenek completed the score of his grand opera *Karl V*, in which he first applied the twelve-tone technique. The young composer of the frivolous international success *Jonny spielt auf* had thereby joined the fraternity of dodecaphonists.

Chapter XXIV   Turn of fortunes (1934)

1. While a performance never materialized, the Singverein rehearsed this work as late as 1 February 1934, according to a diary note of Roland Leich, one of Webern's pupils.

2. Webern, as president of the Vienna section of the ISCM, officially accepted Pisk's resignation. The letter of acknowledgement, dated 5 May 1934, is reproduced in facsimile in Hans Moldenhauer, "Paul Amadeus Pisk and the Viennese Triumvirate" in *Paul A. Pisk, Essays in His Honour*, p. 216.

3. H. H. Stuckenschmidt, *Schönberg*, p. 386.

4. *Arnold Schoenberg Letters*, p. 195.

5. Webern's letter to Mrs Emil Hertzka of 12 July 1934, in which he enlists her collaboration in the project, is reproduced in facsimile in Hans Moldenhauer, *The Death of Anton Webern*, plate 4.

6. Webern's letters to Otto Jokl (1891–1963) were found among that composer's voluminous correspondence, which also included numerous letters by Berg. Jokl's entire creative legacy (compositions, plays, poems, and paintings) is in the Moldenhauer Archives.

7. Later Mrs E. Beller of Princeton, New Jersey.

8. The full texts of this and the following letter to Mrs Hertzka are contained in Hans Moldenhauer, *The Death of Anton Webern*, pp. 27–30.

9. Schoenberg's birthday tribute to Bach was a three-voiced canon on one of his own poems. He composed it after Webern made known to him, as well as to Berg, that Bach was very eager to have a work dedicated to him.

10. Comprising 99 pages, the notebook contains many musical examples. WA.

Chapter XXV   Opera 22–25—Schubert and Bach transcriptions (1928–1935)

1. In his commentary to *Anton von Webern: Sketches (1926–1945)*, Ernst Krenek analyses (on page 4) the string quartet fragment as follows:

> The first line (seven bars, obviously for violin) shows Webern's predilection for reversible models: from bar 4 on, the melody retraces its steps. Since the twelve-tone row that he ultimately employs appears in all four basic forms only three and four lines later, one might assume that he at first conceived a melodic line as a basic idea and then derived and fashioned from it a formal tone-row. Of course at that time his thinking was already so dodecaphonically conditioned that his spontaneous ideas were very nearly twelve-tone patterns. . . . They [the sketches] are mainly interesting because of the persistent sub-division of the series into three and two-tone patterns, such as became a characteristic feature of his later works, and because of the tendency to squeeze the contrapuntal strands into a very narrow band of pitches.

2. During September 1927, Webern had been introduced to Mrs Coolidge, under whose auspices two chamber music concerts were given in Vienna. On 13 June 1930, after Adolph Weiss had suggested that Webern might gain her financial support by offering a work to her, the composer responded: "It indeed would be a joy for me to dedicate to Mrs Coolidge my Quartet for violin, clarinet, saxophone, and piano!!! Naturally I will wait for further news about this before I hand the work over to the publishers (U.E.)! To be sure, I am not finished with it yet." In the meantime, however, Weiss had already received a negative reply from Mrs Coolidge, who wrote to him on 31 May:

> I regret that I am not able to respond as you would like to your recent letter on behalf of Mr von Webern. It is not that I do not appreciate his talent nor that I have anything but a feeling of friendship for him whom I met so pleasantly when I was in Vienna nearly three years ago, but I have in mind at present nothing further in the way of commissions. . . . Mr von Webern is so well known everywhere that it seems to me he should certainly be able to find the right patrons and the right audiences for his music.

However, I shall hope that he will find someone nearer home who can assist him in the way you indicate and I hope that neither you nor he will interpret this letter as unfriendly or unappreciative to him.

(In 1938, Mrs Coolidge was to honour Webern by commissioning his String Quartet, Op. 28, which is dedicated to her.) In early October of 1930, Webern offered his Quartet, Op. 22, to Henry Cowell. Undoubtedly the $100 honorarium received for the print of "Liebste Jungfrau" in *New Music* encouraged him to hope that his Quartet might also be accepted. However, in November he told Weiss that he had received only a "vague answer," and subsequently he gave the work to Universal Edition.

   3. *The Path to the New Music*, p. 57.

   4. When Webern presented Hildegard Jone with the published score, he wrote underneath the printed dedication: "What belongs to you, as well as to me, dear Hildegard, herewith receive, together with Humplik, from your Webern, May 1936." On the lower margin of the page, the poetess added a distich, the epigrammatic form into which she cast her sentiments on virtually every special occasion: "Alle die Künste sind wahrlich Geschwister: Form, Klang, Vers und Farbwelt. Sucht sie zur Einheit im Sein!" ("All the arts are truly brothers and sisters: form, sound, verse, and colour cosmos. Seek them for unity in being!")

   5. The first phrase is from René Leibowitz, *Schoenberg et son école*, p. 223, the second from his *Introduction à la musique de douze sons*, p. 239.

   6. The text of the palindrome had been known since Biblical times. It poses an enigma as far as the name "Arepo" is concerned. Philological research has linked it with an Old Testament passage in which the prophet Ezekiel speaks of an angel who, commanded by God, gathers fiery coals ("Arripuit" in the Latin translation of the Hebrew text) to strew them over the sinful city. The early Christians, spreading their new faith only at the cost of mortal danger, used the palindrome as a means of making themselves known to each other, and also as a symbol of warning to their persecutors that God's judgement was impending. Besides this menacing connotation, an additional symbolism was attached to the word-square: the 24 letters of the palindrome surrounding the centre letter N can be so arranged that "Pater Noster," the first two words of the Lord's Prayer, appear once vertically and once horizontally, crossing each other at that centre N, denoting in this context "Nazarenus, King of the Jews." The remaining letters, two times A and O, have become the symbol of Christian faith, "Alpha" and "Omega," the beginning and the end. The letter T has the shape of the antique form of the cross. The first extant specimen of the palindrome stems from a house wall in Pompeii, the luxurious Roman city destroyed in AD 79 by an eruption of Vesuvius. The fragment can be viewed in the museum there.

   7. *Anton von Webern: Sketches (1926–1945)*, p. 5.

   8. *The Path to the New Music*, p. 56.

   9. *Anton von Webern: Sketches (1926–1945)*, plates 33 ff.

   10. Published later in Hildegard Jone, *Anima, Gedichte des Gottesjahres* (Vienna: Verlag Herder, 1948).

   11. Ernst Krenek describes the unexpected intermezzo as follows:

At face value, it is hard to believe that Webern actually wished to incorporate these ten bars of chorus into an otherwise purely instrumental composition. Or did he plan to go on setting the whole poem to music, using the twenty-five bars—fruit of assiduous labour—as an introduction to a cantata? The possibility should not be ruled out, for at the very end of all the sketches he did just that. [The reference is to Webern's last unfinished composition, also begun as a concerto and then converted into a cantata.] There is no doubt that the choral setting of page 71 was meant to continue the twenty-five bars of the Concerto that far worked out. Not only the context of measure numbers and *vi-de* symbols proves it, but also the fact that the choral voices employ the same tone-row as does the Concerto. However, only four days later, on 15 May 1934, he picks up another *vi*—from page 49 of the sketchbook, at measure 24, skips from measure 25 to 37, which is identical with measure 26 of the printed score—as if nothing had happened. . . . It is remarkable that the continuity of so intricate a design remained vividly enough in the composer's mind for him to be able to take it up after more than two years while at the same time he seemed to contemplate the possibility of overthrowing the basic idea of the whole work. *Anton von Webern: Sketches (1926–1945)*, p. 6.

12. *Storia della dodecafonia*, p. 125.

13. *Variation über neue Musik* (Munich: Nymphenburger Verlag 1959), p. 189.

14. *The Path to the New Music*, pp. 55–56.

15. In Hildegard Jone's personal copy (WA), she commemorated the receipt of the publication, on 21 April 1957, by writing on the inside cover a four-line poem, beginning "Vom Freund vertont 'Wie bin ich froh!'" ("Set to music by my friend 'How happy I am!'"). The verses celebrate spring as the eternal fountain of life, as the affirmation of man's rejuvenation within the perennial rebirth of nature. The poetess added the note: "The poem 'How happy I am!' gave Ferdinand Ebner joy just before his early death: for him 'everything became green once more.'" Ebner, the Austrian writer-philosopher, had esteemed Hildegard Jone's poetry. She cared for him during his final illness and, after his death on 17 October 1931, assumed guardianship of his literary estate, making arrangements for its later publication.

16. Letter fragment, undated.

17. *The Musical Offering* is a compendium of contrapuntal studies written by Bach in 1747. The composer had been invited that year by Frederick II, King of Prussia, to appear at the court in Potsdam. During his visit, the monarch, himself an accomplished composer and flutist, had given his guest one of his own themes for extemporization. After returning to Leipzig, Bach made that royal theme the vehicle for a rigorous contrapuntal discourse, comprising fugues, canons, and a trio sonata. His dedication to Frederick the Great was: "*R*egis *I*ussu *C*antio *E*t *R*eliqua *C*anonica *A*rte *R*esoluta" (By command of the king, the theme and other things developed in canonical art). Read acrostically, the inscription results in the word *Ricercar*, a term not only denoting the learned character of the entire study but also applying to the specific type of fugues included in it.

18. Memoirs of Arnold Elston. Typescript. WA.

19. Webern used his own manuscript for both performances. The score, in the archives of Universal Edition, bears his conductor's markings.

20. Published in *die Reihe 2*, p. 19.

21. When Scherchen conducted the Ricercar for the first time in Germany, in a concert of the 1954 Kranichsteiner Ferienkurse in Darmstadt, a violent controversy on the subject of Bach arrangements broke out. It was sparked by a shrill whistle from within the audience that disrupted the performance of Schoenberg's transcription of Bach's Organ Prelude and Fugue.

22. A facsimile reproduction of the first page of the letter is contained in *Anton von Webern: Perspectives*, p. 38.

23. Webern's Ricercar transcription fascinated Igor Stravinsky so much that he copied it out by hand. When the author visited the Stravinsky apartment in New York in 1972, Robert Craft showed him this manuscript and informed him that Stravinsky had also made a copy of the closing movement of Webern's Second Cantata (see Chapter XXXII, Note 18).

Chapter XXVI   Last conducting appearances in Vienna—Berg's death—Crisis at Barcelona (1935–1936)

1. Letter to the author.

2. "Mendelssohn's music is inadmissible in the Third Reich, where the unshatterable law of racial purity must be uncompromisingly maintained," Wilhelm Herzog had written in *Die Musik* (1 November 1934). This journal, Germany's most scholarly musical monthly, had been forced to become a mouthpiece for Nazi doctrine when it was converted, on 1 April 1934, into the official organ of the Reichsjugendführung. Its editor pledged to serve the ideals of Hitler's youth organization. To replace Mendelssohn's incidental music to *A Midsummer Night's Dream*, that old familiar standby of German theatres and concert halls, Rudolf Wagner-Régeny and Julius Weismann were commissioned to write new scores. These were introduced in June during the Reichstagung of the National Socialist Kulturgemeinde at Düsseldorf. Such radical excisions of salient parts of the German cultural heritage were not always possible in the pursuit of "racial purity." Heinrich Heine's poem "Die Lorelei," part and parcel of German tradition, was simply retained, but the name of its Jewish author was deleted and replaced with the attribution "Volkslied." Such absurdity and deceit became commonplace in carrying out the policies of the Third Reich.

3. Letter to the author.

4. At a time when the tidal wave of radical nationalism swept his native country, Karl Amadeus Hartmann (1905–1963) was one of the first to profess a pacifist creed and to engage in underground resistance against the Hitler régime. *Miserae*, conducted in its Prague première by Hermann Scherchen, bears this dedication: "To my friends who had to die a hundred times, who sleep for all eternity, we do not forget you (Dachau 1933–1934)." The inscription pledged allegiance to the hapless prisoners in the first of Nazi Germany's notorious concentration camps. The holograph score of *Miserae* is in the Moldenhauer Archives, as are other manuscripts by Hartmann, including his last work, the *Gesangsszene*, for baritone and orchestra, which is dedicated to the author.

5. Berg's *Lulu* Suite had been premièred on 30 November 1934 in a concert of the Berliner Staatskapelle in the opera house Unter den Linden. With this performance, conductor Erich Kleiber had courageously defied Germany's cultural dictators, who branded any Schoenberg follower as a "Judenknecht" and "Kulturbolschewik." Four days later, Kleiber was forced to resign his position as General Music Director of the State Opera. He emigrated to South America in open protest against the National Socialist régime. Although the *Lulu* Suite was promptly and officially denounced in Germany, the work quickly received performances in countries still free from Fascist domination. Berg, like Webern, increasingly experienced the bitter taste of discrimination. His symphonic fragments from *Wozzeck* had been scheduled for the Biennale in Venice, held during September of 1934, and he himself was a member of the festival committee. However, because of political intrigue, Berg's name was dropped both from the programme and the roster of directors. Only by the intervention of Italian colleagues like Alfredo Casella and Gian Francesco Malipiero was the Fascist-engineered decision reversed, and Berg was personally able to witness the successful performance of his concert aria *Der Wein* (replacing the *Wozzeck* fragments) in the Teatro Fenice on 11 September. It was the composer's last trip abroad.

6. Published as "Incontro con Anton Webern" in *Il Mondo* (Florence, 3 November 1945). Translated for this biography by Mario Castelnuovo-Tedesco.

7. In 1970 Helene Berg gave an account of her husband's last illness in a signed document which she entrusted to this author for later publication. It is a bitter denunciation of the medical profession.

8. Letter to the author.

9. This information and the report on his part in the Barcelona episode were communicated by Egon Wellesz in a letter to the author.

10. Letter to the author.

11. The recollections of Brunswick, as well as those of Krasner, were personally communicated to the author.

12. There exists a recording of this broadcast, of which Krasner has a copy.

13. Letter to the author.

Chapter XXVII   Webern as a conductor—Schoenberg in Los Angeles—Before the Anschluss (1936–1938)

1. Quoted from Gunther Schuller, "A Conversation with Steuermann," *Perspectives of New Music* 3 (Fall-Winter 1964), p. 28.

2. The observation was made during an evening's conversation with this author a few weeks before Steuermann's death in 1964.

3. Letter to the author.

4. Josef Polnauer, ed., *Anton Webern Letters to Hildegard Jone and Josef Humplik*, p. 72, n. 6/3.

5. Hans W. Heinsheimer, *Best Regards to Aida* (New York: Alfred A. Knopf, 1968), p. 15.

6. Letter to the author.

7. Letter to the author.

8. Letter to the author.

9. Ernst Krenek, "Anton von Webern: A Profile," *Anton von Webern: Perspectives*, p. 6.

10. Josef Polnauer, "In Gedenken an Anton Webern," *Mitteilungsblatt des Landes Wien des Österreichischen Arbeiter-Sängerbundes* 4 (1963), p. 1.

11. In 1975 Humpelstetter made a tape recording of his recollections, simulating Webern's dialect in direct quotations. WA.

12. Quoted by Linde Dietz in "Anton Webern als Leiter der Arbeiter-Symphoniekonzerte und des Arbeiter-Singvereins," *Almanach der Wiener Festwochen 1969* (Vienna: Verlag Jugend & Volk), pp. 105–108.

13. Conversation Brunswick with the author.

14. The reference pertains to Fritz Busch (1890–1951).

15. Memoirs of Arnold Elston. Typescript. WA. Later quotations are from the same source.

16. Frederick Deutsch-Dorian, "Webern als Lehrer," *Melos* 27 (April 1960), p. 102.

17. Conversation with the author. The conductor Fritz Mahler (1901–1973) was a distant relative of Gustav Mahler. He wrote the first published analysis of Berg's *Wozzeck*.

18. Letter to the author.

19. The scarf is extant, as are several other personal mementoes, such as Webern's glasses, the pocket knife he used for erasures, his cigarette case, a wallet made of crocodile leather, and the large travel bag he had inherited from his father. WA.

20. The Suite in G Major, Schoenberg's first purely tonal composition since his Second String Quartet (1907–08), was conceived primarily for the use of school orchestras. Such pragmatic considerations, also manifest in the Theme and Variations for Wind Band, Op. 43A, caused a stir at the time, since Schoenberg's return to tonality in these works was misinterpreted by some as a renunciation of his own progressive theories. The steady flow of large and important compositions in the twelve-tone idiom that followed provided ample refutation.

21. *Arnold Schoenberg Letters*, p. 198.

22. Webern's acquaintance with Klemperer dated back several years. He had first met him privately at the home of Mark Brunswick, where the conductor used to stay during his Vienna visits. From their first encounter there was little affinity between the very tall,

ebullient, and loquacious maestro and the slightly built, retiring, and soft-spoken composer. Brunswick recalled an episode when Klemperer suddenly fired the question at Webern: "What do you think of Puccini?" Webern quietly replied: "Nothing whatever!"

23. Letter to the author.

24. Peter Stadlen, "Serialism Reconsidered," *The Score* 22 (Feb. 1958), p. 12. Klemperer's own opinion of Webern's work was expressed in an interview published many years later:

> *Heyworth:* "What about Webern's music?"
> *Klemperer:* "I don't understand it. I know it, of course. I conducted his symphony in Berlin, as well as in Vienna. But I couldn't find my way into it. I found it terribly boring. So I asked Webern—I was staying in Vienna—to come and play it to me on the piano. Then perhaps I would understand it better. He came and played every note with enormous intensity and fanaticism."
> *Heyworth:* "Not coolly?"
> *Klemperer:* "No, passionately! When he had finished, I said, 'You know, I cannot conduct it in that way. I'm simply not able to bring that enormous intensity to your music. I must do as well as I can'. I did so, and it went quite well. I think that Webern was happy when anyone played his music at that time—that was about 1931. And I am sure that he was a very good musician. Stravinsky had the greatest admiration for him. He said something to the effect that for us Webern is an extract of genius. But I don't believe that. I think that Webern's music is perhaps a sign of the time of crisis in which it appeared. I also believe in his absolute integrity. But that I was very eager to conduct his music, that I can't say."

(Peter Heyworth, ed., *Conversations with Klemperer*, London, Victor Gollancz, 1973, p. 76.)

25. The programme also included compositions by Honegger and Weill, the première of Krenek's *Vier Bagatellen* for piano, four hands, played by the composer and Peter Stadlen, and Stravinsky's *L'Histoire du soldat*.

26. In a secret annex to the Austro-German treaty of 11 July 1936, Chancellor Schuschnigg had made far-reaching concessions to Hitler's followers in Austria. Since that time, Franz von Papen, the special German ambassador in Vienna, had bent all his efforts towards undermining Austria's independence, the country's fusion with Nazi Germany being the ultimate objective. Financed and motivated by their German chieftains, the Austrian Nazis became increasingly bold. Having already assassinated Schuschnigg's predecessor, Dollfuss, they plotted a like fate for the new leader. In their systematic campaign of terror, bombings occurred almost daily throughout the provinces.

27. A torchlight parade by thousands of students ended on a square opposite the university, where the books of all those considered subversive or striking at the roots of German thought and the German home became the fuel for a huge bonfire. Among the German authors were Thomas Mann, Stefan Zweig, Erich Maria Remarque, Lion Feuchtwanger, the scientist Albert Einstein, and such political writers as Walther Rathenau and Hugo Preuss (the latter had drafted the Weimar Constitution). Austrian authors included Sigmund Freud and Arthur Schnitzler. Those of other nationalities were Jack London, Upton Sinclair, H. G. Wells, André Gide, Emil Zola, and Marcel Proust.

28. Conversation with the author.

29. Letter to the author.

30. Conversation with the author.

31. Conversation with the author.

32. On 6 December 1934 Goebbels, indignantly referring to the bathtub aria in Hindemith's opera *Neues vom Tage*, had condemned the moral decay of "atonal

composers." Denounced as a "cultural Bolshevik," Hindemith, under fire almost from the start, was taken to task for his continued association with Jewish musicians. When the attacks grew menacing, Wilhelm Furtwängler rose to the composer's defence, writing on 25 November 1934 in the *Allgemeine Musikzeitung* that Germany could ill afford to reject a musician of Hindemith's powers. Almost immediately, Furtwängler himself was officially denounced, and on 4 December he resigned as conductor of the Berlin Philharmonic, Deputy President of the Reichsmusikkammer, and Director of the Berlin State Opera. This act of protest was embarrassing to the régime, and a personal meeting with Goebbels was arranged on 28 February 1935. During the confrontation Furtwängler expressed regret that his public defence of Hindemith's music had been interpreted politically. Under pressure he apologized for having encroached on a domain now controlled by the leadership of the Reich. On 25 April Furtwängler was reinstated. As to Hindemith, he accepted in 1935 an invitation of the Turkish government to organize that country's institutes of music study and research according to western models. In his official capacity he was able to bring several Jewish colleagues out of Germany. (The pianist Eduard Zuckmayer, who together with Maurits Frank had given the première of Webern's Cello Pieces, Op. 11, in 1924, rose to directorship of Ankara's Institute for Music Pedagogy.) After three prolonged stays in Turkey, during which he taught at the conservatory in Ankara, Hindemith made his first American appearance in April 1937 during the Coolidge Festival at the Library of Congress. He subsequently settled in the United States.

33. These included the works of Cézanne, Chagall, Gauguin, van Gogh, Matisse, and Picasso, among others. The German school of expressionists, with such representatives as Ernst, Grosz, Kirchner, Kokoschka, and Nolde, fared no better.

34. Before long, Hitler's cultural edicts were to become the law of the land in Austria also. An unofficial boycott of Jewish artists had already made itself felt. According to K. H. Lehrigstein, Webern's junior colleague on the teaching staff of the Israelitic Institute for the Blind, a 1937 recital by the pianist Artur Schnabel, world-renowned for his interpretation of Beethoven, was attended by no more than 50 persons, many of whom had been given free tickets.

35. In his postwar testimony, President Miklas denied that Schuschnigg had acted with his approval when he capitulated. Rising to great strength in the hour of decision, Miklas held firm, never resigning as president of the Republic and refusing to sign the document ratifying the annexation of his country.

Chapter XXVIII   Opera 26–28 (1935–1938)

1. The deepening friendship between Webern and the Humpliks had led shortly before to their use of the familiar address "Du" instead of the formal "Sie."

2. In March 1938 Zenk submitted his arrangement to Webern, who returned the manuscript with his alterations and an annotation lauding the "magnificent reduction." The composer sent a copy of the printed vocal score to Hildegard Jone, inscribing it ". . . 'und strömt als Freude sanft zurück' [and gently flows back as joy], to you, dear Hildegard and to Humplik from your Webern, May 1938."

3. The draft of the programme notes was found among Webern's papers. Although not in his handwriting, it no doubt reflected his ideas. WA.

4. Conversation with the author. The memoirs of Luigi Dallapiccola appearing in Note 11 of Chapter XXIX contain that composer's reaction to *Das Augenlicht* following its première in 1938.

5. Peter Stadlen, "Serialism Reconsidered," p. 12.

6. *Ibid.*

7. Gunther Schuller, "A Conversation with Steuermann," p. 28.

8. Peter Stadlen, "Serialism Reconsidered," p. 12. The following quotations are from the same source, pp. 14–16.

9. The letter to which Webern refers was unfortunately lost in the turmoil of the post-war period. Only 47 letters and postcards that Hildegard Jone wrote to Webern between 1939 and 1945 are extant. WA.

10. Mrs Coolidge wanted to have the work performed by George Barrère's wind ensemble at the 1938 Pittsfield Festival.

11. The holograph of Webern's Quartet is now in the Library of Congress, Washington, D.C., as part of the Coolidge Collection, in which Webern's correspondence with Mrs Coolidge is also housed. In May of 1938 Webern entered in his income book the amount received from Mrs Coolidge for the Quartet: 1,850.41 Reichsmarks, German currency having become the monetary standard in Austria since the Anschluss. In converting the $750 actually paid by Mrs Coolidge, Webern lost close to one-third of the value as a result of the reduced exchange rate just then decreed by Germany. Webern bemoaned the loss at length in two letters to Kolisch in the hope that Mrs Coolidge might make up the difference.

12. The terms for the work's publication that Webern suggested to Stein were very moderate: an outright payment of £25–30, plus royalties that Webern hoped could be as high as 20 per cent (those paid by Universal Edition were fifteen per cent). Eventually, Webern had to settle for £15 and fifteen per cent. In the course of the preliminary correspondence, Stein had transmitted a question from Dr Alfred A. Kalmus, director of Universal Edition's London branch, as to whether the Quartet could be arranged for string orchestra in the manner of the Five Movements, Op. 5. That point was not pursued further, however. The arrangements with Boosey & Hawkes, in which Dr Kalmus participated, included an understanding for the later transfer of the copyright to Universal Edition, Vienna, who, from 1955 on, issued the work under its own imprint.

13. The pertinent passages in Webern's letter to Stein read: "As my directions within the musical text, tempos, etc., presumably will be given in *German* (I hardly can assume anything different, or else we would first have to communicate in minute detail about the translation), the title, too, should in my opinion be in *German*. This is naturally not so important to me, but it would be more uniform. Letter type: *Antiqua*!!! Such as I have had for years in my Universal Edition publications. Cover and inside title page completely identical. The dedication is to be placed, if the layout permits, on a separate leaf and in the centre; if this is not possible, it is to appear on top of the inside title page or, better yet, on the verso! May the dedication, too, be in German? Do the publishers employ ornamentations on their covers? Then I plead for sacrificing them as an exception. And, generally, I beg you that the publication conform as much as possible to the previous editions of my compositions."

14. In that letter Webern informed Stein that he himself was distributing copies to Schoenberg, Jalowetz, Bach, and Polnauer, and that he would like to have further copies sent to Brunswick, Krenek, Wellesz, Rosbaud, Scherchen, Ansermet, Steuermann, and Winter. Copies inscribed to the Humpliks and Zenk are extant. WA.

15. The autograph of Webern's analysis is in an unidentified Swiss collection.

16. "Reviews of Music: Webern, Anton, String Quartet, Op. 28," *Music Review* 1 (May 1940), pp. 177–178.

17. *Klangfiguren*, p. 176.

Chapter XXIX   Consequences of the Anschluss—Webern as a teacher (1938)

1. William L. Shirer, *The Rise and Fall of the Third Reich* (Greenwich, Conn.: Fawcett Publications, 1964), p. 477.

2. This office was set up by Hitler's deputy, Reinhard Heydrich, and administered by the notorious Austrian Nazi, Karl Adolf Eichmann.

3. Baron Rothschild, for example, was forced to sign over his steel mills to the Hermann Goering Works.

4. Kurt Manschinger left Vienna a few hours after Schuschnigg's resignation. Boarding a train at 6 am on 12 March, the same morning German troops entered Austria, he managed to cross into Czechoslovakia only because his actress wife, feigning hysterics and a fainting spell, succeeded in duping the border officials.

5. Letter to the author, dated 29 April 1969. The manuscript was a fair copy of the third movement of the Variations, Op. 27, which Webern inscribed "Auf baldiges Wiedersehen, lieber Dr Kurzmann. Immer Ihr Anton Webern 18 Juli 1938." Dr Kurzmann later presented the autograph to Robert Mann of the Juilliard Quartet. It is now in the collection of Robert Owen Lehman at the Pierpont Morgan Library, New York City.

6. Peter von Webern enlisted in the Reichsarbeitsdienst and received training for leadership in that government-controlled work organization, a civilian equivalent of military service. The camp to which he was assigned was located in Bernburg by the River Saale. In a letter to his sister Amalie, dated 30 October 1938 (WA), Peter described his severe schooling as a future Truppführer (platoon leader): "On duty, as well as outside of duty hours, the strictest and most faultless discipline is demanded of us. . . . Our trainers and teachers are all Prussians. Therefore you can imagine how things go. Our field master is from Berlin. He is so loud-mouthed that one gets really hot under the collar when he lets his voice ring out. For us Austrians, this school is certainly very hard, but it will surely not harm us, for we are being educated by it to become tough and resolute men."

7. Conversation with the author.

8. Conversation with the author.

9. On New Year's Day of 1938, Webern wrote to Scherchen:

It makes me very happy that you will do "my" (I think I may call it that) Bach Fugue on the BBC. And more particularly that you have written to tell me so, which, anyway for me, re-opens the contact between us that appeared to be broken after the unhappy days in Barcelona. To think that absolutely nobody should have understood me then! How I felt right after Berg's passing, and that I simply could no longer endure the stresses connected with the task of premièring his last work so soon after his death! Right up to the last moment I had hoped to be able to stand it. But it just could not be done! (Published in *die Reihe 2*, p. 19.)

10. Published in Willi Reich, "Berg und Webern schreiben an Hermann Scherchen," *Melos* 33 (July–August 1966), p. 227.

11. Published in "Incontro con Anton Webern," *Il Mondo* (3 November 1945). The following passages were translated by Mario Castelnuovo-Tedesco:

Webern's music is too new to reveal at first sight all its qualities of tone-colour. The wish to approach the work of a master with whom I was not familiar enough was, in fact, one of the main reasons for my trip. To hear *Das Augenlicht* was worth going all the way through green France and across the Channel, amidst the screeching of the seagulls. . . . Anton Webern is a lonely flower who does not resemble anyone. He is completely different from Arnold Schoenberg, his teacher, and completely different from Alban Berg, his brotherly friend. It would be enough to consider such difference to conclude that the twelve-tone system is not, after all, a blind alley, as so many pretend; it is not that malefic influence that would reduce the music of all countries to a minimum common denominator, as has been affirmed too often and repeated thoughtlessly; it is instead a language that has possibilities of the most varied differentiations, the results of which we perhaps won't be able to witness. What struck me mainly in *Das Augenlicht*, at a first and—alas—single audition, was the quality of sound. The thin orchestral score, which at first reading seems to present thousands of problem-passages, would by itself be enough to demonstrate the fallacy of so many rules that the various treatises of orchestration have perpetuated almost by heredity. I mean, first of all, that almost superstitious terror that paralyses the treatise-writers at the prospect of those thin spots in the texture of a score that are called, in professional slang, *holes*. The theorists, instead of advising the study of the later Bach, the thoughtful and humble consideration of the *Canones diversi* in the *Musical Offering* or of the *Art of the Fugue*, instead of speaking of counterpoint and polyphony, to preserve the young student from the danger of "quicksands" in orchestration, suggest the *filling parts*: precisely those parts that have encumbered thousands of scores in the second half of the XIXth century, and too many in our own times.

Webern proves to me, even when he does not work in a strictly contrapuntal direction, that two notes by the celesta, a light touch of the glockenspiel, a barely audible tremolo in the mandolin, are able to bridge abysses that at first sight seem to be separated by incalculable distances.

The instruments of the orchestra are limited to the essential. And this certainly not because of a mania for originality, nor the wish to depart, as much as possible, from the sound of the orchestra of Wagner and Strauss. Webern has studied the possibilities of all instruments and is able to write for those combinations that, at a given moment, seem to him indispensable.

Das Augenlicht, on first hearing, reveals itself to be poetic and harmonious. The voices and the instruments, often at great distance, seem to oppose each other's sonorous planes. The orchestral score seems to be enriched by mysterious vibrations as though performed under a glass bowl. The musical construction has an inner rhythm, which has nothing in common with the mechanical rhythm. Certain refinements of writing deserve a separate study: as for instance how Webern avoids that sudden call to reality that is given by the accent on the *strong beat* of the measure, and that here—inevitably—would wipe out the dreamy atmosphere pervading this most poetic composition. The sound, for the time being, is the most powerful emotional impression I received from this work. A sound, by itself, that makes me consider *Das Augenlicht* as one of the fundamental works of our time. And in particular one should mention the *musical allusions* that seem to arise, as distant overtones, from the twelve-tone row and its ramifications.

12. Kurt List and Humphrey Searle, Webern's pupils.

13. Willi Reich, "Berg und Webern schreiben an Hermann Scherchen," pp. 227–228.

14. The *Daily Telegraph and Morning Post* of 16 March 1938 reported the incident under the headline "Why Cellist Walked Out":

Mr James Whitehead, cellist of the Philharmonic Trio, who walked off the stage at Wigmore Hall on Tuesday night at the start of the first English performance of Webern's String Trio, Op. 20, gave his version of the incident yesterday to a representative of the *Daily Telegraph and Morning Post*. "The Philharmonic Trio were playing in the third Adolph Hallis chamber concert. Mr Whitehead, after playing a few bars, exclaimed, 'Oh, I can't play this thing,' and walked off, followed shortly by his two colleagues. 'I am afraid I felt no sympathy with the piece and acted on the spur of the moment,' he said yesterday. 'When I first saw the score I refused to play it. Then I was persuaded to work on it and felt even more certain. To me it is not music, but a nightmare and nonsense.' The committee of the Adolph Hallis Chamber Music Concerts, in a statement signed by Mr Adolph Hallis, Mr Edward Clark, Mr Christian Darnton, and Mr Alan Rawsthorne, said that the concerts were a cooperative venture in which artists were invited to take a financial share and agreed to play works recommended by the committee. The Philharmonic Trio, it is stated, agreed last May to play Webern's string trio, and it was not until Sunday that any reluctance to play the work was shown. The committee describes Mr Whitehead's conduct as 'inexcusable' and a 'breach of faith with the public'.''

15. Robert later became a member of the music faculty at the University of New Mexico. Among his memorabilia was a large notebook containing his harmony lessons with Webern. WA.

16. "Vienna since the Anschluss," *Modern Music* 23 (Spring 1946), p. 95.

17. *Arnold Schoenberg Letters*, p. 195.

18. In addition to the comments cited in this section, the reminiscences of Karl Amadeus Hartmann appear in Chapter XXXI.

19. Kurt Manschinger (1902–1968) adopted the name of Ashley Vernon after settling in New York in 1940. The list of his compositions is extensive and includes several operas and symphonic works. Manschinger's entire musical estate is in the Moldenhauer Archives.

20. In one of his courses Webern admitted, however: "Die 'Salome' bleibt" ('Salome' will remain). Quoted from Frederick Deutsch-Dorian, "Webern als Lehrer," *Melos* 27 (April 1960), p. 104.

21. Stefan Wolpe (1902–1972) was of Russian-Jewish and Austrian parentage. He was on his way to Palestine, from where he was to emigrate to America in 1938. In the United States he became well known as a composer. His comments on Webern are contained in a letter to the author.

22. Oehlgiesser and Spira, both of Jewish birth, fled Austria after Hitler's takeover. Oehlgiesser escaped to Switzerland, where he settled in Zürich. Spira, a native of Poland, emigrated to England. Oehlgiesser's recollections were communicated in a letter to the author.

23. Arnold Elston (formerly Elstein, 1907–1971), a native of New York City, had a career leading to professorships at the Universities of Oregon and California. At the same time he established a reputation as a composer and author. His memoirs of Webern as a teacher were written especially for this biography.

24. Roland Leich (b. 1911), who rose to a professorship at the Carnegie-Mellon Institute in Pittsburgh, went to Webern on the advice of a former fellow student at the Curtis Institute of Music in Philadelphia. There he had received four years of rigorous training in counterpoint under the conservative Rosario Scalero, but he was inexperienced in writing in the larger forms. His comments on Webern's teaching are contained in a letter to the author.

25. Returning to America in 1935, Gordon Claycombe (b. 1909) first worked as a music teacher and journalist, then as a radio executive and hospital administrator. His memoirs were written especially for this biography.

26. Humphrey Searle (b. 1915) came to Webern with a background of classics and philosophy received at Oxford University. At the same time he had been tutored at London's Royal College of Music by John Ireland and Reginald Owen Morris. In his compositions Searle was to employ a modified serial technique. *Put Away the Flutes*, for tenor and six instruments, was written in 1947 in memory of Webern, as was his Fifth Symphony in 1964. (The latter score is in the Moldenhauer Archives.) Searle was the author of the article on Webern in the fifth edition of *Grove's Dictionary of Music and Musicians*.

27. Humphrey Searle, "Conversations with Webern," *The Musical Times* 81 (October 1940), pp. 405–406.

28. *Ibid.*

29. Humphrey Searle, "Webern the Evolutionist," *Sunday Telegraph* (London, 16 April

1961). The excerpts quoted are from Searle's original manuscript (WA), which varies slightly from the printed text.

30. Friedrich Deutsch (b. 1902) changed his name to Frederick Dorian when, in 1936, he emigrated to the United States, where he assumed a professorship at Carnegie-Mellon University in Pittsburgh. He is the brother of the Schoenberg pupil, Max Deutsch, a conductor and teacher who settled in Paris.

31. Frederick Deutsch-Dorian, "Webern als Lehrer," pp. 102–106. English translation by Dorian.

Chapter XXX   Webern and "The Third Reich" (1938–1941)

1. On 7 November 1938 the seventeen-year-old Herschel Grynszpan entered the German embassy in Paris with the intention of assassinating the ambassador. His purpose was to protest before the world the German persecution of the Jews, more particularly the recent treatment of 10,000 of them, including his own father, who had been deported in boxcars to Poland. Ironically, the youth did not kill the ambassador, but his third secretary, Ernst vom Rath, himself suspected of anti-Nazi attitudes because of his refusal to endorse the excesses in the implementation of the Nuremberg laws.

2. The atrocities included rape. Since the Nuremberg laws had long made sexual intercourse between Aryans and Jews a crime, the rapists were duly expelled from the Nazi party; all other excesses were condoned as compliance with orders.

3. *The Rise and Fall of the Third Reich*, p. 586.

4. Besides being an accomplished composer, Otto Jokl (1891–1963) held a doctorate in philology and was an authority on classical Latin. After settling in New York City, he became an editor for Associated Music Publishers.

5. The baptismal certificate and Webern's letters to Jokl are extant. WA.

6. In America, Julius Schloss (1902–1972) was again thwarted from pursuing a musical career. Unable to find employment in his profession, he worked for the next fourteen years in factories and attended an engineering college at night. Not until his retirement could he return to composing and earn a measure of recognition.

7. The BBC programme of 7 February was entitled "The Composer as Arranger."

8. This is the earliest extant letter of Hildegard Jone to Webern.

9. Webern's new passport, issued on 10 January 1940, bears the swastika of the Third Reich on the cover. WA.

10. On 7 February 1940 Webern, using the opportunity to send messages to his friends abroad, wrote to David Josef Bach: "Has it [the Passacaglia] perhaps become already a piece of history (after 32 years)?"

11. Three premières of Bartók's works had been given in Basel: Music for String Instruments, Percussion, and Celesta (in 1937), Sonata for Two Pianos and Percussion (in 1938), and Divertimento for String Orchestra (on 11 June 1940, one week before Webern's letter to Reich).

12. Letter to the author.

13. Eduard Steuermann recalled: "I found out later that he [Zenk] was at the same time a convinced Nazi. That was just a brand of the Viennese 'double counterpoint'." (Gunther Schuller, "A Conversation with Steuermann," p. 28).

14. The episode was related to the author by Polnauer, who also made available his correspondence with Webern. WA.

15. Communicated to the author by Steuermann shortly before his death.

16. Schoenberg's last surviving message to Webern was the announcement, on 28 January 1941, of the birth of his son Lawrence the day before. In several essays written during his years in America Schoenberg listed Webern in first place when referring to his disciples. In "How One Becomes Lonely" (1937) he spoke of "that small group of faithful friends, my pupils, among them my dear friend Anton von Webern, the spiritual leader of the group, a veritable hotspur in his principles, a real fighter, a

friend whose faithfulness can never be surpassed, a real genius as a composer."
(Arnold Schoenberg, *Style and Idea*, p. 41)

Chapter XXXI   Wartime vignettes—Webern's 60th birthday—
Iconography (1940–1943)

1. Reproduced in facsimile in *die Reihe 2*, plate 3.
2. Webern's manuscript is in the archive of Universal Edition, Vienna.
3. Published in *die Reihe 2*, p. 22.
4. "Incontro con Anton Webern," *Il Mondo*, Florence, 3 November 1945.
5. Conversation with the author.
6. In 1936 his First String Quartet won the first prize in the Geneva *Carillon* contest and was heard at the London ISCM festival of 1938. In 1937 his cantata *Anno 48-Friede* received an award from the Emil Hertzka Memorial Foundation. His early compositions also included an opera, *Simplicius Simplicissimus*. Karl Amadeus Hartmann was a man of buoyant temperament and great charm. Politically, he belonged to a small group of Germans who, from the beginning, had adamantly opposed the Hitler régime. He escaped military service by going into hiding for long periods of time, and with a few trusted friends he formed the nucleus of a resistance movement. After the war, he organized the Musica Viva concerts in his native Munich. His eight symphonies have established him as a prominent representative of the German symphonic tradition.
7. Quoted from "Lektionen bei Anton Webern," *Karl Amadeus Hartmann, Kleine Schriften*, pp. 26–32.
8. In accounts by Borris, Craft, Kolneder and others.
9. Conversation with the author.
10. Letter to the author.
11. Letter to the author.
12. Conversation with the author.
13. The next day Webern dispatched a letter to Munich to reach the young couple, who were en route to Garmisch-Partenkirchen. With touching concern, he offered Peter detailed advice for his trip, in particular how he might best find quarters, which were scarce because of the wartime conditions. Addressing the envelope "Peter von Webern," the father, here as always, made it a point to uphold the noble family tradition, which he never failed to impress upon his progeny. WA.
14. On 15 May 1935.
15. On 2 February 1943, 330,000 Axis troops had been forced to surrender to the Russians.
16. Quoted from Schoenberg's Preface to Webern's Six Bagatelles, Op. 9.
17. One of those observing Webern's anniversary without his knowledge was Luigi Dallapiccola, whose diary contained this entry: "Fiesole, 3 December 1943. Today Anton Webern is sixty years old. *A solitary soul who clings to faith.* . . . In Florence, as by now in all Italian cities, persecution takes on a perturbing rhythm. I feel myself, more than ever, *a solitary soul.* . . . I decide to dedicate to the master the *Six Carmina Alcaei*, which I am going to present him, when the war is over, with the trepidation well known to one who submits his own work to the judgement of somebody so far his superior." (Published in "Incontro con Anton Webern")
18. Its genesis had begun during Advent of 1941 when the poetess had sent Webern the photograph of a self-portrait, inscribing the picture with the first lines of "Schöpfen aus Brunnen des Himmels," one of the poems to find use in the new cantata. On the back she penned a message: "Actually, I do not know at all whether drawings can convey to you something close to your own nature—for me they are at present the most necessary form of expression." In his Christmas letter of that year, Webern responded with a musical quotation from "Freundselig ist das Wort," the opening choral passage

of the cantata movement on which he was then working. During the following summer
(1942), Hildegard Jone began to concentrate on lithographs. She referred to them when
writing to Webern on 9 July: "There really are decades of life embodied in such a few
lines. To express clarity—this demands time and, if it succeeds here or there, it is perhaps
a moment of eternity. One could say it still more simply: that which is timeless consumes
much time in one's life."

19. The artist died on 5 April 1941 at Spandau as a political prisoner of the Nazis.

20. Hildegard Jone created this famous painting in the autumn of 1945, fresh under
the impact of Webern's death. The portrayal is filled with an atmosphere of terrifying
explosiveness (the artist stated that she painted it in the middle of a furious
thunderstorm). From the same experience sprang several poems which this author, at
the request of the poetess, combined in 1963 into a cycle entitled *Requiem in memoriam
Anton von Webern*.

21. All these art works are housed in the Webern Archive except the following:
Kokoschka's oil portrait (collection Charlotte Knize, New York City), Dolbin's drawings
(collections Benedikt F. Dolbin, New York City, and Andre Meyer, Paris), the Rederer
drawing (Margit Rederer, Zürich), and the Schiele drawing of 1917 (Jacob Kaplan, New
York City). The other Schiele drawing (1918) and the Kokoschka drawing (1912) are in
undisclosed private collections.

Chapter XXXII   Opera 29–31 (1938–1944)

1. The manuscript Webern sent is one of the most beautiful of his holographs, all of
which are distinguished by exquisite calligraphy. Ten years earlier, at the beginning of
their acquaintance, the composer had presented the poetess with another handsome
score, the fair copy of his double canon "Fahr hin, o Seel'" from the Five Sacred Songs,
Op. 15. In May 1962 she gave both autographs, as well as those of the Second Cantata,
to the author on the occasion of the First International Webern Festival in Seattle.

2. Undated letter, in which Hildegard Jone requested that the movement be called
simply "Kleiner Flügel," rather than "Kleiner Flügel Ahornsamen."

3. The texts read:

"Blitz und Donner"
Zündender Lichtblitz des Lebens schlug ein aus der Wolke des Wortes.
Donner, der Herzschlag, folgt nach, bis er in Frieden verebbt.

"Das Prisma"
Wird Dir das Herz zum Christall, so lässt es leicht sich bewegen:
wird so zum Prisma des Lichts, das alle Farben umfasst.

"Doppelte Gabe"
Alles war doppelt geschenkt mir was je mir als Freude gegeben:
ging mit der Träne des Lids über zum Thau meines Lieds.

4. The translation, by Eric Smith, appears in the printed score of the Cantata.

5. The première was given in London during the first ISCM festival after the war.
Again it was England that led in the recognition of Webern's genius and restored his
music to the concert halls as soon as the fury of battle subsided. The work was presented
on 12 July 1946 by the BBC Orchestra and Chorus under the leadership of Webern's
former pupil, Karl Rankl, then newly appointed as conductor of the Covent Garden
Opera. Emelie Hooke was the soprano soloist. The performance was generally acclaimed
as the highlight of the festival. Humphrey Searle commented in *The Monthly Musical Record*
(December 1946): ". . . throughout the whole work, one is fascinated by the remarkable
sonorities achieved. Like most of Webern's later music, the work is built up like a mosaic
from small fragments contributed by the different instruments; yet this is done not in

any impressionist or pointillist manner, but architecturally, and the crystal-clear structure holds together as logically as any Bach fugue."

6. Hildegard Jone, "A Cantata," *die Reihe 2*, p. 7.

7. Ten years after the composer's death, Hildegard Jone was asked to contribute to the commemorative Webern issue of *die Reihe*, a periodical devoted to serial music. Her essay, entitled "A Cantata," was based on her recollection of that intimate gathering in August of 1940. Transcending the bitterness of Webern's tragic death, she defined the essence of her "Chariten" text: "The poem says what the word 'grace' means to me; above all, it means infinitely more to me than something not quite reconcilable with complete seriousness. For grace can itself be all that is purest and deepest in the seriousness of life, not only the breath of beauty in what is well and whole, but also the healing of the wound and the cheerful acceptance of the wound that cannot be healed. . . . Grace is courage to try to put the world in order through love."

8. This estimate, as well as that of twenty minutes given to Hildegard Jone, far exceeds the duration of the work as it is generally performed.

9. Less technical was the description of the Variations Webern gave Hildegard Jone the same month that he sent his commentary to Reich. On 19 May 1941 the poetess asked him to tell her in detail about his new work, saying: "It is really so marvellous to articulate what one has discovered. In my painting I always experience it this way." Elated, the composer replied on 26 May:

How I value your request! Imagine this: six notes are given, in a *shape* determined by the sequence and the rhythm, and what follows (in the course of the piece, which lasts about twenty minutes) is nothing other than this shape over and over again!!! To be sure, in continual "metamorphosis" (the musical term for this process is "variation")—but it is nevertheless the same over and over. Goethe says of the "primeval phenomenon":

> ideal as the ultimate that can be perceived,
> real as that which has been perceived,*
> symbolic because it comprehends every case,
> identical with every case.**

* That is what it really is in my piece, *namely the shape mentioned*! (The comparison, to be sure, serves only to clarify the *process*).

** Namely in my piece! This is what it does!

First this *shape* becomes the "theme" and then six variations of this theme follow. However, the "theme" itself represents, as stated above, nothing but variations (metamorphoses of this first shape). As a *unit* it again becomes the point of departure for new "variations." But this theme with its six variations finally produces, in *formal* respect, a structure that is equivalent to that of an "adagio," but in *character* —according to content—my piece is not that at all—only according to form. Think of something like a classical "overture." So even though I have entitled the piece "Variations," yet these for their part are fused again into a new unit (in the sense of a different form). Such and such a number of metamorphoses of the first shape produce the "theme." This, as a new unit, passes again through such and such a number of metamorphoses; these again, fused into a new unit, produce the form of the whole. *This, approximately then, is the shape of the whole piece.* Perhaps these comments do give you some idea.

10. In his letter to Reich, dated 23 August 1941, Webern gave vent to his frustration:

Should a man like Sacher really be entirely inaccessible to such thought processes? [Webern refers to the laws of nature, with which he considered twelve-tone composition to conform.] If he has no "audience" for the *truth*, as he maintains (in his letter to UE), only he himself is guilty. For that matter, I was not that much surprised by the negative result and therefore am not particularly disappointed, either. At any rate, my quite special thanks to you for your efforts, dear friend, and by no means be resentful: we will yet be proven right! Convey my cordial greetings to Sacher. Tell him: I know that *he*, too, will yet say that I was right.

11. In Hildegard Jone's manuscript, the poem's title is spelled "Freund-selig," a mannerism with which she often tried to give new meaning to familiar words like "Er-leben" or "Neu-werden."

12. Hildegard Jone's manuscript of the text (from the cycle *Alle Glocken*, part of the unpublished collection *Der Mohnkopf*) bears the heading "Ne avertas faciem tuam a me" (May you not turn your face away from me). The two opening lines had appeared under the photographs of the self-portrait that Hildegard Jone sent the Weberns during Advent of 1941. She then cited the verses as a motto for the holiday season, under the title "Glocken der Weihnacht," and Webern had responded with a musical quotation from "Freundselig ist das Wort," the movement in progress at that time.

13. The scores which Webern sent the Humpliks after completing each movement were preserved by Hildegard Jone in a folder inscribed "Die grosse Kantate, die 2. Kantate 1944 Freundseligkeit." WA.

14. Facsimile reproduction in *Anton von Webern: Sketches (1926–1945)*, plate 40.

15. The recording by Pierre Boulez (Westminster) lasts a little over twelve minutes and that by Robert Craft (Columbia) takes only ten minutes, thirty seconds.

16. Polnauer, in his annotations to the published correspondence, erroneously ascribes both references to Webern's last unfinished cantata, the presumptive Opus 32.

17. Theodor W. Adorno, *Klangfiguren*, p. 178.

18. Stravinsky, intrigued with the chorale movement, made a manuscript copy for himself (as he had done earlier with the Bach Ricercar transcription). Robert Craft related that Stravinsky "reduced the music to a single metrical unit, not to 'correct' Webern, but to facilitate reading the music for himself." (Letter to the author)

Chapter XXXIII   The war comes home—Peter's death (1943–1945)

1. The child was born on 13 September, Schoenberg's birthday, a circumstance to which Webern attached much significance.

2. Edwin Komauer, "Kurze Selbstbiographie," *Jahresbericht des Musikvereins für Kärnten* (1943), p. 18.

3. She later married the Haydn scholar C. Robbins Landon. Subsequently she became a Schubert authority in her own right.

4. In that letter, Hildegard Jone quoted what the eminent architect, Rudolf Schwarz, had written to her when his magnificent home, that he himself had designed, was completely destroyed in another attack on 20 July: "Such blows can hardly be felt at a time when what is so indescribably more valuable dies or is threatened. One does not consider it when so much worse is befalling us. If it were only hard or bitter things that are destined to come, then one could take them like the easy ones, each in its own time. But what is about to come is woven into the *mysterium iniquitatis* [mystery of evil]. May God grant that we all are in the right place when they happen."

5. The inventory was found in Webern's estate. WA.

6. Humplik's studio had suffered extensive damage in two previous attacks. After the second one, Hildegard Jone had written to Webern on 2 October: "We are gravely concerned over Seppi's new sculpture which stands day and night under water now."

7. Hildegard Jone asked Webern to supply her with copies of the particular texts, as her manuscripts had been stored in an air-raid shelter. The composer's fair copies were later found in the estate of the poetess, who had preserved them in a brocade cover. WA.

8. At first Hildegard Jone had wanted Webern himself to be the reader, reasoning in her letter of 25 April 1944: "Somehow the words, when spoken by you, are already full of the music that you hear in them." Not wishing to appear actively on the programme, Webern declined. He reminded the poetess of the deep impression she had made on him and his wife recently with recitations from Goethe and her own writings, and he urged her to be the reader. She refused, however.

9. The thoroughness with which Webern prepared that small affair is evident from four extant letters to Riemerschmid. On 3 December 1944 Webern told him of his pleasure that the reading had so markedly corresponded with his own conception of the lyrics.

10. Peter von Webern was buried in an unmarked mass grave. It was by a strange stroke of fate that the last to bear the family name would be laid to rest in the same town where his great-great-grandfather, Josef Eduard von Webern, was married in 1812, and from where the later generations had gone forth.

11. All of Hermine von Webern's recollections, documented by her diaries and correspondence, were imparted to the author in a series of conversations in 1968.

12. Together with the printed death announcement, Webern sent personal messages to his closest relatives and friends. All dated 8 March 1945 and almost identical in wording, the letters to Webern's sister Rosa and her husband, to Ludwig Zenk, and to the Humpliks are extant. The text is reproduced in *Anton Webern Letters to Hildegard Jone and Josef Humplik*, p. 59.

Chapter XXXIV   *Catastrophe and flight (1945)*

1. After the closing of all Vienna theatres in September 1944, including the Theater in der Josefstadt, where he had been employed, Zenk had to register first for the army and then for labour in an armament plant. But a nervous ailment that paralysed his left hand rendered him unfit. At Christmas-time he was assigned as a night air-raid warden for the Gesellschaft der Musikfreunde, which was housed in the same building as Universal Edition. In the middle of February 1945, he found himself suddenly drafted into the Volkssturm, a corps consisting of men unsuited for regular military service.

2. Letter Ludwig Zenk to Ernst Diez, written on 10 December 1946.

3. Earlier, in January, the Russians had entered East Prussia and Czechoslovakia. They soon conquered all the territories east of the Oder River and prepared for their assault on Berlin.

4. The stringent discipline exercised by the air-raid wardens almost led to the detection of Josef Polnauer, who had been living in hiding since 1943. He sought the safety of a public shelter during a particularly heavy bombing attack. After the doors had been shut, there was an unexpected check of identity cards. Polnauer was terrified. But the all-clear signal was sounded just before the control reached him and everyone was released. Polnauer thus narrowly escaped arrest and certain deportation to a concentration camp. (The anecdote was related to the author by Polnauer himself.)

5. Letter to the author.

6. The train ticket for this journey was preserved by Webern among his papers. WA.

7. This and following quotations from Amalie Waller's account were first published in Hans Moldenhauer, *The Death of Anton Webern.*

8. One of these fugitives was Heinrich Walz, in private life a famous goldsmith in Dresden, who had been a sergeant in the Waffen SS, the combat unit of Hilter's notorious bodyguard. He had sought refuge in a remote shepherd's hut high above the Felber Valley. Learning of the decree that would automatically subject him, because of his political past, to 20 years' imprisonment at hard labour, he shot his beautiful wife and then himself. Their bodies, buried in a mountain meadow by a shepherd boy, were transferred years later (1962) to the cemetery in Mittersill.

9. For two decades, the relics, including a cache of manuscripts, lay forgotten in the hideaway. For the full story of their discovery in 1965, see Hans Moldenhauer, "In Quest of Webern," *Saturday Review* (New York, 27 August 1966), pp. 47–49, 60, and Hans Moldenhauer, "A Webern Pilgrimage," *Musical Times* (London, February 1968), pp. 122–127.

10. Conversation with the author.

11. That ten-word message is extant, as are similar ones sent the same day to the Humpliks and Ludwig Zenk. They were all incredibly delayed. Postmarked Salzburg, 12 October, over three months after they had left Mittersill, they did not reach their recipients until the middle of October, a full month after Webern had died. The text of the card to the Humpliks is reproduced in *Anton Webern Letters to Hildegard Jone and Josef Humplik*, p. 60.

12. Published in *die Reihe 2*, p. 21.

Chapter XXXV   Mittersill notebook—The presumptive Opus 32 (1944–1945)

1. Magda von Graedener-Hattingberg, *Rilke und Benvenuta/Ein Buch des Dankes* (Vienna: Wilhelm Andermann Verlag, 1943). The Rilke passages quoted in this chapter are from this source, with the exception of the last two. Eng. tr. Cyrus Brooks *Rilke and Benvenuta/ A Book of Thanks* (London: William Heinemann Ltd., 1949)

2. Also included was her cycle *Enthüllte Form (Distichen um 5 im Kriege entstandene Plastiken von 1941–44)*.

3. *Anton von Webern: Perspectives*, pp. 111–112.

4. In the brochure accompanying the record album *Anton Webern: The Complete Music*, Robert Craft erroneously quotes one of the earlier versions of the row.

5. Hildegard Jone shared with Webern a consuming admiration for that work. Her estate contained a nine-page manuscript in her handwriting entitled "Passages copied by Anton Webern from Goethe's *Farbenlehre*." The excerpts afford an insight into the scientific precepts that moved the composer to draw analogies for his own aesthetic conclusions.

6. Polnauer's quotation of this text, contained in his annotations to Webern's published letters to the Humpliks, differs in several places; no doubt he found it difficult to decipher Webern's handwriting in the sketchbook, which was his only source.

7. Postcard dated 23 December 1944.

Chapter XXXVI   Webern's death (15 September 1945)

1. This was related to the author by Webern's daughters Amalie and Maria.

2. Cesar Bresgen, "Webern's Last Months in Mittersill," *Anton von Webern: Perspectives*, pp. 111–115. The following quotations are from the same source.

3. 1 kilogram = 2·2 English pounds.

4. 1 decagram = 10 grams.

5. Letter to the author, dated 17 May 1960.

6. For complete documentation see Hans Moldenhauer, *The Death of Anton Webern: A Drama in Documents*. All letters and documents quoted in the book have been deposited in the Webern Archive.

7. Translated into English by Martin U. Heiman, the interpreter at the inquest.

8. *Wiener Kurier*, 10 October; *Österreichische Volksstimme, Zentralorgan der Kommunistischen Partei Österreich* 12 October; *Österreichische Zeitung, Zeitung der Roten Armee für die Bevölkerung Österreichs*, 20 October 1945.

9. By this author.

10. Letter to the author, dated 7 April 1960.

Epilogue: Wilhelmine—Renaissance

1. Later Boelke-Bomart, Inc., Hillsdale, New York.

2. The original drawing is in the Webern Archive.

3. On 19 August 1949, shortly before her death, the widow wrote to Hildegard Jone: "I love my other grandchildren very much, too, but these three are really my favourites. They were for my husband also. Karin, especially, he idolized."

4. After Wilhelmine's death, the family moved to Argentina where Mattel soon succeeded in amassing great wealth.

5. Wilhelmine's letters to Hildegard Jone were found in the estate of the poetess. WA. Hildegard Jone lived out her years in the rambling house at Wintergasse 13 in Purkersdorf, surrounded by her paintings and Josef Humplik's sculptures. Her husband died on 5 April 1958, and the poetess, ailing and impoverished, was left alone in the dilapidated villa. There she spent her remaining years painting and writing. A large cupboard, filled to overflowing with unpublished manuscripts, was what she called her "Noah's Ark," a vessel for posterity. She died on 28 August 1963 and was buried beside her husband and her mother, whom she had venerated, in a cemetery nestled in the Vienna Woods on a hillside above Purkersdorf. The grave is marked by a heart, sculptured in pink marble, that she had designed herself for her "old age home," as she would refer to her last resting place with a serene smile.

6. Letter undated.

7. In 1950 Herbert Häfner conducted the première of the Second Cantata in Brussels.

8. It was this sculpture that, two decades later, led to the dramatic discovery of important manuscripts (see Introduction).

9. Letter Riemerschmid to Polnauer, dated 9 March 1947.

10. In 1968 the ownership of these letters became the subject of litigation. Because of the long time lapse, the judge could only settle the dispute by dividing the correspondence between Webern's heirs and Riemerschmid's widow. The parties then agreed to place all the letters in the archives of Vienna's Stadtbibliothek.

11. Instead, Hermine kept the instrument and had it repaired. She subsequently deposited the relic in the Webern Archive.

12. That renaissance, which became known as "The Age of Webern," started when the international avant-garde of composers lifted Webern on their shield. Spokesmen such as Pierre Boulez and Karlheinz Stockhausen hailed him as the originator of a music that was to become for them the point of departure for an altogether new aesthetic and technique. An entire generation of disciples emulated Webern, and a host of theoreticians divulged his influence on the new trends. In 1955, the veteran master Igor Stravinsky, then 73 years of age, joined his young colleagues in their acclaim. He paid homage to Webern with a eulogy that opened the special issue of the periodical *die Reihe*, published on the tenth anniversary of the composer's death. "The 15th of September 1945, the day of Anton Webern's death, sh●uld be a day of mourning for any receptive musician," Stravinsky wrote. "We must hail not only this great composer but also a real hero. Doomed to a total failure in a deaf world of ignorance and indifference he inexorably kept on cutting out his diamonds, his dazzling diamonds, the mines of which he had such a perfect knowledge." In a later essay, Stravinsky declared that Webern was, for him, "le juste de la musique." In 1957, Stravinsky's close associate, Robert Craft, produced a set of recordings under the title *Anton Webern, The Complete Music*, which contained all of the then known compositions. Craft's pioneering achievement was instrumental in bringing Webern's music to widest awareness.

13. Letter to the author.

14. The First International Webern Festival was staged under the auspices of the University of Washington in Seattle, Washington, on 25–29 May 1962. On that occasion the International Webern Society was organized. Hans Moldenhauer, the festival's instigator and chairman, was elected president, and Gertrud Schoenberg, Helene Berg,

Hildegard Jone and Amalie Waller (who was in attendance) were named honorary members. Five more festivals followed: Salzburg/Mittersill, as part of the Salzburg Festival (1965); State University of New York at Buffalo (1966); Dartmouth College at Hanover, New Hampshire (1968); Vienna, under the auspices of the Austrian Society for Music, a government sponsored agency (1972); and Louisiana State University at Baton Rouge, with a closing concert in New Orleans (1978). During these events, various Webern compositions that were discovered by the authors during the 1960s had their first performances.

APPENDICES
SELECTED BIBLIOGRAPHY
INDEX

APPENDIX 1

Work List

THE WORK LIST is organized in five sections:

A. Published Works with Opus Numbers
B. Published Works without Opus Numbers
C. Other Works and Projects
D. Arrangements (1. Webern's own works   2. Works of other composers)
E. Writings

Each section is arranged chronologically within itself (the two versions of Opus 6 in Section A, listed successively, are a notable exception). The Chronological Index preceding the Work List encompasses all compositions (Sections A–D) and assigns a number to each of them. This numerical system interrelates the four groups and establishes an exact chronology of Webern's œuvre. The numbers provide, in particular, a tool for the ready identification of Webern's many posthumous compositions and projects. They may also prove useful in designating individual songs or movements for performance (Webern himself suggested such practice on several occasions). The section indicator following each Index caption facilitates tracing the particular entry in the Work List. The Index also helps to locate the cross references occurring in the "Remarks" column of the Work List.

In the cycles employing serial technique, the chronological ordering of the component parts aids in ascertaining the primary row. The practice of individually listing the songs or movements of cyclic works is not observed in Section D, because arrangements would obviously follow the already established sequence of a given work. Within each year, compositions having a specific date are listed first, followed by those for which only the year is marked on the manuscript and, lastly, by those for which the time of origin must be assumed. All data based on conjecture are placed in brackets. In general, the dates given indicate when the draft of a composition was completed, but in a number of cases the beginning dates also are provided. The work chapters contain supplemental information.

All works in Section B were published posthumously. Asterisks denote that the titles of the particular compositions, as well as the sequence within cycles, were not established by Webern, but designated by the editors for the purposes of performance and publication.

Materials included in Section C range from finished scores to sketches and fragments. To indicate the extent of the various works and projects, measure numbers are provided (except for the sketches which have been published). In most cases the measure count represents consecutive musical material, but it sometimes also includes redrafts of certain passages. The distinction between ink and pencil writing is to somewhat convey the nature of the manuscripts; Webern generally employed ink only as his musical thought approached a degree of finality. Instruments are specified, except for the orchestral song projects of 1914–1924 (grouped according to poetic sources) where designations in the sketches are not sufficiently conclusive. Several works listed in this section are projected for publication.

Section E, not included in the Chronological Index, contains Webern's literary products: poems, a stage play, essays, tributes, and analyses. His posthumously published lectures and correspondence are not listed in this section, but appear in the Bibliography.

HANS MOLDENHAUER

Abbreviations

anon = anonymous
arr = arrangement
BWV = Wolfgang Schmieder,
  . . . Bach-Werke-Verzeichnis (Leipzig,
  1950, Breitkopf & Härtel)
CF = Carl Fischer, New York
compl = complete
cond = conductor
D = Otto Erich Deutsch, Schubert,
  Thematic Catalogue . . . (London,
  1951, Dent)
instr = instruments
IWF = International Webern Festival
mm = measures
MS = manuscript
mvt = movement
orch = orchestra
perf = performance
prob = probably
qu = quartet
Sketches = Anton von Webern: Sketches
  (1926–1945) (New York, 1968,
  Carl Fischer)
UE = Universal Edition, Vienna
v = voice

Instruments:
afl = alto flute
asax = alto saxophone

bcl = bass clarinet
bn = bassoon
btrp = bass trumpet
btuba = bass tuba
cbn = contrabassoon
cel = celesta
cl = clarinet
db = double bass
Ehn = English horn
fl = flute
glock = glockenspiel
guit = guitar
harm = harmonium
hn = horn
hp = harp
mand = mandolin
ob = oboe
perc = percussion
picc = piccolo
pn = pianoforte
str = string or strings
timp = timpani
trb = trombone
trp = trumpet
tsax = tenor saxophone
va = viola
vc = cello
vn = violin
xyl = xylophone

Chronological Index
(Sections A–D)

136	Im Morgentaun Op. 3/IV	A
137	Kahl reckt der Baum Op. 3/V	A
138	Eingang Op. 4/I	A
139	Noch zwingt mich Treue Op. 4/II	A
140	Ja Heil und Dank dir Op. 4/III	A
141	So ich traurig bin Op. 4/IV	A
142	Ihr tratet zu dem Herde Op. 4/V	A
143	Erwachen aus dem tiefsten Traumesschosse	B
144	Kunfttag I	B
145	Trauer I	B
146	Das lockere Saatgefilde	B

1909

147	Five Movements Op. 5/I	A
148	Five Movements Op. 5/II	A
149	Five Movements Op. 5/III	A
150	Five Movements Op. 5/IV	A
151	Five Movements Op. 5/V	A
152	Six Pieces Op. 6 (original) I	A
153	Six Pieces Op. 6 (original) II	A
154	Six Pieces Op. 6 (original) III	A
155	Six Pieces Op. 6 (original) IV	A
156	Six Pieces Op. 6 (original) V	A
157	Six Pieces Op. 6 (original) VI	A
158	Two Piano Pieces (atonal) I	C
159	Two Piano Pieces (atonal) II	C
160	Schoenberg: Gurrelieder, Prelude and Interludes (arr)	D

1910

161	Four Pieces Op. 7/I	A
162	Four Pieces Op. 7/II	A
163	Four Pieces Op. 7/III	A
164	Four Pieces Op. 7/IV	A
165	Die sieben Prinzessinnen	C
166	Schoenberg: Six Orchestral Songs Op. 8 (arr)	D
167	Du, der ichs nicht sage Op. 8/I	A
168	Du machst mich allein Op. 8/II	A

1911

169	Five Pieces Op. 10/I	A
170	Five Pieces Op. 10/IV	A
171	Six Bagatelles Op. 9/II	A
172	Six Bagatelles Op. 9/III	A
173	Six Bagatelles Op. 9/IV	A
174	Six Bagatelles Op. 9/V	A

175	Schoenberg: Verklärte Nacht Op. 4 (arr)	D
176	Schoenberg: Pelleas und Melisande Op. 5 (arr)	D

1912

177	Schoenberg: Five Orchestra Pieces Op. 16 (arr)	D

1913

178	Six Bagatelles Op. 9/I	A
179	Schmerz, immer blick nach oben	C
180	Six Bagatelles Op. 9/VI	A
181	Five Pieces Op. 10/III	A
182	Five Pieces Op. 10/II	A
183	Orchestra Pieces (1913) III	B
184	O sanftes Glühn der Berge	B
185	Five Pieces Op. 10/V	A
186	Orchestra Pieces (1913) V	B
187	Orchestra Pieces (1913) I	B
188	Orchestra Pieces (1913) II	B
189	Orchestra Pieces (1913) IV	B
190	Eight Orchestra Fragments I	C
191	Eight Orchestra Fragments II	C
192	Eight Orchestra Fragments III	C
193	Eight Orchestra Fragments IV	C
194	Eight Orchestra Fragments V	C
195	Eight Orchestra Fragments VI	C
196	Eight Orchestra Fragments VII	C
197	Eight Orchestra Fragments VIII	C
198	Schien mir's (chorus)	C

1914

199	Die Einsame Op. 13/II	A
200	Leise Düfte	B
201	Kunfttag III	B
202	Cello Sonata	B
203	Three Little Pieces Op. 11/I	A
204	Three Little Pieces Op. 11/II	A
205	Three Little Pieces Op. 11/III	A
206	Entflieht auf leichten Kähnen Op. 2 (arr)	D
207	In einer lichten Rose	C
208	String Quartet Movement	C
209	Meiner Mutter	C
210	In tiefster Schuld	C
211	Mutig trägst du die Last	C

1915

212	Der Tag ist vergangen Op. 12/I	A
213	Schien mir's Op. 12/III	A

1926
286 Weiss wie Lilien Op. 19/I   A
287 Ziehn die Schafe Op. 19/II   A
288 Auf Bergen, in der reinsten
     Höhe   C

1927
289 String Trio Op. 20/II   A
290 String Trio Op. 20/I   A
291 String Trio Op. 20/(III)   C

1928
292 Two Songs Op. 19 (arr)   D
293 Symphony Op. 21/II   A
294 Symphony Op. 21/I   A
295 Symphony Op. 21/(III)   C
296 Six Pieces Op. 6 (revised) I   A
297 Six Pieces Op. 6 (revised) II   A
298 Six Pieces Op. 6 (revised) III   A
299 Six Pieces Op. 6 (revised) IV   A
300 Six Pieces Op. 6 (revised) V   A
301 Six Pieces Op. 6 (revised) VI   A

1929
302 Five Movements Op. 5 (arr)   D
303 Nun weiss man erst   C
304 String Quartet Movement   C

1930
305 Quartet Op. 22/II   A
306 Cirrus (voice-piano)   C
307 Der Spiegel sagt mir   C
308 Quartet Op. 22/I   A
309 Quartet Op. 22/(III)   C

1931
310 Orchesterstück (Ouvertüre)   C
311 Schubert: German Dances (arr)   D

1933
312 Herr Jesus mein Op. 23/III   A
313 Es stürzt aus Höhen Frische
     Op. 23/II   A

1934
314 Das dunkle Herz Op. 23/I   A
315 Wie kann der Tod   C
316 Concerto Op. 24/I   A
317 Wie bin ich froh Op. 25/I   A
318 Instrumental Movement   C
319 Concerto Op. 24/II   A
320 Concerto Op. 24/III   A
321 Sterne, Ihr silbernen Bienen
     Op. 25/III   A

322 Des Herzens Purpurvogel
     Op. 25/II   A

1935
323 Bach: Fuga (Ricercata) (arr)   D
324 Das Augenlicht Op. 26   A

1936
325 Variations for Piano Op. 27/III   A
326 Variations for Piano Op. 27/I   A
327 Variations for Piano Op. 27/II   A

1937
328 String Quartet Op. 28/III   A

1938
329 String Quartet Op. 28/I   A
330 String Quartet Op. 28/II   A
331 Kleiner Flügel Op. 29/II   A

1939
332 Zündender Lichtblitz
     Op. 29/I   A
333 Wagner-Régeny: Johanna
     Balk (arr)   D
334 Tönen die seligen Saiten Apolls
     Op. 29/III   A

1940
335 Variations for Orchestra
     Op. 30   A

1941
336 Leichteste Bürden
     Op. 31/IV   A

1942
337 Schoeck: Das Schloss Dürande
     (arr)   D
338 Freundselig ist das Wort
     Op. 31/V   A
339 Gelockert aus dem Schosse
     Op. 31/VI   A
340 Casella: Paganiniana (arr)   D

1943
341 Schweigt auch die Welt
     Op. 31/I   A
342 Sehr tiefverhalten
     Op. 31/II   A
343 Schöpfen aus Brunnen
     Op. 31/III   A

Chrono-logical No.	Title and/or first line of text; performance directions	Dedication	Medium
127	Passacaglia for Orchestra, Op. 1 "Sehr mässig"		orch (3 each fl (1 picc), ob (1 Ehn), cl (1 bcl), bn (1 cbn); 4 hn, 3 trp, 3 trb, btuba, timp, perc, hp, str)
129	"Entflieht auf leichten Kähnen," Op. 2 "Zart bewegt"		mixed chorus *a cappella*
	Five Songs from *Der siebente Ring* by Stefan George, Op. 3		v & pn
133	I. "Dies ist ein Lied"		
134	II. "Im Windesweben"		
135	III. "An Bachesranft"		
136	IV. "Im Morgentaun"		
137	V. "Kahl reckt der Baum"		
	Five Songs on Poems of Stefan George, Op. 4	Werner Reinhart	v & pn
138	I. *Eingang* ("Welt der Gestalten")		
139	II. "Noch zwingt mich Treue"		
140	III. "Ja Heil und Dank dir"		
141	IV. "So ich traurig bin"		
142	V. "Ihr tratet zu dem Herde"		
	Five Movements for String Quartet, Op. 5		str qu
147	I. "Heftig bewegt"		
148	II. "Sehr langsam"		
149	III. "Sehr bewegt"		
150	IV. "Sehr langsam"		
151	V. "In zarter Bewegung"		
	Six Pieces for Large Orchestra, Op. 6 (original)	Arnold Schoenberg	orch (4 fl (also 2 picc, 1 afl), 2 ob, 2 Ehn, 3 cl (1 also E♭) 2 bcl, 2 bn (1 also cbn), 6 each hn, trp, trb; btuba, 2 hp, cel, timp, perc, str)
152	I. "Etwas bewegte ♪"		
153	II. "Bewegt"		
154	III. "Zart bewegt"		
155	IV. "Langsam (♩) marcia funebre"		
156	V. "Sehr langsam"		
157	VI. "Zart bewegt"		

Text	Place and date of composition	Published	Place and date of first performance; remarks
	Vienna, [spring] 1908	UE 1922	Vienna, 4 Nov. 1908, Tonkünstlerverein Orch., Anton von Webern cond; see also 234
Stefan George *Das Jahr der Seele* (*Traurige Tänze* cycle)	Vienna, [autumn] 1908	UE 1921	Fürstenfeld (Austria), 10 Apr. 1927; see also 206
Stefan George *Der siebente Ring* (*Lieder* cycle)	[Vienna or Preglhof] 1908–1909	Verlag des Vereins für musikalische Privataufführungen 1919; UE 1921	Vienna, 6 June 1919, Felicie Hüni-Mihacsek v, Eduard Steuermann pn (compl); individual songs Vienna, 8 Feb. 1910; see also 143, 144
Stefan George *Der siebente Ring* (*Traumdunkel* cycle) *Das Jahr der Seele* (*Waller im Schnee* cycle) *Das Jahr der Seele* (*Nach der Lese* cycle)	[Vienna or Preglhof] 1908–1909; definitive version 1920	UE 1923 (compl)	Basel, 10 Feb. 1940, Marguerite Gradmann-Lüscher v, Erich Schmid pn (compl); individual songs Vienna, 8 Feb. 1910; see also 145, 146
Das Buch der Sagen und Sänge (*Sänge eines fahrenden Spielmanns* cycle)			IV. New York, 18 Jan. 1925, Greta Torpadie v, Rex Tillson pn
Das Jahr der Seele (*Traurige Tänze* cycle)		V. *Der blaue Reiter*, May 1912	
	Preglhof, spring 1909	UE 1922	Vienna, 8 Feb. 1910; see also 302
	Preglhof, summer [end Aug.] 1909	Selbstverlag 1913 (as "Op. 4"); UE 1961	Vienna, 31 March 1913, Arnold Schoenberg cond; see also 243

Chrono- logical No.	Title and/or first line of text; performance directions	Dedication	Medium

296
297
298
299
300
301
	Six Pieces for Orchestra, Op. 6 (revised)
	  I. "Langsam"
	  II. "Bewegt"
	  III. "Mässig"
	  IV. "Sehr mässig"
	  V. "Sehr langsam"
	  VI. "Langsam"
		Arnold
		Schoenberg
			orch (2 fl (picc), 2 ob, 3 cl,
			2 bn (cbn), 4 each hn,
			trp, trb; btuba, hp, cel,
			timp, perc, str)

161
162
163
164
	Four Pieces for Violin and Piano, Op. 7
	  I. "Sehr langsam"
	  II. "Rasch"
	  III. "Sehr langsam"
	  IV. "Bewegt"
			vn & pn

167
168
	Two Songs on Poems of Rainer Maria Rilke,
	Op. 8
	  I. "Du, der ichs nicht sage"
	  II. "Du machst mich allein"
			v & instr (cl (bcl), hn, trp,
			cel, hp, vn, va, vc)

178
171
172
173
174
180
	Six Bagatelles for String Quartet, Op. 9
	  I. "Mässig"
	  II. "Leicht bewegt"
	  III. "Ziemlich fliessend"
	  IV. "Sehr langsam"
	  V. "Äusserst langsam"
	  VI. "Fliessend"
			str qu

169
182
181
170
185
	Five Pieces for Orchestra, Op. 10
	  I. "Sehr ruhig und zart"
	  II. "Lebhaft und zart bewegt"
	  III. "Sehr langsam und äusserst ruhig"
	  IV. "Fliessend, äusserst zart"
	  V. "Sehr fliessend"
			orch (fl (picc), ob, cl
			(bcl), E♭ cl, hn, trp,
			trb, harm, cel, hp,
			mand, guit, perc, 1 each
			solo str)

Text	Place and date of composition	Published	Place and date of first performance; remarks
	Mödling, Aug.–Sept. 1928	UE 1956	Berlin, 27 Jan. 1929, Hermann Scherchen cond
	Preglhof, [June] 1910; definitive version summer 1914	UE 1922 (compl) I. *Der Ruf*, March 1912	Vienna, 24 Apr. 1911, [Fritz Brunner vn, Etta Jonas-Werndorff pn]
Rainer Maria Rilke *Die Aufzeichnungen des Malte Laurids Brigge*	Preglhof, [10] Aug. and [30] Aug., 1910 (original); undated second version; spring 1921, new instrumentation (third version); Jan. 1925, revised for publication (fourth version)	UE 1926	First public perf. unknown. Columbia Masterworks, 1957: Grace-Lynne Martin v, ensemble Robert Craft cond; see also 285
	Mürzzuschlag, June–July 1913 Preglhof, summer 1911 Preglhof, summer 1911 Preglhof, summer 1911 Preglhof, summer 1911 Mürzzuschlag, June–July 1913	UE 1924 (compl) IV. *Der Ruf*, May 1913	Combined from *II. Streichquartett* (II, III, IV, V) and *Drei Stücke für Streichquartett* (I & VI); 1st perf. of Six Bagatelles: Donaueschingen, 19 July 1924, Amar Quartet; 1st perf. of *Drei Stücke* in original form: New York, 11 April 1964, Juilliard String Quartet with Adele Addison v; see also 179
	Preglhof, 28 June 1911 Vienna, 13 Sept. 1913 Vienna, 8 Sept. 1913 Preglhof, 19 July 1911 Vienna, 6 Oct. 1913	UE 1923	Zürich, 22 June 1926, Tonhalle Orch, Anton von Webern cond; see also 241

Chrono-logical No.	Title and/or first line of text; performance directions	Dedication	Medium
	Three Little Pieces for Violoncello and Piano, Op. 11		vc & pn
203	I. "Mässige♩"		
204	II. "Sehr bewegt"		
205	III. "Äusserst ruhig"		
	Four Songs for Voice and Piano, Op. 12		v & pn
212	I. "Der Tag ist vergangen"		
217	II. *Die geheimnisvolle Flöte* ("An einem Abend")		
213	III. "Schien mir's, als ich sah die Sonne"		
216	IV. *Gleich und Gleich* ("Ein Blumenglöckchen")		
	Four Songs for Voice and Orchestra Op. 13	Norbert Schwarzmann	
221	I. *Wiese im Park* ("Wie wird mir zeitlos")		v & instr (fl, cl, bcl, hn, trp, trb, cel, glock, hp; solo vn, va, vc, db)
199	II. *Die Einsame* ("An dunkelblauem Himmel")		v & instr (as above, with picc for fl)
223	III. *In der Fremde* ("In fremdem Lande")		v & instr (picc, cl, bcl, trp, cel, hp; solo vn, va, vc)
231	IV. *Ein Winterabend* ("Wenn der Schnee")		v & instr (cl, bcl, trp, trb, cel, hp; solo vn, va, vc, db)
	Six Songs on Poems of Georg Trakl, Op. 14		
251	I. *Die Sonne* ("Täglich kommt die gelbe Sonne")		v & B♭ cl, vn, vc
240	II. *Abendland I* ("Mond, als träte ein Totes")		v & bcl, vn, vc
237	III. *Abendland II* ("So leise sind die grünen Wälder")		v & B♭ cl, vn, vc
222	IV. *Abendland III* ("Ihr grossen Städte")		v & E♭ cl, bcl, vc
239	V. *Nachts* ("Die Bläue meiner Augen")		v & E♭ cl, bcl, vn
238	VI. *Gesang einer gefangenen Amsel* ("Dunkler Odem im grünen Gezweig")		v & B♭ cl, bcl, vn, vc

Text	Place and date of composition	Published	Place and date of first performance; remarks
	Vienna, spring–summer [June], 1914	UE 1924	Mainz, 2 Dec. 1924, Maurits Frank vc, Eduard Zuckmayer pn
folk song	Vienna, 13 Jan. 1915	UE 1925 (compl) I. *Musikblätter des Anbruch*, May 1922	January 1927 (compl) (diary entry Webern)
Li-Tai-Po (Hans Bethge *Die chinesische Flöte*)	Vienna, 10 Apr. 1917		
August Strindberg *Gespenster Sonate*	Vienna, 31 Jan. 1915		
Johann Wolfgang von Goethe *Lieder*	Vienna, 31 March 1917		IV. October 1926 (diary entry Webern)
		UE 1926	Winterthur, 16 Feb. 1928, Clara Wirz-Wyss v, Hermann Scherchen cond; see also 264
Karl Kraus *Worte in Versen*, Part I	Klagenfurt, 16 June 1917		
Wang-Seng-Yu (Bethge *Die chinesische Flöte*)	Vienna, 16 [Feb.] 1914		
Li-Tai-Po (Bethge *Die chinesische Flöte*)	Klagenfurt, [4 July] 1917		
Georg Trakl (*Der Herbst des Einsamen* cycle)	Mödling, 10 July 1918; revised Mödling, March 1922		
Georg Trakl (*Siebengesang des Todes* cycle)	Mödling, 12 Aug. 1921	UE 1924	Donaueschingen, 20 July 1924, Clara Kwartin v, ensemble headed by Rudolf Kolisch, Anton von Webern cond; see also 262
(*Gesang des Abgeschiedenen* cycle)	Mürzzuschlag, 28 July 1919		
(*Gesang des Abgeschiedenen* cycle)	Mürzzuschlag, 7 July 1919		
(*Gesang des Abgeschiedenen* cycle)	Klagenfurt, 23 June 1917		
(*Sebastian im Traum* cycle)	Mürzzuschlag, 18 July 1919		
(*Gesang des Abgeschiedenen* cycle)	Mürzzuschlag, 11 July 1919		

Chrono-logical No.	Title and/or first line of text; performance directions	Dedication	Medium
	Five Sacred Songs, Op. 15		
252	I. "Das Kreuz, das musst' er tragen"		v & fl, bcl, trp, hp, va
256	II. *Morgenlied* ("Steht auf, ihr lieben Kinderlein")		v & bcl, trp, hp, vn
253	III. "In Gottes Namen aufstehn"		v & cl, trp, va
257	IV. "Mein Weg geht jetzt vorüber"		v & fl, cl
224	V. "Fahr hin, o Seel'"		v & fl, cl, trp, hp, vn
	Five Canons on Latin Texts, Op. 16		
270	I. "Christus factus est"		v & cl, bcl
259	II. "Dormi Jesu"		v & cl
260	III. "Crux fidelis"		v & cl, bcl
261	IV. "Asperges me"		v & bcl
269	V. "Crucem tuam adoramus"		v & cl, bcl
	Three Traditional Rhymes, Op. 17		
268	I. "Armer Sünder, du"		v & cl, bcl, vn
275	II. "Liebste Jungfrau"		v & cl, bcl, vn
274	III. "Heiland, unsre Missetaten"		v & cl, bcl, va
	Three Songs, Op. 18		v & E♭ cl, guit
281	I. "Schatzerl klein"		
282	II. *Erlösung* ("Mein Kind, sieh an")		
283	III. "Ave, Regina coelorum"		

Text	Place and date of composition	Published	Place and date of first performance; remarks
anon.	Mödling, 28 Aug. 1921	UE 1924	Vienna, 9 Oct. 1924, Felicie Hüni-Mihacsek v, members of the Vienna Opera orch, Anton von Webern cond; see also 263
from *Des Knaben Wunderhorn*	Traunkirchen, 22 July 1922		
anon.	Mödling, 3 Sept. 1921		
anon.	Traunkirchen, 26 July 1922		
anon. [Peter Rosegger?]	Klagenfurt, 20 July 1917		V. On his handwritten copy of the text, Webern gives Peter Rosegger's *Erdsegen* as source
Gradual from the Solemn evening Mass for Maundy Thursday	Mödling, 12 Nov. 1924	UE 1928	New York, 8 May 1951, Bethany Beardslee v, Everett Matson cl, Robert Olisar bcl, Jacques Monod cond
from *Des Knaben Wunderhorn*	Mödling, July 1923		
Hymn from the Solemn afternoon Liturgy for Good Friday	Mödling, 8 Aug. 1923		
Psalm 50 (8, 1)	Mödling, 21 Aug. 1923		
Antiphon from the Solemn afternoon Liturgy for Good Friday	Mödling, 29 Oct. 1924		
anon.	Mödling, autumn 1924	UE 1955 (compl)	New York, 16 March 1952, Bethany Beardslee v, Jeffrey Lerner cl, Anthony Gilio bcl, Abram Loft vn-va (compl);
anon.	Mödling, 17 July 1925	II. *New Music* 1930 (as *Geistlicher Volkstext*)	II. New York, 8 May 1951, Bethany Beardslee v, Everett Matson cl, Robert Olisar bcl, Abraham Shevelov vn, Jacques Monod cond
anon.	Mödling, 11 July 1925		
folk song	Mödling, 10 Sept. 1925	UE 1927	Los Angeles, 8 Feb. 1954, Grace-Lynne Martin v, Hugo Raimondi cl, Jack Marshall guit, Robert Craft cond
from *Des Knaben Wunderhorn*	Mödling, 27 Sept. 1925		
Marian Antiphon	Mödling, 28 Oct. 1925		

Chrono- logical No.	Title and/or first line of text; performance directions	Dedication	Medium
	Two Songs, Op. 19	David Josef Bach	mixed chorus & instr (cel, guit, vn, cl, bcl)
286	I. "Weiss wie Lilien"		
287	II. "Ziehn die Schafe"		
	String Trio, Op. 20		vn, va, vc
290	I. "Sehr langsam"		
289	II. "Sehr getragen und ausdrucksvoll"		
	Symphony, Op. 21	Christine von Webern	chamber ensemble (cl, bcl, 2 hn, hp, 1. & 2. vn, va, vc)
294	I. "Ruhig schreitend"		
293	II. Variationen ("Sehr ruhig")		
	Quartet, Op. 22	Adolf Loos	vn, cl, tsax, pn
308	I. "Sehr mässig"		
305	II. "Sehr schwungvoll"		
	Three Songs from Viae inviae, Op. 23	Hildegard Jone	v & pn
314	I. "Das dunkle Herz"		
313	II. "Es stürzt aus Höhen Frische"		
312	III. "Herr Jesus mein"		
	Concerto, Op. 24	Arnold Schoenberg	chamber ensemble (fl, ob, cl, hn, trp, trb, pn, vn, va)
316	I. "Etwas lebhaft"		
319	II. "Sehr langsam"		
320	III. "Sehr rasch"		

Text	Place and date of composition	Published	Place and date of first performance; remarks
Johann Wolfgang von Goethe (*Chinesisch-deutsche Jahres- und Tageszeiten* cycle)	Mödling, Dec. 1925–Jan. 1926 Mödling, 8 July 1926	UE 1928	First public perf. unknown. Columbia Masterworks, 1957: Marni Nixon, Grace-Lynne Martin, Richard Robin, Charles Scharbach (vocal quartet), ensemble Robert Craft cond; see also 292, 288
	Summer 1926—end of June 1927 Mödling, spring 1927 Mödling, summer 1926–early 1927	UE 1927	Vienna, 16 Jan. 1928, members of the Vienna String Quartet (Rudolf Kolisch vn, Eugen Lehner va, Benar Heifetz vc); see also 291
	Nov. 1927–June 1928 Mödling, 27 June 1928 Mödling, 27 March 1928	UE 1929	New York, 18 Dec. 1929, Alexander Smallens cond; see also 295
	Sept. 1928–Aug. 1930 Mödling, 14 Aug. 1930 Mödling, 12 Apr. 1930	UE 1932	Vienna, 13 Apr. 1931, Rudolf Kolisch vn, Johann Löw cl, Leopold Wlach tsax, Eduard Steuermann pn; see also 309
Hildegard Jone *Viae inviae*	Maria Enzersdorf, 15 March 1934 Maria Enzersdorf, 18 Aug. 1933 Maria Enzersdorf, 14 July 1933	UE 1936	Basel, 5 Dec. 1943, Marguerite Gradmann-Lüscher v, Paul Baumgartner pn
	Jan. 1931–Sept. 1934 Maria Enzersdorf, 25 June 1934 Maria Enzersdorf, 4 Aug. 1934 Maria Enzersdorf, 4 Sept. 1934	UE/Editions Dynamo (Liège), 1948	Prague, 4 Sept. 1935, Heinrich Jalowetz cond; begun at Mödling as *Orchesterstück* (*Ouvertüre*); see also 310, 315, 318

Chrono-logical No.	Title and/or first line of text; performance directions	Dedication	Medium
	Three Songs on Poems of Hildegard Jone, Op. 25		v & pn
317	I. "Wie bin ich froh!"		
322	II. "Des Herzens Purpurvogel"		
321	III. "Sterne, Ihr silbernen Bienen"		
324	*Das Augenlicht*, Op. 26 ("Durch unsre offnen Augen")	Amalie Waller	mixed chorus & orch (fl, ob, cl, asax, hn, trp, trb, timp, perc, cel, hp, mand, 8 vn, 4 va, 4 vc)
	Variations for Piano, Op. 27	Eduard Steuermann	pn
326	I. "Sehr mässig"		
327	II. "Sehr schnell"		
325	III. "Ruhig fliessend"		
	String Quartet, Op. 28	Elizabeth Sprague Coolidge	str qu
329	I. "Mässig"		
330	II. "Gemächlich"		
328	III. "Sehr fliessend"		
	First Cantata, Op. 29		soprano solo, mixed chorus & orch (fl, ob, cl, bcl, hn, trp, trb, timp, perc, hp, cel, mand, vn, va, vc)
332	I. "Zündender Lichtblitz"		
331	II. "Kleiner Flügel"		
334	III. "Tönen die seligen Saiten Apolls"		
335	Variations for Orchestra, Op. 30 "Lebhaft"	Werner Reinhart	orch (fl, ob, cl, bcl, hn, trp, trb, btuba, timp, hp, cel, str)

Text	Place and date of composition	Published	Place and date of first performance; remarks
Hildegard Jone (*Die Freunde* cycle)	Maria Enzersdorf, 16 July 1934 Maria Enzersdorf, 15 Nov. 1934 Maria Enzersdorf, 8 Oct. 1934	UE 1956	New York, 16 March 1952, Bethany Beardslee v, Jacques Monod pn
Hildegard Jone *Viae inviae*	Maria Enzersdorf, Feb.–13 Sept. 1935	UE 1956	London, 17 June 1938, BBC Orch & Chorus, Hermann Scherchen cond. Piano-vocal score by Ludwig Zenk (UE 1938)
	Maria Enzersdorf, Oct. 1935–Sept. 1936 19 August 1936 5 Sept. 1936 8 July 1936	UE 1937	Vienna, 26 Oct. 1937, Peter Stadlen pn
	Maria Enzersdorf, Nov. 1936–March 1938 21 Jan. 1938 26 March 1938 20 August 1937	Boosey & Hawkes (Hawkes & Sons) 1939; UE 1955	Pittsfield (Mass.), 22 Sept. 1938, Kolisch Quartet
Hildegard Jone Blitz und Donner (*Der Mohnkopf* cycle) in *Enthüllte Form*	Maria Enzersdorf July 1938–Nov. 1939 25 April 1939	UE 1954	London, 12 July 1946, Emelie Hooke v, BBC Orch & Chorus, Karl Rankl cond; see also 345
(*Fons hortorum* cycle)	14 Dec. 1938		
from *Verwandlung der Chariten*	26 Nov. 1939		
	Maria Enzersdorf, April 1940–25 Nov. 1940	UE 1956	Winterthur, 3 March 1943, Stadtorchester, Hermann Scherchen cond

Chrono-logical No.	Title and/or first line of text; performance directions	Dedication	Medium
	Second Cantata, Op. 31		soprano solo, bass solo, mixed chorus & orch (picc, fl, ob, Ehn, cl, bcl, asax, bn, hn, trp, trb, btuba, perc, hp, cel, str)
341	I. "Schweigt auch die Welt"		
342	II. "Sehr tiefverhalten"		
343	III. "Schöpfen aus Brunnen"		
336	IV. "Leichteste Bürden"		
338	V. "Freundselig ist das Wort"		
339	VI. "Gelockert aus dem Schosse"		

Text	Place and date of composition	Published	Place and date of first performance; remarks
Hildegard Jone	Maria Enzersdorf, [April] 1941–Nov. 1943	UE 1949, choral score UE 1956, full score	Brussels, 23 June 1950, Ilona Steingruber & Otto Wiener v, NIR chamber orch & chorus (Radio Belgium), Herbert Häfner cond; see also 346, 344
Strahl und Klang (*Licht und Lied* cycle)	21 Jan. 1943		
Die Stille um den Bienenkorb (*Das Feldpostpäckchen* cycle)	6 July 1943		
Alle Glocken (*Der Mohnkopf* cycle)	3 Nov. 1943		
Der Wind (*Das Feldpostpäckchen* cycle)	31 July 1941		
(*Freundseligkeit* cycle)	2 July 1942		
Das Neugeborene (*Alltag* cycle)	26 Aug. 1942		

Chrono-logical No.	Title and/or first line of text; performance directions	Medium	Text
1 2	*Two Pieces (1899) I. "Langsam" (G major) II. "Langsam" (F major)	vc & pn	
3	Three poems for Voice and Piano I. *Vorfrühling* ("Leise tritt auf")	v & pn	Ferdinand Avenarius *Stimmen und Bilder* (*Jahrbuch* cycle; first poem of *Vorfrühling* group)
13	II. *Nachtgebet der Braut* ("O Welt, wann darf ich")		Richard Dehmel
12	III. *Fromm* ("Der Mond scheint")		Gustav Falke *Mit dem Leben*
7	*Eight Early Songs I. *Tief von fern* ("Aus des Abends")	v & pn	Richard Dehmel *Erlösungen*, Zweiter Abschnitt
15	II. *Aufblick* ("Über unsere Liebe")		Richard Dehmel
21	III. *Blumengruss* ("Der Strauss, den ich")		Johann Wolfgang von Goethe *Lieder*
62	IV. *Bild der Liebe* ("Vom Wald umgeben")		Martin Greif *Neue Lieder und Mären*
16	V. *Sommerabend* ("Du Sommerabend")		Wilhelm Weigand
64	VI. *Heiter* ("Mein Herz ist wie ein See")		Friedrich Nietzsche
19	VII. *Der Tod* ("Ach, es ist so dunkel")		Matthias Claudius *Sämtliche Werke des Wandsbecker Boten*, Sechster Teil
18	VIII. *Heimgang in der Frühe* ("In der Dämmerung")		Detlev von Liliencron *Bunte Beute*
60	*Three Songs after Poems by Ferdinand Avenarius I. *Gefunden* ("Nun wir uns lieben")	v & pn	Ferdinand Avenarius *Stimmen und Bilder* (*Ehe* cycle)
20	II. *Gebet* ("Ertrage du's")		(*Stimmungen* cycle)
59	III. *Freunde* ("Schmerzen und Freuden")		(*Ehe* cycle)
63	*Im Sommerwind* ("Idyl for large orchestra after a poem by Bruno Wille") "Ruhig bewegt"	orch (3 fl, 2 ob, E hn, 2 A cl, 2 B♭ cl, bcl, 2 bn, 6 hn, 2 trp, timp, perc, 2 hp, str)	

Place and date of composition	Published	Place and date of first performance; remarks
Preglhof, 17 Sept. 1899 [Preglhof], 1899	CF 1975	Cleveland, 3 June 1970; Gregor Piatigorsky vc, Victor Babin pn
Klagenfurt, 1899	CF 1965	Seattle, 26 May 1962 (1st IWF), Esther LaBerge v, Rudolph Ganz pn. The first of two mss. of *Vorfrühling* is dated Klagenfurt 1899, the second, Klagenfurt, 12 Jan. 1900; see also 5
Preglhof, 10 April 1903		
Preglhof, 11 Sept. 1902		
Klagenfurt, 21 Apr. 1901	CF 1965	Seattle, 27 May 1962 (1st IWF), Esther LaBerge v, Rudolph Ganz pn
Preglhof, 12 Aug. 1903		
Vienna, 1903		
Preglhof, 11 Sept. 1904		
Preglhof, 7 Sept. 1903		
[Vienna or Preglhof], 1904		
Vienna, 24 Nov. 1903		
Vienna, 21 Nov. 1903		
[Vienna or Preglhof], 5 April 1904	CF 1965	Seattle, 26 May 1962 (1st IWF), Esther LaBerge v, Rudolph Ganz pn
Preglhof, 1903		
[Vienna], 6 Jan. 1904		
Preglhof, 16 Sept. 1904	CF 1966	Seattle, 25 May 1962 (1st IWF), Philadelphia Orch, Eugene Ormandy cond

Chrono-logical No.	Title and/or first line of text; performance directions	Medium	Text
78	*Langsamer Satz* "Langsam, mit bewegtem Ausdruck"	str qu	
79	String Quartet (1905) "Düster und schwer"	str qu	
112	* *Satz für Klavier* "Lebhaft"	pn	
114	*Sonatensatz (Rondo) für Klavier* "Bewegt"	pn	
115	Rondo "Bewegt"	str qu	
	*Five Songs after Poems by Richard Dehmel	v & pn	Richard Dehmel
83	I. *Ideale Landschaft* ("Du hattest einen Glanz")		*Weib und Welt*
130	II. *Am Ufer* ("Die Welt verstummt")		*Weib und Welt*
131	III. *Himmelfahrt* ("Schwebst du nieder")		*Weib und Welt*
119	IV. *Nächtliche Scheu* ("Zaghaft vom Gewölk")		*Aber die Liebe*
132	V. *Helle Nacht* ("Weich küsst die Zweige")		*Weib und Welt*
118	Quintet "Mässig"	2 vn, va, vc, pn	
	*Four Stefan George Songs	v & pn	Stefan George
143	I. "Erwachen aus dem tiefsten Traumesschosse"		*Das Jahr der Seele* (Nacht-wachen cycle)
144	II. *Kunfttag I* ("Dem bist du Kind")		*Der siebente Ring* (Maximin cycle)
145	III. *Trauer I* ("So wart, bis ich dies")		*Der siebente Ring* (Maximin cycle)
146	IV. "Das lockere Saatgefilde"		*Der siebente Ring* (Gezeiten cycle)

Place and date of composition	Published	Place and date of first performance; remarks
Vienna, June 1905	CF 1965	Seattle, 27 May 1962 (1st IWF), University of Washington String Quartet
Preglhof, 25 Aug. 1905; revised ending Vordernberg, 12 Sept. 1905	CF 1965	Seattle, 26 May 1962 (1st IWF), University of Washington String Quartet
[Vienna, 1906]	CF 1970	Vienna, 2 Dec. 1958, Else Stock-Hug pn
[Vienna, 1906]	CF 1969	Hanover (N. H.), 2 Aug. 1968 (4th IWF), Noël Lee pn
[Vienna, 1906]	CF 1970	Hanover, 1 Aug. 1968 (4th IWF), Philadelphia String Quartet
	CF 1966	Seattle, 26 May 1962 (1st IWF), Grace-Lynne Martin v, Leonard Stein pn
Vienna, Easter 1906		
Vienna, 1908		
[Vienna or Preglhof], 1908		
[Vienna or Preglhof], 1907		
[Vienna or Preglhof], 1908		
Vienna, spring 1907	Boelke-Bomart 1953	Vienna, 7 Nov. 1907, Oskar Adler 1. vn, George Heim 2. vn, Heinrich Jalowetz va, Heinrich Geiger vc, Etta Jonas pn
[Vienna or Preglhof], 1908–1909	CF 1970	Buffalo, 29 Oct. 1966 (3rd IWF), Ethel Casey v, Cornelius Cardew pn
		} originally planned for Op. 3
		} originally planned for Op. 4

Chrono-logical No.	Title and/or first line of text; performance directions	Medium	Text

187 188 183 189 186	*Orchestra Pieces (1913)
	    I. "Bewegt"
	    II. "Langsam (sostenuto)"
	    III. "Sehr bewegte Viertel"
	    IV. "Langsame Viertel"
	    V. "(Alla breve)"
		orch (picc, 2 fl, 2 ob, E hn, E♭ cl 2 B♭ cl, bcl, 2 bn, cbn, 4 hn, 3 B♭ trp, E♭ btrp, 3 trb, btuba, guit, hp, cel, harm, timp, perc, solo & tutti str)	

200 201 184	Three Orchestral Songs (1913/14)
	    I. "Leise Düfte, Blüten so zart"
	    II. *Kunfttag III* ("Nun wird es wieder Lenz")
	    III. "O sanftes Glühn der Berge"
		v & orch (fl (picc), ob, Ehn, cl, bcl, hn, trp, 2 trb, harm, cel, hp, mand, guit, timp, perc, solo vn, va, vc, 2 db)	Anton von Webern
			
			Stefan George *Der siebente Ring* (*Maximin* cycle)
			Anton von Webern

202	Cello Sonata "Sehr bewegt"	vc & pn	
267	*Kinderstück* "Lieblich"	pn	
277	*Klavierstück* "Im Tempo eines Menuetts"	pn	
278	*Satz für Streichtrio* "Ruhig fliessend"	vn, va, vc	

Place and date of composition	Published	Place and date of first performance; remarks
	CF 1971	Compl: Cologne, 13 Jan. 1969, West German Radio Orch, Friedrich Cerha cond
[Vienna, 1913]		I, III, V: Philadelphia, 14 April 1967,
[Vienna, 1913]		Philadelphia Orch, Eugene Ormandy cond
[Vienna], 21 Sept. 1913		
[Vienna, 1913]		
[Vienna], 2 Dec. 1913		
	CF 1968	Buffalo, 30 Oct. 1966 (3rd IWF), Marni Nixon v,
[Vienna], 23 March 1914		Buffalo Philharmonic Orch, Lukas Foss cond
[Vienna], 2 April 1914		
[Vienna], 30 Sept. 1913		
Vienna, 9 May 1914	CF 1970	Cleveland, 3 June 1970, Gregor Piatigorsky vc, Victor Babin pn
Mödling, autumn 1924	CF 1967	New York, 22 July 1966, Caren Glasser pn
Mödling, [summer] 1925	UE 1966	Vienna, 8 Feb. 1963, Ivan Eröd pn
Mödling, 9 Aug. 1925	UE 1966	Vienna, 8 Feb. 1963, Viktor Redtenbacher vn, Eugenie A.'tmann va, Friedrich Hiller vc

Chrono-logical No.	Title and/or first line of text; performance directions	Medium	Text
4	*Wolkennacht* ("Nacht, dem Zauber")	v & pn	Ferdinand Avenarius *Stimmen und Bilder*
6	*Vorfrühling II* ("Doch schwer hinschnaubend")	v & pn	Ferdinand Avenarius *Stimmen und Bilder* (*Jahrbuch* cycle; second poem of *Vorfrühling* group)
8	*Wehmut* ("Darf ich einer Blume still")	v & pn	Ferdinand Avenarius *Stimmen und Bilder* (*Jahrbuch* cycle)
9	"Du bist mein, ich bin dein"	v & pn	anon., Minnelied, *ca.* 12th century
10	"Du träumst so heiss im Sommerwind"	v & pn	?
11	*Dämmerstunde* ("Im Sessel du, und ich zu deinen Füssen")	v & pn	Theodor Storm *Gedichte* (second of two poems with the same title)
17	*Siegfrieds Schwert* ("Jung Siegfried war ein stolzer Knab'")	v & orch (2 each fl, ob, cl, bn; cbn, 4 hn, 3 trp, 3 trb, timp, perc, str)	Ludwig Uhland *Balladen und Romanzen*
22	Theme and Variations A minor	pn; str qu	
	Variations on "Der Winter ist vergangen"		
23	I. G major	pn	
24	II. G major–G minor	str qu	
25	String Quartet Variations F major–F minor	str qu	
26	String Quartet Movement E minor	str qu	
27	String Quartet Movement G major	str qu	
28	String Quartet Movement C minor	str qu	
29	Piano Piece C major	pn	

Place and date of composition	Published	Place and date of first performance; remarks
Klagenfurt, 1900	MS	46 mm pencil
[1900]	MS	26 mm pencil Buffalo, 29 Oct. 1966 (3rd IWF), Ethel Casey v, Cornelius Cardew pn
Preglhof, 15 July 1901	MS	23 mm pencil Buffalo, 29 Oct. 1966 (3rd IWF), Ethel Casey v, Cornelius Cardew pn
[1901]	MS	20 mm pencil
[1901]	MS	whereabouts of MS unknown
[1901]	MS	33 mm pencil
Preglhof, 25 Sept 1903	MS	94 mm finished ink score
[1903]	MS	21 numbered variations (No. 21 for str qu), 188 mm ink
[1903]	MS	theme based on a folksong 72 mm ink; 10 mm pencil 82 mm ink
[1903]	MS	*ca.* 107 mm pencil
[1903]	MS	14 mm ink; 21 mm pencil
[1903]	MS	13 mm pencil
[1903]	MS	17 mm ink & pencil
[1903]	MS	34 mm ink; *ca.* 80 mm pencil

Chrono-logical No.	Title and/or first line of text; performance directions	Medium	Text
30	Piano Piece Ab major	pn	
31	Piano Piece C major	pn	
32 33	Two Piano Pieces I. E major II. E minor	pn	
	Eleven Short Piano Pieces	pn	
34	I. Bb major		
35	II. G major		
36	III. D major		
37	IV. A minor		
38	V. F major		
39	VI. C major		
40	VII. A minor		
41	VIII. C major		
42	IX. G major		
43	X. D major		
44	XI. E major		
45	Piano Piece A major	pn	
46	Piano Piece C major	pn	
47	String Orchestra Movement C# minor	vn I, vn II, va, vc, db	
48	String Orchestra Movement C major	vn I, vn II, va, vc, db	
61	*Liebeslied* ("Ob ich lach")	v & pn	Hans Böhm
65	*Hochsommernacht* ("Stille ruht die weite Welt")	vocal duet (soprano, tenor) & pn	Martin Greif
66	String Quartet Movement C major	str qu	
67	Quartet Movement E minor; "Mässig bewegt"	cl, vn, va, pn	

Place and date of composition	Published	Place and date of first performance; remarks
[1903]	MS	24 mm ink; *ca.* 40 mm pencil
[1903]	MS	30 mm ink; 10 mm pencil
[1903]	MS	151 mm ink; 38 mm pencil *ca.* 40 mm ink
[1903]	MS	In addition to the ink scores listed below, there are pencil sketches totalling *ca.* 245 mm 8 mm ink 12 mm ink 16 mm ink 21 mm ink 20 mm ink 27 mm ink 25 mm ink 31 mm ink 20 mm ink 11 mm ink 23 mm ink
[1903]	MS	80 mm ink; 140 mm pencil
[1903]	MS	62 mm ink; *ca.* 90 mm pencil
[1903]	MS	20 mm pencil
[1903]	MS	*ca.* 133 mm pencil
24 April 1904	MS	18 mm pencil
[1904]	MS	29 mm ink & pencil Buffalo, 29 Oct. 1966 (3rd IWF), Ethel Casey & Warren Hoffer v, Cornelius Cardew pn
[1904]	MS	*ca.* 138 mm ink
[1904]	MS	32 mm pencil

Chrono-logical No.	Title and/or first line of text; performance directions	Medium	Text
68	Scherzo and Trio A minor	str qu	
69	*Zum Schluss* ("Wen'ge sinds, die mich verstehen")	v & orch (2 each fl, ob, cl, bn, trp; Ehn, bcl, cbn, 4 hn, 3 trb, btuba, timp, hp, str)	?
70	String Quartet Movement B♭ major; "Schwer"	str qu	
71	Orchestra Movement F major	orch (ob, cl, hn, & str indicated)	
72	Orchestra Movement D major; "Sehr bewegt"	orch (picc, 2 fl, 2 ob, Ehn, D cl, 2 B♭ cl, bcl, 2 bn, cbn, 6 hn, 3 trp, 3 trb, btuba, timp, perc, hp, str)	
73	Orchestra Movement F major; "Kräftig bewegt"	orch (picc, 2 fl, 2 ob, Ehn, E♭ cl, 2 B♭ cl, 2 bn, cbn, 4 hn, 3 trp, 3 trb, timp, perc, hp, str)	
74	String Orchestra Movement D minor	str orch	
75	Piano Piece A minor; "Schnell"	pn	
76	Piano Piece G major; "Langsam"	pn	
77	Piano Piece E♭ major–E♭ minor	pn	
80	String Quartet Movement D major–D minor	str qu	
81	Piano Quintet G minor	pn & str qu	

Place and date of composition	Published	Place and date of first performance; remarks
[1904]	MS	2 versions, 90 & 71 mm finished ink scores Baton Rouge, 17 Feb. 1978 (6th IWF), Concord String Quartet
[1904]	MS	22 mm full score, ink
[1904]	MS	26 mm pencil
[1904]	MS	*ca.* 86 mm condensed score, pencil
[1904]	MS	59 mm full score, ink; 518 mm condensed score, pencil
[1904]	MS	36 mm full score, ink; 470 mm condensed score, pencil
[1904]	MS	142 mm full score, ink; 276 mm condensed score, pencil
[1904]	MS	14 mm ink
[1904]	MS	21 mm ink; also sketched for str qu, 21 mm ink
[1904]	MS	14 mm pencil
[1905]	MS	*ca.* 66 mm pencil
[1905]	MS	*ca.* 36 mm pencil

Chrono- logical No.	Title and/or first line of text; performance directions	Medium	Text
82	Orchestra Variations D major–D minor	orch (not specified)	
84	Eighteen German Chorale Settings I. "Komm heil'ger Geist, du Tröster mein"	a 4	
85	II. "Christus, der ist mein Leben"		
86	III. "Christ lag in Todes- banden"		
87	IV. "Nun freut euch, Gottes Kinder all"		
88	V. "O Ewigkeit, du Donner- wort"		
89	VI. "Herr Jesu Christ, dich zu uns wend'"		
90	VII. "Nicht so traurig, nicht so sehr"		
91	VIII. "Gib dich zufrieden und sei stille"		
92	IX. "O Traurigkeit, o Herzeleid"		
93	X. "Wenn wir in höchsten Nöten sein"		
94	XI. "Nun ruhen alle Wälder"		
95	XII. "Danket dem Herren, denn er ist sehr freundlich"		
96	XIII. "Nun komm, der Heiden Heiland"		
97	XIV. "Herr Jesu Christ, du höchstes Gut"		
98	XV. "Von Gott will ich nicht lassen"		
99	XVI. "Heut' ist, o Mensch, ein grosser"		
100	XVII. "Jesus, meine Zuversicht"		
101	XVIII. "Erschienen ist der herrliche Tag"		
102	Orchestra Movement B minor; "Sehr lebhaft"	2 cl, hn, str	
103	Orchestra Movement E major	not specified	
104	Piano Quintet Movement C minor	pn & str qu	

Place and date of composition	Published	Place and date of first performance; remarks
[1905]	MS	522 mm condensed score, pencil
[Preglhof, summer 1906]	MS	
		28 mm finished ink score Source: Zahn, *Die Melodien der deutschen Kirchenlieder*, Vol. 1 (1889), No. 38 BWV 281
		BWV 277
		BWV 387
		BWV 397
		BWV 332
		BWV 384
		BWV 315
		BWV 404
		BWV 431
		BWV 392 BWV 286
		BWV 36
		BWV 334
		BWV 417
		BWV 341
		BWV 365 BWV 145
[1906]	MS	7 mm full score, ink & pencil
[1906]	MS	20 mm condensed score, pencil
[1906]	MS	65 mm pencil

Chrono-logical No.	Title and/or first line of text; performance directions	Medium	Text
105	String Quartet Movement D major–A major	str qu	
106	String Quartet Movement D major; "Sehr lebhaft"	str qu	
107	String Quartet Movement C major	str qu	
108	String Quartet Movement E minor	str qu	
109	String Quartet Movement D minor	str qu	
110	String Quartet Movement A major–E major	str qu	
111	String Quartet Movement D minor	str qu	
113	Piano Movement F major	pn	
116	Piano Piece C minor	pn	
117	Violin–Piano Movement E minor; "Sehr lebhaft"	vn & pn	
120	Theme and Variations C♯ minor; "Langsam"	str qu	
121	String Quartet A minor	str qu	
122	String Quartet C minor–C major; "Sehr bewegt"	str qu	
123	Instrumental Piece G major	only 2nd vn specified	

Place and date of composition	Published	Place and date of first performance; remarks
[1906]	MS	*ca.* 112 mm pencil
[1906]	MS	*ca.* 93 mm pencil
[1906]	MS	53 mm pencil
[1906]	MS	19 mm ink & pencil
[1906]	MS	46 mm pencil
[1906]	MS	48 mm pencil
[1906]	MS	68 mm pencil
[1906]	MS	134 mm ink
[1906]	MS	16 mm ink; 25 mm pencil
[1906]	MS	113 mm ink; 385 mm pencil
[1907]	MS	theme 15 mm ink; three variations 46 mm pencil; sketches 55 mm pencil
[1907]	MS	269 mm ink & pencil; full score was reconstructed from sketches & extant vn II & vc parts Baton Rouge, 16 Feb. 1978 (6th IWF), Concord String Quartet
[1907]	MS	109 mm ink; 574 mm pencil
[1907]	MS	*ca.* 36 mm condensed score, pencil

Chrono-logical No.	Title and/or first line of text; performance directions	Medium	Text
	Three Orchestra Studies on a Ground	orch	
	A minor		
124	I. "Ruhig bewegt"	2 fl, 2 ob, Ehn, 2 A cl, bcl, 2 bn, cbn, 4 hn, 3 trp, 3 trb, btuba, hp, timp, perc, str	
125	II.	2 fl, Ehn, 2 A cl, bcl, bn, 4 hn, hp, timp, str	
126	III.	A cl, 4 hn, hp, timp, str	
128	*Alladine und Palomides*	opera project	Maurice Maeterlinck (second of *Drei mystische Spiele*)
	Two Piano Pieces (atonal)	pn	
158	I.		
159	II.		
165	*Die sieben Prinzessinnen*	opera project	Maurice Maeterlinck (first of *Drei mystische Spiele*)
179	"Schmerz, immer blick nach oben"	v & str qu	
	Eight Orchestra Fragments	orch (picc, fl,	
190	I. "Andante"	ob, cl, bcl, hn,	
191	II. "Langsam"	B♭ trp, E♭ btrp,	
192	III.	trb, mand,	
193	IV.	guit, cel, hp,	
194	V.	glock, xyl,	
195	VI.	bells, harm,	
196	VII.	perc, solo vn, vn, solo va,	
197	VIII. "Rasch"	vc, db)	
198	"Schien mir's, als ich sah die Sonne"	women's chorus & instr	August Strindberg *Gespenster Sonate*
207	"In einer lichten Rose"	v & orch	Dante *Divine Comedy*, Canto XXXI of Book III, *Paradise*

Place and date of composition	Published	Place and date of first performance; remarks
[1907]	MS	
		19 mm finished ink score
		19 mm finished ink score
		19 mm finished ink score
[Spring–summer] 1908	MS	Prelude, beginning of Act I, 15 mm pencil
[1909–1910]	MS	19 mm pencil 7 mm pencil
Preglhof, summer 1910	MS lost	
Mürzzuschlag, June–July 1913	MS	13 mm finished ink score New York, 11 April 1964, Adele Addison v, Juilliard String Quartet Originally No. II of *Drei Stücke für Streich-quartett*, see also 178, 180
[Preglhof, summer 1911] Vienna, autumn 1913	MS	6 mm condensed score, pencil 3 mm full score, ink 4 mm full score, ink 2 mm condensed score, pencil 3 mm condensed score, pencil 3 mm condensed score, pencil 3 mm full score, ink; possibly an early version of Op. 10, No. 4 8 mm condensed score, pencil Vienna, 16 March 1972 (5th IWF), ensemble *die reihe*, Friedrich Cerha cond
[Vienna], winter 1913–1914	MS	5 mm pencil
1914	MS	20 mm condensed score, pencil

Chrono-logical No.	Title and/or first line of text; performance directions	Medium	Text
208	String Quartet Movement "Lebhaft"	str qu	
209	*Meiner Mutter* ("Wie oft sah ich die blassen Hände nähen")	v & pn	Detlev von Liliencron *Adjutantenritte und andere Gedichte*; subsequently in *Sizilianen* (*Kampf und Spiele*)
210	"In tiefster Schuld vor einem Augenpaar"	v & cl, vn, harm	?
211	"Mutig trägst du die Last"	v & pn; also v & vn, ob, harm	?
	Eight Trakl Songs		Georg Trakl
214	I. *In der Heimat* ("Resedenduft durchs kranke Fenster irrt")	v & pn	(*Im Dorf* cycle)
215	II. *In den Nachmittag geflüstert* ("Sonne, herbstlich dünn und zag")	v & instr	(*Traum des Bösen* cycle)
218	III. "Mit silbernen Sohlen"	v & orch	*Offenbarung und Untergang* Part VI
225	IV. *Verklärung* ("Wenn es Abend wird")	v & instr; v & pn	(*Siebengesang des Todes* cycle)
227	V. *Siebengesang des Todes* ("Bläulich dämmert der Frühling")	v & orch	(*Siebengesang des Todes* cycle)
247	VI. *Nachtergebung* ("Mönchin! schliess mich in dein Dunkel")	v & orch; also v & pn	(*Offenbarung und Untergang* cycle)
248	VII. *Die Heimkehr* ("Die Kühle dunkler Jahre")	v & orch	(*Gesang des Abgeschiedenen* cycle)
254	VIII. *Jahr* ("Dunkle Stille der Kindheit")	v & cl, va, vc	(*Gesang des Abgeschiedenen* cycle)
219	Orchestral Song (no text)	v & orch	?
	Two Goethe Songs		Johann Wolfgang von Goethe
220	I. *Gegenwart* ("Alles kündigt dich an!")	v & pn	*Lieder*
235	II. *Cirrus* ("Doch immer höher steigt der edle Drang!")	v & orch	*Gott und Welt* (*Howards Ehrengedächtnis* cycle)
	String Quartet Movements	str qu	
226	I. "Spiccato"		
228	II. "Sanft bewegt"		
229	III.		
230	IV. "Mässig bewegt"		

Place and date of composition	Published	Place and date of first performance; remarks
[1914]	MS	20 mm pencil
[1914 or later]	MS	9 mm pencil
[1914 or later]	MS	9 mm pencil
[1914 or later]	MS	5 mm pencil; 10 mm pencil
1915–1921	MS	
Vienna, 1915		28 mm pencil
Vienna, 1915		12 mm condensed score, pencil
Vienna, 1917		2 sketches, 11 & 2 mm condensed score, pencil
Klagenfurt, 1917		5 sketches, 4 to 13 mm pencil
1917		16 mm condensed score, pencil
1920		3 sketches, 9 & 4 mm condensed score, pencil; 8 mm (v & pn) pencil
[1920]		2 sketches, 8 & 6 mm condensed score, pencil
1921		3 mm pencil
Hietzing, 1917	MS	13 mm condensed score, pencil; voice line left blank
1917–1918	MS	
Vienna, 1917		38 mm pencil
Mödling, 1918		4 sketches, 6 to 13 mm condensed score, pencil
1917–1918	MS	
Klagenfurt 1917		12 mm pencil
Vienna, end of Jan. 1917– Mödling, 1918		*ca.* 45 mm pencil
1917–1918		14 mm pencil
Mödling, 5 July 1918		12 mm pencil

Chrono-logical No.	Title and/or first line of text; performance directions	Medium	Text
	Three Kraus Songs	v & orch	Karl Kraus
232	I. *Vallorbe* ("Du himmlisches Geflecht")		*Worte in Versen*, Part III
236	II. *Vision des Erblindeten* ("So, Mutter, Dank!")		*Worte in Versen*, Part III
246	III. *Flieder* ("Nun weiss ich doch")		*Worte in Versen*, Part IV
	Two Songs from Bethge's *Die chinesische Flöte*		
233	I. *Nächtliches Bild* ("Vom Wind getroffen")	v & orch	Tschan-Jo-Su
244	II. *Der Frühlingsregen* ("Der holde liebe Früh-lingsregen")	v & orch; also v & pn	Thu-Fu
242	Trio Movement	cl, trp, vn	
245	"Christkindlein trägt die Sünden der Welt"	v & pn	?
265	"Morgenglanz der Ewigkeit"	v & orch	Christian Knorr von Rosen-roth, 1684 (*Freylingshausen Gesangbuch*, 1704)
266	Children's piece "Lieblich"	pn	
273	String Trio Movement "Ruhig"	vn, va, vc	
276	"Dein Leib geht jetzt der Erde zu"	v & cl, bcl, va	?
279	String Quartet Movement	str qu	
280	Piano Piece	pn	
284	"Verderben, sterben—ich leb' ohne Trost"	v & instr	?
288	"Auf Bergen, in der reinsten Höhe"	mixed chorus *a cappella*	Johann Wolfgang von Goethe *Gott, Gemüt und Welt*

Place and date of composition	Published	Place and date of first performance; remarks
1918–1920	MS	
Mödling, 5 Aug. 1918		3 sketches, 63, 17 & 7 mm condensed score, pencil
Mürzzuschlag, 2 July 1919		·39 mm condensed score, pencil
Mödling, 1920		4 sketches, 8 to 15 mm condensed score, pencil
1918–1920	MS	
Mödling, autumn 1918		2 sketches, *ca.* 27 & 26 mm condensed score, pencil
1920		9 mm condensed score, pencil; 2 sketches 11 & 4 mm pencil
Mödling, 21 Aug. 1920	MS	17 mm pencil Baton Rouge, 17 Feb. 1978 (6th IWF), David DeFoe cl, Alan Sierichs trp, Dinos Constantinides vn
1920	MS	10 mm pencil
Mödling, spring 1924	MS	Also "Vorspiel" to same; 3 sketches, 4 to 8 mm condensed score, pencil
Mödling, autumn 1924	MS	9 mm pencil
Mödling, spring 1925	MS	24 mm pencil Baton Rouge, 17 Feb. 1978 (6th IWF), members of the Concord String Quartet (Mark Sokol vn, John Kochanowski va, Norman Fischer vc)
[Summer] 1925	MS	7 mm pencil
Mödling, 24 Aug. 1925	MS	9 mm pencil
Mödling [late Aug.] 1925	MS	4 sketches, 3 to 10 mm pencil
[1925]	MS	9 mm condensed score, pencil
Mödling, autumn 1926	*Sketches*	projected for Op. 19

Chrono-logical No.	Title and/or first line of text; performance directions	Medium	Text
291	String Trio Movement "Sehr lebhaft"	vn, va, vc	
295	Symphony Movement	orch	
303	"Nun weiss man erst, was Rosenknospe sei"	v & pn	Johann Wolfgang von Goethe (*Chinesisch-deutsche Jahres- und Tageszeiten* cycle)
304	String Quartet Movement	str qu	
306	*Cirrus* ("Doch immer höher steigt der edle Drang")	v & pn	Johann Wolfgang von Goethe *Gott und Welt* (*Howards Ehrengedächtnis* cycle)
307	"Der Spiegel sagt mir: ich bin schön!"	4-part women's chorus	Johann Wolfgang von Goethe (*Der West-östliche Divan* cycle)
309	Quartet Movement	vn, cl, tsax, pn	
310	*Orchesterstück (Ouvertüre)*	orch (fl, ob, cl, hn, trp, trb, hp, cel, pn, timp, perc, vn, va, vc)	
315	"Wie kann der Tod so nah der Liebe wohnen?"	mixed chorus	Hildegard Jone, *Der Schnee*
318	Instrumental Movement "Sehr rasch"	woodwinds, vn, va, pn	
344	"Kleiner sind Götter geworden"	mixed chorus	Hildegard Jone, *Verwandlung der Chariten*
347	*Konzert*, evolving into presumptive Third Cantata ("Das Sonnenlicht spricht")	solo v, chorus & instr	Hildegard Jone (*Lumen* cycle)

Place and date of composition	Published	Place and date of first performance; remarks
Hafning, [July–August] 1927	*Sketches*	Vienna, 16 March 1972 (5th IWF), Viktor Redtenbacher vn, Eugenie Altmann va, Leonhard Wallisch vc; projected for Op. 20
Mödling, Aug. 1928	*Sketches*	projected for Op. 21
Mödling, 7 March 1929	*Sketches*	
Mödling, 30 June 1929	*Sketches*	
Mödling, 29 June–9 July 1930	*Sketches*	
Mödling, 7–[14] July 1930	*Sketches*	
Mödling, 20 Aug.–[12] Sept. 1930	*Sketches*	projected for Op. 22
Mödling, 16 Jan.–22 Feb. 1931	*Sketches*	evolving into Op. 24
Maria Enzersdorf, 11–[14] May 1934	*Sketches*	projected for Op. 24?
Maria Enzersdorf, 21 July 1934	*Sketches*	projected for Op. 24?
Maria Enzersdorf, Dec. 1943–Jan. 1944	*Sketches*	projected for Op. 31
Maria Enzersdorf, 26 Jan. 1944–[1945?]	*Sketches*	

(1) *Webern's own works*

Chrono-logical No.	Composer and title	Medium
5	*Vorfrühling*	v, ob, 2 E♭ hn, hp
206	"Entflieht auf leichten Kähnen" (Op. 2)	mixed chorus & instr (vn, va, vc, harm, pn)
234	Passacaglia for Orchestra (Op. 1)	2 pn, 6 hands
241	Five Pieces for Orchestra (Op. 10)	chamber ensemble (vn, va, vc, harm, pn)
243	Six Pieces for Large Orchestra (Op. 6)	chamber ensemble (fl, ob, cl, 1. & 2. vn, va, vc, perc, harm, pn)
262	Six Songs on Poems of Georg Trakl (Op. 14)	v & pn
263	Five Sacred Songs (Op. 15)	v & pn
264	Four Songs for Voice and Orchestra (Op. 13)	v & pn
285	Two Songs on Poems of Rainer Maria Rilke (Op. 8)	v & pn
292	Two Songs (Op. 19)	mixed chorus & pn
302	Five Movements for String Quartet (Op. 5)	str orch
345	First Cantata (Op. 29)	pn-vocal score
346	Second Cantata (Op. 31)	pn-vocal score

Place and date of composition	Published	Place and date of first performance; remarks
[Klagenfurt, 1900]	MS	opening 4 mm; see also 3
Vienna, spring 1914	MS	Saarbrücken, 14 March 1969, Schola Cantorum Stuttgart & members of the Saarländisches Rundfunk Orch, Friedrich Cerha cond
[Mödling, late 1918]	MS presumably lost	private: Vienna, 2 Feb. 1919, Society for Private Musical Performances public: Vienna, 6 June 1919, same organization, Eduard Steuermann, Ernst Bachrich, Paul A. Pisk pn
[Mödling 1919]	MS	Vienna, 30 Jan. 1920, Society for Private Musical Performances, Rudolf Kolisch vn, Walter Seligmann va, Maria Lazansky vc, Hans Neumann harm, Karl Hein pn, Anton von Webern cond
Mödling 1920	MS	Vienna, 16 March 1970, ensemble *die reihe*, Friedrich Cerha cond
Mödling, Oct.–Nov. 1923	MS	Seattle, 26 May 1962 (1st IWF), Grace-Lynne Martin v, Leonard Stein pn
[Mödling 1923]	MS	
Mödling, Feb. 1924	UE 1926	
[Mödling 1925]	MS	
I. Mödling, 29 Feb 1928 II. Mödling, 3 March 1928	UE 1928	
Mödling, summer 1928, first version; Mödling, Jan.–Feb. 1929, second version	UE 1961	Philadelphia, 26 March 1930, Philadelphia Chamber String Sinfonietta, Fabien Sevitzky cond
Vienna, autumn 1944	UE 1954	
Vienna, autumn 1944	UE 1951	

D. *Arrangements*
(2) *Works of other composers**

Chrono-logical No.	Composer and title	Medium
	Hugo Wolf: Three Songs	
14	I. *Denk es, o Seele* (Mörike Songs, 16)	v & orch (2 each fl, ob, cl, bn, hn, trp; 3 trb, hp, perc, str)
49	II. *Lebe wohl* (Mörike Songs, 29)	v & orch (2 each fl, ob, cl, bn, hn; str)
50	III. *Der Knabe und das Immlein* (Mörike Songs, 2)	v & orch (2 each fl, ob, cl, bn, hn; str)
	Franz Schubert: Five Songs	v & orch (2 each fl, ob, cl, bn, hn; str)
51	I. *Thränenregen* (*Die schöne Müllerin*, D 795, No. 10)	
52	II. *Ihr Bild* (*Schwanengesang*, D 957, No. 9)	
53	III. *Romanze aus* Rosamunde (D 797, No. 3a)	
54	IV. *Der Wegweiser* (*Winterreise*, D 911, No. 20)	
55	V. *Du bist die Ruh'* (D 776)	
56	Franz Schubert: Piano Sonatas	orch (2 each fl, ob, cl, bn, hn; str)
56	I. Op. 42 (D 845), 2nd mvt.	
57	II. Op. 122 (D 568), 3rd mvt.	
58	III. Op. 147 (D 575) 2nd mvt. 3rd mvt.	
160	Arnold Schoenberg: *Gurrelieder*, Prelude and Interludes	2 pn, 8 hands
166	Arnold Schoenberg: Six Orchestral Songs, Op. 8	v & pn
175	Arnold Schoenberg: *Verklärte Nacht*, Op. 4	pn
176	Arnold Schoenberg: *Pelleas und Melisande*, Op. 5	pn
177	Arnold Schoenberg: Five Orchestra Pieces, Op. 16	2 pn, 4 hands
249	Johann Strauss: *Schatzwalzer* (*Zigeunerbaron*)	pn, harm, 1. vn (2), 2. vn, va, vc

* Not included among Webern's Schoenberg arrangements are his adjustment in the orchestration of *Lied der Waldtaube* from *Gurrelieder* (Prague, Jan. 1916) and his augmentation of the instrumental accompaniment to *Friede auf Erden*, Op. 13 (Vienna, Nov. 1928).

Place and date of composition	Published	Place and date of first performance; remarks
Preglhof, 16 April 1903	MS	
[Vienna, 1903]	MS	last 20 mm extant
[Vienna, 1903]	MS	mm 1–36 extant
[Vienna, 1903]	MS	Buffalo, 30 Oct 1966 (3rd IWF), Marni Nixon v, Buffalo Philharmonic Orch, Lukas Foss cond
[Vienna, 1903]	MS	
		mm 1–52
		mm 1–36
		mm 1–13
		mm 1–53
Vienna, [winter 1909–1910]	MS	Vienna, 14 Jan. 1910, Anton von Webern, Etta Jonas-Werndorff, Rudolf Weirich, Arnold Winternitz pn
Preglhof, July–Aug. 1910	UE 1911 (singly) 1913 (compl)	
[Berlin-Zehlendorf 1911–1912]	MS	pencil sketch, mm 105–115
[Berlin-Zehlendorf 1911–1912]	MS	pencil sketch, mm 89–92 & mm 330–340
Berlin-Zehlendorf, April-May 1912	C. F. Peters 1912	
Mödling, [spring] 1921	MS	Vienna, 27 May 1921, Society for Private Musical Performances, Eduard Steuermann pn, Alban Berg harm, Rudolf Kolisch & Arnold Schoenberg 1. vn, Karl Rankl 2. vn, Othmar Steinbauer va, Anton von Webern vc

Chrono-logical No.	Composer and title	Medium
250	Arnold Schoenberg: *Die glückliche Hand,* Op. 18	chamber orch (fl (picc), cl (bcl), trp, hn, harm, pn, 2 vn, va, vc, db)
255	Arnold Schoenberg: Four Songs, Op. 22	v & instr (pn, harm, vn, va, vc)
258	Arnold Schoenberg: Chamber Symphony, Op. 9	fl (or 2. vn), cl (or va), vn, vc, pn
271	Franz Liszt: *Arbeiterchor*	bass solo, mixed chorus & orch (2 each fl, ob, cl, bn; 4 hn, 2 trp, 3 trb, timp, perc, str)
272	Franz Liszt: *Arbeiterchor*	pn–vocal score
311	Franz Schubert: German Dances (D 820)	orch (2 each fl, ob, cl, bn, hn; str)
323	J. S. Bach: *Fuga (Ricercata) a 6 voci* (No. 2 from the *Musical Offering*, BWV 1079, No. 5)	orch (fl, ob, Ehn, cl, bcl, bn, hn, trp, trb, timp, hp, str)
333	Rudolf Wagner-Régeny: *Johanna Balk* (opera)	pn–vocal score
337	Othmar Schoeck: *Das Schloss Dürande* (opera)	pn–vocal score
340	Alfredo Casella: *Paganiniana*, Op. 65 (orchestral suite)	pn

Place and date of composition	Published	Place and date of first performance; remarks
Mödling, July 1921	MS presumably lost	projected for performance during the 1921–22 season of the Society for Private Musical Performances
[Mödling, 1921?]	MS?	projected for performance during the 1921–22 season of the Society for Private Musical Performances
Mödling, 3 Nov. 1922–Jan. 1923	UE 1968	Barcelona, 29 April 1925, Franz Wangler fl, Viktor Polatschek cl, Rudolf Kolisch vn, Joachim Stutschewsky vc, Friedrich Wührer pn, Arnold Schoenberg cond
[1924]	MS	Vienna, 13 March 1925 (Workmen's Symphony Concert), Walter Berry v, Singverein, Anton von Webern cond
[1924]	Verlag des Reichsverbandes der Arbeiter-gesangvereine Österreichs	
Mödling, May–[16] June 1931	UE 1931	Berlin, 25 Oct. 1931, Hermann Scherchen cond
Maria Enzersdorf, Nov. 1934–21 Jan. 1935	UE 1935	London, 25 April 1935, BBC Orch, Anton von Webern cond; the transcription is dedicated to Edward Clark
Maria Enzersdorf, [October] 1939	UE 1941	Webern's name as arranger is not given in the printed score
Maria Enzersdorf, Aug. 1941–Feb. 1942	UE 1942	Webern's name as arranger is not given in the printed score
Maria Enzersdorf, [Sept–Oct] 1942	MS	

Five early poems [Klagenfurt or Preglhof 1902]
    1. "Waldweg"   2. "Sonnenaufgang"   3. "An den Preglhof"   4. "Frauen-Schönheit"   5. "Traum" (For texts of the first four poems, see Chapter III.)

"Einleitung," Heinrich Isaac *"Choralis Constantinus." Zweiter Teil. Graduale in mehrstimmiger Bearbeitung (a cappella), bearbeitet von Anton von Webern* [Vienna 1905–6]. *Denkmäler der Tonkunst in Österreich,* Jg. XVI/1–Bd. 32, pp. [vii]–xii. (Excerpts in *die Reihe* 2 (1955), 30–32 (German) and *die Reihe* 2 (1959), 23–25 (English).)

"Schönbergs Musik" [Berlin-Zehlendorf, autumn 1911], in *Arnold Schönberg.* Munich, 1912, Piper, 22–48. Also published (under the title "Über Arnold Schönberg" and with additional text) in *Rheinische Musik- und Theaterzeitung* (Cologne) 13 (February 1912).

"Der Lehrer" [Berlin-Zehlendorf, autumn 1911], in *op. cit.,* 85–87.

Three poems [Klagenfurt or Mürzzuschlag, summer 1913].
    1. "Schmerz, immer blick nach oben" (see Work List 179).
    2. "O sanftes Glühn der Berge" (see Work List 184).
    3. "Leise Düfte" (see Work List 200).

Stage play *Tot, Sechs Bilder für die Bühne* [Vienna] October 1913. MS (see Chapter XII).

"Über Arnold Schönberg als Dirigent" [Vienna, spring 1914], in Rudolf Stephan, "Ein unbekannter Aufsatz Weberns über Schönberg," *Österreichische Musikzeitschrift* 27, no. 3 (March 1972), 127–130.

"Passacaglia für grosses Orchester" [Mödling, spring 1922], *Allgemeine Musikzeitung* 49 (1922). (For reprint, see Bibliography: Stephan, "Weberns Werke auf deutschen Tonkünstlerfesten," 123–124.)

["Zum 50. Geburtstag"], *Musikblätter des Anbruch* 6 (August–September 1924) (*Arnold Schönberg zum fünfzigsten Geburtstag, 13. September 1924*), 272.

Contribution [Mödling, October 1930] to *Adolf Loos zum 60. Geburtstag am 10. Dezember 1930.* Vienna, 1930, R. Lányi, 67.

"'Sechs Orchesterstücke' [Op. 6]" [Maria Enzersdorf, spring 1933], *Zeitschrift für Musik* 100, no. 6 (June 1933), 566–567. (For reprint, see Bibliography: Stephan, "Weberns Werke auf deutschen Tonkünstlerfesten," 126.)

"Aus Schönbergs Schriften" [Maria Enzersdorf, spring 1934], *Musikblätter des Anbruch* 16 (September 1934) (*Arnold Schönberg zum 60. Geburtstag, 13. September 1934*), 11–14. A selection of excerpts from Schoenberg's writings compiled and prefaced by Webern.

Analysis of String Quartet Op. 28 [Maria Enzersdorf, May 1939]. (See Appendix 2.)

N.B. For Webern's published lectures and correspondence, see Bibliography.

Anton von Webern: Analysis of the String Quartet, Op. 28

The analysis of his String Quartet Op. 28 is Webern's longest known essay on one of his own works. He sent it to Erwin Stein during the summer of 1939. The best estimate that can be made of the actual date of writing places it between 8 May and 2 June of that year (see Chapter XXVIII).

In the following translation I attempted to capture the peculiar flavour of Webern's writing, as well as his idiosyncratic use of the analytical terminology.* For the sake of greater clarity, however, at times I found it necessary to re-arrange the order of Webern's clauses, and to alter and supplement his punctuation.

My translation was based on a typewritten transcript of Webern's text, secured by Hans Moldenhauer in 1968 through the late Mario Uzielli of Liestal, Switzerland (the original is in an unidentified Swiss collection). I compared this text with those given by Friedhelm Döhl (Döhl, *Weberns Beitrag* . . . , pp. 443ff; see Bibliography) and Ursula von Rauchhaupt (Rauchhaupt, *Die Streichquartette der Wiener Schule*, pp. 137ff.). The three texts differ from each other only in minor details. Briefer analytical remarks contained in a letter from Webern to Rudolf Kolisch (19 April 1938; in Rauchhaupt, *op. cit.*, pp. 131, 133) enabled me to check on, and verify my interpretation of a number of the composer's ideas and expressions. Finally, Eugene Hartzell's earlier translation (in *ibid.*/English edition, pp. 132ff.) provided a welcome touchstone.

Zoltan Roman

---

*For a detailed and perceptive treatment of this matter, see Döhl, "Zum Formbegriff Weberns".

First Movement

The first movement is a *variation movement*; however, the fact that the variations also constitute an *adagio form* is of *primary* significance. That is to say, *it* is the basis of the movement's formal structure, and the variations have come into being *in accordance* with it. Thus, the shaping of an adagio form on the basis of variations. In my opinion, the slow movement of Beethoven's Quartet Op. 135 is something similar, only on a smaller scale, i.e. it is limited to the form of a *three-part song*. But, *that is the primary consideration*—the fact that it consists of variations is *formally* not decisive. My design, however, did not derive from that example; I found it only subsequently, recently, and had great pleasure from this verification!

The theme of the movement extends to Measure 16. The first variation, in the sense of a repetition of the theme, begins with Measure 16—but in the manner of an upbeat! (further, see below!). The theme itself is *periodically* structured: antecedent to Bar 9.

It must be noted right at the beginning (viola—1st and 2nd violin—cello) that what takes place here is the augmentation and diminution of the figures. This is elevated into a *"principle"* for all variations. One will find this to be the basis for every one of them. It would be going too far to demonstrate this now in every separate instance. Here, I only would like to specify the *functions* that are to be fulfilled by the individual variations within the framework of the *adagio* form. As was stated earlier, then, the first variation is a repetition of the theme. How does it come to a repetition of the theme in an adagio? Well, because its first statement, despite its strict periodic form, still has something *introductory* about it.

The 1st Variation extends to Measure 33. But now Measure 16, in which it begins, counts as an *upbeat*! That is, basically the theme consists of *16 bars*, but this sixteenth bar plays a different role each time. The 2nd Variation commences in Measure 33 and extends to 49. Bar 48 is the sixteenth measure and, again, it contains an "upbeat" to the 3rd Variation (2nd violin). The 2nd Variation represents the transition to the "second theme" that is presented in the 3rd Variation, and finds its repetition in the 4th one. Here, at the juncture of these two variations, the earlier one—i.e. the 3rd Variation—extends beyond its sixteenth bar—to Measure 66, that is. However, this will be made up again, since the 4th Variation has its sixteenth bar in Measure 80. With the upbeat therein to Measure 81 begins the 5th Variation, and therewith the reprise of the "Adagio." The sixteenth bar of this variation is Measure 96; it is the upbeat to the 6th Variation which represents the *Coda* of the piece. Thus, theme and six variations. The variations are purely *canonic* in nature! And yet, I also make use of *variants* on occasion, in keeping with more important considerations! But the sum of the durations, including *rests*, remains *absolutely* the same, naturally! ! !

About the treatment of the "rows" later, since it is valid for *every movement*!

That is to say, the rows always run *linearly* and horizontally. At *not a single* point are notes stacked vertically from *the same row*! The voice-leading always coincides with the course of the row, and it also remains *predominantly* in the same *instrument*!

Second Movement

It is a "Scherzo" in miniature.

"Scherzo" to Measure 19 ("bewegt"); followed by the "Trio," to Measure 37 ("wieder gemächlich"), where the *reprise*—i.e. the *da capo*—of the Scherzo begins.

"Miniature" means that neither "Scherzo" nor "Trio" have development sections, but only a theme that is repeated; this is stipulated by repeat signs in the "Scherzo" as well as in its reprise, and it is written out in the "Trio." The *theme of the Scherzo* is a *perpetual* four-part canon in a "subject"-like form.

Everything is *canonic* in the Trio as well. Observe how, through the doubled tempo, the *conclusion of the canon* in the reprise of the "Scherzo" (starting with the second ending) takes on the *function* of a stretto-coda.

The fact that there is a repeat also in the reprise of the "Scherzo" may be attributed to a formal rounding-off, and to the need for bringing the *"perpetuity"* of the canon to bear once more.

The construction of the "Trio," however, is not rigid but *"developmental"*; therefore the model—that which I meant above by the "theme" of the Trio, so to speak—extends to Bar 27. Then the repetition in a completely new form.

"Developmental": that is, one can also grasp the form of the *whole piece* as a *three-part song form*. In that case, the Trio appears as the *"second"* *part* of the total structure.

And that is possibly even the *over-riding* function of this section, in the sense of a total *"developing* form" [*"Wuchs*form"]. I found this word recently in a splendid book with the title "Vom Bau der Kirche," by Rudolf Schwarz.*

Third Movement

Well, to explain this movement to you—yes, that really makes me quite excited. Within the work it must be the "crowning fulfilment," so to speak, of the *"synthesis"* of *"horizontal"* and *"vertical"* construction (Schoenberg!) I strove for already in the first and second movements. As is known, the classical cyclic forms—sonata, symphony, and so forth—evolved on the basis of the former, while *"polyphony"* and its associated practices (canon, fugue, and so on) derived from the latter. And now, here I have attempted not only to comply with the principles of both styles in general, but also specifically to combine *the forms* themselves: as already through the use of *"canons"* in the preceding movements, so here in this movement through the *"fugue!"*

What we are dealing with *primarily* is a "scherzo"-form; that is, its *subject-development-reprise*. In this respect, the principles of the "horizontal" style were decisive. But the "development" consists of a *fugue*, the third "exposition" of which is the reprise of the *scherzo subject*, the fulfilment of the scherzo form!

With reference to the scherzo form, therefore, the fugue comprises the "development" as well as the reprise. But, as was mentioned, this reprise also constitutes the third exposition of the fugue. Accordingly, therefore, the

---

* German architect (1897–1961); master of modern Catholic church architecture, planner of the rebuilding of Cologne after World War II; *Vom Bau der Kirche* (1937, 1949²).

"scherzo" subject is already so designed that when it is recapitulated, it is capable of serving as the third exposition of a fugue.

And now to the subject! It extends to Measure 16; it is strictly periodically designed: antecedent (1st violin) Bars 1 to 7 inclusive; consequent Measures 8 to 13 inclusive—I mean, as it is given in the first violin part. But now, the *consequent* is the *rhythmic retrograde* of the antecedent—occasionally varied!—, and its inversion according to the "row." This periodic structure is also found in the *other three parts: canonically*, but in the following canon-formation. *Cello*: its antecedent presents *in retrograde* the pitches of the antecedent in the 1st violin; it is also its *rhythmic retrograde*. The consequent in the cello has the same *rhythmic* relationship to the consequent played by the 1st violin, but its pitches are the retrograde of the consequent as it appears in the viola! ! !

The viola and the 2nd violin relate to each other in the same way (thus there are two pairs: 1st violin and cello; viola and 2nd violin): *retrograde* of the rhythm and melody in the antecedent; in the consequent, rhythmic retrograde; but with respect to the pitches: in the 2nd violin, retrograde of the 1st violin's consequent, and in the viola, melodic retrograde of the cello's consequent. This may well be described as a *double canon in retrograde*!

Formwise, this structure is but a *periodic scherzo subject* in the shape of the third exposition of a *double fugue*; that is to say (with reference to my fugue subject which begins in the development of the Scherzo): a stretto of "subject" and "countersubject." As far as I know, this had *never* been done before; as a double canon in *retrograde, moreover*, it had, in point of fact, never been done at all! ! ! Therefore, does this not justifiably constitute also the third exposition of a double fugue? And to repeat it once more, it is yet but nothing other than a period, in compliance with the principles of construction of a *scherzo subject*, as in Beethoven. Thus, it obeys the laws of *horizontal* construction. But as the stretto, the third exposition of a double fugue, *at the same time* it is also in compliance with the principles of *vertical* construction, as in Bach. Now then, is this or is this not a *synthesis* of the two styles?

Now to proceed: with Measure 16 begins the development section of the Scherzo, that is to say in this case the fugue! The subject subdivides into *three motives* [*Gestalten*]: cello (Bar 16), 2nd violin (Bar 17) and viola (Bars 18 and 19). "Answer" in the 1st violin (Bars 19 and 20), 2nd violin (Bars 20 and 21) and viola (Bars 21 and 22). How does this "answer" follow, then, since here, indeed, the former principle (in the sense of the *tonic-dominant contrast*), the transposition to the other hexachord, **can no longer be applied?** Well, then, what was the *primary* rôle of the "answer" in the old fugue? The first *repetition* of the subject, in the sense mentioned above. Exactly because it is no longer possible to accomplish this, *another* means of this repetition must be found: therefore, *here* I selected the form of the melodic *retrograde* (but *motive by motive*) of the *three motives* which make up my subject. Compare the 1st violin with the cello, the 2nd violin with itself, and the same way with the viola! The *third* and last entry of the subject—the fugue has three voices—in the "exposition" (or first statement, as it is also called): surely, in the past it had been always, or for the most part, once again in the tonic. So with me, too, the subject is repeated right away—*cello*: Measures 22 (upbeat, "pizz." F) and 23; viola: Bar 24; and 2nd violin: Measures 24 (upbeat) and 25. To be sure, the motives are varied! But this is a double fugue! The "countersubject" appears with the "answer," as is customary. With me—and now the relationship between "scherzo" subject and third statement will become clear—the "countersubject" presents the *rhythmic* retrograde of the subject. Here, too, the three motives are distinguished from each other melodically: the first motive of the countersubject (cello, Bar 20 with upbeat and Bar 21) is like the second one of the subject at its first appearance; the second motive of the countersubject (1st violin, Bar 22 with upbeat) is like the first one of the subject; the third motive of the countersubject (2nd violin, Measures 22 and 23) is like the *retrograde* of the third motive of the subject. But that resulted automatically from the nature of the row. Thus, a rhythmic retrograde, even with the occasional variation of the three motives of the subject. At the third entry of the subject, the countersubject behaves likewise: 1st violin (Measures 23 and 24), cello (Bar 25), and viola (Bars 25 and 26) in rhythmic retrograde, but *again another* exchange of the notes.

Thus, the exposition extends up to, and includes Bar 26 in the viola. Commencing in this bar in the 1st violin, there follows the first *"episode"*; it extends to Measure 38 ("gewichtig"). It is a *strict four-part canon*: the 1st violin begins it and presents the theme in retrograde rhythmic motion to Measure 34. That is, once again the "countersubject," but in a varied *new form*: the second motive enters in the first bar in 3/32 metre, but in spite of this *it is preserved intact in its note values*, as is the third motive; it is the same in the other three voices.

The second exposition of the fugue begins with Bar 38!: subject in the 2nd violin (the upper auxiliaries of the trills *are* part of it, e f d e-flat). Again there are three motives, Bars 38–39, 40–41 and 42–43; coupled with them in the viola is the "countersubject" for the same measures, presenting the precise *rhythmic retrograde* and naturally also the retrograde of the *intervals*. Thus, here the subject itself is also presented *twice*; that is, in this way already two statements have been made, with the same holding true also for the countersubject. However, the third entry of the subject and countersubject begins already in the last two measures (42–43), hence already at this point there is a stretto: 1st violin with countersubject and cello with subject and, for that matter, with the same notes with which the first pair of voices conclude. Therefore this doubling of the 1st and 2nd violin, and what transpires in the viola and cello are no "jests of instrumentation," but have purely thematic significance! With Measure 44 ("sehr ruhig"), however, this third statement of the subject and countersubject changes into the second "episode." Again it is a four-part canon, also in contrary motion, commencing in the 1st violin and extending to Bar 52. However, the 1st violin *completes the subject* with the remaining 8 pitches of the "row" begun in Measure 42, from its second motive onward in a new tempo and with a different character, yet precisely according to the note values. The same thing happens with the remaining pitches of the row which started with the entry of the subject in the cello (Measures 42 and 43), except that they are taken over by the viola. Two new "rows" begin with the entries of the 2nd violin and the cello in canon (in Bars 46 and 47, respectively); their last four notes—taken over by the viola and the 1st violin—provide the material for Measures 52 and 53. These two bars represent the *transition* to the reprise of the scherzo subject, in keeping with its form at the beginning.

The question could be raised how this is possible, I mean in the canon just described: one pair of voices has Notes 5–12 and the other pair Notes 1–8. And is a strict canon among all four parts possible in spite of this? Well, now I must finally reveal how the "row" is constructed; this is, indeed, one of the most important concerns in this Quartet, perhaps the most fundamental one! You see, the second four notes of the row fashion their *intervals* from the *retrograde* of the first four, and the last four notes relate to the second four in the same way. But this means that the entire Quartet is based on nothing else than this specific *succession of four pitches*! Now it so happens that the first four notes of the "original" form of the row, transposed to b-flat, yield the four letters B [b-flat] A C H [b-natural]. Thus, my fugue subject presents this name three times (with the subject's three motives of four notes each making up the 12 notes of the row), but only *secretly* because, on the other hand, the original form **never** occurs in this ostentatious transposition!!! All the same though, the *four notes* do underlie the *entire Quartet*!!

But to proceed: we have now arrived at the reprise of the scherzo subject: from *Meaure 54 to the end*! But, in a different sense, we have also arrived at the *third exposition of my double fugue*, or else at the *second* one, depending on whether one speaks of "statement" or of 1st Exposition. Now follow events that are exactly the same in the relationship of the four voices to one another as they were at the first appearance of the "subject," only everything is completely differently organized. The whole is constructed in such a way that it also provides for the *Coda* of the piece; that is, taking into account also the rules of finale construction. Thus, this reprise fulfills *three functions*! Still, observe how the **character** of the subject also changes completely (especially at its first appearance, as in the canon), due to the continual change of metre which causes each voice to fall differently in the measure; that is to say, it has an *entirely different centre of gravity*. And yet, all these occurrences add up to nothing other than a simple, and I believe quite self-contained, strictly periodically structured scherzo subject.

Perhaps one could ask: what does the fugue subject "really" have in common with the scherzo subject, so that the reprise of the latter can also function as the third exposition of the fugue? Answer: in both cases the 12 notes of the row; that is, what rules here is altogether the **most far reaching relationship** which can exist between two forms: they are *identical*!!! In both cases, moreover, the grouping of 3 × 4 notes; for it is also present in the subject of the Scherzo, even if it is not so conspicuous there. But it is there—and this I still would like to say in closing—, even reaching as far as it does in the row itself. Namely, as each successive four notes in the row constitute the *retrograde* of the preceding four, so is such a relationship given also in the scherzo subject's *rhythmic structure* from four-note group to four-note group, even if it does not become so clearly visible there because of the variations. For such a relationship within the row must also carry an obligation for everything else that follows! And with this I am saying that the subject is based not only on a group of **four pitches,** but also on their rhythmic configuration!

SELECTED BIBLIOGRAPHY

IN SELECTING ITEMS for the Bibliography, the demands posed by a Webern-literature which has undergone well-nigh phenomenal growth during the past two decades had to be reconciled with the practical limitations inherent in a bibliography that is basically an appendage to a larger work, rather than an independent publication. Generally, I was guided by the dual consideration of supporting the content of the book through the inclusion of the most important biographical sources, and complementing it by providing a wide-ranging sampling of the valuative and analytical literature. Aside from a few items possessing historical interest, writings of a journalistic nature (e.g. reviews and critiques) had to be excluded; didactic and survey-type books and articles were included only if I felt that they contribute significantly to an understanding of Webern and his music.

The task of the bibliographer is greatly lightened if he is able to draw on the work and advice of other scholars. Accordingly, it is with pleasure that I acknowledge my indebtedness to, among others, William Austin, Ann Phillips Basart, Célestin Deliège, Friedhelm Döhl, Michael Fink, Walter Kolneder, Wallace McKenzie, Hans Moldenhauer, Hans Ferdinand Redlich and, above all, Rosaleen Moldenhauer, who compiled a basic bibliography during the book's preparation.

Finally, a word of sincere appreciation is due to the publishers of this book. In an age of unparalleled production costs they encouraged the inclusion of a sizeable bibliography, in order to enhance the book's value to the reader.

Zoltan Roman

ABBREVIATIONS

AfMw	*Archiv für Musikwissenschaft*
AWP	Moldenhauer, *Anton von Webern. Perspectives* (see main entry)
BÖGM	*Beiträge der Österreichischen Gesellschaft für Musik*
CM	*Current Musicology*
diss.	dissertation
DA	*Dansk Aarbog for Musikforskning*
DB	*Darmstädter Beiträge zur Neuen Musik*
DJM	*Deutsches Jahrbuch der Musikwissenschaft*
ed.	editor(s) or edition
IM	*Incontri Musicali*
JMT	*Journal of Music Theory*
M	*Melos*
MB	*Musik und Bildung*
MbA	*Musikblätter des Anbruch*
ME	*Music in Education* (London)
Mf	*Musikforschung*
MM	*Modern Music*
MQ	*Musical Quarterly*
MR	*Music Review*
MT	*Musical Times*

NZM   *Neue Zeitschrift für Musik*
ÖMZ   *Österreichische Musikzeitschrift*
PNM   *Perspectives of New Music*
Pisk Fs   John Glowacki, ed. *Paul A. Pisk: Essays in his honor.* Austin, Texas, 1966,
           University of Texas Press.
R   *die Reihe*
RaM   *La Rassegna Musicale*
RB   *Revue Belge de Musicologie*
RM   *La Revue Musicale*
Sc   *The Score*
SMZ   *Schweizerische Musikzeitung*
T   *Tempo*
tr.   translator(s)
VINMD   Veröffentlichungen des Instituts für Neue Musik und Musikerziehung
           Darmstadt
ZMT   *Zeitschrift für Musiktheorie*
23 WM   *23, eine Wiener Musikzeitschrift*

Adorno, Theodor Wiesengrund. "Anton von Webern," *Merkur* 13, no. 3 (March 1959),
    201–214. Reprinted in *Klangfiguren* (Musikalische Schriften I). Berlin, 1959,
    Suhrkamp; and in *Nervenpunkte der Neuen Musik.* Reinbeck bei Hamburg, 1969,
    Rowohlt (Rowohlts deutsche Enzyklopädie, 333).
——— "Anton Webern: zur Aufführung der fünf Orchesterstücke in Zürich," *MbA* 8
    May 1926), 280–282.
——— "Berg and Webern—Schoenberg's heirs," *MM* 8 (January 1931), 29–38.
——— *Der getreue Korrepetitor.* Frankfurt/Main, 1963, Fischer.
——— "Form in der Neuen Musik," *DB* 10 (1966), 9–21.
——— *Impromptus (Zweite Folge neu gedruckter musikalischer Aufsätze).* Frankfurt/Main, 1968,
    Suhrkamp.
——— "[Meister und Jünger]," *23 WM* No. 14 (February 1934) (Anton Webern zum 50.
    Geburtstag), 9.
Anthony, Donald Bruce. "A general concept of musical time with special reference to
    certain developments in the music of Anton Webern." Ph.D. diss., Stanford
    University, 1968.
"Anton Webern: Trio für Geige, Bratsche und Violoncell, op. 20 (komp. 1927),"
    Allgemeine Musikzeitung 55 (1928), 603, 605.
Archibald, Bruce. "Some thoughts on symmetry in early Webern: Op. 5, No. 2," *PNM*
    10, no. 2 (1972), 159–163.
Asuar, José Vicente. "Una incursión por el Op. 5 de Anton Webern," *Revista musical
    chilena* 12 (March–April 1958), 19–41.
Austin, William. *Music in the 20th century: From Debussy through Stravinsky.* New York, 1966,
    Norton.
——— "Webern and the tradition of the symphony," in *AWP,* 78–85.
Babbitt, Milton. "Contemporary music composition and music theory as contemporary
    intellectual history," in Barry S. Brook, ed. *Perspectives in Musicology.* New York, 1972,
    Norton, 151–184.
——— "Since Schoenberg," *PNM* 12, no. 1–2 (1973/74), 3–28.
——— "Some aspects of twelve-tone composition," *Sc* No. 12 (June 1955), 53–61.
——— "Twelve-tone invariants as compositional determinants," *MQ* 46, no. 2 (April
    1960), 246–259.
Bach, David Josef. *Anton Webern zum 50. Geburtstag.* Vienna, 1934, Verlag der IGNM
    (Sektion Österreich). Reprinted in Reich, ed. *Anton Webern* (1961). English in
    Wildgans, *Anton Webern.*

Bach, David Josef. "New music by Berg, Webern, Krenek," *MM* 12 (November–December 1934), 31–38.

Bach, Hans-Elmar. "Struktur und Ausdruck im geistlichen Liedschaffen Anton Weberns," *Musica Sacra* 85 (1965), 207–219.

Bailey, Kathryn. "Formal and rhythmic procedures in Webern's Opus 30," *Journal of the Canadian Association of University Schools of Music* 2, no. 1 (1972), 34–52.

—— "The evolution of variation form in the music of Webern," *CM* No. 16 (1973), 55–70.

Ballif, Claude. "Points, mouvement," *RM* No. 263 (1968) (*Claude Ballif: Essais—Études—Documents*), 53–75.

Banks, M. "Anton Webern: serial technique and formal principles." Ph.D. diss., University of Glasgow, 1967/68.

Barkin, Elaine. "[Analysis symposium] Webern, Orchestra Pieces (1913): Movement I (Bewegt)," *JMT* 19, no. 1 (Spring 1975), 48–64.

Basart, Ann Phillips. *Serial Music: A classified bibliography of writings on twelve-tone and electronic music.* Berkeley, Los Angeles, 1961, University of California Press. Reprinted Westport, Connecticut, 1976, Greenwood Press.

Batstone, Philip. "Musical analysis as phenomenology," *PNM* 7, no. 2 (1969), 94–110.

Bauer, Hans-Joachim. "Interpretation durch Instrumentation: Bachs sechsstimmiges Ricercar in der Orchestrierung Anton von Weberns," *NZM* 135, no. 1 (1974), 3–6.

Bauman, Jon Ward. "*The Cantata Number Two* of Anton Webern." D.M.A. diss., University of Illinois, 1972.

Baur, Jürg. "Über Anton Weberns 'Bagatellen für Streichquartett'," in Lars Ulrich Abraham *et al.*, *Neue Wege der musikalischen Analyse.* Berlin, 1967, Merseburger, 62–68. (VINMD, 6).

Beale, James. "Webern's musical estate," in *AWP*, 15–30.

Beckmann, Dorothea. *Sprache und Musik im Vokalwerk Anton Weberns.* Regensburg, 1970, Bosse. (Kölner Beiträge zur Musikforschung, 57) (Originally Ph.D. diss., University of Cologne, 1970.)

Bell, Digby Bernard. "The Variations for Piano, Op. 27 of Anton Webern [. . .]." D.M.A. diss., North Texas State University, 1973.

Berg, Alban. *Briefe an seine Frau.* Munich, Vienna, 1965, Albert Langen, Georg Müller. English: *Letters to his Wife* (ed., tr. and annotated by Bernard Grun). New York, 1971, St. Martin's Press; London, 1971, Faber & Faber.

"Bibliographie: Anton Webern," *MB* 5 (June 1973), 330–333.

Blume, Joachim. *Komposition nach der Stilwende. Begriffe und Beispiele.* Wolfenbüttel, Zürich, 1972, Möseler.

Boehmer, Konrad. "Material—Struktur—Gestalt; Anmerkungen zu einer analytischen Methodik neuer Musik," *Mf* 20, no. 2 (1967), 181–193.

Boretz, Benjamin. "Meta-variations, part IV: analytic fallout (I)," *PNM* 11, no. 1 (1972), 217–223.

Borkowski, Marian. "Zagadnienie formy muzycznej w utworach dodekafonicznych Weberna" ["The problem of musical form in Webern's dodecaphonic works"; in Polish], *Res Facta* 6 (1972), 48–64.

Borris, Siegfried. "Stilistische Synopsis—Analogien und Kontraste," in Siegfried Borris *et al.*, *Stilporträts der Neuen Musik.* Berlin, 1961, Merseburger, 74–95. (VINMD, 2.)

—— "Structural analysis of Webern's Symphony Op. 21," in *Pisk Fs*, 231–242.

—— "Weberns Symphonie Op. 21—Strukturanalyse," *MB* 5 (1973), 324–329.

Boulez, Pierre. "Alea," *DB* 1 (1958), 44–56. Italian in *IM* No. 3 (August 1959), 3–15.

—— "Anton Webern," in *Relevés d'apprenti* (ed. Paule Thévenin). Paris, 1966, Éditions de Seuil, 367–379. English in *Notes of an Apprenticeship* (tr. Herbert Weinstock). New York, 1968, Knopf, 377–391.

—— "Für Anton Webern," *R* 2 (1955), 45–46. English: "The threshold," *R* 2 (2nd, revised ed., 1959), 40–41.

Boulez, Pierre. "Moment de Jean-Sébastien Bach," in *Relevés d'apprenti* (ed. Paule Thévenin). Paris, 1966, Éditions de Seuil, 9–25. English: "A time for Johann Sebastian Bach," in *Notes of an Apprenticeship* (tr. Herbert Weinstock). New York, 1968, Knopf, 3–20.

—— *Penser la musique aujourd'hui.* Geneva, Paris, 1963, Gonthier. German: "Musikdenken heute 1," *DB* 5 (1963), complete issue; English: *Boulez on Music Today* (tr. Susan Bradshaw and Richard Rodney Bennett). Cambridge, Massachusetts, 1971, Harvard University Press; London, 1975, Faber.

—— "Webern, Anton von," in *Encyclopédie de la musique* 3 (Paris, 1961, Fasquelle), 907–912.

Bour, Ernest. "Die richtige Antwort," *M* 26, no. 6 (June 1959), 169–173.

Boykan, Martin. "The Webern Concerto revisited," *Proceedings of the American Society of University Composers* 3 (1968), 74–85.

Bracanin, Philip Keith. "Analysis of Webern's 12-note music—fact and fantasy," *Studies in Music* (Australia) No. 2 (1968), 103–110.

—— "The palindrome; its applications in the music of Anton Webern," *Miscellanea Musicologica* (Adelaide) 6 (1972), 38–47.

Bradshaw, Merrill K. "Tonal structure in the early works of Anton Webern." D.M.A. diss., University of Illinois, 1962.

Bresgen, Cesar. "Gibt es eine Webern-Nachfolge?," *BÖGM 1972/73,* 146–152.

—— "Webern's last months in Mittersill," in *AWP,* 111–115.

Briner, Andres. "An den Wurzeln eines neuen musikalischen Stils; zu einer Vortragsreihe von Anton v. Webern," *SMZ* 101, no. 1 (1961), 15–20.

Brinkmann, Reinhold. "Die George-Lieder 1908/09 und 1919/23—ein Kapitel Webern-Philologie," *BÖGM 1972/73,* 40–50.

Broekema, Andrew J. "A stylistic analysis and comparison of the solo vocal works of Arnold Schoenberg, Alban Berg and Anton Webern." Ph.D. diss., University of Texas, 1962.

Brown, Robert Barclay. "The early atonal music of Anton Webern: sound material and structure." Ph.D. diss., Brandeis University, 1965.

Buccheri, John Stephen. "An approach to twelve-tone music: articulation of serial pitch units in piano works of Schoenberg, Webern, Krenek, Dallapiccola, and Rochberg." Ph.D. diss., Eastman School of Music, University of Rochester, 1975.

Buchanan, Herbert H. "An investigation of mutual influences among Schoenberg, Webern and Berg (with an emphasis on Schoenberg and Webern, *ca.* 1904–08)." Ph.D. diss., Rutgers University, The State University of New Jersey, 1974.

Budde, Elmar. "Anton Webern: Op. 5/IV—Versuch einer Analyse," in Lars Ulrich Abraham, ed. *Erich Doflein. Festschrift zum 70. Geburtstag.* Mainz, 1972, Schott, 58–66.

—— *Anton Weberns Lieder Op. 3 (Untersuchungen zur frühen Atonalität bei Webern).* Wiesbaden, 1971, Steiner. (Beihefte zum Archiv für Musikwissenschaft, 9.) (Originally Ph. D. diss., University of Freiburg, 1967.)

—— "Bemerkungen zum Verhältnis Mahler–Webern," *AfMw* 33, no. 3 (1976), 159–173.

—— "Metrisch-rhythmische Probleme im Vokalwerk Weberns," *BÖGM 1972/73,* 52–60.

Burde, Wolfgang. "Anton von Weberns instrumentale Miniaturen," *NZM* 132 (June 1971), 286–289.

Cappelli, Ida. "Storiografia weberniana dal dopoguerra ad oggi," *RaM* 31, no. 4 (1961), 459–465.

—— "Webern e l'Espressionismo," *Musica Università* (Rome) 2 (September 1964), 8–10.

Carner, Mosco. "Alban Berg and Anton Webern," in Martin Cooper, ed. *The Modern Age (1890–1960).* London, 1974, Oxford University Press, 362–386. (New Oxford History of Music, 10.)

Castiglioni, Niccolò. "Sul rapporto tra parole e musica nella Seconda Cantata di Webern," *IM* No. 3 (August 1959), 112–127.

Cerha, Friedrich. "Die Wiener Schule und die Gegenwart," *ÖMZ* 16 (June–July 1961), 303–314.

Chase, Gilbert. "Webern in America: the growth of an influence," *BÖGM 1972/73*, 153–166.

Chittum, Donald. "Some observations on the row technique in Webern's Opus 25," *CM* No. 12 (1971), 96–101.

Cholopov, Juri. "Die Spiegelsymmetrie in Anton Weberns Variationen für Klavier Op. 27," *AfMw* 30, no. 1 (1973), 26–43.

Claycombe, Gordon. "Personal recollections of Webern in Vienna 1929–1934," *BÖGM 1972/73*, 29–35.

Cohen, David. "Anton Webern and the magic square," *PNM* 13, no. 1 (1974), 213–215.

Colding-Joergensen, Gunnar. "Konstruktion og klingende resultat; 2. sats af Weberns klavervariationer" [in Danish], *Dansk Musiktidsskrift* 44, no. 2 (1969), 39–43.

Collaer, Paul. *La musique moderne, 1905–1955* (3rd, revised ed.). Brussels, 1963, Éditions Meddens. English: *A History of Modern Music* (tr. by Sally Abeles from the 2nd, revised ed., Brussels, 1958). Cleveland, 1961, World Publishing Co. German: *Geschichte der modernen Musik*. Stuttgart, 1963, Kröner.

Cone, Edward T. "Webern's apprenticeship," *MQ* 53, no. 1 (1967), 39–52.

Cooper, Martin Du Pré. "Atonality and 'Zwölftonmusik' (Written after attending a course of lectures by Dr. Anton Webern)," *MT* 74 (June 1933), 497–500.

Cowell, Henry. "Current chronicle: New York," *MQ* 35 (January 1949), 106–111.

Craft, Robert. "Anton Webern," *Sc* No. 13 (September 1955), 9–22. Reprinted with minor revisions in the booklet (ed. Kurt Stone) accompanying the record album "Anton Webern—The complete music" (Columbia Masterworks no. K4L-232).

Dahlhaus, Carl. "Analytische Instrumentation. Bachs sechstimmiges Ricercar in der Orchestrierung Anton Weberns," in Martin Geck, ed. *Bach Interpretationen. Walter Blankenburg zum 65. Geburtstag*. Göttingen, 1969, Vanderhoeck & Ruprecht, 197–206.

—— "Rhythmische Strukturen in Weberns Orchesterstücken op. 6," *BÖGM 1972/73*, 73–80.

Dallapiccola, Luigi. "Incontro con Anton Webern. Pagine di diario," *Il Mondo* (Florence), 3 November 1945. German: "Begegnung mit Anton Webern," *M* 32, no. 4 (April 1965), 115–117. (Omits entry for 2 January 1942.) English (expanded): "Meeting with Anton Webern (Pages from a diary)," *T* No. 99 (1972), 2–7. French: "Rencontre avec Anton Webern—Pages de journal," *SMZ* 115, no. 4 (July–August 1975), 165–168.

Deliège, Célestin. "Bibliographie [de la musique atonale et sérielle]," *RB* 13 (1959), 132–148.

—— "Webern: op. 10 no. 4, un theme d'analyse et de reflexion," *Revue de musicologie* 61 (1975), 91–112.

Denisow, Edison. "Wariacje op. 27 na fortepian Antona Weberna" [in Polish], *Res Facta* 6 (1972), 75–108.

Deppert, Heinrich. "Rhythmische Reihentechnik in Weberns *Orchestervariationen* Op. 30," in Erhard Karkoschka, ed. *Festschrift Karl Marx zum 70. Geburtstag*. Stuttgart, 1967, Ichthys, 84–93.

—— *Studien zur Kompositionstechnik im instrumentalen Spätwerk Anton Weberns*. Darmstadt, 1972, Tonos. (Musikbücher von Tonos, 3)

—— "Zu Weberns klanglich-harmonischem Bewusstsein," *BÖGM 1972/73*, 61–72.

"Der Dirigent Anton Webern," *R* 2 (1955), 18. English: "Anton Webern as a conductor," *R* 2 (2nd, revised ed, 1959), 11.

Deri, Otto. *Exploring Twentieth Century Music*. New York, 1968, Holt, Reinhart, and Winston.

Deutsch-Dorian, Frederick. "Webern als Lehrer," *M* 27, no. 4 (April 1960), 101–106.

Dimond, Chester A. "Fourteen early songs of Anton Webern." D.M.A. diss., University of Oregon, 1971.

Dimov́, Boschidar. "Webern und die Tradition," *ÖMZ* 20 (August 1965), 411–415.

Döhl, Friedhelm. "Die Welt der Dichtung in Weberns Musik," *M* 31, no. 3 (March 1964), 88–90.

—— *Weberns Beitrag zur Stilwende der Neuen Musik. Studien über Voraussetzungen, Technik und Ästhetik der "Komposition mit 12 nur aufeinander bezogenen Tönen."* Munich, Salzburg, 1976, Katzbichler. (Berliner Musikwissenschaftliche Arbeiten, 12.) (Originally Ph.D. diss., University of Göttingen, 1966.)

—— "Weberns Opus 27," *M* 30, no. 12 (December 1963), 400–403.

—— "Zum Formbegriff Weberns. Weberns Analyse des Streichquartetts op. 28 nebst einigen Bemerkungen zu Weberns Analyse eigener Werke," *ÖMZ* 27, no. 3 (March 1972), 131–148.

Drew, James. "Information, space, and a new time-dialectic," *JMT* 12, no. 1 (Spring 1968), 86–103.

Eimert, Herbert. "Die notwendige Korrektur," *R* 2 (1955), 35–41. English: "A change of focus," *R* 2 (2nd, revised ed., 1959), 29–36.

—— "Intervallproportionen—Streichquartett, 1. Satz," *R* 2 (1955), 97–102. English: "Interval proportions: String Quartet, 1st movement," *R* 2 (2nd, revised ed., 1959), 93–99.

—— "Von der Entscheidungsfreiheit des Komponisten," *R* 3 (1957), 5–12. English: "The composer's freedom of choice," *R* 3 (1959), 1–9.

Elston, Arnold. "The formal structure of Op. 6, No. 1," in "Some views of Webern's Op. 6, No. 1," *PNM* 6, no. 1 (1967) 63–66.

Fábián, Imre. "Die Wiener Schule und ihre geistige Auswirkung in Ungarn," *BÖGM 1970/71*, 78–83.

Fant, Göran. "Mest om Anton Weberns kantater" [in Swedish], *Nutida Musik* 8, no. 1 (1964), 25–35. (Includes work list, compiled by Ove Nordwall, 33–35.)

Fennelly, Brian. "Structure and process in Webern's Op. 22," *JMT* 10, no. 2 (1966), 300–328.

Fiehler, Judith Marie. "Rational structures in the late works of Anton Webern." Ph.D. diss., Louisiana State University, 1973.

Fink, Michael (compiler). "Anton Webern: Supplement to a basic bibliography," *CM* No. 16 (1973), 103–110.

Finney, Ross Lee. "Webern's Opus 6 No. 1," in "Some views of Webern's Op. 6, No. 1," *PNM* 6, no. 1 (1967), 74.

Fiore, Mary E. "The formation and structural use of vertical constructs in selected serial compositions." Ph.D. diss., Indiana University, 1963.

—— "Webern's use of motive in the *Piano Variations*," in Harry B. Lincoln, ed. *The Computer and Music.* Ithaca, New York, and London, 1970, Cornell University Press, 115–122.

Forte, Allen. "A theory of set-complexes for music," *JMT* 8, no. 2 (1964), 136–183.

Forte, Allen and Roy E. Travis. "Analysis symposium: Webern, 'Orchestral Pieces (1913): Movement I (Bewegt)'," *JMT* 18, no. 1 (1974), 2–43.

Fortner, Wolfgang. "Anton Webern und unsere Zeit," in *Wolfgang Fortner—Eine Monographie* (ed. Heinrich Lindlar). Rodenkirchen/Rhein, 1960, Tonger, 140–143. (Kontrapunkte, 4)

Fuller, Ramon Conrad. "An information theory analysis of Anton Webern's Symphonie, Op. 21." D.M.A. diss., University of Illinois, 1965.

—— "Toward a theory of Webernian harmony, via analysis with a digital computer," in Harry B. Lincoln, ed. *The Computer and Music.* Ithaca, New York, and London, 1970, Cornell University Press, 123–131.

Gallaher, Christopher Summers. "Density in twentieth-century music." Ph. D. diss., Indiana University, 1975.

Gerhard, Roberto. "Apropos Mr. Stadlen," *Sc* No. 23 (July 1958), 50–57.

—— "Some lectures by Webern," *Sc* No. 28 (January 1961), 25–28.

—— "Tonality in twelve-tone music," *Sc* No. 6 (May 1952), 23–35.

Gerlach, Reinhard. "Anton Webern: 'Ein Winterabend' Op. 13, Nr. 4: zum Verhältnis von Musik und Dichtung; oder, Wahrheit als Struktur," *AfMw* 30, no. 1 (1973), 44–68.

—— "Die Dehmel-Lieder von Anton Webern. Musik und Sprache im Übergang zur Atonalität," in *Jahrbuch des Staatlichen Instituts für Musikforschung Preussischer Kulturbesitz 1970*, Berlin, 1971, Merseburger, 45–100.

—— "Die Handschriften der Dehmel-Lieder von Anton Webern: Textkritische Studien," *AfMw* 29, no. 2 (1972), 93–114.

—— "Kompositionsniederschrift und Werkfassung am Beispiel des Liedes 'Am Ufer' (1908) von Webern," *BÖGM 1972/73*, 111–126.

—— "Mystik und Klangmagie in Anton von Weberns hybrider Tonalität (Eine Jugendkrise im Spiegel von Musik und Dichtung der Jahrhundertwende)," *AfMw* 33, no. 1 (1976), 1–27.

Glück, Franz. "Briefe von Anton von Webern und Alban Berg an Adolf Loos." *ÖMZ* 30, no. 3 (March 1975), 110–113.

Godwin, Paul Milton. "A study of concepts of melody, with particular reference to some music of the twentieth century and examples from the compositions of Schoenberg, Webern and Berg." Ph.D. diss., Ohio State University, 1972.

Goebel, Walter F. "Anton Weberns Sinfonie," *M* 28, no. 11 (November 1961), 359–362.

Goldthwaite, Scott. "Historical awareness in Anton Webern's *Symphony*, Op. 21," in Gustave Reese and R. J. Snow, ed. *Essays in musicology: In honour of Dragan Plamenac on his 70th birthday*. Pittsburgh, 1969, University of Pittsburgh Press, 65–81.

Gredinger, Paul. "Das Serielle," *R* 1 (1955), 34–41. English: "Serial technique," *R* 1 (1958), 38–44.

Grube, Gustav. "Sonstige Konzerte: [. . .] Schüler der Kompositionsschule Arnold Schönberg [. . .]," *Musikalisches Wochenblatt/NZM* No. 47 (21November 1907), 963.

Gruhn, Wilfried. "Bearbeitung als kompositorische Reflexion in Neuer Musik," *Musica* 28, no. 6 (1974), 522–528.

—— "Reihenform und Werkgestalt bei Anton Webern," *ZMT* 2, no. 2 (1971), 31–38.

Grüss, Hans. "Zu Weberns Quartett, Op. 22," *Beiträge zur Musikwissenschaft* 8, no. 3–4 (1966), 241–247.

Halen, Walter. "An analysis and comparison of compositional practices used by five contemporary composers in works titled 'Symphony'." Ph.D. diss., Ohio State University, 1969.

Hamilton, Iain. "Alban Berg and Anton Webern," in Howard Hartog, ed. *European Music in the Twentieth Century* (revised ed.). London, 1961, Pelican Books, 107–130.

Hampton, Christopher. "Anton Webern and the consciousness of the time," *MR* 20 (February 1959), 45–51.

Hartmann, Karl Amadeus. "Lektionen bei Anton Webern. Briefe an meine Frau," in *Kleine Schriften* (ed. Ernst Thomas). Mainz, 1965, Schott, 26–32.

Häusler, Josef. *Musik im 20. Jahrhundert. Von Schönberg zu Penderecki*. Bremen, 1969, Schünemann.

Hijman, Julius. *Nieuwe oostenrijkse musiek*. Amsterdam, 1938, Bigot en van Rossum.

Hiller, Lejaren and Ramon Fuller. "Structure and information in Webern's Symphonie, Op. 21," *JMT* 11, no. 1 (Spring 1967), 60–115.

Hilmar, Ernst. "Arnold Schönberg an Anton Webern: Eine Auswahl unbekannter Briefe," in Ernst Hilmar ed. *Arnold Schönberg Gedenkausstellung 1974*, Vienna, 1974, Universal Edition 44–67.

Hitchcock, H. Wiley. "A footnote on Webern's Variations," *PNM* 8, no. 2 (1970), 123–126.

Hodeir, André. "La musique occidentale post-webernienne," *Esprit* 28 (January 1960), 65–74.

Hoffmann, James Avery. "A study of tripartite forms in the compositions of Anton Webern." D.M.A. diss., University of Illinois, 1963.

Hoffmann, Richard. "Webern: Six Pieces, Opus 6 (1909)," in "Some views of Webern's Op. 6, No. 1," *PNM* 6, no. 1 (1967), 75–78.

Huber, Nicolaus A. "Die Kompositionstechnik Bachs in seinen Sonaten und Partiten für Violine solo und ihre Anwendung in Weberns op. 27, II," *ZMT* 1, no. 2 (1970), 22–31.

Huff, Jay A. "Webern's Op. 28; serial organization of time spans in the last movement," *MR* 31, no. 3 (1970), 255–256.

Humplik, Josef. "[Dem Freundel]," *23 WM* No. 14 (February 1934) (Anton Webern zum 50. Geburtstag), 13.

Hupfer, Konrad. "Webern greift in die Reihenmechanik ein," *M* 34, no. 9 (September 1967), 290–294.

Jackson, Roland John. "Harmony before and after 1910: a computer comparison," in Harry B. Lincoln, ed. *The Computer and Music*. Ithaca, New York, and London, 1970, Cornell University Press, 132–146.

Jalowetz, Heinrich. "Anton Webern wird 50 Jahre alt," *MbA* 15, no. 9–10 (November–December 1933), 135–137. Excerpts reprinted in Reich, ed. *Anton Webern* (1961) (German) and in Wildgans, *Anton Webern* (1966) (English translation).

Johnson, Martha. "A Study of Linear Design in Gregorian Chant and Music written in the Twelve-tone Technique" in E. Krenek, ed. *Hamline Studies in Musicology* (1945), 69–99.

Jone, Hildegard. "Dem Freunde," *23 WM* No. 14 (February 1934) (Anton Webern zum 50. Geburtstag), 12–13.

—— "Eine Kantate," *R* 2 (1955), 14–15. English: "A Cantata" (2nd, revised ed., 1959), 7–8.

Jones, James Rives. "Some aspects of rhythm and meter in Webern's Opus 27," *PNM* 7, no. 1 (1968), 103–109.

Kandinsky, Wassily and Franz Marc, ed. *Der blaue Reiter*. Munich, 1912, Piper. Reissued Munich, 1965, Piper; Klaus Lankheit, ed. English tr. by Henning Falkenstein, with M. Terzian and G. Hinderlie; London, 1974, Thames and Hudson.

Karkoschka, Erhard. "Hat Webern seriell komponiert?," *ÖMZ* 30, no. 11 (1975), 588–594.

—— "Studien zur Entwicklung der Kompositionstechnik im Frühwerk Anton Weberns." Ph.D. diss., University of Tübingen, 1959.

—— "Weberns op. 11 unter neuen analytischen Aspekten," *BÖGM 1972/73*, 81–92.

Kaufmann, Harald. "Figur in Weberns erster Bagatelle," in Lars Ulrich Abraham *et al.*, *Neue Wege der musikalischen Analyse*. Berlin, 1967, Merseburger, 69–72. (VINMD, 6)

—— "Struktur bei Schönberg, Figur bei Webern," in *Spurlinien. Analytische Aufsätze über Sprache und Musik*. Vienna, 1969, Lafite, 159–174.

—— "Versuch über die Wiener Schule," in *Hans Erich Apostel*. Vienna, [n.d. 1965?], Lafite, 7–18, 69–70. (Österreichische Komponisten des XX. Jahrhunderts, 4.)

—— "Zum Verhältnis zweier Musen. Über das Wort-Ton-Problem: Dallapiccolas 'Prigioniero,' Weberns Trakllied 'Die Sonne'," in *Spurlinien. Analytische Aufsätze über Sprache und Musik*. Vienna, 1969, Lafite, 65–80.

Kirchmeyer, Helmut and Hugo Wolfram Schmidt. *Aufbruch der jungen Musik. Von Webern bis Stockhausen*. Cologne, 1970, Hans Gerig.

Klammer, Armin. "Weberns Variationen für Klavier, op. 27, 3. Satz," *R* 2 (1955), 85–96. English: "Webern's Piano Variations, op. 27, 3rd movement," *R* 2 (2nd, revised ed., 1959), 81–92.

Klemm, Eberhardt, ed. "Der Briefwechsel zwischen Arnold Schönberg und dem Verlag C. F. Peters," *DJM 1970* 15, Leipzig, 1971, Peters, 5–66.

Klemm, Eberhardt. "Symmetrien im Chorsatz von Anton Webern," *DJM 1966* 11, Leipzig, 1967, Peters, 107–120.

—— "Zur Theorie einiger Reihen-Kombinationen," *AfMw* 23, no. 3 (1966), 170–212.

Kolneder, Walter. "Anton Webern," in Siegfried Borris *et al.*, *Stilporträts der Neuen Musik*. Berlin, 1961, Merseburger, 56–64 (VINMD, 2).

—— *Anton Webern. Einführung in Werk und Stil*. Rodenkirchen, 1961, Tonger. (Kontrapunkte, 5). English: *Anton Webern. An introduction to his works* (tr. Humphrey Searle). Berkeley and Los Angeles, 1968, University of California Press.

—— "Anton Webern—Gedanken zum 15. September 1945," *BÖGM 1970/71*, 55–70.

—— *Anton Webern. Genesis und Metamorphose eines Stils*. Vienna, 1974, Lafite/Österreichischer Bundesverlag. (Österreichische Komponisten des XX. Jahrhunderts, 19.)

—— "Hat Webern seriell komponiert?," *BÖGM 1972/73*, 167–172.

—— "Klang in Punkt und Linie: Anton Weberns Variationen op. 27," in Siegfried Borris *et al.*, *Vergleichende Interpretationskunde*. Berlin, 1963, Merseburger, 49–55 (VINMD, 4).

—— "Klangtechnik und Motivbildung bei Webern," in *Festgabe für Joseph Müller-Blattau zum 65. Geburtstag*. Saarbrücken, 1960, 27–50. (Annales Universitatis Saraviensis, Phil. Fakultät IX/1.)

—— "Webern und die Klangfarbenmelodie," *ÖMZ* 27, no. 3 (March 1972), 148–152.

Kramer, Jonathan D. "The row as structural background and audible foreground: the first movement of Webern's First Cantata," *JMT* 15, no. 1–2 (1971), 158–181.

Krellmann, Hanspeter. *Anton Webern in Selbstzeugnissen und Bilddokumenten*. Reinbeck bei Hamburg, 1975, Rowohlt. (Rowohlts Monographien, 229).

Krenek, Ernst. "Anton von Webern: a profile," in *AWP*, 3–14.

—— "Anton Weberns magisches Quadrat," *Forum* 12 (August–September 1965), 395–396.

—— "Commentary," in [Moldenhauer], *Anton von Webern: Sketches*, 1–7.

—— "Freiheit und Verantwortung," *23WM* No. 14 (February 1934) (Anton Webern zum 50. Geburtstag), 10–11. Reprinted in *Zur Sprache gebracht*, Munich, 1958, Albert Langen/Georg Müller; and in Reich, ed. *Anton Webern* (1961).

—— "New dimensions of music," in *AWP*, 102–107.

Kudrjašov, Jurij. "[Some features of the artistic world outlook of Anton Webern]" [in Russian], in Lev Raaben, compiler and ed. [*The Crisis of Bourgeois Culture and Music*, II]. Moscow, 1973, Muzyka.

Kudrjašova, I. "[The character and form of the early works of Webern]" [in Russian], in H. Orlov *et al.*, compilers. [*Problems in Musicology*, II]. Moscow, 1973, Sovetskij Kompozitor.

Leibowitz, René. "Innovation and tradition in contemporary music: II. The tragic art of Anton Webern," *Horizon* (London) 15 (May 1947), 282–293.

—— *Introduction à la musique de douze sons*. Paris, 1949, L'Arche.

—— "La musique: Anton Webern," *L'Arche* 2, no. 11 (November 1945), 130–134.

—— *Qu'est-ce que la musique de douze sons? Le Concerto pour neuf instruments, op. 24, d'Anton Webern*. Liège, 1948, Éditions Dynamo.

—— *Schoenberg et son école: l'étape contemporaine du langage musical*. Paris, 1947, J. B. Janin. English: *Schoenberg and His School: the contemporary stage of the language of music* (tr. Dika Newlin). New York, 1949, Philosophical Library.

Lesure, François. *Exposiçao Darius Milhaud*. Lisbon, 1968, Fundaçao Calouste Gulbenkian.

Lewin, David. "A metrical problem in Webern's Op. 27," *JMT* 6, no. 1 (1962), 124–132.

—— "Some applications of communication theory to the study of twelve-tone music," *JMT* 12, no. 1 (1968), 50–84.

Ligeti, György. "Die Komposition mit Reihen und ihre Konsequenzen bei Anton Webern," *ÖMZ* 16 (June–July 1961), 297–302.

—— "Über die Harmonik in Weberns erster Kantate," *DB* 3 (1960), 49–64.

Ligeti, György. "Weberns Melodik," *M* 33, no. 4 (April 1966), 116–118.

List, Kurt. "Anton von Webern," *MM* 21 (November–December 1943), 27–30.

Little, Jean. "Architectonic levels of rhythmic organization in selected twentieth-century music." Ph.D. diss., Indiana University, 1971.

Luckman, Phyllis. "The sound of symmetry: a study of the sixth movement of Webern's *Second Cantata*," *MR* 36, no. 3 (1975), 187–196.

Machabey, Armand. "Notes sur la musique allemande contemporaine, V: Webern," *Le Ménestrel* 92 (14 November 1930), 477–479.

Maegaard, Jan. "Some formal devices in expressionistic works," *DA* 1 (1961), 69–75.

Mason, Colin. "Webern's later chamber music," *Music and Letters* 38 (July 1957), 232–237.

Mayer, Harry. "De liedkunst van Anton Webern," *Mens en Melodie* 14 (April 1959), 114–117.

Mazzoni, A. "I maestri della scuola di Vienna," *Chigiana* 9 (1975), 207–217.

McKenzie, Wallace C., Jr. "The music of Anton Webern." Ph.D. diss., North Texas State College, 1960.

—— "Webern's posthumous music," *BÖGM 1972/73*, 185–197.

—— "Webern's technique of choral composition," in *AWP*, 62–77.

McLean, Barton Keith. "An analysis of Anton Webern's Six Songs' [. . .] op. 14." D.M.A. diss., Indiana University, 1969.

Mersmann, Hans *et al.* "Neue Musik aus dem Schönbergkreise," *M* 25, no. 1 (January 1958), 20–22. Reprinted from *M* (September 1928).

Metzger, Heinz-Klaus. "Analyse des Geistlichen Liedes op. 15 Nr. 4," *R* 2 (1955), 80–84. English: "Analysis of the Sacred song, op. 15, no. 4," *R* 2 (2nd, revised ed., 1959), 75–80.

—— "Webern und Schönberg," *R* 2 (1955), 47–50. English: "Webern and Schoenberg," *R* 2 (2nd, revised ed., 1959), 42–45.

Miller, D. Douglas. "Analysis for performance of Anton von Webern's choral works with opus numbers." D.M.A. diss., Indiana University, 1973.

Moldenhauer, Hans. "Anton von Webern—Neue Sichten. Ein Gespräch mit Harald Goertz," *BÖGM 1972/73*, 93–98.

—— "Anton von Webern: Neue Sichten—über einige posthume Werke," *ÖMZ* 27, no. 3 (March 1972), 114–121.

[—— compiler]. *Anton von Webern: Sketches (1926–1945)*. New York, 1968, Carl Fischer. "Foreword," [iii].

—— "A Webern archive in America," in *AWP*, 117–166.

—— "A Webern pilgrimage," *MT* 109 (February 1968), 122–127.

—— "Das Webern-Archiv in Amerika," *ÖMZ* 20, no. 8 (August 1965), 422–424.

—— "In quest of Webern," *Saturday Review*, 27 August, 1966, 47–49, 60.

—— "[Notes on Webern's *Im Sommerwind* and *Six Pieces for Orchestra*, Op. 6]," in *Performing Arts* (Los Angeles Philharmonic) 4, no. 2 (February 1970), 43–44, 47.

—— "Paul Amadeus Pisk and the Viennese triumvirate," in *Pisk Fs*, 208–216.

—— *The Death of Anton Webern: a drama in documents*. New York, 1961, Philosophical Library. German: *Der Tod Anton von Weberns* (tr. Gerd Sievers, with a Foreword by Igor Stravinsky). Wiesbaden, 1970, Breitkopf & Härtel.

—— "Webern, Anton von," in *Encyclopaedia Britannica* (15th ed., Chicago, London, etc. 1974), 19 (Macropaedia), 717–718.

—— "Webern as teacher," *Music Educators Journal* 57, no. 3 (November 1970), 30–33, 101–103.

—— "Webern's projected Op. 32," *MT* 111 (August 1970), 789–792.

—— "Weberns letzte Gedanken," *M* 38, no. 7–8 (July–August 1971), 273–281.

Moldenhauer, Hans, compiler and Demar Irvine, ed. *Anton von Webern; Perspectives*. Seattle and London, 1966, University of Washington Press; London, 1967, Sidgwick & Jackson. Reprint, New York, 1978, Da Capo Press.

Moroi, Makoto, "[A study on Webern]" [in Japanese], *Ongaku-Geijutsu* [Music-Art] (Tokyo) 19 (1961), no. 1, 54–64; no. 3, 22–25; no. 5, 26–31; no. 6, 20–28; no. 7, 19–21; no. 9, 18–21; no. 10, 38–41; no. 11, 42–44; no. 12, 24–29; 20 (1962), no. 2, 10–14; no. 3, 20–27; no. 5, 28–33; no. 6, 47–49.

Moschetti, Giorgio. "Postromanticismo ed espressionismo nelle prime opere di Anton Webern," *Il convegno musicale* 1 (January–March 1964), 39–44.

Nelson, Gary Lee. "Anton Webern's *Five Canons*, Opus 16: a test case for computer-aided analysis and synthesis of musical style." Ph.D diss., Washington University, 1974.

Nelson, Robert U. "Webern's path to the serial variation," *PNM* 7, no. 2 (1969), 73–93.

Nielsen, Henning. "Zentraltonprinzipien bei Anton Webern," *DA* (1966/67), 119–138.

Nieman, Alfred. "A fresh look at Webern," *Composer* (London) No. 30 (Winter 1968/69), 1, 3–6, 8–9.

Nono, Luigi. "Die Entwicklung der Reihentechnik," *DB* 1 (1958), 25–37.

Oana-Pop, Rodica. "Particularități stilistice în creația pianistică a celei de a doua școli viereze" ["Stylistic characteristics in the piano works of the second Viennese school"; in Rumanian, summaries in French, Russian, German], *Lucrări de muzicologie* 4 (1968), 157–174.

Oesch, Hans. "Alban Berg, Arnold Schönberg und Anton Webern—ihr Werk für die 'Neue Musik'," *Universitas* (Stuttgart) 28, no. 7 (July 1973), 713–722.

Ogdon, Wilbur Lee. "A Webern analysis," *JMT* 6, no. 1 (Spring 1962), 133–138.

—— "Series and structure: an investigation into the purpose of the twelve-note row in selected works of Schoenberg, Webern, Krenek and Leibowitz." Ph.D. diss., Indiana University, 1955.

Olah, Tiberiu. "Muzică grafică sau o nouă concepție despre timp și spațiu?—însemnări despre perioada preserială a lui Webern" ["Graphic music, or a new concept of time and space: a short account of Webern's pre-serial period"; in Rumanian], *Muzica* 19, no. 2 (December 1969), 13–21.

—— "Weberns vorserielles Tonsystem," *M/NZM* 1, no. 1 (January–February 1975), 10–13. (Fold-out of musical examples at the back of the periodical.)

Oliver, Harold. "Structural functions of musical material in Webern's Op. 6, No. 1," in "Some views of Webern's Op. 6, No. 1," *PNM* 6, no. 1 (1967), 67–73.

Op de Coul, Paul. "Unveröffentlichte Briefe von Alban Berg und Anton Webern an Daniel Ruyneman," *Tijdschrift voor Muziekwetenschap* (formerly *Tijdschrift van de Vereeniging voor Nederlandse Muziekgeschiedenis*) (Utrecht) 20, no. 3 (1972), 201–220.

Payne, Elsie. "The theme and variation in modern music," *MR* 19 (May 1958), 112–124.

Perle, George. *Serial Composition and Atonality: an introduction to the music of Schoenberg, Berg and Webern* (4th ed., revised). Berkeley and Los Angeles, 1977, University of California Press.

—— "Webern's twelve-tone sketches," *MQ* 57, no. 1 (1971), 1–25.

Persky, Stanley. "A discussion of compositional choices in Webern's 'Fünf Sätze für Streichquartett,' Op. 5, first movement," *CM* No. 13 (1972), 68–74.

Pestalozzi, Luigi. "Storicità di Anton Webern," *RaM* 28 (December 1958), 303–321.

Pisk, Paul Amadeus. "Anton Webern: profile of a composer." *Texas Quarterly* 5, no. 4 (Winter 1962), 114–120.

—— "New music in Austria during the 1920's," *Orbis Musicae: Studies in Musicology* (Israel) 1, no. 1 (1971), 83–87.

—— "Webern's early orchestral works," in *AWP*, 43–52.

[Ploderer, Rudolf]. "Ecce poeta!," *23 WM* No. 3 (March 1932), 1–2.

Pohlmann, Peter. "Die harmonischen Ordnungsprinzipien der neuen Musik, dargestellt an ihren Hauptvertretern." Ph.D. diss., University of Hamburg, 1956.

Polnauer, Josef. "Paralipomena zu Berg und Webern," *ÖMZ* 24, no. 5–6 (May–June 1969), 292–296.

Poné, Gundaris. "Webern and Luigi Nono; the genesis of a new compositional morphology and syntax," *PNM* 10, no. 2 (1972), 111–119.

Pousseur, Henri. "Anton Weberns organische Chromatik—1. Bagatelle, op. 9," *R* 2 (1955), 56–65. English: "Webern's organic chromaticism," *R* 2 (2nd, revised ed., 1959), 51–60.

—— "Da Schoenberg a Webern: una mutazione," *IM* No. 1 (December 1956), 3–39.

—— "Forme et pratiques musicales," *RB* 13 (1959), 98–116. German: "Musik, Form und Praxis. (Zur Aufhebung einiger Widersprüche)," *R* 6 (1960), 71–86. English: "Music, form and practice (an attempt to reconcile some contradictions)," *R* 6 (1964), 77–93.

—— "Stravinsky selon Webern selon Stravinsky," *Musique en Jeu* No. 4 (October 1971), 21–47, and No. 5 [n.d.], 107–126. English: "Stravinsky by way of Webern; the consistency of a syntax," *PNM* 10, no. 2 (1972), 13–51, and 11, no. 1 (1972), 112–145.

—— "Theorie und Praxis in der neuesten Musik," *DB* 2 (1959), 15–29.

—— "The question of order in new music," *PNM* 5, no. 1 (1966), 93–111.

—— "Vers un nouvel univers sonore," *Esprit* 28 (January 1960), 52–64.

—— "Webern und die Theorie," *DB* 1 (1958), 38–43.

—— "Zur Methodik," *R* 3 (1957), 46–87. English: "Outline of a method," *R* 3 (1959), 44–88.

Pütz, Werner. *Studien zum Streichquartettschaffen bei Hindemith, Bartók, Schoenberg und Webern.* Regensburg, 1968, Bosse. (Kölner Beiträge zur Musikforschung, 36.) (Originally Ph.D. diss., University of Cologne, 1968.)

Rabe, Folke. "Anton Webern—Fem satser för strakkvartett" [in Swedish], *Nutida Musik* 5, no. 1 (1961/62), 21–24.

Raiss, Hans-Peter. "Analyse der Bagatelle Op. 9, 5 von Anton Webern," in Rudolph Stephan, ed. *Versuche musikalischer Analysen.* Berlin, 1967, Merseburger, 50–60. (VINMD, 8).

—— "[Anton Webern:] Symphonie op. 21, 2. Satz," in Hans Vogt et al., *Neue Musik seit 1945.* Stuttgart, 1972, Reclam, 205–218.

Rauchhaupt, Ursula von, ed. *Die Streichquartette der Wiener Schule. Schoenberg, Berg, Webern. Eine Dokumentation.* Munich, 1971, H. Ellermann. English: *Schoenberg, Berg, Webern: the string quartets. A documentary study* (tr. Eugene Hartzell). Hamburg, 1971, Deutsche Grammophon Gesellschaft.

Redlich, Hans Ferdinand. "Anton (von) Webern," in *Die Musik in Geschichte und Gegenwart*, vol. 14 (Kassel, 1968, Bärenreiter), cols. 339–350.

Reich, Willi. "Alban Berg und Anton von Webern in ihren neuen Werken," *Der Auftakt* 10, no. 5–6 (1930), 132–135.

—— "Anton von Webern," *Die Musik* 22 (August 1930), 812–816, 832. Dutch: in *De Muziek* 4 (1929–30), 249–253.

—— "Anton Webern," *Der Auftakt* 13, no. 11–12 (1933), 164–166.

—— "Anton Webern: the man and his music," *T* No. 14 (March 1946), 8–10.

—— ed. *Anton Webern: Weg und Gestalt; Selbstzeugnisse und Worte der Freunde.* Zürich, 1961, Verlag der Arche.

—— "Anton Weberns letzte literarische Arbeit," *SMZ* 107, no. 3 (1967), 149.

—— "Berg und Webern schreiben an Hermann Scherchen," *M* 33, no. 7–8 (July–August 1966), 225–228.

—— "Briefe aus Weberns letzten Jahren," *ÖMZ* 20 (August 1965), 407–411.

—— "Der 'Blaue Reiter' und die Musik," *SMZ* 85, no. 8–9 (September 1945), 341–345.

[——] "Die Presse," *23 WM* No. 14 (February 1934) (Anton Webern zum 50. Geburtstag), 22–23.

—— "Ein verschollener Webern-Text," *M* 36, no. 1 (January 1969), 9. Webern's text was originally published in the *Rheinische Musik- und Theaterzeitung* (Cologne) 13 (February 1912).

—— "Eine neue Sinfonie von Anton Webern," *M* 11 (1930), 146–147.

[Reich, Willi]. "Jenseits von Gut und Böse," *23 WM* No. 7 (December 1932), 1–9.

—— "Versuch einer Geschichte der Zwölftonmusik," *Alte und neue Musik: das Basler Kammerorchester (1926–1951)*. Zürich, 1952, Atlantis, 106–132.

—— "Weberns Musik," *23WM* No. 14 (February 1934) (Anton Webern zum 50. Geburtstag), 5–8.

—— "Weberns Vorträge," *23WM* No. 14 (February 1934) (Anton Webern zum 50. Geburtstag), 17–22.

Reid, E. J. "The music of Anton Webern [. . .]." Ph.D. diss., University of Aberdeen, 1961/62.

Reid, John W. "Properties of the set explored in Webern's Variations, Op. 30," *PNM* 12, no. 1–2 (1973/74), 344–350.

Riley, Howard. "A study in constructivist procedures: Webern's Variations for Piano, Op. 27, first movement," *MR* 27, no. 3 (1966), 207–210.

Rimmer, Frederick. "Sequence and symmetry in twentieth-century melody," *MR* 26, no. 1 (1965), 28–50, and no. 2 (1965), 85–96.

Ringger, Rolf Urs. *Anton Weberns Klavierlieder.* Zürich, 1968, Juris Verlag. (Part of Ph.D. diss., University of Zürich, 1964.)

—— "Orchesterstücke des Expressionismus," *NZM* 129 (October 1968), 441–443.

Rochberg, George. "The new image of music," *PNM* 2, no. 1 (1963), 1–10.

—— "Webern's search for harmonic identity," *JMT* 6, no. 1 (Spring 1962), 109–122.

Rognoni, Luigi. *Espressionismo e dodecafonia.* Turin, 1954, Einaudi.

—— "Meditazione su Anton Webern," *Quadrivium* 14 (1973), 405–411.

Rohwer, Jens. *Neueste Musik; ein kritischer Bericht.* Stuttgart, 1964, E. Klett.

—— "Zur Analyse neuer Musik," *Mf* 21, no. 1 (1968), 69–73.

Rostand, Claude. *Anton Webern, l'homme et son œuvre.* Paris, 1969, Éditions Seghers. (Musiciens de tous les temps, 40.)

Rubin, Marcel. "Webern und die Folgen," *Musik und Gesellschaft* 10 (August 1960), 463–469.

Ruwet, Nicolas. "Contradictions du langage sériel," *RB* 13 (1959), 83–97. German: "Von den Widersprüchen der seriellen Sprache," *R* 6 (1960), 59–70. English: "Contradictions within the serial language," *R* 6 (1964), 65–76.

Salazar, Adolfo. *La música moderna; las corrientes directrices en el arte musical contemporáneo.* Buenos Aires, 1944, Editorial Losada. English: *Music in Our Time; trends in music since the romantic era* (tr. Isabel Pope). New York, 1946, Norton; London, 1948, Bodley Head; reprinted Westport, Connecticut, 1970, Greenwood Press.

Saturen, David. "Symmetrical relationships in Webern's First Cantata," *PNM* 6, no. 1 (1967), 142–143.

Schaefer, Hansjürgen. ". . . nicht nur von historischem Interesse—Bemerkungen zum Werk Anton Weberns, Karl Amadeus Hartmanns und Paul Hindemiths," *Musik und Gesellschaft* 23 (December 1973), 734–740.

Schäffer, Boguslaw. "Präexistente und inexistente Strukturen," *Kongressbericht Kassel 1962*, Kassel, 1963, Bärenreiter, 263–268.

Scherchen, Hermann. "Dépassement de l'orchestre," *RM* No. 236 (Pierre Schaeffer, ed. *Vers une musique expérimentale.*), 56–59.

Schiller, Henryk. "Faktura chóralna utworów Weberna" ["Choral technique in Webern's works"; in Polish], *Muzyka* 10, no. 3 (1965), 63–75.

—— "Kantata 'Das Augenlicht' Antona Weberna" [in Polish], *Ruch Muzyczny* 2, no. 19 (1958), 20–25.

Schmidt-Garré, Helmut. "Webern als Angry Young Man. Aus alten Zeitungskritiken über Anton Webern," *NZM* 125, no. 4 (1964), 132–137.

Schmitt, Ingo. "Harmonische Gesetzmässigkeiten in Weberns Spätwerk," in *42. Deutsches Bachfest Wuppertal 1967*, Hannover, 1967, Neue Bach-Gesellschaft, 38–47.

Schnebel, Dieter. "Anleitung zum Hören," in *Denkbare Musik. Schriften 1952–1972* (ed. Hans Rudolf Zeller). Cologne, 1972, M. DuMont Schauberg, 156–170.

Schnebel, Dieter. "Konzept über Webern," in *Denkbare Musik. Schriften 1952–1972* (ed. Hans Rudolf Zeller). Cologne, 1972, M. DuMont Schauberg, 42–54.

Schoenberg, Arnold. *Briefe* (ed. Erwin Stein). Mainz, 1958, Schott. English: *Letters* (tr. Eithne Wilkins and Ernst Kaiser). London, 1964, Faber & Faber; New York, 1965, St. Martin's Press.

—— *Style and Idea* (ed. Leonard Stein). New York, 1975, St Martin's Press; London, 1975, Faber & Faber.

—— ["Foreword"], in Anton Webern. *Sechs Bagatellen für Streichquartett, op. 9*. Vienna, 1924, Universal Edition, [2]. Reprinted in *23 WM* No. 14 (Anton Webern zum 50, Geburtstag), 8 and in *R 2* (1955), 15 (German); in *R 2* (2nd, revised ed., 1959), 8 (English).

Schollum, Robert. *Die Wiener Schule; Schönberg, Berg, Webern. Entwicklung und Ergebnis.* Vienna, 1969, Lafite.

—— "Stilistische Elemente der frühen Webern-Lieder", *BÖGM 1972/73*, 127–134.

Schreker-Bures, Haidy. *El caso Schreker*. Buenos Aires, 1968, Editorial Talia.

Schuller, Gunther. "A conversation with Steuermann," *PNM* 3 (Fall-Winter 1964), 22–35.

Schwarz, Richard. "Webern und Berg," *MbA* 6, no. 9 (October 1924), 381.

Searle, Humphrey. "Conversations with Webern," *MT* 81 (October 1940), 405–406.

—— "Studying with Webern," *Royal College of Music Magazine* (London) 54 (Summer 1958), 39–40.

—— "Webern, Anton (von)," *Grove's Dictionary of Music and Musicians* (5th ed.), vol. 9 (London, 1954, Macmillan), 225–228.

—— "Webern's last works," *Monthly Musical Record* 76 (December 1946), 231–237.

Self, George. "The old and the new: Anton Webern," *ME* 31, no. 323 (January–February 1967), 345–348.

Siedentopf, Henning. "Das Motiv B-A-C-H und die neue Musik—Dargestellt an Werken Regers, Schönbergs und Weberns," *Musica* 28, no. 5 (1974), 420–422.

Siegele, Ulrich. "Entwurf einer Musikgeschichte der sechziger Jahre," in Rudolf Stephan, ed. *Die Musik der sechziger Jahre*. Mainz, 1972, Schott, 9–25 (VINMD, 12).

Slonimsky, Nicolas. *Music since 1900* (4th ed., revised and enlarged). New York, 1971, Charles Scribner's Sons.

Small, Christopher. "Webern: Concerto for Nine Instruments," *ME* 39 (January–February 1975), 19–22.

—— "Webern: String Quartet Op. 28," *ME* 39 (May–June 1975), 114–116, 118–119.

Smalley, Roger. "Rarità di Schoenberg, Webern, Zenk," *Chigiana* 9 (1975), 218–221.

—— "Webern's sketches," *T* 112 (1975), 1–12; 113 (1975), 29–40; 114 (1975), 14–22.

Smith, Leland. "Composition and precomposition in the music of Webern," in *AWP*, 86–101.

Smith, Robert. "This Sorry Scheme of Things . . . ," *MR* 22, no. 3 (1961), 212–219.

Somfai, László. "Rhythmic continuity and articulation in Webern's instrumental works," *BÖGM 1972/73*, 100–110.

—— *Webern* [in Hungarian]. Budapest, 1968, Gondolat. (Kis Zenei Könyvtár, 40.)

Spinner, Leopold. "Analyse einer Periode—Konzert für 9 Instrumente, op. 24, 2. Satz," *R 2* (1955), 51–55. English: "Analysis of a period: Concerto for 9 instruments, op. 24, 2nd movement," *R 2* (2nd, revised ed., 1959), 46–50.

—— "Anton Weberns Kantate Nr. 2, Opus 31. Die Formprinzipien der kanonischen Darstellung (Analyse des vierten Satzes)," *SMZ* 101, no. 5 (1961), 303–308.

Spitzmüller, Alexandre de. "Le triomphe de la sensibilité," *Contrepoints* 2 (February 1946), 71–73.

Stadlen, Peter. "Das pointillistische Missverständnis," *BÖGM 1972/73*, 173–184.

—— "No real casualties?," *Sc* No. 24 (November 1958), 65–68.

—— "Serialism reconsidered," *Sc* No. 22 (February 1958), 12–27. German: "Kritik am Seriellen," *Musica* 13 (February 1959), 89–98.

Starr, Mark. "Webern's palindrome," *PNM* 8, no. 2 (1970), 127–142.

Stein, Erwin. "Alban Berg and Anton von Webern," *The Chesterian*, New Series, No. 26 (October 1922), 33–36. German in *MbA* 5 (1923), 13–16.

—— "Anton Webern," *Neue Musikzeitung* 49 (1928), 517–519.

—— "Anton Webern," *MbA* 13 (June–July 1931), 107–109.

—— "Anton Webern," *MT* 87 (January 1946), 14–15. Reprinted in *Orpheus in New Guises*. London, 1953, Rockliff, 99–102.

—— "Fünf Stücke für Orchester von Anton Webern," *Pult und Taktstock* 3 (1926), 109–110.

—— "Webern's new Quartet," *T* No. 4 (July 1939), 6–7.

Stein, Leonard. "The *Privataufführungen* revisited," in *Pisk Fs*, 203–207.

—— "Webern's *Dehmel Lieder* of 1906–8," in *AWP*, 53–61.

Steiner, Ena. "In Memoriam: Alban Berg and Anton Webern," *Journal of the Canadian Association of University Schools of Music* 5, no. 2 (Autumn 1975), 76–92.

Stephan, Rudolf. "Anton von Webern," *Deutsche Universitäts-Zeitung* 11, no. 13–14 (July 1956), 26–29.

—— "Ein unbekannter Aufsatz Weberns über Schönberg," *ÖMZ* 27, no. 3 (March 1972), 127–131. (See Work List E. "Über Arnold Schönberg als Dirigent.")

—— "Über einige geistliche Kompositionen Anton von Weberns," *Musik und Kirche* 24 (July–August 1954), 152–160.

—— "Weberns Werke auf deutschen Tonkünstlerfesten. Mit zwei wenig beachteten Texten Weberns," *ÖMZ* 27, no. 3 (March 1972), 121–127. (See Work List E. "Passacaglia"; " 'Sechs Orchesterstücke'.")

—— "Zu einigen Liedern Anton Weberns," *BÖGM 1972/73*, 135–144.

Stockhausen, Karlheinz. "Struktur und Erlebniszeit," *R* 2 (1955), 69–79. Reprinted in *Texte zur elektronischen und instrumentalen Musik* (ed. Dieter Schnebel), vol. 1, Cologne, 1963, M. DuMont Schauberg. (DuMont Dokumente.) English: "Structure and experiential time," *R* 2 (2nd, revised ed., 1959), 64–74.

—— "Weberns Konzert für 9 Instrumente op. 24—Analyse des ersten Satzes," *M* 20, no. 12 (December 1953), 343–348. Reprinted in *Texte zur elektronischen und instrumentalen Musik*, vol. 1 (1963).

—— "Zum 15. September 1955," *R* 2 (1955), 42–44. English: "For the 15th of September, 1955," *R* 2 (2nd, revised ed., 1959), 37–39.

Stravinsky, Igor. "A decade later (an interview)," in *AWP*, xix–xxvii.

Stravinsky, Igor and Robert Craft. *Themes and Episodes*. New York, 1966, Knopf.

Strobel, Heinrich. "Die Wiener Schule," *M* 30, no. 11 (November 1963), 369–377.

—— "So sehe ich Webern," *M* 32, no. 9 (September 1965), 285–290.

Stroh, Wolfgang Martin. *Anton Webern. Historische Legitimation als kompositorisches Problem*. Göppingen, 1973, Kümmerle. (Göppinger Akademische Beiträge, 63).

—— "Über die Bedeutung von Weberns Kompositionsskizzen," *NZM* 131, no. 9 (September 1970), 434–438.

Stuckenschmidt, Hans Heinz. "Anton Webern," *Ricordiana* [nuova serie] 3 (June 1957), 274–277.

—— "Contemporary techniques in music," *MQ* 49, no. 1 (1963), 1–16.

—— *Schönberg. Leben, Umwelt, Werk*. Zürich, Freiburg, 1974, Atlantis.

—— *Schöpfer der neuen Musik: Portraits und Studien*. Frankfurt/M, 1958, Suhrkamp.

—— "Was ist musikalischer Expressionismus?," *M* 36, no. 1 (January 1969), 1–5.

Swanay, John Lee. "Romantic style characteristics which led to the rise of dodecaphonic techniques." Ph.D. diss., University of Texas, 1963.

Swarowsky, Hans. "Anton von Webern: Bemerkungen zu seiner Gestalt," *BÖGM 1972/73*, 14–22.

Szmolyan, Walter. "Webern in Mödling und Maria Enzersdorf," *BÖGM 1972/73*, 36–39.

—— "Webern-Stätten in Österreich," *ÖMZ* 27, no. 3 (March 1972), 162–166.

Teitelbaum, Richard. "Intervallic relations in atonal music," *JMT* 9, no. 1 (1965), 72–127.

Travis, Roy. "Directed motion in Schoenberg and Webern," *PNM* 4, no. 2 (1966), 85–89 (preceded by 8 unnumbered pages of music examples with the title "Directed motion in two brief piano pieces by Schoenberg and Webern"). Reprinted in part as "Directed motion in Webern's Piano Variations, Op. 27/II," *Proceedings of the American Society of University Composers* 2 (1967), 54–60.

Venus, Dankmar. "Vergleichende Untersuchungen zur melischen Struktur der Singstimmen in den Liedern von A. Schönberg, A. Berg, A. Webern und P. Hindemith." Ph.D. diss., University of Göttingen, 1965.

—— "Zum Problem der Schlussbildung im Liedwerk von Schönberg, Berg und Webern," *MB* 4, no. 3 (March 1972), 117–123.

Vlad, Roman. "Anton Webern," *La Musica (Enciclopedia Storica)*, vol. 4 (Turin, 1966, Unione Tipografica-Editrice Torinese), 853–861.

—— *Storia della dodecafonia*. Milan, 1958, Zerboni.

Vojtěch, Ivan. "Arnold Schönberg, Anton Webern, Alban Berg—Unbekannte Briefe an Erwin Schulhoff," *Miscellanea Musicologica* (Prague) 18 (1965), 31–83.

Waller, Amalie. "Mein Vater Anton von Webern," *ÖMZ* 23, no. 6–7 (June–July 1968), 331–333.

Webern, Anton von. "An die Redaktion der *Muziek* in Amsterdam," *De Muziek* 5, no. 1 [October 1930], 22. Reprinted in Willi Reich, "Anton Webern über Alban Berg," *NZM* 124, no. 4 (April 1963), 143.

—— "Aus dem Briefwechsel," *R* 2 (1955), 20–28. English: "From the correspondence," *R* 2 (2nd revised ed., 1959), 13–21.

—— "Aus unveröffentlichten Briefen," *Der Turm* 1, no. 12 (1945/46), 390–391.

—— "Brief an Frau Schreker," in *Programmheft des Staatstheaters Kassel 1964/65*, No. 1, 8.

—— "Ein Brief Anton Weberns an Hanns Eisler," *Musik und Gesellschaft* 8 (1958), 338–340.

—— *Briefe an Hildegard Jone und Josef Humplik* (ed. J. Polnauer). Vienna, 1959, Universal Edition. English: *Letters to Hildegard Jone and Josef Humplik* (tr. Cornelius Cardew). Bryn Mawr, Pennsylvania, 1967, Th. Presser, in association with Universal Edition, London.

—— "Briefe an zwei Freunde," *M* 26, no. 12 (December 1959), 377–379.

—— "Briefe der Freundschaft (1911–1945)," in *Die Stimme der Komponisten*, Rodenkirchen, 1958, Tonger, 126–133. (Kontrapunkte, 2)

—— "Der UE-Lektor. Aus Gutachten Weberns für die Universal-Edition," *R* 2 (1955), 29. English: "The U.E. reader. Extracts from opinions given by Webern to Universal Edition," *R* 2 (2nd, revised ed., 1959), 22.

—— *Der Weg zur neuen Musik* (ed. Willi Reich). Vienna, 1960, Universal Edition. English: *The Path to the New Music* (tr. Leo Black). Bryn Mawr, Pennsylvania, 1963, Th. Presser; London, 1963, Universal Edition.

—— "Previously unpublished composers' letters as written to Claire R. Reis," *Musical America* 83, no. 1 (January 1963), 16.

—— *Verso la nuova musica. Lettere a Hildegard Jone e Josef Humplik*. Milan, 1963, Bompiani. (Portico, 42)

—— "Zwei Briefe an Hanns Eisler," *Sinn und Form* (Deutsche Akademie der Künste, Berlin) 16 (1964), 108–109.

Webern, Anton von and Arnold Schoenberg. "Letters of Webern and Schoenberg (to Roberto Gerhard)," *Sc* No. 24 (November 1958), 36–41.

See also Work List, Section E, and the following entries:

Döhl, "Zum Formbegriff Weberns.[. . .]."

Glück, "Briefe von Anton von Webern und Alban Berg [. . .]."

Klemm, "Der Briefwechsel zwischen Arnold Schönberg und dem Verlag C. F. Peters."

Krellmann, *Anton Webern in Selbstzeugnissen* [. . .].
[Moldenhauer, compiler], *Anton von Webern: Sketches* [. . .].
Op de Coul, "Unveröffentlichte Briefe [. . .]."
Rauchhaupt, *Die Streichquartette der Wiener Schule.*[. . .].
Reich, *Anton Webern: Weg und Gestalt;*[. . .].
—— "Berg und Webern schreiben an Hermann Scherchen."
—— "Briefe aus Weberns letzten Jahren."
Schreker-Bures, *El caso Schreker.*
Vojtěch, "Arnold Schönberg, Anton Webern, Alban Berg [. . .]."
Wildgans, *Anton Webern.*

Wellesz, Egon. "Anton von Webern, a great Austrian," in *AWP*, 108–110.
—— "Anton von Webern: Lieder opus 12, 13, 14," *M* 2 (1921), 38–40.
—— "Begegnungen in Wien," *M* 33 (1966), 6–12.
—— "Reviews of music: Webern, Anton, String Quartet, op. 28," *MR* 1 (May 1940), 177–178.
Wen-Chung, Chou. "Asian concepts and twentieth-century Western composers," *MQ* 57, no. 2 (April 1971), 211–229.
Westergaard, Peter. "On the problems of 'reconstruction from a sketch': Webern's 'Kunfttag III' and 'Leise Düfte'," *PNM* 11, no. 2 (1973), 104–121.
—— "Some problems in rhythmic theory and analysis," *PNM* 1, no. 1 (1962), 180–191.
—— "Toward a twelve-tone polyphony," *PNM* 4 (1966), 90–112.
—— "Webern and 'total organization': an analysis of the second movement of Piano Variations op. 27," *PNM* 1, no. 2 (1963), 107–120.
Whittall, Arnold. "On summarizing Webern," *Soundings* (Cardiff) 1 (1970), 54–57.
Wildgans, Friedrich. "Anton von Webern; zu seinem 75. Geburtstag am 3. Dezember 1958," *ÖMZ* 13 (November 1958), 456–460.
—— *Anton Webern. Eine Studie.* Tübingen, 1967, Rainer Wunderlich. English: *Anton Webern* (tr. Edith Temple Roberts and Humphrey Searle). London, 1966, Calder & Boyars; New York, 1969, October House.
—— "Gustav Mahler und Anton von Webern," *ÖMZ* 15, no. 6 (June 1960), 302–306.
Wille, Rudolf. "Reihensymmetrien und Reihenquadrate," *Mf* 21, no. 1 (1968), 47–50.
Wilsen, William. "Equitonality as a measure of the evolution toward atonality in the pre-Opus 1 songs of Anton Webern." Ph.D. diss., Florida State University, 1975.
Wittlich, Gary E. "An examination of some set-theoretic applications in the analysis of non-serial music." Ph.D. diss., University of Iowa, 1969.
Wolff, Christian. "Kontrollierte Bewegung," *R* 2 (1955), 66–68. English: "Movement," *R* 2 (2nd, revised ed., 1959), 61–63.
Zenk, Ludwig. "Mein Lehrer," *23 WM* No. 14 (February 1934) (Anton Webern zum 50. Geburtstag), 13. Reprinted in Reich, ed. *Anton Webern* (1961).
Zielinski, Tadeusz Andrzej. "Ekspresjonizm Schoenberga i Weberna" [in Polish], *Ruch Muzyczny* 14, no. 18 (1970), 3–7.

Index

The Introduction was excluded from the Index, except for references to the history of the Webern Archive. The indexing of the Work List (Appendix 1) was limited to locating the compositions and arrangements discussed or mentioned in the main text. The Bibliography was indexed as to topics only.

Letters—quoted or mentioned, and understood to include all forms of written communication—were listed only under the name of the writer. Music, literature, and visual art works were indexed under their creator's name.

Articles were disregarded in the alphabetization of work lists.

Z. R.